HANDBOOK OF EARLY CHILDHOOD INTERVENTION,
Second Edition

The second edition of the much-heralded *Handbook of Early Childhood Intervention* is a core text for students and experienced professionals who are interested in the health, development, and well-being of young children and their families. It is intended to serve as a comprehensive reference for service providers, policy makers, researchers, graduate students, and advanced trainees in such diverse fields as child care, early childhood education, child health, and early intervention programs for children with developmental disabilities as well as for those who live in high-risk environments (e.g., poverty and parental mental illness) that jeopardize their development. This book will be of interest to professionals in a broad range of disciplines including psychology, child development, early childhood education, social work, pediatrics, nursing, child psychiatry, physical and occupational therapy, speech and language pathology, and social policy. Its main purpose is to provide a scholarly overview of the knowledge base and practice of early childhood intervention. With fifteen entirely new chapters and thirteen extensively revised chapters, it is unique in its balance between breadth and depth and its integration of the multiple dimensions of the field.

Jack P. Shonkoff is Dean of the Heller Graduate School and Samuel F. and Rose B. Gingold Professor of Human Development at Brandeis University. He also serves as Chair of the Board on Children, Youth, and Families at the Institute of Medicine and the National Research Council/National Academy of Sciences, Chair of the NRC/IOM Committee on Integrating the Science of Early Childhood Development, and member of the scientific core group of the John D. and Catherine T. MacArthur Foundation and James S. McDonnell Foundation Research Network on Early Experience and Brain Development.

Samuel J. Meisels is Director of the Assessment Projects and Professor in the School of Education and a Research Scientist at the Center for Human Growth and Development at the University of Michigan. He is president-elect of the Board of Directors of Zero To Three: The National Center for Infants, Toddlers, and Families. He is also a senior principal investigator for the national Early Childhood Longitudinal Study and the Center for the Improvement of Early Reading Achievement.

HANDBOOK OF EARLY CHILDHOOD INTERVENTION

SECOND EDITION

Edited by

JACK P. SHONKOFF
Brandeis University

SAMUEL J. MEISELS
The University of Michigan

CAMBRIDGE
UNIVERSITY PRESS

PUBLISHED BY THE PRESS SYNDICATE OF THE UNIVERSITY OF CAMBRIDGE
The Pitt Building, Trumpington Street, Cambridge, United Kingdom

CAMBRIDGE UNIVERSITY PRESS
The Edinburgh Building, Cambridge CB2 2RU, UK   http://www.cup.cam.ac.uk
40 West 20th Street, New York, NY 10011-4211, USA   http://www.cup.org
10 Stamford Road, Oakleigh, Melbourne 3166, Australia
Ruiz de Alarcón 13, 28014 Madrid, Spain

First published 2000

Printed in the United States of America

Typeface Stone Serif 9/12   *System* LaTeX 2_ε [TB]

A catalog record for this book is available from the British Library.

Library of Congress Cataloging in Publication Data
Handbook of early childhood intervention / edited by Jack P. Shonkoff,
    Samuel J. Meisels. – 2nd ed.
        p.   cm.
    Includes bibliographical references.
    ISBN 0-521-58471-X (hbk.)

    1. Developmental disabilities – Prevention Handbooks, manuals, etc.
    2. Child health services Handbooks, manuals, etc.   I. Shonkoff,
    Jack P.   II. Meisels, Samuel J.
    RJ135.H46   2000
    362.1'9892 – dc21   99-25362
                                                         CIP

ISBN 0 521 58471 X hardback
ISBN 0 521 58573 2 paperback

To our families

Contents

Foreword   *page* xi
      EDWARD F. ZIGLER, YALE UNIVERSITY

Preface   xvii

Contributors   xix

PART ONE. INTRODUCTION

1   Early Childhood Intervention: A Continuing Evolution   3
    SAMUEL J. MEISELS AND JACK P. SHONKOFF

**PART TWO. CONCEPTS OF DEVELOPMENTAL VULNERABILITY
AND RESILIENCE**

2   The Biology of Developmental Vulnerability   35
    JACK P. SHONKOFF AND PAUL C. MARSHALL

3   Adaptive and Maladaptive Parenting: Perspectives on Risk and Protective Factors   54
    JOY D. OSOFSKY AND M. DEWANA THOMPSON

4   The Human Ecology of Early Risk   76
    JAMES GARBARINO AND BARBARA GANZEL

5   Cultural Differences as Sources of Developmental Vulnerabilities and Resources   94
    CYNTHIA GARCÍA COLL AND KATHERINE MAGNUSON

6   Protective Factors and Individual Resilience   115
    EMMY E. WERNER

PART THREE. THEORETICAL FRAMEWORKS FOR INTERVENTION

7   Transactional Regulation: The Developmental Ecology of Early Intervention   135
    ARNOLD J. SAMEROFF AND BARBARA H. FIESE

8   Guiding Principles for a Theory of Early Intervention:
   A Developmental–Psychoanalytic Perspective   160
    ROBERT N. EMDE AND JOANN ROBINSON

9   Behavioral and Educational Approaches to Early Intervention   179
    MARK WOLERY

10   The Neurobiological Bases of Early Intervention   204
      CHARLES A. NELSON

PART FOUR. APPROACHES TO ASSESSMENT

11   The Elements of Early Childhood Assessment   231
      SAMUEL J. MEISELS AND SALLY ATKINS-BURNETT

12   Assessment of Parent–Child Interaction: Implications for Early Intervention   258
      JEAN F. KELLY AND KATHRYN E. BARNARD

13   Family Assessment Within Early Intervention Programs   290
      MARTY WYNGAARDEN KRAUSS

14   Measurement of Community Characteristics   309
      FELTON EARLS AND STEPHEN BUKA

PART FIVE. SERVICE DELIVERY MODELS AND SYSTEMS

15   Preventive Health Care and Anticipatory Guidance   327
      PAUL H. DWORKIN

16   Early Care and Education: Current Issues and Future Strategies   339
      SHARON L. KAGAN AND MICHELLE J. NEUMAN

17   Early Intervention for Low-Income Children and Families   361
      ROBERT HALPERN

18   Services for Young Children with Disabilities and Their Families   387
      GLORIA L. HARBIN, R. A. McWILLIAM, AND JAMES J. GALLAGHER

19   Early Childhood Mental Health Services: A Policy and Systems
      Development Perspective   416
      JANE KNITZER

20   Paraprofessionals Revisited and Reconsidered   439
      JUDITH MUSICK AND FRANCES STOTT

21   Personnel Preparation for Early Childhood Intervention Programs   454
      NANCY K. KLEIN AND LINDA GILKERSON

PART SIX. MEASURING THE IMPACT OF SERVICE DELIVERY

22   An Expanded View of Program Evaluation in Early Childhood
      Intervention   487
      PENNY HAUSER-CRAM, MARJI ERICKSON WARFIELD, CAROLE C. UPSHUR,
      AND THOMAS S. WEISNER

23   Another Decade of Intervention for Children Who Are Low Income
      or Disabled: What Do We Know Now?   510
      DALE C. FARRAN

24   Early Childhood Intervention Programs: What About the Family?   549
      JEANNE BROOKS-GUNN, LISA J. BERLIN, AND ALLISON SIDLE FULIGNI

25   Economics of Early Childhood Intervention   589
      W. STEVEN BARNETT

**PART SEVEN. NEW DIRECTIONS FOR THE TWENTY-FIRST
CENTURY**

26   Early Childhood Intervention Policies: An International Perspective   613
      SHEILA KAMERMAN

27   Evolution of Family–Professional Partnerships: Collective
      Empowerment as the Model for the Early Twenty-First Century   630
      ANN P. TURNBULL, VICKI TURBIVILLE, AND H. R. TURNBULL

28   Resilience Reconsidered: Conceptual Considerations, Empirical Findings,
      and Policy Implications   651
      MICHAEL RUTTER

Name Index   683

Subject Index   708

Foreword

If the earlier edition of the handbook represented the coming of age of the field of early childhood intervention, the presentation of this edition surely marks the beginning of its maturity. As developmental psychologists know well, each stage of development brings characteristic triumphs and challenges, with occasional setbacks and recurrences of the previous stage's struggles, not entirely abandoned as the young move forward into new stages along their growth trajectory. Our young field is no exception. A decade later, we are stronger, wiser, and capable of more complex tasks and deeper understanding than we were, yet old difficulties reassert themselves and continue to beset us, and there is still much to learn. Just as social expectations increase as the individual reaches maturity, the responsibilities of the field of early intervention have been accruing apace. We know more now; we have a great deal to do.

Throughout the 1990s, we have witnessed great breakthroughs in the field of brain development. Recent brain research has demonstrated with unprecedented certainty the importance of early experience in influencing the actual growth and development of neural pathways in the individual (Kotulak, 1996). During the years from 3 to 10, the brain is more densely "wired" than at any other time in the child's life. This means that there is literally a profusion of synapses connecting brain cells that are present in the growing child. Moreover, we have learned that the early years are a particularly sensitive time for that portion of the brain that controls such essential complex functions as language acquisition and the processes that facilitate logical thinking. It has been suggested that brain activity in children of this age exceeds that of adults (Shore, 1997).

These revolutionary insights into the workings of the brain have tremendous implications for the field of early childhood intervention. Investigation has shown that as the young child's brain grows, a particular economy of demand and supply prevails: Connections that receive stimulation tend to be reinforced, while unstimulated connections tend to be eliminated. Thus, the human brain is constructed to be quite efficient at acquiring a range of skills early in life and at disposing of neural capacity that is seemingly unneeded. After that time, learning certainly continues, but remediation becomes more challenging once the dense neural net of early life has diminished (Carnegie, 1996). Although scholars and practitioners in the field have long championed the value of intervening early in the child's life, we now know with virtual certainty that the quality of the environment in which young children spend their early years is a critical influence on their capacity to develop an adequate foundation for later learning, as well as for emotional regulation. Over the years, the field has struggled to demonstrate conclusively the efficacy of early intervention as a means to combat the damaging effects of poverty on young children. We have argued that children who are able to form strong, trusting relationships with caregivers in their early years are more likely to learn, develop healthy self-esteem, and acquire the coping skills they will need in later life. With advances in brain imaging research techniques, we are now in a position to begin to support our empirical program research findings with views of actual brain structures. In the future, there is the potential for comparing the effects of different levels and forms of stimulation on these structures.

Along with advances in knowledge about brain development, the 1990s has brought considerable progress in modes of empirical analysis. In the introduction to the previous edition to this book, I observed that the great empirical task of the future would be to identify what processes mediate the long-term effects of early intervention for economically disadvantaged children. With time, our analytic capacity has evolved to the point that we are beginning to perform this kind of investigation, as well as forms of analysis permitting a far more refined approach to identifying factors that contribute to program efficacy. From its origins in the mid-1970s, with Smith and Glass's (1977) study of psychotherapy outcomes, the era of meta-analysis has reached its prime, enabling us to undertake, as it were, "evaluative studies of evaluative studies" – systematic research on an ambitious scale that affords previously unattainable refinements in our knowledge of treatment effects (Lipsey & Wilson, 1993).

The meta-analysis performed by Lipsey and Wilson (1993) constitutes a dramatic milestone in the statistical evolution of early intervention research. In their masterful study, more than 300 reports of psychological, educational, and behavioral treatment programs were examined. Following an exhaustive and analytically sophisticated investigation of the treatment effects reported, Lipsey and Wilson's meta-analysis revealed "stark, dramatic patterns of evidence for the general efficacy of such treatment" (1993, p.1182). The authors noted that their findings stand in contrast to previous conventional reviews of research dealing with the issue of treatment efficacy, in which considerable variation among studies has prevented firm conclusions about the effectiveness of intervention in a broad sense.

Obviously, the analysis noted here cannot speak to the issue of relative efficacy among treatment models; not all treatments are equally effective. Nevertheless, the Lipsey and Wilson (1993) meta-analysis determined unequivocally that nearly every treatment examined had positive effects, even after the researchers accounted for methodological or availability biases or even placebo effects that may have

acted to skew the results in a positive direction. Their conclusions remained firm: Well-developed behavioral, educational, and psychological interventions generally have positive effects in terms of their intended outcomes.

Lest these results make us overly bold, however, we must remember the limits of this form of analysis, which is, as Lipsey and Wilson (1993) pointed out, only as powerful as the studies it attempts to examine in aggregate. In the decade to come, the need for more fine-grained analysis will continue, as will the imperative that we cast more light upon mediating processes. With the advent of this breakthrough work, however, research questions may now be more meaningfully framed. As Wilson and Lipsey, among others, concur, now that we have a clearer picture of general program efficacy, the major task is to identify which programs work best and how these results are achieved, as well as which components of programs are most essential to achieve maximum benefit. This latter question is critical, given the limited funding with which most intervention programs must be mounted and sustained. We still must grapple with the questions surrounding why some participants, albeit in similar circumstances, benefit more than others from similar programs.

Along with advances in knowledge and methodology throughout the 1990s, the intervention field has found itself revisited by some familiar arguments that many workers believed had long ago been put to rest. For decades, we in early intervention have been fighting the good fight over the true goals of Head Start, not to increase IQ per se but to increase social competence, help the child meet social expectancies, and assist children living in poverty to prepare for formal schooling. During these decades, I and my colleagues have resisted formidable attempts to make Head Start a program with solely a cognitive emphasis, and we have encouraged program evaluators to investigate other, broader program benefits for participant children and their families, in addition to possible cognitive gains. To a large extent we have been successful in bringing attention back to the program's original goals, as I and the other founders perceived them. Recent evaluative efforts have expanded the scope of inquiry considerably beyond cognitive achievement-style tests. Notably, the ongoing Family and Child Experiences Survey (FACES) is undertaking an assessment of the effects and possible benefits of the Head Start program in which a nationally representative sample is being used. The study focuses on both parent and child outcomes and includes such assessment tools as child observation, as well as measures of social awareness and social skills, story concepts, and the ability to engage successfully in activities with peers. The survey will be completed in 2001.

Against this background, in which intervention programs generally and a number of well-known projects (e.g., the Chicago Child Parent Center program [Reynolds, in press] in particular) have been and continue to be shown to have significant far-reaching benefits for children and their families, it is extraordinary to come upon a recurrence of the following two arguments. These are 1) that changes in IQ, academic achievement, or both constitute the only proper measures of an intervention program's success and 2) that no study has revealed that substantial long-term changes in these areas have been produced by early educational intervention (Detterman & Thompson, 1997). Thus, we face a new controversy in the field of early intervention, yet it is reminiscent of the controversies of old, from which we so recently seemed to have emerged.

The 1997 article by Detterman and Thompson that has given rise to the controversy focuses on the field of special education, yet its arguments are extended to all intervention programs, under which category we may place special education. Detterman and Thompson hold that a fair measure of the efficacy of special education and of early intervention programs generally is the programs' ability to raise IQ, the level of academic achievement, or both. As a seasoned worker in the mental retardation as well as the early intervention fields, I must take issue with both the manner in which these authors frame the question of program efficacy and how they purport to answer it. Having stated the avowed and actual purpose of such programs incorrectly, Dettermen and Thompson then assail all special education and other intervention programs in terms of failure to meet goals that they themselves, not those who designed the programs, identify (see Symons & Warren, 1998). The authors stated that there are only two goals special education can have: raising the mean level of performance on IQ tests, reducing the standard deviation of performance, or both (Detterman & Thompson,

1997). Briefly, I believe that few, if any, individuals working in the special education field would countenance such a narrow and even rather mechanistic representation of the field's aspirations for the individuals it serves. Rather than attempt a full refutation of the arguments and research interpretations of Detterman and Thompson here, I refer to the excellent points raised by my colleagues (Ramey & Landesman-Ramey, 1998; Symons & Warren, 1998; Keogh, Forness, & MacMillan, 1998).

This is not the place to enter the fray or rather to re-enter a former battleground. The point I would like to raise is that the field of intervention as a whole has moved beyond the limited considerations of IQ and academic competence. At one time, measures of cognitive performance were, I believe, overused in the evaluation of program effectiveness. More than 20 years ago, I encouraged our colleagues to look beyond the narrow cognitive focus to the broader bases of human functioning in society – the cluster of skills that make up the construct of social competence (Zigler & Trickett, 1978). Early intervention programs that have succeeded in achieving long-term benefits are not narrowly focused. They are typically comprehensive broad-based programs with strong parental involvement components (Center for the Future of Children, 1985; Seitz, 1990). Thus, such programs frequently benefit two generations.

One exemplar among several highly successful programs, the Prenatal Early Childhood Nurse Home Visitation Program, has demonstrated long-term positive effects on the life course of both parents and children. The program's effects include an 80% reduction in child abuse, as well as positive effects on birth spacing and a reduction in substance abuse and criminality (Olds, 1997). Another well-known intervention program, the Perry Preschool Project, has followed its participant children for more than 20 years. The benefits shown include reduced rates of criminality, decreased teen pregnancy, increased high school graduation rates and employment, as well as higher academic achievement (Schweinhart, Barnes, & Weikart, 1993). Particularly when both parent and child reap benefits, program effectiveness is extended to the community as a whole, in economic as well as in quality of life terms. Another advance in the field of early intervention has been the rise of economic cost-benefit analysis of programs. The benchmark study of the Perry

Preschool Project, which identified a $4 savings for every dollar invested in preschool education (Barnett, 1985), marked the beginning of a new era of demonstrable economic advantage associated with high-quality intervention programs. A more recent follow-up of the Perry Preschool children at age 27 determined that the savings totaled $7 for every dollar spent on the program (Schweinhart, Barnes, & Weikart, 1993). A description of the current status of this developing field is found in this edition of the handbook.

As social competence has grown into its rightful place in the world of early intervention, we have welcomed another still somewhat ambiguous construct – school readiness. These two foci are not dissimilar, and I believe the acceptance of school readiness as a focus for organizing our efforts marks a wholesome trend in the evolution of the field. Originally presented as the first of the National Education Goals, school readiness is likely to include, as its definition evolves, many of the abilities we recognize as essential facets of social development: the capacity to communicate and interact positively with peers and adults, a healthy self-concept, the ability to self-regulate, the ability to use language, and the like. Our responsibility must be to watch over the development of the idea of readiness, to guide its progress to insure that it is used in an inclusive manner, and to nurture the growth of all children and not to segregate them.

The publication of this volume is an extraordinary achievement. It is not merely a revision of the former edition; it is a compendium representative of current work by the best thinkers in our field. This handbook builds on the sound foundation of the prior effort, yet it goes well beyond it in examining developing areas of knowledge. Noteworthy among these areas are investigations of topics as diverse and essential as community characteristics, mental health issues in early childhood, and the neurobiology of early intervention. The topics addressed in this volume are clearly at the forefront of our knowledge, in which growth is most vigorous and most exciting to witness. In some cases, as in the study of the economics of early intervention, we eagerly await the newest findings; in others, as in the chapter on transactional regulation and program ecology, we are given the opportunity to deepen our understanding of subtle new ways of approaching and interpreting the

life of a program. These are stimulating chapters indeed, which together should have the dual effect of making the field proud of its accomplishments while invigorating its workers for the challenging tasks that lie ahead. The authors have my enthusiastic congratulations, as well as my admiration and gratitude for producing what will certainly prove the essential early intervention guidebook for the next decade.

Edward F. Zigler
Yale University

REFERENCES

Barnett, W. S. (1985). *The Perry Preschool Project and its long-term effects: A benefit-cost analysis.* High/Scope Early Childhood Policy Papers (No. 2) Ypsilanti, MI: High/Scope Press.

Carnegie Corporation of New York. (1996). *Years of promise. The Report of the Carnegie Task Force on Learning in the Primary Grades.* New York: Author.

Center for the Future of Children. (1995). *Long-term outcomes of early childhood programs.* David and Lucile Packard Foundation: Author.

Detterman, D. K., & Thompson, L. A. (1997). What is so special about special education? *American Psychologist, 52,* 1082–90.

Keogh, B. K., Forness, S. R., & MacMillan, D. L. (1998). The real world of special education. Comment on Detterman & Thompson. *American Psychologist, 53,* 1161–62.

Kotulak, R. (1996). *Inside the brain: Revolutionary discoveries of how the mind works.* Kansas City, MO: Andrews and McNeel.

Lipsey, M., & Wilson, D. B. (1993). The efficacy of psychological, educational, and behavioral treatment: Confirmation from meta-analysis. *American Psychologist, 48,* 1181–209.

Olds, D., Eckenrode, J., Henderson, C., Kitzman, H., Powers, J., Cole, R., Sidora, K., Morris, P., Pettitt, C., & Luckey, D. (1997). Long-term effects of home visitation on maternal life course and child abuse and neglect: Fifteen year follow-up of a randomized trial. *Journal of the American Medical Association, 278,* 637–43.

Ramey, C. T., & Landesman-Ramey, S. (1998). In defense of special education. Comment on Detterman and Thompson. *American Psychologist, 53,* 1159–60.

Reynolds, A. J. (in press). *Success in early intervention: The Chicago Child–Parent Centers and youth through age 15.* Lincoln: University of Nebraska Press.

Schweinhart, L. J., Barnes, H. V., & Weikart, D. P. (1993). *Significant benefits: The High/Scope Perry Preschool study through age 27*. Monographs of the High/Scope Educational Research Foundation (No. 10) Ypsilanti, MI: The High/Scope Press.

Seitz, V. (1990). Intervention programs for impoverished children: A comparison of educational and family support models. *Annals of Child Development, 7*, 73–103.

Shore, R. (1997). *Rethinking the brain: New insights into early development.* New York: Families and Work Institute.

Smith, M. L., & Glass, G. V. (1997). Meta-analysis of psychotherapy outcome studies. *American Psychologist, 52*, 752–60.

Symons, F. J., & Warren, S. F. (1998). Straw men and strange logic: Issues and pseudo-issues in special education. Comment on Detterman & Thompson. *American Psychologist, 53*, 1160–1.

Zigler, E. F., & Trickett, P. K. (1978). IQ, social competence, and the evaluation of early childhood intervention programs. *American Psychologist, 33*, 789–98.

Preface

Like the first edition, the second edition of this *Handbook of Early Childhood Intervention* is designed to integrate the science, policy, and practice of early childhood intervention in order to serve as a comprehensive vehicle for communication across the many disciplines and perspectives that contribute to this complex and continually evolving field. Since the 1960s, we have witnessed the transformation of this arena from a modest collection of pilot projects with a primitive empirical foundation, precarious funding, and virtually no public mandate, to a multidimensional domain of theory, research, practice, and policy. Today, the world of early childhood intervention contains a growing knowledge base, a dynamic service enterprise, and a highly significant policy agenda.

Early childhood intervention is based on three underlying assumptions. The first is rooted in a set of fundamental principles of contemporary biological and psychological research – namely, that all organisms are designed to adapt to their environment and that behavior and developmental potential are neither predetermined at birth by fixed genetic factors nor immutably limited by a strict critical period beyond which change is impossible.

The second assumption is that the development of young children can only be fully appreciated and understood within a broad ecological context. Beginning with a core understanding of the family as a dynamic system, this perspective extends outwards to include the complex, interactive influences of the child's immediate community and the broader social, economic, and political environment in which

he or she lives. This contextual framework sets the stage for all aspects of intervention from prevention and identification of developmental concerns through assessment, service delivery, program evaluation, and the formulation of policy.

The third assumption reflects the essential interdisciplinary nature of the field. Because the developmental opportunities and challenges confronting young children are so diverse, the range of services and supports required to meet their needs is extensive. Consequently, the practice of early intervention incorporates a host of program models, providers, and systems that combine a wide range of professional disciplines, including education, psychology, medicine, social work, child care, speech and language pathology, occupational and physical therapy, nursing, and public health. A thorough understanding of early childhood intervention requires a willingness to engage in professional pluralism, a recognition that no single prescription can be applied universally, and a realization that a univariate research focus cannot capture adequately all of its dynamics.

These three assumptions inform the following general definition for the field:

Early childhood intervention consists of multidisciplinary services provided to children from birth to 5 years of age to promote child health and well-being, enhance emerging competencies, minimize developmental delays, remediate existing or emerging disabilities, prevent functional deterioration, and promote adaptive parenting and overall family functioning. These goals are accomplished by providing individualized developmental, educational, and therapeutic services for children in conjunction with mutually planned support for their families.

The basic design and organization of this handbook reflect these underlying assumptions and definition. Designed as a core textbook for those who are interested in young, vulnerable children and their families, this volume is addressed to a diverse audience involved in academic training programs, research and scholarly endeavors, policy development, and sevice provision.

The book is divided into seven sections. The first consists of an introductory chapter that places the concept of early childhood intervention in a historical context and identifies new challenges to be addressed by the field in the coming years. The second section examines multiple sources of vulnerability (biological, familial, and sociocultural) that can have deleterious effects on human development, as well as protective factors that serve as buffers against risk. The next section explores four theoretical frameworks that present a strong rationale for early childhood intervention, including transactional, psychodynamic, behavioral–educational, and neurobiological approaches. The following section examines current challenges to assessment in four domains: the child, the parent–child relationship, the family, and the community.

Next, several models of service delivery are explored in depth. These chapters reflect the multiple approaches to systems organization that mark the contemporary landscape of early childhood intervention. They range from universally required services (e.g., preventive health care), to high prevalence societal needs (e.g., early child care and education), and to specialized programs for targeted populations (e.g., developmental disabilities and mental health services). The section concludes with chapters on the roles of paraprofessionals and current approaches to personnel preparation.

Although every chapter in the handbook carefully reviews relevant research in depth, the sixth section identifies four discrete areas of efficacy and effectiveness research for more systematic scrutiny. The first chapter in this section critically analyzes a range of investigative approaches to the evaluation of service impacts. The second comprehensively reviews current knowledge about the effects of programs on children. The third chapter in this section examines research on family outcomes, and the last considers research concerning the economic costs and benefits of intervention.

The book's final section explores a selection of policy and programmatic challenges facing the field. Included are chapters on international approaches to early childhood policies, services, and family support programs; reflections on evolving models of family–professional relationships; and a comprehensive analysis of the multidimensional concept of developmental resilience. These chapters are intended to highlight emerging issues and to examine some of the complex interactions among knowledge, policy, and advocacy that are central to the future development of the field's scope and impact.

The contributors to this handbook include many of the most distinguished leaders in the field. The breadth of scholarship contained in this volume reflects the diversity and the richness of the early childhood knowledge base at the dawn of the twenty-first century. Our hope is that this book will cast both the past and the present in sharp relief and will promote a dynamic interaction between science and practice that will assure the continued vitality and growth of the field and will lead to improved outcomes for vulnerable young children and their families.

One of the special pleasures of working in the world of early childhood intervention is the opportunity it affords to develop an abundance of personal and professional relationships, reflected in no small measure by the equally shared editorial responsibility (and alternating order of authorship) that has characterized the creation of both the first and second editions of this handbook. To the many mentors, colleagues, trainees, students, parents, and children who have taught us so much over the years (and whose names, if listed, would fill many pages), we want to express our deepest gratitude. Above all, we are highly indebted to the talented contributors to this book, without whom this project could not have come to fruition. Finally, to our families, Fredi, Michael, and Adam Shonkoff and Alice, Seth, and Reba Meisels, we express our deepest appreciation for teaching us about the magic of parenting and the treasures of family relationships – from conception through the emergence of adulthood.

Jack P. Shonkoff
Samuel J. Meisels

Contributors

Sally Atkins-Burnett, School of Education, The University of Michigan

Kathryn E. Barnard, Ph.D., Child Development and Mental Retardation Center, University of Washington

W. Steven Barnett, Ph.D., Graduate School of Education, Rutgers University

Lisa J. Berlin, Ph.D., Teachers College, Columbia University

Jeanne Brooks-Gunn, Ph.D., Teachers College, Columbia University

Stephen Buka, Ph.D., School of Public Health, Harvard University

Cynthia García Coll, Ph.D., Department of Pediatrics, Brown University

Paul H. Dworkin, M.D., Department of Pediatrics, Saint Francis Hospital and Medical Center, University of Connecticut School of Medicine

Felton Earls, M.D., School of Public Health, Harvard University

Robert N. Emde, M.D., Department of Psychiatry, School of Medicine, University of Colorado Health Science Center

Dale C. Farran, Ph.D., Peabody College, Vanderbilt University

Barbara H. Fiese, Ph.D., Department of Psychology, Syracuse University

Allison Sidle Fuligni, Teachers College, Columbia University

James J. Gallagher, Ph.D., Frank Porter Graham Child Development Center, University of North Carolina-Chapel Hill

Barbara Ganzel, Family Life Development Center, Cornell University

James Garbarino, Ph.D., Family Life Development Center, Cornell University

Linda Gilkerson, Ph.D., Erikson Institute

Robert Halpern, Ph.D., Erikson Institute

Gloria Harbin, Ph.D., Frank Porter Graham Child Development Center, University of North Carolina-Chapel Hill

Penny Hauser-Cram, Ed.D., School of Education, Boston College

Sharon Lynn Kagan, Ph.D., Bush Center for Child Development and Social Policy, Yale University

Sheila Kamerman, Ph.D., School of Social Work, Columbia University

Jean F. Kelly, Ph.D., Child Development and Mental Retardation Center, University of Washington

Nancy K. Klein, Ph.D., College of Education, Cleveland State University

Jane Knitzer, Ph.D., National Center for Children in Poverty, Columbia University

Marty Wyngaarden Krauss, Ph.D., The Heller Graduate School, Brandeis University

Katherine Magnuson, Institute for Policy Research, Northwestern University

Paul C. Marshall, M.D., Department of Pediatrics, University of Massachusetts Medical School

R. A. McWilliam, Ph.D., Frank Porter Graham Child Development Center, University of North Carolina-Chapel Hill

Samuel J. Meisels, Ed.D., School of Education, The University of Michigan

Judith Musick, Ph.D., Ounce of Prevention Fund

Charles A. Nelson, Ph.D., Institute of Child Development, University of Minnesota

Michelle J. Neuman, Bush Center for Child Development and Social Policy, Yale University

Joy D. Osofsky, Ph.D., Departments of Pediatrics and Psychiatry, Louisiana State University Medical Center

JoAnn Robinson, Ph.D., Department of Psychiatry, School of Medicine, University of Colorado Health Science Center

Sir Michael Rutter, M.D., MRC Child Psychiatry, University of London

Arnold J. Sameroff, Ph.D., Center for Human Growth & Development, The University of Michigan

Jack P. Shonkoff, M.D., The Heller Graduate School, Brandeis University

Frances Stott, Ph.D., Erikson Institute

M. Dewana Thompson, Departments of Pediatrics and Psychiatry, Louisiana State University Medical Center

Vicki Turbiville, School of Education, University of Kansas

Ann Turnbull, Ph.D., School of Education, University of Kansas

H. R. Turnbull, J.D., School of Education, University of Kansas

Carole C. Upshur, Ph.D., University of Massachusetts-Boston

Marji Erickson Warfield, Ph.D., Department of Pediatrics, University of Massachusetts Medical School

Thomas S. Weisner, Ph.D., Departments of Psychiatry & Anthropology, University of California at Los Angeles

Emmy E. Werner, Ph.D., Department of Human & Community Development, University of California at Davis

Mark Wolery, Ph.D., Frank Porter Graham Child Development Center, University of North Carolina-Chapel Hill

PART ONE

INTRODUCTION

CHAPTER ONE

Early Childhood Intervention:

A Continuing Evolution

SAMUEL J. MEISELS AND JACK P. SHONKOFF

Children are the touchstone of a healthy and sustainable society. How a culture or society treats its youngest members has a significant influence on how it will grow, prosper, and be viewed by others. In the words of the Carnegie Corporation's 1996 report, entitled *Starting Points: Meeting the Needs of Our Youngest Children*, it is these children

whose boundless energy is matched only by their curiosity and creativity, whose agility is the envy of their parents and teachers, [and] whose openness and expressiveness are always remarkable and occasionally breathtaking. Watching them, it is easy to believe that they can do anything they want to do, be anyone they want to be; it is easy to summon the optimism that yet a new generation is rising to fuel this nation's historical belief in endless possibility. (p. 3)

Nevertheless, not all children are born healthy; not all children have access to good nutrition, adequate health care, and acceptable housing; not all children are raised by parents who can comfort, nurture, and challenge them appropriately; and not all children are born free of disabilities or other biological vulnerabilities. It is the mission of early childhood intervention to help young children and their families to thrive. The fundamental challenge that faces early intervention services is to merge the knowledge and insights of scholars and practitioners with the creative talents of those who design and implement social policy initiatives and to invest the products of this alliance in the future of our children and thereby in the well-being of our society as a whole.

The mandate to provide support and to intervene on behalf of infants and young children – especially those who are vulnerable, disabled, or at risk – appears, at first glance, to be a straightforward goal. One would think that a child with a disability, or one whose early life experiences are dominated by the material deprivations of poverty or by the caregiving of an overwhelmed, isolated, or abusive parent, would be the uncontested beneficiary of adequately funded public services. Indeed, many researchers and advocates have proposed that the allocation of resources for this most vulnerable and disenfranchised population group should be based simply on its moral imperative (e.g., Caldwell, 1986; Children's Defense Fund, 1998; Edelman, 1987; National Commission on Children, 1991; Schorr, 1988; Turnbull & Turnbull, 1985). Moreover, evidence is emerging that an "investment" in the health and development of young children will also return monetary dividends in the subsequent, decreased need for special education, custodial care, welfare support, and incarceration for delinquent behavior (Barnett, 1985; Barnett, this volume; Council of Economic Advisers, 1997; Karoly et al., 1998; Warfield, 1994; Zigler, Taussig, & Black, 1992).

Despite its intrinsic appeal, however, early childhood intervention has not been embraced uniformly or supported consistently. It has endured battles over the delineation of its goals and objectives (Casto & White, 1993; Clarke & Clarke, 1976; Ferry, 1981; White, Taylor, & Moss, 1992), specification of program models and methods (Anastasiow & Mansergh, 1975; Meisels, Dichtelmiller, & Liaw,

3

1993), and selection of service providers and recipients (Bricker & Slentz, 1988; Gallagher, Malone, Cleghorne, & Helms, 1997; Neuman, Hagedorn, Celano, & Daly, 1995). It has tried to respond to the challenge to document its effectiveness while struggling with the methodological and logistical constraints of inadequate outcome measures, unavoidable sample attrition, limited funds to sustain long-term longitudinal studies, and ethical barriers to the maintenance of untreated control groups of children with documented problems (Meisels, 1985a; Shonkoff, 1992; Shonkoff & Hauser-Cram, 1987; Shonkoff, Hauser-Cram, Krauss, & Upshur, 1988).

The history of early childhood intervention in the United States illustrates the power of an idea and set of practices that continue to evolve over time. Whereas its early roots were established in a variety of fields that have converged over the past four decades, its theoretical foundation continues to grow and mature from both its successes and disappointments. On the threshold of the twenty-first century, the concept of early childhood intervention faces a formidable array of political, practical, and theoretical challenges and opportunities. Its antecedent pathways and their links to the tasks of the present and the future are the focus of this chapter.

The chapter is divided into four sections. The first explores the diverse origins of the field of early childhood intervention prior to the 1960s. The second section provides an overview of the dramatic advances of the past four decades. The third focuses on the provisions of the landmark federal special education law that mandates comprehensive family-centered services for young children with developmental disabilities and delays. Finally, the chapter closes with an examination of the conceptual and programmatic challenges facing the field at the beginning of the twenty-first century.

HISTORICAL ROOTS AND EARLY FOUNDATIONS

The overall framework of contemporary early childhood intervention has evolved from multiple sources. This section focuses on the historical contributions of four related domains: early childhood education, maternal and child health services, special education, and child development research.

Early Childhood Education

The intellectual roots of early childhood education can be traced to the relatively recent historical recognition of childhood as a unique period of life and to the writings of the European philosophers of the seventeenth and eighteenth centuries (Aries, 1962). Comenius (1592–1670) characterized the "School of the Mother" as the most appropriate vehicle for education in the first six years of life and advocated that the child learn "spontaneously . . . in play whatever may be learned at home" (Eller, 1956, p. 116, cited by Clarke-Stewart & Fein, 1983). John Locke (1632–1704) popularized the notion of the tabula rasa, suggesting that children from birth are a blank slate, thereby challenging the commonly held concept of genetically predetermined behavior and competence. Jean-Jacques Rousseau (1712–78), an even stronger advocate of a child's unspoiled nature, urged a laissez-faire approach to the early childhood years to allow for the natural unfolding of individual talents. These views were largely echoed by the nineteenth-century educational experiments of Tolstoy (1967) and by those of A. S. Neill (1960) and other school reformers in the latter half of the twentieth century. In contrast to the humanistic child development attitudes of eighteenth- and nineteenth-century Europe, child-rearing practices in the American colonies during the seventeenth and eighteenth centuries were dominated by a harsh Puritan influence, which focused on spiritual salvation and advocated rigid discipline in early education to counteract the innate "sinful" tendencies of young children (Greven, 1973; Wishy, 1968).

KINDERGARTEN. The first formal kindergarten classes, which were based on a philosophy grounded in traditional religious values and in a belief in the importance of learning through supervised play, were established in Germany by Friedrich Froebel in the early 1800s (Brosterman, 1997). During the latter half of the nineteenth century, these ideas were transported across the Atlantic and stimulated the proliferation of experimental programs throughout the United States (Cuban, 1992). Shortly after the first public school kindergarten was established in St. Louis in 1872, the National Education Association made an official recommendation that kindergarten become a regular part of the public school system (Peterson, 1987).

The interactive influences of industrialization, urbanization, and secularization provided the social context in which the kindergarten movement developed in the nineteenth-century United States. With much early support coming from private agencies and philanthropic groups, advocates of formal kindergarten programs emphasized the potential benefits for poor children and focused particularly on recent U.S. immigrants and those who were living in urban slums (Braun & Edwards, 1972; Cremin, 1988).

Within a few decades of its early popularization in the United States, however, the kindergarten movement was beset with a series of battles over goals and curricula. Traditionalists remained loyal to the philosophy of Froebel and defended their value-driven educational practices. In contrast, reformists worked to liberalize the kindergarten experience and looked beyond its moralistic foundation to the emerging discipline of child psychology for more empirically derived principles based on the systematic observations, data collection, and analyses of early child development researchers (Hill, cited in Braun & Edwards, 1972). During the early 1900s, G. Stanley Hall's developmental approach to early childhood curriculum and John Dewey's pragmatic emphasis on the functional purposes of education were particularly influential.

As research about the developmental process progressed, and as social and political forces shifted, sharp disagreements over the goals of kindergarten persisted throughout the twentieth century (Bredekamp & Copple, 1997; Hirsch, 1996). Its primary objectives alternated between an emphasis on early academic achievement and an emphasis on social and emotional development, including exploration and discovery of the world. Although publicly supported kindergarten programs are not yet mandated in all parts of the country, kindergarten is considered a standard component of the American education system and has become instrumental in introducing child development ideas to the educational mainstream.

NURSERY SCHOOLS. Similar to kindergartens, nursery schools originated in Europe. In 1910, Rachel and Margaret MacMillan established the first nursery school in London, which began as a health clinic that was later expanded into an open-air school. This experimental program was designed to provide comprehensive prevention-oriented services to meet young children's social, physical, emotional, and intellectual needs. Unlike the religious orientation of Froebel's kindergarten, the MacMillans' curriculum was based on secular social values and focused on the development of self-care, individual responsibility, and educational readiness skills (Peterson, 1987).

While the MacMillans developed their model of early medical–educational intervention in England, Maria Montessori opened the first nursery school in the slums of Rome. Montessori, a physician and former director of an institution for children with mental retardation, applied the methods she had developed for training children with intellectual impairments to the preschool education of nondisabled, urban, poor children. The Montessori method departed significantly from traditional early childhood curricula in its emphasis on individualized self-teaching by children within a carefully prepared classroom environment (Elkind, 1967).

The initial introduction of the Montessori approach to preschool education in the United States had minimal impact, as it was lost amidst the battles then being waged among the Froebelian conservatives, the liberal–progressive adherents of the philosophy of Dewey, and the newly emerging "American" positivism championed by such prominent psychologists as Thorndike and Kilpatrick (Braun & Edwards, 1972). Consequently, interest in the Montessori method remained essentially dormant in the United States until the 1960s. The rise in its popularity in the latter half of this century, however, has been greatest among the middle classes, rather than among those who work with poor or disabled children – the populations for whom the method was originally designed (Peterson, 1987).

The nursery school movement first gained popularity in the United States in the 1920s, based upon an adaptation of the MacMillans' model that attached a great deal of importance to parent involvement within the school program. In contrast to the kindergarten focus on school readiness, early nursery school programs were designed to nurture exploration and to facilitate social–emotional development. By the early 1930s, approximately 200 nursery schools existed in the United States, half of which were associated with colleges and universities, including some of the most productive child development laboratories in the country. The remaining programs were operated as private schools or were sponsored by child welfare agencies (Peterson, 1987).

During the Depression of the 1930s, the number of nursery schools increased dramatically as federal relief programs were developed to subsidize unemployed teachers. With the onset of World War II, the need for women to work in defense plants led to further expansion of the schools and to the establishment of federally supported day care centers under the Lanham Act of 1940 (Morgan, 1972). Prior to this period, child care services were utilized primarily by the working poor. The employment of large numbers of middle-class women to support the war effort blurred the distinctions between day care programs and nursery schools. After the war ended, however, federal support for child care terminated, large numbers of women left the workforce to raise families, and many programs closed. Without public resources, nursery schools drifted from their early mission of serving poor children and became increasingly available only to those who could afford private tuition.

In recent years, as women have chosen or been compelled by circumstances to combine both child rearing and employment outside the home, the distinctions between child care programs and nursery schools have become blurred once again (see Kamerman, this volume). In this social context, the debate about the balance between "care" and "education" in the early preschool years has resumed with considerable intensity (see Barnett & Frede, 1993; Hauser-Cram, Pierson, Walker, & Tivnan, 1991; Kahn & Kamerman, 1987; Kamerman & Kahn, 1995; Provence, Naylor, & Patterson, 1977).

SUMMARY. An examination of the historical roots of early childhood education in the United States tells us much about our enduring traditions and changing values. First, it reveals a willingness to explore ideas that were developed in other societies and a determination to adapt them to our own perceived needs. Second, it emphasizes the extent to which the interests of young children and their families are always addressed within the constraints of concurrent political and social demands. Third, it highlights the degree to which early childhood

programs have alternatively been developed to meet the needs of poor children or middle-class children and their families. Finally, it underlines the extent of inevitable overlap that exists among the generic health, educational, and social needs of all young children regardless of socioeconomic status.

Early childhood intervention services have been influenced significantly by our history of education for young children prior to traditional school entry. The central features of these early programs that have become firmly embedded in current intervention efforts include a child-centered curriculum focus; an emphasis on early socialization of the child outside of the family; an enhanced understanding of child development and the practical applications of developmental theory; and a belief in the importance of the early years as a foundation for later social, emotional, and intellectual competence. This conceptual legacy, in conjunction with the wealth of materials, resources, and techniques that have been refined over the years, is woven throughout the day-to-day activities of contemporary early intervention programs.

Maternal and Child Health Services

In much the same way that the industrialization and secularization of the nineteenth century provided fertile ground for the development of new concepts in early childhood education, persistently high mortality rates among young children promoted greater concern for their physical health. In fact, many pediatric authorities in the late 1800s urged a de-emphasis on educational stimulation before five years of age to prevent the diversion of "vital forces" from activities that promoted physical well-being (Griffith, 1895; Holmes, 1857). In a classic textbook, one of the most prominent pediatricians at the turn of the century wrote:

Great injury is done to the nervous system of children by the influences with which they are surrounded during infancy, especially during the first year... Playing with young children, stimulating to laughter and exciting them by sights, sounds, or movements until they shriek with apparent delight may be a source of amusement to fond parents and admiring spectators, but it is almost invariably an injury to the child... It is the plain duty of the physician to enlighten parents upon this point, and insist that the infant shall be kept quiet, and that all such playing and romping as has been referred to shall, during the first year at least, be absolutely prohibited. (Holt, 1897, p. 5)

THE CHILDREN'S BUREAU. In 1912, in an attempt to address the widespread problems of high infant mortality, poor physical health, and exploitation of working children, Congress established a Children's Bureau in the Department of Labor "to investigate and report . . . upon all matters pertaining to the welfare of children and child life among all classes of our people" (quoted in Lesser, 1985, p. 591). In its first annual report, the Bureau acknowledged its responsibility to serve all children but noted that particular attention would be focused on "those who were abnormal or subnormal or suffering from physical or mental ills" (Bradbury, 1962, cited in Lesser, 1985, p. 591). On the basis of a decision to emphasize the concept of prevention, and having addressed the issue of infant mortality as the object of its first investigation, the Children's Bureau proceeded to conduct early studies in such subject areas as day care, institutional care, mental retardation, the health of preschool children in selected cities, and the care of "crippled children" (Lesser, 1985).

As the first official acknowledgment of a federal responsibility for children's welfare, the establishment of the Children's Bureau provided a foundation for governmental data collection and federal grants to promote the health and development of the nation's most vulnerable children. In its earliest studies, the Bureau highlighted striking correlations between socioeconomic factors and infant and maternal deaths. These data established a firm justification for programs supported by the Sheppard-Towner Act during the 1920s that increased public health nursing services and stimulated the creation of state child hygiene divisions and permanent maternal and child health centers throughout the country (Steiner, 1976).

Although the development of programs for children with disabilities progressed more slowly than services for those who were poor, data collected by the Children's Bureau through its state surveys served to highlight marked unmet needs in this area as well. Consequently, the 1930 White House Conference on Child Health and Protection recommended that federal funds be made available to each of the states to establish programs for "crippled children" that reflected cooperation among medical, educational, social welfare, and vocational rehabilitation agencies to provide a comprehensive array of diagnostic and treatment services (Lesser, 1985).

TITLE V. When the Social Security Act was enacted in 1935, the importance of a federal responsibility for the well-being of children and their mothers was reinforced explicitly. Title V of this landmark legislation contained three major components that established the framework for resource allocation and program development that has influenced national health policy for children and families over the succeeding half century (see Magee & Pratt, 1985).

Part I (Maternal and Child Health Services) authorized financial assistance to states to develop services designed to promote the general health of mothers and children, with special emphasis on program initiatives for rural and economically depressed areas. The most common activities supported by such funds included prenatal care, well-baby clinics, school health services, immunization programs, public health nursing, nutrition services, and health education.

Part II (Services for Crippled Children) created the first federal program in which state funds were matched by federal funds in the provision of medical services to a targeted patient group. The law was clear in its intent to develop a comprehensive service system, including case finding, diagnosis, treatment, and follow-up care. The prevention of "crippling" diseases and the amelioration of secondary handicaps were highlighted as central goals, and each state was required to promote cooperative efforts between health and welfare groups to achieve such ends. The definition of crippled children was left to the states and, although more than three-quarters of those who received services in the 1930s and 1940s had orthopedic problems, by the mid-1950s that proportion had dropped to less than 50% as increasing numbers of children with other chronic disabilities (e.g., heart disease, seizure disorders, and so forth) were identified.

Part III (Child Welfare Services) of the Title V program authorized funding to state welfare agencies to develop programs (especially in rural areas) for the care and protection of homeless, dependent, and neglected children, as well as children considered to be in danger of becoming delinquents (Lesser, 1985).

In 1939, nonmatching Title V funds were appropriated for "special projects of regional and national significance" (SPRANS grants), thus enabling states to develop innovative programs beyond the core of mandated services. Subsequently, these grants provided support for such wide-ranging initiatives as improved care for premature infants, training of professionals, and applied research on children with a wide variety of chronic illnesses and disabling conditions, including sensory impairments, seizure disorders, and congenital heart disease.

EPSDT. In 1965, the Medicaid provisions of the Social Security Act (Title XIX) were signed into law to improve the quality and accessibility of medical services for all those living in poverty. Although designed primarily as a medical reimbursement program to be administered by the states and jointly financed by state and federal funds, Medicaid does include mandated programs that reflect specific federal interest in early childhood intervention for poor children. One of the best known of these efforts is the Early and Periodic Screening, Diagnosis, and Treatment Program (EPSDT).

EPSDT was initiated in the late 1960s as part of a national effort to improve the health and welfare of poor children. It mandated the early and periodic medical, dental, vision, and developmental screening, diagnosis, and treatment of all children and youth under 21 years of age whose families qualified for Medicaid eligibility. Recognition of the wide-ranging and apparently preventable problems among the nation's youth was one of the incentives for formulating and enacting this new program (Foltz, 1982). Thus, EPSDT was designed to ensure early identification of such problems and to provide funds for subsequent intervention. Indeed, this program was conceived as an attempt to break the cycle of poverty, to remedy the health consequences of uneven economic circumstances, and to improve poor children's health by providing services designed to have a high payoff in later well-being (Meisels, 1984). Unfortunately, EPSDT's record of success has been uneven, and as it continues into its fourth decade of existence – especially with recent changes in the welfare and Medicaid laws – its effectiveness has been impaired (Foltz,

1982; Margolis & Meisels, 1987; Meisels & Margolis, 1988; Ohlson, 1998).

SUMMARY. Unlike education, which is accepted as a traditional responsibility of state and federal government, health care services in the United States are provided by a complex amalgamation of public and private resources and delivery systems. Thus, any attempts on the part of the federal government to regulate or otherwise influence the organization or delivery of medical services are always met with some degree of organized opposition, noncompliance, or both, in the private sector. In this context, the early history and subsequent growth of publicly supported maternal and child health and crippled children's services are striking. Indeed, within the American political system, there is a persistent, powerful, underlying consensus that the care and protection of children's health is too important to be left to the "wisdom" of the free market, particularly for those who are poor or those who have a chronic disabling condition. The creation in 1997 of the State Children's Health Insurance Program (SCHIP) under Title XXI of the Social Security Act, during a period of marked public resistance to increased government spending, further underscores the political salience of child health concerns. Furthermore, as the single largest federal commitment to child health since the enactment of Medicaid, SCHIP moved beyond the domain of poverty to include the needs of uninsured children of low-income working families. Whether recent changes in health care management and reduced public health and welfare benefits will both have an adverse impact on child health and well-being have yet to be seen.

Special Education

The history of special education services for children with disabilities provides a third lens through which we can examine the evolution of early childhood intervention services. In ancient times, young children with physical anomalies or obvious disabilities were often the victims of active or passive euthanasia. During the Middle Ages and in succeeding centuries, individuals with mental retardation were either tolerated as court jesters or street beggars (see Ariès, 1962) or imprisoned or otherwise institutionalized (see Chase, 1980).

Most historical overviews of the field of special education begin with the attempts by Itard, in the late eighteenth century, to teach the "wild boy of Aveyron," using a set of sensory training techniques and what is currently characterized as behavior modification. However, Itard's student, Edouard Seguin, is generally acknowledged as the most important pioneer in this field. As director of the Hospice des Incurables in Paris, Seguin developed a "physiological method of education" for children with disabilities. This method was based on a detailed assessment of individual strengths and weaknesses and a specific plan of sensorimotor activities designed to correct discrete difficulties. Through painstaking observations, Seguin described the early signs of developmental delay and emphasized the importance of early education (Crissey, 1975). As noted earlier, his methods were later adapted by Montessori for the education of poor preschool children in Rome.

Seguin's pessimism about the benefits of special education initiated later in life was complemented by his belief in the critical importance of early intervention. He stated, "If the idiot cannot be reached by the first lessons of infancy, by what mysterious process will years open for him the golden doors of intelligence?" (quoted in Talbot, 1964, p. 62). Seguin was, indeed, one of the first "early interventionists."

RESIDENTIAL PLACEMENTS. Inspired by Seguin's work in Paris, educational programs for persons with mental retardation proliferated throughout the world during the early 1800s. In the latter half of the nineteenth century, residential institutions were built in the United States, and, stimulated by Seguin's immigration to this country, his teaching techniques were incorporated into many of these newly opened facilities. In 1876, the Association of Medical Officers of American Institutions for Idiotic and Feeble-Minded Persons was formed, with Seguin as its first president, to provide a mechanism for communication among those interested in the education of persons with mental retardation. (In 1906, the name of the organization was changed to the American Association for the Study of the Feeble-Minded; in 1933, it was changed again to the American Association on Mental Deficiency; and in 1987, the name was changed for the third time to the American Association on Mental Retardation). By the end of the nineteenth century,

residential institutions in the United States were well established, highly invested in the development of teaching strategies, and firmly committed to the integration, albeit in limited form, of persons with disabilities into community life (Crissey, 1975).

In the early decades of the twentieth century, however, residential institutions changed their mission from training and planned social integration to custodial supervision and isolation. Among the forces that influenced this dramatic shift were the activities of such prominent psychologists as Henry Goddard and Louis Terman, who embraced the prejudices of the eugenics movement and employed the newly developed technology of individual intelligence testing to identify specific groups for discrimination, if not systematic exclusion, from American society (Chase, 1980). Data providing "scientific validation" of the link between mental retardation and criminal behavior were disseminated, and intelligence test scores were used to justify the legislation of racist immigration restrictions and compulsory sterilization procedures for the "mentally defective" (Kamin, 1974). The psychology community's harsh rhetoric challenged the early optimism of special education, and residential institutions were transformed into dreary warehouses for neglected and forgotten individuals.

PUBLIC SCHOOL PROGRAMS. In the public schools, the development of special education programs began slowly and served relatively small numbers of children. Children with moderate-to-severe disabilities were either sent to institutions or kept at home, and most children with mild disabilities were simply enrolled in regular classes from which they ultimately dropped out at very high rates. During the Depression and the World War that followed, special education resources for the public schools were curtailed, and greater reliance was placed on already overcrowded and educationally limited residential institutions.

During the postwar period, children with disabilities began to receive more benevolent attention. This renewed interest in the needs of developmentally vulnerable children was stimulated in part by the results of massive testing of military personnel during World War II, which revealed the striking prevalence of young men and women with physical, mental, or behavioral disabilities. This interest was also stimulated by changes in societal attitudes toward disabled persons, in general, brought about by the large numbers of wounded veterans who returned with physical impairments. In 1946, a Section for Exceptional Children was established within the United States Office of Education, which later (in 1966) became the Bureau of Education for the Handicapped and then (in 1980) the Office of Special Education and Rehabilitation Services. By the late 1950s, state and federal legislation began to promote greater access to special education for wider segments of the population (Hobbs, 1975).

SUMMARY. Shifts in attitudes and practices regarding the education of children with disabilities have been described in evolutionary terms by Caldwell (1973), who identified three major historical periods. The first, labeled "Forget and Hide," refers to the practice in the first half of this century through which children with significant physical or intellectual handicaps were kept out of public view, presumably to avoid embarrassing their families. The second period corresponds to the prevailing attitudes of the 1950s and 1960s and is called "Screen and Segregate." In this period, children with disabilities were tested, labeled, and then isolated once again in special facilities, based on the assumption that they needed protection and could not function independently in the mainstream. Caldwell named the third period "Identify and Help." Beginning in the mid-1970s, with the passage of landmark special education legislation, this stage was marked by efforts to screen for special needs in the early years of life in the hopes of providing appropriate intervention services at as young an age as possible. We might add a fourth evolutionary period to describe the past 15 years in special education services, calling it "Educate and Include." The goals of this period (see Gartner & Lipsky, 1987; Turnbull, Turbiville, & Turnbull, this volume) are to contain the consequences of disabling conditions, prevent the occurrence of more severe disorders, empower the families of children with special needs, and increase the opportunities for all children to reach their full potential by integrating them as fully as possible into regular classrooms and society at large.

Child Development Research

Although fundamental decisions regarding program design and resource allocation are typically motivated by sociopolitical considerations, the evolving conceptual context of early childhood services has been influenced substantially by the scholarly study of the development of young children. Thus, a fourth lens through which the history of early childhood intervention can be examined focuses on the contributions of the academic child development community. Although a comprehensive overview of the history of child development research is beyond the scope of this chapter, a brief mention of several influential theoretical and empirical contributions is essential. In this regard, two critical research themes are addressed: the nature–nurture controversy and the importance of the caregiver–child relationship.

THE NATURE–NURTURE DEBATE. Interest in the determinants of competence in young children is a relatively modern phenomenon. Although systematic evaluations of the emerging abilities of infants were conducted by a New Orleans physician in the late nineteenth century (Chaille, 1887), the cataloguing of early achievements and the methods of childhood assessment were not well developed until the early decades of the twentieth century.

The dominant figure in the emerging field of child developmental evaluation was Arnold Gesell, a pediatrician and psychologist. As the director of one of several child study centers supported by the Laura Spelman Rockefeller Memorial Fund, Gesell conducted extensive studies of the skills of normally developing children, the abilities of youngsters with Down syndrome, and the developmental accomplishments of those who were born prematurely or who sustained perinatal injuries (Gesell, 1925, 1929). His observational methods produced a wealth of data that continue to influence to this day the construction of developmental assessment instruments.

Gesell's theoretical orientation was clear, and his impact on the clinical study of children was enormous. He strongly believed in the primacy of biologically determined maturation. He disdained the relative impact of experience on the developmental process, and he viewed the alteration of this process by early intervention as futile. Gesell's maturational perspective generated a linear model of human development that was used by clinicians to predict long-term outcomes based on the rate of acquisition of specific developmental milestones in early infancy. During the 1950s, this model was linked to the growing recognition of a correlation between adverse perinatal events and later neurodevelopmental disorders, which resulted in the popularization of an influential paradigm of biological determinism known as the "continuum of reproductive casualty" (Lilienfeld & Parkhurst, 1951; Lilienfeld & Pasamanick, 1954).

As the maturationist view of development attracted support during the first half of the twentieth century, its influence was countered by the comparably powerful concepts of behaviorism. The behaviorists believed that, in the absence of significant brain damage, developmental outcomes in children are controlled largely by environmental forces. John B. Watson, an early supporter of the interventionist approach to human development and a prominent psychologist, wrote:

Since the behaviorists find little that corresponds to instincts in children, since children are made not born, failure to bring up a happy child, a well adjusted child – assuming bodily health – falls upon the parents' shoulders. The acceptance of this view makes child rearing the most important of all social obligations. (Watson, 1928, p. 8)

The controversy over the relative impact of nature and nurture on the developmental process in early childhood has been an enduring one. While the maturationists championed the belief in biological determination, the behaviorists advocated the tenets of operant conditioning and environmental manipulation. Each position has had strong support. Yet, when examined in isolation, both perspectives have been found to be quite limited.

With the advent of Piaget's "cognitive revolution" in the 1950s and 1960s (Cairns, 1983), the stage was set for a rapprochement between the polarities of nature and nurture. This was facilitated by a recognition that biological and experiential factors in development mutually influence one another, thereby creating a need to go beyond the traditional

nature–nurture debate. In fact, research findings even led some scholars to adopt the paradoxical position that all behavior is completely inherited as well as completely determined by experience. As Goldberg (1982) noted, "Unless capacities for behavior are inherited, a behavior can never occur (e.g., chimpanzees will never talk regardless of what experiences are provided). But . . . the actual occurrence of behavior depends on appropriate experience (e.g., a human infant will not learn to speak without hearing the speech of others)" (pp. 35–6). In other words, many researchers began to acknowledge that the distinctions between biological and environmental explanations for developmental outcomes are, if not arbitrary and incomplete, at least ambiguous.

Sameroff and Chandler (1975) articulated one of the most influential conceptualizations of the reciprocal relationship between nature and nurture. In a challenge to the previously popular paradigm of a "continuum of reproductive casualty," they formulated the notion of a "continuum of caretaking casualty" to describe the transactional effects of familial, social, and environmental factors on human development. In Sameroff's (1975) terms, "Although reproductive casualties may play an initiating role in the production of later problems, it is the caretaking environment that will determine the ultimate outcome" (p. 274). For the field of early childhood intervention, acceptance of the transactional model of development meant that biological insults could be modified by environmental factors and that developmental vulnerabilities could have social and environmental etiologies. This focus on the bidirectionality of environmental and biological factors proved to have a major impact on both research and service delivery (Sameroff, Seifer, Baldwin, & Baldwin, 1993).

Concurrent with the growing interest in theories about the transactional nature of the developmental process, some researchers began to emphasize the importance of broader contextual factors to better understand the determinants of a child's growth, development, and learning (Bell, 1974; Bronfenbrenner, 1974; Werner, Bierman, & French, 1971; Werner & Smith, 1977). In a monograph entitled "Is Early Intervention Effective?" Bronfenbrenner (1974) approached these issues not from the point of view of the child in isolation but of the child in context. He concluded that a common thread linking successful intervention programs is their treatment of children as individuals situated within a family rather than as isolated experimental subjects or narrowly defined targets of nativist or nurturist theories. Contemporary theorists view children as members of multilayered social systems that are often remarkably nurturant but that may also be potentially disturbed or dysfunctional. Therefore, to intervene effectively on behalf of children is to intervene in context, and nothing less is deemed to be sufficient if the goal is to establish meaningful and durable change (Guralnick, 1998; Liaw, Meisels, & Brooks-Gunn, 1995; Ramey & Ramey, 1998).

THE IMPORTANCE OF EARLY RELATIONSHIPS. As the child development community first began to explore the process through which developmental outcomes could be affected by the child-rearing environment, several investigators began to study the adverse consequences of deprivation in early human relationships. Guided by a psychoanalytic framework, these ground-breaking "natural experiments" first focused attention on the effects of institutionalization on the cognitive and socioemotional development of infants (Provence & Lipton, 1962; R. A. Spitz, 1945). Such studies documented the developmentally destructive impact of the sustained isolation and understimulation typical of life in many orphanages, poorly staffed hospital wards, and other institutional settings. The features of this syndrome, which Spitz (1945) characterized as "hospitalism," included growth retardation, maladaptive social relationships, and health-related problems in young and otherwise normal children. These issues have continued to be studied throughout this century (Fenichel & Provence, 1993).

A complementary set of seminal studies in this area focused on the degree to which the developmental sequelae of early deprivation are modifiable. Beginning with a classic experiment with children institutionalized for mental retardation (Skeels & Dye, 1939), investigators manipulated living arrangements and levels of stimulation for a range of deprived populations and demonstrated that a responsive and stimulating environment could reverse the effects of negative, isolated, and otherwise deleterious experiences in early infancy (Dennis,

1960, 1973; Skeels, 1966). The growing empirical literature generated by such studies highlighted the malleability of early human development, thereby establishing a rationale for intervention within the early years of life (also see Kirk, 1958; Richardson & Koller, 1996; H. H. Spitz, 1986).

On a conceptual level, John Bowlby's work provided a theoretical framework for the empirical findings of the early deprivation studies. With support in the 1950s from the World Health Organization, Bowlby investigated the problems of homelessness and maternal deprivation and examined their consequences for mental health in children. In his classic monograph on maternal and child health, Bowlby (1951) called attention to the critical importance of the mother–child relationship for healthy child development. He subsequently formulated the attachment construct, which then provided a theoretical foundation for researchers studying young children's socioemotional adaptation (Ainsworth, 1969; Ainsworth, Blehar, Waters, & Wall, 1978; Bowlby, 1969; Bretherton & Waters, 1985; NICHD Early Child Care Research Network, 1997; Sroufe, 1983, 1996).

Much of the empirical research that demonstrated the marked influence of the caretaking environment and thereby supported the validity of the transactional model of development emerged from a number of landmark longitudinal studies initiated in the 1950s and 1960s. Two of these investigations focused on the growth and development of large birth cohorts; the others delineated the emerging abilities of young children with specifically defined risk factors.

The Collaborative Perinatal Project of the National Institute of Neurological Diseases and Blindness generated the most extensive longitudinal data on the developmental impact of biological and social risk factors in a birth cohort. A national sample of more than 53,000 pregnant women was enrolled in the study, and researchers followed these women's children after childbirth through the early school years (Broman, Bien, & Shaughnessy, 1985; Broman, Nichols, & Kennedy, 1975; Nichols & Chen, 1981). A second, remarkably rich investigation, known as the Kauai Studies, collected longitudinal data from the neonatal period through adulthood on more than 1,000 children born on the Hawaiian island of Kauai (Werner, Bierman, & French, 1971; Werner

& Smith, 1977, 1982, 1992). Both of these studies documented the significant influence on developmental outcomes of maternal education and the quality of the caregiving environment, except in cases of severe brain damage.

A number of pioneering prospective studies of the development of infants with documented risk factors or diagnosed disabilities were similarly enlightening. Investigations of young children with histories of perinatal anoxia, for example, revealed the extent to which adverse neurological sequelae were often found to be transient, as many at-risk children displayed normal development over the ensuing preschool years (Graham et al., 1962; Graham et al., 1957). Similarly, detailed longitudinal assessments of young children with diagnosed developmental disorders such as Down syndrome and phenylketonuria (PKU) provided reliable databases for assessing individual outcomes, highlighted the extent to which levels of disability varied within diagnostic categories, and demonstrated the limitations of early developmental predictions (Fishler, Graliker, & Koch, 1964; Share, Webb, & Koch, 1961). The data generated by these diverse studies contributed important insights to the growing interest in early intervention services for vulnerable children. The developmental process was found to be complex and transactional, and it was becoming increasingly clear that outcomes are mediated by the mutual effects of both nature and nurture (see Osofsky & Thompson, this volume; Garbarino and Ganzel, this volume; Shonkoff & Marshall, this volume; Werner, this volume).

SUMMARY. During the early decades of the twentieth century, questions regarding child development were framed within relatively simple paradigms reflecting the competing influences of organic endowment and individual experience. Subsequent research on young children extended our knowledge of the essential transactional nature of the developmental process and of the potential benefits of early intervention services. The degree to which the quality of the caregiving environment influences the effects of biological risk factors has provided substantial support for the development of intervention strategies to modify that environment. The design of such interventions has reflected a range of cultural and conceptual perspectives and

has been founded on a wide variety of empirically and theoretically based practices (see Garcia Coll & Magnuson, this volume; Emde & Robinson, this volume; Rutter, this volume; Sameroff & Fiese, this volume; Wolery, this volume). Recent research on early brain development has provided significant insights into the neurobiological substrate of both cognitive and social development in young children, which also have important implications for early intervention (Nelson, this volume; Schore, 1994).

FOUR DECADES OF GROWTH AND DEVELOPMENT

The philosophical and pragmatic roots of early childhood intervention prior to the 1960s emerged from a variety of sources. In each domain – early childhood education, maternal and child health, special education, and child development research – interactions between professional expertise and sociopolitical circumstances helped lay a foundation for the educational, psychological, public health, and public policy developments of the past forty years. Consistent themes persisting throughout the early years, despite occasional opposition, are as follows: a belief in society's responsibility to provide care and protection for young children; a commitment to the special needs of children who are particularly vulnerable as a result of a chronic disabling condition or as a consequence of growing up in poverty; and a sense that prevention is better than treatment and that earlier intervention is better than later remediation. These three themes reflect the spiritual foundation of early childhood intervention. They also provide an organizing framework for examining the major initiatives that have unfolded during the last four decades and that are likely to influence the field as it enters the twenty-first century.

The Sixties: A Broad Agenda with an Ambitious Promise

The 1960s mark the beginning of the modern era in early childhood intervention. It was a time of optimism and creative program development. Public support for investing in human services was broad-based, and resources flowed from the federal government to promote the achievement of ambitious social goals. Within this context, the convergence of several critical social issues served to frame the agenda for early childhood services. These included President Kennedy's interest in mental retardation, the political impact of the civil rights movement, and President Johnson's commitment to wage war on the sources and consequences of poverty.

Affected by his family's personal experience with mental retardation, in 1961 President John F. Kennedy appointed a presidential commission to explore current knowledge in this area and to develop a national strategy for prevention. In 1963, Public Law 88-156 provided new federal funding under Title V of the Social Security Act for special projects for children with mental retardation. Screening programs for inborn errors of metabolism, such as PKU, and Maternity and Infant Care Projects, implemented to help reduce the incidence of mental retardation caused by childbearing complications, are examples of such projects.

As the decade opened with President Kennedy's interest in the prevention of mental retardation, it closed with President Johnson's commitment to the educational needs of young children with disabilities. In 1968, Public Law 90-538, the Handicapped Children's Early Education Assistance Act, authorized funds to stimulate the development, evaluation, refinement, and dissemination of model demonstration programs for the education of eligible infants, preschoolers, and their parents. Through grants to demonstration programs, and with the initiation of federal support to specialized university teacher-training programs, a new field of study was born.

Closely related to this new discipline of early childhood special education in many of its underlying principles, but distinct and separate in its political beginnings, the concept of early childhood intervention also received considerable support in the 1960s as a potential weapon in the war on poverty. As a result of the efforts of civil rights activists, progressive politicians, and social scientists, Americans became painfully aware of the extent of poverty in the United States and the degree to which the consequences of marked socioeconomic inequalities threatened the nation's well-being (Chase-Lansdale & Vinovskis, 1995; deLone, 1979).

In its analysis of the "poverty cycle," the President's Panel on Mental Retardation echoed the prevailing stereotype of "cultural deprivation" as a major cause of recurrent, multigenerational retardation (Albee, 1968). On the basis of its belief that education was the key to breaking this cycle, the panel recommended the widespread establishment in economically disadvantaged communities of preschool programs designed to foster "the specific development of the attitudes and aptitudes which middle-class culture characteristically develops in children, and which contributes in large measure to the academic and vocational success of such children" (The President's Panel on Mental Retardation, 1963, quoted in Zigler & Valentine, 1979, p. 12; see also Halpern, this volume).

The theoretical rationale to intervene in disadvantaged children's lives emerged from a growing body of evidence questioning previous widely accepted assumptions regarding the immutable genetic determination of intelligence. Supported by the recently published scholarly work of J. McVicker Hunt (1961) and Benjamin Bloom (1964), social activists emphasized the powerful influence of experience on the development of competence in young children and focused on the particular vulnerability and malleability of the first years of life. In the decade of social experimentation that followed, interactions between academic researchers and program developers flourished.

Experimental preschool programs were created in the laboratories of child development researchers and tested in communities across the country . . . . Developmental psychologists were ready to change the world; their proposals to structure children's experiences in ways different from those traditionally accomplished by untutored parents at home were made with enthusiasm and optimism. (Clarke-Stewart & Fein, 1983, p. 918)

In 1965, the most far-reaching experiment of the decade, Project Head Start, began as an 8-week pilot program for children in more than 2,500 communities around the country. Originally developed under the auspices of the Office of Economic Opportunity, Head Start flourished under the leadership of Julius B. Richmond, a prominent pediatrician, and Edward F. Zigler, a distinguished academic psychologist appointed as the first director of the Office of Child Development. Head Start was based on a belief in the crucial impact of early childhood experiences on later development. Its founders assumed that socioeconomically impoverished environments contain biological (e.g., poor health and nutritional status) and experiential (e.g., understimulation and reduced motivation) risk factors that can affect early childhood adversely. They were convinced that compensatory programs in the preschool period could facilitate better school adjustment and performance for children who were disadvantaged by the consequences of poverty and social disorganization (Zigler & Muenchow, 1992; Zigler & Valentine, 1979).

Head Start was conceived as a multidimensional, comprehensive service system designed to strike at the roots of disadvantage for poor families with young children (Zigler, Styfco, & Gilman, 1993). It harnessed the expertise of a broad array of professionals to provide educational, medical, dental, nutritional, psychological, and social services. The program invested a great deal of energy in parent involvement at both the volunteer and the decision-making levels and included training programs for low-income adults from the community to facilitate employment mobility. Head Start provided a bold and dramatic model of early childhood intervention that continues to the present day (Peters & Kontos, 1987; Reese, 1985; Takanishi & deLeon, 1994; Zigler & Styfco, 1993). Its insistence on combining health, education, and social services was critical; its provisions for parent participation in both the classroom and on the administrative policy committees were unprecedented in American education policy; and its approach to the client–professional relationship as a vehicle for shared decision making was revolutionary.

The achievements and political resilience of Head Start have been well documented (Hubbell, 1983; Zigler & Muenchow, 1992; Zigler & Valentine, 1979). In its triumphs and in its disappointments, it provides a microcosm of the 1960s. The beneficial effects on children, families, and their communities have been extolled frequently (Lazar & Darlington, 1982). The program has not, however, resulted in the elimination of school failure, welfare dependency, delinquent behavior, or any of the other social consequences of poverty (Vinovskis, 1993; see also Farran, this volume). Perhaps one of the greatest lessons that Head Start has to teach the field of early childhood intervention is that programs must establish explicit and realistic goals and objectives. The legacy of the 1960s has taught us to be cautious about the promises we make and has served to remind us that there are no magic solutions to complex social problems.

The Seventies: The Political Ascendance of Developmental Disabilities

While much of the creative intervention energies of the 1960s were channeled into the War on Poverty, the 1970s witnessed a greater investment in the needs of children with disabilities. As the social and political upheavals of the previous decade subsided and the nation worried more about the effects of inflation on the middle class than about the effects of poverty on the development of young children, increased attention was focused on the social status and legal rights of persons with handicapping conditions (Gliedman & Roth, 1980).

Federally supported demonstration and outreach projects proliferated at a rapid rate (DeWeerd, 1981; Martin, 1989). Funds from both the Bureau of Education for the Handicapped and the Division of Maternal and Child Health supported multidisciplinary training programs at university-affiliated facilities across the country and produced new cadres of professionals to work with children with disabilities. Early childhood special education became a higher priority as the demand increased for teachers of preschool children with special needs and as state departments of education began to develop guidelines for certification in this new area of specialization (Stile, Abernathy, Pettibone, & Wachtel, 1984).

In 1972, Public Law 92-424 (the Economic Opportunity amendments) mandated that all Head Start centers reserve at least 10% of their enrollment for children with identified disabilities. In 1973, the Division for Early Childhood (DEC) was established as a new entity within the Council for Exceptional Children (CEC), thereby reflecting the sense of a distinct professional identity felt by early childhood special educators. In 1974, the federal government earmarked separate funding for state implementation grants to assist states in the planning and development of services for infants and preschoolers with disabilities.

In 1975, with the passage of Public Law 94-142 (the Education for All Handicapped Children Act), the right to a free and appropriate public education was established for all children of school age, regardless of the presence of a disability. This landmark legislation mandated the development of individualized education plans (IEPs) based on the results of a nondiscriminatory assessment; specified requirements for parent involvement in the construction of such plans; spelled out principles of due process for both children and parents in the planning and implementation of educational services; and articulated requirements that IEPs be carried out in the least restrictive environment (Hobbs, 1975; Singer & Butler, 1987). Although the P.L. 94-142 provisions did not require states to offer services for infants, toddlers, or preschoolers with disabilities, the new federal law endorsed the importance of such services and provided financial incentives for states to serve children as young as 3 years of age. During this period of cautious interest in infant intervention, the National Center for Clinical Infant Programs (renamed Zero To Three: The National Center for Infants, Toddlers, and their Families in the 1990s) was founded in order to focus the nation's attention on the needs of the very youngest children and their families.

Complementing their achievements in the area of public education, advocates for persons with disabilities borrowed some of the strategies used so successfully by civil rights groups during the 1960s and brought their message to both the Congress and the court system in a battle to end discrimination on the basis of disability in all aspects of society (Gliedman & Roth, 1980). The first federal civil rights law specifically directed toward the rights of persons with disabilities (Public Law 93-112, the Vocational Rehabilitation Act, Sec. 504), which focused primarily on employment, was passed in 1973. The following year it was amended under Public Law 93-516 to establish rights for nondiscrimination in employment, admission into institutions of higher learning, and access to public facilities. Supportive legislation, multiple successful class-action suits, and a rising public consciousness about the injustice of discrimination against people with disabilities characterized much of the 1970s legacy.

The Eighties: Governmental Retrenchment and the Formation of New Alliances

The 1980s began with the presidential inauguration of Ronald Reagan, who brought with him a national mandate based on a different set of values about government's role. In 1981, the Omnibus Budget Reconciliation Act was passed by a coalition of politically conservative forces bent on reducing the investment of federal resources in social programs and on shifting the responsibility for such efforts (and the concomitant financial burden) to the states. Consequently, while Congress endorsed substantial reductions in federal taxes (in conjunction with the sharpest increases in military expenditures ever recorded during peacetime), many domestic programs began to be dismantled and others sustained significant decreases in funding (Edelman, 1987; Schorr, 1988). Formula grants to the states were consolidated into block grants, and overall appropriations for social programs were reduced. The newly conceived Maternal and Child Health Block Grant, for example, incorporated funding for eight categorical programs that previously received separate grants, with an overall budget reduction of 18% in the first two years (Lesser, 1985). The eight programs whose previous support was combined into a single block grant included crippled children's, maternal and child health, and genetic disease testing and counseling services; prevention programs for lead paint poisoning, sudden infant death syndrome, and adolescent pregnancy; hemophilia diagnostic and treatment centers; and Supplemental Security Income for children with disabilities. The immediate result of their consolidation into a block grant was the pitting of categorical programs against each other in a fight for a fair share of the smaller amount of government social spending.

The fact that early childhood intervention programs survived the federal policies of the 1980s attests to the depth of their political and social strength and to the breadth of their constituency groups. At a time when the war on poverty was all but eliminated from federal policy making, Head Start was included in the Reagan administration's so-called safety net and continued to receive federal funds. In an era when presidential advisers talked about the advisability of abolishing the U.S.

Department of Education, federal expenditures for the education of young children with special needs continued to grow. P.L. 99-457 (described later in this chapter), the most sweeping piece of legislation for children with disabilities since P.L. 94-142, was enacted, despite the opposition of the Secretary of Education and the threat of a presidential veto. The explanation for the survival of Head Start and for the continued progress of early intervention services for young children with disabilities was clear. Each had developed and nurtured a powerful array of advocates and constituency groups both within and outside government, and the basic principles of early intervention for vulnerable children and their families had gained wide national support (Schorr, 1988).

The Nineties: Seeking Market Solutions to Human Needs Amidst Growing Financial Constraints

The political context of the 1990s was marked by harsh, contentious, highly polarized debate about the balance between public and personal responsibility for the health and well-being of children and families. The decade also witnessed the continuing ascendance of a conservative political philosophy committed to low taxes, limited government, extensive cuts in federal funding for social welfare programs, and a reliance on market solutions to human needs. This was a period of unprecedented economic prosperity but also one of growing disparities between the "haves" and the "have nots." It was a decade in which the interests of children with disabilities attracted relatively modest attention, and the care of children living under conditions of poverty or economic hardship became increasingly tenuous. Indeed, the 1990s reflected a stunning paradox. At a time when the economy was robust and the science of early childhood development was maturing, rhetoric on behalf of young children was strong, but creative advances in service delivery and program evaluation were scarce. Standing on the threshold of a major economic and technological transformation that demands a highly skilled and well-educated workforce (which will bear significant responsibility for an aging population that is growing rapidly), public concern about school readiness grew, but investment in the well-being of vulnerable young children sputtered.

The mixed status of early childhood intervention in the 1990s was reflected most dramatically in the sharp contrast among several important federal initiatives. The implementation of the landmark special education law, P.L. 99-457, opened the decade with a major investment in the development of comprehensive state systems of family-centered services for highly vulnerable infants and toddlers. Several other initiatives were built on this foundation, although their modest accomplishments failed to match their initially high promise. Finally, in marked contrast to the popular principles of family support, the decade ended with the enactment of the Omnibus Personal Responsibility and Work Opportunity Reconciliation Act, which terminated a sixty-year federal commitment to "aid for families with dependent children" and abandoned the concept of a safety net for poor women and their young children.

WELFARE REFORM. The Omnibus Personal Responsibility and Work Opportunity Reconciliation Act of 1996 abolished the guarantee of federal aid to children and families living in poverty that had endured for more than six decades, which thereby fundamentally altered our nation's commitment to its neediest citizens. Stated simply, the concept of public assistance for poor mothers with dependent children was transformed from an entitlement that assured modest financial support to a time-limited period of eligibility for financial assistance linked to a work requirement. In place of Aid to Families with Dependent Children (AFDC), the new law offered Temporary Assistance to Needy Families (TANF). This new program, designed as a capped block grant, provides states with level funding through the end of the decade to support poor families with young children. Among its many provisions and sanctions, TANF requires that recipients of public assistance participate in work preparation programs and find jobs within two years. Although some contingency funds were established for a small number of families who cannot meet the law's requirements, hardship exemptions are limited. Moreover, these provisions are likely to be inadequate to meet the needs of families who have children with significant disabilities or families in which one or more of the parents is disabled or otherwise unable to work.

The marked contrast between the supportive goals of early childhood intervention and the punitive reformulation of the welfare rules is not simply about whether parents of young children should work. The problem with TANF for families of children who are disabled or developmentally at risk is that its sanctions and limitations impose considerable burdens on poor families who are already stressed significantly (Ohlson, 1998). Examples of these greater hardships include: 1) reductions in funds available for Supplementary Security Income (SSI) insurance and redefined eligibility criteria that have resulted in the termination of cash allowances for many children who had qualified previously; 2) greater difficulty for poor families to qualify for Medicaid coverage because of changes in the application process and modifications in the SSI eligibility guidelines; and 3) elimination of federal child-care assistance for families who take part in welfare-to-work activities or who are making a transition from welfare dependence to gainful employment (Ohlson, 1998). In short, changes in the welfare law are destined to result in greater stress for those members of society who are most at risk – specifically, very young, developmentally vulnerable children and their families who are living in poverty. To the extent that the new welfare policies further undermine the ability of poor families to meet the needs of their young children, they are sure to create significant additional challenges for the field of early childhood intervention in the decades to come.

SCHOOL READINESS. Framed as the first of the National Education Goals established at the beginning of the decade ("All children in America will start school ready to learn," National Education Goals Panel, 1991), attention to school readiness emerged as a major national policy issue in the 1990s. Buttressed by strong public endorsement, the National Education Goals Panel appointed a Resource Group and two Technical Review Panels to clarify the meaning of this deceptively simple concept, and many states held "Goal 1 Conferences" to report on their progress in garnering support for activities intended to improve young children's readiness for school. The "Readiness Goal," as it came to be known, was even credited with providing an overall framework and incentive for the National Center for Education Statistics as it began

planning an Early Childhood Longitudinal Study of more than 23,000 children from kindergarten through fifth grade, beginning in the fall of 1998 (Meisels, 1999).

Unfortunately, despite the benefits of drawing greater national attention to the condition of children and schools at the outset of formal education, numerous questions remained unresolved. Considerable debate ensued about whether children's readiness for school can be assessed without doing them harm through excessive labeling or stigmatization. Also of concern were questions about whether readiness testing can capture the unique characteristics of early development and learning, and whether a finding that large numbers of children are not ready for school would be viewed as a problem in the child or within the community. Although the challenge of defining school readiness was not resolved during the 1990s, the Readiness Goal served to keep the early childhood years at the forefront of the nation's education policy agenda.

EARLY HEAD START. The concept of Early Head Start emerged from discussions among policy makers, service providers, politicians, and researchers concerning the need to provide comprehensive, intensive, and continuous year-round child development services for low-income families with children under age three. Similar to Head Start programs for 3- and 4-year-olds, Early Head Start was designed to enhance children's physical, social, emotional, and intellectual development; to assist and support parents in caring for their children; and to enable parents to become more self-sufficient. Early Head Start embodied the following principles: high program quality; health promotion and disease prevention; positive relationships among children, parents, families, and staff; active parent involvement; inclusion of children with special needs; understanding of various cultures; comprehensiveness of service models; support during transition to Head Start or other preschool programs; and collaboration among community sources of support and early intervention. Begun in 1995, following the reauthorization of the Head Start Act, Early Head Start initially had fewer than 40 sites and grew to more than 600 programs before the decade's end. Data on the program's effectiveness are due shortly after the turn of the century. This evaluation, which will provide critically important information on the short- and long-term benefits of a broad-based, national program for infants, toddlers, and their families, has the potential to influence policies affecting young children and families for many years to come.

WHITE HOUSE CONFERENCES. In 1997, two major White House Conferences were convened – one focused on early childhood development and learning (including the relation between early experience and brain development) and the other on critical issues related to child care. Both served to stimulate widespread public discussion about the importance of the first years of life and the need for strategic investments in early childhood development. In a manner somewhat reminiscent of the collaboration that flourished between academics and policy makers in the 1960s, the blending of cutting-edge science and political commitment suggested the possibility of a creative renaissance in early childhood intervention. In sharp contrast to the accomplishments of the 1960s, however, the bold vision set by the Clinton White House in the 1990s generated a relatively modest legislative agenda, which dissipated in the face of strong political opposition and the distractions of a major scandal. Despite their meager political impact, however, these two landmark White House Conferences served to expand the national consciousness about the critical influence of early experiences on the development of young children. In focusing on the neurobiology of brain development, the conferences also captured the public's imagination and laid important groundwork for renewed faith in the value of a science-based approach to early childhood policy.

PUBLIC ACCOUNTABILITY AND AN EMERGING SCIENTIFIC BASE. The close scrutiny of all public expenditures for health and human services in the 1990s placed a strong premium on the value of efficacy data and the need for an integrative synthesis of the substantial evaluation literature on early intervention that had been amassed over the preceding decades. Guralnick (1998), the editor of a major volume on the effectiveness of early intervention services (Guralnick, 1997), noted: "There now exists unequivocal evidence that the declines in intellectual development that occur in the absence of systematic early intervention can be substantially

reduced by interventions implemented and evaluated *during the first 5 years of life*" (Guralnick, 1998, p. 321, italics in original). Ramey and Ramey (1998, p. 115) also pointed out the "remarkable consistencies in the major findings derived from early interventions," and others (e.g., Barnett, 1995; Reynolds, Mann, Miedel, & Smokowski, 1997) reinforced the notion that participation in early childhood programs is associated consistently with positive outcomes. In addition, the costs and benefits of early intervention were analyzed by the Rand Corporation (Karoly et al., 1998) and the Council of Economic Advisors (1998) and were found to be a wise public investment on behalf of children and families.

Despite a strong consensus regarding the overall value of early intervention services, however, the emerging research base concerning their specific impacts has not been uniformly positive (Farran, this volume; Halpern, this volume). Indeed, as service systems have evolved and longitudinal data have been collected, a number of limitations have been highlighted. One of the most important realizations to emerge from the research literature is the recognition that program efficacy demands sound implementation. That is to say, a potentially effective service model cannot be expected to demonstrate positive effects if it is not delivered appropriately (whether because of insufficient funding, substandard delivery, or inadequate staff training) or if the intended service recipients do not participate fully in the program. In such circumstances, it is not possible to make a judgment about how effective an intervention *would* be if it had been both delivered and received as intended.

A second problem that affects much of the early intervention efficacy literature has been the continued focus on global questions about whether programs "work," despite long-standing pleas for a more focused research strategy that investigates "where," "how," and "for whom" specific interventions are differentially effective, based on specific child, family, community, and program characteristics (Guralnick, 1997; Meisels, 1985b; Meisels, Dichtelmiller, & Liaw, 1993; Shonkoff, 1992; Shonkoff, Hauser-Cram, Krauss, & Upshur, 1988, 1992). Consequently, as another decade of early childhood intervention research comes to a close, three basic findings provide an important starting point for the next generation of investigators.

First, there is considerable documentation of the positive impacts of services that are designed to address explicit goals and that are delivered as planned. Second, there is extensive evidence about programs with only modest impacts, thus underscoring the need for realistic expectations based on the match between the services that are provided and the nature and magnitude of the vulnerabilities (both biological and environmental) they are intended to ameliorate. Third, there is a growing recognition of the methodological and practical challenges facing meaningful program evaluation in this field, particularly as scholars devote increasing attention to the problems encountered in previous large-scale assessments (see Hauser-Cram, Warfield, Upshur, & Weisner, this volume).

THE INDIVIDUALS WITH DISABILITIES EDUCATION ACT (IDEA).

The legislative predecessor to IDEA – the Education for All Handicapped Children Act Amendments of 1986 (P.L. 99-457) – was the most important legislation ever enacted for developmentally vulnerable young children in the United States. Proposed, passed, and signed into law within a six-month period, the statute calls for "a statewide, comprehensive, coordinated, multidisciplinary, interagency program of early intervention services for all handicapped infants and their families" (P.L. 99-457, Sec. 671). Although the law did not mandate universal services for all children younger than 6 years of age, it strengthened incentives for states to serve 3–6-year-olds and established a program (Part H of the statute, now known as Part C) to provide services for children from birth to 3 years. Though passed in 1986, the full implementation of the law did not unfold until the early 1990s.

In the 1997–98 reauthorized version of IDEA (P.L. 105-17), the law contains three main provisions. The first part (formerly known as Part H and designated Part C since mid-1998) established a requirement for states to facilitate the development of comprehensive systems of early intervention services for infants and toddlers with developmental delays or disabilities. All children from birth through 2 years of age who are experiencing developmental delays, as measured by appropriate assessments and procedures (see Kelly & Barnard, this volume; Meisels & Atkins-Burnett, this volume), were

deemed entitled to services. The second part (Part B, Section 619) required states to provide free and appropriate public education and related services for all eligible children with disabilities from the age of 3 to 5 years. The last part of the law reauthorized a number of federal discretionary programs, such as services for deaf-blind children, early childhood research institutes, and grants for personnel training.

Early intervention is defined narrowly under the new law as "developmental services which... are designed to meet a handicapped infant's or toddler's developmental needs in any one or more of the following areas: physical development; cognitive development; language and speech development; psychosocial development; or self-help skills." Although the language in Part C (which refers to the "development" rather than the "education" of the infant or toddler with disabilities) reinforces a spirit of comprehensiveness, health services are included only to the extent that they are "necessary to enable the infant or toddler to benefit from the other early intervention services." Nevertheless, the statute clearly recognizes that effective early intervention services will require the contributions of professionals from many different disciplines and orientations. Thus, multiple perspectives are woven throughout the planning and implementation of the law, and the activities prescribed under Part C must be guided by a State Interagency Coordinating Council.

As a federal initiative, the law provides for states to exercise considerable discretion regarding organizational and programmatic decision making. In fact, the range of implementation options is sufficiently broad that there could eventually be as many different service systems in place as there are states (Harbin, Gallagher, Lillie, & Eckland, 1992). Nevertheless, the law prescribes a number of critical components that each state must plan and make operational (see Gallagher, Trohanis, & Clifford, 1989; Hauser-Cram, Upshur, Krauss, & Shonkoff, 1988).

Lead Agency

To receive Part C funds, each state is required to select a lead agency to administer its service system and must appoint an Interagency Coordinating

Council to assist in its planning, development, and implementation. The intent of this requirement is to overcome the typically fragmented systems of services found within most states (Meisels, 1985a; Meisels, Harbin, Modigliani, & Olson, 1988). At the time of the passage of P.L. 99-457, services for infants and toddlers with disabilities were delivered through a wide variety of programs supported by local and state taxes, Medicaid, and the U.S. Public Health Service (e.g., Developmental Disabilities programs or the Maternal and Child Health Block Grant) and through a similar diversity of programs supported by the U.S. Department of Education (e.g., demonstration projects funded through the Handicapped Children's Early Education Program; Meisels, Harbin, Modigliani, & Olson, 1988). Although Part C, like Part H, is administered by the federal Department of Education, each state is given full authority to designate its own lead agency. In the first year of implementation, about one-third of the states chose departments of education as their lead agency, slightly fewer selected departments of health, and the remainder designated other agencies, such as departments of mental health or human services (Garwood, Fewell, & Neisworth, 1988). This distribution has changed over the years, with an increase in lead agencies in the health area and a concomitant reduction in education.

Health and Education Collaboration. Traditional relations between the health care (public and private) and education communities concerning the care of infants and toddlers with disabilities have been uneven and complex. Thus, coordination between health care and education agencies at the local, state, and federal levels is viewed as particularly critical to the successful implementation of early intervention services (Ireys & Nelson, 1992; Smith & Strain, 1988). Although physicians are usually the professionals best situated to identify very young children with disabling conditions, initial attitudes toward early intervention services within the pediatric community were variable (Green, Ferry, Russman, Shonkoff, & Taft, 1987; Guralnick, Heiser, Eaton, Bennett, Richardson & Groom, 1988). Nevertheless, because many infants with disabilities have associated health problems (e.g., seizures, sensory impairments, and growth disorders) that require sophisticated medical

management to assure optimal early intervention efficacy (see Shonkoff & Marshall, this volume), successful medical–educational collaboration has evolved slowly and deliberately over the past decade (Gartner & Lipsky, 1987; see Dworkin, this volume).

To counteract jurisdictional boundaries and disputes over funding responsibilities between health and education agencies, the law urges collaborative efforts, and formal interagency agreements have been negotiated at the federal level between the Bureau of Maternal and Child Health in the Department of Health and Human Services, and the Office of Special Education Programs in the Department of Education. The need to develop local service systems based on functional medical–educational cooperation in the context of the bureaucratic division of medical and educational resources, however, remains a perplexing policy challenge for the next decade (Butler, Starfield, & Stenmark, 1984; see Knitzer, this volume).

Programmatic Decisions. Beyond their influence on bureaucratic organization, the provisions of the federal law create a framework within which a number of crucial state-level programmatic decisions must be made about the evolving nature of early childhood intervention services. Each state, for example, is required to develop its own definition of developmental delay, which must be based on appropriate diagnostic procedures that cover five areas of performance (cognitive, physical, language and speech, self-help, and psychosocial development). Numerous problems remain in the development of appropriate and meaningful eligibility criteria (Shonkoff & Meisels, 1991). Although the numbers of infants and toddlers with disabilities who have been identified and served in the various intervention systems created by the states has been highly variable (Bowe, 1995; Kochanek & Buka, 1998; Meisels & Wasik, 1990), systematic efforts have been put in place to find eligible children and families and to establish appropriate services (see Harbin, McWilliam, & Gallagher, this volume).

A second issue related to service eligibility involves the problem of developmental risk. The law requires that early intervention services be made available for two major target groups: those experiencing *developmental delay* at the time of referral and assessment, and those who have a diagnosed condition that has a high probability of resulting in subsequent delay (i.e., *established conditions*). Each state has the additional option of including children who are "at risk of having substantial developmental delays if early intervention services are not provided." Children in this discretionary third category have traditionally been characterized as "biologically at risk," "environmentally at risk," or both (Tjossem, 1976). Difficulties in identifying such children, however, have been monumental and continue to present a significant challenge to states (Meisels & Wasik, 1990). The financial implications related to definitions that increase the potential size of the service population are a particular focus of contention, although ironically preventive interventions for children living in high-risk environments offer the highest potential cost savings over the long term.

A third major task presented by the law is the requirement that an individualized family service plan (IFSP) be developed by a multidisciplinary team, which must include a parent or guardian for each child and family enrolled in an early intervention program. Based on an assessment of the needs of the entire family, the IFSP must articulate specific child and family goals; describe the criteria, methods, and timing to be used to evaluate goal attainment; specify the services needed to meet each goal; and identify a case manager who is responsible for insuring the implementation of the plan. The most recent reauthorization of the law (P.L. 105-17) calls for an assurance in IFSPs that intervention services take place in such natural environments as the home.

The Role of the Family. In explicitly acknowledging the family (rather than the child in isolation) as the central focus of the service, the concept of an IFSP reflects contemporary theoretical perspectives about child development (Brooks-Gunn, Berlin, & Fuligni, this volume; Emde & Robinson, this volume; Osofsky & Thompson, this volume; Sameroff & Fiese, this volume), current practices in many early childhood programs (Kagan & Neuman, this volume; Musick & Stott, this volume; Wolery, this volume), and empirically based findings regarding enhanced outcomes for children whose parents and communities are involved actively in their program experiences (Earls & Buka, this volume; Krauss, this volume; Shonkoff & Hauser-Cram, 1987). The IFSP

provision, however, has generated considerable controversy as a matter of public policy. On the one hand, it is both a logical extension of the mandated parental involvement for school-age children embedded within P.L. 94-142 and a formal endorsement of the family-oriented approach that characterizes the current state of the art for services in the early years of life (Brooks-Gunn, Berlin, & Fuligni, this volume; Healy, Keesee, & Smith, 1985; Turnbull, Turbiville, & Turnbull, this volume). On the other hand, the IFSP can also be viewed as a catalyst for radical change in early childhood programs that impose a significant intrusion into family life (Krauss, 1990). The selection of sensitive evaluation strategies to identify family needs (see Krauss, this volume), and the development of appropriate new training experiences to enable existing and future service providers to conduct, interpret, and utilize such assessment protocols constructively (see Klein & Gilkerson, this volume), will determine how well the IFSP achieves its statutory promise.

Transition. The transition across service systems at 3 years of age presents another potential dilemma in the implementation of the law. The proposed regulations require that the IFSP include a plan to support the transfer of service responsibility from the early intervention system to a preschool program, and that a case manager must be responsible for the development of such a plan. Disputes over the determination of appropriate educational plans, delays in starting services, and disagreements about whether all children enrolled in early intervention programs necessarily qualify for special education classes at age 3 years have all been reported (Association for Retarded Citizens, 1986; Kerns, 1988). Therefore, development of effective transition procedures will continue to require considerable thought and effort (Hanline & Knowlton, 1988).

Summary

From the perspective of public policy, P.L. 99-457 and its subsequent reauthorizations represent a bold initiative that raises a number of critical challenges for the field of early childhood intervention (Hauser-Cram et al., 1988; Meisels, 1989). This law combines an enduring national commitment to the needs of vulnerable young children with the "new federalism" that began in the 1980s to transfer responsibility for many social programs into the hands of state policy makers. Under the law, each state must make independent decisions about the definition of developmental delay, the service eligibility of children at risk for developmental disabilities, the criteria and methods to be used for family assessment, and the strategies needed to identify a lead service agency. States must also constitute an Interagency Coordinating Council and facilitate a smooth transition of children and families from early intervention programs to preschool special education services. How these decisions are reached, whose views are solicited by state policy makers, how research is used to inform and defend specific decisions, and how the impacts of existing state practices are assessed require the participation of diverse constituencies from the academic, policy, and service delivery arenas. The task is formidable, but the rewards are potentially great.

CHALLENGES FOR THE NEW MILLENNIUM

As we experience the end of the twentieth century and the beginning of a new millennium, the health and development of young children in the United States, and the well-being of their families, are threatened by a broad array of political, economic, and social forces. Challenges to children and families, to society at large, and to early intervention programs in particular provide a multilevel framework for reflection. In their broadest sense, these issues have critical implications for the future of American society, and they highlight an increasingly complex agenda for the field of early childhood intervention.

Challenges Facing Young Children and Their Families

Three challenges face young children and their families. The first is embedded in the emergence of increasingly diverse structures and definitions of "family," the continuing evolution of gender roles, and fundamental changes in the nature of adult work. The complex interactions among these dynamic social and economic transformations have important implications for the lives of both women and men and, most assuredly, for the care and protection of their children. The period from birth to school entry for America's children has changed in fundamental and dramatic ways over the past few decades. With the concept of family-centered service delivery now firmly established in the culture of early childhood intervention, programs must respond creatively to the fact that the definition of "family" and the meaning of "family-centered" are not always entirely clear.

The second challenge facing children and families is the growing gap between the wealthy and the poor, its underlying causes, and the multidimensional stresses on those who live under conditions of poverty or economic insecurity. The impacts of poverty on child health and development have been documented extensively for decades. This does not present a new challenge. However, the number of children living in poverty in the United States remains unacceptably high, and the nature of that experience appears to be more debilitating than ever. Moreover, the poorest segment of the population is augmented by an increasing number of children who are growing up under circumstances characterized by "near poverty." These children are faced with the stresses experienced by hard-working, low-income families whose earning power is diminishing and whose job security is highly tenuous. The growing gap between the secure "haves" and the insecure "have nots" has become dramatic in the first five years of life. The comfortable middle class has discovered the benefits of enriched early childhood experiences for their young children prior to enrollment in school, whereas the working poor find that increasingly large portions of their wages must be devoted to basic child care, which is often of lower quality than can be purchased by families with greater income.

The third challenge facing children and families in the United States is the increasing racial and ethnic diversity of the population and the continuing effects of racism and discrimination on human development. Demographers project that, within the next few decades, more than half of the population of the United States will be nonwhite, not of European origin, or both. Much of this population shift is related to current immigration from Latin America and Asia. As the nation seeks ways to incorporate these cultural differences into its social fabric, the delicate balance between individual acculturation and the preservation of distinct ethnic group identities will have an impact on the environments in which young children are socialized. Although there is considerable rhetoric in the field of early childhood intervention about the importance of "cultural competence," much remains to be learned about the meaning of these social changes and how they can best be addressed in formal service delivery systems.

Challenges Facing Society

As it grapples with the challenges of changing family structures, evolving gender roles, major transformations in the nature of work and their relation to family life, complex economic inequalities, and growing racial, ethnic, and cultural diversity, the field of early childhood intervention must also contend with a complex political environment. Several cross-cutting themes can be identified.

Perhaps the most important feature of the changing political culture in the United States over the past decade is its increased polarization and the contentious nature of contemporary public discourse. Prominent in this respect are the social and political tensions related to contrasting views about the balance between public and personal responsibility, the devolution of political authority from the federal to state and local levels, and conflicting opinions on the role of government and the private sector in providing a "safety net" for vulnerable children and their families. In this context, many of the core principles of early childhood intervention have been subjected to serious challenge. Stated simply, whether we maintain a shared commitment to a sense of communal responsibility for the well-being of all young children presents a critical challenge for early childhood intervention as an effective public service.

A second cross-cutting theme is the increased demand for outcomes accountability, management innovation, and new financing strategies for all health and human services. In a society focused increasingly on cost containment, efficiency, tax cutting, and market solutions to social problems, the delivery of health and human services is subjected to increased, and at times unforgiving, scrutiny. Where management expertise is deficient, program survival is in jeopardy. Where business control is paramount, the core service mission may be under-

mined. The balance between these forces, and the need to blend the cultures of business and human services, characterize a critical frontier for the early intervention field.

A third cross-cutting theme concerns the need to understand how the pervasive experiences of persistent poverty, racism, and social disadvantage can be overcome and how the resulting cycle of hopelessness, violence, and self-destructive behavior can be broken. The intergenerational poverty and social exclusion of the past several decades present a much more challenging environment within which early intervention programs must operate than was previously the case. The growing and changing burdens of substance abuse, and the increasing epidemic of community violence, intensify the tasks facing intervention efforts. Despite greater knowledge and significant progress in a broad range of service contexts, the entrenchment of deep poverty, complicated by racial/ethnic discrimination that relegates a part of the population to the status of "other people's children," remains a formidable challenge.

Fourth, and perhaps most fundamental to the concept of early childhood intervention, is the need to find new and more effective ways to shift the political culture away from a search for simplistic remedial or punitive approaches to complex human problems and toward a positive, preventive investment in the care and protection of children and support for competent family functioning. In simple terms, we must determine how to focus public attention on the need for proactive policies that promote positive human adaptation and that sustain preventive interventions in order to counteract the roots of individual failure. Within this context, the greatest challenge facing the early intervention field reaches far beyond the boundaries of current service delivery systems and demands that we address the broad social, economic, and political fabric of contemporary American society.

Challenges Facing Early Intervention Systems

The science of early childhood development has grown considerably over the past several decades. This continually expanding knowledge base has been informed by a rich diversity of academic disciplines, including developmental psychology, psycholinguistics, anthropology, and sociology, among others. Although much of our current understanding of the early roots of human competence is derived from the social sciences, a recent surge of interest in the biology of brain development, and the extent to which it is influenced by individual experience, has underscored the need for a thoughtful, cross-disciplinary assessment of what we know and how to apply that knowledge constructively to promote human well-being (Nelson, this volume).

Within this context, questions concerning the concepts of neuroplasticity and sensitive (or critical) periods in the development of cognitive, linguistic, and social–emotional competence are particularly compelling and have important implications for policy decisions regarding the provision of early intervention services. Are there windows of opportunity when particular experiences are necessary for optimal development? What are these experiences, and, if missed, can compensatory actions be taken later in life? What is the cumulative impact of varying experiences over the first few years of life? What are their implications for later developmental trajectories?

Awareness of this emergent knowledge base now extends far beyond academia to the general public, where its application to the tasks of child rearing has been facilitated by the proliferation of a diversity of dissemination vehicles, including parenting and "women's" magazines, television and radio talk shows, and a range of popular books authored by such respected authorities as T. Berry Brazelton and Penelope Leach. The consequences of this broadly disseminated knowledge explosion include greater public awareness of the importance of the early years, thoughtful concern about the degree to which misuse of available knowledge can lead to unnecessary elevations in parental anxiety, and increased interest in the potential impact of integrated, family-centered support services.

Beyond the basic care and protection provided by parents and other primary caregivers, formal services designed to promote the health and development of young children in the United States are widespread. However, these services have evolved within a highly fragmented infrastructure of categorical programs embedded in a broad array of public and private systems. Examples of these separate service streams include the following: 1) health pro-

motion and primary medical care for all children (Dworkin, this volume); 2) child care for children of working parents (Kagan & Neuman, this volume); 3) preventive intervention and family support for children living under conditions of poverty, social disadvantage, or both (Halpern, this volume; Osofsky & Thompson, this volume); 4) therapeutic/educational interventions and family support for children with developmental delays or diagnosed disabilities (Harbin, McWilliam, & Gallagher, this volume; Wolery, this volume); and 5) specialized mental health services for children experiencing a wide variety of clinical conditions including child physical, emotional, or sexual abuse; child neglect; maternal and child psychopathology (e.g., psychosis, depression, and behavior disorders); and maternal substance abuse (Knitzer, this volume).

Despite their long-standing tradition of independent operation, all human service systems for young children and their families are currently challenged to provide greater integration and to define best practices in order to guide the allocation of finite public resources. These pressures, in turn, have underscored the need to draw upon a strong, unified knowledge base about the fundamental developmental tasks and needs of young children to guide the design and delivery of new service initiatives, to inform both pre- and in-service training and professional development efforts, and to formulate well-grounded standards of practice. As demonstrated throughout this volume, the challenge for researchers is to contribute to the creation of an enhanced, integrated science of early childhood intervention by asking and answering the right questions in practically and empirically meaningful ways that cut across diverse service systems. To address this challenge, the Board on Children, Youth, and Families of the National Research Council and the Institute of Medicine convened the Committee on Integrating the Science of Early Childhood Development. Its report will be released in the year 2000.

CONCLUSIONS

In summary, at the dawn of the twenty-first century, the field of early childhood intervention faces an exciting mix of opportunities and challenges. The extent to which the opportunities can be realized and the challenges can be mastered will depend ultimately on our ability to negotiate the dynamic tensions among science, policy, practice, and advocacy (Shonkoff, in press). In practice, these contrasting perspectives are unlikely partners. Advocates are mobilized by passionate conviction. Scientists are driven by cool skepticism. Advocates have little interest in what is unknown. Scientists draw their lifeblood from the excitement of uncertainty. Advocates demand action. Scientists call for reflection and restraint. Advocates have no patience for the deliberate pace of science. Scientists disparage the short attention span of politics.

Notwithstanding their credentials as an "odd couple," the marriage of advocacy and science represents the best hope for the future of early childhood intervention. If the commitment of a true marriage presents too much of a challenge, these two cultures must at least be willing to live together for the sake of the children – to accommodate to each other's needs in order to serve a greater good. In a society whose social and political roots are deeply embedded in the concepts of limited government and personal responsibility, the battles over finite public resources will always be fierce, and the role of effective advocacy for those who are vulnerable will always be critical. Nevertheless, there are dangers inherent in any enterprise that does not subject itself to serious self-assessment in the service of continuous improvement. History teaches us the danger of assuming that state-of-the-art knowledge represents the last word. Indeed, the future vitality of all early childhood intervention efforts depends on the extent to which we can improve what we do rather than maintain the status quo.

In short, both advocates and scholars of early childhood intervention must embrace Campbell's (1987) notion of the "experimenting society." We must think of evaluation research not only as a vehicle for documenting success but also as a tool for finding out more about where and how we are falling short. The field of early childhood intervention, broadly defined, serves a markedly diverse population of children and families. For some, currently available interventions represent a lifeline that facilitates dramatic gains. For others, conventional efforts may have little measurable impact in the face of overwhelming adversity. For those interventions that are successful, we must secure adequate funding to assure high quality and sustained implementation and obtain full access for all who may benefit from them. For those efforts that appear to have more modest impact, we need to find a better way.

In the end, the major question facing the field of early childhood intervention is not whether young children are worthy of public investment. The critical challenge is how to capitalize on current knowledge and mobilize our collective resources to ensure better health and developmental outcomes. Our task is not to choose between supportive advocacy or critical research. Our mandate is to bring these two perspectives together to promote the well-being of all our children.

REFERENCES

Ainsworth, M. D. S. (1969). Object relations dependency and attachment: A theoretical review of the mother-infant relationship. *Child Development, 40*, 969–1025.

Ainsworth, M. D. S., Blehar, M. D., Waters, E., & Wall, S. (1978). *Patterns of attachment: A psychological study of the Strange Situation.* Hillsdale, NJ: L. Erlbaum.

Albee, G. W. (1968). Needed – a revolution in caring for the retarded. *Transaction, 3*, 37–42.

Anastasiow, N. J., & Mansergh, G. P. (1975). Teaching skills in early childhood programs. *Exceptional Children, 41*, 309–17.

Ariès, P. (1962). *Centuries of childhood: A social history of family life.* New York: Knopf.

Association for Retarded Citizens. (1986). *Transition practices for handicapped youngsters in early childhood settings.* Boston: Author.

Barnett, W. S. (1985). Benefit-cost analysis of the Perry Preschool Program and its policy implications. *Educational Evaluation and Policy Analysis, 7*, 333–42.

Barnett, W. S. (1995). Long-term effects of early childhood programs on cognitive and school outcomes. *The Future of Children, 5* (3), 25–50.

Barnett, W. S., & Frede, E. C. (1993). Early childhood programs in the public schools: Insights from a state survey. *Journal of Early Intervention, 17* (4), 396–413.

Bell, R. Q. (1974). Contributions of human infants to caregiving and social interaction. In M. Lewis & L. A. Rosenblum (Eds.), *The effect of the infant on its caregiver* (pp. 1–19). New York: Wiley.

Bloom, B. S. (1964). *Stability and change in human characteristics.* New York: Wiley.

Bowe, F. G. (1995). Population estimates: Birth-to-5 children with disabilities. *The Journal of Special Education, 20*, 461–71.

Bowlby, J. (1951). *Maternal care and mental health.* Geneva: World Health Organization.

Bowlby, J. (1969). *Attachment and loss* (Vol. I). New York: Basis Books.

Braun, S. J., & Edwards, E. P. (1972). *History and theory of early childhood education.* Worthington, OH: Charles A. Jones.

Bredekamp, S., & Copple, C. (1997). *Developmentally appropriate practice* (rev. ed.). Washington, DC: National Association for the Education of Young Children.

Bretherton, I., & Waters, E. (1985). Growing points of attachment: Theory and research. *Monographs of the Society for Research in Child Development, 50* (1-2, Serial No. 209).

Bricker, D., & Slentz, K. (1988). Personnel preparation: Handicapped infants. In M. C. Wang, M. C. Reynolds, & H. J. Walberg (Eds.), *Handbook of special education: Research and practice* (Vol. 3, pp. 319–45). Elmsford, NY: Pergamon Press.

Broman, S. H., Bien, E., & Shaughnessy, P. (1985). *Low achieving children: The first seven years.* Hillsdale, N.J.: Lawrence Earlbaum Associates.

Broman, S. H., Nichols, P. L., & Kennedy, W. A. (1975). *Preschool IQ: Prenatal and early developmental correlates.* Hillsdale, NJ: Lawrence Erlbaum Associates.

Bronfenbrenner, U. (1974). *Is early intervention effective?* Washington, DC: Office of Human Development.

Brosterman, N. (1997). *Inventing kindergarten.* New York: Harry N. Abrams, Inc.

Butler, J. A., Starfield, B., & Stenmark, S. (1984). Child health policy. In H. W. Stevenson & A. E. Siegel (Eds.), *Child development research and social policy* (pp. 110–88). Chicago: University of Chicago Press.

Cairns, R. B. (1983). The emergence of developmental psychology. In W. Kessen (Ed.), *History, theory, and methods: Vol I. Handbook of child psychology* (pp. 41–102). New York: Wiley.

Caldwell, B. M. (1973). The importance of beginning early. In M. B. Karnes (Ed.), *Not all little wagons are red: The exceptional child's early years* (pp. 2–10). Arlington, VA: Council for Exceptional Children.

Caldwell, B. M. (1986). Education of families for parenting. In M. W. Yogman & T. B. Brazelton (Eds.), *In support of families* (pp. 229–41). Cambridge: Harvard University Press.

Campbell, D. T. (1987). Problems for the experimenting society in the interface between evaluation and service providers. In S. L. Kagan, D. R. Powell, B. Weissbourd, & E. F. Zigler (Eds.), *America's family support programs* (pp. 345–51). New Haven: Yale University Press.

Carnegie Task Force on Meeting the Needs of Young Children. (1996). *Starting points: Meeting the needs of our youngest children.* New York: Carnegie Corporation.

Casto, G., & White, K. R. (1993). Longitudinal studies of alternative types of early intervention: Rationale and design. *Early Education and Development, 4* (4), 224–37.

Chaille, S. (1887). Infants. Their chronological process. *New Orleans Medical and Surgical Journal,* 14, 893–902.

Chase, A. (1980). *The legacy of Malthus: The social costs of the new scientific realism.* New York: Knopf.

Chase-Lansdale, P., & Vinovskis, M. A. (1995). Whose responsibility? An historical analysis of the changing roles of mothers, fathers, and society. In P. Chase-Lansdale & J. Brooks-Gunn (Eds.), *Escape from poverty: What makes a difference for children?* (pp. 11–37). New York: Cambridge University Press.

Children's Defense Fund. (1998). *The state of America's children: Yearbook 1998.* Washington, DC: Author.

Clarke, A. M., & Clarke, A. D. B. (1976). *Early experience: Myth and evidence.* New York: The Free Press.

Clarke-Stewart, A., & Fein, G. (1983). Early childhood programs. In P. Mussen (Ed.), *Handbook of child psychology* (Vol. 2, pp. 917–99). New York: Wiley.

Council of Economic Advisers. (1997). *The first three years: Investments that pay.* Washington, DC: Author.

Cremin, L. (1988). *American education: The metropolitan experience, 1876–1980.* New York: Harper & Row.

Crissey, M. S. (1975). Mental retardation – past, present, and future. *American Psychologist, 30,* 800–8.

Cuban, L. (1992). Why some reforms last: The case of the kindergarten. *American Journal of Education, 100,* 166–94.

deLone, R. H. (1979). *Small futures: Children, inequality, and the limits of liberal reform.* New York: Harcourt, Brace, Jovanovich.

Dennis, W. (1960). Causes of retardation among institutionalized children: Iran. *The Journal of Genetic Psychology, 96,* 47–59.

Dennis, W. (1973). *Children of the creche.* New York: Appleton-Century-Croft.

DeWeerd, J. (1981). Early education services for children with handicaps: Where have we been, where are we now, and where are we going? *Journal of the Division for Early Childhood, 2,* 15–23.

Edelman, M. W. (1987). *Families in peril: An agenda for social change.* Cambridge: Harvard University Press.

Elkind, D. (1967). Piaget and Montessori. *Harvard Educational Review, 37* (4), 535–45.

Eller, E. (Ed.). (1956). *The school of infancy by John Amos Comenius.* Chapel Hill: University of North Carolina Press.

Fenichel, E., & Provence, S. (Eds.). (1993). *Development in jeopardy: Clinical responses to infants and families.* Madison, CT: International Universities Press.

Ferry, P. C. (1981). On growing new neurons: Are early intervention programs effective? *Pediatrics, 67,* 38–41.

Fishler, K., Graliker, B. V., & Koch, R. (1964). The predictability of intelligence with Gesell developmental scales in mentally retarded infants and young children. *American Journal of Mental Deficiency, 69,* 515–25.

Foltz, A. M. (1982). *An ounce of prevention: Child health politics under Medicaid.* Cambridge: MIT Press.

Gallagher, J. J., Trohanis, P. L., & Clifford, R. M. (Eds.). (1989). *Policy implementation & P. L. 99-457.* Baltimore, MD: Paul H. Brookes.

Gallagher, P., Malone, D. M., Cleghorne, M., & Helms, K. A. (1997). Perceived inservice training needs for early intervention personnel. *Exceptional Children, 64* (1), 19–30.

Gartner, A., & Lipsky, D. K. (1987). Beyond special education: Toward a quality system for all students. *Harvard Educational Review, 57,* 367–595.

Garwood, S. G., Fewell, R. R., & Neisworth, J. T. (1988). Public Law 94–142: You can get there from here! *Topics in Early Childhood Special Education, 8,* 1–11.

Gesell, A. (1925). *The mental growth of the preschool child.* New York: Macmillan.

Gesell, A. (1929). *Infancy and human growth.* New York: Macmillan.

Gliedman J., & Roth, W. (1980). *The unexpected minority: Handicapped children in America.* New York: Harcourt, Brace, Jovanovich.

Goldberg, S. (1982). Some biological aspects of early parent-infant interaction. In S. G. Moore & C. R. Cooper (Eds.), *The young child: Review of research* (Vol. 3, pp. 35–56). Washington, DC: National Association for the Education of Young Children.

Graham, F. K., Ernhart, C. B., Thurston, D. L., & Craft, M. (1962). Development three years after perinatal anoxia and other potentially damaging newborn experiences. *Psychological Monographs, 76* (3, Whole No. 522).

Graham, F. K., Pennoyer, M. M., Caldwell, B. M., Greenman, M., & Hartmann, A. T. (1957). Relationships between clinical status and behavior test performance in a newborn group with histories suggesting anoxia. *Journal of Pediatrics, 50,* 177–89.

Green, M., Ferry, P., Russman, B., Shonkoff, J., & Taft, L. (1987). Early intervention programs: When do pediatricians fit in? *Contemporary Pediatrics, 4,* 92–118,

Greven, P. (Ed.). (1973). *Child rearing concepts, 1628–1861.* Itasca, IL: F. E. Peacock.

Griffith, J. P. C. (1895). *The care of the baby – A manual for mothers and nurses.* Philadelphia: Saunders.

Guralnick, M. J. (Ed.). (1997). *The effectiveness of early intervention.* Baltimore, MD: Paul H. Brookes.

Guralnick, M. J. (1998). Effectiveness of early intervention for vulnerable children: A developmental perspective. *American Journal on Mental Retardation, 102* (4), 319–45.

Guralnick, M. J., Heiser, K. E., Eaton, A. P., Bennett, F. C., Richardson, H. B., & Groom, J. M. (1988). Pediatricians' perceptions of the effectiveness of early intervention for at-risk and handicapped children. *Journal of Developmental and Behavioral Pediatrics, 9,* 12–18,

Hanline, M. F., & Knowlton, A. (1988). A collaborative model for providing support to parents during their child's transition from infant intervention to preschool special education public school programs. *Journal of the Division for Early Childhood, 12,* 116–25.

Harbin, G., Gallagher, J. J., Lillie, T., & Eckland, J. (1992). Factors influencing state progress in the implementation of Public Law 99-457, Part H. *Policy Sciences, 25,* 103–15.

Hauser-Cram, P., Pierson, D. E., Walker, D. K., & Tivnan, T. (1991). *Early education in the public schools: Lessons from a comprehensive birth-to-kindergarten program.* San Francisco: Jossey-Bass.

Hauser-Cram, P., Upshur, C., Krauss, M., & Shonkoff, J. (1988). Implications of Public Law 99-457 for early intervention services for infants and toddlers with disabilities. *Social Policy Report of the Society for Research in Child Development, 3* (3), 1–16.

Healy, A., Keesee, P., & Smith, B. (1985). *Early services for children with special needs: Transactions for family support.* Iowa City: The University of Iowa.

Hirsch, E. D. (1996). *The schools we need and why we don't have them.* New York: Doubleday.

Hobbs, N. (1975). *The futures of children.* San Francisco: Jossey-Bass.

Holmes, D. (1857). *The child's physician: A popular treatise on the management of diseases of infancy and childhood.* Providence, RI.

Holt, L. E. (1897). *The diseases of infancy and childhood.* New York: D. Appleton and Company.

Hubbell R. (1983). A *review of Head Start research since 1970.* Washington, DC: U.S. Department of Health and Human Services.

Hunt, J. M. (1961). *Intelligence and experience.* New York: Ronald Press.

Ireys, H. T., & Nelson, R. P. (1992). New federal policy for children with special health care needs: Implications for pediatricians. *Pediatrics, 90,* 321–7.

Kahn, A. J., & Kamerman, S. B. (1987). *Child care: Facing the hard choices.* Dover, MA: Auburn House.

Kamerman, S. B., & Kahn, A. J. (1995). *Starting right: How America neglects its youngest children and what we can do about it.* New York: Oxford University Press.

Kamin, L. (1974). *The science and politics of I.Q.* Potomac, MD: L. Erlbaum.

Karoly, L. A., Greenwood, P. W., Everingham, S. S., Hoube, J., Kilburn, M. R., Rydell, C. P., Sanders, M., & Chiesa, J. (1998). *Investing in our children: What we know and don't know about the costs and benefits of early childhood interventions.* Santa Monica, CA: RAND.

Kerns, G. M. (1988). *Transition for young children with special needs in New Hampshire: Perceptions of parents and early intervention program directors.* Paper presented at the 112th Annual Meeting of the American Association on Mental Retardation, Washington, DC.

Kirk, S. A. (1958). *Early education of the mentally retarded.* Urbana, IL: The University of Illinois Press.

Kochanek, T. T., & Buka, S. L. (1998). Patterns of early intervention service utilization: Child, maternal, and provider factors. *Journal of Early Intervention, 21* (3), 217–31.

Krauss, M. (1990). New precedent in family policy: Individualized family service plan. *Exceptional Children, 56* (5), 388–95.

Lazar, I., & Darlington, R. (1982). Lasting effects of early education: A report from the Consortium for Longitudinal Studies. *Monographs of the Society for Research in Child Development, 47*, (2–3, Serial No. 195).

Lesser, A. J. (1985). The origin and development of maternal and child health programs in the United States. *American Journal of Public Health, 75*, 590–8.

Liaw, F., Meisels, S. J., & Brooks-Gunn, J. (1995). The effects of experience of early intervention on low birthweight, premature children: The Infant Health and Development Program. *Early Childhood Research Quarterly, 10*, 405–531.

Lilienfeld, A. M., & Parkhurst, E. (1951). A study of the association of factors of pregnancy and parturition with the development of cerebral palsy: A preliminary report. *American Journal of Hygiene, 53*, 262–82.

Lilienfeld, A. M., & Pasamanick, B. (1954). Association of maternal and fetal factors with the development of epilepsy, I: Abnormalities in the prenatal and paranatal periods. *Journal of the American Medical Association, 155*, 719–24.

Magee, E. M., & Pratt, M. W. (1985). *1935–1985: 50 years of U.S. federal support to promote the health of mothers, children, and handicapped children in America*. Vienna, VA: Information Sciences Research Institute.

Margolis, L. H., & Meisels, S. J. (1987). Barriers to the effectiveness of EPSDT for children with moderate and severe developmental disabilities. *American Journal of Orthopsychiatry, 57*, 424–30.

Martin, E. W. (1989). Lessons from implementing P.L. 94-142. In J. J. Gallagher, P. L. Trohanis, & R. M. Clifford (Eds.), *Policy implementation & P.L. 99-457* (pp. 19–32). Baltimore, MD: Paul H. Brookes.

Meisels, S. J. (1984). Prediction, prevention, and developmental screening in the EPSDT program. In H. W. Stevenson & A. E. Siegel (Eds.), *Child development research and social policy* (pp. 267–317). Chicago: University of Chicago Press.

Meisels, S. J. (1985a). A functional analysis of the evolution of public policy for handicapped young children. *Educational Evaluation and Policy Analysis, 7*, 116–26.

Meisels, S. J. (1985b). The efficacy of early intervention: Why are we still asking this question? *Topics in Early Childhood Special Education, 5*, 1–8.

Meisels, S. J. (1989). Meeting the mandate of Public Law 99-457: Early childhood intervention in the nineties. *American Journal of Orthopsychiatry, 59*, 451–60.

Meisels, S. J. (1999). Assessing readiness. In R. C. Pianta & M. M. Cox (Eds.), *The transition to kindergarten.* (pp. 39–66). Baltimore, MD: Paul H. Brookes.

Meisels, S. J., Dichtelmiller, M., & Liaw, F. (1993). A multidimensional analysis of early childhood intervention programs. In C. Zeanah (Ed.), *Handbook of Infant Mental Health* (pp. 361–85). New York: Guilford Press.

Meisels, S., Harbin, G., Modigliani, K., & Olson, K. (1988). Formulating optimal state early childhood intervention policies. *Exceptional Children, 55*, 159–65.

Meisels, S. J., & Margolis, L. H. (1988). Is EPSDT effective with developmentally disabled children? *Pediatrics, 81*, 262–71.

Meisels, S. J., & Wasik, B. A. (1990). Who should be served? Identifying children in need of early intervention. In S. J. Meisels & J. P. Shonkoff (Eds.), *The handbook of early childhood intervention* (pp. 605–32). New York: Cambridge University Press.

Morgan, G. (1972). The Kaiser child service centers. In S. J. Braun & E. P. Edwards (Eds.), *History and theory of early childhood education* (pp. 368–72). Worthington, OH: Charles A. Jones.

National Commission on Children. (1991). *Beyond rhetoric: A new American agenda for children and families*. Washington, DC: U.S. Government Printing Office.

National Education Goals Panel (1991). *The national education goals report*. Washington, DC: Author.

Neill, A. S. (1960). *Summerhill: A radical approach to child rearing*. New York: Hart Publishing.

Neuman, S. B., Hagedorn, T., Celano, D., & Daly, P. (1995). Toward a collaborative approach to parent involvement in early education: A study of teenage mothers in an African-American community. *American Educational Research Journal, 32*, 801–27.

NICHD Early Child Care Research Network. (1997). The effects of infant child care on infant-mother attachment security: Results of the NICHD study of early child care. *Child Development, 68* (5), 860–79.

Nichols, P. L., & Chen, T. (1981). *Minimal brain dysfunction: A prospective study*. Hillsdale, NJ: Lawrence Erlbaum Associates.

Ohlson, C. (1998) Welfare reform: Implications for young children with disabilities, their families, and service providers. *Journal of Early Intervention, 21* (3), 191–206.

Peters D. L., & Kontos, S. (1987). Continuity and discontinuity of experience: An intervention perspective. In D. L. Peters and S. Kontos (Eds.), *Continuity and discontinuity of experience in child care* (pp. 1–16). Norwood, NJ: Ablex Publishing.

Peterson, N. (1987). *Early intervention for handicapped and at-risk children: An introduction to early childhood-special education*. Denver: Love Publishing.

Provence, S., & Lipton, R. C. (1962). *Infants in institutions*. New York: International Universities Press.

Provence, S., Naylor, A., & Patterson, J. (1977). *The challenge of day care*. New Haven: Yale University Press.

Ramey, C. T., & Ramey, S. L. (1998). Early intervention and early experience. *American Psychologist, 53* (2), 109–20.

Reese, C. (1985). Head Start at 20. *Children Today, 14*, 6–9.

Reynolds, A. J., Mann, E., Miedel, W., & Smokowski, P. (1997). The state of early childhood intervention: Effectiveness, myths, and realities, new directions. *Focus: Newsletter of the University of Wisconsin Institute for Poverty, 19* (1), 5–11.

Richardson, S. A., & Koller, H. (1996). *Twenty-two years: Causes and consequences of mental retardation*. Cambridge, MA: Harvard University Press.

Sameroff, A. J. (1975). Early influences on development: Fact or fancy? *Merrill-Palmer Quarterly of Behavior and Development, 21,* 267–94.

Sameroff, A. J., & Chandler, M. J. (1975). Reproductive risk and the continuum of caretaking casualty. In F. D. Horowitz, M. Hetherington, S. Scarr-Salapatek, & G. Siegel (Eds.), *Review of child development research* (Vol. 4, pp. 187–244). Chicago: University of Chicago Press.

Sameroff, A. J., Seifer, R., Baldwin, A., & Baldwin, C. (1993). Stability of intelligence from preschool to adolescence: The influence of social and family risk factors. *Child Development, 64,* 80–97.

Schore, A. N. (1994). *Affect regulation and the origin of the self: The neurobiology of emotional development.* Hillsdale, NJ: Lawrence Erlbaum Associates.

Schorr, L. B. (1988). *Within our reach: Breaking the cycle of disadvantage.* New York: Anchor Press.

Share, J., Webb, A., & Koch, R. (1961). A preliminary investigation of the early developmental status of mongoloid infants. *American Journal of Mental Defi ciency, 66,* 238–41.

Shonkoff, J. P. (1992). Early intervention research: Asking and answering meaningful questions. *Zero to Three, 12* (3), 7–9.

Shonkoff, J.P. (in press). Science, policy, and practice: Three cultures in search of a shared mission. *Child Development.*

Shonkoff, J. P., & Hauser-Cram, P. (1987). Early intervention for disabled infants and their families – A quantitative analysis. *Pediatrics, 80,* 650–8.

Shonkoff, J. P., Hauser-Cram, P., Krauss, M. W., & Upshur, C. C. (1988). Early intervention efficacy research: What have we learned and where do we go from here? *Topics in Early Childhood Special Education, 8,* 81–93.

Shonkoff, J. P., Hauser-Cram, P., Krauss, M. W., & Upshur, C. C. (1992). Development of infants with disabilities and their families. *Monographs of the Society for Research in Child Development, 57* (6, Serial No. 230).

Shonkoff, J. P., & Meisels, S. J. (1991). Defining eligibility for services under P. L. 99-457. *Journal of Early Intervention, 15* (1), 21–5.

Singer, J., & Butler, J. A. (1987). The Education for All Handicapped Children Act: Schools as agents of social reform. *Harvard Educational Review, 57,* 125–52.

Skeels, H. M. (1966). Adult status of children with contrasting early life experiences. *Monographs of the Society for Research in Child Development, 31,* 1–65.

Skeels, H. M., & Dye, H. B. (1939). A study of the effects of differential stimulation on mentally retarded children. *Proceedings of the American Association of Mental Deficiency, 44,* 114.

Smith, B. J., & Strain, P. S. (1988). Early childhood special education in the next decade; Implementing and expanding P.L. 99-457. *Topics in Early Childhood Special Education 8,* 37–47.

Spitz, H. H. (1986). *The raising of intelligence: A selected history of attempts to raise retarded intelligence.* Hillsdale, NJ: Lawrence Erlbaum Associates.

Spitz, R. A. (1945). Hospitalism: An inquiry into the genesis of psychiatric conditions in early childhood. In R. S. Eissler (Ed.), *Psychoanalytic study of the child.* New Haven, CT: Yale University Press.

Sroufe, L. A. (1983). Infant-caregiver attachment and patterns of adaptation in preschool: The roots of maladaptation and competence. In M. Perlmutter (Ed.), *The Minnesota symposia on child psychology* (Vol. 16, pp. 41–84). Hillsdale, NJ: Lawrence Erlbaum.

Sroufe, L. A. (1996). *Emotional development: The origins of emotional life in the early years.* New York: Cambridge University Press.

Steiner, G. Y. (1976). *The children's cause.* Washington, DC: The Brookings Institution.

Stile, S., Abernathy, S., Pettibone, T., & Wachtel, W. (1984). Training and certification for early childhood special education personnel: A six-year follow-up study. *Journal of the Division for Early Childhood, 11,* 66–73.

Talbot, M. E. (1964). *Edward Seguin – A study for an educational approach to the treatment of mentally defective children.* New York: Columbia University Teachers College.

Takanishi, R., & deLeone, P. (1994). A Head Start for the 21st century. *American Psychologist, 49,* 120–2.

Tjossem, T. (1976). Early intervention: Issues and approaches. In T. Tjossem (Ed.), *Intervention strategies for high risk infants and young children* (pp. 3–33). Baltimore, MD: University Park Press.

Tolstoy, L. (1967). *Tolstoy on education.* Chicago: University of Chicago Press.

Turnbull, A. P., & Turnbull, H. R. (1985). Stepping back from early intervention; An ethical perspective. *Journal of the Division for Early Childhood, 10,* 106–17.

Vinovskis, M. A. (1993). Early childhood education: Then and now. *Daedalus, 122* (1), 151–76.

Warfield, M. E. (1994). A cost-effectiveness analysis of early intervention services in Massachusetts: Implications for policy. *Educational Evaluation and Policy Analysis, 16* (1), 87–99.

Watson, J. (1928). *Psychological care of infant and child.* New York: Norton.

Werner E. E., Bierman, J. M., & French, F. E. (1971). *The children of Kauai: A longitudinal study from the prenatal period to age ten.* Honolulu: University of Hawaii Press.

Werner, E. E., & Smith, R. S. (1977). *Kauai's children come of age.* Honolulu: University of Hawaii Press.

Werner, E. E., & Smith, R. S. (1982). *Vulnerable but invincible: A longitudinal study of resilient children and youth.* New York: McGraw-Hill.

Werner, E. E., & Smith, R. S. (1992). *Overcoming the odds: High risk children from birth to adulthood.* Ithaca, NY: Cornell University Press.

White, K. R., Taylor, M. J., & Moss, V. (1992). Does research support claims about the benefits of involving parents in early intervention programs? *Review of Education Research, 62* (1), 91–125.

Wishy, B. (1968). *The child and the republic – The dawn of modern American child nurture.* Philadelphia: University of Pennsylvania Press.

Zigler, E. F., & Muenchow, S. (1992). *Head Start: The inside story of America's most successful educational experiment.* New York: Basic Books.

Zigler, E. F., & Styfco, S. J. (Eds.). (1993). *Head Start and beyond: A national plan for extended childhood intervention.* New Haven, CT: Yale University Press.

Zigler, E. F., Styfco, S. J., & Gilman, E. (1993). The national Head Start program for disadvantaged preschoolers. In E. F. Zigler & S. J. Styfco (Eds.) (1993). *Head Start and beyond: A national plan for extended childhood intervention* (pp. 1–42). New Haven, CT: Yale University Press.

Zigler, E. F., Taussig, C., & Black, K. (1992). Early childhood intervention: A promising preventative for juvenile delinquency. *American Psychologist, 47,* 997–1006.

Zigler, E. F., & Valentine, J. (Eds.). (1979). *Project Head Start: A legacy of the War on Poverty.* New York: The Free Press.

PART TWO

CONCEPTS OF DEVELOPMENTAL VULNERABILITY AND RESILIENCE

CHAPTER TWO

The Biology of Developmental Vulnerability

JACK P. SHONKOFF AND PAUL C. MARSHALL

Human development and behavior unfold through a complex and highly interactive process in which both biological regulation and experiential influences are substantial. Although most attention in the field of early childhood intervention has been focused on the role of experience, the contribution of the biological substrate requires equal scrutiny. To achieve a balanced understanding of the transaction between nature and nurture, it is essential that we examine the normal development of the central nervous system (CNS) and explore the effects of specific abnormalities and injuries on its functioning.

Extensive research conducted over the past few decades has resulted in a dramatic increase in our knowledge about the normal development of the brain (Sarnat, 1996; Nelson, this volume). This research shows that the biology of neuromaturation is controlled by genetic mechanisms whose timing is regulated precisely and whose unfolding is sensitive to a variety of environmental influences. As our understanding of the mechanisms involved in the evolution of brain structure and function has become more sophisticated, nowhere has this been more striking than in the identification of genes that program cellular growth, differentiation, and maturation. Indeed, the elucidation of cellular and intracellular signal mechanisms has not only resulted in greater knowledge of overall brain development but it also has reflected a breakthrough in our understanding of operational mechanisms of brain function. Significant progress in the fields of neuropsychology, neuroanatomy, neurophysiology, and neural-imaging has also added remarkably to the

base of our knowledge (Nelson & Bloom, 1997). As a result, we are better able to generate more sophisticated hypotheses about the neurological basis of such complex behaviors as attention, problem solving, communication, and creative thinking.

The immediate and long-term consequences of specific biological insults and malformations that impinge on the developing brain continue to be studied and are highlighted in this chapter. It is clear, however, that even when such variables as the individual nature of the injurious agent, the dosage of the insult, and its timing in the sequence of brain development are taken into account, there is considerable variability in the functional impact on any given individual. Although knowledge in this area continues to evolve, our current understanding of the impact of insults to the central nervous system rests more on a concept of increased developmental vulnerability than on inevitable disability.

In contrast to the adult nervous system, the developing brain possesses an initial redundancy of developing neurons that acts as a neurological reserve against possible injury (Sarnat, 1996). The ultimate outcome of any specific injury to the central nervous system is mediated potentially by a broad range of protective factors, both within the child and in the environment in which he or she is reared. Some fetuses, for example, may be highly resistant on a genetic basis to the adverse effects of a high level of maternal alcohol ingestion during pregnancy. Others may be born with some of the features of the fetal alcohol syndrome after only a moderate exposure to this potential teratogen (Clarren & Smith, 1978). Some newborns may be quite resilient and survive an asphyxiating delivery without sequelae, whereas others who appear to sustain a comparable degree of oxygen deprivation may manifest the signs of cerebral palsy early in the first year (Nelson & Ellenberg, 1979, 1981). A premature infant who struggles through multiple medical complications and is discharged from the neonatal intensive care unit to a nurturing home with excellent social supports is likely to do well developmentally; another baby with an identical medical history who is reared in an unstable environment by an isolated, disorganized, and highly stressed single parent is likely to have a host of developmental disabilities (see Osofsky & Thompson, this volume). Thus, biological insults to the central nervous system have variable effects on the development of a young child. This diversity in outcomes reflects the impact of individual differences in the constitutional resilience of children and the critical influence of the caregiving environment on early childhood development. Indeed, there is increasing and compelling experimental laboratory data on the developing mammalian nervous system to support the hypothesis that appropriate environmental supports are crucial to recovery from genetic and physical injury. In essence, earlier views of the immutability of brain injury have given way to greater appreciation of the mutual impact of nature and nurture.

This chapter focuses on the neurological basis of developmental disability in early childhood. It begins with an overview of the normal process of development and maturation of the central nervous system from conception through infancy. Next, neurological determinants of disability and dysfunction are examined, with particular consideration given to the nature of the specific pathological influence, the timing of the insult, and the range and variety of subsequent consequences it may have for later developmental and behavioral competence. The chapter concludes with a recapitulation of the extent to which neurological vulnerabilities interact with environmental factors to produce variable functional outcomes in the early years of life.

DEVELOPMENT OF THE CENTRAL NERVOUS SYSTEM

The orderly progression of human development from a fertilized egg to a highly differentiated yet immature infant is determined by an exquisitely tuned sequence of events that is controlled by genetic regulation and influenced both by intrauterine and postnatal environmental factors. This section provides a broad overview of the embryogenesis and early maturation of the central nervous system. Interested readers can find more detailed accounts elsewhere (Lemire, Loeser, Leech, & Alvord, 1975; Volpe, 1995).

The human nervous system begins its differentiation as a simple plate of neuroectodermal cells that is present as early as sixteen days after fertilization. During the next two weeks, this neural plate folds into a tube or cylinder whose rostral (head) end will develop into the upper spinal cord and brain. By day 28 of gestation, the neural tube is completely closed, and major subdivisions of the nervous system are identifiable. Although most biological insults during this early stage of brain development result in spontaneous miscarriage, a localized failure of closure of the neural tube can have nonfatal, but significant, consequences. If, for example, the rostral end fails to close, the child may be born with *anencephaly*, an invariably fatal condition in which there is an absence of the cerebral cortex. Failure of closure of the caudal (tail) end of the neural tube can result in *myelodysplasia* (spina bifida), a nonfatal disorder with a variable prognosis.

By five weeks of gestational age, the neural tube will have divided lengthwise to form two cerebral hemispheres with paired bilateral ventricles. Further cleavage and folding in other planes result in structural differentiation of the major parts of the central nervous system. At this point in embryogenesis, specific insults or interruptions of development are likely to result in severe anomalies. An example of such a malformation is *holoprosencephaly*, or single-sphered brain, in which there is a failure of cleavage of the developing brain into hemispheres. Holoprosencephaly may result from a chromosomal abnormality (e.g., trisomy 13) and results invariably in death in infancy. This abnormality, similar to many early malformations, so disrupts brain development that intrinsic reparative and adaptive mechanisms are overwhelmed.

With closure and differentiation of the neural tube completed by the end of the first six weeks of pregnancy, the brain is a primitive but recognizable organ. At this point, the nervous system proceeds rapidly through a contemporaneous and time-limited process of cellular proliferation and migration. Any significant interference with this process may result in a marked reduction in the number of viable neurons available for later brain function. Radiation exposure, genetic disorders, or infection (e.g., rubella) represent the types of insults known to interfere with this process of extensive cell division. When the insult is extensive, and there is a marked decrease or destruction of cerebral tissue, it leads to a condition termed *microcephaly* (which means literally, "small brain").

As primitive neural and supporting (glia) cells multiply, they migrate to proximal (adjacent) or distal (distant) parts of the brain where further differentiation takes place. This migration process is highly regulated. For example, in the cortex the neurons are guided to their final destination by specialized glia that provide the ladder on which the neurons climb into position. The first neurons to reach the evolving cerebral cortex reside in the lower cellular level, followed by further waves of neurons that migrate to layers that are closer to the brain's surface, thereby resulting in an inside-out topography of cortical development. Biological triggers that regulate the initiation and termination of this precisely controlled migration of cells are just beginning to be elucidated (Sarnat, 1996). Interference with this process of migration can result in neurons and their processes not arriving in their appropriate location in the brain, thereby producing a disruption of neuronal interconnections and networks.

A dramatic example of a disorder of neuronal migration is *agenesis* (failure of formation) of the *corpus callosum*. The corpus callosum is a broad band of white matter that serves as the major connecting link between the two hemispheres. Corpus callosum formation generally begins at 11–12 weeks of gestation and is complete by 20 weeks. If a significant insult affects callosal development in its early stages, complete agenesis results. If the disruption occurs somewhat later, a lesser degree of interhemispheric connection is lost, resulting in partial agenesis and generally a lesser disability. Another example of a migrational disorder, which is more common and increasingly recognized with the advent of sophisticated neuroimaging techniques, is *cortical dysplasia*. This is a more localized disruption of brain architecture that can lead to loss of function, often

associated with seizures, because the normal neural network is not able to develop as a result of the abnormal geography of the affected neurons. In some disorders, a combination of genetically determined abnormalities of both neuronal migration and differentiation takes place. An example is children with certain neurocutaneous syndromes (e.g., *neurofibromatosis* or *tuberous sclerosis*) who, through different mechanisms, show evidence of dysplastic neurons and glia overgrowth and disorganization. The resultant architectural abnormality of the brain is assumed, at least in part, to explain the mental retardation and seizures that often accompany these disorders (North, 1997).

By six months gestation, under normal circumstances, the adult complement of neurons is achieved. Beyond this period, however, and extending into adult life, the process of neuronal differentiation continues, with considerable variability from one part of the nervous system to another. Although the genetic programming of this process is substantial, environmental influences mediated by signals among cells have significant impact as well (Bayer & Altman, 1991; Sarnat, 1996).

Maturing neurons differentiate primarily by the growth of appendages (i.e., axons and dendrites) that are the connecting links through which nerve cells communicate with each other. The elaboration of axons and dendrites, which can be visualized as a process of arborization or treelike branching, is accompanied by a parallel process called *synaptogenesis*, which involves the development of synaptic spines (i.e., the sites of connection) between the appendages of adjacent neurons. These resultant synapses represent the final step in the establishment of the basic circuitry of the central nervous system. The single synapse is the basic unit of anatomical and functional connection between neurons, which collectively generate the full neural network. Each is highly specialized in its morphology and chemical specificity but has the capacity to be modified.

Synaptogenesis continues at a brisk pace well into the first year of postnatal life to the point where there is an overabundance of connections. At this stage, there begins a process of selective elimination of synapses and neuronal branches that results in a more highly organized and efficient brain. This process of selective pruning is accompanied by programmed neuronal death (apoptosis). Thus, an immature brain begins with an abundance of synapses and neurons, many of which will be eliminated as the brain matures. It is this redundancy of neurons and synapses that plays a central role in the plasticity and capacity for adaptation that is characteristic of a young brain (see Nelson, this volume). This process, although beginning in prenatal life, continues throughout childhood and requires environmental stimulation as a key determinant for effective and normal brain development (Volpe, 1995).

Parallel to the process of neuronal differentiation and the establishment of synapses, the supporting tissue network (which is composed of glial cells) also undergoes dramatic proliferation and differentiation. In addition to their important role in neuronal migration, glial cells appear to provide neurons with the appropriate metabolic milieu for normal function. In producing the myelin sheath that surrounds axons, these cells make a critical contribution to the process of neuromaturation. Myelination involves the encasement of axons in an insulating material that serves to facilitate the capacity of the central nervous system to transmit messages in a more efficient manner. Although myelination begins in the prenatal period, it becomes most significant in the first year of postnatal life and continues into the third decade. Certain inborn errors of metabolism, such as *metachromatic leukodystrophy*, can disturb the myelination process, leading to significant brain dysfunction.

In summary, the process of brain development and overall neuromaturation is highly complex and is programmed precisely. It unfolds through a series of interactive steps that are regulated genetically, according to a highly predictable timetable, and that are influenced by factors in both the intrauterine and extrauterine environments. The early stages of this process are characterized by the rapid proliferation and migration of neurons. Subsequent stages are characterized by cell differentiation, synapse formation, programmed cell death, and pruning of synapses. Disruptions in brain development can be caused by intrinsic factors (such as genetic disorders) or by a wide variety of extrinsic influences (such as infection, toxins, or asphyxia), whose ultimate impact is determined by the nature, dose, and timing of the insult; by individual differences in susceptibility; and by the subsequent interplay between the resulting biological vulnerability and early life experiences.

ORIGINS OF CENTRAL NERVOUS SYSTEM DYSFUNCTION AND DISABILITY

Although the manifestations of neurological dysfunction can be diagnosed on the basis of a comprehensive clinical examination, an understanding of the specific etiology or underlying pathophysiological mechanism is often limited. In some cases, a structural abnormality of the brain can be identified through sophisticated diagnostic procedures, such as computerized tomography (CT) or magnetic resonance imaging (MRI). In many conditions, however, the brain itself appears normal under conventional imaging, and even by sophisticated neurophysiological evaluation techniques, despite its impaired functioning. Some disabilities, such as Down syndrome, are known to be associated with a well-defined chromosomal abnormality, yet we do not understand how additional or incomplete chromosomal material results in atypical physical features and mental retardation. Under other circumstances, such as after a prenatal infection from cytomegalovirus, the causal mechanisms of the neurological sequelae may be more clear, but we are still left with unanswered questions about the wide variations in individual susceptibility and differential outcomes in children who sustained apparently comparable infection in utero (Demmler, 1994). More commonly, however, the precise etiology of a neurologically based disability is completely unknown. The following sections provide a selected overview of some of the malformations and insults that have been demonstrated to affect the central nervous system adversely.

Genetic Disorders

Developmental disabilities can result from abnormalities of the genetic code and the interplay of human genes and environmental factors. The recent explosion of knowledge in molecular genetics is generating a more detailed understanding of the mechanisms of both normal and abnormal development, and is leading to an expansion of the borders of what is considered genetic in origin. Consequently, the categories of genetic disorder have expanded into at least five groups: 1) chromosomal abnormalities, 2) single gene defects, 3) mitochondrial disorders, 4) multifactorial disorders, and 5) somatic genetic disorders. This last category, which refers to mutations arising in cells that may eventuate in tumor development in the genetically predisposed individual, has been studied primarily in the context of malignancy and is not discussed in this chapter.

CHROMOSOMAL ABNORMALITIES. These conditions arise from a loss, gain, or abnormal arrangement of the human chromosome complement. Although the diagnosis of a chromosomal anomaly is specific and unambiguous, its developmental manifestations can be quite variable. In an autosomal, (i.e., involving chromosomes other than X or Y) chromosomal disorder, developmental disabilities and mental retardation generally are the rule. When there are anomalies of the sex (X or Y) chromosomes, the results can be more variable.

Down Syndrome. Also known as *trisomy 21* (i.e., triplicate instead of the normal duplicate copies of chromosome 21), Down syndrome is the most common known chromosomal disorder, with an estimated frequency of 1 in 600 live births. At birth, children with this disorder are hypotonic and present fairly recognizable physical features, including a protruding tongue in a small mouth, narrow and upward slanting palpebral fissures (eyelids), and characteristic hand and eye formations. Children with Down syndrome have a higher incidence of cardiac and gastrointestinal anomalies that can be life-threatening, particularly in the neonatal period. Although most children with Down syndrome have significant mental retardation, some may function in the borderline range of ability (Iannaleone & Rosenberg, 1996; Pueschel, 1978).

Fragile-X Syndrome. The observation of a high proportion of males in the population of individuals with mental retardation, and the predominance of males in diagnoses of familial mental retardation, led to an early hypothesis that an abnormality of the X-chromosome may be related to a significant proportion of biologically based intellectual impairment. In 1991, an unstable DNA fragment on the X-chromosome was identified, and further studies located an abnormal gene, termed the *FMR-1 gene,* at this site. This gene is abnormally long and consists of an unusually large number of repeated three base-pair sequences (i.e., triplet repeats) (Kramer et al., 1991). The genetic misinformation that results from this chromosomal anomaly produces a syndrome characterized by large testes, elongated palpebral fissures, large head, prominent ears, and variable mental retardation. The frequency of the Fragile-X syndrome is 1 in 1,500 boys, making it a relatively common cause of mental retardation (Goldson & Hagerman, 1992). The range of IQ scores among individuals with this syndrome extends from 20 to 80, although learning disabilities and attentional problems with normal intelligence have been reported (Hagerman, Kemper, & Hudson, 1985). Many of the female carriers of the Fragile-X chromosome also have intellectual deficits, and the degree of mental retardation generally correlates directly with the number of triplet repeats (Taylor et al., 1994). In addition to the triplet repeats, the FMR-1 gene can sustain point mutations and deletions (i.e., localized abnormalities along the chromosome), which present another mechanism in the etiology of the syndrome (Warren & Nelson, 1994).

Prader-Willi Syndrome and Angelman Syndrome. These two different syndromes are an example of the recently described mechanism of imprinting. Both parents are normal, but during chromosomal replication a mutation develops at a particular site on chromosome 15, resulting in a deletion of chromosomal material. If the abnormality arises from the maternal chromosome, Angelman syndrome results; if it is located in the paternal chromosome, the child will have Prader-Willi syndrome (Knoll et al., 1989). Although classical genetic principles maintain that parental origin of the chromosome is not relevant to clinical expression, this example of genomic imprinting represents an important exception (Brock, 1993). Angelman syndrome is characterized by hypotonia, seizures early in infancy, and severe mental retardation. Affected children have a tendency to smile and laugh frequently, and their movements have been described as similar to those of a marionette (thereby leading to the unfortunate use of the term "Happy Puppet syndrome"). Prader-Willi syndrome has an incidence of 1 in 20,000 and is characterized by hypotonia, small hands and feet, initial failure to thrive and later obesity, hypogonadism, and distinctive facial features (Holm et al., 1993).

Rett Syndrome. This syndrome, which occurs only in girls, is presumed to be related to an abnormality on the X-chromosome. However, the actual site of the anomaly has not yet been established. The prevalence rate of the syndrome is approximately 1 in 15,000 female births (Sekul & Percy, 1992). Unlike most of the other disorders noted in this chapter, Rett syndrome is progressive. Early development may be normal, but by the end of the first year there is a slowing of developmental progress and a clear deceleration in head growth. In the second year, children with the syndrome exhibit developmental regression, seizures, hyperventilation, and loss of purposeful hand movement. Later, the child develops a characteristic wringing of the hands, followed by spasticity and frequent loss of ambulation (Perry, 1991). Familial recurrence is unusual.

Turner Syndrome and Klinefelter Syndrome. In contrast to persons with an abnormal number of autosomal chromosomes, individuals with an abnormal number of sex (X or Y) chromosomes are likely to have normal intelligence. Girls with Turner syndrome, in which there is a single X-chromosome, generally have IQs in the normal range, although they appear to be vulnerable to specific learning disabilities, particularly in the area of visual-spatial skills (Rovet, 1993). Affected youngsters also tend to have difficulties with social skills and can be hyperactive and inattentive (McCauley, Ito, & Key, 1986). Boys with Klinefelter syndrome have an extra X-chromosome (XXY). Although IQ scores typically are normal, there can be significant problems with expressive language, auditory processing, and memory, which often lead to disabilities in reading and spelling (Graham et al., 1988). Similar to girls with Turner syndrome, boys with Klinefelter syndrome have difficulties with social and peer relationships, although their personality styles are quite different.

SINGLE-GENE DEFECTS. Single-gene abnormalities may be inherited through a variety of genetic patterns, including autosomal dominant (transmitted by either parent alone), autosomal recessive (transmitted by both parents together), X-linked dominant (transmitted by either parent alone), or X-linked recessive (asymptomatic in females and symptomatic in males) mechanisms. A number of inborn errors of metabolism, for example, are inherited as autosomal recessive disorders. Many of

these conditions are accompanied by moderate or severe retardation, and the known disorders in this category are responsible for approximately 4–6% of all severe mental retardation (Moser, 1985). Some metabolic disorders, such as Tay-Sachs disease, result in progressive neurological impairment and death with no treatment options available at the present time. Others, such as phenylketonuria (PKU), whose toxic effects are also produced by a specific enzyme deficiency, can be treated through dietary therapy that prevents potential complications, including seizures and mental retardation. Many inborn errors of metabolism are detectable through prenatal diagnosis. The separation of chromosomal-deletion syndromes from single-gene abnormalities is arbitrary. In single-gene abnormalities, the gene is aberrant and therefore its expression is modified to render it dysfunctional. This same functional outcome may occur if the gene is actually deleted physically and is not simply abnormal.

MITOCHONDRIAL DISORDERS. Not all of the genetic message is delivered by chromosomal DNA. There is a small amount of DNA that is found in a cellular structure called the *mitochondrion*. Because sperm are small and consist almost entirely of nuclear DNA, mitochondrial DNA is passed exclusively by the mother. In the 1980s and 1990s, there has been a rapid expansion in our knowledge of disorders resulting from abnormal mitochondrial DNA. For the most part, these disorders are rare and are characterized by progressive developmental deterioration, seizures, metabolic disturbance, and, less commonly, progressive hearing and visual loss. The rarity of these disorders precludes more extensive discussion here; reviews are available (Shapira & DiMauro, 1994).

MULTIFACTORIAL DISORDERS. The least well-understood genetic pattern, multifactorial inheritance, refers to the process whereby the presence of a disorder is determined by the interactive effects of one or more minor genes and by specific environmental facilitators. Neural tube defects (Carter, 1974) and schizophrenia (Kety, 1978) are important examples of disorders that appear to have a multifactorial genetic basis. Spina bifida, for example, has been reported both to occur with greater frequency in some families and to have a two to four times higher incidence among lower socio-economic groups (Nevin, Johnston, & Merritt, 1981). These data led to the hypothesis that suboptimal maternal nutrition may be a contributing factor in the pathogenesis of myelodysplasia among those women who have a genetic predisposition toward bearing children with this disorder (Smithells et al., 1981). Subsequently, a landmark therapeutic trial of folate supplementation in the early weeks of pregnancy showed a clear reduction of neural tube defects from 3.6% to 0.6% (MRC Vitamin Research Study Group, 1991). These data were so convincing that the U.S. Centers for Disease Control and Prevention recommended that folic acid be given to women daily in the first three months of pregnancy. In general, however, understanding multifactorial disorders is difficult because of the complexity of potential interactions among genes and the environment.

SUMMARY. Many specific developmental or behavioral disabilities, with or without associated mental retardation, have a genetic basis. The variability of expression among these inherited conditions, however, is considerable. Despite their underlying biological etiology, the marked extent to which environmental influences may affect the ultimate outcome for children with genetic disorders is substantial. Consequently, firm generalizations about the genetic basis of developmental disabilities are problematic.

Early Brain Malformations

Detectable malformations of the central nervous system may be associated with known genetic disorders that are predetermined from the moment of conception or with random yet identifiable prenatal insults. Their etiology may also be completely obscure. Although they reflect a specific structural departure from normal brain development, the functional consequences of central nervous system malformations can be extremely variable, ranging from profound disability to essentially normal development.

MYELODYSPLASIA. Also known as *myelomeningocele* or *spina bifi dq* myelodysplasia is the most commonly encountered anatomical malformation of the central nervous system. As described earlier in the chapter, this condition generally results from an incomplete closure of the caudal portion of the neural tube during the first month of pregnancy. As a consequence of defective closure, the skeletal and soft tissue coverings of the spinal cord do not develop, and the spinal cord itself and the nerves that exit the spinal canal at that location are dysplastic (abnormal), covered only by a thin membrane. This membrane can rupture easily, leading to meningitis, if surgical repair is not instituted promptly after birth. When meningitis does occur, the risk for additional complications, such as hearing impairment and mental retardation, is increased significantly.

The nature of the neurological handicap associated with myelomeningocele is determined by the location of the spinal defect. More than 80% of affected children have their lesion in the lumbar or lumbosacral region, which results in varying degrees of lower extremity motor impairment (paraparesis), sensory loss, and bowel and bladder dysfunction, depending on the location of the defect and the integrity of the underlying dysplastic neural elements. If the lesion is located in the thoracic region, a severe curvature of the spine (kyphoscoliosis) develops as a frequent result of the malfunction of the adjacent (paraspinal) muscle groups. Almost 90% of children with lumbosacral myelomeningocele have an associated malformation of the brain stem and cerebellum (known as the *Chiari malformation*) with secondary hydrocephalus.

Despite the multiplicity of clinical problems that are associated with myelodysplasia, developmental outcomes are extremely variable and are, in part, determined by the availability of aggressive medical and surgical treatment. A classic review of 200 consecutive, unselected patients with myelomeningocele and hydrocephalus (all of whom received aggressive treatment) found a mortality rate by 3 to 7 years of 14%, with nearly three-quarters of the survivors having IQ scores greater than 80 and a comparable number reported to be ambulatory (McClone et al., 1985). Cesarean section delivery prior to the onset of labor, early closure of the back lesion, and the use of prophylactic antibiotics in the first 24 hours of life represent key elements in the management of children with this disorder (Volpe, 1995). When associated cerebral anomalies of greater severity are present, the mortality and morbidity rates are higher. Thus, the simple diagnosis of myelomeningocele does not necessarily imply a poor developmental prognosis. Rather, associated anomalies (over which we have little control), and the quality of the medical and surgical care (over which we have substantial control), contribute additional elements of risk and protection, which interact with factors in the child's caregiving environment to determine ultimate outcome.

HYDROCEPHALUS. A common clinical problem among children with myelodysplasia, hydrocephalus can be caused by a variety of other lesions that interrupt the circulation and/or reabsorption of cerebrospinal fluid. Such interruptions can arise from other malformations, such as aquaductal stenosis (narrowing of the passage between the third and fourth ventricles of the brain), or from scarring secondary to infection or hemorrhage within the ventricular system.

Under normal circumstances, spinal fluid is produced continuously within the cerebral ventricles. The fluid circulates through the ventricular system and then exits the brain into the subarachnoid space, where it bathes the spinal cord and the brain surface before it is reabsorbed. Any interruption in the continuous circulation of cerebrospinal fluid results in fluid backup, increased intracranial pressure, and eventual expansion of the ventricles. If the ventricles expand slowly, the brain can compensate, at least initially. Under such circumstances, through either spontaneous resolution or surgical placement of a shunt (which drains fluid from the cerebral ventricles to the abdominal cavity), there is little, if any, functional impairment. Prolonged hydrocephalus, on the other hand, which results in marked compression of the cerebral cortex, can produce significant developmental consequences. This problem is particularly striking among children surviving with intrauterine hydrocephalus, who demonstrate a 54% rate of intellectual impairment (McCullough & Balzer-Martin, 1982). The extent of disability, however, is not simply determined by the degree to which the cerebral cortex is thinned as a result of prolonged elevation of intracranial pressure. Thus, on an individual basis, brain adaptation is variable and accurate prediction of ultimate cognitive outcomes is extremely difficult, even when cerebral imaging techniques offer the option of measuring the thickness of the cortex.

Children with hydrocephalus who are identified early and treated appropriately can have a reasonably optimistic prognosis for the future. In a study of children with myelomeningocele and hydrocephalus, in which youngsters with and without shunt infection were compared, those who had not had infected shunts demonstrated a mean IQ on follow-up of 95, and those with shunt infections had a mean IQ of 73. A controlled population of children with myelomeningocele without hydrocephalus had a mean IQ of 102 (McClone et al., 1982). Thus, it appears that hydrocephalus that is treated promptly and is not complicated by infection does not necessarily lead to significant cognitive limitations.

MICROCEPHALY. Microcephaly, a less common malformation, may be suspected when measured head circumference is greater than three standard deviations below the mean for age. Although significant reductions in head size can reflect abnormal brain development or brain injury, a head circumference below the second percentile is not a guarantee of neurological disability or intellectual impairment. In fact, most individuals with a head circumference just below the normal range are quite normal intellectually (Sells, 1977). In some cases, a small head circumference without disability may be a familial trait. A brain that is pathologically small at birth can be caused by any number of intrauterine insults, including congenital infection, intracranial infarction, or, more rarely, excessive exposure to radiation. Familial microcephaly with mental retardation is a genetic disorder presumably related to deficient neuronal proliferation and is diagnosed on the basis of family history.

MEGALENCEPHALY. Megalencephaly is defined operationally as a head circumference greater than the 98th percentile for age. Once again, this physical finding by itself does not necessarily imply neurological dysfunction (Lorber & Priestly, 1981). A large head can be associated with a genetically large brain or it can be secondary to hydrocephalus or a space-occupying lesion, such as a tumor or subdural fluid collection. Neuroimaging techniques, a thorough review of family history, and a careful clinical examination for associated anomalies usually help with the differential diagnosis. Once again, no developmental prognosis can necessarily be attached to this clinical finding without further investigation.

AGENESIS OF THE CORPUS COLLOSUM. In its partial or complete form, agenesis of the corpus collosum is among the more common major structural defects of the brain itself. This malformation is usually part of a syndrome of associated findings and is seen frequently in conjunction with other anomalies of midline structures, such as cleft lip and cleft palate. Despite the severity of the anatomical disruption, at least 15% of individuals with this diagnosis have normal intelligence. Of those identified with disabilities, impairments range from mild to severe (Lemire et al., 1975).

SUMMARY. Although a number of specific anatomical malformations of the brain have been described, their developmental consequences are variable and often difficult to predict during early infancy. It is likely that differences in both biological adaptability and early childhood experiences contribute to the diversity of outcomes.

Infections of the Central Nervous System

Acute or chronic infections of brain tissue (encephalitis), or of the meninges (the covering membrane for the central nervous system) and contiguous brain structures (meningitis), are an important cause of chronic neurological impairment. During the prenatal period, a number of organisms have been demonstrated to produce recognizable congenital syndromes with a range of adverse neurological sequelae. Postnatally, bacterial meningitis remains a potentially devastating illness whose consequences can range from negligible to severe.

CYTOMEGALOVIRUS (CMV). CMV is the most common cause of congenital infection that can lead to neurological impairment. The frequency of infection among newborns ranges from 0.2% to 8.0% of all births worldwide, with an average in the United States of 1% (Demmler 1991; Hanshaw, 1981). Fetal damage usually occurs after a maternal primary infection, but recurrent infection, presumably with a different strain, can also have untoward effects (Demmler, 1991). Of those infants born with active infection, 5–10% show evidence of clinically

overt disease. Affected children demonstrate multiple organ system involvement characterized by intrauterine growth retardation, chorioretinitis (damage to the eyes), pneumonia, anemia, and hepatosplenomegaly (enlargement of the liver and spleen). They also show signs of brain injury that can result in microcephaly, hypotonia or hypertonia, weakness, visual loss, and hearing impairment. In this group, 10% will not live past infancy, and most of the survivors will have significant neurological impairments, including mental retardation and cerebral palsy (Pass, Stango, Myers, & Alford, 1980).

More than 90% of children infected in utero with CMV are relatively asymptomatic at birth. However, 5–15% will eventually develop sensorineural hearing impairment, which can become progressive over time (Connolly, Jerger, & Williamson, 1992; Williamson et al., 1992). Although data regarding the prognosis for neurocognitive outcomes for children without hearing loss are mixed, replicated studies have demonstrated the likelihood of normal intellectual function (Conboy et al., 1986; Hanshaw et al., 1976; Kashden et al., 1998). Thus, it is prudent for asymptomatic infants to have close developmental surveillance and periodic hearing evaluations extending into school age. Specific treatment of congenital CMV thus far has been confined to infants with life-threatening or sight-threatening disease. However, antiviral agents are not without significant risk, and therefore prevention through immunization remains an important goal.

CONGENITAL RUBELLA. Although encountered less frequently because of successful immunization programs, rubella was once the prototypic example of the consequences of congenital infection (Cooper & Krugman, 1966). Unfortunately, there remains a significant pool of unimmunized young women of child-bearing age in the United States, which results in periodic increases in the number of diagnosed cases of congenital rubella syndrome (Centers for Disease Control, 1991). Generally speaking, congenital rubella syndrome is unlikely to occur after 17 weeks of gestation, and the earlier the infection the more severe the outcome (Miller, Craddock-Watson, & Pollack, 1982). In its symptomatic form, congenital rubella is manifested by growth retardation, cataracts and retinitis (eye inflammation), microcephaly, hepatosplenomegaly, petechiae (a rash related to a blood-clotting dysfunction), and congenital heart disease. In the most severe cases, active signs of central nervous system infection with seizures may be seen. Only 25% of children with congenital rubella, however, demonstrate neurological symptoms at birth. Such neonates present with marked irritability, diminished head size, and hypotonia as the predominant features of the syndrome. By the end of the first year, over one-third of children with congenital infection demonstrate signs of psychomotor retardation. Behavior disorders are also common, and a small percentage of children show features of autism (Chess, 1974). Although the most severe hearing impairments are associated with earlier presentations, progressive hearing loss and other developmental disabilities may evolve over time. Therefore, close follow-up for all children with a confirmed diagnosis of congenital rubella is essential. Progressive visual deficits, secondary to retinitis or cataracts, are also common and are usually obvious. In rare cases, a progressive and fatal brain infection (panencephalitis) has been reported. Although 75% of infected children do not appear to have symptoms at birth, many demonstrate progressive impairment over the first few years. In view of the marked range of individual differences in susceptibility and outcome, vigilant long-term follow-up is necessary.

TOXOPLASMOSIS. Congenital toxoplasmosis is caused by the protozoan parasite *Toxoplasma gondii*. Pregnant women may become infected by ingesting contaminated, undercooked meat or by contact with the excreta of infected cats. About 40% of infections in pregnant women result in active infection in the fetus, and, as with other congenital infections, the earlier the insult the more severe the sequelae. About 10% of children with congenital toxoplasmosis are symptomatic with severe disease in the newborn period. The clinical picture consists of hydrocephalus, seizures, chorioretinitis (inflammatory injury to the eye), and intracranial calcifications (Desmonts & Couvreur, 1979; Swisher, Boyer, & McLeod, 1994). Affected children develop severe disabilities, and the mortality rate is high (Stray-Pederson, 1980). About 30% develop generalized disease with hepatosplenomegaly (enlarged liver and spleen), jaundice, lymph node swelling, anemia, and

fever (Eichenwald, 1960; Swisher, Boyer, & McLeod, 1994). Although most children with toxoplasmosis are asymptomatic at birth, almost all will eventually develop significant sequelae, including choreoretinitis (often resulting in blindness), seizures, motor disability, deafness, and mental retardation (Wilson, Remington, Stagno, & Reynolds, 1980). The development of improved diagnostic and therapeutic modalities, however, has changed the outlook for congenital toxoplasmosis significantly. More effective diagnosis during pregnancy, neonatal screening, and antimicrobial therapy have resulted in markedly improved outcomes (McAuley et al., 1994). Prompt antimicrobial treatment, beginning at birth and continuing through the first year, has led to a vastly improved neurological outcome, with 70% of such children achieving IQ scores above 70, and 80% demonstrating normal routine neurological examinations. Despite its improving prognosis, however, the prevention of congenital toxoplasmosis remains a considerable challenge. Although improved public education and earlier recognition of the disease are important, the development of vaccines to protect humans and livestock still remains a critical goal.

CONGENITAL HIV-1 INFECTION. Human Immunodeficiency Virus-Type I infection has become an increasing problem over the past decade, as it has spread from sub-Saharan Africa to virtually every populated area of the world. HIV in women is acquired through intravenous drug use and increasingly via heterosexual contact. The rate of transmission of the virus from mother to child averages approximately 30%, but studies of HIV-infected pregnant women treated with Zidovudine have shown that the infection rate can be reduced substantially (Connor, Sperling, & Gelber, 1994). In about 20% of children with HIV infection, the clinical presentation starts in early infancy with failure to thrive and a subacute encephalopathy characterized by loss of developmental milestones, apathy, and asymmetrical spasticity (Koch, 1996). These findings usually are accompanied by other signs of immunologic deficiency, but the expression of central nervous system involvement is often delayed for several years. In such children, subtle changes in behavior, such as deterioration in play and mood or intellectual impairment, may mark the onset of neurological regression. Despite the initially grave prognosis for children with HIV infection, there is some optimism about the emergence of effective strategies for both prevention and treatment in the future (Koch, 1996).

SUMMARY. Infections of the central nervous system can be associated with a variety of outcomes ranging from normal function to severe disability. In some cases, devastating sequelae are immediate and dramatic. Under other circumstances, the impact of an infectious assault on the brain can be more insidious and may be characterized by the gradual appearance of a subtle or increasingly significant impairment. Although the actual injury from a congenital infection may be nonprogressive, symptoms may not emerge until later, as in the case of a motor disability. In other circumstances, the infectious insult may be ongoing and cumulative, as in the case of a progressive impairment of vision or hearing. As with other injuries to the central nervous system, the timing of the infection and differences in fetal susceptibility account for marked variability in developmental outcomes.

Toxic Insults to the Central Nervous System

Although the number of exposures to potentially toxic substances during an average pregnancy is undoubtedly high, specific birth defects (teratogenic effects) attributed to particular chemicals or drugs have been well documented in only a small number of instances. In general, attempts to understand the relation between individual toxic exposures and their possible link to subsequent developmental disability are plagued by methodological challenges. Confounding variables – such as poor nutrition, low socioeconomic status, and multiple agent exposure – make clinical studies difficult to conduct and interpret. As noted previously, the timing of the toxic exposure to the developing brain might also be reasonably expected to affect the outcome. Difficulty in collecting reliable data regarding the amount of alcohol consumed or cigarettes smoked during a pregnancy presents one of the many examples of the challenges in this area of research. Variations in clinical expressivity, given a presumed comparable

degree of insult, also represent a serious impediment to formulating hypotheses about the relation between a toxin and a cluster of signs and symptoms. One example is the discrepancy noted frequently in the outcomes of fraternal twins born to mothers who have abused alcohol, although this may be explained by multifactorial inheritance and a toxin with a variable effect, depending on the genomic substrate. This section provides a brief overview of selected putative toxins and their presumed effects on the immature central nervous system, with full realization that a final understanding of the influence of these agents on human development has not yet been achieved.

FETAL ALCOHOL SYNDROME (FAS). This syndrome is seen in about 2.5% to 4% of children of mothers who drink heavily and has an estimated worldwide incidence of nearly 2 per 1,000 live births (Abel & Sokol, 1987). It is characterized by craniofacial anomalies, pre- and postnatal growth deficiency, and psychomotor retardation with microcephaly (Clarren & Smith, 1978). The craniofacial anomalies, although striking, are not unique and have been noted with other presumed toxins, especially cocaine and marijuana (Astley, Clarren, & Little, 1992; Hingson, Alper, & Day, 1982). The mean IQ scores of affected individuals appear to fall between 65 and 70, but variation is considerable (Streissguth et al., 1991). In fact, some children demonstrate normal intelligence, although they have greater problems with attention and learning (Shaywitz, Cohen, & Shaywitz, 1980); others show mild-to-severe speech impairments with or without behavioral problems (Iosub, Fuchs, Bingol, & Gromish, 1981). Pre- and postnatal growth retardation is seen in over 80% of affected children (Clarren & Smith, 1978). In general, children with FAS have decreased brain size, and neuronal migrational abnormalities have been documented. Although these neuropathological findings certainly could explain the range of disability observed in FAS, the lack of understanding of precisely how alcohol causes problems in neuronal growth and migration makes further study necessary. The marked variability of outcome and the relatively low incidence of FAS in children of mothers with chronic alcoholism continue to obscure the understanding of alcohol's effects on fetal development. Although there are new data emerging about fetal alcohol syndrome, it is difficult to conclude anything more definitive than to say that alcohol remains a potent risk factor for subsequent developmental disability in offspring of mothers who drink heavily.

COCAINE. As for alcohol, the literature regarding cocaine and its effects on the developing central nervous system is plagued with problems. Because women who use cocaine during pregnancy are more likely to be involved in a complex, multirisk lifestyle, other factors must be considered when analyzing the specific effects of fetal cocaine exposure. Affected women also have higher rates of HIV infection and lower use of prenatal services. Nonetheless, there are some specific effects on pregnancy that appear to be cocaine related, such as a higher incidence of spontaneous abortions, stillbirths, and premature delivery. Low birth weight, small head size, and intrauterine growth retardation have also been reported in affected newborns, as well as an increased incidence of midline brain abnormalities such as agenesis of the corpus collosum. Neonates exposed to cocaine in utero tend to be tremulous and generally have increased muscle tone, the latter of which may continue into infancy. Affected newborns also seem to show significant differences in organizational responses in their active behavior when compared to controls (Chiriboga, 1991; Zuckerman et al., 1989). In experimental animals, cocaine has been shown to exert a potent vasoconstrictor effect on cerebral blood vessels, which may explain the increased incidence of neonatal stroke (Dominquez, Vila-Coro, & Slopis, 1991). For the present, however, outcome data remain relatively meager, especially for the long term. Thus, although cocaine exposure must be considered a potential risk factor in brain development, definitive outcomes cannot be predicted on the basis of current knowledge.

In addition to alcohol and cocaine, there have been numerous studies of the effects of other agents on the developing fetus, including cigarettes, opiates, and marijuana, among others (Brust, 1996). As for all other causes of potential brain injury, the emphasis should be on both primary prevention and ongoing support for children who have been exposed to toxic agents. Perhaps most important is the fact that the adverse impacts of an impoverished environment are often more detrimental to human brain development than the effects of any single specific agent (Brust, 1996).

Malnutrition

The association between malnutrition in infancy and subsequent intellectual abilities has been well documented, particularly in developing countries (Pollitt, 1994). When severe calorie and protein deprivation exist during the prenatal period and into early childhood, mental retardation and behavioral disorders have been frequent and irreversible. The effects of moderate or chronic low-grade malnutrition, however, are less well understood (Scrimshaw & Gordon, 1968). Extensive research on laboratory animals suggests that the timing of a nutritional insult relative to the maturational state of the brain will have important influence on ultimate developmental outcome. Studies in rats, for example, have shown that comparatively mild nutritional restrictions during periods of rapid cell proliferation result in permanent changes in the adult brain that cannot be reversed subsequently by a better diet, but significant undernutrition before or after the growth-spurt period produces no detectable effect that has not been demonstrated to be reversible by later dietary supplementation (Dobbing & Sands, 1971). In addition, growth and proliferation of synapses in the developing cortex are reduced significantly by undernutrition during periods of dendritic development (Cragg, 1972). Although studies of nutritionally deprived human infants and children are quite limited, they have shown similar findings of decreased brain weight, reduced myelination, and abnormalities in dendritic arborization that parallel findings in the experimental animal (Cordero et al., 1993; Fishman, Prensky, & Dodge, 1969).

The sensitive period of rapid brain growth in human development appears to include two important phases. The first extends from midpregnancy until the end of the second year of life, and this phase is characterized by early neuronal proliferation and later increase in glial numbers. The second phase extends well into the third and fourth years, and this phase is characterized by rapid myelination in association with the continuous elaboration of increasingly complex dendritic branching and synaptic connections (Dobbing, 1974). Thus, current evidence suggests that the periods of human growth that are vulnerable to the effects of malnutrition exist both before and after birth.

In a review of seven studies, Chase (1973) reported significant intellectual impairment among malnourished children ages 2–14 in all but one study. Other investigators noted greater deficits in behavioral characteristics – such as attentiveness, curiosity, activity, and social responsiveness – than in measured intelligence per se. Several epidemiological studies have documented significant nutritional vulnerabilities among poor children in the United States that suggest increased risk for developmental sequelae (Livingston, Calloway, MacGregor, Fisher, & Hastings, 1975; Owen, Kram, Garry, Lowe, & Lubin, 1974; Select Panel for the Promotion of Child Health, 1981).

The most obvious methodological problem in human studies on the effects of malnutrition has been the almost universal association of poor nutrition with poverty, whose correlates typically have an independent negative influence on intellectual development (McKay, Sinisterra, McKay, Gomez, & Lloreda, 1978). A few studies, however, have reported instances of malnutrition in the absence of significant socioeconomic deprivation. Lloyd-Still, Hurwitz, Wolff, and Shwachman (1974) studied 41 middle-class children, aged 2–21 years, who were substantially malnourished in infancy secondary to cystic fibrosis or congenital defects of the gastrointestinal tract. Significant differences in scores on the Merrill-Palmer Scales were found up to age 5 years, but no differences were observed on the Wechsler scales administered to the older subjects. Klein, Forbes, and Nader (1975) reported a follow-up study of 50 children, aged 5–14 years, who had brief periods of starvation in early infancy as a result of pyloric stenosis. When compared to siblings and matched controls, these children showed no significant difference in measures of global intelligence but did demonstrate significantly lower scores on subtests related to short-term memory and attention.

The risks for later developmental disabilities among children subjected to malnutrition in early life present a clear example of the synergistic effects of both biologic and environmental vulnerability. Differential sensitivity to the biological impact of inadequate nutrition on the basis of the maturational status of the brain is

particularly noteworthy. Experimental studies in animals generally show no evidence of reversal of the behavioral effects of undernutrition by environmental enhancements (Bedi & Bhide, 1988; Sara, King, & Lazarus, 1976). Human studies, however, suggest the relative preservation of intellectual function when undernutrition is buffered by a stable home environment and appropriate stimulation (Beardslee, Wolff, & Hurwitz, 1982), although some have demonstrated preservation of cognitive abilities but lower performance than expected in the areas of short-term memory and attention (Klein, Forbes, & Nader, 1975). Finally, any discussion of human nutrition must go beyond addressing the simple provision of adequate proteins and calories, as diets deficient in specific nutrients (such as essential fatty acids, vitamins, and minerals) can produce neurological sequelae that may be only partially reversible if a timely diagnosis is not made. There is little disagreement that significant malnutrition in the form of reduced calories, protein, or specific supplements will have an adverse impact on brain development, but there is little consensus as to the inevitability or reversability of mild deficiencies. One area for which there has been extensive investigation, however, is the developmental impact of iron deficiency anemia.

Children with iron deficiency anemia demonstrate a variety of symptoms including increased fatigue and irritability, decreased motivation, shortened attention span, and cognitive impairments (Deinard, List, Lindgren, Hunt, and Chang, 1986; Lozoff et al., 1987; Lozoff, Wolf, Urrutia, & Viteri, 1985; Oski, Honig, Helu, & Howanitz, 1983). Studies in Latin America (Lozoff, 1990) and Asia (Seshadri & Gopaldas, 1989) have confirmed the potentially significant adverse developmental impacts of iron-deficient states, and some investigators have found that children with moderately severe iron-deficiency anemia during the infancy period are at greater risk for persistent developmental difficulties up to the time of school entry (Lozoff, Jimenez, & Wolf, 1991). It remains unclear, however, whether the behavioral differences related to iron deficiency are secondary to chronic deficits in tissue oxygenation, abnormalities in iron-dependent central nervous system neurotransmitters, the consequences of associated general malnutrition, or the result of adverse environmental influences on poorly nourished children who live under conditions of poverty or significant social disorganization. The extent to which the negative impacts of iron deficiency anemia are age dependent is also unclear at this time. In addition, children with iron deficiency anemia are more likely to have elevated blood lead levels, secondary to increased absorption of lead from the gastrointestinal tract, which leads to greater developmental vulnerability (Yip, 1989). Double-blind, randomized clinical trials provide evidence that therapeutic treatments that replenish iron stores and normalize hemaglobin levels result in improved performance on developmental assessments (Idjradinata & Pollitt, 1993). Therefore, the continued prevalence of iron deficiency anemia, particularly among children growing up under conditions of poverty, makes this an important source of developmental vulnerability that demands prompt identification and effective medical treatment.

Prenatal and Perinatal Brain Injury

In 1862, W. J. Little noted the link between the development of cerebral palsy and a history of injury to the brain at the time of delivery. Over the ensuing century, much has been learned about the etiology of cerebral palsy, and it is now increasingly apparent that the causative neurological injury is more related to prenatal (before birth) than perinatal (at the time of birth) factors (Kuban & Leviton, 1994). Although cerebral palsy generally refers to a nonprogressive motor impairment, associated disability beyond the motor domain is common. The fact that motor skill development is documented more easily than other areas of function in the first year probably explains the motor emphasis to this date. In reality, however, it is important to remember that both pre- and perinatal brain injury can result in a wide spectrum of disability.

PERINATAL INJURY. As indicated, Little's original thesis was that cerebral palsy is a consequence of physical trauma at the time of delivery. However, with the development of improved fetal monitoring and obstetrical techniques, physical injury is now rare (Rosen, 1985). With the elimination of physical trauma as a major cause of perinatal injury, attention has turned to the phenomenon of hypoxic (inadequate oxygen)–(inadequate blood supply) ischemic

encephalopathy. This conclusion seems logical because the pattern of injury seen clinically appears to correlate well with neuropathological findings, such as selective necrosis (destruction) of neurons, white matter injury, and cystic changes (Volpe, 1995). Among the neuropathological sequelae of hypoxic–ischemic injury, neuronal necrosis is the most common. It can be widespread, involving not only the cerebral cortex but also the brain stem, basal ganglia, and cerebellum. White matter injury is often concentrated near the ventricles (i.e., periventricular leukomalacia [PVL]), but it also is widespread and can be related to other prenatal factors, including maternal infection (Gilles, 1985). PVL is associated most commonly with prematurity. The widespread cystic changes found in the brain are the result of severe ischemia in the perinatal period, but the origins of less extensive lesions are not known definitively in most cases. The clinical outcomes for children with any of these major perinatal insults are variable.

The early clinical signs of hypoxic–ischemic encephalopathy in the newborn period are also variable. They range from relatively minor differences in state control to a number of serious signs and symptoms, including seizures and abnormalities in muscle tone, posture, reflexes, respiratory patterns, and autonomic function. However, of all the full-term neonates who demonstrate signs of hypoxia or ischemia in the perinatal period, 85% have been shown to demonstrate no evidence of cerebral palsy at follow-up (Nelson & Ellenberg, 1979). For many years, it was believed that oxygen deprivation during delivery led to cerebral palsy, often with associated mental retardation. There are now abundant data to indicate that the pathogenesis of cerebral palsy is far more complicated, and that a simple cause–effect relation with perinatal difficulties has not been substantiated (Freeman, 1985; Freeman & Nelson, 1988). Even Apgar scores below 3 (of a possible 10) at 5 minutes have not been shown to be predictive of cerebral palsy (Nelson & Ellenberg, 1981; Thomson, Searle, & Russell 1977). Indeed, a study of surviving children with Apgar scores of 3 at 15 minutes reported a rate of cerebral palsy of only 9% (Nelson & Ellenberg, 1981). Stated simply, hypoxic–ischemic encephalopathy at birth appears to be responsible for only a small percentage of children with cerebral palsy, but when it does occur in children born at term, the outcome is generally not good.

Premature babies have a much higher rate of cerebral palsy than term infants. In fact, one-third of infants later identified as having cerebral palsy had birth weights of less than 2,500 grams (Kuban & Leviton, 1994). Two particular etiologic findings appear to be important in the premature infant: PVL and intracranial (primarily intraventricular) hemorrhage (IH).

The pathogenesis of PVL seems to be related to a number of factors that are prominent in the premature infant. For example, the fact that premature white matter is in the arterial border zones, coupled with the pressure of passive cerebral circulation and the intrinsic vulnerability of white matter itself, makes this area susceptible to the adverse effects of hypoxia and particularly ischemia (Volpe, 1995). Hypoxic–ischemic insult, however, does not appear to account for all cases of PVL. Nevertheless, when diagnostic criteria are applied rigorously, PVL can be diagnosed by ultrasound in the newborn period and can predict cerebral palsy accurately in a high percentage of cases (Levene, 1990).

IH and germinal matrix hemorrhage remain the most common types of intracranial bleeding. Despite the fact that their incidence has decreased dramatically in the 1980s and early 1990s, from approximately 40% to 20% of infants weighing less than 2,250 grams (Paneth, Pinto-Martin, & Gardiner, 1993), the number of affected infants remains high because of the overall improved survival rates of low-birth-weight babies (Volpe, 1995). The germinal matrix is an area of brain adjacent to the rostral-medial aspect of the lateral ventricle. This region serves as a center for neuronal proliferation. The character of its blood supply probably contributes substantially to its vulnerability to local bleeding and even to rupture in the adjacent ventricle. IH is graded presently on a scale of 1 to 3, and is diagnosed most often by cranial ultrasound. Grades 1 and 2 are characterized by bleeding that is confined to the subependymal region on less than half of the ventricular area. Grade 3 hemorrhage, in contrast, is characterized by more extensive bleeding with rupture into the substance of the cerebral cortex and, in the most serious cases, is accompanied by hydrocephalus and PVL. Low-grade IH is often unrecognizable clinically, but, with more extensive hemorrhage, it is much more likely to be associated with alterations in level of consciousness, muscle tone, and spontaneous movement. Although mortality rates are higher among infants who sustain any degree of hemorrhage, it is clear that low-grade (i.e., mild) bleeds have a substantially better prognosis. Volpe (1995), in his review of long-term outcome studies, suggests that the prognosis depends primarily on the degree of brain injury (i.e., PVL and infarction, or cell death due to lack of blood supply) and to a lesser degree on the amount of ventricular hemorrhage. Overall, Grade 1–2 hemorrhage has an incidence of significant neurological sequelae in the neighborhood of 5%–15%, whereas individuals with more severe bleeding have an incidence of neurological sequelae of 35–90%, again depending on the amount of brain tissue involved (Volpe, 1995). The majority of premature infants who survive and sustain only mild hemorrhage ultimately have a long-term prognosis that is good. Improvements in neuroimaging with MRI and cranial ultrasound have increased the ability to predict outcomes more precisely.

PRENATAL FACTORS. The major causes of cerebral palsy are not related to perinatal injury, as noted earlier, but are more likely to have been determined earlier in the pregnancy. Unfortunately, however, available data do not permit us to determine the etiology in many, if not most, cases. Nevertheless, a number of factors have been identified in epidemiologic studies as being associated with a higher incidence of cerebral palsy (Kuban & Leviton, 1994). Low-income mothers and those with a history of repeated miscarriages or long menstrual cycles have a higher incidence of having children with cerebral palsy. Fetal growth retardation, congenital malformations, twin gestation, abnormal fetal presentation, congenital infection, and toxins are also associated with greater risk for this disorder. Unfortunately, many perturbations in pregnancy that can result in fetal injury are not well understood, and our knowledge of the underlying pathophysiology of prenatal injury remains remarkably limited.

SUMMARY: THE DEVELOPMENTAL IMPACT OF NEUROLOGIC INSULT

The process of adaptation that follows a specific insult to the brain is exceedingly complex. On the one hand, many severe disabilities demonstrate the limitations of the central nervous system for recovery. On the other hand, the ability of the brain to adapt to a wide variety of assaults, with relatively minor residual sequelae, has been well documented. In most circumstances of neurological dysfunction, however, we have limited ability to determine the precise nature, severity, and timing of the presumed insult with any reasonable accuracy and, therefore, are constrained significantly in our capacity to predict its ultimate developmental impact.

Clearly, the immature brain of the young child is capable of adaptive recovery to a far greater degree than the more differentiated and mature brain of an adult (see Nelson, this volume). Although the central nervous system may be limited in its ability to replace damaged neurons after the early stage of cell proliferation is completed, changes in the communication network among functioning cells can take place. That is to say, axons and dendrites that transmit and receive impulses from one cell to another are capable of undergoing a process of "rewiring," although explaining how this process is initiated and controlled remains a challenge to neurobiologists.

Neurological insult can take many forms. Specific injury to the brain may result from infection, exposure to a toxic substance, malnutrition, or a hypoxic–ischemic event. The sequelae of these adverse influences on the central nervous system are variable and often unpredictable on an individual basis. In some cases, alterations of brain structure or functional relationships result in substantial disability within a narrow range of variability. In other circumstances, highly specific cortical insults seemingly can produce a wide variety of outcomes. Young children vary in their apparent vulnerability to noxious biological experiences. The burden of an insult to the central nervous system may be insurmountable or simply a risk factor that can be neutralized by individual resilience or a nurturant, caregiving environment. The process of development is transactional and complex. All humans are endowed with a reservoir of biological adaptability, as well as sources of vulnerability. Many of these characteristics are determined genetically.

The development of competence is not determined by biology alone. Rather, it unfolds under the mutual influences of nature and nurture. Indeed, the maturation of the central nervous system itself is affected by the experiences that characterize each individual's personal environment. For the very young child, interactions and evolving relationships with her or his caregivers are the most crucial elements in that environment. When such relationships are dysfunctional, the most biologically resilient youngster will be at risk for later problems. When such relationships are supportive of adaptive development, the young child with extensive neurological vulnerabilities may still have an opportunity to thrive.

The field of early childhood intervention faces a number of critical challenges. Among these is the need to increase our ability to identify biological risk factors and to reduce their deleterious effects. Major advances in this area will require significant breakthroughs in the basic science of neurobiology, including a greater understanding of the molecular bases of neurological function and the prevention of neurological damage. In those circumstances in which biological insult cannot be avoided, the task before us is to enhance our understanding of human adaptation. This will require more extensive investigation of how protective factors in the child and in her or his environment can mitigate the adverse developmental impact of brain injury. Identifying and facilitating such protective factors are central components of early childhood intervention.

REFERENCES

Abel, E. L., & Sokol, R. J. (1987). Incidence of fetal alcohol syndrome and economic impact of FAS anomalies. *Drug and Alcohol Dependency, 11,* 51–70.

Astley, S. J., Clarren, S. K., & Little, R. E. (1992). Analysis of facial shape in children gestationally exposed to marijuana, alcohol, and/or cocaine. *Pediatrics, 89,* 67–8.

Bayer, S. A., & Altman, J. (1991). *Neocortical development.* New York: Raven Press.

Beardslee, W. R., Wolff, P. H., & Hurwitz, I. (1982). The effects of infantile nutrition on behavioral development: A follow-up study. *American Journal of Clinical Nutrition, 35,* 1437–41.

Bedi, K. S., & Bhide, P. G. (1988). Effects of environmental diversity on brain morphology. *Early Human Development, 17,* 107–44.

Brock, D. J. H. (1993). *Molecular genetics for the clinician.* New York: Cambridge University Press.

Brust, J. C. M. (1996). Disorder of the nervous system secondary to substance abuse. In B. O. Berg (Ed.), *Principles of child neurology* (pp. 1343–62). New York: McGraw Hill.

Carter, C. (1974). Clues to the aetiology of neural tube malformations. *Developmental Medicine and Child Neurology, 32* (Suppl.), 3–15.

Centers for Disease Control. (1991). Increase in rubella and congenital rubella syndrome–United States, 1988–1990. *Morbidity and Mortality Weekly Report, 40,* 93–9, 105.

Chase, H. (1973). The effects of intrauterine and postnatal undernutrition on normal brain development. *Annals of the New York Academy of Science, 205,* 231–44.

Chess, S. (1974). The influence of defect on development in children with congenital rubella. *Merrill-Palmer Quarterly, 20,* 255–74.

Chiriboga, C. A. (1991) Abuse of children: Fetal and pediatric AIDS, fetal alcohol syndrome, fetal cocaine effects, and the battered child syndrome. In L. P. Rowland (Ed.), *Merritt's textbook of neurology, 9th ed.* (pp. 995–1000). Baltimore, MD: Williams and Wilkins.

Clarren, S., & Smith, D. (1978). The fetal alcohol syndrome. *New England Journal of Medicine, 288,* 1063–7.

Conboy, T. J., Pass, R. F., Stagno, S., Britt, W., Alford, C., McFarland, C., & Boll, T. (1986). Intellectual development in school-aged children with asymptomatic congenital cytomegalovirus infection. *Pediatrics, 77,* 801–6.

Connolly, P., Jerger, S., Williamson, W., Smith, R. J. H., & Demmler, G. (1992). Evaluation of higher level auditory function in children with asymptomatic CMV infection. *American Journal of Otology, 13,* 185–93.

Connor, E. M., Sperling, R. S., & Gelber, R. (1994). Reduction of maternal–infant transmission of human immuno deficiency virus type 1 with zidovudine therapy. *New England Journal of Medicine, 331,* 1173–80.

Cooper, L. Z., & Krugman, S. (1966). Diagnosis and management: Congenital rubella. *Pediatrics, 37,* 335–8.

Cordero, M. E., D'Acuna, E., Benveniste, S., Prado, R., Nunez, J. A., & Colombo, M. (1993). Dendritic development in the neocortex of infants with early life under nutrition. *Pediatric Neurology, 9,* 457–264.

Cragg, B. G. (1972). The development of cortical synapsis during starvation of the rat. *Brain, 95,* 143–50.

Deinard, A., List, A., Lindgren, B., Hunt, J., & Chang, P. (1986). Cognitive deficits in iron-deficient and iron-deficient anemic children. *Journal of Pediatrics, 108,* 681–9.

Demmler, G. (1991). Summary of a workshop on surveillance for congenital cytomegalovirus disease. *Review of Infectious Disease, 13,* 315–29.

Demmler, G. (1994). Congenital cytomegalovirus infection. *Seminars in Pediatric Neurology, 1,* 36–42.

Desmonts, G., & Couvreur, J. (1979). Congenital toxoplasmosis: A prospective study of the offspring of 542 women who acquired toxoplasmosis during pregnancy. In O. Thalhammer, K. Baumgarten, & A. Pollak (Eds.), *Perinatal medicine, Sixth European Congress,* Vienna, 1978 (pp. 51–60). Stuttgart: Georg Thieme Publishers.

Dobbing, J. (1974). The later growth of the brain and its vulnerability. *Pediatrics, 53,* 2–6.

Dobbing, J., & Sands, J. (1971). Vulnerability of the developing brain: IX. The effect of nutritional growth retardation on the timing of the brain growth-spurt. *Biology of the Neonate, 19,* 363–78.

Dominquez, R., Vila-Coro, A. A., & Slopis, J. M. (1991). Brain and ocular abnormalities in infants with in utero exposure to cocaine and other street drugs. *American Journal of Diseases of Children, 145,* 688–95.

Eichenwald, H. G. (1960). A study of congenital toxoplasmosis with particular emphasis on clinical manifestations, sequelae, and therapy. In J. C. Sim (Ed.), *Human toxoplasmosis* (pp. 40–9). Copenhagen, Denmark: Munksgard.

Fishman, M. A., Prensky, A. L., & Dodge, P. R. (1969). Low content of cerebral lipids in infants suffering from malnutrition. *Nature, 221,* 552–5.

Freeman, J. (1985). *Prenatal and perinatal factors associated with brain disorders.* (National Institute of Health Publication No. 85-1149). Washington, DC: U.S. Department of Health and Human Services.

Freeman, J., & Nelson, K. (1988). Intrapartum asphyxia and cerebral palsy. *Pediatrics, 82,* 240–9.

Gilles, F. H. (1985). Neuropathologic indicators of abnormal development. In J. Freeman (Ed.), *Prenatal and perinatal factors associated with brain disorders.* (National Institute of Health Publication No. 85-1149, pp. 53–108). Washington, DC: U.S. Department of Health and Human Services.

Goldson, E., & Hagerman, R. J. (1992). The Fragile-X Syndrome. *Developmental Medicine and Child Neurology, 34,* 822–32.

Graham, J. M., Bashir, A., Stark R., Silbert, A., & Walzer, S. (1988). Oral and written language abilities of XXY boys: Implications for anticipating guidance. *Pediatrics, 81,* 795–806.

Hagerman, R., Kemper, M., & Hudson, M. (1985). Learning disabilities and attentional problems in boys with the Fragile-X syndrome. *American Journal of Diseases of Children, 139,* 674–8.

Hanshaw, J. (1981). Cytomegalovirus infections. *Pediatrics in Review, 2,* 245–51.

Hanshaw, J., Scheiner, A., Moxley, A., Gaev, L., Abel, V., & Scheiner, B. (1976). School failure and deafness after "silent" congenital cytomegalovirus infection. *New England Journal of Medicine, 295,* 468–70.

Hingson, R., Alper, T. T., & Day, N. (1982). Effects of maternal drinking and marijuana use on fetal growth and development. *Pediatrics, 70,* 539–46.

Holm, V., Cassidy, S., Butler, M., Hanchett, J., Greenswag, L., Whitman, B., & Greenberg, F. (1993). Prader-Willi Syndrome: Consensus diagnostic criteria. *Pediatrics, 91,* 398–402.

Iannaleone, S. T., & Rosenberg, R. N. (1996). Principles of molecular genetics and neurological disease. In B. O. Berg (Ed.), *Principles of child neurology* (pp. 551–7). New York: McGraw Hill.

Idjradinata, P., & Pollitt, E. (1993). Reversal of developmental delays in iron-deficient anaemic infants treated with iron. *Lancet, 341* (8836), 1–4.

Isoub, S., Fuchs, M., Bingol, N., & Gromish, D. S. (1981). Fetal alcohol syndrome revisited. *Pediatrics, 68,* 475–9.

Kashden, J., Frison, S., Fowler, K., Pass, R., & Boll, T. (1998). Intellectual assessment of children with asymptomatic congenital cytomegalovirus infection. *Journal of Developmental and Behavioural Relations, 19,* 254–9.

Kety, S. (1978). Genetic and biochemical aspects of schizophrenia. In A. Nicholi (Ed.), *Harvard guide to modern psychiatry.* Cambridge, MA: Belknap Press.

Klein, P., Forbes, G., & Nader, P. (1975). Effects of starvation in infancy (pyloric stenosis) on subsequent learning abilities. *Journal of Pediatrics, 87,* 8–15.

Knoll, J. H. M., Nichols, R. D., Magenis R. E., Graham, J. M., Lalande, M., & Latt, S. A. (1989). Angelman and Prader Willi Syndromes share a common chromosome 15 deletion, but differ in parental origin of the deletion. *American Journal of Medical Genetics, 32,* 285–90.

Koch, T. (1996). Neurological complications of pediatric HIV infection. In B. O. Berg (Ed.), *Principles of child neurology* (pp. 869–88). New York: McGraw Hill.

Kramer, E. J., Pritchard, M., Lynch M., Yu, S., Holman, K., Baker, E., Warren, S. T., Schlesinger, D., Sutherland, G. R., & Richards, R. I. (1991). Mapping of DNA susceptibility at the fragile X site to a trinucleotide repeat sequence (CGG). *Science, 252,* 1711–14.

Kuban, K., & Leviton, A. (1994). Cerebral palsy. *New England Journal of Medicine, 330,* 188–94.

Lemire, P. J., Leoser, J. D., Leech, R. W., & Alvord, E. C. (1975). *Normal and abnormal development of the human nervous system.* New York: Harper & Row.

Levene, M. I. (1990). Cerebral ultrasound and neurological impairment: Telling the future. *Archives of Disease in Childhood, 65,* 469–71.

Livingston, R., Calloway, D., MacGregor, J., Fisher, G., & Hastings, A. (1975). U.S. poverty impact on brain development. In M. Brazier (Ed.), *Growth and development of the brain* (pp. 377–94). New York: Raven Press.

Lloyd-Still, J., Hurwitz, I., Wolff, P., & Shwachman, H. (1974). Intellectual development after severe malnutrition in infancy. *Pediatrics, 54,* 306–12.

Lorber, J., & Priestly, B. L. (1981). Children with large heads: A practical approach to diagnosis in 557 children, with special reference to 109 children with megalencephaly. *Developmental Medicine and Child Neurology, 23,* 494–504.

Lozoff, B. (1990). Has iron deficiency been shown to cause altered behavior in infants? In J. Dobbing (Ed.), *Brain, behavior, and iron in the infant diet* (pp. 107–31). London: Springer-Verlag.

Lozoff, B., Brittenham, G., Wolf, A., McClish, D., Kuhnert, P., Jimenez, E., Jimenez, R., Mora, L., Gomez, I., & Krauskoph, D. (1987). Iron deficiency anemia and iron therapy effects on infant developmental test performance. *Pediatrics, 79,* 981–95.

Lozoff, B., Jimenez, E., & Wolf, A. (1991). Long-term developmental outcome of infants with iron deficiency. *New England Journal of Medicine, 325,* 687–94.

Lozoff, B., Wolf, A., Urrutia, J., & Viteri, F. (1985). Abnormal behavior and low developmental test scores in iron-deficient anemic infants. *Journal of Developmental and Behavioral Pediatrics, 6,* 69–75.

McAuley, J. B., Boyer, K. M., Patel, D., Mets, M., Swisher, C., Roizen, N., Walters, V., Stein, L., Stein, M., Schay, W., Remington, J., Meier, P., Johnson, D., Heydeman, P., Holpel, P. Winters, S., Mack, D., Brown, C., Patton, D., & McLeod, R. (1994). Early and longitudinal evaluations of treated infants and children and untreated historical patients with congenital toxoplasmosis: The Chicago treatment trial. *Clinical Infectious Disease, 18,* 38–72.

McCauley, E., Ito, J., & Key, T. (1986): Psychosocial functioning in girls with Turner Syndrome and short stature. *Journal of American Academy of Child Psychiatry, 25,* 105–12.

McClone, D. G., Czyzurski, D., Raimondi, A. J., & Sommers, R. C. (1982). Central nervous system infections as a limiting factor in the intelligence of children with myelomeningocoele. *Pediatrics, 70,* 338–42.

McClone, D. G., Dias, L., Kaplan, W. E., & Sommers, M. W. (1985). Concepts in the management of spina bifida. *Concepts in Pediatric Neurosurgery, 5,* 97–105.

McCullough, P., & Balzer-Martin, L. (1982). Current prognosis in overt neonatal hydrocephalus. *Journal of Neurosurgery, 57,* 378–83.

McKay, H., Sinisterra, L., McKay, A., Gomez, H., & Lloreda, P. (1978). Improving cognitive ability in chronically deprived children. *Science, 200,* 270–8.

Miller, E., Craddock-Watson, J. E., & Pollock, T. M. (1982). Consequences of confirmed maternal rubella and successive stages of pregnancy. *Lancet, 2,* 781–4.

Moser, H. (1985). Biologic factors of development. In J. Freeman (Ed.), *Prenatal and perinatal factors associated with brain disorders* (National Institute of Health publication No. 85-1149, pp. 121–61). Washington, DC: U.S. Department of Health and Human Services.

MRC Vitamin Study Research Group. (1991) Prevention of neural tube defects: Results of the Medical Research Council Vitamin Study. *Lancet, 338,* 131–7.

Nelson, C., & Bloom, F. (1997). Child development and neuroscience. *Child Development, 68,* 970–87.

Nelson, K. B., & Ellenberg, J. H. (1979). Neonatal signs and predictors of cerebral palsy. *Pediatrics, 74,* 225–32.

Nelson, K. B., & Ellenberg, J. H. (1981). Apgar scores as predictors of chronic neurologic disability. *Pediatrics, 68,* 36–44.

Nevin, N. C., Johnston, W. P., & Merritt, J. D. (1981). Influence of social class on the risk of recurrence of anencephalus and spina bifida. *Developmental Medicine and Child Neurology, 23,* 155–9.

North, K. (1997). *Neurofibromatosis Type 1 in Childhood.* London: MacKeith Press.

Oski, F., Honig, A., Helu, B., & Howanitz, P. (1983). Effect of iron therapy on behavior performance in nonanemic, iron-deficient infants. *Pediatrics, 71*, 877–80.

Owen, G., Kram, K., Garry, P., Lowe, J., & Lubin, A. (1974). A study of nutritional status of preschool children in the United States, 1968–1970. *Pediatrics, 53*, 597–646.

Paneth, N., Pinto-Martin J., & Gardiner, A. (1993). Incidence and timing of germinal matrix/intraventricular hemorhage in low birth weight infants. *American Journal of Epidemiology, 137*, 167–76.

Pass, R., Stagno, S., Myers, G., & Alford, C. (1980). Outcome of symptomatic congenital cytomegalovirus infection: Results of long-term longitudinal follow-up. *Pediatrics, 66*, 758–62.

Perry A. (1991). Rett's Syndrome: A comprehensive review of the literature. *American Journal of Mental Retardation, 96*, 275–90.

Pollitt, E. (1994). Poverty and child development: Relevance of research in developing countries to the United States. *Child Development, 65*, 283–95.

Pueschel, J. (Ed.). (1978). *Down syndrome: Growing and learning.* Kansas City, KS: Andrews & McMeel.

Rosen, M. G. (1985). Factors during labor and delivery that influence brain disorders. In J. Freeman (Ed.), *Prenatal and perinatal factors associated with brain disorders* (National Institute of Health Publication No. 85-1149, pp. 237–62). Washington, DC: U.S. Department of Health and Human Services.

Rovet, J. (1993). The psychoeducational characteristics of children with Turner syndrome. *Journal of Learning Disabilities, 26*, 333–41.

Sara, V. R., King, T. L., & Lazarus, L. (1976). The influence of early nutrition and environmental rearing on brain growth and behavior. *Experientia, 32*, 1538–40.

Sarnat, H. B. (1996). Neuroembryology. In B. O. Berg (Ed.), *Principles of child neurology* (pp. 607–28). New York: McGraw Hill.

Scrimshaw, N., & Gordon, J. (Eds.). (1968). *Malnutrition, learning, and behavior.* Boston: MIT Press.

Sekul, E. A., & Percy, A. K. (1992). Rett syndrome: Clinical features, genetic considerations and search for a biological marker. *Currents in Neurology, 12*, 173.

Select Panel for the Promotion of Child Health. (1981). *Report to the U.S. Congress and the Secretary of Health and Human Services on better health for our children.* Washington, DC: U.S. Department of Health and Human Services.

Sells, C. J. (1977). Microcephaly in a normal school population. *Pediatrics, 59*, 262–5.

Seshadri, S., & Gopaldas, T. (1989). Impact of iron supplementation on cognitive functions in preschool and school-aged children: The Indian experience. *American Journal of Clinical Nutrition, 50* (Suppl.), 675–86.

Shapira, H. V., & DiMauro, S. (1994). *Mitochondrial disorders in neurology.* Oxford: Butterworth Heinemann.

Shaywitz, S., Cohen, D., & Shaywitz, B. (1980). Behavior and learning difficulties in children of normal intelligence born to alcoholic mothers. *Journal of Pediatrics, 96*, 978–82.

Smithells, R. W., Sheppard, S., Schorah, C. J., Seller, M. J., Nevin, N. C., Harris, R., Read, A. P., & Fielding, D. W. (1981). Apparent prevention of neural tube defects by preconceptual vitamin supplementation. *Archives of Disease in Childhood, 56*, 911–18.

Stray-Pedersen, B. (1980). Infants potentially at risk for congenital toxoplasmosis. *American Journal of Diseases of Children, 134*, 638–42.

Streissguth, A. P., Aase, J. M., Clarren, S. T., Randeis, S. P., LaDue, R. A., & Smith, D. F. (1991). Fetal alcohol syndrome in adolescents and adults. *Journal of American Medical Association, 265*, 1961–7.

Swisher, C. N., Boyer, K., & McLeod, R. (1994). Congenital toxoplasmosis. *Seminars in Pediatric Neurology, 1*, 4–25.

Taylor, A. K., Safanda, J. Fall, M. Z., Quince, C., Lang, K. A., Hull, C. E., Carpenter, I., Staley, L. W., & Hagerman, R. J. (1994). Molecular predictors of cognitive development in female carriers of Fragile-X syndrome. *Journal of American Medical Association, 271*, 507–14.

Thomson, A.J., Searle, M., & Russell, G. (1977). Quality of survival after severe birth asphyxia. *Archives of Disease in Childhood, 52*, 620–6.

Volpe, J. J. (1995). *Neurology of the newborn.* Philadelphia: W. B. Saunders.

Warren, S. T., & Nelson, D. L. (1994). Advances in molecular analysis of fragile X syndrome. *Journal of American Medical Association, 271*, 536–42.

Williamson, W., Demmler, G., Percy, A., & Catlin, F. (1992). Progressive hearing loss in infants with asymptomatic congenital cytomegalovirus infection. *Pediatrics, 90*, 862–6.

Wilson, C. B., Remington, J. S., Stagno, S., & Reynolds, D. W. (1980). Development of adverse sequelae in children born with subclinical congenital toxoplasma infection. *Pediatrics, 66*, 767–74.

Yip, R. (1989). The interaction of lead and iron. In L. J. Filer, Jr. (Ed.), *Dietary iron: Birth to two years.* New York: Raven.

Zuckerman, B., Frank, D. A., Hingson, R., Amaro, H., Levenson, S. M., Kayne, H., Parker, S., Vinci, R., Aboagye, K., Fried, L. E., Cabral, H., Timperi, R., & Bauchner, H. (1989). Effects of maternal marijuana and cocaine on fetal growth. *New England Journal of Medicine, 320*, 762–8.

CHAPTER THREE

Adaptive and Maladaptive Parenting:

Perspectives on Risk and Protective Factors

JOY D. OSOFSKY AND M. DEWANA THOMPSON

Professionals who think about parenting often focus on the many social ailments that burden families, including the effects of single parenting, the problem of teenage pregnancies, the increasing number of children being raised in violent environments, the negative effects of substance abuse, and the impact of these factors on the psychological well-being of children and families. Less frequently, discussions center around the adaptive aspects of parenting or the conditions under which children raised with problematic or maladaptive parenting prove to be resilient.

In considering adaptive and maladaptive parenting, it is important that the latter not be viewed as a permanent state for families but be recognized as a situation that can be altered, given improved circumstances. This leads to two critically important questions: 1) What circumstances foster adaptive parenting? and 2) Which circumstances lead to resilience in situations of risk? We argue that parents who have positive relationships with multiple systems that provide organization and support in their environments exhibit more adaptive parenting styles than those who lack these significant relationships. Positive relationships and communication between the parent and child, and between the parents and members of their support network, have all been shown to be beneficial in fostering adaptive parenting. Some parents, even when living under conditions of high psychosocial risk, who are able to maintain positive reciprocal relationships, adequate support networks, and have the added benefit of sharing parenting with someone else, can alter their behaviors and engage in enhanced caregiving.

The environmental circumstances in which families live, and the relationships that are nurtured within these environments, influence the behaviors and attitudes of parents. Systems theorists support the notion that individuals can form mutually beneficial relationships with their environments, which can in turn translate into positive or negative parenting behaviors (Belsky, 1984; Bronfenbrenner, 1989).

ENVIRONMENTAL INFLUENCES ON PARENTING

Parenting is largely defined by the environments in which families live. Although the microsystem encompasses the most basic and direct level of interaction within the environment, indirect relationships between the parent and distal factors are significant as well. Parenting, therefore, can be understood not only in terms of the dyadic relationship between the parent and child but also in a broader context. As described by Bronfenbrenner (1989), parent–child interactions exist within the context of multiple relationships and milieus. It is essential to understand that an individual's environment can encompass significant influential factors and relationships that affect overall development and that families are involved in reciprocal and mutually beneficial relationships with their environments. In these relationships, the influence is transactional. Parents both influence and are affected by their environments. The manner in which an individual parents his or her children, therefore, is largely a result of the patterns that are evident in the existing systems and the overall environment in which that person resides (Bronfenbrenner, 1989).

Socioeconomic factors, culture, the psychological well-being of the parent, child characteristics, and community climates are all factors that may influence patterns of behaviors (Belsky, 1984). Bronfenbrenner (1989) warned against solely considering demographic characteristics, or such personal attributes as IQ levels, when examining determinants of parenting. He believes that there is a need to examine jointly the characteristics of the environment and those of the individual. Using a person/context model allows for such an examination of parents' personal characteristics in the context of various ecological niches. Bronfenbrenner (1989) raised a question about which ecological niches are favorable for psychological growth. We also ask, which ecological niches or environmental conditions are favorable for adaptive parenting? Several factors have consistently been found to foster adaptive parenting environments. In this chapter, we focus on the importance of reciprocity, the existence of social networks in the parents' lives, and the significant role of the father.

In the first edition of the *Handbook of Early Childhood Intervention*, Beckwith (1990) highlighted the parent–infant relationship and the many microlevel influences on parenting. In this edition, we focus on more meso-, exo-, and macrolevel influences. From this perspective, the discussion moves from influences on adaptive parenting to considerations of resilience and protective factors in situations of risk. Lynch and Cicchetti (1998) have proposed that, in situations of risk, compensatory factors that are enduring and proximal (as contrasted to transient and distal) can serve as buffers in the parenting process. The existence of these factors appears to have the longest and most profound influence on children's overall development. Therefore, an essential component of this discussion is the recognition that unique circumstances within their environment may allow parents who are at risk for maladaptive parenting to develop and facilitate positive and healthy relationships with their children.

CHARACTERISTICS OF ADAPTIVE PARENTING

Importance of Reciprocity

Reciprocity, involving shared or complementary affects and experiences, is extremely important for the developing infant and his or her relationships. Winnicott (1965) proposed that there is no such thing as a baby. By this he meant that, psychologically, there is only a baby with a mother. In fact, there is no such thing as a parent without a child. Thus, the reciprocal, complementary relationship goes both ways. Winnicott (1953) characterized the commitment of parent to child in terms of primary maternal preoccupation. As such, the behaviors, needs, moods, intentions, and place of the infant should fill the parents' minds and help motivate them to respond appropriately to the child. Clinicians have long viewed affect as a crucial part of both understanding and facilitating the relationship that is so important for effective clinical work. In infancy, emotions play a particularly meaningful role in the evolving relationship between the parent and the child as they are a primary means of communication for both the infant and caregiver. Emotions in the caregiver–infant relationship are the basis for building important aspects of reciprocity. Attempts by parents to regulate their emotions are important for understanding parental effectiveness on both a theoretical and a practical basis (Dix, 1991).

Reciprocity, or building mutually satisfying relationships between the developing infant or young child and parent, influences both behavioral and affective development. Historically, the notion of affective reciprocity has been key for understanding the development of the early relationship. Some of the pioneer observers in this area presented an extreme and grim picture that may be useful in considering factors that are important for adaptive parenting. For example, data gathered by Spitz (1945, 1946), through his clinical observations of infants separated from their mothers in institutions, suggested that a predominance of negative affect, and, in severe cases, anaclitic depression (behavior marked by crying, withdrawal, and a frozen rigidity of expression and affect), may accompany disruptions in the early parent–infant relationship. In a similar way, Bowlby (1973, 1980) emphasized the importance of early separation and loss as potentially disruptive for the development of the parent–child relationship. In addition to traumatic events, children may also experience rejecting or overly frustrating events in their families, such as abuse or neglect, both of which can lead to disruptions in the development of reciprocity. Both the anaclitically depressed infants described by Spitz, and the children who have warded off painful affects according to Bowlby's theory, experience significant problems in achieving affective reciprocity that is important for positive psychosocial development. In a similar way, Erikson (1950) described the infant's need to develop basic trust. These ideas are closely related to the sensitive work of Fraiberg and colleagues (Fraiberg, Adelson, & Shapiro, 1975), which dealt with disturbed mothers' neurotic patterns of repetitions that occurred as they attempted to parent their infants. Fraiberg et al. termed these repetitions and maladaptive patterns "ghosts in the nursery" because of their tendency to be repeated generation after generation if no reparative work is done.

Several researchers and clinicians have added to our understanding of reciprocity through a combination of empirical work with infants and families and the development of new theoretical perspectives. Stern (1985), in his classic book, *The Interpersonal World of the Infant*, discussed how an infant forms a predictable and dependable representation of a parent–infant relationship. Infants use this parent representation to monitor their own behavior in relationship to their parent. As the infant develops more affective and intellectual capacities, it is possible to observe a matching of mental states between the infant and the parent as well as both parties' abilities to share feelings. Stern coined a now much-used phrase, "affect attunement," to describe this occurrence, meaning the ability of parents to be resonant with their infants by sharing affectual states. The ability to share emotions is extremely important for affective development because it is through the sharing of emotions with the infant that a feeling state is understood. If the parent is unable to share the infant's affective states, then one will observe a lack of reciprocity in the relationship. This will be described later as part of the risk situations that contribute to maladaptive parenting. In Stern's (1990) book *The Diary of a Baby*, the concepts of reciprocity and affect attunement are woven throughout his sensitive descriptions and observations of the development of the earliest relationship.

Another type of reciprocity, "emotional availability," focuses on the parent's accessibility and capacity for reading the emotional cues and meeting the emotional needs of the infant. Emde (1980) suggested that emotional availability may be one of the keenest barometers of how development proceeds in early childhood. Under optimal circumstances, one would expect to view a range of emotions, with a balance of the positive emotions of interest and pleasure between infant and parent. Emotional availability has been illustrated empirically in interesting research on a form of emotional referencing characterized as social referencing (Sorce, Emde, Campos, & Klinnert, 1985). In these experiments, an infant encounters a situation of uncertainty. When through normal exploration he or she looks to the mother for help in dealing with the uncertainty, the mother signals either fear/anger or joy/interest. When presented with the positive signal, the infant approaches and explores; in response to the negative signal, the infant avoids the new situation. Thus, the mother's facial expression or verbal signal significantly affects both the infant's affective response and his or her behavior. Social referencing illustrates a general developmental process that a person uses to gain information from a significant other about an uncertain or ambiguous situation. Clearly, emotional availability is important not only for the development of basic trust but also for the facilitation of positive exploration and for the development of competent behaviors. This response from a parent or significant caregiver plays a key role in the infant's development of a positive internalized sense of self. Empirical work on affect exchanges (Osofsky, 1993) provides similar examples of the importance not only of affective mirroring but also of sensitivity to the other's cues and feelings. Positive affect sharing is an early sensitive indicator that all is going well with development and with the relationship. This emotional differentiation in the development of children in high-risk groups is one that we return to in the maladaptive parenting sections of this chapter.

The Role of Fathers

The parenting literature often focuses on the mother–child dyad, suggesting implicitly that this dyadic relationship is the most significant in a child's life. Less frequent is the inclusion of fathers in the discussion of parenting. However, the dynamics of the father–child relationship are unique in their own regard and significant in a child's overall development. Thus, the distinct contributions of fathers should not be omitted in considering adaptive parenting.

Whether in single or married households, the presence of the father in the lives of both the mother and the child is clearly evident. Although there has been an increase in the number of children being raised by single mothers, a large proportion of children are also parented by their fathers. Moreover, a significant number of children raised primarily by their mothers have positive and healthy relationships with their fathers. Still another facet of fatherhood is the paternal role that many men choose to undertake, despite the fact that they are not the biological father. These relationships are often assumed by surrogate fathers who have consanguineal ties to the child (grandfathers, uncles, cousins) or significant others in the lives of mothers (boyfriends or friends) who make a personal commitment to serve in the fathering role. These relationships are less clearly defined and much harder to quantify, but they exist and must be recognized as significant and influential. We discuss briefly the significant role of fathers in the adaptive parenting relationship in married and in single-headed family systems.

The father's unique role in parenting has been clearly defined as beneficial in the lives of children. Supporting the earliest relationship between father and infant fosters strong ties for the later father–child relationship (Horn, in press; Parke, 1995). Regardless of the status of the relationship between the mother and the father, the relationship between the father and child and the influences that coparenting can have on a child's development are clear. Lamb, Hopps, and Elster (1987) outlined three ways in which fathers are involved in the parenting role. The first is the *interactive* component in which the father shares in specific activities and child-care routines. The second, the *availability* component, refers to the father's level of direct or indirect accessibility to the child. Third, the *responsibility* component refers to the fathers' acquisition of the provider role in which he ensures that the child's primary needs are met and that the necessary resources are available to him or her. Others have contended that there are additional ways in which father's levels of involvement are delineated. Involvement, for example, can be defined in terms of activities in which fathers participate with their children. These include play, leisure time, and child-care activities (Radin, 1993). The benefits

of these varied levels of paternal involvement with children have been well documented in the literature (Collins & Russell, 1991; Crockett, Eggebeen, & Hawkins, 1993; Horn, in press; Grossman, Pollack, & Golding, 1988; Lamb, 1987; Lamb, Hopps, & Elster 1987; Lamb, Plecke, & Levine, 1985; Parke, 1981, 1995).

In terms of the types of interactions that take place between fathers and their children, fathers generally tend to be less involved in caregiving interactions than are mothers. Several studies have shown that fathers are more likely to be engaged in interactions that evolve around play with their infants (Clarke-Stewart, 1980; Palm, 1997; Power & Parke, 1982; Yogman, 1983). These playful interactions – which include physical play, movement games, bouncing, and generally stimulating play – have been linked to higher levels of infant arousal (Clarke-Stewart, 1980; Power & Parke, 1982; Yogman, 1983). Fathers also have been found to promote assertiveness in their children and to participate in structured physical activities such as scouting and Little League (Palm, 1997). Mothers more often focus on socioemotional stimulation in their play with infants (e.g., playing peekaboo). For single noncustodial fathers, the amount of involvement in their children's lives proves to be just as important as in coparenting situations and more frequent than most would expect. Lerman (1993) found that almost half of the 600 young unwed fathers who were included in his study reported having at least weekly contact with their infants. Involvement, however, appears to decline as the infant becomes older.

Fathers' competence to provide nurturing and stimulating interactions with their children has been studied by many investigators. Fathers appear to be responsive and sensitive to their infants' needs and to continue to be able to manage and supervise their children's behaviors throughout their development (Parke, 1995; Russell & Russell, 1987). The presence of a male figure in the home has also been linked to more secure attachment in lower-income families (McLoyd, 1995). This reciprocal and mutually beneficial relationship between fathers and children is a key component found in families in which children tend to be healthy, successful, and competent and who have a secure sense of self. The added component of paternal influence providing the opportunity for children to interact and form an affective bond with both parents fosters adaptive parenting environments that aid in the promotion of healthy child development. Regardless of the dynamics between the mother and father, the added effort from other systems in children's lives is essential for ensuring that fathers are welcomed and not excluded from the parenting experiences of their children.

The Problem of Categorizing Single-Headed Families as "At Risk"

Weinraub and Gringlas (1995) suggested that children raised in single parent families are increasingly considered at risk. This status, however, is often determined by the social conditions faced frequently by single parents and not the demographic category of single parenthood itself. Single parents are more often women and, therefore, are paid lower wages than their male counterparts. They often face problems finding suitable employment and are more likely to live in deteriorated and violent communities with diminished access to community resources. An additional consequence is the lack of adequate educational opportunities that are available to their children. These combined factors place children living in these ecological niches at risk. A distinction exists, however, within the realm of single parenthood. At one end of the continuum are those parents who are unable to negotiate their environments or protect their children from being affected negatively. At the other end are those parents who are able to meet the challenges that their environments pose and who foster positive and healthy socializing contexts for their children. Thus, many single parents successfully meet and master significant challenges on a daily basis, despite adverse life circumstances, with adaptive parenting therefore the result. This is often accomplished with the help of additional members of their social systems, the added support of paternal involvement, the benefits of healthy reciprocal relationships with their children, and the utilization of religious and spiritual ties.

Bronfenbrenner (1989) warned that theorists should be careful not to use social addresses or demography in isolation to characterize individual behavior patterns. Alternatively, cumulative ecological effects should be examined. Because we recognize the challenges facing many single-headed families in America, and the consequences of such life circumstances, we choose not to define single parenthood itself as a risk factor. Instead, we address some of the social conditions affecting many families across demographic lines that can lead to maladaptive parenting. From this perspective, we address why some groups are disproportionately at risk and how resilience is often found in families who are challenged by adverse social conditions.

Social Networks and the Role of Supportive Relationships in Adaptive Parenting

Social networks have a significant influence on the lives of parents (Cochran & Niego, 1995). Personal social networks are defined as "those people outside the household who engage in activities and exchanges of an affective and/or material nature with members of the immediate family" (Cochran & Niego, 1995, p. 396). In examining the influence of social networks on adaptive parenting, it is important to distinguish between this concept and that of social support. Social support can be described in terms of the instrumental, informational, or emotional help provided by members of one's social network (Crockenberg, 1987). Members of a social network may offer support to a parent by taking on child care responsibilities, giving child care advice, or simply offering encouragement. However, some researchers argue that social networks should not merely be defined in terms of their supportive or nonsupportive roles or functions in the lives of parents (Cochran, 1993; Cochran & Brassard, 1979). This dichotomy ignores the additional positive and negative roles that members of a social network can fulfill. A much broader view of the role of social networks may include the previously mentioned modes of assistance, in addition to offering material assistance and serving as role models for both parents and children. However, members of a social network are not always supportive. When conflict arises among members, or when there is an overload of information and interaction, networks can contribute to stressful home environments for parents (Cochran & Niego, 1995). Nevertheless, the supportive role that network members serve often outweighs the stress that they may impose on a parent. Thus, social support is more appropriately defined as one of many functions served by the individuals in one's social network.

The role that social networks play in the lives of parents has been measured in four primary ways. The composition, density, and size of the overall network, as well as the number of interactions that take place between the individual and the network are all factors that influence the impact of a social network on a family system (Burchinal, Follmer, & Bryant, 1996). The network composition refers to the categories into which each member falls. This can include a spouse, family members, members of the community, friends, or professional acquaintances. The network density is measured by the interrelationships among individuals. This can be assessed, for example, by examining the relationship between the spouse and the grandparent (Burchinal, Follmer, & Bryant, 1996). MacPhee, Fritz, and Miller-Heyl (1996) found that the network size was far less important than whether the network members met the parents' needs. Therefore, on an individual level, the specific characteristics of members of the network, the number of social exchanges that take place between the individual and a particular member, and the perceived intensity of these relationships are all factors that may make greater contributions to parenting than the actual size of the network. The synergistic effect that both these structural and functional components of a social network have on the parent-child dyad ultimately fosters adaptive parenting environments.

The presence of social networks that are extensive and supportive has been linked to adaptive parenting in many ways (Burchinal, Follmer, & Bryant, 1996; Cochran & Niego, 1995). Supportive social networks have been found to reduce stress by serving as a buffer against threatening events, influencing the coping strategies of parents, and providing emotional support (Crockenberg, 1987). The presence of supportive environments improves parents' general dispositions, assists them in feeling less overwhelmed by parenting tasks, and allows them to have additional tangible and intangible resources from which to draw information (Crnic & Greenberg, 1987; McLoyd, 1995). Two of the most significant types of information provided by members of social networks include child-rearing advice and information regarding community resources. Tangible sources of support include child care assistance and financial support (Cochran & Niego, 1995). Riley (1990) found that fathers relied on the child-rearing advice of several significant members of their social network. These networks appear to guide parents in positive directions and offer additional resource information regarding their children.

Parents who have supportive social networks available to them have also been shown to be better equipped with resources that buffer stressful life events (Cochran, Lerner, Riley, Gunnarsson, & Henderson 1990; Voight, Hans, & Bernstein, 1996). Hanshaw and Frazier-Thompson (1996) found that fathers who were raising children with disabilities were better able to cope and accept their children's disability when they had supportive family networks available to them. Despite additional hardships that parents may face, punitive, harsh, and controlling parenting styles are less likely to be found in families in which there is a supportive and extensive network (Hashima & Amato, 1994; Jennings, Stagg, & Connors, 1991). This finding has been demonstrated across both racial and economic lines, in which individuals are able to use their social network as a source of strength. In family situations in which there are stressors, but also the existence of a strong network, there tends to be a lower incidence of child abuse and violence (Crockenberg, 1987) and, for teenage mothers in particular, higher levels of psychological well-being (Thompson & Peebles-Wilkins, 1992). In contrast, the absence of such systems can lead to social isolation and conditions that foster maladaptive parenting. Researchers have found that abusive parents, when compared with nonabusive parents, are more likely to be isolated from both formal and informal support networks, tend to be newer to their neighborhoods, and are less likely to have a relative living in close proximity (McLoyd, 1995). Abusive parents also report having less access to informal support and not being satisfied with the social networks available to them (MacPhee, Fritz, & Miller-Heyl, 1996).

Supportive social networks are related positively to adaptive parenting behaviors. More specifically, parents who have supportive networks available tend to have more nurturant styles of parenting, display more positive affect and responsiveness with their infants, and foster more stimulating home environments (Burchinal, Follmer, & Bryant, 1996; Crnic, Greenberg, & Slough, 1986; MacPhee, Fritz,

& Miller-Heyl, 1996). Such parents are more sensitive to their children's needs and exhibit less coercive modes of discipline than those who do not have access to such systems (McLoyd, 1995). The presence of supportive social networks has been related to less punitive and more responsive behaviors in teenage mothers (Nitz, Ketterlinus, & Brandt, 1995). In Crockenberg's (1987) study, poor adolescent mothers who had access to more family members who helped with child care and who took on household responsibilities were more responsive to their infants and showed higher levels of sensitivity to them as compared with those who had less support. Adolescent mothers frequently identify grandmothers as the primary members of their social networks on whom they depend the most, particularly for child care assistance (Hunter, 1997; Nitz, Ketterlinus, & Brandt, 1995; Wilson & Tolson, 1990). Grandparents play a significant role in the lives of parents as well as children. The presence of grandmothers in the home of single African American mothers is related positively to higher levels of emotional adjustment in their children (McLoyd, 1995; Wilson & Tolson, 1990). Children generally benefit from the existence of familial support. High levels of support in families have been related to greater levels of social interaction in children, higher levels of academic achievement, and overall enhanced social and emotional well-being (Gonzales, Cauce, Friedman, & Mason, 1996; Homel, Burns, & Goodnow, 1987; Taylor, 1997; Tietjen, 1985). In contrast, lower levels of social support are related to insecure attachment in infants, including both resistant and avoidant behaviors (Crockenberg, 1981). Although the individual characteristics children bring to the parent–child relationship may contribute to these outcomes, supportive environments generally enhance the likelihood of these positive outcomes.

Contextual influences are key factors to consider when examining social networks. For poor and uneducated parents, personal social networks are often determined by those individuals to whom they have access in their immediate environment. Because of a limited pool of resources, these parents may have access to fewer social network members (Cochran, 1993). For example, parents with less education may not be as socially active as parents with higher educational attainment. The former may have fewer social ties, whereas more educated parents may have relationships that extend into various geographic areas and are able to incorporate a wider range of network members. Parents' ethnicity has also been shown to influence their network membership. Ethnic groups that rely on a collectivist orientation, such as Hispanics and Native Americans, have been found to depend more heavily on close family members and fictive kin for emotional support (MacPhee, Fritz, & Miller-Heyl, 1996). African Americans also tend to rely heavily on extended support networks (Hunter, 1997; Kohn & Wilson, 1995; McAdoo, 1988; Taylor, Chatters, Tucker, & Lewis, 1990). Cross (1990) reported that African Americans often have larger social networks that they utilize more frequently than do European Americans. It is essential to take such contextual influences into consideration when examining the factors that influence parenting.

By and large, supportive networks benefit parenting skills in three ways. First, parents are able to gain additional information about developmentally appropriate methods of parenting (Bronfenbrenner & Crouter, 1983). Second, support networks often offer tangible resources in terms of child care or financial assistance when needed (Cochran & Niego, 1995). Finally, networks often serve as buffers against maladaptive parenting and stressful life situations (Voight, Hans, & Bernstein, 1996). These modes of assistance often translate into adaptive parenting environments that contribute to positive outcomes in infants and children.

RISK FACTORS FOR MALADAPTATION IN PARENTING

Both biological and environmental factors can lead to risk for maladaptive parenting. In this section we review four selected areas in which there is much current interest, including substance abuse, violence exposure, adolescent parenting, and parental psychopathology.

Substance Abuse

The role that substance abuse plays in the lives of parents and their children has been examined in a number of ways, including its effects on infants, parents, and the parent–infant relationship. To understand the overall effect on parenting, it is necessary to recognize the complexity of each of these factors.

Much is known about the detrimental effects of cocaine, alcohol, marijuana, heroin, and other drugs on a child when they are introduced early in life. Prenatally, the use of drugs and alcohol may result in birth defects, growth retardation, and developmental problems in infancy, including lower levels of information processing, attentional disturbances, and decreased interactions (Das Eiden & Leonard, 1996; Jacobson, Jacobson, Sokol, Martier, & Ager, 1993; Lester & Tronick, 1994; Margura & Laudet, 1996; Mayes, 1995; Mayes & Bornstein, 1996; Mayes, Feldman, Granger, Haynes, Bornstein, & Schottenfeld, 1997; Mejta & Lavin, 1996; Struthers & Hansen, 1992). However, it is not possible to evaluate the ultimate effects on the infant without taking into account both the overall environment into which the child is born and in which he or she is raised and the effects on the parent–infant relationship. Reciprocity, discussed earlier in this chapter, influences the behavioral and affective development of infants. Its presence, in the form of emotional availability, is particularly important for the parent's ability to read the infant's cues and meet his or her emotional needs. In most cases, addiction prevents a mother from responding to her infant's needs because her primary focus is on her drug of choice, not her infant (Brooks, Zuckerman, Bamforth, Cole, & Kaplan-Sanoff, 1994). Mothers who abuse drugs show much lower levels of interaction with their infants (Mayes & Bornstein, 1996). Their lack of ability to parent effectively is influenced by their current preoccupation with drugs and by the fact that many of these mothers were raised in dysfunctional families themselves, where substance abuse, psychopathology, and violence in many forms were part of everyday life.

The lack of reciprocity observed so often between mothers who have abused drugs and their infants is influenced by three factors. First, the exposure of the infant to drugs prenatally may lead to both developmental impairments and lability in states and moods, both of which may contribute to making the infant more difficult to parent. Thus, positive, healthy interactions between the parent and the infant are less likely. Second, long-term drug use (specifically cocaine) has been found to affect an individual's neuropsychological functioning. These effects often include deterioration of short-term memory, impaired task orientation, altered attention levels, and lowered levels of concentration (Mayes, 1995). Increased risk of psychiatric disorders is also present, including extremely high rates of depression in individuals who abuse drugs and alcohol. These impairments inevitably affect a parent's ability to meet effectively the physical and emotional demands of an infant. The parent in such situations is frequently physically present but is psychologically unavailable to her infant. Finally, as mentioned earlier, substance abuse is frequently associated with such other high-risk factors as elevated levels of violence, poverty, homelessness, social isolation, and noncompletion of high school (Mayes, 1995). The combined effects of these factors, along with chronic or acute drug use, are likely to have a significant impact on parenting.

As with other maladaptive parenting situations, substance abuse in a parent will have differential impacts on children of different ages. However, some developmental needs that are basic for all children may be influenced remarkably by being raised by a parent who uses drugs (Kaplan-Sanoff, 1996). The cycle of trauma that accompanies substance abuse affects children's daily lives. When parents abuse substances, unpredictability and chaos characterize the household. Emotional unavailability and abandonment are recurring themes. Out-of-home placements are also prevalent while the mother struggles with her addiction. Similarly, a child of a teenage or depressed mother must deal with changing and confusing roles – at one time being infantilized and at another being given the responsibility of taking care of the parent (known as parentification). As Kaplan-Sanoff (1996) and Brooks et al. (1994) emphasized, living with a parent with an addiction challenges the child's development of trust, attachment, autonomy, and self-esteem and affects the child's ability to develop appropriate behavioral control and affect regulation (Beeghley & Tronick, 1994). Lester and Tronick (1994) discussed lifestyle factors that lead women to abuse substances and the resultant family and neighborhood conditions in which children are reared. Children raised by a parent who abuses drugs or alcohol most often have a chaotic, disorganized lifestyle that may include inadequate and disruptive parenting, poverty, stress, and exposure to violence. Any of these conditions can contribute to poor developmental outcomes. When they are combined with prenatal drug exposure, children are at extremely high risk for learning and behavior problems (Lester & Tronick, 1994; Kaplan-Sanoff, 1996).

In a more general way, studies have indicated that substance abuse impairs parenting abilities (Mayes, 1995). Parental substance abuse has been associated with 1) other psychiatric disorders, including depression and antisocial personality; 2) multigenerational transmission of both substance abuse patterns and psychiatric disorders; 3) a high incidence of violence, both between adults and toward children; 4) an increased risk for abandonment and neglect; and 5) a generally poor sense of competence as a parent and a poor understanding of the needs of children. Furthermore, and consistent with these associations, studies have demonstrated that without ongoing support, mothers who have managed to stop using drugs are more likely to resume their drug habits (see Mayes, 1995). It is most likely that, because there may be significant physiological and biological effects on infants born to parents who are addicted to drugs or alcohol, the negative effects on the child relate to an interaction between the characteristics or problems of the infant and those of the parent. Thus, the depressed behaviors, intrusiveness, erratic responses, and violence observed as negative parenting in mothers who abuse drugs may be a result of both the substance abuse problem and a cumulative effect of the many parental risk factors that affect this mother. Because the problem is a transactional one with many individuals – infant, parent, extended family, broad social network – contributing, effective intervention efforts must also be individual-, family-, and community-centered. Therefore, it is important to address the individual needs of the infant and the parent, provide appropriate interventions and support, and recognize the very important dimension of developing a trusting relationship with the addicted parent. Only if the parent learns to trust him- or herself will he or she then be able to parent the child sensitively and effectively.

Violence

Parenting is, at best, a complex process, and in situations of high risk, it is even more so. For some parents and children, the stress associated with violence exposure and the necessary coping with violence as an everyday event affect both the mother's ability to parent and the child's capacity to form healthy attachment relationships (Osofsky & Fenichel, 1994). Because early relationships form the basis for all later relationship experiences, such difficult early interactions may be problematic for the child's later development. Poverty, job and family instability, and environmental violence add immeasurably to the inherent difficulties. Although systematic research has not yet been conducted concerning the effects of violence exposure on parenting and the caregiving environment, we know from anecdotal reports that parents who live with violence frequently describe a sense of helplessness and frustration about their inability to protect their children and keep them safe, even in their own neighborhoods (Garbarino, Dubrow, Kostelny, & Pardo, 1992; Lorion & Saltzman, 1993; National Survey of Children and Parents, 1991; Osofsky & Fenichel, 1994; Osofsky, Wewers, Hann, & Fick, 1993; Richters & Martinez, 1993). A constant barrage of violence in the community may lead parents to communicate helplessness and hopelessness to their children.

Protecting children and facilitating their development is a family's most basic function. Regardless of their composition, families are uniquely structured to provide the attention, nurturance, and safety that children need to grow and develop. An important psychological aspect of parenting an infant or toddler is being able to provide a "holding environment" (Winnicott, 1965) in which a parent can both protect a child and allow and encourage appropriate independence. Parents who are aware that they may not be able to protect their children from violence are likely to feel frustrated and helpless. In addition, when parents witness violence or are themselves victims of violence, they are likely to have difficulty being emotionally available, sensitive, and responsive to their children. In trying to help children and parents who have been traumatized by violence exposure, it becomes clear that parents must cope with their own trauma before they are able to deal with their children's needs. Furthermore, when parents live in constant fear, their children often lack the sense of basic trust and security that is the foundation of healthy emotional development (Osofsky, 1995; Osofsky, Cohen, & Drell, 1995).

Parents may experience additional burdens because children's traditional societal protectors, including schools, community centers, and churches, are also overwhelmed and are not able to assure safe environments for their children. A recent survey was designed to identify issues of trust and safety among a group of African American parents and children living in an inner-city environment with a high rate of violence according to police homicide statistics. Thirty-five percent of the parents reported that they did not feel their children were safe walking to school, and 54% did not feel they were safe playing in their neighborhood. Only 17% of these parents felt that the children were very safe doing these activities. However, the majority (62%) felt that the children were very safe at home, and 30% felt they were very safe at school (Fick, Osofsky, & Lewis, 1997). These data are consistent with the responses of 250 African American elementary schoolchildren, ages 8–12, from the same neighborhoods, who reported that they felt much safer at home and in school than walking to school or playing in their neighborhood. Ninety percent of their parents felt that violence was a serious problem or crisis in their neighborhood. In clinical work with traumatized young children and their families, one of the first issues that must be dealt with before any treatment can begin is whether the child and the family feel safe. There is a dual problem, however, in dealing with chronic community violence: 1) the continued physical reality of the violent environment and 2) the continued posttraumatic reality for the young child and caregivers.

Exposure to violence may interfere with normal developmental transitions for both parents and children. If violence occurs in their neighborhood, to their child, or to a child they know, parents may become overprotective, hardly allowing their children out of their sight. Under such circumstances, parents have difficulty behaving in any other than a controlling, or even authoritarian, manner. Yet, encouragement of autonomy is important for development and comes with trust in the safety of the environment (Erikson, 1950). For families living with violence, children's growing independence and normal exploration may be anything but safe and, therefore, are not allowed. Parents who are exposed to chronic violence may also become depressed and unable to provide for their young children's needs.

Even with heroic efforts, if parents are sad and anxious, it will be more difficult for them to respond positively to the smiles and lively facial expressions of their young children. Depressed parents may be more irritable and may talk less often and with less intensity. All of these factors, although understandable, may influence young children to be less responsive themselves and feel that they may have done something "bad" to contribute to this state of affairs. Thus, supports outside of the family are very important for parents and children exposed to violence.

Teenage Mothers

Parenting risks for adolescent mothers (here referred to as 16 years and younger) often begin early in their infants' lives because the cognitive as well as socioemotional caregiving environment is often problematic. Adolescent mothers generally initiate verbal interactions less often and are less responsive to their infants and young children than older mothers (Furstenberg, Brooks-Gunn, & Morgan, 1987; Chase-Lansdale, Brooks-Gunn, & Palkoff, 1991; Crockenberg, 1987; Culp, Appelbaum, Osofsky, & Levy, 1988; Field, Widmayer, Stringer, & Ignatoff, 1980; Osofsky, 1991; Osofsky et al., 1992; Osofsky & Eberhart-Wright, 1988, 1992). When observing interactions between adolescent mothers and their infants, one is frequently struck with the stillness of the interaction. Many of the mothers talk very little to their infants and young children, and the children verbalize relatively little. When the mothers do talk, they give short commands, or discipline the child, rather than giving elaborated responses or statements. Thus, many of these children grow up in impoverished cognitive as well as economic and socioemotional environments (Chase-Landsdale, Brooks-Gunn, & Palkoff, 1991; Osofsky, 1996). The increased risk when they enter the organized school setting is obvious.

Research examining adolescent mother–child interactions has shown that adolescent mothers' parenting practices may increase their children's risk for less adaptive developmental outcomes. When compared to the interactions of adult mothers with their infants and toddlers, interactions between adolescent mothers and their children differ in terms of both the amount and quality of the behaviors displayed. Studies of mother–child interactions conducted in the home as well as in homelike laboratory situations have found adolescent mothers to engage in less verbal and more physical forms of interaction (Culp, Appelbaum, Osofsky, & Levy, 1988; Garcia-Coll, Hoffman, & Oh, 1987; Osofsky & Osofsky, 1970). The paucity of talking between adolescent mothers and their infants combined with the less descriptive and articulate verbal interactions of adolescent mothers and their toddlers (Osofsky, 1996) may contribute to the poorer cognitive and linguistic outcomes associated with teenagers' children (East & Felice, 1990; Furstenberg, Brooks-Gunn, & Chase-Landsdale, 1989). In addition, adolescent mothers and their toddlers are more likely to engage in misregulated patterns of affective interaction in which either negative affects are emphasized (e.g., child cries and mother yells) or affective cues are misread by the dyad (e.g., child becomes angry and mother laughs). Participation in misregulated patterns of affect was found to be most characteristic of teenage mother–toddler interactions in comparison to both socially advantaged and socially disadvantaged older mothers and toddlers (Hann, Robinson, Osofsky, & Little, 1991).

The developmental ramifications of the less optimal interaction patterns associated with adolescent mothers and their children may be detected early in the social–emotional development of these children. Lamb, Hopps, and Elster (1987) found the distribution of infant attachment classifications differed between infants of adolescent and adult mothers. Infants of adolescent mothers showed significantly more avoidant behavior and were more likely to be classified as avoidantly attached. More recent attachment research that has included disorganized patterns of attachment in addition to secure and insecure patterns (Main & Solomon, 1989) indicates that the offspring of adolescent mothers may also be at high risk for developing disorganized attachment relationships with their mothers (Hann, Castino, Jarosinski, & Britton, 1991; Hann, Osofsky, & Culp, 1996; Speiker, 1989). The finding that children of adolescent mothers are at higher risk for developing insecure attachment relationships is consistent with previous research concerning the etiology of avoidant and disorganized attachment, both of which have been associated with earlier insensitive, negative, and emotionally unavailable

caregiving (Main & Hesse, 1990). These patterns have been observed frequently with adolescent mothers and their children. The increased risk among adolescent mothers' children for developing less optimal patterns of interaction and insecure and disorganized attachment relationships may contribute to the poorer social and emotional outcomes seen in these children (Brooks-Gunn & Furstenberg, 1986; Furstenberg, Brooks-Gunn, & Chase-Landsdale, 1989; Osofsky & Eberhart-Wright, 1988; Osofsky, Eberhart-Wright, Ware, & Hann, 1992). Further research, however, is needed to establish the links between early patterns of mother–child interaction and infant attachment and later socioemotional outcomes in adolescent mothers and their children.

Mental health risks for adolescent mothers and their offspring may have been overlooked in previous research. In a recent study conducted in New Orleans on the effects of chronic community violence on 58 elementary-school-age children, ages 9–12 years old, we found that almost half of the children included in the sample were born to mothers who became parents as teenagers (Osofsky, Wewers, Hann, & Fick, 1993). Furthermore, there was a significant relation between reported behavior problems of these children on the Child Behavior Checklist (Achenbach, 1979) and their having been parented by an adolescent mother. In addition to reported exposure to community violence and family violence, and because of the age and immaturity of the young mothers, as well as lack of support, children of adolescent mothers are frequently victims of child abuse and neglect. Thus, being born and raised in the family of an adolescent mother may increase the risk of a child's being exposed to environmental and family factors that increase mental health risks.

In our experience in developing interventions with adolescent mothers, we found that it is most helpful to use strategies that assist the mother in developing empathy for her baby. Adolescence is a developmental period when individuals tend to focus mainly on themselves rather than on another person. Thus, a child interferes with a teenager's egocentric focus. For a teen mother, her own feelings are crucial, not those of others. Even if a young woman is already a mother, she will continue with her own personal struggle to determine "Who am I?" Thus, helping the mother become attuned to her baby's feelings is difficult but crucial, for both the child and the relationship. Video recordings and other techniques may help the mothers to focus playfully on their babies' feelings and to recognize the impact of their behaviors on the baby (Carter, Osofsky, & Hann, 1991b). It should be noted, however, that teen mothers who live in healthy, supportive environments where they themselves are nurtured and where they receive both tangible and intangible support from family, friends, and community resources often foster positive home environments and have healthy relationships with their children (Brooks-Gunn & Chase-Landsdale, 1991, 1995; Osofsky, 1996). Factors that have been found to influence the positive outcomes of teen mothers and their children include completing high school and moving into the workforce and having fewer subsequent pregnancies, the support of family members and a significant other, and positive role models in their lives whom they can emulate (Brooks-Gunn & Chase-Landsdale, 1995). The presence of these individual and combined factors can often trigger adaptive parenting situations for the youngest of mothers.

Parental Psychopathology

Parental psychopathology is a risk factor for caregiving that often occurs in conjunction with other risk factors including substance abuse, child maltreatment, exposure to violence, and adolescent pregnancy. By definition, child maltreatment, which frequently accompanies parental psychopathology, constitutes a severe dysfunction in parenting that can lead to serious maladjustment and behavior problems (Rogosch, Cicchetti, Shields, & Toth, 1996).

Because maternal depression has been studied and observed most frequently as a risk factor that affects parenting – often in lower socioeconomic and highly stressed groups – we focus on this area of parental psychopathology. Maternal depression contributes to less adequate and even negative parenting behavior that can lead to problems in the adjustment of infants and children (Field, Murrow, & Adelstein, 1993; Gelfand & Teti, 1990; Gopfert, Webster, & Seeman, 1996; Tronick & Gianino, 1986; Weinberg & Tronick, 1997). It has been associated with such undesirable parenting practices as

unresponsiveness, inattentiveness, intrusiveness, inept discipline, and negative perceptions of children (Gelfand & Teti, 1990). Although, some of the studies have methodological limitations, Gelfand and Teti (1990) reported age-typical forms of child psychopathology accompanying maternal depression and such associated stressors as marital discord. Earlier, as part of our review of the role of reciprocity in adaptive parenting, we discussed the importance of emotional regulation, including sharing and complementary affects between the parent and the developing infant. This topic is highly relevant in considering the impact of depression on parenting effectiveness. Emotional availability and a sense of emotional consistency include the idea of "good enough" mothering (Winnicott, 1965), affect attunement and sensitivity (Bowlby, 1973; Cramer & Brazelton, 1990; Osofsky & Eberhart-Wright, 1988; Stern, 1985), and parental "mirroring" of affective states (Kohut, 1977; Stolorow, Brandchaft, & Atwood, 1987). (A "good enough" parent is one who is not "perfect" but provides sufficient nurturance and caregiving – both physically and emotionally – to support healthy child development.) Three types of interaction patterns have been observed with depressed low-income mothers and their infants: 1) withdrawn-unavailable; 2) hostile-intrusive; and 3) mainly positive (Murray & Cooper, 1997a,b). The two negative patterns of interaction have been shown to interfere with healthy cognitive and emotional development. A longitudinal study conducted in Germany (Laucht, Esser, & Schmidt, 1994) showed how disturbed patterns of mother–infant interaction for a sample of 353 mothers and infants mediated the negative effects on cognitive and emotional development.

Empirical research, in addition to clinical observations, has shown that depressed mothers have difficulty with affect regulation and tend to be dysynchronous with their infants rather than resonating sensitively to emotional states (Field, 1995; Osofsky, 1993; Weinberg & Tronick, 1997). Furthermore, these mothers match negative states more often than positive behaviors when compared with nondepressed mothers (Field, 1995). Using the "still-face" situation (an experimental paradigm during which the caregiver is asked first to be normally responsive to her or his infant and then to stop being responsive and show a still face with flat affect for several minutes), Tronick and his colleagues (Cohn & Tronick, 1983; Weinberg & Tronick, 1997) found that when mothers were asked to "look depressed" for a short period of time during face-to-face interaction, infants of nondepressed mothers became distressed very quickly, whereas infants of chronically depressed mothers did not. The latter group seemed to tune out both when their mothers were responsive and when they were nonresponsive (Field, 1995). Field, Healy, Goldstein, and Guthertz (1990) described several patterns in depressed mothers that include the more typical withdrawn, flat affect pattern as well as one that is intrusive and overstimulating. Depressed mothers, similar to adolescent mothers (who may also be depressed), tend to talk less to their infants, show fewer positive facial expressions, vocalize less, and display less positive physical affection (Field et al., 1993; Murray & Cooper, 1997a). Indeed, there is increasing evidence indicating that adolescent mothers are more likely to be depressed than older mothers (Field, 1995; Hann, Castino, Jarosinski, & Britton, 1991; Osofsky, 1996; Osofsky & Eberhart-Wright, 1988).

Depressed mothers have been reported to be less available emotionally to their infants and children, thereby providing a less empathic and responsive environment (Field, 1995; Osofsky, 1996). Zuravin (1989) emphasized the link between maternal depression and mother-to-child aggression, finding that moderately, but not severely, depressed low-income mothers are at increased risk for child abuse and physical aggression. Several caveats are necessary in interpreting the results of this study, including the method used to measure depression and the sample studied. However, it is important not to underestimate the effect that maternal depression may have on the quality of the interactive relationship between mother and child. For low-income, already stressed dyads, maternal depression may place infants and children at much greater risk for depression. Substantial research (Carter, Osofsky, & Hahn, 1991a,b; Field et al., 1990; Hann, Castino, Jarosinski, & Britton, 1991; Osofsky & Eberhart-Wright, 1988; Radke-Yarrow et al., 1985; Tronick & Gianino, 1986; Zahn-Waxler et al., 1990) suggests that the children of depressed mothers are at higher risk for problems in affect regulation, including both increased depression, or subdued affect, and inappropriate aggression. According to Tronick and Gianino (1986),

if the infant is able to cope with a nonresponsive environment and maintain both self- and interactive regulation simultaneously, then the outcome is likely to be positive mental health. In contrast, if the infant cannot maintain interactive regulation, then self-regulation will be the primary means of coping and the outcome is likely to be problematic. The combination of depression in the mother and difficulties with affect regulation in the child results in less emotional availability and increases the risk for other problems in the relationship.

In general, either as a result of the depression or as a contributing factor, depressed mothers have less support available to them and more restricted social networks. Thus, an important mediating factor for resilience in parenting may be absent for these mothers. One study (Hossain et al., 1994) suggested that, in some cases, fathers may buffer the negative effects of maternal depression on infants. The investigators observed that infants' interactions with their nondepressed fathers were more positive than those with their depressed mothers. Field (1995) reported a similar finding with familiar nondepressed child care providers. These infants' interactions with the child care workers showed increased arousal with more stimulation and positive affective exchanges than were observed with their depressed mothers.

Infants may also contribute to the negative patterns of interaction observed with depressed mothers. Because infants of depressed mothers may show fewer affective responses early in their development, increased irritability, and lower activity levels, they may contribute to interactional disturbances. Zuckerman et al. (1990) noted that newborns of depressed mothers are more difficult to console. Yet, it is not clear whether these behavioral reactions were due to environmental or to genetic prenatal influences. Thus, there may be an unfortunate negative reverberating cycle for depressed mothers and their infants. In fact, mothers may perceive their infants more negatively (Field, 1995; Field et al., 1993) and interact less with them. At the same time, the infants may be more irritable and less responsive because of pre- or perinatal risk factors. Early identification of risk and the potential benefits of preventive interventions are imperative, including early home visitation models that have been shown to be effective for such high-risk mothers (Olds, Henderson, & Kitzman, 1994; Olds, Henderson, Tatelbaum,

& Chamberlain, 1988; Olds, Kitzman, Henderson, Hanks et al., 1997; Werner, 1984, 1994). Lyons-Ruth, Connell, and Grunebaum (1990) pointed to both the negative developmental consequences associated with severe social risk conditions and to the buffering effects of developmentally oriented home visiting services for infants at greatest social risk. When infants of depressed mothers received home visiting services, they outperformed an unserved group on the Bayley Scales of Infant Development at 18 months of age and were twice as likely to be classified as securely attached in their relationship with their mother. These differences were found with home visiting services that involved a concerted outreach and a strong social service component, with focus on the mother–infant relationship (with 13 months of home visiting services involving forty-six completed home visits). There is much yet to be learned about parental psychopathology and its effects on parenting. However, it is clear that an important first step is a recognition of the potentially negative effects of parental psychopathology and a commitment to address them before the effects on children become too severe or difficult to remediate.

Importance of Resilience

Recent years have witnessed an increased emphasis on resilience; that is, factors that may improve conditions directly affecting a child's coping ability. One of the most important resilience factors is effective parenting. A substantial body of theoretical and research work has been conducted on resilience in infants and children. This research is important to our consideration of adaptive and maladaptive parenting.

Werner (1984) carried out a landmark study on resilience, conceptualizing this phenomenon as the ability to recover from or adjust easily to misfortune or sustained life stress. Resilience is often used to describe the following outcomes in children: 1) good outcomes despite risk status, 2) sustained competence under stress, and 3) recovery from trauma (Werner, 1994). Many studies, including those of Werner (1994) and Masten (1997), define a resilient child as one who is more likely to have an adaptable easy temperament and who is more intelligent than nonresilient children. A resilient child is also more likely to have a supportive person – often a parent or caregiver – in his or her environment, a person with whom the child has a trusting relationship.

Werner (1984) discovered that resilient children who adapted successfully to adult life had the following protective factors: 1) an adaptable temperament that allowed them to elicit positive responses from caring adults, 2) skills and values that allowed for an assessment of the child's abilities in order to develop realistic educational and vocational goals, and 3) parents or caregivers who reflected competence and fostered self-esteem in their children or other supportive adults who fostered trust. Furthermore, resilient children sought out environments that reinforced and rewarded their competencies and helped them handle life's transitions successfully.

Much can be learned from Werner's (1984) remarkable longitudinal research. In her study with 698 babies born on the Hawaiian island of Kauai, resilient youth (about one-third of the group) at the time of high school graduation had developed a positive self-concept and an internal locus of control. They displayed a more nurturant, responsible, and achievement-oriented attitude toward life than did their high-risk peers who had developed problems in their teens. These boys and girls had grown up in families in which they had not experienced prolonged separations from their primary caregivers during the first year of life. All had the chance to establish a close bond with at least one caregiver from whom they received much positive attention when they were infants. Some of this nurturance came from caregiver substitutes, such as grandparents or older siblings, or other members of their extended family. Both parents and surrogate parents served as important role models with whom the children identified.

A second major body of research on resilience has been conducted as part of Project Competence, a longitudinal study directed by Masten, Hubbard, Gest, Tellegen, Garmezy, and Ramirez (in press) that followed Garmezy's pioneering work in this area (Garmezy & Rutter, 1983; Masten, 1997; Masten, Best, & Garmezy, 1990). This study includes competent children growing up with little adversity, resilient children growing up with high levels of adversity, and maladaptive children who have not been able to overcome hardship successfully. They found that the role of a "good-enough" parent is crucial for positive outcomes in these children. Successful children, whether from low- or high-risk circumstances, have a history of access to more resources than maladaptive children, including better intellectual skills and good parenting.

Resilience in children and youth is not fostered in a vacuum, even with good-enough parenting. Promoting positive development depends on creating healthy external systems in addition to healthy individuals. Thus, parents need support from the broader environment for parenting, educating, and socializing their children. Furthermore, Masten and colleagues (in press), recently suggested that future understanding of the impact of parenting on developmental outcomes could benefit from disaggregating global resources such as "parenting quality" into such meaningful components as the dimensions of structure, warmth, and expectations that may relate to conduct, achievement, and social functioning with peers under different conditions. For example, Baldwin, Baldwin, and Cole (1990) determined that the "structure" dimension of parenting, rather than warmth, differed for parents of competent children, depending on whether they lived in dangerous or safe neighborhoods. Other studies have shown that stricter parenting may be especially protective in unsafe environments (Osofsky & Fenichel, 1994).

The development of resilience begins in infancy, and longitudinal studies point consistently to factors in very young children that contribute to such strengths. Werner (1994) reported that 10% of the Asian and Polynesian cohort she studied who had experienced four or more risk factors – including perinatal complications, parental psychopathology, family instability, and chronic poverty before the age of 2 years – developed into competent, confident, caring adults. These resilient young children were described by their caretakers as active, affectionate, cuddly, easy infants with few problematic early behaviors. Similar observations of resilient infants were part of the Coping Project conducted by the Menninger Foundation (Murphy & Moriarity, 1987) in which clinical assessments of thirty-two Caucasian infants revealed an active, easygoing nature and few feeding and sleeping problems. These babies were also notably responsive to people and objects in their environment. Such resilient babies are often characterized by responsiveness and warmth as well as by an ability to seek out and relate to others in

their environment. Similar positive behaviors were observed in studies of infants of teenage mothers who did better as they developed (Osofsky, 1996).

Rutter (1993) refined the issue of resilience further as it relates to parenting. He cites evidence from behavioral genetics indicating that in many circumstances, nonshared environmental influences tend to have a greater effect than shared ones. Thus, features that equally affect all children in a family may be less important than those that affect differentially, in which one child may be affected more than others. Therefore, it is not uncommon to see in a relatively well-organized family one child in the family being scapegoated or favored over others. How does a child manage to be resilient under such circumstances? He or she may distance him- or herself from what is happening. For example, in some families, quarrels and fights occur and one child may be drawn into the disagreement or dispute while another remains uninvolved. In a family with parental mental illness, a less vulnerable child may manage to find emotional support outside of the home. Children – even very young children – can do a great deal to influence what happens to them. Rutter (1978, 1993) indicated that protective effects may result from people actively planning how they deal with what happens to them, thus feeling as if they have more control of their lives. Younger children may protect themselves by withdrawing and finding support outside the family. Older children may be able to plan actively in ways that make them feel less vulnerable.

Thus, results from many studies of resilient infants, young children, and youth identify consistently a small number of crucial protective factors for development (Masten, 1997; Masten et al., 1990; Werner, 1994; Werner & Smith, 1982). The most important protective resource is a strong relationship with a competent, caring, positive adult – most often a parent. The most important personal quality is average or above-average intellectual development with good attention and interpersonal skills. Although catastrophic stressors such as premature birth, war, trauma, or loss can threaten the integrity of a child's ability to think and solve problems, good parenting by either a parent or another significant adult that supports both emerging competence and healthy relationships will help a child proceed positively in the face of adversity. Additional protective factors include other positive role models, feelings of self-esteem and self-efficacy, attractiveness to others in both personality and appearance, individual talents, religious affiliation, socioeconomic advantage, opportunities for good schooling and employment, and ability to seek out people and environments that are positive for development (Garmezy & Rutter, 1983; Masten, 1997; Osofsky, 1996; Werner, 1994). It is crucial to emphasize, however, that adult behavior, especially good-enough parenting, plays a central role in a child's risks, resources, opportunities, and, therefore, his or her resilience.

CONCLUSION

In this review of adaptive and maladaptive parenting, we discussed various factors that lead to positive outcomes, including effective social networks, social support, reciprocity in early relationships, and other circumstances that contribute to resilience. We have also considered conditions that lead to negative outcomes, including substance abuse, exposure to violence, teen pregnancy, and parental psychopathology. In this concluding section, we highlight a perspective on preventive intervention that focuses on programmatic directions that may protect a child and family and that can lead to more positive outcomes, even under conditions of significant adversity. There is considerable agreement that preventive interventions have the potential to be beneficial to infants and children and their families in terms of both their immediate impact and their long-term consequences (Fonagy, 1998; Osofsky, 1997). The immediate outcomes of such interventions may include improved prenatal, perinatal, and early and later developmental outcomes for infants and young children (Olds, Henderson, Tatelbaum, & Chamberlain, 1988; Olds et al., 1997), as well as more opportunities for education, employment, and demonstrated competence for parents. In the long term, early preventive interventions have the potential to diminish future behavior problems, child maltreatment, delinquency, and violence (Chalk & King, 1998; Osofsky, 1997; Prothrow-Stith, 1998).

The types of preventive interventions that appear to be most effective for all high-risk groups are those that start early and are comprehensive, utilizing a systems approach involving multiple types of intervention that affect the individual, family, and community levels. To build adaptive rather than maladaptive parenting patterns, preventive strategies that are likely to be most effective will engage families at points in their lives when they are most available for intervention. Such interventions do well not only to instill parenting skills but also to help parents with issues surrounding their personal life, including health care, stress, job training, nutrition, building communication skills, and identifying available community resources. Parents are better able to be effective in parenting their children when their own individual needs are recognized and met. Interventions should also build on the strengths that parents have and not take a deficit approach by focusing only on their weaknesses. Inviting parents to share their insights and their parenting expertise will allow them to feel good about themselves, while potentially helping other parents to observe alternative modes of parenting. Furthermore, the contacts need to take place in multiple settings, including homes, hospitals, schools, churches, and other community sites during the prenatal and perinatal periods and during the early years of the child's life. Intervention methods include home visitation, parent education, and support for parents and the impacts on parent–infant–child relationships that have been shown to be most effective when they focus on groups at highest risk for problems in development and in the relationship. It is unrealistic to expect that effective preventive intervention efforts can be conducted primarily at a designated site to which parents must come. Effectiveness requires that the intervenors be flexible and willing to engage the parents on their own terms and in settings where they are most comfortable. Several models that incorporate many of these factors have longitudinal data showing positive outcomes (Lally, Mangione, Honig, & Wittmer, 1988; Olds et al., 1994; Schweinhart, Barnes, & Weikart, 1993; Werner, 1994; Werner & Smith, 1982).

Several related, but slightly different, approaches to preventive intervention have emerged as a result of increased concern for children who witness violence in their communities and in their homes. These programs are designed to provide help for traumatized children and families and to address the problem of violence prevention broadly, with a focus on supportive systems within communities

(Groves & Zuckerman, 1997; Marans & Adelman, 1997; Murphy, Pynoos, & James, 1997; Osofsky, 1997). The programs provide services for children and families and they interface with the police, schools, courts, community programs, health-care settings, and others that help children by providing education about violence prevention and community resources in order to reach children earlier after the trauma occurs. These preventive intervention approaches provide models of how police and other systems within communities can be integrated into a preventive intervention network for children and families.

In considering interventions, it is important to note that earlier approaches contributing to adaptive parenting focused almost exclusively on the individual; that is, the parent or child and their individual needs. Currently, more emphasis is placed on the importance of the relationship and how to provide support for individuals in a relationship context. For all high-risk groups, the establishment of meaningful relationships providing support and stability is crucial. Many adolescent mothers come from families that have lacked consistent, stable relationships. Certainly, families with members who are addicted to drugs are characterized by relationship problems, inconsistency, and unpredictability that frequently exist for more than one generation. With children and families exposed to violence, it is crucial to establish a sense of safety in a relationship for recovery to take place. Difficulties with parenting resulting from parental psychopathology are also helped by a supportive relationship for both parent and child that can help them build a better relationship together. Thus, relationship strengthening is likely to be extremely helpful, whether the problem is inadequate or insensitive child care due to age or debilitating condition, harsh or negative discipline, psychiatric illness, or some other difficulty.

Finally, it is important to recognize the importance of "the match" in developing intervention efforts. Each baby and mother is different, and sometimes the most helpful information that can be imparted to the mother, whether young or old, is just that message. By recognizing the individuality of her baby, the match may become less important as a test of her mothering ability. This issue is particularly important for adolescent mothers and others at high psychosocial risk who may be focusing more on their own needs than on those of the baby. It is very reassuring for a mother to hear that she may not always be responsible for the difficult behaviors manifested by her baby. Encouraging the recognition and acceptance of the child's individuality can increase the mother's acceptance of the child.

In short, we want to emphasize that an understanding of adaptive and maladaptive parenting requires a dynamic perspective. In some situations, factors that usually lead to maladaptation can be mediated by personal and environmental circumstances that help an individual or family overcome adversity. Conversely, some families may have many resources and advantages, but a mismatch in expectations and perceptions, or difficulties with a particular developmental period, may lead to increased risk and maladaptation. Thus, the process of parenting is best understood as dynamic and changing, and one that can be greatly influenced and supported by sensitive and appropriate preventive intervention strategies.

REFERENCES

Achenbach, T. M. (1979). The Child Behavior Profile: An empirically based system for assessing children's behavioral problems and competencies. *International Journal of Mental Health, 7,* 24–42.

Baldwin, A. L., Baldwin, D., & Cole, R. E. (1990). Stress-resistance families and stress resistant children. In J. Rolf, A. S. Masten, D. Cicchetti, K. H. Nuechterlein, & S. Weintraub (Eds.), *Risk and protective factors in the development of psychopathology* (pp. 257–80). New York: Cambridge University Press.

Beckwith, L. (1990). Adaptive and maladaptive parenting: Implications for intervention. In S. J. Meisels & J. P. Shonkoff (Eds.), *Handbook of early childhood intervention* (1st ed., pp. 53–77). New York: Cambridge University Press.

Beeghley, M., & Tronick, E. Z. (1994). Effects of prenatal exposure to cocaine in early infancy: Toxic effects on the process of mutual regulation. *Infant Mental Health Journal, 15,* 158–76.

Belsky, J. (1984). The determinants of parenting. *Child Development, 55,* 83–96.

Bowlby, J. (1973). *Attachment and loss* (Vol. 2). New York: Basic Books.

Bowlby, J. (1980). *Attachment and loss* (Vol. 3). New York: Basic Books.

Bronfenbrenner, U. (1989). Ecological systems theory. In R. Vasta (Ed.), *Annals of child development* (Vol. 6, pp. 187–249). Greenwich, CT: Jason Aronson Press.

Bronfenbrenner, U., & Crouter, A. C. (1983). The evolution of environmental models in developmental research. In P. H. Mussen (Series Ed.) & W. Kessen (Eds.), *Handbook of child development: Vol. 1. History, theories, and methods* (pp. 358–414). New York: Wiley.

Brooks, C. S., Zuckerman, B., Bamforth, A., Cole, J., & Kaplan-Sanoff, M. (1994). Clinical issues related to substance-involved mothers and their infants. *Infant Mental Health Journal, 15,* 202–17.

Brooks-Gunn, J., & Chase-Landsdale, L. (1991). Teenage childbearing: Effects on children. In R. M. Lerner, A. C. Peterson, & J. Brooks-Gunn (Eds.), *Encyclopedia of adolescence* (pp. 103–6). New York: Garland.

Brooks-Gunn, J., & Chase-Landsdale, L. (1995). Adolescent parenthood. In M. Bornstein (Ed.), *Handbook of parenting* (pp. 113–50). New York: Wiley.

Brooks-Gunn, J., & Furstenberg, F. F. (1986). The children of adolescent mothers: Physical, academic, and psychological outcomes. *Developmental Review, 6,* 224–51.

Burchinal, M. R., Follmer, A., & Bryant, D. M. (1996). The relations of maternal social support and family structure with maternal responsiveness and child outcomes among African American families. *Developmental Psychology, 32,* 1073–83.

Carter, S., Osofsky, J. D., & Hann, D. M. (April, 1991a). *Maternal depression and affect in adolescent mothers and their infants.* Paper presented at the Biennial Meeting of the Society for Research in Child Development, Seattle.

Carter, S., Osofsky, J. D., & Hann, D. M. (1991b). Speaking for baby: Therapeutic interventions with adolescents mothers and their infants. *Infant Mental Health Journal, 12,* 291–301.

Chalk, R., & King, P. (1998). *Violence in families: Assessing prevention and treatment programs.* Washington, DC: National Academy Press.

Chase-Landsdale, L., Brooks-Gunn, J., & Palkoff, R. L. (1991). Research programs for adolescent mothers: Missing links and future promises. *Family Relations, 40,* 1–8.

Clarke-Stewart, K. A. (1980). The father's contribution to children's cognitive and social development in early childhood. In F. Pederson (Ed.), *The father–infant relationship.* New York: Praeger.

Cochran, M. (1993). Parenting and personal social networks. In T. Luster & L. Okagaki (Eds.), *Parenting: An ecological perspective* (pp. 149–78). Hillsdale, NJ: Lawrence Erlbaum Associates, Inc., Publishers.

Cochran, M., & Brassard, J. (1979). Child development and personal social networks. *Child Development, 50,* 609–15.

Cochran, M., Lerner, M., Riley, D., Gunnarsson, L., & Henderson, C. R., Jr. (1990). *Extended families: The social networks of parents and their children.* New York: Cambridge University Press.

Cochran, M., & Niego, S. (1995). Parenting and social networks. In M. Bornstein (Ed.), *Handbook of parenting* (pp. 393–418). Mahwah, NJ: Erlbaum.

Cohn, J. F., & Tronick, E. Z. (1983). Three-month-old infants' reaction to simulated maternal depression. *Child Development, 54,* 185–93.

Collins, W. A., & Russell, G. (1991). Mother-child and father-child relationships in middle childhood and adolescence: A developmental analysis. *Developmental Review, 11,* 91–136.

Cramer, B., & Brazleton, T. B. (1990). *The earliest relationship.* New York: Addison Wesley.

Crnic, K., & Greenberg, M. (1987). Maternal stress, social support, and coping: Influences on early mother–child relationship. In C. Boukydis (Ed.), *Research on support for parents and infants in the postnatal period* (pp. 25–40). Hillsdale, NJ: Erlbaum.

Crnic, K. A., Greenberg, M. T., & Slough, N. (1986). Early stress and social support influences on mothers' and high-risk infants' functioning in late infancy. *Infant Mental Health Journal, 7,* 19–33.

Crockenberg, S. (1981). Infant irritability, mother responsiveness, and social support influences on the security of infant–mother attachment. *Child Development, 52,* 857–65.

Crockenberg, S. (1987). Support for adolescent mothers during the postnatal period: Theory and research. In C. F. Z. Boukydis (Ed.), *Research on support for parents and infants in the postnatal period* (pp. 3–24). Hillsdale, NJ: Erlbaum.

Crockett, L. J., Eggebeen, D. J., & Hawkins, A. J. (1993). Fathers' presence and young children's behavioral and cognitive adjustment. *Journal of Family Issues, 14,* 355–77.

Cross, W. E. (1990). Race and ethnicity: Effects on social networks. In M. Cochran, M., Lerner, D., Riley, I., Gunnarson, & C. Henderson (Eds.), *Extending families: The social networks of parents and their children* (pp. 67–85). New York: Cambridge University Press.

Culp, R. E., Appelbaum, M. I., Osofsky, J. D., & Levy, J. A. (1988). Adolescent and older mothers: Comparison between prenatal maternal variables and newborn interaction measures. *Infant Behavior and Development, 11,* 353–62.

Das Eiden, R., & Leonard, K. E. (1996). Paternal alcohol use and the mother–infant relationship. *Development and Psychopathology, 8,* 307–23.

Dix, T. (1991). The affective organization of parenting. *Psychology Bulletin, 110,* 3–25.

East, P. L., & Felice, M. E. (1990). Outcomes and parent-child relationships of former adolescent mothers and their 12-year-old children. *Developmental and Behavioral Pediatrics, 11,* 175–83.

Emde, R. N. (1980). Emotional availability: A reciprocal reward system for infants and parents with implications for prevention of psychosocial disorders. In P. M. Taylor (Ed.), *Parent–infant relationships* (pp. 87–115). New York: Grune & Stratton.

Erikson, E. H. (1950). *Childhood and society.* New York: Norton.

Fick, A., Osofsky, J. D., & Lewis, M. L. (1997). Perceptions of violence: Children, parents, and police officers. In J. D. Osofsky (Ed.), *Children in a violent society* (pp. 261–76). New York: Guilford Publishers.

Field, T. (1995). Psychologically depressed parents. In M. Bornstein (Ed.), *Handbook of parenting* (Vol. 4, pp. 85–100). Mahwah, NJ: Erlbaum.

Field, T., Healy, B., Goldstein, S., & Guthertz, M. (1990). Behavior-state matching and synchrony in mother-infant interactions on nondepressed versus depressed dyads. *Developmental Psychology, 26,* 7–14.

Field, T., Morrow, C., & Adelstein, D. (1993). "Depressed" mothers' perceptions of infant behavior. *Infant Behavior and Development, 16,* 99–108.

Field, T. M., Widmayer, S. M., Stringer, S., & Ignatoff, E. (1980). Teenage, lower class, black mothers and their pre-term infants: An intervention and developmental follow-up study. *Child Development, 51,* 426–36.

Fonagy, P. (1998, April). *Early influence on development and social inequalities: An attachment theory perspective.* Paper presented at Kansas Conferences on Health and Its Determinants, Wichita, Kansas.

Fraiberg, S., Adelson, E. & Shapiro, V. (1975). Ghosts in the nursery: A psychoanalytic approach to the problems of impaired infant-mother relationships. *Journal of the American Academy of Child Psychiatry, 14,* 387–421.

Furstenberg, F. F., Jr., Brooks-Gunn, J., & Chase-Landsdale, L. (1989). Teenaged pregnancy and childbearing. *American Psychologist, 44,* 313–20.

Furstenberg, F. F., Jr., Brooks-Gunn, J., & Morgan, P. (1987). *Adolescent mothers in later life.* New York: Cambridge University Press.

Garbarino, J., Dubrow, N., Kostelny, K., & Pardo, C. (1992). *Children in danger: Coping with the consequences of community violence.* San Francisco, CA: Jossey-Bass.

Garcia-Coll, C. T., Hoffman, J., & Oh, W. (1987). The social ecology and early parenting of Caucasian adolescent mothers. *Child Development, 58,* 955–62.

Garmezy, N., & Rutter, M. (Eds.). (1983). *Stress, coping and development.* New York: McGraw-Hill.

Gelfand, D. M., & Teti, D. M. (1990). The effects of maternal depression on children. *Child Psychology Review, 10,* 329–53.

Gonzales, N. A., Cauce, A. M., Friedman, R. J., & Mason, C. A. (1996). Family, peer, and neighborhood influences on academic achievement among African-American adolescents: One-year prospective effects. *American Journal of Community Psychology, 24,* 365–87.

Gopfert, M., Webster, J., & Seeman, M. V. (1996). *Parental psychiatric disorders.* New York: Cambridge University Press.

Grossman, F. K., Pollack, W. S., & Golding, E. (1988). Fathers and children: Predicting the quality and quantity of fathers' involvement. *Developmental Psychology, 24,* 82–91.

Groves, B. M., & Zuckerman, B. (1997). Interventions with parents and caregivers of children who are exposed to violence. In J. D. Osofsky (Ed.), *Children in a violent society* (pp. 183–201). New York: Guilford Publishers.

Hann, D. M., Castino, R. J., Jarosinski, J., & Britton, H. (1991, April). Relating mother-toddler negotiation patterns to infant attachment and maternal depression with an adolescent mother sample. In J. D. Osofsky & L. Hubbs-Tait (Chairs), *Consequences of adolescent parenting: Predicting behavior problems in toddlers and preschoolers.* Symposium conducted at the biennial meeting of the Society for Research in Child Development, Seattle.

Hann, D. M., Osofsky, J. D., & Culp, A. M. (1996). Relating the adolescent mother-child relationship to preschool outcomes. *Infant Mental Health Journal, 17,* 302–9.

Hann, D. M., Robinson, J. L., Osofsky, J. D., & Little, C. (1991, April). *Emotional availability in two caregiving environments: Low risk adult mothers and socially at-risk adolescent mothers.* Paper presented at the biennial meeting of Society for Research in Child Development, Seattle.

Hanshaw, C., & Frazier-Thompson, M. D. (1996, November). *Fathers raising children with special needs: The role of social capital.* Paper presented at the National Council on Family Relations, 58th Annual Conference, Kansas City, Missouri.

Hashima, P. Y., & Amato, P. R. (1994). Poverty, social support, and parental behavior. *Child Development, 65,* 394–403.

Homel, R., Burns, A., & Goodnow, J. (1987). Parental social networks and child development. *Journal of Social and Personal Relationships, 4,* 159–77.

Horn, W. (in press). Fathering Infants. In J. D. Osofsky & H. Fitzgerald (Eds.), *WAIMH handbook of infant mental health.* New York: Wiley.

Hossain, Z., Field, T., Gonzales, J., Malphurs, J., del Valle, C., & Pickens, J. (1994). Infants of "depressed" mothers interact better with their nondepressed father. *Infant Mental Health Journal, 15,* 348–57.

Hunter, A. G. (1997). Counting on grandmothers: Black mothers' and fathers' reliance on grandmothers for parenting support. *Journal of Family Issues, 18,* 251–69.

Jacobson, J. L., Jacobson, S. W., Sokol, R. J., Martier, S. S., & Ager, J. W. (1993). Prenatal alcohol exposure and infant information processing ability. *Child Development, 64,* 1706–21.

Jennings, K. D., Stagg, V., & Connors, R. E. (1991). Social networks and mothers' interactions with their preschool children. *Child Development, 62,* 966–78.

Kaplan-Sanoff, M. (1996). The effects of maternal substance abuse on young children: Myths and realities. In E. Erwin (Ed.), *Putting children first* (pp. 77–103). Baltimore, MD: Paul Brookes Publishers.

Kohn, M., & Wilson, M. N. (1995). Social support networks in the African American family: Utility for culturally compatible intervention. In M. N. Wilson (Ed.), *New directions for child development: Vol 68. African American family life: Its structural and ecological aspects* (pp. 5–21). San Francisco: Jossey-Bass Publishers.

Kohut, H. (1977). *The restoration of the self.* New York: International Universities Press.

Lally, J. R., Mangione, P. L., Honig, A. S., & Wittmer, P. S. (1988). More pride, less delinquency: Findings from the ten-year follow-up study of the Syracuse University Family Development Research Program. *Zero to Three, 8*(4) 13–18.

Lamb, M. E. (Ed.). (1987). *The father's role: Cross-cultural perspectives.* Hillsdale, NJ: Erlbaum.

Lamb, M. E., Hopps, K., & Elster, A. B. (1987). Strange situation behavior of infants with adolescent mothers. *Infant Behavior and Development, 10,* 39–48.

Lamb, M. E., Plecke, J. H., & Levine, J. A. (1985). The role of the father in child development: The effects of increased paternal involvement. In B. Lahey & E. E. Kazdin (Eds.), *Advances in clinical child psychology* (Vol. 8). New York: Plenum.

Laucht, M., Esser, G., & Schmidt, M. H. (1994). Parental mental disorder and early child development. *European Child and Adolescent Psychiatry, 3,* 124–37.

Lerman, R. I. (1993). A national profile of young unwed fathers. In R. I. Lerman & T. J. Ooms (Eds.), *Young unwed fathers* (pp. 27–51). Philadelphia: Temple University Press.

Lester, B. M., & Tronick, E. Z. (1994). Prenatal drug exposure and child outcome. *Special Issue of Infant Mental Health Journal, 15.*

Lorion, R., & Saltzman, W. (1993). Children's exposure to community violence: Following a path from concern to research to action. In D. Reiss, J. E. Richters, M. Radke-Yarrow, & D. Scharff (Eds.), *Children and Violence* (pp. 55–65). New York: Guilford.

Lynch, M., & Cicchetti, D. (1998). An ecological-transactional analysis of children and context: The longitudinal interplay among child maltreatment, community violence, and children's symptomatology. *Development and Psychopathology, 10,* 235–57.

Lyons-Ruth, K., Connell, D. B., & Grunebaum, H. U. (1990). Infants at social risk: Maternal depression and family support services as mediators of infant development and security of attachment. *Child Development, 61,* 85–98.

MacPhee, D., Fritz, J., & Miller-Heyl, J. (1996). Ethnic variations in personal social networks and parenting. *Child Development, 67,* 3278–95.

Margura, S., & Laudet, A. B. (1996). Parental substance abuse and child maltreatment: Review and implications for intervention. *Children and Youth Services Review, 18,* 193–220.

Main, M., & Hesse, E. (1990). Parent's unresolved traumatic experiences are related to infant disorganized attachment stories: Is frightened and/or frightening parental behavior the linking mechanism? In M. T. Greenberg, D. Cicchetti, & E. M. Cummings (Eds.), *Attachment in

the preschool years: Theory, research, and intervention* (pp. 161–82). Chicago: University of Chicago Press.

Main, M., & Solomon, J. (1989). Procedures for identifying infants as disorganized disoriented during the Ainsworth Strange Situation. In M. T. Greenberg, D. Cicchetti, & E. M. Cummings (Eds.), *Attachment in the preschool years: Theory, research, and intervention* (pp. 121–60). Chicago: University of Chicago Press.

Marans, S., & Adelman, A. (1997). Experiencing violence in a developmental context. In J. D. Osofsky (Ed.), *Children in a violent society* (pp. 202–22). New York: Guilford Press.

Masten, A. (1997). *Resilience in children at risk.* In Research/Practice: A Publication from the Center for Applied Research and Educational Improvement. Minneapolis: College of Education and Human Development, University of Minnesota.

Masten, A. S., Best, K. M., & Garmezy, N. (1990). Resilience and development: Contributions from the study of children who overcome adversity. *Development and Psychopathology, 2,* 425–44.

Masten, A., Hubbard, J. J., Gest, S. D., Tellegen, A., Garmezy, N., & Ramirez, M. (in press). Competence in the context of adversity: Pathways to resilience and maladaptation from childhood to late adolescence. *Development and Psychopathology.*

Mayes, L. C. (1995). Substance abuse in parenting. In M. Bornstein (Ed.), *Handbook of parenting* (pp. 101–25). Mahwah, NJ: Erlbaum.

Mayes, L. C., & Bornstein, M. H. (1996). The context of development for young children from cocaine-abusing families. In P. M. Kato, & T. Mann (Eds.), *Handbook of diversity issues in health psychology* (pp. 69–95). New York: Plenum Press.

Mayes, L. C., Feldman, R., Granger, R. H., Haynes, O. M., Bornstein, M. H., & Schottenfeld, R. (1997). The effects of polydrug use with and without cocaine on mother-infant interaction at 3 and 6 months. *Infant Behavior and Development, 20,* 489–502.

McAdoo, H. P. (1988). Transgenerational pattern of upward mobility in African-American families. In H. P. McAdoo (Ed.), *Black families* (pp. 139–62). Newbury Park, CA: Sage.

McLoyd, V. C. (1995). Poverty, parenting and policy: Meeting the support needs of poor parents. In H. Fitzgerald, B. Lester, & B. Zuckerman (Eds.), *Children of poverty: Research, health, and policy issues* (pp. 269–303). New York: Garland Press.

Mejta, C. L., & Lavin, R. (1996). Facilitating healthy parenting among others with substance abuse or dependence problems: Some considerations. *Alcoholism Treatment Quarterly, 14,* 33–46.

Murray, L., & Cooper, P. (1997a). *Postpartum depression and child development.* New York: Guilford Press.

Murray, L., & Cooper, P. (1997b). The role of infant and maternal factors in post-partum depression, mother-infant interactions and infant outcome. In L. Murray &

P. Cooper (Eds.), *Post-partum depression and child development* (pp. 111–35). New York: Guilford Press.

Murphy, L., & Moriarity, A. (1987). *Vulnerability, coping, and growth from infancy to adolescence.* New Haven, CT: Yale University Press.

Murphy, L., Pynoos, R. S., & James, C. B. (1997). The trauma/grief-focused group psychotherapy module of an elementary school-based violence prevention/ intervention program. In J. D. Osofsky (Ed.), *Children in a violent society* (pp. 223–55). New York: Guilford Press.

National Survey of Children and Parents. (1991). *"Speaking of kids."* National Commission on Children, Washington, DC.

Nitz, K., Ketterlinus, R. D., & Brandt, L. J. (1995). The role of stress, social support, and family environment in adolescent mothers' parenting. *Journal of Adolescent Research, 10,* 358–82.

Olds, D. L., Henderson, C. R., & Kitzman, R. N. (1994). Does prenatal and infancy nurse home visitation have enduring effects on qualities of parental caregiving and child health at 25 to 50 months of life? *Pediatrics, 93,* 89–98.

Olds, D. L., Henderson, C. R., Tatelbaum, R., & Chamberlain, R. (1988). Improving the life-course development of socially disadvantaged mothers: A randomized trial of nurse home visitation. *American Journal of Public Health, 78,* 1436–45.

Olds, D. L., Kitzman, H., Henderson, C., Hanks, C., Cole, R., Tatelbaum, R., McConnochie, M., Sidora, K., Luckey, D., Shaver, D., Engelhardt, K., James, D., & Barnard, K. (1997). Effect of prenatal and infancy home visitation by nurses on pregnancy outcomes, childhood injuries, and repeated childbearing. *Journal of the American Medical Association, 278,* 644–52.

Osofsky, H. J., & Osofsky, J. D. (1970). Adolescents as mothers: Results of a program for low-income pregnant teenagers with some emphasis upon infants' development. *American Journal of Orthopsychiatry, 40,* 825–34.

Osofsky, J. D. (1991). *A preventive intervention program for adolescent mothers and their infants.* Final report to the Institute of Mental Hygiene, New Orleans.

Osofsky, J. D.(1993). Applied psychoanalysis: How research with infants and adolescents at high psychosocial risk informs psychoanalysis. *Journal of the American Psychoanalytic Association, 41* (Supp.), 193–207.

Osofsky, J. D. (1995). The effects of exposure to violence on young children. *American Psychologist, 50,* 782–88.

Osofsky, J. D. (1996). Psychosocial risk for adolescent parents and infants: Clinical implications. In J. Noshpitz, S. Greenspan, S. Weider, & J. D. Osofsky (Eds.), *Handbook of child and adolescent psychiatry* (Vol. 1, pp. 177–90). New York: Wiley.

Osofsky, J. D. (1997). *Children in a violent society.* New York: Guilford Press.

Osofsky, J. D., Cohen, G., & Drell, M. (1995). The effects of

trauma on young children: A case of two year old twins. *International Journal of Psychoanalysis, 76,* 595–607.

Osofsky, J. D., & Eberhart-Wright, A. (1988). Affective exchanges between high risk mothers and infants. *International Journal of Psychoanalysis, 69,* 221–32.

Osofsky, J. D., & Eberhart-Wright, A. (1992). Risk and protective factors for parents and infants. In G. Suci & S. Robertson (Eds.), *Human development: Future directions in infant development research* (pp. 29–35). New York: Springer-Verlag.

Osofsky, J. D., Eberhart-Wright, A., Ware, L. M., & Hann, D. M. (1992). Children of adolescent mothers: A group at risk for psychopathology. *Infant Mental Health Journal, 13,* 119–31.

Osofsky, J. D., & Fenichel, E. (Eds.) (1994). *Caring for infants and toddlers in violent environments: Hurt, healing, and hope.* Arlington, VA: Zero to Three/National Center for Clinical Infant Programs.

Osofsky, J. D., Wewers, S., Hann, D. M., & Fick, A. C. (1993). Chronic community violence: What is happening to our children? *Psychiatry, 56,* 36–45.

Palm, G. F. (1997). Promoting generative fathering through parent and family education. In A. J. Hawkins & D. C. Dollahite (Eds.), *Current issues in the family series: Vol. 3, Generative fathering: Beyond deficit perspectives* (pp. 167–82). Thousand Oaks, CA: Sage.

Parke, R. D. (1981). *Fathers.* Cambridge, MA: Harvard University Press.

Parke, R. D. (1995). Fathers and families. In M. H. Bornstein (Ed.), *Handbook of parenting* (Vol. 3, pp. 27–63). Mahwah, NJ: Erlbaum.

Pellegrini, D. S., Masten, A. S., Garmezy, N., & Ferrarese, M. J. (1987). Correlates of social and academic competence in middle childhood. *Journal of Child Psychology and Psychiatry, 28*(5), 699–714.

Power, T. G., & Parke, R. D. (1982). Play as a context for early learning: Lab and home analyses. In I. E. Siegal & L. M. Laosa (Eds.), *The family as a learning environment* (pp. 147–78). New York: Plenum.

Prothrow-Stith, D. (1998, May). *Violence prevention: A public health mandate to save our children.* Paper presented at the American Psychiatric Association Meeting, Toronto, Canada.

Radin, N. (1993). Primary caregiving fathers in intact families. In A. Gottfried & A. Gottfried (Eds.), *Redefining families* (pp. 11–54). New York: Plenum.

Radke-Yarrow, M., Cummings, E. M., Kuczynski, L., & Chapman, M. (1985). Patterns of attachment in two- and three-year-olds in normal families and families with parental depression. *Child Development, 56,* 884–93.

Richters, J. E., & Martinez, P. (1993). The NIMH community violence project: I. Children as victims of and witnesses to violence. *Psychiatry, 56,* 7–21.

Riley, D. (1990). Network influences on father involvement in childrearing. In M. Cochran, M. Larner, D. Riley, L. Gunnarson, & C. Henderson, Jr. (Eds.), *Extending families:*

The social networks of parents and their children (pp. 131–53). New York: Cambridge University Press.

Rogosch, F. A., Cicchetti, D., Shields, A., & Toth, S. (1996). Parenting dysfunction in child maltreatment. In M. Bornstein (Ed.), *Handbook of parenting* (Vol. 4, pp. 127–62). Mahwah, NJ: Erlbaum.

Russell, G., & Russell, A. (1987). Mother–child and father–child relationships in middle childhood. *Child Development, 58*, 1573–85.

Rutter, M. (1993). Resilience: Some conceptual considerations. *Contemporary Pediatrics, 11*, 36–48.

Schweinhart, J. L., Barnes, H., & Weikart, D. P. (1993). *Significant benefits: The High/Scope Perry School Study through Age 27*. Ypsilanti, MI: High/Scope Press.

Sorce, J., Emde, R. N., Campos, J., & Klinnert, M. D. (1985). Maternal emotional signaling: Its effect on the visual cliff behavior of 1-year-olds. *Developmental Psychology, 21*, 337–41.

Spieker, S. (1989). *Mothering in adolescence: Factors related to infant security*. (Grant No. MC-J-50535). Washington, DC: The Maternal and Child Health and Crippled Children's Services.

Spitz, R. (1945). Hospitalism: An inquiry into the genesis of psychiatric conditions in early childhood. *Psychoanalytic Study of the Child, 1*, 53–74.

Spitz, R. (1946). Anaclitic depression: An inquiry into the genesis of psychiatric conditions in early childhood II. *Psychoanalytic Study of the Child, 2*, 313–42.

Stern, D. (1985). *The interpersonal world of the infant*. New York: Basic Books.

Stern, D. (1990). *The diary of a baby*. New York: Basic Books.

Stevens, J. H., Jr. (1984). Child development knowledge and parenting skill. *Family Relations, 33*, 237–44.

Stolorow, R. D., Brandchaft, B., & Atwood, G. E. (1987). *Psychoanalytic treatment: An intersubjective approach*. Hillsdale, NJ: Analytic Press.

Struthers, J. M., & Hansen, R. L. (1992). Visual recognition memory in drug exposed infants. *Journal of Developmental and Behavioral Pediatrics, 13*, 108–11.

Taylor, R. D. (1997). The effects of economic and social stressors on parenting and adolescent adjustment in African-American families. In R. D. Taylor & M. C. Wang (Eds.), *Social and emotional adjustment and family relations in ethnic minority families*. Mahwah, NJ: Erlbaum.

Taylor, R. J., Chatters, L. M., Tucker, M. B., & Lewis, E. (1990). Developments in research on Black families: A decade review. *Journal of Marriage and the Family, 52*, 993–1014.

Thompson, M. S., & Peebles-Wilkins, W. (1992). The impact of formal, informal, and societal support networks on the psychological well-being of Black adolescent mothers, *Social Work, 37*, 322–8.

Tietjen, A. (1985). Relationships between the social networks of Swedish mothers and their children. *International Journal of Behavioral Development, 8*, 195–216.

Tronick, E. Z., & Gianino, A. F., Jr. (1986). The transmission of maternal disturbance to the infant. In E. Z. Tronick & T. M. Field (Eds.), *Maternal depression and infant disturbance, new directions for child development* (pp. 61–82). San Francisco: Jossey-Bass.

U.S. Department of Commerce. (1993). *We the American children*. Economics and Statistics Administration, Bureau of the Census. Washington DC: Government Printing Office.

Voight, J. D., Hans, S. L., & Bernstein, V. J. (1996). Support networks of adolescent mothers: Effects on parenting experience and behavior. *Infant Mental Health Journal, 17*, 58–73.

Weinberg, K., & Tronick, E. Z. (1997). Maternal depression and infant maladjustment: A failure of mutual regulation. In J. Noshpitz, S. Greenspan, J. D. Osofsky, & Weider, S. (Eds.), *Handbook of child and adolescent psychiatry* (Vol. 1, pp. 177–90). New York: Wiley Publishers.

Weinraub, M., & Gringlas, M. B. (1995). *Single parenthood*. In M. H. Bornstein (Ed.), *Handbook of parenting* (Vol. 3, pp. 65–87). Hillsdale, NJ: Lawrence Erlbaum Associates, Inc., Publishers.

Werner, E. E. (1984). Resilient children. *Young Children, 40*, 68–72.

Werner, E. E. (1994). Overcoming the odds. *Journal of Developmental and Behavioral Pediatrics, 15*, 131–6.

Werner, E. E., & Smith, R. S. (1982). *Vulnerable but invincible: A study of resilient children*. New York: McGraw-Hill.

Wilson, M. N., & Tolson, T. F. J. (1990). Familial support in the Black community. *Journal of Clinical Child Psychology, 19*, 347–55.

Winnicott, D. (1953). *Collected papers: Through pediatrics to psychoanalysis*. New York: Basic Books.

Winnicott, D. (1965). *The maturational processes and the facilitating environment*. Madison, CT: International Universities Press.

Yogman, M. W. (1983). Development of the father-infant relationship. In H. Fitzgerald, B. Lester, & M. W. Yogman (Eds.), *Theory and research in behavioral pediatrics* (Vol. 1) New York: Plenum.

Zahn-Waxler, C., Kochanska, G., Krupnick, J., & McKnew, D. (1990). Patterns of guilt in children of depressed and well mothers. *Developmental Psychology, 26*, 51–9.

Zuckerman, B., Bauchner, H., Parker, S., & Cabral, H. (1990). *Maternal depressive symptoms during pregnancy and newborn irritability*. Unpublished manuscript, Boston Medical Center.

Zuravin, S. J. (1989). Severity of maternal depression and three types of mother-to-child aggression. *American Journal of Orthopsychiatry, 59*, 377–89.

CHAPTER FOUR

The Human Ecology of Early Risk

JAMES GARBARINO AND BARBARA GANZEL

An ecological perspective on developmental risk directs our attention simultaneously to two kinds of interactions. The first is the interaction of the child as a biological organism with the immediate social environment as a set of processes, events, and relationships. The second is the interplay of social systems in the child's social environment. This dual mandate to look both outward to the forces that shape social contexts and inward to the day-to-day interaction of the child in the family is both the beauty and the challenge of human ecology. It demands much of us intellectually and ideologically, if it is to be more than an academic exercise.

Ecology is the study of relationships between organisms and environments. Ecologists explore and document how the individual and the habitat shape the development of each other. Like the biologist who learns about an animal by studying its habitat, sources of food, predators, and social practices, the student of human development must address how people live and grow in their social environment. Whereas all students of animal ecology must understand the purposeful actions of the organism, the human ecologist must go further and seek to incorporate the phenomenological complexity of the organism–environment interaction – the social and psychological maps that define human meaning.

We must recognize that the habitat of the child at risk includes family, friends, neighborhood, church, and school, as well as less immediate forces that constitute the social geography and climate (e.g., laws, institutions, and values) and the physical environment. The interplay of these social forces and

physical settings with the individual child defines the range of issues in the forefront of an ecological perspective. The most important characteristic of this ecological perspective is that it both reinforces our inclination to look inside the individual and encourages us to look beyond the individual to the environment for questions and explanations about individual behavior and development. The ecological perspective emphasizes development in context.

An ecological perspective constantly reminds us that child development results from the interplay of biology and society, from the characteristics children bring with them into the world and the way the world treats them, from nature and nurture. In this it reflects what Pasamanick (1987) called "social biology." In contrast to sociobiology, which emphasizes a genetic origin for social behavior (Wilson, 1978), social biology concentrates on the social origins of biological phenomena (e.g., the impact of poverty on infant morbidity). Nevertheless, the two perspectives are not mutually exclusive. Indeed, we can see the historical origins of biological phenomena in social phenomena. Gene pools change through the social behavior of individual organisms that carry those genes (Wilson, 1978). The social impact of biologically rooted traits affects the survival of organisms and thus the likelihood that those particular genetic patterns will be passed along to surviving offspring.

Children face different opportunities and risks for development because of their mental and physical makeup and because of the social environment they inhabit. Moreover, social environment affects the very physical makeup of the child. These effects may be negative (e.g., the impact of poverty on birth weight or the mutagenic influence of industrial carcinogens) or positive (e.g., intrauterine surgery or nutritional therapy for a fetus with a genetic disorder). When these social influences operate in psychological or sociological terms, we refer to them as *sociocultural opportunities and risks.*

When we refer to opportunities for development we mean relationships in which children find material, emotional, and social encouragement compatible with their needs and capacities as they exist at a specific point in their developing lives. For each child, the best fit must be worked out through experience, within some broad guidelines of basic human needs, and then renegotiated as development proceeds and situations change. Windows of opportunity for intervention appear repeatedly across the life course. What may be a critical threat at one point may be benign or even developmentally enhancing at another. For example, Elder's (1974) analyses revealed that the effects of the 1930s economic crisis were felt most negatively by young children. In fact, some adolescents even benefited from the fact that paternal unemployment often meant special opportunities for enhanced responsibility for teenage sons and daughters. Bronfenbrenner (1986) confirmed that the stress of urban life associated with family adversity is most negative and potent for young children, yet it may stimulate some adolescents.

Risks to development can come both from direct threats and from the absence of normal, expectable opportunities. Besides such obvious biological risks as malnutrition or injury, there are sociocultural risks that impoverish the developing individual's world of essential experiences and relationships and thereby threaten development, what we term *social toxicity* (Garbarino, 1995). For example, economic inequality, mass media legitimization of aggression, and racism may deprive children of the affirmation they need to thrive. When sociocultural risks threaten, appropriate early intervention can help the child find new routes for adaptive development. Understanding the consequences of both sociocultural risks and opportunities and the role of social support networks is a central concern of human ecology.

Our goal here is to make use of a systems approach to clarify the complexity we face in attempting to understand the interplay of biological, psychological, social, and cultural forces in early developmental risks and their amelioration. A systems approach helps us discover the connections among what might at first seem to be unrelated events. It can also help us see that what often seems like an obvious solution may actually only make the problem worse. Forrester (1969) noted that some urban *renewal* initiatives actually produced urban *decay* by disabling the social environment of the urban neighborhoods as a by-product of reconstructing the physical environment. He concluded that because systems are linked, and therefore influence each other (feedback), many of the most effective solutions to social problems are not readily apparent, and may even be counterintuitive. According to Hardin (1966), the first law of ecology is "You can never do just one thing."

For example, the relation between the foster care system and the former Aid to Families with Dependent Children (AFDC) was largely ignored by policy makers, even though federal funds from AFDC supported out-of-home placement through foster care programs since 1961 (Courtney, 1995). Over the past two decades, the need for foster care has increased in parallel with increases in reports of child maltreatment and with the rise of crack cocaine use. In California, there was an 82% rise in the number of children in foster care between 1979 and 1989 (Yancey, 1992), and there were nearly a half-million children in foster care nationwide in 1992 (Courtney, 1995). It has been suggested that reductions in funding due to welfare reform (P.L. 104–193, Personal Responsibility and Work Opportunity Reconciliation Act of 1996) will have a catastrophic effect on the current child welfare system because most of the funding remaining in individual states' Child Protection Block Grants will need to be diverted to out-of-home care (Meezan & Giovannoni, 1995). Intersystem feedback ensures that any single action may reverberate and produce unintended consequences. This becomes apparent as we proceed further.

As individuals develop, they play more active roles in an ever-widening world. Newborns shape the feeding behavior of their mothers but are confined largely to cribs or laps and have limited means of communicating their needs and wants. Ten-year-olds, on the other hand, influence many adults and other children in many different settings and have many ways of communicating. The adolescents' world is still larger and more diverse, as is their ability to influence that world. Individuals and environments negotiate their relationships over time through a process of reciprocity. Neither is constant; each depends on the other. When asked, "Does *X* cause *Y*?" the answer is always, "It depends" (Garbarino & Associates, 1992). We cannot reliably predict the future of one system without knowing something about the other systems with which it is linked. And even then this may be very difficult. We see this when we ask, Does early child care enhance or harm development? It depends on the child's age, quality of parent–child attachment, the child-care provider's relationship to the child's parents, and the child-care provider's motivations and training, as well as the more obvious question of what exactly constitutes the experience of child care. In short, it depends (cf. Belsky, 1986).

We see this in all aspects of development. Thus, for example, the link between early developmental delay and later IQ deficit appears to differ across social-class groupings in the kind of social system present in most United States communities. In one classic study, 13% of the lower-class children who were developmentally delayed at 8 months showed an IQ of 79 or less at 4 years of age. In contrast, only 7% of the middle-class children who were delayed at 8 months of age were retarded at 4 years of age. For the upper-class children, the figure was only 2% (Willerman, Broman, & Fiedler, 1970). Does developmental delay predict IQ deficit? It would seem that it depends on the family and community environment in which the child is growing up. We might hypothesize that the social-class effect linked to family status would be exaggerated in some communities, whereas it might be diminished in others.

Drawing on the work of Urie Bronfenbrenner, we see the individual's experiences as subsystems within systems within larger systems "as a set of nested structures, each inside the next, like a set of Russian dolls" (Bronfenbrenner, 1979, p. 22). In asking and answering questions about development, we can and should always be ready to look at the next level of systems beyond and within to find the questions and answers (Garbarino & Associates, 1992). If we see parents and visiting nurses in conflict over the use of physical punishment in early childhood

(the family system), we need to look to the community that establishes laws and policies about child abuse. We should also look to the culture that defines physical force as an appropriate form of discipline in early childhood. We must also look within the individual, as a psychological system that is affected by conscious and changing roles, unconscious needs, and motives, to know why and how each adjusts in ways that generate conflict. In addition, we must look *across* to see how the several systems involved (family, social services, social network, and economy) adjust to new conditions. Interaction among these social forces is the key to an ecological analysis of early developmental risk. They exist as linked social systems, implying that intervention can take place at each system level *and* that intervention at one level may well spill over to others.

This system approach examines the environment at four levels beyond the individual organism – from the micro to the macro. These systems have been catalogued in detail elsewhere (Bronfenbrenner, 1979, 1986; Garbarino & Associates, 1992). The goal here is to introduce them briefly in order to provide a context for discussing the ecology of early developmental risk.

ECOLOGICAL CONTEXTS FOR HUMAN DEVELOPMENT

Microsystems

Microsystems are the immediate settings in which individuals develop. The shared experiences that occur in each setting provide a record of the microsystem and offer some clues to its future. Microsystems evolve and develop much as do individuals themselves from forces generated both within and without. The quality of a microsystem depends on its ability to sustain and enhance development and to provide a context that is emotionally validating and developmentally challenging. This ability to enhance development in turn depends on the capacity to operate in what Vygotsky (1934) called "the zone of proximal development;" that is, the distance between what the child can accomplish alone (the level of actual development) and what the child can do when helped (the level of potential development).

Children can handle (and need) more than infants. Adolescents can handle (and need) more than children. We measure the social richness of an individual's life by the availability of enduring, reciprocal, multifaceted relationships that emphasize playing, working, and loving. And we do that measuring over time, because, similar to individuals, relationships change over time. Risk, on the other hand, lies in patterns of abuse, neglect, resource deficiency, and stress that insult the child and thwart development (Garbarino, Guttmann, & Seeley, 1986).

The "same" child-care center is very different in June from what it was in September for the same infants who, of course, are themselves not the same as they were at the beginning of the year. The family setting, as the first-born child experiences it, is different from that experienced by subsequent offspring. Naturally, children themselves change and develop, as do others in the setting. It is also important to remember that our definition speaks of the microsystem as a pattern *experienced by* the developing person. Individuals influence their microsystems, and these microsystems influence them in turn. Each participant acts on the basis of an emergent social map: a phenomenological record and projection.

Mesosystems

Mesosystems are relationships *between* microsystems in which the individual experiences reality. These links themselves form a system. We measure the richness of a mesosystem in the number and quality of its connections. One example is the case of an infant's child care group and his or her home. We ask, Do staff visit the child at home? Do the child's parents know his or her friends at child care? Do parents of children at the center know each other? A second example concerns a hospital and the home for a chronically ill child. What role do the parents play in the hospital regime? Do the same health care professionals who see the child in the hospital visit the home? Is the child the only one to participate in both? If he or she is the only linkage, the mesosystem is weak, and that weakness may place the child at risk. Research suggests that the strength of the mesosystem linking the setting in which an intervention is implemented with the settings in which the individual spends most significant time is crucial

to the long-term effectiveness of the intervention and to the maintenance of its effects (Whittaker, 1983).

Exosystems

Exosystems are settings that have a bearing on the development of children, but in which those children do not play a direct role. For most children, the key exosystems include their parents' workplace (in general, most children are not participants there) and power centers such as school boards, church councils, and planning commissions that make decisions affecting their day-to-day life. The concept of an exosystem illustrates the projective nature of the ecological perspective, for the same setting that is an exosystem for a child may be a microsystem for the parent, and vice versa. Thus, one form of intervention may aim at transforming exosystems into microsystems by initiating greater participation in important institutions for isolated, disenfranchised, and powerless clients (e.g., by getting parents to visit the family child care home or by creating on-site child care at the workplace).

In exosystem terms, both risk and opportunity come about in two ways. The first is when the parents or other significant adults in a child's life are treated in a way that impoverishes (risk) or enhances (opportunity) their behavior in the microsystems they share with children. Examples include elements of the parents' working experience that impoverish family life on the one hand – unemployment, low pay, long or inflexible hours, traveling, or stress – or enhance family life on the other hand – an adequate income, flexible scheduling, an understanding employer, or subsidies for child care (Bronfenbrenner & Crouter, 1982).

The second way risk and opportunity flow from the exosystem lies in the orientation and content of decisions made in those settings that affect the day-to-day experience of children and their families. For example, when the state legislature suspends funding for early intervention programs, it jeopardizes development. When public officials expand prenatal health services or initiate specialized child care in high-risk communities, they increase developmental opportunities (and may reduce infant mortality or morbidity).

Albee (1980) identified powerlessness as the primary factor leading to impaired development and mental disability. It certainly plays a large role in determining the fate of groups of individuals by means of public policy and may even be important when considering individual cases, such as whether parents have the influence to get a medically vulnerable child enrolled in a special treatment program. In many cases, risk and opportunity at the exosystem level are essentially political matters.

One of the most useful aspects of the ecological approach is its ability to highlight situations in which the actions of people with whom the individual has no direct contact significantly affect development. The following example illustrates the relationship between social policy and individual child development. Because of a leveraged corporate takeover, a board of directors decides to shift operations from one plant to another. Hundreds of families with young children are forced to move to new locations. Local services are underfunded in a period of escalating demand. Parents lose their jobs and thus their health insurance. The quality of prenatal and well-baby care declines; infant mortality increases. This is a classic illustration of an exosystem effect. It highlights the fact that exosystem events may establish much of the agenda for day-to-day early intervention on behalf of children at risk.

It is worth emphasizing that the ecological perspective forces us to consider the concept of risk beyond the narrow confines of individual personality and family dynamics. In the ecological approach, both are causes of the child's developmental patterns and reflections of broader sociocultural forces. Mark Twain wrote, "If the only tool you have is a hammer you tend to treat every problem as if it were a nail." Inflexible loyalty to a specific focus (e.g., the parents) is often a stumbling block to effective intervention. However, the obverse must also be considered: If you define every problem as a nail, the only tool you will seek is a hammer. Viewing children at risk only in terms of organismic and interpersonal dynamics precludes an understanding of the many other avenues of influence that might be open to us as helpers or that might be topics of study for us as scientists. This message provides a crucial guide to our discussion of early intervention.

Macrosystems

Meso- and exosystems are set within the broad ideological, demographic, and institutional patterns of a particular culture or subculture. These patterns are the *macrosystems* that serve as the master blueprints for the ecology of human development. These blueprints reflect a people's shared assumptions about how things should be done, as well as the institutions that represent those assumptions. Macrosystems are ideology incarnate. Thus, we contrast societal blueprints that rest on fundamental institutional expressions, such as a collective versus individual orientation. Religion provides a classic example of the macrosystem concept because it involves both a definition of the world and a set of institutions reflecting that definition: both a theology and a set of roles, rules, buildings, and programs.

Macrosystem refers to the general organization of the world as it is and as it might be. Historical change demonstrates that "might be" is real and occurs through either evolution (many individual actions guided by a common reality) or through revolution (dramatic change introduced by a small cadre of decision makers). In 1989, the fall of the Iron Curtain dramatically altered social welfare systems and social and mental health services across Central and Eastern Europe, as newly autonomous governments struggled to establish market economies. In the past, social problem solving occurred from the top down through the central ministries of the Soviet Union. Now each government faces the task of constructing relevant social programs while also coping with deepening poverty within the population because of the loss of both guaranteed employment and price controls (Fried, 1995; Atherton, Raymond, & Roff, 1993). For example, two-thirds of the Bulgarian population now have incomes or pensions below the minimum social level, and the communist regime has left the current government seriously in debt. As a result of this new social and economic climate, Bulgarian social services are distributed to meet the requirements of biological survival rather than being used as a means of rewarding those who strengthened the communist regime politically (Fried, 1995). In China, too, modernization efforts have included a massive shift from collective reward to private initiative as the dominating economic force. More directly relevant still is China's one-child policy that has altered the demography of the family and appears to be altering the social fabric at each level of the human ecology (Schell, 1982).

In the United States, the increasing concentration of high-risk families in a geographically concentrated "underclass" (Lemann, 1986; Wilson, 1987) is exerting dramatic influences on the need and prognosis for early interventions. Pockets of marked vulnerability show poverty and infant mortality rates many times the average found in unafflicted communities. For early intervention services to be plausible in such high-risk ecological niches, they must target ecological transformation as the program goal. For example, the Cornell Family Life Development Center's Prenatal and Early Infancy Project conducted a randomized trial of intensive nurse home visitation to women in Elmira, New York, a region that at the time was the most economically depressed in the county, with the highest rates of child abuse and neglect in the state (Olds, Henderson, Tatelbaum, & Chamberlin, 1988). The study provided free sensory and developmental screening and referrals for regular prenatal and well-child care to all participating families. In the comparison group receiving the most services, nurse home visitors also provided broad family support during pregnancy and through the child's second year of life. These families received services designed to improve the mothers' health-related behaviors, parents' care of their children, parents' own personal development, and formal and informal family support systems (Olds, Henderson, Chamberlin, & Tatelbaum, 1994).

A fifteen-year follow-up (Olds, Eckenrode, Henderson, Kitzman, Powers, Cole, Sidora, Morris, Pettitt, & Luckey, 1997; Olds, Henderson, Cole, Eckenrode, Kitzman, Luckey, Pettitt, Sidora, Morris, & Powers, 1998) found that nurse-visited children in families receiving the most intensive support were identified as victims in 58% fewer verified reports of abuse and neglect and they were arrested 54% fewer times than the comparison group, which had no home visitors. Poor, unmarried mothers in the group with the most intensive home visitation also had 0.5 fewer subsequent children, 69% fewer arrests, 79% fewer convictions, and were reported to spend 30 fewer months receiving Aid to Families with Dependent Children. Thus, when such efforts are conducted in

the context of thoughtful evaluation research, they can serve as the kind of transforming experiments that advance an ecologically valid science of early intervention (Bronfenbrenner, 1979).

An ecological perspective has much to contribute to the process of formulating, evaluating, and understanding early intervention. It gives us a kind of social map for navigating a path through the complexities of programming. It helps us see the relations (potential and actual) among programs – how, for example, some programs are complementary, whereas others may be competitive. It aids us in seeing the full range of alternative conceptualizations of problems affecting children and points us in the direction of multiple strategies for intervention. An ecological perspective provides a kind of checklist to use in thinking about what is happening and what to do about it when faced with developmental problems and social pathologies that affect children. It does this by asking us always to consider the micro-, meso-, exo-, and macrosystem dimensions of developmental phenomena and interventions. It constantly suggests the possibility that context is shaping causal relationships. It always tells us "it depends" and stimulates an attempt to find out "on what."

THE ECONOMIC AND DEMOGRAPHIC CONTEXT OF EARLY CHILDHOOD IN THE UNITED STATES

Having identified the four social systems in which child development occurs, we turn next to identifying current sources of risk in the human ecology of the young child. To accomplish this, a brief social history of early risk must be considered in the context of recent economic trends in the United States, particularly as they affect the experience and developmental prognosis of young children.

In assessing the greatest social–environmental threats to families in the 1970s, several blue-ribbon panels identified economic deprivation as the principal villain (e.g., the National Academy of Sciences, 1976, Keniston, 1977, which was suggested by the Carnegie Corporation). In the space of two decades, as the relative economic position of young children has deteriorated these reports have come to seem mild. Reversing the traditional pattern for the

United States, in which poverty had been concentrated among the elderly, economic deprivation is now most common among families with young children. In 1993, for example, about 26% of America's children under age 6 were living in poverty (Hembroke, Morris, & Bronfenbrenner, 1996), as compared with 13% of the general population, including the elderly (McClelland, 1996). For African Americans and Hispanics, the rates are higher. In 1994, the poverty rate for children under 6 was about 20% for White children, 45% for Hispanic children, and 53% for African American children (Hembroke et al., 1996). The social concern of the 1980s focused attention on these latter (and growing) groups, now often called the "underclass"; but the larger group remains at risk, particularly if a period of temporary impoverishment coincides with the birth of a child. Of course, because there are so many more White families in the general population, 60% of all children in poverty are White (Hembroke et al., 1996).

Although chronic impoverishment poses a serious threat to child welfare, so does acute episodic impoverishment, which is much more prevalent in our society. In the late 1980s, many studies projected that one in four young children would live in poverty, particularly in single-parent households (Garbarino, 1995). This projection also expected single parenthood, a major correlate of poverty, to continue as a social phenomenon for one in two children at some point in their first 18 years of life. It also reflected the expectation that outbreaks of unemployment would continue above and beyond the chronic unemployment and underemployment characterizing the inner-city "underclass." These concerns have been borne out in the 1990s.

In 1993, one-quarter of all children under the age of 6 lived below the poverty line (5.5 million children). The number of families in need of cash assistance went up 10% between 1970 to 1995, and the average amount of public assistance per family dropped more than $650 per month in the same time period (Hembroke, Morris, & Bronfenbrenner, 1996). These figures reflect the period prior to the Welfare Reform Act of 1996 (P.L. 104–193), which is expected to reduce the average amount of public assistance per family much further. New York, for example, plans to cut assistance almost in half over the first four years of the new policy (Kilborn, 1996).

There is considerable debate about the exact processes that translate unemployment into developmental risk for children, but there is consensus that acute economic deprivation represents a challenge to the coping resources of individuals, families, and communities (Fisher & Cunningham, 1983). The connection between unemployment and developmental crisis is mainly indirect, but it is real nonetheless.

Unemployment tends to diminish resources and precipitate problems in mental health and welfare. Male identity and parental status have traditionally been tied to occupational position. Unemployment diminishes that identity and gives rise to ambiguity or even outright conflict in the family. This psychic threat is compounded by the practical fact that employment is the principal source of basic health and welfare services. Unemployment thus precipitates crises in both the psychic and the fiscal economy of the family. Both increase the likelihood of risky conditions for children and decrease the likelihood that such risky conditions will be observed and attended to effectively.

This dynamic is particularly important for workers in financially marginal employment, in which reserves are minimal or nonexistent – one paycheck away from disaster, as they are often described. This financial vulnerability heightens the importance of social resources of the kind discussed later in this chapter. One source of concern is the growing recognition that there has been a steady increase in the politically tolerable level of "normal" unemployment, from 4% in 1950 to 6.8% in 1993 (McClelland, 1996). Indeed, it may go even higher, because of methods of public accounting that do not include those too discouraged to seek work and others who are not fully employed. As recessions occur, they produce double-digit levels of unemployment (i.e., 10% or more), with localized hot spots in excess of 20%. These deteriorating economic conditions, characterized by increases in the number of people falling below the poverty level, are a major force driving the human ecology of early risk (Bronfenbrenner, Moen, & Garbarino, 1984).

In addition to the well-established connection between poverty and infant mortality, researchers have identified a link between economic deprivation and child maltreatment, certainly a primary indicator of child welfare and family functioning (see Garbarino

& Crouter, 1978a; Garbarino & Sherman, 1980; Garbine, Eckenrode, & the Family Life Development Center, 1996; Pelton, 1978; Steinberg, Catalano, & Dooley, 1981). Briefly, these studies report a correlation between low income and the risk for child maltreatment on both the individual level and the community level. Thus, the rate of maltreatment (all forms of abuse and neglect combined) computed as part of the federally financed National Incidence Study (which dealt with many of the issues of class-biased reporting) ranges from 27.3 per 1,000 children among families with 1979 incomes of under $7,000, to 14.6 per 1,000 for families in the $15,000 to $24,999 range, and 2.7 per 1,000 for families with annual incomes in excess of $25,000 (Garbarino et al., 1996). Studies of rates at the community level tell the same story (Garbarino & Crouter, 1978b), as discussed in greater detail later.

Inflation-adjusted wages dropped 13% between 1979 and 1989 for workers in the poorest tenth of the workforce, even though they increased 5% in the wealthiest tenth over the same period (McClelland, 1996). A further disturbing trend is that the economic recovery of the 1980s and 1990s did not (and in all likelihood will not) reach the growing "underclass," in which unemployment, poverty, and demographic adversity are becoming ever more entrenched and chronic (Wilson, 1987). These families and the neighborhoods they inhabit remain the hot spots for all early intervention services. For example, at-birth foster care placements tripled between 1986 and 1988 in New York City overall (Wulcyn & Goerge, 1992), reflecting much higher localized increases within some neighborhoods because of drug addiction and poverty.

Most industrialized societies entitle all families to maternal and infant health care and basic child support subsidies; ours does not (Kahn & Kamerman, 1975; Kamerman & Kahn, 1976; Miller, 1987). As noted by Bronfenbrenner (1986), this may explain why correlations between measures of income or socioeconomic status and basic child outcomes are often higher in the United States than in other modern societies. That is, low income is a better predictor of deficits in the United States than in other countries because our social policies tend to exaggerate rather than minimize the impact of family income on access to preventive and rehabilitative services.

The phenomenology of poverty is dominated by the experience of deprivation and is exacerbated by widespread promulgation of highly monetarized affluence as the standard. Low-paying jobs can come to be interpreted as an affront in such a context, the accoutrements of affluence a right. We must add to this the geographic concentration of economically marginal families as communities become more homogeneous (e.g., in Cleveland, the proportion of poor people living in neighborhoods that are predominantly poor went from 23% in 1960 to 65% in 1990). Children cost too much when their caregivers cannot generate enough income to meet popular expectations for participating in the monetarized economy of day-to-day life.

In a nation where everything costs money and continues to cost more, most families need two incomes to keep up, although because of divorce and single parenthood, more and more families have only one potential wage earner. This was not the case at the outset of the economic depression in the 1930s. Most families with children at that time contained two adults, and wives represented a largely untapped resource that could be and was mobilized to generate cash income in response to the unemployment and income loss experienced by male workers (Elder, 1974). Now this resource has already been tapped to meet basic family expenses and, therefore, does not represent a reserve in the sense that it did in the 1930s. By 1992, 75% of married women with children had entered the workforce, and most of these had children under the age of 6 (Cherlin, 1996). Furthermore, children are increasingly an economic burden, directly because of what it costs to raise them and indirectly because of what they cost in lost parental income (i.e., time away from the job that over a childhood comes to tens of thousands if not hundreds of thousands of dollars).

Conventional Economics

The relationship between developmental risk and economic crisis flows from both the current political climate and the conventional economic thinking that undergirds our political economy (Garbarino, 1995). The problem is thus both our political ideology and the conventional economic thinking that guides our institutions. Conventional economics was built and continues to rest on a foundation of ecologically flawed assumptions about prices, costs, and values.

Conventional economics does not recognize the real material and social basis of production. Capital and labor are fully interchangeable only in the abstract calculations of conventional economics. For example, farmers farm not only to earn an income but also because of their attachment to a particular kind of life. One person farming 10,000 acres using robots is not the same as 100 people each farming 100 acres using minimal mechanization. Standard economics proceeds on the assumption that acts that do not have an immediate cash price (such as dumping pollutants into rivers or closing enterprises that are the lifeblood of a community because they do not return a high enough dividend) are free. Economists call these factors that are outside an enterprise's direct costs *externalities*. Social and material costs are pushed onto the public in general, and specific communities and families in particular. Conventional economists tell us to assume that these costs are accounted for automatically in the marketplace and result in the general good.

The invalidity of this assumption is ever more apparent as the scale of human economic enterprise grows to the point at which it is sufficiently powerful to degrade the earth on global proportions. In the social domain, this invalid assumption is evident in the increasingly unrealistic character of conventional economic analyses of the threats posed to children by the monetarily inadequate resource base for child care. Current policy initiatives aimed at welfare reform and improving child care do not consider fully the true costs. There are limits to the number of children that one caregiver can serve without compromising development. Family child care providers who serve less than affluent families are usually in a difficult position because they cannot generate sufficient income per child served to set a proper limit on the number of children in their care. Issues such as this must be at the top of our agenda when we speak of the economics of child development. We also need to ask such questions as, How can we afford to pay $2,000 a day for neonatal intensive care for one child but not $2,000 per family in intensive prenatal care to prevent low birth weight and neonatal risk?

Some knowledge of economic motivation and analysis is essential for an adequate understanding of the human ecology of early risk and the prospects for intervention. The implications of this analysis are counter to the laissez-faire themes put forward during the 1990s by political forces demanding less rather than more governmental responsibility for families and early childhood, thereby exacerbating the dynamics of family vulnerability and economic hardship (Garbarino, 1995).

The politics of early childhood risk and opportunity in the 1990s portend a long series of battles pitting the basic well-being of some children and their families against the affluence of others. The politics of choosing between those two thrusts will intensify as they become more clearly mutually competitive. The internal situation in the United States will thus mirror the global choices to be made between more luxuries for the "haves" versus more necessities for the "have nots." If the Bureau of Labor Statistics numbers are adjusted to account for inflation since the data were last compiled in the mid-1980s, a family of four requires about $48,000 to live at a "high" level. The same family requires about $25,000 to live at a "lower" (struggling) level, and about $14,000 to live at poverty level.

Should the majority of the population be brought up to $25,000 or should the prospects of those who have reached the $48,000 level be enhanced? The former goal is much more germane to early intervention and the prevention of developmental risks; the latter may be more in keeping with the spirit of the times.

Economic issues play a large role in the dynamics of early risk. At the microsystem level, family structure and activities interact with the parents' participation in the workforce. Macrosystem issues provide a context for this. To the degree to which the community's day-to-day life is monetarized, families as microsystems will be drawn or driven into the cash economy. If the exosystems of the community (local government, philanthropic institutions, etc.) remain aloof from this process, those who cannot generate sufficient cash income to participate in basic activities will become ever poorer. Impoverished microsystems will begin to form systematic patterns of deprivation: family, school, and social network will reinforce developmental delay and deviant socialization. This is played out in the human ecology of infant mortality and child maltreatment, particularly in socially impoverished urban areas where the entire human ecology seems to operate in a concerted attack upon the foundations for successful

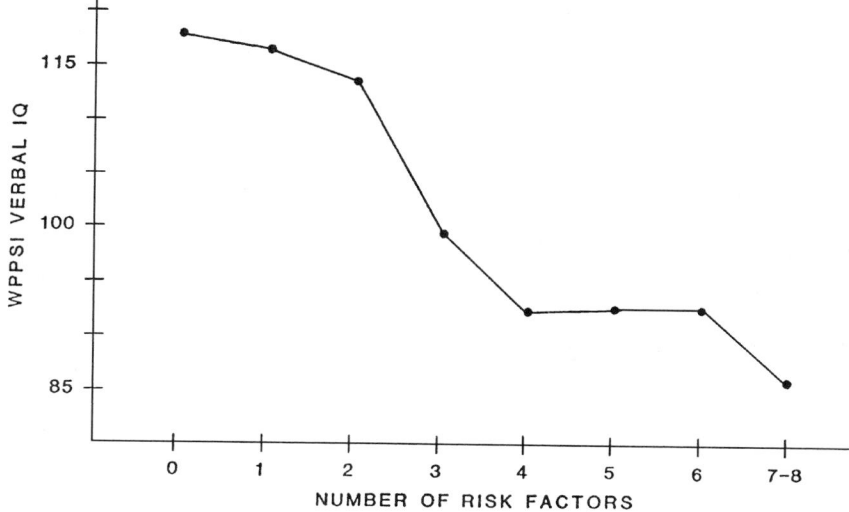

child development. In this sense, the "underclass" represents a kind of ecological conspiracy against children.

Figure 4.1. Effects of multiple risk scores on preschool intelligence (Sameroff et al., 1987).

THE CLINICAL SOCIOLOGY OF EARLY RISK: AN EMPIRICAL MODEL OF CHILD MALTREATMENT, INFANT MORTALITY, AND EARLY INTERVENTION IN HIGH-RISK COMMUNITIES

Sameroff and his colleagues (1987) examined the relation between a child's IQ at age 4 and the presence of risk factors across a variety of systems (including poverty, father absence, low parental education, a rigid and punitive child-rearing style, minority group status, parental substance abuse, maternal mental illness, and large family size). Figure 4.1 presents their results, which show that the effect of any two risk factors on a child's intelligence is small.

Surprisingly, this suggests, for example, that for a child of 4 years, there are no *intellectual* effects of living in poverty with a drug-abusing mother (all other risks being absent). However, as the risks accumulate, so does the effect. The largest drop (and the drop that takes the child below average) in associated IQ is noted between two and three risk factors. The children in this study with seven or eight risk factors had an average IQ that was 30 points lower than children with no risk factors at all. These results suggest that we need not make life risk free for children to protect them from serious harm, but rather

we must prevent the accumulation of risk beyond the coping capacity of the child.

There is, though, more than just the accumulation of risk; there is the compensating force of opportunity. Some children experience more than "not risk;" they experience opportunity. It is more than their father is not absent; their father is intensely involved with them. It is more than their mother is avoiding alcoholism; their mother is modeling how to manage alcohol effectively (and by implication, everything else as well). Dunst and Trivette (1992) have looked at the relative accumulation of risk versus opportunity and found that a child with four risk factors and four opportunity factors has a much better statistical chance of doing better intellectually than a child with four risk factors and only one opportunity factor.

Applying these data to children today make it clear why so many are struggling. Half of them bear the risk factor of an absent parent because of divorce, separation, or single motherhood. A sizable proportion (perhaps as many as 30%) are living with a mother who has a history of serious depression, and one in four lives in poverty. Moreover, the risks are not distributed evenly; more than 50% of African American children are poor (Hembroke et al., 1996). The Center on Addiction and Substance Abuse reported that 28% of parents on welfare (who are thus also poor and are often single parents) have substance-abuse problems (Garbarino, 1995). Of all children, those who are burdened by an accumulation of risk need a safe neighborhood most, but neighborhood safety and stability have declined most in the areas in which they live.

In contrast to the socially rich family environment stands the socially impoverished one, in which the parent–child relationship is denuded of enduring supportive relationships and protective behaviors. It is thus deprived of the essential elements of social support: nurturance and positive feedback systems (Caplan, 1974; Whittaker et al., 1983). The socially rich environment includes people who are "free from drain" (Collins & Pancoast, 1976). Such individuals can afford to give to and share with others because the balance of needs and resources in their own lives markedly favors the latter. They offer services that do not involve cash transactions. Thus, these individuals stand outside the monetarized human service sector (i.e., the services that involve salaries and wages, prices and financial contracts); they find nonmonetarized payoff in helping others.

What do these people who are free from drain do? One thing they do is provide "protective behaviors" for children. Emlen (1977) used this concept to refer to what neighbors and friends may do to keep children safe: from keeping an eye on them while they play outside, to offering assistance to parents with day-to-day or emergency care, to intervening on the child's behalf when threatened (even to reporting child maltreatment to protective service agencies). These individuals become one aspect of the socially rich neighborhood. Kromkowski (1976) put it this way:

A neighborhood's character is determined by a host of factors, but most significantly by the kinds of relationships that neighbors have with each other . . . . A healthy neighborhood has some sort of cultural and institutional network that manifests itself with pride in the neighborhood, care of homes, security for children, and respect for each other. (p. 288)

Socially impoverished neighborhoods, in contrast, lack people who are free from drain and therefore tend to operate on a scarcity economy when it comes to social relations. Mutuality is suppressed by fears of exploitation and of being a burden and excessively beholding. For example, residents may fear acts of neighboring such as generalized offers of shared child care because such open-ended acts can open a Pandora's box of requests and may lead to the expectation of reciprocity – a negative prospect if one distrusts the caregiving practices of one's neighbors.

This social impoverishment can occur independently of economic impoverishment. When it does, however, its consequences for young children are likely to be blunted because affluent families can gain access to monetarized services to compensate. Nonetheless, the affluent but socially impoverished environment may catch up with children and families as they face the transition to adolescence, when the need for social stability increases to compensate for the intrinsic psychological and physiological challenges of puberty (Garbarino & Associates, 1985). Thus, even a financially affluent social environment may lack the kind of enduring support systems that provide adolescents with positive role models, caring adult supervision, and a sense of personal validation. The same may be true for the parents of those adolescents who may feel acutely embarrassed to admit difficulty with their adolescents in a community in which there is a presumption of competence and high expectations for achievement.

The greatest risks come when families lack the financial resources to purchase support services in the marketplace and are cut off from the informal helping relationships. It is when the monetarized and nonmonetarized economics are both impoverished, however, that child maltreatment and infant mortality flourish and early intervention challenges are greatest (Garbarino, Stocking, & Associates, 1980). This condition is seen most clearly in the urban underclass that has become the focal point for emergency intervention. Marginal or submarginal economic resources interact with diminished psychosocial resources born of violence, academic failure, exploitation, despair, fear, and deteriorated community infrastructure. For example, in a recent study focusing on preschoolers' lives in an inner-city public housing project, all of the mothers cited "shooting" as their greatest fear for their children (Dubrow & Garbarino, 1987).

In this inner-city area, every child has had a firsthand encounter with gunfire, including being in the arms of someone when that person was shot and having bullets come through apartment windows nearby while playing. In such environments, most women experience their first pregnancy while still an unmarried teenager, living with little prospect of economic self-sufficiency or two-parent family status. Many of these pregnancies result from sexual exploitation by much older men (Barclay-McLaughlin, 1987). These are the environments in which prenatal care is inadequate, intervals between births are often too short, beliefs about child care too often dysfunctional, access to and utilization of well-baby care inadequate, early intervention for child disabilities inadequate, and thus in which child mortality and morbidity are high.

Research has shown that some individuals and families create and sustain patterns of interaction that generate infant mortality and child maltreatment (Belsky, 1980; Garbarino, 1977; Gaudin & Polansky, 1985; Polansky, Chalmers, Buttenwieser, & Williams, 1981). However high-risk families are not the whole story. To understand the forces that create and sustain early developmental risk, we must go further to identify and investigate high-risk environments in which such families live. Understanding infant mortality and child maltreatment is thus an issue for clinical sociology (see Pavenstedt, 1967; Roman & Trice, 1974) as much as for clinical psychology. Families both shape their social surroundings and are shaped by them. This interactive process can enhance or undermine family functioning (Garbarino, 1977; Martin, 1976). More systematic efforts to study and serve families in context can enrich research and intervention, both preventive and rehabilitative. For many practical purposes, this means examining high-risk neighborhoods as well as high-risk families (see Sattin & Miller, 1971).

Previous research has sought to explore and validate the concept of social impoverishment as a characteristic of high-risk family environments. The links between child maltreatment and social impoverishment are well known (Garbarino, 1977). Similarly, it has long been well known, and recently affirmed, that infant mortality rates serve as social indicators of impoverishment. The environmental correlates of child maltreatment (Garbarino, 1976; Garbarino, Crouter, & Sherman, 1977) have provided an empirical basis for identifying high- and low-risk neighborhoods. This research has been extended to incorporate infant mortality as well. In Chicago, for example, public health data document infant mortality rates in the poorest third of the city's neighborhoods five to ten times the

rate observed in the most affluent third (Kostelny & Garbarino, 1987).

Multiple regression analyses employing measures of socioeconomic and demographic resources have been used to illuminate two meanings of high risk (Garbarino & Crouter, 1978b). The first, of course, refers to areas with a high absolute rate of child maltreatment and infant mortality (based on cases per unit of population). In this sense, concentrations of socioeconomically distressed families are most likely to be at high risk. In one city (Omaha, Nebraska), socioeconomic status accounts for about 40% of the variation across neighborhoods in child maltreatment ($r = .64$). Similar results are obtained when infant mortality is the dependent variable of interest. In Chicago, for example, these same conditions account for some 60–75% of the variation among seventy-seven community areas in child maltreatment and infant mortality (Kostelny & Garbarino, 1987).

We should note that the magnitude of these correlations may reflect a social policy effect. It seems reasonable to assume that in a society in which low income is not correlated with access to basic human services (e.g., where there is universal availability of maternal–infant health care), these correlations would be smaller; in a society totally devoid of policies to ameliorate the impact of family-level differences in social class, the correlations might be even larger. The key is how social class (a status variable) is translated into the experiences of children and parents (i.e., the process variables).

Tukinn (1972) classic analysis of the concept of "cultural deprivation" made this clear. On the one hand, it is not the culture of those living in poverty in some general sense that matters most. Rather, it is those aspects of that culture that translate into an inability to meet the basic developmental needs of children that matter; for example, whether caregivers accept infant attachment, whether they give up too quickly on sick children, and whether it is normative to reject children with disabilities (Scheper-Hughes, 1987).

The community plays a vital role in deciding this issue. By establishing a strong and aggressive system of prenatal and maternal and child health care, and by making it easy to gain access and difficult to avoid it, a community can do much to dissociate poverty and infant mortality (Miller, 1987). By adopting a passive stance and by allowing the free market to rule, a community can strengthen the links between poverty and early child death (Garbarino, 1995).

This hypothesis merits empirical exploration, but it is consistent with the observation that socioeconomic status is a more potent predictor of child development outcomes in the United States than in some European societies. Furthermore, a replication of the Omaha study conducted in Montreal revealed a weaker association of socioeconomic status and child maltreatment rates, presumably because of that city's welfare policies that diminish the link between income and basic services (Bouchard, 1987). The direct correlational links between social class and social pathology constitute the first meaning of high risk; that is, the finding that poverty is a risk

factor because it is associated with rates of infant mortality, child abuse, and so on.

However, it is the second meaning of high risk that may be of greatest relevance here. High risk can also be taken to mean that a social environment has a higher rate of child maltreatment or infant mortality than would be predicted knowing its socioeconomic character. Thus, two areas with similar socioeconomic and demographic profiles may have different rates of child maltreatment and infant mortality. In this sense, one is high risk while the other is low risk, although both may have higher rates than other more affluent areas. Figure 4.2 illustrates this.

Areas A and B have high actual observed rates of child maltreatment (36 per 1,000 and 34 per 1,000, respectively). Areas C and D have lower rates (16 per 1,000 and 14 per 1,000). However, areas A and C

Figure 4.2. Two meanings of "risk" in assessing community areas.

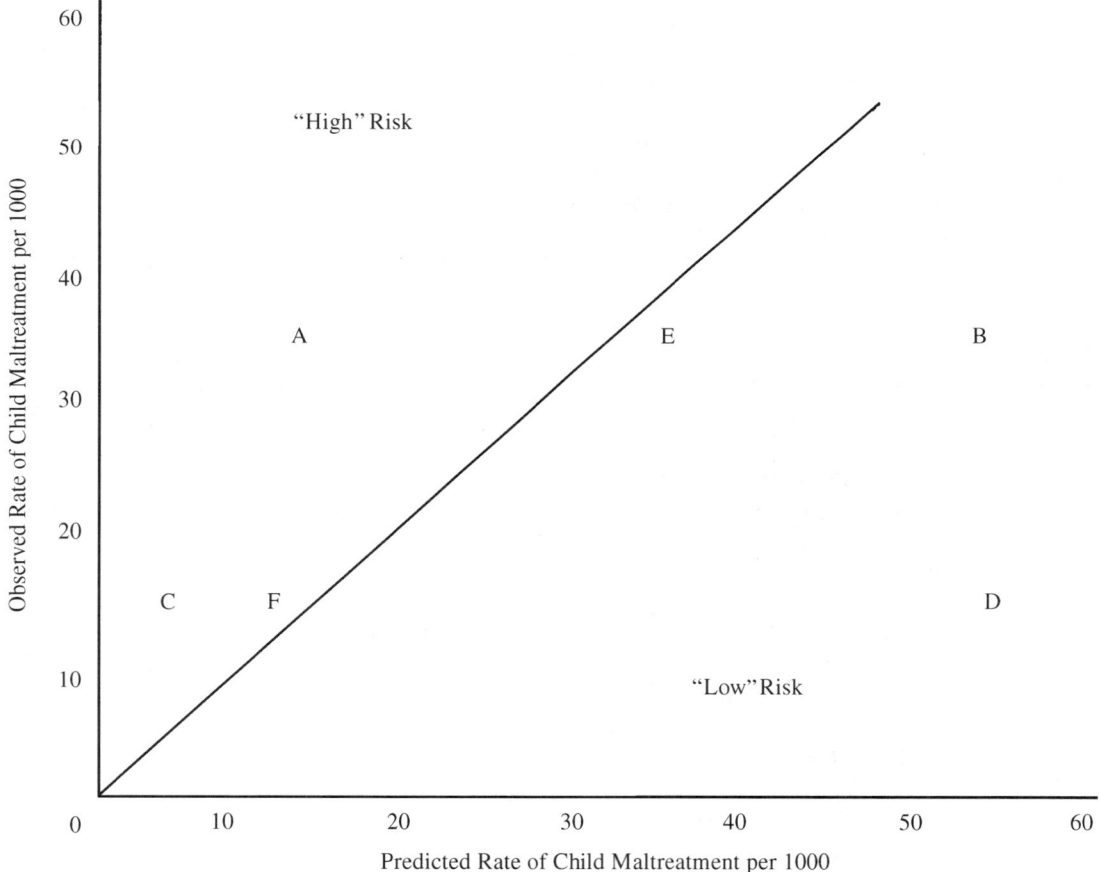

have higher actual observed rates than would be predicted (10 per 1,000 predicted for A, 7 per 1,000 for C), whereas areas B and D have lower actual observed than predicted rates (55 per 1,000 for B and 54 per 1,000 for D). In this sense, A and C are both high risk, whereas B and D are both low risk. Areas E and F evidence a close approximation between predicted and actual rates. This classification system can provide the basis for identifying contrasting social environments, as seen later.

What do low- and high-risk social environments look like? One way to answer this question is to examine a pair of neighborhoods with the same predicted but different observed rates of child maltreatment (i.e., one high risk and the other low risk for child maltreatment). This approach provides a test of the hypothesis that the two neighborhoods present contrasting environments for child rearing (Garbarino & Sherman, 1980). Relative to a low-risk area, and even though it is socioeconomically equivalent (i.e., has the same poverty level), a high-risk neighborhood represents a socially impoverished human ecology in the sense discussed earlier; that is, it has few people who are free from drain, a generalized fear of being exploited in neighborly interactions, and a lot of highly stressed and emotionally needy families.

To complement demographic and socioeconomic data from census records and individual perceptions from face-to-face interviews with parents, investigators can interview a wide range of "informants" – people who are familiar with a neighborhood in their professional roles as police, visiting nurses, principals, clergy, mail carriers, and the like. These observers are asked to provide information about the following domains: neighborhood public image, neighborhood appearance, social characteristics, neighborhood change, neighborhood quality of life, child abuse and neglect, neighborhood involvement, and informal supports. The results obtained through blind open-ended questions are subjected to a content analysis and validate the identification of one area as being relatively more socially impoverished than the other (Garbarino & Sherman, 1980).

The observers may describe the high-risk neighborhood as deteriorated interpersonally and physically, as a dangerous place, as disorganized, and as distrustful. In one study, there was less positive neighboring and more stressful day-to-day interactions for families in the high-risk area (Garbarino & Sherman, 1980).

In a study of Chicago neighborhoods, Garbarino and Kostelny (1992) applied this approach. Figure 4.3 shows the results. In 1980, North and West had similar actual maltreatment rates. However, North's actual maltreatment rate was below the rate predicted by its compound social and demographic factors. West's actual rate was slightly above its predicted rate. By 1986, however, the two areas had changed dramatically in relation to each other. North's actual maltreatment rate soared, whereas West's rate increased only slightly and fell far below the predicted rate of maltreatment by 1986. North became a very high-risk area, and West became a low-risk area. Why did North become a deteriorating environment for children, while West did not?

Interviews showed that there was a clear difference in climate between North and West, with the general tone of North being depressed and negative. People in North had a difficult time finding anything good to say about their community and had little or no community identity. They knew less about what community services were available, and they demonstrated little evidence of a network or support system or political leadership. In West, people were eager to talk about their communities, they reported strong political leadership, and they knew more about what services were available. Although they listed serious problems, most of them felt that their communities were poor but decent places to live and they felt a strong, informal community network of support. In short, even though North had equal economic status with the low-risk area West, it violated all of Kromkowski's (1976) requisites for a good neighborhood: pride in the neighborhood, care of homes, security for children, and respect for each other.

Further research in metropolitan Chicago sought to place evaluation of community-based prevention programs within an ecological perspective (Garbarino, Schellenbach, & Kostelny, 1986). This was done by focusing on the operation and impact of child abuse prevention, infant mortality reduction, and family support programs in four high-risk community areas. This provides a case study for applying human ecology concepts to the practice of evaluating the impact of early intervention.

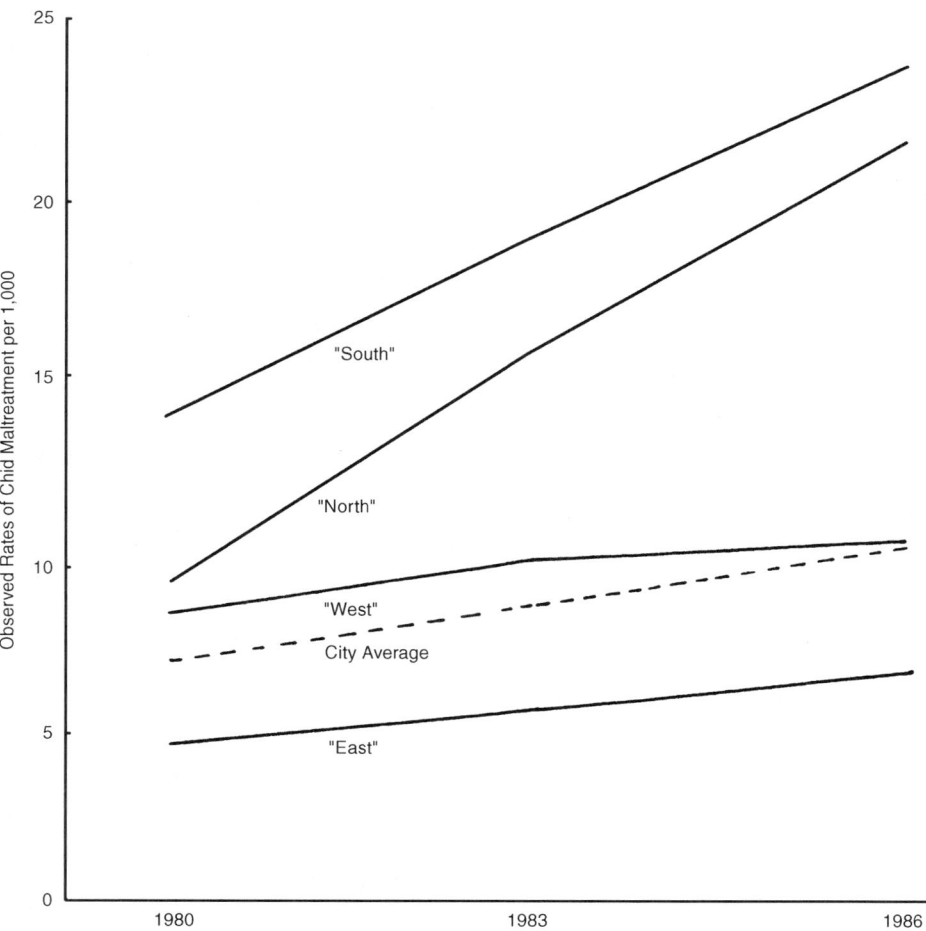

Figure 4.3. Child maltreatment rates in four community areas.

The net result of these analyses has documented the degree to which program operation is conditioned by community factors. This is an important issue for the field of early intervention, in which family support programs seek to be community based (cf. Kagan, Powell, Weissbourd, & Zigler, 1987). Such analyses can shed light on the degree to which program effectiveness is conditioned by community characteristics and thus provide guidance for early interventionists, program managers, and community development specialists. Such analyses can serve as a model for the kind of program evaluation needed to make sense of the issues we face in making a community commitment to deal

with developmental risk and can provide the operational basis for understanding the human ecology of early developmental risk.

The clinical sociology of early risk is one of the important underdeveloped resources for improving the life prospects of children. It requires further efforts to operationalize the concepts of social richness and social impoverishment, to use these concepts to understand the impact of social class on development, and to operationalize a community-based program evaluation model for assessing early intervention efforts. Clinical sociology can be a useful tool in our efforts to promote the ecological insight that understands that when one is asked, Does X cause Y?, the answer is always, It depends. Finding out the precise who, what, where, and when of that assertion of the importance of context is one of the major challenges we face in making further progress in a science of early intervention on behalf of children at risk.

CONCLUSION

In the Middle Ages, half of all living children died by age 5. Now, child death is relatively rare. As standards and expectations for the care and life prospects of children have improved throughout the twentieth century, developmental risk has become a growing focal point for research and policy. Thus, our focus has shifted from sheer quantitative concern with child survival to a qualitative concern with development. This is a major accomplishment.

This chapter has explored the sources of developmental risk in the social environment. Its ecological perspective provides a challenge to researchers, policy makers, and clinicians. The challenge is both intellectual and spiritual. The intellectual challenge is to insist on analytic models that are ecologically valid, which incorporate (or at least address) the full range of influences on children: from the organismic to the macrosocial. This strains our intellectual resources to their limits and sometimes beyond. The spiritual challenge is to refuse to despair when faced with the ecological "conspiracies" that envelop children in high-risk social environments. Similarly, we must refuse to despair and refuse to capitulate to narrow intervention approaches, single-variable models, and other efforts to deny the importance of ecological validity. This is the agenda before us.

REFERENCES

Albee, G. (1980). Primary prevention and social problems. In G. Gerbner, C. J. Ross, & E. Zigler (Eds.), *Child abuse: An agenda for action* (pp. 106–17). New York: Oxford University Press.

Atherton, C. R., Raymond, G. T., Roff, L. L. (1993). The transition in Eastern Europe: Implications for both East and West. *International Social Work, 36,* 197–206.

Barclay-McLaughlin, G. (1987). *The Center for Successful Child Development.* Chicago, IL: The Ounce of Prevention Fund.

Belsky, J. (1980). Child maltreatment: An ecological interaction. *American Psychologist, 35,* 20–335.

Belsky, J. (1986). Infant day care: A cause for concern? *Zero to Three, 6,* 1ff.

Bouchard, C. (1987). *Child maltreatment in Montreal.* Montreal: University of Quebec.

Bronfenbrenner, U. (1979). *The ecology of human development: Experiments by nature and design.* Cambridge: Harvard University Press.

Bronfenbrenner, U. (1986). Ecology of the family as a context for human development research perspectives. *Developmental Psychology, 22,* 723–42.

Bronfenbrenner, U., & Crouter, A. (1982). Work and family through time and space. In S. N. Kamerman & C. D. Hayes (Eds.), *Families that work: Children in a changing environment of work, family and community* (pp. 138–56). Washington, DC: National Academy of Sciences.

Bronfenbrenner, U., Moen, P., & Garbarino, J. (1984). Families and communities. In H. R. Parke (Ed.), *Review of child development research* (pp. 251–78). Chicago: University of Chicago Press.

Caplan, G. (1974). *Support systems and community mental health.* New York: Behavioral Publications.

Cherlin, A. J. (1996). *Public and private families.* New York: McGraw-Hill.

Collins, A., & Pancoast, D. (1976). *Natural helping networks.* Washington, DC: National Association of Social Workers.

Courtney, M. (1995, summer). The foster care crisis and welfare reform: How might reform efforts affect the foster care system? *Public Welfare, 53,* 3, 27–33.

Dubrow, N., & Garbarino, J. (1987). *Living in the war zone: Mothers and children in public housing developments.* Chicago: Erikson Institute.

Duncan, G., Coe, R., & Hill, M. (1981). *The dynamics of poverty.* Ann Arbor: University of Michigan.

Dunst, C., & Trivette, C. (1992). *Risk and opportunity factors influencing parent and child functioning.* Paper presented at the Ninth Annual Smoky Mountain Winter Institute, Asheville, NC.

Elder, G. H. (1974). *Children of the great depression.* Chicago: University of Chicago Press.

Emlen, A. (1977, November). *If you care about children, then care about parents.* Paper presented at the Tennessee Association for Young Children, Nashville, TN.

Fisher, K., & Cunningham, S. (1983). The dilemma: Problem grows, support shrinks. *APA Monitor, 14,* 2, Iff.

Forrester, J. (1969). *Urban dynamics.* Cambridge, MA: MIT Press.

Fried, A. O. (1995). Bulgarian social services and social work education. *International Social Work, 38,* 39–51.

Garbarino, J. (1976). A preliminary study of some ecological correlates of child abuse: The impact of socioeconomic stress on mothers. *Child Development, 47,* 178–85.

Garbarino, J. (1977). The human ecology of child maltreatment: A conceptual model for research. *Journal of Marriage and the Family, 39,* 721–36.

Garbarino, J. (1995). *Raising children in a socially toxic environment.* San Francisco: Jossey-Bass.

Garbarino, J., & Associates. (1992). *Children and families in the social environment.* (2nd ed.) Hawthorne, NY: Aldine.

Garbarino, J., & Associates (1985). *Adolescent development: An ecological perspective.* Columbus, OH: Merrill.

Garbarino, J., & Crouter, A. (1978a). Defining the community context of parent-child relations. *Child Development, 49,* 604–16.

Garbarino, J., & Crouter, A. (1978b). A note on assessing the construct validity of child maltreatment report data. *American Journal of Public Health, 68,* 598–9.

Garbarino, J., Crouter, A., & Sherman, D. (1977). Screening neighborhoods for intervention: A research model for child protective services. *Journal of Social Service Research, 1,* 135–45.

Garbarino, J., Eckenrode, J., and the Family Life Development Center. (1996). *Understanding abusive families.* San Francisco: Jossey-Bass.

Garbarino, J., Guttmann, E., & Seeley, J. (1986). *The psychologically battered child.* San Francisco: Jossey-Bass.

Garbarino, J., & Kostelny, K. (1992). Child maltreatment as a community problem. *Child Abuse and Nelgect, 16,* 455–64.

Garbarino, J., Schellenbach, C., & Kostelny, K. (1986). *A model for evaluating the impact of family support and child abuse prevention programs in high-risk communities.* Chicago: Erikson Institute.

Garbarino, J., & Sherman, D. (1980). High-risk neighborhoods and high-risk families: The human ecology of child maltreatment. *Child Development, 51,* 188–98.

Garbarino, J., Stocking, S. H., & Associates (Eds.). (1980). *Protecting children from abuse and neglect.* San Francisco: Jossey-Bass.

Gaudin, J., & Polansky, N. (1985). Social distancing of the neglectful family. *Social Service Review, 58,* 245–53.

Hardin, G. (1966). *Biology: Its principles and implications.* San Francisco: Freeman.

Hembroke, H., Morris, P., & Bronfenbrenner, U. (1996). Poverty and the next generation. In U. Bronfenbrenner, P. McClelland, E. Wethington, P. Moen, & S. J. Ceci (Eds.), *The state of Americans.* New York: Free Press.

Kagan, S., Powell, D., Weissbourd, B., & Zigler, E. (Eds.). (1987). *Family support programs.* New Haven, CT: Yale University Press.

Kahn, A., & Kamerman, S. (1975). *Not for the poor alone: European social services.* Philadelphia: Temple University Press.

Kamerman, S., & Kahn, A. (1976). *Social services in the United States: Policies and programs.* Philadelphia: Temple University Press.

Keniston, K. (1977). *All our children.* New York: Harcourt Brace Jovanovich.

Kilborn, P. T. (1996). The nation: Welfare all over the map. *The New York Times.* December 8, 1996.

Kostelny, K., & Garbarino, J. (1987). *The human ecology of infant mortality: An analysis of risk in 76 urban communities.* Chicago: Erikson Institute.

Kromkowski, J. (1976, August). *Neighborhood deterioration and juvenile crime* (U.S. Department of Commerce). South Bend, IN: The South Bend Urban Observatory. (NTIS No. PB-260 473).

Lemann, N. (1986). The origins of the underclass. *Atlantic Monthly, 257,* 31–61.

Martin, H. (Ed.). (1976). *The abused child: A multidisciplinary approach to developmental issues and treatment.* Cambridge, MA: Ballinger.

McClelland, P. (1996). Economic developments. In U. Bronfenbrenner, P. McClelland, E. Wethington, P. Moen, & S. J. Ceci (Eds.), *The state of Americans.* New York: Free Press.

Meezan, W., & Giovannoni, J. (1995). The current threat to protective services and the child welfare system. *Children and Youth Services Review, 17,* 4, 567–74.

Miller, A. (1987). *Maternal health and infant survival.* Washington, DC: National Center for Clinical Infant Programs.

National Academy of Sciences. (1976). *Towards a national policy for children and families.* Washington, DC: U.S. Government Printing Office.

Olds, D., Eckenrode, J., Henderson, C. Jr., Kitzman, H., Powers, J., Cole, R., Sidora, K., Morris, P., Pettitt, L., Luckey, D. (1997). Long-term effects of home visitation on maternal life course and child abuse and neglect: 15-Year follow-up of a randomized trial. *Journal of the American Medical Association, 278,* 637–643.

Olds, D., Henderson, C., Chamberlin, R., & Tatelbaum, R. (1994). Does prenatal and infancy nurse home visitation have enduring effects on qualities of parental caregiving and child health at 25 to 50 months of life? *Pediatrics, 93,* 89–98.

Olds, D., Henderson, C., Cole, R., Eckenrode, J., Kitzman, H., Luckey, D., Pettitt, L., Sidora, K., Morris, P., & Power, J. (1998). Long-term effects of nurse home visitation on children's criminal and antisocial behaviour: 15 years follow-up of a randomized trial. *The Journal of the American Medical Association, 280*(14), 1238–1244.

Olds, D., Henderson, C., Tatelbaum, R., & Chamberlin, R. (1988). Improving the life-course development of socially disadvantaged mothers: A randomized trial of nurse home visitation. *American Journal of Public Health, 78,* 11, 1436–45.

Pasamanick, B. (1987, Winter). Social biology and AIDS. *Division 37 newsletter.* Washington, DC: American Psychological Association.

Pavenstedt, E. (1967). *The drifters: Children of disorganized lower-class families.* Boston: Little, Brown.

Pelton, L. (1978). The myth of classlessness in child abuse cases. *American Journal of Orthopsychiatry, 48,* 569–79.

Polansky, N., Chalmers, M., Buttenwieser, E., & Williams, D. (1981). *Damaged parents.* Chicago: University of Chicago. Press.

Roman, R., & Trice, H. (Eds.). (1974). *Exploration in psychiatric sociology.* Philadelphia: Davis.

Sameroff, A. J., Seifer, R., Barocas, R., Zax, M., & Greenspan, S. (1987). Intelligence quotient scores of 4-year-old children: Social–environmental risk factors. *Pediatrics*, *79*, 343–50.

Sattin, D., & Miller, J. (1971). The ecology of child abuse. *American Journal of Orthopsychiatry*, *41*, 413–25.

Schell, J. (1982). *The fate of the earth*. New York: Knopf.

Scheper-Hughes, N. (1987). Culture, scarcity, and maternal thinking: Mother love and child death in northeast Brazil. In N. Scheper-Hughes (Ed.), *Child survival* (pp. 187–210). Boston: Reidel.

Steinberg, L., Catalano, R., & Dooley, D. (1981). Economic antecedents of child abuse and neglect. *Child Development*, *52*, 975–85.

Tukinn, S. (1972). An analysis of the concept of cultural deprivation. *Developmental Psychology*, *6*, 326–39.

Vygotsky, L. S. (1934). *Thought and language*. Cambridge, MA: MIT Press.

Whittaker, J. (1983). Social support networks in child welfare. In J. Whittaker, J. Garbarino, & Associates, *Social support networks* (pp. 167–87). Hawthorne, NY: Aldine.

Whittaker, J., Garbarino, J., & Associates. (1983). *Social support networks*. Hawthorne, NY: Aldine.

Willerman, L., Broman, S. H., & Fiedler, M. (1970). Infant development, preschool IQ, and social class. *Child Development*, *41*, 69–77.

Wilson, E. (1978). *On human nature*. Cambridge, MA: Harvard University Press.

Wilson W. (1987). *The truly disadvantaged: The inner city, the underclass, and public policy*. Chicago: University of Chicago Press.

Wulcyn, F., & Goerge, R. (1992). Foster care in New York and Illinois: The challenge of rapid change. *Social Service Review*, *66*, 278–94.

Yancey, A. K. (1992). Identity formation and social maladaptation in foster adolescents. *Adolescence*, *27*, 188, 819–31.

CHAPTER FIVE

Cultural Differences as Sources of Developmental Vulnerabilities and Resources

CYNTHIA GARCÍA COLL AND KATHERINE MAGNUSON

Developmentalists have had an ongoing, albeit uneasy, relationship with the constructs of culture, ethnicity, "race," and minority status (Cole, 1996; Duckitt, 1992). As their influence becomes recognized, these constructs have often proved difficult to conceptualize and even harder to incorporate as key sources of influence in all children's lives. This has led some academics and clinicians to ignore their role in human development, and others to inappropriately apply these constructs peripherally to their work; whereas a few academics and clinicians have placed these constructs at the core of their research questions and service delivery.

The push to understand the role of culture in children's development began in the middle of the twentieth century with the work of such anthropologists and cross-cultural psychologists as John and Beatrice Whiting (Whiting & Whiting, 1975), Robert Levine (Levine, 1977), and Michael Cole (Cole & Bruner, 1974; Cole, 1996), followed more recently by Sarah Harkness and Charles Super (Super & Harkness, 1980), as well as Barbara Rogoff (Mistry & Rogoff, 1994; Rogoff & Morelli, 1989), among others. Unfortunately, though well regarded in its own niche, this work has been relegated to the margins of mainstream developmental work (García Coll & Magnuson, 1999b; Slaughter-Defoe, Nakagawa, Takanishi & Johnson, 1990). Most developmentalists have continued to pursue implicit universal trends and truths; this detracts from our understanding of phenomena that are culturally bound and the influence of other sociocultural factors on development, thus affecting programming efforts on behalf of children and their families.

In addition, culture was, and to a large extent still is, conceptualized as something that other groups, societies, and nations possess. Consequently, the role of culture in development within the United States has been neglected (Harkness, 1980). This is in keeping with our society's and with developmental scientists' often nearly exclusive focus on individuals as the developmental unit of analysis (Caplan & Nelson, 1973). We tend to place the individual child at the center of our explanatory and theoretical models of development and then seek to understand developmental outcomes as mediated by immediate personal, individual, or familial contextual factors. Therefore, it is no surprise that early intervention efforts with high-risk infants and children considered the child historically to be the primary object of intervention and then set forth the goal of maximizing cognitive or neurological outcomes (Meyer et al., 1994), disregarding sociocultural factors.

More recent conceptual models of development have increasingly proposed sociocultural influences on infant and child development (Bronfenbrenner, 1979; Sameroff & Fiese, this volume). This shift has been driven by a compelling combination of scholarly and clinical contributions that have indicated that universal assumptions about development do not equally explain all processes and pathways of development for all populations. The variation in causal roots of outcomes between and within populations of different backgrounds suggests, for example, that what might cause a Hispanic child to display certain behaviors in a particular context can be significantly different from what might cause a Black child to display the same behaviors in a comparable situation.

Consequently, the significance of sociocultural constructs to the development of children and the field of early intervention is receiving increasing attention both in the conceptual and the clinical arenas. Through discussions of contextual influences on development, theoretical models have begun to make room for the role of culture and other sociocultural factors in child development. Nevertheless, most models have been defined too narrowly and applied to explicate successfully the processes by which these factors affect development. Therefore, these models do not constitute optimal frameworks with which to approach the development of children from diverse backgrounds.

As a response, more specific conceptual frameworks have been proposed to describe the strengths of diverse cultural populations and the mechanisms by which macrostructural forces and social stratification influence development (e.g., Boykin & Toms, 1985; García Coll, Thorne, Cooper, Scott-Jones, Eccles, & Nakashima, 1996; Harrison, Wilson, Pine, Chan, & Buriel, 1990; McLoyd, 1990b; Ogbu, 1981). These models address the developmental processes specific to such populations as children of color and to such contexts as poverty. Although these efforts have not yet brought about a paradigm shift, they have led scholars to several critical points of interpretation that are gaining increasing acceptance. Perhaps most important, it is now widely accepted that to gain a thorough understanding of a child's development, it is necessary to understand the child and family in relation to both the immediate and larger sociocultural environment. In addition to a child's immediate family, his or her neighborhoods, communities, and societal structures are considered worthy of examination. This has resulted in calls for more accurate and thorough information about the characteristics of study samples by such journals as *Child Development* and by federal funding agencies. Responding to these needs, Entwisle and Astone (1994) presented guidelines for collecting, determining, and reporting the ethnic and social category group membership of research participants. They argued that this information can lead to a better understanding of the role of demographic characteristics in children's development by making more studies comparable and able to contribute to aggregate knowledge.

Unfortunately, despite the calls to consider and report this type of social category information, the significance of such data has been better incorporated into theoretical work than into empirical research and clinical intervention. Consequently, significant obstacles remain in the process of distilling the role of culture and other sociocultural factors in child development. We are better able to discuss the role of culture, race, and ethnicity in the abstract than to make it a core or concrete part of our research or clinical practices.

When culture and ethnicity are operationalized as independent variables, the processes through which specific aspects operate are often left unexamined (Whiting, 1976). Consequently, even when culture is taken into account, it is often done so in no more than a perfunctory manner and is typically viewed as a monolithic, nominal, explanatory construct. That is, research is often designed in a manner such that when ethnicity or race is found to be correlated with a specific outcome, the research cannot adequately describe what aspect of being White, for example, accounts for the correlation. Furthermore, generalizations and descriptions are often made from informal observations or clinical experiences rather than from empirical data (Phinney, 1993). These approaches lead to overgeneralizations and to an emphasis on differences rather than on similarities, as well as a disregard for individual differences within groups (García Coll, 1990; McLoyd, 1990a). As such, these approaches leave many areas of influence unexplored, even if they advance our recognition of culture as an important influence on development. As Szapocnik and Kurtines (1993) noted, "If we are interested in studying cultural context, we have to study it as it really occurs, rather than as some idealized concept of indigenous culture" (p. 400). Similarly, Whiting (1976) called upon developmentalists to "unpackage" culture, that is, to consider it as a multidimensional, evolving source of influence that becomes operationalized through developmental processes and specific antecedent variables in any culture (Phinney, 1993; Segall, 1986). This admonishment to examine or tease apart aspects of culture has been a persistent theme throughout the literature dealing with cultural influences on development.

Another crucial obstacle in the process of understanding culture in child development is the way in which cultural differences in the United States are confounded with ethnicity, minority status, and poverty (Huston, McLoyd & García Coll, 1994). In other words, as we seek to understand cultural influences in the United States, we should be aware that this knowledge is specific to a larger sociocultural context that is often intolerant of diversity. In academic, policy, and clinical settings, conceptualizations of cultural differences for the most part reflect the stereotypes and prejudices that are dominant in our society. As an example, Slaughter-Defoe et al. (1990) argued that culture is invoked inconsistently and inaccurately as a causal mechanism when discussing the success or failure of Asian American and African American students in school. That is, the explanations that have been used to explain the successes of Asian American students have been very different from those used to explain the failures of African American students. The success of some Asian populations in school is attributed to their cultural values of hard work and familial duty, whereas the lack of school success of some African American students is attributed to father absence and a "culture-as-social-class" perspective.

Stereotypes and prejudices have real consequences for the socioeconomic status of some culturally different populations. In the United States, discriminatory practices have been more the norm than the exception and have contributed to the disproportionate overrepresentation of members of various cultural groups among the poor. This is most notably the case for children of color, who usually also represent culturally different populations.

However, even when the influences of such constructs as socioeconomic status are controlled through either the selection of a sample or the statistical technique used to address the confounding of "race," culture, ethnicity, and social class, researchers run the risk of using indices that are more or less valid or comparable between groups (Steinberg & Fletcher, 1998). Banks (1988) has argued that social scientists must also consider generational middle-class status as a variable when studying minority group subjects. Many African American study participants who are classified as middle class have achieved recent social mobility and consequently will exhibit significant behavioral differences caused by the persistence of social class effects. This notion is especially relevant for researchers engaging in cross-ethnic research. For example, a Black family that has recently reached middle class status is not comparable to a White family that has been established as middle class for several generations. A difference in outcomes and behaviors might also lead researchers to attribute outcome differences inaccurately to the participants' ethnic status because the ethnicity and generational social class variables are confounded.

This chapter addresses the role of culture, ethnicity, race, and minority status as distinct but also additive influences to developmental risks and resources. It is our position that these factors operate in conjunction and therefore require simultaneous consideration (García Coll et al., 1996). Furthermore, we contend that culture itself does not constitute a source of vulnerability or risk. Most parents of diverse cultural backgrounds act in what they perceive to be the best interest of their children, and most children develop appropriate competencies in most cultural settings. Nevertheless, cultural differences have become a source of vulnerability in the United States for various reasons, the most significant of which is that historically they have been conceptualized as a source of risk. To this end, governmental policies as well as research and clinical strategies have promoted the view that minority cultural differences are deficits within individual families that need to be remedied or fixed. In this chapter, we argue that in order for early intervention services to be successful for children and families from diverse backgrounds, these conceptualizations and policies must be reframed to take into account extant resources for children and families within these populations.

Another source of developmental risk is the result of cultural mismatch between service providers and clients. Differing cultural values and goals, as well as diverse communication and interaction styles, may influence the way in which development is understood and interventions are approached by both parents and professionals. Relevant culturally bound constructs might include the identification of a problem, beliefs about its causal roots, and the appropriate course of action (Groce & Zola, 1993).

When parents' conceptions of development differ from those of the intervention system, the cultural mismatch can constitute an additional source of risk, thus rendering services less effective for children of culturally different backgrounds. Again, reframing interventions to better suit parental goals and values, or working with parents to increase their understanding of our conventional intervention approaches, will transform these differences into assets on behalf of the child.

A final way in which culture can become a source of vulnerability emerges from the confound in the United States between diverse cultural backgrounds and minority status. The experience of being an ethnic minority within the U.S. culture is a source of risk to a child's development. Racism, discrimination, and diminished life opportunities related to segregation constitute a source of risk for children of color (McAdoo, 1981). Experiences of exclusion at various societal levels constitute insults to children's healthy social and cognitive development (Brookins, 1993). Again, recognition of the impacts of these forces on family life might be used to mobilize necessary resources to intervene within the family system on behalf of the children. This chapter examines the conceptualization of culture and other related sociocultural constructs, explores these three sources of vulnerability, and considers the necessary reframing of culture as a resource.

CONCEPTUAL CLARIFICATIONS

Culture is a complex construct that is often intertwined with the concepts of ethnicity and race, two overlapping terms that also require clarification. Culture refers to a distinct system of meaning or a cognitive schema that is shared by a group of people or an identifiable segment of the population (Betancourt & Lopez, 1993). These diverse meanings are learned, shared, and transmitted generationally within a population. Culture is given force by values and beliefs that are operationalized through daily interactions (Rogoff, 1990; Rogoff, Mistry, Goncu, & Mosier, 1993; Weisner, 1996). For example, in Puerto Rican culture, *respeto* (respect) for parents and family is highly valued. In research, this value has been found to be translated into differential patterns of play behavior between Puerto Rican

mothers and their infants. Harwood et al. (1997) and García Coll, Ramos, Magnuson, Halpern, and Valcarel (1997) have found that Puerto Rican mothers use more commanding and less questioning techniques than Anglo mothers. In this example, the cultural value of respect is part of the fabric of daily life in the earliest social interactions. Nevertheless, the implicit and procedural aspects of these culturally defined schemas often render them transparent to members of the cultural group. Ironically, the transparency of cultural schemas is often the source of their strength (Weisner, Metheson, & Bernheimer, 1996).

The family is recognized as the primary vehicle for the transmission of culture, serving to mediate cultural beliefs from one generation to the next (McCubbin et al., 1993). For the most part, children absorb and learn their cultural schemas from their parents and extended families. Families are a strong force in the transmission of culture in part because child rearing is so strongly organized by each culture. Aspects of cultural schemas that are particularly important to child developmental outcome, and therefore to early intervention, include the following: child-rearing beliefs and practices, conceptualizations about children's growth and development, definition and role of family members, and meaning of both parental and children's behavior. These all fall under the rubric of parental ethno-theories, cultural belief systems, and organized understandings that translate into daily routines, interaction patterns, and advice-seeking behaviors (Harkness & Super, 1996). For example, it is a part of ethno-theory in U.S. society that children should not be employed outside of the home and that their participation in housework should be limited. However, throughout history and in many other societies, children have been an important part of the family economic system and, as such, their participation within the household economy has been and remains a usual, acceptable, and often necessary occurrence.

Ethnicity, on the other hand, is typically used to describe a group defined by a common nationality, culture, or language. The term is often used to demarcate the affiliation of a group that is defined by a particular culture. Thus, ethnicity is a broad grouping to which members have a subjective sense of belonging (Phinney, 1993). However, ethnicity itself does not constitute culture, although it may be that affiliative ethnic interactions contribute to the transmission of culture (Betancourt & Lopez, 1993). That is, for a child who is ethnically a Russian Jew, interacting with other Russian Jews will inculcate Russian Jewish heritage. However, belonging to a Russian Jewish community will not necessarily lead a child to adopt the Russian Jewish culture. Even if ethnicity and culture are overlapping but distinctive sources of influence, when we address cultural differences in the United States we are often referring to values and behaviors displayed by different ethnic groups.

Ethnicity is also often mistakenly used interchangeably with "race." The term *race* is used in the United States to describe a group that typically is defined solely by its members' physical characteristics and phenotypical traits such as skin color, hair type, and other racially identified characteristics. Historically, racial classifications have been dominated in the United States by a black-and-white binary formula and steeped in a discourse and rhetoric of biological or cultural deficiency and superiority. This legacy has been maintained, even as it has been demonstrated that racial groups are more alike, both genetically and biologically, than they are different (Lewontin, 1982). Racial groups, which are artificially defined by physical traits, are highly heterogeneous. One source of heterogeneity within the United States is the large numbers of people who are of mixed race descent, yet still racially categorized as either White or Black. Historically, an individual's racial classification was based on the *one-drop rule*, which held that a person having "one drop" of Black blood was racially Black. Recently a movement to recognize and claim biracial heritage has emerged in a variety of public and political arenas, including the U.S. Census Bureau. Consequently, the viability of racial classifications is vehemently resisted, contested, and criticized as a social construction in need of revision and critical analysis (García Coll et al., 1996).

Given overwhelming similarities in the genetic constitution of "races," significant differences in development and in health status among different racial or ethnic groups should not be primarily determined biologically, although in some instances this can clearly be the case (Krieger, Avery, Rowley, Phillips, & Herman, 1993). Nevertheless, socially constructed racial groups have been forceful organizers of social systems in our society, as well as primary sources of resources, and consequently they must be considered critical influences on development. Thus, "race" might play an explanatory role in certain aspects of development, especially as it influences how children are perceived and reacted to by others, and how these interactions might in turn relate to their life chances (García Coll et al., 1996). We must acknowledge that a child whose appearance would have others perceive him as racially Black in a context where being Black is seen as deficient will have very different experiences growing up from a child whose appearance would lead others to perceive him as White, regardless of the child's actual or chosen ethnicity or "race." Kreiger and colleagues (1993) explained, "At issue is how health is influenced by injurious social divisions based on race and by cultural differences linked to ethnicity" (p. 85). They use the concept of racism rather than race as the central explanatory construct for understanding differential outcomes. Although the viability of genetically determined racial classifications is both resisted and contested, the social constructions associated with them persist as forceful influences on children's development.

Conceptual distinctions and a recognition of the powerful intersections among culture, ethnicity, and "race" are most important, given the increasing diversity of the U.S. population. In fact, minority populations, once easily identifiable numerically, can now be referred to collectively as an emerging majority. Differing birth rates among groups and increasing immigration from Asia and Latin America have contributed to an increase in the size of ethnically diverse populations, and within the next century, non-Hispanic Whites will be the minority of children within the United States. The family contexts of these ethnic populations are different from those of Euro-American families, and tend to be characterized by younger mothers, a higher percentage of single parents, and larger extended families (García Coll, 1990).

INDIVIDUAL DIFFERENCES AMONG MEMBERS OF A PARTICULAR CULTURE

Although ethnic/racial/minority groups residing within the United States might possess distinct cultural codes and family contexts, it is important to keep in mind that there are probably as many overlaps among cultural groups as there are differences. For example, we have argued elsewhere that developmental processes should be similar among different ethnic and cultural groups (García Coll et al., 1996) but that their particular expressions might differ given the different promoting and inhibiting environments to which they are exposed. Language acquisition, attachment to primary caregivers, and emergence of major emotional and cognitive systems are relevant processes in all populations. However, the particular language, the number of important attachment figures, and the expression of emotions and cognitive skills in particular contexts might differ.

Likewise, it is as important to recognize the differences between ethnic groups as it is to recognize the diversity within each group. As Phinney (1993) reminded us, it is not "clear whether particular individuals or samples actually reflect the culture they are thought to represent." As a matter of fact, cultures' and individuals' positioning on a cultural continuum are not static but highly variable and changing, depending on the contextual influences (McDermott & Varenne, 1995). A first-generation Mexican American child living in a Hispanic enclave might have a very different level of involvement in his or her culture than a fourth-generation Mexican American child living in a predominantly White community. This difference might be relevant to the assumptions that we make and the approach that we take in our work as researchers or clinicians.

Similarly, some differences that are labeled cultural might actually be better understood as adaptations to unique socioeconomic and historical contexts. As we have argued elsewhere, a delicate balance must be found between understanding the traditional child-rearing attitudes, values, and practices of a group and more recent adaptations to specific needs and circumstances (García Coll, Meyer, & Brillon, 1995). For example, families might differ in their investment in maintaining their traditional culture versus adopting more "modern" practices. The fact that their children speak their native language might be important for some, whereas for others being identified with a particular ethnic group through the use of interpreters might be repudiated.

Acculturation levels are just as important as sources of variability as are cultural differences (Phinney, 1996; Vasquez García et al., in press). Through examining acculturation levels, researchers and clinicians can begin to understand individuals' positioning within a culture or across various cultures. Acculturation is generally defined as the extent to which an individual has maintained a culture of origin versus adapted to the new society's culture. Instrument development in the area of acculturation has recently progressed from the use of single indicators (e.g., language use, place of birth, and so forth) to the measurement of multiple sociocultural characteristics (e.g., self-identification, language and social group preferences, and culturally defined behaviors and attitudes; Phinney, 1996). Multidimensional assessment instruments enable investigators to understand an individual's level of acculturation on an orthogonal continuum that encompasses both the addition of the new culture's values and behaviors as well as the persistence of the traditional culture's beliefs (García Coll et al., 1995).

Individuals and populations of different cultural backgrounds often vary in their decisions regarding which aspects of their traditional culture they maintain (if given a choice, which does not always happen) and which aspects of the new culture they acquire. A recent study of Latino adolescents (Vasquez García et al., in press) found that two strong values of traditional family systems (respect and familism) were upheld differentially by adolescents in comparison to their parents. Both groups were high on familism (i.e., they considered family obligations and ties as very important), although only parents considered respect as important in their interactions with others, whereas their children held more egalitarian views. Consequently, it is important to assess the extent to which a particular family and child have become acculturated to the dominant culture.

It is even more crucial to recognize that different members of a family might be at different levels of acculturation. That is, as children grow up and are exposed to more varied institutions of the dominant society, it is quite possible that their level of acculturation might vary significantly from that of other family members. Similarly, as employment opportunities and differential contacts with the mainstream culture differ by gender and age, adult family members might be at different levels of acculturation.

This acculturation dissonance can be a source of strain on family functioning, program participation, and adherence to interventions (Szapocnik, Kurtines, & Fernandez, 1980).

One particularly important aspect of assessment might be the extent to which a family has accepted or adopted the dominant culture's perspective on child development. For example, Gutierrez, Sameroff, and Karrer (1988) have pointed out that both socioeconomic status and acculturative levels influence Mexican American mothers' concepts of development. Using a questionnaire to examine differences in parental reasoning, these investigators sorted mothers into three conceptual levels ranging from perspectivistic to categorical. At one extreme, *perspectivistic* mothers conceptualize child development as multidetermined and look at a particular outcome or behavior as potentially having a variety of causal factors. In contrast, mothers at the *categorical* level reason from a single determinant to a single outcome, seeing few if any variations in cause. Controlling for socioeconomic status, Gutierrez, Sameroff, and Karrer (1988) found that mothers who were more acculturated were more perspectivistic than those who were less acculturated. This work underscores the importance of looking at the acculturative levels of the individuals being served rather than considering ethnicity and culture as a discrete or homogeneous category.

The call to consider cultural and ethnic influences on child development and behavior does not suggest that these constructs constitute the sole or even primary source of variability in parenting or family functioning. In contrast, culture interacts with many other contextual and individual level characteristics. For example, Laosa's (1978, 1980) research with Chicana mothers indicated that child-rearing techniques are related not only to cultural background but also to formal education. Arguing that formal education is a noncultural change that might contribute to behavioral changes, Laosa (1980) examined the teaching strategies used by Anglo and Chicana mothers with their young children. Although Chicana mothers as a group historically have completed fewer years of school, this study afforded an opportunity to examine whether differences in teaching techniques between Chicana and Anglo mothers "would persist or disappear as a result of social change toward educational and socioeconomic

equality" (p. 760). The findings demonstrated that Anglo mothers most frequently used praise, whereas Chicana mothers most often used modeling and visual cues to teach their children. When the mothers' formal level of education was held constant, however, this variation disappeared.

The increasingly diverse cultural mosaic of ethnic groups in the United States, and their respective place in the racial spectrum, are pushing researchers and service providers to understand the complexity of child development as it is influenced by both individual and sociocultural forces. In this regard, universal assumptions and generalizations are no longer serving scientific, explanatory, or clinical purposes. Consequently, it is crucial to take into consideration not just the child's ethnic, racial, or cultural group but also the child's and family's level of acculturation within the dominant mainstream society.

HISTORICAL CONSTRUCTION OF CULTURE AS A RISK FACTOR

Historically, developmental research and its clinical applications in the United States have considered the child-rearing values, attitudes, practices, and norms of the dominant White, Anglo-Saxon middle-class culture to be optimal for child development (García Coll & Meyer, 1993). These parenting and developmental characteristics have served as the yardstick against which all populations are compared and contrasted (Patterson & Blum, 1993). Parents from diverse backgrounds have been urged to adopt these characteristics of parenting and have been admonished when their children's development has not mirrored that of White, Anglo, middle-class children.

Using Anglo middle-class behaviors as the normative standard has been a disservice to both scientific inquiry and to the interests of populations of color on several counts. Bronfenbrenner (1985) argued that when minority groups are compared to majority groups, they are most typically judged as inferior. Thus, the classification of cultural differences as deviance has dominated most of the child development literature (Thomas, 1992), despite the fact that what is considered normative parenting and development for White, Anglo, middle-class populations has changed over time (Young, 1990). As Patterson and Blum (1993) noted, "The continuing prevalence of racism in our society has contributed to equating difference with deviance" (p. 1025).

Through the process of comparing and contrasting diverse populations with Anglo experiences, minority populations' child rearing has generally been found to be inadequate and in need of remedial services. A striking example of this phenomenon was the term *cultural deprivation*, which was used in the 1960s to describe "disadvantaged" populations. For example, Bloom, Davis, and Hess (1964) traced the roots of disadvantaged children to "their experiences in their homes that do not transmit the cultural patterns necessary" for success in mainstream institutions (p. 3). This view of "deviance or deprivation," in turn, contributed to the conceptualization of minority families as a social problem in need of correction and requiring further scholarly attention (Slaughter & McWorter, 1985).

The continuing problematization of minority families has served to perpetuate researchers' fixation on documenting and understanding the deviant behaviors of ethnic minority groups to the exclusion of studying their normative behavior. Thus, Barbarin (1993) found that most research on African American and Latino school-age children focused on aggression, delinquency, attention deficits, and hyperactivity. The desire to understand the "deviance" of populations of color has both skewed and limited our knowledge base concerning the adaptive development. Graham (1992) has proposed that "it is not clear at all that we have achieved a better understanding of the intellectual potential of black children and their repertoires of adaptive social behaviors while relying on empirical literatures that simply chart their gains and losses relative to those of a white comparison group." Barbarin, like Graham, found that research has not informed such areas as normative emotional development and resiliency. Normative studies of Native American and Asian children are largely unavailable (García Coll, 1990).

The approach of most researchers to foreign-born or recent immigrant populations has been no more insightful than their approach to native-born minorities. The immigration and acculturation experience has been conceptualized and researched largely as a stressful experience with profound negative consequences. Studies have been concerned with documenting and understanding the maladjustment of immigrant children through such measurable indicators as behavioral or psychiatric disorders (García Coll & Magnuson, 1996; Koplow & Messinger, 1990). Immigrant children have been characterized as caught between their parents' traditional culture and that of the new society, belonging to neither. The adaptability of children and the benefits that might be accrued from either balanced bilingualism or biculturalism are often overshadowed by the assumed difficulties and negative consequences of negotiating two different languages or cultures.

The assumed inferiority of ethnic minority parents has perpetuated the notion that their children have an impairment that could be corrected through resocialization and compensatory programs (Bronfenbrenner, 1985; García Coll & Magnuson, 1996). During President Johnson's War on Poverty in the 1960s, new intervention programs were created to address the "deficiencies" of low-income populations, that were disproportionately populations of color. These remedial and compensatory programs reflected two strategies: first, early childhood education and then, somewhat later, parenting education classes. These programs differed in their approach but shared the assumption that the relatively poor performance of low-income children (who were most often children of color) could be attributed to their parents' patterns of child rearing and their failure to provide the experiences necessary for optimal achievement, whether it was teaching a child a social skill, such as sitting still for a long time, or an academic skill, such as knowledge of numbers and letters (Laosa, 1984; Siegal, 1983). Thus, early childhood education programs were designed to provide disadvantaged children with direct supplemental experiences.

Parenting education classes evolved as a response to disappointing results from early childhood education programs and were constructed as a more fundamental type of intervention (Florin & Dokeki, 1983). These classes attempted to teach mothers how to provide developmentally enhancing experiences for their young children. Consequently, the classes sought to modify the ways in which low-income and minority-population parents interacted with their children, encouraging them to act more like White, Anglo, middle-class parents (García Coll & Magnuson, 1999b).

The effort to resocialize ethnic minorities has been most blatant for immigrant populations, although these efforts have been formulated differently from traditional early childhood education or parenting classes. Throughout its history, U.S. society has promoted an assimilationist ideology that has sought to minimize individual and group-level differences between recent immigrants and the native born population. This melting-pot ideology has asked wave after wave of immigrants to discard the ways of their homelands, to homogenize, and to adopt White, Anglo, middle-class ideals and values. This push for "Americanization" has operated through such policies as refugee relocation programs and English as a Second Language (ESL) education programs (García Coll & Magnuson, 1999b).

In summary, any discussion of culture as a source of vulnerability (and resources) must be understood against this historical backdrop. Both conventional ideology and scientific inquiry have explicitly and implicitly conceptualized cultural difference as a fundamental source of vulnerability in children. Consequently, ethnic and minority parenting practices, values, and beliefs have been viewed as a source of developmental risk. These conceptualizations have often driven intervention efforts to resocialize culturally different children by providing them with compensatory experiences. In contrast, rather than seeing cultural differences as inherently deficient, child vulnerability could be viewed as a consequence of cultural mismatch and the burden of minority status. Clearly, alternative modes of intervention would then become more appropriate as a product of this reframing.

CULTURAL MISMATCH AS A SOURCE OF RISK

How do parents know when their children might need more help than they can provide for them? How do they come to recognize that they should seek out the assistance of a professional for evaluation and possible treatment? How do they choose the best intervention when presented with many options? These are difficult questions that few parents are completely prepared to answer. When a parent has a perception of normative development that is incongruent with that of the broader society and its service providers, this begins to constitute a source of developmental risk that we call "cultural mismatch."

Culture as a schema and a source of values shapes definitions of what behaviors and symptoms merit intervention. It also molds beliefs about the causal root of a "problem" and about what course of action should be taken (García Coll & Meyer, 1993; Groce & Zola, 1993). A marker of risk, delay, or disability in one culture may or may not be recognized as meriting intervention in another. We know about what behavior is developmentally appropriate only because we have a wealth of information provided by the surrounding community. Therefore, the culture of our collective communities defines what is disabled, delayed, and nonnormative in contrast to what is abled, advanced, and normative. As described by McDermott and Varenne (1995), culture provides us with the guidelines to notice, identify, and make consequential both the contextual and developmental differences of others. These differences, as prescribed by our culture, then become the root from which we either enable or disable individuals and judge them to be at risk or not. McDermott and Varenne noted, "For every skill that people gain, there is another that is not developed; for every focus of attention, something is passed by; for every specialty a corresponding lack . . . . Perceptions of ability organize perceptions of disability" (p. 331).

The parameters that are used to identify problems or potential difficulties are culturally bound and constructed by a nation's history, legal system, and social structure (Groce & Zola, 1993). In the past, U.S. society has utilized the dominant Anglo culture to define what is developmentally appropriate and to determine what behaviors and circumstances are worthy of intervention (Weiss, 1993). Thus, professional service providers within the United States have preconceived notions of what constitutes the normative processes of development and which contexts pose a risk to development. These notions are often not explicit nor are they well communicated to parents. Furthermore, these parameters are most often described and supported by scientific inquiries that follow a biomedical approach to development and health that may not be endorsed by all cultural groups (Kraut, 1990). Consequently, when parents and families of diverse cultural backgrounds raise children within the United States, the mismatch between the families' perspective and the existing early intervention system might create an additional source of risk to the child's development.

Recent laws guiding our intervention system for children who are developmentally delayed or at risk for disabilities have recognized the importance of cultural influences (Meisels and Shonkoff, this volume), and the mandate to tailor intervention efforts to families' needs (i.e., a family-centered approach to intervention) reflects this understanding. Thus, an *individualized family service plan* (IFSP) that is based on a family's strengths and weaknesses and that helps a family gain access to services across multiple agencies must take into account the family's cultural background as it influences and organizes the family's functioning (García Coll & Meyer, 1993). This is viewed as important both for the design of more effective care and to increase the likelihood of better adherence to a plan of treatment.

Keeping the potential dangers of cultural mismatch in mind, it is important for developmental assessments not only to gain an accurate evaluation of a child's abilities and skills but also to assess the family's perspective on why the child is being referred for services. For example, Widmayer et al. (1990, 1992) found that Haitian parents living in Florida did not think of infants as being able to respond to language or to be cognitively capable. Consequently, the Haitian mothers spoke to their children predominantly in order to discipline them rather than to stimulate their language. In an assessment of the children's development, the quality of parent–child interactions, as measured by the HOME score, predicted cognitive performance, as indicated by the Bayley Scales of Infant Development (BSID). In this study, the Haitian mothers' perceptions of their young children's limited cognitive potential reduced their interactions with their children and affected their development adversely, as measured by the BSID. When a service provider or clinician brings alternative expectations for the child's cognitive development, these differences in beliefs influence the ways each would identify or approach the developmentally delayed child.

If a child's family perceives a problem, it is crucial to establish agreement between the family and service provider on the scope or severity of the concern. Even if the family first identifies the problem, they might not consider it worthy of immediate attention or formal intervention. In contrast, it is also possible that a family might identify a child problem and seek help in circumstances that service providers do not consider problematic (García Coll & Meyer, 1993). It has been observed, for example, among Hispanic families that the lack of prescription medication for a physical ailment denotes "bad" medical treatment. Some families will continue to seek out different health providers (including alternative non-Western ones) until a medication is prescribed.

Cultural differences can also emerge within the context of interactions and relationships with service providers. These issues may go beyond communication or language barriers, although these too can be significant sources of difficulty (Harwood, 1981; Hoang & Erickson, 1985). For example, in many cultures parents are not the sole decision makers for their children. In some cases, a member of the extended family, such as the grandfather, might be the ultimate authority. Alternatively, the decision-making process might involve the entire family, based on the best interests of the family unit rather than on those of the individual child. Likewise, some cultures have a strict gender hierarchy that makes service delivery dependent on the support, approval, and involvement of the male head of household. Trying to secure approval or information from the mother, rather than both parents or the father, may prove much more difficult in such circumstances (García Coll & Meyer, 1993). Thus, adherence to an early intervention plan might not be maintained if other family members are excluded from the decision-making process.

Interactive patterns also might be affected by families' perceptions of the service provider's social status. For example, in some Asian cultures, doctors are highly honored and respected; therefore, Asians are often deferential to their health-care providers (Hoang & Erickson, 1985). Thus, members of an Asian family might be uncomfortable sharing information that they think might be met with disapproval by professional service providers. Hmong parents have been characterized as shy, leery, and likely to answer service providers in a way that they feel will please them (Faller, 1985). Similarly, Mexican Americans and Puerto Ricans may expect their service providers to display *respeto* and *personalismo* as well as to spend a considerable amount of time speaking with them. These cultural expectations can stand in stark contrast to some North Americans' expectations for their service providers to assume a professional role that is characterized by an honest, candid, impersonal, and detached approach (García Coll & Magnuson, 1996).

Even when families recognize a developmental delay or a need for intervention, they will not necessarily agree on the cause of the problem or the degree to which a child's developmental outcome might be modified (Gutierrez & Sameroff, 1990). When a family is faced with the stress of a child who is displaying a problem, turning to familiar cultural or religious resources might provide comfort and order in an otherwise mystifying and chaotic process (Comeroff & McQuire, 1981). Consequently, parents may develop a different perception of the etiology of the problem and a different understanding of how (if at all) the course of their child's development may be altered or improved (Korbin & Johnston, 1982).

Families' explanatory models may vary considerably, depending on their sociocultural background and the extent to which they have adopted Western perspectives on child development. A study of Haitian American and Cuban American mothers found that the two groups had different understanding of the etiology of illnesses that affect infants and preschoolers (DeSantis, 1989). The Cuban sample had a Westernized biomedical approach to early childhood diseases and their causes, and they most frequently cited visiting physicians and giving prescribed medications as the appropriate treatment. In contrast, Haitian mothers did not identify disease or its causes with biomedical terminology. Rather, they described illnesses as caused by external circumstances, such as bad air, dirty objects, or a spell. For example, one mother reported that diarrhea was caused by swallowing saliva during teething. Although the Haitian mothers also reported taking their child to a physician for treatment, this was indicated less often than it was by the Cuban mothers. Haitian mothers also listed home remedies more frequently and were more likely to take their child to a traditional healer. Their choices of treatment were based on their understanding of the causes of the illnesses, and over half did not think the conditions they mentioned were preventable (DeSantis, 1989).

Some traditional cultures espouse supernatural explanations of problems. Members of these cultures attribute their conditions to the influence of gods, malevolent spirits, and spells. Similarly, some cultures interpret problems as retribution for wrongdoing, either for their own or their ancestors' behavior.

It is also possible, in such circumstances, that families may consider a child's difficulties as fated. In these instances, intervention is often disregarded because it is considered futile.

Another culturally prevalent conceptualization of developmental difficulties attributes problems to an imbalance of "hot and cold." Although often framed in corporeal terms, this notion of hot and cold incorporates little of the physiological concerns of North American biomedical science. It refers instead to an imbalance of a natural order between hot and cold elements in the universe (Hoang & Erickson, 1985). All of these ethno-theories of disease and treatment need to be taken into account when services are sought or considered necessary.

Finally, even if a family and service provider agree on the existence and nature of a problem, they might differ on the decision about what course of action to take, as well as on the process by which that course of action is decided (García Coll & Meyer, 1993). These differences are often linked closely to the families' beliefs about the etiology of the problem, as well as to their expectations about the purpose of the intervention. If the family has a supernatural understanding of the problem, it is unlikely that they will seek a biomedical approach for treatment and more likely that they will accept their child's difficulty as fated. Furthermore, when clients' expectations are not met, they continue to seek alternative treatments. For example, Scott (1974) described a Puerto Rican mother who took her child to a physician yet would not accept the prescribed pills because she believed that the child needed an injection to be cured, and continued to visit multiple clinics until her child was given a shot.

No matter how long a family has lived in the United States, many continue to use traditional folk medicines and home remedies. These can range from serving as the primary source of treatment to a complementary one (Scott, 1974), and practices range from intensive herbal treatments to dietary restrictions to topical treatments. It also is possible that a family will seek both traditional treatment and mainstream Western intervention, relying on the former to treat the cause of the problem and the latter to treat the symptoms. If clients sense disapproval from service providers about their use of traditional folk treatment, it is quite possible that they will withhold information about its use (Korbin &

Johnston, 1982). The effectiveness or danger associated with these treatments is unclear. Scott (1974) concluded that "these beliefs although perhaps running counter to the scientific medical systems, have survived in these populations for generations and may indeed be measurably effective" (p. 531). Similarly, Stafford (1978) suggested that when families are strongly committed to folk practices, service providers will be more effective if they accept or incorporate the family's belief system into their course of treatment, including the use of traditional treatments as long as they are not harmful.

Finally, service providers who must rely on parents to participate actively in the intervention must take into account the probability that parents might not expect a change in their daily routines to be part of the treatment (García Coll & Meyer, 1993). Although parents may accept that their child needs an intervention, they might not necessarily agree that their own behavior should be modified. This resistance to changing one's own behavior, whether it be an interaction pattern or family diet, may be a significant barrier to effective service delivery. Furthermore, families often have varying access to formal and informal support networks, and the responsibilities for an intervention effort within support networks might also be disparate. In some families, grandparents and relatives play an essential role in the caretaking of the children, whereas in other families this is not the case. Likewise, the involvement of both mothers and fathers in single-parent families can vary greatly. Consequently, service providers may be unable to make accurate assumptions about the importance of the responsibilities, or strict role definition of family members or support givers, and must endeavor to use the information available about the family's functioning to create an effective and acceptable intervention plan (García Coll & Meyer, 1993).

In summary, three key issues must be considered when providing intervention for a family from a different culture: 1) whether the family believes that a problem exists, 2) what the family beliefs are about the cause of the problem, and 3) what different family members think about the course of action that should be taken. In service provision settings, families' explanatory models must not only be elicited but must be taken into account and respected. Parents and other significant family members, such as health-care and intervention brokers for their children, play a crucial role in supporting their development. Although service providers may have difficulty trusting the judgment of parents and other important caregivers, the design of an intervention that respects their explanatory model will in turn provide a course of treatment that is more likely to be accepted and consequently to facilitate the intervention effort.

MINORITY STATUS AS A SOURCE OF RISK

What is the cost to the development of a child who is teased or even hit or kicked by other children in school because he or she has darker skin, slanted eyes, or an accent? What is the cost of coming to know that people of your cultural background are considered dumb, no good, ugly, or lazy? What is the cost of growing up in a neighborhood that is predominantly non-Anglo and poor? What is the cost of thinking that your teachers do not care if you learn and do not expect you to succeed because of your cultural background? What is the cost of consistently fighting stereotypes and prejudices that are saturated with negative images and demeaning conceptualizations of the culturally different? What are the costs associated with these experiences to an individual's health, well-being, and developmental outcome. What are the benefits, if any?

Although cultural differences are conceptually distinct from minority status, the two circumstances are often confounded in U.S. society. Consequently, when discussing culture as a source of risk, it is also necessary to remember that minority status is a related but distinct source of vulnerability for children from diverse cultural backgrounds.

The racism that pervades society in the United States, although often perceived as a Black-and-White dichotomy, is manifested in many different ways. In recent years, some research has found that prejudicial and stereotypic attitudes toward minority populations, and particularly toward Blacks, have been diminishing (Dovidio & Gaertner, 1991; for a discussion of this work, see Devine & Elliot, 1995). However, another body of work posits that a more covert and subtle form of racism persists (Devine & Elliot, 1995). Thus, the stereotypes held about Blacks in the United States may have changed in nature rather than diminished. Furthermore, this modern racism allows, and in fact requires, Americans to rationalize prejudicial behavior in nonracial terms (McConahay, 1983; McConahay, Hardee, & Batts, 1981). For example, discriminatory hiring practices that were once openly attributed to a potential employee's race now continue, but employers no longer use an applicant's race as a justification for their decisions. Consequently, although prejudicial attitudes may be expressed directly less often, this does not signify a decrease in discriminatory practices but rather a shift toward a more covert and subtle form of racism.

There are several ways in which racism and discrimination can become consequential in the lives of families and children. In an integrative model for the study of developmental competencies in minority children we have postulated that three types of segregation are central to understanding a family's and child's ongoing transactions with the environment: residential, economic, and social–psychological (García Coll et al., 1996). In each circumstance, segregation refers to the systematic separation of groups and individuals on the basis of attributions made about their social position. Although no longer legitimized by law, separation and segregation remain pervasive and ongoing aspects of life in the United States.

Most research on segregation has focused on the first two types. Residential segregation is an inhibiting and limiting factor to the extent that the location of a family's residence has a direct and constraining effect on the resources (e.g., health care, employment, and so forth) available to the population that lives within the area. In the United States, one of the most important resources allocated by residence is public education. Although the 1954 Supreme Court decision in *Brown v. Board of Education* legally required school districts to desegregate, many public schools remain highly segregated to this day. Furthermore, the higher concentration of populations of color relative to Whites who live in impoverished neighborhoods suggests that children of color are more likely to live in dangerous communities and be exposed to violence, inadequate housing, and other environmental health risks such as lead (Krieger et al., 1993).

Economic segregation, perpetuated by the persistence of employment discrimination in both salary levels and hiring practices, has contributed to the

disadvantage experienced by minority populations. Although a full discussion of the impact of poverty on children is beyond the scope of this chapter, it is important to note that children of color from diverse cultural backgrounds are disproportionately represented among the poor and are more likely than White children to face persistent poverty (Huston, McLoyd, & García Coll, 1994).

In comparison to work on residential and economic segregation, little research has addressed developmentally related aspects of segregation or ways in which the psychological inputs of racism overlap with those of other sources of oppression, such as sexism (Kreiger et al., 1993). One issue that has been suggested as potentially demonstrative has been the higher rate of infant mortality among African Americans. The main contributing factors to this higher rate are high incidence of preterm delivery, low birth weight, and frequency of postnatal mortality among normal birth weight babies. Even among better educated and financially secure African American women who have ready access to the health care system, infant mortality rates associated with preterm delivery and low birth weight remain high. Consequently, some researchers have suggested that environmental stressors associated with being African American might provide a causal mechanism. Rowley (1990) argued that experiences with racism and its associated coping mechanisms might involve physiological responses to environmental stresses that occur before, during, and after pregnancy and that might affect the process of pregnancy adversely and thus influence the mother's and child's subsequent health (Rowley, 1990).

Social and psychological segregation also occur when families and children of color are not permitted access to important social and emotional resources as a result of social stratification mechanisms. Such social and emotional isolation among groups only serves to widen the gap between them. As the emotional intensity of discord between groups escalates, their separation increases, fostering feelings of distrust and fear (García Coll et al., 1996; Harry, 1992).

All of these sources of segregation, and the experiences of discrimination associated with them, not only place the child at risk but can also contribute to significant mistrust among populations of diverse cultural backgrounds. In the early 1980s, Terrell and

Terrell (1981) coined the term *cultural mistrust* to describe the feelings of Blacks toward Whites, and developed the Cultural Mistrust Inventory to measure the specific characteristics of Black individuals in three different settings: educational, interpersonal, and social. This mistrust is thought to develop in response to experiences with discrimination and prejudice. It has been argued that even in the absence of direct individual experiences with discrimination, an African American family might facilitate the development of mistrust by giving definitional information, parameters, and cautions of what it means to be Black in a White society (Biafora, Taylor, Warheit, Zimmerman, & Vega, 1993).

In an early intervention setting, parents' previous experiences with racism might contribute to a certain amount of distrust toward mainstream professionals, thereby rendering their interactions much more difficult. Levy (1985) argued that Blacks do not know how they will be received by Whites in new situations and that their "past experiences of humiliation and discrimination produce feelings of anxiety and resentment" (p. 639). Consequently, some Black individuals become convinced that experiences with White institutions most often end in frustration and have learned to anticipate poor treatment and poor results from their interactions with White Americans. Similarly, Kraut (1990) asserted that foreign-born patients are separated from American physicians by complex cultural differences that often "lead to misunderstandings on one side, intimidation on the other and deep frustration on both" (Kraut, 1990, p. 1807). This inclination toward mistrust of individuals from different cultural backgrounds can clearly have a negative effect on an individual parent's relationship with early intervention programs and providers.

Most studies in this area have been conducted with African American Blacks; little research has determined whether a comparable level of mistrust is present among more recent immigrant populations from Asia or Latin America, as well as in other native populations of color such as Native Americans. Theorists who acknowledge the existence of a minority or castelike experience in the United States (e.g., Boykin & Toms, 1985; Ogbu, 1981) would perhaps argue that there is a clear, direct translation of these patterns of behavior across minority groups. However, it has also been suggested that the variety

of contexts that minority populations experience indicate that we should be cautious about generalizing from one population to another. Even under similar circumstances, it is possible for one individual to perceive treatment as discriminatory while another might not. Thus, the relationship between minority status and cultural mistrust is complex (García Coll & Magnuson, 1996).

Finally, undocumented immigrant populations might have a clear and immediate reason to avoid intervention services, and their fear of deportation might even keep them from seeking necessary medical care. Research with Haitian immigrants in Miami has found that many pregnant women arrive to give birth at the hospital without having seen a doctor during the course of their pregnancy (Widmayer et al., 1992). Illegal immigrant Mexican mothers in San Diego were also found to seek out prenatal care much later and much less often than legal immigrants (Chavez, Cornelius, & Jones, 1986), leading to an increase in infant mortality and serious complications in childbirth. This pattern of behavior is based on the fear that service providers will not only refuse to help them but will also turn them over to immigration authorities.

In short, minority status, though encompassing many ethnicities, can serve as a common source of developmental risk across groups. Minority status segregates many families of color in living conditions that may create high-risk conditions for their children's development. Experiences within a racist and discriminatory society operationalized through both interpersonal and structural interactions may also constitute unique sources of vulnerability for minority populations. Although insufficient research and attention have been devoted to understanding the impacts of these macrolevel influences, some lines of investigation indicate that in order to understand the development of children of color more fully, increased attention must be focused on the processes by which minority status becomes a risk factor in their lives.

CULTURE AS A DEVELOPMENTAL RESOURCE

We present culture as a resource because it is our contention that this is often not considered. We rarely think about how parents from a culturally different background promote their child's development or how it might be to a child's detriment if he or she is raised incongruently to his or her parents' cultural background. Stated simply, culture, as it serves to delineate the social context in which children develop, can be a growth-promoting influence.

Levine (1977) has provided a useful framework for understanding the development of caregiving environments in different cultures. He posited that child-rearing techniques depend to a certain extent on the nature of the instrumental competencies that individuals are expected to master in a given culture. Thus, adults try either consciously or unconsciously to inculcate the cognitive, linguistic, motivational, and social competencies that are deemed relevant to their cultural milieu. Levine also suggested that parental care reflects the opportunities as well as the hazards of their historically constructed environments and represents a compromise that has been reached in the pursuit of multiple goals.

Within this framework, Levine gave credence to the notion of a universal hierarchy of parental goals delineated as follows:

1. the physical survival of the child;
2. the development of the child's behavioral capacity for economic self-maintenance in maturity; and
3. the development of the child's behavioral capacity for maximizing other cultural values (e.g., morality).

The hierarchical structure of the goals indicates that if the first goal of parenting (i.e., the health or survival of the child) is threatened, parents will concentrate their efforts in this direction, because subsequent objectives can only follow the achievement of the primary goal. The goals are also structured by a developmental sequence. In the first year of an infant's life, physical survival and health are of the greatest concern. This model suggests that populations that inhabit varying environmental niches or that have differing economic resources may have different goals. Levine (1988) referred to child-rearing goals as parental investment strategies for allocating time, attention, and domestic resources. Furthermore, he argued that each type of human socioeconomic adaptation (e.g., agricultural, industrial, etc.) is assumed to have an optimal strategy that reflects its specific incentives and hazards. For example, in the United States considerable emphasis is placed on developing skills and traits in children that will

lead to financial success in a technologically advanced marketplace. Consequently, our educational systems promote such cognitive skills as memory recall and reasoning and such personality characteristics as independence and competitiveness. These values clearly differ from the skills needed for success in a traditional agricultural society. In either situation, the skills of one society would be less valuable in another.

The underlying premise of Levine's framework is that, regardless of the specific techniques employed, most parenting practices are designed to be beneficial to children. For example, in Africa the physical mobility of walking infants is often restricted as an adaptation to the hazards of open fires for cooking (Levine, 1977). In North America, on the other hand, we value freedom of action and mobility, and playpens are now considered too restrictive because it is argued that children should be allowed to navigate their surroundings so that they will be more stimulated through exploration. In both situations, values and goals that are determined to be beneficial to children are translated into specific practices that support the attainment of that goal (García Coll & Meyer, 1993).

Although this type of contrast in child-rearing goals is clear when examining another nation's culture, some empirical work is emerging that looks at Black populations' parenting practices in the United States within a similar framework. Ogbu's (1981) research echoes that of Levine and provides a broad framework that brings contextual factors explicitly into our understanding of development. Ogbu argued that a society's effective environment, those aspects of the environment that directly affect subsistence quests and protection from physical violence, shapes its child-rearing behaviors. Thus, much like Levine's framework, he suggested that parents inculcate and that children acquire instrumental competencies that are determined by the context in which they develop. In applying this framework to inner-city ghettoes in the United States, Ogbu claimed that

the marginal participation of ghetto residents in the conventional economy and their participation in the street economy affect the way in which they organize their child rearing . . . ghetto blacks indeed acquire different rules of behavior for achievement and related competencies because such is a requirement for their cultural/subsistence tasks and not merely because ghetto parents lack white middle class capability in child rearing (pp. 424–5).

The conclusion is that a Black child raised by middle-class White parenting strategies would have a difficult time surviving and succeeding in his or her neighborhood.

Jarrett (1996) discussed the way in which low-income African American parents living in dangerous neighborhoods restrict the activities of their children in a manner that generally is inconsistent with most mainstream middle-class parents' notions of appropriate parenting. In fact, inner-city parents often go to great lengths to confine their children to the immediate household and forbid them from going outside during their nonschool time for any reason, especially to play. However, this imposed isolation can be promoted in a more subtle manner and accompanied by family chaperoning. In such instances, parents may selectively discourage their children from being friends with "bad kids" or they may accompany them on their activities throughout the neighborhood (Jarrett, 1996). These protective strategies allow parents to control their children's exposure to dangerous neighborhood influences.

Deater-Deckard, Dodge, Bates, and Petit (1996) examined the relations between harsh parental control and such child-externalizing behaviors as hostility and aggression. In previous theories and empirical research, parents' use of physical discipline was linked to children's aggression, and, over time, coercive parent–child transactions were thought to lead to externalizing behavior problems (Maccoby & Martin, 1983). Yet, the preponderance of this research has been carried out with middle-class European-American families. In contrast, Deater-Deckard et al. (1996) looked at harsh parenting correlates and the development of preschool children in a four-year study of both African American and Euro-American families. They found that the harshness of physical discipline (in the nonabusive range) was associated with higher externalizing problems as rated by peers and teachers in the sample of Euro-American children, but their researchers found no association between harsh

discipline and externalizing behavior problems in the African American sample. In fact, the trend showed that harsh parenting for African American children was related to lower externalizing behaviors and aggression, suggesting that children across ethnic and cultural groups might have differing interpretations of their parents' behaviors and that African American children in particular may not interpret their parents' strict discipline as a lack of warmth or concern. This study demonstrates that what might contribute to negative outcomes in one cultural or ethnic group of parents and children might have a different impact in another group. Consequently, what we designate as "wrong" in one population might actually be "right" and to the benefit of children in another cultural milieu.

Just as most parents engage in behaviors that they think will benefit their children, most children demonstrate remarkable consistency in some areas of development. Even given the wide variation in context and the instrumental competencies defined by mainstream U.S. culture, most children acquire the skills they need to be effective members of their cultural group. These competencies encompass cognitive, communicative, and social skills. For example, although children may be exposed to multiple caregivers, most infants form primary attachments and the quality of these attachments is predictive of the quality of subsequent interactions between the children and other adults and peers (Bretherton & Waters, 1985). In other words, despite the wide variety in cultural backgrounds and subsequent parenting strategies, most families are competent at raising children and most children develop into competent members of their society.

Some aspects of development may vary in timing, content, or expression, depending on the cultural context. For example, studies by cross-cultural psychologists point out the ways in which memory and cognitive skills may be culturally determined by the contexts of elicitation and practice (Rogoff & Morelli, 1989). Schooling, in particular, has been found to be related to many cognitive activities such as memory, logical reasoning, and classification. For example, classifying lists of unrelated objects may be an unusual activity outside of literate school-related activities (Rogoff & Waddell, 1982), and participants might perform poorly on such classification tasks if they have not had formal schooling experiences (Rogoff & Morelli, 1989). Similarly, work by Mistry and Rogoff (1994) and Greenfield and Lave (1982) demonstrated that a participant's performance on memory skill tasks may reflect the way in which the task has been constructed rather than the ability of the individual. If the stimuli and situation presented in a memory task are familiar to the child, his or her performance will be better than if the subject or situation constructed in the task is unknown. This literature has informed us that the role of the cultural environment is to facilitate the development of specific cognitive skills and to determine the application of these skills to particular contexts and not others, rather than to promote the development and use of abstract, context-free cognitive abilities (Rogoff & Morelli, 1989).

The increasing number of ethnic minority and immigrant children in the United States highlights the fact that many children are members of more than one cultural group. Although the experience of navigating two cultural and possibly two linguistic systems is often conceptualized as a barrier or obstacle to a child's healthy development, the potential benefits of this experience have been documented. For example, balanced bilingualism may promote cognitive growth by contributing to a metalinguistic awareness and language proficiency in children (for a review, see Diaz 1985; Diaz & Klinger, 1991). In addition, Ramirez (1983) has argued that individuals with bicultural competencies have a greater adaptability and flexibility of coping and enhanced ability to relate and empathize with a variety of people from different backgrounds. LaFromboise, Coleman, and Gerton (1993) have provided a useful review of the literature on the psychological impact of biculturalism.

In summary, regardless of the child-rearing techniques employed, most practices are considered by parents to be beneficial to their children. Likewise, most children, despite wide variations in child-rearing environments, demonstrate remarkable consistency in some areas of development, whereas others may vary in timing, content, or expression, depending upon the sociocultural context. Furthermore, bilingualism and biculturalism can be beneficial to children. These observations refocus the discussion of culture as an inevitable source of developmental risk by suggesting that culture

fundamentally shapes the practices of diverse groups to specific environmental demands, and that biculturalism might have some advantages that have long been overlooked.

CONCLUSION

As the number of families of diverse cultural backgrounds increases in the United States, the role of culture in children's developmental outcomes must receive more serious consideration. It is crucial that we reframe the notion of cultural difference so that it is no longer defined as deviance but rather viewed as a source of risk for other reasons, such as cultural mismatch and its confound with minority status. Three conclusions follow from this reframing. First, the limited amount of both theoretical and empirical work that has examined the possible positive impact of culture on development must be given further consideration. Diverse populations should be understood in light of the strengths and protective factors that their cultural backgrounds provide. Traditional cultural schemas and parental ethnotheories are compelling and have been effective in a variety of contexts and domains over here. It is important to investigate those contexts and domains in which traditional schemas serve as protective factors and as sources of strength.

Second, service providers must contend explicitly with the cultural mismatches that occur between families' and professionals' expectations of the intervention experience. This requires service providers to recognize how their own culture constructs conceptualizations of development. The assumptions that the early intervention system in the United States draws from these conceptualizations must be made explicit if we are to recognize and address differences due to cultural frameworks. Although easy to suggest, this is often a difficult, lifelong process for professionals, requiring greater knowledge as well as respect for different cultures' disparate beliefs and practices. Nevertheless, the potential benefits of making a concerted effort to incorporate the influence of culture and cultural mismatches into our early intervention system are great. The consequent partnerships that will emerge among delivery systems, communities, and families will ultimately assure that interventions will be more effective. To this end, working with the beliefs and strengths of the families that we are trying to serve will improve our own work and thus the lives of the children.

Finally, the persistence of minority status as a risk factor for development demands that we improve our early intervention and prevention delivery systems by taking a broad and multilevel approach to supporting families. Efforts to resocialize culturally "deviant" families have been misguided, have met with limited success, and will continue to fall short until we are able to identify and contend with the larger macrostructural forces that are sources of developmental risk. The racist and discriminatory treatment and the segregation that minority populations typically face are highly consequential to their well-being. If our intention is to improve the life prospects for children and families, we must ameliorate the negative circumstances that are imposed upon them as a consequence of their minority status.

REFERENCES

Banks, J. A. (1988). Ethnicity, class, cognitive, and motivational styles: Research and teaching implications. *Journal of Negro Education, 57,* 452–66.

Barbarin, O. A. (1993). Coping and resilience: Exploring the inner lives of African American children. *Journal of Black Psychology, 19,* 423–46.

Betancourt, H., & Lopez, S. R. (1993). The study of culture, ethnicity, and race in American psychology. *American Psychologist, 48,* 629–37.

Biafora, F. A., Taylor, D. L., Warheit, G. J., Zimmerman, R. S., & Vega, W. A. (1993). Cultural mistrust and racial awareness among ethnically diverse black adolescent boys. *Journal of Black Psychology, 19,* 266–81.

Bloom, B. S., Davis, A., & Hess, R. (1964). *Compensatory education for cultural deprivation.* Chicago: Department of Education, University of Chicago.

Boykin, A. W., & Toms, F. D. (1985). Black child socialization: A conceptual framework. In H. P. McAdoo & J. H. McAdoo (Eds.), *Black children: Social, educational, and parental environments* (pp. 33–51). Newbury Park, CA: Sage.

Bretherton, I., & Waters, E. (Eds.) (1985). Growing points of attachment theory and research. *Monographs of the Society for Research in Child Development, 50* (1–2, serial number 209).

Bronfenbrenner, U. (1979). *The ecology of human development: Experiments by nature and design.* Cambridge, MA: Harvard University Press.

Bronfenbrenner, U. (1985). Summary. In M. B. Spencer, G. K. Brookins, & W. R. Allens (Eds.), *Beginnings: The social and affective development of black children* (pp. 67–73). Hillsdale, NJ: Erlbaum.

Brookins, G. K. (1993). Culture, ethnicity, and bicultural competence: Implications for children with chronic illness and disability. *Pediatrics, 91* (5-Suppl.), 1056–62.

Caplan, N., & Nelson, S. D. (1973). On being useful: The nature and consequences of psychological research on social problems. *American Psychologist, 38,* 199–211.

Chavez, L. R., Cornelius, W. A., & Jones, O. W. (1986). Utilization of health services by Mexican women in San Diego. *Women's Health, 11*(2), 3–20.

Cole, M. (1996). *Cultural psychology: A once and future discipline.* Cambridge, MA: Harvard University Press.

Cole, M., & Bruner, J. S. (1974). Cultural differences and indifferences about psychological processes. In J. W. Berry & P. R. Dasen (Eds.), *Culture and cognition: Readings in cross cultural psychology* (pp. 231–46). London: Methuen & Co. Ltd.

Comeroff, J., & McQuire, P. (1981). Ambiguity and the search for meaning: Childhood leukemia in the modern clinical context. *Social Science and Medicine, 1513,* 115–23.

Deater-Deckard, K., Dodge, K. A., Bates, J. E., & Petit, G. S. (1996). Physical discipline among African American and European American mothers: Links to children's externalizing behaviors. *Developmental Psychology, 6,* 1065–72.

DeSantis, L. (1989). Health care orientation of Cuban and Haitian immigrant mothers: Implications for health care professionals. *Medical Anthropology, 12,* 69–89.

Devine, P., & Elliot, A. (1995). Are racial stereotypes really fading? The Princeton trilogy revisited. *Personality and Social Psychology Bulletin, 21,* 1139–50.

Diaz, R. M. (1985). Bilingual cognitive development: Addressing three gaps in current research. *Child Development, 56,* 1376–88.

Diaz, R. M., & Klinger, C. (1991). Towards an explanatory model of interaction between bilingualism and cognitive development. In E. Bialystok (Ed.), *Language processing in bilingual children* (pp. 167–92). New York: Cambridge University Press.

Dovidio, J. F., & Gaertner, S. L. (1991). Changes in the expression of racial prejudice. In H. Knopke, J. Norrell, & R. Rogers (Eds.), *Prejudice, discrimination, and racism* (1–34). New York: Academic Press.

Duckitt, J. (1992). Psychology and prejudice. *American Psychologist, 47,* 1182–93.

Entwisle, D. R., & Astone, N. M. (1994). Some practical guidelines for measuring youth's race/ethnicity and socioeconomic status. *Child Development, 65,* 1521–40.

Faller, H. S. (1985). Perinatal need of immigrant Hmong women: Surveys of women and health care providers. *Public Health Report, 100,* 341–3.

Florin, P. R., & Dokeki, P. R. (1983) Changing families through parent and family education. In I. E. Siegal &

L. Laosa (Eds.), *Changing families* (pp. 23–64). New York: Plenum Press.

García Coll, C. T. (1990). Developmental outcome of minority infants: A process oriented look into our beginnings. *Child Development, 61*, 270–89.

García Coll, C. T., & Magnuson, K. (1996). The psychological experience of immigration: A developmental perspective. In A. Booth, A. C. Crouter, & N. Landale (Eds.), *Immigration and the family: Research and policy on US immigrants* (pp. 91–131). Hillsdale, NJ: Erlbaum.

García Coll, C., & Magnuson, K. (1999a). Cultural influences on child development: Are we ready for a paradigm shift? In C. Nelson & A. Masten (Eds.), *Cultural processes in child development*. Minnesota symposium on child psychology, vol. 29 (pp. 1–24). New Jersey, Erlbaum.

García Coll, C., & Magnuson, K. (1999b). Theory and research with children of color: Implications for social policy. In H. Fitzgerald (Ed.), *Children of color: Research, health, and policy issues*. New York: Garland.

García Coll, C. T., & Meyer, E. (1993). The socio-cultural context of infant development. In C. H. Zeanah (Ed.), *Handbook of infant mental health* (pp. 56–69). New York: Guilford Press.

García Coll, C. T., Meyer, E. C., & Brillon, L. (1995). Ethnic and minority parents. In M. H. Bornstein (Ed.), *Handbook of parenting, vol. II* (pp. 189–209). Hillsdale, NJ: Erlbaum.

García Coll, C. T., Ramos, A., Magnuson, K., Halpern, L., & Valcarel, M. (1997). *Puerto Rican and Anglo mothers and infants: Similarities and differences in developmental goals and processes*. Society for Research on Child Development, April 3, Washington, DC.

García Coll, C. T., Thorne, B., Cooper, C., Scott-Jones, D., Eccles, J., Nakashima, C. (1996). Paper presented at Third National Symposium of Head Start Research. June 23, Washington, DC.

Graham, S. (1992). "Most of the subjects were white and middle class." *American Psychologist, 47*, 629–39.

Greenfield, P., & Lave, J. (1982). Cognitive aspects of informal education. In D. A. Wagner & H. W. Stevenson (Eds.), *Cultural perspectives on child development* (pp. 146–65). San Francisco: Freeman.

Groce, N. E., & Zola, I. K. (1993). Multiculturalism, chronic illness, and disability. *Pediatrics, 91* (5-Suppl.), 1048–55.

Gutierrez, J., & Sameroff, A. (1990). Determinants of complexity in Mexican-American mothers' conceptions of child development. *Child Development, 61*, 384–94.

Gutierrez, J., Sameroff, A., & Karrer, B. (1988). Acculturation and SES effects on Mexican-American parents' concepts of development. *Child Development, 59*, 250–5.

Harkness, S. (1980). The cultural context of child development. *New Directions for Child Development, 8*, 7–14.

Harkness, S., & C. M. Super (Eds.). (1996). *Parents' cultural belief systems*. New York: Guilford.

Harrison, A. O., Wilson, M. N., Pine, C. J., Chan, S. Q., & Buriel, R. (1990). Family ecologies of ethnic minority children. *Child Development, 61*, 347–62.

Harry, B. (1992). Restructuring the participation of African-American parents in special education. *Exceptional Children, 59*, 123–131.

Harwood, A. (1981) Guidelines for culturally appropriate health care. In Harwood A., (Ed.), *Ethnicity and medical care* (pp. 482–507). Cambridge, MA: Harvard University Press.

Harwood, R. L., Schoelmerich, A., Schulze, P. A., & Wilson, S. P. (1997). *Mother-infant interactions and long-term socialization goals in San Juan and the U.S.* Society for Research on Child Development, April 3, Washington, DC.

Hoang, G. N., & Erickson R. V. (1985). Cultural barriers to effective medical care among Indochinese patients. *Annual Review of Medicine, 36*, 229–39.

Huston, A., McLoyd, V. C., & García Coll, C. (1994). Children and poverty: Issues in contemporary research. *Child Development, 65*, 275–82.

Jarrett, R. (1996). African American family and parenting strategies in impoverished neighborhoods. *Qualitative Sociology, 20*, 275–88.

Koplow, L., & Messinger, E. (1990). Developmental dilemmas of young children of immigrant parents. *Child and Adolescent Social Work, 7*, 121–34.

Korbin, J. E., & Johnston, M. (1982). Steps toward resolving cultural conflict in a pediatric hospital. *Clinical Pediatrics, 21*, 259–63.

Kraut, A. M. (1990). Healers and strangers: Immigrant attitudes toward the physicians in America: A relationship in historical perspective. *Journal of American Medical Association, 263*, 1807–11.

Krieger, N., Avery, B., Rowley, D. L., Phillips, M. T., & Herman, A. A. (1993). Racism, sexism, and social class: Implications for studies of health, disease, and well-being. *American Journal of Preventative Medicine, 9*, 82–122.

LaFromboise, T., Coleman, H. L. K., & Gerton, J. (1993). Psychological impact of biculturalism: Evidence and theory. *Psychological Bulletin, 114*, 395–412.

Laosa, L. (1978). Maternal teaching strategies in Chicano families of varied educational and socioeconomic levels. *Child Development, 49*, 1129–35.

Laosa, L. (1980). Maternal teaching strategies in Chicano and Anglo-American families: The influence of culture and education on maternal behavior. *Child Development, 51*, 759–65.

Laosa, L. (1984). Social policies toward children of diverse ethnic, racial, and language groups in the United States. In H. W. Stevenson & I. E. Siegal (Eds.), *Child development research and social policy* (pp. 1–109). Chicago: University of Chicago Press.

Levine, R. (1977). Child rearing as cultural adaptation. In P. Liedermen, S. R. Tulkin, & A. Rosenfeld (Eds.), *Culture and infancy: Variations in the human experience* (pp. 15–27). New York: Academic Press.

Levine, R. (1988). Human parental care: Universal goals, cultural strategies, individual behavior. *New Directions for Child Development, 1988*, 3–12.

Levy, D. R. (1985). White doctors and black patients: Influence of race on the doctor-patient relationship. *Pediatrics, 75*, 639–43.

Lewontin, R. C. (1982). *Human diversity.* New York: Freeman & Company.

Maccoby, E. E., & Martin, J. (1983). Socialization in the context of the family: Parent-child interaction. In M. Hetherington (Vol. Ed.), *Handbook of child psychology* (pp. 1–102). New York: Wiley.

McAdoo, H. P. (1981). Upward mobility and parenting in middle-income black families. *Journal of Black Psychology, 8*, 122.

McConahay, J. B. (1983). Modern racism and the modern discrimination: The effects of race, racial attitudes, and context on simulated hiring decisions. *Personality and Social Psychology Bulletin, 9*, 551–8.

McConahay, J. B., Hardee, B. B., & Batts, V. (1981). Has racism declined in America? It depends on who is asking and on what is asked. *Journal of Conflict Resolution, 25*, 563–79.

McCubbin, H., Thompson, E. A., Thompson, A. I., McCubbin, M. A., & Kaston, A. J. (1993). Culture, ethnicity and the family: Critical factors in childhood chronic illnesses and disabilities. *Pediatrics, 91*, 1063–70.

McDermott, R., & Varenne, H. (1995). Culture as disability. *Anthropology & Education Quarterly, 26*, 324–48.

McLoyd, V. C. (1990a). Minority children: Introduction to a special issue. *Child Development, 61*, 311–46.

McLoyd, V. C. (1990b). The impact of economic hardship on black families and children: Psychological distress, parenting, and socio-emotional development. *Child Development, 61*, 311–46.

Meyer, E., García Coll, C., Lester, B., Boudykis, Z., McDonough, S., & Oh, W. (1994). Family based intervention improves maternal psychological well-being and feeding interaction of preterm infants. *Pediatrics, 93*, 241–6.

Mistry, J., & Rogoff, B. (1994). Remembering in cultural context. In W. L. Lonner & R. Malpass (Eds.), *Psychology and culture* (pp. 139–44). Needham Heights, MA: Allyn & Bacon.

Ogbu, J. U. (1981). Origins of human competence: A cultural-ecological perspective. *Child Development, 52*, 413–29.

Patterson, M., & Blum, R. W. (1993). A conference on culture and chronic illnesses in childhood: Conference summary. *Pediatrics, 91* (5- Suppl.), 1025–30.

Phinney, J. S. (1993). A three-stage model of ethnic identity development in adolescence. In M. E. Bernal & G. P. Knight (Eds.), *Ethnic identity: Formation and transmission among Hispanics and other minorities* (pp. 61–79). Albany, NY: State University Press.

Phinney, J. (1996) When we talk about American ethnic groups, what do we mean? *American Psychologist, 51*, 918–27.

Ramirez, M. (1983). *Psychology of the Americas: Mestizo perspectives on personality and mental health.* Elmsford, NY: Pergamon.

Rogoff, B. (1990). *Apprenticeship in thinking: Cognitive development in social context.* Oxford: Oxford University Press.

Rogoff, B., Mistry, J. J., Goncu, A., & Mosier, C. (1993). Guided participation in cultural activity by toddlers and caregivers. *Monographs of the Society for Research in Child Development, 58*, 7, Serial No. 236.

Rogoff, B., & Morelli, G. (1989). Perspectives on children's development from cultural psychology. *American Psychologist, 44*, 343–8.

Rogoff, B., & Waddell, K. (1982). Memory for information organized in a scene by children from two cultures. *Child Development, 53*, 1224–8.

Rowley, D. (1990). Research issues in the study of very low birthweight and preterm delivery among African American women. *Journal of the National Medical Association, 85*, 761–5.

Scott, C. (1974). Health and healing practices among five ethnic groups in Miami, Florida. *Public Health Report, 6*, 524–32.

Segall, H. M. (1986). Culture and behavior: Psychology in a global perspective. *Annual Review of Psychology, 37*, 523–64.

Siegal, I. E. (1983). The ethics of intervention. In I. E. Siegal & L. Laosa (Eds.), *Changing families* (pp. 1–22). New York: Plenum Press.

Slaughter, D. T., & McWorter, G. A. (1985). Social origins and early features of the scientific study of black American families and children. In M. B. Spencer, G. K. Brookins, W. R. Allens (Eds.), *Beginnings: The social and affective development of black children* (pp. 5–18). Hillsdale, NJ: Erlbaum.

Slaughter-Defoe, D. T., Nakagawa, K., Takanishi, R., & Johnson, D. R. (1990). Toward cultural/ecological perspectives on schooling and achievement in African American children. *Child Development, 61*, 363–83.

Spencer, M.B., & Sanford, D. (1990). Challenges in studying minority youth. In S. Feldman & G. Elliot (Eds.), *At the threshold: The developing adolescent* (pp. 121–246). Cambridge, MA: Harvard University Press.

Stafford, A. (1978). The application of clinical anthropology to medical practice: A case study of recurrent abdominal pain in a preadolescent Mexican-American female. In E. Brauwens (Ed.), *The anthropology of health* (pp. 12–22). St. Louis, MO: C. V. Mosby.

Steinberg, L., & Fletcher, A. (1998). Data analytic strategies in research on ethnic minority youth. In V. McLoyd and L. Steinberg (Eds.), *Research on minority adolescents.* Hillsdale, NJ: Erlbaum.

Super, C. M., & Harkness, S. (1980). Anthropological perspectives on child development [Special issue]. *New Directions for Child Development, 8.*

Szapocnik, J., & Kurtines, W. M. (1993). Family psychology and cultural diversity: Opportunities for theory research and application. *American Psychologist, 48,* 400–7.

Szapocnik, J., Kurtines, W. M., & Fernandez, T. (1980). Bicultural involvement and adjustment in Hispanic-American youths. *International Journal of Intercultural Relations, 4,* 353–65.

Terrell, F. T., & Terrell, S. (1981). An inventory to measure cultural mistrust among blacks. *The Western Journal of Black Studies, 5,* 180–5.

Thomas, D. D. (1992). *Cultural diversity: Understanding the variability within.* Paper presented at the Eighth National Conference of Parent Care, New Orleans, LA.

Vasquez García, H. A., García Coll, C. T., Erkut, S., Alarcon, O., & Tropp, L. (in press). Family values of Latino adolescents. In F. A. Villarruel (Ed.), *Latino adolescents: Building on Latino diversity.* New York: Garland Press.

Weisner, T. S. (1996). *Successful pathways and the daily routine: An ecological family project.* (An outline proposal for the MacArthur research network on successful pathways through middle childhood.)

Weisner, T. S., Metheson, C. C., & Bernheimer, L. P. (1996).

American cultural models of early influence and parent recognition of developmental delays: Is earlier always better? In S. Harkness & C. M. Super (Eds.), *Parents' cultural belief systems* (pp. 496–531). New York: Guilford Press.

Weiss, H. B. (1993). Home visits: Necessary but not sufficient. *The Future of Children, 3* (3), 113–28.

Whiting, B. (1976). The problem of the packaged variable. In K. F. Riegal & J. A. Meacham (Eds.), *The developing individual in a changing world.* The Hague, Netherlands: Mouton & Co.

Whiting, B. B., & Whiting, J. W. M. (1975). *Children of six cultures: A psychocultural analysis.* Cambridge, MA: Harvard University Press.

Widmayer, S. M., Peterson, L. M., Calderon, A., Carnahan, S., Wingerd, J., & Marshall, R. (1992). The Haitian perinatal intervention project: Bridge to a new culture. In M. Larner, R. Halpern, & O. Harkavy (Eds.), *Fair start for children: Lessons learned from seven demonstration projects* (pp. 115–35). New Haven, CT: Yale University Press.

Widmayer, S. M., Peterson, L. M., Larner, M., Carnahan, S., Calderon, A., Wingerd, J., & Marshall, R. (1990). Predictors of Haitian-American infant development at twelve months. *Child Development, 61,* 410–15.

Young, K. (1990). American conceptions of infant development from 1955–1984: What the experts are telling parents. *Child Development, 61,* 17–28.

CHAPTER SIX

Protective Factors and Individual Resilience

EMMY E. WERNER

It is man's role
in this evolving universe
to teach the terrors of his nature
and his world to sing.

Lillian Smith, *The Journey*

Since the publication of the first edition of *The Hand-book of Early Childhood Intervention*, a rapidly grow-ing body of literature dealing with the phenomenon of resilience and the role of protective factors in the lives of individuals who were born and raised un-der adverse conditions has appeared (Werner, 1990, 1995). Most research in this area has focused on short-term studies in middle childhood and adoles-cence. There has also been a growing interest in the life histories of adults who managed to overcome a cruel past successfully. Published accounts are usu-ally retrospective or based on clinical samples (Hig-gins, 1994; Rubin, 1996). Surprisingly, despite the current popularity of the term resilience, relatively few prospective longitudinal studies have examined this phenomenon in infancy and the preschool years.

A lively debate has taken place over conceptual issues, centering on whether resilience is a state or trait, whether successful coping in the face of adver-sity is domain specific, and what the psychic costs are for at-risk children who manage to grow into competent, confident, and caring adults (Klohnen, 1996; Luthar & Cushing, 1999; Luthar & Zigler, 1991; Masten, Best, & Garmezy, 1990; Rutter, 1994; Zimmerman & Arunkumar, 1995). Some of these is-sues can be clarified by focusing on the few longi-tudinal studies that have examined resilience as a

transactional process between the child and his or her environment. As we look at the findings, we may gain a better understanding of the relations among risk and protective factors, both internal and exter-nal, and their impact on the individual at different stages of development.

The first objective of this chapter is a clarification of the concepts of "resilience" and "protective fac-tors" on the basis of a brief description of the major longitudinal studies of infants and preschool chil-dren that have examined these phenomena over time. The second objective is to provide an overview of what is presently known about the role of protec-tive factors – both internal and external resources – in the successful adaptation of children at risk. The chapter concludes with a discussion of the implica-tions of these findings for early intervention, as well as suggestions of avenues for future research across cultures and generations which may help us better understand the roots of resilience.

THE CONCEPTS OF RESILIENCE AND PROTECTIVE FACTORS

Since the mid-1980s, a number of investigators from different disciplines – child development, pediatrics, psychology, psychiatry, and sociology – have pub-lished findings from longitudinal studies of infants and preschool children who grew up under adverse conditions. Several of these studies have recently come of age and now provide us with a database that extends over several decades.

Researchers have used the term *resilience* to de-note three classes of phenomena. The first type of study focuses on good developmental outcomes in children from high-risk backgrounds who have overcome great odds. Risk factors whose impact on child development have been studied across time include *economic hardships* (Egeland, Carison, & Sroufe, 1993; Elder, Caspi, & Van Nguyen, 1985; Werner & Smith, 1989, 1992), *parental mental illness* (Anthony, 1987; Musick, Stott, Spencer, Goldman, & Cohler, 1987; Radke-Yarrow & Brown, 1993; Seifer, Sameroff, Baldwin, & Baldwin, 1992), *substance abuse* (Johnson, Glassman, Fisk, & Rosen, 1990; Werner, 1991; Werner & Johnson, in press), *child abuse and neglect* (Farber & Egeland, 1987; Herrenkohl, Herrenkohl, & Egolf, 1994), *teenage motherhood* (Furstenberg, Brooks-Gunn, & Morgan, 1987; Werner & Smith, 1992), and *perinatal complications* (Werner & Smith, 1989, 1992). Children in these studies often were exposed to multiple risks, which increased their vulnerability.

The second type of investigation examines sustained competence under conditions of stress. A number of such studies focused on divorce as a common stressor in American children's lives (Emery & Forehand, 1994), with two major longitudinal investigations examining the long-term effects on young children of the breakup of their parents' marriages (Hetherington, Stanley-Hagan, & Anderson, 1989; Wallerstein & Kelley, 1980; Wallerstein & Blakeslee, 1989). In a promising new avenue of research, Boyce and his associates have looked at psychobiologic factors that moderate the adaptation of preschool and kindergarten children to *child-care stressors* (Barr, Boyce, & Zeltzer, 1994).

The third type of study focuses on individuals who have successfully recovered from such serious childhood traumas as war and political violence (Burnette, 1996; Richman, 1993). Noteworthy are two follow-up studies in midlife of child survivors of World War II concentration camps (Moskovitz, 1983) and young children whose mothers were political prisoners during the Greek Civil War (Dalianis, 1994).

Under each of these conditions, behavioral scientists focused their attention on protective factors and mechanisms that buffered or ameliorated a child's reaction to a stressful situation or chronic adversity so that his or her adaptation was more successful than would be the case if the protective factors were not present (Masten, 1994). The term *protective factors* is used in this context as a generic term for

moderators of risk and adversity that enhance good, that is, developmentally appropriate outcomes. *Resilience* is conceived as an end product of buffering processes that do not eliminate risks and stress but that allow the individual to deal with them effectively (Rutter, 1987).

In the longitudinal studies that are the focus of this chapter, developmental outcomes are usually defined in terms of multiple criteria. These include the absence of significant developmental delays or serious learning and behavior problems and the mastery of developmental tasks (Havighurst, 1972) or psychosocial stages (Erikson, 1959) that are appropriate for a given age and culture, including the attainment of a sense of trust, autonomy, and initiative by the time a child reaches age 6. Follow-up studies of at-risk children in adolescence and adulthood indicate that the mastery of these early developmental tasks can serve as a strong and enduring protective buffer in the face of later adversity (Egeland, Carison, & Sroufe, 1993; Werner & Smith, 1992).

Garmezy, Masten, and Tellegen (1984) hypothesized that protective factors may operate through three different mechanisms: compensation, challenge, and immunization. In the compensatory model, stress factors and protective factors combine additively in the prediction of outcome, and severe stress can be counteracted by personal qualities or sources of support. In the challenge model, stress can potentially enhance competence (provided the degree of stress is not excessive), and the relation between stress and competence may therefore be curvilinear. In the immunity model, there is a conditional relation between stressors and protective factors. Such factors moderate the impact of stress on the quality of a child's adaptation but may have no detectable effects in the absence of a stressor. The compensatory, challenge, and immunity models of stress resistance are not mutually exclusive. They may operate simultaneously or successively in the adaptive repertoire of a resilient individual, depending on his or her stage of development.

Just as risk factors and childhood stressors may co-occur within a particular population (Seifer & Sameroff, 1987) or within a particular developmental period, protective factors are also likely to occur together to some degree (Gore & Eckenrode, 1994). Assessing the overall pattern of external and internal resources alerts us to the possibility of one resource substituting for another in coping with adversity. It is possible that different protective factors, such as social support and positive experience in preschool, for example, may produce similar results, such as an increase in the child's self-esteem. Protective factors not only help account for individual differences in reactivity to environmental or biological risks at any given point but the presence of certain protective factors also determines the emergence of other protective mechanisms at some later point. That is, a preschool child with high self-esteem may make peer friends more easily when he or she enters kindergarten or first grade. The task of delineating such interconnections should become an important agenda in longitudinal studies of at-risk children and in early intervention programs.

METHODOLOGICAL ISSUES IN THE STUDY OF RESILIENCE AND PROTECTIVE FACTORS

Our current understanding of the roots of resilience in young children comes from about a dozen longitudinal studies that have been conducted in different geographic regions of the country: from Hawaii and California to the Midwestern heartland (Illinois, Kansas, Minnesota, Missouri) and the Eastern parts of the United States (New York, Maryland, Pennsylvania). The studies include Asian American, African American, and Caucasian children who have been followed from infancy and the preschool years to middle childhood, adolescence, young adulthood, and midlife.

Data analyses exploring the interplay among multiple risk and protective factors at several levels – the individual, the immediate family, and the larger social context in which he or she lives – are still rare and have only been employed by a handful of prospective studies (Egeland et al., 1993; Elder et al., 1985; Furstenberg et al., 1987; Seifer et al., 1992; Werner & Smith, 1992). The availability of data for more complex analyses should increase in the near future, as several longitudinal studies with large numbers of children and multiple assessments are coming of age.

Methodological issues that have confronted researchers who study the buffering process of protective factors in the lives of at-risk children include 1) the selection of age-appropriate measures of adaptation; 2) the need to use multiple criteria to determine successful outcome in high-risk groups; 3) the need for low-risk control groups; and 4) the need to observe children at multiple measurement points in time. In a number of investigations, individual-based approaches to studying resilience have yielded both quantitative and qualitative measurements. Descriptive profiles of highly competent high-risk children have been a useful supplement to variable-based analyses (for examples, see Moriarty, 1987; Radke-Yarrow & Brown, 1993; Werner & Smith, 1989, 1992).

Despite the heterogeneity of these studies, one can begin to discern a common core of individual dispositions and sources of support that contribute to resilience in individual development. These protective buffers appear to transcend ethnic, social class, and geographic boundaries. They also appear to make a more profound impact on the life course of children who grow up in adversity than do specific risk factors or stressful life events. Our discussion turns to the major protective factors that have been replicated in longitudinal studies of young children who grew up in high-risk conditions in the United States (see Table 9.1).

PROTECTIVE FACTORS WITHIN THE CHILD

Infancy

Beginning in the prenatal period, the Kauai Longitudinal Study monitored the impact of a variety of biological and psychosocial risk factors, stressful life events, and protective factors on the development of 698 Asian and Polynesian children born in 1955 on the northwestern-most island in the Hawaiian chain. Half of the cohort lived in chronic poverty. Data on the children and their families were collected at birth, in the postpartum period, and at ages 1, 2, 10, 18, 32, and 40 years (Werner & Smith, 1989, 1992; Werner, Randolph, & Masten, 1996).

One of three children in this birth cohort developed learning or behavior problems in the first two decades of life. Most children with such problems had been exposed to multiple risk factors that included perinatal complications, parental psychopathology, family instability, and chronic poverty. A group of seventy-two children (some 10% of the cohort), who had experienced four or more such risk factors before the age of 2, however,

TABLE 6.1. Protective Factors Within Individuals, Replicated in Two or More Longitudinal Studies of At-Risk Children First Identified Before the Age of Six.

Protective Factors	Developmental Period	Risk Factors
Low distress/ low emotionality	Infancy–Adulthood	Child abuse/neglect Poverty Multiple risks
Active; alert; high vigor; drive	Infancy	Poverty Multiple risks
Sociability	Infancy	Child abuse/neglect Parental mental illness Poverty Multiple risks
"Easy," engaging temperament (affectionate; cuddly)	Infancy–Childhood	Child abuse/neglect Divorce Parental substance abuse Poverty Multiple risks
Advanced self-help skills	Early childhood	Poverty Multiple risks
Average–above average intelligence (language and problem-solving skills)	Childhood–Adulthood	Child abuse/neglect Parental mental illness Parental substance abuse Poverty Multiple risks
Ability to distance oneself; impulse control	Childhood–Adulthood	Parental mental illness Parental substance abuse Poverty Multiple risks
Internal locus of control	Childhood–Adolescence	Parental mental illness Child abuse/neglect Poverty Multiple risks
Strong achievement motivation	Childhood–Adolescence	Parental mental illness Parental substance abuse Poverty Multiple risks
Special talents, hobbies	Childhood–Adolescence	Parental mental illness Poverty Multiple risks
Positive self-concept	Childhood–Adolescence	Divorce Poverty Multiple risks
Planning, foresight	Adolescence–Adulthood	Teenage parenthood Poverty Multiple risks
Strong religious orientation, Faith	Childhood–Adulthood	Parental mental illness Parental substance abuse Poverty Multiple risks

TABLE 6.2. Protective Factors within the Family and Community Replicated in Two or More Longitudinal Studies of At-Risk Children First Identified Before the Age of Six

Protective Factors	Developmental Period	Risk Factors
Small family size <4 children	Infancy	Teenage motherhood Poverty Multiple risks
Mother's education	Infancy–Adulthood	Teenage motherhood Poverty Multiple risks
Maternal competence	Infancy–Adolescence	Child abuse/neglect Poverty Parental mental illness Multiple risks
Close bond with primary caregiver (who need not be biological parent)	Infancy–Adolescence	Child abuse/neglect Poverty Parental mental illness Parental substance abuse Teenage motherhood Multiple risks
Supportive grandparents	Infancy–Adolescence	Child abuse/neglect Divorce Parental substance abuse Teenage motherhood Poverty Multiple risks
Supportive siblings	Childhood–Adulthood	Child abuse/neglect Divorce Parental substance abuse Poverty Multiple risks
For girls: emphasis on autonomy with emotional support from primary caregiver	Childhood–Adolescence	Poverty Multiple risks
For boys: structure and rules in household	Childhood–Adolescence	Divorce Poverty Multiple risks
For both boys and girls: assigned chores: "required helpfulness"	Childhood–Adolescence	Parental psychopathology Poverty Multiple risks
Close, competent peer friends who are confidants	Childhood–Adolescence	Divorce Poverty Multiple risks
Supportive teachers	Preschool–Adulthood	Divorce Parental mental illness Parental substance abuse Poverty Multiple risks
Successful school experiences	Preschool–Adulthood	Divorce Parental mental illness Poverty Multiple risks
Mentors (elders, peers)	Childhood–Adulthood	Poverty Multiple risks

developed instead into competent, confident, and caring adults. The majority of these resilient boys and girls were characterized by their caregivers as very active, affectionate, cuddly, good-natured, and easy to deal with when they were infants. Few had distressing feedings or sleeping habits. Low distress and emotionality characterized these same individuals on temperament ratings in adulthood as well.

The Coping Project of the Menninger Foundation in Topeka, Kansas, reported strikingly similar findings on the basis of clinical assessments of thirty-two middle-class Caucasian infants at 4–32 weeks. Observers noted a consistent positive relation among good energy resources, easy vegetative functioning, and resilience. An intense drive and vigor, and a notable responsiveness to people and objects, characterized the successful copers in that study (Moriarty, 1987; Murphy, 1987).

Moriarty (1987) illustrated the characteristics of a resilient infant in her case study of a boy with sensory deficits (hearing loss and divergent strabismus). Even as early as 4 weeks, this child showed a high energy level and was able to express clear-cut preferences, such as being held upright rather than laid supine. He expressed protest forcefully by crying but recovered quickly from discomfort. He utilized support well, cuddled comfortably, and responded positively to physical contact. Throughout his first year of life, in repeated home observations, he gave reliable evidence that he was an active and assertive baby with a great deal of social responsiveness and a distinct capacity for self-expression through motor and preverbal channels.

Similarly, Farber and Egeland (1987) reported from the Minnesota Mother–Child Project that securely attached infants of abusing mothers who lived in poor dysfunctional families were especially robust and able to elicit support from other caregivers. They appeared alert, easy to soothe, and socially responsive. Secure attachments in these infants were found to be associated with the availability of a caring adult – if not the mother, then a grandmother or an older sibling.

At the University of Chicago, Musick et al. (1987) found similar interaction styles in babies of mentally ill mothers who profited from the availability of a therapeutic nursery when their mothers underwent treatment as part of their Risk and Recovery Study. In spite of separations and family discord during their earliest months, these infants had relationships with their mothers that were, at least some of the time, characterized by responsiveness and warmth. They also actively reached out for others – the well parent or grandparents.

Early Childhood

The resilient toddlers in the Kauai Study met familiar adults and strangers (examining pediatricians and psychologists) on their own terms. During a potentially stressful situation, such as a series of developmental tests, they were described by the examiners as more alert, cheerful, responsive, self-confident, and independent than children of the same age and sex who later developed serious learning or behavior problems. The Kauai toddlers were also more advanced in communication, locomotion, and self-help skills and engaged in more social play than the toddlers who later developed problems (Werner & Smith, 1989).

Here is an example of a resilient toddler from our case records: Jenny, a preterm infant whose mother had a difficult pregnancy and delivery, was a small, frail-looking child at 20 months. She appeared to be active and very alert to examiners. Her score on the Cattell Infant Intelligence Scale was in the average range (97), but she demonstrated superior self-help skills on the Vineland Social Maturity Scale (SQ 132). Jenny was perceived by her mother as an assertive and determined little girl who could occasionally be disagreeable if she did not get her way. In spite of her physical frailty, her independence and autonomy were quite apparent.

Farber and Egeland (1987) noted that abused children who were securely attached tended to be less vulnerable to the detrimental effects of abuse from their mothers when they were 42 months old. They were also more competent in their dealings with problem-solving tasks in a frustrating situation, such as the Barrier Box, than children who were insecurely attached. These competent children had been rated as more alert and attentive as newborns by independent observers.

Wallerstein and Kelley (1980) and Hetherington et al. (1989) found similar characteristics among preschool children who weathered successfully the stresses of parental divorce. Such children related to both peers and teachers without excessive anxiety or need for attention. They were more socially mature than preschoolers who had difficulty coping with the marital breakup and were able to distance themselves from their parents' conflict by establishing routines and order in their lives.

An exciting new avenue of research has recently focused on the role of psychobiologic factors as moderators of young children's vulnerability to stress (Barr, Boyce, & Zeltzer, 1994). Noteworthy are two studies conducted by Boyce and his colleagues at the University of California, San Francisco Department of Pediatrics. In the first, preschool children attending four child-care centers were followed for 1 year, during which both child-care-related stressors and teacher-reported injuries were prospectively ascertained. Laboratory sessions at the onset of the study year provided independent measures of cardiovascular reactivity. Results showed that children who displayed exaggerated reactivity in the laboratory setting had injury rates comparable with their minimally reactive peers under low-stress conditions but significantly greater injury rates under high-stress conditions. Low cardiovascular reactivity thus functioned as a moderator variable, making preschool children less vulnerable to injury under high stress (Boyce, Chesney, Kaiser, Alkon-Leonard, & Tschann, 1992).

In the second study, 5-year-old children were assessed twice – 1 week before and 1 week following primary school entry – in order to examine changes in immune competence occurring in the transition to kindergarten. After completion of the immunologic assays, children were prospectively followed for 12 weeks, ascertaining the incidence and severity of respiratory tract infections. By chance, the 1989 San Francisco Area Loma Prieta earthquake occurred at the midpoint of the surveillance period, thus creating a natural experiment with predisaster measures of immunologic competence. The children of parents reporting high levels of disaster-related stress showed widely divergent illness rates: Children with low immune reactivity had strikingly lower postearthquake illness rates than children with high immune reactivity (Boyce, Chestermaen, Wara, Cohen, Folkman, & Martin, 1991).

Psychobiologic differences in stress vulnerability may be similar to those that render young children pain-vulnerable or pain-resistant. Barr, Boyce, and Zeltzer (1994) reviewed evidence that young children differ in the way they tolerate pain during clinical tests. Among children with cancer, "distractors" – those who diverted their attention away from the induced sensations of cold pressor testing and lumbar puncture – had higher pain tolerance than "attenders" – those who primarily focused their attention on the clinical procedures. Attenders also reported less anxiety prior to the tests and less variability in heart rate and systolic blood pressure. Both distractors and attenders demonstrated high within-child stability in the choice of their coping styles.

Clearly, further research on the role of psychobiologic reactivity to *both* physical and emotional stressors should become an important item on the research agenda of behavioral scientists interested in resilience and protective factors in young children's lives.

Middle Childhood

At present, we have more data on characteristics of resilience in middle childhood than for any other developmental period. Longitudinal studies of competent children who experienced stressful life events, such as the breakup of their parents' marriage, and follow-up studies of resilient children who were exposed to high-risk conditions, such as poverty and parental psychopathology, have yielded similar results in a variety of cultural and geographical contexts: from rural areas and suburbia to inner city slums and from the Pacific Coast to the Midwestern heartland to the Atlantic seaboard. A sense of competence and self-efficacy appears to be the general hallmark of these children.

The "vulnerable, but invincible" 10-year-olds in the Kauai Longitudinal Study were neither unusually talented nor intellectually gifted. They did, however, possess well-developed problem-solving and communication skills that they put to good use. Their teachers noted that they were not only sociable but also remarkably independent. They were able to control their impulses and concentrate on their schoolwork, even if they grew up in homes marred by chronic discord, parental alcoholism, or psychosis. Parental and self-reports indicated that these resilient children displayed a healthy androgyny in their interests and activities and engaged in hobbies that were not narrowly sex-typed. Such activities gave them solace in adversity and provided them with a sense of mastery and pride. This was especially true for the resilient children of parents with alcoholism (Werner, 1991; Werner & Smith, 1989).

Both resilient boys and girls shared a number of common strengths: 1) they were well liked by peers and adults; 2) their dominant cognitive style was reflective rather than impulsive; 3) they demonstrated an internal locus of control, a belief that they were capable of influencing their environment positively; and 4) they were able to use flexible coping strategies in overcoming adversity. Similarly, Anthony (1987) noted that the children he studied in the St. Louis Risk Project resisted becoming engulfed in the parental psychopathology, showed curiosity in understanding what it was that troubled the psychotic parent, maintained a compassionate but detached approach to the mentally ill parent, and often discovered a refuge and source of self-esteem in the pursuit of hobbies and creative interests with schoolmates or friends.

In a 10-year longitudinal study of the offspring of parents with affective disorders conducted at the National Institute of Mental Health, Radke-Yarrow and Brown (1993) found that children with the most constant pattern of resilience were assertive and highly achievement oriented. They were better equipped than their troubled peers to reach out for support from others, especially from teachers and peers.

In the Rochester Longitudinal Study, competence, internal locus of control, and social support were also potent protective factors in the lives of 4- to 13-year-old children who succeeded despite poverty and maternal mental illness (Seifer et al., 1992). The elementary-age children who coped well with the stresses of parental divorce in the Wallerstein and Kelley (1980) study displayed similar characteristics. These children enjoyed their classmates and teachers, tended to be good students, and had a positive self-concept.

Adolescence and Adulthood

Among the personality characteristics that differentiated high-risk youths on Kauai at age 17–18 from their peers with serious delinquencies and mental problems were a more internal locus of control, a more positive self-concept, and higher scores on the California Psychological Inventory (CPI) scales for Responsibility, Socialization, Achievement via Conformance, and Femininity for both sexes (Werner & Smith, 1989). Resilient youths who coped successfully in spite of chronic poverty, parental psychopathology, and family discord were more responsible and achievement-oriented than their troubled teenage peers. These youths were more socially mature and had internalized a positive set of values. They were also more nurturant, empathic, and socially perceptive than their age-mates who had difficulty coping. These characteristics differentiated them from their peers in adulthood (age 32) and midlife (age 40) as well (Werner & Smith, 1992).

Investigations of other resilient high-risk groups revealed similar personality dispositions. These groups included adolescents who coped well with the trauma of parental divorce (Wallerstein & Blakeslee, 1989; Wallerstein & Kelley, 1980) and teenage mothers who established stable relationships with a man and improved their educational and financial status after the birth of their baby (Furstenberg et al., 1987; Werner & Smith, 1992).

Youths in both groups were more responsible, independent, and socially mature than their peers who coped unsuccessfully under similar circumstances. A sense of self-worth and a more internal locus of control also characterized the well-functioning youngsters from maltreating homes who were followed from early childhood to late adolescence in the Lehigh Longitudinal Study (Herrenkohl, Herrenkohl, & Egolf, 1994).

Intelligence and Resilience

Even though there is little evidence that high intelligence alone promotes more effective coping, most longitudinal studies of resilient children and youths report that intelligence (especially communication and problem-solving skills) and scholastic competence (especially reading skills) are associated positively with the ability to overcome adversity. Correlations between measures of intelligence and effective adaptation tend to increase from early to middle childhood and adolescence (Block & Kremen, 1996).

It stands to reason that youngsters who are better able to appraise stressful life events correctly are also better able to figure out effective strategies for coping with adversity, either through their own efforts or by actively reaching out to other people for help. This finding has been replicated with children from all socioeconomic groups and from diverse ethnic backgrounds, in studies of African American, Asian American, and Caucasian children who grew up under a variety of high-risk conditions, including poverty, parental mental illness, and substance abuse, as well as family discord and child abuse (Egeland et al., 1993; Herrenkohl et al., 1994; Radke-Yarrow & Brown, 1993; Seifer et al., 1992; Werner & Smith, 1992).

In summary, protective factors that have been observed repeatedly in children who coped well in adverse situations include at least average intelligence and positive temperamental characteristics, such as activity level, sociability, and low emotionality – dispositions that have a strong genetic base (Scarr & McCartney, 1983). As infants, these children are successful in eliciting positive attention from other people and are able to recover quickly from discomfort. By the time they are preschoolers, they have evolved a strong sense of autonomy coupled with the ability to ask for support when needed. From repeated experiences in successfully overcoming frustrating situations, either on their own initiative or with the help of others, they derive in childhood and adolescence a sense of self-efficacy and confidence that leads to a strong belief that they are able to influence their environment positively. These youngsters tend to employ a wide range of flexible coping strategies that are not narrowly sex typed. They select what they need from their environment, make active use of it, or change or restructure a situation so it meets their needs.

PROTECTIVE FACTORS WITHIN THE FAMILY

Despite the burdens of parental psychopathology, family discord, or chronic poverty, most children identified as resilient have had the opportunity to establish a close bond with at least one person who provided them with stable care and from whom they received adequate and appropriate attention during the first year of life (see Table 6.2). The resilient offspring of alcoholic parents on Kauai, the resilient infants of abusive mothers in Minnesota and Pennsylvania, and the resilient babies of psychotic parents

in Chicago, Rochester, and St. Louis all had enough good nurturing to form secure attachments and to develop a basic sense of trust. So did the child survivors of concentration camps and political persecutions who made a successful adaptation in later life (Dalianis, 1994; Moskovitz, 1983).

Maternal Competence

Among the most powerful protective factors associated with the successful adaptation of high-risk children in the Kauai Longitudinal Study were their mother's education level and their exposure to a competent caregiver in the first year of life. The model of a mother who was gainfully employed after her child reached preschool age was an especially potent protective factor for high-risk girls in this predominantly Asian American study population (Werner & Smith, 1989, 1992).

Similar findings have been reported for Caucasian samples by Elder et al. (1985) in their life history analyses of preschool children who grew up in the Great Depression and by Egeland et al. (1993) and Seifer et al. (1992) in their studies of contemporary children who grew up in multi-risk families in the midst of poverty and parental psychopathology. Furstenberg et al. (1987) found a similar positive association between maternal competence and children's successful adaptation in their follow-up studies of Black teenage mothers who lived in the inner-city of Baltimore. Furstenberg and his associates also replicated another finding first reported in the Kauai Longitudinal Study: that a low birth order (single, first-, or second-born) and a small family size (fewer than 4 children) seemed to ameliorate the developmental risk of growing up in poverty and social disorganization, especially when children are spaced at least 2 years apart.

Affectional Ties with Alternative Caregivers

In high-risk families in which a parent may be absent or incapacitated, some of the nurturing often comes from alternative caregivers – the "kith and kin" who have remained relatively invisible in the child development literature. Among family members who play important roles as providers of stable care and positive models of identification, grandparents and older siblings emerge as important stress buffers in the lives of many children.

GRANDPARENTS. In the Kauai Longitudinal Study, grandparents played an important role as caregivers and sources of emotional support for children whose parents were mentally ill or alcoholic (Werner, 1991). Even as adults, children who were well cared for by their grandparents under these circumstances maintained strong emotional ties to them (Werner & Smith, 1992).

Both Farber and Egeland (1987) in Minnesota and Herrenkohl and her associates in Pennsylvania (1994) observed that resilient children from maltreating homes often developed a secure attachment to grandparents who became their substitute caregivers. Musick and her associates (1987) and Radke-Yarrow and Brown (1993), in their longitudinal studies of psychotic mothers' resilient offspring, noted that children were more likely to bounce back from the effects of multiple separations from an ill parent if the grandparents joined with the well parent in providing loving care.

Furstenberg et al. (1987) also demonstrated the positive impact of caring grandparents in their longitudinal study of low-income teenage mothers from the Baltimore area who kept their babies. When the cognitive development of their offspring was assessed at ages 3–4 years, the children of these unmarried teenage mothers tended to have higher scores if they were cared for by more than one adult – in most cases by the maternal grandmother. Furthermore, unmarried teenage mothers who remained with their own parents were more likely to return to school, graduate from high school, and be employed and off welfare than teenage mothers who did not have such (grand)parental support (Furstenberg et al., 1987).

Several studies have shown that grandparents can also be a significant source of support for children of divorce. Whether they are preschoolers or adolescents, youngsters who cope well during and after the parental breakup often have ongoing relationships with grandparents who are attentive to their needs (Wallerstein & Kelley, 1980). When grandparents live nearby, they may provide financial support, child care, and emotional sustenance. Grandfathers can play a particularly important role in skills training and in the provision of activities for young

grandsons in divorced families (Hetherington et al., 1989).

SIBLINGS. Sibling caregiving seems to be another protective buffer for children who grow up in high-risk families. In cases of permanent father absence as a result of death, desertion, or divorce or in homes with an alcoholic parent, such caregiving contributed to the pronounced sense of responsibility and social maturity we observed among the resilient youth on Kauai. Involvement in sibling caregiving, either as a provider or as a recipient, proved to be one of the major protective factors in their stressful lives (Werner, 1991; Werner & Smith, 1989).

Siblings were also found to be major sources of emotional support for children who survived the breakup of their parents' marriage. They remained models of commitment and loyalty in the midst of marital upheaval (Wallerstein & Blakeslee, 1989). There is evidence that female siblings of divorced parents may also act as buffers and fill the emotional void left by unresponsive parents after divorce (Hetherington et at., 1989).

Sibling caregiving tends to be more effective when it is supplementary rather than substitute parenting. Under some traumatic circumstances (such as those found in abusive homes or during wars), however, children have also served as surrogate parents for each other. A classic example is the six orphans of Terezin whose parents died in a concentration camp. When brought to a therapeutic nursery in England at the end of World War II, these children did not trust any adult. They had, however, developed strong attachments to each other and looked out for each other with fierce loyalty. Extremely sensitive to each other's needs, they provided mutual emotional support. Remarkable in their resilience as children, they have remained so as adults (Moskovitz, 1983).

In the long term, the availability of supplemental adult resources seems to be a crucial determinant of whether an older sibling will help or hinder a younger brother or sister. Among the resilient children of Kauai, when a parent was absent, alcoholic, or mentally ill, other concerned adults, relatives, and neighbors acted as such protective buffers (Werner & Smith, 1989). Resilient children seem to be especially adept at actively recruiting such surrogate parents.

Socialization Practices

Both the Berkeley Study of ego-resiliency and the Kauai Longitudinal Study have noted characteristic child-rearing orientations that appear to promote resilience differentially in boys and girls (Block & Gjerde, 1986; Werner & Smith, 1989). Resilient girls tend to come from households that combine an absence of overprotection, an emphasis on risk-taking and independence, and reliable emotional support from the primary caregiver, whether she be mother, grandmother, sister, or aunt. Resilient boys, on the other hand, appear to come from households where there is greater structure, rules, parental supervision, and the availability of a male who serves as a model of identification (father, grandfather, older brother, or uncle) and where there is encouragement of emotional expressiveness. Socialization factors that emphasize independence and an absence of overprotection appear to have a greater impact on the resilience of girls than of boys (Block & Gjerde, 1986).

Required Helpfulness

Assigned chores and the need to take on domestic responsibilities and part-time work to help support the family have proved to be sources of strength and competence for resilient children. On Kauai, many of the high-risk resilient youths had responsibility for the care of younger siblings. Some managed the household when a parent was ill or hospitalized; others worked part-time after school to support their family (Werner & Smith, 1989).

Such acts of "required helpfulness" (Rachman, 1979) have also been noted by Anthony (1987) in his clinical studies of the resilient offspring of psychotic parents, by Johnson, Glassman, Fisk, and Rosen (1990) and Werner (1991) among the competent offspring of alcoholic parents, and by Moskovitz (1983) among resilient orphans of war. Studies of children who lived during the Great Depression (Elder et al., 1985) have shown that such productive roles of responsibility, when associated with close family ties, are important protective factors during times of adversity.

Faith: A Sense of Coherence

A number of studies of resilient children from a wide variety of socioeconomic and ethnic back-grounds noted that their families held religious beliefs that provided stability and meaning to their lives, especially in times of hardship and adversity (Anthony, 1987; Dalianis, 1994; Moskovitz, 1983; Werner & Smith, 1989; 1992). The content of their beliefs varied from Buddhism to Mormonism to Catholicism and fundamental and liberal versions of Protestantism and Judaism. Such faiths appear to give resilient children a sense of rootedness and coherence (Antonovsky, 1987), a conviction that their lives have meaning, and a belief that things will work out in the end, despite unfavorable odds. This sense of meaning persists, even among children uprooted by wars or scattered throughout the world as refugees, and enables them to love despite hate and to behave compassionately toward other persons (Dalianis, 1994; Moskovitz, 1983). In adulthood and midlife, such a faith was considered one of the most important protective factors among the men and women who had overcome great odds (Werner & Smith, 1992).

PROTECTIVE FACTORS IN THE COMMUNITY

Several longitudinal studies have suggested that resilient children obtain a great deal of emotional support from outside their own family, and they tend to rely on friends, neighbors, and teachers for counsel and comfort in times of transition or crisis.

Friends

Even though they may come from poor, chaotic, and discordant homes, resilient children tend to be well liked by their playmates and classmates and to have one or more close friends. These children tend to keep their childhood friends into adulthood and rely on them for ongoing emotional support, which is more prevalent for women than for men (Werner & Smith, 1992).

Association with friends and the parents of friends who come from stable families can help resilient children gain a perspective and maintain a constructive distance between themselves and their own households, which may be marred by discord, parental psychopathology, or alcoholism (Anthony, 1987; Werner, 1991; Werner & Smith, 1989). Investigators who have studied the role of friends in the lives of children whose parents become divorced have noted that peers may enrich and expand the quality of a resilient child's life, but, like siblings, they are more effective as supplements rather than as substitutes for a close and stable relationship with at least one adult in the home or neighborhood (Wallerstein & Kelly, 1980).

School

Most studies have noted that resilient children enjoy school, whether nursery school, grade school, or high school (Musick et al., 1987; Werner & Smith, 1989). Even if they are not unusually gifted, those who ultimately show the greatest resilience tend to put whatever abilities they have to good use. In many cases, such children make school into a home away from home, a refuge from a disordered household.

Hetherington et al. (1989) found a remarkable similarity in the characteristics of both home and school environments that were associated with greater resilience among children of divorced families. In both settings, a greater degree of adaptive behavior among children was associated with a more responsive and nurturant atmosphere and a more organized and predictable environment, which clearly defined and consistently enforced standards, rules, and responsibilities. In fact, structure, organization, rule enforcement, and assignment of responsibilities were more important for children from divorced than from nondivorced families. Structure and control appeared more salient for fostering resilience in boys; nurturance and the assumption of responsibility were more important for girls (Wallerstein & Kelly, 1980).

Teachers and Mentors

Among the most frequently encountered positive role models in the lives of the children of Kauai, outside of the family circle, was a favorite teacher. For the resilient youngster, a special teacher was not just an instructor for academic skills but also a confidant and positive role model (Werner & Smith, 1989). Studies that have explored the role of teachers as protective buffers in the lives of children who grew up in homes marred by poverty, parental mental illness, alcoholism, and domestic strife tend to agree in their findings that teachers or mentors

can have a significant positive impact on at-risk children (Freedman, 1993; Radke-Yarrow & Brown, 1993; Wallerstein & Blakeslee, 1989; Werner, 1991; Werner & Smith, 1992).

Two investigations deserve special note. One is a follow-up study of twenty-four child survivors of the Nazi Holocaust who were sent from concentration camps and orphanages to a therapeutic nursery school in England at the close of World War II (Moskovitz, 1983). Excerpts from follow-up interviews after 30–40 years reveal an extraordinary affirmation of life. Furthermore, all of the resilient survivors considered one woman to be among the most potent influences in their lives – the nursery school teacher who provided warmth and caring and who taught them "to behave compassionately."

The other is a follow-up study at midlife of men and women who had spent their infancy and early childhood years with their mothers in a maximum-security prison during the Greek Civil War (Dalianis, 1994). Most children had lost their fathers who had been killed as resistance fighters; their mothers were awaiting execution. The people who sustained these children were fellow prisoners – mostly professional women – who taught these youngsters how to read, sang and played with them, and sustained their health and their spirits until they were liberated. Now middle-aged, these former child prisoners have grown into competent and caring adults who have children of their own and established roots in their respective communities.

PROTECTIVE FACTORS: A SUMMARY

Several protective factor clusters emerge as recurrent themes in longitudinal studies of young children who managed to overcome great odds. Some protective factors are internal resources that the individual brings to his or her encounter with stressful life events; others are external sources of support in the family and community.

Resilient children, as a whole, are engaging to other people, adults and peers alike. They have good communication and problem-solving skills, including the ability to recruit substitute caregivers actively; they have a talent or special skill that is valued by their peers; and they have faith that their own actions can make a positive difference in their lives.

Resilience is enhanced by external resources as well; foremost are affectional ties that encourage trust, autonomy, and initiative in the child. These ties are often provided by alternate caregivers, among them members of the extended family. There are also support systems in the community that reinforce and reward the competencies of such youngsters and that provide them with positive role models. Among them are caring neighbors, teachers, mentors, and peer friends.

The data reviewed here suggest that these protective factors may have a more generalized effect on children's adaptation than those of specific risk factors or stressful life events. The buffering processes that shape resilience have been demonstrated in children of all races and in a variety of social contexts.

The Shifting Balance Between Vulnerability and Resilience

Just as vulnerability is relative, depending on complex interactions among constitutional factors and life's circumstances, resilience is governed by a similar dynamic interaction among protective factors within the individual, his or her family environment, and the larger social context in which he or she lives (Cohler, 1987). Longitudinal studies following children from birth to adulthood have found a shifting balance between stressful life events that heighten children's vulnerability and protective factors that enhance their resilience. This balance changes not only with different stages of the life cycle but also varies with sex and cultural context.

In our adult follow-up in the Kauai Longitudinal Study, for example, we found a few offspring of psychotic parents who had managed to cope successfully with a variety of stressful life events in childhood and adolescence, but whose mental health began to deteriorate in the third decade of life. Other high-risk individuals had grown into competent, confident, and caring adults but felt a persistent need to detach themselves from parents and siblings whose domestic and emotional problems still threatened to engulf them. This was especially true for the adult children of alcoholic parents, some of whom had been physically and emotionally abused when they were growing up (Werner, 1991; Werner & Smith, 1992). The balancing act between forming new attachments to loved ones of their choice and the loosening of old family ties that evoked painful memories had exacted a toll in their adult lives. The price they paid varied from stress-related health problems to a certain aloofness in their interpersonal relationships. Anthony (1987) also noted the same detachment in his follow-up of the adult offspring of psychotic parents.

On the positive side, we found that the opening of opportunities at major life transitions (high school graduation, entry into the world of work, marriage) enabled the majority of the high-risk individuals who had a troubled adolescence to rebound in their twenties and thirties. Among the most potent second chances for such youths were adult education programs, voluntary military service, active participation in a church community, and a supportive friend or marital partner.

The same protective buffers were also observed by Elder et al. (1985) in the adult lives of children of the Great Depression and by Furstenberg et al. (1987) in the later lives of Black teenage mothers whose prospects improved in the third and fourth decades of life. Those whose life trajectories shifted in a positive direction, from vulnerability to resilience, were generally more women than men. Individuals who were of average or above average intelligence, and who had been rated as more affectionate and less anxious as children, managed this shift more easily than those who had difficulties availing themselves of external sources of emotional support in adulthood (Werner & Smith, 1992).

Links Between Protective Factors and Successful Adaptation in High-Risk Children and Youths

When we examined the links between protective factors within the individual and outside sources of support or stress, we noted a certain continuity that appeared in the life courses of the high-risk men and women in the Kauai Longitudinal Study who successfully overcame a variety of childhood adversities. Their individual dispositions led them to select or construct environments that, in turn, reinforced and sustained their active, outgoing dispositions and that rewarded their competencies (Werner, 1993).

Although parental competence and the sources of support available in the childhood home were modestly linked to the quality of adult adaptation, they made less of a direct impact in adulthood than did the individual's competencies, self-esteem, self-efficacy, and temperamental dispositions. Many resilient high-risk youths left the adverse conditions of their childhood homes (and their island community) after high school and sought environments they found more compatible. In short, they picked their own niches. We noted, however, that protective factors within the individual (such as temperament, cognitive skills, self-esteem, and locus of control) tended consistently to make a greater impact on the quality of adult adaptation for the high-risk women than for the high-risk men. In contrast, outside sources of support tended to make a greater difference in the lives of the high-risk men than in lives of the high-risk women.

Our findings lend some empirical support to Scarr and McCartney's (1983) theory concerning how people make their own environment. They proposed three different effects of people's genes on their environment: passive, evocative, and active. Because parents provide both genes and rearing environments, children's genes are necessarily correlated with their own environments, which is the passive type of genotype–environment effect. The evocative type refers to the fact that a person's partially heritable characteristics, such as intelligence, temperament, and physical attractiveness, evoke certain responses from other people. Finally, a person's interest and special talents (genetically variable traits) may lead him or her to select or create particular environments, which is an active genotype–environment effect. In line with this theory, there was a shift from passive to active effects as the youths and young adults in the Kauai study left stressful home environments and sought extrafamilial environments that they found more compatible and stimulating. Genotype–environment effects of the evocative sort tended to persist throughout the different life stages we studied, as individuals' physical characteristics, temperament, and intelligence elicited differential responses from other people: parents, teachers, and peers.

IMPLICATIONS FOR EARLY INTERVENTION

What then are some of the implications that we can draw from the longitudinal studies of resilient children? Most of all, they provide us with a more hopeful perspective than can be gleaned from reading only the literature on children who succumb to the negative consequences of biological insults, caregiving deficits, and ecological stressors. Research on protective factors and individual resilience gives us an awareness of the self-righting tendencies that move children toward normal development under all but the most persistent adverse circumstances.

As long as the balance between stressful life events and protective factors is favorable, successful adaptation is possible even for young children who live in high-risk conditions. However, when stressful life events outweigh the protective factors, even the most resilient child can develop problems. Intervention may thus be conceived as an attempt to shift the balance from vulnerability to resilience, either by decreasing exposure to risk factors and stressful life events or by increasing the number of available protective factors (e.g., competencies and sources of support) in vulnerable children's lives.

It needs to be kept in mind that, with very few exceptions, research on individual resilience and protective factors has focused on children who muddled through on their own, with informal support from kith and kin, not children who were recipients of early intervention services. Yet, there are some lessons such children can teach us about effective early intervention.

1. There are large individual differences among high-risk children in their responses to both negative and positive circumstances in their environment. The very fact of individual variation among infants and young children who live in adverse conditions suggests the need for greater assistance to some than to others.
2. We need to set priorities, to make hard choices, if we cannot extend early intervention services to every child from birth to 6 years of age. Such programs need to focus especially on infants and young children who appear most vulnerable because they lack, temporarily or permanently, some of the essential social bonds that appear to buffer stress. Among these vulnerable children are the survivors of neonatal intensive care; hospitalized children who are separated from their families for extended periods of time; young offspring of alcoholic or psychotic parents; infants and toddlers whose mothers work full time in the labor market, without access

to stable child care; babies of single or teenage parents with no other adult in the household; and young migrant, homeless, or refugee children with no roots in a permanent community. Above all, we need to focus on young children who are poor.

3. Assessment and diagnosis, the initial part of early intervention, need to focus not only on risk factors in the lives of children and families they serve but also on the protective factors. These include the competencies and sources of informal support that already exist that can be utilized to enlarge a young child's repertoire of problem-solving skills and that can enhance his or her self-esteem.

4. Research on resilient children has shown repeatedly that if a parent is incapacitated or unavailable, other significant people in a young child's life can play an enabling role, whether they are grandparents, older siblings, child-care providers, or nursery school teachers. In many situations, it may make better sense to strengthen such available informal ties to kin and community than to introduce additional layers of bureaucracy into the delivery of services, and it might be less costly as well.

5. For any early intervention program to be effective, a young child needs enough consistent nurturance within that program to trust in its availability. Research on resilient children has shown that they had at least one person in their lives who accepted them unconditionally, regardless of temperamental idiosyncrasies, physical attractiveness, or intelligence level.

6. Research has also shown that the promotion of resilience in young children by caring adults does not rely on removing stress and adversity completely from their lives but rather in helping them encounter graduated challenges that enhance their competence and confidence.

7. Such challenges appear to be most effective for young children in the context of an organized and predictable environment that combines warmth and caring with a clearly defined structure and an established setting of explicit limits that are consistently enforced.

Project Head Start, the largest nationwide early intervention program established for children of poverty, even today, serves only one out of three of those who are eligible for the program. Especially in high-quality programs, it can foster many of the protective factors that have brought about positive

changes in the lives of the at-risk children who have been the focus of this review.

A promising example of a Head Start–based peer treatment program has been reported by Fantuzzo and his associates (Fantuzzo, Coolahan, & Weiss, in press). These investigators paired maltreated and socially withdrawn preschool children with more socially adept and responsive peers in Head Start programs that were supervised by parent assistants. In their study, Fantuzzo et al. demonstrated a significant and lasting increase in positive social interactions and a decrease in solitary play for these at-risk children under the influence of their more outgoing peers.

Several national evaluation studies have also documented positive effects on both at-risk youngsters and foster grandparents who are participants in the Domestic Volunteer Service. Infants with foster grandparents were easily comforted and became strongly attached to their foster grandmothers; toddlers showed improvement in motor and social development; and preschool children made gains in cognitive development and social competence. For the foster grandparents, in turn, the experience with the children in their care was associated with improved life satisfaction, health, and vigor (Werner, 1997).

The positive effects of one-to-one mentoring on the lives of older at-risk children has been demonstrated in a nationwide evaluation study by the Philadelphia-based Public/Private Venture (P/PV), a policy research organization. In 1995, Big Brothers/Big Sisters operated all across the country and maintained 75,000 active matches between adult volunteers and children. On average, the adult–youth pairs met for three to four hours, three times a month, for at least a year. Researchers from P/PV examined 959 10- to 16-year-olds who had applied to Big Brothers/Big Sisters programs in 1992 and 1993. More than 60% of the sample youths were boys; more than half were minorities, mainly Black, and almost all lived with a single parent. More than 80% came from poor households, 40% from homes with a history of substance abuse, and nearly 30% from homes with a history of serious domestic violence. Half of these youths were randomly assigned to a group for which Big Brother/Big Sister matches were made; the other half were assigned to waiting lists.

The results were striking. The addition of a Big Brother or Big Sister to a youngster's life for 1 year cut first-time drug use by 46%, lowered school absenteeism by 52%, and reduced violent behavior by 33%. Participants in the Big Brothers/Big Sisters program were significantly less likely to start using alcohol, less likely to assault someone, more likely to do well in school, and much more likely to relate well to friends and family. The effects held across races, for both boys and girls (Tierney, Grossman, & Resch, 1995).

In *Within Our Reach: Breaking the Cycle of Disadvantage*, Schorr (1988) isolated a set of common characteristics of programs that successfully prevented poor outcomes for children who grew up in high-risk families. Such programs typically offer a broad spectrum of health, education, and family support services; cross professional boundaries; and view the child in the context of the family and the family in the context of the community. These programs provide children with sustained access to competent and caring adults, both professionals and volunteers, who teach them problem-solving skills, enhance their communication skills and self-esteem, and provide positive role models for them (Pless & Stein, 1994).

The life stories of resilient individuals have taught us that competence, confidence, and caring can flourish even under adverse circumstances, if young children encounter persons who provide them with a secure basis for the development of trust, autonomy, and initiative. However, we also need to examine the price exacted from such children, for some protective factors (such as the ability to detach oneself from a dysfunctional home environment) may promote positive adaptation in one context at one time but have negative effects in another context, at a later developmental stage (such as difficulties in forming intimate relationships in adolescence or adulthood).

Future research on risk and resiliency needs to acquire a cross-cultural perspective as well as focus on developing-world children and on immigrant children from these countries, whose daily lives are confronted with many biological and psychosocial risk factors that increase their vulnerability far beyond that of their peers who were born in affluent industrialized countries. We need to know more about individual dispositions and sources of support that transcend cultural boundaries and operate effectively in a variety of high-risk contexts.

Finally, future risk and resilience research must direct its attention to causal-relationship hypotheses by making use of behavior and genetic strategies. Many stressful experiences, such as parental discord, parental mental illness, substance abuse, or divorce, impinge differently on different siblings in the same family. Thus, we need to look more carefully at the contributions of shared versus nonshared family environments to the vulnerability and resiliency of high-risk children (Rende & Plomin, 1993).

Ultimately, the most powerful tests of protective factor and individual resilience hypotheses may come from intergenerational studies of siblings in high-risk families who differ in developmental outcomes and from evaluation studies of early intervention programs whose objective is to change the course of development in children who have been exposed to potent biological, psychosocial, or both, risk factors. Both types of studies should have high priority for research in the next century.

REFERENCES

Anthony, E. J. (1987). Children at high risk for psychosis growing up. In E. J. Anthony & B. J. Cohler (Eds.), *The invulnerable child* (pp. 147–84). New York: Guilford Press.

Antonovsky, A. (1987). *Unraveling the mystery of health: How people manage stress and stay well*. San Francisco: Jossey-Bass.

Barr, R. G., Boyce, T., & Zeltzer, L. K. (1994). The stress-illness association in children: A perspective from the biobehavioral interface. In R. J. Haggerty, L. R. Sherrod, N. Garmezy, & M. Rutter (Eds.), *Stress, risk, and resilience in children and adolescents* (pp. 182–224). New York: Cambridge University Press.

Block, J. (1993). Studying personality the long way. In D. Funder, R. Parke, C. Tornlinson-Keasey, and K. Widaman (Eds.), *Studying lives through time: Personality and development* (pp. 9–41). Washington, DC: American Psychological Association.

Block, J., & Gjerde, P. (1986, August). *Early antecedents of ego-resiliency in late adolescence*. Paper presented at the American Psychological Association Meeting, Washington, DC.

Block, J., & Kremen, A. M. (1996). IQ and ego-resiliency: Conceptual and empirical connections and separateness. *Journal of Personality and Social Psychology 70*, 349–61.

Boyce, W. T., Chesney, M., Kaiser, P., Alkon-Leonard, A., & Tschann, B. (1992). Child care stressors, cardiovascular reactivity, and injury incidence in preschool children. *Pediatric Research, 32,* 9A.

Boyce, W. T., Chesterman, E. A., Wara, D., Cohen, F., Folkman, S., & Martin, N. (1991). Immunologic changes occurring at kindergarten entry predict respiratory illness following the Lorna Prieta earthquake. *Pediatric Research, 29* (4), 8A.

Burnette, E. (1996). Research looks at how children fare at times of war. *APA Monitor* (January).

Cohler, B. S. (1987). Adversity, resilience, and the study of lives. In E. J. Anthony & B. J. Cohler (Eds.), *The invulnerable child* (pp. 363–424). New York: Guilford Press.

Dalianis, M. K. (1994). *Early trauma and adult resiliency: A mid-life follow-up study of young children whose mothers were political prisoners during the Greek Civil War.* Doctoral dissertation, Karolinska Institute, Stockholm, Sweden.

Egeland, B., Carison, L., & Sroufe, L. A. (1993). Resilience as process. Special issue: Milestones in the development of resilience. *Development and Psychopathology, 5,* 517–28.

Elder, G. H., Caspi, A., & Van Nguyen, T. (1985). Resourceful and vulnerable children: Family influence in hard times. In R. Silbereisen & H. Eyferth (Eds.), *Development in context* (pp. 167–86). Berlin: Springer Verlag.

Emery, R. E., & Forehand, R. (1994). Parental divorce and children's well-being: A focus on resilience. In R. J. Haggerty, L. R. Sherrod, N. Garmezy, & M. Rutter (Eds.), *Stress, risk, and resilience in children and adolescents* (pp. 64–99). New York: Cambridge University Press.

Erikson, E. H. (1959). Identity and the life cycle. *Psychological Issues, 1,* 1–171.

Fantuzzo, J., Coolahan, K. C., & Weiss, A. D. (in press). Resiliency partnership-directed intervention: Enhancing the social competence of preschool victims of physical abuse by developing peer resources and community strengths. In D. Cicchetti & S. L. Toth (Eds.), *Rochester symposium on developmental psychopathology, Vols. 8 & 9: The effects of trauma on the developmental process.* Rochester, NY: University of Rochester Press.

Farber, E. A., & Egeland, B. (1987). Invulnerability among abused and neglected children. In E. J. Anthony & B. J. Cohler (Eds.), *The invulnerable child* (pp. 253–88). New York: Guilford Press.

Freedman, M. (1993), *The kindness of strangers.* San Francisco: Jossey-Bass

Furstenberg, F. F., Brooks-Gunn, J., & Morgan, S. P. (1987). *Adolescent mothers in later life.* New York: Cambridge University Press.

Garmezy, N., Masten, A. S., & Tellegen, A. (1984). The study of stress and competence in children: Building blocks for developmental psychopathology. *Child Development, 55,* 97–111.

Gore, S., & Eckenrode, J. (1994). Context and process in research on risk and resilience. In R. J. Haggerty, L. R. Sherrod, N. Garmezy, & M. Rutter (Eds.), *Stress, risk, and resilience in children and adolescents* (pp. 19–63). New York: Cambridge University Press.

Havighurst, R. J. (1972). *Developmental tasks and education.* New York: David McKay.

Herrenkohl, F. C., Herrenkohl, R. C., & Egolf, B. (1994). Resilient early school-age children from maltreating homes: Outcomes in late adolescence. *American Journal of Orthopsychiatry, 64,* 301–9.

Hetherington, E. M., Stanley-Ragan, M., & Anderson, E. R. (1989). Marital transitions: A child's perspective. *American Psychologist, 44,* 303–12.

Higgins, G. O. (1994). *Resilient adults: Overcoming a cruel past.* San Francisco: Jossey-Bass.

Johnson, H. L., Glassman, M. B., Fisk, K. B., & Rosen, T. S. (1990). Resilient children: Individual differences in developmental outcomes of children born to drug abusers. *Journal of Genetic Psychology, 151,* 523–39.

Klohnen, P. C. (1996). Conceptual analysis and measurement of the construct of ego-resiliency. *Journal of Personality and Social Psychology, 70,* 1067–79.

Luthar, S., & Zigler, E. (1991). Vulnerability and competence: A review of research on resilience in childhood. *American Journal of Orthopsychiatry, 61,* 6–22.

Luthar, S., & Cushing, G. (1999). Measurement issues in the empirical study of resilience: An overview. In M. D. Glantz, J. Johnson, & L. Huffman (Eds.), *Resiliency and development: Positive life adaptations* (pp.). New York: Plenum Press.

Masten, A. S. (1994). Resilience in individual development: Successful adaptation despite risk and adversity. In M. C. Wang & E. W. Gordon (Eds.), *Educational resilience in inner-city America: Challenges and prospects* (pp. 1–25). Hillsdale, NJ: Erlbaum.

Masten, A. S., Best, K. M., & Garmezy, N. (1990). Resilience and development: Contributions from the study of children who overcame adversity. *Development and Psychopathology, 2,* 425–44.

Moskovitz, S. (1983). *Love despite hate: Child survivors of the Holocaust and their adult lives.* New York: Schocken.

Moriarty, A. (1987). John, a boy who acquired resilience. In E. J. Anthony & B. J. Cohler (Eds.), *The invulnerable child* (pp. 106–43). New York: Guilford Press.

Murphy, L. B. (1987). Further reflections on resilience. In E. J. Anthony & B. J. Cohler (Eds.), *The invulnerable child* (pp. 84–105). New York: Guilford Press.

Musick, S. S., Stott, F. M., Spencer, K. K., Goldman, S. et. al. (1987). Maternal factors related to vulnerability and resiliency in young children at risk. In E. J. Anthony & B. J. Cohler (Eds.), *The invulnerable child* (pp. 229–52). New York: Guilford Press.

Pless, I. B., & Stein, R. E. K. (1994). Intervention research: Lessons from research on children with chronic disorders. In R. J. Haggerty, L. R. Sherrod, N. Garmezy, & M. Rutter (Eds.), *Stress, risk, and resilience in children and adolescents* (pp. 317–52). New York: Cambridge University Press.

Rachman, S. (1979). The concept of required helpfulness. *Behavior Research and Therapy 12*, 1–16.

Radke-Yarrow, M., & Brown, F. (1993). Resilience and vulnerability in children of multiple-risk families. *Development and Psychopathology, 5*, 581–92.

Rende, R., & Plomin, R. (1993). Families at risk for psychopathology: Who becomes affected and why? *Development and Psychopathology , 5*, 529–40.

Richman, N. (1993). Children in situations of political violence. *Journal of Child Psychology and Psychiatry, 34*, 1286–1302.

Rubin, L. (1996). *The transcendent child*. New York: Basic Books.

Rutter, M. (1987). Psychosocial resilience and protective mechanism. *American Journal of Orthopsychiatry, 57*, 316–31.

Rutter, M. (1994). Stress research: Accomplishments and tasks ahead. In R. J. Haggerty, L. R. Sherrod, N. Garmezy, & M. Rutter (Eds.), *Stress, risk, and resilience in children and adolescents* (pp. 354–86). New York: Cambridge University Press.

Scarr, S., & McCartney, L. (1983). How people make their own environments: A theory of genotype–environment effects. *Child Development, 54*, 424–35.

Schorr, L. (1988). *Within our reach: Breaking the cycle of disadvantage*. New York: Anchor Press.

Seifer, R., & Sameroff, A. J. (1987). Multiple determinants of risk and invulnerability. In E. J. Anthony & B. J. Cohler (Eds.), *The invulnerable child* (pp. 51–69). New York: Guilford Press.

Seifer, R., Sameroff, A. J., Baldwin, C. P., & Baldwin, A. (1992). Child and family factors that ameliorate risk between 4 and 13 years of age. *Journal of the American Academy of Child and Adolescent Psychiatry, 31*, 893–903.

Tierney, J. P., Grossman, J. B., & Resch, N. L. (1995). *Making a difference: An impact study of Big Brothers/Big Sisters*. Philadelphia: Private/Public Ventures.

Wallerstein, J. S., & Blakeslee, S. (1989). *Second chances: Men, women, and children a decade after divorce*. New York: Ticknor and Fields.

Wallerstein, J. S., & Kelley, J. B. (1980). *Surviving the breakup: How children and parents cope with divorce*. New York: Basic Books.

Werner, E. E. (1990). Protective factors and individual resilience. In S. J. Meisels & J. P. Shonkoff (Eds.), *Handbook of early childhood intervention* (pp. 97–116). New York: Cambridge University Press.

Werner, E. E. (1991). *The role of caring adults and religious coping efforts in the lives of children of alcoholics*. Final Report to the Lilly Endowment, Inc., Indianapolis, IN.

Werner, E. E. (1993). Risk, resilience, and recovery: Perspectives from the Kauai Longitudinal Study. *Development and Psychopathology, 5*, 503–15.

Werner, E. E. (1995). Resilience in development. *Current Directions in Psychological Science, 4* (3), 81–5.

Werner, E. E. (1997). The value of applied research for Head Start: A cross-cultural and longitudinal perspective. *National Head Start Association Journal of Research and Evaluation 1* (1).

Werner, E. E., & Johnson, J. L. (in press). Can we apply resilience? In M. D. Glantz, J. Johnson, & L. Huffman (Eds.), *Resiliency and development: Positive life adaptations*. New York: Plenum Press.

Werner, E. E., & Smith, R. S. (1989) *Vulnerable but invincible: A longitudinal study of resilient children and youth*. New York: Adams, Bannister, Cox.

Werner, E. E., & Smith, R. S. (1992). *Overcoming the odds: High risk children from birth to adulthood*. Ithaca, NY: Cornell University Press.

Zimmerman, M. A., & Arunkumar, R. (1995). Resiliency research: Implications for schools and policy. *Society for Research in Child Development Social Policy Reports, 8*, 1–19. Ann Arbor, MI: Society for Research in Child Development.

PART THREE

THEORETICAL FRAMEWORKS FOR INTERVENTION

CHAPTER SEVEN

Transactional Regulation:

The Developmental Ecology of Early Intervention

ARNOLD J. SAMEROFF AND BARBARA H. FIESE

The prevention of children's psychosocial disorders has not been an easily accomplished task. During the years since we wrote this last sentence in our chapter for the first edition of this book (Sameroff & Fiese, 1990), the lives of children in the United States have not improved. The Children's Defense Fund (1995) estimates that between 3 and 10 million children experience domestic violence yearly, with more than a million confirmed child abuse or neglect cases in 1993. Mental health also continues to be a major problem, with approximately 20% of children having diagnosable disorders (U.S. Department of Health and Human Services, 1990). Surveys of child health found that 13.4% of children in the United States have emotional or behavioral disorders, 6.5% have learning disabilities, and 4% have developmental delays (Zill & Schoenborn, 1990). Decreasing these numbers requires a clear understanding of the causes of these childhood problems. One of the clear correlates of increases in child problems is the decline in the quality of children's environments.

Concurrent with the high level of problems among children, family resources for coping with these problems have diminished. In 1991, 22% of children lived in families with incomes below the poverty line, the highest rate since the early 1960s (Children's Defense Fund, 1992). During the same period, the percentage of female-headed single-parent homes increased from 7% to more than 21% (McLanahan, Astone, & Marks, 1991). Moreover, 75% of mothers of school-age children are in the workforce now compared to about 50% in 1970 (U.S. Department of Health and Human Services, 1993).

Declines in family resources for supporting child development have often been offset by social programs that offer compensatory professional or economic support. Unfortunately, we are living in a historical period in which these resources are also in decline. For all these reasons, if we are to utilize beneficially the intervention resources that are still available, it is of the utmost importance to have a clear understanding of the sources of problems in child development. The first edition of this handbook made a major contribution in emphasizing that the context of development is as important as the characteristics of the child in determining successful development. We shall continue this theme by delineating an ecological model of development and the dynamic processes by which children and their environments interact. Through this presentation we identify a number of requirements necessary for successful intervention to support child development. The first is to recognize that child development has multiple contributors at multiple levels of the child's ecology. The second is that at each of these levels, multiple processes are represented in family thought and cultural symbols and are enacted in family interactions and social services. The third requirement is that intervention processes be targeted at a particular problem for a particular child in a particular family in a particular culture. Unfortunately, there are no universal treatments for all children.

In this chapter, we use an ecological model (Bronfenbrenner, 1977; Garbarino, 1990) to enumerate a variety of factors that affect child competence, ranging from parent practices that have direct influence on the child to community and economic factors that impinge on the child through the action of others. Depending on disciplinary background, different factors have been proposed to explain children's problems. Economists focus on poverty and deprivation as the roots of social maladjustment; sociologists implicate problems in the community and family structure as the variables that promote deviancy; educators seek to repair problems in the school system; and psychologists focus on processes within the family and its members as the environmental influences that most profoundly affect successful development. We have accepted all of these proposals but, rather than viewing them as competing, we see them as additive contributors to a positive or negative trajectory through life.

No single factor is damaging or facilitating for children. Rather, the power of an individual factor or set of factors lies in their accumulation in the life of any one child. Children reared in families with a large number of negative influences will do worse than children in families with few risk factors. Such a view militates against any simplistic proposal that by changing one thing in society, we will change the fate of our children. Competence is the result of a complex interplay of children with a range of personalities in different kinds of families in communities with varying economic and social resources. Only by attending to such complexity will the development of competence be understood and perhaps altered for the better.

Unfortunately, intervention programs are seldom equipped to deal with the full range of factors that influence successful development. To the extent that there is a range of options within a program, decisions must be made as to which families need which options. To the extent that appropriate options are not available, decisions have to be made concerning where families can obtain needed resources. In either event, there is a need to understand the social influences on development and, in turn, which of them can be improved upon. It is the purpose of this chapter to provide a perspective on social influences that can help with such decisions.

We begin with an overview of traditional concepts of intervention and prevention. When these ideas are used to interpret causal factors in disease, a variety of paradoxes emerge that require a contextual systems analysis of developmental processes for their understanding. A transactional model is described that explains behavioral outcomes as the mutual effects of context on child and child on context. The transactional model is shown as embedded in a regulatory system that is characteristic of all developmental processes. Based on the regulatory system, a number of intervention strategies are described that are theoretically driven and that enhance the possibility of providing optimal outcomes for children. Several of these ideas have been presented at greater length in the first edition of this handbook. In portions of the text where we have abbreviated the presentation, the reader is referred to the earlier reference (Sameroff & Fiese, 1990).

DEFINING PREVENTION

Intervention efforts are typically divided into primary, secondary, and tertiary categories (Leavell & Clark, 1965). Primary prevention is practiced prior to the origin of the disease. Secondary prevention is practiced after the disease has been identified but before it has caused disability. Tertiary prevention occurs after disability has been experienced with the goal of reducing further deterioration.

However, these distinctions among prevention categories are less clear when one turns from the primary prevention of biological diseases, the source of the formulation of these definitions, to the primary prevention of psychological disease, the source of the increasing complexity of the problem. Although clear linkages have been found between some germs and specific biological disorders (e.g., diplococci and diptheria), this is not true for behavioral disorders. Much promise is emanating from progress in genetic research. However, translations into effective intervention programs are yet to be achieved.

Primary prevention of psychological disorders, in the sense of deterring a single biological factor, may have meaning in a small percentage of instances, but these are usually the most severe and profound cases. In the vast majority of cases, behavioral or developmental disturbances are the result of combined factors that are more strongly associated with the environment than with any intrinsic characteristics of the affected individuals. The one major genetic success story is the prevention of the effects of phenylketonuria (PKU). However, the prevention strategy is an environmental one, changing the child's diet rather than changing the child.

Traditionally, early intervention programs have been based on stable models of development in which children who were identified as doing poorly early in life were expected to continue to do poorly. Early childhood education, as exemplified in Head Start, was designed to improve the learning and social competence of children during the preschool years with the expectation that these improvements would be maintained later in life. Unfortunately, follow-up research of Head Start children has shown only moderate gains in measurable intellectual competence being maintained through adolescence (Zigler, Styfco, & Gilman, 1993), although there were reduced rates of school failure and need for special education in other early intervention programs (Lazar, Darlington, Murray, Royce, & Snipper, 1982; Schweinhart & Weikart, 1980).

From a different perspective, children who were identified early in life as being at risk because of such biological circumstances as birth complications were thought to have generally negative developmental outcomes. But longitudinal research in this area has demonstrated that the majority of children who experienced such biological conditions did not have intellectual or social problems later in life (Sameroff, 1986; Sameroff & Chandler, 1975).

We can draw two conclusions that have major implications for intervention programs. The first is that the child's level of competency at any point in early development, whether reached through normal developmental processes or some special intervention efforts, is not linearly related to the child's competence later in life. The second point is that in order to complete an equation predictive of later development, one needs to add the effects of the child's social and family environment that act to foster or impede the continuing positive developmental course of the child. In short, intervention programs cannot be successful if changes are made only in the individual child. Corollary changes in the environment must occur that will enhance the existing competencies of the child and buffer the child from stressful life events in the future.

ECOLOGICAL RISK FACTORS

Let us turn for a moment to research aimed at identifying representative risk factors in the development of cognitive and social–emotional competence. Such competencies of young children have been found to be strongly related to family mental health and especially social class (Broman, Nichols, & Kennedy, 1975; Werner & Smith, 1982). However, social classes differ in many of the characteristics that foster or impede psychological development in their children. These factors range from such proximal variables as the mother's interaction with the child, to such intermediate variables as the mother's mental health, to distal variables such as the financial resources of the family.

An ecological model emphasizes the complexity of development and the large number of environmental influences on children. Although causal models have been sought in which singular variables uniquely determine aspects of child behavior, a series of studies in a variety of domains has found that, except at the extremes of biological dysfunction, it is the number rather than the nature of risk factors that is the best determinant of outcome. For example, Parmelee and Haber (1973) found this to be true for neurological factors in samples of infants with many perinatal problems, and Rutter (1979) for family factors in samples of children with many psychosocial problems. We have followed this theme in a series of developmental studies of children and found that attention to the full array of contextual factors provides a better picture of each child's development as well as identifying those children in greatest need of intervention efforts.

The Rochester Study

In a longitudinal study of children in Rochester, New York, Sameroff, Seifer, Barocas, Zax, and Greenspan (1987) assessed a set of 10 environmental variables when the children were 4 years old. They tested whether poor development was a function of low SES or the compounding of environmental risk factors found more frequently in lower SES groups. The ten environmental risk variables were chronicity of maternal mental illness; maternal anxiety; a parental perspectives score derived from a combination of measures that reflected rigidity or flexibility in the attitudes, beliefs, and values that mothers had in regard to their child's development; spontaneous positive maternal interactions with the child during infancy; occupation of head of household; maternal education; disadvantaged minority status; family support; stressful life events; and family size.

When these risk factors were related to social–emotional and cognitive competence scores, major differences were found between those children with low multiple risk scores and those with high scores. In terms of intelligence, children with no environmental risks scored more than thirty points higher than children with eight or nine risk factors. Similarly, the range in scores on an assessment of the social and emotional competencies of the children showed a similar spread (Sameroff, Seifer, Zax, & Barocas, 1987).

Several conclusions from this study are relevant to intervention efforts. One conclusion is that the number of risk factors was the prime determinant of outcome within each socioeconomic level, not the socioeconomic level itself. The second and more important conclusion for intervention strategies is that the same outcomes were the result of different combinations of risk factors. Preschool cognitive development was not different for groups of children with the same number of risks. No single factor was regularly related to either poor or good outcomes. If this is the case, it is unlikely that universal interventions can be found for the problems of children. For every family situation, a unique analysis of risk factors will require a unique set of intervention strategies embedded within a developmental model.

The Philadelphia Study

The Rochester Study (Sameroff et al., 1987) was somewhat exploratory in that risk factors were chosen from those already available in the data set and were not fully representative of the many contexts in which children are influenced. In a newer study of adolescents in Philadelphia, Pennsylvania, Furstenberg, Cook, Eccles, Elder, and Sameroff (1999) were more planful and included factors in six different ecological domains. They examined variables within systems that affected the adolescent, ranging from those microsystems (Bronfenbrenner, 1977) in which the child was an active participant, such as parent–child interactions, to those systems more distal to the child, such as community characteristics.

Twenty variables were selected from six groupings reflecting different ecological relations to the adolescent (see Table 7.1), twice as many as in the Rochester

TABLE 7.1. Ecological Risk Variables in Philadelphia Study

Domain	Variables
Family process	Support for autonomy, discipline effectiveness, parental investment, and family climate
Parent characteristics	Education, efficacy, resourcefulness, and mental health
Family structure	Marital status, household crowding, and welfare receipt
Management of community	Institutional involvement, informal networks, social resources, and economic adjustment
Peers	Prosocial and antisocial
Community	Neighborhood SES, neighborhood problems, and school climate

Study. The intention was to have multiple factors in each of the six ecological levels. *Family Process* was the first grouping and included variables in the family microsystem that were directly experienced by the child. These included support for autonomy, behavior control, parental involvement, and family climate. The second grouping was *Parent Characteristics*, which included the mother's mental health, sense of efficacy, resourcefulness, and level of education. This group included variables that influenced the child but, generally speaking, were less influenced by the child. The third grouping was *Family Structure*, which included the parents' marital status, and socioeconomic indicators of household crowding and receiving welfare payments. The fourth grouping was *Family Management of the Community* and comprised variables that characterized the family's management of its relationship to the larger community as reflected in variables of institutional involvement, informal networks, social resources, and adjustments to economic pressure. The fifth grouping, *Peers*, included indicators of another microsystem of the child, the extent to which the youth was associated with prosocial and antisocial peers. *Community* was the sixth grouping representing the ecological level most distal to the youth and the family. It included a census tract variable reflecting the average income and educational level of the neighborhood the family lived in, a parental report of the number of problems in the neighborhood, and the climate of the adolescent's school.

In the Philadelphia Study (Furstenberg et al., 1999), in addition to the larger number of ecological variables, we had a wider array of assessments available for interpreting developmental competence. The five outcomes that were thought to characterize successful adolescence were parent reports of adolescent *Psychological Adjustment* on a number of mental health scales; youth reports of *Self-Competence* measures and *Problem Behavior* with drugs, delinquency, and sexual behavior; combined youth and parent reports of *Activity Involvement* in sports, religious, extracurricular, and community projects; and *Academic Performance* as reflected in grade reports submitted by the parent and adolescent.

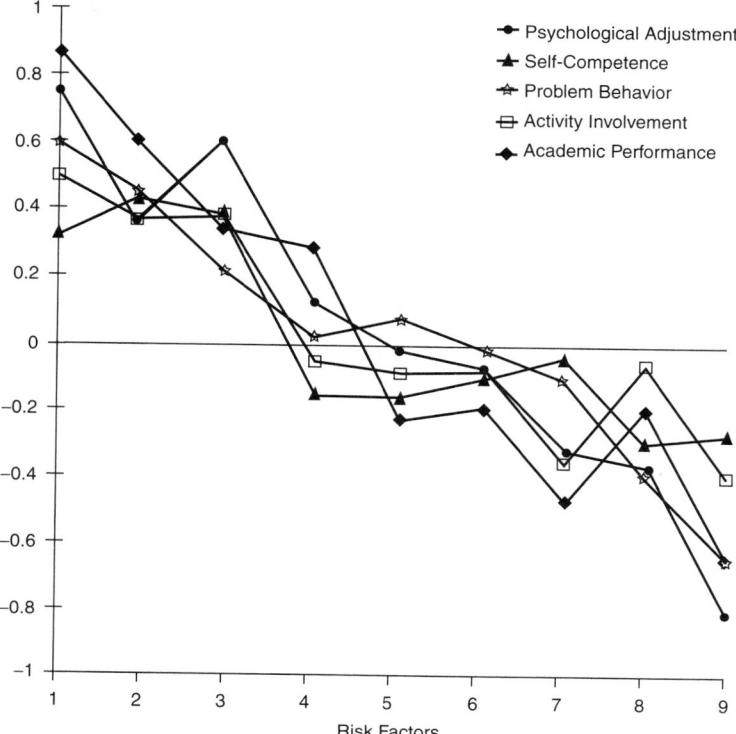

Figure 7.1. Relation of five youth outcomes to multiple risk scores in Philadelphia study.

In the Philadelphia data, there were risks at every ecological level associated with child outcomes. It was not only the parent or the family that had an influence on child competence but also the peer group, neighborhood, and community, together with their interactions with the family. Some of the variables were risks for each of our five outcomes. These included lack of support for autonomy, a negative family climate, and few prosocial peers. At the other extreme were variables that affected only a few outcomes such as having parents who lacked education and resourcefulness, single marital status and significant economic adjustment, a lack of informal networks, and low census tract socioeconomic status.

The important question was whether there would be the same effect of multiple risk factors in Philadelphia as was seen in Rochester. When the five normalized adolescent outcome scores were plotted against the number of risk factors, a large decline in outcome was found with increasing risk. As can be seen in Figure 7.1, the maximum effect of cumulative risk was on Psychological Adjustment and

Academic Performance with smaller relations to the youth's report of Self Competence and Activity Involvement.

ODDS-RATIO ANALYSIS. Whether the cumulative risk score meaningfully increases the predictive efficiency of risk variables can be demonstrated by an odds-ratio analysis. The odds of having a bad outcome in a high-risk neighborhood could be compared with the odds in a low-risk environment. To simplify the report, we examined the relation between the negative outcomes and adolescent environmental risk scores in four multiple-risk groups: a low-risk group defined as three or fewer, two moderate risk groups of four-to-five and six-to-seven risks, and a high-risk group with eight or more (see Figure 7.2).

The relative risk in the high-risk group for each of the negative outcomes was substantially higher than in the low-risk group. The strongest effects were for Academic Performance, in which the relative risk for

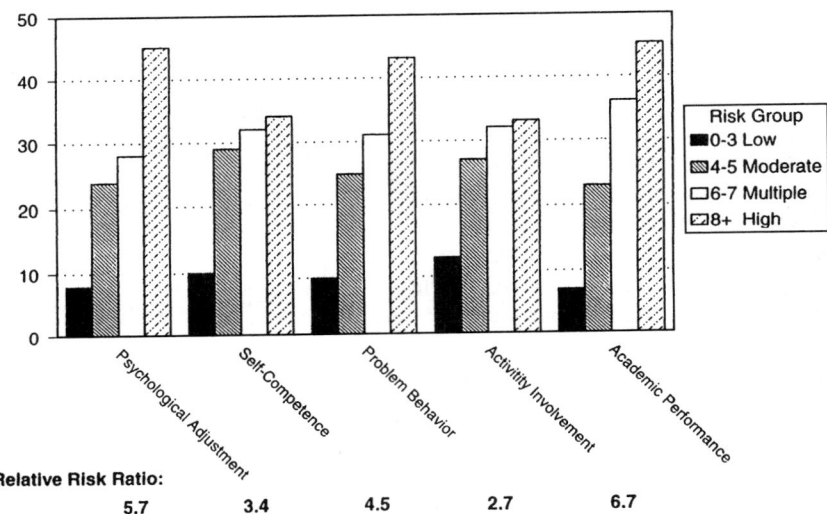

Figure 7.2. Percentage of youth in lowest quartile for five youth outcomes in the Philadelphia study separated into four multiple risk groups. Odds are calculated as the ratio between percent of youth in the lowest quartile in the high-risk and low-risk groups.

a bad outcome increased from 7% in the low-risk group to 45% in the high-risk group – an odds ratio of 6.7 to 1. The weakest effect was for Activity Involvement, in which the relative risk only increased from 12 to 33% – an odds ratio of 2.7 to 1. In some sense this is not unexpected because, although everyone would agree that academic failure and poor mental health are bad outcomes, there might be some dispute whether an adolescent's desire not to participate in scouts, religious activities, or sports reflects a lack of competence. In any case, for the important cognitive and social–emotional outcomes of youth, there seem to be powerful negative effects of the accumulation of environmental risk factors.

PROMOTIVE FACTORS

The concern with preventing developmental failures has often clouded the fact that the majority of children in every social class and ethnic group are not failures. They get jobs, have successful social relationships, and raise a new generation of children. The concern with the source of such success has fostered an increasing concern with the development of competence and the identification of protective factors (Garmezy, Masten, & Tellegen, 1984). However, the differentiation between risk and protective factors is far from clear (Seifer & Sameroff, 1987), and there continue to be many theoretical and methodological limitations in their identification (Luthar & Zigler, 1991).

Although some have argued that protective factors can only have meaning in the face of adversity (Rutter, 1987), in most cases protective factors simply appear to be the positive pole of risk factors (Stouthamer-Loeber et al., 1993). In this sense, a better term for the positive end of the risk dimension would be *promotive* rather than protective factors. To test this simplification, we created a set of promotive factors by subdividing each of our risk dimensions at the top quartile (Sameroff, Bartko, Baldwin, Baldwin, & Seifer, 1998). For example, when a negative family climate had been a risk factor, a positive family climate now became a promotive factor, or when a parent's poor mental health was a risk factor, her good mental health became promotive. We then summed these promotive factors and examined their relation to our five outcomes. The results mirrored our analysis of the effects of multiple risks. A similar range of promotive factors was found from families with none to families with 15 out of a possible 20 and a similar relation to outcomes; families with many promotive factors did substantially better than those from contexts with few promotive factors. For the youths in the Philadelphia sample, there does not seem to be much difference between the influence of risk and promotive variables. The greater the risk factors, the worse the outcomes; the more promotive factors, the better the outcomes. In short, when taken as part of a constellation of environmental influences on child development, most contextual variables in the parents, the family, the neighborhood, and the culture at large seem to be dimensional, aiding in general child development at one end and inhibiting it at the other.

IDENTIFYING INTERVENTION TARGETS

Multirisk analyses emphasize the many factors that influence child development, yet most political policy is devoted to changing single factors in children's lives. Two factors that have received great attention are the *effects of poverty* and the *effects of living in a single-parent home*. Although one would think that these factors should have powerful effects on the fate of children, we did not find such differences when these single variables were put into a broader multi-risk ecological framework. Differences in effects on child competence disappeared when we controlled for the number of other environmental risk factors in each family. To test the effects of different amounts of financial resources, we split our sample of families into those with higher, middle, and lower income levels. For the family structure comparison, we divided the sample into groups of children living in two-parent versus single-parent families. To simplify the analysis further, we combined the five youth outcomes into one overall adolescent competence score reflecting general adaptation across personal, academic, and social domains. In each case, there were no differences in the relation to child competence when we compared groups of children with the same number of risk factors raised in rich or poor families or families with one or two parents.

The reason that income and marital status seem to make major differences in child development is not because they are overarching variables in themselves but because they are strongly associated with a combination of other risk or promotive factors.

For example, we found that although 39% of poorer children lived in high-risk families with more than seven risk factors, only 7% of more affluent children did. Similarly, although 29% of single-parent families lived in high-risk social conditions, only 15% of two-parent families did.

Our analyses of the data reveal that single environmental factors rarely make a major difference by themselves; rather, the constellation of risks in each family's life does make a difference. In the Philadelphia study, the effects of income level or marital status taken alone were small or nonexistent in comparison with the effects of the accumulation of multiple negative influences that characterize our high-risk groups. The overlap in outcomes for youths in high- and low-income families, and in single- and two-parent families, is substantial for any and all psychological outcomes. There are many successful adults who were raised in poverty and unsuccessful ones who were raised in affluence. There are many healthy and happy adults who come from broken homes, and there are many unhappy ones who were raised by two parents.

What these analyses tell us is that income level and marital status taken alone may have some effects on adolescent behavior but that these differences pale in comparison with the accumulation of multiple negative influences that characterize our high-risk groups. The overlap in outcomes for youths in low-income versus high-income families and families with one or two parents is substantial for most psychological outcomes, but the overlap is far less in comparisons of groups of children reared in conditions of high versus low multiple risk, in which income and number of parents in the home are only single factors. The important implication of this research is that a focus on individual characteristics of families can never explain more than a tiny proportion of variance in behavioral development. To truly appreciate the determinants of successful development requires that attention be paid to a broad constellation of ecological factors in which these individuals and families are embedded.

TRANSACTIONAL MODEL

In our ecological analyses, we have emphasized the role of the environment in affecting child development and have argued that planning effective

MOTHER

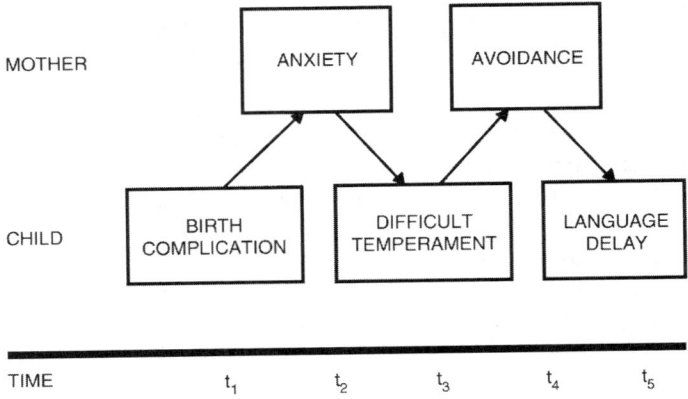

CHILD

TIME t_1 t_2 t_3 t_4 t_5

Figure 7.3. Example of transactional process leading to developmental problem.

interventions requires a sophisticated view of environmental action that includes attention to many factors. Within this contextual emphasis, we cannot lose sight of the important role individual differences in the child play in terms of what the child elicits from the environment and what the child is able to take from the environment.

One such developmental model that appears to apply in a number of scientific domains is the transactional model (Sameroff, 1983, 1993; Sameroff & Chandler, 1975). In this approach, developmental outcomes are neither a function of the individual alone nor of the experiential context alone. Outcomes are a product of the combination of an individual and his or her experience. To predict outcome, a singular focus on the characteristics of the individual, in this case the child, frequently will be misleading. An analysis and assessment of the experiences available to the child need to be added.

Within this transactional model, the development of the child is seen as a product of the continuous dynamic interactions of the child and the experience provided by his or her family and social context. What is innovative about the transactional model is the equal emphasis placed on the effects of the child and the environment so that the experiences provided by the environment are not viewed as independent of the child. The child may have been a strong determinant of current experiences, but developmental outcomes cannot be systematically described without an analysis of the effects of the environment on the child. A concrete example

of such a transactional outcome can be seen in Figure 7.3.

In Figure 7.3, the child's outcome is neither a function of the initial state of the child nor the initial state of the environment but is a complex function of the interplay of child and environment over time. For example, complicated childbirth may have made an otherwise calm mother somewhat anxious. The mother's anxiety during the first months of the child's life may have caused her to be uncertain and inappropriate in her interactions with the child. In response to such inconsistency, the infant may have developed some irregularities in feeding and sleeping patterns that give the appearance of a difficult temperament. This difficult temperament decreases the pleasure that the mother obtains from the child, so she tends to spend less time with her child. If adults are not actively interacting with the child, and especially speaking to the child, the child may not meet the norms for language development and may score poorly on preschool language tests.

What determined the poor outcome in this example? Was the poor linguistic performance caused by the complicated childbirth, the mother's anxiety, the child's difficult temperament, or the mother's avoidance of verbal and social interaction? If one were to design an intervention program for this family, where would it be directed? If one were to select the most proximal cause, it would be the mother's avoidance of the child, yet one can see that such a view would oversimplify a complex developmental sequence. Would primary prevention be directed at eliminating the child's difficult temperament, changing the mother's reaction, or providing alternative sources of verbal stimulation for the child? Each of these would eliminate a potential dysfunction at some contemporary point in the developmental system. But would any of these efforts ensure the verbal competence of the child or, perhaps more important, ensure the continued progress of the child after the intervention was completed?

The series of transactions described earlier is an example of how developmental achievements are rarely sole consequences of immediate antecedents and even more rarely sole consequences of distal antecedents. Not only is the causal chain extended over time but it is also embedded in an interpretive framework. The mother's anxiety is based on an interpretation of the meaning of a complicated childbirth, and her avoidance is based on an interpretation of the meaning of the child's irregular feeding and sleeping patterns. To understand the effects of interventions on the way parents behave toward their infants, there is a need to understand this interpretive framework. What follows is a description of the organization and operation of this interpretive scheme that offers the possibility of a richer understanding of why past intervention strategies were more or less successful. The ultimate goal of this description is to provide a theoretical basis for the design of future intervention strategies that can be targeted at a level of developmental regulation appropriate to the desired change in a child's development.

THE ENVIRONTYPE

Just as there is a biological organization, the genotype, which regulates the physical outcome of each individual, there is a social organization that regulates the way human beings fit into their society. This organization operates through family and cultural socialization patterns and has been postulated to compose an *environtype* analogous to the biological genotype (Sameroff, 1995). The importance of identifying the sources of regulation of human development is obvious if one is interested in manipulating that development, as in the case of prevention or intervention programs. It is beyond the scope of even the most ambitious intervention program to manipulate all of the parameters that influence child development. The alternative is to understand determinants of development in sufficient degree to choose a level of complexity appropriate to the problem to be solved, the developmental stages of the child and family, and available supports. The failures of intervention efforts can only be understood in terms of a failure to understand these regulatory systems. Each individual's environtype contains these regulatory patterns.

For our purposes, we restrict the discussion to levels of environmental factors contained within the culture, the family, and the individual parent. These subsystems not only transact with the child but also transact with one another. Developmental regulations at each of these levels are carried within codes:

the cultural code, the family code, and the individual code of the parent. These codes regulate cognitive and social–emotional development so that the child ultimately will be able to fill a role defined by society. They are hierarchically related in their evolution and in their current influence on the child. The experience of the developing child is partially determined by the beliefs, values, and personality of the parents; partially by the family's interaction patterns and transgenerational history; and partially by the socialization beliefs, controls, and supports of the culture. However, there is a distinction between codes and behaviors. The environtype is no more a description of the experiential environment than the genotype is a description of the biological phenotype. In each case, the code must be actualized through behavior. The codes have an organizational and regulatory influence on parent behavior, but the behavior is not the same as the codes.

Most behavioral research on the effects of the environment has been limited to the study of mother–child interaction patterns, which is only one component of the environtype. Another component is parental belief systems (Sigel, McGillicuddy-De-Lisi, & Goodnow, 1992). These beliefs include parent understanding of child behavior, the sources of developmental change (Sameroff & Feil, 1983), and child-rearing values (Kohn, 1969).

To summarize the overall model of developmental regulation, the child's behavior is a product of the transactions between the phenotype (i.e., the child), the environtype (i.e., the source of external experience) and the genotype (i.e., the source of biological organization; see Figure 7.4). Traditional research on child development has emphasized the child's utilization of biological capacities to gain experience and the role of experience in shaping child competencies, but there has been far less attention to how

Figure 7.4. Regulation model of development with transactions among genotype, phenotype, and environtype.

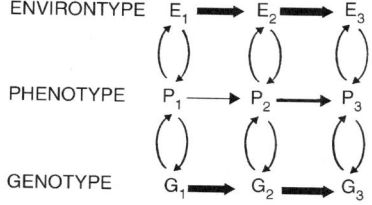

that experience is organized. Indeed, the organization of experience is explicit in the great amount of attention given to curriculum development and behavior modification plans, but far less attention is given to the implicit organization of experience found in the environtype to be described later.

Cultural Code

The ingredients of the cultural code are the complex characteristics that organize a society's child-rearing system and that incorporate elements of socialization and education. These processes are embedded in sets of social controls and social supports. They are based on beliefs that differ in the amount of community consensus ranging from mores and norms to fads and fashions. It would be beyond the scope of this chapter to elucidate the full range of cultural regulatory processes that are potentially relevant to intervention efforts. As a consequence, only a few points are highlighted to clarify the dimensions of the cultural code.

Many common biological characteristics of the human species have acted to produce similar developmental agendas in most cultures. For example, in most cultures formal education begins between the ages of 6 and 8 when most children have developed the cognitive ability to learn from such structured experiences (Rogoff, 1981). However, there are historical and cross-cultural differences in which changes in child behavior are emphasized or ignored. For example, informal education can begin at many different ages, depending on the culture's attributions to the child. For example, some middle-class parents have been convinced that prenatal experiences will enhance the cognitive development of their children and consequently begin stimulation programs during pregnancy, whereas others believe it best to wait until the first grade before beginning formal learning experiences. Such examples demonstrate the variability of human developmental contexts and the openness of the regulatory system to modification.

Family Code

The family code regulates child development through combinations of factors that extend across generations, include the coordinated efforts of more than two people, and provide a sense of belonging to a group. Traditional approaches to regulation in the family system have focused on the directly observable interaction patterns that are associated with such individual adaptations as sensitive, intrusive, or neglectful behaviors directed toward the child (e.g., Clarke-Stewart, 1973). In these cases, repetitive patterns of neglect or intrusiveness are proposed to lead to maladaptive development. Recent extensions to family management and dyadic interaction have also been proposed (Grych & Fincham, 1990; Parke & Bhavnagri, 1989). Regulation in the family system has also been approached from the perspective that family beliefs affect behavior directly through working models that guide behavior and impart expectations to children. This approach is evident in the attachment literature as well as in generational influences on development (Bowen, 1976; Main & Goldwyn, 1984). Both approaches may account for variability in child development and need not be considered incompatible heuristics. Intervention with families of young children demands attention to both the direct effects of interaction patterns that are proximal to the child's experience and family beliefs that may be more distal to the child.

To appreciate the effects of family interactions and beliefs on child development, it is important to identify the central tasks of the family. Family life extends across a variety of domains, and families are responsible for multiple aspects of their members' development. Landesman, Jaccard, and Gunderson (1991) proposed six domains of family functioning: 1) physical development and health, 2) emotional development and well-being, 3) social development, 4) cognitive development, 5) moral and spiritual development, and 6) cultural and aesthetic development. Families organize their behavior around these goals, and adaptation is linked to whether they are reached successfully. Families also change over the life span with shifts in membership through marriage, divorce, birth, and death that are often accompanied by changes in roles and responsibilities that affect individual adaptation (McGoldrick, Heiman, & Carter, 1993). We propose that the family code regulates development so that the tasks of the family may be fulfilled.

THE REPRESENTED AND PRACTICING FAMILY. Families organize experience through the beliefs that they hold and the ways in which they interact with each other. Reiss (1989) has theorized that family regulation can be detected and observed through the study of family practices and representations. The represented family highlights the internal representation of relationships and how working memories provide a sense of stability. Working models of relationships develop within the context of the family, are retained in memory, and guide the individual's behavior over time. To study the represented family, we must explore how families impart values and make sense of personal experiences. The practicing family, in contrast, stabilizes and regulates family members through observable interactions. The interaction patterns are repetitive and serve to provide a sense of family coherence and identity. Family life resides not only in the minds of individuals but also comes to life in the observed coordinated practices of the group (Grych & Fincham,1990; Reiss, 1981).

Representations are time-linked recollections of past experiences that are often reconstructed to include future expectations (Stern, 1989). For example, a parent's recollection of past childhood experiences may be influenced by the age of children in the family and current child-raising demands (Fiese, Hooker, Kotary, Schwagler, & Rimmer, 1995; Miller & Moore, 1989). Family practices are momentary exchanges that are repeated over time. They may serve as the foundation for some representations as interaction patterns become predictable, expectable, and a source of comment. For example, repetitive interactions among family members at the dinner table may become the source of a family story for the next generation (Byng-Hall, 1995).

The family code is a cause and a consequence of what families do on a regular basis and how family values and beliefs are directly imparted to children. One way to access the family code, while considering family ecology, is to examine family stories as part of the represented family and family rituals as part of the practicing family. Family stories and rituals are integrated into the developmental demands of raising young children and reflect transactional processes over time.

FAMILY STORIES. Family stories deal with how the family makes sense of its world, expresses rules of interaction, and creates beliefs about relationships. When family members are called upon to recount an experience, they set an interpretive frame reflecting how individuals grapple with understanding events, how the family works together, and how the ascription of meaning is linked to beliefs about relationships in the family and social world. The stories that families tell about their personal experiences aid in constructing a meaningful picture of the family's theory of how the world works and their expectations for family members' behavior (Bruner, 1990). Family stories may be examined by their thematic content on the one hand and by the process of storytelling itself on the other.

The formation of close interpersonal relationships and striving for success are two central themes in adult and child development (Erikson, 1950; Gilligan, 1982; McAdams & de St. Aubin, 1992). How the family goes about imparting values of relationships and achievement will be tempered by the developmental stage of the family and personal values held by the family. Family stories about one's own childhood may aid in integrating generational factors with the current demands of parenting. In addition, these themes are sensitive to the developmental life cycle of the family. In a study of parents whose oldest child was either an infant or preschooler, several developmental and parent gender differences were found in the thematic content of family stories (Fiese et al., 1995). Fathers tended to talk about their childhood experiences with an emphasis on achievement themes and mothers tended to talk about childhood experiences with an emphasis on affiliation themes. Furthermore, parents of infants were more likely to tell family stories with strong affiliation themes, and parents of preschoolers were more likely to tell family stories with achievement themes.

Parents may use stories as a means to highlight expected developmental tasks of family members. During the early stages of parenting, mothers and fathers both told stories of an affiliative nature, focusing on the needs of others and being close. Consistent with the demands of raising an infant, parents recall experiences that incorporate themes of belonging. However, when the oldest child is of preschool age and is gaining a sense of autonomy, parents' stories begin to include themes of personal success and achievement, perhaps preparing the child for roles as a student and achiever. In addition to the thematic content of family stories, the relative coherence of family narratives may impart to children that the world can be understood and mastered. The importance of family stories for early intervention is highlighted by the kinds of stories imparted by high-risk parents. In a study of psychiatrically ill parents, Dickstein and colleagues found that depressed mothers told stories that provided a less coherent image of family life (Dickstein et al., 1999). In this regard, the child in a depressed family may not only be at risk because of inconsistent interaction patterns but also because of the transmission of family messages that are inconsistent and poorly organized and that demonstrate a mismatch between affect and content. One only has to speculate what it is like for a child to be raised in an environment that is marked by difficulties in creating coherent images of personal experiences.

FAMILY RITUALS. Family rituals are powerful organizers of family life and are associated with both the practicing and represented aspect of the family code. Family rituals range from highly stylized religious observances, such as first communion, to less articulated daily interaction patterns, such as dinnertime, to problem-solving routines such as anger management. Family rituals appear to affect family life by pairing meaning and affect with patterned interactions (Fiese, 1992, 1995). During the child-rearing years, creating and maintaining rituals on a daily basis are an integral part of family life (Bennett, Wolin, & McAvity, 1988). The organized experience of the family in its daily practices is sensitive to developmental changes in the family and may aid in the preservation of close relationships during periods of transition. In families with young children, it was found that families of preschool-age children establish more dinnertime, weekend, and annual celebration rituals than parents of infants. Furthermore, families of preschool-age children also report the occurrence of more family rituals, a greater attachment of affect and symbolic significance to family rituals, and more deliberate planning around ritual events, with a stated commitment to continue the family rituals into the future (Fiese, Hooker, Kotary, & Schwagler, 1993). As children are able to take on a more active role in the family, daily activities appear to be reorganized to incorporate the child's participation (Goodnow & Delaney, 1989). Over time, these practices have meaning for the family and aid in the creation of a family identity.

Family rituals may also preserve relationships during times of transition and may protect couples from marital dissatisfaction during the early stages of parenthood. Couples who are able to practice meaningful family rituals in the context of raising children are more satisfied in their marriage than couples who find their family practices hollow and lacking in meaning (Fiese et al., 1993). Families who are faced with the care of a family member with a chronic illness may also find that rituals provide a sense of stability and meaning associated with family adaptation. Bush and Pargament (1997) reported that for adults with chronic pain, the regularity of family routines provided a sense of predictability associated with positive adaptation. For the spouse of the patient, the meaning of the ritual was linked to feelings of family competence, suggesting a sense of belongingness and preservation of family relationships in the face of caring for someone with chronic pain. Whether a similar pattern holds for families with children with chronic conditions has yet to be determined. However, taken together, these findings suggest that the stability of family rituals as well as the meaning associated with family practices is related to family adaptation.

SYNTHESIZING FAMILY PRACTICES AND REPRESENTATIONS. From a transactional perspective, both the practicing and the represented family code behavior across time and affect one another. Family practices come to have meaning over time and become translated into the symbolic aspect of the represented family. The represented family, in turn, may affect how the family regulates and interprets its practices. As an example, consider negative affect at the dinner table in the context of a parent with generational patterns of abuse and neglect. The parent does not expect relationships to be rewarding and has created a representation of family as unfulfilling and disappointing (Cicchetti & Toth, 1995). Negative affect at the dinner table confirms the parent's expectation of unrewarding family interactions. Direct exposure to negative affect may then lead to acting-out behaviors (Katz & Gottman, 1993). The acting-out behaviors may serve to reinforce the parent in the belief that he or she cannot expect his or her offspring to behave in a positive manner, and a family story is then created labeling the child as "bad" and uncontrollable. This transactional process results in escalation of problem behavior and an entrenchment of beliefs that makes it

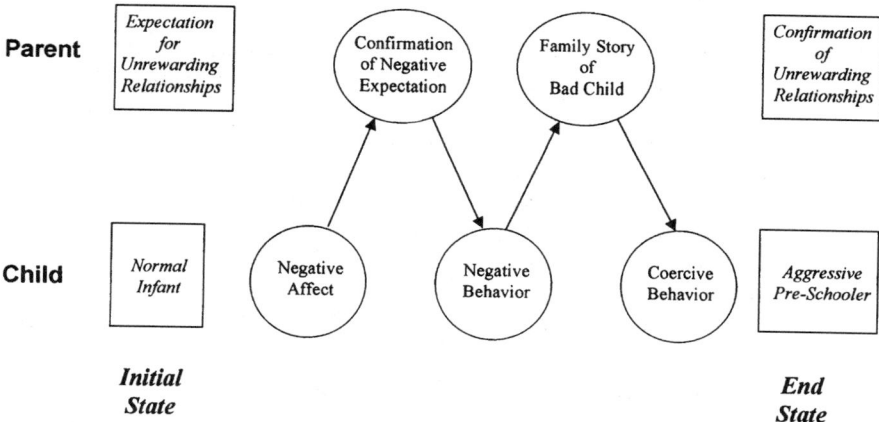

Parent

| Expectation for Unrewarding Relationships | Confirmation of Negative Expectation | Family Story of Bad Child | Confirmation of Unrewarding Relationships |

Child

| Normal Infant | Negative Affect | Negative Behavior | Coercive Behavior | Aggressive Pre-Schooler |

Initial State   *End State*

Figure 7.5. Transactional process leading from parent expectations of unrewarding relationships to child conduct problems.

more difficult to alter maladaptive patterns of interaction. The storied representation of family behavior becomes tainted with expectations for unfulfilling family relationships confirmed in the directly observable interaction among family members (Fiese & Marjinksy, 1999). This transactional process is illustrated in Figure 7.5.

As with other transactional systems, there is no direct causal link between parental expectations for unrewarding relationships and child coercive behavior. The relation is mediated by a chain of reciprocal events that could lead to many other outcomes with appropriate interventions. Changing parental behavior at dinnertime, negative expectations of the child, or family stories may significantly alter the outcome for the child. A transactional understanding of such processes helps in identifying both problematic developmental processes and potential interventions.

Individual Parental Code

There is clear evidence that parental behavior is influenced by the family context. When operating as part of a family, the behavior of each member is altered (Parke & Tinsley, 1987), frequently without awareness of the behavioral change (Reiss, 1981). However, there is no doubt that individuals also contribute to family interactions. The contribution of parents has much more complex origins than that of young children, given the multiple levels that organize their behavior. We have discussed the socializing regulations embodied in the cultural and family codes. We have not discussed the individualized

interpretations that each parenting figure imposes on these codes. To a large extent, these interpretations are conditioned by each parent's past participation in his or her own family's coded interactions, but they are captured uniquely by each member of the family. These individual influences further condition each parent's responses to his or her own child. Main and Goldwyn (1984) have identified adult attachment categories that reflect parents' encoding of their interpretation of their attachment to their own parents. What is compelling about these adult attachment categories is that they operate across generations and are predictive of the attachment categories of the infant.

The richness of both health and pathology embodied in these parental responses is well described in the clinical literature. In terms of early development, Fraiberg (1980) and her colleagues provided many descriptions of the attributions that parents bring to their parenting. These "ghosts" of unresolved childhood conflicts have been shown to "do their mischief according to a historical or topical agenda, depending upon the vulnerabilities of the parental past" (Fraiberg, Adelson, & Shapiro, 1975, pp. 387–421).

The effect of parental deviance has long been recognized as a contributor to the poor developmental status of children (Sameroff, Seifer, & Zax, 1982). One of the major steps forward in current early intervention programs is the effort to facilitate the parent's caregiving behavior because of its importance for the development of the child. Although we acknowledge that influence, we must also be careful to add the importance of the contexts in which parental behavior is rooted – the family and cultural codes. To ignore these contexts that organize parental behavior would permit only limited additional success when parent involvement is added to intervention efforts that foundered when the child was the sole target of treatment. It is important to understand the parent as a major regulating agent, but it is equally important to recognize that parental behavior is itself embedded in regulatory contexts that may require additional intervention strategies.

Regulations

The description of the contexts of development is a necessary prologue to the understanding of developmental problems and to the eventual design of intervention programs. Once an overview of the complexity of systems is obtained, we can turn to the search for nodal points at which intervention strategies can be directed. These points will be found in the interfaces among the child, the family, and the cultural systems, especially when regulations are occurring.

Despite a tendency to see infants as objects existing in a material world where their talents unfold in some maturational sequence, the reality is that from conception the infant is embedded in relationships with others who provide the nutrients for both physical and psychological growth. In Figure 7.6, the developmental changes in this relationship between individual and context are represented as an expanding cone. The balance between other-regulation and self-regulation shifts as the child is able to take on

Figure 7.6. Changing balance between other-regulation and self-regulation as child develops into adult.

REGULATION MODEL

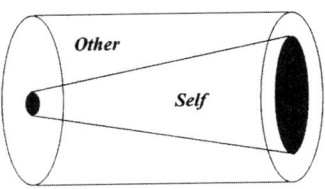

Development ⟶

increasing responsibility for his or her own well-being. At birth the infant could not survive without the environment providing nutrition and warmth. Later the child is able to put on a jacket and find the refrigerator, although someone else still has to buy the clothing and food for the family. The child eventually reaches adulthood and becomes part of the other-regulation of a new infant, beginning the next generation.

To complete the picture of the developmental system, one must appreciate the complexity of regulatory processes reflected in their time span, purposiveness, level of representation, and the nature of the child's contribution. We have divided developmental regulations into three categories on the basis of these considerations: macroregulations, miniregulations, and microregulations (Sameroff, 1987; Sameroff & Fiese, 1990). Macroregulations are predominantly purposive major changes in experience that continue for long periods of time – such as weaning or entry into school. Miniregulations are predominantly caregiving activities that occur on a daily basis and include dressing, feeding, or disciplining. Microregulations are almost automatic patterns of momentary interactions. Examples include attunement (Stern, 1977) on the positive side or coercion (Patterson, 1986) on the negative.

The three sources of regulation are organized at different levels of the environtype. *Macroregulations* are the modal form of regulation within the cultural code. Many cultural codes are written down or memorized and may be passed on to individual members of society through customs, beliefs, and mythologies, in addition to actual laws that are aimed at regulating child health and education. *Miniregulations* are modal within the family code in which less formal interactions condition the caregiving behavior of family members. *Microregulations* come into play at the individual level in which differences in personality and temperament balance with commonalities in human species-specific behavior in regulating reactions to the child.

The operation of the family code is characterized by a series of regulated transactions. Parents may hold particular concepts of development that influence their caretaking practices. As children are exposed to different role expectations and listen to the family stories, they make their own contribution by their particular styles. The child's acting out of roles within the family is incorporated into family stories, rituals, and myths. By becoming an active transactor in the family code, the child ultimately may affect the child rearing practices of the parents and even influence the code to be passed down to the next generation.

TARGETING INTERVENTION EFFORTS

A sensitivity to the complexities of child development has encouraged the implementation of intervention strategies to include multiple members of the child's family (Turnbull, Summers, & Brotherson, 1983), as well as multiple disciplines concerned with early childhood (Bagnato & Neisworth, 1985; Bricker, 1986; Bricker & Dow, 1980). Increasingly, early intervention programs designed today are based on a team approach that addresses the many facets of childhood problems. As it becomes less acceptable to focus on isolated aspects of developmental disorders, the total environmental context of the child is considered (Sameroff, 1982). Once multiple determinants have been recognized as being associated with childhood problems, a more targeted approach to implementing intervention is in order, which is based on the specific determinants identified in a specific situation.

A frequent problem in planning intervention strategies is deciding where to concentrate therapeutic efforts. As outlined earlier, developmental regulatory systems may include individual, family, and cultural codes. Not only do economic and personnel limitations preclude global interventions across systems, but all these regulatory codes also incorporate different aspects of the child's development and imply different intervention strategies. A careful analysis of the regulatory systems is necessary to define what may be the most effective avenue and form of intervention. The cultural, familial, and individual codes are embedded in temporal and behavioral contexts that vary in magnitude of time and scope of behavior. A basic point that emerges from this analysis is that there will never be a single intervention strategy that will solve all developmental problems. Cost-effectiveness will not be found in the universality of a treatment but in the individuation of programs that are targeted at the relevant nodal points for a specific child in a specific family in a specific social context.

In consideration of the temporal dimensions of regulation, what are the implications for intervention? Frequently, models of intervention attempt to cover a wide range of contexts for a single identified problem. Some early intervention programs for disabled infants are designed to intervene on the level of the child, family, and occasionally the larger context of social support systems (Dunst, Trivette, & Cross, 1986). Although well intentioned, a great deal of effort may be expended with minimal results. A more precise understanding of regulatory systems and diagnostic decision making may provide more effective forms of intervention.

TRANSACTIONAL MODEL OF INTERVENTION

The transactional model has implications for early intervention, particularly for identifying targets and strategies of intervention. The nonlinear premise that continuity in individual behavior is a systems property rather than a characteristic of individuals provides a rationale for an expanded focus of intervention efforts. According to the model, changes in behavior are the result of a series of interchanges among individuals within a shared system following specifiable regulatory principles. Emphasis is placed on the multidirectionality of change while pinpointing regulatory sources that mediate change. By examining the strengths and weaknesses of the regulatory system, targets can be identified that minimize the necessary scope of the intervention while maximizing cost efficiency. In some cases, small alterations in child behavior may be all that is necessary to reestablish a well regulated developmental system. In other cases, changes in the parents' perception of the child may be the most strategic intervention. A third category includes cases that require improvements in the parents' ability to take care of the child. These categories have been labeled *remediation*, *redefinition*, and *reeducation*, respectively, or the "three *R*s" of intervention (Sameroff, 1987).

An abstraction of the regulatory model that focuses only on the three *R*s of early intervention can be seen in Figure 7.7. Remediation changes the way the child behaves toward the parent. For example, in cases in which children are diagnosed with known organic disorders, intervention may be directed primarily toward remediating biological dysregulations. By improving the child's physical status, the child will be better able to elicit caregiving from the parents. Redefinition changes the way the parent interprets the child's behavior. Attributions

3-Rs of Intervention

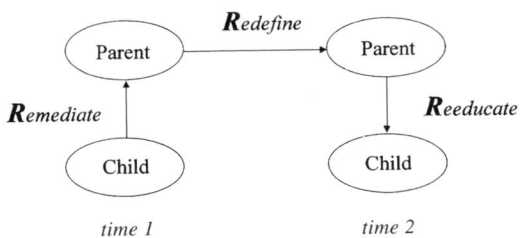

Figure 7.7. The 3-Rs of early intervention within a transactional model.

to the child of difficulty or willfulness may deter a parent from positive interactions. By refocusing the parent on other, more acceptable, attributes of the child, positive engagement may be facilitated. Reeducation changes the way the parent behaves toward the child. Providing training in positioning techniques for parents of physically handicapped children is an example of this form of intervention. Each category of intervention is described further, with examples of early intervention techniques used for each regulatory code.

Intervening with Low-Birth-Weight Infants

In the previous edition of this handbook, we described the transactional model of intervention as applied to children with failure to thrive (Sameroff & Fiese, 1990). For this edition, we have chosen another condition of interest to early interventionists, that of low birth weight (LBW). LBW is associated with a variety of developmental problems and represents a significant portion of health care costs. LBW infants have been described as more difficult to care for and less responsive to parent interaction attempts (Field, 1987; Spiker, Ferguson, & Brooks-Gunn, 1993), having difficulty regulating distress (Crnic, Greenberg, Ragozin, Robinson, & Basham, 1983), and being at risk for cognitive and social–emotional difficulties (Achenbach, Phares, Howell, Rauh, & Nurcombe, 1990). It is estimated that of the $11 billion spent on health care for infants, approximately 35% is spent on the 7% of infants who are LBW (Shiono & Behrman, 1995). Various early intervention programs have been developed to address the needs of LBW infants and their families and may

be used to illustrate the transactional model of early intervention. This nonexhaustive review highlights individual programs that focus on a particular aspect of the transactional model and, when taken together, have implications for future intervention efforts.

REMEDIATION. As represented in Figure 7.7, the strategy of remediation is the class of intervention techniques designed to change the child, with eventual changes occurring in the parent (upward arrow). Remediation is not aimed at changing the family or cultural codes. The intervention goal is to fit the child to preexisting caregiving competencies that could operate adequately, given appropriate infant triggering responses. Remediation is typically implemented outside of the family system by a professional whose goal is to change an identifiable condition in the child. Once the child's condition has been altered, intervention is complete.

One form of remediation aimed at LBW infants is the prevention of early delivery. There are, however, few proven ways to safely delay delivery. Pharmacological interventions in the final stages of pregnancy have been found to suppress preterm labor, but typically these drugs are effective for only a brief period of time and often have serious side effects for the mother and infant (Nathanielsz, 1995; Ricciotti, Chen, & Sachs, 1995).

LBW, premature infants are born ill-equipped to deal with the sensory environment outside of the womb (Als, 1992). Infants placed in neonatal intensive care units (NICUs) are exposed to a variety of sensations, including multiple people involved in the direct care of the infant, mechanical support systems, and round the clock activity and light exposure. Whereas it was previously thought that LBW infants needed added stimulation to catch up with healthy infants, current NICU procedures support the notion that sensory stimulation needs to be decreased for LBW infants in order to optimize development. Field and colleagues have demonstrated that for LBW infants, gentle stroking in a prone position and passive movement of the limbs in a supine position decrease the stress associated with being in a NICU (Field et al., 1986). On follow-up, infants who received the touch intervention showed more weight gain, mature habituation, orientation, and spent more time awake than LBW infants who did not receive the touch intervention. The positive effects of the intervention extended one year post-discharge, with the intervention infants scoring higher on the Bayley Scales of Infant Development. Field et al. (1986) suggested that the intervention facilitates the motor activity and alertness of the infants, which in turn facilitates parent–infant interaction that contributes to later mental and psychomotor development.

This example of remediation is an intervention aimed at changing the child, with the expectation that the child will become a more responsive interaction partner. In this regard, remediation allows the child to participate more fully in the practicing family. Remediation is indicated when there is a reasonable expectation that the child's condition can be altered and that the family and cultural code do not prevent implementation of the intervention. Remediation is most effective when there is a time-limited intervention aimed at the child with the support and assurance that the family can take over routine caregiving activities once the intervention is complete. There are instances, however, in which the cultural or familial code cannot operate successfully and a second strategy needs to be implemented – the strategy of redefinition.

REDEFINITION. Redefinition as an intervention strategy is indicated when existing family codes do not fit with the child's behavior. Redefinition is represented by the horizontal arrow between the parents at Time 1 and Time 2 in Figure 7.7. Redefinition strategies are directed primarily toward the facilitation of more optimal parenting interactions through an alteration in parental beliefs and expectations. Redefinition is warranted when the parents have defined the child as abnormal and are unable or unwilling to provide normal caregiving. Difficulties in caregiving may arise from a variety of sources, including a failure of parents to adapt to a disabling condition in the child, failure of the parents to distinguish between their emotional reactions to the child and the child's actual behavior, and maladaptive patterns of care that extend across generations. Examples of the first kind of problem are parents who disqualify themselves as adequate caregivers by automatically translating a child's physical or mental handicap into a condition that can only be treated by professionals (Roskies, 1972). Examples of the second kind

are parents who become disenchanted with child rearing because they find a poor fit between their expectations of child behavior and the child's actual performance. The third situation is marked by caregiving that is constrained by childhood experiences of the parents that prevent them from distinguishing current caregiving demands from their past experiences.

LBW infants are often sent home in a biologically vulnerable state. Parents may be called upon to continue massage techniques provided in the NICU, monitor the child's sleep patterns, and adjust feeding practices to meet the needs of a small infant. Although parents may feel competent to care for a healthy infant, they may feel overwhelmed by the demands of caring for a vulnerable LBW infant. In this instance, the parents define caregiving as an extraordinary experience that they are unable to manage. Redefinition interventions may be aimed at normalizing the care of the infant and decreasing the emphasis on "special care" the child demands. Highlighting the normal developmental tasks of sleeping, eating, and play would redefine the parents' role as one that is familiar and consistent with the parents' image of caregiving. Once parents consider the normative aspect of raising an LBW infant, they may then be able to proceed with their intuitive parenting (Barnard, Morisset, & Spieker, 1993; Papousek & Papousek, 1987).

In some cases, the need for redefinition extends beyond normalizing the parents' experience of caregiving. In these cases, the parents' attributions of the child's behavior prevents them from engaging in sensitive caregiving. The Vermont Intervention Program for Low Birthweight Infants (Achenbach, Phares, Howell, Rauh, & Nurcombe, 1990; Nurcombe et al., 1984) was aimed at enhancing the mother's adjustment to the care of an LBW infant by enabling her to appreciate her infant's individual temperament and sensitizing her to the behavioral cues of the child. By redefining the infant's behavior to fit the mother's expectation for normal development, the mothers were able to engage in more reciprocal interaction patterns related to optimal development (Rauh, Achenbach, Nurcombe, Howell, & Teti, 1988).

Occasionally, parents are unresponsive to programs aimed at redefining the child's behavior because of beliefs that are entrenched across generations. Recent work of attachment researchers has demonstrated that current caregiving activities are framed in light of the parents' relationship with their own caregivers (Crowell & Feldman, 1988; Main & Goldwyn, 1984). Mothers whose working models of attachment are tempered by inconsistent, unreliable, or abusive relationships are more likely to form insecure attachments with their children. The current relationship between mother and child is proposed to be a partial reenactment of the mother's relationship with her mother, and current behavior is guided by generational patterns of relating. Attachment relationships are malleable, however, and interventions aimed at redefining the attachment relationship have been found to be effective in a sample of high-risk infants and their mothers. Lieberman, Weston, and Pawl (1991) conducted infant–parent psychotherapy sessions with mothers and infants who had been classified as anxiously attached. Anxious attachments are characterized by inconsistent parental response to infant distress and a resistance on the part of the infant to be soothed by familiar caregivers. Insecure attachments are overrepresented in LBW infants (Easterbrooks, 1989; Wille, 1991). However, there is some question as to whether low birth weight in itself is a risk factor for attachment disorders or if associated features of low birth weight such as low SES, alcohol and drug abuse, or disrupted education may be more directly related to attachment classification in LBW infants. Infant–parent psychotherapy aimed at redefining the current caregiving relationship has been shown to affect a mother's responsiveness to her child's signals and increase active engagement between mother and child. Redefinition interventions are aimed at distinguishing the current relationship between mother and child from the mother's own upbringing. By casting out the "ghosts in the nursery" (Fraiberg, Adelson, & Shapiro, 1975), it is possible to redefine the current relationship in order that more sensitive forms of interaction may be maintained. Mothers who feel that their current caregiving interactions will be appreciated are more likely to engage in positive and reciprocal interactions than mothers who believe that their child is unlikely to be a source of reward and positive esteem.

Redefinition interventions aimed at parents often incorporate the represented aspects of the family code. Family stories offer one avenue to access the parent's current beliefs about their child. The story that parents tell about their child's birth may reveal symbolic images of family life that are related to relationship adaptation (Oppenheim, Wamboldt, Gavin, Renouf, & Emde, 1996) and may offer clues to effective interventions. Contrast these two stories told by mothers of LBW infants as to how they involve the infant in the story.

It was horrible. I remember. It was terrible. The whole experience was just . . . We had a terrible maternity ward nurse. I had camelbacked in contractions, I mean, it was horrible. And then it wasn't my OB that delivered, his coverage came in and was a real jerk, just a jerk. He was like, "What do you want to do?" I was like, "I don't think we're paying you the money for me to make the decision," and then my baby was delivered and developed a lung infection. I didn't see him until the following day. It was just terrible all the way around. I can remember right when they took him. I was wondering where he was. It seemed like hours and I was alone in the room. I'm like, "Shouldn't somebody be paying attention to me?"

In this brief vignette, the image of the child is pushed away to accommodate the mother's need to be the central focus. Redefinition interventions may be aimed at bringing the child back into the picture and exploring the mother's feelings about placing caregiving needs of the baby above her needs for personal attention. A traumatic birth experience does not necessarily mean that the parent is not able to accept the child as part of a normative experience, as highlighted in the second story.

My water bag broke really early and I was scared because, you know, usually your water bags don't break that early. So, I went to the doctor and he wanted me to go, you know, home for bed rest. I was thinking, I've got two young children at home and I'm supposed to bed rest? And I started to have contractions so they told me to come in and they put me on medication that helps your contractions stop. I was in there for three days. And then I started having more contractions and I said this kid is going to come out tonight and they go "No, no, it's not." And they say, "Well she's dilated to three so we have to take her to the delivery room." I don't know but the contractions were really weird because they would start and then they would stop and then there was like nothing and, you know, she finally came out. And they told me to breathe correctly and she just came out. And was I ever glad. They told me it was a girl. I thought I was going to have a boy but it didn't matter to me, you know, if I was going to have a boy or a girl. And she was breathing on her own, which with preemies they don't breathe on their own, and with her she did. I was just happy and glad that she was okay. She had five fingers and five toes.

In this case, the mother's story of the child concluded with a normative statement, "She had five fingers and five toes." The mother had performed her own redefinition, paving the way for a normative integration of the child into the family. Redefinition interventions are aimed at altering parents' beliefs and expectations about their child. If beliefs that the child is deviant are changed, then normative caregiving can begin or resume. The parents are free to use the skills that are already in their repertoire. There are cases, however, in which the parents do not have the requisite skills or knowledge base for effective parenting. In this case reeducation is indicated.

REEDUCATION. Reeducation refers to teaching parents how to raise their children. Reeducation is represented by the downward arrow from parent to child at Time 2 in Figure 7.7. It is directed toward parents who do not have the knowledge base to use a cultural code to regulate their child's development. Reeducation is typically aimed at families and individuals who are considered at risk because of environmental conditions or characteristics of the parents (e.g., teenage mothers, alcoholic parents, and failure to complete high school). Public health initiatives have been used on occasion to reeducate large segments of society to change their caregiving behaviors. Instructional materials such as Keys to Caregiving (Spietz, Johnson-Crowley, Sumner, & Barnard, 1990) are aimed at instructing parents about what to expect from infants at different ages in terms of their behaviors, cues, state modulation, and feeding interactions. A target for reeducation efforts is weight gain during pregnancy. In the case of LBW, restricted maternal weight gain has been found to be associated with premature and LBW deliveries. Despite this, in a recent survey, one-quarter of the pregnant women questioned reported that they believed they should not gain more than 20 pounds during pregnancy, reasoning that a smaller baby is easier to deliver and that it would be difficult to lose more than 20 pounds after delivery (Carruth & Skinner, 1991). Reeducation interventions targeted to pregnant women may reduce the incidence of LBW in

those cases in which mothers intentionally restrict weight gain.

The majority of reeducation efforts are directed toward the family or individual parent and serve to provide information about specific caregiving skills. The Infant Health and Development Program (IHDP, 1990) was one such reeducation intervention aimed at enhancing the development of LBW premature infants. The IHDP was a multisite clinical trial that combined family and home-based educational interventions with child-focused center interventions. For the purposes of this illustration, we limit our discussion to the home-based educational component. The families enrolled in the program received interventions over a period of three years. Weekly home visits were provided for the first year, with twice per month thereafter. The home visits provided parents with information on child development, instruction in the use of age-appropriate games, and family support for identified problems. Intervention effects improved cognitive development and reduced reports of child behavior problems two and three years after the intervention (Brooks-Gunn, Klebanow, Liaw, & Spiker, 1993). Intervention effects also improved the quality of maternal assistance, the child's persistence and enthusiasm, and dyadic mutuality in a laboratory setting (Spiker, Ferguson, & Brooks-Gunn, 1993).

In contrast to large center-based reeducation interventions are interventions tailored to meet the needs of individual families. McDonough (1993) described the use of feedback to parents while viewing videotapes of family interactions to guide positive family interactions. Infants and their entire family are videotaped during a weekly play session. Afterward the family views the videotape with the therapist. The feedback portion of the session serves to facilitate the parents' understanding of child development and to identify interactive behaviors that are reinforcing to the parents, as well as patterns of interaction that lead to less enjoyable exchanges. The interaction guidance treatment approach focuses on existing adaptive patterns of interaction and builds on the family's strengths.

Reeducation interventions are typically aimed at the practicing aspect of the family code. These interventions focus on the immediate and momentary exchanges between parent and child that are associated with optimal development. It is assumed that once parents have the requisite knowledge about their child's behavior that caregiving will proceed to facilitate development in accord with the cultural code. To date, interventions aimed at directly changing family practices and routines have not been a central part of early intervention programs. However, McDonough (1993) speculated that regularly scheduled play sessions provide a comforting routine to chaotic families. Future efforts are warranted to identify other family practices such as mealtimes that may be amenable to reeducation interventions.

SPECIFICITY OF INTERVENTIONS. Remediation, redefinition, and reeducation have been described as distinct forms of interventions aimed at targeting specific aspects of the transactional process. However, development is part of a system that is organized to include influence from multiple aspects of the cultural, family, and individual code. An examination of instances in which interventions do not work or have differential effectiveness may point to how choosing a form of intervention needs to be aligned with resources and characteristics of individual families and children. Spiker, Ferguson, and Brooks-Gunn (1993) commented on the IHDP findings that educational interventions were more effective for some mothers than for others. Mothers who expressed very low supportive presence during a laboratory task tended to react to their children in a hostile, detached, or highly inconsistent manner. The authors proposed that there are likely to be at least two types of mothers involved in early intervention programs: those who provide inadequate affective and instructional support to their children and those who lack instructional skills but possess positive affective qualities. In the first case, reeducation would not be sufficient and would warrant redefinition interventions to alter the parents' affective response to their children. In the same regard, redefinition efforts aimed at current interactions between parent and child may stimulate childhood experiences and require a more historical consideration of caregiving (Lieberman & Pawl, 1993). Spillover effects from one area of functioning to another, such as between the practicing and represented family, have been documented in therapeutic interventions with families (Zuckerman, Kaplan-Sanoff, Parker, & Young, 1997). Whether a similar pattern occurs in early intervention programs deserves further attention. For example, during the McDonough (1993) program of interaction guidance, it would be difficult to imagine that increasing the satisfaction of parents in their interactions with their infant through reeducation would not also redefine their attitudes and beliefs about the child.

When faced with limited resources for early intervention programs, it is beneficial to consider the most cost-effective form of intervention that would affect multiple domains of adaptation. If education efforts aimed at parents also influence how they interact with their children and the beliefs they hold about development, then focused education programs may be offered to large groups of parents. However, if the parent is unable to make use of the educational efforts because of a past history of poor caregiving or lack of social support, more intensive redefinition programs would be warranted. It is possible to frame the three forms of intervention in the form of a transactional diagnosis process.

Transactional Diagnosis and Environtype Codes

We have argued that it may be helpful to focus intervention efforts according to problem identification and type of environtype code that is applicable to the problem. Such categorization would not only lead to better program design but to better evaluation models and research designs as well. In the case of remediation, the child is defined as developmentally atypical and interventions would be necessary with any parent. The focus of remediation is to change the child, with little alteration in the cultural or family code. Redefinition interventions are prescribed when the parents' relationship with the child inhibits the child's normal growth and development. Intervention is necessary because of the particular relationship between the parent and child and involves alterations in the family code (most notably the represented family). Finally, in the case of reeducation, the parent has been identified as being deficient in certain skills or knowledge, whereas the child's condition is not in need of change. Here the purpose of intervention is to change the parent's knowledge of all children or their child's particular condition and also involves alteration in the family code (most notably the practicing family).

A decision tree can be described for choosing the appropriate form of transactional early intervention. Because in almost every case the child is brought into a program because he or she is perceived as having a problem, the first decision to be made is whether remediation is appropriate or viable. For infants, remediation may take the form of medical interventions and is typically provided by health professionals outside of the context of the family. Remediation cannot be achieved in at least two instances: a case in which there is no procedure to modify the condition of the child or a situation in which nothing can be found in the child that needs changing. In such cases, the parents' knowledge of the developmental agenda and their reactions to the child must be examined. When parents show evidence of knowing the cultural code but are not using it with their child, redefinition is necessary. When the child's problems can be identified as a result of the parent's lack of knowledge about the cultural code, reeducation is indicated.

Redefinition requires parents to identify areas of normal functioning in their child to counter their focus on aspects of the child they see as deviant. For redefinition in the case of a biologically vulnerable child, the parents need to identify the developmental aspects of their child that are normative and cast aside perceptions that may be influenced by their personal histories or beliefs about caregiving. In the case of redefinition, the parents need to recognize that their child possesses the qualities necessary to be a rewarding interaction partner. Their current relationship with the child should be seen as distinct from past insults and unfulfilled expectations in the lives of the parents.

Reeducation is evident in programs that provide direct or indirect instructional support to parents.

In the case of LBW infants, instructions about developmental timetables, age-appropriate games, and methods for identifying sources of support fall within the realm of reeducation interventions. Reeducation allows parents to perform the tasks of caregiving once armed with sufficient developmental information.

When taking a systems perspective, it is tempting to consider intervention always occurring at the level of the family. However, the transactional model of diagnosis and intervention proposed here pinpoints how intervention at the level of the child or parent alone may affect other aspects of the caregiving system. Table 7.2 summarizes the interventions that we have described, focusing on LBW infants as examples. The three types of intervention correspond to different aspects of the environtype. Although singular interventions may be aligned more closely with specific aspects of the cultural, family, or parental codes, it should be evident that interventions in one area may influence other parts of the developmental agenda. Remediation aimed at the individual child may affect the family code by facilitating parent–infant interaction while stimulating redefinition of the child.

SUMMARY

This chapter has been aimed at understanding the impact of contextual influences on development. Through an ecological analysis, some aspects of the environtype were highlighted as providing the regulatory framework for healthy child development. These factors included the cultural and family codes.

TABLE 7.2. Transactional Interventions Applied to Levels of Environtype Codes

	Transactional interventions (Three *R*s)		
Environtype code	Remediation	Redefinition	Reeducation
Cultural			Media promotion of adequate weight gain during pregnancy
Family		Redefine family representations of past caregiving and current child	
Parent	NICU touching of infant to stimulate growth		

A case was made that the environment is an active force in shaping outcomes. However, the shaping force is constrained by the state and potentialities of the individual (Sameroff, 1983). In an attempt to incorporate both aspects in a coherent model of development, the utility of the transactional model for designing programs to prevent cognitive and social–emotional problems was explored. The development of these problems has been interpreted as deviations in a child-rearing regulatory system. The prevention of these problems has been defined as the adjustment of the child to better fit the regulatory system or the adjustment of the regulatory system to better fit the child.

Within this regulatory framework, transactions are ubiquitous. Whenever parents change their way of thinking about or behaving toward the child as a result of something the child does, a transaction has occurred. Most of these transactions are normative within the existing cultural code and facilitate development. Intervention only becomes necessary when these transactions are nonnormative. In our progress toward effective intervention programs, we have reached a key theoretical breakthrough. The problems of children are no longer seen as restricted to children. Social experience is now recognized as a critical component of all behavioral developments, both normal and abnormal. Unfortunately, we have not yet reached the level of sophistication in theory and research that would connect childhood problems with corollary regulatory problems. There are many possible regulations to solve the same problem and, therefore, many possible interventions. Future research should test the relative efficacies of interventions at the individual, family, or cultural level.

The complex model that characterizes our modern understanding of the regulation of development seems an appropriate one for analyzing the etiology of developmental disorders. It permits the understanding of intervention at a level necessary to identify targets of intervention, and it helps us to understand why initial conditions do not determine outcomes, either positively or negatively. The model also helps us to understand why early intervention efforts may not determine later outcomes. There are many points in development in which regulations can facilitate or retard the child's progress. The hopeful part of this model is that these many points in time represent opportunities for changing the course of development.

In summary, models that focus on singular causal factors are inadequate for the study or manipulation of developmental outcomes. The evolution of living systems has provided a regulatory model that incorporates feedback mechanisms between the individual and the regulatory codes. These cultural and genetic codes are the context of development. By appreciating the workings of this regulatory system, we can obtain a better grasp of the process of development and how to change it.

REFERENCES

Achenbach, T. M., Phares, V., Howell, C. T., Rauh, V. A., & Nurcombe, B. (1990). Seven-year outcome of the Vermont intervention program for low-birthweight infants. *Child Development, 61,* 1672–81.

Als, H. (1992). Individualized, family-focused developmental care for the very low birthweight preterm infant in the NICU. In S. L. Friedman & M. D. Sigman (Eds.), *The psychological development of low birthweight children* (pp. 341–88). Norwood, NJ: Ablex.

Bagnato, J. J., & Neisworth, J. T. (1985). Efficacy of interdisciplinary assessment and treatment for infants and preschoolers with congenital and acquired brain injury. *Analysis and Intervention in Developmental Disabilities: Vol. 1,* 107–28.

Barnard, K. E., Morisset, C. E., & Spieker, S. (1993). Preventive interventions: Enhancing parent-infant relationships. In C. H. Zeanah (Ed.), *Handbook of infant mental health* (pp. 386–401). New York: Guilford Press.

Bennett, L. A., Wolin, S. J., & McAvity, K. J. (1988). Family identity, ritual and myth: A cultural perspective on life-cycle transitions. In C. J. Falicov (Ed.), *Family transitions,* (pp. 211–34). New York: Guilford Press.

Bowen, M. (1976). Principles and techniques of multiple family therapy. In P. J. Guerin (Ed.), *Family therapy: Theory and practice.* New York: Gardner Press.

Bricker, D. D. (1986). *Early education of at-risk and handicapped infants, toddlers, and preschool children.* Glenview, IL: Scott, Foresman and Company.

Bricker, D. D., & Dow, M. (1980). Early intervention with the young severely handicapped child. *Journal of the Association for Severely Handicapped, 5,* 130–8.

Broman, S. H., Nichols, P. L., & Kennedy, W. A. (1975). *Preschool IQ: Prenatal and early developmental correlates.* New York: Erlbaum.

Bronfenbrenner, U. (1977). Toward an experimental ecology of human development. *American Psychologist, 32,* 513–31.

Brooks-Gunn, J., Klebanow, P. K., Liaw, F., & Spiker, D. (1993). Enhancing the development of low-birthweight premature infants: Changes in cognition and behavior over the first three years. *Child Development, 64,* 736–53.

Bruner, J. (1990). *Acts of meaning*. Cambridge, MA: Harvard University Press.

Bush, E. G., & Pargament, K. I. (1997). Family coping with chronic pain. *Family, Systems, and Health, 15*, 147–60.

Byng-Hall, J. (1995). *Rewriting family scripts*. New York: Guilford Press.

Carruth, B. R., & Skinner, J. D. (1991). Practitioners beware: Regional differences in beliefs about nutrition during pregnancy. *Journal of the American Dietetic Association, 4*, 435–40.

Children's Defense Fund. (1992). Child poverty hits 25-year high, growing by nearly 1 million children in 1991. *CDF Reports, 13*(12), 2.

Children's Defense Fund. (1995). *The state of America's children: 1995*. Washington, DC: Children's Defense Fund.

Cicchetti, D., & Toth, S. L. (1995). Developmental psychopathology and disorders of affect. In D. Cicchetti & D. J. Cohen (Eds.), *Developmental psychopathology: Vol. 2* (pp. 369–420). New York: Wiley.

Clarke-Stewart, A. (1973). Interactions between mothers and their young children: Characteristics and consequences. *Monographs of the Society for Research in Child Development, 38* (5–6, Serial No. 153).

Crnic, K. A., Greenberg, M. T., Ragozin, A. S., Robinson, N. M., & Basham, R. B. (1983). Social interaction and developmental competence of preterm and full-term infants during the first year of life. *Child Development, 54*, 1199–210.

Crowell, J. A., & Feldman, S. S. (1988). Mothers' internal model of relationships and children's behavioral and developmental status: A study of mother–child interaction. *Child Development, 59*, 1273–85.

Dickstein, S., St. Andre, M., Sameroff, A. J., Seifer, R., & Schiller, M. M. (1999). Maternal depression, family functioning, and child outcomes: A narrative assessment. In B. H. Fiese, A. J. Sameroff, H. D. Grotevant, F. S. Wamboldt, S. Dickstein, & D. L. Fravel (Eds.), *The stories that families tell: Narrative coherence, narrative interaction and relationship beliefs*. Monographs of the Society for Research in Child Development (Serial No. 257, *64*, No. 2, pp. 84–104). Malden, MA: Blackwell.

Dunst, C. J., Trivette, C. M., & Cross, A. H. (1986). Mediating influences of social support: Personal, family and child outcomes. *American Journal on Mental Deficiency, 90*, 403–17.

Easterbrooks, M. A. (1989). Quality of attachment to mother and father: Effects of perinatal risk status. *Child Development, 60*, 825–30.

Erikson, E. H. (1950). *Childhood and society*. New York: Norton.

Field, T. M. (1987). Affective and interactive disturbances in infants. In J. D. Osofsky (Ed.), *Handbook of infant development*, 2nd ed. (pp. 972–1005). New York: Wiley.

Field, T. M., Schanberg, S. M., Scafidi, F., Bauer, C. R., Vega-Lahr, N., Garcia, R., Nystrom, J., & Kuhn, C. M. (1986). Tactile/kinesthetic stimulation effects on preterm neonates. *Pediatrics, 77*, 654–8.

Fiese, B. H. (1992). Dimensions of family rituals across two generations: Relation to adolescent identity. *Family Process, 31*, 151–62.

Fiese, B. H. (1995). Family rituals. In D. Levinson (Ed.), *Encyclopedia of marriage and the family* (pp. 275–8). New York: Macmillan.

Fiese, B. H., Hooker, K. A., Kotary, L., & Schwagler, J. (1993). Family rituals in the early stages of parenthood. *Journal of Marriage and the Family, 55*, 633–42.

Fiese, B. H., Hooker, K. A., Kotary, L., Schwagler, J., & Rimmer, M. (1995). Family stories in the early stages of parenthood. *Journal of Marriage and the Family, 57*, 763–70.

Fiese, B. H., & Marjinksy, K. A. T. (1999). Dinnertime stories: Connecting family practices with relationship beliefs and child adjustment. In B. H. Fiese, A. J. Sameroff, H. D. Grotevant, F. S. Wamboldt, S. Dickstein, & D. L. Fravel (Eds.), *The stories that families tell: Narrative coherence, narrative interaction and relationship beliefs*. Monographs of the Society for Research in Child Development (Serial No. 257, *64*, No. 2, pp. 52–68). Malden, MA: Blackwell.

Fraiberg, S. (1980). *Clinical studies in infant mental health: The first year of life*. New York: Basic Books.

Fraiberg, S., Adelson, E., & Shapiro, V. (1975). Ghosts in the nursery. *Journal of the American Academy of Child Psychiatry, 14*, 387–421.

Furstenberg, F. F., Jr., Brooks-Gunn, J., & Morgan, S. P. (1987). *Adolescent mothers*. Cambridge, England: Cambridge University Press.

Furstenberg, F. F., Jr., Cook, T., Eccles, J., Elder, G. H., & Sameroff, A. J. (1999). *Urban families and adolescent success*. Chicago: University of Chicago Press.

Garbarino, J. (1990). The human ecology of early risk. In S. J. Meisels & J. P. Shonkoff (Eds.), *Handbook of early childhood intervention* (pp. 78–96). New York: Cambridge University Press.

Garmezy, N., Masten, A. S., & Tellegan, A. (1984). The study of stress and competence in children: A building block of developmental psychopathology. *Child Development, 55*, 97–111.

Gilligan, C. (1982). *In a different voice: Psychological theory and women's development*. Cambridge, MA: Harvard University Press.

Goodnow, J. J., & Delaney, S. (1989). Children's household work: Task differences, styles of assignment, and links to family relationships. *Journal of Applied Developmental Psychology, 10*, 209–26.

Grych, J. H., & Fincham, F. D. (1990). Marital conflict and children's adjustment: A cognitive-contextual framework. *Psychological Bulletin, 108*, 267–90.

Infant Health and Development Program (IHDP). (1990). Enhancing the outcomes of low-birthweight, premature infants. *Journal of the American Medical Association, 263* (22), 3035–42.

Katz, L. F., & Gottman, J. M. (1993). Patterns of marital conflict predict children's internalizing and externalizing behaviors. *Developmental Psychology, 29*, 940–50.

Kohn, M. L. (1969). *Class and conformity: A study in values.* Homewood, IL: Dorsey.

Landesman, S., Jaccard, J., & Gunderson, V. (1991). The family environment: The combined influence of family behavior, goals, strategies, resources, and individual experiences. In M. Lewis & S. Feinman (Eds.), *Social influences and socialization in infancy* (pp. 63–96). New York: Plenum.

Leavell, H. R., & Clark, E. G. (1965). *Preventive medicine for a doctor in his community: An epidemiological approach,* (3rd ed.) New York: McGraw-Hill.

Lieberman, A. F., & Pawl, J. H. (1993). Infant-parent psychotherapy. In C. H. Zeanah (Ed.), *Handbook of infant mental health* (pp. 427–42). New York: Guilford Press.

Lieberman, A. F., Weston, D. R., & Pawl, J. H. (1991). Preventive intervention and outcome with anxiously attached dyads. *Child Development, 62*, 199–209.

Luthar, S. S., & Zigler, E. (1991). Vulnerability and competence: A review of research on resilience in childhood. *American Journal of Orthopsychiatry, 61*, 6–22.

Main, M., & Goldwyn, R. (1984). Predicting rejection of their infant from mother's representation of her own experience: Implications for the abused and abusing intergenerational cycle. *Child Abuse and Neglect, 8*, 203–17.

McAdams, D. P., & de St. Aubin, E. (1992). A theory of generativity and its assessment through self report, behavioral acts, and narrative themes in autobiography. *Journal of Personality and Social Psychology, 62*, 1003–15.

McDonough, S. C. (1993). Interaction guidance: Understanding and treating early infant-caregiver relationship disturbances. In C. H. Zeanah (Ed.), *Handbook of infant mental health* (pp. 414–26). New York: Guilford Press.

McGoldrick, M., Heiman, M., & Carter, B. (1993). The changing family life cycle: A perspective on normalcy. In F. Walsh (Ed.), *Normal family processes* (2nd ed., pp. 405–43). New York: Guilford Press.

McLanahan, S. S., Astone, N. M., & Marks, N. F. (1991). The role of mother-only families in reproducing poverty. In A. C. Huston (Ed.), *Children in poverty* (pp. 51–78). Cambridge, England: Cambridge University Press.

Miller, P., & Moore, B. B. (1989). Narrative conjunctions of caregiver and child: A comparative perspective on socialization through stories. *Ethos, 17*, 428–49.

Nathanielsz, P. W. (1995). The role of basic science in preventing low birth weight. *The Future of Children 5*, 57–70.

Nurcombe, B., Howell, D. C., Rauh, V. A., Teti, D. M., Ruoff, P., & Brennan, J. (1984). An intervention program for mothers of low-birthweight infants: Preliminary results. *The Journal of the American Academy of Child Psychiatry, 23*, 319–25.

Oppenheim, D., Wamboldt, F. S., Gavin, L. A., Renouf,

A. G., & Emde, R. N. (1996). Couples' co-construction of the story of their child's birth: Association with marital adaptation. *Journal of Narrative and Life History, 6*, 1–21.

Papousek, H., & Papousek, M. (1987). Intuitive parenting: A dialectic counterpart to the infant's integrative competence. In J. D. Osofsky (Ed.), *Handbook of infant development* (2nd ed., pp. 669–720). New York: Wiley.

Parke, R. D., & Tinsley, B. J. (1987). Family interaction in infancy. In J. Osofsky (Ed.), *Handbook of infancy* (2nd ed., pp. 579–641). New York: Wiley.

Parke, R. D., & Bhavnagri, N. P. (1989). Parents as managers of children's peer relationships. In D. Belle (Ed.), *Children's social networks and social supports* (pp. 241–59). New York: Wiley.

Parmelee, A. H., & Haber, A. (1973). Who is the at risk infant? *Clinical Obstetrics and Gynecology, 16*, 376–87.

Patterson, G. R. (1986). Performance models for antisocial boys. *American Psychologist, 41*, 432–44.

Rauh, V. A., Achenbach, T. M., Nurcombe, B., Howell, C. T., & Teti, D. M. (1988). Minimizing adverse effects of low birthweight: Four-year results of early intervention program. *Child Development, 59*, 544–53.

Reiss, D. (1981). *The family's construction of reality.* Cambridge, MA: Harvard University Press.

Reiss, D. (1989). The represented and practicing family: Contrasting visions of family continuity. In A. J. Sameroff & R. N. Emde (Eds.), *Relationship disturbances in early childhood: A developmental approach* (pp. 191–220). New York: Basic Books.

Ricciotti, H. A., Chen, K. T. H., & Sachs, B. P. (1995). The role of obstetrical medical technology in preventing low birth weight. *The Future of Children* (Vol. 5, pp. 71–86). Los Altos, CA: The Center for the Future of Children, The David and Lucille Packard Foundation.

Rogoff, B. (1981). Schooling and the development of cognitive skills. In H. C. Triandis & A. Heron (Eds.), *Handbook of cross-cultural psychology: Developmental psychology.* Vol. 4 (pp. 233–94). Boston: Allyn & Bacon.

Roskies, E. (1972). *Abnormality and normality: The mothering of thalidomide children.* Ithaca, NY: Cornell University Press.

Rutter, M. (1979). Protective factors in children's responses to stress and disadvantage. In M. W. Kent & J. E. Rolf (Eds.), *Primary prevention of psychopathology (Vol. 3): Social competence in children.* Hanover, NH: University Press of New England.

Rutter, M. (1987). Continuities and discontinuities from infancy. In J. Osofsky (Ed.), *Handbook of infant development* (2nd ed., pp. 1256–96). New York: Wiley & Sons.

Sameroff, A. J. (1982). The environmental context of developmental disabilities. In D. Bricker (Ed.), *Intervention with at-risk and handicapped infants: From research to application* (pp. 141–52). Baltimore, MD: University Park Press.

Sameroff, A. J. (1983). Developmental systems: Contexts and evolution. In W. Kessen (Ed.), *History, theories, and methods.* In P. H. Mussen (Ed.), *Handbook of child psychology* (Vol. 1, pp. 238–94). New York: Wiley.

Sameroff, A. J. (1986). Environmental context of child development. *Journal of Pediatrics, 109,* 192–200.

Sameroff, A. J. (1987). The social context of development. In N. Eisenberg (Ed.), *Contemporary topics in developmental psychology* (pp. 273–91). New York: Wiley.

Sameroff, A. J. (1993). Models of development and developmental risk. In C. H. Zeanah (Ed.), *Handbook of infant mental health* (pp. 3–13). New York: Guilford Press.

Sameroff, A. J. (1995). General systems theories and developmental psychopathology. In D. Cicchetti & D. Cohen (Eds.), *Manual of developmental psychopathology* (Vol. 1, pp. 659–95). New York: Wiley.

Sameroff, A. J., Bartko, W. T., Baldwin, A., Baldwin, C., & Seifer, R. (1998). Family and social influences on the development of child competence. In M. Lewis & C. Feiring (Eds.), *Families, risk, and competence* (pp. 161–86). Hillsdale, NJ: Erlbaum.

Sameroff, A. J., & Chandler, M. J. (1975). Reproductive risk and the continuum of caretaking casualty. In F. D. Horowitz, M. Hetherington, S. Scarr-Salapatek, & G. Siegel (Eds.), *Review of child development research* (Vol. 4, pp. 187–244). Chicago: University of Chicago Press.

Sameroff, A. J., & Feil, L. (1983). Parental concepts of development. In I. Sigel (Ed.), *Parent belief systems: The psychological consequences for children* (pp. 83–104). Hillsdale, NJ: Erlbaum.

Sameroff, A. J., & Fiese, B. H. (1990). Transactional regulation and early intervention. In S. J. Meisels & J. P. Shonkoff (Eds.), *Handbook of early childhood intervention* (pp. 119–49). New York: Cambridge University Press.

Sameroff, A. J., Seifer, R., Barocas, B., Zax, M., & Greenspan, S. (1987). IQ scores of 4-year-old children: Social-environmental risk factors. *Pediatrics, 79*(3), 343–50.

Sameroff, A. J., Seifer, R., & Zax, M. (1982). *Early development of children at risk for emotional disorder.* Monographs of the Society for Research in Child Development, *47* (7, Serial No. 199).

Sameroff, A. J., Seifer, R., Zax, M., & Barocas, R. (1987). Early indicators of developmental risk: The Rochester Longitudinal Study. *Schizophrenia Bulletin, 13:* 383–93.

Schweinhart, L., & Weikart, D. (1980). *Young children grow up: The effects of the Perry preschool program on youths through age 15.* Monographs of the High/Scope Educational Research Foundation, No. 7.

Seifer, R., & Sameroff, A. J. (1987). Multiple determinants of risk and vulnerability. In E. J. Anthony & B. J. Cohler (Eds.), *The invulnerable child* (pp. 51–69). New York: Guilford Press.

Shiono, P. H., & Behrman, R. E. (1995). Low birth weight: Analysis and recommendations. *The Future of Children*

(Vol. 5, pp. 4–18). Los Altos, CA: The Center for the Future of Children, The David and Lucille Packard Foundation.

Sigel, I. E., McGillicuddy-De-Lisi, A. V., & Goodnow, J. (Eds.) (1992). *Parental belief systems.* Hillsdale, NJ: Lawrence Erlbaum Associates.

Spietz, A., Johnson-Crowley, N., Sumner, G., & Barnard, K. E. (1990). *Keys to Caregiving: Study guide.* Seattle: NCAST, University of Washington School of Nursing.

Spiker, D., Ferguson, J., & Brooks-Gunn, J. (1993). Enhancing maternal interactive behavior and child social competence in low birthweight premature infants. *Child Development, 64,* 754–68.

Stern, D. (1977). *The first relationship: Infant and mother.* Cambridge, MA: Harvard University Press.

Stern, D. N. (1989). The representation of relational patterns. In A. Sameroff & R. N. Emde (Eds.), *Relationships and relationship disorders* (pp. 52–69). New York: Basic Books.

Stouthamer-Loeber, M., Loeber, R., Farrington, D. P., Zhang, Q., van Kammen, W., & Maguin, E. (1993). The double edge of protective and risk factors for delinquency: Interrelations and developmental patterns. *Development and Psychopathology, 5,* 683–701.

Turnbull, A., Summers, J., & Brotherson, M. (1983). *Working with families with disabled members: A family systems approach.* Lawrence: University of Kansas Research and Training Center.

U.S. Department of Health and Human Services. (1990). *Child health USA '90.* Washington, DC: U.S. Government Printing Office.

U.S. Department of Health and Human Services (1993). *Child health USA '92.* Washington, DC: U.S. Government Printing Office.

Werner, E. E., & Smith, R. S. (1982). *Vulnerable but invincible: A longitudinal study of resilient children and youth.* New York: McGraw-Hill.

Wille, D. E. (1991). Relation of preterm birth with quality of infant-mother attachment at one year. *Infant Behavior and Development, 14,* 227–40.

Zigler, E., Styfco, S. J., & Gilman, E. (1993). The national Head Start program for disadvantaged preschoolers. In E. Zigler & S. S. Styfco (Eds.), *Head Start and beyond* (pp. 1–41). New Haven, CT: Yale University Press.

Zill, N., & Schoenborn, C. A. (1990). *Developmental, learning, and emotional problems: Health of our nation's children, United States, 1988.* Hyattsville, MD: U.S. Department of Health and Human Services, Centers for Disease Control and Prevention, National Center for Health Statistics.

Zuckerman, B., Kaplan-Sanoff, M., Parker, S., & Young, K. T. (1997). The healthy steps for young children program. *Zero-to-Three, 17*(6), 20–5.

CHAPTER EIGHT

Guiding Principles for a Theory of Early Intervention:

A Developmental–Psychoanalytic Perspective

ROBERT N. EMDE AND JOANN ROBINSON

This chapter presents some guiding principles for a theory of early intervention that result from a developmental psychoanalytic systems perspective. Psychoanalytic thinking has provided important incentives for such a perspective, but recent research has taken this thinking in surprising directions. Our goal is to articulate basic principles, relate them to traditional concerns of psychoanalysis, and update them with current perspectives from the developmental sciences.

A number of dialectical themes pervade our principles. First among these is the interplay of biology and culture. Development includes aspects of both domains, and it includes their dynamic influences on each other. All principles of intervention include this interplay. A second theme is the interplay of affiliation and control. Attachment research has emphasized the dimension of affiliation in the developing individual but, equally important, is the dimension of control or the child's developing sense of boundaries. From early infancy on the interventionist must consider both dimensions. A third can be thought of as the interplay of science and mystery in our work. We gain knowledge from our science, but the gain is always to some extent uncertain and singular because we as observers

Robert N. Emde's work is supported by the National Institute of Mental Health Project Grant MH22803 and Research Scientist Award 5 K02 MH36808. JoAnn Robinson's work is supported in part by grants from The Colorado Trust and The Robert Wood Johnson Foundation. The work reflected in this chapter has been supported by grants from the Administration for Children, Youth, and Families for Research in Early Head Start.

participate in creating that knowledge. Because of our transactions, there is always a zone of mystery. We attempt to minimize uncertainty in our knowledge by using multiple windows of observation and by applying differing methods and points of view. However, uncertainty continues to exist because events are unpredictable, and much of the experience of others remains private and unavailable to us. As interventionists we must, of necessity, remain humble in the face of what we cannot know.

A fourth pervasive theme is the interplay of what is unique about early development and what is common to development throughout life. Although it is true that there are unique aspects of early development that must be attended to in our interventions – including crucial needs for caregiving and formative experiences necessary for socioemotional competencies – it is also true that there are general aspects of developmental processes that we use in our interventions. As we demonstrate here, these include motives that are remarkably salient early but persist throughout life.

The principles discussed here focus on how we think about intervention. The first set highlights how we think about the developing child, the second set how we think about the child's interactions, and the third set how we think about the process of intervention itself. Wherever possible throughout the discussion we recommend recognizing and building on strengths in development at the same time we as interventionists recognize and struggle with difficulties facing the child.

THE STRENGTHS OF INDIVIDUALITY
AND MEANING

A continuing contribution from the psychoanalytic tradition has been its focus on individuality and personal meaning. Exploring what is important for the individual in particular circumstances and pursuing the complexities of meaning have been central in psychoanalytically based interventions. Exploring meaning in this way can generate respect, increase self-confidence, and promote a sense of new beginnings that can take advantage of newly envisioned possibilities – especially when the wider meanings of struggles are taken into account along with an appreciation of one's strengths (Emde, 1990, 1992).

The principle of building on the strengths of individuality and meaning in our interventions is highlighted by our increasing knowledge about complexity. Perspectives from developmental systems work highlights that not only is the developing child best understood in terms of complexity that is organized, but that such complexity is increasingly organized with development. Developmental processes, by definition, "run up" to gain increasing levels of structure (negentropy); contrary to previous psychoanalytic and other drive-reduction views (Freud, 1920; Rapaport, 1959), developmental processes do not "run down" to lose structure and dissipate energy (entropy). Interventions, therefore, must deal with personal meaning that is expanding, transforming, and reorganizing. Moreover, the developing individual who is immersed in a particular culture organizes meaning in unique ways that to some extent carve out individual pathways for adaptation (see references from developmental systems work that highlight these points such as Bertalanffy, 1968; Boulding, 1956; Platt, 1966; Werner, 1957; and, more recently, Gottlieb, 1992; Hinde, 1992; Sameroff, 1983; Thelen & Ulrich, 1991).

Some psychoanalytic clinicians have made use of this line of thinking as they have noted that the complexities of individuality take account of health as well as illness, and they have discussed the need for "systems sensitivity" in therapeutic work (Fleming & Benedek, 1966; Lennard & Bernstein, 1960). Systems sensitivity, in their view, refers to an intuitive registration by a therapist of the quality of complex personality subsystems and their interactions; it provides the kind of sensitivity that allows a clinician to focus on a felt problem area that can be worked on while appreciating its connection with other areas. We strongly support this notion. Systems sensitivity can represent an important creative skill of the early interventionist. It can allow one to attend to a system appropriate to a problem while taking into account the dialectical relations between levels of complexity in other systems, as Hinde (1992) has put it. Such a skill may also enable us to reflect upon ourselves and the qualities of our participation. We return to this idea when we discuss our principle of "using relationships to advantage."

As we think about building on the strengths of individuality, it is worth reminding ourselves that the term *individuality* has several connotations. In its sociocultural sense, it refers to an experience of self in relation to others, reminding us of the importance of cultural variation of what is experienced as individuality, both in the United States and elsewhere. Indeed, cultures vary considerably in the degree to which individuality is experienced in terms of one's connectedness with others as contrasted with one's autonomy from others (see Doi, 1992; Gilligan, 1982; Hermans, Kempen, & van Loon, 1992; Sampson, 1988; Shweder & Bourne, 1982). Such matters are important when we think about intervention, for as Erik Erikson brought to our attention some time ago, culture provides the rootedness for the child's sense of identity (Erikson, 1950).

Another sense of the term *individuality* includes biology and is brought to mind by our accelerating knowledge of genetics. We are immersed in an age of revolutionary discoveries in human genetics wherein both the complexity of individuality and the new possibilities of how we can build on the strengths of individuality can be envisioned. Earlier simplified ways of thinking are no longer valid. Nature and nurture, or genetic and environmental influences, work together in development – not separately. Yet, very often our habitual thoughts trap us into assuming there is some opposition between such influences. Two recent phrases are corrective, especially when thinking about influences among differing levels of systems complexity for developing individuals. Gottlieb (1992) used the phrase "co-action of genes with the environment," and Hinde (1992) spoke of a "continuous interplay."

Dynamic relations among such influences are remarkable and may also be thought of as encouraging for interventionists. The developing individual is known to influence which genes he or she expresses and is able to affect his or her environment, which can in turn influence genetic expression (Plomin, 1986; Scarr, 1992).

Gottlieb (1992) reminded us that genetic expression is influenced through the environment at multiple levels of interaction and that there are two types of potential for what might be considered "hidden" genetic–environmental coactions in development. On the one hand, there is the large "hidden genetic store for phenotypic variation" (p. 151) that may not be expressed in a particular environment. Genetically identical twins reared apart can look and act very differently, especially if one is raised in an environment with inadequate nutrition and the other is not. More subtle influences may be apparent in unexpressed genetic influences on mental competencies that depend on adequate environmental factors. Skeels (1966), in his classic intervention follow-up study of orphanage children who suffered early deprivation of emotional and social stimulation, concluded that children who were provided with a corrective intervention in the form of a change in environment and subsequent adoption were able to achieve an average range of mental functioning; a comparison group of early deprived children who did not have such an intervention were not able to achieve an average level of mental functioning. On the other hand, there may be hidden environmental coactions simply because they are so widespread that they may be unappreciated, even though necessary for normative genetic expression. A variety of nutritional and caregiving factors are widespread, and it is only when we discover instances of particular absence in extreme or isolated environments that we realize their potential coactions for genetic expression, either physical or mental (also see discussion in Emde, 1991).

The above might be taken as a hopeful indicator for upcoming genetic knowledge that can benefit intervention strategies. As we learn more about biological variation (e.g., through genetic discoveries), we can also learn more about environmental variations that can strengthen developmental competencies, correct vulnerabilities, or prevent disorder.

Recent analyses from our MacArthur Longitudinal Twin Study (Emde et al., 1992; Plomin et al., 1993) provide an illustration of the dynamic and changing qualities of genetic and environmental influences during the second and third years of life. It is worth remembering that there are several sources of genetic change throughout development. Genes can contribute directly to the process of change because they "turn on" in development, triggering a cascade of biological events that result in other major events (such as the onset of upright locomotion or puberty) as well as more subtle events (such as a tendency toward a greater or lesser degree of shyness in the developing child). Genes can also influence a behavior at one age but not another because genes "turn off" during development or because of changes in developmental systems across age such that some genes no longer have an influence while others do (Plomin et al., 1993). Our twin comparison analyses of observed empathy are illustrative of this point. There is genetic influence, for example, at 14 and 20 months – as indicated by substantially higher similarities in empathic responses of identical twins as compared to fraternal twins and there is also substantial environmental influence – especially of the nonshared sort, as indicated by substantial amounts of nonsimilarity in both types of twins – but the pattern of genetic influence on component responses is different at the two aforementioned ages. Our longitudinal results at 24 and 36 months of age reveal continued genetic influence on empathic responses (i.e., showing cognitive, emotional, and behavioral arousal in response to the distress of another) but with a dramatic influence of testing conditions (Robinson, Zahn-Waxler, & Emde, in press). A predominantly genetic influence on children's empathic responses was found when an unfamiliar tester was the source of distress. But when mother was the source of the distress, predominant influences were of the shared environmental type. In other words, context made a big difference. Presumably, strong socialization influences shared by the twins in their day-to-day interactions with parents and others were a major influence with mothers but not with testers.

What can interventionists take from this? Developing individuals are unique and they become increasingly complex. Moreover, development takes place in a biological and sociocultural context wherein mutual influences occur. Individuality is constructed and co-constructed; the strengths of particular endowments become integrated with the values of particular cultures. As we learn more about the role of genetic variation in the near future and about which contexts activate particular behavioral strengths and which ones activate vulnerabilities, it seems clear that opportunities for intervention will be enhanced.

Although we pose the rest of our principles in general terms, we fully expect the interventionist-reader to apply these principles with keen attention to the child's individuality in particular circumstances. It is the uniqueness of a child that fascinates us; that is, a child who is energized and coursing through development in special ways, actively discovering the world, and co-constructing meaning from what is provided by a culture of significant others.

BASIC MOTIVES IN EARLY DEVELOPMENT

Another contribution from the psychoanalytic tradition has been its focus on motivations. In terms of intervention in early development, the psychoanalytic theory of motivation has taken some surprising directions. It has moved away from an emphasis on the motives of sexuality and aggression (the latter motives stemming from clinicians working with older children and adults) and has taken account of the special features of early development (see, for example, Kernberg, 1993). Bowlby (1969, 1973, 1980); Fraiberg (1980); Mahler, Pine, and Bergman (1975); and Spitz (1959, 1965) have emphasized the embeddedness of early development in caregiving relationships, the importance of direct observations and participation in working with caregivers and infants, and the child's developing autonomy along with the child's developing interconnectedness with others. Bowlby broadened considerations of motivation by bringing in contributions from ethology and comparative animal behavior as he articulated how the human infant is born preadapted by evolution for social interactions. Attachment and exploration develop within the context of supportive and consistent caregiving interactions, points that were also enumerated in the observations and theorizing of R. A. Spitz (Emde, 1983). Fraiberg broadened considerations of motivation by bringing cognitive perspectives from Piaget and other developmental

perspectives to her psychoanalytic experience. Perhaps her new motivational theory was more implicit than explicit as she wrote so compellingly of her new approaches to infant–parent psychotherapy in which the infant was present during psychodynamic explorations with the mother. In an often-quoted phrase, she commented, "It's a little bit like having God on your side" when considering the rapid development of the infant over the course of the early months of life (Fraiberg, 1980). A positive developmental impetus could be experienced, appreciated, and acknowledged as part of the mother's caregiving. In other words, this impetus could be used by the interventionist to help bolster the mother's esteem and, by implication, add incentives to her own development as well.

It is with this background that we summarized recent multidisciplinary research according to a set of basic motives of infancy, motives that can be built upon in our interventions (Emde, 1988a, 1988b). These motives are inborn tendencies, present in earliest infancy, that are fostered by caregivers who are emotionally available. Such basic motives continue throughout life, however, and can therefore also be thought of as fundamental modes of development (Emde, 1990). In other words, we believe, as Fraiberg (1980) hinted, that these motives are aspects of developmental processes that become consolidated during the experiences of early caregiving and can also be mobilized in interventions. It may be useful to list these motives and indicate some of their particulars.

Activity is a first basic motive. It is included in all contemporary theories that summarize knowledge about development. Given a consistent caregiving environment, the infant is active, exploratory, and motivated to master the world and realize developmental agendas (Emde, 1991; Emde, Biringen, Clyman, & Oppenheim, 1991). *Self-regulation* is identified as a second basic motive, referring to the fact that there is an inborn propensity for regulation of behavior as well as physiology. Such regulation includes cycles of sleep, wakefulness, and attentiveness, as well as a longer term built-in propensity for an individual's attaining species-important developmental goals such as self-awareness, representational thinking, and language. *Social-fittedness*, a third basic motive, summarizes research that indicates the extent to which infants are motivated and preadapted for initiating, maintaining, and terminating human interactions. Many researchers have documented the extent to which there is biological preparedness for the dynamic complexities of human interaction, provided there are caregiving experiences to support this and to foster its development (see, for example, Papousek & Papousek, 1979; Stern, 1985).

Affective monitoring is a fourth basic motive referring to research that indicates there is a propensity from early infancy to monitor experience according to what is pleasurable or unpleasurable. From the mother's point of view, infant affective expressions guide caregiving. The reader needs only to think of the messages conveyed by an infant's cry; an interested, alert expression; or a bright, beaming smile. During the middle of the first year, a momentous development takes place from the infant's point of view. The infant begins to monitor emotional expressions of others in a new way. When confronted with a situation of uncertainty, the infant engages in social referencing, searching out emotional expressions of significant others in order to guide behavior accordingly. Thus, if mother smiles, the infant is encouraged to approach an odd-looking toy or a stranger; if mother looks fearful or angry, the infant holds back. Social referencing adds a new level of shared meaning to the infant's affective monitoring.

Cognitive assimilation is designated as a fifth basic motive. This refers to research indicating that, from the beginning, the infant has a tendency to explore the environment, seeking what is new in order to make it familiar. This motive overlaps with the first motive of activity, but it is added so that we can bring emphasis to a more directed tendency of the child to "get it right" about the environment. Many readers will recall that the phrase *cognitive assimilation* comes from Piaget (1952), who referred to it as a "basic fact of life." This designated motive incorporates a line of research concerning mastery motivation (Harmon & Murrow, 1995; MacTurk & Morgan, 1995) and the child's experience of pleasure in performing newly acquired behaviors and skills.

These motives are universal features of normal development, and perhaps their ubiquity accounts for why they are generally assumed by our theories and are not specified as motivations. Still, when such motives are experienced by an infant with an emotionally available parenting figure, they facilitate the development of important psychological structures prior to 3 years of age. Among these are a set of what we may consider basic moral motives. These are also motives that interventionists can assess and build upon.

BASIC MORAL MOTIVES

The principle that early intervention can build on moral motives provides another set of surprises against the background of a psychoanalytic tradition. Classic psychoanalytic theory maintained that moral development began with the preschooler, during the *oedipal period* when the child's awareness of urges and struggles with triangular family relationships ultimately led to developmental resolutions in the form of a conscience or *superego*, the latter acquisition being expectable around 5 or 6 years of age. Much has changed in recent psychoanalytic thinking to modify these traditional views. Not only has there been increasing appreciation of earlier dyadic (i.e., caregiver–child relationship) contributions to both the child's sense of self in relation to others and the child's emergence of conscience (for a review, see Emde, Johnson, & Easterbrooks, 1987), but there has also been increasing appreciation that important aspects of moral development occur earlier than previously thought and in a broader domain. Morality contains positive aspects that become internalized (what might be referred to as the "do's" of early moral development), as well as negative aspects that become internalized (what might be referred to as the "don'ts" of early moral development). The "do's" are prominent in the infant's early experience and can be thought of as coming quite naturally from the basic motives we have described. For example, the basic motive of social fittedness or a propensity for social interactions involves a reciprocity in exchanges. Inclinations of this sort result in the internalization of rules for turn-taking that are learned in the course of games and other social interactions with caregivers. These rules can be observed in gestural sequences by 4 to 5 months of age in the infant's participation and turn-taking in the "So-o-o BIG" game (Bruner, 1986; Kaye, 1982). How is this an aspect of moral development? One need only reflect that expectations and internalized rules about turn-taking are early forms of reciprocity that find their way into all moral systems (such as in the Golden Rule of "Do unto others as you would have them do unto you" and its variations). Similarly, the basic motive of cognitive assimilation, of getting it right about the world, results in the internalization of many rules that become accepted by the child during the course of everyday experience. Much of the early moral internalizations with respect to the do's involve shared meaning with emotionally available caregivers, a point that is emphasized in the next two principles. During the latter half of the first year, for example, the infant engages in social referencing to seek guidance from the emotions of caregivers during situations of uncertainty and begins to show compliance to caregiver requests as a result, as well as inhibition of previously prohibited behaviors.

During the second year, toddlers develop further moral inclinations. When confronted by another's distress, the 1 1/2-year-old may respond empathically – resonating with distress and attempting to comfort, soothe, or share something with the distressed other (Zahn-Waxler, Radke-Yarrow, & King, 1979; Zahn-Waxler, Robinson, & Emde, 1992). Another aspect of early morality also becomes apparent toward the end of the second year when the tendency for getting it right shows itself in a new affective way. The child sometimes shows anxiety when internal standards are violated. When faced with a familiar object that is drastically changed, flawed, or dirty, the child may evidence distress and there may be a tendency to repair or to make it better (Kagan, 1981). Such knowledge adds to previous psychoanalytic observations that indicated early moral development during this age; these included the toddler's use of a semantic "no" (Spitz, 1957) and a developing sense of "good" and "bad" (Mahler et al., 1975; Sander, 1985).

The infant's sense of initiative and self-directedness takes on a new level with the onset of walking, something Erikson captured earlier with his psychoanalytic notion of a phase characterized by "autonomy versus shame and doubt" (Erikson, 1950). The internalization of prohibitions, or "don'ts", occurs through repeated interactions with caregivers, wherein rules of safety and family culture are imposed. Such a process not only involves negative features but also takes into account aspects of "do's" in terms of the toddler's desire to get it

right. Processes of social referencing mediate what is internalized and facilitate the development of self-control and emotional regulation. Research suggests that during parental prohibitions, the child's internalization of rules does not take place in any simple way. Instead, it involves a motivated child who with repeated experiences of back-and-forth exchanges learns strategies of negotiation in the midst of emotional communications from parents, as well as the consequences of these learned strategies (Emde et al., 1987). Recent studies of 2- and 3-year-olds by Kochanska and her group are instructive. In one study, sensitivity to "violations of standards" (e.g., when a toy is broken or a chair placed upside down or a favorite blanket is suddenly washed) was linked in many children to a sense of having done something wrong (Kochanska, Casey, & Fukamoto, 1995). In two other studies, parental practices were seen to involve many "do demands" ("come sit here and eat" or "put your shirt on") in addition to "don't demands" (such as "don't put your finger there" or "don't spill your juice"). When parental practices emphasized "do's" as well as positive affect, enhanced child compliance was observed (Kochanska & Aksan, 1995; Kuczynski & Kochanska, 1995). Home observations also highlight processes of negotiation. Dunn (1988) emphasized that conflicts with caregivers and siblings provide an important arena for the internalization of expectations, rules, and inclinations about how to negotiate or cope with conflicts involving possession, sharing, destruction, and caring.

A striking feature of early morality is that its internalized rules, expectations, and inclinations are mostly nonconscious. Rules about turn-taking, reciprocity, empathy, and repair are learned in the course of everyday procedures and practices with family members. Such rules are learned in the same manner that one learns the rules of grammar for a first language. One operates according to these rules, even though one cannot state what they are (unless one later learns such rules in school, where children most experience them as somewhat superfluous and artificial). Similarly, much of what the young child learns, and wants to continue, is "practicing knowledge" as David Reiss has put it (Reiss, 1989), knowledge that is activated when particular people come together in family or group routines or rituals.

Procedural and practical knowledge are forms of nonconscious mental activity that were not envisioned by traditional psychoanalysis; they go beyond the psychodynamic constructs of the preconscious and the dynamic unconscious. Thus, more recent results from cognitive scientists (see Clyman, 1991; Horowitz, 1988; Horowitz, Fridhandler, & Stinson, 1992; Kihlstrom, 1987) have provided another surprise: Freud, although during his lifetime was heavily criticized for elaborating a psychology that emphasized operations beyond consciousness, may have underestimated the extent to which mental activity is not conscious!

How does the interventionist make use of this information? Again, individuality in the child and in the child's experience in co-constructing the meaning of gestures, words, and actions within the caregiving environment will produce variation that may need to be assessed. In addition to gauging the child's level of affiliation, shared meaning, and emotional availability with significant others (which is discussed in more detail as part of the next principle), a child needs to establish a sufficient degree of regulation of biological and emotional states and behavioral control. An assessment of the child's moral motives (to reciprocate, to repair, and to follow rules) in the context of the family and the engagement of these motives as strengths for intervention are, we believe, an untapped resource. Many of the neediest children have not been provided the consistent caregiving routines and practices to support these early moral motives. Intervention work in these instances can benefit from addressing basic ground-building activities in the family that will foster consistency during mealtimes, bedtimes, play, and other daily routines.

Finally, we believe it important to address the issue of values as an aspect of culture. Although it is true that cultures emphasize different values that are important to identify for building strengths and interventions, we believe it is also true that the early moral motives we have discussed are important for adaptation, and in their basic forms are in some degree held universally. Thus, we believe all cultures value the child's being able to explore and be open to new experiences as compared with being closed and constricted to such experiences (although some cultures may delay when this happens as in extensive swaddling or the restriction of the onset of self-produced locomotion). We also believe all cultures value the child's developing a "we" orientation as opposed to a narrow egocentric orientation that does not engage in social reciprocity or exchange. Finally, we believe that all cultures value the child's ability to develop a capacity for engaging larger views and thinking about alternative possible worlds (e.g., in planning, imagination, art, and spiritual matters). The task of the interventionist is to understand the meaningful cultural variations in these areas and support their strengths insofar as they contribute to developmental gains.

Although the earlier discussion focuses on the early years, in considering a broader time span for child development, we believe we can say more about values (Emde, 1994). All cultures deal with such values as 1) promoting mastery learning and effectance; 2) promoting social reciprocity (fairness and sense of equity and the rules that govern them); 3) caring (including the parenting of children as well as emotional responsiveness and empathy in human relationships); 4) values of citizenship (the sense of community and the respect for traditions and rules that govern social change); and 5) recognition of conflict and its management (e.g., the conditions of discovering shared meaning, compromises for a community's greater good, and negotiation). Finally, many cultures (including those in all democratic societies) address values regarding respect for individuality, personal integrity, and differences (including human rights and the diversity of peoples).

USING OUR EMOTIONS TO ADVANTAGE

The previous principle illustrated that early moral motives – such as social reciprocity, a tendency to get it right about the world, a tendency to repair and correct standards, as well as a tendency to empathy – may provide additional bases for an interventionist's work. Children and their families will bring such motives and capacities to intervention settings in varying degrees. Such motives may also be mobilized in the course of the intervention's empathic work, giving more impetus for favorable change.

Regulation of the emotional communicative system is one of the most important tasks facing the parent and infant. Initially, the emotional availability of the parent to the child provides the main basis for regulation. Being emotionally available means communicating an openness toward and acceptance of the other's feelings and expressed needs (Biringen & Robinson, 1991). Emotional availability reflects a quality of the developing relationship that is continually re-created in face-to-face interaction, anticipating what will bring relief from distress, what will bring pleasure, or when a response is needed to flow from the sensitive, available parent (Emde, 1980). Regulating actions are required of parents initially because, although there is a biological capacity for self-regulation of many physiological and behavioral systems at birth, the development of self-regulation for the infant requires external regulation by the caregiver. Emotional signals in the young infant serve to arouse caregivers to respond and, over time, they shape motivations to act on behalf of the child (Dix, 1991). Infants can become disorganized by too much excitement or distress, and communicative signals can become aversive and disruptive for caregivers. Managing their own arousal to infant signals is thus one of the challenges for caregivers in sustaining availability to their infants.

The forward thrust of the infant's development means that the relationship between baby and caregiver will undergo revision many times. Within the context of the caregiving relationship, the infant's emotions become more complex and differentiated across the first year. Infant signals of joy, anger, fear, and surprise, for example, take on particular meanings and expectations for response from the parent. Through repeated experiences with emotionally available caregivers, especially during the second year, the child also learns skills of self-control, emotional regulation and negotiation, empathy, and helping others. Correspondingly, pride and shame typically develop during the child's second year. For interventionists, the richness of early emotional development offers repeated opportunities to re-engage or enhance attunement to the child by highlighting the toddler's new skills and emotional reactions. With effective regulation, the child's communicative skills increase and contribute to a parent's sense of effectiveness and competence. The child's increasing communicative competence permits rich expression of his or her emotional availability to the parent.

The experience and expression of positive emotions are vital aspects of communication and adaptive regulations. Positive emotions such as joy have the function of maintaining behavior for both caregiver and infant (Emde, 1980). They accompany successful progress toward goal attainment and thus serve to acknowledge and reward interventions by the parent as well as initiatives by the child. Positive emotions sustain a relationship over time, and their cultivation by parents and interventionists provide a base for emotionally available caregiving. Interactive guidance can provide opportunities for allowing more fragile parents to practice the cultivation of positive engagement with their infants. A curriculum, such as the Partnership in Parenting Education (PIPE; Dolezol, Butterfield, & Grimshaw, 1994; Butterfield, Dolezol, & Knox, 1995; Butterfield, Pagano, & Dolezol, 1997), recognizes that some parents need concrete direction in how to set the stage for positive interactions with an infant. For such parents, an intuitive basis for emotionally available engagement is not present, and explicit techniques must be taught so that they have some idea of what getting it right feels like. Once having experienced a positive response from the infant, the inherent reward that pleasing another instills can motivate the parent to try again. In this way, infant emotions reward parents and keep them coming back for more, so to speak.

As we have discussed, empathy for the child's experience motivates caregiving actions. The early parent–child relationship rests on the biologically based social-fittedness of parent and newborn. Most parents are intuitively dedicated to and capable of responding to their individual infant's cues and providing consistent caregiving. For many parents, this empathic engagement flows naturally from having experienced an empathically engaged parent themselves. For others who have not had an experience of empathic caregiving adults in their own lives, empathic failures can create repeated risks for the child throughout development. Intervention that seeks to bolster fragile parents of this sort with a secure base and that keeps the infant's individuality in focus for the parent may provide opportunities for repair and engagement of a parent–infant bond.

The empathic interventionist who communicates an emotional availability to the parent can provide the conditions for corrective experiences to take place. Communicating an understanding of painful past experiences and how they might motivate actions in the present conveys an empathic and open presence to the family. Maintaining a consistent, supportive alliance may also serve to challenge a mother's view of herself as undeserving of care, a stance that she may unconsciously generalize to her infant. When the interventionist is able to help the parent view a child's motives and capacities more clearly (perhaps seeing them in a more positive light), the "ghosts" from the past that may distort perception (Fraiberg, Adelson, & Shapiro, 1975) may slowly give way to an appreciation of the child's individuality and uniqueness. Thus, the availability of the interventionist for the parent and for the developing parent–infant relationship becomes a crucial model for the needy parent. Availability can also contribute to the regulation of the parent–infant relationship by correcting the parent's unavailability for the child.

USING RELATIONSHIPS TO ADVANTAGE

The child's relationship with a caregiver is the essential vehicle for allowing the child's individuality to develop while enhancing the motives we have described. Relationship strengthening at this level must therefore be a core consideration for early interventions. A recent statement contained in the guidelines for launching Early Head Start programs in the United States – a new Head Start program for birth to 3-year-olds and their families – articulates this view. It is worth quoting at length.

Child caregiver relationships...are critical for providing infants and toddlers support, encouragement, continuity and emotional nourishment necessary for healthy development and the development of healthy attachments...Within the context of caregiving relationships, the infant builds a sense of what is expected, what feels right in the world, as well as skills and incentives for social turn-taking, reciprocity, and cooperation. The infant's activities are nourished and channeled in appropriate ways so as to encourage a sense of initiative and self-directedness. During the toddler period, the child, through repeated interactions with emotionally available caregivers, also begins to learn basic skills and self-control, emotional regulation and negotiation. Empathy for others and prosocial tendencies for caring and helping also develop during toddlerhood as well as the emotions of pride and shame; experiencing and learning about these capacities require responsive caregiving relationships in the midst of life's inevitable stresses and challenges...A sense of pleasure, interest and exploration, early imaginative capacities, and the sharing of positive emotions also begin in infancy – all of which require repeated and consistent caregiver relationship experiences and form a basis for social competence that carries through toddlerhood and the preschool period... (Department of Health and Human Services, 1994, p. 7)

The psychoanalytic tradition has emphasized the importance of relationships in psychological development not only in the experience of early mothering and dealing with later family conflicts but also in the experience of making use of therapy and intervention. The contributions of Bowlby (1969, 1973, 1980) and Spitz (1957, 1959, 1965) to the significance of early formative caregiving relationships and the emotional underpinnings of these relationships have previously been mentioned. Additionally, psychoanalysis has focused on relationship phenomena such as therapeutic matches and alliances as well as transferences and countertransferences as the arena for therapeutic action. Most recently, both clinical theory and research have emphasized that psychoanalysis is as much an interpersonal as an intraindividual psychology (see Shapiro & Emde, 1994).

This information seems straightforward and useful as we think about early interventions. There is room, however, for further expansion of our theory. All interventions – from short term to long term and from crisis to analysis – involve the influence of relationships on other relationships. We believe that this has at least two implications. If we acknowledge and assess these influences, we may further strengthen our interventions by discovering other supportive relationships and conflicting ones that can use attention. A second implication is that our efforts may often be misplaced. In our infancy work, we make use of our relationship to the mother, but what seems most important is the relation we have to the mother–infant relationship. Thus, our efforts may need to be concentrated on fostering that relationship instead of focusing on the mother or on the child.

When we think of interventions as the influences of relationships on relationships, we realize that there are different levels we may address in developing systems, and it is often strategic to choose a level for working that offers maximum leverage. And our goals may differ, depending on the circumstances.

For example, we may have a long-term goal to influence the internalized represented relationships in the child (such as to improve "working models of attachments") or goals to influence internalized relationships within the mother's representational world. Other targeted goals might include improving father–child and mother–father relationships within the family in the course of our interventions. Still other goals might address the level of enhancing other supportive relationships for the mother who is in a relationship with her infant – goals that are often prioritized in family support programs. Or we may target a more direct and immediate level for our goal-setting that concentrates on improving the repeated interactions between mother and infant in order to make such interactions more satisfying. In all instances, it seems clear that our intervention relationship is part of one or more other relationships that we hope to influence for the better. More thought should be given to these points in order to achieve a better understanding of familial systems and our relationship to these. Family systems approaches currently come closest to addressing these matters but, with a few exceptions (cf. Byng-Hall, 1995; Scharff & Scharff, 1987), they seldom consider relations to internalized representations of relationships and they usually do not consider development. What is needed is an intervention theory that probes further into this area and that can specify schemes for assessing leverage points in developing systems – one that can yield opportunities for influencing the effects of relationships on relationships and their consequences for intervention in particular circumstances.

Another quality of the infant–caregiver relationship is noteworthy. In contrast to later relationships in life, early caregiver relationships are formative; they are the child's first (Stern, 1977). Moreover, as we have already noted, many of the child's adaptive functions are embedded in the context of such relationships and cannot be seen as independent of them. Thus, the early relationship experiences of caregiving are qualitatively different than later relationship experiences, and behavior regulation and dysregulation are often more characteristic of the caregiving relationship than they are of either partner alone (Sameroff & Emde, 1989). This has led to an aspect of our changing view of diagnosis during early development, which is our next topic.

DIAGNOSIS IS AN ONGOING PROCESS: A CHANGING ORIENTATION

Diagnosis in the course of early developmental interventions represents a special challenge. Since the time of Hippocrates, diagnosis has been linked to prognosis and the clinician's desire to make predictive statements about outcomes. Infancy, however, is a time of rapid change, and the interventionist is occupied at all times with facilitating favorable developmental change. Thus, the task of predicting continuities in disorder across time is difficult, if not paradoxical. Another difficulty with traditional medical diagnosis is the presumed search for diagnoses that are linked to simple lines of causation, especially with regard to biologically based disturbances of the brain. Simple lines of causation seem rare in infant mental health problems, wherein most are found to result from multiple etiologic factors that involve interactions of environmental and intrinsic elements in varying combinations and degrees. Still another difficulty in the diagnostic tradition is the tendency of most classification systems to designate disorder in categorical terms, wherein disorders are viewed as either present or absent. Most early interventionists believe that evidence favors the usefulness of regarding common emotional and behavioral disorders as existing on continua of adaptation rather than as present-or-absent categories (Achenbach, 1988; Rutter & Tuma, 1988). Another difficulty is the assumption inherent in most medically based classification schemes that disorder resides within individuals. The family relationship context is central in evaluating behavior and functioning in early development, and dysfunction that needs correction is often seen in that context. To be more specific, when disturbances are embedded in caregiving relationships, and may even be specific to such relationships, how are they to be classified?

The principle we advocate in this area describes an approach that is intended to assist with these difficulties. It reflects a changing orientation that regards diagnosis not as fixed and final but as ongoing. The diagnostic process, in this view, is one in which periodic reevaluations are expected and applied. Moreover, the diagnostic process is usefully regarded as consisting of two aspects: 1) the assessment of individuals and 2) the classification of disorders. The assessment of individuals involves a variety of evaluations of an individual's functioning and symptoms within the context of family relationships, culture, and stresses that are both biological and environmental. The classification of disorder involves a way of ordering knowledge about symptom patterns and linking it to what is known in general about classified syndromes that may provide links to etiology, prognosis, and treatment outcomes. Clinical classification also allows for communication among professionals, but it is important to remind ourselves that we classify disorders, not individuals (Rutter & Gould, 1985).

The diagnostic process begins with assessment and subsequently moves to considerations of classification. Because of the multidisciplinary nature of early intervention activities, and the diverse background of practitioners, multiple paradigms and methods of assessment may be applied. Psychoanalytic contributions to early assessment include those of Brazelton and Cramer (1990); Cramer et al. (1990); Fraiberg (1980); Gaensbauer and Harmon (1981); Greenspan (1981, 1997); and Stern and Stern-Bruschweiler (1987). Psychoanalytic concepts have contributed to assessments and to observational ratings, but they have not led to classifications that are reliable and valid. A similar comment can be made about family systems contributions that have led to useful schemes for assessment (Minuchin, 1974; Scharff & Scharff, 1987). Similarly, contributions to assessment from other disciplines are also noteworthy and are discussed elsewhere in this volume.

A recent advance has been the publication of *Diagnostic Classification of Mental Health and Developmental Disorders of Infancy and Early Childhood* (DC: 0–3; Zero To Three, 1994). This diagnostic classification represents the work of a national task force of clinicians. It reflects the changing orientation about diagnosis in that it recommends a process of assessment prior to classification, incorporates the strategies of a multiaxial system that allows for features of assessment, and pays special attention to the evaluation of the caregiver relationship. The DC: 0–3 system arose in order to include common problems and symptom configurations encountered in the first three years in a diagnostic scheme that had coverage and usefulness for interventionists. It is a new scheme intended to supplement the *Diagnostic and Statistical Manual of Mental Disorders* (*DSM–IV*; American Psychiatric

Association, 1994), which does not have adequate coverage of the early age period.

As with the *DSM–IV* current approaches, DC: 0–3 attempts insofar as possible to have operationally based criteria that can be subject to evaluation and research. The DC: 0–3 scheme has added a special axis dealing with relationship disorder. The relationship disorder axis also contains the recommended use of a parent–infant relationship global assessment scale, which provides anchor points for clinical judgments. It must be said, however, that the relationship disorder axis as well as the DC: 0–3 classification scheme itself is the first of its kind and awaits evaluation in terms of terms of trials of reliability and validity.

PREVENTING COMPROMISES IN DEVELOPMENT AND STRENGTHENING COMPETENCIES

Another principle reflects a changing orientation about preventive interventions. The developmentalist sees such interventions in broader terms than those linked to preventing a diagnosable disorder. These consist of 1) preventing developmental compromises and problems of adaptation, and 2) strengthening individual pathways for development. These two dimensions link aspects of traditional prevention of disorder with aspects of health promotion. Table 8.1 presents these two dimensions for thinking about prevention in five developmental areas and links them to current classifications of disorder.

We developed our approach to preventive interventions for mental health, but Table 8.1 suggests the scheme may be relevant for fields in addition to psychiatry, social work, psychology, and occupational therapy. That such a line of thinking may include interventions in early childhood education is illustrated in our next section.

SCIENCE POLICY: THE IMPORTANCE OF A LONG-TERM DEVELOPMENTAL PERSPECTIVE FOR EARLY INTERVENTION

There are vital reasons for scientists to advocate a long-term developmental perspective for evaluating early intervention effects. Policy makers and funders of evaluations often rely on short-term answers

---

TABLE 8.1. Developmental Scheme for Thinking About Prevention

What are we preventing?
Developmental compromises and problems of adaptation in:
  Learning (e.g., learning inhibitions and failures)
  The formation and maintenance of relationships (e.g., relationship disturbances –
    DC: 0–3 Axis II)
  Emotional regulation (e.g., internalizing problems in behavior – DC: 0–3 Axis I
    Disorders of Affect)
  Behavioral conduct (e.g., externalizing problems in behavior – such as planning
    difficulties, dysregulation of aggression, and problems of reciprocity and empathy)
  Risk-taking behaviors and exposure to physical illness (e.g., accidents and
    injuries, lack of immunization, poor utilization of health services, poor
    nutrition, and substance abuse)

What are we strengthening?
Individual pathways for development, including:
  Motivation for learning and positive experiences with exploration
  Motivation for reciprocity in relationships, communicating, and positive
    experiences with caring and support
  Confidence in the use of emotions for self and other; consistent emotional
    experiences with significant others that includes shared positive emotions and
    conflict, as well as play and imagination
  Character-sense that includes planning skills, confidence in mastering
    challenges, effectiveness in social exchanges, and a sense of conscience or
    responsibility
  Safety and health

---

without interest in the long term, but such approaches, as we indicate later, can be misleading. A short time ago, we were asked to prepare a policy statement for evaluating effects of interventions related to Early Head Start (EHS). We came to an inescapable conclusion about the importance of a long-term developmental perspective. We would like to summarize our thinking about this because it illustrates features about evaluating early interventions in general.

We were attracted to a theories of change approach proposed by Connell and Kubisch (1996). These authors recommended a step-by-step approach in order to "unpack" interventions in circumstances wherein community initiatives are being evaluated. Step I of their recommended scheme involves identifying the long-term outcomes program planners hope to observe. Long-term outcomes such as graduation from high school are easier to identify and agree about than are earlier intermediate outcomes such as academic success in the fourth grade. This is so for a variety of reasons. These include the complexities and uncertainties of contextual variables that can influence intermediate outcomes (such as

family moves, crises, and changes in welfare policy), as well as the operation of threshold effects and nonlinear relations between causes and outcomes. Thus, it is only after identifying long-term outcomes as Step I of the scheme, that one proceeds to the process of articulating an appropriate theory of change by moving backwards in time to Step II for penultimate outcomes, then to intermediate outcomes, which can be specified as steps in varying degree, then to early outcomes, and then, as a final step in the scheme, to initial activities (i.e., to the intervention itself).

In thinking about evaluating the interventions of EHS, we found this approach to be liberating. Whereas early outcomes such as cognitive development and language may be variable and more difficult to predict with certainty (particularly when we focus on the child), we realized we could see desirable long-term outcomes with clarity.

A developmental perspective indicates why this is so, and it may be useful to review some of its aspects. First, there are different qualities of the child's early development as compared with the child's later development. Early development is characterized by a relative lack of differentiation, with many of the child's adaptive functions embedded in formative caregiving relationships; correspondingly, what we know about developmental plasticity and the possibility of different adaptive pathways existing for important developmental functions make straightforward outcomes difficult to specify. Second, the nature of the developmental process adds further, related, reasons that explain why long-term outcomes can be specified with more clarity than intermediate ones. Nonlinearity in development is demonstrated by longitudinal observation of those with developmental disabilities, for example, in which there are multiple pathways in achieving developmentally important later outcomes. Thus, children who are born blind, deaf, or with severe motor handicaps all have different sensorimotor experiences in infancy – and yet all can achieve Piaget's representational intelligence as well as the expectable postinfancy milestones of emotional development; such children accomplish this by making use of developmental pathways that are quite different from those that Piaget or others had imagined in their theories.

A third consideration follows from this and adds to the necessity of seeking long-term outcomes. It seems highly likely that any evaluations of intervention will find meaningful variation in the functionally significant contexts in which early development can take place. This is especially relevant for the contexts of poverty and other forms of environmental risk, such as community violence. Cultural variation, it should be emphasized, has much to teach us about the appropriate strengths and risks for intermediate processes of development in the midst of such challenging contexts.

Thus, any scheme for outcomes must be sufficiently long term to allow for the appropriate operation of program or intervention impacts on multiple developmental pathways that are brought forth in the midst of varying biological and environmental challenges. Premature closure should be assiduously avoided wherein intermediate outcomes could be misleading (e.g., outcomes that are temporarily puzzling because they are different, seemingly absent, or unexpected).

Many things fell into place once we began with long-term outcomes, worked out our parameters, and moved to our intermediate steps. We assumed the developing child in the context of the family

provided the most appropriate target for evaluating outcomes, although other goals of EHS (e.g., parental work sufficiency, family harmony, community support, or staff development) might also have been addressed. We further assumed that two domains of an individual's adaptive functioning seemed most relevant for evaluating the interventions of EHS (as well as the interventions of Head Start). These are 1) learning competencies and 2) social competencies. These two competency domains are dynamic, having much to do with one's motivation, sense of efficacy, and engagement with the world. Although somewhat awkward, we decided to designate each of these domains in the plural form to indicate that they encompass multiple features that can in turn contribute to ongoing development in multiple contexts. Longitudinal research can usefully assess these two domains through multiple pathways of development in varying cultural contexts as individuals move toward the long-term desirable outcomes we have identified.

What was our chosen long-term outcome point? Once we had thought this through, the answer seemed clear: *Early adulthood is the most appropriate period for assessing the long-terms outcomes of EHS.* Early adulthood outcomes, as Figure 8.1 illustrates, can be specified in our domains as 1) gainful employment or engagement in education beyond high school and 2) intimacy in personal relationships (i.e., commitment, trust, and reciprocity with selected others). Moreover, we also highlight parenting as a central long-term outcome in early adulthood. For both conceptual and empirical-research reasons, healthy and engaged parenting can be considered the most powerful outcome for early programs of psychosocial intervention. Conceptually, we know that all of our helpful interventions involve the effects of relationships on other relationships; that relationship experiences are internalized by individuals according to locally meaningful contexts; and that in EHS interventions, relationships have their effect by strengthening caregiving patterns, which in turn will generate experiences that are internalized by the child. Empirically, some of the most powerful influences of early experience that show continuities to later experience have been demonstrated across generational time in the parenting realm (Fonagy, 1995; Main, 1993; Rutter & Gould, 1985; Sroufe &

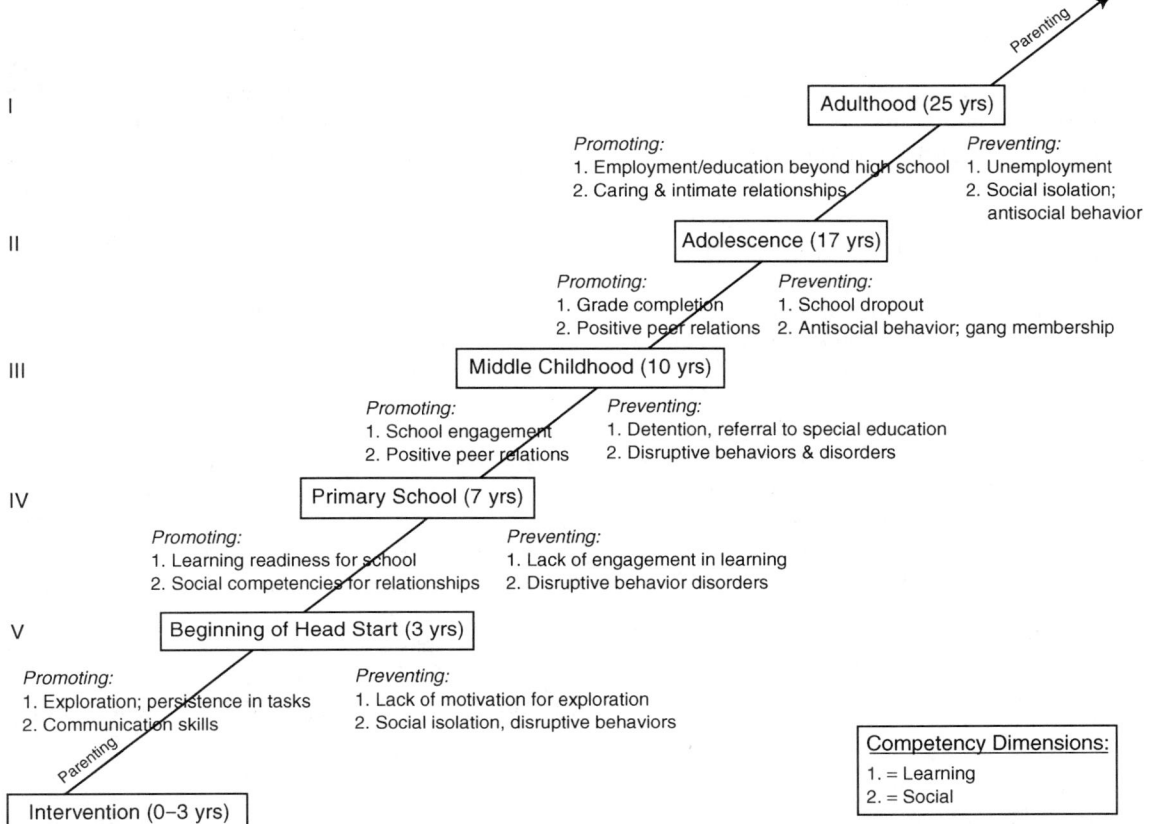

I

Adulthood (25 yrs)

Promoting:
1. Employment/education beyond high school
2. Caring & intimate relationships

Preventing:
1. Unemployment
2. Social isolation; antisocial behavior

II

Adolescence (17 yrs)

Promoting:
1. Grade completion
2. Positive peer relations

Preventing:
1. School dropout
2. Antisocial behavior; gang membership

III

Middle Childhood (10 yrs)

Promoting:
1. School engagement
2. Positive peer relations

Preventing:
1. Detention, referral to special education
2. Disruptive behaviors & disorders

IV

Primary School (7 yrs)

Promoting:
1. Learning readiness for school
2. Social competencies for relationships

Preventing:
1. Lack of engagement in learning
2. Disruptive behavior disorders

V

Beginning of Head Start (3 yrs)

Promoting:
1. Exploration; persistence in tasks
2. Communication skills

Preventing:
1. Lack of motivation for exploration
2. Social isolation, disruptive behaviors

Competency Dimensions:
1. = Learning
2. = Social

Intervention (0–3 yrs)

Figure 8.1. A parenting-to-parenting developmental perspective for Early Head Start.

Fleeson, 1988). There is also implicit support for this parenting-to-parenting outcome perspective. Improving parenting outcomes in the next generation is implied by many social policy statements but is seldom made explicit. An adage that clinicians have used for years captures an intuitive wisdom that makes the point: "Treat your children the way you would like your grandchildren to be."

Intermediate outcomes are best conceptualized in our scheme at points following developmental transitions. Times of consolidation (following such transitions) can better allow for assessment of individual differences that might result from interventions, especially when comparing groups with and without interventions under varying conditions. Times of developmental transition are important in that they set in motion pervasive and enduring changes within the child and also major changes in the child's roles with parents and others. Although times of developmental transition represent windows of

opportunity for positive intervention, they also represent periods of vulnerability as developmental systems are reorganizing. Moreover, times of developmental transition, as McCall (1979) has indicated, contain variation in individual differences as a consequence of maturation and associated contextual factors. Therefore, for meaningful assessments of intervention effects across individuals, it is strategic to choose age points following well-studied developmental transitions in order to track intermediate outcomes.

Finally, in accordance with the principle outlined in the previous section of this chapter, we found it useful to specify the outcomes in our scheme according to dimensions of 1) what we are promoting and strengthening in the above domains as well as 2) what we are preventing (in terms of developmental compromises and problems of adaptation) in these domains.

Taken together, we believe the parenting-to-parenting developmental perspective has a number of advantages. Among these are the following:

1. Alternative developmental pathways and varying contexts are highlighted; this allows opportunities for discovering individual and cultural strengths in the midst of adversity and biological handicap; it also helps us avoid errors in judgment about intermediate outcomes.
2. This perspective keeps the importance of longitudinal evaluation in the forefront. All we know from past research and from the best thinking of developmentalists emphasizes that longitudinal study is essential, yet it is difficult to fund in the midst of political pressures for quick answers.
3. The perspective helps us keep in mind why the study of variations across time (i.e., "What leads to what under what circumstances") is important and can lead to discoveries about the impact of interventions on meaningful developmental outcomes.

In summary, the parenting-to-parenting longitudinal perspective provides a scope that is respectful of what we know about developmental processes and relevant research concerning continuities from early experience and intervention. It is a perspective that can allow for the identification of both important developmental outcomes relevant to particular cultural settings, as well as features that are relevant across cultures.

A CONCLUDING EPILOGUE: FOSTERING ALTERNATIVES AND ENCOURAGING IMAGINATION

Our essay has emphasized that a developmental–psychoanalytic perspective has directed attention to certain areas for guiding early intervention. Among these are individuality and meaning, the importance of motives and morality, the significance of emotions, and the centrality of caring relationships. Identifying domains of competence in each of these areas allows the interventionist to design programs for strengthening developmental pathways and for

preventing both compromises in development and problems of adaptation. We have reviewed how diagnosis in early childhood is an ongoing process that is expectant of developmental change and that consists of assessing individuals within their circumstances, as well as the classification of any identified disorder. We have also emphasized that psychoanalytic thinking, while directing attention to these areas, has itself been led in some surprising directions by recent developmental research.

We would like to conclude with an additional area of thinking that exemplifies the latter point. Traditional psychoanalytic approaches to intervention have often emphasized the role of thinking about the past, of avoiding repetitions of misery, and of "putting the past in its place" in order to overcome one's current struggles (Fenichel, 1945; Freud, 1937). More recent psychoanalytic approaches provide another emphasis, namely, that of thinking about the future. Psychotherapy and other interventions enable "new beginnings" (Loewald, 1960) and can mobilize the basic developmental motives we have enumerated in this essay (Emde, 1990). As the previous discussion highlighted, new beginnings may involve alternative developmental pathways. Individuals can discover meaning in different ways as they build on developmental motives. Developmental pathways may differ substantially for those children who were challenged by a biological handicap, and they may differ for those children who were challenged by environmental stress. Thus, in the long-term sense, the interventionist's work is future-oriented and has a goal of fostering alternatives. The interventionist makes it possible for individual children who are in difficulty or at risk to find particular adaptive pathways, and the interventionist makes it possible for children to make use of strengths in family and culture that may be different from what we expect.

There is also a more immediate sense in which early intervention aims to foster alternatives. It aims to provide the conditions wherein the young child can envision alternatives in the everyday challenges of life and gain experience in making use of chosen options. To highlight the importance of this point, we need only recall that the ability to envision alternative possibilities has long been accepted by clinicians as a hallmark of adaptation. Rigidity, or a lack of imagination, is a key element of pathology;

this occurs when an individual shows an inability to adapt to new situations.

Imagination as an adaptive psychological function, and the circumstances under which we can foster imagination, deserve more attention in our work. It is through imaginative capacities that the child, the parent, and the interventionist can envision new combinations and better possibilities. One might say that what we have enumerated as our first guiding principle, namely, "building on the strengths of individuality and meaning," reaches a high level when the interventionist is able to encourage or engage imaginative activity. As adults, we realize that imaginative activity in literature and the arts adds enrichment to our lives by showing us alternative worlds, but we often lose sight of a more mundane truth in our work with children. Viewing alternative possibilities is also vital for social exchange and everyday functioning. The child, for example, needs to see another's view for effective communication. The child also needs to see other views in order for effective action to take place when a goal is blocked or when a conflict is encountered.

The reader might wonder about imaginative abilities in the young child. Fostering imaginative alternatives might seem reasonable as a focus for the interventionist's work with family members who are older than 3 years – but what about at younger ages? Surprisingly, recent research has made us aware of the extent to which imaginative capacities develop in important ways at the dawn of language. Most children at 3 years of age have narrative capacities that allow them to organize meaningful alternative possible worlds and to express them to others (Bretherton, 1983; Bruner, 1986, Wolf, Rygh, & Altshuler, 1984). Children as young as 2 are able to transform reality in play without being confused and can experience pleasure with their caregivers when doing so. All of this is quite different from the traditional psychoanalytic view that the young child normally has difficulty distinguishing fantasy and imagination from reality.

We end with a vignette from a 24-month-old who was videotaped and recorded in one of our studies. The child is seated between his parents eating dinner at home and begins making motions and sounds with his bread. The transcript that follows is one among many we have recorded that illustrate early imaginative transformations at 2 years of age. We

refer to the vignette as "A horse made from bread." This vignette, along with others, is discussed in more detail in Emde, Kubicek, and Oppenheim (1997). The words in brackets describe behaviors, whereas the other words are verbatim; x refers to child vocalizations that were not intelligible to transcribers; C = child; M = mother.

C : [clicks tongue, looks at bread] [more of same]
M : Boy, Mike, you're eatin' a really nice dinner.
C : [plays with bread, "gallops" across table] Look a horsie, look horsie mama; [holds bread towards M]
M : Does that look like a horsie?
C : Yeah. My bread horsie.
M : [chuckles] Is that your bread horsie?
C : xxx fall off.
M : Uh-oh.
C : Put him together.
M : Well, I don't know, once you take bread apart I don't know that you can put it back together again.
C : xxx
M : Kinda like Humpty Dumpty.

We have documented other examples of early play with such imaginative transformations. To be sure, such imaginative activity at a young age is more prominent in children whose language development is early and who have families who delight in such activities during shared play routines. Research on early imaginative capacities and their variations is only beginning. It seems likely, however, that such variations are considerable and that many children, particularly under conditions of environmental deprivation and stress, show less of such abilities. It also seems likely that children who are stressed may, at times, confuse elements of the imaginary with what is real, especially when they feel not in control, frightened, ill, or sleepy. Overall, one might say that being able to imagine alternatives is of major adaptive importance in that it may appear as soon as the toddler strings words together. But we must also say that the significance of early variations in this ability for intervention are unclear. What does seem clear is that interventionists will be faced with increasing opportunities for learning about variations and fostering alternatives for clinicians and families. This will occur as we encounter the particulars of biological variation from advances in molecular genetics and the cognitive neurosciences and as we encounter the particulars of cultural variation in our increasingly diverse and interconnected society.

REFERENCES

Achenbach, T. M. (1988). Integrating assessment and taxonomy. In M. Rutter, A. H. Tuma, & I. S. Lann (Eds.), *Assessment and diagnosis in child psychopathology* (pp. 300–46). New York: Guilford Press.

American Psychiatric Association. (1994). *Diagnostic and statistical manual of mental disorders* (*DSMIV*). Washington, DC: Author.

Bertalanffy, L. von (1968). *General system theory: Foundations, development, applications.* New York: Braziller.

Biringen, Z., & Robinson, J. L. (1991). Emotional availability in mother-child dyads. *American Journal of Orthopsychiatry, 61,* 258–71.

Boulding, K. (1956). General systems theory: the skeleton of science. *Management Science, 2,* 197–208.

Bowlby, J. (1969). *Attachment and loss: Vol. I (Attachment).* New York: Basic Books.

Bowlby, J. (1973). *Attachment and loss: Vol. II (Separation, Anxiety, and Anger).* New York: Basic Books.

Bowlby, J. (1980). *Attachment and loss: Vol. III (Loss, Sadness, and Depression).* New York: Basic Books.

Brazelton, T. B., & Cramer, B. G. (1990). *The earliest relationship.* Reading, MA: Addison-Wesley.

Bretherton, I. (1983). Representing the social world in symbolic play: Reality and fantasy. In I. Bretherton (Ed.), *Symbolic play: The representation of social understanding* (pp. 3–41). New York: Academic Press.

Bruner, J. (1986). *Actual minds, possible worlds.* Cambridge, MA: Harvard University Press.

Butterfield, P. M., Dolezol, S., & Knox, R. M. (1995). *Love is layers of sharing.* Denver, CO: Read Your Baby.

Butterfield, P. M., Pagano, B., & Dolezol, S. (1997). *Playing is learning.* Denver, CO: Read Your Baby.

Byng-Hall, J. (1995). *Rewriting family scripts: Improvisation and systems change.* New York: Guilford Press.

Clyman, R. B. (1991). The procedural organization of emotions: A contribution from cognitive science to the psychoanalytic theory of therapeutic action. *Journal of the American Psychoanalytic Association, 39*(Suppl.), 349–82.

Connell, J. P., & Kubisch, A. T. (1996). *Applying a theories of change approach to the evaluation of comprehensive community initiatives: Progress, prospects, and problems.* Unpublished manuscript. Second Draft.

Cramer, B., Robert-Tissot, C., Stern, D. N., Serpa-Rusconi, S., DeMuralt, M., Besson, G., Palacio-Espapa, F., Bachmann, J. Knauer, D., Berney, C., & D'Arcis, U. (1990). Outcome evaluation in brief mother–infant psychotherapy: A preliminary report. *Infant Mental Health Journal, 11,* 278–300.

Department of Health and Human Services. (1994, September). *The Statement of the Advisory Committee on Services for Families with Infants and Toddlers.* Washington, DC: Author.

Dix, T. (1991). The affective organization of parenting: Adaptive and maladaptive processes. *Psychological Bulletin, 110,* 3–25.

Doi, T. (1992). On the concept of amae. *Infant Mental Health Journal, 13,* 7–11.

Dolezol, S., Butterfield, P. M., & Grimshaw, J. (1994). *Listen, listen, listen.* Denver, CO: Read Your Baby.

Dunn, J. (1988). *The beginnings of social understanding.* Cambridge, MA: Harvard University Press.

Emde, R. N. (1980). Emotional availability: A reciprocal reward system for infants and parents with implications for prevention of psychosocial disorders. In P. M. Taylor (Ed.), *Parent–infant relationships* (pp. 87–115). Orlando, FL: Grune & Stratton.

Emde, R. N. (1988a). Development terminable and interminable: I. Innate and motivational factors from infancy. *International Journal of Psycho-Analysis, 69,* 23–42.

Emde, R. N. (1988b). Development terminable and interminable: II. Recent psychoanalytic theory and therapeutic considerations. *International Journal of Psycho-Analysis, 69,* 283–96.

Emde, R. N. (1990). Mobilizing fundamental modes of development: An essay on empathic availability and therapeutic action. *Journal of the American Psychoanalytic Association, 38,* 881–913.

Emde, R. N. (1991). Positive emotions for psychoanalytic theory: Surprises from infancy research and new directions. *Journal of the American Psychoanalytic Association, 39*(Suppl.), 5–44.

Emde, R. N. (1992). Individual meaning and increasing complexity: Contributions of Sigmund Freud and René Spitz to developmental psychology. *Developmental Psychology, 28,* 347–59.

Emde, R. N. (1994). Individuality, context, and the search for meaning. *Child Development, 65,* 719–37.

Emde, R. N. (Ed.). (1983). *Rene A. Spitz: Dialogues from infancy. Selected papers* (with commentary). New York: International Universities Press.

Emde, R. N., Biringen, Z., Clyman, R. B., & Oppenheim, D. (1991). The moral self of infancy: Affective core and procedural knowledge. *Developmental Review, 11,* 251–70.

Emde, R. N., Johnson, W. F., & Easterbrooks, M. A. (1987). The do's and don'ts of early moral development: Psychoanalytic tradition and current research. In J. Kagan & S. Lamb (Eds.), *The emergence of morality in young children* (pp. 245–77). Chicago: University of Chicago Press.

Emde, R. N., Kubicek, L., & Oppenheim, D. (1997). Imaginative reality observed during early language development. *International Journal of Psycho-Analysis.*

Emde, R. N., Plomin, R., Robinson, J., Reznick, J., Campos, J., Corley, R., DeFries, J., Fulker, D. W., Kagan, J., & Zahn-Waxler, C. (1992). Temperament, emotion, and cognition at 14 months: The MacArthur longitudinal twin study. *Child Development, 63*, 1437–55.

Erikson, E. (1950). *Childhood and society.* New York: Norton.

Fenichel, O. (1945). *The psychoanalytic theory of neurosis.* New York: Norton.

Fleming, J., & Benedek, T. (1966). *Psychoanalytic supervision.* New York: Grune & Stratton.

Fonagy, P. (1995). Psychoanalytic and empirical approaches to developmental psychopathology: An object-relations perspective. In T. Shapiro & R. N. Emde (Eds.), *Research in psychoanalysis: Process, development, outcome* (pp. 245–60). Madison, CT: International Universities Press.

Fraiberg, S. (1980). *Clinical studies in infant mental health.* New York: Basic Books.

Fraiberg, S., Adelson, E., & Shapiro, V. (1975). Ghosts in the nursery: A psychoanalytic approach to the problems of impaired infant-mother relationships. *Journal of American Academy of Child Psychiatry, 14,* 387–421.

Freud, S. (1920). Beyond the pleasure principle. In J. Strachey (Ed. and Trans.), *The standard edition of the complete psychological works of Sigmund Freud* (Vol. 18, pp. 7–64). London: Hogarth Press.

Freud, S. (1937). Analysis terminable and interminable. In J. Strachey (Ed. and Trans.), *The standard edition of the complete psychological works of Sigmund Freud* (Vol. 23, pp. 209–53). London: Hogarth Press.

Gaensbauer, T. J., & Harmon, R. J. (1981). Clinical assessment in infancy utilizing a structured playroom situation. *Journal of the American Academy of Child Psychiatry, 20,* 264–80.

Gilligan, C. (1982). *In a different voice: Psychological theory and women's development.* Cambridge, MA: Harvard University Press.

Gottlieb, G. (1992). *Individual development and evolution.* New York: Oxford University Press.

Greenspan, S. I. (1981). *Psychopathology and adaptation in infancy and early childhood.* New York: International Universities Press.

Greenspan, S. (1997). *The growth of the mind.* Reading, MA: Addison-Wesley. (With Beryl Lieff Benderly.)

Harmon, R. J., & Murrow, N. S. (1995). The effects of prematurity and other perinatal factors on infants' mastery motivation. In R. H. MacTurk & G. A. Morgan (Eds.), *Advances in applied developmental psychology: Vol. 12. Mastery motivation: Origins, conceptualizations, and applications* (pp. 237–56). Norwood, NJ: Ablex.

Hermans, H. J. M., Kempen, H. J. G., & van Loon, R. J. P. (1992). The dialogical self. *American Psychologist, 47,* 23–33.

Hinde, R. A. (1992). Developmental psychology in the context of older behavioral sciences. *Developmental Psychology, 28,* 1018–29.

Horowitz, M. J. (Ed.). (1988). *Psychodynamics and cognition.* Chicago: The University of Chicago Press.

Horowitz, M., Fridhandler, B., & Stinson, C. (1992). Person schemas and emotion. In T. Shapiro & R. N. Emde (Eds.), *Affect: Psychoanalytic perspectives* (pp. 173–208). Madison, CT: International Universities Press.

Kagan, J. (1981). *The second year: The emergence of self-awareness.* Cambridge: Harvard University Press.

Kaye, K. (1982). *The mental and social life of babies: How parents create persons.* Chicago: University of Chicago Press.

Kernberg, O. F. (1993). The psychopathology of hatred. In T. Shapiro, & R. N. Emde (Eds.), *Affect: Psychoanalytic perspectives* (pp. 209–38). Madison, CT: International Universities Press.

Kihlstrom, J. F. (1987). The cognitive unconscious. *Science, 237*(4821), 1445–52.

Kochanska, G., & Aksan, N. (1995). Mother-child mutually positive affect, the quality of child compliance to requests and prohibitions, and maternal control as correlates of early internalization. *Child Development, 66,* 236–54.

Kochanska, G., Casey, R. J., & Fukamoto, A. (1995). Toddlers' sensitivity to standard violations. *Child Development, 66,* 643–56.

Kuczynski, L., & Kochanska, G. (1995). Function and content of maternal demands: Developmental significance of early demands for competent action. *Child Development, 66,* 616–28.

Lennard, H. L., & Bernstein, A. (1960). *The anatomy of psychotherapy.* New York: Columbia University Press.

Loewald, H. W. (1960). On the therapeutic action of psycho-analysis. *International Journal of Psycho-Analysis, 41,* 16–33.

MacTurk, R. H., & Morgan, G. A. (Eds.). (1995). *Advances in applied developmental psychology: Vol. 12. Mastery motivation: Origins, conceptualizations, and applications.* Norwood, NJ: Ablex.

Mahler, M. S., Pine, F., & Bergman, A. (1975). *The psychological birth of the human infant: Symbiosis and individuation.* New York: Basic Books.

Main, M. (1993). Discourse, prediction, and recent studies in attachment: Implications for psychoanalysis. In T. Shapiro & R. N. Emde (Eds.), *Research in psychoanalysis: Process, development, outcome* (pp. 209–44). Madison, CT: International Universities Press.

McCall, R. B. (1979). The development of intellectual functioning in infancy and the prediction of later I.Q. In J. Osofsky (Ed.), *Handbook of infant development* (pp. 707–741). New York: Wiley.

Minuchin, S. (1974). *Families and family therapy.* Cambridge, MA: Harvard University Press.

Papousek, H., & Papousek, M. (1979). Early ontogeny of human social interaction: Its biological roots and social dimensions. In K. Foppa, W. Lepenies, & D. Ploog (Eds.), *Human ethology: Claims and limits of a new discipline* (pp. 456–89). Cambridge University Press.

Piaget, J. (1952). *The origins of intelligence in children* (2nd ed.). New York: International Universities Press.

Platt, J. R. (1966). *The step to man*. New York: Wiley.

Plomin, R. (1986). *Development, genetics, and psychology*. Hillsdale, NJ: Erlbaum.

Plomin, R., Emde, R. N., Braungart, J. M., Campos, J., Corley, R., Fulker, D. W., Kagan, J., Reznick, J. S., Robinson, J., Zahn-Waxler, C., & DeFries, J. C. (1993). Genetic change and continuity from 14 to 20 months: The MacArthur Longitudinal Twin Study. *Child Development, 64*, 1354–76.

Rapaport, D. (1959). The structure of psychoanalytic theory: A systematizing attempt. *Psychological Issues, Monograph #6*. New York: International Universities Press.

Reiss, D. (1989). The represented and practicing family: Contrasting visions of family continuity. In A. J. Sameroff & R. N. Emde (Eds.), *Relationship disturbances in early childhood: A developmental approach* (pp. 191–220). New York: Basic Books.

Robinson, J., Zahn-Waxler, C., & Emde, R. N. (in press). Relationship context as a moderator of sources of individual differences in empathic development. In R. N. Emde & J. K. Hewitt (eds.), *The transition from infancy to early childhood: Genetic and environmental influences in the MacArthur Longitudinal Twin Study*. New York: Oxford University Press.

Rutter, M., & Gould, M. (1985). Classification. In M. Rutter & L. Hersov (Eds.), *Child and adolescent psychiatry: Modern approaches* (pp. 304–21). London: Blackwell Scientific Publications.

Rutter, M., & Tuma, A. H. (1988). Diagnosis and classification: Some outstanding issues. In M. Rutter, A. H. Tuma, & I. S. Lann (Eds.), *Assessment and diagnosis in child psychopathology* (pp. 437–52). New York: Guilford Press.

Sameroff, A. J. (1983). Developmental systems: Contexts and evolution. In E. M. Hetherington (Ed.), P. H. Mussen (Series Ed.), *Handbook of child psychology, Vol. 1. Socialization, personality, and social development* (pp. 237–94). New York: Wiley.

Sameroff, A. J., & Emde, R. N. (Eds.) (1989). *Relationship disturbances in early childhood: A developmental approach*. New York: Basic Books.

Sampson, E. E. (1988). The debate on individuality. *American Psychologist, 43*, 15–22.

Sander, L. (1985). Toward a logic of organization in psychobiological development. In K. Klar & L. Siever (Eds.), *Biologic response styles: Clinical implications*. Monograph Series of the American Psychiatric Press.

Scarr, S. (1992). Developmental theories for the 1990s: Development and individual differences. *Child Development, 63*, 1–19.

Scharff, D. E., & Scharff, J. S. (1987). *Object relations family therapy*. New Jersey and London: Jason Aronson.

Shapiro, T., & Emde, R. N. (Eds.). (1994). *Research in psychoanalysis: Process, development, outcome*. Madison, CT: International Universities Press.

Shweder, R. A., & Bourne, E. (1982). Does the concept of the person vary cross-culturally? In A. J. Marsella & G. White (Eds.), *Cultural concepts of mental health and therapy* (pp. 97–137). Boston: Reidel.

Skeels, H. M. (1966). Adult status of children with contrasting early life experiences: A follow-up study. *Monographs of the Society for Research in Child Development, 31*(3 Serial No. 105), 1–65.

Spitz, R. A. (1957). *No and yes: On the genesis of human communication*. New York: International Universities Press.

Spitz, R. A. (1959). *A genetic field theory of ego formation*. New York: International Universities Press.

Spitz, R. A. (1965). *The first year of life*. New York: International Universities Press.

Sroufe, L. A., & Fleeson, J. (1988). The coherence of family relationships. In R. A. Hinde & J. Stevenson-Hinde (Eds.), *Relationships within families: Mutual influences* (pp. 27–47). Oxford, England: Clarendon Press.

Stern, D. (1985). *The interpersonal world of the infant*. New York: Basic Books.

Stern, D. N. (1977). *The first relationship: Mother and infant*. Cambridge, MA: Harvard University Press.

Stern, D., & Stern-Bruschweiler, N. (1987). *The mother's representation of her infant: Considerations of its nature*. Unpublished manuscript, University of Geneva.

Thelen, E., & Ulrich, B. D. (1991). Hidden skills. *Monographs of the Society for Research in Child Development, 56*(1, Serial No. 223).

Werner, H. (1957). *Comparative psychology of mental development*. New York: International Universities Press.

Wolf, D. P., Rygh, J., & Altshuler, J. (1984). Agency and experience: Actions and states in play narratives. In I. Bretherton (Ed.), *Symbolic play: The development of social understanding* (pp. 195–217). Orlando, FL: Academic Press.

Zahn-Waxler, C., Radke-Yarrow, M., & King, R. A. (1979). Child rearing and children's prosocial initiations toward victims of distress. *Child Development, 50*, 319–30.

Zahn-Waxler, C., Robinson, J., & Emde, R. N. (1992). The development of empathy in twins. *Developmental Psychology, 28*, 1038–47.

Zero To Three: The National Center for Infants, Toddlers, and Families (1994). DC: Zero To Three (Diagnostic Classification of Mental Health and Developmental Disorders of Infancy and Early Childhood). Washington, DC: Author.

CHAPTER NINE

Behavioral and Educational Approaches to Early Intervention

MARK WOLERY

A wide range of factors can have powerful, enduring adverse impacts on children's developmental and educational achievement. Among others, these include genetic disorders, physiological and metabolic disorders, ill health, infections, central nervous system insults, and disordered environments with a number of counterproductive influences. These factors, separately and in combination, can produce disabilities and substantial risks for developmental difficulties. Those disabilities in turn often negatively affect children's adaptation and learning as well as threaten their families' functioning and well-being. Society's response to children with disabilities and those at severe risk for disabilities includes funding for basic and applied research to understand more completely and precisely the causes, course, and treatment of disabling conditions; actions and policies designed to prevent the occurrence of disabilities; and programs to address children's developmental problems.

This chapter presents a rationale for the use of educational programs for young children who have disabilities. In addition, the chapter describes the behavioral perspective that is used as a foundation for many educationally oriented intervention programs, discusses the contributions derived from that orientation, and identifies the challenges faced by

those programs. The chapter then describes additional models for conceptualizing intervention efforts and draws implications from those perspectives. The chapter concludes by discussing how such programs are likely to be structured in the future. This chapter focuses primarily on infants and young children who have identifiable disabilities rather than on children who are solely at environmental risk for developmental problems. This latter issue has been addressed in other sources (e.g., Bryant & Maxwell, 1997; Guralnick, 1998; Ramey & Ramey, 1998).

RATIONALE FOR EDUCATIONAL INTERVENTION PROGRAMS

Formal education usually begins sometime after children's fifth or sixth birthdays. Thus, a legitimate question arises about why educational programs emerged for young children with developmental delays and disabilities. The answer is due, in large part, to historical factors and to the nature of children's needs.

Historical Precedents for Early Educationally Oriented Intervention Programs

Organized intervention programs for young children with disabilities are relatively new endeavors and have become visible only during the last four decades of the twentieth century. Despite the fact that free, appropriate public education became available for school-age children with disabilities in the

Preparation of this chapter was supported by the U.S. Department of Education, Office of Special Education and Rehabilitative Services (Grant Number HO24Q70001 to the University of North Carolina at Chapel Hill). However, the opinions here expressed do not necessarily reflect the policy of the U.S. Department of Education, and no official endorsement should be inferred.

mid-1970s through Public Law 94-142, this legislation did not mandate services for infants, toddlers, or preschoolers with disabilities. Such services were not required until subsequent amendments in 1986 and did not become operational in most states until the early 1990s (Gallagher, 1996).

In the 1960s, several factors converged to set the stage for using educational programs to address the needs of young children with disabilities (Bailey & Wolery, 1992). First, the civil rights movement called attention to the rights and needs of individuals who were different from the majority population. These actions laid the groundwork for other groups (e.g., women and individuals with disabilities) to seek their rights and to prompt governmental action. Concomitantly, education was seen as a primary means for addressing the ills of society. For example, racial integration of schools was the mechanism used to bridge the racial divisions in the country. Also, children from economically disadvantaged families were failing in elementary education; thus, Head Start was funded to reduce school failure with the hope that it would subsequently eradicate poverty in the United States. Head Start set the precedent for delivering public educational services below the usual school-entry age in the United States.

Families of children with disabilities initiated litigation and lobbied legislators on behalf of their children, sometimes with the support of professionals and professional organizations. These actions resulted in passage of P.L. 94-142. However, as noted earlier, this law did not require services for young children with disabilities, but it set the stage for the notion that children with disabilities needed educational services. Another federal initiative that influenced the development of educationally oriented intervention programs was the Handicapped Children's Early Education Program, which was funded in 1968. This program, later named the Early Education Program for Children with Disabilities, supported different types of projects. Over the years, more than 500 model demonstration projects were funded to develop, evaluate, and disseminate information about how to serve young children with disabilities (Smith & McKenna, 1994). The program also funded efforts to train personnel through in-service and outreach projects to provide services to young children with disabilities and their families. Finally, the program supported larger research institutes to study specific issues related to educating young children with disabilities.

Thus, the civil rights movement gave credence to the notion that individuals who were different from the norm had rights to services. Society had faith in education to solve the problems it faced, and educational services were granted to school-age children with disabilities. Head Start highlighted the importance of children's early years and suggested that educational programs could have positive influences. Furthermore, model demonstration programs provided evidence that services were potentially beneficial. As a result, it is not surprising that educationally oriented programs emerged for young children with disabilities.

Nature of Children's Disabilities

In addition to the forces and events noted earlier, the disabilities of children called for a response beyond usual child rearing practices. Different disabilities can have profoundly different effects on children's functioning, and the same disability (e.g., blindness) can have differential effects at different levels of severity (Hatton, Bailey, Burchinal, & Ferrell, 1997). Nonetheless, four general effects can be noted across a range of disabilities and severity levels (Wolery, Strain, & Bailey, 1992). First, children's disabilities often make them dependent upon others. For example, if a child cannot feed herself, then someone must feed her. If a child cannot crawl, walk, or otherwise move from one place to another, someone must move him if a change in location is needed. If a child cannot communicate his or her wants and needs through some understandable means, then someone else must anticipate the child's needs and wants. While young, typically developing children are also dependent upon others; their independence within the range of safe activities is encouraged and promoted in many families. For young children with disabilities, this dependence can maintain well beyond usual age expectations, beyond the reasonable limits of safety, and beyond those children's ability to learn the skills needed for independence. In addition to these obvious undesirable outcomes, children's continued dependence may contribute to learned helplessness that has other negative consequences (Utley, Hoehn, Soraci, & Baumeister, 1993).

Second, children's disabilities often result in delayed development that becomes increasingly great as children grow older. These delays in development may be evident in the social, communicative, intellectual, and physical domains and appear to occur in most high incidence disabilities (e.g., mental retardation). The discrepancies in the developmental abilities of children with disabilities and their age-mates tend to increase with age, which results in children with disabilities becoming progressively more behind and unlike their typically developing peers. Stark ability distinctions may well lead to less social acceptance by peers, greater stigmatization, more social isolation, and less participation in activities with their age-mates.

Third, children's disabilities often interfere with how well they can learn from usual environmental structures and interactions. For example, some young children with disabilities do not imitate their peers; thus, observational learning from those peers' models is not an avenue of learning. Other young children with disabilities do not engage in complex play with toys and objects in their physical environment, and this absence of play reduces their ability to acquire and refine their knowledge about the world. Other young children with disabilities do not engage in social or communicative interactions with their peers; thus, their ability to learn from the social environment is reduced. Still other young children with disabilities engage in interactions with toys and others, but they do so for fleeting periods of time, which limits their ability to acquire meaningful skills through sustained engagement and interactions.

Fourth, left without intervention, children's disabilities can lead to the emergence of additional or secondary disorders. For example, some young children with cerebral palsy will develop contractures if range of motion exercises are not performed. Many children with severe communication disorders appear to develop problematic behaviors because of their inability to communicate effectively. Similarly, children with more mild communication disorders may talk less, which leads to additional delays in language and communicative skills (Warren & Kaiser, 1986).

In short, few good reasons can be proposed for allowing children to remain dependent upon others, particularly when independence is possible, age

appropriate, and safe. Similarly, few good reasons can be proposed for allowing children to fall farther and farther behind their age-mates developmentally, for having ineffective and inefficient modes of learning, and for letting secondary disorders appear. Thus, programs were designed with an educational emphasis, often from the behavioral perspective, to minimize the realization of these negative outcomes.

BEHAVIORAL PERSPECTIVE

In this section, the foundations of the behavioral perspective are discussed. The contributions and programs that emerged from this view are identified. Finally, some of the challenges faced by programs derived from the behavioral view are presented.

Foundations of the Behavioral Perspective

The behavioral model has its roots in the experimental analysis of human behavior as articulated by Skinner (1953). Skinner and other behaviorists maintained that behavior was a result of one's physiology, learning history, and current situation. In the middle portion of the twentieth century, behavioral theory was applied to human behavior outside of the laboratory and became known as *applied behavior analysis* (Baer, Wolf, & Risley, 1968; see Cooper, Heron, and Heward, 1987, for an accessible description of this history). A behavioral description of child development has been given (Bijou & Baer, 1961, 1965, 1978), as has a behavioral account of atypical development (Bijou, 1981; Kozloff, 1994a). Although the behavioral perspective is often seen as a totally mechanistic model, it assumes children influence their environments as well as being influenced by those settings; thus, it is an interactive model (Bijou & Baer, 1978). The perspective also recognizes the existence of ideas, thoughts, expectations, and other mentalistic processes but chooses to focus primarily on observable responses and their relationships to environmental events (Cooper et al., 1987).

The behavioral perspective is concerned with the relationships between the organism's behavior (e.g., child's behavior) and the environment or, more precisely, relationships between behavior and stimuli in the environment – given, of course, the limitations and propensities of the individual's learning history and physiology. Two broad types of behavior are recognized: respondent behavior and operant behavior. Respondent behavior refers to responses that are elicited by specific stimuli. The stimulus temporally comes before the behavior and appears to cause the response to occur. This relationship is often called a *reflex*. The stimulus that elicits the behavior is called the *unconditioned stimulus* because its effect on the behavior is not a result of conditioning or experience (i.e., learning history). Other stimuli, which do not originally have the power to elicit specific responses, can be made to do so through respondent conditioning, sometimes called *classical conditioning. Respondent conditioning* involves presenting the unconditioned stimulus with (i.e., in close temporal relationship to) a neutral stimulus – one that does not elicit the behavior. Over repeated exposures, the neutral stimulus will acquire the ability to elicit the response. When this occurs, the stimulus then is called the *conditioned stimulus* because through conditioning (experience) the neutral stimulus now has the eliciting properties of the unconditioned stimulus; it can produce the response. Although respondent learning is well recognized and is used in some intervention practices, its applications are not as extensive as those associated with *operant behavior and learning.*

With operant behavior, the relationship between the behavior and the environmental stimuli occurs in the context of a contingency that has three elements: "1) a precise definition of the limits and range of response topographies that will produce 2) a specific consequence and 3) the environmental situation . . . in which that occurrence influences future probability of response" (Cooper et al., 1987, p. 21). In short, a behavior occurs in some context (i.e., some situation), and a consequence of the behavior influences the likelihood that the behavior will occur again in that context. The consequence is a change in the environment after the behavior occurs. This change can take two forms: the addition or presentation of a new stimulus or the termination or removal of an existing stimulus. The result of the consequence on the rate of the behavior is also twofold: the probability of the behavior recurring may either increase or decrease. Thus, four direct relationships may occur. First, the probability of the behavior recurring is increased by the addition of the new stimulus; this is called *positive reinforcement.*

Second, the probability of the behavior recurring is increased by the removal or termination of an existing stimulus; this is called *negative reinforcement.* Third, the probability of the behavior recurring is decreased by the addition of the new stimulus; this is called *Type I punishment.* Fourth, the probability of the behavior recurring is decreased by the removal or termination of an existing stimulus; this is called *Type II punishment* (Wolery, Bailey, & Sugai, 1988).

These four behavior–consequence relationships can only be said to exist if there are clear effects on the occurrence of the behavior. The two reinforcement procedures result in maintenance of, or increase in, the occurrence of the behavior in question; the two punishment procedures result in a decrease in the occurrence of the studied behavior. A given stimulus may be added regularly and contingently upon the occurrence of the behavior; however, if the behavior does not increase, then that stimulus cannot be called a positive reinforcer – no relationship is present between this consequence and the rate of the behavior. The consequent event must produce a measurable effect on the behavior's occurrence before the conclusion can be made that a relationship exists between the behavior and the consequence. Given a reinforcer, several factors influence the likelihood that a relationship will be established. Specifically, the proportion of the behavior's occurrences that result in the consequent event and the timing of the addition or removal/termination of the consequent event are important factors. Generally, when nearly every occurrence of the behavior results in the consequence, there is an increased likelihood that a relationship will be established. Similarly, when the consequent event is added or removed immediately after the occurrence of the behavior, there is a greater likelihood that a relationship will be developed.

In terms of implications for intervention, some general assumptions must be noted (Cooper et al., 1987; Wolery et al., 1988). The behavioral perspective assumes that the principles of behavior (e.g., reinforcement or punishment) are operating in the natural environment with or without our knowledge. The behaviors of young children, their parents, and their interventionists are subject to the influence of these behavior–consequence relationships. Thus, a child's actions on the environment may result in predictable consequences that influence the likelihood of the child's behavior occurring again. Similarly, the child's actions may influence the environment, which could have the function of producing predictable behavior in the adults within the child's environment, and those predictable behaviors may have consistent consequences that influence the likelihood that the adult's behavior will recur. This situation, of course, constitutes bidirectional influences between children and others (parents, caregivers, interventionists, etc.).

It is important to note that the consequences that influence behavior are often natural outcomes that occur as a result of the behavior and are tied directly to the behavior. For example, the positive reinforcer for asking questions is often the answer containing the information that was sought in the questions; the positive reinforcer for locomotion is often arriving at a given destination. In short, these consequences are built into the social and physical world and often occur predictably without particular intention or intervention by others in the individual's environment. The implication for intervention is that we should structure young children's environments to increase the probability that they will engage in the behaviors that result in predictable but natural consequences, which in turn allow adaptive behavior to be learned.

Another implication for practice is that the value of particular consequences may vary from individual to individual and over time within each individual. Thus, a consequent event that functioned as a positive reinforcer for one child may not do so for another child. Likewise, a consequent event that functioned as a positive reinforcer for a given child at one point in time may not do so later. In short, consequent events must be individually selected for each person, and the relative power of those events may change over time because of differences in the individual's physiology and learning history – including repeated use of those consequences.

As noted previously, the behavior–consequence relationships occur in the context of other stimulus conditions in the environment. Each time the behavior occurs, some stimuli (other than the consequences of the behavior) are present in the environment (situation). These stimuli can occur in at least two forms: setting events and antecedent events. Setting events have different definitions but are those features and characteristics of environments that

are relatively stable (for a more extensive discussion of setting events, see Carr, Reeve, & Magito-McLaughlin, 1996, and Horner, Vaughn, Day, & Ard, 1996; for a discussion of establishing operations, see Michael, 1982, 1993). Antecedent events are stimuli that may be added to the environment before the behavior occurs; things that happen or are present immediately before the behavior. Both setting and antecedent events may acquire discriminative properties, meaning that they increase the probability of the behavior occurring again. When setting and antecedent events have discriminative power, they appear to cue the individual that reinforcement is probable if the behavior is performed. This increased probability is a result of the history of the behavior–consequence relationship when the setting or antecedent event is present. When a behavior consistently occurs more frequently in the presence of a given setting or antecedent event, then stimulus control has been established. Stimulus control simply means that a given behavior is more likely to occur when a given setting event or antecedent stimulus is present and the behavior is less likely to occur when that same setting event or antecedent stimulus is absent. Controlled is the foundation from which complex behavioral repertoires are derived.

Stimulus control is established when a given consequent event (e.g., positive reinforcer) is consistently and contingently provided when the behavior occurs in the presence of the setting or antecedent event and when that consequent event is consistently withheld when the behavior occurs in the absence of the setting or antecedent event (Wolery, Ault, & Doyle, 1992). For example, to increase the frequency with which a child uses a given word to name a particular object, reinforcement would occur when the child uses that word in the object's presence and reinforcement would be withheld when the child uses the word in the object's absence. In nearly all cases, stimulus control is not established by one occurrence of a behavior in the presence of a given stimulus; usually, multiple occurrences of the behavior are necessary. Establishing stimulus control is the basic goal of instructional programs at any level; specifically, the intent of teaching is to ensure that new behavior will reliably and predictably occur when a given stimulus or stimulus constellation is present. This new behavior may be some discrete response, a chain of responses, or responses that are indicative of and consistent with given rules (i.e., rule-governed behavior), as in concept formation. Stimulus control, of course, is established, strengthened, and weakened by naturally occurring events and is operational with or without our awareness and knowledge.

In summary, the behavioral perspective views individuals' behavior as a function of their physiology, learning history, and current situation. The perspective assumes the child influences and is influenced by environmental events, including the behavior of others. Furthermore, four general relationships exist between individuals' behavior and the consequences of those behaviors. These relationships describe the effects of consequent events on the likelihood that the behavior will recur. Other environmental stimuli can also acquire influence over the behavior through the process of stimulus control – the behavior is reinforced when the environmental stimuli are present and it is not reinforced when the environmental stimuli are absent.

Contributions of the Behavioral Perspective to Educationally Oriented Interventions

The behavioral model has made at least five significant contributions to intervention programs for young children with disabilities. First, the perspective has been used as an explanation for how behaviors, particularly problematic social behaviors, are established and maintained. As such, it provides explanations for behavior that are based on natural laws of learning and that lead directly to potential interventions or actions adults can take to address the problematic behaviors (Baer, 1978; Kozloff, 1994a). This contribution has merit to the extent that interventionists help parents understand some of their children's behavior in this light.

Second, the principles of reinforcement and punishment have been used widely to address children's problematic behaviors (Singh, 1997). Practice in this area has undergone substantial revision and advancement in the last fifteen years of the twentieth century. In the past, these principles were translated directly into intervention techniques, a large number of techniques emerged, and the techniques had wide application across many groups of individuals with disabilities and in various settings

(Singh, 1997; Wolery et al., 1988). Examples of reinforcement procedures included differential reinforcement of other behaviors (Repp & Deitz, 1974), differential reinforcement of alternative behaviors (Ogier & Hornby, 1996), and differential reinforcement of incompatible behaviors (Luiselli, Colozzi, Helfen, & Pollow, 1980). Instances of punishment procedures included various types of time out. Examples are *contingent observation*, in which reinforcement is withheld for a given period of time while the child watches other children behave appropriately (Mace & Heller, 1990), *nonexclusionary* time out, in which reinforcement is withheld for a specific period of time but the child remains in the activity (Yeager & McLaughlin, 1995), and *exclusionary* time out, in which reinforcement is withheld while the child is removed from the activity (Twyman, Johnson, Buie, & Nelson, 1994). Other punishment procedures include the contingent application of aversive stimuli (Guess, Helmstetter, Turnbull, & Knowlton, 1987) and overcorrection (Doke & Epstein, 1975; Foxx & Azrin, 1973). There are two types of overcorrection: positive practice and restitution. *Positive practice* involves requiring the child to practice an alternative positive behavior contingent upon each occurrence of a problematic behavior; for example, if a child inappropriately threw a wooden block, the child would be required to stack a certain number of blocks or to stack blocks for a given amount of time (e.g., two minutes). *Restitution* involves making the child restore the environment to a state better than it was before the problematic behavior occurred; for example, if a child aggressively grabbed a toy from another child, the offending child would be required to give the other child two or three toys. Applications of these techniques resulted in at least three distinct findings: 1) in many cases, the problematic behaviors were treated successfully and the problem situation was resolved; 2) in some occasional cases, the problematic behaviors continued or worsened despite careful implementation of the selected technique (Solnick, Rincover, & Peterson, 1977); and 3) in some cases, the techniques were not used appropriately or were used inconsistently and did not produce the desired effects (Taylor & Miller, 1997).

In light of these findings, professionals and caregivers became concerned about the punishment procedures. These concerns focused on the punitive nature of the aversive procedures, the potential for violating the basic human rights of individuals with disabilities, and the perception that aversive procedures were being used indiscriminately and that there was an overreliance on their use (Guess et al., 1987). These concerns led professional organizations (e.g., The Association for Persons with Severe Handicaps, The Association for Behavior Analysis, and The American Association on Mental Retardation) to pass position statements about the use of aversive procedures and about the right to treatment for persons with disabilities (see Singh, Lloyd, & Kendall, 1990, for a listing of these position statements). Concomitant with the increasing concern about the use of aversive procedures was a growing realization that the same problematic behavior (e.g., self-injury) across different individuals may have different motivational properties (could occur for different reasons; Carr, 1977). These forces converged to cause a re-analysis of practice (Repp & Singh, 1990).

A central outcome of this re-analysis was a return of the field to its analytical roots as evidenced by greater attention to the factors that controlled or contributed to the occurrence of the problematic behaviors. Efforts became focused on identifying the communicative intent of the problematic behaviors (Donnellan, Mirenda, Mesaros, & Fassbender, 1984), the actual function served by the problematic behavior (Day, Horner, & O'Neill, 1994; Horner & Day, 1991), and the identification and control of setting events or other conditions that contributed to the occurrence of the behavior (Kennedy & Meyer, 1996). This emphasis on variables associated with the problematic behavior led to assessment techniques to identify those factors. As a result, scales for assessing motivational factors emerged (Durand & Crimmins, 1988), observational systems were devised to identify when and under what conditions the behaviors occurred (Touchette, MacDonald, & Langer, 1985), interview protocols supplemented with direct observational procedures were developed for assessing these factors (Arndorfer, Miltenberger, Woster, Rortvedt, & Gaffaney, 1994; O'Neill, Horner, Albin, Storey, & Sprague, 1990), and procedures were devised for evaluating the effects of hypothesized reasons for the occurrence of the problematic behaviors (Iwata, Dorsey, Slifer, Bauman, & Richman, 1982; Wacker et al., 1990).

This emphasis on assessment contributed directly to the use of nonaversive approaches for dealing with problematic behaviors. Specifically, the assessment results are used to devise more proactive treatment plans than had been the case in the past. These plans include such activities as attempting to prevent the use of the problematic behaviors by focusing on skill building (Dunlap, Johnson, & Robbins, 1990), providing children with more choices about activities (Dyer, Dunlap, & Winterling, 1990), and teaching communicative behavior as an alternative to the problematic behavior – known as functional communication training (Dyer & Larsson, 1997) – and new applications of reinforcement procedures such as *behavioral momentum* (Davis & Reichle, 1996). Behavioral momentum involves rapidly reinforcing behaviors that have a high probability of occurring and then providing the child with an opportunity to engage in a behavior that has a low probability of occurring (Davis & Brady, 1993). For example, if a child generally does not comply with adult requests to clean up or to change activities, the adult might ask the child to engage in three or four behaviors that are likely to result in compliance (e.g., "give me a hug" and "give me five"), reinforce the child for doing these behaviors, and then tell the child to clean up or change activities. In addition to changes in the types of interventions used with children, greater attention is now given to supporting families and other caregivers and accounting for the contributing features in the settings and contexts in which children live and spend time (Koegel, Koegel, & Dunlap, 1996).

Third, application of the behavioral model has produced a conceptualization of learning and instruction that includes at least four separate phases: *acquisition, fluency, maintenance,* and *generalization* (Haring, White, & Liberty, 1978). Acquisition was seen as learning the basic requirements of a skill (i.e., learning how to do the skill); fluency was seen as learning to perform the skill smoothly at natural or rapid rates; maintenance was seen as continued performance of the skill after instruction stopped; and generalization was seen as learning to perform the skill in noninstructional situations such as across persons, settings, and materials (Wolery, Ault, & Doyle, 1992). These phases of learning appear applicable across different types of skills including social, communicative, motor, play, and cognitive domains. The importance of this conceptualization rested in a central assumption:

Performance in each phase requires slightly different intervention techniques and strategies. To promote acquisition, children needed information on how to do the behavior; to promote fluency, children needed multiple and repeated opportunities to practice with motivation for engaging in that practice; to promote maintenance, children needed overlearning, thin reinforcement schedules, and use of naturalistic reinforcers; and to promote generalization, a number of strategies were used such as teaching with multiple types of materials, using materials from the natural environment, delaying reinforcement, employing varied instructional conditions, duplicating the natural environment in the instruction setting, teaching in the natural environment, and using self-control techniques (Wolery et al., 1988).

This conceptualization carried three major implications for intervention programs. First, interventionists needed to understand the phase of learning represented by the child's performance on each important skill. Second, interventionists needed to use intervention techniques and strategies that matched children's level of performance. Third, intervention was not complete until children's use of the skill was demonstrated when and wherever it was needed and did so well after initial learning was completed. These implications call for increased monitoring of children's performance, an awareness of performance outside of the instructional context, and making decisions about techniques and strategies based on children's performance. Although specific decision rules exist for guiding changes in instruction (Wolery, 1996), relatively few applications of these rules have been reported with young children beyond documenting that different interventions are necessary to influence children's acquisition, maintenance, and generalization (Bailey & Wolery, 1992).

Fourth, the processes used to establish and transfer stimulus control have been employed to develop instructional strategies (Wolery, Ault, & Doyle, 1992). Early intervention practice is replete with strategies based on stimulus control processes. Examples include milieu language teaching procedures; that is, strategies involving relatively brief instructional exchanges that are focused on the child's attention or communicative attempts in the context of ongoing activities (Kaiser, Yoder, & Keetz, 1992); peer-mediated strategies, group friendship activities, and

structured play routines for promoting social interactions and social play (McEvoy, Odom, & McConnell, 1992); direct instructional procedures for promoting language, cognitive, and motor behavior (Wolery et al., 1992); and procedures for promoting response-contingent behaviors and engagement with the environment (Dunst, Lowe, & Bartholomew, 1990; Dunst, Mahoney, & Buchan, 1996).

Stimulus control, as noted earlier, involves providing contingent and differential reinforcement of the desired behavior or skill in the presence of the target stimulus or stimulus complex. The interventionist's task is to ensure that the behavior occurs when the stimulus is present so that the behavior can be reinforced. This is often accomplished by manipulating the environment to make the occurrence of the behavior more likely. For example, to increase children's language initiations, teachers place preferred toys on shelves where children can see them but must ask an adult to get the toy, or to increase the likelihood of child comments, teachers present novel materials or experiences (Ostrosky & Kaiser, 1991). This sets the stage for the behavior to occur in contextually relevant situations, which in turn allows reinforcement for building stimulus control. Another means of building stimulus control is to use *response shaping* – differential reinforcement of successive approximations of the desired response (Cooper et al., 1987). Response shaping is quite useful with many responses and can be used to increase the complexity of existing behaviors. For example, if a goal is to promote more creativity (e.g., in block building or painting), then using response shaping differentially to reinforce variations in design can result in predictable increases in children's more elaborate and diverse products (Goetz, 1982). Similarly, to increase children's social initiations, playing social games and responding to their social alertness during diapering can result in more social interactions (Venn & Wolery, 1992).

Another highly useful process is transferring stimulus control. *Transfer of stimulus control* involves, as the name implies, shifting the control exerted by one stimulus to the new or desired stimulus. The most salient example of this is the use of adult assistance (e.g., prompts or models). If an adult's prompt will already produce the desired response, then the task of intervention is to shift that control to the new stimulus. For example, if a child vocally imitates adult words, then the adult verbal model has stimulus control of the child's verbal behavior. Presenting new objects, modeling the names of those objects, providing children with opportunities to imitate the model, and fading the model over repeated exposures while reinforcing the occurrence of the behavior will result in transfer of stimulus control from the model to the actual objects (Wolery et al., 1992). Several procedures exist for transferring stimulus control; these include such naturalistic language teaching procedures as incidental teaching and mand-model procedures (Kaiser & Hester, 1994; Warren & Gazdag, 1990). Incidental teaching involves modifying environments to increase children's initiations to adults, asking for more elaborate language contingent upon a child's initiation, providing a model if more language is not forthcoming, and responding to the content of the child's initiation. The mand-model procedure involves identifying the child's focus of attention, asking a non-yes/no question, waiting for the child's response, and modeling an appropriate response if the child does not initiate one. Other procedures for transferring stimulus control include the *time delay procedures, constant time delay* (Holcombe, Wolery, & Snyder, 1994), and *progressive time delay* (Venn, Wolery, Werts, et al., 1993). Both time delay procedures involve two types of learning trials: zero-second and delay trials. The zero-second trials are used during initial instruction and involve asking the child to make a response and immediately prompting (assisting) the child in making that response. The *delay* trials involve asking the child to make a response and then delaying the prompt (assistance). With the constant time delay procedure, the interval between asking for a response and providing the assistance is of a fixed (constant) duration (e.g., four seconds). With the progressive time delay procedure, the interval between asking for a response and providing the assistance is gradually (progressively) lengthened (e.g., by one-second increments) throughout repeated learning trials. Another procedure for transferring stimulus control is *graduated guidance* (Schoen, Lentz, & Suppa, 1988). This procedure involves immediately providing prompts as the child needs, them and immediately removing them as independent performance occurs. This procedure is almost always used with skills requiring several steps that must be completed in sequence. Another frequently used procedure is the system of *least prompts* (Filla, Wolery, & Anthony, in press). This procedure involves providing children with at least three levels of assistance, each of which progressively provides more information on how to do the behavior. The first level always involves doing the behavior independently, the second level involves minimal assistance, and each subsequent level involves more assistance. The child is able to select the level of assistance needed to perform the behavior.

With each of these procedures, adult assistance is used that already controls responding, and the control of that assistance is transferred to some natural or target stimulus. The differences in the procedures deal with the means used to fade the adult prompts (assistance). It should be noted that, in many cases, siblings (Hancock & Kaiser, 1996) and peers (Venn, Wolery, Fleming, et al., 1993; Wolery, Werts, Snyder, & Caldwell, 1994) have been taught to use these procedures with other young children who have disabilities.

Fifth, the principles of behavior have been used, often in combination with other orientations and literatures, as a foundation for developing broad intervention approaches. Examples include the development of curriculum packages (Tawney, Knapp, O'Reilly, & Pratt, 1979), comprehensive assessment and intervention tactics (Kozloff, 1994a, 1994b), programs for addressing the problematic and communicative behavior of children (Dunlap & Fox, 1996; Fox, Dunlap, & Philbrick, 1997), and comprehensive intervention program models (Hoyson, Jamieson, & Strain, 1984; Kohler, Strain, & Shearer, 1996; Strain & Cordisco, 1994).

Challenges Faced by the Educationally Oriented Intervention Programs

Despite the contributions of the behavioral approach discussed earlier, intervention programs that adopt this perspective as their guiding emphasis face a number of challenges. In this section, these challenges are considered. In some cases, these challenges are unique to programs using a behavioral approach; in others, they apply to all early intervention programs that adopt educationally oriented philosophies.

CHALLENGE OF SPECIFYING GOALS/OUTCOMES. Educationally oriented intervention programs by definition have a curriculum. Although different definitions of curriculum exist, most include 1) the content to be learned, 2) the instructional methods or experiences for learning that content, 3) a means of identifying those parts of the content that are important for given learners, and 4) a theoretical perspective for organizing the other three elements (Bailey, Jens, & Johnson, 1983; Dunst, 1981). The behavioral perspective focuses primarily on the second element (i.e., the instructional methods) and can be used for assessing an individual's performance against a specified content. However, the behavioral perspective does not specify the content of the curriculum – it does not suggest a particular sequence of skills to be learned. As a result, programs adopting a behavioral perspective must solve the challenge of what is to be learned.

To solve this problem, two approaches have been used. First, and perhaps most frequently, behavioral programs adopt a sequence of skills from various developmental theories (Bailey & Wolery, 1992). As noted by Dunst (1981), the behavioral perspective can be merged successfully with dialectic approaches to development (e.g., Piaget and Vygotsky), but not with the maturational theory (i.e., Gesell) because these perspectives hold fundamentally different assumptions. In such programs, children receive developmental assessments, goals are established, those goals are task analyzed (broken into small steps for instruction), and the behavioral methods are used to teach the goals.

The second approach for identifying the content of the curriculum is represented by Thurman's (1997) ecological congruence model. This model is concerned with "both the development of the child and the fit between the characteristics of the child and the environment." He suggests that "educational interventions must be concerned not only with changing the child to fit the environment but also with changing the environment to fit the child" (Thurman & Widerstrom, 1990, p. 210). The approach has three dimensions that represent three separate continua: deviance, competency, and tolerance for difference. They are depicted in Figure 9.1.

The *deviance* continuum ranges from low to high deviance. This dimension refers to the extent to which the child's behaviors, characteristics, or both

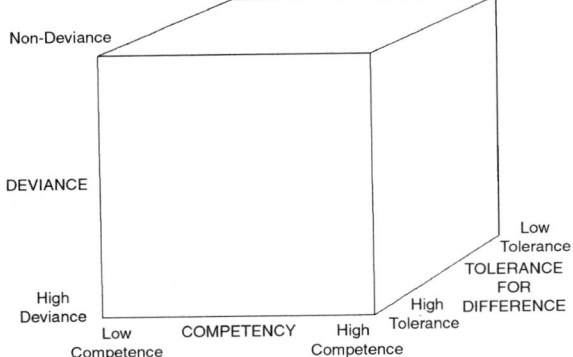

Figure 9.1. Schematic of Thurman's ecological congruence model. From S. K. Thurman (1997). Systems, ecologies, and the context of early intervention. In S. K. Thurman, J. R. Cornwell, & S. R. Gottwald (Eds.), *Contexts of early intervention: Systems and settings* (pp. 3–17). Baltimore, MD: Paul H. Brookes; p. 10; reprinted with permission.

differ from those that occur in the child's environment. Deviance is not a static or an inherent characteristic because a behavior is not necessarily in and of itself deviant. Rather, judgments of deviance are based on social comparisons and the values and perspectives of those in the social environment who make those judgments (Thurman, 1997). The *competency* dimension ranges from low to high competence. This dimension refers to the extent to which the child has the ability to engage in functional behavior (Thurman, 1997). In this model functional behaviors are those that are needed for specific tasks, jobs, or activities that occur within specific settings of the environment. Nonperformance of functional behaviors should not be confused with lack of competence, because performance is tied to motivational properties and environmental demands and constraints (Thurman & Widerstrom, 1990). A child may be capable of performing a given skill, but there may be no motivational factors (internal or external) to encourage performance. Also, a given setting within the environment may preclude the performance of the skill; for example, a child may not initiate communicative attempts because the caregivers anticipate his or her needs or because of a substantial history of unresponsiveness to his or her previous attempts to communicate. The *tolerance for difference* dimension also ranges from low to high tolerance. This dimension refers to the "goodness of fit between the individual and the environmental/social context" (Thurman & Widerstrom, 1990, p. 211). The range of difference that is acceptable varies by context and by individual. For environments, the tolerance of difference applies both to the deviance of the individual's behaviors and characteristics and to the individual's competence for performing specific tasks within the environment. Lack of congruence (or fit) may occur when the social context does not tolerate the deviance or the lack of competence. For the individual, the degree of acceptance of the environment may vary across settings and across activities within settings. Lack of congruence occurs when the individual (e.g., the child) does not tolerate the environment. That is, the individual may not tolerate the manner in which the environment is structured, various features of the environment, or the manner in which the tasks and activities are operated within the settings.

An "adaptive fit results from mutual acceptance between the individual and the environment" (Thurman, 1997, pp. 11–12). Using this definition, it is clear that adaptive fit does not imply "normal" or "usual" behavior; rather, it speaks to mutual adaptation of the individual to the environment and the environment to the individual. Fit or congruence, of course, is not static. As individuals and environments change, the degree or amount of adaptive fit may fluctuate. Congruence implies there is a mutual base from which the individual and environment can change as interactions occur between the two. These changes may reflect increases in competence, greater acceptance of the individual by the social context, and greater tolerance of the environment by the individual.

According to Thurman and Widerstrom (1990), processes and interventions designed to promote ecological congruence (adaptive fit), have "three objectives: 1) to change individual patterns of behavior, 2) to change the tolerance for systemic difference of these individuals, and 3) to change the tolerance of the system for individual differences in competency and perceived deviance" (p. 211). To carry out these objectives, Thurman and Widerstrom identified and described, in detail, nine steps for using the ecological congruence model when planning intervention programs. These steps are listed in Table 9.1.

The steps shown in Table 9.1 involve a process similar to that advocated by Brown et al. (1979) for planning instructional programs for adolescents with significant disabilities. Compared to using a purely developmental approach to intervention

---

TABLE 9.1. Procedures for Planning Intervention Programs by Applying the Ecological Congruence Model

1. Identify the major environmental settings that are important to the child's life
2. Develop an inventory of critical tasks in those settings (i.e., those that make the setting function)
3. Assess the child's competence to perform those tasks
4. Assess motivational variables (i.e., contingency structures) and other factors that affect the child's ability to perform tasks
5. Assess the child's tolerance of the environment
6. Determine which of the child's behaviors and characteristics are outside the level of tolerance of the system. (These behaviors and characteristics may be those labeled as deviant, or they may be the result of insufficient development of the child to perform necessary tasks.)
7. Identify objectives for each component of the ecology (i.e., child and system) that, when accomplished, will lead to increased ecological congruence.
8. Identify strategies for accomplishment of the objectives.
9. Establish a means by which interventions are to be monitored and their effectiveness assessed.

From S. K. Thurman and A. H. Widerstrom (1990). *Infants and young children with special needs: A developmental and ecological approach* (2nd ed.). Baltimore, MD: Paul H. Brookes, p. 212; used with permission.

planning, the processes advocated by Thurman and Widerstrom (1990) and Brown et al. (1979) hold at least three major advantages. First, this approach requires the intervention team to view the child's performance and competence in context. This fact allows teams to plan programs to promote the child's independence and mastery of his or her unique settings and to facilitate adaptive fit between the child and the settings. Thus, greater individualization of intervention efforts should result. Second, this approach allows the team to identify features of the environment that interfere with acceptance (adaptive fit), independence, and mastery. When such environmental features are identified, the team can develop plans and address changing these environmental features. This would be impossible with, or would occur accidentally from, a developmental assessment approach. Third, because the child's competence is viewed in context, the team can analyze performance across settings and across activities or tasks within settings. A recurring issue with young children who have disabilities is the lack of skill transfer or generalization from one setting or situation to another. By assessing both child competence and contextual features, the team can identify skills that are needed across settings as well as characteristics of those settings that may interfere with or promote skill generalization. Thus, the ecological congruence model holds direct and important implications for intervention planning.

In summary, the behavioral perspective does not specify the content of the curriculum. Educationally oriented intervention programs using the behavioral perspective must derive the content from some other method. One approach is to use a developmental theory and resulting assessments; a second approach is to analyze the child's behavior in terms of its congruence with the environmental demands and expectations.

CHALLENGE OF INFLUENCING A SUFFICIENT AMOUNT OF THE CHILD'S INTERACTIONS WITH THE ENVIRONMENT. Development appears to be a result of the ongoing interactions and transactions between a biologically maturing organism with a specific genetic endowment and the social and physical dimensions of the environment embedded within a complex ecological system. Despite the influences of the child's genetics, biology, and his or her ecology, children's experiences are important factors in shaping their learning and development. Some of these experiences may make positive contributions to children's development and others may make negative contributions (Bijou, 1981). Furthermore, children's experiences that occur throughout the day may positively or negatively influence their learning. As a result, intervention programs for young children with disabilities should be designed to minimize experiences that have negative effects on development and to promote experiences that have positive effects. A clear finding from the early intervention literature with children from economically disadvantaged families indicates that more intense interventions (i.e., more hours per day, more days per week, and so forth) are likely to result in greater benefit than less intense interventions (Bryant & Maxwell, 1997; Ramey & Ramey, 1998). By extension, this notion suggests that programs for young children with disabilities should seek to influence positively a major proportion of children's interactions each day. The question, however, is how can this be accomplished?

Programs based on the behavioral perspective have chosen to respond to this question in two primary ways. First, in some cases, a highly intense intervention is provided. For example, the University of California at Los Angeles Young Autism Project provided at least forty hours per week of intervention by a therapist for each child with autism. This one-on-one intervention occurred in the child's home and occasionally in the child's community preschool. At age 7, about half of the participating children were at normal age ranges on the measures used (Lovaas, 1987; Lovaas & Buch, 1997). Subsequent evaluation several years later indicated maintenance of positive results for most children (McEachin, Smith, & Lovaas, 1993). Such programs, however, are the exception rather than the rule. Most programs for young children with disabilities are not that intense.

The second approach is to provide children with daily experiences in a center-based intervention program and to provide their parents and other caregivers with training and support in influencing the remainder of the children's interactions with the environment. For example, in Project LEAP, children attend an integrated preschool with a high staff-to-child ratio and a behaviorally oriented curriculum based on children's individual needs (Hoyson, Jamieson, & Strain, 1984). Their parents also receive regular and ongoing training in how to support their children's learning outside of the center (Strain & Cordisco, 1994). Despite the success of some programs in providing training and support to families in influencing children's interactions with the environment (Fox et al., 1997), concerns are expressed about such approaches. Clearly such training must not supplant a parent's relationship with the child, must preserve sharing of positive affect and responsiveness, and probably should not impose therapist-type behaviors on parents' interactive styles. Although such outcomes are attainable, some parents may not have the energy, time, or inclination to assume a major intervention role.

Thus, to minimize interactions that contribute negatively and to maximize interactions that contribute positively to children's development, intervention programs based on the behavioral perspective have provided either intense one-on-one intervention or used a combination of center-based programs and parent training. This need to influence a major proportion of children's interactions with the environment is not unique to programs based on the behavioral model; it applies to all approaches that adopt an educational orientation.

CHALLENGE OF THE NEGATIVE PERCEPTION OF THE BEHAVIORAL APPROACH. Although the behavioral perspective has been used to devise a number of useful intervention techniques and to provide a base for organizing intervention programs, many professionals have adverse reactions to the view (Strain et al., 1992). Such responses to the perspective appear to exist for a number of reasons, including 1) lack of complete understanding of the theory, 2) negative reactions to the assumed mechanistic and deterministic features of the theory, 3) prevailing interest in the mentalistic aspects of development, 4) inaccurate perceptions about the limitations of behavioral theory (e.g., useful only for "behavior management"), 5) assumption that the theory cannot be combined with other world views, 6) the precise and prescribed nature of some of the intervention practices, and 7) ineffective and often imposing and arrogant description of the theory and practices by its proponents. These factors may

make adoption and use of behavioral principles and practices less likely, may lead to hesitation to recommend behavioral practices, and may interfere with the adoption of behavioral models. Nonetheless, investigators using behavioral theory have developed some practices that are readily received and are used by some practitioners.

CHALLENGE OF ADDRESSING BROAD ECO-LOGICAL INFLUENCES. As noted earlier, children live in ecologies broader than their immediate social and physical environments. These broader ecologies are made up of multiple interrelated systems (Bronfenbrenner, 1977, 1992). Changes in one of these systems can influence the operation of the other systems. In these broader ecological systems, many factors can positively and negatively influence children's developmental outcomes. As is widely known, many factors in children's ecologies (e.g., poverty, unemployment, lack of education, and inadequate housing) can place children at risk for negative outcomes, particularly when they live in ecologies where multiple risk factors are operating (Sameroff, Seifer, Barocas, Zax, & Greenspan, 1987). Similarly, many factors in children's ecologies (e.g., economic advantage, high maternal education levels, and adequate housing) can provide children and their families with opportunity factors that have positive effects on children's outcomes, particularly when multiple opportunity factors are present and operating (Dunst, 1993). Because of the negative influences of risk factors and the positive influences of opportunity factors, intervention programs should be aimed, at least in part, at minimizing risk factors and maximizing opportunity factors.

Although the behavior model may be useful for analyzing behavior between entities within ecological systems, it has not been used widely – perhaps because of practical reasons – in devising broad-based, community-wide intervention programs. The behavioral model is much more useful in understanding and manipulating children's immediate interactions with their social and physical environments. Thus, educationally oriented intervention programs using the behavioral model may be addressing only part of the issues that should be addressed if large and enduring impacts are desired. As a result, such intervention programs should seek additional conceptualizations to minimize risk factors and to maximize use of opportunity factors.

In summary, despite the utility of the behavioral perspective in designing interventions for children's immediate environments and for understanding children's behavior within these settings, behaviorally oriented intervention programs face some challenges. To define the content of their curriculum, they must merge the behavioral perspective with a developmental theory, must analyze the extent to which children's behavior is consistent with the demands and expectations of the settings in which children live and spend time, or both. To minimize the occurrence of negative child–environment interactions and to maximize the occurrence of positive interactions, educationally and behaviorally oriented intervention programs must influence a major proportion of children's daily interactions. Programs accomplish this by providing either highly intense interventions or daily center-based programs supplemented with parent training to influence the out-of-center interactions children have with their environments. Behaviorally oriented programs also face a milieu in which behavioral theory and practices are suspect or are openly resisted. Finally, application of the behavioral theory is not practical for minimizing risk factors and promoting opportunity factors. Thus, behaviorally oriented intervention programs need to combine their efforts with broader conceptualizations of the ecology to ensure that their impacts are substantial and lasting.

ALTERNATIVE CONCEPTUALIZATIONS OF THE ENVIRONMENT

This section describes two conceptualizations of the environment that can be used to supplement or replace behaviorally oriented intervention programs. Specifically, these conceptualizations present a context for early intervention that is broader than the behaviorally oriented educational programs. Although other models could be discussed, these are described because they appear to present two decidedly different approaches to intervention. As noted previously, these models are consistent with ecological systems theory (Bronfenbrenner, 1992); are consistent and compatible with Thurman's (1997) ecological congruence model; and are compatible with, but broader and more comprehensive, than behaviorally oriented intervention models.

Guralnick's Early Development and Risk Factors Model

Guralnick (1997, 1998) presented "a model that links factors influencing early childhood development to the components of early intervention programs. This linkage is accomplished by conceptualizing risk and disability status in terms of stressors capable of adversely affecting family interaction patterns that govern the development of outcomes of children" (1997, p. 3). This model proposes to connect "program features, child and family characteristics, and outcomes" (1997, p. 4). Guralnick maintained that this model could be used for organizing existing knowledge and for guiding future research.

Guralnick's (1997) model of early developmental outcomes for children with disabilities and for those who are at biological risk for disabilities has three major components: family patterns, family characteristics, and potential stressors. These are depicted in Figure 9.2. Two of these components, family characteristics and potential stressors, tend to be distal to the child, whereas the family patterns are proximal factors that influence children's outcomes directly.

The *family patterns* component is seen as primarily responsible for child outcomes, and the other components influence the extent to which the family patterns are beneficial and optimal for development to occur. The family patterns component consists of three elements: quality of parent–child transactions, child experiences that are arranged by the family, and environments that promote child health and safety. Several features of parent–child interactions/transactions, drawn from existing developmental literature, are thought to be useful for all children, including those with disabilities and those who are at risk for disabilities. Guralnick (1997) stated these transactions should be "contingent, encouraging, affectively warm, nonintrusive, appropriately structured, discourse-based, and developmentally sensitive" (p. 6). The family-orchestrated experiences refer to things families do to provide meaningful experiences for children. These include providing responsive and stimulating social and physical environments as well as carrying out special events such as recreational activities during the preschool years, forming play groups, and engaging in enriching activities (e.g., going to the zoo or participating in cultural celebrations). The third element of the family patterns component involves the family providing the child with a safe environment, engaging in appropriate and preventive health care practices such as well-baby check-ups and immunizations, and ensuring adequate diet and appropriate daily routines (e.g., sleep and activity). These three factors in combination are seen as directly responsible for children's developmental outcomes.

The family patterns, however, do not occur in a vacuum. They are influenced by the other two components of the model, specifically the family characteristics and the potential stressors. The *family characteristics* component includes two broad contextual factors: the personal characteristics of the parents and the characteristics of the child that are not related to his or her disability. The family characteristics occur within the context of historical and current events and conditions. Examples of these include "the interpersonal characteristics of the parents (e.g., degree of depression, level of education, intergenerational parenting experiences including cultural expectations) and characteristics not related to the child's disability or risk status (e.g., quality of the marital relationship, child temperament, available supports including family resources and social support networks)" (Guralnick, 1997, p. 6). These characteristics influence how well the family can carry out the family patterns (discussed earlier). When these characteristics are subject to risk (e.g., lack of financial resources, social isolation, and poor mental health), then the family's ability to perform the family patterns may be impaired. The degree of impairment, of course, depends on the severity of the risk as well as the cumulative number of risk factors.

The third component, *potential stressors due to the child's disability*, may also interfere with the family carrying out the family patterns. Guralnick (1997) classified these potential stressors in four broad

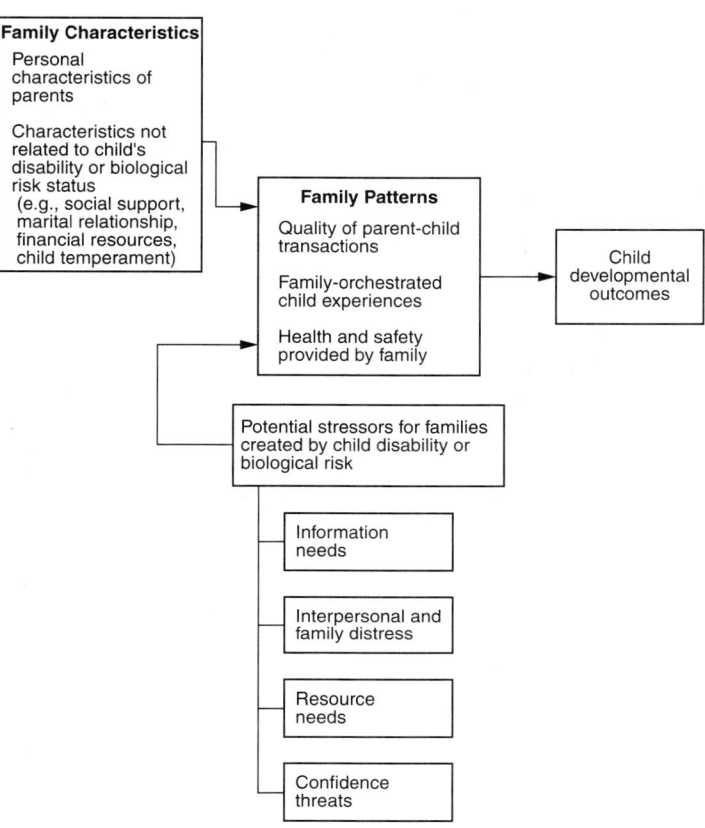

Figure 9.2. Schematic of Guralnick's model of factors influencing children's developmental outcomes. From M. J. Guralnick (Ed.), *The effectiveness of early intervention.* Baltimore, MD: Paul H. Brookes; p. 7; reprinted with permission.

categories. The first is information needs that arise as a result of the child's disability. Parents may have information needs in a number of areas, including, among others, basic information about their child's diagnosis and prognosis, information about how to interact with and care for the child, and information about potential educational and therapeutic approaches. The second category of stressors is the interpersonal reactions and family distress that may occur as a result of the child's disability. This category includes, among others, the potential for marital problems, negative reactions of individuals outside of the family, and difficulties related to caring for the child. The third category of stressor is resource needs. Examples in this category include the demands on parents' energy and time to care for the child, difficulties securing appropriate services, and financial demands that may arise. The final category of stressor is confidence threats. This category refers to the notion that having a child with disabilities may interfere with the family's ability to make decisions and solve the day-to-day problems that arise and as a result may cause them to question their actions and judgments. These categories of stressors separately and together can negatively influence the family's ability to carry out family patterns in a manner that would promote optimal development.

As noted previously, Guralnick's (1997) model includes an interface among the three components and the early intervention program. Specifically, he proposed that the intervention program should contain three major components: resource supports, social supports, and information and services. Each of these components is designed to address the categories of stressors listed earlier. The assumption is that by addressing or alleviating the various stressors, the early intervention program will help families carry out the family patterns that directly influence children's developmental outcomes.

Figure 9.3. Schematic of the resource-based model of Dunst and Trivette. From Trivette, C. M., Dunst, C. J., & Deal, A. G. (1997), Resource-based approach to early intervention. In S. K. Thurman, J. R. Cornwell, & S. R. Gottwald (Eds.), *Contexts of early intervention: Systems and settings* (pp. 73–92). Baltimore, MD: Paul H. Brookes; p. 84; reprinted with permission.

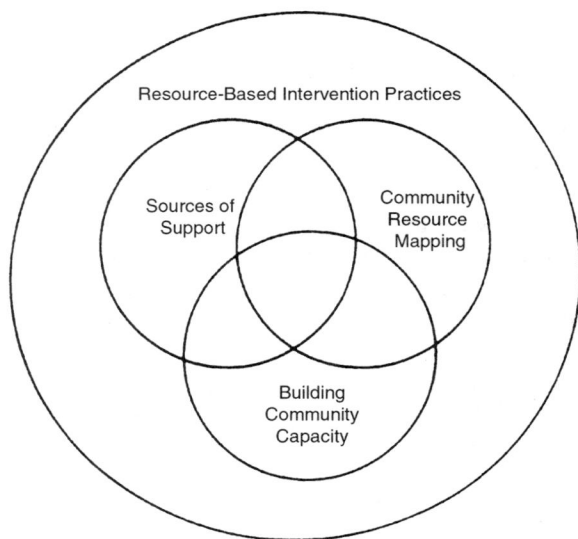

This model's primary feature is the conceptual connection of the early intervention program with a description of how families influence children's development. For example, if the child's disability primarily places stress on the family in the area of resource needs, then the model calls for the intervention program to be composed primarily of the resource supports. Ideally, the model will assist the field in understanding the interactions and connections among child and family characteristics and intervention program features on child outcomes.

Dunst and Trivette's Resource-Based Approach

The resource-based approach to early intervention (Trivette, Dunst, & Deal, 1997) grew from the work of Dunst and his colleagues as well as the research of other investigators. Dunst drew on a number of literatures and defined early intervention as follows:

Early intervention can be defined as the provision of support to families of infants and young children from members of informal and formal social support networks that impact both directly and indirectly upon parental, family, and child functioning. Stated differently, early intervention can be conceptualized as an aggregation of the many different types of help, assistance, and services that are provided to families by individuals and groups. Involvement in a home-based or center-based special education program is one type of early intervention, but so is compassion from a friend, advice from a physician, baby sitting by a neighbor, participation in a parent-to-parent support program, and role-sharing between a husband and wife. (Dunst, 1985, p. 179)

Dunst and his colleagues have conducted a substantial amount of research based on this definition and the assumptions on which it is built (e.g., Dunst, Trivette, & Deal, 1988, 1994; Dunst, Trivette, Starnes, Hamby, & Gordon, 1993). This research has led to the resource-based model shown in Figure 9.3. The fundamental assumptions underlying the model and its components are described next.

This definition and the resource-based model of early intervention assume families and children are embedded within a number of influential ecological systems – as proposed by Bronfenbrenner (1977). This definition also recognizes, however, that "families of young children experience events *in addition to* those provided by early intervention programs that can and do influence child development and family functioning" (Trivette et al., 1997, p. 73; italics added for emphasis). The definition also states explicitly that informal supports, and by extension resources, positively influence child and family outcomes. This definition and the resource-based model assume that families as well as communities have assets and strengths. The model seeks to promote the use of those strengths. Emphasis is placed on developing partnerships with families as contrasted to promoting paternalism and on empowering families to make decisions and be independent of early interventionists as compared to professionals making decisions and usurping the family's role in determining their own paths of action (Dunst, 1985). Furthermore, the model recognizes that how support and assistance are provided is highly related to perceptions of how effective it is. Specifically, how the helping relationship is established will predict how useful that help was (see Dunst et al., 1994, chapter 14). As a result, Dunst and his colleagues have identified important beliefs, attitudes, and behaviors of the helping relationship.

Although the model recognizes the presence – perhaps increasing presence and saliency – of many risk factors, it also recognizes that communities and potentially intervention programs can provide families with opportunity factors (Dunst & Trivette, 1997). Opportunity factors are facilitative influences within and external to families that assist them in supporting their children's development and promoting their children's competence (Dunst, 1993). Examples of opportunity factors include "maternal positive well-being and psychosocial health, maternal locus of control (internal), maternal education (>15 years), occupation of the head of household (professional), positive life events, presence of a spouse or partner, and parenting style (facilitative)" (Dunst & Trivette, 1997, p. 161). These factors and their total number are related to positive developmental outcomes for children (Dunst & Trivette, 1997). The assumption is that resource-rich communities have many accessible opportunity factors for families.

This model also makes a distinction between resources and services. It argues that resources are located in the community, whereas services are based in professional expertise. Resources in the community are seen as varied and renewable, whereas services tend to be scarce and are often available only through means-testing. Resource models give emphasis, as described earlier, to informal and formal supports, but service models give emphasis to providing formal supports. Resource models tend to be asset-driven, whereas service models tend to focus on deficits; and in resource models, "outside resources are used in ways that are responsive to local agenda building" but in the service models, "solutions tend to be prescribed by 'outsiders' as an infusion of expertise" (Trivette et al., 1997, p. 77). The community is a central feature of the resource model. Community, as used here, is not restricted to a physical location (e.g., neighborhood) but refers to a broader unit in which there is a sense of membership and belonging. "The term community resources is used ... to mean community people, groups, organizations, programs, and so on that can be used by families of preschool-age children" (Trivette et al., 1997, p. 76). Most of the community resources are not specialized for families of children with disabilities but are available for all families who have young children. Furthermore, the community resources may involve opportunities for parents as well as for children.

The resource-based model has three components as identified in Figure 9.3: sources of support, community resource mapping, and building community capacity. In terms of *sources of support*, Trivette et al. (1997, pp. 82–86) listed four broad categories: personal social network members, associational groups, community programs and professionals, and specialized services. The personal social network may include persons from whom the family seeks assistance, guidance, and nurturing. Examples of these are a spouse, friends, relatives, religious leaders, and others with whom the family has regular contact (e.g., through work or other activities). Associational groups include a range of potential community organizations such as "church groups, civic events, ... community support groups, ... ethnic associations, ... service clubs, social cause groups" and so forth (Trivette et al., 1997, p. 82). Community programs and professionals refer to a range of programs and organizations that are integral parts of most communities. Examples include child care programs, community colleges, hospitals, medical services, employment agencies, libraries, and so forth. These are programs and professionals who serve the community as compared to families of children with disabilities. Specialized professional services are those services designed specifically for families, children, or both, such as mental health agencies, specialists (e.g., special educators and therapists), respite care programs, referral services, and many others. These four categories of potential sources of support expand considerably the sources of support commonly associated with early intervention programs.

The second component of the community resources model is *community resource mapping* (Trivette et al., 1997). Developing a community map involves identifying the various kinds of resources that exist in a given locale (neighborhood, village, and county). Mapping also involves identifying the location of each resource. This serves as a source from which families of children with disabilities can find and access resources they deem important. This mapping can be done in collaboration with families and should be an ongoing activity for identifying existing sources of support for families.

The third component of the resource-based model involves *building community capacity* (Trivette et al., 1997). Building community capacity begins with recognizing the strengths and assets of a community. Trivette et al. recommended a three-step process: "1) identifying the strengths of community people and groups, 2) demonstrating how these strengths address child and family desires, and 3) eliminating barriers through use of other resources" (p. 86).

The resource-based model of early intervention has existed in various forms for a number of years. Different early intervention programs have adopted selected portions of the model; however, it seems that most early intervention programs have not fully adopted a resource-based approach. The empirical evidence supporting the model is strong (Dunst & Trivette, 1997; Trivette et al., 1997). The strength of the model is that it relies, in large part, on assisting families in addressing their priorities in the context of their existing and potential relationships with available and accessible community resources and sources of support. The model seeks to promote families' participation in opportunity factors as well as to reduce the impacts of risk factors.

Conclusions About Conceptualizations for Early Intervention

The behavioral perspective described earlier in the chapter, Guralnick's (1997) model, and the resource-based model of Dunst and Trivette (1997) place different emphases on various aspects of the intervention process. Guralnick's model and the resource-based model were presented because the behaviorally oriented educational approach does not provide a framework for addressing broader issues that are important in early intervention. The approaches described by Guralnick and by Dunst and Trivette are based in part on Bronfenbrenner's (1977) ecological systems framework, but the behavioral approach is not. Guralnick's approach and the Dunst and Trivette resource-based model recognize the existence of interrelated systems, place an emphasis on the family, and acknowledge that risk factors can have detrimental effects on family functioning and child outcomes. Both of these models articulate how the early intervention system can conceptualize its activities in the context of the ecological system. Guralnick's model views families as the primary source of proximal influence on children's outcomes, although external risk factors are acknowledged (Guralnick, 1998). His model further suggests that the role of intervention programs is to address stressors (risk factors) that the family experiences, particularly those that occur as a result of the child's needs and disabilities or that are due to family characteristics. The resource-based model by Dunst and Trivette also assumes families are a major source of influence on children's outcomes but views intervention options in a broader sense than that proposed by Guralnick. Specifically, Dunst and Trivette place emphasis on helping families access opportunity factors within their community rather than assuming intervention is to reduce stressors or to eliminate sources of risk. Although Guralnick's model seems to recognize the value of informal supports for families and children, the resource-based model employs those supports more systematically and intentionally. Thus, while both of these models provide precise blueprints of intervention activities on the basis of Bronfenbrenner's work, the two appear to lead to decidedly different early intervention programs. Specifically, the resource-based model draws more heavily on the assets in the community, values inclusion of families in community life, and relies more directly and intentionally on informal supports for families.

The models described by Guralnick (1997) and by Dunst and Trivette (1997) recognize the likelihood of intervention programs working directly with children (e.g., child-care programs and center-based intervention programs). However, these models provide relatively little guidance about how staff should structure and manipulate such settings. By extrapolation, we can assume Guralnick's model suggests using variations in the family patterns that are assumed to be proximal to promoting children's developmental outcomes. The resource-based model by Dunst and Trivette, however, advocates using community programs that are available to children without disabilities as sources of support and opportunity for children with disabilities. In such cases, the intervention staff then assist in mapping the community resources and building community capacity. The behavioral model, on the other hand, includes precise intervention methods for influencing child–environment interactions directly – given, of course, identification of goals through a developmental approach or through Thurman's (1997) ecological congruence framework. The behavioral methods are compatible with both Guralnick's approach and the resource-based model, although it is not necessary for the implementation of either model.

IMPLICATIONS

Implications from these approaches can be drawn for practice and for future research. In this section, some obvious implications are presented. Many others could be included; these are not proposed as an exhaustive list. Rather they represent some of the more important implications for researchers to address.

Implications for Early Intervention Programs

Across each approach presented earlier, an implicit or explicit assumption is made: Children's experiences are significant factors in their outcomes. Behaviorally oriented programs attempt to influence

a major proportion of children's experiences with one of two options: 1) providing highly intense one-on-one programs or 2) using center-based programs with concomitant parent training designed to influence interactions outside of the center. The resource-based model described by Dunst and Trivette (1997) provides an alternative or supplement to these approaches by assisting families in using community resources that can provide children with a number of nonintervention yet extremely facilitative experiences. Gurlanick's notion of family-orchestrated child experiences may be an avenue for supplementing usual intervention-promoted experiences.

Clearly, some of children's experiences promote positive outcomes and other experiences promote undesirable outcomes. Several types of child experiences are known to have negative effects; among others, these include persistent child abuse, lack of contact with caring adults, unresponsive social environments, lack of multiple response-contingent experiences, environments devoid of language, and environments that promote helplessness (Bijou, 1981). Thus, a major implication is that intervention programs must ensure that children's experiences fulfill facilitative as contrasted to impeding functions. These perspectives provide some guidance in this area: promoting contact between families and children with social support networks and with opportunity factors in the community (Dunst & Trivette, 1997), reducing stressors to promote facilitative family patterns (Guralnick, 1997), and using the ecological congruence approach to identify goals for behaviorally oriented programs. Another implication, however, is that some experiences provided by intervention programs may unwittingly promote negative outcomes. Intervention programs often contend that they engage in facilitative practices; however, given our incomplete knowledge and imperfect application of that knowledge, some programs undoubtedly produce child or family experiences that impede positive outcomes. Dunst (1985) suggested that practices using a deficit approach, usurping parental decision making, and promoting paternalism (including a view of families that assumes pathology) are counterproductive to the aims of early intervention. Similarly, practices that impede child initiations, interfere with exploration, discourage independence, are not response-contingent, and are overly directive may have undesirable consequences for children (Bailey & Wolery, 1992, chapter 7). Thus, a major implication is that programs should examine carefully their practices to identify any that are inconsistent with their goals.

Ecological factors outside of child–environment experiences may influence outcomes for families and for children. This includes many factors that are well recognized as risk factors for poor family and child outcomes (e.g., poverty, low maternal education, underemployment, prenatal and ongoing substance abuse, single-parent households, and poor paternal mental health). It now seems clear that it is not just the presence of these factors but the cumulative effect of multiple factors that have increased probability of negative outcomes (Dunst, 1993). However, environmental factors outside of the child–environment experiences may also enhance outcomes for children (i.e., opportunity factors; Dunst, 1993; Dunst & Trivette, 1997). There is emerging evidence that having multiple opportunity factors may well have cumulative positive effects on children's developmental outcomes (Dunst, 1993). The major implications for early intervention programs are threefold. First, interventions should be structured to reduce the impacts of risk factors, particularly when multiple risk factors are present. The models by Guralnick (1997) and Dunst and Trivette (1997) provide some guidance for doing this. Second, intervention activities should promote families' contacts with opportunity factors. The resource-based model seems to be the initial example of how to accomplish this effort. Third, early intervention efforts, even those associated with building community capacities for providing multiple opportunity factors, are likely to be insufficient. To reduce risk factors and to promote opportunity factors, political and social action is needed. This extends beyond the content and practices of early intervention programs; it focuses on what we as a society find acceptable and what we decide to do.

Implications for Future Research

The models discussed in this chapter raise questions that can occupy many years of research by many investigators, but some issues seem particularly noteworthy. An important area of study is *opportunity factors*. We do not have a clear picture of how to assist families in procuring opportunity factors through early intervention or how to assist communities in using their resources to provide families with opportunity factors. Furthermore, we need basic information about opportunity factors, including how to identify and measure some of those factors, whether and how opportunity factors interact with risk factors, and what combinations of opportunity factors (if any) are sufficient to ensure adequate developmental outcomes in children with disabilities. Research in these areas is useful on multiple levels, because implications may arise for practice, policy, and how we understand children and families.

Little is known as well about the effects of the resource-based model. Although promising, we do not know how positive outcomes accrue to children from participating in nonintervention community groups and activities. The logic is sound, but we need research about whether such participation enhances developmental outcomes, acceptance in the social environment, and longitudinal participation in community life. We do not know the extent to which families of children with disabilities already participate in such activities and whether or how intervention programs can facilitate such participation when families view it as desirable.

A driving motivation behind Guralnick's (1997) model is to explicate the effects of specific features of intervention programs on family and child outcomes. Relatively little research has focused on this question. A logical assumption is that some program features and practices are likely to be more or less effective in producing particular outcomes, but we have insufficient empirical evidence to guide practitioners in structuring their programs to operate on this assumption. An equally logical assumption, however, is that how program personnel conduct intervention activities and interact with families will be as powerful, if not more so, than the specific program features. An open question, of course, is whether the existing models sufficiently operationalize the relevant program features and program practices. Similarly, we have insufficient empirical knowledge to argue for particular types of program features for families who display given characteristics, including such characteristics as belonging to specific language or ethnic groups. We continue to have substantial knowledge deficits related to devising intervention programs that are acceptable and accessible to families with long histories, including intergenerational histories, of exposure to multiple risk factors.

Despite substantial advances in assessment and intervention practices throughout the 1990s, research is needed that focuses on how child care and other early childhood programs can actually promote the competence of children with disabilities in the context of those programs. This research should build upon the ecological congruence approach and on the practices that have emerged from the behavioral approach, including how to embed instructional practices in ongoing activities and routines in the natural environment. Despite some efforts, we do not have a complete understanding of how to assist families in making usual daily routines and play activities less demanding for parents and more facilitative for children. In addition, we have relatively little information about how to address the caregiving and learning needs of children with the most profound disabilities.

Finally, a substantial need exists to ensure that usual practice in intervention programs reflects the most recent advances in knowledge. In part, the continuing gap between research knowledge and practice deals with how findings are disseminated, practitioners are prepared, and intervention systems support innovation and application of new practices. However, a substantial contributor to the gap is that research may not speak to the perceived needs of practitioners. This issue deals not only with how findings are packaged for practitioners but also with which research questions are asked and how the research is conducted.

EARLY INTERVENTION PROGRAMS OF THE FUTURE

The brief history of early intervention has taught us a great deal about how to think about the environment, how to structure individual–environment interactions, and the effects of environmental factors on family and child functioning. Early intervention history has also taught us that environmental entities, systems, and forces are tremendously complex. We have learned that families and young children with disabilities are not homogeneous groups but are often different from

one another on nearly every dimension. Although we currently develop individualized family service plans, future early intervention programs are likely to be even more individualized – assuming that logic and research guide program development. This individualization will be promoted by 1) a growing awareness that one intervention program is not appropriate for all children and families; 2) increasing diversity of families on racial, ethnic, religious, and value dimensions; and 3) additional reliance on resource-based models. These forces may embed early intervention activities into families' communities, but this will occur at a time when community cohesion and activity appear to be declining in American life. Resolving this tension will be a major challenge to early intervention personnel.

Families in increasing numbers are likely to need out-of-home care for their young children with disabilities. Child care programs of various types will increasingly be asked to include children with disabilities in their programs, and some of those children will have fairly significant disabilities. A major challenge will be how those programs can provide children with experiences that promote development and learning. Initial attempts to use the behavioral model in such contexts indicate that this is feasible (Wolery & Wilbers, 1994); however, these applications have often occurred in high-quality child care programs with adequate child-to-staff ratios. Standard child care in the United States remains undersupported and of uneven quality. Thus, a major task of early interventionists will be to assist in enhancing the quality of child care while incorporating children with significant needs into those contexts.

REFERENCES

Arndorfer, R. E., Miltenberger, R. G., Woster, S. H., Rortvedt, A. K., & Gaffaney, T. (1994). Home-based descriptive and experimental analysis of problem behaviors in children. *Topics in Early Childhood Special Education, 14*, 64–87.

Baer, D. M. (1978). The behavioral analysis of trouble. In K. E. Allen, V. J. Holm, & R. L. Schiefelbusch (Eds.), *Early intervention – A team approach* (pp. 57–93). Baltimore, MD: University Park Press.

Baer, D. M., Wolf, M. M., & Risley, T. (1968). Current dimensions of applied behavior analysis. *Journal of Applied Behavior Analysis, 1*, 91–7.

Bailey, D. B., Jens, K. G., & Johnson, N. (1983). Curricula for handicapped infants. In S. G. Garwood & R. R. Fewell

(Eds.), *Educating handicapped infants: Issues in development and intervention* (pp. 387–419). Rockville, MD: Aspen.

Bailey, D. B., & Wolery, M. (1992). *Teaching infants and preschoolers with disabilities* (2nd ed.). Englewood Cliffs, NJ: Prentice Hall.

Bijou, S. W. (1981). The prevention of retarded development in disadvantaged children. In M. J. Begab, H. C. Haywood, & H. L. Garber (Eds.), *Psychosocial influences in retarded performance. Volume I: Issues and theories in development.* Baltimore, MD: University Park Press.

Bijou, S. W., & Baer, D. M. (1961). *Child development: Vol 1: A systematic and empirical theory.* New York: Appleton-Centry-Crofts.

Bijou, S. W., & Baer, D. M. (1965). *Child development: Vol 2: Universal stage of infancy.* New York: Appleton-Centry-Crofts.

Bijou, S. W., & Baer, D. M. (1978). *Behavior analysis of child development.* Englewood Cliffs, NJ: Prentice Hall.

Bronfenbrenner, U. (1977). Toward an experimental ecology of human development. *American Psychologist, 32,* 32, 513–31.

Bronfenbrenner, U. (1992). *Ecological systems theory.* London: Jessica Kingsley Publishers.

Brown, L., Branston, M. B., Hamre-Nietupski, S., Pumpian, I., Certo, N., & Gruenewald, L. (1979). A strategy for developing age appropriate and functional curricular content for severely handicapped adolescents and young adults. *Journal of Special Education, 13,* 81–90.

Bryant, D., & Maxwell, K. (1997). The effectiveness of early intervention for disadvantaged children. In M. J. Guralnick (Ed.), *The effectiveness of early intervention* (pp. 23–46). Baltimore, MD: Paul Brookes.

Carr, E. G. (1977). The motivation of self-injurious behavior: A review of some hypotheses. *Psychological Bulletin, 84,* 800–16.

Carr, E. G., Reeve, C. E., & Magito-McLaughlin, D. (1996). Contextual influences on problem behavior in people with developmental disabilities. In L. K. Koegel, R. L. Koegel, & G. Dunlap (Eds.), *Positive behavioral support: Including people with difficult behavior in the community* (pp. 403–23). Baltimore, MD: Paul H. Brookes.

Cooper, J. O., Heron, T. E., & Heward, W. L. (1987). *Applied behavior analysis.* Columbus, OH: Merrill.

Davis, C. A., & Brady, M. P. (1993). Expanding the utility of behavioral momentum with young children: Where we've been, where we need to go. *Journal of Early Intervention, 17,* 211–23.

Davis, C. A., & Reichle, J. (1996). Variant and invariant high-probability requests: Increasing appropriate behaviors in children with emotional-behavioral disorders. *Journal of Applied Behavior Analysis, 29,* 471–82.

Day, H. M., Horner, R. H., & O'Neill, R. E. (1994). Multiple functions or problem behaviors: Assessment and intervention. *Journal of Applied Behavior Analysis, 27,* 279–89.

Doke, L. A., & Epstein, L. H. (1975). Oral overcorrection: Side effects and extended applications. *Journal of Experimental Child Psychology, 20,* 496–511.

Donnellan, A. M., Mirenda, P. L., Mesaros, R. A., & Fassbender, L. L. (1984). Analyzing the communicative functions of aberrant behavior. *Journal of the Association for Persons with Severe Handicaps, 9,* 201–12.

Dunlap, G., & Fox, L. (1996). Early intervention and serious problem behaviors. In L. K. Koegel, R. L. Koegel, & G. Dunlap (Eds.), *Positive behavioral support: Including people with difficult behavior in the community* (pp. 31–50). Baltimore, MD: Paul H. Brookes.

Dunlap, G., Johnson, L. F., & Robbins, F. R. (1990). Preventing serious behavior problems through skill development and early intervention. In A. C. Repp & N. N. Singh (Eds.), *Perspectives on the use of nonaversive and aversive interventions for persons with developmental disabilities* (pp. 273–86). Sycamore, IL: Sycamore Publishing.

Dunst, C. J. (1981). *Infant learning: A cognitive-linguistic intervention strategy.* Hingham, MA: Teaching Resources.

Dunst, C. J. (1985). Rethinking early intervention. *Analysis and Intervention in Developmental Disabilities, 5,* 165–201.

Dunst, C. J. (1993). Implications of risk and opportunity factors for assessment and intervention practices. *Topics in Early Childhood Special Education, 13,* 143–53.

Dunst, C. J., Lowe, L. W., & Bartholomew, P. C. (1990). Contingent social responsiveness, family ecology, and infant communicative competence. *National Student Speech Language Hearing Association Journal, 17,* 39–49.

Dunst, C. J., Mahoney, G., & Buchan, K. (1996). Promoting the cognitive competence of young children with or at risk for developmental disabilities. In S. L. Odom & M. E. McLean (Eds.), *Early intervention/early childhood special education* (pp. 159–96). Austin, TX: PRO-ED.

Dunst, C. J., & Trivette, C. M. (1997). Early intervention with young at-risk children and their families. In R. Ammerman & M. Hersen (Eds.), *Handbook of prevention and treatment with children and adolescents: Intervention in the real world* (pp. 157–80). New York: Wiley.

Dunst, C. J., Trivette, C. M., & Deal, A. G. (1988). *Enabling and empowering families: principles and guidelines for practice.* Cambridge, MA: Brookline Books.

Dunst, C. J., Trivette, C. M., & Deal, A. G. (1994). *Supporting and strengthening families: Vol. 1: Methods, strategies and practices.* Cambridge, MA: Brookline Books.

Dunst, C. J., Trivette, C. M., Starnes, A. L., Hamby, D. W., & Gordon, N. J. (1993). *Building and evaluating family support initiatives: A national study of programs for persons with developmental disabilities.* Baltimore, MD: Paul H. Brookes.

Durand, V. M., & Crimmins, D. B. (1988). Identifying the variables maintaining self-injurious behavior. *Journal of Autism and Developmental Disorders, 18,* 99–117.

Dyer, K., Dunlap, G., & Winterling, V. (1990). Effects of choice making on the serious problem behaviors of students with severe handicaps. *Journal of Applied Behavior Analysis, 23,* 515–24.

Dyer, K., & Larsson, E. V. (1997). Developing functional communication skills: Alternatives to severe behavior problems. In N. N. Singh (Ed.), *Prevention and treatment of severe behavior problems: Models and methods in developmental disabilities* (pp. 121–48). Pacific Grove, CA: Brooks/Cole.

Filla, A., Wolery, M., & Anthony, L. (in press). Promoting children's conversations during play with adult prompts. *Journal of Early Intervention.*

Fox, L., Dunlap, G., & Philbrick, L. A. (1997). Providing individual supports to young children with autism and their families. *Journal of Early Intervention, 21,* 1–14

Foxx, R. M., & Azrin, N. H. (1973). The elimination of autistic self-stimulatory behavior by overcorrection. *Journal of Applied Behavior Analysis, 6,* 1–14.

Gallagher, J. J. (1996). Policy development and implementation for children with disabilities. In E. F. Zigler, S. L. Kagan, & N. W. Hall (Eds.), *Children, families, and government: Preparing for the twenty-first century* (pp. 171–87). New York: Press Syndicate.

Goetz, E. M. (1982). A review of functional analyses of preschool children's creative behaviors. *Education and Treatment of Children, 5,* 157–77.

Guess, D., Helmstetter, E., Turnbull, H. R., III, & Knowlton, S. (1987). Use of aversive procedures with persons who are disabled: A historical review and critical analysis. *TASH Monograph Series, No. 2.* Seattle, WA: The Association for Persons with Severe Handicaps.

Guralnick, M. J. (1997). Second generation research in the field of early intervention. In M. J. Guralnick (Ed.), *The effectiveness of early intervention.* Baltimore, MD: Paul H. Brookes.

Guralnick, M. J. (1998). Effectiveness of early intervention for vulnerable children: A developmental perspective. *American Journal on Mental Retardation, 102,* 319–45.

Hancock, T., & Kaiser, A. P. (1996). Siblings' use of milieu teaching at home. *Topics in Early Childhood Special Education, 16,* 168–90.

Haring, N. G., White, O. R., & Liberty, K. A. (1978). *An investigation of phases of learning and facilitating instructional events for the severely handicapped: Annual progress report 1977–1978.* Seattle: University of Washington, College of Education.

Hatton, D. D., Bailey, D. B., Burchinal, M. R., & Ferrell, K. A. (1997). Developmental growth curves of preschool children with vision impairments. *Child Development, 64,* 788–806.

Holcombe, A., Wolery, M., & Snyder, E. (1994). Effects of two levels of procedural fidelity with constant time delay on children's learning. *Journal of Behavioral Education, 4,* 49–73.

Horner, R. H., & Day, H. M. (1991). The effects of response efficiency on functionally equivalent competing behaviors. *Journal of Applied Behavior Analysis, 24,* 719–32.

Horner, R. H., Vaughn, B. J., Day, H. M., & Ard, W. R. (1996). The relationship between setting events and problem behavior: Expanding our understanding of behavioral support. In L. K. Koegel, R. L. Koegel, & G. Dunlap (Eds.), *Positive behavioral support: Including people with difficult behavior in the community* (pp. 381–402). Baltimore, MD: Paul H. Brookes.

Hoyson, M., Jamieson, B., & Strain, P. S. (1984). Individualized group instruction of normally developing and autistic-like children: The LEAP curriculum model. *Journal of the Division for Early Childhood, 8,* 157–72.

Iwata, B. A., Dorsey, M. F., Slifer, K. J., Bauman, K. E., & Richman, G. S. (1982). Toward a functional analysis of self-injury. *Analysis and Intervention in Developmental Disabilities, 2,* 3–20.

Kaiser, A. P., & Hester, P. P. (1994). Generalized effects of enhanced milieu teaching. *Journal of Speech and Hearing Research, 37,* 1320–40.

Kaiser, A. P., Yoder, P., & Keetz, A. (1992). Evaluating milieu teaching. In S. F. Warren & J. Reichle (Eds.), *Causes and effects in communication and language intervention* (pp. 9–47). Baltimore, MD: Paul H. Brookes.

Kennedy, C. H., & Meyer, K. A. (1996). Sleep deprivation, allergy symptoms, and negatively reinforced problem behavior. *Journal of Applied Behavior Analysis, 29,* 133–5.

Koegel, L. K., Koegel, R. L., & Dunlap, G. (1996). *Positive behavioral support: Including people with difficult behavior in the community.* Baltimore, MD: Paul H. Brookes.

Kohler, F. W., Strain, P. S., & Shearer, D. D. (1996). Examining levels of social inclusion within an integrated preschool for children with autism. In L. K. Koegel, R. L. Koegel, & G. Dunlap (Eds.), *Positive behavioral support: Including people with difficult behavior in the community* (pp. 305–32). Baltimore, MD: Paul H. Brookes.

Kozloff, M. A. (1994a). *Improving educational outcomes for children with disabilities: Principles of assessment, program planning, and evaluation.* Baltimore, MD: Paul H. Brookes.

Kozloff, M. A. (1994b). *Improving educational outcomes for children with disabilities: Guidelines and protocols for practice.* Baltimore, MD: Paul H. Brookes.

Lovaas, O. I. (1987). Behavioral treatment and normal educational and intellectual functioning in young autistic children. *Journal of Consulting and Clinical Psychology, 55,* 3–9.

Lovaas, O. I., & Buch, G. (1997). Intensive behavioral intervention with young children with autism. In N. N. Singh (Ed.), *Prevention and treatment of severe behavior problems: Models and methods in developmental disabilities* (pp. 69–86). Pacific Grove, CA: Brooks/Cole.

Luiselli, J. K., Colozzi, G. A., Helfen, C. S., & Pollow, R. S. (1980). Differential reinforcement of incompatible behavior (DRI) in treating classroom management problems of developmentally disabled children. *Psychological Record, 30,* 261–70.

Mace, F. C., & Heller, M. (1990). A comparison of exclusion time-out and contingent observation for reducing severe disruptive behavior in a 7-year-old boy. *Child and Family Behavior Therapy, 12,* 57–68.

McEachin, J. J., Smith, T., & Lovaas, O. I. (1993). Long-term outcomes for children with autism who received early intensive behavioral treatment. *American Journal on Mental Retardation, 97,* 359–72.

McEvoy, M. A., Odom, S. L., & McConnell, S. R. (1992). Peer social competence interventions for young children with disabilities. In S. L. Odom, S. R. McConnell, & M. A. McEvoy (Eds.), *Social competence of young children with disabilities: Issues and strategies for intervention* (pp. 113–33). Baltimore, MD: Paul H. Brookes.

Michael, J. (1982). Distinguishing between discriminative and motivational functions of stimuli. *Journal of the Experimental Analysis of Behavior, 37,* 149–55.

Michael, J. (1993). Establishing operations. *Behavior Analyst, 16,* 191–206.

Ogier, R., & Hornby, G. (1996). Effects of differential reinforcement on the behavior and self-esteem of children with emotional and behavioral disorders. *Journal of Behavioral Education, 6,* 501–10.

O'Neill, R. E., Horner, R. H., Albin, R. W., Storey, K., & Sprague, J. R. (1990). *Functional analysis of problem behavior: A practical assessment guide.* Sycamore, IL: Sycamore Publishing.

Ostrosky, M. M., & Kaiser, A. P. (1991). Preschool classroom environments that promote communication. *Teaching Exceptional Children, 23*(4), 6–10.

Ramey, C. T., & Ramey, S. L. (1998). Early intervention and early experience. *American Psychologist, 53,* 109–20.

Repp, A. C., & Deitz, S. M. (1974). Reducing aggressive and self-injurious behavior of institutionalized retarded children through reinforcement of other behaviors. *Journal of Applied Behavior Analysis, 7,* 313–25.

Repp, A. C., & Singh, N. N. (1990). *Perspectives on the use of nonaversive and aversive interventions for persons with developmental disabilities.* Sycamore, IL: Sycamore Publishing.

Sameroff, A. J., Seifer, R., Barocas, B., Zax, M., & Greenspan, S. (1987). IQ scores of 4-year-old children: Social–environmental risk factors. *Pediatrics, 79,* 343–50.

Schoen, S. F., Lentz, F. E., Jr., & Suppa, R. J. (1988). An examination of two prompt fading procedures and opportunities to observe in teaching handicapped preschoolers self-help skills. *Journal of the Division for Early Childhood, 12,* 349–58.

Singh, N. N. (Ed.). (1997). *Prevention and treatment of severe behavior problems: Models and methods in developmental disabilities.* Pacific Grove, CA: Brooks/Cole.

Singh, N. N., Lloyd, J. W., & Kendall, K. A. (1990). Nonaversive and aversive interventions: Issues. In A. C. Repp & N. N. Singh (Eds.), *Perspectives on the use of nonaversive and aversive interventions for persons with developmental disabilities* (pp. 3–16). Sycamore, IL: Sycamore Publishing.

Skinner, B. F. (1953). *Science and human behavior.* New York: Macmillan.

Smith, B. J., & McKenna, P. (1994). Early intervention public policy: Past, present, and future. In L. J. Johnson, R. J. Gallagher, & M. J. LaMontagne (Eds.), *Meeting early intervention challenges: Issues from birth to three* (pp. 251–64). Baltimore, MD: Paul Brookes.

Solnick, J. V., Rincover, A., & Peterson, C. R. (1977). Some determinants of the reinforcing and punishing effects of time-out. *Journal of Applied Behavior Analysis, 10,* 415–24.

Strain, P. S., & Cordisco, L. K. (1994). LEAP preschool. In S. Harris & J. Handleman (Eds.), *Preschool education programs for children with autism.* Austin, TX: PRO-ED.

Strain, P. S., McConnell, S. R., Carta, J. J., Fowler, S. A., Neisworth, J. T., & Wolery, M. (1992). Behaviorism in early intervention. *Topics in Early Childhood Special Education, 12,* 121–41.

Taylor, J., & Miller, M. (1997). When timeout works some of the time: The importance of treatment integrity and functional assessment. *School Psychology Quarterly, 12,* 4–22.

Tawney, J. W., Knapp, D. S., O'Reilly, C. D., & Pratt, S. S. (1979). *Programmed environments curriculum.* Columbus, OH: Merrill.

Thurman, S. K. (1997). Systems, ecologies, and the context of early intervention. In S. K. Thurman, J. R. Cornwell, & S. R. Gottwald (Eds.), *Contexts of early intervention: Systems and settings* (pp. 3–17). Baltimore, MD: Paul H. Brookes.

Thurman, S. K., & Widerstrom, A. H. (1990). *Infants and young children with special needs: A developmental and ecological approach* (2nd ed.). Baltimore, MD: Paul H. Brookes.

Touchette, P. E., MacDonald, R. F., & Langer, S. N. (1985). A scatter plot for identifying stimulus control of problem behavior. *Journal of Applied Behavior Analysis, 18,* 343–51.

Trivette, C. M., Dunst, C. J., & Deal, A. G. (1997). Resource-based approach to early intervention. In S. K. Thurman, J. R. Cornwell, & S. R. Gottwald (Eds.), *Contexts of early intervention: Systems and settings* (pp. 73–92). Baltimore, MD: Paul H. Brookes.

Twyman, J. S., Johnson, H., Buie, J. D., & Nelson, M. (1994). The use of a warning procedure to signal a more intrusive timeout contingency. *Behavioral Disorders, 19,* 243–53.

Utley, C. A., Hoehn, T. P., Soraci, S. A., & Baumeister, A. A. (1993). Span of apprehension in mentally retarded children: An initial investigation. *Journal of Intellectual Disability Research, 37,* 183–7.

Venn, M. L., & Wolery, M. (1992). Increasing day care staff members' interactions during caregiving routines. *Journal of Early Intervention, 16,* 304–19.

Venn, M. L., Wolery, M., Fleming, L. A., DeCesare, L. D., Morris, A., & Sigesmund, M. H. (1993). Effects of teaching preschool peers to use the mand-model procedure during snack activities. *American Journal of Speech-Language Pathology, 2*(1), 38–46.

Venn, M. L., Wolery, M., Werts, M. G., Morris, A., DeCesare, L. D., & Cuffs, M. S. (1993). Embedding instruction in art activities to teach preschoolers with disabilities to imitate their peers. *Early Childhood Research Quarterly, 8,* 277–94.

Wacker, D., Steege, M., Northup, J., Reimers, T., Berg, W., & Sasso, G. (1990). Use of functional analysis and acceptability measures to assess and treat severe behavior problems: An outpatient clinic model. In A. C. Repp & N. N. Singh (Eds.), *Perspectives on the use of nonaversive and aversive interventions for persons with developmental disabilities* (pp. 349–59). Sycamore, IL: Sycamore Publishing.

Warren, S. F., & Gazdag, G. (1990). Facilitating early language development with milieu intervention procedures. *Journal of Early Intervention, 14,* 62–83.

Warren, S. F., & Kaiser, A. P. (1986). Incidental language teaching: A critical review. *Journal of Speech and Hearing Disorders, 51,* 291–9.

Wolery, M. (1996). Monitoring child progress. In M. McLean, D. B. Bailey, & M. Wolery (Eds.), *Assessing infants and preschoolers with special needs* (pp. 519–60). Englewood Cliffs, NJ: Prentice Hall.

Wolery, M., Ault, M. J., & Doyle, P. M. (1992). *Teaching students with moderate and severe disabilities: Use of response prompting strategies.* White Plains, NY: Longman.

Wolery, M., Bailey, D. B., & Sugai, G. M. (1988). *Effective teaching: Principles and procedures of applied behavior analysis with exceptional students.* Boston: Allyn and Bacon.

Wolery, M., Strain, P. S., & Bailey, D. B. (1992). Reaching the potentials of children with special needs. In S. Bredekamp & T. Rosegrant (Eds.), *Reaching potentials: Appropriate curriculum and assessment for young children* (pp. 92–111). Washington, DC: National Association for the Education of Young Children.

Wolery, M., Werts, M. G., Snyder, E. D., & Caldwell, N. K. (1994). Efficacy of constant time delay implemented by peer tutors in general education classrooms. *Journal of Behavioral Education, 4,* 415–36.

Wolery, M., & Wilbers, J. S. (1994). *Including children with special needs in early childhood programs.* Washington, DC: National Association for the Education of Young Children.

Yeager, C., & McLaughlin, T. F. (1995). The use of a time-out ribbon and precision requests to improve child compliance in the classroom: A case study. *Child and Family Behavior Therapy, 17,* 1–9.

CHAPTER TEN

The Neurobiological Bases of Early Intervention

CHARLES A. NELSON

The goal of this chapter is to lay the foundation for considering the possible neurobiological mechanisms that may underlie the success of early childhood intervention. The view espoused here is that the efficacy of any given intervention will depend on the capacity of the nervous system (at the cellular, metabolic, or anatomic levels) to be modified by experience. This process, referred to throughout the chapter as *neural plasticity*, is often bounded by time; that is, there may be a window of opportunity, or critical period, for altering neural function. However, it will also become apparent that critical periods often interact with different neural systems, such that some neural systems remain open to modification longer than others. Moreover, there is evidence that critical periods and neural systems may interact at yet a third level, that of the individual. Thus, there may be individual differences in both the timing and the extent to which neural systems can be modified by experience.

To demonstrate that neural plasticity lies at the heart of early childhood intervention, it is necessary to begin this chapter with an exposition of the pre-

The views expressed in this chapter have profited from discussions I have had about neural plasticity with Floyd Bloom, Bill Greenough, and David Kupfer. I would also like to thank Emma Adam, Patricia Bauer, Ron Dahl, and Ann Masten for reading and commenting on a draft of this chapter. The writing of this chapter was made possible, in part, by grants from the National Institutes of Health (NS NS32755 and NS32976) and from the John D. and Catherine T. MacArthur Foundation's Research Network on Psychopathology and Development.

cise embryonic and fetal events that give rise to the human brain. Although much of this chronology is orchestrated by genetic and humoral (hormonal) signals, experience can exert its influence even on the embryonic and fetal brain. The examples that are provided also illustrate the vulnerability of this phase of the life cycle; specifically, how compromised prenatal environments (e.g., poor nutrition) may lead to poor neurodevelopmental outcomes.

The next section turns to the postnatal development of the brain, beginning with a few broad brush strokes and then shifting attention to the development of those regions of the brain that may underlie the focus of many early intervention programs. Although intervention can be aimed at many levels (social, cognitive, emotional, etc.), the chapter focuses on two areas that have implications for cognitive development: the neural systems that underlie memory (located in the medial temporal lobe) and those that underlie executive functions, such as planning, problem solving, and working memory (subserved by the prefrontal cortex).

Finally, having laid a foundation for the possible neurobiological substrate of early childhood intervention, the chapter concludes with a discussion of underlying mechanisms. After defining what is meant by the term neural plasticity, examples of both positive and negative outcomes are described (i.e., how the brain can adapt to deleterious as well as beneficial conditions). The discussion focuses not only on the very young organism but on the mature organism as well, in order to demonstrate that plasticity is possible in many neural systems well beyond childhood.

HUMAN BRAIN DEVELOPMENT

Gross Anatomical Development

By approximately the fourth week of gestation, the human embryo has divided into the *ectodermal* (outer), *endodermal* (inner), and *mesodermal* (middle) layers. For present purposes, we are most concerned with the ectoderm, as that is what eventually will become the nervous system.

On approximately the eighteenth day of gestation, a protein-like stimulus triggers the dorsal side (toward the rear) of the ectoderm to thicken and form a pear-shaped neural plate. In the center of this structure, a longitudinal neural groove appears, which then deepens and folds over onto itself. This process begins at the midpoint of the groove and extends rostrally (anterior) and caudally (posterior), with both ends of the groove remaining open. At about the twenty-fourth day, the rostral end begins to close, followed by the caudal end two days later. This conversion of neural plate to neural tube is called *neurulation* and is the first external sign of the development of a bilaterally symmetrical craniocaudal axis.

Unfortunately, neurulation does not always proceed flawlessly. The variety of errors that can occur during the time the neural tube is forming are referred to collectively as *neural tube defects*. The most severe example of such a defect is *anencephaly*, a disorder that results from failure of the rostral end of the neural tube to close, probably before the twenty-fourth day. The most common abnormality in this disorder involves the forebrain and varying portions of the brain stem. The majority of infants who receive no intensive care die shortly after birth, whereas those receiving such care generally die within two weeks. The incidence of anencephaly is approximately two infants per 1,000 live births (see Volpe, 1995, for discussion).

A less severe and more common neural tube defect is *myelomeningocele* (or spina bifida), a condition in which a more caudal portion of the neural tube (i.e., what will be the spinal cord) fails to close completely, with 80% of such infants having lesions in the lumbar, thoracolumbar, or lumbosacral regions. The expression of such a condition is largely manifested in motor limitations determined by the height of the lesion on the cord itself. The incidence of this disability is approximately two to four infants per 1,000 live births (see Volpe, 1995, for discussion).

Assuming the neural tube closes normally, its subsequent growth is greatest at the cranial end, where the actual brain will appear. Toward the end of the fourth week, three primary vesicles are formed – the *forebrain* (prosencephalon), *midbrain* (mesencephalon), and *hindbrain* (rhombencephalon). The remainder of the neural tube becomes the spinal cord. By the fifth week of gestation, the forebrain develops into the *telencephalon* and *diencephalon*, while the hindbrain forms the *metencephalon* and *myelencephalon*, and the midbrain changes very little. These structures are illustrated in Figure 10.1.

The *myelencephalon* will become the future *medulla oblongata*, whose rostral portion contains the motor nuclei, whereas the walls of the *metencephalon* will form the *pons* and the *cerebellum*. The fourth ventricle will also evolve out of the metencephalon, and its roof will generate the choroid plexuses, which are microstructures that line the ventricles and produce cerebral spinal fluid (CSF). Later, during the midfetal period, the roof of the fourth ventricle ruptures and forms permanent openings (*foramina luschkae*), through which CSF passes to the outer surface of the brain. The ventricles are illustrated in Figure 10.2.

The midbrain changes less during development than other parts of brain. Some parts will become the *superior colliculus* (for vision) and *inferior colliculus* (for hearing), while others develop into the *red nucleus* and *substantia nigra* (the latter being involved in dopamine production).

Let us now discuss the development of the forebrain, which consists of the *diencephalon* and *telencephalon*. By the sixth prenatal week, the diencephalon proper grows from three swellings of the lateral walls of the third ventricle, which in turn become the *epithalamus*, the *thalamus*, and the *hypothalamus*, which is attached to the *pituitary gland*. The *telencephalon*, in turn, develops into the two cerebral hemispheres, which comprise about 75% of all cells in the central nervous system. These first appear as two lateral diverticula of the *prosencephalon*. The cranial end of each hemisphere becomes the frontal

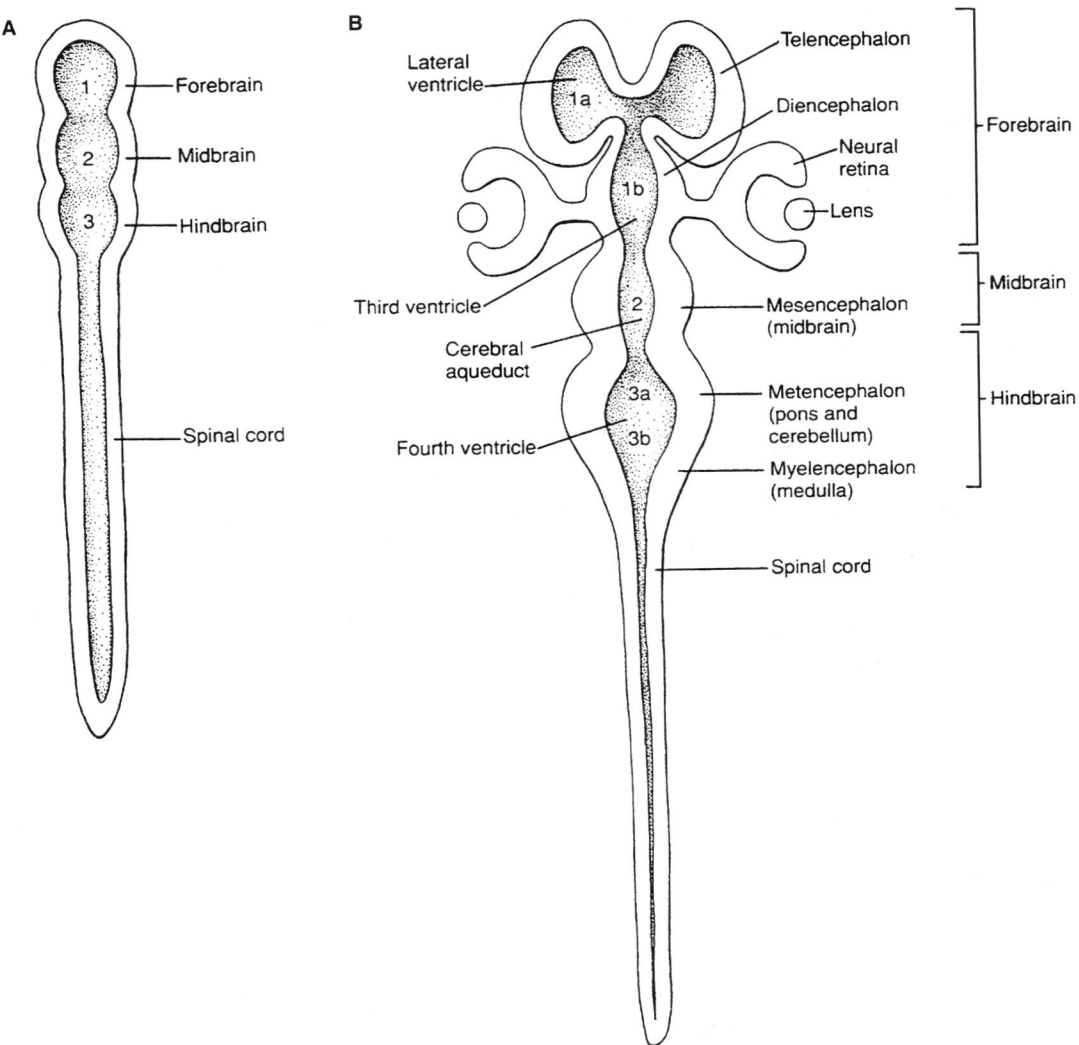

Figure 10.1. On the left (top and bottom) are shown the three primitive vesicles (forebrain, midbrain, and hindbrain) that evolve from the rostral end of the neural tube; on the right (top and bottom) is shown the 5 vesicle stage (forebrain evolves into telencephalon and diencephalon, midbrain remains the same, and hindbrain become the metencephalon and myelencphalon). (From *Principles of Neural Science*, 3rd ed., by E. R. Kandel, J. H. Schwartz, & T. M. Jessell. Copyright 1991 by Springer-Verlag; reprinted with permission.)

pole, and this region then turns ventrally, eventually to form the temporal pole. The occipital pole emerges as a new outgrowth of the hemisphere.

Cellular Development

CELL MIGRATION. The major anatomical milestones just described actually are derived from a series of cellular and molecular events that begin with the closure of the neural tube. To understand the key physiological events that transpire later in gestation and subsequently after birth, it is necessary to describe these events.

The walls of the recently closed neural tube consist of a single layer of *epithelial* cells, which are connected to each other and extend over the entire thickness of the wall, forming a pseudostratified

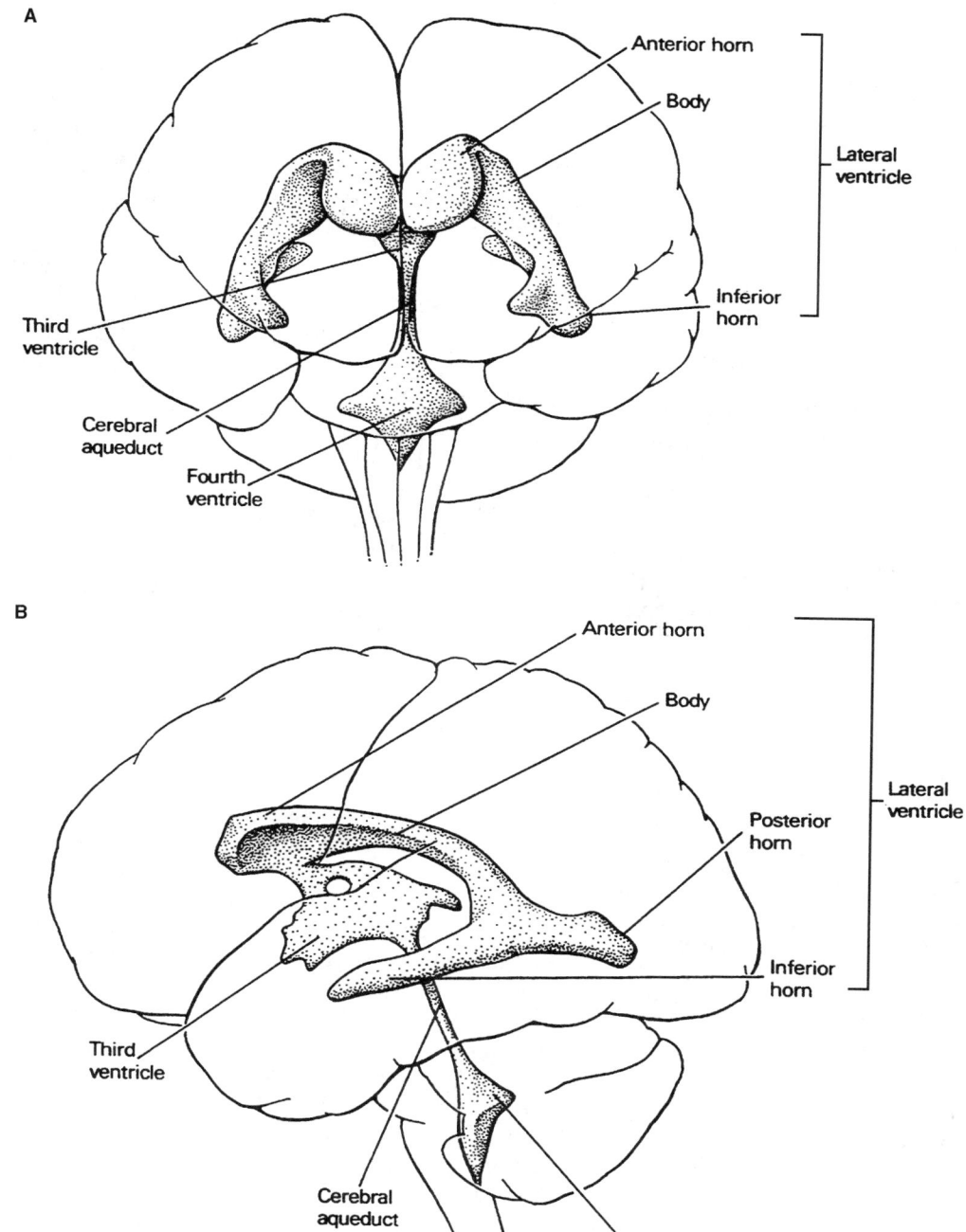

Figure 10.2. The mature ventricular system shown in frontal (A) and lateral (B) views. (From *Principles of Neural Science*, 3rd ed., by E. R. Kandel, J. H. Schwartz, & T. M. Jessell. Copyright 1991 by Springer-Verlag; reprinted with permission.)

epithelium. At a very rapid pace, these cells proliferate and the layer thickens. Within this layer, there are two zones: the *ventricular* zone of cells still undergoing mitosis (i.e., division) and a *marginal* zone of

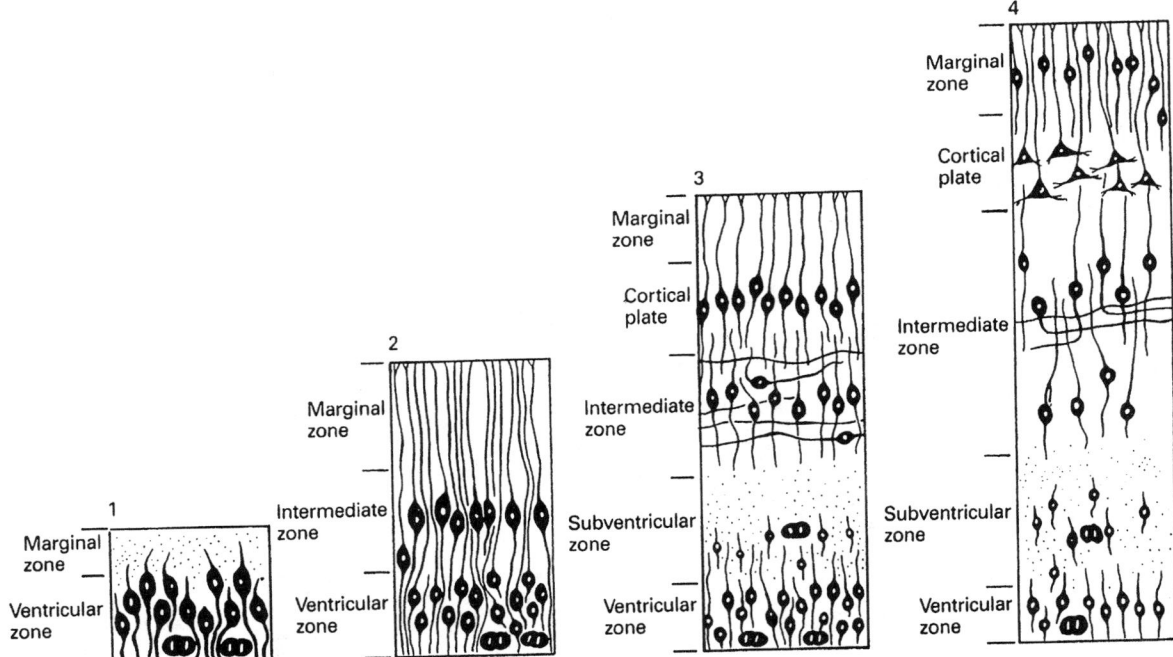

Figure 10.3. Progressive thickening of the wall of the developing brain. At the earliest stage (1) the wall consists only of a simple epithelium, in which the ventricular zone contains the cell bodies, and the marginal zone contains only the extended outer cell processes. As some of these cells withdraw from the mitotic cycle, they form a second layer, the intermediate zone (2). In the forebrain, the cells that pass through this zone form the cortical plate, the region in which the various layers of the cerebral cortex will develop (3). As discussed in the text, the cortical cell layers develop in an inverted fashion, such that cells in the deeper layers (e.g., VI) develop first. The cells in the superficial layers must migrate past older cells to reach their appropriate position. At the last stage (4), the original ventricular zone remains as the ependymal lining of the cerebral ventricles, and the comparatively cell-free region between the lining and the cortex becomes the subcortical white matter, through which nerve fibers enter and leave the cortex. (From *Principles of Neural Science*, 3rd ed., by E. R. Kandel, J. H. Schwartz, & T. M. Jessell. Copyright 1991 by Springer-Verlag; reprinted with permission.)

the cellular processes (e.g., primitive axons). As cell proliferation continues and migration begins, an *intermediate* zone of neurons is formed. By 8 to 10 weeks, this intermediate zone has enlarged to form the region from which the cortex develops. This region, in turn, is composed of two zones: the *cortical plate* and the *subventricular* zone (also known as the

subependymal zone). This *subventricular* zone is really a secondary zone, which some think is responsible for the development of glia. These zones are illustrated in Figure 10.3.

At this point in development, cells trapped between the ectodermal wall and the neural tube are referred to as *neural crest cells*. This band of cells will extend effectively from the prosencephalon downward along an axis. The cells on each side of this axis migrate to the dorsolateral side of the neural tube (i.e., they each go to one side of the tube or the other) and eventually give rise to the *sensory ganglia* (or dorsal root ganglia) of the spinal cord and a number of the cranial nerves.

To return to cortical development, the initial formation of the *cortical plate* occurs through the migration of cells to the deepest layer (layer VI) of the cortex, with subsequent migrations following in what is called an *inside-out* pattern. Migration occurs by primitive neurons (neuroblasts) attaching themselves to *radial glial fibers*, which are stretched across the chasm created by the expanding epithelial layer of cells. Once a migrating neuroblast reaches its target destination, it detaches itself from the fiber and comes to occupy a given location. In this manner, young (postmitotic) neurons leave their zone of origin and typically migrate past older cells to reach their final position. As a result, the earliest formed cells inhabit the deepest cortical layer (VI), whereas progressively later formed cells occupy positions at progressively more superficial layers. The exception to this rule is in the *cerebellum,* where granule cells are formed in the external germinative layer and move in an *internal* direction, resulting in an *outside-in* pattern of development.

In general, the central nervous system has many different types of cells and subtypes (e.g., neurons, such as *interneurons* and *motor neurons*, and glia, such as *astrocytes* and *oligodendrocytes*). Each type of cell is generated only during one period of development, and each type is likely to be determined by a sequence of molecular-genetic events. The generative zone of origin determines *what* cells will be produced and *where* ultimately they will wind up in the nervous system. (For discussion of these events, see Rakic, 1971, 1972, 1974.)

In general, both cell proliferation and migration vary from area to area, but as a rule proliferation is complete by six months. The exceptions to this rule include the *cerebellum,* whose development is more prolonged, *glial cells,* which continue to be produced in the subventricular zone after birth, and *granule* in the dentate gycus of the hippocampus, which continue to be produced throughout the life span.

ERRORS OF CELL MIGRATION. It should be noted that errors of cell migration are not uncommon, and the hallmark of such errors is an aberration of gyral development (gyri are the convolutions that lie at the surface of the brain). *Schizencephaly,* a condition in which part of the cortex is missing entirely, is perhaps the most severe form of a migrational error. The onset of this disorder appears to be as late as the third prenatal month. Symptoms include seizures, spasticity, and mental retardation as well as motor disabilities. A second example is *Lissencephaly-pachygyria.* As contrasted to the former example, in which the brain has no gyri, in this condition there are only a few abnormally broad gyri and the cortex itself is thick and consists of only four layers that are themselves abnormal. Here it is assumed that development was normal until the 13–15 week of gestation, when the migration of neurons along radial glial processes was interrupted. Finally, perhaps occurring most commonly,

is *agenesis of the corpus callosum,* or the absence of the bundle of fibers that connects the two hemispheres and permits interhemispheric communication. This error likely occurs between the third and fifth prenatal month. Interestingly, given the dramatic anatomical abnormality, some children are nevertheless asymptomatic (for discussion of migrational errors, see Volpe, 1995).

Synaptogenesis

Perhaps the most notable and functionally significant event to occur postnatally (although it begins prenatally) is the formation of synapses (*synaptogenesis*). A great deal is known about the phenomenon of synaptogenesis in the monkey, which provides a good model for understanding human brain development. Rakic and colleagues (e.g., Bourgeois & Rakic, 1993; Rakic et al., 1986) studied synaptogenesis from visual, somatosensory, motor, prefrontal, and hippocampal cortex in the rhesus macaque and calculated the number and density of synapses per unit area. They predicted that synaptogenesis in these areas would follow a timetable corresponding to a functional hierarchical model rather than be dictated by anatomical location. Thus, it was hypothesized that sensory areas would develop the earliest, while association areas (prefrontal in particular) would develop last, based on the assumption that sensory function precedes higher-level cognitive functions. However, the results did not confirm these predictions. Rather, the timing and the rate of increase in the formation of synapses were found to be similar for each area studied, with synaptic density increasing rapidly during the last third of gestation and this increase continuing until the fourth postnatal month at an identical rate for each area. Furthermore, each area passed through a phase of excess synapses, higher than adult levels, at roughly the same postnatal ages. This synapse overproduction was particularly high between the second and fourth postnatal months, after which synapse elimination increased and the number of synapses declined to adult numbers. This decline was steepest during the first year, followed by a more gradual rate of decline over the next several years.

Another finding of interest was that not only was synaptogenesis the same in each area studied but it also was the same for all six layers of cortex. This suggests that synaptogensis, because it follows a similar time course in diverse regions and layers of the cortex and ultimately stabilizes at the same absolute density of synapses throughout the cortex, is orchestrated by common genetic or humoral signals.

The pattern described for monkeys is slightly different for humans. Based on work by Huttenlocher (1979, 1990, 1994), it has been observed that there is a rapid burst of synapses in the visual cortex between 3 and 4 postnatal months, with maximum density reached at 4 months. Synaptogenesis in the primary auditory cortex (Heschl's gyrus) follows a similar timetable and is 80% complete by 3 months. Similar early overshoot is found in the middle frontal gyrus, but maximum density is not reached until 1 year. In contrast, retraction of synapses differs in these three areas: adult levels of synapses in the visual and auditory cortices are reached early in childhood (2 to 6 years), whereas adult levels are not attained in the middle frontal gyrus until adolescence. In more recent work, Huttenlocher (1994) found more synapses in the auditory area than in language and master speech areas at 3 months postnatally, but by 4 years synaptic density was the same across areas, although it was still twice as high as in the adult brain.

Collectively, synapse elimination in the human brain appears to occur late in gestation and early in the postnatal period, during a period when the nervous system is highly sensitive to environmental influences. We return to this issue later in the chapter.

ERRORS OF SYNAPTOGENESIS. As Volpe (1995) noted, relatively little is known about errors in synaptogenesis, primarily because of the inadequacy in the methods used to evaluate neural circuitry in general and the pathology of such circuitry in particular. Errors in synapses have been observed in a variety of disorders, including Down syndrome (e.g., Purpura, 1975), Fragile-X syndrome (e.g., Hinton et al., 1991), and other forms of mental retardation (e.g., Huttenlocher, 1975). However, perhaps most relevant to this volume is the observation that infants who have experienced a variety of pre- and perinatal difficulties also demonstrate problems in process (axons, dendrites) development. For example, Takashima and Mito (1985) reported abnormal dendrites and decreased numbers of dendritic spines in premature infants who were dependent on ventilators. The implication that early intervention might attenuate the expression of such problems is apparent, although supportive data are not yet available (Volpe, 1995).

Myelination

Like synapse development, the development of myelin is a protracted developmental process extending well into the postnatal period. Myelin (a lipid and protein substance that wraps itself around the axon) is produced from Schwann cells (a type of glial cell termed *oligodendroglia*). The principal purpose of myelin is to insulate the cell and to increase conduction velocity (i.e., the speed at which nerve impulses are transmitted from one cell to another). The formation of myelin is a genetically defined process that is preceded by the proliferation and differentiation of glial cells proximate to the pathways to be myelinated and is most prominent during the period of rapid brain growth. It is important to note that although this process is genetically determined, it can be influenced by environmental factors, such as diet, during the postnatal period. In terms of human development, this translates to approximately 2 months after the differentiation of neurons and the growth of nerve fibers.

It is possible to divide the myelinated cortex into three fields or zones. *Primordial* or premature fields are those that myelinate before birth, about 2 months after the differentiation of neurons and the growth of nerve fibers. The first part of the brain to myelinate is the peripheral nervous system (derived from neural crest tissue), whose motor roots myelinate before sensory roots, followed by myelination of the primary somesthetic (sense of touch), visual, and auditory cortices. The *intermediate* or postmature fields myelinate during the first 3 postnatal months. These include secondary association areas that surround the primary sensory or motor cortices. Finally, *terminal* fields are the last to myelinate, between the fourth postnatal month and possibly as late as midadolescence. These include the classic association areas that are involved with higher cortical functions, most notably in the frontal cortex. It is important to note, however, that although myelination is not complete until the second decade of life, it is likely that most myelinated pathways are laid down in the first 10 years. Aside from influencing the speed at which information travels through the brain, little is known about what other functions myelin might subserve.

ERRORS OF MYELINATION. One example of a myelination error is *cerebral white matter hypoplasia*, a rare disorder that is accompanied by seizures and other abnormal neurological findings. Here there is a lack of myelin in particular areas (e.g., centrum ovale, including the corpus callosum), which appears to have a genetic basis, as it is commonly observed in other family members. A second example is the consequence of *undernutrition*, because diets that are overly restricted in lipids tend to result in undermyelination, especially during the first 4 years of postnatal life. A third example is *periventricular leukomalacia*, which affects a significant number of extremely low-birth-weight premature infants. This is a disorder in which there is a disruption of the distribution of white matter (i.e., myelinated axons) in the region surrounding the lateral ventricles, presumably because of an interruption of the blood flow to this area, which in turn appears to cause injury to oliogodendroglia.

The Development of Specific Structures Relevant to Early Intervention

Two key cognitive systems are likely to be central to the success of early intervention efforts that target intellectual development: the ability to remember and recall events, and the ability to engage in planning and strategic activities (i.e., executive functions). With regard to the former, we are concerned with the capacity to encode new information into memory and to retrieve this information at some later date. The current term that best describes this ability is explicit or declarative memory (for discussion of the ontogeny of this type of memory, see Nelson, 1995, 1996). It is now well documented that explicit memory depends on structures that lie in the medial temporal lobe, including the hippocampus, the amygdala, and the rhinal cortex (see Meunier, Hadfield, Bachevalier, & Murray, 1996). The inferior temporal cortex may also play a role in explicit memory, particularly after the infancy period.

With regard to executive functions, it is known that the prefrontal cortex plays a principal role in their orchestration. As Robbins (1996) has described, executive functioning is required when one must formulate a new plan of action and when appropriate sequences of responses must be selected and scheduled. Some of the components of executive functioning include working memory (the ability to hold information on-line until some action is taken; see Goldman-Rakic, 1987); the mounting and implementation of attentional resources (e.g., Shallice, 1982); the inhibition of inappropriate responses (e.g., Shallice & Burgess, 1993); and the ability to monitor one's behavior in the context of one's affective or motivational state (see Damasio, 1994; Petrides, 1996; for elaboration on executive functioning in general, including its neural bases, see Robbins, 1996). In neuropsychological terms, these functions are all subserved by different regions of the prefrontal cortex, an enormous expanse of cortical tissue that receives inputs from throughout the brain and sends signals to many remote sites. The material that follows is limited to those areas that have been most studied in the development of the monkey or human.

DEVELOPMENT OF THE MEDIAL TEMPORAL LOBE. There are several key structures of the medial temporal lobe (MTL) that are considered to play a role in explicit memory. These include the hippocampal region, the amygdala, the entorhinal cortex, and the inferior temporal cortex. Each of these will be discussed in turn.

Hippocampus. The distribution of muscarinic receptors (i.e., receptors for acetylcholine) in the monkey limbic cortex are adultlike at birth, in contrast to those in the cortex, which mature later (O'Neil, Friedman, Bachevalier, & Ungerleider, 1986). In the human brain, the volume of limbic cortex and the size of relevant limbic structures (e.g., hippocampus) rapidly become adultlike in the second half of the first year of life (Kretschmann et al., 1986). Indeed, most of the structures that comprise the hippocampal formation are cytoarchitecturally mature before birth, except for the dentate (Janas, 1994; see also Berger, Alvarez, & Goldman-Rakic, 1993; Berger & Alvarez, 1994). The subiculum (which links the entorhinal cortex with the hippocampus) and the hippocampus proper mature relatively early in postnatal development (Humphrey, 1966), and dendritic development in the hippocampus precedes that of the visual cortex (Paldino & Purpura, 1979), a structure known to be functional by the second half of the first year of life (Bourgeois & Rakic, 1993). Metabolic activity (as inferred from glucose uptake using positron emission tomography [PET]) in the temporal lobes increases substantially by the third postnatal month and precedes that of the prefrontal cortex by several months (Chugani, 1994; Chugani & Phelps, 1986). In fact, the only area within the hippocampal formation that is protracted in development is the dentate gyrus, in which adult levels of synapses are not attained until ten months in the monkey, which is the equivalent to approximately three to four years in the human (Eckenhoff & Rakic, 1991; however, most dentate cells originate *prenatally* in the monkey; see Seress & Ribak, 1995).

Collectively, then, the hippocampus and the surrounding region appear to mature relatively early in life. Based on the best available evidence, it seems reasonable to propose that at least some hippocampal function emerges in the first few months of life, followed by more adultlike function by one year of age, possibly sooner (for discussion, see Nelson, 1995, 1996).

Amygdala. Although the role of the amygdala in memory continues to be debated, its role in emotion is assured, as it appears to mediate the formation of emotional associations that are attached to central representations of stimulus events (Aggleton & Mishkin, 1986; Jones & Mishkin, 1972). Unfortunately, much less is known about the development of this structure than the hippocampus, although it would appear that it, like the hippocampus, develops early. This argument is based on the observation that both the hippocampus and the amygdala are structures that lie deep in the cortex, and thus their cell migration would be complete earlier than structures that lie in more superficial laminae. What we do know is that the cells of the human amygdala are differentiated by the third prenatal month, and by the fourth month they have distinct nuclei. In the sixth month, all areas are well distinguished, and cell differentiation seems to be complete at birth (for discussion, see Sidman & Rakic, 1982).

Entorhinal Cortex. The entorhinal cortex seems to play an important role in the general neural circuitry of the hippocampal formation. More importantly, several investigators have carefully documented its role by demonstrating profound disruptions in memory in both the infant and the adult monkey when it is the only structure lesioned (e.g., Webster, Ungerleider, & Bachevalier, 1991a,b; 1995). The rhinal cortex has already begun to form synapses and express neurotransmitters by midgestation in the monkey and may already have begun to form extrinsic connections (Berger & Alvarez, 1994; Berger et al., 1993).

Inferior Temporal Cortex. Another area thought to be critically involved in explicit memory is the inferior temporal cortex (area TE in the monkey). However, several investigators have demonstrated that although lesions of area TE in the adult animal result in significant disruptions in memory, similar lesions in the infant animal apparently have little or no effect (Bachevalier, 1990, 1992; Bachevalier, Hagger, & Mishkin, 1991; Bachevalier & Mishkin, 1992; Webster et al., 1995). These findings suggest that this structure is immature or at least not online early in life. This speculation is supported by anatomical studies in the Rhesus monkey, which indicate that adult levels of glucose utilization are not obtained in area TE until approximately 4 months of age (the equivalent to approximately 12–16 months in the human; see Jacobs et al., 1995). In contrast, and as reviewed earlier, the hippocampus appears to be functionally developed within the first month or so of life. It has been reported by Webster and colleagues (e.g., Webster et al., 1991b; Webster et al., 1995) that in normal unlesioned monkeys, a transient projection is observed from area TEO (the region of the temporal lobe that borders the occipital lobe; see Figure 10.4) to the lateral basal nucleus of the amygdala; this projection is retracted later in development and is not present in the adult. However, when area TE is removed during the neonatal period, this normally transient projection is seen in the adult. Webster et al. (1995) have speculated that the sparing in performance on certain memory tasks (e.g., delayed non-match to sample [DNMS]) that has been observed in animals that experienced lesions of area TE as young infants may be due to the retention of these early transient projections. The DNMS task involves presenting an animal with a sample stimulus, after which a delay is imposed. After the delay (which can range from seconds to minutes), the animal is then presented with the sample stimulus alongside a novel stimulus.

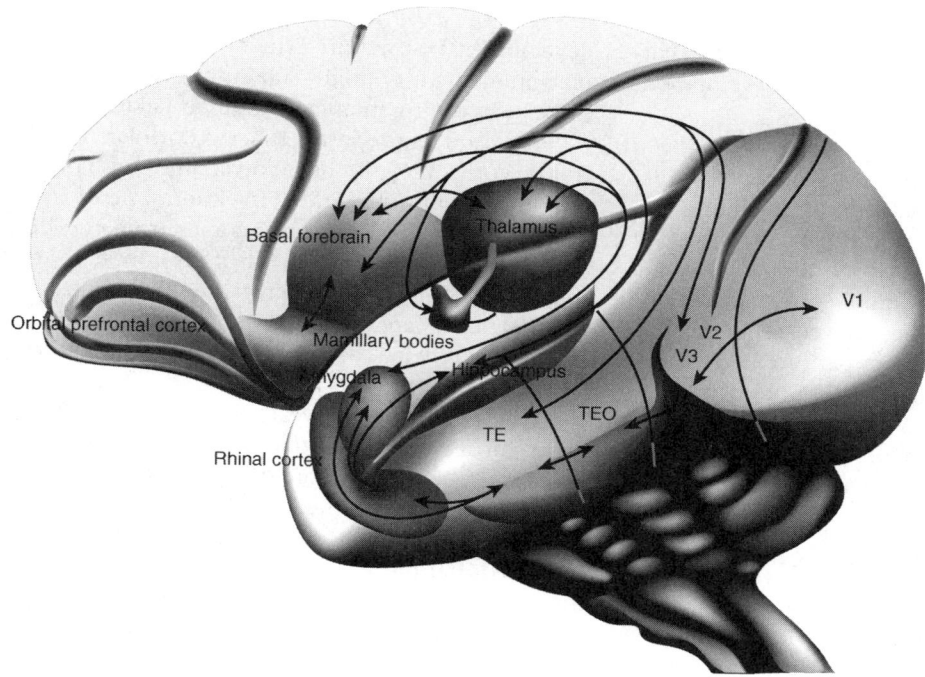

Reaching to the novel stimulus is considered the correct response. The number of trials required to learn this task, and the performance obtained once criterion has been met, are often the key parameters looked at by the investigator. This form of plasticity may ultimately account for why young human infants who experience catastrophic brain injury before or after birth may in some instances be spared catastrophic behavioral deficits.

Summary. Collectively these data suggest that much of the hippocampal formation (with the possible exception of the dentate; see Eckenhoff & Rakic, 1991), the amygdala, and the surrounding rhinal cortex develop fairly early in life, possibly within the first 2 years. This early development likely makes possible the impressive forms of memory that have been demonstrated in the infancy period (for review, see Bauer, 1996; Nelson, 1995, 1996; Rovee-Collier, 1996). In contrast, cortical area TE is on a later developmental trajectory and may not become adultlike until the preschool period. The development of this area, along with the prefrontal cortex (see next section), may possibly be responsible for some of the memory milestones that occur later in the preschool period (e.g., improved memory span)

Figure 10.4. A schematic view of the structures thought to be involved in explicit memory, including the hippocampus, rhinal cortex, and area TE. (Adapted from Bachevalier, Pascalis, & Overman, 1995, with permission.)

and may explain why we rarely remember life events prior to the age of 3 years (i.e., the concept of *infantile amnesia*). Be that as it may, early anatomical development, coupled with the observation that impressive feats of memory are possible in the first 2 years of life, points to this time period as potentially profiting from intervention efforts (i.e., we may view this period as a window of opportunity for experience-dependent effects on the brain).

DEVELOPMENT OF THE PREFRONTAL CORTEX. As discussed previously, the prefrontal cortex is thought to play a critical role in a variety of capacities broadly subsumed under the term *executive* function. In view of the fact that such skills as the ability to hold things in working memory, engage in strategic planning activities, and inhibit inappropriate responses are central to many early childhood interventions, a view of the development of the prefrontal cortex seems appropriate. Unfortunately, with the exception of the dorsolateral prefrontal cortex and, to a limited degree, the orbitoprefrontal cortex, relatively little is known about the development of this large expanse of neural tissue.

Dorsolateral Prefrontal Cortex. It has been known for some time that the dorsolateral prefrontal cortex is involved in spatial working memory (i.e., the ability to remember the location of an object that briefly disappears from view). For example, lesions of the adult dorsolateral prefrontal cortex profoundly impair performance on the delayed-response (DR) task, and similar lesions affect performance on the Piagetian A not B task (Diamond & Goldman-Rakic, 1989).

The DR task typically involves presenting an animal with two wells, one of which is baited (testing usually occurs when the animal is motivated by hunger). The bait is then moved from one well to the other. A delay is then imposed (generally less than 10 seconds), after which the baited and nonbaited wells are presented again. Reaching to the baited well is considered correct, whereas reaching to the nonbaited well is considered incorrect. The number of trials required to master the task is one of several parameters used by investigators to gauge performance. This task is fundamentally similar to the Piagetian A not B task used with human infants. Instead of baiting wells, in the A not B task the infant must observe where an object is hidden and, after some delay, reach for the correct location. The A not B error reflects reaching to the incorrect location (generally the next to last place the object was hidden). Diamond and Doar (1989) have demonstrated that these tasks are comparable in the demands they place on working memory.

Goldman-Rakic and colleagues (e.g., Goldman, 1971) investigated the role of the dorsolateral prefrontal cortex in DR performance in infant monkeys. It was initially demonstrated that neonatal lesions in this area had little effect on performance during the later infancy period (i.e., at 8 months). More recently, however, Diamond and Goldman-Rakic (see Diamond, 1990; Diamond & Goldman-Rakic, 1989) demonstrated that when lesions occur later in the infancy period (4$^1/_2$ months), DR and A not B performance are impaired. Although this finding suggests that this region of the brain is functional early in monkey life and mediates performance on these

tasks, it must be kept in mind that other more developmentally mature structures in the general prefrontal circuitry might subserve performance on these tasks during infancy (Goldman-Rakic, 1985).

One reason for proposing that the dorsolateral prefrontal cortex may not be involved in A not B or DR performance until the end of the infancy period (see Nelson, 1995, for discussion) comes from the human data on the development of prefrontal cortex in general. First, it has been reported that adult levels of synapses are not obtained until adolescence; prior to this there is an overabundance of synapses, which peaks at about 6 years and gradually declines over the next 10 or so years (Huttenlocher, 1979, 1990; for review, see Huttenlocher, 1994). Second, myelination in the prefrontal cortex is slow, continuing through adolescence (Jernigan & Tallal, 1990; Yakovlev & LeCours, 1967). Third, PET studies have indicated that metabolic activity in the frontal cortex lags behind all other cortical regions, only approaching adult values by 1 year, and continuing to develop over the next decade or more (Chugani, 1994; Chugani & Phelps, 1986).

Orbitoprefrontal Cortex (OFC). This region of the prefrontal cortex receives multimodal, integrated sensory information from distal uni- and multisensory cortices and also receives emotional associations formed by the amygdala. The OFC is thought to hold these associations on-line in representational memory and then dictates how the organism should behave (see Goldman-Rakic, 1987). For example, the OFC may initiate or inhibit motor, autonomic, and neurohumoral responses to specific sensory events. Through its connectivity to a variety of subcortical structures, the OFC may also play a role in selecting and initiating appropriate behavioral responses. Within the OFC also lie neural networks devoted to the production of emotional expressions. Collectively, the OFC, through its complex array of connections, regulates the adaptation of emotional behavior across environmental contexts.

Unlike the dorsolateral prefrontal cortex, relatively little is known about the development of the orbitoprefrontal cortex. Schore (1994) reviewed the literature on this subject, although most of the work on development is concerned with the more molecular aspects of transmitter release and function, primarily in the rat. What little is known is that myelin develops in the orbital prefrontal regions before the dorsolateral region (Orzhekhovskaya, 1975, as cited in Fuster, 1990). In addition, the cytoarchitecture of the orbital surfaces of the OFC appears to precede dorsolateral maturation (Pandya & Barnes, 1987). Finally, on the basis of the emergence of various emotional behaviors in infancy, Luria (1973), and more recently Schore (1994), argued that the first 2 postnatal years witness tremendous development in the OFC.

Collectively, although relatively little is known about this region of the brain, it appears that many functions subserved by the OFC and related circuitry are coming on-line during the infancy period, and presumably they continue on a steep upward trajectory through the elementary school years (inferred, in part, by the improved ability over this period of time to regulate emotion and to use stored information for action). Accordingly, one might argue that intervention efforts that target executive functions could begin as late as the toddler period but should be maintained through middle childhood.

Summary of Human Brain Development

The development of the brain has an enormously long trajectory, beginning within a few weeks after conception and, at the cellular level, continuing through adolescence. Arguably the most dramatic development – that of structures, sulci, gyri, and so forth – occurs during the first few years of life. Here we witness everything from the creation of the primitive neural tube, and the formation and then migration of primitive neuroblasts that will eventually give rise to the laminae of the cortex, to the development of mature neurons that will go on to sprout processes (axons and dendrites). However, the *functional* development of the brain is made possible by, in lay terms, the completion of the wiring diagram: the local and distal connections that are formed between and among areas by way of synapses and entire neural circuits. Nevertheless, as the following section on plasticity makes clear, the term *completion* may be inaccurate, because evidence is presented to suggest that such connections continue to be made and remade well into the life span. As a segue to this discussion, the next section illustrates several of the ways experience exerts its influence on

brain development, even at the embryonic and fetal stages.

ENVIRONMENTAL FACTORS INFLUENCING BRAIN DEVELOPMENT

Although the primary focus of this chapter is to illustrate the biological mechanisms that are responsible for modifying the nervous system through the life span, it must be acknowledged that the environment plays a critical role in regulating and determining both prenatal and early postnatal brain development. It is well known that a variety of environmental factors play a significant role in modulating prenatal neurological and behavioral development. These include maternal nutritional status, drug use, and stress, to name just a few.

Effects of Maternal Malnutrition

Both undernourished and malnourished mothers are at greater risk for delivering infants who develop neurological sequelae. The effects of nutritional deficits on the fetus vary, however, as a function of fetal anatomical and biochemical maturity (see Dobbing & Sands, 1971, for discussion). For example, nutritional deprivation in the second trimester has been shown to result in deficient numbers of neurons, whereas deprivation in the last trimester has been shown to lead to deficient numbers of glial cells and to influence the maturation of now-differentiated neurons (e.g., Dickerson, 1981). Finally, poor nutrition during the first several years of postnatal life has been shown to affect a wide range of both behavioral and neurological functions as a result of its adverse impact on myelination, which in turn has been shown to affect conduction velocity (Dickerson, 1981). Severely malnourished children (suffering from either marasmus, a form of caloric and nutrient deficiency, or Kwashiorkor, a form of protein deficiency) during the first 2 to 3 years of postnatal life have been shown to sustain impairments in brain growth. Specifically, the earlier the malnutrition occurs, the greater the reduction in brain size, and the longer the malnutrition continues, the greater the effect on the brain (Morgan & Winick, 1985; Winick, 1976). Because the brains of malnourished children are not only smaller but contain less DNA, they therefore contain fewer neurons (e.g., Winick & Rosso, 1969).

With respect to the behavioral effects of postnatal malnourishment (some of which would expect to be related to neurological impairment), Pollitt and Gorman (1994) have reported convincingly that, at a global level, protein energy malnutrition and iron deficiency can both affect cognitive development adversely. Malnourishment need not be only general, however, to exert deleterious effects; it can also be quite specific. For example, deficiencies in folic acid early in pregnancy (i.e., the first few months) have been linked to neural tube defects (Winick, 1989), and iodine or thyroid hormone deficiencies throughout pregnancy have been linked to mental retardation via congenital hypothyroidism (see Omaye, 1993; Zhang & Mahoney, 1993).

Fortunately, unlike other deleterious aspects of the pre- and postnatal environment (see next section), many of the effects of undernutrition or malnutrition can be reversed if a program of nutritional intervention is implemented in the first years of life and then continued thereafter (see Pollitt & Gorman, 1994). This is particularly true if nutritional supplementation is combined with environmental stimulation and emotional support (Lloyd-Still, 1976; Yatkin, McLaren, Kanawati, & Sabbach, 1971).

Effects of Teratogens

In addition to nutritional deficiencies, there are a host of teratogenic effects that can occur prenatally that may seriously compromise many aspects of behavioral and neurological development. Perhaps the best illustration is alcohol. For example, 43% of the pregnancies of chronically alcoholic women have adverse outcomes (Jones, Smith, & Hanson, 1976; for discussion, see Dodson, 1992). In 80% of children diagnosed with fetal alcohol syndrome, the central nervous system is affected, with microcephaly as the most common anomaly. Beyond the specifics of the neurological insult, infants with full-blown fetal alcohol syndrome typically demonstrate various levels of intellectual retardation (Dodson, 1992). Consistent with the effects of poor nutrition, there generally is a dose-dependent relationship with alcohol, such that greater exposures are associated with higher risks.

Effects of Stress

As is the case with nutrition and drugs, the literature on the relation between psychological stress and early childhood development is too extensive to review here in detail. A few observations are worth noting, however. For example, repeated or prolonged separations of the pre-weaned rat from its mother result in a host of physical and behavioral effects, including: 1) inhibition of cellular development with subsequent retardation of many body organs (e.g., heart, lung; see Lau et al., 1992) and 2) elevated baseline levels of glucocorticoids (i.e., stress hormones; see Suchecki et al., 1993b). In addition, Robbins, Jones, and Wilkinson (1996) reported that isolation rearing also results in a host of behavioral impairments, including hyperactivity, abnormal responses to novelty and stressors, and cognitive deficits in adulthood. Research on monkeys has demonstrated that even brief periods of maternal stress (imposed by the imposition of sudden, unpredictable loud noises) have serious and sustained effects on the newborn and older monkey as evidenced by greater distractibility, poor coordination, and slower response speed (e.g., Clarke, Soto, Bergholz, & Schneider, 1996; Schneider, 1992). Importantly, the measured effects of stress on physiology and behavior may not be restricted to the fetal or early postnatal animal. For example, mature monkeys exposed to the stress of improper caging show increases in glucocorticoids and damage to the hippocampus (see Uno et al., 1989). Adult humans who have undergone traumatic stress (and who suffer from posttraumatic stress disorder) also show smaller hippocampal volumes and demonstrate correspondingly poorer memories (Bremner et al., 1995). Collectively, exposure to stress prenatally, or even postnatally, can have severe and prolonged neurological and behavioral effects.

Summary

Overall, it is clear that a variety of factors can have deleterious effects on the prenatal brain. Examples include teratogens other than alcohol (e.g., heroin, cocaine, and lead), maternal medical conditions such as diabetes, fetal conditions such as intrauterine growth retardation, and so forth. It is beyond the scope of this chapter to discuss these factors in detail (see Shonkoff & Marshall, this volume, for further illustrations). Rather, this chapter focuses on the myriad *postnatal* factors that can influence the brain. The goal is to demonstrate not only that brain development depends critically on postnatal experience but also that brain *function* in general depends on such experience and may do so well into old age. The next section begins by offering a conceptual framework to explain how the nature of experience is incorporated into the structure of the brain.

MODELS OF NEURAL PLASTICITY

An unfortunate misconception of developmental neurobiology is that most aspects of brain development during the prenatal and immediate postnatal periods are under strict maturational control. In addition to the examples already provided (e.g., the effects of prenatal stress on the brain), the fallacy of this view can also be illustrated in the elegant models of brain–environment interactions offered by Greenough and colleagues (for review, see Greenough & Black, 1992). These investigators have proposed two mechanisms whereby synapses are formed. The first, *experience-expectant* synaptogenesis, refers to processes by which synapses form after some minimal experience has been obtained. A good example is the development of stereoscopic depth perception, in which normal visual input is necessary for ocular dominance columns (which represent the connections between each eye and layer IV of the visual cortex) to develop. If for some reason the two eyes are not properly aligned, thereby preventing them from converging effectively on a distant target, then the ocular dominance columns that support normal stereoscopic depth perception will fail to develop normally. If this condition is not corrected by the time the number of synapses begins to reach adult values (generally by the end of the preschool or early elementary school period), the child will not develop normal stereoscopic vision.

Experience-dependent synaptogenesis, in contrast, is a process that optimizes the individual's adaptation to specific and possibly unique features of the environment. A good example might be the information acquired by specific learning. Thus, depending on the individual's learning history, diverse information will be obtained and stored for use at a later

time, giving rise to individual differences in a variety of cognitive domains. The fundamental difference between experience-expectant and experience-dependent development is that the former applies in a similar fashion (presumably) to all members of a species, whereas the latter applies differentially to individual members.

In general, Greenough (e.g., Greenough & Black, 1992) has proposed that the structural substrate of "expectation" is the unpatterned, temporary overproduction of synapses dispersed within a relatively wide area during a sensitive period, with the subsequent "pruning" of synapses that have not formed connections at all or that have formed connections that are abnormal. The expected experience produces predictable patterns of neural activity, targeting those synapses that will be selected for preservation. The assumption is that synaptic contacts are initially transient and require some type of confirmation for their continued survival. If such confirmation is not obtained, synapses will be retracted according to a developmental schedule or as a result of competition from synapses that are clearly established. Support for this model comes from the observation that in both humans (e.g., Huttenlocher, 1994) and monkeys (e.g., Rakic et al., 1986) synapses are massively overproduced early in life, only to be followed later (postnatally) by a pruning back of exuberant or unused connections (see earlier section on synaptogenesis). Presumably the purpose of overproducing synapses is to prepare the nervous system for a broad range of possible experiences by overproducing connections on a widespread basis so that experience-related neural activity can select a functionally appropriate subset for further refinement.

MECHANISMS OF PLASTICITY

Prior to discussing examples of neural plasticity, it is useful to review some of the principles by which it is assumed the brain is sculpted by experience.

As a rule, plasticity is thought to reflect anatomic, neurochemical, or metabolic changes at the neural level. Anatomic changes illustrate the ability of existing synapses to modify their activity by the sprouting or regeneration of axons, or by the expansion of dendritic surfaces. Two examples will suffice. First, it has been observed that the loss of axonal fibers in the corpus callosum may cause a loss of synapses that is subsequently compensated for by an increase in thalamic synapses into the vacated space, thereby restoring interhemispheric communication (see Kolb & Whishaw, 1990, for discussion). Second, recovery of spinal cord function has recently been demonstrated in the rat by using peripheral nerve implants (Cheng, Cao, & Olson, 1996).

A second purported mechanism of plasticity exists at the neurochemical level. This account of plasticity demonstrates the ability of existing synapses to modify their activity by increasing neurotransmitter synthesis or by elevating the postsynaptic response to the transmitter. Finally, neural plasticity can also be manifested in metabolic changes. Metabolic explanations point to fluctuations in cortical and subcortical metabolic activity (e.g., glucose utilization) both ipsilateral (same side) and contralateral (opposite side) to the site of injury. Thus, if one area of the brain is damaged, the blood flow, and thus nutrient supply (e.g., glucose, oxygen), is increased in the neighboring region.

Ideally, one would like to speculate that if brain damage occurs early enough there will be significant regrowth of neurons. However, the only areas of the mammalian brain currently known to possess the capacity to regenerate neurons on a regular basis are the olfactory bulb and the dentate region of the hippocampus. Nevertheless, there is evidence that the experimental regrowth of neurons might be possible. For example, Reynolds and Weiss (1992) removed the striatum (an area of the brain known to be involved in regulating movement) from 3- to 18-month-old adult mice. Cells were cultured, and the epidermal growth factor was applied. Although many of the cells died, a small percentage multiplied to make new cells. The implications of this finding are enormous, as they suggest that it is possible for brain cells to make new neurons and that this mitotic process occurred in an *adult* animal, not in a juvenile.

Overall, there are a number of ways that the brain may be modified at the anatomic, cellular, or metabolic levels. These are necessitated by the fact that the brain does not repair itself or respond to environmental stimulation by generating new neurons. With these mechanisms in mind, in conjunction with the models of plasticity discussed earlier, a number of examples illustrating plasticity in the developing organism, as well as in the mature adult, are described.

Neural Plasticity in the Developing Organism

There are now numerous illustrations from a variety of species that demonstrate the influence of positive or negative early life experiences on both the function and the structure of the brain. One example has already been provided: the effects of stress on the developing rat brain. It is also known that rats raised in isolation exhibit neurochemical and behavioral abnormalities in their mesolimbic dopamine (DA) systems suggestive of hyperactivity. Isolation rearing may therefore provide a nonpharmacological way to induce in rats a deficit in sensorimotor gating (i.e., the inability to regulate incoming sensory signals) – a deficit that has also been observed in persons with schizophrenia (for elaboration of these points, see Geyer et al., 1993; Jones et al., 1990, 1991, 1992; Phillips et al., 1994a,b; Wilkinson et al., 1994). Finally, it has been demonstrated that brief maternal deprivation in the rat pup permanently alters the sensitivity of the hypothalamic pituitary axis (see Rots et al., 1995; Suchecki et al., 1993a), which presumably results in long-term abnormalities in the capacity to mediate stress responses. This hypothesis currently is being tested in humans, by studying children who have been removed from maternal care and placed in orphanages early in life (e.g., Earls, 1996).

In terms of the beneficial effects of experience, it is known that rats raised in complex laboratory environments outperform isolation-reared rats on certain cognitive tasks (e.g., the former make fewer errors on tasks of spatial cognition; Greenough, Madden, & Fleischmann, 1972). At the cellular level, some of the changes observed among rats raised in enriched environments include 1) several regions of the dorsal neocortex are heavier and thicker and have more synapses per neuron; 2) dendritic spines and branching patterns increase in number and length; and 3) there is increased capillary branching, thereby increasing blood and oxygen volume (for examples, see Black et al., 1989; Greenough & Black, 1992; Greenough, Juraska, & Volkmar, 1979; Greenough et al., 1972; for recent review, see Black et al., 1999).

Neural Plasticity in the Mature Organism

As reviewed by Nelson and Bloom (1997), it was assumed for many years that large-scale neural reorganization following injury is limited to the infancy period, with only modest reorganization possible in the adult. Within the past few years, however, this model of restricted adult plasticity has been reexamined. Precipitating this trend was a follow-up study published by Pons and colleagues (Pons et al., 1991) of a group of monkeys that 12 years earlier had received deafferentations of an upper limb (i.e., the fibers sending signals from the upper arm to the somatosensory cortex had been severed). After a lengthy experimental perturbation, the investigators examined the response of the brain to the loss of limb sensations and elicited neuronal responses from area SI, the region of the somatosensory cortex that normally would have represented the portion of the limb that had been deafferented, including the fingers, palm, and adjacent areas. Surprisingly, this region of the brain now responded to stimulation of a region of the face that normally borders the region innervated by the deafferented limb. For the face to occupy the region previously represented by the limb suggests a reorganization of somatosensory cortex of approximately 10–14 mm.

This study demonstrated that large-scale cortical reorganization can occur following injury, even in the mature animal. Equally impressive were subsequent reports of comparable findings in human adults. For example, one team of investigators reasoned that an individual who had experienced a limb amputation (e.g., such as the forearm) would show sensitivity on the area of the body represented by the area of the brain adjacent to the amputated limb (see Ramachandran et al., 1992). In the case of one such patient, whose left arm was amputated several centimeters above the elbow, sensation was experienced in the limb that had been amputated (i.e., phantom limb phenomenon) as well as along the regions of the face that are known to innervate the area of somatosensory cortex adjacent to the area previously innervated by the missing limb. That is to say, when this region of the face was lightly stimulated, the patient reported sensation in both the face and the missing limb. By carefully mapping out the stimulated area, Ramachandran et al. (1992) were able to determine the degree to which the cortical surface had been reorganized to subsume the area previously occupied by the missing limb. In these studies, changes at the neural level were inferred from overt behavior and were not examined directly. However, recent work using cortical magnetoencephalography (MEG) in combination with high resolution magnetic resonance imaging (i.e., magnetic source imaging [MSI]) confirmed Ramachandran's interpretation of the findings. For example, separate groups of investigators have now mapped the somatosensory cortex in normal, intact individuals using MEG (e.g., Yang et al., 1993, 1994a,b) as well as in adult human amputees (e.g., Elbert et al., 1994). Essentially, the region of the brain that previously represented the missing limb expands to represent the area adjacent to the limb, such as the cheek in the case of forearm amputation.

The logical conclusion of the monkey and human amputee studies is that the motor system is able to reorganize itself following injury. In an extension of this logic, Nudo et al. (1996) mapped the motor cortex of squirrel monkeys by using intracortical microstimulation (ICMS) before and after an ischemic lesion was induced (i.e., blood supply was interrupted, resulting in a loss of oxygen, followed by tissue damage). The induced infarct resulted in a pronounced deficit in the animal's ability to retrieve food pellets with the hand. The animals then received intensive training in hand use, which resulted in performance comparable to pre-injury levels. ICMS was used again to map the motor cortex, revealing substantial rearrangement of the area of the brain that represented the hand surrounding the lesion site. These findings, coupled with those reviewed earlier, suggest that the representation of the limbs in the adult primate can be altered as a function of experience. It is presumably this mechanism that underlies the success of some forms of stroke rehabilitation.

In summary, there is now evidence in support of the thesis that cortical reorganization is possible following peripheral nervous system injury in the adult human. In response to the question of whether this phenomenon is restricted to cases in which an injury has occurred (i.e., Could such reorganization be observed in a noninjured "healthy" individual?), the answer appears to be yes. For example, in a study reported by Elbert et al. (1995), the somatosensory cortex of adults with and without experience playing a stringed instrument (e.g., guitar, violin) was mapped using MEG. The investigators reported that the area of the somatosensory cortex in the musicians that represented the fingers of the left hand (the hand used on the fingerboard, which by default required greater fine motor skill) was larger than the area represented by the right hand (which was used, for example, to bow, a *relatively* gross motor skill) and larger than the left hand area in the nonmusicians. Moreover, there was a tendency for this effect (i.e., greater cortical representation) to be larger in individuals who had begun their musical training before the age of 10 years. This work suggests that the brain of the adult human can reorganize on the basis of positive experiences in the environment (e.g., training) as well as negative ones (e.g., response to injury).

To supplement these findings, let us now consider a study of cortical reorganization in the language domain following a specific training experience. Tallal and colleagues have speculated that children with language learning impairments (LLI) have difficulty in parsing phonetic elements (phonemes) embedded in ongoing speech, particularly when these elements are presented rapidly. This deficit results in difficulty discriminating speech sounds, a problem that may be unconscious and originate in the auditory thalamocortical pathway (see Kraus, McGee, Carrell, Zecker, & Koch, 1996, for discussion and evidence). In earlier work, Tallal reported that performance could be improved if the rate of change of the phonetic transitions was slowed down (e.g., Tallal & Piercy, 1973). Tallal and Merzenich (e.g., Merzenich et al., 1996; Tallal et al., 1996) have reported that when LLI children were given four weeks of intensive training in the temporal processing of speech, significant improvements (e.g., a gain of two years) in both speech discrimination and language comprehension were noted. In one instance, these gains persisted six weeks beyond the training period (Tallal et al., 1996). Although the investigators did not examine structural or physiological changes in the brains of these children, it is not unreasonable to hypothesize that such changes were at the heart of the improved performance (for evidence with monkeys in support of this hypothesis, see Merzenich & Jenkins, 1994, 1995; Recanzone, Merzenich, & Jenkins, 1992; Recanzone, Merzenich, & Schreiner, 1992).

Collectively, then, it appears that reorganization of cortical pathways in the adult human brain is possible beyond childhood and that such reorganization is not limited to motor or sensory pathways but may also include cognitive (e.g., language) systems. In this context, it is useful to question the simplistic notion that the brain is fixed and increasingly difficult to modify beyond the first few years of life. Although much of brain development clearly occurs late in gestation and through the first years of postnatal life, it is far from set in its trajectory. Indeed, there is now strong evidence that at least some regions of the brain, at least under some conditions, are able to incorporate the structure of experience into the structure of the neural substrate throughout much of the life span.

IMPLICATIONS FOR EARLY INTERVENTION

In reviewing the evidence on neural plasticity, the goal of this chapter is to demonstrate that the developing brain is capable of being modified by both deleterious (e.g., early stress) and beneficial (e.g., enriched environments) experiences. It has been shown that stressors that occur as early as the fetal stage of development can have long-term adverse consequences for the developing brain, whereas positive experiences, such as being raised in a complex environment, can have long-term beneficial impacts. Clearly, there is a sound neurophysiological basis for early childhood intervention, particularly in those circumstances in which early life experiences may be less than optimal and therefore not represent the "expected" environment.

The theme of neural plasticity was also carried forward to include the "mature" organism, in which research has shown that reorganization of an injured motor cortex is possible through activities of daily living (as revealed by work with amputees; see Ramachandran et al., 1992) and through rehabilitation (as revealed by work with squirrel monkeys that had incurred strokes; see Nudo et al., 1996). The research on stroke rehabilitation is particularly dramatic, as it provides concrete physiological evidence of motor cortex reorganization in an animal before and following injury.

When viewed in its entirety, research on neural plasticity raises two intriguing motifs. First, it is clear that there are neurophysiological events that unfold in response to experience, which permit the brain to reorganize itself. This argues strongly in favor of intervention efforts, as such experiences result in concrete changes at the level of the nervous system as well as at the level of behavior. Second, there also is evidence that modifications in the nervous system are not limited to the early part of the life span. Paradoxically, this raises a question about whether intervention needs to occur early or can in fact be effective at many points in the life span.

In formulating a response to this question, it is important to note that the evidence for neural plasticity in the mature organism is predominantly (although not exclusively) limited to the motor domain. In some respects, the fact that the motor system is capable of adaptation throughout much of the life span should not be surprising, given the lengthy period of input that this system receives. In other words, from the moment a child is born, the motor system is continually challenged, thereby keeping it "open" to new experience. Arguably, this process could begin as early as the fifth prenatal month. In contrast, we know that the ability to acquire oral language may have a considerably shorter period of modifiability. We know, for example, that English-speaking adults who have not been exposed to such languages as Swedish or Thai are unable to discriminate speech contrasts from these languages, in contrast to the ceiling-level ability to discriminate speech contrasts from their own (English) language (e.g., "ba" versus "ga"). Kuhl demonstrated that between 6 and 12 months of life, infants' ability to discriminate phonemes from languages to which they are not exposed diminishes greatly. Thus, although a 6-month-old infant raised in an English-speaking home may be able to discriminate contrasts from English as well as those from Swedish or Thai, by 12 months of age, such infants become more like English-speaking adults. That is, they lose the ability to discriminate contrasts from their nonnative language (for discussion, see Kuhl, Williams, Lacerda, Stevens, & Lindblom, 1992; Kuhl, 1993). The argument that Kuhl and others have proposed is that the speech system remains open to experience for a certain period of time, but if experience in a particular domain (such as hearing speech contrasts in different languages) is not forthcoming, the window begins to close early in life.

One might argue that, unlike the speech system, the motor system is challenged continually from birth, thereby keeping it open for much of the life span (which could be responsible for the success witnessed in stroke rehabilitation). Even in the motor domain, however, there are limitations. For example, although adults with experience playing a stringed instrument showed evidence of cortical reorganization, there was a trend for this reorganization to be more pronounced in those individuals who had begun their musical training before the age of 10 (Elbert et al., 1995). Presumably, the constraint here was not motor training per se but the acquisition of the syntax of music.

Outside of the motor domain, there is a paucity of information on neural plasticity in the mature organism. Thus, it is not possible to answer definitively the question of whether there are critical periods for early intervention in domains outside of motor rehabilitation. Nevertheless, it stands to reason that the likelihood of success for any given intervention would vary as a function of whether the challenged domain has had the "right" early experience to "set" the system (such as exposure to normal language) and whether it is challenged continually thereafter. Thus, it may be that the success of the Tallal–Merzenich intervention rests on the fact that the auditory input these children received early in life was normal (although their brain did not respond normally to this input) and that this input was maintained. On the other hand, one might argue that if appropriate early experiences are lacking, then the challenge of intervention may be more difficult. Under such circumstances, if the expected social–emotional environment is not met (e.g., as for neglected or abused infants and young children), the adverse impact of these experiences on the brain may create a situation whereby intervention must be provided early and intensively to be successful. Similarly, one might also argue that if the expected early environment was present, thereby setting the system correctly, but that the subsequent environment was lacking, then presumably intervention could come later and still be successful. Of course, these are hypothetical examples that remain to be evaluated.

One additional point should be addressed in the context of neural plasticity – whether intervention should be targeted specifically at a given function or be applied globally. Ultimately, the answer to this question will rest on the nature of the early experience. Thus, if a child lacks a range of experiences, spanning the gamut from the intellectual (e.g., no experience in problem solving or planning behavior) to the social and emotional (e.g., inconsistent or absent contingent nurturance), then presumably intervention should include as much of the missing experiences as possible. In contrast, if the deficit is specific, then so should be the intervention. Although this would seem intuitively obvious, it is important to emphasize that the ability to target the intervention varies as a function of the ability to identify the missing experience, the deficit, or both. For example, lesions of the caudate nucleus (such as might occur with a Grade III intraventricular hemorrhage) will lead to a different cognitive profile than lesions of the prefrontal cortex (such as might occur by ischemic infarct). Future studies will be needed to develop sophisticated batteries designed to specify deficits (or potential deficits) with greater precision, thereby permitting service programs to target their interventions accordingly.

It may be useful to illustrate the approach just prescribed with a brief example. Recall the discussion of Tallal's work, in which deficits in the ability to parse the speech train have been hypothesized to underlie some forms of language learning impairments. Tallal has further hypothesized that this deficit has its structural–anatomical basis in the auditory thalamocortical pathway. Kraus et al. (1996) utilized a component of the event-related potential (ERP) to evaluate this hypothesis. These authors employed a speech discrimination task while recording the match-mismatch negativity (MMN) from children with and without language learning impairments. The MMN response reflects the allocation of attention to deviant (e.g., rarely presented or unusual) auditory stimuli and has been used extensively to examine a range of auditory and speech discrimination phenomena. Additionally, the MMN is thought to originate in the auditory thalamocortical pathway, and thus can be used to index the integrity of this pathway. Kraus et al. reported that children with language impairments evinced abnormalities in the MMN. Given the neuroanatomical basis thought to underlie this component of the ERP, these findings provide support for the Tallal hypothesis that some language learning deficits are due to problems in the auditory thalamocortical pathway. What is additionally promising about this work is that presumably this same response could be used to index the effectiveness of intervention. For example, if the children in the Kraus et al. study were exposed to some intervention program, could one use the MMN response as a neurological marker of the effectiveness of this intervention; that is, would the MMN normalize with positive changes in behavior?

The point of this example is to underscore the need for developing precise measures of function – structure relations that can be used both to index the nature of a deficit or impairment and, at the same time, to provide a neurological indicator of the effectiveness of an intervention. In the cognitive domain, for example, are there components of the ERP that can be used to reflect deficits in memory or executive functions and that in turn can be used to assess the success of an intervention targeted to improve such functions? In the emotional domain, would it be possible to use functional magnetic resonance imaging (fMRI) both to evaluate the integrity of the structures and circuits thought to underlie emotion regulation and to index the effectiveness of an intervention designed to remediate deficits?

In conclusion, it should be evident that the success of early childhood intervention strategies rests to a great degree on the relative plasticity of the human brain. Although data were reviewed that demonstrate that the brain can be modified by experience, critical periods for intervention are most likely real phenomena based on actual neurobiological principles. In addition, recent advances in the neurosciences have made possible the ability to examine the relation between behavior and neurobiology in children. Hopefully, an understanding of the principles and the methods of developmental neurobiology ultimately will facilitate the design of more effective intervention strategies and more thorough evaluations of their impacts.

REFERENCES

Aggleton, J. P., & Mishkin, M. (1986). The amygdala: Sensory gateway to the emotions. In E. Plutchik & H. Kellerman (Eds.), *Emotion: Theory, research, and experience: Vol. 3. Biological foundations of emotion* (pp. 281–99). New York: Academic Press.
Bachevalier, J. (1990). Ontogenetic development of habit and memory formation in primates. In A. Diamond (Ed.), *Development and neural bases of higher cognitive*

functions (pp. 457–84). New York: New York Academy of Sciences Press.

Bachevalier, J. (1992). Cortical versus limbic immaturity: Relationship to infantile amnesia. In M. R. Gunnar & C. A. Nelson (Eds.), *Minnesota symposia on child psychology: Vol. 24. Developmental behavioral neuroscience* (pp. 129–53). Hillsdale, NJ: Erlbaum.

Bachevalier, J., Hagger, C., & Mishkin, M. (1991). Functional maturation of the occipitotemporal pathway in infant rhesus monkeys. In N. A. Lassen, D. H. Ingvar, M. E. Raichle, & L. Friberg (Eds.), *Brain work and mental activity* (pp. 231–40). Copenhagen: Munksgaard.

Bachevalier, J., & Mishkin, M. (1984). An early and a late developing system for learning and retention in infant monkeys. *Behavioral Neuroscience, 98,* 770–8.

Bachevalier, J., & Mishkin, M. (1992). *Dissociation of the effects of neonatal inferior temporal cortical versus limbic lesions on visual recognition in 10-month-old rhesus monkeys.* Manuscript unpublished.

Bauer, P. (1996). Development of memory in early childhood. In N. Cowan (Ed.), *The development of memory in childhood.* London: University College London Press.

Berger, B., & Alvarez, C. (1994). Neurochemical development of the hippocampal region in the fetal rhesus monkey. II. Immunocytochemistry of peptides, calcium-binding proteins, DARPP-32, and monoamine innervation in the entorhinal cortex by the end of gestation. *Hippocampus, 4,* 85–114.

Berger, B., Alvarez, C., & Goldman-Rakic, P. S. (1993). Neurochemical development of the hippocampal region in the fetal rhesus monkey. I. Early appearance of peptides, calcium-binding proteins, DARPP-32, and monoamine innervation in the entorhinal cortex during the first half of gestation (E47 to E90). *Hippocampus, 3,* 279–305.

Black, J. E., Jones, T. A., Nelson, C. A., & Greenough, W. T. (1999). Neuronal plasticity and the developing brain. In N. Alessi (Ed.), *Handbook of child and adolescent psychiatry. Part III. Developmental neuroscience.*

Black, J. E., Sirevaag, A. M., Wallace, C. S., Savin, M. H., & Greenough, W. T. (1989). Effects of complex experience on somatic growth and organ development in rats. *Developmental Psychobiology, 22,* 727–52.

Bourgeois, J.-P., & Rakic, P. (1993). Changes in synaptic density in the primary visual cortex of the Macaque monkey from fetal to adult stage. *Journal of Neuroscience, 13,* 2801–20.

Bremner, J. D., Randall, P., Scott, T. M., Bronen, R. A., Seibyl, J. P., Southwick, S. M., Delaney, R. C., McCarthy, G., Charney, D. S., & Innis, R. B. (1995). MRI-based measurement of hippocampal volume in patients with combat-related posttraumatic stress disorder. *American Journal of Psychiatry, 152,* 973–81.

Cheng, H., Cao, Y., & Olson, L. (1996). Spinal cord repair in adult paraplegic rats: Partial restoration of hind limb function. *Science, 273,* 510–13.

Chugani, H. T. (1994). Development of regional brain glucose metabolism in relation to behavior and plasticity. In G. Dawson & K. Fischer (Eds.), *Human behavior and the developing brain* (pp. 153–75). New York: Guilford Press.

Chugani, H. T., & Phelps, M. E. (1986). Maturational changes in cerebral function in infants determined by [18]FDG positron emission tomography. *Science, 231,* 840–3.

Clarke, A. S., Soto, A., Bergholz, T., & Schneider, M. L. (1996). Maternal gestational stress alters adaptive and social behavior in adolescent Rhesus monkey offspring. *Infant Behavior and Development, 19,* 451–61.

Damasio, A. (1994). *Descartes' error.* New York: Putnam Press.

Diamond, A. (1990). The development and neural bases of memory functions as indexed by the AB and delayed response tasks in human infants and infant monkeys. In A. Diamond (Ed.), *Development and neural bases of higher cognitive functions* (pp. 267–317). New York: New York Academy of Sciences Press.

Diamond, A., & Doar, B. (1989). The performance of human infants on a measure of frontal cortex function, the delayed response task. *Developmental Psychobiology, 22,* 271–94.

Diamond, A., & Goldman-Rakic, P. S. (1989). Comparison of human infants and rhesus monkeys on Piaget's AB task: Evidence for dependence on dorsolateral prefrontal cortex. *Experimental Brain Research, 74,* 24–40.

Dickerson, J. W. T. (1981). Nutrition, brain growth and development. In K. J. Connolly & H. F. R. Prechtl (Eds.), *Maturation and development: Biological and psychological perspectives* (pp. 110–30). Suffolk, England: Lavenham Press.

Dobbing, J., & Sands, J. (1971). Vulnerability of the developing brain. IX. The effect of nutritional growth retardation on the timing of the brain growth spurt. *Biology of the Neonate, 19,* 363–78.

Dodson, W. E. (1992). Deleterious effects of intrauterine drug exposure on the nervous system. In R. A. Polin & W. W. Fox (Eds.), *Fetal and neonatal physiology* (pp. 1613–23). Philadelphia: W. B. Saunders.

Earls, F. (1996, May). *Recovery from profound early social deprivation.* Paper presented at a meeting entitled Advancing Research on Developmental Plasticity: Integrating the Behavioral Science and the Neuroscience of Mental Health, Washington, DC.

Eckenhoff, M. F., & Rakic, P. (1991). A quantitative analysis of synaptogenesis in the molecular layer of the dentate gyrus in the rhesus monkey. *Developmental Brain Research, 64,* 129–35.

Elbert, T., Flor, H., Birbaumer, N., Knecht, S., Hampson, S., Larbig, W., & Taub, E. (1994). Extensive reorganization of the somatosensory cortex in adult humans after nervous system injury. *NeuroReport, 5,* 2593–7.

Elbert, T., Pantev, C., Wienbruch, C., Rockstroh, B., & Taub,

E. (1995). Increased cortical representation of the fingers of the left hand in string players. *Science, 270*, 305–7.

Fuster, J. M. (1990). *The prefrontal cortex*. New York: Raven Press.

Geyer, M. A., Wilkinson, L. S., Humby, T., & Robbins, T. W., (1993). Isolation rearing of rats produces a deficit in prepulse inhibition of acoustic startle similar to that in schizophrenia. *Biological Psychiatry, 34*, 361–72.

Goldman, P. S. (1971). Functional development of the prefrontal cortex in early life and the problem of neuronal plasticity. *Experimental Neurology, 32*, 366–87.

Goldman-Rakic, P. S. (1985). Toward a neurobiology of cognitive development. In J. Mahler (Ed.), *Neonate cognition* (pp. 285–306). Hillsdale, NJ: Erlbaum.

Goldman-Rakic, P. S. (1987). Circuitry of the prefrontal cortex and the regulation of behavior by representational knowledge. In F. Plum & V. Mountcastle (Eds.), *Handbook of physiology: Section I. The nervous system: Vol. 5. Higher functions of the brain* (pp. 373–417). Bethesda, MD: American Physiological Society.

Goldman, P. S., & Rosvold, H. E. (1972). The effects of selective caudate lesions in infant and juvenile rhesus monkeys. *Brain Research, 43*, 53–66.

Greenough, W. T., & Black, J. E. (1992). Induction of brain structure by experience: Substrates for cognitive development. In M. R. Gunnar & C. A. Nelson (Eds.), *The Minnesota symposia on child psychology: Vol. 24. Developmental behavioral neuroscience* (pp. 155–200). Hillsdale, NJ: Erlbaum.

Greenough, W. T., Juraska, J. M., & Volkmar, F. R. (1979). Maze training effects on dendritic branching in occipital cortex of adult rats. *Behavioral and Neural Biology, 26*, 287–97.

Greenough, W. T., Madden, T. C., & Fleischchmann, T. B. (1972). Effects of isolation, daily handling, and enriched rearing on maze learning. *Psychonomic Science, 27*, 279–80.

Hinton, V. J., Brown, W. T., Wisniewski, K., et al. (1991). Analysis of neocortex in three males with the fragile X syndrome. *American Journal of Medical Genetics, 41*, 289–94.

Humphrey, T. (1966). The development of the human hippocampal formation correlated with some aspects of its phylogenetic history. In S. Hassler (Ed.), *Evolution of the forebrain* (pp. 104–116). Stuttgart, Germany: Thieme.

Huttenlocher, P. R. (1975). Synaptic and dendritic development and mental defect. In N. A. Buchwald & M. A. B. Brazier (Eds.), *Brain mechanisms in mental retardation*. New York: Academic Press.

Huttenlocher, P. R. (1979). Synaptic density in human frontal cortex: Developmental changes and effects of aging. *Brain Research, 163*, 195–205.

Huttenlocher, P. R. (1990). Morphometric study of human cerebral cortex development. *Neuropsychologia, 28*, 517–27.

Huttenlocher, P. R. (1994). Synaptogenesis, synapse elimination, and neural plasticity in human cerebral cortex. In C. A. Nelson (Ed.), *Minnesota symposium on child psychology: Vol. 27. Threats to optimal development: Integrating biological, psychological, and social risk factors* (pp. 35–54). Hillsdale, NJ: Erlbaum.

Jacobs, B., Chugani, H. T., Llada, V., Chen, S., Phelps, M. E., Pollacls, D. B., and Raleigh, M. J. (1995). Developmental changes in brain metabolism in destaed rhesus macaques and vervet monkeys revealed by positron emission tomography. *Cerebral Cortex, 3*, 222–33.

Janas, M. S. (1994). *The developing human foetal brain: A qualitative and quantitative study of the hippocampal formation in the normal, the abnormal, and the potentially abnormal human foetus*. Unpublished doctoral dissertation, Faculty of Health Sciences, University of Copenhagen.

Jernigan, T. L., & Tallal, P. (1990). Late childhood changes in brain morphology observable with MRI. *Developmental Medicine and Child Neurology, 32*, 379–85.

Jones, G. H., Hernandez, T. D., Kendall, D. A., Marsden, C. A., & Robbins, T. W. (1992). Dopaminergic and serotonergic function following isolation rearing in rats: study of behavioural responses and postmortem and in vivo neurochemistry. *Pharmacology Biochemistry and Behavior, 43*, 17–35.

Jones, G. H., Marsden, C. A., & Robbins, T. W. (1990). Increased sensitivity to amphetamine and reward-related stimuli following social isolation in rats: Possible disruption of dopamine-dependent mechanisms of the nucleus accumbens. *Psychopharmacology, 102*, 364–72.

Jones, G. H., Marsden, C. A., & Robbins, T. W. (1991). Behavioural rigidity and rule-learning deficits following isolation-rearing in the rat: neurochemical correlates. *Behavioral Brain Research, 43*, 35–50.

Jones, B., & Mishkin, M. (1972). Limbic lesions and the problem of stimulus-reinforcement associations. *Experimental Neurology, 36*, 362–77.

Jones, K., Smith, D., & Hanson, J. (1976). The fetal alcohol syndrome: Curved delereation. *Study of the New York Academy of Sciences, 273*, 130–9.

Kandel, E. R., & Schwartz, J. H. (1985). *Principles of neural science* (2nd ed.). New York: Elsevier Press.

Kandel, E. R., Schwartz, J. H., & Jessell, T. M. (1991). *Principles of neural science* (3rd ed.). New York: Elsevier Press.

Klebanoff, M. A. et al. (1989). Second generation consequences of small-for-dates birth. *Pediatrics, 84*, 343–47.

Kolb, B., & Whishaw, I. Q. (1990). *Fundamentals of neuropsychology* (3rd ed.). New York: Freeman Press.

Kraus, N., McGee, T. J., Carrell, T. D., Zecker, S. G., & Koch, D. B. (1996). Auditory neurophysiologic responses and discrimination deficits in children with learning problems. *Science, 273*, 971–3.

Kretschmann, J.-J., Kammradt, G., Krauthausen, I., Sauer, B., & Wingert, F. (1986). Growth of the hippocampal formation in man. *Bibthca Anat, 28*, 27–52.

Kuhl, P. K. (1993). Effects of linguistic experience in the first half year of life: Implications for a theory of infant speech perception. In B. de Boysson-Bardies, S. de Schonen, P. Jusczyk, P. MacNeilage, & J. Morton (Eds.), *Developmental neurocognition: Speech and face processing in the first year of life* (pp. 259–74). The Netherlands: Kluwer Academic Press.

Kuhl, P. K., Williams, K. A., Lacerda, F., Stevens, K. N., & Lindblom, B. (1992). Linguistic experience alters phonetic perception in infants by 6 months of age. *Science, 255*, 606–8.

Lau, C., Cameron, A. M., Anrolick, L. L., & Stanton, E. E. (1992). Repeated maternal seperation in the neonatal rat: Cellular mechanisms contributing to brain growth sparing. *Journal of Developmental Physiology, 17*, 265–76.

Lloyd-Still, J. D. (1976). *Malnutrition and intellectual development*. Littleton, MA: Publishing Sciences Group.

Luria, A. R. (1973). *The working brain*. New York: Basic Books.

Merzneich, M. M., & Jenkins, W. M. (1994). Cortical representation of learned behaviors. In P. Anderson, O. Hvalby, O. Paulsen, & B. Hokfelt (Eds.), *Memory concepts* (pp. 437–51). Amsterdam: Elsevier.

Merzneich, M. M., & Jenkins, W. M. (1995). Cortical plasticity, learning, and learning dysfunction. In B. Julesz & I. Kovacs (Eds.), *Maturational windows and adult cortical plasticity* (pp. 247–72). Reading, MA: Addison-Wesley.

Merzneich, M. M., Jenkins, W. M., Johnston, P., Schreiner, C., Miller, S. L., & Tallal, P. (1996). Temporal processing deficits of language-learning impaired children ameliorated by training. *Science, 271*, 77–81.

Meunier, M., Hadfield, W., Bachevalier, J., & Murray, E. A. (1996). Effects of rhinal cortex lesions combined with hippocampectomy on visual recognition memory in Rhesus monkeys. *Journal of Neurophysiology, 75*, 1190–1205.

Morgan, B. L. G., & Winick, M. (1985). Pathologic effects of malnutrition on the central nervous system. In H. Sidransky (Ed.), *Nutritional pathology – Pathobiochemistry of dietary imbalances* (pp. 161–206). New York: Dekker.

Nelson, C. A. (1995). The ontogeny of human memory: A cognitive neuroscience perspective. *Developmental Psychology, 31*, 723–38.

Nelson, C. A. (1996). The neurobiological basis of early memory development. In N. Cowan (Ed.), *The development of memory in childhood*. University College London Press: London.

Nelson, C. A., & Bloom, F. E. (1997). Child development and neuroscience. *Child Development, 68*, 970–87.

Nudo, R. J., Wise, B. M., SiFuentes, F., & Milliken, G. W. (1996). Neural substrates for the effects of rehabilitative training on motor recovery after ischemic infarct. *Science, 272*, 1791–4.

Omaye, S. T. (1993). Nutrient deficiencies and pregnancy outcome. In R. P. Sharma (Ed.), *Dietary factors and birth defects* (pp. 12–41). San Francisco: Pacific Division, AAAS.

O'Neil, J. B., Friedman, D.P., Bachevalier, J., & Ungerleider, L. G. (1986). Distribution of muscarinic receptors in the brain of a newborn rhesus monkey. *Society for Neuroscience Abstracts, 12*, 809.

Orzhekhovskaya, N. S. (1975). Comparative study of formation of the frontal cortex of the brain of monkeys and man in ontogenesis. *Arkhiv, Anatomii, Gistologii, Embriologii, 68*, 43–9.

Paldino, A. M., & Purpura, D. P. (1979). Branching patterns of hippocampal neurons of human fetus during dendritic differentiation. *Experimental Neurology, 64*, 620–31.

Pandya, D. N., & Barnes, C. L. (1987). Architecture and connections of the frontal lobes. In E. Perecman (Ed.), *The frontal lobes revisited* (pp. 41–72). Hillsdale, NJ: Erlbaum.

Petrides, M. P. (1996). Lateral frontal cortical contribution to memory. *Seminar in the Neurosciences, 8*, 57–63.

Phillips, G. D., Howes, S. R., Whitelaw, R. B., Robbins, T. W., & Everitt, B. J. (1994a). Isolation rearing impairs the reinforcing efficacy of intravenous cocaine or intra-accumbens d-amphetamine: Impaired response to intra-accumbens D1 and D2/D3 dopamine receptor antagonists. *Psychopharmacology, 115*, 419–29.

Phillips, G. D., Howes, S. R., Whitelaw, R. B., Wilkinson, L. S., Robbins, T. W., & Everitt, B. J. (1994b). Isolation rearing enhances the locomotor response to cocaine and a novel environment, but impairs the intravenous self-administration of cocaine. *Psychopharmacology, 115*, 407–18.

Pollitt, E., & Gorman, K. S. (1994). Nutritional deficiencies as developmental risk factors. In C. A. Nelson (Ed.), *Minnesota symposia on child psychology: Vol. 27. Threats to optimal development: Integrating biological, psychological, and social risk factors* (pp. 121–44). Hillsdale, NJ: Erlbaum.

Pons, T. (1995). Abstract: Lesion-induced cortical plasticity. In B. Julesz & I. Kovacs (Eds.), *Maturational windows and adult cortical plasticity* (pp. 175–8). Reading, MA: Addison-Wesley.

Pons, T. P., Garraghty, P. E., Ommaya, A. K., Kaas, J. H., Taub, E., & Mishkin, M. (1991). Massive cortical reorganization after sensory deafferentation in adult macaques. *Science, 252*, 1857–60.

Purpura, D. P. (1975). Dendritic differentiation in human cerebral cortex: Normal and aberrant developmental patterns. In G. W. Kreutzberg (Ed.), *Advances in neurology*. New York: Raven Press.

Rakic, P. (1971). Guidance of neurons migrating to the fetal monkey neocortex. *Brain Research, 33*, 471–6.

Rakic, P. (1972). Mode of cell migration to the superficial layers of fetal monkey neocortex. *Journal of Comparative Neurology, 145*, 61–84.

Rakic, P. (1974). Neurons in rhesus monkey visual cortex: Systematic relation between time of origin and eventual disposition. *Science, 183*, 425–7.

Rakic, P., Bourgeois, J.-P., Eckenhoff, M. F., Zecevic, N., & Goldman-Rakic, P. S. (1986). Concurrent overproduction of synapses in diverse regions of the primate cerebral cortex. *Science, 232*, 232–5.

Ramachandran, V. S., Rogers-Ramachandran, D., & Stewart, M. (1992). Perceptual correlates of massive cortical reorganization. *Science, 258,* 1159–60.

Recanzone, G. H., Merzenich, M. M., & Jenkins, W. M. (1992). Frequency discrimination training engaging a restricted skin surface results in an emergence of a cutaneous response zone in the cortical area 3a. *Journal of Neurophysiology, 67,* 1057–70.

Recanzone, G. H., Merzenich, M. M., & Schreinder, C. E. (1992). Changes in the distributed temporal response properties of S1 cortical neurons reflect improvements in performance on a temporally based tactile discrimination task. *Journal of Neurophysiology, 67,* 1071–91.

Reynolds, B. A. & Weiss, S. (1992). Generation of neurons and astrocytes from isolated cells of the adult mammalian central nervous system. *Science, 255,* 1707–10.

Robbins, T. W. (1996, March). *Dissociating executive functions of the prefrontal cortex.* Paper presented at the Royal Society Discussion Meeting on Executive and Cognitive Functions of the Prefrontal Cortex, London, UK.

Robbins, T. W., Jones, G. H., & Wilkinson, L. S. (1996). Behavioural and neurochemical effects of early social deprivation in the rat. *Journal of Psychopharmacology, 10,* 39–47.

Rots, N. Y., Workerl, J. O., Sutanto, W., Cools, A. R., Levine, S., de Kloet, E. R., & Oitzl, M. S. (1995). Maternal deprivation results in an enhanced pituitary-adrenal activity and an increased dopamine susceptibility at adulthood. *Society for Neuroscience Abstracts, 21,* 524.

Rovee-Collier, C. (1996). Development of memory in infancy. In N. Cowan (Ed.), *The development of memory in childhood.* London: University College London Press.

Schneider, M. L. (1992). The effect of mild stress during pregnancy on birthweight and neuromotor maturation in Rhesus monkey infants (Macaca mulatta). *Infant Behavior and Development, 15,* 389–403.

Schore, A. N. (1994). *Affect regulation and the origin of the self: The neurobiology of emotional development.* Hillsdale, NJ: Lawrence Erlbaum Associates.

Seress, L., & Ribak, C. E. (1995). Postnatal development and synaptic connections of hilar mossy cells in the hippocampal dentate gyrus of rhesus monkeys. *Journal of Comparative Neurology, 355,* 93–110.

Shallice, T. (1982). Specific impairments of planning. *Philosophical Transactions of the Royal Society of London: B, 298,* 199–209.

Shallice, T., & Burgess, P. (1993). Supervisory control of action and thought selection. In A. Baddeley & L. Weiskrantz (Eds.), *Attention: Selection, awareness, and control* (pp. 171–87). Oxford, England: Clarendon Press.

Sidman, R. L., & Rakic, P. (1982). Development of the human central nervous system. In W. Haymaker & R. D. Adams (Eds.), *Histology and histopathology of the nervous system* (pp. 3–145). Springfield, MA: C. C. Thomas.

Suchecki, D., Mozaffarian, D., Gross, G., Rosenfeld, P., Levine, S. (1993b). Effects of maternal deprivation on the ACTH stress response in the infant rat. *Neuroendocrinology, 57,* 204–12.

Suchecki, D., Rosenfeld, P., & Levine, S. (1993a). Maternal regulation of hypothalamic-pituitary axis in the infant rat: The role of feeding and stroking. *Developmental Brain Research, 75,* 185–92.

Takashima, S., & Mito, T. (1985). Neuronal development in the medullary reticular formation in sudden infant death syndrome and premature infants. *Neuropediatrics, 16,* 76–9.

Tallal, P., & Piercy, M. (1973). Defects of non-verbal auditory perception in children with developmental aphasia. *Nature, 241,* 468–9.

Tallal, P., Miller, S. L., Bedi, G., Byma, G., Wang, X., Nagarajan, S. S., Schreiner, C., Jenkins, W. M., & Merzenich, M. M. (1996). Language comprehension in language-learning impaired children improved with acoustically modified speech. *Science, 271,* 81–4.

Uno, H., Tarara, R., Else, J. G., Suleman, M. A., & Sapolsky, R. M. (1989). Hippocampal damage associated with prolonged and fatal stress in primates. *Journal of Neuroscience, 9,* 1705–11.

Volpe, J. V. (1995). *Neurology of the newborn* (3rd ed.). Philadelphia: W. B. Saunders.

Webster, M. J., Bachevalier, J., & Ungerleider, L. G. (1995). Development and plasticity of visual memory circuits. In B. Julesz & I. Kovacs (Eds.), *Maturational windows and adult cortical plasticity.* Reading, MA: Addison-Wesley.

Webster, M. J., Ungerleider, L. G., & Bachevalier, J. (1991a). Lesions of inferior temporal area TE in infant monkeys alter cortico-amygdalar projections. *Developmental Neuroscience, 2,* 769–72.

Webster, M. J., Ungerleider, L. G., & Bachevalier, J. (1991b). Connections of inferior temporal areas TE and TEO with medial temporal-lobe structures in infant and adult monkeys. *Journal of Neuroscience, 11,* 1095–116.

Wilkinson, L. S., Killcross, S. S., Humby, T., Hall, F. S., Geyer, M. A., & Robbins, T. W. (1994). Social isolation in the rat produces developmentally specific deficits in prepulse inhibition of the acoustic startle response without disrupting latent inhibition. *Neuropsychopharmacology, 10,* 61–72.

Winick, M. (1976). *Malnutrition and brain development.* New York: Oxford University Press.

Winick, M. (1989). *Nutrition, pregnancy, and early infancy.* Baltimore, MD: Williams & Wilkins.

Winick, M., & Rosso, P. (1969). The effect of severe early malnutrition on cellular growth of the human brain. *Pediatric Research, 3,* 181–4.

Yakovlev, P. I., & LeCours, A.-R. (1967). The myelogenetic cycles of regional maturation of the brain. In A. Minkowski (Ed.), *Regional development of the brain in early life* (pp. 3–70). Oxford, England: Blackwell Scientific.

Yang, T. T., Gallen, C. C., Schwartz, B. J., & Bloom, F. E. (1993). Noninvasive somatosensory homunculus mapping in humans by using a large-array biomagnetometer. *Proceedings of the National Academy of Sciences, 90,* 3098–102.

Yang, T. T., Gallen, G., Schwart, B., Bloom, F. E., Ramachandran, V. S., & Cobb, S. (1994a). Sensory maps in the human brain. *Nature, 368,* 592–3.

Yang, T. T., Gallen, C. C., Ramachandran, V. S., Cobb, S., Schwartz, B. J., & Bloom, F. E. (1994b). Noninvasive detection of cerebral plasticity in adult human somatosensory cortex. *Neuroreport, 5,* 701–4.

Yatkin, U. S., McLaren, D. S., Kanawati, A. A., & Sabbach, S. (1971). Undernutrition and mental development: A one year follow-up. In D. S. McLaren & N. J. Daghir (Eds.), *Proceedings of the 6th symposium on nutrition and health in the Near East* (pp. 277–81). Beirut: American University.

Zhang, D., & Mahoney, A. W. (1993). Iron status during pregnancy. In R. P. Sharma (Ed.), *Dietary factors and birth defects* (pp. 73–108). San Francisco: Pacific Division, AAAS.

PART FOUR

APPROACHES TO ASSESSMENT

CHAPTER ELEVEN

The Elements of Early Childhood Assessment

SAMUEL J. MEISELS AND SALLY ATKINS-BURNETT

Early childhood assessment is a field in transition. Dominated from its inception by psychometric models and measurement strategies used with older children and adults, it is only now beginning to forge a methodology that is unique to very young children. Much of the early work in infant assessment was directed at determining whether infant behavior could predict later child performance (Brooks-Gunn & Weinraub, 1983; Honzik, 1983). In Nancy Bayley's first monograph concerning mental development, she attempted to specify those infant behaviors that could be tied empirically to later mental functioning. She posed such questions as "What specific behavior precedes later mental achievements? To what extent are these later achievements dependent on the earlier? Can we predict later development from early behavior? How do individual growth rates compare with the norm for a group of infants? To what extent are these rates affected by environmental conditions?" (Bayley, 1933, p. 7). The instrument that she developed, which has been revised twice since its experimental versions (Bayley, 1969, 1993), was intended to answer these questions.

The Bayley Scales of Infant Development II (BSID-II; Bayley, 1993) are used primarily to sample the intellectual and motoric growth of infants and toddlers. The scales are most successful in sorting, categorizing, and ranking children according to demonstrable parameters of infant behavior. Despite its widespread use, few researchers, including Bayley, believed that mental functioning in the first few months and years of life provides us with accurate information about children's later intellectual development or performance (see Bayley 1970; McCall,

1981; McCall, Hogarty, & Hurlburt, 1972; but for a differing opinion about the long-term predictability of infant characteristics, see Fagan & McGrath, 1981, and Fagan, Singer, Montie, & Shepherd, 1986). It seems that all we know with certainty is that the relationship is poorly defined between early-appearing, preverbal cognitive and psychomotor functions and typical intellectual performance that is manifested at school age and beyond.

This chapter focuses on research concerning perspectives that broaden the prevailing, normative paradigm in assessment and describes other assessment purposes besides normative ranking and short- and long-term predictions. It begins with a brief presentation of the principles of responsive assessments and then suggests alternative approaches to assessing the developmental status of young children. Five elements of early childhood assessment are discussed: 1) the target of assessment, 2) the context in which assessments occur, 3) limitations of conventional methods of assessment, 4) varied roles of personnel in assessments, and 5) the relationship of assessment to intervention. Consideration of these elements is central to the appraisal of existing methods of assessment and to the development of future models of evaluation and intervention for young children.

PRINCIPLES OF ASSESSMENT

In 1992, the Zero to Three Working Group on Developmental Assessment, a multidisciplinary group of professionals and parents, convened to identify "problems and promising approaches in current

---

TABLE 11.1. Principles of Assessment in Infancy and Early Childhood

1. Assessment must be based on an integrated developmental model.
2. Assessment involves multiple sources of information and multiple components.
3. An assessment should follow a certain sequence.
4. The child's relationship and interactions with his or her most trusted caregiver should form the cornerstone of an assessment.
5. An understanding of sequences and timetables in typical development is essential as a framework for the interpretation of developmental differences among infants and toddlers.
6. Assessment should emphasize attention to the child's level and pattern of organizing experience and to functional capacities, which represent an integration of emotional and cognitive abilities.
7. The assessment process should identify the child's current competencies and strengths, as well as the competencies that will constitute developmental progression in a continuous growth model of development.
8. Assessment is a collaborative process.
9. The process of assessment should always be viewed as the first step in a potential intervention process.
10. Reassessment of a child's developmental status should occur in the context of day-to-day family or early intervention activities, or both.

Adapted from: Greenspan & Meisels (1996, pp. 17–22).

assessment paradigms, policies, and practices" (Meisels & Fenichel, 1996, p. 5). Their discussions led to the establishment of a set of principles for guiding the assessment of young children in the realms of intellect, affect, and psychomotor development (Greenspan & Meisels, 1996, pp. 17–25). These principles are presented in Table 11.1. They serve as touchstones for future activity in the area of early childhood assessment.

In general, the goal of early childhood assessment is to acquire information and understanding that will facilitate the child's development and functional abilities within the family and community. Developmental assessment in particular is

A process designed to deepen understanding of a child's competencies and resources, and of the caregiving and learning environments most likely to help a child make fullest use of his or her developmental potential. Assessment should be an ongoing, collaborative process of systematic observation and analysis. This process involves formulating questions, gathering information, sharing observations, and making interpretations in order to form new questions. (Greenspan & Meisels, 1996, p. 11)

The assessment principles listed in Table 11.1 assume this definition of assessment. We examine these assessment principles below and offer examples of instruments and practices that utilize them.

Interdependence of Development

The child is an integrated being – not a collection of articulated skills, acquisitions, or elements – and the development of each area of functioning is dependent on other areas (cf. Emde, Biringen, Clyman, & Oppenheim, 1991). For example, the child's skill in naming a picture is an indication of sensory, cognitive, and motor abilities, as well as language acquisition. Underlying all of this is the emotional capacity that enables children to relate to others and to organize their world. To consider only one area of development in isolation from others leaves unrecognized the influence of the other areas and may obscure our understanding of the child's abilities and challenges. The child's functional capacities should be examined in a variety of contexts in order to comprehend fully how children integrate skills into their repertoire of behaviors and responses.

In-depth examination of a child's skills in a single area of development proceeds from the more complete picture of the child's overall skills and knowledge acquisitions, recognizing the interdependence of the systems in development. Examples of assessment tools that focus on functional capacities in an integrated fashion include the Functional Emotional Assessment Scale (FEAS; Greenspan, 1992) and the structured and nonstructured play observations that are part of the Transdisciplinary Play-Based Assessment (TPBA; Linder, 1993).

Multiple Sources and Multiple Components

The ability to take into account a variety of perspectives – what may be called "polyocular vision" – is essential for providing a complete view of the child's strengths and capacities and is the optimal means of promoting further development. Information can be obtained from a variety of contexts with different tools guiding the process and informing the assessment. Members of assessment teams must make evident to one another their perspective on the child and the underlying assumptions of that perspective. As each member, including the parent, shares his or her understanding of the child's abilities, predispositions, and challenges, a more complete, informed, and multidimensional profile of the child emerges (McCune, Kalmanson, Fleck, Glazewski, & Sillari, 1990). The expertise of the different members of the team sheds light on the various interpretations that can be given to observed behaviors and the ways in which emerging abilities can be supported and new abilities fostered. An example of an assessment that accounts for multiple sources and that is composed of multiple components is the Infant–Toddler Developmental Assessment (IDA; Provence, Erikson, Vater, & Palmeri, 1995).

Assessment Sequence

Assessments should follow a sequence that begins with the establishment of reliable, working alliances with significant individuals in the child's life. These individuals hold important information about the child and his or her capacities. To create a reliable alliance with parents, the development of mutual trust and respect is necessary (Turnbull & Turnbull, 1996), as are sensitive listening skills, responsivity to requests and concerns, openness to the family's interpretations, and honesty in interactions. Mutual respect for the family involves understanding the family's strengths, challenges, problem-solving strategies, as well as awareness and communication of the cultural assumptions undergirding assessment and professional recommendations. Hirshberg (1996) described precisely this kind of parent–professional relationship in his presentation of clinical interviewing. He noted that human connectedness is essential for the process of assessment and intervention. This connectedness occurs at many levels: between parent and child, parent and clinician, and clinician and child.

Subsequent to establishing this relationship, the assessment can begin to focus on practical outcomes. Assessment is not an end in itself. Rather, its goals are to obtain useful and accurate information about the child and the child's nurturing environment, including the resources and obstacles inherent in that environment, in order to find or create the most optimal situation for supporting and enhancing the child's development. Numerous assessment methods are available to assist in accomplishing these goals, as this chapter demonstrates. Beyond information gathering, assessments are intended to assist families and caregivers in creating practical solutions to problems of significance. In short, the sequence of an assessment begins with the family, moves through multiple means of data collection, and results in the creation of plans of action. Ultimately, the validity of assessment is determined in terms of its application.

Child–Caregiver Relationships

The interactions and relationship between child and caregiver form the foundation of the child's ability to organize and respond to his or her world (Weston, Ivins, Heffron, & Sweet, 1997). Parents are usually more skilled at reading and responding to their child's cues than even the most sensitive professionals. However, when the relationship between parent and child is strained or maladaptive and there is no substitute relationship, the long-term consequences for the child can be very negative (Williamson, 1996). Observations of interactions between the child and parent allow professionals to learn methods of intervention from the parent that have proven successful for the family and child, as well as ways in which the professional can offer support for more successful interactions.

Parker and Zuckerman (1990) suggested that one of the goals of the assessment process should be to determine the level of involvement in the intervention process that is most beneficial for the family. For some families, it is constructive to have a very active role in the intervention process. Other families are so overwhelmed by their own and their child's demands that additional roles cannot easily be assumed and are often an added burden that might seriously strain existing resources. For all families, interventions that build upon and support existing strengths in the child–caregiver relationship are most likely to succeed.

Bailey (1991) noted that every interaction with a family constitutes an assessment. Moreover, every assessment can be viewed as an intervention. Greater awareness of realistic developmental expectations for children at different ages may be all the intervention some families require. Although research clearly shows that the family relationship is central to children's development (Barnard, Morisset, & Spieker, 1993; Crnic, Greenberg, Ragozin, Robinson, & Basham, 1983; Rauh, Achenbach, Nurcombe, Howell, & Teti, 1988; Sameroff, 1993; Sameroff & Fiese, 1990), families vary. No single intervention that would be applicable to all situations is meaningful or desirable. Of those assessments that are designed to focus specifically on these issues, the Nursing Child Assessment Feeding and Teaching Scales (Barnard, 1994; Morisset, 1994) are particularly effective in highlighting the different styles of interaction between parents and very young children.

Framework of Typical Development

Early intervention requires an understanding of child growth and development. Growth in the early years is rapid and is accompanied by large variations in when and how children manifest different skills and behaviors. Cultural influences that may affect opportunities for learning may alter the arrival and appearance of developmental milestones. By viewing the development of all children on a continuum, most children who are born with disabilities or developmental delays can be viewed from the perspective of children who are not yet functioning as expected in given areas, rather than children who are unable to acquire the skills of typically developing children. Assessment frameworks that exemplify this view of development provide important information for parents and interventionists because they place the child's achievements within a normal continuum of accomplishments. They suggest a series of steps or experiences that must be rendered, rather than a set of milestones the child has failed to reach. A productive approach to assessing typical development is to observe the child in naturally occurring play situations that are both structured and unstructured. Some methods of play-based assessment are well developed and can be used as highly effective methods of obtaining critical information about children's development and their relationships to people and objects in their world (see the Transdisciplinary Play-Based Assessment [TPBA; Linder, 1993], as well as the methods of interpreting unstructured play described by Segal & Webber [1996] and Wieder [1996]).

Emphasis on Organizing and Functional Capabilities of the Child

As children learn to organize their experiences, they are increasingly able to learn about the world and to participate in it actively. Skills or behaviors with no functional application, learned and tested out of context, have no place in early intervention (Goodman & Pollak, 1993). The goal should be to help children make meaning of their world and help them to participate in it. Toward that end, assessment of discrete areas of functioning (e.g., auditory discrimination or visual-motor integration) or specific skills (e.g., acquisition of pincer grasp or number of words used) should take place only to inform our understanding of the child's attempts to master a given area or to better learn about the resources the child brings to the learning situation. In short, knowledge of a child's skills or abilities is only part of the challenge. Knowledge about how the child uses those skills and abilities, what motivates the child, what is frustrating, and what is satisfying, as well as the availability of experiences for eliciting, supporting, and extending skills and abilities, are also necessary.

Greenspan's (1992) approach to assessing children's development – particularly their emotional development – focuses directly on the functional capacities of the child. Called the *Functional Emotional Assessment Scale (FEAS)*, this approach embeds assessment in the context of structured play interactions with the child's caregivers. Among the core capacities of the child that are evaluated are "the child's capacity for self-regulation, engagement, elaborating symbols and representations, and creating logical bridges or differentiations within his or her emerging symbolic world ('emotional thinking')" (Greenspan, 1996, p. 232). The child's interactions with adults are evaluated in terms of a number of specific expected primary emotional capacities. Greenspan's goal is to use this information to devise interventions that will build strong and supportive relationships between the child and his or her caregivers and to enhance the child's core capacities to explore, utilize, and master challenges in the extrafamilial environment.

Identify Current and Emerging Competencies and Strengths

The traditional model of assessment operates in terms of deficits by sorting and sifting children into different categories of disability or pathology. Identifying children's competencies and examining how those competencies emerge is an integral part of more recently developed assessments (Meisels & Fenichel, 1996). The child's strengths and competencies alert us to the personal and ecological resources that a child may be able to call upon to meet subsequent developmental challenges. They also aid us in fashioning interventions that make good use of available strengths and resources (see Provence, Erikson, Vater, & Palmeri, 1995).

How a child manifests a particular skill or behavior is equally and sometimes more important than the mere quantitative presence or absence of the ability (Meisels, 1994). For example, a child with motoric challenges may be able to walk but may have difficulty scanning the environment for obstacles or stopping and turning when necessary. For such a child, walking may not be very functional, even though it is a skill he or she has acquired. The context in which the child can perform the skill is also critical for understanding the child's capacities and challenges. Can the child get around on different floor surfaces? Does the child play and explore on calm days but tend to sit, watch, and suck his or her thumb when things get confusing? Can the child draw a circle on a horizontal surface but not on an easel? Does the child need to master a simple gestural symbol system in order to communicate with peers, although family members respond to different, highly familiar cues from the child? Answers to these questions lead to a more differentiated view of the child's skills and resources, and ultimately to a more individualized set of interventions. These qualitative observations may also suggest the shape

of the child's trajectory in acquiring more stable, adaptable, and well-differentiated skills.

Many of the assessments described in this chapter adopt this functional approach to recognizing stable and emergent skills and capacities, as seen in the IDA (Provence et al., 1995), the FEAS (Greenspan, 1992), the TPBA (Linder, 1993), and naturalistic play observations (Segal & Webber, 1996). These approaches begin with a recognition of what the child can do and with an attempt to understand the context in which the child is most familiar. The child's functional capabilities and the child's natural environment form the anchors from which it becomes possible to learn more about the child's areas of difficulty in everyday functioning and relationships, as well as the areas in which skills are in the process of consolidation and emergence.

Collaborative Process

Assessment of young children should be based on the quality of the working relationship between parents and professionals (Weston, Irvins, Heffron, & Sweet, 1997). The professional's job is not to promote her or his view of the child to the parent but to join the parents and other professionals in viewing the child multidimensionally in order to contribute to the generation of strategies that will help the child make developmental advances and organize his or her world more adequately.

A variety of parent report instruments and protocols for parent interviews is available to help inform the assessment process (see, for example, the AEPS Family Report [Bricker, 1993], the Vineland Scales of Adaptive Behavior [Sparrow, Balla, & Cicchetti, 1984], and the Minnesota Child Development Inventory [Ireton, 1992]). These instruments provide different perspectives on a child's behaviors. Designed to be easily understood by most parents, they allow for active parental participation in the assessment process and give parents an awareness of the normative lens through which professionals view children. They can provide a starting point in the conversation between parents and professionals.

Parents play a vital role in helping the professional understand how familial and cultural contexts influence the child's repertoire of skills. Professionals must maintain positions of cultural reciprocity when interpreting assessment findings and making recommendations to families (Barrera, 1996; Harry, 1992; Kalyanpur, 1996). This means that the professional must identify the values inherent in professional interpretations and recommendations, determine if these values are congruent with the value system of the family, and explain to families the assumptions underlying these recommendations. Professionals need to take into account the cultural differences identified and, together with the child's family, find the most effective means of adapting professional recommendations to meet the needs of the child in a manner that is culturally relevant (Barrera, 1996). Parents are most apt to follow through on recommendations when they and the professional hold similar perceptions of the child's needs and strengths, the professional is perceived by the family as a caring individual, information is presented clearly and precisely, and when possible, both parents are involved in conferences or consultations (Human & Teglasi, 1993).

Overall, the key to a successful assessment goes well beyond "establishing rapport" – the first step described in most test manuals. Successful relationships require rapport as a necessary condition, but rapport is not sufficient for learning about a child and family's needs and strengths. Other features of the relationship include respect, reciprocity, and flexibility. These characteristics are key to establishing a framework in which honest and meaningful interactions can take place.

Assessment as the Beginning of Intervention

A complete assessment includes information about how to facilitate the child's development and the supports that are needed to help the child exhibit desirable behaviors. When assessment occurs in isolation from intervention, particularly when it is dependent on traditional norm-referenced instruments, the outcome of assessment may be confusing, misleading, and ultimately counterproductive. It is only by testing the hypotheses uncovered during the assessment that we can fully evaluate the validity of an assessment. The intervention not only confirms or disconfirms the assessment hypotheses, it also elicits new hypotheses – new information – that is in itself an assessment of "current functioning" (Meisels, 1996).

However, the notion of current functioning is extremely narrow. A child's current functioning changes from moment to moment. The success of an assessment can be viewed in part as a function of its predictive invalidity. That is, as the information acquired from an assessment alters the context and content of the intervention, the current functioning of the child changes and is transformed. Needed is continuous assessment that is incorporated into the intervention so that the two functions become virtually seamless.

Reassessment as an Ongoing Process

This chapter strongly supports the view that assessment and intervention should be interactive processes in which each informs the other. For this to occur, reassessments must take place. Reassessments are written into state and federal laws in order to prevent children from being abandoned in special classes or programs, never to make a transition to a more appropriate or less restrictive environment.

However, reassessments, or reevaluation, can have another meaning that is more functional and potentially even more critical for the overall growth and development of children. Reevaluation can serve as an opportunity to reflect on the effect of the intervention. Every intervention provides some information that can be used as part of an assessment to create a new and more differentiated intervention. The metaphor that may be most powerful here is that of a moving target and of successive approximations to that target. Children's development is a moving target of skills, knowledge, experiences, dispositions, and personality variables. As we begin the process of assessing children, we draw a bead on these elements or targets, but each time that we do so they seem to change before our very eyes. This is especially true as we begin to transfer the knowledge acquired through assessment into the arena of intervention. Here we are dealing with a set of dynamic variables that simply will not remain fixed. Every intervention alters the child in some way – sometimes for the better, as when the child breaks through to a new skill, and sometimes for the worse, as when the child's motivation to learn is diminished by continuing experiences of failure and frustration. Reevaluation on a continuing basis is essential if parents and professionals are to understand what they should try to do next with the child. Information about the child's prior history is useful but quickly loses its power and relevance with very young children. Constant infusions of new assessment information, acquired in the process of intervention, are essential to maximize the relationship between the child, the child's family, and professionals.

ELEMENTS OF EARLY CHILDHOOD ASSESSMENT

The following sections describe five elements of early childhood assessment that build on the research of recent years and the principles noted earlier. Reflecting an outlook on assessment that reaches out to the next generation of research and development of new procedures, approaches, and instruments (see Meisels, 1996, for background about these elements), the five elements are as follows:

1. Target of assessments
2. Context of assessments
3. Methods of assessments
4. Assessment personnel
5. Fusion of assessment and intervention

Each element is discussed in turn, and research supporting and elaborating the elements is presented. Assessment methods that exemplify each element are also discussed.

Target of Assessment

Traditionally, assessments focused primarily on the child in isolation. With the passage of IDEA, practitioners began to address both the child and the family in an additive rather than an integrative approach. Today, assessments are considered incomplete unless they view the child in relation to his or her family and caregivers; that is, a child within a family within a larger ecosystem. The extensive research about the impact of parent–child relationships on development is key to this point of view. Children's growth and development are highly influenced by the caregiving environment in which the child is reared, and the child in turn influences caregivers' interactions. We have known for many years that parental socioeconomic status (SES) and education are key predictors of childhood developmental outcomes (Beckwith, 1990). Sameroff

and his colleagues (Sameroff, 1993; Sameroff & Chandler, 1975; Sameroff & Fiese, 1990; Sameroff, Seifer, Barocas, Zax, & Greenspan, 1987), as well as other researchers, have highlighted the importance of family variables in numerous studies with varied samples and data collected under both short- and long-term conditions (Barnard, Morisset, & Spieker, 1993; Crnic, Greenberg, Ragozin, Robinson, & Basham, 1983; Rauh, Achenbach, Nurcombe, Howell, & Teti, 1988).

Research by Bernstein and his colleagues made this point quite dramatically. Focusing on low-income, multiproblem families, they demonstrated that mother–infant interaction is a helpful marker of infants who are experiencing difficulties in development and who are at risk for optimal growth (Bernstein, Jeremy, & Marcus, 1986). Bernstein, Hans, and Percansky (1991) noted that the parent–child relationship mediates the effects of risk. In fact, even such perinatal insults as intraventricular hemorrhage are more closely associated with social and interactional factors than with biological variables. Introducing Goldberg's (1997) construct of *mutual competence*, which includes contingent responsivity on the part of the parent and efforts to make maximal use of environmental and personal resources in order to help the child begin to acquire a sense of self as an effective agent, Bernstein et al. suggested that the development of increasingly effective interactions and communication patterns between parent and infant are linked directly to more positive child outcomes. This is seen clearly in a study that Bernstein and Hans (1994) conducted with a group of forty-two 2-year-olds who were born exposed to methadone and a group of nonexposed children. The mothers of children in both groups also participated in this two-year longitudinal study. The investigators found that poorer developmental outcomes among the infants were predicted by cumulative environmental risk factors and not by methadone exposure per se. They concluded that women who used methadone and who had communication problems with their children had children with particularly problematic outcomes. The combination of biological risk (methadone) and maternal substance abuse combined to limit development.

Other studies provide additional data that demonstrate the futility of assessments that target the child alone or even the child primarily. Cardon and Fulker

(1991) used structural equation models with a longitudinal data set of 208 twin pairs followed from 7–36 months to study the sources of continuity between nine measures of infant cognitive processing and later childhood IQ. In this study of the relation between specific infant measures and general mental ability tests administered later in infancy and early childhood, the authors found evidence of discontinuity between skills assessed by infant measures and later general ability or IQ scores. The specific skills measured by the infant assessments were apparently not incorporated into later general ability measurements. Instead, they seemed to be related to general cognitive ability in only a relatively unstable manner. Furthermore, Cardon and Faulker noted that neither the genetic nor the environmental sources of variance in the longitudinal measurements adequately explain the outcomes they observed. Rather, continuity in development is a result of both children's genetic makeup and the features of the infant's home environment. A single target of assessment is likely to be "off target."

Several researchers who have studied high-risk children beyond infancy have concluded that the child's embeddedness in a context is key to understanding and evaluating the child's potential for achievement in school. Fowler and Cross (1986) followed 210 preschoolers and their parents. Using regression techniques they examined the relation to achievement scores in reading and mathematics of maternal education, results of two brief screening tests, age and sex of the child, and history of learning problems in the child's family. They found that maternal education, family history of learning problems, physician ratings of the child's attention span for academic activities, and developmental screening tasks that tapped cognitive and visual motor skills were highly related to early academic achievement and successful grade completion. Their study demonstrated that environmental factors and SES variables have a much higher correlation with school achievement than variables that are defined typically as biological or medical in origin. Fowler and Cross concluded their research by emphasizing an approach to evaluating preschoolers for academic risk that does not reduce that risk to a single variable.

Gorman and Pollitt (1996) also examined the relationship among a variety of environmental, medical, and developmental risk factors and children's risk for academic problems. They studied rural Guatemalan children in order to understand better the role of schooling in buffering risk. The subjects were part of a sample of 222 children who had been studied for more than twenty years. Now in their adolescence, these subjects were considered extremely high risk for biological and environmental deficits.

Gorman and Pollitt (1996) reported three major findings. First, exposure to increasing numbers of risk factors during early childhood was clearly related to lower school achievement and poorer test performance in adolescence; second, early risk exposure and performance in school are associated independently with adolescent test performance; and third, good schooling exerts a "buffering effect . . . for those exposed to high levels of early risk" (p. 322). As others have found (cf. Rutter, 1987; Sameroff, Seifer, Barocas, Zax, & Greenspan, 1987; Werner, 1990), developmental outcomes are highly associated in a linear fashion with the number of risk factors in a child's life. The greater the number of risks, the greater the adverse impact on children's development. Schooling was found to be a buffer for children with numerous risk factors in their lives, but schooling alone could not compensate for the effects of severe risk. The conclusion of this highly significant study echoes earlier research: Development is multiply determined. It is not the result of singular variables or isolated factors. Only when children are studied in context can we hope to understand the forces that affect them, the likelihood that these forces will alter their trajectory of growth and development, and the ways in which we might support families and children.

Even among children who are considered to be at low risk biologically, the prevalence of familial psychosocial problems and environmental risks can have negative impacts on their health and development. Kemper, Osborn, Hansen, and Pascoe (1994) surveyed a sample of more than 400 "low-risk" mothers of children younger than age 6 and found that psychosocial problems were prevalent. This research focused primarily on demographic factors, dysfunction in the mother's family of origin, maternal depression, and maternal substance abuse. The findings suggest that children may be at risk for environmental and familial difficulties even when they are not members of typical high-risk groups. Early identification of adverse factors in children's lives requires a multidimensional approach that is not limited to any single variable, whether that variable includes biological and constitutional factors, environmental and SES elements, or familial influences. A focus on the broad context that makes up a child's world is called for in this and other research in order to advance our understanding of risk and protective factors.

Examples of such multidimensional approaches are to be found in a number of programs of early identification. Nord, Zill, Prince, Clarke, and Ventura (1994) created a composite risk index based on data collected as part of the National Longitudinal Study of Youth. Their purpose was to develop a new child health index that would relate to children's readiness to learn upon entry to school. The risk index included the following information, all available from standard birth certificates:

1. Late (third trimester) or no prenatal care
2. Low maternal weight gain (<21 lbs.)
3. Closely spaced birth (within 18 months to same mother)
4. Three or more older siblings
5. Maternal smoking during pregnancy
6. Maternal alcohol during pregnancy

Nord and her colleagues showed that this index significantly predicted children's school success at age 4 and 5, even after controlling for such important confounding factors as maternal education, race, ethnicity, and mothers' own mental ability. This study provides additional evidence concerning the importance of incorporating environmental and familial data into assessments of children's well-being.

Additional support can be derived from other forms of assessment that incorporate risk indexes but that also go beyond them. Kochanek and Buka (1991) described a population-based screening model designed to identify infants and toddlers with developmental disabilities and those who are substantially at risk. This model was designed to obtain information about child and family needs and to create linkages with community-based resources and programs. It contains the four components shown in Table 11.2.

Implementing this system, Kochanek and Buka (1991) found that both child- and family-centered screening components made a unique contribution to the identification of vulnerable children. However, family environmental factors accounted for a much greater proportion of those children who performed poorly on follow-up. On a nearly 3:1 basis, family-related variables were implicated in follow-up decisions, as compared with child-related variables. This study thus fulfills a dual purpose: It shows that vulnerability can occur within both the biologic and ecologic systems, and it presents a model of infant/toddler/family screening that is built on the premise that the child should not be the sole target of assessment in the first years of life.

In short, there is strong support for the contention that "the traditional model of diagnosis/placement has little or no bearing within early childhood special education...because the focus of the diagnosis/placement model is on the child and not on the family within which the child lives" (Shriver, Kramer, & Garnett, 1993, p. 268). A change in assumptions is needed wherein child assessment is understood to mean child-within-family assessment. We cannot know the child in isolation from his or her family. Without viewing the child within the familial context, inferences about young children's developmental status will be incomplete, and generalizations about children's developmental trajectories may be seriously flawed.

Context of Assessment

Traditionally, assessments of young children have taken place under controlled circumstances in highly structured environments that were as similar to one another as possible. In recent years, we have begun to witness an emphasis on conducting assessments within naturalistic settings that are comfortable, familiar, nonthreatening, and of interest to the child (cf. Meisels & Provence, 1989). By definition, such settings are not homogeneous. Considerations of the context of assessment bring with them issues of social validity. Bagnato and Neisworth (1994) defined social validity in assessment as the "ecological characteristics of assessment information, the acceptability of the methods employed, and the importance of the data derived" (p. 82). When social validity is ignored, the probability of obtaining accurate assessment results is diminished.

TABLE 11.2. Components of a Population-Based Screening Model

1. *Multifaceted screening components* (i.e., screening data are collected about the infant's biological circumstances and developmental competence as well as family needs, strengths, resources, support systems, and quality and quantity of the child–parent relationship);
2. *Multiple information sources* (i.e., parents, professionals, other family, or community members who know the child and family well);
3. *Periodicity* (screening should occur on multiple occasions in the first 3 years of life to account for the wide variability in child development and because of late-appearing manifestations of risk);
4. *Dual level screening.* Level 1 screening is very brief and is intended to capture highly significant, macro–scopic components that can be used to identify children in need of more in-depth follow-up. Level 2 screening is conducted within the home. It is a comprehensive process that includes information on the child's developmental competence; family strengths, needs, and support systems; and the generic quality of the caregiving environment.

Adapted from: Kochanek & Buka, 1991.

Bracken (1987) suggested that discrepancies between two or more assessments that seek to assess similar skills may be attributable to the context of assessment: the ecology in which the assessments occur. Some elements of this context include the following:

1. Motivation, state of arousal, disposition, and health of the child
2. Examiner–examinee differences in rapport or race, culture, sex, or even size
3. Examiner differences in level of competence
4. Environmental differences in terms of physical and emotional comfort for the child
5. Familiarity with the examiner or the materials used in assessment

Other factors that are associated more closely with the developmental capacities of children rather than with factors exogenous to the child play a role in evaluating the social ecology of assessments. For example, young children have a restricted ability to comprehend assessment cues. Cues consist of verbal instructions, visual stimuli, situational clues, or other instructions and stimuli. Young children have a great deal of difficulty attending to such cues. Culture may play a role in determining which cues are most salient to children (Rogoff, 1990). Further, traditional assessments require that examiners elicit and children respond. The child is rarely the initiator. Elicited language in particular may be qualitatively different from language that is used functionally in everyday contexts and

thus is not representative of the child's functioning. Second, young children's verbal and perceptual-motor response capabilities are limited when compared with older children. Young children's emergent verbal abilities often require that examiners make inferences based on the child's overt motor behaviors, or parent report, rather than direct response. Third, some types of questions require complex information-processing skills that young children do not possess. Multistep instructions or requests for information from young children are generally highly inappropriate. Finally, young children may have difficulty understanding the demand characteristics of the measurement situation, and they may not be able to control their behavior to meet these demands. Many factors, including cultural background, experience in similar situations, and associations with previous assessments, can play a role in influencing children's behavior in such settings (see Meisels, 1994, for an elaboration of these points).

All of these factors contribute to the instability of early childhood measurement results. When we develop assessments that take social validity into account, we find that designations of risk may change dramatically. Hall and Barnett (1991) showed that estimates of who is at risk can be altered by using alternative measures for assessing risk status or by focusing on family characteristics rather than limiting ourselves to information about the child's developmental level. In short, assessments that take context into account provide very different information from those that attempt to be context- or culture-free.

Of great concern is what has come to be called "ethnic validity" (or "cultural competence") – the "relevance of traditional assessment procedures and special education services to children of different ethnic groups" (Barnett, MacMann, & Carey, 1992, p. 30). Overall, ethnic or cultural issues are given serious consideration all too infrequently when young children are assessed, although we ignore ethnic validity only at our peril and that of the children we are assessing. For example, most assessments are based on a cultural perspective that values independence rather than collectivity. Thus, a 2-year-old is usually expected to be performing some self-care activities such as feeding or even dressing him- or herself. Yet, in some cultures, children this young are not encouraged to achieve independence in self-care until much later (Lynch & Hanson, 1992).

The social and cultural validity of an assessment has significant implications for classifications among children aged 3–21 years. Andrews, Wisniewski, and Mullick (1997) pointed out that African American children are more likely to be classified as mildly mentally retarded than learning disabled. For Caucasians, though, the opposite finding holds. They are more likely to be classified as having a specific learning disability rather than mild mental retardation. In other words, contextual variables can influence how children are assessed, the conclusions that are drawn from those assessments, and the interventions that are ultimately delivered to them.

The assessment of social–ecological process is sometimes called "ecobehavioral analysis" – a method that "focuses on natural systems such as families, classrooms, schools, and communities. . . . It establishes a broad context for understanding adjustment and planning interventions by requiring multiple perspectives for each stage of problem solving" (Barnett, MacMann, & Carey, 1992, p. 35). This approach carries with it several implications about how assessments should be constructed. When we engage in ecobehavioral analysis and contextual assessment, and when we are concerned about ethnic validity, it follows that our assessments will be marked by multiple sources and multiple methods; by recognition of the need to assess the child within the context of the family; and by inclusion of information about the home environment, parent–

child interactions, and family social support networks (Sexton, Thompson, Perez, & Rheams, 1990). Moreover, these assessments will take place over time, rather than on a single occasion.

Researchers who have adopted this broad contextual view have reported findings that are fairly striking. For example, in Brooks-Gunn, Klebanov, and Duncan's (1996) study of the links among poverty, ethnicity, and intelligence test scores, they found that IQ differences between Black and White 5-year-olds were eliminated almost completely when they adjusted for such contextual variables as difficulty of neighborhood economic conditions, family poverty, maternal education, and prior learning experiences. Their study highlights differences in the meaning of tests and test items for subgroups of children who are not White and middle class. Brooks-Gunn et al. concluded that intelligence tests and other cognitive tests are culturally biased and are not equivalent across cultures.

Another perspective on this issue emerges from a study that examined age versus schooling effects on the development of intelligence. Cahan and Cohen (1989) evaluated children's IQ scores at the end of elementary school in terms of their age and amount of schooling. They found that increases in intelligence scores were highly associated with length of schooling and that schooling had a significant impact on gains in verbal rather than in nonverbal scores. The significance of these findings for this discussion about the context of assessment is that schooling and intervention in general represent a marker for a plethora of environmental variables that are all but ignored when we consider age-based norms alone, as is commonly done when children are assessed outside of their lived contexts. Such norms penalize children with less optimal experience. If attention is not paid to these contextual variables, accurate conclusions about development will be unattainable. With limited resources available, it is essential to identify those children and families who can benefit most optimally from intervention, and this requires a broad view of the child in context.

The Transdisciplinary Play-Based Assessment (TPBA; Linder, 1993) is one example of a contextually sensitive assessment. The TPBA is a comprehensive transdisciplinary approach to developmental assessment that is based on the premise that developmental functions are interdependent and that children's development is influenced by a variety of factors. TPBA reflects a functional approach to assessing young children with disabilities, or those at risk for developmental delay, by actively involving the child, the child's parents, and other professionals in a natural environment of assessment and intervention. TPBA is organized around the planning of a play session that is based on information about the child's developmental status acquired from the parents. Materials that are appropriate for the child's developmental level are used to encourage the child to play using various play strategies and developmental skills. One team member is assigned to facilitate the child's play and to encourage the expression of optimal abilities. Guidelines are provided for observing the cognitive, social-emotional, communication and language, and sensorimotor capacities of the child. Fundamental to this assessment is the ecobehavioral validity of its methods, materials, and techniques.

Because the assessment is planned with the family, and information is acquired from family members as well as from others who are familiar with the child, the baseline for the assessment is close to the family's experience. Multiple opportunities for the child to interact with new and familiar materials are provided, and many observers are included in the assessment in order to capture as many perspectives as possible. Parents complete a preassessment inventory that provides valuable information about the child's developmental level and skills and also assists the team in preparing an environment that will elicit the child's optimal abilities. The assessment itself involves several phases: 1) unstructured facilitation in which the examiner follows and expands on the child's lead; 2) structured facilitation in which the examiner attempts to elicit behaviors that were not demonstrated spontaneously in phase one; 3) introduction of a peer in order to observe child-to-child interaction; 4) parental play with the child in both structured and unstructured ways; 5) structured and unstructured motor play; and 6) snack, which allows for screening of oral-motor capacities as well as social and adaptive development. Throughout the observation period a staff member discusses with the parent the representativeness of the child's behaviors, some of the professional interpretation of behaviors, and the parent's perception of the child's performance. Observers are guided in their observations by questions that address both quantitative and qualitative aspects of the child's behavior rather than just the presence or absence of behavior. Once the assessment is complete, and the guidelines provided are reviewed in terms of the child's behavior and accomplishments, transdisciplinary recommendations are developed and a program-planning meeting is convened to provide additional feedback for the child's parents and others working with the child. This experience is designed to be highly respectful of the child, the child's family, and the culture in which the child is reared.

Methods of Assessment

As the TPBA demonstrates, assessment methods have changed dramatically from highly specialized procedures administered in formalized environments in a constrained manner to approaches that make use of everyday experiences that more adequately enable children to show what they know, what they can do, and what they are experiencing (Meisels, 1996). Many reasons can be advanced to explain these changes, not the least being the motivation to design assessments that are ecologically more valid. Other reasons for the change in methodology, however, can be found in the dissatisfaction among professionals concerning the conventional model of norm-referenced assessment.

In a study of several hundred psychologists who work with young children, Bagnato and Neisworth (1994) found that only 4% of their respondents supported the use of norm-referenced, standardized intelligence tests for young children with developmental problems. Most respondents to their survey emphasized the importance of flexibility in choice of assessment methods, the potential for modification of the instruments, and the need for a multidimensional, team-based assessment approach.

Problems with the use of norm-referenced tests with special populations are legion. According to Fuchs, Fuchs, Benowitz, and Barringer (1987), some of the major difficulties include the following:

1. Inappropriateness of test content for certain subgroups of the population
2. Inadequate technical characteristics of the instruments
3. Biases against low SES examinees

4. Irrelevance of the assessment to the intervention process
5. Errors by examiners in selecting appropriate tests
6. Inaccuracies of examiners in administration and scoring
7. Poor fit between intervention recommendations and the assessment data
8. Absence of children with disabilities from the samples used to develop test norms

Fuchs et al. (1987) suggested that before a test may be considered nondiscriminatory, or unbiased, it is necessary to demonstrate that it measures with equal accuracy the skills and abilities of children both with and without disabilities. Few norm-referenced tests can make this claim legitimately, however. At best, most instruments include small studies with children who represent only one or two disability categories, and the analyses seem limited to showing the instruments' ability to discriminate these children from those who are developing typically.

Other researchers have described a host of other problems attributable to the use of conventional psychometric instruments with special populations. Meltzer and Reid (1994) listed six criticisms of psychometric techniques. These include 1) emphasizing the end product of learning and ignoring the processes and strategies children use for problem solving; 2) failing to distinguish between a child's current level of performance and his or her ability to learn and acquire new skills and information; 3) not providing information that is useful for intervention; 4) ignoring the role of motivation, personality, social factors, and cultural issues; 5) not measuring qualitative and quantitative changes that are consequent upon development; and 6) misclassification and incorrect special education placements.

In addition to these problems, assessments of young children – whether the children are disabled, high risk, or developing typically – are vulnerable to numerous psychometric problems. These problems manifest themselves in lack of agreement across measures, unreliability of instruments, circularity of the criterion measures (i.e., one test is used to establish the validity of another, which in turn is validated with the first measure), and problems of treatment validity (the relationship of the assessment to beneficial treatment outcomes) (Barnett, MacMann, & Carey, 1992).

Bracken (1988) described in detail some of the psychometric problems associated with standardized, norm-referenced tests. In particular, he addressed a set of problems that is critical to early intervention. Nearly all states mandate that eligibility be based on a percentage of delay on a norm-referenced or criterion-referenced test or a predetermined standard deviation of scores from the mean. However, most tests that seem to be similar to one another nevertheless produce dissimilar results. This has enormous implications for this method of assigning eligibility. Bracken listed ten reasons that explain the psychometric differences among tests. After a brief summary of these reasons, we use the Battelle Developmental Inventory (BDI; Newborg, Stock, Wnek, Guidabaldi, & Svinicki, 1984) to illustrate some of these issues.

First, tests may have different *floor effects*. The floor is the lower range of standard scores. If the floor is too high, it will not be possible for low-functioning children to respond to questions correctly, and thus it is impossible to measure their abilities. Second, tests usually have different *ceilings*. A test with a low ceiling will not distinguish between a highly able child and a child who is only average or slightly above average. Third, tests differ by *item gradients*. This relates to the content validity of a test, because a test should be able to sample the full range of content across all difficulty levels. If the gradients between items are too steep, then elements of a domain will be missed and a child's full performance will not be tapped. Some instruments may use seven to ten items to determine whether a child is performing significantly below average, whereas other instruments may use only one or two items. Fourth, *norm tables* are not similar across instruments. The arrangement of dates for establishing norms is a critical element in establishing scores. If the "anniversary dates" (i.e., when the child passes from one norm table to another) differ between instruments, the results of the two tests are usually incompatible.

Fifth, some tests use *age* or *grade equivalents* for making comparisons among children. Such statistics, however, do not possess the psychometric characteristics of standard scores and should not be used for diagnostic or placement decisions. These equivalents are often derived from but not supported by empirical evidence. The sixth reason for psychometric differences between apparently similar tests concerns *reliability differences*. Tests that do not have high reliabilities – that are not stable and consistent – contain much more measurement error than tests with high reliability. Seventh, differences in *skills assessed across tests* can produce significantly different scores because of lack of overlap in the specific skills measured by each instrument. Eighth, *content differences* often occur in tests that purportedly measure equivalent constructs or domains, with concomitant implications for comparisons between tests and test takers. Ninth, *publication dates* play a role in the ability to compare performance across tests, because norms shift over time. Finally, the *representativeness of the norming sample* must be taken into account: "When a sample is drawn in such a way that it does not accurately represent the population, an unknown amount of error results in the development of the norms" (Bracken, 1988, p. 164). Because children with disabilities are rarely included in such samples, the likelihood of these instruments being accurate for such children is low.

BATTELLE DEVELOPMENTAL INVENTORY. Considered norm-referenced and curriculum compatible, the Battelle is widely used in both eligibility decisions and program planning in early childhood intervention (Bagnato, Neisworth, & Munson, 1997; Goodman & Pollak, 1993). It consists of 341 items grouped in five domains: Adaptive, Cognitive, Communication, Motor, and Personal–Social. It is one of the few measures that includes children with disabilities in its standardization group. The BDI spans the age range from birth to 8 years and thus can be used to assess children who tend to fall between infant and preschool measures. The BDI items can be administered directly or through parent interview. It also has a screening version consisting of items selected from the larger BDI.

Despite its wide use, many problems have been noted with both its psychometric integrity and its applicability to curriculum. Some researchers claim that the BDI overestimates the number of preschoolers classified as developmentally delayed (Bagnato, Neisworth, & Munson, 1997). The concerns raised about the BDI are explored in order to illustrate some of the more general problems already identified in using norm-referenced tests to establish eligibility for services for children with special needs.

Standardization. The BDI's standardization sample included only 100 children at each 6-month age range from birth to 24 months. Assuming a normal distribution among these 6-month periods, each month is represented by fewer than seventeen children. Knowing the rapid growth and developmental change that takes place in the first 2 years of life, this sample size is insufficient to represent the diversity that is found in a national population. After the age of 23 months, only 100 children compose the norming sample for the entire year; that is, slightly more than eight children per month if evenly distributed by age. This contrasts with the Bayley Scales of Infant Development II, which includes 100 children per month until age 6 months, then 100 children for every two months until age 12 months. From 12–30 months, the Bayley's standardization sample incorporates 100 children for every three months (i.e., 400 children per year after the first year). Clearly, greater confidence can be placed in the norms obtained from the Bayley II than from the BDI.

Reliability. There are many problems in obtaining reliable scores with the BDI. In a statewide implementation study of the Battelle in North Carolina, Bailey, Vandiviere, Dellinger, and Munn (1987) conducted an investigation with seventy-six teachers of 247 two- to five-year olds with disabilities. Teachers rated the Battelle as being less helpful for children with more severe handicapping conditions than for those with less significant impairments, and many errors were made in scoring the BDI. Because of its complicated scoring procedures, about one half-hour is required to score each protocol, and the scoring process resulted in many errors. Only eleven teachers (14.5%) and fifty protocols (20.2%) had no scoring errors. The most common errors were simple mistakes in arithmetic (44.7% of the teachers; 21.9% of the protocols), followed by difficulties establishing the basal (47% of the protocols; 43.4% of the teachers), and problems crediting the child for items below the basal (11.4% of the protocols; 28.9% of the teachers).

Validity. Although correlations between the Battelle and the Bayley have been reported in independent studies of samples of children with special needs, validity has not been confirmed with high-risk samples. Gerkin, Eliason, and Arthur (1994) did not find significant correlations between standard scores on the BSID and the BDI total or between the Mental Development Index on the BSID and all of the BDI domain scores with a sample of at-risk infants. These findings are consistent with the findings of Boliek and Obrzut (1991), who studied fifty typically developing infants and toddlers and obtained correlations between the BDI and the BSID that ranged from $r = .097$ to $.683$. The item gradients on the BDI are so steep that it does not discriminate easily among children who are within two standard deviations of the mean. In addition, for children more than two standard deviations below the mean, the developmental quotient is derived from a formula that occasionally results in negative developmental quotients.

Convergent validity was established for most of the domains (i.e., items in the same subscale are correlated with one another and so appear to measure related skills), but discriminant validity (i.e., the property of separating one group or one set of items from another) is problematic. In some domains, items within the subscales are more highly correlated with items in other subscales than with items in the same subscale. For example, the language and cognitive domains are highly intercorrelated ($r = .84$), and several of the subdomains in the cognitive domain are more highly correlated with the communication domain than with other areas in the cognitive domain. Gerkin et al. (1994) acknowledged problems with discriminant validity in the younger age group: "BDI factors (domains) tend to be more accurate with children over the age of two. For children under the age of two, there are only three factors which tend to be general" (p. 59). Despite this, the manual permits use of the subscale scores to determine eligibility for children aged 24 months and younger.

The criterion-related validity studies reported in the BDI manual use scales that are not normed on infants (Wechsler Intelligence Scale for Children – Revised [WISC–R] and Stanford–Binet) or instruments that measure discrete areas of functioning (e.g., the Vineland). No age data are reported for the validity studies, but given the criterion measures that were used, it is doubtful that infants were included in the sample. Ershler and Elliot (1992) also questioned the validity of the Battelle, pointing out problems with BDI's cutoff scores, its inconsistent representation of subdomains across age levels, unequal succession of items in terms of their difficulty

level across age categories, and absence of evidence of content validity.

Norms Tables. Strong "birthday effects" with the BDI were noted by several researchers (Boyd, 1989; Gerkin, Eliason, & Arthur, 1994; McLinden, 1989). Because of the configuration of the norms tables, children who score in the normal (average) range (DQ = 100) on the BDI two weeks before their 6-month birthday will qualify for special education services immediately following their birthday. Therefore, most children can qualify for special services if the assessment is timed close to a cutoff.

The 1988 recalibration of norms included in the BDI manual was intended to correct the skewed nature of the score distribution by using the median age performance for the age-equivalency norms. However, examination of the age-equivalency tables and the percentile rank tables indicate continuing problems with severe birthday effects and an incongruence between age equivalencies and standard scores. For example, a 24-month-old with a raw score of 39 on the communication domain would be at the 14th percentile (more than two standard deviations below the mean and eligible for service if the norms tables are used). However, if the age-equivalent table is used, the raw score of 39 can be transformed into an age equivalent of 23, thus rendering the child ineligible for services.

Similarly, a 12-month-old with a raw score of 24 on the communication domain ranks at the 13th percentile, which is more than two standard deviations below the mean. This would entitle him or her to be eligible for service in virtually all states. However, the age-equivalent table would place her at 12 months, rendering her ineligible: Same child, same raw score, same time of test administration, but different tables within the same instrument giving very different results.

This type of problem is true not just of the domain scores but also of the total score. If a 12-month-old had a total raw score of 173, he or she would be in the 12th percentile (more than two standard deviations below the mean and definitely eligible according to state requirements). However, if the age-equivalent tables are used, his or her age-equivalent total score would be set at 13 months, and thus would not be eligible.

Sexton and colleagues (1988) used age-equivalent BDI scores rather than standard scores to study the performance of children with special needs and found the age-equivalent scores to be more reliable in describing the actual levels of young children. Boyd et al. (1989) also compared age-equivalent and standard scores for children with special needs and found correlations to be higher with the age equivalencies than studies using standard scores. These results are highly anomalous from a psychometric perspective.

The birthday effects continue as children grow older. On the BDI, standard scores are converted from percentiles by using a table. At every point in time from birth to 3 years, the mean raw score of one age group in the percentile rank tables falls more than two standard deviations below that of the next age group.

Subscales. Using the BDI, Newborg et al. (1994) did not report internal consistency coefficients for any of the subscales or complete scales. They argued that in order to compute these reliability coefficients, it is necessary that all of the test items measure the same skill or trait, but the BDI domains or subdomains do not have this characteristic. Attempts to replicate the factor structure reported in the Battelle for children with special needs were unsuccessful (Snyder, Lawson, Thompson, Stricklin, & Sexton, 1993). Only two to three factors were found – all different from those reported in the manual.

When comparing the Battelle to other preschool instruments, problems with the subscales are again highlighted. The fine motor domain on the Battelle correlates more highly with the Stanford–Binet than does the cognitive or communication domain ($r = .50$ for cognitive versus $r = .61$ with fine motor). Similarly, the WISC–R verbal intelligence score correlates with the BDI cognitive at only .43 and with communication at .46, although it correlates .68 with the fine motor.

Criterion-Reference. If we accept that there are problems with using the BDI to establish eligibility, what are the advantages of using it as a criterion-referenced instrument? This use is also arguable. Reviews of items found on IEPs indicate that the BDI and other developmental inventories influence IEP construction at the preschool level (Goodman & Pollak, 1993). However, the IEPs of children with severe mental impairments are similar to those of moderately and mildly mentally impaired students, indicating a lack of sensitivity to the range of individual needs. In a statewide study of the BDI, teachers reported that only two-thirds of the items correspond to important instructional targets (Bailey et al., 1987).

Summary. Arguments against clinically based instruments contend that they are not sufficiently objective and that their lack of standardization limits the reliability of the judgments based upon them. Most states require that standardized instruments be used to determine eligibility for special services. The BDI, however, demonstrates that standardization alone cannot guarantee reliable, valid estimates of children's developmental levels. Even when such instruments as the Battelle include individuals with disabilities in the normative group and attempt to target functional skills, problems remain that reduce its value in determining eligibility for service and in planning for intervention.

Assessment Personnel

Traditional models of assessment are dyadic: They include a subject who is assessed and an examiner who administers the test or assessment. This approach assumes a highly structured and formalized set of procedures that is followed uniformly, regardless of the examiner or the subject.

Current models of assessment – especially those used with young children – depart substantially from the traditional view. Since the passage of Public Law 94-142 in 1975 and its reauthorizations over the succeeding decades, assessments of individuals with disabilities have involved multiple examiners representing multiple disciplines. In addition, these multidisciplinary team evaluations incorporate active participation of the child's parents and they are scheduled on a recurrent basis, rather than on only one occasion.

In best practice, this multidisciplinary team discusses the observations of each participant and shares perspectives on the child's behaviors. This allows for the development of a more complete portrait of the child's strengths and abilities. Unfortunately, this collaboration does not always occur. Children may be examined by multiple professionals who come together only in order to give a report of their assessment of the child's functioning. Parents do not often have an active role in these meetings and function more as passive recipients of information. These so-called team meetings are sometimes reminiscent of the fable of the three blind men and the elephant – each of the three blind men goes forward to examine an elephant. The men then argue over their interpretation of the elephant. One has examined the trunk of the elephant and speaks of its strength and adaptive movement. One examines the leg and describes the breadth of this limb and the remarkable stability and balance it provides. The final blind man examines the tail and speaks of the narrow limb with quick movements. Each individual gives a true representation of what he examined, but none of the three portrays the whole and none can appreciate the influence of one part on the other. Mandates regarding team evaluations do not always translate into cooperative ventures.

DEVELOPMENTAL MONITORING AND DEVELOP-MENTAL SURVEILLANCE. Despite these mandates and other statements of best practice regarding early intervention that call for multidisciplinary evaluation (Beckman, 1996), there is encouragement within pediatrics to adopt a single-source approach to early identification in the primary health care setting. In recent years, the popularity of this approach (characterized as developmental surveillance, opportunistic surveillance, or developmental monitoring – although these terms are not necessarily equivalent), has grown within primary care pediatric practice.

According to Dworkin (1989, and also see this volume), developmental monitoring refers to "the process of closely watching children's development, without implying any specific process or technique. Monitoring may be periodic or continuous, systematic or informal, and may or may not involve such processes as screening, surveillance, or assessment" (p. 1001). First introduced in Great Britain, the rationale for developmental monitoring is tied to the purported limited validity of developmental screening instruments and the amount of time, effort, and money required to conduct such screenings, especially in the primary care medical setting (cf. Bain, 1989; Houston & Davis, 1985; Hutchison & Nicoll, 1988; Sturner, Funk, & Green, 1994).

Although few studies of the cost of developmental screening are available, Glascoe, Foster, and Wolraich (1997) studied the relative cost effectiveness of various approaches to early detection of

developmental disabilities in nearly 250 parents and their birth to 6-year-old children. Not surprisingly, they found that costs decreased as screening instruments increased in sensitivity and specificity. Overall, Glascoe et al.'s study supported the economic value of early detection and intervention. In a study of the use of the Ages and Stages Questionnaires (Bricker, Squires, Kaminski, & Mounts, 1988), a parent–report screening tool, Squires (1996) also reported on a number of methods for collecting screening data at low expense.

From another perspective, the expense associated with developmental screening can be viewed within a preventive framework of costs and benefits. Developmental screening represents a secondary level of prevention. It consists of actions taken to prevent a condition from becoming more severe or actions intended to halt the progress of a condition before it becomes debilitating (Meisels, 1988). Although only 5–7% of an unselected preschool population is actually at risk, the savings to society of identifying these children is significant in terms of avoidance of special education, later ability to pursue productive livelihoods, and general support for children and families.

From another perspective, evidence has been mounting for some time that screening can take place with substantial accuracy. Published reports of a variety of developmental screening instruments demonstrate sensitivity and specificity that is highly acceptable (see Glascoe & Byrne, 1993; Meisels et al., 1997; Meisels, Liaw, Henderson, Browning, & Ten Have, 1993; Squires, 1996; Squires & Bricker, 1991; Squires, Nickel, & Bricker, 1990), although the use of some screening instruments is still highly questionable (see, for example, Glascoe, Byrne, Ashford, Johnson, Chang, & Strickland's [1992] analysis of the Denver-II). The lack of valid and reliable screening instruments is no longer a barrier to engaging in this type of data gathering with young children.

But the crux of the argument for developmental surveillance is closely connected to the issue of personnel in assessments. It assumes that most pediatricians can make accurate informal evaluations of children's development. Unfortunately, evidence supporting this statement is not strong. Costello et al. (1987) reported data on psychosocial disorder in a group of 789 children, aged 7–11, who were seen in standard pediatric primary care facilities; about half of the children were followed up with a detailed psychiatric assessment. The study showed that the clinical judgments of pediatricians and primary care physicians were highly inaccurate. The pediatricians diagnosed the presence of emotional and behavioral problems in only 5.6% of children, representing only 17% of the children who actually had such problems. They missed 83% of the diagnoses of problems in the sample being studied.

Similar results are available from other studies. In a provocatively titled article called "Psychosocial problems during child health supervision visits: Eliciting, then what?" Sharp, Pantell, Murphy, and Lewis (1992) demonstrated that pediatricians do not often respond to parents' expressions of concern regarding their child's psychosocial and developmental problems during routine health supervision visits. The authors reviewed videotapes of child health visits by thirty-four children aged 5–12 years to thirty-four pediatric and family medicine residents. Sharp et al. found that physicians responded with information, reassurance, guidance, or referral in only 40% of the cases. "Of interest, experienced board-certified pediatricians in private practice and a prepaid clinic responded to fewer than half the psychological concerns of mothers during audiotape-recorded well-child visits" (Sharp et al., 1992, p. 622). These authors suggest that this type of unresponsiveness contributes to the advent of "an unheeded new morbidity" in which a large proportion of learning, behavioral, and emotional problems are not detected at an early age.

A study of private practice pediatricians who treated preschoolers aged 2 to 5 years displayed similar results. Lavigne et al. (1993) included data on 3,876 children and 68 pediatricians. The children were screened by the health providers during routine child health visits. Subsequently, 495 children, representing equal numbers of children who scored high and low on the Child Behavior Checklist (Achenbach & Edelbrock, 1983), participated in a second-stage evaluation in which they were interviewed by trained clinical psychologists. The results showed a high rate of underreferral on the part of the pediatricians. More than half of the children who had an emotional–behavioral disorder, as determined by the psychologist, were overlooked by the pediatrician. This occurred among children who typically visit their pediatricians annually and who were seen by their own doctors for routine health supervision visits "when the opportunity to detect such problems is presumably the greatest" (Lavigne et al., 1993, p. 653).

The clear view from the field about personnel in assessment is that no single professional preparation is ideally suited or unsuited for the tasks of evaluation and identification. Rather, multiple perspectives from parents (see Diamond & Squires, 1993; Henderson & Meisels, 1994; Sexton, Thompson, Perez, & Rheams, 1990) and from other professionals (Ireton, 1996; Meisels & Provence, 1989) contribute to reasonable and responsible views of children's emerging skills, abilities, and difficulties. Despite the practical problems of trying to perform developmental screening in a busy pediatric practice, developmental surveillance may not be a solution to the challenge of early identification. Because of the risk of its overreliance on a single professional perspective, as well as its setting (a busy clinic or pediatric facility), timing (children who are ill or who are anxious because of visiting a physician and the brevity of the visit), and the absence of a standardized protocol (see Kemper, Osborn, Hansen, & Pascoe, 1994), it is likely that developmental surveillance may result in large numbers of errors of over- and underidentification. It is only as a supplement, rather than as a replacement for other personnel and other perspectives and methods, that developmental monitoring and surveillance can play an important role in early assessment.

CLINICAL JUDGMENT. One element of developmental monitoring and developmental surveillance that is highly consistent with recent trends in assessment concerns its reliance on clinical judgment. Fleischer, Belgredan, Bagnato, and Ogonosky (1990) defined this as "a type of assessment through which the perceptions of many individuals, including parents, teachers, school psychologists, and others who have contact with the child, are collected and used to evaluate the functional capabilities of the child" (pp. 13–14). Physicians' judgments in the process of developmental surveillance are part of the information that goes into clinical judgment, but not all of it. When clinical judgment is undertaken systematically – what some call *Judgment-Based Assessment* (see Neisworth, 1990)—it provides a structure for collecting and evaluating a range of information that organizes the diverse impressions of professionals and caregivers concerning a child. The rationale for using judgment-based assessment is to overcome various functional limitations that prevent valid and reliable administrations of standardized instruments. It also allows for judgments regarding how a child performs a given task (e.g., fluidity, control, hesitancy, or spontaneity of responses). It relies on the perceptions of raters but it recognizes the importance of obtaining evidence to support clinical impressions through collecting both confirmatory and potentially disparate data prior to drawing conclusions. It must be used with skill and great care and preferably in a multidisciplinary setting, lest reliability and validity be sacrificed.

The Infant–Toddler Developmental Assessment (IDA; Provence, Erikson, Vater, & Palmeri, 1995) is one systematic approach to early assessment that combines clinical judgment with more conventional means of childhood evaluation. The IDA goes beyond traditional measures by addressing health, family, and social aspects of development as well as developmental dimensions. "The IDA is anchored in theoretical constructs and clinical perspectives which acknowledge the variety and interdependence of factors that influence the health and development of young children" (Erikson, 1996). The six phases of this assessment process provide a guide for team process, decision making, and the inclusion of parents in the assessment. A minimum of two professionals, who function as developmental generalists and who also contribute their own disciplinary expertise, form a team. The team may include social workers, developmental nutritionists, nurses, special educators, physicians, and physical, occupational, or speech therapists. The IDA helps these individuals organize information from multiple sources about the health, development, and social supports of the child and family. It may be used in clinics, schools, or other specialized settings and is appropriate for children at risk, as well as those with established handicapping conditions. Team members share responsibility and work to develop confidence in each other's judgment. "The team model opens up opportunities for co-observing and mutual support, and the goal of the team is to obtain high reliability in shared observations and findings. The team shares responsibility for gathering, organizing, integrating, and synthesizing information, and for the problem

solving inherent in all clinical work" (Erikson, 1996, p. 19). The team roles include family interviewer and primary family liaison, health reviewer, child evaluator, and assessment coordinator. When practitioners are learning the IDA, it is recommended that every team member experience each of the major roles and all phases of the assessment be co-observed so that interdisciplinary and multidisciplinary assessments become a reality and not just an ideal. The IDA is an assessment that is based upon obtaining multiple perspectives on the wide variety of elements that make up children's performance, learning, and relationships.

Fusion of Assessment and Intervention

Perhaps the most significant change to take place in early childhood assessment in recent years concerns the *fusion* of assessment and intervention. Unlike other modifications in assessment that were transposed from work with older children or adults, the idea that assessment and intervention are inextricably linked, or fused, is something that has its origins in work with children and families in the first few years of life (see Meisels, 1996, for an elaboration of the continuum of assessment and intervention). Several assessments described in this chapter (e.g., the Transdisciplinary Play-Based Assessment and the IDA) share in this model to some extent. A new infant–toddler assessment (described in Meisels, 1996, as the Infant–Toddler Assessment Scale and now known as the Ounce of Prevention Scale) is under development. It will be briefly described in order to highlight some of the characteristics of this approach.

The idea behind the fusion of assessment and intervention is relatively simple and rests on three fundamental assumptions. The first assumption is that assessment is a dynamic enterprise that calls on information from multiple sources collected throughout numerous time points reflecting a wide range of child experiences and caregiver interpretations. The second assumption is that the formal act of assessment is only the first step in the process of acquiring information about the child and family. Through intervention – by putting into practice the ideas or hypotheses raised by the initial assessment procedures – more information will be acquired that can serve the dual purpose of refining the assessment and enhancing the intervention. Third, assessment is of limited value in the absence of intervention. The meaning of an assessment is closely tied to its utility, which is its contributions to decision making about practice or intervention or its confirmation of a child's continuing progress.

The rationale for a fusion-oriented, utility-focused assessment model has already been suggested. To review briefly, we know that all too often children at risk and those with special needs are exposed to assessment techniques that ignore context, the special learning requirements of these children, critical features of early childhood development, and the special talents that these children and their families may have developed in order to compensate for their special needs (see Bagnato & Neisworth, 1994). The importance of developing context-rich, responsive assessments for young children with disabilities or those who are at risk for developmental disorders is even greater than for the general population because of the more complex learning needs and requirements of these children and families.

The notion that assessment and intervention can be fused into a single set of procedures shares a legacy with an approach to assessment that is growing in use outside of the field of early intervention: performance assessment. These assessments provide an alternative approach to documenting the social, emotional, physical, and cognitive–academic accomplishments of children. They constitute actual examples of criterion performances rather than highly inferential estimates of learning accomplishments such as those found on most conventional tests. Known also as *authentic* assessments when they are embedded in the curriculum rather than used on demand to elicit specific types of performances, these assessments are potentially nonstigmatizing (i.e., they are not designed to sort and categorize children), enhance children's motivation, assist teachers and other caregivers in making decisions about intervention, and are effective means of engaging families in their children's intervention progress.

Several features or criteria that are common to performance assessment are potentially of great value to the assessment of young children with special needs (cf. Calfee, 1992; Herman, Aschbacher, & Winters, 1992; Shepard, 1991; Wiggins, 1989), including the following:

1. documenting children's daily activities as well as their initiative and creativity,
2. providing an integrated means for evaluating the quality of children's performance and behavior,
3. reflecting an individualized approach to intervention,
4. evaluating those elements of learning and development that most conventional assessments do not capture very well,
5. utilizing the information acquired in the intervention to further elaborate the evaluative picture of the child that is emerging from the assessment, and
6. focusing the caregiver's attention and activity away from the typical content of test-taking and onto the learning of the child and the environment in which intervention is taking place.

Epistemology is another feature of performance assessment that is noteworthy (see Meisels, Dorfman, & Steele, 1995). In performance assessment, we focus on "evidence of knowing" (Wiggins, 1989, p. 705). Competence is not assessed on the basis of a single performance. Rather, a child's behavior and performance are assessed repeatedly through a variety of documentation methods (e.g., a portfolio, a set of systematic checklists, or both). Over time and in the context of numerous performances, we observe "the *patterns* of success and failure and the reasons behind them" (Wiggins, 1989, p. 705). These patterns constitute the evidence on which the assessment is based. Invidious comparisons between children are minimized, because children are evaluated according to how their specific levels of performance conform to the aims of the intervention, rather than on how closely their overall performance conforms to the average performance of a normative group.

From a theoretical perspective, this approach to assessment is consistent with a view of knowledge development that is often called "constructivist." However, the critical point is that we are concerned not only with the child's acquisition of knowledge, skills, and abilities but also with the knowledge about the child by the assessor or intervenor – who, in the case of infants and toddlers, is often the same individual. This approach to assessment is thus concerned with both the knower (the assessor–intervenor) and the known (the child). Piaget says this well:

To know an object, to know an event, is not simply to look at it and make a mental copy or image of it. To know an object is to act on it. To know is to modify, to transform the object, and to understand the process of this transformation, and as a consequence to understand the way the object is constructed. (Piaget, 1964, quoted in Goodman & Pollak, 1993, p. 200)

To "know" a child is a far more dynamic process than learning about objects and events. It is through interacting in different ways and observing the child's interactions with us and others that we begin to learn about the child's skills, knowledge, interests, and achievements. Assessment should not be just a matter of our acting on the child but the child acting on us.

Intervention is at best an approximation of the knowledge that is really required to assist in a child's development, because in the process of intervention changes occur in the child and the intervenor's knowledge about the child and relationships with the child are concomitantly altered. Hence, assessment becomes a process that is ongoing and continuous and that is linked to intervention. Without assessment, intervention is blind and purposeless; without intervention, assessment is static and of limited relevance and utility.

A new performance assessment under development for infants, toddlers, and their families illustrates these tenets. Previously described as the Infant–Toddler Assessment Scale, it is now called the Ounce of Prevention Scale (see Meisels, 1996). The Ounce Scale is being designed as a method of focusing on parent, child, and professional development through documenting, evaluating, and assessing child growth and development within a caregiving context. Designed for use in such intervention programs as Early Head Start, early intervention programs for disabled and at-risk infants and toddlers, and other home- and center-based infant programs for typically developing children, its purposes are several:

1. Encouraging active engagement between parents and their infants through focusing on interactions rather than on the achievement of milestones;
2. assessing children in their caregiving and environmental contexts by providing systematic methods of keeping track and evaluating their growth and development;

3. helping parents obtain information to promote optimal development in their children;
4. designing interventions that are responsive to the child's skills, knowledge, interests, dispositions, and changing abilities;
5. helping professionals work with families by forging collaborative relationships with them that focus on their child's growth and development; and
6. using assessment information to help families and professionals better understand the challenges to a child's development and the strengths that may help in finding solutions to overcome obstacles.

As families and caregivers share information and observations about the child, communication between them is enhanced. Indeed, to some extent, this assessment is being developed as a relationship-building tool intended to strengthen parent and caregiver knowledge and control and to lead to shared empowerment. The Ounce Scale blends assessment and intervention and helps structure interactions that support the baby's growth. It fosters positive relationships between families and caregivers and helps both parents and providers formulate a picture of the whole baby, not just splinter skills and macrolevel milestones. Fundamentally, this scale helps to differentiate and expand parents' and providers' perceptions of babies so that every child is treated as an individual and so that the unique character of the relationship with that baby can be appreciated and fostered.

Nearly 30 years ago, Nancy Bayley wrote that for children without severely compromised genetic or neurological potential, the best environment for facilitating mental growth is "a supportive, 'warm' emotional climate, together with ample opportunities for the positive reinforcement of specific cognitive efforts and success" (Bayley, 1970, p. 1203). The approach to assessment described here expands this notion to all areas of development and to all stages of development in the first 3 years of life. Moreover, it creates a role for three main actors in this developmental drama: the baby, the family, and the caregivers–interventionists. All three help define the environment in which the baby can thrive, and all three are central to accomplishing the overall purpose of early childhood assessment: to answer questions about how specific children can be helped, how their accomplishments can be enhanced, and how they can more adequately meet their potential.

CONCLUSION: THE SOCIAL UTILITY OF EARLY CHILDHOOD ASSESSMENT

Of all the changes in assessment currently underway, perhaps the most dramatic and far-reaching is a burgeoning emphasis on *social utility*. The social utility of an assessment concerns its value in planning, executing, and evaluating a treatment or intervention. Social utility, also known as *treatment utility*, refers to the degree to which an assessment or assessment process is shown to contribute to beneficial treatment or intervention outcomes (Hayes, Nelson, & Jarrett, 1987).

Ironically, the high status that testing and measurement enjoy is virtually independent of any demonstrated relationship to intervention. Rather, the value of testing and measurement is tied to psychometric principles that sort children by age or diagnostic category. As Neisworth and Bagnato (1992) pointed out in their critique of intelligence testing in early childhood, the process of norming and refining item content allows only those items that are empirically consistent or psychometrically useful to survive, but these items are generally of little or no instructional utility. The twin towers of the psychometric edifice – reliability and validity – are based on the consistency of measurement. Consistency is considered the sine qua non of quality assessment. However, many assessment devices that are highly reliable and valid have virtually no treatment utility. Conversely, it is possible for an assessment process to lack internal consistency, as defined by conventional standards of reliability and validity, but still have high treatment utility. Nevertheless, some researchers point out that it is impossible to build a science of assessment on treatment utility alone. "Knowing the effect on treatment outcome itself requires assessment, and that means that treatment utility must ultimately be based on measures that are themselves not validated in this manner" (Hayes, Nelson, & Jarrett, 1987, p. 971).

This issue of broadening the meaning of validity has been raised in studies of performance assessments of older children. An approach to the use and interpretation of measurement information that has gained prominence recently in studies of performance assessment is known as "consequential validity." Building on the work of Messick (1989), and going beyond the traditional validity categories of construct-content-criterion (Moss, 1992), the consequential basis of test use is concerned with the reactions of the participants to the assessment program (cf. Miller & Legg, 1993; Miller & Seraphine, 1993). Consequences can be positive, as in the improvement of instruction or the enhancement of a child's sense of control over his or her environment, or negative, as in the homogenizing of intervention options and the reduction in perceived autonomy of caregivers.

Consensus is growing among researchers that alternative criteria of validation must be considered to understand fully the meaning and effectiveness of performance assessments (Linn, Baker, & Dunbar, 1991; Messick, 1994; Moss, 1992). Linn et al. suggested that such criteria should include intended and unintended consequences of the assessment, the degree to which performance on specific assessment tasks transfers to other situations, fairness, content quality, comprehensiveness, cost and effectiveness, cognitive complexity demonstrated by children, and the meaningfulness of the intervention for children and caregivers.

A focus on consequential validity and treatment utility changes our question from "Is this particular diagnosis correct?" to "Is this assessment useful in practice?" or "Does this assessment contribute to beneficial treatment outcomes?" (Hayes, Nelson, & Jarrett, 1987, p. 964). We are no longer forced to use a narrow psychometric model of internal consistency or comparison to an external criterion that is itself divorced from practice. Rather, we have available to us a wide range of measures of social utility and application.

This focus on social utility of assessment has major implications for the content of assessments. As we begin to associate the design of interventions with the measurement of developmental skills, neglected aspects of adaptive and developmental measurement will begin to be considered (Poth & Barnett, 1988). These include descriptions of the contexts in which developmental skills are acquired and performed in specific settings. For this to occur, both parental and interventionist roles are fundamental to the assessment process.

In short, the model for assessment that is being proposed here is one that uses assessment to inform intervention but then takes information from the intervention context to help refine the assessment. This is not a one-time event that initiates the intervention and then does not recur until it is time for reevaluation a year or more later. Rather, this model is based on a continuous, functional design that is iterative and even autocatalytic. That is, every change increases the rate of change. Every assessment that contributes to intervention increases the information available for further assessment in a recurring pattern that maintains a focus on improving children's well-being and on optimally utilizing the resources available in the child's environment.

A further implication of this focus on social utility and consequential validity concerns the type of interventions that will meet the standards spelled out throughout this chapter. Adopting a dynamic view of assessment suggests that our interventions as well as our assessments must be multidimensional. We will learn very little about a child's skills, approaches to learning, areas of strength, or areas of weakness if the intervention model is narrow and one-dimensional. Referring to children residing in extremely deprived economic backgrounds, Gorman and Pollitt (1996) pointed out that "unifocal interventions which are limited in scope will fall far short of meeting the needs of children growing up in poverty; long-term optimal development will require multifocal investments that include infants, children, families, and schools" (p. 324). Although this statement refers specifically to children living in poverty, it applies to children of all backgrounds. If our goal is to create a responsive performance-based system of assessment and intervention that is evaluated in terms of its beneficial effects on development, then it is critical that the interventions themselves reflect values described in this chapter for assessment.

The research reviewed here suggests a change from a policy of assessment in the absence of intervention to the use of assessments that actually acquire their meaning and significance from intervention. This type of transformation lends support to the development of a wide range of assessments and different methods of collecting information from children and families. Sternberg (1991) noted that "our best assessments will almost certainly involve converging operations, where a number of different kinds of measurements are made in order to assess the performance of each individual. There is no one kind of

assessment that will be optimal...under every circumstance" (p. 267). It is clear that assessment must include active participation of the child's family, information about the broad context in which the child and family live, expanded methods of collecting assessment data, use of varied personnel including the family, and intervention-oriented applications of assessment data that will advance our goal of helping all children and families reach their potential. These elements of early childhood assessment will continue to evolve as we learn more about them and as they assist us in learning more about the children in our care.

REFERENCES

Achenbach, T. M., & Edelbrock, C. S. (1983). *Manual for the Child Behavior Checklist.* Burlington, VT: University of Vermont.

Andrews, T. J., Wisniewski, J. J., & Mullick, J. A. (1997). Variables influencing teachers' decisions to refer children for school psychological assessment services. *Psychology in the Schools, 34,* 239–43.

Bagnato, S. J., & Neisworth, J. T. (1994). A national study of the social treatment "invalidity" of intelligence testing for early intervention. *School Psychology Quarterly, 9,* 81–102.

Bagnato, S. J., Neisworth, J. T., & Munson, S. M. (1997). *Linking assessment and early intervention: An authentic curriculum-based approach.* Baltimore, MD: Paul H. Brookes.

Bailey, D. B. (1991). Issues and perspectives on family assessment. *Infants and Young Children, 4,* 26–34.

Bailey, D. B., Vandiviere, P., Dellinger, J., and Munn, D. (1987). The Battelle Developmental Inventory: Teacher perceptions and implementation data. *Journal of Psychoeducational Assessment, 5*(3), 217–26.

Bain, J. (1989). Developmental screening for pre-school children: Is it worthwhile? *Journal of the Royal College of General Practitioners, 39,* 133–7.

Barnard, K. E. (1994). What the Feeding Scale measures. In G. S. Sumner & A. Spietz (Eds.), *NCAST: Caregiver/parent–child interaction feeding manual* (pp. 98–121). Seattle: University of Washington NCAST Publications.

Barnard, K. E., Morisset, C. E., & Spieker, S. (1993). Preventive interventions: Enhancing parent–infant relationships. In C. H. Zeanah (Ed.), *Handbook of infant mental health* (pp. 386–401). New York: Guilford Press.

Barnett, D. W., MacMann, G. M., & Carey, K. T. (1992). Early intervention and the assessment of developmental skills: Challenges and directions. *Topics in Early Childhood Special Education, 12,* 21–43.

Barrera, I. (1996). Thoughts on the assessment of young children whose sociocultural background is unfamiliar to the assessor. In S. J. Meisels & E. Fenichel (Eds.), *New visions for the developmental assessment of infants and young children* (pp. 69–84). Washington, DC: Zero to Three.

Bayley, N. (1933). Mental growth during the first three years. *Genetic Psychology Monographs, 14*, 1–92.

Bayley, N. (1969). *The Bayley scales of infant development.* San Antonio, TX: Psychological Corporation.

Bayley, N. (1970). Development of mental abilities. In P. H. Mussen (Ed.), *Carmichael's manual of child psychology* (pp. 1163–1209). New York: Wiley.

Bayley, N. (1993). The Bayley scales of infant development–II. San Antonio, TX: Psychological Corporation.

Beckman, P. (Ed.) (1996). *Strategies for working with families of young children with disabilities.* Baltimore, MD: Paul H. Brookes.

Beckwith, L. (1990). Adaptive and maladaptive parenting–Implications for intervention. In S. J. Meisels & J. P. Shonkoff (Eds.), *Handbook of early childhood intervention* (pp. 53–77). New York: Cambridge University Press.

Bernstein, V. J. & Hans, S. L. (1994). Predicting the developmental outcome of two-year-old children born exposed to methadone: Impact of social–environmental risk factors. *Journal of Clinical Child Psychology, 23*, 349–59.

Bernstein, V. J., Hans, S. L., & Percansky, C. (1991). Advocating for the young child in need through strengthening the parent–child relationship. *Journal of Clinical Child Psychology, 20*, 28–41.

Bernstein, V. J., Jeremy, R. J., & Marcus, J. (1986). Mother-infant interaction in multi-problem families: Finding those at risk. *Journal of the American Academy of Child Psychiatry, 25*, 631–40.

Boliek, C. A., & Obrzut, J. E. (1991). Assessment of infant and toddlers: A comparison of two developmental inventories. *Proceedings of the National Association of School Psychologists.* Dallas: NASP.

Boyd, R. D. (1989). What a difference a day makes: Age-related discontinuities and the Battelle Develpmental Inventory. *Journal of Early Intervention, 13*(2), 114–19.

Boyd, R. D., Welge, P., Sexton, D., & Miller, J. H. (1989). Concurrent validity of the Battelle Developmental Inventory: Relationship with the Bayley Scales in young children with known or suspected disabilities. *Journal of Early Intervention, 13*, 14–23.

Bracken, B. A. (1987). Limitations of preschool instruments and standards for minimal levels of technical adequacy. *Journal of Psychoeducational Assessment, 4*, 313–26.

Bracken, B. A. (1988). Ten psychometric reasons why similar tests produce dissimilar results. *Journal of School Psychology, 26*, 155–66.

Bricker, D. (1993). Family report. In D. Bricker (Ed.), *Assessment, evaluation, and programming system* (AEPS; pp. 295–313). Baltimore, MD: Paul H. Brookes.

Bricker, D., Squires, J., Kaminski, R., & Mounts, L. (1988). The validity, reliability, and cost of a parent-completed questionnaire system to evaluate at-risk infants. *Journal of Pediatric Psychology, 13*(1), 55–68.

Bricker, D., Squires, J., & Mounts, L. (1995). Ages and stages questionnaires. Baltimore, MD: Paul H. Brookes.

Brooks-Gunn, J., Klebanov, P. K., & Duncan, G. J. (1996). Ethnic differences in children's intelligence test scores: Roles of economic deprivation, home environment, and maternal characteristics. *Child Development, 67*, 396–408.

Brooks-Gunn, J., & Weinraub, M. (1983). Origins of infant intelligence testing. In M. Lewis (Ed.), *Origins of intelligence: Infancy and early childhood* (pp. 25–66). New York: Wiley.

Cahan, S. & Cohen, N. (1989). Age versus schooling effects on intelligence development. *Child Development, 60*, 1239–49.

Calfee, R. (1992). Authentic assessment of reading and writing in the elementary classroom. In M. J. Dreher & W. H. Slater (Eds.), *Elementary school literacy: Critical issues* (pp. 211–26). Norwood, MA: Christopher-Gordon.

Cardon, L. R. & Fulker, D. W. (1991). Sources of continuity in infant predictors of later IQ. *Intelligence, 15*, 279–93.

Costello, E. J., Edelbrock, C., Costello, A. J., Dulcan, M. K., Burns, B. J., & Brent, D. (1987). Psychopathology in pediatric primary care: The new hidden morbidity. *Pediatrics, 82*, 415–24.

Crnic, K. A., Greenberg, M. T., Ragozin, A. S., Robinson, N. M., & Basham, R. B. (1983). Social interaction and developmental competence of preterm and full-term infants during the first year of life. *Child Development, 54*, 1199–1210.

Diamond, K. E., & Squires, J. (1993). The role of parental report in the screening and assessment of young children. *Journal of Early Intervention, 17*(2), 107–15.

Dworkin, P. H. (1989). British and American recommendations for developmental monitoring: The role of surveillance. *Pediatrics, 84*, 1000–10.

Emde, R. M., Biringen, Z., Clyman, R. B., & Oppenheim, D. (1991). The moral self of infancy: Affective core and procedural knowledge. *Developmental Review, 11*, 251–70.

Erikson, J. (1996). The Infant-Toddler Developmental Assessment (IDA): A family-centered transdisciplinary assessment process. In S. J. Meisels & E. Fenichel (Eds.), *New visions for the developmental assessment of infants and young children* (pp. 147–68). Washington, DC: Zero to Three.

Ershler, J., & Elliot, S. N. (1992). Review of the Battelle Developmental Inventory Screening Test. In J. J. Kramer & J. C. Conoley (Eds.), *The eleventh mental measurements yearbook* (pp. 67–72). Lincoln, NE: Buros Institute of Mental Measurement.

Fagan, J. F., & McGrath, S. K. (1981). Infant recognition memory and later intelligence. *Intelligence, 5*, 121–30.

Fagan, J. F., Singer, L. T., Montie, J. E., & Shepherd, P. A. (1986). Selective screening device for the early detection of normal or delayed cognitive development in infants at risk for later mental retardation. *Pediatrics, 78*, 1021–6.

Fleischer, K. H., Belgredan, J. H., Bagnato, S. J., & Ogonosky, A. B. (1990). An overview of judgment-based assessment. *Topics in Early Childhood Special Education, 10*, 13–23.

Fowler, M. G., & Cross, A. W. (1986). Preschool risk factors as predictors of early school performance. *Developmental and Behavioral Pediatrics, 7*(4), 237–41.

Fuchs, D., Fuchs, L. S., Benowitz, S., & Barringer, K. (1987). Norm-referenced tests: Are they valid for use with handicapped students? *Exceptional Children, 54*(3), 263–71.

Gerkin, K. C., Eliason, M. J., & Arthur, C. A. (1994). The assessment of at-risk infants and toddlers with the Bayley Mental Scale and the Battelle Developmental Inventory: Beyond the data. *Psychology in the Schools, 31*, 181–7.

Glascoe, F. P., & Byrne, K. E. (1993). The accuracy of three developmental screening tests. *Journal of Early Intervention, 17*(4), 368–79.

Glascoe, F. P., Byrne, K. E., Ashford, L. G., Johnson, L. L., Chang, B., & Strickland, B. (1992). Accuracy of the Denver-II in developmental screening. *Pediatrics, 89*, 1221–5.

Glascoe, F. P., Foster, M., & Wolraich, M. L. (1997). An economic analysis of developmental detection methods. *Pediatrics, 99*(6), 830–7.

Goldberg, S. (1997). Social competence in infancy: A model of parent–infant interaction. *Merrill-Palmer Quarterly, 23*, 163–78.

Goodman, J. F., & Pollack, E. (1993). An analysis of the core cognitive curriculum in early intervention programs. *Early Education and Development, 4*, 193–203.

Gorman, K. S., & Pollitt, E. (1996). Does schooling buffer the effects of early risk? *Child Development, 67*, 314–26.

Greenspan, S. I. (1992). *Infancy and early childhood: The practice of clinical assessment and intervention with emotional and developmental challenges.* Madison, CT: International Universities Press.

Greenspan, S. I. (1996). Assessing the emotional and social functioning of infants and young children. In S. J. Meisels & E. Fenichel (Eds.), *New visions for the developmental assessment of infants and young children* (pp. 231–66). Washington, DC: ZERO TO THREE.

Greenspan, S. I., & Meisels, S. J. (1996). Toward a new vision for the developmental assessment of infants and young children. In S. J. Meisels & E. Fenichel (Eds.), *New visions for the developmental assessment of infants and young children* (pp. 11–26). Washington, DC: ZERO TO THREE.

Hall, J. D., & Barnett, D. W. (1991). Classification of risk status in preschool screening: A comparison of alternative measures. *Journal of Psychoeducational Assessment, 9*, 152–9.

Harry, B. (1992). Developing cultural self-awareness: The first step in values clarification for early interventionists. *Topics in Early Childhood Special Education, 12*(3), 333–50.

Hayes, S. C., Nelson, R. O., & Jarrett, R. B. (1987). The treatment utility of assessment: A functional approach to evaluating assessment quality. *American Psychologist, 42*, 963–74.

Henderson, L. W., & Meisels, S. J. (1994). Parental involvement in the developmental screening of their young children: A multiple source perspective. *Journal of Early Intervention, 18*, 141–54.

Herman, J. L., Aschbacher, P. R., & Winters, L. (1992). *A practical guide to alternative assessment.* Alexandria, VA: Association for Supervision and Curriculum Development.

Hirshberg, L. M. (1996). History-making, not history-taking: Clinical interviews with infants and their families. In S. J. Meisels & E. Fenichel (Eds.), *New visions for the developmental assessment of infants and young children* (pp. 85–124). Washington, DC: Zero to Three.

Honzik, M. P. (1983). Measuring mental abilities in infancy: The value and limitations. In M. Lewis (Ed.), *Origins of intelligence: Infancy and early childhood* (pp. 67–106). New York: Wiley.

Houston, H. L. A., & Davis, R. H. (1985). Opportunistic surveillance of child development in primary care: Is it feasible? *Journal of the Royal College of General Practitioners, 35*, 77–9.

Human, M. T., & Teglasi, H. (1993). Parents' satisfaction and compliance with recommendations following psychoeducational assessment of children. *Journal of School Psychology, 31*(4), 449–67.

Hutchison, T., & Nicoll, A. (1988). Developmental screening and surveillance. *British Journal of Hospital Medicine*, 22–9.

Ireton, H. (1992). *The Child Development Inventory Manual.* Minneapolis, MN: Behavior Science Systems.

Ireton, H. (1996). The child development review: Monitoring children's development using parents' and pediatricians' observations. *Infants and Young Children, 9*, 42–52.

Kalyanpur, M. (April 12–13, 1996). Multicultural aspects of disability and abuse: Building respect for differences. Paper presented at a conference entitled "Light the Shadows: Responding to abuse and neglect of persons with disabilities across the lifespan." Kansas City: University of Kansas Medical Center.

Kemper, K. J., Osborn, L. M., Hansen, D. F., & Pascoe, J. M. (1994). Family psychosocial screening: Should we focus on high-risk settings? *Developmental and Behavioral Pediatrics, 15*, 336–41.

Kochanek, T. T., & Buka, S. L. (1991). Using biologic and ecologic factors to identify vulnerable infants and toddlers. *Infants and Young Children, 4*, 11–25.

Lavigne, J. V., Binns, H. J., Christoffel, K. K., Rosenbaum, D., Arend, R., Smith, K., Hayford, J. R., McGuide, P. A., and Pediatric Practice Research Group (1993). Behavioral and emotional problems among preschool children in pediatric primary care: Prevalence and pediatricians' recognition. *Pediatrics, 91*(3), 649–55.

Linder, T. W. (1993). *Transdisciplinary play-based assessment* (Rev. ed.). Baltimore, MD: Paul H. Brookes.

Linn, R. L., Baker, E. L., & Dunbar, S. B. (1991). Complex, performance-based assessment: Expectations and validation criteria. *Educational Researcher, 20*(8), 15–21.

Lynch, E. W., & Hanson, M. J. (Eds.)(1992). *Developing cross-cultural competence: A guide for working with young children and their families.* Baltimore, MD: Pauett, Brookes.

McCall, R. B. (1981). Early predictors of later IQ: The search continues. *Intelligence, 5,* 141–7.

McCall, R. B., Hogarty, P. S., & Hurlburt, N. (1972). Transitions in infant sensorimotor development and the prediction of childhood IQ. *American Psychologist, 27,* 728–48.

McCune, L., Kalmanson, B., Fleck, M. B., Glazewski, B., & Sillari, J. (1990). An interdisciplinary model of infant assessment. In S. J. Meisels & J. P. Shonkoff (Eds.), *Handbook of early childhood intervention* (pp. 219–45). New York: Cambridge University Press.

McLinden, S. E. (1989). An evaluation of the Battelle Developmental Inventory for determining special education eligibility. *Journal of Psychoeducational Assessment, 7*(1), 66–73.

Meisels, S. J. (1988). Developmental screening in early childhood: The interaction of research and social policy. In L. Breslow, J. E. Fielding, & L. B. Lave (Eds.), *Annual review of public health* (pp. 527–50). Palo Alto, CA: Annual Reviews.

Meisels, S. J. (1994). Designing meaningful measurements for early childhood. In B. L. Mallory & R. S. New (Eds.), *Diversity in early childhood education: A call for more inclusive theory, practice, and policy* (pp. 205–25). New York: Teachers College Press.

Meisels, S. J. (1996). Charting the continuum of assessment and intervention. In S. J. Meisels & E. Fenichel (Eds.), *New visions for the developmental assessment of infants and young children* (pp. 27–52). Washington, DC: ZERO TO THREE.

Meisels, S. J., Dorfman, A., & Steele, D. (1995) Equity and excellence in group-administered and performance-based assessments. In M. Nettles & A. Nettles (Eds.), *Equity in educational assessment and testing* (pp. 195–211). Boston: Kluwer Academic.

Meisels, S. J., & Fenichel, E. (Eds.). (1996). *New visions for the developmental assessment of infants and young children.* Washington, DC: ZERO TO THREE.

Meisels, S. J., Liaw, F., Henderson, L. W., Browning, K., & Ten Have, T. (1993). New evidence for the effectiveness of the Early Screening Inventory. *Early Childhood Research Quarterly, 8,* 327–46.

Meisels, S. J., Marsden, D. B., Wiske, M. S., & Henderson, L. W. (1997). *The Early Screening Inventory-Revised (ESI-R).* Ann Arbor, MI: Rebus.

Meisels, S. J., & Provence, S. (1989). *Screening and assessment: Guidelines for identifying young disabled and developmentally vulnerable children and their families.* Washington, DC: National Center for Clinical Infant Programs.

Meltzer, L., & Reid, D. K. (1994). New directions in the assessment of students with special needs: The shift toward a constructivist perspective. *The Journal of Special Education, 28*(3), 338–55.

Messick, S. (1989). Validity. In R. L. Linn (Ed.), *Educational measurement* (3rd ed., pp. 13–104). New York: Macmillan.

Messick, S. (1994). The interplay of evidence and consequences in the validation of performance assessments. *Educational Researcher, 23,* 12–23.

Miller, M. D., & Legg, S. M. (1993). Alternative assessment in a high-stakes environment. *Educational Measurement: Issues and Practice, 12,* 9–15.

Miller, M. D., & Seraphine, A. E. (1993). Can test scores remain authentic when teaching to the test? *Educational Assessment, 1,* 119–29.

Morriset, C. E. (1994). What the Teaching Scale measures. In G. S. Sumner & A. Spietz (Eds.), *NCAST: Caregiver/parent–child interaction feeding manual* (pp. 53–80). Seattle: University of Washington NCAST Publications.

Moss, P. A. (1992). Shifting conceptions of validity in educational measurement: Implications for performance assessment. *Review of Educational Research, 62,* 229–58.

Neisworth, J. T. (1990). Judgment-based assessment and social validity. *Topics in Early Childhood Special Education, 10*(3).

Neisworth, J. T., & Bagnato, S. J. (1992). The case against intelligence testing in early intervention. *Topics in Early Childhood Special Education, 12*(1), 1–20.

Newborg, J., Stock, J., Wnek, L., Guidabaldi, J., & Svinicki, J. (1984). *Battelle Developmental Inventory: Examiner's Manual.* Dallas: DLM/Teaching Resources.

Nord, C. W., Zill, N., Prince, C., Clarke, S., & Ventura, S. (1994). Developing an index of educational risk from health and social characteristics known at birth. *Bulletin of the New York Academy of Medicine, 71*(2), 167–87.

Parker, S. J., & Zuckerman, D. S. (1990). Therapeutic aspects of the assessment process. In S. J. Meisels & J. P. Shonkoff (Eds.), *Handbook of early childhood intervention* (pp. 350–70). New York: Cambridge University Press.

Poth, R. L., & Barnett, D. W. (1988). Establishing the limits of interpretive confidence: A validity study of two preschool developmental scales. *School Psychology Review, 17,* 322–30.

Provence, S., Erikson, J., Vater, S., & Palmeri, S. (1995). *Infant–Toddler Developmental Assessment: IDA.* Chicago: Riverside Publishing.

Rauh, V. A., Achenbach, T. M., Nurcombe, B., Howell, C. T., & Teti, D. M. (1988). Minimizing adverse effects of low birthweight: Four-year results of early intervention program. *Child Development, 59,* 544–53.

Rogoff, B. (1990). *Apprenticeship in thinking: Cognitive development in social context.* New York: Oxford University Press.

Rutter, M. (1987). Continuities and discontinuities from infancy. In J. Osofsky (Ed.), *Handbook of infant development* (2d ed., pp. 1256–96). New York: Wiley.

Sameroff, A. J. (1993). Models of development and developmental risk. In C. H. Zeanah, Jr. (Ed.), *Handbook of infant mental health* (pp. 3–13). New York: Guilford Press.

Sameroff, A. J., & Chandler, M. (1975). Reproductive risk and the continuum of caretaking casualty. In

F. D. Horowitz, M. Hetherington, S. Scarr-Salapatek, & G. Siegel (Eds.), *Review of child development research* (Vol. 4, pp. 187–244). Chicago: University of Chicago Press.

Sameroff, A. J., & Fiese, B. H. (1990). Transactional regulation and early intervention. In S. J. Meisels & J. P. Shonkoff (Eds.), *Handbook of early childhood intervention* (pp. 119–49). New York: Cambridge University Press.

Sameroff, A. J., Seifer, R., Barocas, B., Zax, M., & Greenspan, S. I. (1987). IQ scores of 4-year-old children: Social-environmental risk factors. *Pediatrics, 79*(3), 343–50.

Segal, M., & Webber, N. T. (1996). Nonstructured play observations: Guidelines, benefits, and caveats. In S. J. Meisels & E. Fenichel (Eds.), *New visions for the developmental assessment of infants and young children* (pp. 207–30). Washington, DC: Zero to Three.

Sexton, D., McLean, M., Boyd, R., Thompson, B., & McCormick, K. (1988). Criterion-related validity of a new standardized developmental measure for use with infants who are handicapped. *Measurement and Evaluation in Counseling and Development, 21*, 16–24.

Sexton, D., Thompson, B., Perez, J., & Rheams, T. (1990). Maternal versus professional estimates of developmental status for young children with handicaps: An ecological approach. *Topics in Early Childhood Special Education, 10*, 80–95.

Sharp, L., Pantell, R. H., Murphy, L. O., & Lewis, C. C. (1992). Psychosocial problems during child health supervision visits: Eliciting, then what? *Pediatrics, 89*, 619–23.

Shepard, L. A. (1991). Interview on assessment issues. *Educational Researcher, 20*, 21–3, 27.

Shriver, M. D., Kramer, J. J., & Garnett, M. (1993). Parent involvement in early childhood special education: Opportunities for school psychologists. *Psychology in the Schools, 30*, 264–71.

Snyder, P., Lawson, S., Thompson, B., Stricklin, S., & Sexton, D. (1993). Evaluating the psychometric integrity of instruments used in early intervention research: The Battelle Developmental Inventory. *Topics in Early Childhood Special Education, 13*(2), 216–32.

Sparrow, S. S., Balla, D. A., & Cicchetti, D. V. (1984). Vineland Scales of Adaptive Behavior. Circle Pines, MN: American Guidance Service.

Squires, J. (1996). Parent-completed developmental questionnaires: A low-cost strategy for child-find and screening. *Infants and Young Children, 9*, 16–28.

Squires, J., & Bricker, D. (1991). Impact of completing infant developmental questionnaires on at-risk mothers. *Journal of Early Intervention, 15*(2), 162–72.

Squires, J., Nickel, R., & Bricker, D. (1990). Use of parent-completed developmental questionnaires for child-find and screening. *Infants and Young Children, 3*(2), 46–57.

Sternberg, R. J. (1991). Death, taxes, and bad intelligence tests. *Intelligence, 15*, 257–69.

Sturner, R. A., Funk, S. G., & Green, J. A. (1994). Simultaneous technique for acuity and readiness testing (START): Further concurrent validation of an aid for developmental surveillance. *Pediatrics, 93*, 82–8.

Turnbull, A. P. & Turnbull, H. R. (1996). *Families, professionals, and exceptionality: A special partnership* (3d ed.). Upper Saddle River, NJ: Merrill/Prentice Hall.

Werner, E. (1990). Protective factors and individual resilience. In S. J. Meisels & J. P. Shonkoff (Eds.), *Handbook of early childhood intervention* (pp. 97–116). New York: Cambridge University Press.

Weston, D. R., Ivins, B., Heffron, M. C., & Sweet, N. (1997). Formulating the centrality of relationships in early intervention: An organizational perspective. *Infants and Young Children, 9*, 1–12.

Wieder, S. (1996). Climbing the "Symbolic Ladder": Assessing young children's symbolic and representational capacities through observation of free play interaction. In S. J. Meisels & E. Fenichel (Eds.), *New visions for the developmental assessment of infants and young children* (pp. 267–88). Washington, DC: Zero to Three.

Wiggins, G. (1989). A true test: Toward more authentic and equitable assessment. *Phi Delta Kappan, 70*, 703–13.

Williamson, G. G. (1996). Assessment of adaptive competence. In S. J. Meisels & E. Fenichel (Eds.), *New visions for the developmental assessment of infants and young children* (pp. 193–206). Washington, DC: Zero to Three.

CHAPTER TWELVE

Assessment of Parent–Child Interaction:

Implications for Early Intervention

JEAN F. KELLY AND KATHRYN E. BARNARD

Traditionally, those working with children who have special needs and their parents have focused on helping the child master cognitive, language, and motor goals in which functionally based curricula are used. This approach has centered on the child because of parental concerns about the child's ability to accomplish developmental milestones and because of the emphases of professional training programs on remediating the child's skill deficits. Evaluations of intervention programs demonstrate, however, that focusing on family interactions, as well as on children's skills, may have a greater effect on child development than focusing solely on the child (e.g., Brofenbrenner, 1975; Shonkoff, Hauser-Cram, Krauss, & Upshur, 1992). As a result, the importance of encouraging reciprocal and motivating parent–child interaction is now increasingly recognized (e.g., Bernstein, Hans, & Percansky, 1991; Glovinsky, 1993; Greenspan, 1988; Kelly & Barnard, 1990; McCollum & Hemmeter, 1997; McLean & McCormick, 1993; Thorp & McCollom, 1994).

Previous research has shown that the quality of the early parent–child relationship has important consequences for a child's development (e.g., Bakeman & Brown, 1980; Beckwith & Rodning, 1996; Bee et al. 1982; Belsky, Goode, & Most, 1980; Brazelton, 1988; Coates & Lewis, 1984; Farran & Ramey, 1980; Hann, Osofsky, & Culp, 1996; Kelly, Morisset, Barnard, Hammond, & Booth, 1996; Papousek & Bornstein, 1992; Redding, Harmon, & Morgan, 1990; Tamis-LeMonda & Bornstein, 1989, Wachs & Gruen, 1982). Additionally, federal legislation relating to early intervention programs (Part C, the Early Intervention Section of IDEA) mandates a stronger

emphasis on family involvement and reflects the recognition that parents and other family members are critical to the success of any early intervention effort. To develop appropriate methods for strengthening the relationship between a parent and child, it is important to assess the quality of the parent–child interaction.

In this chapter, we discuss several issues related to the assessment of parent–child interaction when the child has special needs. First, we describe past studies that have identified important elements of parent–child interaction. Second, we discuss research on parent–child interaction when the infant is disabled or at risk for developing disabilities, and we discuss the potential significance of this research in shaping assessment and intervention practices. Third, we introduce several approaches to the assessment of parent–child interaction that can be used to guide intervention efforts. Fourth, we discuss a selection of current assessments designed to measure early parent–child interaction. Finally, we conclude with suggestions for future research and professional training efforts.

Although this chapter addresses the general concept of parent–child interaction, most studies have collected data on mothers, rather than fathers, interacting with their young children. This does not negate the importance of the father's role but reflects the fact that the parent available for observation is most often the mother. Recent interaction research points to the importance of the father's role (e.g., Black & Logan, 1995; Bridges, Connell, & Belsky, 1988; Girolametto & Tannock, 1994; Yogman, Kindlon, & Earls, 1995) and should encourage researchers to broaden the study of interaction to include observations of both mothers and fathers.

IDENTIFICATION OF IMPORTANT ELEMENTS OF PARENT–CHILD INTERACTION

Substantial research throughout the 1970s, 1980s, and 1990s has concentrated on the nature of early parent–child interaction. Investigators have used a variety of measurement techniques to identify the important elements in that interaction and have demonstrated the strong relationship between early parent–child interaction and child competence (Barnard et al., 1989; Beckwith & Cohen, 1984; Bee et al., 1982; Bell & Ainsworth, 1972; Bradley & Caldwell, 1976a, 1976b; Clarke-Stewart, 1973; Coates & Lewis, 1984; Engel & Keane, 1975; Nelson, 1973; Olson, Bates, & Bayles, 1984; Ramey, Farran, & Campbell, 1978; Snow et al., 1974; Tulkin & Covitz, 1975; Wachs, Uzgiris, & Hunt, 1971). These elements include the behavioral repertoire of both the child and the parent and the reciprocity that develops in an interaction as both partners respond and adapt to one another. We describe several classic studies that provide a foundation for current research as well more recent research studies that add to our knowledge of parent–child interaction.

Behavioral Repertoire of Child and Parent

Important research during the 1970s focused attention on the individual characteristics of the child and parent and explored how these characteristics relate to the formation of interactional patterns. Research showed that infants contribute their own unique behaviors to the interaction (e.g., Bell, 1974; Brazelton, Koslowski, & Main, 1974; Cohen & Beckwith, 1979; Lewis & Rosenblum, 1974; Robson & Moss, 1970). As early as 1959, Chess, Thomas, and Birch hypothesized that various child-care practices were determined not only by what the mother feels and does but also by the specific pattern of behavioral responses that characterize the individual child. Korner (1971) stated that individual infant differences at birth may affect later development, including the manner in which different infants perceive the world around them. She suggested that for mutuality to develop between the mother and

child, the individual infant behaviors must evoke differences in mothering. In summarizing her research and that of others, Korner reported that individual characteristics of the newborn – such as amount of crying behavior, soothability, and capacity to take in and synthesize sensory stimuli – will affect short- and long-range adaptation to the environment. She emphasized that parents must tune in to the infant and deal with his or her behavior differentially.

Stern (1977) concluded that "the infant arrives with an array of innately determined perceptual predilections, motor patterns, cognitive and thinking tendencies, and abilities for emotional expressiveness and perhaps recognition" (p. 10). Beebe and Stern (1977) described the infant's coping behaviors that let the caregiver know when he or she is ready for interaction. Infant engagement and disengagement allow the infant to manage stimulation within a comfortable range or to prompt the responsive mother to alter her behavior if it is uncomfortable. Booth (1985) found that both social status and neonatal state regulation (such behaviors as cuddliness, consolability, hand-to-mouth facility, and self-quieting activity) predicted the amount of synchrony in mother–infant interaction at 10–12 months. Hess (1970) and Bell (1974) proposed that the infant's physical appearance affects maternal responsiveness. Hess described features, called "babyishness," that heighten visual attention and serve as innate releasers for other parental behaviors.

In addition to the effect of individual infant characteristics, researchers have also examined the influence of maternal characteristics on interaction. Lewis and Goldberg (1969) found positive correlation between maternal responsiveness to infant behavior and the cognitive development of the infant at 3 months of age. They observed twenty mothers and infants in two situations: a controlled naturalistic setting and an experimental situation. Maternal responsiveness was measured by recording the occurrence of various behaviors (e.g., mother looking at, smiling at, vocalizing to, holding, or touching the infant). Each time the infant exhibited specific behaviors (e.g., eyes opened or closed, movement, crying, or vocalizing), the observer rated the nature and intensity of the maternal response. The data consistently indicated that there was a positive correlation between maternal response to infant behavior and the cognitive development of the infant as measured by response decrement in a habituation paradigm. This research suggested that the mother's increasing importance as a reinforcer of behaviors is one indication that the infant has learned to expect rewards from environmental interactions, which is the basis for future learning.

Stern et al. (1973) conducted a factor-analytic study concerned with learning more about mutually influential patterns of social behavior. Data were collected from clinic interviews and observations of thirty mothers and their infants. Seventy-nine items were designed to rate mother and infant characteristics. The factor analysis of the items yielded nine factors based on composites of the mother's and child's personality and behavior and the child's mental and motor development. The authors stated that the patterns of the factor loadings in each case suggest a causal sequence of relationships between the personality characteristics of the mother, the modes of maternal behavior she adopts, and the responses and development of the child. For example, one factor represented mothers who were loving, attentive, skillful, and emotionally involved; the infants shared only one thing in common, accelerated development. In contrast, a different factor described mothers who were indifferent and disorganized in their interactions; their infants' behaviors were similarly lacking in purpose and plan.

Beckwith (1971) showed that maternal verbal and physical responsiveness was related positively to Cattell scores in adopted middle-class infants, whereas maternal restriction of exploration was correlated negatively with developmental status. Ainsworth (1973) demonstrated that infants acquire a sense of security through the countless interactions they have with their mothers during the first year. When mothers demonstrate sensitive responsiveness to infants in the first months of life, the infants demonstrate secure attachment later and are able to use the parent as a secure base for exploration and as a source of comfort in time of stress. In a study with a sample of socially high-risk mothers and their infants, maternal and infant behaviors during a teaching interaction were measured with the Nursing Child Assessment Satellite Training (NCAST) Teaching Scale. The Teaching Scale score at 3 months correlated positively with secure attachment at 12 months (Barnard et al., 1989).

There is evidence that negative patterns of mother–child interaction are more likely to occur in families that are at high social risk due to social or economic disadvantages. Booth, Barnard, Mitchell, and Spieker (1987) pointed out that, in general, mothers in difficult circumstances (e.g., those with a low educational level, little support, multiple chronic problems, or high life stress) tend to have interactions with their infants that are less optimal than do mothers who do not have such difficulties (see also Barnes, Gutfreund, Satterly, & Wells, 1983; Crnic, Greenberg, Robinson, & Ragozin, 1984; Egeland & Sroufe, 1981; Kelly, Morisset, Barnard, & Patterson, 1996; Ramey, Farran, & Campbell, 1978).

Importance of Reciprocity in Parent–Child Interaction

The research literature substantiates that the parent and child each comes to the interaction with unique characteristics. It is the merging of the parent's and child's individual styles that determines the success of the mother–child relationship. Several authors have described and labeled the development of this relationship. Spitz (1964) spoke of the interaction as a dialogue composed of action cycles. The dialogue can be impaired by meaningless exchange or inappropriate reactions. Spitz further emphasized that the breakdown of a dialogue in infancy had consequences for each subsequent developmental state. He pointed out that the newborn cannot understand the parent's inner processes; therefore, the mother's role is to interact in ways that demonstrate an understanding of her baby's behaviors. Only with this empathic parent perspective will the interaction be meaningful; without this perspective, the parent is likely to initiate actions that might not apply to the child's needs or might interrupt responses before completion.

Stern (1984) also discussed empathy as an important aspect of the parent–child relationship, labeling this *affect attunement*, the ability to know what another is experiencing subjectively. The mental state of one partner must first become visible through his or her overt behaviors. Attunement occurs when the other partner perceives this state and produces a meaningful response. This takes place, for example, when a child tenses his or her body to make the final effort to grab a toy (overt behavior) and the mother at this precise time says "uuuuuh...uuuuuh!" with her vocal effort matching the child's physical effort. Although affect attunement is a matching process, it goes beyond simple matching and focuses on the internal state of the partner (Beckwith, 1990).

Sander (1964) described the parent–infant relationship as a process of adaptation. He identified five stages during the first two years that are differentiated by the predominant behaviors of the child. It is the active tendencies of both parent and child that determine the development of a positive reciprocal relationship, marked by harmony and "turn-taking." At each stage, a type of refitting must be negotiated. The stages defined for the first year are primary modulation (birth–3 months); social–affective (3–6 months); initiative (6–9 months); and focalization (9–19 months). The final stage, which occurs after one year, is characterized as self-assertion and is related directly to the development of autonomy and independent action. Sander's work reminds us that this independence is coordinated and achieved through an adaptive parent–child interaction.

Brazelton et al. (1974) studied the communication system that develops between infants and their caregivers within the first few months of life. They videotaped caregiver and infant behaviors simultaneously and reported that rhythmicity between the primary caregiver and the infant is an essential characteristic of the developing relationship; that is, there is a positive interaction when each member of the dyad responds to the needs of the other. When one member is out of phase with the other, there appears to be a negative quality to the interaction. The strength of the interdependence of the dyad seems to be more powerful in shaping each member's behavior than does any other factor.

Thoman (1975) also reported on the mother–infant adaptation process, concluding that each baby has his or her own capabilities for providing cues to the mother and that each mother has unique ways of responding to her baby. Thoman described the process of adaptation as a behavior pattern developed in a three-part cue–response sequence: 1) cue giving by the baby, 2) cue-responsiveness by the mother, and 3) the response of the baby to the mother's action.

Kaye (1975, 1976) described the process of turn-taking, in which each partner learns the rules for beginning and ending his or her turn from the other partner's feedback. Both mother and infant behaviors are mutually shaped over time, and each becomes more competent at influencing the other partner's behavior. Stern (1974) observed gaze behavior of 3- and 4-month-old infants and their mothers, and Strain and Vietze (1975) studied vocal behaviors of 3-month-old infants and their mothers. Both research groups found evidence of this mutual regulation of mother and child behaviors during interaction.

Barnard et al. (1989) described four necessary features of the mutually adaptive "dance" between partners. First, each of the partners must possess a sufficient repertoire of behaviors. If either partner lacks important qualities, the dance may be less satisfying. Among the crucial skills the child brings are the abilities to see, hear, and visually attend to the mother; smiling; body adaptation to holding or movement; soothability; and regularity with predictability of response. The parent brings the ability and willingness to read and respond appropriately to infant cues and a repertoire of behaviors to stimulate and engage the infant. Second, partner responses need to be contingent on one another. The contingent quality of parental responsiveness appears to be significant in the development of a secure attachment to the parent (Ainsworth, Blehar, Waters, & Wall, 1978; Belsky et al., 1984; Blehar, Lieberman, & Ainsworth, 1977; Crockenberg, 1981) and affects the subsequent development of competency in the child (Beckwith & Cohen, 1984; Coates & Lewis, 1984; Goldberg, 1977; Lewis & Coates, 1980). Third, there needs to be a richness of the interactive content. The amount of time the mother spends with the child and the range of toys and activities presented are examples of measures of the level of richness. Fourth, the specific adaptive patterns between parent and child must change over time. Studies have noted that the ways mothers and children interact with each other change with the child's development (Belsky et al., 1984; Olson et al., 1984).

A study of intervention effects with low-birth-weight, premature children by Liaw, Meisels, and Brooks-Gunn (1995) highlighted the importance of examining parent and child joint involvement in interaction activities. They related exposure (number of intervention contacts), rate (number of activities presented to the parent–child dyad), and active experience (parental interest in interaction and child's mastery of tasks) and found that the best predictor of children's one-to-three-year outcomes was active experience, the combination of parental interest in interaction activities, and the child's mastery of intervention activities. Liaw et al.'s research suggests that it is important to consider both the parent's and the child's participation levels in assessment and intervention efforts.

The studies described in this review contribute to an understanding of the importance of parent–child interaction to optimal child development and of the specific elements in the parent–child interaction. These elements include the individual behavioral repertoire of both the infant and parent and the reciprocity that develops as both partners in an interaction respond and adapt to each other. Research shows that infants come to the interaction with a unique set of characteristics. For a synchronous relationship to develop, these individual characteristics must evoke differences in mothering. For example, work with premature infants and their mothers demonstrates the need for mothers to adjust the amount of their stimulation to the infant's capacity to tolerate sensory input (Field, 1982; Lyons, 1981). In addition to infant characteristics, the individual characteristics of the parent affect the interaction. Barnard and Martell (1995) pointed out that parents' awareness of their child's development and abilities and the parents' level of energy in using this awareness are major factors in the development of a growth-fostering interaction. Finally, the reciprocity that develops as both partners in an interaction respond and adapt to each other is the basis for a mutually satisfying relationship between the parent and child. The research discussed in this review described this process of developing reciprocity in many different ways. Spitz (1964) spoke of *action cycles*; Stern (1984) discussed *affective attunement*; Sander (1964) developed five stages of adaptation; and Brazelton (1988) explained the reciprocity model as a feedback process that allows for flexibility, disruption, and organization. Thoman (1975) had previously described a similar process as a cue–response sequence, and Kaye (1975, 1976) described the process of turn-taking. Barnard et al. (1989) suggested the term *mutually adaptive dance* and described four necessary features of the dance.

In all of these studies, researchers defined the process of mutual regulation and adaptation that occurs in optimal interactions. For assessment purposes, the description of these elements facilitates the construction of assessment procedures that make it possible to identify the important strengths and needs of the individual parent–child relationship. This resulting assessment information can be used to further research efforts and to plan appropriate intervention techniques.

PARENT–CHILD INTERACTION WHEN THE CHILD HAS SPECIAL NEEDS

As the importance of early childhood intervention gained recognition in the 1970s, researchers had begun to examine the interaction of parents and children when the child was disabled or at risk for developmental problems. Investigators found differences in the interactive characteristics of both infants and mothers and the resulting reciprocity between the two members of the dyad.

Behavioral Repertoire of the Parent and the Child with Disabilities or the Child Who Is At Risk

Data support the assumption that delayed infants' cues are less frequent and more subtle than nondelayed infants. Richard (1986) reviewed the literature comparing infants without disabilities and those with Down syndrome on several infant characteristics and found evidence of significant differences in temperament (Rothbart & Hanson, 1983), gaze behavior (Gunn, Berry, & Andrews, 1979; Krakow & Kopp, 1983; Rothbart, 1984), gestures (Bricker & Carlson, 1980; Cicchetti & Sroufe, 1978; Dunst, 1980; Jens & Johnson, 1982), vocalization (Gisel, Lange, & Niman, 1984; Harris, 1983; Smith & Oller, 1981; Stevenson, Leavitt, & Silverberg, 1985), and proximity to caregivers (Smith & Hagen, 1984).

Shonkoff et al. (1992), in their study of 190 infants with disabilities, found that young children with atypical development demonstrated delayed interactive behaviors. In comparison to parents of children without disabilities, mothers had greater difficulty in reading the children's signals and in facilitating their learning. Shonkoff et al. identified a subgroup of twenty-three mothers, however, who demonstrated an increase in their growth-promoting behaviors with their children. Although their children did not differ significantly from other children on outcome measures at the initial measurement point, they did show significant differences one year later. Their analysis points to an association between substantial improvement in mother–child interactive behavior and increasing developmental gains for children.

Studies of differences between term infants and preterm infants have reported that the premature infant has a decreased level of behavioral responsiveness and less organization of sleep–wake activity (Kang & Barnard, 1979; Telzrow, Kang, Mitchell, Ashworth, & Barnard, 1982). Initially, parents of preterm infants try harder to stimulate their infant, yet preterm infants are less responsive (Beckwith & Cohen, 1980; Divitto & Goldberg, 1979; Field, 1977, 1979; Goldberg, Brachfeld, & Divitto, 1980). Field (1983) studied whether high-risk infants are less attentive and show less positive affect and game-playing during interaction. Her data showed that preterm and postterm infants were less attentive to their mothers and appeared to have less fun in early interactions than full-term infants.

Researchers have attempted to characterize differences in maternal characteristics by comparing groups of mothers with delayed and nondelayed infants. Eheart (1982) compared mother–child dyads with both mentally retarded and cognitively normal infants on interaction patterns demonstrated during free-play sessions. She found that mothers of children with mental retardation dominated the play sessions and perceived themselves as trying to change their children's behavior more often than did mothers of cognitively normal infants. The children with retardation responded less frequently to their mother's initiations and initiated less than half as many interactions as control children. Mothers of disabled children were noted to be more dominating, and their infants correspondingly seemed less involved than what was observed for the nondelayed child–parent dyads. Brooks-Gunn and Lewis (1982) studied play behavior in disabled and normal infants. Among many findings, they concluded that mothers tailor play interaction to their child's ability and behavior. However, mothers of infants with disabilities may not encourage independent or infant-initiated toy play because of their perceptions of their children's deficits. For example, maternal initiation of toy play occurred much more often with the disabled children, reinforcing the belief that these mothers were controlling the interaction much longer than were mothers of normal children. Jones (1977) compared the interactional exchanges between mothers and their nondelayed infants with those between mothers and infants with Down syndrome. He found that the children in the two groups showed no difference in their frequency of participation in interactive exchanges; there was a trend, though, toward more mother-directed interactions in the group with Down syndrome as contrasted to more child-directed interactions in the nondelayed group.

Later research attempted to determine the underlying reasons for mothers' increased control and its effect on children's behavior. Investigators suggest that maternal directives may be an adaptive response on the part of the mother to the child's handicapping condition (Marfo, 1990); may promote the development of children with delays (Davis, Stroud, & Green, 1988); and may have the positive benefit of facilitating the child's engagement in interaction (Tannock, 1988). Crawley and Spiker (1983) examined the relationship between individual differences in mother–child interactional patterns and child competence within a sample of 2-year-old children with Down syndrome. They concluded that it was not possible to typify the mother–child interaction because there were notable individual differences in interaction patterns. The mothers in Crawley and Spiker's study showed wide variation along such dimensions as directiveness, sensitivity, and elaborativeness. Some mothers had a highly directive style, whereas others spent most of the free-play period observing and commenting on their child's activities. Their results further indicated that mothers could be both directive and highly sensitive with their children or, conversely, insensitive and nondirective. Mothers who received high ratings for stimulation had children with higher Bayley MDI scores, and mothers who were both sensitive and directive were rated high on stimulation. Perhaps there is an optimal combination of sensitivity and directiveness for children with Down syndrome, or perhaps the relationship between the mother's stimulation and the elevated MDI scores reflects the infant's effect on the mother.

Several studies have indicated that it is the mother's intentions that drive the interaction rather than the infant's characteristics that drive it. Mahoney, Fors, and Wood (1990) suggested that group differences in maternal directive behavior cannot be explained on the basis of children's behavior but appear to reflect differences in maternal interactive intentions. In their comparison of children with Down syndrome and nondelayed children, mothers of delayed children had a higher number of requests for children to perform actions, requested actions that were relatively difficult, and asked children to attend to information that was not related to the children's current focus of attention. Their results supported previous investigations (Mahoney, Finger, & Powell, 1985; Mahoney & Powell, 1988) that suggested maternal directiveness was negatively correlated with responsiveness.

Rosenberg and Robinson (1988) maintained that if maternal directiveness has positive effects on the development of children with delays, such effects are influenced by the rate of maternal responsiveness. The findings of Cielinski (1993) support the belief that a mother's directive behavior can have positive developmental effects if it is used in combination with maternal responsive behavior. To determine if directiveness leads to a reduction in cognitive development, she compared the interactions of a group of mothers and nondelayed infants with a group of mothers and their children with Down syndrome. Lielinski found that mothers of children with Down syndrome were more directive and slightly more intrusive, but they were not less responsive than the mothers of nondelayed infants. For children with Down syndrome, the mother's directive behavior lengthened the child's attention-duration during play; for the nondelayed group, in contrast, maternal directiveness enhanced the complexity of play repertoire for the children. This conclusion suggests the need to examine both the responsive and the contingent nature of the dyadic interaction (reciprocity) when the infant is delayed.

Reciprocity in Dyads When the Child Has a Disability or Is At Risk

The following section reviews many of the studies that have examined differences in the development of reciprocity in dyads with delayed infants.

Past research tended to typify mothers of children with delays as being nonresponsive and overly controlling. To study this, Spiker, Boyce, and Price (1996) rated the interactions of 238 mothers and their 2-year-old children with disabilities. All dyads were participants in a longitudinal study of early intervention from six sites across the United States. Notably, 62% of the mothers were rated as highly developmentally appropriate in responding to child cues. Spiker et al.'s research demonstrates that reciprocity patterns vary according to the individual characteristics of each mother and infant; that is, mothers of children with delays are not a homogeneous group. Given this understanding, it is important to identify potential problems in the development of reciprocity between mothers and their delayed or at-risk infants and to examine how these negotiations between parent and child continue or impede the developmental process.

Fraiberg (1974) found that in a sample of ten mothers and their blind infants, only two mothers were able to establish good communication systems through tactile means without some professional guidance. She explained that the infants seemed to be less responsive, to vocalize less, and to be slower than sighted children in learning to localize objects by sound. Fraiberg's intervention efforts sensitized parents to the subtle cues that blind infants display in communication attempts. These intervention strategies were possible to use only after carefully observing the infants' specific behavioral cues (e.g., signs of pleasure, interest, discomfort, or need).

In normal interactions, turn-taking increases with the developmental age of the child while the relative frequency of simultaneous vocalizations decreases, indicating that turn-taking is the more appropriate form for the development of mature communication (Schaffer, Collis, & Parson, 1977; Stern, Jaffe, Beebe, & Bennett, 1975). Berger and Cunningham (1983) recorded the vocal interactions of six infants with Down syndrome and seven nondisabled infants with their mothers during the first six months of life. They found a qualitative difference in the turn-taking behaviors of the two groups of mother–infant dyads, which reflected more than the different rates of the infants' vocal development. Their data suggest that there is an increasing age-related trend toward vocal "clashing" versus turn-taking in the interaction between infants with Down syndrome and their mothers when compared to dyads without disabled infants. Perhaps the delayed language development of children with Down syndrome caused mothers to form a pattern of simultaneous vocalization rather than turn-taking. As the developmental age of the child increased, it was difficult for mothers to alter the well-established pattern to accommodate the child's newly learned verbal skills.

Vietze, Abernathy, Ashe, and Stich (1978) studied infants with and without delays and identified a different pattern of maternal behavior. Results for the delayed and nondelayed groups at 1 year of age were strikingly similar, in that both showed a great deal of reciprocal vocal interaction. When the infants with delays were divided into two groups, however, one having scored higher on the Bayley Scales than the other, the failure of the lower scoring group to differentiate between the presence and the absence of maternal vocalizations eventually affected the interactive style of the mothers. The authors maintained that this failure on the part of the lower functioning infants may lead to less contingent maternal responses. Goldberg (1977) suggested that as parents become more sensitive to infant cues and better at predicting the outcomes of an act, they become more self-confident as parents. She stressed, however, that there are broad individual differences among infants in the clarity of their cues, so that even the most sensitive parent can have interactions that are noncontingent and chaotic if the infant is less readable or predictable. Goldberg's conclusions are similar to those reached by Vietze et al., (1978).

An important goal of intervention, therefore, is to help parents become good observers of their own babies. Bromwich (1981), in describing her intervention program, stated that the kinds of comments that accompanied observations of the child's play, language, affective cues, social responses, and motor behavior called the parent's attention to the details of behavior that revealed important developmental changes in the child, no matter how small. The discussions that ensued from the observations motivated the parent to continue these observations, and they gave the parent additional ideas about what was important to look for in order to help the mother interact more pleasurably and effectively with her child.

Field (1982) concluded from her studies with premature infants that it is important to find an optimal level of stimulation, because low levels do not elicit responses from premature infants and high levels may result in gaze aversion and fussiness. In general, a mother's stimulating behavior can best be defined as overstimulating, overcontrolling, or overdominating if it results in subtle or potent disengagement cues from the infant. The result of such behaviors can only be determined by assessing the individual dyad's interactions. Barnard (1994) summarized studies with parents and preterm infants by using the NCAST Feeding Scale and noted that the absence of selected parental behaviors may develop in response to a lower sensory threshold for the infant. Parents' observations of the infants' immature systems and lower states of arousal may lead to maladaptive responses on the part of the parent.

These studies emphasize the importance of examining reciprocity in terms of the level of mutual accommodation present in the interaction. Perhaps what is critical in the interaction is not the number of parental directives, the duration of parental control, or the level of maternal stimulation but the degree to which each member is responding to the other in contingent, sensitive, and empathetic ways. Helping parents to recognize infant cues and to respond contingently may be one of the most important intervention goals. Additionally, it is important to conceptualize parent–child assessment as an ongoing process in intervention efforts. As the developing child matures, parents should recognize changing cues and adjust their behaviors and interactions accordingly. The development of reciprocity is not a static process; it is continually changing according to the individual behavioral characteristics of the parent and young child.

Parent–Child Interaction in Families At Risk for Environmental Reasons

Among the early environmental characteristics that have been identified as early risk factors contributing to poor outcomes in children are low maternal intelligence (Kelly, Morisset, Barnard, & Patterson, 1996; Longstreth et al., 1981; Yeates, MacPhee, Campbell, & Ramey, 1983); low maternal educational achievement (Dubow & Luster, 1990; Furstenberg, Brooks-Gunn, & Morgan, 1987;

Sameroff, Seifer, Barocas, Zax, & Greenspan, 1987; Werner, 1985); maternal depression or low self-esteem (Dubow & Luster, 1990; Sameroff et al., 1987; Werner, 1985); low maternal age at time of child's birth (Baldwin & Cain, 1980; Dubow & Luster, 1990; Furstenberg, Brooks-Gunn, & Morgan, 1987); large family size (Blake, 1989; Dubow & Luster, 1990; Rutter, 1978; Sameroff et al., 1987); and poverty (Dubow & Luster, 1990; Furstenberg et al., 1987; McLoyd, 1990; Werner, 1985). Children exposed to several risk factors at the same time are especially vulnerable to developing learning or behavioral difficulties (Dubow & Luster, 1990; Furstenberg et al., 1987; Lester et al., 1995; Sameroff & Seifer, 1995).

In families with identified environmental risk elements, researchers have attempted to describe how the young child experiences risk by observing the parent's behavior in the parent–child interaction. Interaction research, therefore, has focused more on identifying the behavioral patterns of the parent rather than the child. For example, researchers have noted that mothers from socioeconomically disadvantaged environments are less stimulating and less responsive (Barnes, Gutfreund, Satterly, & Wells, 1983; Ramey, Farran, & Campbell, 1978; Tulkin & Cohler, 1973) and more restrictive and controlling (Bee, Van Egren, Streissguth, Nyman, & Leckie, 1969; Clarke-Stewart, 1973) of their children's needs than mothers from middle-class environments. In families with deficits in psychosocial resources, the deficits can serve to restrict the mother's emotional availability and skill in responding to her infant (Emde, 1983). Parents with cognitive deficits have difficulties providing stimulating home environments and interacting in developmentally appropriate and nurturing ways (Feldman, 1994). Adolescent mothers have been found to be less verbally expressive, less sensitive, express less positive affect, and more frequently endorse punitive child-rearing attitudes and show more negative affect (Culp, Appelbaum, Osofsky, & Levy, 1988; Field, Widmayer, Stringer, & Ignatoff, 1980; Garcia-Coll, Hoffman, & Oh, 1987; Hann, Osofsky, Barnard, & Leonard, 1994; Osofsky, Hann, & Peebles, 1993; Reis, 1989).

Preventive intervention with high social risk families is an effort to prevent developmental compromise and problems of adaptation by strengthening individual pathways for development (Emde, 1996). Studies of children's resiliency in the face of adversity show that positive parent–child interaction and attachment (Easterbrooks, Davidson & Chazan, 1993, Werner, 1985) are correlates of resilient outcomes. Interventionists increasingly recognize that the basis for strengthening developmental outcomes is building strong early parent–child relationships that are the foundation for later socioemotional development (Early Headstart Guidelines, DHHS, 1994; Emde, 1996).

Summary

It is important to apply knowledge cautiously in interpreting assessment information and in designing resulting intervention efforts. It is possible, however, to draw some initial conclusions on the basis of current research.

First, individual parent and child characteristics need examination. Research indicates that young children with delays often initiate interaction less frequently and give cues that are more subtle and difficult to read. Parents tend to compensate for infant behavior by more directive behavior in their interactions. Parents experiencing adverse environmental conditions tend to be less responsive and sensitive in their interactions. Because each member of the dyad comes to the interaction with unique characteristics, these individual characteristics must be closely observed and discussed as part of the intervention process.

Second, reciprocity between the parent and child must be assessed. The literature shows that individual infant and parent cues affect the interaction and that the ability of the infant and parent to merge their unique styles into a contingent and reciprocal relationship determines the success of the interaction. It is important to view each interaction as a system in which each element is seen in terms of its effect on other elements. Thus, the ability of the parent to adjust her or his own behavior in response to the child's engagement and disengagement cues is a determining factor in the success of the interaction and should help shape intervention goals.

Third, the assessment must measure adaptations and changes over time. Several studies indicate that parent–infant interaction changes during the first year (Barnard et al., 1984; Beckwith & Cohen, 1983; Berger & Cunningham, 1983; Vietze et al., 1978). These studies suggest that the behaviors of the dyad are affected by individual infant and parent characteristics and that the interaction can be affected adversely over time if mutuality is not established. Additionally, infant and parent characteristics and the resulting degree of mutuality are not static elements, and each degree of change affects the other elements in the interaction. Individual assessment must therefore be repeated at regular intervals so that intervention strategies that encourage and sustain the relationship can be adjusted to the current interaction.

APPROACHES TO ASSESSING EARLY PARENT–CHILD INTERACTION

Assessment approaches are used to advance our empirical knowledge about the importance and nature of interaction and to design and evaluate intervention efforts. In this section, we briefly discuss setting and contextual issues in the assessment of parent–child interaction. We then make recommendations about the best practices for incorporating assessment information into intervention efforts designed to facilitate mutually satisfying parent–child interaction. Finally, we use case vignettes to illustrate how these assessment and intervention practices can be tailored to the individual needs of parents and young children.

Decisions About the Setting and Context for Assessment

THE SETTING. Assessing parent–child interaction in the familiar home setting reflects the field's growing awareness of and respect for family interactions, patterns, and relationships as they occur naturally in the child's daily environment (Miller & Robinson, 1996). Kelly et al. (1996) suggested that the home setting is the optimal place for assessing needs in order to develop appropriate intervention goals that may include restructuring the physical environment and family routines. The assessment should include a combination of nonjudgmental verbal interviews and home observational techniques that involve the mother in joint assessment and intervention plans. For intervention purposes, Bromwich (1983) pointed out that it is important to build rapport with the family, to observe spontaneous parent–infant interaction, and to talk informally with the parent in order to gather information to be used in an ongoing intervention program. She suggested that the assess-

ment period include two home visits to observe and interact with the family in a natural setting and a third clinic session to collect additional information.

Although home observations provide an ecologically valid picture of everyday interactions, they can be more expensive and difficult to arrange (Segal & Webber, 1996). Additionally, Berman and Shaw (1996) pointed out that although some families are comfortable with professionals coming to their homes, other parents may prefer to meet at the program site. They concluded that it is important for families to have a choice in the setting, timing, and personnel for all assessment experiences.

THE CONTEXT. Mahoney, Spiker, and Boyce (1996) pointed out that the context in which observations are made can have a substantial impact on how parents and infants behave. For example, parents may behave differently in a play versus a teaching interaction. Similarly, a parent attempting to soothe a distraught child may use a different style than when she or he is interacting with a happy, contented child. Additionally, the length of the observation may contribute to different outcomes, as will the familiarity between the parent–infant dyad and the person conducting the observation. Kalmanson (1996) suggested that assessment for intervention purposes should be viewed as the first step in the treatment process. The assessment period should occur during a four-to-five-week period and include, among other things, numerous interviews with the mother revealing the mother's historical perspective on mothering and her current view of her baby and their interaction.

In summary, for intervention purposes, it is important to observe behaviors as they occur naturally, within a broad array of situations, with an observer who has already established rapport and trust with the parent and child. The use of prior knowledge about the dyad serves to enrich assessment information and adds to the appropriateness of intervention activities.

Recommendations for Assessment of Parent–Child Interaction

In an article seeking to identify problems with the reliability and validity of assessment instruments, Mahoney, Spiker, and Boyce (1996) cautioned that standardized assessment procedures may not be developed sufficiently to be included as part of the developmental assessment process, may lead to a significant number of errors in judgments and conclusions about the parent–child relationship, and may be potentially harmful to the parents and the parent–professional relationship. They noted that because of the personal nature of the parent–child relationship, it is necessary to address the relationship with the utmost tact, respect, and sensitivity. At the same time, as mentioned earlier, professionals are increasingly cognizant of the importance of viewing the young child as part of a social milieu that includes the primary caregiver and the home environment. Indeed, the interaction between parent and child is most often the primary influence on cognitive, linguistic, and social–emotional development during the first 3 years of life, and the encouragement of healthy interaction must be considered if a program's goals are to support child development. The research discussed earlier supports the need to design intervention practices that promote and sustain parent–child relationships necessary for optimal child development. Additionally, professional training programs should include competencies that address the ability of the practitioner to promote interaction between parent and child (Thorp & McCollum, 1994). It is critical, therefore, to develop guidelines that help professionals use appropriate culturally sensitive assessment practices, interpret resulting assessment information in ways that are helpful for parents, and translate the assessment information into parent–professional jointly designed intervention goals and services.

Recognizing that all young children function within a partnership that is critical to their development, program developers and service providers cannot afford to ignore this critical relationship in their intervention efforts. We have developed the following recommendations for obtaining assessment information about parent–child interactions in sensitive and appropriate ways and including the assessment information in subsequent intervention efforts.

RECOGNIZE THE IMPORTANCE OF THE PARENT–PROFESSIONAL RELATIONSHIP. The relationship between the parent and the service provider is the most potent predictor of the success of intervention

(Kalmanson & Seligman, 1992; Kalmanson, 1996). The success of a parent–professional relationship may depend on the ability to be empathic and responsive. Primary concerns that are within the scope of the program should be acknowledged and dealt with first so that help with the interaction can proceed. For example, if a parent is concerned with the baby's health or the ability to access needed medical services, respite, or child care, the provider should listen and help with these concerns and then focus on the parent–child interaction. Our ability to listen to primary concerns, validate their importance, and help parents access other services is vital to the success of our intervention efforts.

Hirshberg (1996) urged professionals to remember that human connectedness is essential in the assessment process. Unless a parent and professional form a personal relationship, parents may not develop a sense of trust or share feelings and observations that are essential to accurate assessment and development of treatment plans. Treatment, developed as a result of assessment, only succeeds if parents choose to carry it out. If parents feel blamed, criticized, not heard, rejected, and so forth, they will be much less likely to follow through on treatment plans. Hirshberg further cautioned that many times professionals let time constraints, prior professional knowledge, and feelings of helplessness get in the way of truly listening to the parent. He advised that the important question in assessment is to determine how the parent is going to handle the situation – what does he or she want to do and what stands in his or her way. Finally, if the professional has strongly negative attitudes about a parent, the professional needs to consider the feelings to be a sign that he or she needs to reflect carefully on his or her own experience or history as well as the experience of the family.

DETERMINE WHAT ASSISTANCE IS NEEDED. As stated earlier, professionals should first listen to the primary concerns of the parent and help with those concerns, then focus on the parent–child interaction. Second, professionals must recognize that not all families requesting early intervention services have parent–child interactions that are at risk or problematic. Professionals should be prepared to recognize and support relationships that are filled with sensitive, responsive, and growth-promoting interactions. Third, professionals should assist parents with parent–child interaction when symptoms appear that are disruptive in daily life, parental interactions appear notably inflexible and insensitive, or it is clear that the relationship is an obstacle to the developmental progress of the child.

ASSESS INDIVIDUAL PARENT AND CHILD CHARACTERISTICS AND RECIPROCITY. Intervention efforts should be guided by assessment practices that are designed to examine the individual characteristics in the dyadic interaction. Preconceptions about elements in the interaction that are still only partly understood (e.g., the role of parental directive behavior or the use of praise) can stand in the way of recognizing mutuality in the relationship. We suggest that the individual characteristics of the parent and child and the development of reciprocity should be the focus of attention in assessment practices. Specifically, the parent's and child's initiating and responding behaviors should be examined, as well as the contingency and mutuality present in the interaction. Does the child display behavioral cues that indicate interest, alertness, satisfaction, resistance, disengagement, or distress? Does the child show signs of underactivity or overactivity? Observe the child's attempts to self-regulate: Is the process smooth and integrated or disorganized and unpredictable? What are the child's responses to auditory and visual stimulation: Does he or she enjoy it or become overstimulated, or is it difficult to interest the child in activities? How do the child's functional characteristics affect the interaction? For example, a child with visual problems may need more auditory and tactile cues to help him or her interpret the environment. How does the individual parent demonstrate an understanding or lack of understanding of realistic developmental expectations? Are the individual parent's responses determined by infant cues and characteristics? Or is the parent intrusive as defined by her child's negative responses (disengagement) to her or his behaviors? What are the parent's responses to conflict and anger? How does the parent express love and affection? Finally, what is the degree of compatibility between the parent and child: Does the relationship seem to be mutually satisfying with each member accommodating the other to keep the developmental process moving, or does it

stagnate, turn negative, and fail to progress along developmental lines?

RESPECT INDIVIDUAL VALUES AND PREFERENCES. Berman and Shaw (1996) cautioned that not everyone shares the same values about what constitutes appropriate child development, and some milestones that professionals consider universal may actually conflict with what some families expect and want for their child. Hanson, Lynch, and Wayman (1990) discussed four critical elements for developing respect for individual cultural differences: 1) clarification of the interventionist's own values and assumptions, 2) collection and analysis of ethnographic information related to the community in which the family resides, 3) determination of the degree to which the family operates transculturally, and 4) examination of the family's orientation to specific child-rearing issues.

Professionals engaging in either assessment or treatment plans must have the communication skills that enable them to establish positive relationships with parents from different cultural backgrounds. These skills include the ability to respect individual differences; make continual efforts to understand differences; adjust one's own expectations with new knowledge and understanding; and relay these attitudes of respect, open-mindedness, and flexibility to parents.

Finally, the child's experiences must be understood within the cultural context of the child and family (Greenspan & Meisels, 1996). Specific ways of relating and interacting and the content of interactions (what is communicated with behavior, play, and words) may vary considerably from culture to culture.

USE AN APPROACH IN WHICH THE PARENT REMAINS IN CONTACT WITH THE CHILD. The traditional assessment and intervention approach usually involves the professional working directly with the baby while the parent observes the professional teaching or interacting with the child. This approach is presented as an educational model for the parent to imitate in the home environment. Designing the assessment and resulting intervention so that the parent instead of the professional remains in contact with her or his child reinforces the concept that what is important is the unique and important relationship that exists between parent and child, not a model that may seem culturally irrelevant to the parent. Additionally, designing the assessment and intervention so the parent remains in contact with the child helps strengthen the parent's belief that the parent is the most important source of knowledge about her or his child, not the professional. It would be difficult, indeed, to assess accurately children's relational capabilities unless the parent is the interactive partner instead of the professional.

USE A JOINT PARENT–PROFESSIONAL ASSESSMENT PROCESS. We suggest that assessment be a joint process between the parent and the professional, in which both parent feedback during interviews and the parents' assessment of their relationship with their child are used. This approach builds on information from parents and avoids cultural bias and mistaken assumptions. Greenspan and Meisels (1996) stated that assessment should include the parents' description of the child's abilities and developmental history and the observations of the child within the family context. Discussions with parents can identify ways parents have found to support their child as well as interactional patterns that are of concern to them.

During informal and open-ended interviews, the parent needs to be asked what her or his views of her baby are, what she or he thinks about the relationship with the baby, and how a professional can help. Professionals need to avoid jargon and ask questions with genuine interest. Professionals should avoid reaching hasty conclusions that may be based on their own biases. The use of follow-up questions can be used to explore a parent's meaning. The professional can clarify with the parent that he or she has unique knowledge about her or his baby that is vital to the intervention: Namely, the parent knows the child in ways that others do not and that the professional will benefit from this parental expertise. In turn, the professional has knowledge in specific areas used to assist the parent.

We suggest an approach for joint assessment of the interaction that is similar to those successfully used in previous assessment and intervention efforts (e.g., Bernstein, Hans, & Percansky, 1991; Glovinsky, 1993; Kelly, 1982; Koniak-Griffin, Verzemnieks, & Cahill, 1992; McDonough, 1993). With this approach, the parent(s) and child are videotaped during a brief interaction episode. Together the parent and professional review the tape, while the parent comments on the positive aspects of the interaction and what she or he likes about the interaction and relationship. The parent controls the pace, adding additional information about the relationship if she or he chooses. The tape is reviewed again with the parent noting anything about the interaction that seems problematic. The professional adds input at this point, concentrating first on the positive aspects, before addressing any concerns. Segment(s) of the parent and child interacting together can be used to illustrate examples of positive behavioral cues and reciprocal interactions. Parental feelings and comments about the assessment process are discussed.

From information in the videotape and from parental input during interviews, the parent and professional jointly design the intervention goals. The success of the intervention can be monitored with later videotapes and parental reports. If goals are designed together, the parent and professional are more likely to form a close alliance based on mutual respect and purpose.

EMPHASIZE THE POSITIVE. Feedback to the parent about the interaction should be as positive and nonjudgmental as possible; general negative appraisals should never occur. Feedback to parents during the parent–child interaction should be sensitively paced, in which the parent's behavioral cues are used as feedback. Information about child development should be given within the context of the interaction, not as part of a didactic curriculum. Professionals should avoid authoritarian perspectives and adopt a spirit of discovery with the parent as a partner in the assessment and subsequent intervention.

Hirshberg (1996) suggested that it is particularly important to single out for comment the experiences with the infant during the assessment that signal positive functioning and attachment and to explore them with the parents. Parents may have trouble recognizing these positive feelings of closeness; exploring the details of these moments can boost parental self-esteem, confidence, and recognition of the important aspects of her or his relationship with the child.

ADDRESS THE LIMITATIONS OF INTERVENTION BASED ON ASSESSMENT INFORMATION. The parent's and professional's definition of intervention goals, intervention success, and the limitations of intervention should be addressed clearly. The professional needs to recognize his or her own limitations, and if issues pertaining to the parent's own unresolved conflicts arise, the professional should listen and validate the importance of those issues for both the parent and the child. The success of a parent–professional relationship may depend on the ability to be empathic and responsive during the assessment process. However, the ability to provide therapeutic treatment to resolve conflicts and relationship problems (e.g., marital problems) often falls outside the expertise of the professional and the scope of an intervention program. This limitation should not result in hesitancy to include assessment and facilitation of parent–child interaction as a general program goal. Rather, when the treatment identified by the assessment process cannot be offered by the program professional, an available list of resources and financial costs should be available for referral. It is often helpful for the professional to assist the parent in making the initial contact.

MAKE ASSESSMENT AN ONGOING PROCESS. Assessment is the first step in the intervention and should be an ongoing process throughout the intervention. Parental needs and the parent–child relationship can change over time. The professional should continue to check with the parent about her or his perceptions of what is happening and should also be a close observer of behavioral changes during intervention and how such changes may affect the relationship. The professional should ask the parent how her or his view of the baby has changed over time and how this has affected the parenting experience. Through observations and interviews, the professional can assess whether the parent responds to changes in flexible and appropriate ways or whether the changes in child behavior are seen as unwelcome challenges. Parents initially may be reluctant to discuss their feelings about their child and their relationship with their child. The provider should be sensitive when a parent is hesitant to discuss a topic and responsive when the parent decides

to trust the provider by revealing more information and feelings. When issues of abuse or neglect are present, however, the professional should not hesitate to discuss these issues with the parent and make appropriate referrals.

Case Vignettes

The following three vignettes illustrate how the recommendations discussed earlier can be applied in the early intervention setting. The vignettes were chosen because they illustrate different perspectives a professional can take, on the basis of identified family needs. In the first situation, the mother requests assistance with the interaction, and the professional is able to proceed immediately with joint assessment and development of intervention goals. In the second case, the mother's primary concern is anxiety and grief over a recent diagnosis. The professional responds first to this parent-identified need and is then able to work with the parent on strengthening the parent–child relationship. In the final episode, the interruption of the child's developmental trajectory necessitates an environmental assessment that includes in-depth interviews with the mother. The disruption of the healthy parent–child interaction is due to relationship issues beyond the scope of the intervention program. After the mother and professional work together to identify the needs, the professional recognizes program limitations and makes appropriate referrals.

Chris and Patti: Joint assessment with resulting intervention based on the concepts of recognizing and responding to child cues.

Chris, a 9-month-old boy with Down syndrome, lived with his mother, father, and two older siblings in a rural community. His mother, Patti, managed to drive 1 1/2 hours weekly to a parent–infant program. During a parent discussion, she described Chris as increasingly fussy. When probed, she related her increasing frustration in trying to teach him new skills and said she was enjoying their time together less and less. She felt he was also frustrated during their interactions. Patti was also worried about his physical health, because he had frequent respiratory infections and had recent eye surgery, with good prognosis but requiring him to wear an eye patch over one eye at all times. She felt she had the necessary medical services she needed but still felt concerned about Chris's long-term health and frustrated with their increasing communication problems.

The professional validated Patti's concerns about Chris's health by empathizing with her worry. The professional avoided dismissive comments such as "I am sure he'll be fine" or "You're doing all you can, you just can't worry about it." Additionally, the professional talked with her about the recent surgery and its effects on Patti, Chris, and the resources of an already busy family far from the hospital. The professional asked how Patti and Chris were adapting to the eye patch and what effect that may have on the interaction. The professional then asked Patti if she would be interested in spending time concentrating on the interactions in her weekly visits and explained the video feedback method in which they would jointly look at the interaction and plan an intervention approach. Patti seemed relieved that some action would come about as a result of her expressed concern and wanted to begin immediately. A 10-minute videotape was made of Chris and Patti. Patti began the interaction by playing with Chris and then, when signaled, moved to a teaching situation. Patti and the professional watched the tape together, and then Patti was asked to note the positive aspects of the interaction and any concerns.

It was clear from Patti's comments that she was invested in the relationship with her baby and able to express her concern and love verbally. She pointed out how quickly Chris seemed to tire of the interaction, especially during the teaching phase, in which he had ended up crying and signaling to be held. The professional commented on Patti's ability to observe carefully, and together they again watched the tape. This time the professional pointed out the times during play that Patti had responded appropriately to Chris's cues of interest and engagement. Chris's subtle disengagement cues during the teaching were pointed out, and Patti was soon able to recognize Chris's move from subtle (turning away or frowning) to potent (fussing or crying) cues. Together they discussed the importance of recognizing those cues and responding to the cues by a change of pace or toy or by stopping the teaching altogether. The professional noted Chris's clarity of cues and his ability to respond clearly in the interaction. Patti left the first

session better able to watch for these cues and better able to adjust her own behavior accordingly. During subsequent intervention, Patti learned to slow her pace considerably, position Chris more comfortably, respond to his cues by adjusting her own behavior, and let him take the lead in determining the focus. She was motivated from the start to learn more about Chris's behavior, and the professional's job was to guide this process. After six more sessions in which the professional gave verbal feedback to Patti as she interacted with Chris, another videotape was made, and Patti was excited to see how much more both of them seemed to be enjoying each other. She later expressed the recognition that she had felt compelled to "catch him up" because of his regression after eye surgery, and she now recognized that their "give and take" during the interaction was more important than her "teaching one more skill."

This vignette illustrates the use of several of the recommendations outlined earlier. First, the assessment took place as part of an ongoing intervention program. The service provider was quick to recognize the change in Patti's and Chris's interaction and to listen to the mother's concerns. Second, the professional's assessment and intervention strategies began with a recognition of the parent and child strengths in the interaction. The professional recognized Patti as the best source of information about her child and interpreted Patti's concern as a demonstration of her investment in the parent–child relationship. The professional pointed out Chris's clarity of cues as a developmental strength and helped Patti to recognize the cues and adjust her own behavior accordingly. A joint parent–professional assessment process in which videotapes of Patti and Chris interacting together were used was useful in identifying the unique characteristics of the interaction. Lastly, the intervention was recognized as being within the scope of the intervention program, and the concerns of the mother were addressed immediately.

Laura and Teresa: Dealing with a parent's primary concern and then moving to joint assessment of the interaction and resulting intervention.

Laura was a 4-month-old recently diagnosed with a rare genetic syndrome resulting in significant cognitive and motor delays. She lived with her mother, Teresa, and an older brother close to the center where the diagnosis was determined. Laura and Teresa were soon enrolled in a home-based local intervention program. Teresa was a single mother and welcomed the professional into her home, although she seemed unenthusiastic and detached during the initial visit. During the first visit, the professional spoke with Teresa about Teresa's views of Laura. The visitor asked Teresa what Laura liked and did not like, what they enjoyed doing together, and what kind of schedule Laura and she had during a typical day. It was difficult for Teresa to describe Laura. She did not know what Laura enjoyed and found it easier to describe the differences between Laura and her older brother. Teresa was hesitant to talk about their daily routines but welcomed a conversation about the diagnosis and what this meant for Laura.

The professional realized that it was not possible to reach any immediate conclusions about Laura and Teresa's relationship, because it was very difficult for Teresa to relate her feelings about Laura. The professional's job at this time was to establish rapport, gain Teresa's trust, and attempt to infuse her visits with value for Teresa. Teresa asked for more reading material about Laura's delay, and the professional promised to bring it to the next visit. At the next visit, the professional offered to read through the selected material with Teresa and answer any questions she might have. As they read the material, it was clear that the extent of Laura's disabilities and the poor prognosis had been upsetting to Teresa since the diagnosis. She wondered aloud about her abilities to care for Laura and the effect it would have on their family's limited resources. As she talked, it was clear that Teresa was filled with grief and anxiety, and even though professional services were available to her, she felt alone and scared. She wondered what difference she really could make in Laura's life; as an extension of this feeling, she expressed doubts about any difference professionals could make in Laura's or her life. At this point, the professional validated the concerns the mother had, offered to get in touch with a parent support network for Teresa, and continued to listen to Teresa's doubts and pain. The professional stated that over the next few weeks they would talk more about the possible ways she could help, and the professional realized that she would need to watch closely for the need to refer Teresa to a counselor if her own help seemed insufficient.

Over the course of the next few weeks, Teresa accepted the support of friends, extended family, and the parent network and continued to discuss her feelings about Laura with the professional. Teresa took good care of Laura's physical needs but admitted she did not feel as emotionally available to Laura as she wanted to be. She was beginning to feel guilty about her lack of emotional involvement and reported that her feelings for Laura felt much different than her attachment to her older son. The professional asked Teresa if she would be interested in examining her interaction with Laura using videotapes of herself and Laura interacting. Teresa was hesitant but willing to try. During the course of the assessment, it became clear that Teresa did not think Laura recognized any of her initiations or responses. Although Laura's cues were weak, they were present, and the professional and Teresa worked to interpret these cues and decide on appropriate responses. Gradually, Teresa found it rewarding to watch for Laura's cues and Laura became more responsive, although her ability to initiate remained static. By the end of the three-month intervention, Teresa was feeling less guilt and more satisfaction in her interactions with Laura. Teresa realized that she was the most important person in Laura's life, and she felt better able and willing to meet Laura's needs. Teresa also recognized that although Laura's development was delayed, it was progressing.

The professional recognized the importance of establishing a long-term, positive relationship with Teresa and that the success of the intervention efforts depended on the quality of the parent–professional relationship. She responded to Teresa's primary need to grieve and receive support, and she allowed Teresa time and encouragement in forming a relationship with Laura. She remained nonjudgmental and affirmed that Teresa's and Laura's relationship was the foundation for Laura's development. Rather than intervening by modeling the interaction, the professional took the time with the mother to assess jointly the mother–child interaction and then base the intervention on the joint assessment. She allowed the mother to set the agenda and proceeded at the mother's pace in the intervention. The professional also watched for the need to refer the mother for additional services while providing information requested by the mother.

Lisa and Deborah: Ongoing assessment of needs and recognition of the limits of the intervention program.

Lisa was a 2 1/2-year-old living with her mother and new stepfather. She had a severe motor impairment due to cerebral palsy diagnosed in the first 6 months of life, and she had been enrolled in the same center-based intervention program for two years. Her father and mother divorced soon after Lisa's diagnosis had been made, and Lisa lived alone with her mother, Deborah, until she was 2 years old, when her mother remarried. Lisa had established a close and reciprocal relationship with her mother, and her relationships with other adults in her life (her grandmother, grandfather, and center providers) were close and warm. Even though Lisa had extremely atypical motor development that prevented her from sitting, reaching and grasping, or talking, her cognitive abilities appeared to be close to normal. She managed to send clear cues to people in her daily environment. Shortly before she was 2 1/2 years old, Lisa began to develop eating problems, and she refused to eat at home or at the center. Deborah did not identify any problems in her environment that might be causing Lisa's eating problems, and a doctor who examined Lisa could not identify any new health problem that might be a contributing factor. Lisa's strength continued to deteriorate, and the interventionist closest to the family asked to visit Lisa and Deborah at home. During the next two home visits, Deborah was asked to describe Lisa's routines and interactions in very concrete ways. "What happened when Lisa woke up in the morning? Who put her to bed? How long did she sleep? Where did she sleep? Where did she eat her meals? How did Deborah feel about Lisa and their current relationship? Had there been a change in Lisa's level of communication? What activities did Lisa enjoy? What activities seemed to cause distress? Had there been any recent changes in the amount of time Lisa spent in any of these activities? How did Lisa show she was happy or distressed?"

During the two-week period of home visits, Deborah realized that Lisa's routines had changed substantially since her recent marriage, and Lisa's eating problems and behavior could be a response to these changes. Deborah realized she spent a great deal of time with her new husband and less time with Lisa. Lisa's father, who had expressed concerns about raising Lisa, had abandoned Deborah, and Deborah was determined to protect her relationship with her new husband. Her new husband was irritated by the amount of time Deborah devoted to Lisa's substantial physical needs and her emotional relationship with Lisa. Deborah was now conflicted between the attention Lisa was demanding and the attention she felt her new husband deserved. Lisa was entangled in these conflicts and exhibited her own powerful means of resistance by refusing food. The professional recognized her limitations in helping Deborah resolve her feelings of past abandonment and her current conflicted feelings about how to divide her attentions and maintain her relationships. She discussed the possibility of introducing Deborah to a mental health professional whom she knew and trusted. The psychologist worked in confidence with Deborah and subsequently with all three members of the family. Deborah's family remained intact, and Lisa's eating problems receded. The emotional connection between Lisa and Deborah was repaired, although the family constellation required adjustments for Lisa as well as for Deborah and her new husband.

It was important for the professional first to assess Lisa's and Deborah's current needs as they began to interfere with Lisa's developmental progress. The professional knew the parent was the best source of information about her child, visited the home to increase understanding, and probed for concrete details about changes in the home environment. The professional recognized the problem, validated the mother's concern, and also recognized her own limitations in providing services. She introduced another professional into the picture who was trained in this area while continuing to support Deborah and Lisa in the intervention setting.

The vignettes provided here illustrate the variability of family needs and the necessity to design assessment strategies tailored to the unique needs of each dyad. Professional training efforts must prepare program professionals for developing and implementing these strategies effectively.

A discussion of personnel preparation is included in the final section of this chapter.

SPECIFIC MEASURES USED TO ASSESS PARENT–CHILD INTERACTION

Use of Standardized Assessments of Parent–Child Interaction

We have emphasized the value of including parent–child interaction in the menu of assessments and in the context of early intervention plans. Our guidelines encourage the use of an individualized approach as the best way to intervene in parent–child interaction. Many programs want to offer a more general evaluation of their program's efforts, however. To do this, it is helpful to consider first what standardized approaches are best for a given population or a given program's approach.

Despite an increasing amount of work on developing and testing scales of parent–child interaction, use of these scales in early intervention programs is not widespread. Recently, investigators have included children with special needs or developmental delays in validating the instruments; this is vital to the field. Munson and Odom (1996) reviewed a number of published rating scales. Their review provides a convenient source of information on the scales and their reliability, validity, and training issues. Munson and Odom suggested that the process of identifying an appropriate observational tool can, in and of itself, be a good learning experience for early intervention staff and researchers. We have emphasized two aspects of the parents' behavior: their control or directiveness and their responsiveness. For the child, the most frequently emphasized behaviors are attention, readiness, and responsiveness.

Does the available research inform us about the validity of parent–child interaction with children in early intervention programs? Evidence is emerging about the developmentally delayed population. In a multisite study, Boyce et al. (1996) evaluated the Maternal Behavior Rating Scales (Mahoney, 1992); the Mother–Child Rating Scale (Crawley & Spiker, 1982); and the Multi-Pass system (Marfo, 1991). The sample included 238 mothers and children videotaped while playing at home or at an early intervention center. All children demonstrated developmental delay and scored two standard deviations below the mean on a developmental test. The children's age averaged 31.7 months. Using a factor analysis on the scales items, Boyce et al. developed parent affect, responsiveness, sensitivity, directiveness, and topic control factors. The child factors were play maturity, emotional responsiveness, compliance, and topic control. The results indicated a pattern of moderate positive correlation between child developmental level and maternal responsiveness and a negative correlation with maternal directiveness. There was no association demonstrated with child interaction measures and the child's developmental level.

Likewise, Shonkoff and colleagues (1992) used the Nursing Child Assessment Teaching Scale (NCATS) to measure parent–child interaction in a nonexperimental longitudinal study of developmental change in 190 children with developmental disabilities and their families. The children were from early intervention programs in Massachusetts and New Hampshire. The average age at enrollment was 10.6 months, and the sample included fifty-four children with Down syndrome, seventy-seven with motor impairment, and fifty-nine with developmental delays of uncertain etiology. Data were collected during two home visits within six weeks of program entry and twelve months later and included the Mental Scale of the Bayley Scales of Infant Development and observations of mother–child interaction during teaching and play. At the first home visit, the children's scores on the Teaching Scale were significantly lower than a sample of unimpaired children of the same chronological age. At the second home visit (12 months later), the children's scores had improved significantly and approached the mean of nondisabled children. There also was a significant positive association between the children's outcome measures and the Time 2 measure of the child's interaction score. Gains made at Time 2 in mental age, level of spontaneous play, and adaptive behavior were associated with a higher child total score on the Teaching Scale. Changes in the children's Teaching Scale scores were also associated negatively with the presence of cardiac or seizure disorders. Interestingly, the mothers' scores at Time 2 were significantly correlated with the children's scores.

Palisano et al. (1993) reported a similar finding for a sample of infants with motor delays; the infants' NCAT scores predicted the mothers' scores on the interaction scale.

In three independent and diverse samples – one normal, one in which children were at social risk, and a third with preterm infants – the twelve-month and twenty-four-month NCAT scores were related to both mental development and language (Morisset, 1994). The twelve-month maternal score showed a positive correlation with thirty-six-month language performance for the social risk group and with cognitive scores at five years for the social risk and preterm samples, but not for the normal group. The twenty-four-month measure of mothers' interactions showed consistent positive association with the concurrent two-year Bayley measure, the thirty-six-month language, and the WPPSI at sixty months; correlations with the sixty-month IQ and the twenty-four-month measure of mothers' interaction for all three samples ranged from .45–.52. There is evidence that both parent and child behaviors as measured in interactions are associated with later IQ, which parallels the findings with nonhandicapped samples. Therefore, the value of using the assessment of parent–child interaction as a focus for assisting the parent with interaction patterns that are supportive of the child's subsequent development seems justified from the standpoint that the interaction is a dynamic stage for the child's learning.

Next, we summarize four interactional scales that hold promise for all disciplines in early intervention. The measures chosen all have basic psychometric data on samples of children with special needs, have developed means for others to learn the assessment procedure, and have current literature about the validity of the assessment. The first scales are measures of parent–child interaction that assess the structure and process of dyadic communication during a feeding and teaching episode. These scales are the Nursing Child Assessment Feeding and Teaching Scales (Sumner & Spietz, 1994). The second assessment method is the Parent–Child Early Relational Assessment (Clark, 1985). This scale was developed to evaluate the experience of the child and parent with each other and taps the affective climate of the dyad quite well. The final two scales were developed specifically for samples of children with disabilities and are focused on concepts related to the parent's style and response and the child's involvement in play interaction. These scales are the Mother–Child Rating Scale (Crawley & Spiker, 1982) and the Maternal Behavior Rating Scale (Mahoney, 1992).

A Measure of the Structure and Process of Dyadic Communication: Parent–Child Interactional Scales

The Nursing Child Assessment Feeding and Teaching Scales were developed in the late 1970s as a means to capture the dynamic process of interaction between the parent and child. Since that time they have been used in many research and clinical studies. The samples have included children with developmental delays as well as children at risk because of biological and environmental risks (Barnard, 1994; Morisset, 1994).

The model for both the Feeding and Teaching Scales is the same and is based on the premises that the communication process between a child and parent is reciprocal, each partner needs a repertoire of behaviors, and parent–child interaction is a basic platform for learning about each other as well as about the larger environment. These scales are particularly relevant to the field of early intervention because the interaction with the parent–caregiver in the years from birth to preschool is the major vehicle for experiences that organize the child's developing brain. The parent mediates the child's environment by exposing the child to sounds and sights and provides a field for the child to experience relationships among others and events; these experiences, in turn, influence the brain's cortical pathways, which in turn develop and organize the child's behavior.

Both the Feeding and Teaching Scale items are developed around the model of parent–child interaction. The Feeding Scale has a total of seventy-six items, and the Teaching Scale seventy-three items. Each item has behavioral criteria for rating a yes or no answer. Approximately half of the items in each scale were constructed to reflect reciprocity or contingency, because this concept is vital to the early learning process of the young child. Learning how others respond to your behavior is fundamental in developing a sense of mastery.

There are six elements in the model, and four constitute subscales for the parent–caregiver: Sensitivity to the Child's Cues, Response to Distress, Fostering Social-Emotional Growth, and Fostering Cognitive Growth. The two child-related subscales are Clarity of Cues and Responsiveness to the Caregiver. When children have developmental problems, the capacity to give clear cues and be responsive to the caregiver is often problematic. For example, an infant with poor state control or hypotonia will often not give cues of hunger, happiness, or sadness that the parent can understand.

The parent items are positively correlated with parents' educational level, age, and other measures of competency such as level of community life skills and emotional well-being. The parents' total score is correlated with later measures of child IQ and language at 3–5 years of age. Although the children's scores for a normal sample are not as predictive of later cognitive and language measures, the data demonstrate that for biological or environmental risk groups, the children's scores are predictive of their later language and IQ performance. This may be because of a reduced variance in the children's scores. Parents of preterm infants typically have high scores, whereas the infants initially are compromised as social partners because of their inability to maintain a good alert state. In early intervention, part of the family plan and educational goals involves discovering the match between the parent and the child with immaturity or developmental problems. The Feeding and Teaching Scales are a good means of learning what difficulties the parent is experiencing with a child who has problems communicating because of state control, motor dysfunction, attention difficulties, or altered sensory processing. Many clinicians have reported the usefulness of such a standardized interactional scale for understanding the interaction challenge and then helping guide the parent.

The Feeding Scale has been shown to discriminate on a range of child characteristics, including child temperament (Zeanah et al., 1986); preterm birth (Barnard et al., 1983; Kirgis, 1989; Lyons, 1981); failure to thrive (Lobo et al., 1992); cleft lip and palate (Stock, 1993); congenital heart defect (Lobo et al., 1992); and perinatal and psychosocial high-risk circumstances (Farel et al., 1991). Not all studies reported scores for parents and children separately; those that did reported lower child scores for the preterm infant, the child who was failing to thrive, the child with a cleft lip and palate, and the child with a congenital heart defect. For the Teaching Scale, the measure revealed a lower score for preterm infants who were not being monitored in a follow-up program (Slater et al., 1987) and for children with a developmental disability (Shonkoff et al., 1992).

There are also differences reported on the basis of parent characteristics. Parents' scores are lower on the Feeding Scale for Hispanic mothers (Barnard, 1994); mothers with fewer years of education (Barnard, 1994); mothers with an intrusive play style (Houck et al., 1991); mothers with unfavorable prenatal circumstances (Britton & Gronwaldt, 1988); adolescent mothers (Ruff, 1987; Ruff, 1990; vonWindeguth & Urbano, 1989); and mothers with substance-abuse problems (Blackwell & Kaiser, 1994). For the Teaching Scale, a similar set of parent characteristics discriminates the parents' scores for Hispanic mothers (Barnard, 1994); those with fewer years of schooling (Barnard, 1994); those who use drugs (Blackwell & Kaiser, 1994); those who abuse their child (Bee et al., 1981); those with high family stress (Barnard, Spieker, & Morisset, 1990; Farel et al., 1991; Grace, 1990); and mothers with low IQ (Spieker, 1989). In all instances, the parent characteristic is associated with a lower score on the parent item total.

The Nursing Child Assessment Scales are the most widely taught parent–child interaction scales. Although initially developed for use by nurses, they are now widely used by all disciplines including psychologists, psychiatrists, physical therapists, nutritionists, occupational therapists, social workers, and early childhood educators. Approximately 16,000 individuals have been trained to use the Feeding and Teaching Scales. In several states, such as North Carolina and California, an entire state program uses the scales as part of its early intervention programs. The training consists of about forty hours of video instruction, with tapes for teaching, practice, and reliability. The training material was developed to be self-instructional; it has been shown, however, that group classes taught by certified NCAST instructors are more effective. Information about availability of instructors in the United States and many foreign countries is available from the NCAST Training Office at the University of Washington.

Relationship Assessment: The Parent–Child Early Relational Assessment

The Parent–Child Early Relational Assessment (Clark, 1985) is a standardized way of evaluating the parent–child relationship. It goes beyond assessing the present interaction and is designed to reveal affective exchanges in the past, present, and perhaps future of the relationship. This is similar to the way that the Ainsworth Strange Situation paradigm reveals more about a parent's and child's past experiences than about the specifics of their current interaction. The major concept behind the relational assessment is that maternal affect serves as a regulator of the infant's social development.

The procedure recommended for the Relational Assessment involves videotaping four specific episodes of interaction in a twenty-minute sequence. The episodes include feeding; a structured task chosen to be age appropriate; free play with toys chosen by the assessor; and a brief separation and reunion of parent and child. These four situations were chosen to capture the child's experience with the parent and the parent's experience with the child. Having four distinct situations allows different aspects of experience to come forth. The feeding is a well-rehearsed, habitual experience in which issues of control, sensitivity, and responsiveness are apparent. The teaching situation is slightly novel and could involve scaffolding behavior that is needed to complete an unfamiliar task. The free play calls for balancing the negotiation of an agenda between the parent and the child, and the brief separation demonstrates how the child responds to the stress of the parent's leaving. These four situations provide rich clinical material that the early intervention team can use to assess parenting strengths as well as vulnerabilities.

These videotaped episodes can be used for a video replay interview with the parent. The interviewer must have both a good deal of psychological and clinical sensitivity and also training on this specific technique. The video replay allows the assessor–intervenor to select sections of the tape and use these episodes in provoking the parent to think or "wonder" aloud about her relationship with the child, the meaning of certain behaviors of the child, who the child reminds her of, her sense of competence as a parent, and the enjoyable or difficult parts of the interaction. These techniques are similar to those described in the recommended guidelines; however, the use of these four situations provides a more standardized means of providing a variety of interactional themes.

The objective assessment of the four episodes is aided by a training manual and training from the assessment's developer (Clark, 1985). For assessment of the parent, there are ratings that consider behavioral amount, duration, and intensity of parental affect; attitudes expressed toward the child; involvement; and style. The parental involvement items include physical contact (both positive and negative); visual contact; verbalizations (both quantity and quality); social initiative; contingent responsivity; structure and mediation of the environment; reading and responding to cues; connectedness; and mirroring or emotional availability. The child is rated on affect, motoric and communication skills, social initiation, and responsiveness. The dyad is rated on mutual involvement, joint attention to the task, amount of reciprocity, and enjoyment and tension that exist within the interaction. A rater, who must be trained to establish interrater–observer reliability, performs the evaluation by viewing all four episodes of the relational assessment and by calculating summative ratings on sixty-five items. The rater is expected to view the episodes at least eight times and score no more than ten items on one pass.

Although this relationship construct was developed for use with parents with psychiatric illness, the principles used in deciding on the four episodes and the behaviors rated have universal application. These items define the affective component of the interactive relationship better and in more detail than most currently available. Studies document the scale's ability to discriminate between high-risk mothers and well-functioning mothers (Clark, 1983; Musick, Clark, & Cohler, 1981) as well as between secure infants and insecurely attached infants (Teti, Nakagawa, Das, & Wirth, 1991). Six subscales have been described for the four-month feeding episode and the twelve-month free play episode: 1) Parental Positive Affective, Involvement, Sensitivity and Responsiveness; 2) Parental Negative Affective and Behavior; 3) Infant Positive Affect, Communicative and Social Skills; 4) Infant Dysregulation and

Irritability; 5) Dyadic Mutuality and Reciprocity; and 6) Dyadic Tension. All subscales have alphas above .65, suggesting the items are measuring a unitary construct of behavior (Clark, 1985).

Parent–Child Interaction Scales Focused on Children with Developmental Problems

Two scales for observing parent–child interaction developed specifically for populations of children with developmental problems are the Maternal Behavioral Rating Scale (Mahoney, 1992; Mahoney, Finger, & Powell, 1985), and the Mother–Child Rating Scales (Crawley & Spiker, 1983; Spiker, Crawley & Ferguson, 1995). Mahoney based the Maternal Behavioral Rating Scale on the constructs of the mother's behavioral style, which include child-orientation, quantity of stimulation, and control. The mother is instructed to play with the child in any manner she chooses with toys supplied by the observer; the behavior is videotaped and then rated using Likert-type scales. The original scale had eighteen global maternal behaviors and four child behaviors. Factor analysis yielded three maternal factors: Child-Oriented Maternal Pleasure, Quality of Stimulation, and Control. Those three factors accounted for 23% of the variance in the Bayley Mental Development Index in a sample of sixty children with mental retardation. Children with the highest developmental level had mothers whose interactive styles included a high degree of child orientation and low degrees of control and stimulation (Mahoney & Powell, 1988).

The revised 1992 Maternal Behavioral Rating Scale has twelve behavior subscales: Expressiveness, Enjoyment, Warmth, Sensitivity to the Child's Interest, Responsivity, Achievement Orientation, Inventiveness, Praise, Effectiveness, Acceptance, Pace, and Directiveness. In a study with subjects from five states, 238 mothers and their children were videotaped, and the Maternal Behavioral Rating Scale was scored for each dyad (Boyce et al., 1996). The factor scores used were Affect (Expressiveness, Warmth, Enjoyment, Inventiveness, and Acceptance), Responsiveness (Sensitivity, Effectiveness, and Responsiveness), and Directiveness (Directiveness and Pace). Affect was positively correlated with the child's age;

whereas Responsiveness was positively correlated with the mother's education; the child's developmental level and play maturity; and the child's subsequent developmental level for personal–social skills, cognition, and communication. Directiveness was correlated negatively with the child's developmental level, play maturity, topic control, and subsequent cognitive and communication developmental level. This study confirms the direction of the earlier studies and establishes the importance of the parent's behavior in influencing the child's developmental gains. Behavioral coding criteria and a training manual are available, and the estimated training time is fifty hours (Mahoney, 1992).

The Mother–Child Rating Scales (Crawley & Spiker, 1983) are designed to assess children with developmental delays and their mothers during a play sequence. The scales measure two broad dimensions of maternal behavior: a control dimension and an affective dimension. The focus is on the mother's directiveness and sensitivity, because these qualities discriminate between mothers of children with special needs and mothers of normally developing children. Maternal behavioral items include directiveness, elaborativeness, sensitivity, stimulation value, mood, pacing, developmental appropriateness of play, readability, intrusiveness, and mother appeal; the child ratings focus on social and cognitive maturity in play interaction, affective expression, and level of interest; and the dyadic variable is mutuality. The scales' authors chose to use a global rating rather than behavioral counts, and the scales have a Likert format (five to seven points). Each item is scored from a videotaped play episode in which a set of toys provided by the assessor is used. A coding manual is available from the authors; no specific information on training is available.

The early use of the Mother–Child Rating Scales with a small number of cases ($N = 16$) demonstrated that maternal sensitivity and directiveness were separable dimensions of behavior and that only maternal stimulation value and the dyadic measure of mutuality correlated with the child's mental performance (Crawley & Spiker, 1983). A later study with 150 dyads, all of whom demonstrated developmental delay scoring two standard deviations below the mean, also showed a correlation between maternal behavior and child mental performance. Maternal sensitivity correlated positively both with concurrent and future Battelle total scores, whereas maternal directiveness negatively correlated with the Battelle score (Boyce et al., 1996). The children's scores on each rating – Play Maturity, Social Initiative, Social Responsiveness, Toy Initiative, Object Initiative, Locomotion, Animation, and Appeal – were correlated with the total score on the Battelle Developmental Test (Spiker, Crawley, & Ferguson, 1995).

Summary

These four assessment scales illustrate the similarities and differences of various measurement systems. It is important that researchers continue their efforts to identify the elements of parent–child interaction that are most important to the successful functioning of the child and the family and to develop scales based on those elements that are effective for intervention and evaluation purposes.

FUTURE DIRECTIONS

Although it is increasingly accepted that parent–child interaction should be a focus in early intervention programs, the application of research knowledge to intervention practices is a slow process. It is important to identify future directions that are needed in research and personnel preparation efforts to help shift the focus of early intervention from child-centered practices to family-focused intervention that includes facilitation of healthy parent–child interaction.

First, continued research efforts are needed to demonstrate to program developers and service providers that improving parent–child interaction has significant positive effects on both the development of the child and family functioning. Traditionally, program developers have measured the effects of intervention primarily by showing changes in the child's developmental level as measured by standardized tests of infant and child development. Alternatively, program efforts aimed at improving or sustaining the quality of parent–child interaction need to be measured along a broad spectrum of social, emotional, and communication outcomes. Indeed, several reviews of early intervention efforts have called for a shift in evaluating program

effectiveness, suggesting less concentration on child change measured in terms of IQ or developmental level and greater attention to broader and perhaps more modifiable aspects of the child's early social (interactive) environment (Bricker, Bailey, & Bruder, 1984; Dunst, 1986; Fewell & Vadasy, 1987; Shonkoff et al., 1992; White & Casto, 1985; Zigler & Rescorla, 1985). As Cunningham (1986) pointed out, "We may have some of the emphases in our intervention wrong. The data we have suggest it is the interactions and the adaptation and the attachment processes and some of these social, within family effects that are important." Thus, evaluations of program effectiveness need to concentrate on family outcomes, such as parenting stress and perceptions of parenting roles and satisfaction, as well as child outcomes, such as attachment, communication level, and sociability. If evaluation efforts include these outcomes, it will be more possible to demonstrate intervention effects.

Another consideration in evaluating early intervention is the importance of evaluating latent effects from early interaction intervention. Shonkoff et al. (1992) noted that in previous studies of high-risk groups of infants (e.g., Rauh, Achenbach, Nurcombe, Howell, & Teti, 1988; Ramey, Yeates, & Short, 1984), the effects of the caregiving environment on developmental test scores were not demonstrated before children emerged from the sensorimotor period. Therefore, evaluation models measuring cognitive gains that account for the influences of the early caregiving environment should continue into the preschool years.

Second, professional preparation programs need to include assessment and facilitation of parent–child interaction in their list of professional competencies. Service providers should have a firm understanding not only of child development but also of the parent–child relationship. Aspects of the relationship – such as attachment formation, state and emotional regulation, reading of infant cues, using play and teaching as pathways to learning, positive disciplining, and so forth – should be part of the pre- or in-service curriculum. In addition to a base of knowledge about relationship development, professionals need skills in interaction assessment and facilitation. Communication skills that enable relationship-focused and culturally sensitive interventions need to be addressed. In addition, program developers and administrators need to be able to identify gaps in knowledge in these areas, as well as training strategies to fill such gaps.

Third, professionals need to feel comfortable in their role as facilitators of nurturing parent–child interaction. Assessing and facilitating parent–child interaction are often viewed as overly intrusive and beyond the scope of an early intervention program. If professionals believe their relationship with the parent is critical to their intervention efforts, then putting themselves into a potentially judgmental or critical role may be considered aversive and unprofessional. The recommendations offered earlier can serve as guidelines for avoiding these professional conflicts while, addressing a critical component of early intervention: the parent–child relationship. It is important to design practices that recognize parents' autonomy in making decisions about their very young children. In addition, to avoid judgmental and critical appraisals, the assessment and resulting intervention should be consistently positive and designed jointly with the parent. Parents should be viewed as partners, with parent empowerment as an important goal of any intervention effort. Communication efforts built on trust and honesty, with the goal of reaching mutually agreed objectives, are a necessary foundation for successful intervention (see Able-Boone, 1996, and Dinnebeil, Hale, and Rule, 1996, for discussions of collaborative parent–professional relationships). To create a partnership in which parent knowledge and concerns are respected and valued, flexible and informal assessment and intervention efforts that focus on the individual dyad are more effective than formal interview or questionnaire assessments or curriculum-based intervention strategies.

The enactment of Public Law 99-457 in 1986 amended the Handicapped Children's Education Act so that parents could play an integral role in their child's intervention program. The suggestions for future research and personnel training efforts outlined earlier are consistent with the ecological tenets on which those amendments were based. To maximize children's development within their social milieu, program goals and outcomes must be expanded to encompass family functioning, with special attention to parent–child interaction. Additionally, professional preparation programs need to include competencies and training activities that relate to the development of parent–child and parent–professional relationships.

SUMMARY

Studies described in this chapter demonstrate that there are important links between parent–infant interaction and the child's later social and cognitive development. Specific elements that affect that interaction are derived from the individual behavioral repertoires of both the infant and the parent and the reciprocity that develops as both partners respond and adapt to each other. These identified elements are important because they affect both the emergence of a mutually satisfying relationship between the parent and child and the development of competence in the child. Research that has identified and described these elements in specific terms has facilitated the development of assessment procedures that reflect intervention and program evaluation needs.

Several studies have shown that there are differences in parent–child interaction when the infant is disabled or at risk for disability. There is some evidence that mothers of children with special needs dominate the interchanges and their infants seem to be less involved in the interaction than is the case with mothers and nondisabled infants. Furthermore, data suggest that over time mothers and infants who are disabled or premature are less successful at mutually adapting their behaviors to each other than are dyads without special needs. Finally, mothers experiencing adverse environmental conditions tend to be less sensitive and responsive in their interactions.

Although there is still a great need for more conclusive research to determine why such differences occur and to assess the positive or negative effects of those differences on interactions, it is possible to draw some conclusions on the basis of the available data and to apply this knowledge when selecting and interpreting assessment strategies. In this chapter, we have made several recommendations for obtaining assessment information about parent–child interactions in sensitive and appropriate ways and for including the assessment information in subsequent intervention efforts. The recommendations include designing assessment strategies that recognize the importance of the parent–professional relationship and partnership; use of developmentally relevant, positive, and culturally appropriate strategies; and viewing assessment as an ongoing process. We have presented case vignettes to illustrate the use of the recommendations, and we have also described several measures developed for use in research and in clinical settings to plan individual intervention strategies and to measure their outcomes.

With the general acceptance of the importance of parent–infant interaction, it is now important for investigators to move forward in several ways. There is a need to include facilitation of parent–child interaction routinely in intervention goals and to select the best available assessment strategies to measure the effects of interventions. Additionally, professional preparation programs need to include assessment and facilitation of parent–child interaction in their list of professional competencies, and professionals need to use assessment strategies that allow them to feel comfortable and competent in their role as facilitators of nurturing parent–child interaction. With a better understanding of how to examine areas of individual strengths and concerns in the parent–child relationship, parents and professionals will be able to work together to ensure caregiving environments that help children reach their full developmental potential.

REFERENCES

Able-Boone, H. (1996). Ethics and early intervention: Toward more relationship-focused interventions. *Infants and Young Children, 9*(2), 13–21.

Ainsworth, M. D. (1973). The development of the infant-mother attachment. In B. Caldwell & H. Ricciuti (Eds.), *Review of child development research* (Vol. 3). (pp. 1–94). Chicago: University of Chicago Press.

Ainsworth, M., Blehar, M., Waters, E., & Wall, S. (1978). *Patterns of attachment: A psychological study of the strange situation.* Hillsdale, NJ: Erlbaum.

Bakeman, R., & Brown, J. V. (1980). Early interaction: Consequences for social and mental development at three years. *Child Development, 51,* 437–47.

Baldwin, W., & Cain, V. (1980). The children of teenage parents. *Family Planning Perspectives, 12,* 34–43.

Barnard, K. E. (1994). What the Feeding Scale measures. In G. S. Sumner & A. Spietz (Eds.), *NCAST: Caregiver/parent–child interaction feeding manual* (pp. 98–121). Seattle: University of Washington NCAST Publications.

Barnard, K. E., & Martell, L. K. (1995). Mothering. In M. H. Bornstein (Ed.), *Handbook of parenting: Status and social conditions of parenting* (Vol. 3) (pp. 3–26). Hillsdale, NJ: Erlbaum.

Barnard, K. E., Bee, H. L., & Hammond, M. A. (1984). Developmental changes in maternal interactions with term and preterm infants. *Infant Behavior and Development, 7,* 101–13.

Barnard, K. E., Eyres, S., Lobo, M., & Snyder, C. (1983). An ecological paradigm for assessment and intervention. In T. B. Brazelton & B. M. Lester (Eds.), *New approaches to developmental screening of infants.* New York: Elsevier.

Barnard, K. E., Hammond, M. A., Booth, C. L., Bee, H. L., Mitchell, S. K., & Spieker, S. J. (1989). Measurement and meaning of parent–child interaction. In F. Morrison, C. Lord, & D. Keating (Eds.), *Applied developmental psychology* (Vol. 3). New York: Academic.

Barnard, K. E., Spieker, S., & Morriset, C. E. (1990). *Unpublished raw data.* University of Washington, School of Nursing, Seattle, WA.

Barnes, S., Gutfreund, M., Satterly, D., & Wells, G. (1983). Characteristics of adult speech which predict children's language development. *Journal of Child Language, 10,* 65–84.

Beckwith, L. (1971). Relationships between attributes of mothers and their infants' IQ scores. *Child Development, 42,* 1083–98.

Beckwith, L. (1990). Adaptive and maladaptive parenting: Implications for intervention. In S. J. Meisels & J. P. Shonkoff (Eds.), *Handbook of early childhood intervention* (pp. 53–77). New York: Cambridge University Press.

Beckwith, L., & Cohen, S. E. (1980). Interactions of preterm infants with their caregivers and test performance at age 2. In T. M. Field, S. Goldberg, D. Stern, & M. Sostek (Eds.), *High-risk infants and children: Adult and peer interactions* (pp. 155–178). New York: Academic Press.

Beckwith, L., & Cohen, S. E. (1983, April). *Continuity of caregiving with preterm infants.* Paper presented at the meeting of the Society for Research in Child Development, Detroit, MI.

Beckwith, L., & Cohen, S. E. (1984). Home environment and cognitive competence in preterm children during the first 5 years. In A. W. Gottfried (Ed.), *Home environment and early cognitive development* (pp. 235–71). New York: Academic Press.

Beckwith, L., & Rodning, C. (1996). Dyadic processes between mothers and preterm infants: Development at ages 2–5 years. *Infant Mental Health Journal, 17*(4).

Bee, H. L., Barnard, K. E., Eyres, S. J., Gray, C. A., Hammond, M. A., Spietz, L. A., Snyder, C., & Clark, B. (1982). Prediction of IQ and language skills from perinatal status, child performance, family characteristics, and mother-infant interaction. *Child Development, 53,* 1334–56.

Bee, H. L., Disbrow, M. A., Johnson-Crowley, N., & Barnard, K. E. (1981). *Parent–child interaction during teaching in abusing and nonabusing families.* Paper presented at the biennial meeting of the Society for Research in Child Development, Boston.

Bee, H. L., Van Egren, L. F., Streissguth, A. P., Nyman, B. A., & Leckie, M. S. (1969). Social class differences in maternal teaching strategies and speech patterns. *Developmental Psychology, 1*, 726–34.

Beebe, B., & Stern, D. (1977). Engagement-disengagement early object experiences. In N. Freeman & S. Grand (Eds.), *Communicative structures and psychic structures* (pp. 35–55). New York: Plenum Press.

Bell, R. Q. (1974). Contributions of human infants to caregiving and social interaction. In M. Lewis & L. A. Rosenburg (Eds.), *The effect of the infant on its caregiver* (pp. 1–19). New York: Wiley.

Bell, S. M., & Ainsworth, M. D. S. (1972). Infant crying and maternal responsiveness. *Child Development, 43*, 1171–90.

Belsky, J., Goode, M., & Most, R. (1980). Maternal stimulation and infant exploratory competence: Cross-sectional, correlational, and experimental analyses. *Child Development, 51*, 1163–78.

Belsky, J., Rovine, M., & Taylor, D. G. (1984). The Pennsylvania Infant and Family Development Project, 3: The origins of individual differences in infant-mother attachment: Maternal and infant contributions. *Child Development, 55*, 718–28.

Berger, J., & Cunningham, C. C. (1983). Development of early vocal behaviors and interactions in Down syndrome and non-handicapped infant–mother pairs. *Developmental Psychology, 9*, 322–31.

Berman, C., & Shaw, E. (1996). Family-directed child evaluation and assessment under the Individuals with Disabilities Education Act (IDEA). In S. J. Meisels & E. Fenichel (Eds.), *New visions for the developmental assessment of infants and young children* (pp. 361–90). Washington, DC: Zero to Three.

Bernstein, V. J., Hans, S. L., & Percansky, C. (1991). Advocating for the young child in need through strengthening the parent–child relationship. *Journal of Clinical Child Psychology, 20*(1), 28–41.

Black, B., & Logan, A. (1995). Links between communication patterns in mother–child, father–child, and child–peer interactions and children's social status. *Child Development, 66*(1), 255–71.

Blackwell, P., & Kaiser, M. (1994). *The collaborative approach to nurturing: Mother–infant interaction in cocaine affected dyads.* Unpublished manuscript, Tulane University, New Orleans.

Blake, J. (1989). Number of siblings and educational attainment. *Science, 245*, 32–6.

Blehar, M. C., Lieberman, A. F., & Ainsworth, M. D. S. (1977). Early face-to-face interaction and its relation to later infant–mother attachment. *Child Development, 48*, 182–94.

Booth, C. L. (1985, April). *New and old predictors of cognitive and social outcomes in high social-risk toddlers.* Paper presented at the meeting of the Society for Research in Child Development, Toronto, Ontario, Canada.

Booth, C. L., Barnard, K. E., Mitchell, S. K., & Spieker, S. J. (1987). Successful intervention with multiproblem mothers: Effects on the mother–infant relationship. *Infant Mental Health Journal, 8*, 288–306.

Boyce, G. C., Marfo, K., Mahoney, G., Spiker, D., Price, C., & Taylor, M. J. (1996, March). *Parent–child interaction in dyads with children at risk for developmental delays: A factor analytic study.* Poster presented at the Gatlinberg Conference, Gatlinberg, TN.

Boyce, G. C., Taylor, M. J., Casto, G., Mahoney, G., Spiker, D., Marfo, K., & Wilfong-Grush, E. (1996, July). *An investigation of the individual and contextual factors that relate to maternal interaction behaviors and subsequent child development: A study of mothers and their children with disabilities.* Poster presented at WAIMH.

Bradley, R. H., & Caldwell, B. M. (1976a). Early home environment and changes in mental test performance in children from 6 to 36 months. *Developmental Psychology, 12*, 93–7.

Bradley, R. H., & Caldwell, B. M. (1976b). The relation of infants' home environments to mental test performance at fifty-four months: A follow-up study. *Developmental Psychology, 47*, 1172–4.

Brazelton, T. B. (1988). Importance of early intervention. In E. Hibbs (Ed.), *Children and families: Studies in prevention and intervention* (pp. 107–20). Madison, CT: International Universities Press.

Brazelton, T. B., Koslowski, B., & Main, M. (1974). The origins of reciprocity: The early mother–infant interaction. In M. Lewis & L. A. Rosenblum (Eds.), *The effects of the infant on its caregiver.* New York: Wiley.

Bricker, D., Bailey, E., & Bruder, M. B. (1984). Efficacy of early intervention and the handicapped infant: A wise or wasted resource. *Advances in Developmental and Behavioral Pediatrics, 5*, 373–423.

Bricker, D., & Carlson, L. (1980). *The relationship of object and prelinguistic social-communicative schemes to the acquisition of early linguistic skills in developmentally delayed infants.* Paper presented at the Conference on Handicapped and At-Risk Infants: Research and Applications, Asilomar, Monterey, CA.

Bridges, L. J., Connell, J. P., & Belsky, J. (1988). Similarities and differences in infant-mother and infant-father interaction in the Strange Situation: A component process analysis. *Developmental Psychology, 24*(1), 92–100.

Britton, H., & Gronwaldt, V. (1988). *Birth settings and mother–infant interaction.* Final report Grant MCJ-040523-03-0. National Technical Information Service, U.S. Department of Commerce, Springfield, VA.

Bromwich, R. (1981). *Working with parents and infants: An interactional approach.* Baltimore, MD: University Park Press.

Bromwich, R. (1983). *Parent Behavior Progression – manual and 1983 supplement.* Northridge, CA: The Center for Research Development and Services, Department of Educational Psychology, California State University.

Bronfenbrenner, U. (1975). Is early intervention effective? In U. Bronfenbrenner & M. A. Mahoney (Eds.), *Influences on human development.* Hinsdale, IL: Dryden Press.

Brooks-Gunn, J., & Lewis, M. (1982). Development of play behavior in handicapped and normal infants. *Topics in Early Childhood Special Education, 2,* 14–27.

Chess, S., Thomas, A., & Birch, H. (1959). Characteristics of the individual child's behavior responses to the environment. *American Journal of Orthopsychiatry, 29,* 791–802.

Cicchetti, D., & Sroufe, A. (1978). An organizational view of affect: Illustration from the study of Down's syndrome infants. In M. Lewis & L. A. Rosenblum (Eds.), *The development of affect* (pp. 309–49). New York: Plenum Press.

Cielinski, K. L. (1993). *Differential effects of mother's directive behavior on the play of Down syndrome and normally developing children.* Paper presented at the meeting of the Society for Research in Child Development.

Clark, R. (1983). *Interactions of psychiatrically ill and well mothers and their young children: Quality of maternal care and child competence.* Doctoral Dissertation, Northwestern University.

Clark, R. (1985). *The parent-child early relational assessment instrument and manual.* University of Wisconsin Medical School, Department of Psychiatry, Madison.

Clarke-Stewart, K. A. (1973). Interactions between mothers and their young children: Characteristics and consequences. *Monographs of the Society for Research in Child Development, 38*(153), 6–7.

Coates, D. L., & Lewis, M. (1984). Early mother–infant interaction and infant cognitive predictors of school performance and cognitive behavior in six-year-olds. *Child Development, 55,* 1219–30.

Cohen, S., & Beckwith, L. (1979). Preterm infant interaction with the caregiver in the first year of life and competence at age two. *Child Development, 50,* 767–76.

Crawley, S., & Spiker, D. (1982). *Mother-child rating scale (M-CRS).* Chicago: University of Illinois. (Available from ERIC Document Reproduction Service No. ED 221 978.)

Crawley, S. B., & Spiker, D. (1983). Mother–child interactions involving two-year-olds with Down syndrome: A look at individual differences. *Child Development, 54,* 1312–23.

Crnic, K. A., Greenberg, M. T., Robinson, N. M., & Ragozin, A. S. (1984). Maternal stress and social support: Effects on the mother-infant relationship from birth to eighteen months. *American Journal of Orthopsychiatry, 54,* 224–35.

Crockenberg, S. B. (1981). Infant irritability, mother responsiveness, and social support influences on the security of infant–mother attachment. *Child Development, 52,* 857–65.

Culp, R. E., Appelbaum, M. I., Osofsky, J. D., & Levy, J. A. (1988). Adolescent and older mothers: Comparison between prenatal maternal variables and newborn interaction measures. *Infant Behavior and Development, 11,* 353–62.

Cunningham, C. (1986, April). Patterns of development in Down's syndrome. Paper presented at the Third International Down's Syndrome Congress, Brighton, England. As cited in Fewell, R. R., and Vadasy, P. F. (1987). *Measurement issues in studies of efficacy. Topics in Early Childhood Special Education, 7,* 85–96.

Davis, H., Stroud, A., & Green, L. (1988). Maternal language environment of children with mental retardation. *American Journal of Mental Retardation, 93,* 144–53.

Department of Health and Human Services. (1994). *The statement of the advisory committee on services for families with infants and toddlers.* Washington, DC.

Dinnebeil, L. A., Hale, L. M., & Rule, S. (1996). A qualitative analysis of parents' and service coordinators' descriptions of variables that influence collaborative relationships. *Topics in Early Childhood Special Education, 16*(3), 322–47.

Divitto, B., & Goldberg, S. (1979). The effects of newborn medical status on early parent-infant interaction. In T. M. Field, A. Sostek, S. Goldberg, & H. H. Shuman (Eds.), *Infants born at risk.* New York: Spectrum Publications.

Dubow, E. F., & Luster, T. (1990). Adjustment of children born to teenage mothers: The contribution of risk and protective factors. *Journal of Marriage and the Family, 52,* 393–404.

Dunst, C. (1980, April). *Developmental characteristics of communicative acts among Down's syndrome infants and nonretarded infants.* Paper presented at the biennial meeting of the Southeastern Conference on Human Development, Alexandria, VA.

Dunst, C. J. (1986). Overview of the efficacy of early intervention programs: Methodological and conceptual considerations. In L. Bickman & D. Weatherford (Eds.), *Evaluating early intervention programs for severely handicapped children and their families* (pp. 79–147). Austin, TX: PRO-ED.

Easterbrooks, M. A., Davidson, C. E., & Chazan, R. (1993). Psychosocial risk, attachment, and behavior problems among school-aged children. *Development and Psychopathology, 5*(3), 389–402.

Egeland, B., & Sroufe, L. A. (1981). Developmental sequelae of maltreatment in infancy. In R. Rirley & D. Cicchetti (Eds.), *Developmental perspectives on child maltreatment: New directions for child development.* San Francisco: Jossey-Bass.

Eheart, B. K. (1982). Mother-child interactions with non-retarded and mentally retarded preschoolers. *American Journal of Mental Deficiency, 87,* 20–5.

Emde, R. N. (1983). The pre-representational self and its affective core. *The Psychoanalytic Study of the Child, 38,* 165–207.

Emde, R. N. (1996). Thinking about intervention and improving socio-emotional development: A clinical perspective and recent trends in policy and knowledge. *Zero to Three, 17*(1), 11–16.

Engel, M., & Keane, W. M. (1975, April). *Black mothers and their infant sons: Antecedents, correlates and predictors of cognitive development in the second and sixth year of life.* Paper presented at the biennial meeting of the Society for Research in Child Development, Denver, CO.

Farel, A., Freeman, V. A., Keenan, N. L., & Huber, C. (1991). Interactions between high-risk infants and their mothers: The NCAST as an assessment tool. *Research in Nursing and Health, 14,* 109–18.

Farran, D., & Ramey, C. (1980). Social class differences in dyadic involvement during infancy. *Child Development, 51,* 254–7.

Feldman, M. A. (1994). Parenting education for parents with intellectual disabilities: A review of outcome studies. *Research in Developmental Disabilities, 15*(4), 299–332.

Fewell, R. R., & Vadasy, P. F. (1987). Measurement issues in studies of efficacy. *Topics in Early Childhood Special Education, 7,* 85–96

Field, T. (1977). Effects of early separation, interactive deficits, and experimental manipulations on infant–mother face-to-face interaction. *Child Development, 48,* 763–71.

Field, T. (1979). Interaction patterns of high-risk and normal infants. In T. M. Field, A. Sostek, S. Goldberg, & H. H. Shuman (Eds.), *Infants born at risk* (pp. 333–356). New York: Spectrum Publications.

Field, T. (1982). Interaction coaching for high-risk infants and their parents. *Prevention in Human Services, 1,* 5–54.

Field, T. (1983). High-risk infants "have less fun" during early interactions. *Topics in Early Childhood Special Education, 3,* 77–87.

Field, T. M., Widmayer, S. M., Stringer, S., & Ignatoff, E. (1980). Teenage, lower-class, black mothers and their preterm infants: An intervention and developmental follow-up. *Child Development, 51,* 426–36.

Fraiberg, S. (1974). Blind infants and their mothers: An examination of the sign system. In M. Lewis & L. A. Rosenblum (Eds.), *The effect of the infant on its caregiver* (pp. 215–232). New York: Wiley-Interscience.

Furstenberg, F., Brooks-Gunn, J., & Morgan, S. P. (1987). *Adolescent mothers in later life.* Cambridge, England: Cambridge University Press.

Garcia-Coll, C. T., Hoffman, J., & Oh, W. (1987). The social ecology and early parenting of Caucasian adolescent mothers. *Child Development, 58,* 955–63.

Girolametto, L., & Tannock, R. (1994). Correlates of directiveness in the interactions of fathers and mothers of children with developmental delays. *Journal of Speech and Hearing Research, 37,* 1178–91.

Gisel, E., Lange, L., & Niman, C. (1984). Tongue movement in 4- and 5-year-old Down syndrome children during eating: A comparison with normal children. *American Journal of Occupational Therapy, 38,* 660–5.

Glovinsky, I. (1993). The use of videotaping in the evaluation of preschool-aged children and their parents. *Infants and Young Children, 6,* 60–6.

Goldberg, S. (1977). Social competence in infancy: A model of parent–infant interaction. *Merrill-Palmer Quarterly, 23,* 163–77.

Goldberg, S., Brachfield, S., & Divitto, B. (1980). Feeding, fussing, and play: Parent-infant interaction in the first year as a function of prematurity and perinatal medical problems. In T. M. Field, S. Goldberg, D. Stern, & M. Sostek (Eds.), *High-risk infants and children: Adult and peer interactions* (pp. 133–154). New York: Academic Press.

Grace, J. (1990). Empirical cluster scores and the Nursing Child Assessment Teaching Scale. *NCAST National News, 6*(1), 2–5.

Greenspan, S. (1988). Fostering emotional and social development in infants with disabilities. *Zero to Three, 9*(1), 8–18.

Greenspan, S. I., & Meisels, S. J. (1996). Toward a new vision for the developmental assessment of infants and young children. In S. J. Meisels & E. Fenichel (Eds.), *New visions for the developmental assessment of infants and young children* (pp. 11–26). Washington, DC: Zero to Three.

Gunn, P., Berry, P., & Andrews, R. (1979). Vocalizations and looking behavior of Down syndrome infants. *British Journal of Psychology, 70,* 259–63.

Hann, D. M., Osofsky, J. D., Barnard, K. E., & Leonard, G. (1994). Dyadic affect regulation in three caregiving environments. *American Journal of Orthopsychiatry, 64,* 263–9.

Hann, D. M., Osofsky, J. D., & Culp, A. M. (1996). Relating the adolescent mother–child relationship to preschool outcomes. *Infant Mental Health Journal, 17.*

Hanson, M. J., Lynch, E. W., & Wayman, K. I. (1990). Honoring the cultural diversity of families when gathering data. *Topics in Early Childhood Special Education, 10*(1), 112–31.

Harris, S. (1983). *Improving oral-motor control in young children with motor handicaps: A neurodevelopmental treatment approach.* Unpublished paper.

Hess, E. H. (1970). Ethology and developmental psychology. In P. H. Mussen (Ed.), *Carmichael's manual of child psychology* (Vol. 1). New York: Wiley.

Hirshberg, L. M. (1996). History-making, not history-taking: Clinical interviews with infants and their families. In S. J. Meisels & E. Fenichel (Eds.), *New visions for the developmental assessment of infants and young children* (pp. 85–124). Washington, DC: Zero to Three.

Houck, G. M., Booth, C. L., & Barnard, K. E. (1991). Maternal depression and locus of control orientation as predictors of dyadic play behavior. *Infant Mental Health Journal, 12,* 347–60.

Jens, K., & Johnson, N. (1982). Affective development: A window to cognition in young handicapped children. *Topics in Early Childhood Special Education, 2,* 17–24.

Jones, O. H. M. (1977). Mother–child communication with pre-linguistic Down's syndrome and normal infants. In H. R. Schaffer (Ed.), *Studies in mother-infant interaction* (pp. 379–401). San Diego, CA: Academic Press.

Kalmanson, B. (1996, September). *Overcoming challenges in working with families: A relationship based perspective.* Presentation at Infant Development Association of California, Pleasanton, CA.

Kalmanson, B., & Seligman, S. (1992). Family–provider relationships: The basis of all interventions. *Infants and Young Children, 4,* 23–32.

Kang, R., & Barnard, K. (1979). Using the Neonatal Behavioral Assessment Scale to evaluate premature infants. In *Birth defects: Original article series* (Vol. 15, no. 7, pp. 119–44, The National Foundation). New York: Alan R. Liss.

Kaye, K. (1975, September). *Toward the origin of dialogue.* Paper presented at the Loch Lomond Symposium, University of Strathclyde.

Kaye, K. (1976). Infants' effects on their mothers' teaching strategies. In J. Glidwell (Ed.), *The social context of learning and development.* New York: Gardner Press.

Kelly, J. F. (1982). Effects of intervention on caregiver–infant interaction when the infant is handicapped. *Journal of the Division for Early Childhood, 5,* 53–63.

Kelly, J. F., & Barnard, K. E. (1990). Assessment of parent–child interaction. In S. J. Meisels & J. P. Shonkoff (Eds.), *Handbook of early childhood intervention* (pp. 278–302). New York: Cambridge University Press.

Kelly, J. F., Morisset, C. E., Barnard, K. E., Hammond, M. A., & Booth, C. L. (1996). The Influence of early mother–child interaction on preschool cognitive/linguistic outcomes in a high-social-risk group. *Infant Mental Health Journal, 17*(4), 1–11.

Kelly, J. F., Morisset, C. E., Barnard, K. E., & Patterson, D. L. (1996). Risky beginnings: Low maternal intelligence as a risk factor for children's intellectual development. *Infants and Young Children, 8*(3), 11–23.

Kirgis, C. A. (1989). *Nurse facilitation of mother–preterm infant acquaintance.* Final Progress Report to the National Center for Nursing Research, National Institutes of Health.

Koniak-Griffin, D., Verzemnieks, I., & Cahill, D. (1992). Using videotape instruction and feedback to improve adolescents' mothering behaviors. *Journal of Adolescent Health, 13,* 570–5.

Korner, A. F. (1971). Individual differences at birth: Implications for early experience and later development. *American Journal of Orthopsychiatry, 41,* 608–19.

Krakow, J., & Kopp, C. (1983). The effects of developmental delay on sustained attention in young children. *Child Development, 54,* 1143–55.

Lester, B. M., McGrath, M. M., Garcia-Coll, C., Brem, F. S., Sullivan, M. C., & Mattis, S. G. (1995). Relationship between risk and protective factors, developmental outcome, and the home environment at four years of age in term and preterm infants. In H. E. Fitzgerald, B. M. Lester, & B. Zuckerman (Eds.), *Children of poverty: Research, health, and policy issues* (pp. 197–231). New York: Garland.

Lewis, M., & Coates, D. L. (1980). Mother–infant interaction and cognitive development in twelve-week-old infants. *Infant Behavior and Development, 3,* 95–105.

Lewis, M., & Goldberg, S. (1969). Perceptual-cognitive development in infancy: A generalized expectancy model as a function of the mother–infant interaction. *Merrill-Palmer Quarterly, 15,* 81–100.

Lewis, M., & Rosenblum, L. A. (1974). *The effect of the infant on its caregiver. (Introduction).* New York: Wiley-Interscience.

Liaw, F., Meisels, S. J., & Brooks-Gunn, J. (1995). The effects of experience of early intervention on low birth weight, premature children: The Infant Health and Development Program. *Early Childhood Research Quarterly, 10,* 405–31.

Lobo, M. L., Barnard, K. E., & Coombs, J. B. (1992). Failure to thrive: A parent–infant interaction perspective. *Journal of Pediatric Nursing, 7,* 251–61.

Longstreth, L. E., Davis, B., Carter, L., Flint, D., Owen, J., Rickert, M., & Taylor, E. (1981). Separation of home intellectual environment and maternal IQ as determinants of child IQ. *Developmental Psychology, 17,* 532–41.

Lyons, N. B. (1981). *Behavioral differences in premature and fullterm mother-infant pairs during a feeding interaction.* Master's thesis, University of Washington, Seattle, School of Nursing.

Mahoney, G. (1992). Maternal behavior rating scale (MBRS) (Rev. Ed.). (Available from Family Child Learning Center, 90 W. Overdale Dr., Tallmadge, OH 44278.)

Mahoney, G., Finger, I., & Powell, A. (1985). Relationship of maternal behavioral style to the development of organically impaired mentally retarded infants. *American Journal of Mental Deficiency, 90*(3), 296–302.

Mahoney, G., Finnegan, D., Fors, S., & Wood, S. (1985). *Transactional intervention program suggested activities.* Ann Arbor: University of Michigan.

Mahoney, G., Fors, S., & Wood, S. (1990). Maternal directive behavior revisited. *American Journal on Mental Retardation, 94*(4), 398–406.

Mahoney, G., & Powell, A. (1988). Modifying parent–child interaction: Enhancing the development of handicapped children. *The Journal of Special Education, 22*(1), 82–96.

Mahoney, G., Spiker, D., & Boyce, G. (1996). Clinical assessments of parent–child interaction: Are professionals ready to implement this practice? *Topics in Early Childhood Special Education, 16*(1), 26–50.

Marfo, K. (1990). Maternal directiveness in interactions with mentally handicapped children: An analytic commentary. *Journal of Child Psychology and Psychiatry, 31,* 531–49.

Marfo, K. (1991, April). *Maternal directiveness in interactions with developmentally delayed children: A correlational analysis.* Paper presented at the Biennial Meeting of the Society for Research in Child Development, Seattle, WA.

McCollum, J. A., & Hemmeter, M. L. (1997). Parent-child interaction intervention when children have disabilities.

In M. J. Guralnick (Ed.), *The effectiveness of early intervention* (pp. 549–76) Baltimore, MD: Paul H. Brookes.

McDonough, S. C. (1993). Interaction guidance: Understanding and treating early infant-caregiver disturbances. In C. H. Zeanah (Ed.), *Handbook of infant mental health* (pp. 414–426). New York: Guilford Press.

McLean, M., & McCormick, K. (1993). Assessment and evaluation in early intervention. In W. Brown, S. K. Thurman, & L. F. Pearl (Eds.), *Family centered early intervention with infants and toddlers: Innovative cross-disciplinary approaches* (pp. 43–79). Baltimore, MD: Paul H. Brookes.

McLoyd, V. C. (1990). The impact of economic hardship on black families and children: Psychological distress, parenting and socioemotional development. *Child Development, 61,* 311–46.

Miller, L. J., & Robinson, C. C. (1996). Strategies for meaningful assessment of infants and toddlers with significant physical and sensory disabilities. In S. J. Meisels & E. Fenichel (Eds.), *New visions for the developmental assessment of infants and young children* (pp. 313–28). Washington, DC: Zero to Three.

Morisset, C. E. (1994). What the Teaching Scale measures. In G. S. Sumner & A. Spietz (Eds.), *NCAST: Caregiver/parent–child interaction feeding manual* (pp. 53–80). Seattle: University of Washington NCAST Publications.

Munson, L. J., & Odom, S. L. (1996). Review of rating scales that measure parent-infant interaction. *Topics in Early Childhood Special Education, 16*(1), 1–25.

Musick, J. S., Clark, R., & Cohler, B. J. (1981). The Mother's Project: A clinical research program for mentally ill mothers and their young children. In B. Weissbourd & J. Musick (Eds.), *The social and caregiving environments of infants* (pp. 11–127). Washington, DC: NAEYC.

Nelson, K. (1973). Structure and strategy in learning to talk. *Monographs of the Society for Research in Child Development, 38*(149), 12.

Olson, S. L., Bates, J. E., & Bayles, K. (1984). Mother–infant interaction and the development of individual differences in children's cognitive competence. *Developmental Psychology, 20,* 166–79.

Osofsky, J. D., Hann, D. M., & Peebles, C. D. (1993). Adolescent parenthood: Risks and opportunities for mothers and infants. In C. Zeanah (Ed.), *Handbook of infant mental health* (pp. 106–19). New York: Guilford Press.

Palisano, R. J., Chiarello, L. A., & Haley, S. M. (1993). Factors related to mother–infant interaction in infants with motor delays. *Pediatric Physical Therapy, 5*(2), 55–60.

Papousek, H., & Bornstein, M. H. (1992). Didactic interactions: Intuitive parental support of vocal and verbal development in human infants. In H. Papousek, U. Jurgens, & M. Papousek (Eds.), *Nonverbal vocal communication: Comparative and developmental approaches* (pp. 209–29). Cambridge, England: Cambridge University Press.

Ramey, C. T., Farran, D. D., & Campbell, F. (1978). Predicting IQ from mother–infant interaction. *Child Development, 50,* 804–14.

Ramey, C., Yeates, K., & Short, E. (1984). The plasticity of intellectual development: Insights from preventive intervention. *Child Development, 55,* 1913–25.

Rauh, V., Achenbach, T., Nurcombe, B., Howell, C., & Teti, D. (1988). Minimizing adverse effects of low birth weight: Four-year results from an early-intervention program. *Child Development, 59,* 544–53.

Redding, R., Harmon, R., & Morgan, G. (1990). Relationships between maternal depression and infants' mastery behaviors. *Infant Behavior and Development, 13,* 391–5.

Reis, J. (1989). A comparison of young teenage, older teenage, and adult mothers on determinants of parenting. *The Journal of Psychology, 123,* 141–51.

Richard, N. B. (1986). Interaction between mothers and infants with Down syndrome: Infant characteristics. *Topics in Early Childhood Special Education, 6,* 54–71.

Robson, K. S., & Moss, H. A. (1970). Patterns and determinants of maternal attachment. *Journal of Pediatrics, 7,* 967–85.

Rosenberg, S., & Robinson, C. (1988). Interactions of parents with their young handicapped children. In S. Odom & M. Karnes (Eds.), *Early intervention for infants and children with handicaps* (pp. 159–77). Baltimore, MD: Paul H. Brookes.

Rothbart, M. K. (1984). Social development. In M. Hanson (Ed.), *Atypical infant development* (pp. 207–36). Austin, TX: PRO-ED.

Rothbart, M. K., & Hanson, M. (1983). A caregiver report comparison of temperamental characteristics of Down syndrome and normal infants. *Developmental Psychology, 19,* 766–9.

Ruff, C. (1987). How well do adolescents mother? *American Journal of Maternal–Child Nursing, 12*(4), 249–53.

Ruff, C. (1990). Adolescent mothering: Assessing their parenting capabilities and their health education needs. *Journal of National Black Nurses Association, 4*(1), 55–62.

Rutter, M. (1978). Family, area, and school influences in the genesis of conduct disorder. In L. A. Hersov, M. Berger, & D. Shaffer (Eds.), *Aggression and anti-social behavior in childhood and adolescence* (pp. 95–113). Oxford, England: Pergamon Press.

Sameroff, A. J., & Seifer, R. (1995). Accumulation of environmental risk and child mental health. In H. E. Fitzgerald, B. M. Lester, & B. Zuckerman (Eds.), *Children of poverty: Research, health, and policy issues* (pp. 233–58). New York: Garland.

Sameroff, A. J., Seifer, R., Barocas, R., Zax, M., & Greenspan, S. (1987). Intelligence quotient scores of 4-year-old children: Social–environmental risk factors. *Pediatrics, 79,* 343–50.

Sander, L. W. (1964). Adaptive relationships in early mother–child interaction. *Journal of the American Academy of Child Psychiatry, 3,* 231–63.

Schaffer, H. R., Collis, G. M., & Parson, G. (1977). Vocal interchange and visual regard in verbal and pre-verbal children. In H. R. Schaffer (Ed.), *Studies in mother-infant interaction* (pp. 291–324). London: Academic Press.

Segal, M., & Webber, N. T. (1996). Nonstructured play observations: Guidelines, benefits, and caveats. In S. J. Meisels & E. Fenichel (Eds.), *New visions for the developmental assessment of infants and young children* (pp. 207–30). Washington, DC: Zero to Three.

Shonkoff, J. P., Hauser-Cram, P., Krauss, M. W., & Upshur, C. C. (1992). Development of infants with disabilities and their families. *Monographs of the Society for Research in Child Development, 57*(6).

Slater, M. A., Naqvi, M., Andrew, L., & Haynes, K. (1987). Neurodevelopment of monitored versus nonmonitored very low birth weight infants: The importance of family influences. *Developmental and Behavioral Pediatrics, 8,* 278–85.

Smith, B. L., & Oller, D. K. (1981). A comparative study of pre-meaningful vocalizations produced by normally developing and Down syndrome infants. *Journal of Speech and Hearing Disorders, 46,* 46–51.

Smith, L., & Hagen, V. (1984). Relationship between the home environment and sensorimotor development of Down syndrome and non-retarded infants. *American Journal of Mental Deficiency, 89,* 124–32.

Snow, C. E., Arlman-Rupp, A., Hassing, Y., Jobse, J., Joosten, J., & Vorster, J. (1974). *Mothers' speech in three social classes.* Unpublished paper, Institute for General Linguistics, University of Amsterdam.

Spieker, S. (1989). Adolescent mothers: Parenting skills measured using the NCAST and the HOME. *NCAST National News, 5*(4), 3–4, 8.

Spiker, D., Boyce, G. C., & Price, C. (1996). *Individual differences in the interactions between mothers and their two-year-olds with disabilities.* Poster presented at the International Conference on Infant Studies, Providence, RI.

Spiker, D., Crawley, S. B., & Ferguson (1995, March/April). *The Mother-Child Rating Scales: Use with young children with disabilities.* Poster presented at the Society for Research in Child Development, Indianapolis, IN.

Spitz, R. A. (1964). The derailment of dialogue. *Journal of American Psychoanalytic Association, 12,* 752–75.

Stern, D. N. (1974). Mother and infant at play: The dyadic interaction involving facial, vocal, and gaze behaviors. In M. Lewis & L. A. Rosenblum (Eds.), *The effect of the infant on its caregiver* (pp. 187–214). New York: Wiley-Interscience.

Stern, D. N. (1977). *The first relationship: Infant and mother.* Cambridge, MA: Harvard University Press.

Stern, D. N. (1984). Affect attunement. In J. D. Call, E. Galenson, & R. L. Tyson (Eds.), *Frontiers of infant psychiatry* (pp. 3–14). New York: Basic Books.

Stern, D. N., Jaffe, J., Beebe, B., & Bennett, S. L. (1975). Vocalizing in unison and in alternation: Two modes of communication within the mother–infant dyad. In D.

Aaronson & R. W. Rieber (Eds.), *Developmental psycholinguistics and communication disorders.* New York: New York Academy of Sciences.

Stern, G. G., Caldwell, B. M., Hersher, L., Lipton, E. L., & Richmond, J. B. (1973). Early social contacts and social relations: Effects of quality of early relationship. In L. J. Stone, T. Smith, & L. B. Murphy (Eds.), *The competent infant* (pp. 1097–111). New York: Basic Books.

Stevenson, M. B., Leavitt, L. A., & Silverberg, S. B. (1985). Mother-infant interaction: Down syndrome case studies. In S. Harel & N. J. Anastasiow (Eds.), *The at-risk infant: Psychosocial aspects* (pp. 389–95). Baltimore, MD: Paul H. Brookes.

Stock, J. (1993). The NCAFS and NCATS: Promising research tools in children with craniofacial anomalies, *NCAST National News, 9*(1).

Strain, B. A., & Vietze, P. M. (1975, April). *Early dialogues: The structure of reciprocal infant–mother vocalization.* Paper presented at the meeting of the Society for Research in Child Development, Denver, CO.

Sumner, G. A., & Spietz, A. (Eds.). (1994). *Caregiver/Parent–Child Interaction. Feeding Manual* (pp. 1–176). NCAST Publications, University of Washington, Seattle, WA.

Tamis-LeMonda, C., & Bornstein, M. (1989). Habituation and maternal encouragement of attention in infancy as predictors of toddler language, play, and representational competence. *Child Development, 60,* 738–51.

Tannock, R. (1988). Mothers' directiveness in their interactions with their children with and without Down syndrome. *American Journal on Mental Retardation, 93,* 154–65.

Telzrow, R. W., Kang, R. R., Mitchell, S. K., Ashworth, C. D., & Barnard, K. E. (1982). An assessment of the behavior of the preterm infant at forty weeks conceptional age. In L. P. Lipsitt & T. M. Field (Eds.), *Perinatal risk and newborn behavior.* Norwood, NJ: Ablex.

Teti, D. M., Nakagawa, M., Das, R., & Wirth, O. (1991). Security of attachment between preschoolers and their mothers: Relations among social interaction, parenting stress, and mother's sorts of the Attachment Q-Set. *Developmental Psychology, 27*(3), 440–7.

Thoman, E. B. (1975). *Mother–infant adaptation: The first five weeks.* Paper presented at the Proceedings of Perinatal Nursing Conference, Battelle Seattle Research Center, Seattle, WA.

Thorp, E. K., & McCollum, J. A. (1994). Defining the infancy specialization in early childhood special education. In L. J. Johnson, R. J. Gallagher, M. J. LaMontague, J. B. Jordon, J. J. Gallagher, P. L. Hutinger, & M. B. Karnes (Eds.), *Meeting early intervention challenges: Issues from birth to 3* (pp. 167–83). Baltimore, MD: Paul H. Brookes.

Tulkin, S. R., & Cohler, B. J. (1973). Childrearing attitudes and mother–child interaction in the first year of life. *Merrill-Palmer Quarterly, 19,* 95–106.

Tulkin, S. R., & Covitz, F. E. (1975, April). *Mother–infant interaction and intellectual functioning at age six.* Paper presented at the biennial meeting of the Society for Research in Child Development, Denver, CO.

Vietze, P. M., Abernathy, S. R., Ashe, M. L., & Stich, F. (1978). Contingent interaction between mothers and their developmentally delayed infants. In G. P. Sackett (Ed.), *Observing behavior* (Vol. 1). Baltimore, MD: University Park Press.

von Windeguth, B. J., & Urbano, R. C. (1989). Teenagers and the mothering experience. *Pediatric Nursing, 15,* 517–520.

Wachs, T. D., & Gruen, G. E. (1982). *Early experience and human development.* New York: Plenum.

Wachs, T. D., Uzgiris, I. C., & Hunt, J. (1971). Cognitive development in infants of different age levels and from different environmental backgrounds: An explanatory investigation. *Merrill-Palmer Quarterly, 17,* 283–317.

Werner, E. (1985). Stress and protective factors in children's lives. In A. R. Nicol (Ed.), *Longitudinal studies in child psychology and psychiatry* (pp. 335–55). New York: Wiley.

White, K., & Casto, G. (1985). An integrative review of early intervention efficacy studies with at-risk children: Implications for the handicapped. *Analysis and Intervention in Developmental Disabilities, 5,* 7–31.

Yeates, K. O., MacPhee, D., Campbell, F. A., & Ramey, C. T. (1983). Maternal IQ and home environment as determinants of early childhood intellectual competence: A developmental analysis. *Developmental Psychology, 19*(5), 731–9.

Yogman, M. W., Kindlon, D., & Earls, F. (1995). Father involvement and cognitive/behavioral outcomes of preterm infants. *Journal of the American Academy of Child & Adolescent Psychiatry, 34*(1), 58–66.

Zeanah, C. H., Keener, M. A., & Anders, T. T. (1986). Developing perceptions of temperament and their relation to mother-infant behavior. *Journal of Child Psychology and Psychiatry, 27*(4), 499–512.

Zigler, E., & Rescorla, (1985). Social science and social policy: The case of social competence. In R. Kasschau, L. Rehm, & L. Ullman (Eds.), *Psychology research, public policy and practice: Toward a productive partnership* (pp. 62–94). New York: Praeger.

CHAPTER THIRTEEN

Family Assessment Within Early Intervention Programs

MARTY WYNGAARDEN KRAUSS

This chapter explores the context and processes of family assessment within early intervention programs for children with disabilities or developmental delays. Family assessments are now a routine, indeed mandated, practice in early intervention programs. Three primary reasons can be advanced for the value of family assessment for children with disabilities. First, family assessment recognizes explicitly the need to examine children's development within their most powerful context, that of the family. This requirement acknowledges that the development of young children is not biologically fixed but is conditioned to a large extent by their environment (Bronfenbrenner, 1992). Second, family assessment is grounded in the belief that parents can benefit from focused attention on their capacities for providing a nurturing, informed, and attentive environment for their children, particularly those with disabilities. Families' needs for information, guidance, and reassurance in the face of parenting a child with atypical development is presumed to be aided by a structured assessment of their current strengths, resources, and needs. Third, there is increasing recognition that the intensity and specificity of early intervention programs need to be tailored to the characteristics and functioning of the family in light of the child's disability or risk status (Guralnick, 1998).

Despite the clarity of its rationale, implementation of family assessment reveals deep-seated ambivalence from both parents and early intervention professionals. In its traditional form, family assessment implies a process of fact-finding, evaluation, and professional judgment about the capacities and vulnerabilities of individual families to provide an optimal environment for the growth and development of their children. The goal of such an assessment is to identify specific ways in which external help can be provided that advances the family's natural or acquired abilities to stimulate, nurture, and support a child's development, as defined by the parents, the professionals involved in the child's care, or both. When all parties agree about the optimal conditions for child development, the assessment often proceeds harmoniously and the results reflect a well-negotiated articulation of shared views. When the relevant parties disagree, and express differences in their goals for the child and the means to achieve particular objectives, the family assessment process may constitute a battleground in which deeply held beliefs about family influences and practices produce schisms that must be surfaced, discussed, and reconciled.

For many families, the idea of family assessment as mandated by early intervention programs represents a new phenomenon that they approach skeptically. Others may enter into family assessment quite willingly, explicitly acknowledging that the child's optimal development requires a frontal approach on all spheres of influence. The need to develop a range of assessment methodologies, strategies, or approaches that achieves the goals of family assessment, that are consistent with the skills of intervention professionals, and that can accommodate varying family preferences constitutes a major challenge for the field.

This chapter reviews current practices in family assessment within early intervention programs. It begins with a discussion of the legal and programmatic bases for family assessment and describes their current requirements. It then analyzes three perspectives that undergird the choice and focus of family assessment strategies, including ecological theories of human development, stress and coping approaches to parental adaptation, and family empowerment perspectives for human services. The next section focuses on methods of family assessment, including informal nonstandardized strategies and more formal standardized modalities. The chapter concludes with speculations about the future of family assessment within early childhood programs, focusing particularly on the need to capitalize on the legal mandate for family assessment to inform a variety of theoretically and programmatically relevant questions.

LEGAL AND PROGRAMMATIC FRAMEWORKS FOR FAMILY ASSESSMENT

The passage in 1986 of the Education for the Handicapped Act Amendments (P.L. 99-457) marked a watershed for the legal transformation of early childhood intervention from child-oriented to family-oriented programs. Among the law's provisions was the requirement that plans for children receiving early intervention services be developed within a family context, resulting in the formulation of an Individualized Family Service Plan (IFSP). The IFSP is a written document that an early intervention program must prepare, with family participation; it describes how the program plans to meet the assessed needs of the eligible child and his or her family.

The legacy of increased family involvement in the services provided to young children has been described elsewhere (Krauss & Hauser-Cram, 1992). P.L. 99-457 went much further, however, than previous mandates for parental involvement by redefining the service unit from the child as the primary focus of intervention to the family as the primary focus of services (Krauss, 1990). Legally, services to children in early intervention programs are now required to view the child's needs within the context of the family's strengths and areas in need of development, thus mandating as full an assessment of the family's therapeutic and programmatically relevant issues as was previously provided for the child.

Specific requirements are described for the IFSP's development and content. The IFSP must be prepared within forty-five calendar days from referral and must contain a description of the child's current functioning in five domains: physical development, cognitive development, language and speech development, psychosocial development, and self-help skills. It also must contain the results of a family assessment designed to determine the concerns, priorities, and resources of the family related to enhancing the development of the child. All assessments conducted are voluntary on the part of the family. Intervention plans for both the child and the family are included in the IFSP.

Although many early intervention programs conducted formal and informal assessments of families prior to the enactment of P.L. 99-457 (Krauss & Jacobs, 1990), this landmark legislation and its subsequent reauthorizations (e.g., P.L. 102-119) ushered in a new era in which family assessments are required of all programs serving young children with disabilities. Thus, informal practices have been replaced by mandated, explicit expectations for programmatic activity with parents, a change that has produced considerable consternation within the field of early childhood programs (Slentz & Bricker, 1992). Bailey, Buysse, Edmondson, and Smith (1992) noted the difficulties experienced by early intervention programs in implementing the provisions of the IFSP: 1) the change is perceived as significant; 2) professionals in early intervention programs are experts in child development rather than in family systems; 3) resistance to ceding professional decision-making authority to families exists; and 4) many programs are located within larger agencies that do not require an explicit family focus for assessment and service. Thus, the IFSP requirements signal a range of programmatic challenges that cast the purpose and impact of family assessment into bold relief. Interestingly, the response from the field has been pragmatic. Assessment strategies have been designed that rely on families to define their practical and informational needs. Despite the preponderance of pragmatic approaches toward family assessment that have been developed (and are discussed in the next section), the basis of family assessment rests, in part, on a confluence of theoretical developments concerning family-based influences on child development, stress and coping processes in the caregiving context, and family empowerment as a principle for human services.

THEORETICAL BASES FOR FAMILY ASSESSMENT

The intellectual roots of current family assessment practices can be traced to three pivotal contributions. The first contribution was the articulation of theories of human development that acknowledged environmental influences, such as the family, on the development of the child (Bronfenbrenner, 1979). With respect to children with disabilities or developmental delays, the argument was that the phenotypic expression of genetic or constitutional disorders is varied and conditioned by the context in which development occurs (Hodapp, 1997). Guralnick's (1998) synthesis of the empirical literature regarding the effectiveness of early intervention draws upon a theoretical model of child development that integrates the importance of family characteristics, family interaction patterns, and specific stressors experienced by families of children with disabilities.

The second contribution focuses more specifically on the variability in the most proximate environment inhabited by the developing child, namely, the family. Theories have been advanced to describe and explain those features of the family environment that are most advantageous to the child. This work seeks to explicate the mechanisms that account for individual adaptation to nonnormative events, particularly examining the context of caregiving for dependent family members. Here the subject of study is the caregiver and the processes by which the caregiver adapts to unusual caregiving demands. Among the many theorists who have studied this issue, the work of Pearlin and colleagues (Pearlin, Mullan, Semple, & Skaff, 1990) is useful for describing the stress and coping mechanisms families invoke in the face of challenging events.

The third major contribution to current family assessment practices is the articulation of family empowerment principles on which services should be based. These principles assert that *how* services are provided is as important as *what* is provided. Family-focused service systems, such as early intervention programs, are fueled by a commitment to family empowerment. Among the earliest developers of the rationale for and strategies to promote family empowerment within family-focused services are Dunst

and his colleagues (Dunst & Trivette, 1986; Dunst, Trivette, & Cross, 1986; Dunst, Trivette & Deal, 1988) and Turnbull and Turnbull (1986, 1995). Each of these intellectual roots is discussed in the next section.

Family Influences on Child Development

Family assessment in early childhood programs is based on the conviction that the development of children must be understood within the context of the child's environment. Although some environmental theories suggest that a child's development is affected by the characteristics and contingencies of the immediate context (Sameroff & Feil, 1985), Bronfenbrenner's theory of human ecology advances the idea of reciprocal interactions between the child and the multiple environments in which he or she develops, ranging from proximal to distal influences (Bronfenbrenner, 1992). In addition to asserting the importance of understanding the environmental contexts in which a child develops, Bronfenbrenner focuses on the nature of the interactions between the child and the various environments, noting that different features of the child's behavior instigate or provoke different responses (Sontag, 1996). The reciprocity in the interactions between a child and the environment is perhaps the most compelling aspect of this theory and provides a fundamental rationale for assessing both the child and the family, as the most proximal influence affecting the child.

Guralnick (1998) advanced a developmental theory of child outcomes that incorporates three sets of family patterns of interaction: the quality of the parent–child transactions, family-orchestrated child experiences, and health and safety provided by the family. These patterns are themselves influenced by such family characteristics as parental attitudes and beliefs, psychological functioning, coping styles, social supports, and resources. Guralnick noted that when family characteristics are within normative levels, child development outcomes are generally achieved in an expected manner. Adverse characteristics – such as maternal depression, inadequate support, and so forth – negatively affect familial patterns of interaction, resulting in compromised child development. Guralnick's model of family influences on child outcomes provides an important framework for identifying the qualities and characteristics of the family that warrant assessment within early intervention programs.

Stress and Coping Theories of Parental Adaptation

The second major contribution to the theoretical basis for family assessment comes from the renewed interest over the past twenty years in factors affecting the adaptation of parents to the task of rearing a child with disabilities or developmental delays (Crnic, Friedrich, & Greenberg, 1983; Ramey, Krauss & Simeonsson, 1989; Seltzer & Krauss, 1994). An impressive amount of theoretical and empirical work has been reported that focuses on the mechanisms by which individuals adapt successfully or unsuccessfully to stressors or demands that are unusual, unwanted, or novel (Blacher, 1984; Dunst, Trivette, & Jodry, 1997; Olson & Lavee, 1989; Ryff & Seltzer, 1996). In the context of Bronfenbrenner's theory of human development, this work explores aspects of the microsystem, consisting of the primary caregivers of the child, and the mesosystem, consisting of other systems in which the family lives, and the influences of these systems on familial caregiving practices, which, in turn, affect the child's development.

A comprehensive theoretical and empirical investigation of stress and coping among caregivers was conducted by Pearlin and colleagues (Pearlin, Mullan, Semple, & Skaff, 1990; Pearlin & Schooler, 1978; Pearlin, Lieberman, Menaghan, & Mullan, 1981). Their research focuses on understanding the experiences of family caregivers of persons with Alzheimer's disease. It incorporates many issues resulting from the gradual transformation of the relationship between caregiver and care recipient that characterizes this progressive disease. With Alzheimer's, the requirements of caregiving eventually supersede and dominate all or most aspects of the predisease relationship. Despite the differences in context between their research and studies of parental adaptation to a child with a disability, this conceptual model has general applicability to the study of family experiences during the early childhood period in which the atypical development of a child may challenge anticipated or preexisting parental and familial routines.

Pearlin's model bears resemblance to the Double ABCX Model of McCubbin and colleagues (McCubbin & Patterson, 1981) in its identification of three primary components of the stress and coping paradigm: 1) characteristics of the stressor (the A component); 2) the meaning of the stressor as perceived by the caregiver (the B component); and 3) the resources available to manage the stressful event (the C component). The outcomes in both McCubbin's and Pearlin's conceptualization are the qualities of the adaptations (psychological and behavioral) made by the caregiver.

Pearlin's model provides a map of the process by which caregiving becomes stressful (Pearlin et al., 1990). Specifically, he and his colleagues suggested that the unfolding of the stress process is conditioned initially and pervasively by the background of the caregiver and the context in which caregiving occurs, including the demographic and social characteristics of the caregiver, history of caregiving within the particular family, family and network composition, and availability of services and other resources to aid in caregiving. They noted that "virtually everything we are interested in learning about caregiving and its consequences is potentially influenced by key characteristics of the caregiver. The effects of ascribed statuses, such as age, gender, and ethnicity, along with educational, occupational, and economic attainments are expected to be threaded throughout the entire stress process" (Pearlin et al., 1990, p. 585).

Pearlin's work distinguishes between primary and secondary stressors. Primary stressors include objective indicators of the degree of impairment in the care recipient (i.e., cognitive status, adaptive behavior, and problematic behaviors) and subjective indicators of burden of care in the care provider (i.e., sense of caregiving overload, and relational deprivation). Secondary stressors are those that arise from the caregiving requirements but that are not directly related to the care recipient's need for assistance or the care provider's direct burden of care. Such stressors include family tensions arising from the demands of caregiving, job caregiving conflicts, economic problems created or exacerbated by caregiving, and constriction of the caregiver's social life. Pearlin also conceptualizes secondary intrapsychic strains that arise in the caregiver as a result of primary and secondary stressors. These intrapsychic strains include those related specifically to the caregiving situation (i.e., loss of self, role captivity, competence, and gain), and more global psychological resources that may be challenged by the duration and intensity of caregiving (i.e., self-esteem and mastery). Finally, the outcomes of the stress process include consideration of the mental and physical health of the caregiver (i.e., depression, anxiety, irascibility, cognitive disturbance, physical health, and yielding of role).

The structural elements of the stress process are conditioned, according to Pearlin and colleagues, by two primary mediators: coping and social support. "It is the mediators that are usually called upon to provide the explanation for outcome variability" (Pearlin et al., 1990, p. 589). For example, individuals whose coping strategies are effective in dealing with stressful events (Turnbull et al., 1993) or who have strong social support networks to assist emotionally and instrumentally (Dunst, Trivette, & Jodry, 1997) are more likely to weather the ups and downs of caregiving than individuals whose coping strategies are ineffective or who have unhelpful or negative support networks. According to the model, under conditions of high stress in the caregiving situation, effective coping and satisfying social support can blunt the impact of the stressors and reduce the occurrence of secondary stressors.

Pearlin and colleagues' theoretical framework has been operationalized with a variety of newly constructed instruments and measures (Pearlin et al., 1990). Other standardized, psychometrically sound measures exist that can also be applied to the model (Bailey & Simeonsson, 1988a, 1988b; Krauss & Jacobs, 1990). Although most early childhood programs are not intended or expected to test theories of family adaptation, the elements of Pearlin's theory have strong applicability in identifying specific attributes or resources of families and parents that warrant consideration in the development of intervention programs. Indeed, the powerful mediating influences of coping strategies and social support were among the most common issues investigated in research conducted within early intervention programs during the 1980s and 1990s (Bromwich & Parmelee, 1979; Crnic, Greenberg, Ragozin, Robinson, & Basham, 1983; Krauss, 1997).

Family Empowerment in the Human Services

The third major contribution to the development of current family assessment strategies is the family empowerment model, particularly as articulated by Dunst and colleagues (Dunst, Trivette, & Deal, 1988) and Turnbull and Turnbull (1995). The empowerment model focuses on strategies by which families use assistance to identify and achieve self-defined goals. Its premise is that the most effective interventions are those that are responsive to what the "consumer" of the services deems important. Family empowerment models assert that allowing and assisting families to inventory their own resources, strengths, and needs provides the only valid basis for service delivery. And, most importantly, these models effectively redistribute power from professionals to family members (Turnbull, Turbiville, & Turnbull, this volume).

Drawing on the work of Bronfenbrenner (1975, 1979), Rappaport (1981), Hobbs et al. (1984), and Gottlieb (1983), Dunst and colleagues present a model of parent–professional relationships within early intervention programs that was designed to enhance family functioning through an empowerment process. They identified three conditions that form the core of that process (Dunst et al., 1988, p. 4): 1) a proactive stance in helping relationships, in which it is assumed that people are already competent or have the capacity to become competent; 2) creation of enabling experiences in which competent behavior may be displayed; and 3) recognition that to feel empowered, the help-seeker must attribute behavior change to his or her own actions.

The crux of the empowerment model is a redrafting of the ways in which professionals interact with families (Turnbull, Turbiville, & Turnbull, this volume). A basic tenet is that the most important needs of the family are those that are identified by the family, not by the professional. Furthermore, the empowerment model is based on a goal of the acquisition of self-sustaining and adaptive behaviors that emphasize growth among all family members. In contrast to intervention practices that promote dependencies of the family members on the professional help-givers, the family empowerment model seeks to activate the intrinsic competencies assumed to exist in all families and to utilize natural and formal resources in the many environments of the family to support and sustain their identified goals and capabilities. As noted by Garshelis and McConnell (1993), "By focusing on those needs that are of direct concern to families, interventionists can develop a trusting and collaborative relationship with families, assist families in achieving functional goals, and ultimately enhance the integration of the child with handicaps and other family members" (p. 37).

The empowerment model in human services meshes neatly with the requirement that early intervention programs be family focused. As McBride, Brotherson, Joanning, Whiddon, and Demmitt (1993) noted, family-focused programs establish the family as the unit of services, support and respect family decision making, and provide services designed to strengthen family functioning. This model has also challenged the utility of family assessment strategies that rely on standardized, norm-referenced assessments of various aspects of family functioning, many of which were developed originally for research purposes rather than for service delivery planning (Bailey & Henderson, 1993).

Bailey et al. (1998) offer a framework for assessing family outcomes in early intervention that is based on the empowerment model. They suggested that eight questions be answered to determine whether early intervention has accomplished the goals inherent in a family-centered approach. Three of the outcome questions focus on the family's perceptions of their experiences in early intervention, specifically, 1) Does the family see early intervention as appropriate in making a difference in their child's life? 2) Does the family see early intervention making a difference in their family's life? and 3) Does the family have a positive view of professionals and the service system? The second set of questions focuses on the impact of early intervention on various domains of family life, namely, did early intervention 1) enable the family to help their child grow, learn, and develop? 2) enhance the family's perceived ability to work with professionals and advocate for services? 3) assist the family in building a strong support system? 4) enhance an optimistic view of the future? and 5) enhance the family's perceived quality of life? Although Bailey et al. (1998) acknowledged the need for psychometrically sound instruments to measure the proposed family outcomes, they noted that "the attainment of most family outcomes is a personal experience that can only be reported by family members themselves . . . A better understanding can be attained through interviews or direct observation, but these methods are time-consuming to administer and interpret" (pp. 315–6).

Summary

Bronfenbrenner's enumeration of the hierarchy of environments influencing child development is particularly instructive and illustrates the fact that many of the environments that impinge on a family include those in which the family is not even physically present. For early interventionists, Bronfenbrenner's work has given particular weight to efforts to view the child in the context of the family and to see the family in the context of their social conditions. Guralnick's model of child development illustrates the pivotal role of specific family interaction patterns and characteristics on child outcomes. Thus, one purpose of family assessment within early intervention programs is to identify risk and protective factors within the child's most proximal environment.

Pearlin's articulation of the mechanisms by which caregiving becomes stressful to individuals over time has been helpful in explaining why such resources as social support networks and coping strategies are so crucial among caregivers. Many early intervention programs focus on enhancing parental support networks and on helping parents become skilled advocates for their children; these goals reflect the buffers to caregiving stress posited by Pearlin. The emphasis on coping and social support within the stress process model also fits neatly with the family empowerment model that spotlights the salutary effects of strong social support networks and adaptive coping.

The family empowerment model now has strong roots in early intervention programs. Its emphasis on families as decision makers regarding their family's services and the belief that service providers should elicit and support objectives determined by families is consistent with the general trend toward family-focused services. The family empowerment model, particularly as articulated by Dunst and his colleagues (Dunst, Trivette, & Deal, 1988), focuses on the nature and manner of interactions between families and service providers. In light of the lack of formal training of most early interventionists for working with families, the empowerment model provides useful practice guidelines.

These three major contributions to family assessment strategies – theories of child development, the stress and coping model of caregiving, and the family empowerment model of services – constitute a rich foundation on which the legal mandates for family-focused services rests. However, it has been noted that the dominant question within the early intervention community has shifted over the past twenty years. In its rapid period of expansion during the 1980s, the field of early intervention tried to address the question: What impact does program participation have on families? The methods for investigating family impacts were drawn heavily from the theoretical literature on family processes, family systems, and parental adaptation to unusual caregiving demands. Currently, the dominant question is: To what extent are family goals achieved? (Krauss, 1997). The shift from professionally defined outcomes to family-defined goals may seem subtle, but the implications for assessment strategies are significant. The next section discusses how early intervention programs now approach the task and challenge of family assessment.

CHALLENGES OF FAMILY ASSESSMENT

Prior to the passage of P.L. 99-457 in 1986, family assessment within early intervention programs was not a legally mandated activity. To be sure, many programs conducted informal and formal family assessments as part of the evolution toward family-focused services. However, few programs were guided by theories of family development or behavior. This resulted in an atheoretical approach to family assessment (Krauss & Jacobs, 1990). Many programs avowed a diffuse commitment to family involvement and family-focused services but lacked a clear understanding of why certain services should or could lead to specific outcomes. As Harbin (1993) noted, there is a need for a conceptual framework that translates the results of family research into a comprehensive and systematic view of family intervention. Early interventionists still struggle with developing more ecologically based individualized assessment and intervention programs for families (Beckman, 1996).

With the advent of mandated family assessment in early intervention programs, intensive and extensive activity has resulted in the development of guidelines for the conduct of meaningful family evaluations (Bailey & Simeonsson, 1988a, 1988b; Beckman, 1996). The primary tasks of these guidelines are to develop strategies that both assess family needs and provide practical information for early intervention professionals. Because of the legal requirement to include an explicit statement in the IFSP about the family's needs, resources, and strengths, programs struggle with identifying mechanisms that comply with the legal mandate, are acceptable to families who may be unaccustomed to the requirements of family assessment, yield information of practical value for the program, and conform to the training and capacities of program staff who are often untrained in family processes.

A basic issue faced by early intervention programs has been whether to access the knowledge, methods, and expertise of family therapists, psychologists, and social workers in conducting family evaluations or to develop different approaches and goals for family assessment that are consistent with the essential goals of early intervention programs. Most early intervention programs have chosen the latter approach. The result has been an emphasis on family-focused assessment strategies that allow families to conduct their own evaluations of their strengths, resources, and needs, rather than on professionally driven assessment strategies that are based on theories of child development, family development, and models of caregiver adaptation (Simeonsson, Edmondson, Smith, Carnahan, & Bucy, 1995). One reason for this trend is the absence of appropriately trained professionals within the early intervention system to conduct formalized family evaluations (Krauss & Jacobs, 1990). A more compelling reason, however, is the desire to close the gap between assessment procedures and programmatic utility. As Bailey and Henderson (1993) noted, many of the most sophisticated and well-developed methods of family assessment are ill-suited for early intervention programs, either because the methods were developed primarily for research purposes or because they were designed to be used in therapeutic interventions in family systems. Furthermore, it has been noted that formal family assessment strategies typically focus on uncovering problem areas of family functioning and thus send a deficit message to families in early intervention programs instead of a message that emphasizes family strengths and capabilities (Slentz & Bricker, 1992). Given the context in which family assessment occurs within early intervention programs, the field needs assessment tools and strategies that can be utilized in a straightforward, nonjudgmental fashion, that can be employed by professionals with little or no specific training in family assessment, and that yield readily interpretable and programmatically useful information.

Bailey and Simeonsson (1988a, 1988b) enumerated three primary issues in the development of useful family evaluation procedures for early intervention. The first issue is the articulation of essential domains of family assessment. Based on previous research, the list could be extensive, including psychological attributes (e.g., attitudes, beliefs, and personal traits), patterns of relationships within the family, the ecology of the family, specific family needs, family resources, existing and potential sources of support, current manifestations of family stress, and so forth. Honing in on those family domains that have the most salience for interventionists and that respect family privacy and tolerance for assessment constitutes a major area of program challenge.

The second issue concerns how to conduct family assessments. In contrast to the tradition of formalized, standardized, and norm-referenced assessments of children entering early intervention programs, the guidelines for family assessment are far less fixed. Many options are available, ranging from highly informal conversations about family needs, to direct observation of family practices and interactions, and to formalized rating scales completed by family members. The time requirements, degree of intrusiveness, and quality of information collected vary considerably across the available methods. Furthermore, the methods chosen must match the expertise and skills of the professionals involved in the evaluation, most of whom have had no specialized training in family assessment or family work.

The third issue is to ensure that, whatever methods are chosen, they yield information that has prescriptive utility (Bailey et al., 1998). Because the goal is to link family assessment to family services, strategies that might be useful theoretically in the study of family development but have only vague connections to clinical applications are unlikely to be adopted. Rather, the challenge is to develop methods that identify specific areas of family need and priorities in the areas in which early intervention programs have something to offer.

Although the dominant emphasis in family assessment has been on empowering families to identify their own needs and to match those needs with specific services, concern has also been expressed about the lack of congruence between professionals' assessment of family needs and the family's assessment of those needs (Blackard & Barsh, 1982; Simeonsson et al., 1995; Turnbull & Turnbull, 1985; Wikler, Wasow & Hatfield, 1981). Indeed, this lack of congruence has been cited as a compelling rationale for family-focused assessments. Rather than act on what professionals assume to be the family's needs, it is far better and more effective to let the "consumer" direct the assessment and service provision process. An interesting test of this hypothesis was reported by Garshelis and McConnell (1993), who compared ratings of family needs (using the Family Needs Survey, described later) on a set of families in early intervention programs from three sources of ratings: mothers, individual professionals serving on interdisciplinary intervention teams, and the interdisciplinary teams as a group. They found that both individual professionals and interdisciplinary teams as a whole attributed more needs to mothers than the mothers actually identified. They also found that although interdisciplinary teams as a whole were more consistent with the mothers' identification of needs than were individual professionals, the level of agreement between the teams and the mothers on family needs was less than 60%. The authors recommended that professionals use maternal responses to survey instruments as a guide during subsequent personal interviews regarding service planning. In a related report, Bailey and Blasco (1990) reported that half of the fathers and 40% of the mothers preferred sharing information with early intervention professionals through the use of written surveys instead of parent interviews.

The field of early intervention has focused more on the "how" of family assessment rather than on the "why." The development of methods that are comfortable for families and useful to programs remains a major challenge. The "what" that should be assessed seems to have centered primarily on concrete needs families avow regarding their child's development and their own needs for providing as healthy an environment for the child as possible.

STRATEGIES FOR FAMILY ASSESSMENT: INFORMAL APPROACHES

There is no standard or uniform approach for conducting family assessments in early intervention programs. Three issues tend to dominate, however: 1) developing a "stance" toward family assessment; 2) determining the content of the assessment; and 3) translating the results with respect to service provision. The first issue has received considerable discussion in the literature, particularly with respect to the need to develop a respectful, nonjudgmental, and open attitude toward the diversity of family experiences. The second issue addresses the need to focus the content of family assessment activities on specific concerns that are appropriate for early intervention programs and that are consistent with the families' appraisals of current matters with which they contend. The third issue addresses the need for relevance of family assessment processes to the offerings of intervention programs.

With respect to the stance taken in the conduct of family assessment, guidelines recommend that practitioners preserve a degree of informality in the process and are clear about the purpose, scope, and outcome of the assessment. Assessment is not something to be done "to" or "on" the family; it is something that takes place with the family. Assessment is not a process for exposing the family's deficiencies; it is a process of identifying the family's goals. Assessment is not intended to yield a prescription for remediation of the family's problems; it helps to create an understanding between early interventionists and the family about what types of assistance are desired (if any), as determined by the family. Indeed, family assessment more accurately may be called "family information gathering." Berman and Shaw (1996) noted that "early intervention professionals are not being asked to intrude upon the privacy of families, but are charged with providing opportunities for families to choose to share the challenges for which they want help and support" (p. 365).

Guidelines for the way in which service providers approach families have been enumerated. Beckman, Frank, and Newcomb (1996) suggested six specific skills needed for establishing a relationship with families, including 1) join the family (i.e., listening without judging); 2) use active listening (i.e., listening for both what is said and how it is said); 3) use questions effectively (i.e., balancing between questions that require factual answers and those that are open ended); 4) reflect and clarify (i.e., rephrasing and expanding parent comments); 5) provide information (i.e., offering concrete assistance); and 6) reframe (i.e., redefining problems or information in a positive way). Others have suggested a strategy of "tuning in" to families, in which professionals suspend assumptions about what a family needs or how a family feels about an assessment process (Stepanek, Newcomb, & Kettler, 1996). Because many families feel uncomfortable discussing personal and family issues with professionals, the emphasis on professionals' stance toward families has received considerable attention (Slentz, Walker, & Bricker, 1989).

These strategies can be understood as building blocks for the emerging relationship between service providers and family members. Beckman (1996) identified three cardinal issues: 1) having genuine respect for the family; 2) adopting a nonjudgmental attitude; and 3) conveying empathy for the family's issues. Because family assessment activities typically occur at the beginning of what may well be a long-term relationship between the family and the service provider, the establishment of a collaborative relationship is paramount. Indeed, a major concern among early interventionists is ensuring that parents are equal participants in the development of the IFSP. As Campbell, Strickland, and LaForme (1992) noted, "A quality IFSP is one that uses an individualized family service planning process to produce a written plan that exceeds minimal legal requirements and responds to family concerns, resources, and priorities about their children. Only when parents are involved equally with professionals in the planning and writing of the IFSP can a truly quality plan be written" (p. 113).

For example, Hutchins and Cole (1992) suggested that questions such as Why were you upset by that meeting? may provoke defensiveness, whereas a simple rephrasing to What happened at that meeting that upset you? provides an easier context to provide the requested information. In part, the focus on how information is gathered reflects the belief that families will be more at ease, more responsive, and more forthcoming if they are assured that they will be treated with respect and understanding. It also reflects the need to give service providers, most of whom are untrained in conducting family assessments, some ground rules and guidelines for their work.

The second issue that dominates the literature is the content of family assessment. Beyond the gathering of basic sociodemographic information that is often part of intake procedures, the issue of what to focus upon in family assessment activities remains unresolved. In part, this reflects the atheoretical context in which contemporary family assessment is conducted. In part, the determination of content reflects a carefully balanced appraisal of what should matter for families and what families are willing or able to discuss at the tender juncture of entry into an intervention program.

Two approaches are discussed in the literature with respect to the content of family assessment. One relies on the family revealing its daily routines and concerns through direct questions about patterns of family activities and parenting styles. This approach is based on a belief that family "storytelling" will illuminate specific areas in which interventions may be effective in ameliorating problematic interactions, unsatisfactory routines, or arenas of parental concern. The second approach relies on the interventionist to structure the information gathering according to predetermined areas of probable concerns among families of children with disabilities. For example, Bailey (1987) suggested that service providers organize discussions about resources and concerns by focusing on such specific categories as financial, physical, social, emotional, medical, developmental, and informational issues. These are not mutually exclusive strategies; both may be employed effectively in early intervention programs.

Informal or nonstandardized family assessments usually start with open-ended conversations that focus on family strengths, resources, and needs (Beckman & Bristol, 1991; Winton & Bailey, 1988). Practice guidelines suggest that this conversation should follow the lead of the parent; focus initially on the child and on questions the parent(s) may have about development, management, and prognosis; and then turn to issues affecting the family (Stepanek, Newcomb, & Kettler, 1996). For example,

interventionists may ask about the daily routines in the family, the allocation of caretaking tasks among family members, the times of day most difficult to manage, or the ways that families relax together, as a means of eliciting a general understanding of how a particular family functions, as well as its values and needs. By describing the child in the context of the family, the discussions maintain a child-oriented focus but allow family concerns to surface. These concerns can then be explored with respect to how the early intervention program might assist the family or what other sources of support may be useful.

Bernheimer and Keogh (1995) described an ecocultural approach to family assessment based on the theory that families actively and proactively respond to their life circumstances through the maintenance of routines that support their goals and priorities. Their approach is rooted in Bronfenbrenner's description of the child embedded within a set of interrelated environments that may be conditioned, but not governed, by specific sociodemographic characteristics. The ecocultural approach focuses on the family's ability to "tell their story" as a way of identifying the values, goals, and family patterns that have meaning for them. On the basis of longitudinal research with a diverse sample, Bernheimer and Keogh (1995) identified ten domains of daily family life that are particularly salient in surfacing patterns and issues that may warrant intervention: family subsistence, services, home/neighborhood safety and convenience, domestic workload, child-care tasks, child peer groups, marital roles, instrumental/emotional support, father/spouse role, and parenting information. They noted that "sustainable" interventions are those that are consistent with the family's daily routines and goals. Two aspects of their work are particularly appealing in the context of early intervention programs. First, the interview methods for eliciting family routines are consistent with the preferences of families for informal discussions, conversations, and storytelling as a mechanism for family information gathering (Beckman & Bristol, 1991; Winton, 1988). Second, the methods are applicable to diverse groups of families who may vary along cultural and demographic dimensions (Barnwell & Day, 1996).

Others have noted that although the intent of family interviews or conversations may be to elicit information that has direct impact on services or supports, they bear a resemblance to traditional therapeutic interviews designed to focus on family interactions that reveal psychodynamic material regarding parent–child or other intrafamily relationships. Hirshberg (1996) provided an eloquent description of parent interviews that can reveal a wide range of issues affecting the role of a child with disabilities in the family. He categorized the process as "history making" in contrast to "history taking" in light of his view that the goal of such interviews is to construct a scenario for the articulation of aspirations for the future, based on an understanding of interaction patterns in the past. The sophistication of his approach to interviews with families illustrates a critical difference between family interventions led by highly skilled family therapists and those led by well-meaning but improperly trained early interventionists who are thrust into the realm of "family work."

The third issue is the need for a connection between family assessment and programmatic purposes, namely, the assumption that targeted assistance to families will effect some desired change. As Simeonsson (1988) noted, "The fundamental issue underlying evaluation is clinical and programmatic accountability" (p. 251). Determining the link between assessment and outcomes undoubtedly is complex, insofar as programmatic outcomes for families in early intervention services have never been clearly specified. Most programs rely on measures of satisfaction with services as the most commonly monitored outcome, while acknowledging that satisfaction does not equal effectiveness. The premise is that if the goals identified for and by families are met, the program has achieved some degree of impact or effectiveness. Using informal family-driven modalities for identifying family needs offers excellent possibilities of securing high satisfaction ratings and thus reinforces program practices of individualized assessment and program planning procedures.

In summary, informal assessment procedures constitute the most common method of family assessment in early intervention programs. The literature is more extensively developed on the issues in developing a stance with families, offering many guidelines about how to put families at ease, about good listening and reflecting skills, and about the need to be respectful toward families' individual

histories. There is also considerable discussion about the topic areas that should be covered in family conversations, particularly focused on basic needs of families and on the context in which the child is being reared. The linkage of program activity to outcomes is more tenuous and relies most commonly on general satisfaction measures. The disproportionate concern with *how* to approach family assessment in an informal way, as compared to *what* to discuss or *to what outcomes* assessment should be directed, reflects the field's concern with process rather than outcome.

Given that family assessment and intervention were imposed on a cadre of early interventionists who were not trained for such work, it is imperative that additional tools be made available to those who are called upon to perform such sensitive and critical tasks. In the spirit of providing adequate tools for these roles, several easy-to-administer and clinically valid assessment techniques are available to assess the needs of families of children with suspected or confirmed developmental delays. A sampling of these is described in the next section.

STRATEGIES FOR FAMILY ASSESSMENT: FORMAL METHODS

Formal methods of family assessment are typically used in conjunction with, rather than in lieu of, more informal interview-based assessment strategies. A variety of standardized instruments measuring various aspects of family functioning (i.e., parenting stress, informal support, coping strategies, family cohesion, marital satisfaction, and so forth) are available, many of which were developed initially for research rather than clinical purposes. The selection of instruments is affected by the programmatic orientation of the service setting; the time, energy, and costs associated with different assessment protocols; and the skills and training of the program's staff. An additional selection factor is the acceptability of the protocols to the families being assessed. Important concerns have been expressed about the use of many existing psychometrically tested standardized instruments. Some of these instruments are criticized as "deficit-oriented, value-laden, or intrusive, asking personal questions about lifestyle, spouse support, personal values and feelings. Not only are such questions of little use in program planning, but they may actually be counterproductive by creating resentment and mistrust" (Bailey & Simeonsson, 1988a, p. 7). In response to such concerns, several programmatically relevant instruments have been developed.

Programs that wish to combine standardized structured assessment strategies with more informal methods of information gathering now have the benefit of instruments that have been developed specifically for use in early intervention programs. Other standardized instruments that may have utility in early intervention programs but that were not developed specifically for use in such settings, such as measures of parenting stress, social support, coping strategies, and family environments, have been reviewed elsewhere (Bailey & Simeonsson, 1988a; Claflin & Meisels, 1992; Krauss & Jacobs, 1990). Among the more recently developed instruments appropriate for early intervention programs are measures for the assessment of parent–child interaction, family needs and priorities, family functioning, and social support. Illustrative examples of these measures are given here.

Parent–Child Interaction

Comfort and Farren (1994) developed the Parent/Caregiver Involvement Scale (P/CIS) to monitor the development of social behavior and affect and to identify problems that may interfere with daily life and healthy interpersonal relations. This observation strategy also yields information about the caregiver's interactive style and knowledge of child development. The P/CIS can be used in home visits, laboratory settings, or clinics, and consists of a twenty-minute observation of a free-play interaction between the caregiver and a child between the ages of 3 and 60 months. The observer rates three elements – amount, quality, and appropriateness – for eleven behaviors (physical involvement, verbal involvement, responsiveness of caregiver, playful interaction, teaching behavior, control over child's activities, directives, relationship among activities, positive statements, negative statements/discipline, and goal setting). The reliability of the P/CIS is reported to range from .77–.87 when the scale is administered in a home setting and from .54–.93 when scored from taped observations. Assessment of the validity of the P/CIS revealed moderate-to-high

correlations with behavioral counts of parent–child behaviors and associations with parental and child characteristics (e.g., locus of control, support, and temperament) similar to those presented in the developmental literature (Farren et al., 1987).

The training required for use of the P/CIS includes a four-hour introductory session with a training videotape and workbook. The authors recommend that a consultant be available during the training and that practice sessions be utilized to achieve interrater reliability. They caution that the results of the P/CIS must be interpreted within the context of other relevant information about the family and should be based on multiple observations. Given the reluctance typically experienced by families to be observed or evaluated with respect to their parenting style or skills, it is also urged that the P/CIS (or any other parent–child observational instrument) be used only when a parent or caregiver has expressed concern about the quality of the relationship with the child (Comfort, 1988).

Family Needs and Priorities

To compensate for the perceived inappropriateness of existing instruments, new measures have been developed that are tailored specifically to identify family needs and priorities. In this regard, one of the most promising and widely adopted formal assessment tools is the Family Needs Survey (Bailey & Simeonsson, 1988b). This thirty-five-item self-administered scale can be completed by both mothers and fathers (and presumably, other involved family members). The instrument yields information in six categories: 1) needs for information; 2) needs for support; 3) explaining to others; 4) community services; 5) financial needs; and 6) family functioning. Each item begins with the statement, "I need more . . . [opportunities to meet and talk with other parents of handicapped children]" to which the respondent gives a rating between 1 (*definitely do not need*) and 3 (*definitely need help with this*). The advantage of this phrasing is that it proactively states what the individual needs based on his or her own priorities and has direct applicability to service planning. Test–retest correlations over a six-month period for total scores were reported to be .67 for a sample of mothers and .81 for fathers.

Sexton, Burrell, and Thompson (1992) reported the results of a set of reliability analyses and confirmatory factor analyses of the Family Needs Survey. Cronbach's alpha reliability coefficient was .91 for the total score, with subscale coefficients ranging from .65 to .86. Bailey, Blasco, and Simeonsson (1992) reported that a factor analysis conducted separately for mothers and fathers yielded independent results for both groups. For example, for mothers, the eight social support items loaded onto a single factor, whereas for fathers they loaded onto two factors (differentiating between personal needs for support and family needs for support). They also reported that mothers expressed significantly more needs than did fathers, particularly with respect to the need for help in explaining the child's condition to others. Other studies have also found that the Family Needs Survey yields different results based on parent gender (Cooper & Allred, 1992).

Turnbull and Turnbull (1986) developed the Family Information Preference Inventory (FIPI), a thirty-seven-item tool that covers five informational areas: 1) teaching the child at home; 2) advocacy and working with professionals; 3) planning for the future; 4) helping the whole family relax and enjoy life more; and 5) finding and using more support. The FIPI requires that the respondent indicate the degree of need related to each item using a four-point scale (ranging from *no interest in this information* to *information is a high priority*) and then to identify the desired means of obtaining the information (i.e., a group meeting with other parents, an individual meeting, or written materials). No information on its psychometric properties has been reported. The FIPI was not designed specifically for use in early intervention programs and includes some items regarding sexuality and vocational issues. Its structure, however, is flexible, and additional items geared toward concerns of parents of young children easily could be added.

The Family Resource Scale (FRS; Dunst & Leet, 1987) is intended to measure the adequacy of both physical and human resources, including food, shelter, transportation, time to be with family and friends, health care, money to pay bills, child care, and so forth. The scale consists of thirty-one items ordered from most to least basic. Each item is rated on a five-point scale, ranging from *not at all adequate* to *almost always adequate*. The items are

conceptualized to reflect a needs hierarchy, from basic nutritional resources to interpersonal growth opportunities. Items rated *not at all adequate* or *seldom adequate* can be used clinically as family need identifiers.

Data on the reliability and validity of the scale are based on a study of forty-five mothers of preschool children with special needs in an early intervention program. The alpha reliability coefficient was .92, and the stability of the FRS was .52 based on administration of the scale over a two-to-three-month interval (Dunst & Leet, 1987).

The Family Needs Scale (FNS; Dunst, Cooper, Weeldreyer, Snyder, & Chase, 1985) is formatted similarly to the FRS but focuses specifically on the family's need for any of forty-one types of resources. The resources are grouped into nine major categories (financial, food and shelter, vocation, child care, transportation, communication, etc.). Each item is rated on a five-point scale, ranging from *almost never* to *almost always* a need. The FNS was designed specifically to elicit family-identified needs for intervention purposes. Reliability and validity assessment of the FNS are based on a study of fifty-four parents of preschool children with disabilities in an early intervention program. Coefficient alpha for the scale was .95. The total scale score correlated significantly with measures of locus of control, parental well-being, and decision making (Dunst et al., 1985).

Family Functioning

The Family Functioning Style Scale (Dunst, Trivette, & Deal, 1988) is a self-report measure that can be used in intervention programs to elicit discussions about particular qualities in a family, including family strengths, information-sharing patterns, and coping/resource strategies. According to the authors, there are twelve qualities of strong families that were used to derive the specific items. These include 1) a commitment to growth for all family members; 2) appreciation for individual effort; 3) allocation of time for family activities; 4) sense of purpose in good and bad times; 5) congruence within the family for shared goals; 6) communication emphasizing positive interactions; 7) rules and values regarding acceptable behavior; 8) coping strategies that are positive; 9) problem solving to meet collective needs; 10) positivism in the face of problems; 11) flexibility and adaptability in meeting needs; and 12) balance in using internal and external resources in meeting needs. The scale consists of twenty-six statements rated on a five-point scale, ranging from *not at all like my family* to *almost always like my family*. It can be completed either by individuals or by the family as a whole. No reliablity or validity data are available, although the authors assert that the scale holds promise for clinical utility in its identification of family strengths and resources.

The Family Adaptability and Cohesion Evaluation Scales (FACES I, II, and III; Olson, 1986; Olson, Portner & Bell, 1982) are based on the Circumplex Model of family behavior. The FACES instruments assess the degree of adaptability and cohesiveness within the family system and can be used to identify discrepancies between perceived and idealized qualities in the family. Family cohesion is defined as the emotional bonding that family members have toward one another. Adaptability is defined as the ability of the marital or family system to change its power structure, role relationships, and relationship rules in response to situational and developmental stress (Olson, Portner, & Bell, 1982). According to the Circumplex Model, there are four levels of family cohesion (ranging from disengaged to enmeshed) and four levels of adaptability (ranging from rigid to chaotic). Balanced levels within each dimension are hypothesized to be the most viable for healthy family functioning.

Cohesion is measured with sixteen individual items and adaptability is measured with fourteen individual items, all rated on a five-point scale ranging from *almost never* to *almost always*. Cronbach reliability coefficients were reported as .87 for cohesion, .78 for adaptability, and .90 for the total scale. Test–retest reliability over a 4- to 5-week period was .84 for the total scale (Olson, Portner, & Bell, 1982).

Social Support

The Inventory of Social Support (Dunst, Trivette, & Deal, 1988) is designed to determine the types of help and assistance that different individuals, groups, and agencies provide to a person. The inventory maps the frequency during the past month (ranging from *not at all* to *almost every day*) and method of contact (ranging from *in person, in a group,* or *by telephone*) between the respondent and various

sources of support and ascertains which sources of support are most utilized for different purposes. The respondent is also asked to whom he or she turns for support for twelve different types of aid or assistance. Responses are portrayed in a matrix format that provides a graphical display of the person's personal support network with respect to both source and type of support. Psychometric data on the inventory's properties have not been reported.

The Family Support Scale (Dunst, Jenkins, & Trivette, 1984) focuses on the family as a unit and measures the helpfulness of sources of support to families rearing a young child. It includes eighteen potential sources, such as parents, in-laws, spouse/partner, children, parent groups, church, physicians, service programs, and professional agencies. Each source is rated on a five-point scale, ranging from *not at all helpful* to *extremely helpful* with respect to assistance with parenting. Within an intervention program, the Family Support Scale can be used as the basis for discussions about why and how family support network members may be helpful in meeting basic family needs. Analysis of the scale's reliability resulted in a Cronbach's alpha coefficient of .77. Test–retest reliability over a one-month interval was .75.

Although the regulations governing the implementation of the IFSP state that the assessment must include a personal interview with the family (Winton & Bailey, 1990), the relative efficacy of a personal interview alone or in conjunction with other standardized procedures has been explored only minimally. Sexton, Snyder, Rheams, Barron-Sharp, and Perez (1991) compared the opinions of forty-eight mothers of children in early intervention programs and twenty-five service providers regarding preferences for sharing information through personal interviews or written surveys. The surveys included the Family Needs Survey (Bailey & Simeonsson, 1988a, 1988b), the Family Needs Scale (Dunst, Cooper, Weeldreyer, Snyder, & Chase, 1988), and the Family Functioning Style Scale (Deal, Trivette, & Dunst, 1988). Mothers also participated in family-focused interviews with service providers regarding the development of their IFSPs. They found that about half of the mothers preferred the use of written surveys, and the other half preferred a personal interview. Regardless of personal preference for assessment method, the vast majority of the mothers rated the three written surveys as more useful and user friendly than did service providers. In a related study, Bailey and Blasco (1990) asked almost 230 mothers in ten states to evaluate the utility of the Family Needs Survey. They found that mothers rated the survey highly with respect to its ability to convey their needs to professionals, the utility of the shared information for program planning, and the degree of comfort they experienced in completing the survey. These results were similar for mothers representing different ethnic minorities and those from low-income groups. Bailey and Blasco also found that 60% of the fathers and 40% of the mothers preferred sharing information with early intervention professionals through the use of written surveys in contrast to parent interviews. These results may be attributable to differences in the time required to complete brief surveys as contrasted to engaging in personal interviews, and the sense of clear boundaries provided by standardized questions versus the potential expansiveness of interview situations, and the lack of anonymity provided by interviewers.

SPECULATIONS ON THE FUTURE OF FAMILY ASSESSMENT

Family assessment practices within early intervention programs have become a very complex endeavor. Multiple and often competing forces affect the strategies used by programs, the preferences voiced by families, and the utility of assessments for program planning and service delivery. On the one hand, the mandate for family assessment stems from a sophisticated view of the child's development. Influenced by Bronfenbrenner's work, particularly as it addresses the role of the family system, there are strong theoretical reasons for assessing the qualities and capabilities of those environments most proximate to the child. Understanding the family as an agent in the child's growth legitimizes professional interest in how the family functions, its potential for the promotion of healthy development, and its accommodations to the tasks of rearing a child with atypical development. Coupled with the deepened understanding now available of how families as units, and parents as individuals, manage the unique stressors of caregiving, one would expect a push toward more formalized theoretically grounded assessment strategies that concentrate on specific aspects of family life that are known to explain variability in family environments. Indeed, much of what is known about the adaptation of families with young children to the demands of parenting a child with a disability was learned in the context of early intervention programs that have been eager participants in comprehensive research programs over the past twenty years.

Despite the promise of early intervention programs as a place for the study of families and of the transactional nature of development, the field has taken a different tack. Family assessment strategies are focused on identifying the needs of families in relation to their child with a disability, aiding families to understand the service delivery system on which many will depend over time, and helping families adjust to what "disability" may mean for their future. The mechanisms for such assessments are typically informal, nonstandardized, and highly flexible. Partnerships with parents are valued and an open and accepting stance permeates the early intervention literature. This approach has been accepted enthusiastically by families who, along with early intervention personnel, are uneasy about formal assessment practices for families.

There are two important shortcomings in the current scenario of family assessment. First, there is insufficient interest in investigating the linkage between assessment strategies and service outcomes for families. The focus has been on mechanisms to elicit families' appraisals of their immediate needs – be it through informal unstructured conversations or more standardized instruments. The goal of operationalizing the mandate of family involvement in the development of the IFSP has spawned a healthy investment in diverse ways to match families' needs with service responses. Whether the services that are provided satisfy families' needs or result in changed family functioning is unknown. As with any human service, the need to demonstrate efficacy and appropriateness of public resources that support such services cannot be avoided. Thus, in the future there may be more professional interest in examining critically what early intervention programs actually do for families, how families leaving programs differ from the way they entered such programs, and the efficiency of current practices to produce the changes that may occur. A spirit of inquiry may well lead to more variation in how family assessments are conducted and may result in a more empirically based rationale for how early intervention programs involve, support, and assist families.

Second, it is important to acknowledge that current professionals working in early childhood programs are poorly trained to conduct sophisticated family assessments. Early childhood programs tend to attract personnel whose skills derive from a knowledge of child development, not family functioning. The infusion of substantive family content into the curriculum of graduate programs that produce professionals who will staff early childhood programs is inescapable if this situation is to change. Widening the lens on what matters for children to include what matters for the families in which they live is a natural, yet often neglected, focus in graduate education. We cannot expect early childhood personnel to accomplish tasks for which they are not trained. Family assessment, with all its current imprecision in methodology, constitutes a critical topic that should be incorporated in contemporary professional training programs.

In summary, family assessment within early intervention programs has yet to demonstrate a degree of consistency in practice or clarity in purpose that may well have been expected in the years since the passage of P.L. 99-457. Although the commitment to families as the key context for child development remains strong, the translation of that commitment into assessment procedures that link family needs with program capabilities remains tenuous. Efforts to develop family assessment procedures that are acceptable to families, consistent with program capabilities, and useful for service design and delivery have resulted in program-specific strategies rather than in nationally recognized standards of assessment. The lack of consensus regarding reliable and valid methods for family assessment within a service delivery context suggests that careful monitoring of family assessment strategies is critical. Continued experimentation should be viewed as opportunities to enable early intervention programs to contribute to new understandings of how better to serve vulnerable children and their families.

REFERENCES

Bailey, D. B. (1987). Collaborative goal-setting with families: Resolving differences in values and priorities for services. *Topics in Early Childhood Special Education, 7,* 59–71.

Bailey, D. B., & Blasco, P. M. (1990). Parents' perspectives on a written survey of family needs. *Journal of Early Intervention, 14,* 196–203.

Bailey, D. B., Blasco, P. M., & Simeonsson, R. J. (1992). Needs expressed by mothers and fathers of young children with disabilities. *American Journal on Mental Retardation, 97,* 1–10.

Bailey, D. B., Buysse, V., Edmondson, R., & Smith, T. M. (1992). Creating family-centered services in early intervention: Perceptions of professionals in four states. *Exceptional Children, 58,* 298–309.

Bailey, D. B., & Henderson, L. W. (1993). Traditions in family assessment: Toward an inquiry-oriented, reflective model. In D. M. Bryant & M. A. Graham (Eds.), *Implementing early intervention: From research to effective practice* (pp. 124–47). New York: Guilford Press.

Bailey, D. B., McWilliam, R. A., Darkes, L. A., Hebbeler, K., Simeonsson, R. J., Spiker, D., & Wagner, M. (1998). Family outcomes in early intervention: A framework for program evaluation and efficacy research. *Exceptional Children, 64,* 313–28.

Bailey, D. B., & Simeonsson, R. J. (1988a). *Family assessment in early intervention.* Columbus, OH: Merrill.

Bailey, D. B., & Simeonsson, R. J. (1988b). Assessing needs of families with handicapped infants. *The Journal of Special Education, 22,* 117–27.

Bailey, D. B., Winton, P. J., Rouse, L., & Turnbull, A. P. (1990). Family goals in infant intervention: Analysis and issues. *Journal of Early Intervention, 14,* 15–26.

Barnwell, D. A., & Day, M. (1996). Providing support to diverse families. In P. Beckman (Ed.), *Strategies for working with families of young children with disabilities* (pp. 47–68). Baltimore, MD: Paul H. Brookes.

Beckman, P. (Ed.). (1996). *Strategies for working with families of young children with disabilities.* Baltimore, MD: Paul H. Brookes.

Beckman, P. J., & Bristol, M. M. (1991). Issues in developing the IFSP: A framework for establishing family outcomes. *Topics in Early Childhood Special Education, 11,* 19–31.

Beckman, P. J., Frank, N., & Newcomb, S. (1996). Qualities and skills for communicating with families. In P. Beckman (Ed.), *Strategies for working with families of young children with disabilities* (pp. 31–46). Baltimore, MD: Paul H. Brookes.

Berman, C., & Shaw, E. (1996). Family-directed child evaluation and assessment under the Individuals with Disabilities Education Act (IDEA). In S. J. Meisels and E. Fenichel (Eds.), *New visions for the developmental assessment of infants and young children* (pp. 361–90).

Washington, DC: Zero to Three: National Center for Infants, Toddlers, and Families.

Bernheimer, L. P., & Keogh, B. K. (1995). Weaving interventions into the fabric of everyday life: An approach to family assessment. *Topics in Early Childhood Special Education, 15,* 415–33.

Blacher, J. (Ed.). (1984). *Severely handicapped young children and their families: Research in review.* Orlando, FL: Academic Press.

Blackard, M. K., & Barsh, E. T. (1982). Parents' and professionals' perceptions of the handicapped childs' impact on the family. *Journal of the Association for the Severely Handicapped, 7,* 62–70.

Bromwich, R. M., & Parmelee, A. H. (1979). An intervention program for pre-term infants. In T. M. Field (Ed.), *Infants born at risk* (pp. 389–411). New York: Spectrum.

Bronfenbrenner, U. (1992). Ecological systems theory. In R. Vasta (Ed.), *Annals of child development. Six theories of child development: Revised formulations and current issues* (pp. 187–249). London: Jessica Kingsley.

Bronfenbrenner, U. (1975). Is early intervention effective? In B. Friedlander, G. Sterritt, & G. Kirk (Eds.), *Exceptional infant: Vol. 3. Assessment and intervention* (pp. 449–75). New York: Brunner/Mazel.

Bronfenbrenner, U. (1979). *The ecology of human development: Experiments in nature and design.* Cambridge, MA: Harvard University Press.

Campbell, P. H., Strickland, B., & LaForme, C. (1992). Enhancing parent participation in the individualized family service plan. *Topics in Early Childhood Special Education, 11,* 112–24.

Claflin, C. J., & Meisels, S. J. (1992). Assessment of the impact of very low birthweight infants on families. In N. J. Anastasiow & S. Harel (Eds.), *At-risk infants: Interventions, families, and research* (pp. 57–79). Baltimore, MD: Paul H. Brookes.

Comfort, M. (1988). Assessing parent-child interaction. In D. Bailey & R. Simeonsson (Eds.), *Family assessment in early intervention* (pp. 65–94). New York: Macmillan.

Comfort, M., & Farran, D. C. (1994). Parent–child interaction assessment in family-centered intervention. *Infants and Young Children, 6,* 33–45.

Cooper, C. S., & Allred, K. W. (1992). A comparison of mothers' versus fathers' needs for support in caring for a young child with special needs. *The Transdisciplinary Journal, 2,* 205–21.

Crnic, K. A., Friedrich, W. N., & Greenberg, M. T. (1983). Adaptation of families with mentally retarded children: A model of stress, coping, and family ecology. *American Journal of Mental Deficiency, 88,* 125–38.

Crnic, K. A., Greenberg, M. T., Ragozin, A. S., Robinson, N. M., & Basham, R. B. (1983). Effects of stress and social support on mothers and premature and full-term infants. *Child Development, 54,* 209–17.

Deal, A. G., Trivette, C. M., & Dunst, C. J. (1988). Family Functioning Style Scale. In C. J. Dunst, C. M. Trivette, & A. G. Deal (Eds.), *Enabling and empowering families: Principles and guidelines for practice* (pp. 179–84). Cambridge, MA: Brookline Press.

Dunst, C. J., Cooper, C. S., Weeldreyer, J. C., Snyder, K. D., & Chase, J. H. (1988). Family Needs Scale. In C. J. Dunst, C. M. Trivette, & A. G. Deal (Eds.), *Enabling and empowering families: Principles and guidelines for practice* (p. 151). Cambridge, MA: Brookline Press.

Dunst, C. J., Jenkins, V., & Trivette, C. M. (1984). Family Support Scale: Reliability and validity. *Journal of Individual, Family, and Community Wellness, 1,* 45–52.

Dunst, C. J., & Leet, H. E. (1987). Measuring the adequacy of resources in households with young children. *Child: Care, Health, and Development, 13,* 111–25.

Dunst, C. J., & Trivette, C. M. (1986). Looking beyond the parent–child dyad for the determinants of maternal styles of interaction. *Infant Mental Health Journal, 7,* 69–80.

Dunst, C., Trivette, C., & Deal, A. (1988). *Enabling and empowering families: Principles and guidelines for practice.* Cambridge, MA: Brookline Press.

Dunst, C. J., Trivette, C. M., & Cross, A. H. (1986). Mediating influences of social support: Personal, family, and child outcomes. *American Journal of Mental Deficiency, 90,* 403–17.

Dunst, C. J., Trivette, C. M., & Jodry, W. (1997). Influences of social support on children with disabilities and their families. In M. Guralnick (Ed.), *The effectiveness of early intervention* (pp. 499–522). Baltimore, MD: Paul H. Brookes.

Farren, D. C., Kasari, C., Yoder, P., Harber, L., Huntington, G. S., & Comfort-Smith, M. (1987). Rating mother–child interactions in handicapped and at-risk infants. In T. Tamir (Ed.), *Stimulation and intervention in infant development* (pp. 297–312). London: Freund Publishing House.

Garshelis, J. A., & McConnell, S. R. (1993). Comparison of family needs assessed by mothers, individual professionals, and interdisciplinary teams. *Journal of Early Intervention, 17-1,* 36–49.

Gottlieb, B. H. (1983). *Social support strategies: Guidelines for mental health practice.* Beverly Hills, CA: Sage.

Guralnick, M. J. (1998). Effectiveness of early intervention for vulnerable children: A developmental perspective. *American Journal on Mental Retardation, 102,* 319–45.

Harbin, G. L. (1993). Family issues of children with disabilities: How research and theory have modified practice in intervention. In N. J. Anastasiow & S. Harel (Eds.), *At-risk infants: Interventions, families, and research* (pp. 101–14). Baltimore, MD: Paul H. Brookes.

Hirschberg, L. M. (1996). History-making, not history-taking: Clinical interviews with infants and their families. In S. J. Meisels & E. Fenichel (Eds.), *New visions* for the developmental assessment of infants and young children (pp. 85–124). Washington, DC: Zero to Three, National Center for Infants, Toddlers and Families.

Hobbs, N., Dokecki, P. R., Hoover-Dempsey, K. V., Moroney, R. M. Shayne, M. W., & Weeks, K. H. (1984). *Strengthening families*. San Francisco: Jossey-Bass.

Hodapp, R. M. (1997). Direct and indirect behavioral effects of different genetic disorders of mental retardation. *American Journal on Mental Retardation, 102*, 67–79.

Hutchins, D. E., & Cole, C. G. (1992). *Helping relationships and strategies*. Pacific Grove, CA: Brooks/Cole Publishing.

Krauss, M. W. (1990). New precedent in family policy: The individualized family service plan. *Exceptional Children, 56*, 388–95.

Krauss, M. W. (1997). Two generations of family research in early intervention. In M. Guralnick (Ed.), *The effectiveness of early intervention* (pp. 611–24). Baltimore, MD: Paul H. Brookes.

Krauss, M. W., & Hauser-Cram, P. (1992). Policy and program developments for infants and toddlers with disabilities. In L. Rowitz (Ed.), *Mental retardation in the Year 2000* (pp. 184–196). New York: Springer-Verlag.

Krauss, M. W., & Jacobs, F. (1990). Family assessment: Purposes and techniques. In S. J. Meisels and J. P. Shonkoff (Eds.), *Handbook of early childhood intervention* (pp. 303–25). New York: Cambridge University Press.

McBride, S. L., Brotherson, M. J., Joanning, H., Whiddon, D., & Demmitt, A. (1993). Implementation of family-centered services: Perceptions of families and professionals. *Journal of Early Intervention, 17*, 414–30.

McCubbin, H. I., & Patterson, J. M. (1981). *Systematic assessment of family stress, resources and coping: Tools for research, education and clinical intervention*. St. Paul, MN: Family Social Science.

Olson, D. H. (1986). Circumplex model VII: Validation studies and FACES III. *Family Process, 25*, 337–51.

Olson, D. H., & Lavee, Y. (1989). Family systems and family stress: A family life cycle perspective. In K. Kreppner & R. M. Lerner (Eds.), *Family systems and life-span development* (pp. 165–96). Hillsdale, NJ: Erlbaum.

Olson, D. H., Portner, J., & Bell, R. (1982). *Family Adaptation and Cohesion Evaluation Scales*. Unpublished rating scales. School of Family and Social Sciences, University of Minnesota, St. Paul.

Pearlin, L., Lieberman, M., Menaghan, E., & Mullan, J. (1981). The stress process. *Journal of Health and Social Behavior, 22*, 337–56.

Pearlin, L., Mullan, J., Semple, S., & Skaff, M. (1990). Caregiving and the stress process: An overview of concepts and their measures. *The Gerontologist, 30*, 583–94.

Pearlin, L., & Schooler, C. (1978). The structure of coping. *Journal of Health and Social Behavior, 19*, 2–21.

Ramey, S. L., Krauss, M. W., & Simeonsson, R. (1989). Research on families: Current assessment and future

opportunities. *American Journal on Mental Retardation, 94*, ii–vi.

Rappaport, J. (1981). In praise of paradox: A social policy of empowerment over prevention. *American Journal of Community Psychology, 9*, 1–25.

Ryff, C. D., & Seltzer, M. M. (1996). The unchartered years of midlife parenting. In C. D. Ryff & M. M. Seltzer (Eds.), *The parental experience at midlife* (pp. 3–28). Chicago: University of Chicago Press.

Sameroff, A. J., & Feil, L. (1985). Parental concepts of development. In I. E. Sigel (Ed.), *Parental belief systems: The psychological consequences for children* (pp. 84–104). Hillsdale, NJ: Erlbaum.

Seltzer, M. M., & Krauss, M. W. (1994). Aging parents with co-resident adult children: The impact of lifelong caregiving. In M. M. Seltzer, M. W. Krauss, & M. P. Janicki (Eds.), *Life course perspectives on adulthood and old age* (pp. 3–18). Washington, DC: The American Association on Mental Retardation Monograph Series.

Sexton, D., Burrell, B., & Thompson, B. (1992). Measurement integrity of the Family Needs Survey. *Journal of Early Intervention, 16*, 343–52.

Sexton, D., Snyder, P., Rheams, T., Barron-Sharp, B., & Perez, J. (1991). Considerations in using written surveys to identify family strengths and needs during the IFSP process. *Topics in Early Childhood Special Education, 11*, 81–91.

Simeonsson, R. J. (1988). Evaluating the effects of family-focused interventions. In D. B. Bailey & R. J. Simeonsson (Eds.), *Family assessment in early intervention* (pp. 251–68). Columbus, OH: Merrill.

Simeonsson, R. J., Edmondson, R., Smith, T., Carnahan, S., & Bucy, J. E. (1995). Family involvement in multidisciplinary team evaluation: Professional and parent perspectives. *Child: Care, Health, and Development, 21*, 199–215.

Slentz, K. L., & Bricker, D. (1992). Family-guided assessment for IFSP Development: Jumping off the family assessment bandwagon. *Journal of Early Intervention, 16*, 11–19.

Slentz, K. L., Walker, B., & Bricker, D. (1989). Supporting parent involvement in early intervention: A role-taking model. In G. H. S. Singer & L. K. Irvin (Eds.), *Support for caregiving families: Enabling positive adaptation to disability* (pp. 221–38). Baltimore, MD: Paul H. Brookes.

Sontag, J. C. (1996). Toward a comprehensive theoretical framework for disability research: Bronfenbrenner revisited. *Journal of Special Education, 30*, 319–44.

Stepanek, J. S., Newcomb, S., & Kettler, K. (1996). Coordinating services and identifying family priorities, resources, and concerns. In P. Beckman (Ed.), *Strategies for working with families of young children with disabilities* (pp. 69–90). Baltimore, MD: Paul H. Brookes.

Turnbull, A. P., Patterson, J. M., Behr, S. K., Murphy, D. L., Marquis, J. G., & Blue-Banning, M. J. (Eds.). (1993). *Cognitive coping, families, and disability.* Baltimore, MD: Paul H. Brookes.

Turnbull, A. P., & Turnbull, H. R. (1985). *Parents speak out: Then and now.* Columbus, OH: Merrill.

Turnbull, A. P., & Turnbull, H. R. (1986). *Families, professionals, and exceptionality: A special partnership.* Columbus, OH: Merrill.

Turnbull, A. P., & Turnbull, H. R. (1995). *Families, professionals, and exceptionality: A special partnership* (3rd ed.). Upper Saddle River, NJ: Merrill.

Wikler, L., Wasow, M., & Hatfield, E. (1981). Chronic sorrow revisited: Parent vs. professional depiction of the adjustment of parents of mentally retarded children. *American Journal of Orthopsychiatry, 51,* 63–70.

Winton, P. J. (1988). The family-focused interview: An assessment measure and goal setting mechanism. In D. B. Bailey & R. J. Simeonsson (Eds.), *Family assessment in early intervention* (pp. 185–206). Columbus, OH: Merrill.

Winton, P. J., & Bailey, D. B. (1988). The family-focused interview: A collaborative mechanism for family assessment and goal setting. *Journal of the Division for Early Childhood, 12,* 195–207.

Winton, P. J., & Bailey, D. B. (1990). Early intervention training related to family interviewing. *Topics in Early Childhood Special Education, 10,* 50–62.

CHAPTER FOURTEEN

Measurement of Community Characteristics

FELTON EARLS AND STEPHEN BUKA

Because studying social contexts is arduous and expensive, it is crucial to have both a theoretical and a practical commitment to take on the challenge of measuring community properties with a sense of precision and accuracy. The material covered in this chapter addresses two concerns. While not the primary purpose, the first regards the rationale for studying communities. The second and more central issue regards how to do it. Following the theoretical contributions of Lewin (1954) and Bronfenbrenner (1979), and the empirical approach of Barker and Wright (1949), there has been a rebirth and intensification of interest in community and neighborhood effects on a host of developmental outcomes: from low birth weight and intelligence to rates of high school graduation and violent crime (Brooks-Gunn, Klebanov, & Duncan, 1996; Ensminger, Lamkin, & Jacobson, 1996). As is noted, this research is still in its early phases of evolution, and several methodological and analytical challenges remain to be solved and incorporated systematically into programs of research. By the same token, interventions that are aimed at community-level influences are seldom based on scientifically based information and experience. Commenting on the challenges faced by community-based initiatives, Rosewater noted, "It is clear that the activities are ... outstripping their intellectual and conceptual frameworks. If the initiatives are to fulfill their promise there is a need to sharpen thinking about community development on the one hand, meeting the needs of children and families on the other hand, and the connections between the two" (cited in Aber, 1995, p. 264).

To illustrate the consideration of how best to study communities, experience gained from the Project on Human Development in Chicago Neighborhoods (PHDCN) is highlighted here (Earls & Buka, 1997; Earls & Reiss, 1994). In part, this specific study is chosen because it represents a particularly bold and innovative attempt to advance knowledge about community-level influences, while incorporating research traditions from developmental psychology, pediatrics, child psychiatry, criminology, and public health to examine individual differences in health and behavioral outcomes.

Communities are important to study because economic, geographic, and cultural factors matter in human development. How to determine for which developmental outcomes these influences are most important, and when in development they might have their greatest impact, constitute the types of empirical questions that have led to a renewal of interest in community and neighborhood research. These questions are relevant for acquiring a basic understanding of the strength of community influences and the particular ways in which their effects are exerted. They are also important for judging the effectiveness of interventions that are designed more for the nature of the circumstances and quality of experiences they open to individuals and less with the individual as the primary target of impact. In a society that champions individual effort and achievement, there exists an undeniable proclivity to attribute causal influences on health outcomes and educational achievement to individual differences in personality, motivation, or intellect. Although the circle is often widened to consider family influences,

309

rarely do behavioral scientists engage in deep spec-ulation about impacts that exert themselves beyond the family unit. The same criticism might be applied to clinicians, whose history-taking for a present-ing problem rarely entails asking detailed questions about the patient's or client's social and physical surroundings beyond the immediate home environ-ment.

This concern extends even to those engaged in community-based interventions, both in programs that operate at the community level in an effort to effect individual change and those for which com-munity processes themselves are the focal concern. For the most part, interventions that are based in specific locales and aimed at improving the circum-stances for growth, health, and development are not based on substantive knowledge about the processes involved in transmitting community influences to individual families and children. For example, dur-ing the past fifty years there have been three large community intervention studies aimed at reducing risk factors for cardiovascular disease and improv-ing adult health status. The modest impacts of these large-scale initiatives may be explained by the ob-servation that the investigators "underestimated the complexity of community dynamics, the intricacies of formal, as well as informal community structures, and countervailing societal and economic forces that impact on change processes" (Feinlieb, 1996). Thus, fifty years of experience suggests that the avail-able knowledge base may be insufficient to alter effectively the smoking and dietary behaviors of adults in middle-class communities. How adequate, then, is the knowledge base for influencing the com-plex social and behavioral developmental processes for families and young children in disadvantaged communities?

The paucity of information and knowledge about community influences does not inhibit the desire or effort to better the places where we live. Neverthe-less, throughout the 1990s, there has been an in-creasing recognition that traditional agents of soci-ety are overwhelmed by changes in the social and physical environment. These changes are reflected in the labor market and workplace; the redistri-bution of the population among urban, suburban, and rural areas; the physical landscape of neighbor-hoods; the insertion of vast transportation systems in urban communities; and the introduction of an ever-increasing array of electronic technologies that increase the facility of people to have access to each other, to valuable goods, and to information. This has resulted in a second broad category of commu-nity interventions focused primarily on the func-tioning and social processes of the community and secondarily on the health and behavioral outcomes of its citizens (Freudenberg, 1997).

There is widespread acceptance that the tradi-tional institutions of civil society (e.g., the police, schools, and child welfare agencies) cannot accom-plish their missions alone. Ideally, top-down strate-gies initiated by governments need to be linked to bottom-up strategies from local communities. The new emphasis on community policing, for exam-ple, in which professional training and practices have systematically been changed to better inte-grate the police into the fabric of localities, heralds what we may eventually see happen in other ser-vice sectors (University of Maryland, 1997). Simi-larly, legislation on the Early Head Start Program emphasizes that funded programs should include community capacity-building as one of their man-dates. Yet, what represents a community is not de-fined in this legislation nor is capacity-building. Al-though community change is the goal, the focus of efforts is driven almost exclusively by a concern for child outcomes. In part, this reflects a hesitancy to specify characteristics that may vary so widely as to interfere with program implementation. But it also reflects a deficit in existing research and a need for new and innovative inquiry into the nature and function of communities as they relate to human development.

This chapter presents methods and procedures that will assist in evaluating and building a com-munity's capacity to support its children's develop-ment. For those working at a practical level in com-munities or neighborhoods, it would be desirable to know that measuring a community's contribution to developmental outcomes could be differentiated in some sense from influences that are located within families and from characteristics of individual chil-dren. Because this is a major objective of the PHDCN, reference is made to how multilevel influences on early development are being tackled in its design and execution.

THEORIES OF CONTEXT AND THEORIES OF DEVELOPMENT

Many theories of behavioral, cognitive, and emotional development position the unfolding of human capacities or deficits by taking into account only proximal or intimate features of the social milieu. Characteristics of caretakers and the varieties of stimulation afforded in the home environment are often assumed to be sufficient conditions for development to proceed. This kind of reasoning is, at least in part, a reflection of the academic schism existing between sociology and psychology. Over the years, the fragmentation of reality produced by the specialization of disciplines has been partially compensated for in the work of psychologists such as Lewin, Bronfenbrenner, and Barker, among others. Lewin's (1954) field theory emphasizes the interaction of the person and the environment. He developed formal mechanisms, as manifested by vectors and psychological subsystems, to conceptualize the causal influence played by the environment on behavior. Bronfenbrenner's ecological theory (1979) elaborates the zones of environmental impact in considerable detail: from proximal and intimate influence to distal and relatively remote forces. His theory is sufficiently comprehensive to include all those multiple aspects that operate on the child: from family, peer, and school influences to the impact of material conditions and cultural climate. Although the theory acknowledges reciprocal vectors among levels of organization, its major application has been to emphasize interactions that are largely confined to daily expectable experiences of parents and children. Studies examining neighborhood influences on child maltreatment, for instance, have concentrated on issues of social support available from friends and neighbors (Earls, McGuire, & Shay, 1994; Garbarino & Sherman, 1980). Following yet another scientific doctrine, Barker and Wright's empirical approach (1949) departed so much from the dominant theories of psychologists to conceptualize the mind as an interior phenomenon that he created a new discipline, which he termed *behavioral ecology*. Within this approach, the child's personality is conditioned by the summation of small and large interactions with all aspects of the environment.

Common to all three of these psychologists is a conviction that the child's mind and behavior are strongly conditioned by forces within the external environment. Bronfenbrenner has provided the most complete rendition of how this environment is organized, but the challenges are to measure it with a good approximation to its complexity and to account for its unique and conditional impact on human development. Proposition 8 in Bronfenbrenner's seminal paper (1977) introducing his ecological theory is worth quoting here:

Research on the ecology of human development requires investigations that go beyond the immediate setting containing the person to examine the larger contexts, both formal and informal, that affect events within the immediate environment. (p. 527)

Coulton's (1995) work has been particularly important in moving from general theoretical constructs to empirically grounded research in disadvantaged neighborhoods. She described four perspectives that may help explain how neighborhoods directly affect children or have indirect effects through families, peers, and local organizations. These include 1) compositional effects, 2) stressful neighborhood environments, 3) community context for effective parenting, and 4) community social organization. We describe these here in brief and direct the reader to her more thorough discussion of this topic (Coulton 1995, 1996).

Several decades of research have examined whether the socioeconomic composition of neighborhoods affects individual well-being over and above individual and family factors. Recently, a number of studies found that the presence of affluent neighbors seems to have a positive effect on a range of child and adult outcomes including teen births and IQ among low-birth-weight infants (Brooks-Gunn, Duncan, Klebanov, & Sealand, 1993), as well as school completion (Brooks-Gunn et al., 1993; Crane, 1991; Duncan, 1993; Ensminger et al., 1996). These results hold when taking family characteristics into consideration. Nevertheless, despite mounting evidence for the impacts of neighborhood composition over and above family-level influences taken as a whole, this research "suggests that neighborhood composition is confounded with family characteristics, and when family characteristics are controlled, neighborhood effects are fairly weak" (Coulton, 1996, p. 91). However, the potential to improve developmental outcomes through economic and social integration of neighborhoods should not be dismissed.

The dramatic erosion of the physical condition and presence of institutional resources (e.g., churches, schools, and recreational facilities) in many urban neighborhoods has directed growing attention to the potential impacts of deteriorating and stressful neighborhood environments on child development. These range from increased exposure to physical toxins with known intellectual and behavioral consequences, such as lead in soil and paint, to greater exposure to adverse social and psychological conditions as well. In particular, there is mounting evidence of the deleterious effects on children and youth exposed to community violence, both as witnesses and victims. Our recent review indicated that approximately 25% of urban youth reported seeing someone murdered in their lifetime (Buka et al., in preparation). Similarly, in a sample of Boston pediatric primary care clinic patients, Taylor, Zuckerman, Harik, and Groves (1992) estimated that one of every ten younger children had witnessed a violent event before the age of 6 years. Combining major findings across fourteen studies, we found that males, ethnic minorities, and urban residents are at particularly increased risk for witnessing violence. Various psychiatric problems, including post-traumatic stress disorder, aggression, and externalizing behavioral disorders, are more common among children and youth who witness violence (Cooley-Quille, Turner, & Beidel, 1995; Singer, Anglin, Song, & Lunghofer, 1995).

Coulton also described how parenting styles differ dramatically across neighborhoods and how these may influence child development indirectly. "Communities with more authoritative parents seem to produce better outcomes for children; these beneficial effects may also be conferred on children whose families are compromised by structure, such as single-parent families or other 'limitations'" (Coulton, 1996, p. 95). The available evidence suggests that effective parenting styles have a strong impact on child outcome, that communities differ in patterns of parenting, that troubled neighborhoods elicit less effective parenting, and that the parenting styles of neighbors may compensate for a particular family's limitations (Coulton, 1996; Furstenberg, 1993). Influencing neighborhood patterns and practices of parenting may therefore improve child outcomes throughout the neighborhood.

Finally, Coulton described how the social organization of communities – both through formal structures and such institutions as the police, schools, and clergy, as well as through informal relationships among neighbors, families, and peers – may provide the linkage between macrolevel changes in society and the development of individual children and youth. Community social organization refers to the degree to which local structures are able to accomplish the goals of residents and exert social control from within the community (Sampson, 1992). This perspective has developed in large part from investigations of criminal and delinquent behavior but recently has been expanded to explain other outcomes, such as prosocial youth activities (Freudenburg, 1986) and participation in voluntary organizations (Figueira-McDonough, 1991).

It is essential to point out that an entirely different platform exists from which to understand why social environments look as they do. Theories that assume the primacy of individual-level causation broadly fall under the rubric of social selection models (Scarr, 1992). Here the assumption is that genes, temperament, or early experiences provide such a heavy imprint on the mind and behavior that environmental influences are less consequential or that they essentially become secondary influences. As a function of their intelligence and temperament, it is assumed that children make an active effort to find relationships, skills, and leisure activities that fit their proclivities. Thus, so long as choice operates in these matters, the school or neighborhood environment would matter less. The specific features of these environments and the persons selected from them are what counts.

It is essential to keep in mind the metatheories of social causation and social selection, not so much because one is right and the other is wrong. It is more likely that both are right but not for the same outcome. For example, social selection may account for the socioeconomic plateaus and location of persons with schizophrenia who, because of the impairments associated with this disease, have drifted from their families and neighborhoods of origin to reside in transitional or marginal communities

(Dohrenwend & Lavav, 1992). On the other hand, substance abuse is a problem that is a function of availability and access to the commodities that produce the abusive behavior. Such products are not randomly distributed across environments, so one's location in time and space may be among the major determining factors for this outcome. But it is also understood that availability and access are not alone. A person must still choose (or be persuaded) to take a drug, and not all individuals so exposed will make such a decision. This suggests that behavior is influenced by factors that are both specific to the setting and to the individual. Existing theories are limited in accounting for the nature of this interaction between person and environment.

The incompleteness of current theories of context and development also runs into another problem: the fact that the social and physical environment is in a constant state of flux and that the forces accounting for this dynamic state of affairs are difficult to specify. Economic, political, cultural, and physical forces are always operating on communities and neighborhoods, but with no particular requirement that they be coordinated. Take the labor market as an example. Over much of the twentieth century, the workplace has become increasingly remote from residential neighborhoods. At the same time, the proportion of women in the workforce has increased. These two influences combine to separate parents from their children for many hours of the typical work week. This state of affairs need not be alarming if relationships and activities exist to compensate for the relative absence of the parents. On the other hand, if such surrogate experiences are not present, the child is at risk of social deprivation.

Modern society is producing technologies that will continue to transform our environment in ways that cannot be anticipated. From the automobile to the computer, these inventions provide a means to be less dependent on others. As traditional interdependencies diminish, we must ask if other forms of social organization will take their place (e.g., computer-based websites). As we turn to the measurement and analysis of community influences on early human development, this aspect in which the social environment is in a continual process of creation and re-creation is of fundamental importance if we are to understand how varied and changing circumstances affect children's development and

in another sense circumscribe the institutions and agencies that aim to guide and support that development.

THE COMMUNITY DESIGN OF THE PROJECT ON HUMAN DEVELOPMENT IN CHICAGO NEIGHBORHOODS (PHDCN)

The recommendations of a workshop conducted by the Institute of Medicine (1996), "Youth Development and Neighborhood Influences: Challenges and Opportunities," recapitulate the content of this chapter. In approaching the measurement of neighborhoods, five key issues that require scrutiny and refinement have been identified: 1) establishment of relevant boundaries to facilitate longitudinal studies; 2) creation of reliable and valid measures of the availability of and access to community resources (both formal and informal); 3) selection of adequate community samples to obtain valid measures of resident experiences; 4) examination of the pathways by which socioeconomic status, race/ethnicity, and residential stability influence social settings; and 5) assessment of the mechanisms that connect physical and social environments within communities. All of these recommendations have been incorporated into the community design of the PHDCN.

PHDCN has been explicit in establishing a theoretical framework to guide the study of children's development. First, it recognizes the implications of contrasting social selection with social causation hypotheses. To accomplish this, the same neighborhoods are examined over time to capture changes in the demographic and socioeconomic composition of the population. Second, it adopts the ecological theory of neighborhood social organization, advanced by the Chicago School of Sociology (Sampson, 1992, 1994; Shaw & McKay, 1942), to design measures and to formally test assumptions about how localities interact with characteristics of families and individuals. This theory articulates structural features of neighborhoods as being of prime importance in explaining deviant behavioral development. The three most important structural characteristics are residential mobility, racial or ethnic segregation, and the concentration of poverty among residents. These structural conditions in turn operate to constrain or facilitate neighborhoods to function as organized entities. The theory further

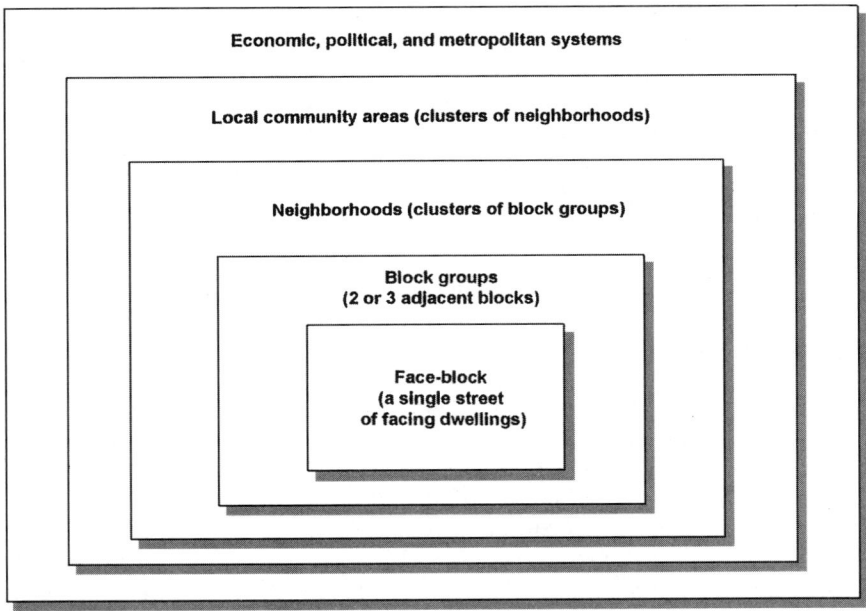

Figure 14.1. Organizational levels of urban areas.

posits that both formal and informal mechanisms exist to regulate and support the activities of residents. Formal mechanisms relate to organized political processes, schools, churches, the police, and commerce. Informal mechanisms are those that arise spontaneously within neighborhoods and reflect trust, reciprocity, friendship, and collective responsibility for children. Such processes also suggest a latent potential to respond to crises that adversely influence the well-being of a large proportion of residents. Such crises can be catastrophic in the form of natural disasters or more chronic, as when an area becomes the target of illegal enterprises.

The reader will have noticed that a transition has occurred from the use of the term *community* to a focus on neighborhood as the unit of interest. In studying the social milieu in which individuals and their families are embedded, the multifaceted connotations of community must be narrowed in order to be operationalized. In the PHDCN, the ecological theory of social organization is a major component of the framework guiding the selection and development of measures of structural and functional characteristics of neighborhoods. But first a strategy to locate and delimit a specific group of

individuals to a bounded geographic space is required. The assumption is that because these residents share a common space, there is a bond formed among them reflecting common interests, and perhaps even common values. It is important not to consider the definition of this unit as fixed at the beginning of an investigation. Having the flexibility to move from smaller to larger units is desirable. A model depicting this way of representing communities and neighborhoods is shown in Figure 14.1 and is referred to in the next section.

Ecological theory does not offer much of an explanation as to how the development of children is influenced by the settings in which they are reared. To complete the framework, a more explicit theory of development needs to be integrated with ideas of formal and informal social organization. While a full discussion of this topic is beyond the scope of this chapter, it is important to note that notions of reciprocity and trust derived particularly from informal social networks are compatible with the development of social competence. Thus, while socioeconomic circumstances and the educational level of one's neighbors may contribute in a major way to an individual's intellectual development and school achievement, from a theoretical perspective the strongest associations between neighborhood ecology and developmental outcomes might be expected in the areas of social competence, self-efficacy, and moral behavior. The negative consequences of growing up in an area that undermines the neighborhood as a setting for human development would not only be reflected in high levels of school underachievement but also in high rates of delinquency, substance use, and early and promiscuous sexual behavior. These pathological behaviors might be viewed as reflections of a failure to promote and sustain developmental trajectories that are marked by prosocial attitudes and behavior.

The following sections relate substantially to the experience of preparing for implementation of the PHDCN. The methods and analytical strategies required to measure neighborhood characteristics are illustrated. While this places some constraint on the range of approaches possible, it is important to acknowledge that this program of research came to fruition after a long period of consultation with an extensive group of behavioral and social scientists (Earls & Buka, 1997; Earls & Reiss, 1994; Tonry et al., 1991).

Choosing Measurement Units: Defining the Neighborhood

Just as one should be warned against generalizing about the nature of child development from studying a few children, the same applies when studying social units, such as neighborhoods. In designing a study to examine the contribution of neighborhoods to children's development, several preliminary decisions warrant that care be taken in selecting areas for study. Neighborhoods could be selected randomly to represent the national profile of urban, suburban, and rural areas. Alternatively, a few large areas could be contrasted to bring out important cultural or regional differences. After examining a variety of such alternatives, the PHDCN's decision was to study a single city that provided a sufficient number of contrasts among its neighborhoods to yield the range of variability needed to examine neighborhood effects on developmental outcomes in a multilevel design. Chicago was chosen because it had both the variety of neighborhoods, contrasting socioeconomic differences and racial/ethnic composition across a broad range, and

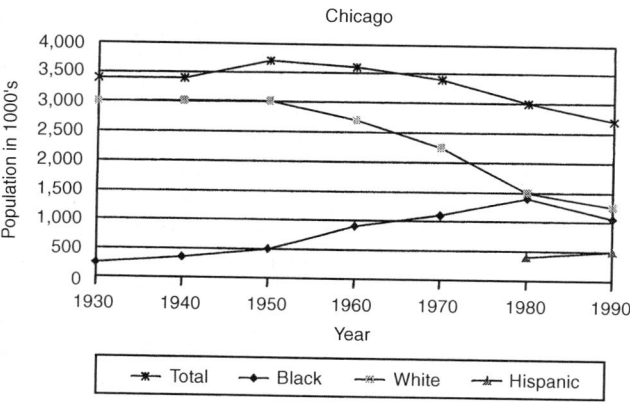

Figure 14.2. Population of Chicago, 1930–1990.

well-defined geographic boundaries to demarcate these areas one from another.

In approaching a city of millions of residents and hundreds of neighborhoods, a historical as well as a demographic perspective is useful. Old neighborhoods decline, new ones are created, and others are reestablished. Any cross-sectional measurement of a neighborhood must bear this in mind, and ideally a data collection effort should find a way to at least capture the direction of change in the areas studied. Figure 14.2 depicts a dramatic level of population change in Chicago over the past thirty years. The in-migration of Blacks from the South, the exodus of Whites and the middle class to suburban areas, and the recent and striking migration of Latinos, especially from Mexico, are features that capture the major demographic changes post–World War II in the United States. These are characteristics suggesting that research on neighborhood life in Chicago should have applicability to other metropolitan areas. This finding also assists one in projecting a picture of what the city may look like in the near future and raises the question of what is determining the overarching relationship between the central city and the much larger metropolitan area in which it has become a part.

Communities vary considerably in size and function, from large sparsely settled farming areas in which just a few households exist to geographically small, densely populated areas as represented in public housing developments in urban centers. As noted in Figure 14.1, one way to array these areas in a large urban area is through a nested model in which the smallest unit is a face-block and the largest is an officially defined entity such as a statistical metropolitan reporting area, as endorsed by the U.S. Bureau of the Census. The most basic unit is the face-block, defined as houses or apartments that allow neighbors to see each other from opposite sides of the same street. Block groups are composed of several adjacent city blocks and may approximate units that most residents would define as their neighborhood. The U.S. Bureau of the Census defines census tracts as units composed of roughly 4,000 to 5,000 residents. These units are typically composed of several block groups. Larger areas are defined for a variety of administrative reasons (e.g., police, school, and park districts) that do not necessarily have any functional integrity to local residents. Thus, the definition of a neighborhood as perceived and lived in by residents may bear little or no similarity to the way city departments provide local services, and each bureaucracy may define units that have little or no similarity to other city departments. For instance, rarely do school and police districts coincide.

One challenge confronting community and neighborhood data collection is the shifting boundaries as defined in these multiple ways. Face-blocks may be the most meaningful unit to study if one is interested in neighborhood effects on young children, but this unit may have decreasing significance as children enter adolescence. Because many infants and toddlers leave their locales to attend child-care facilities, their experience with transportation systems, security devices, recreational facilities, and different languages, foods, and customs may all become a more dominant influence on development than traditionally fashioned theories that view the child as embedded in an intimate setting of a family. The larger units of communities that may encompass tens of thousands of residents may be relevant for issues of service delivery, schooling, and the labor market. In any case, the measurement enterprise must assume a high level of permeability of neighborhood boundaries defined on these multiple levels and must try to achieve a degree of comprehensiveness and flexibility in accumulating data that permit an analysis that is sensitive to exposures at different periods of child and adolescent development.

In the PHDCN, an overriding consideration was given to how the social ecology of the city was demarcated by demographic characteristics of race/ethnicity and socioeconomic status. The census tract provided a convenient and useful point of departure for this analysis. By studying the distribution of income levels and race/ethnic composition across the 847 populated census tracts of the city, tracts were stratified into twenty-one possible types (see Table 14.1). Census tracts were divided into equal

TABLE 14.1. Stratified Sampling Distribution for Chicago Census Tracts, 1990 (N = 847)

Race/Ethnicity	Socioeconomic Status			
	Low	Medium	High	Row Total
Black, 75%+	205	81	27	313 (37.0%)
White, 75%+	0	12	162	174 (20.5%)
Hispanic, 75%+	25	28	1	54 (6.4%)
Hispanic/White, 20%/20%+	8	105	37	150 (17.7%)
Hispanic/Black, 20%/20%+	18	6	0	24 (2.8%)
Black/White, 20%/20%+	5	10	25	40 (4.7%)
Other Heterogeneous	22	39	31	92 (10.9%)
COLUMN TOTAL	283	281	283	847

thirds based on income levels. These arbitrary divisions function to separate areas into those where poverty is concentrated from those where the majority of households are headed by persons in middle- to upper-income levels. When this social class division is cross-classified by race/ethnic homogeneity of neighborhoods, the array includes nearly all types possible in the 3 × 7 grid in Table 14.1. The table reveals a preponderance of poor African American neighborhoods and high social class White neighborhoods. At the same time, the existence of a wide range of socioeconomic levels within the segregated African American neighborhoods (and to a lesser extent in Latino areas) is important to the objective of separating the often confounding influences of race/ethnicity and social class (see García Coll and Magnuson, this volume). For a city widely considered one of the most segregated in the nation, it is also noteworthy that a substantial proportion of neighborhoods are heterogeneous with regard to their race/ethnic composition.

Given this result, it is worth considering how generalizable this picture of geographic demarcation by demographic features may be. There are two related questions. The first asks whether the portrait would change if the entire metropolitan area of Chicago were included. This is unlikely because the majority of residents in suburban areas are not representative of either the lowest social class or race/ethnic minority groups. The second question relates to comparability between Chicago and other American cities. Here again, there is little evidence that the picture would be distinctly different. Thus, a cautious conclusion might be made that the array of neighborhoods provided through systematically sampling the entire city of Chicago broadly reflects the demographic structure of American society.

Methods and Instrumentation

Because the definitions and perceptions of neighborhoods vary in complicated ways, a multimethod approach to gathering data about these units is desirable. In the PHDCN, the decision was reached to collect several types of distinctively different data. These include official and administrative records from federal and local sources; direct observations about the neighborhood's physical setting and social activities; and interviews with residents,

professionals, and service providers who work in the area about their perceptions of the quality of life in the neighborhood. A limited number of settings also were selected for in-depth ethnographic studies aimed at obtaining a detailed understanding of what it is like to grow up in areas undergoing particularly dramatic change (e.g., empowerment zones, immigrant communities, public housing developments, and zones undergoing rapid gentrification).

As described earlier, census data provide a basis for defining neighborhoods according to geographic and demographic characteristics, but to what extent this definition approximates one driven by the way residents perceive its boundaries is open to question. In fact, census data have become the most widely used source of information providing a rich supply of information about population density, the varieties of family structures, and the educational and income levels of residents. Several other types of information can be obtained to characterize land use and real estate values, emergency calls to police and fire departments, incidents and arrests by police, school attendance and achievement levels, and health data about morbidity and mortality trends. But these official and administrative sources should be viewed as crude indicators of the way the neighborhood functions as a unit of habitation or as indirect measures, perhaps crude ones at that, of some deeper social process.

To gather data that address more directly the activities and relationships among residents, their political leaders, and other agents of neighborhoods, observational and interview methods are needed. In the PHDCN, a significant commitment was made to collect these types of data. Administrative or record data were supplemented with three types of information extracted from direct observation and consultation with residents and other key informants.

The observational data were collected using an approach known as *systematic social observation* (SSO). This method is used to record the physical appearance and social behavior of a population or its sampled units by trained observers using a standard protocol. The basic model of the SSO is analogous to that of sample social surveys (Reiss, 1971, 1975). A sampling frame and a sampling plan are selected, one or more samples drawn, a standardized data collection protocol created and pretested, and observers trained. The fundamental difference between

SSO and population censuses or sample surveys is that direct observation by a trained observer replaces respondent reporting to a survey interviewer (Reiss, 1968). The SSO method also differs from ethnography in that it systematizes data collection for all units.

Trained observers look for indications of a neighborhood's level of social organization and objective indicators of quality of life by recording the types of businesses, the degree to which properties are maintained, evidence of graffiti or vandalism, presence and quality of recreational facilities, presence of drug selling and other illegal activities, and the extent to which children are supervised by adults. In the Chicago study, the procedure called for videotaping both sides of a face-block from a van in eighty neighborhoods with some 27,000 block faces. Each videotape was accompanied by an observation log that was completed by two observers, each viewing one side of a block. The items were divided into thirty-five objective items (e.g., Is there a public telephone visible?) and twenty-one subjective items (e.g., Would you characterize the peer group as a gang?).

Structured interviews with randomly selected household residents were used to gather information on how the neighborhood was perceived and used by persons who lived there. The dimensions defined by the ecological theory of social organization, as delineated in Table 14.2, were operationalized in a survey instrument for this purpose, and several steps were taken to assess the reliability, validity, and practical utility of direct survey measurement of multiple aspects of neighborhood social organization within the context of a major American city (Barnes et al., 1997). The interview questions were sequenced for ease of administration. Initial questions cover relationships in the neighborhood, then its physical and observable attributes, presence of institutions and membership of organizations, ideas about values of neighborhood residents, and lastly about demographic aspects of the households. The majority of the items have Likert-type scale responses, and the questions were scored in such a way that a high score represents a better outcome, when directionality could be assumed. The scales with the greatest internal consistency were those describing Informal Social Control ($\alpha = 0.85$) and Social Cohesion ($\alpha = 0.89$). As shown in Table 14.2, these included questions about people being willing to help neighbors in tangible ways such as lending a small amount of money, watching out for trouble, and watching children in the neighborhood (social cohesion); neighbors mixing socially and giving each other advice (social participation); and neighbors having the propensity to intervene when antisocial behavior is noted, such as a fight breaking out, people making graffiti, or seeing children truant from school (informal monitoring/surveillance). Other scales (not shown in the table) in which consistent descriptions were found included neighborhood services and the residential stability of the area (Health Services, 0.74; Neighborhood Stability, 0.79).

The internal consistency analyses indicate that these theoretical constructs lead to consistent patterns of responses from individuals. Questions that ask about ways in which neighbors help one another, relate socially with each other, and are likely to intervene in local predicaments could be aggregated into psychometrically reliable scales. Reports of services available in the local area and the levels of stability and change in the neighborhood also showed substantial reliability. These results give substance to the theoretical constructs of Informal Social Control, Neighborhood Social Cohesion, and Residential Stability. The strong loading of items onto the Social Cohesion factor further suggests that the theoretical distinction between Informal Social Control and Social Cohesion may be one that indicates the degree to which neighbors either help each other or are willing to supervise children other than their own. These findings suggest that where there are people in neighborhoods who help each other, they can also be relied upon to monitor youth and to manifest a high degree of participation in neighborhood activities (Sampson et al., 1997).

Key informants were identified as persons with specialized knowledge about the neighborhood. These individuals included long-time residents or persons who had acquired reputations as activists or civic leaders and representatives of a broad range of professional groups who provided services or ran businesses in the community. This latter group consisted of school administrators, community police, religious leaders, elected officials, and business owners. Each of these groups was systematically sampled from rosters made up of all persons in each of the categories, with the exception of reputational

TABLE 14.2. Result of Factor Analysis and Internal Consistency Checks (Cronbach's Alpha) on Scales of Neighborhood Social Organization

Neighborhood Social Organization	Cronbach's alpha
Informal Social Control	
Local Social Participation	$\alpha = 0.85$
0.75* How often favors exchanged	
0.62 How often watch property	
0.65 How often ask neighbors for advice	
0.63 How often go to neighbors' parties	
0.67 How often visit with neighbors	
Social Cohesion	
Social Capital	$\alpha = 0.89$
0.76 Are people willing to help?	
0.73 Do neighbors watch out for kids?	
0.70 Is this a close-knit neighborhood?	
0.69 Do neighbors watch for trouble?	
0.67 Could you borrow $30 from a neighbor?	
0.65 If there is a problem, will neighbors deal with it?	
0.60 Are there adults to look up to?	
0.56 Can neighbors be trusted?	
0.49 People will take advantage.	
0.46 No one in neighborhood cares (reversed).	
0.38 People go their own way (reversed).	
Recreational and Support Services	$\alpha = 0.81$
0.67 Does neighborhood have recreational/after-school programs?	
0.66 Does neighborhood have after-school program?	
0.62 Does neighborhood have summer recreation program?	
0.52 Does neighborhood have any good parks?	
0.48 Teens can only hang out	
0.48 Does neighborhood have day-care services?	
0.45 No place to play but the street	
0.33 Does neighborhood have a community center?	

*Item/Total Pearson Correlations

leaders. The roster of individuals in this category was nominated by each of the professional groups and selected on the basis of consensus. In comparable fashion to the survey of household residents, an interview method was developed and carefully pretested. Each of the groups was asked several types of questions that tapped their level of awareness of multiple social and political influences and the level at which they could mobilize others to respond to important issues affected by the quality of life in their neighborhoods.

A fourth method is ethnographic in design. This approach provides a way of examining neighborhood processes in greater depth than would be permitted by survey methods. Many ethnographers accomplish this by residing in a neighborhood for some period of time, possibly years, whereas others accomplish data collection through proxies who live in the study area. The types of questions that have been addressed by urban ethnographers concern the role of informal economies and gangs in very poor communities and the impact of policy decisions on the sense of control possessed by residents in such neighborhoods. Newer interests are also emerging. In the PHDCN, attention has been directed to neighborhoods receiving large numbers of recent immigrants. In this effort, the aim is to increase the understanding of attitudes and values of adolescents and young adults that relate to assimilation into American culture and how this process may relate to a worsening of certain health outcomes, such as infant mortality, low birth weight, and deaths resulting from interpersonal violence (Singh & Yu, 1996). Another relevant ethnographic study is situated in an area in which a large public housing complex is undergoing redevelopment. The concern is to learn how local residents, and youth in particular, adapt to and participate in the planning process. In reviewing a broad range of studies, it is interesting to note that the ethnographic approach has not been exploited to study middle class or ethnically heterogeneous neighborhoods.

The challenge is to integrate these various sources of data in a composite, dynamic picture of neighborhoods as social units that capture both horizontal and vertical relationships. Horizontal links reflect characteristic interactions among neighbors, especially regarding the supervision and support of children. Vertical relationships are those between local neighborhoods and large political, administrative, and economic units. The underlying issue regards the capacity of a neighborhood to produce and maintain resources that support a satisfactory standard of living.

Analytical Strategies

A full description of the analytical challenges and statistical models available for studying community or neighborhood influences on development is beyond the scope of this chapter. Interested readers are directed to a separate report that characterizes the major issues being confronted in the PHDCN (Raudenbush, 1997). As improved measures are developed and incorporated into multilevel research designs that permit accurate detection of influences operating at or between neighborhoods, families, and schools, greater confidence will accrue as to how best to design interventions and campaigns to promote well-being. These requirements have been introduced into the PHDCN and, in time, have the promise of providing important new information. For purposes of guiding a comprehensive plan of analysis, the following five issues should be considered. Each was an important criterion to develop and implement in the early stages of executing this project. Their refinement is a matter of continued application as increasing amounts of data become available as the study evolves.

1. Determining the reliability and validity of measures – as in all circumstances in which observations are based on varying degrees of subjective interpretation, measurement characteristics of the assessment tools need to be established and reported. This criterion was established in the preliminary stage of the PHDCN (Raudenbush & Sampson, in press).

2. Capturing within- and between-neighborhood variation – because neighborhoods as a unit of analysis are defined arbitrarily, the level of within-unit variability may be a function of size, and high levels of within-neighborhood variability may mask true differences between locales defined as smaller units.

3. Determining the independent and combined explanatory power of structural versus process neighborhood variables – here we refer to the differences between markers or indicator variables, such as those reflected in demographic or administrative information (e.g., median income or proportion minority), and those reflecting actual social relationships. In other words, it is important to determine the degree to which typical demographic marker variables capture actual social processes. Because administrative and census data are routinely collected, widely available, and much less expensive than survey ethnographic data, it is important to know their limitations and how they can be used best.

4. Moderator and mediator effects on developmental outcomes – both are ways of characterizing indirect effects of neighborhood influences on individuals and families. Moderator effects reflect mechanisms in which neighborhood influences either amplify or dampen other relationships (e.g., the presence of strong gangs); whereas mediator effects suggest that for neighborhood influences to affect human development, they must be filtered through some other set of structures or conditions (e.g., social cohesion).

5. Determining the existence of thresholds in measurement beyond which neighborhoods fail to support human development – this refers to a standard of living index in which some minimal set of conditions is specified.

SUMMARY AND FUTURE APPLICATIONS

Because the formal study of community influences on human development is at an early stage of scientific refinement, it is useful to conclude this chapter with a consideration of future applications, especially as they bear on our principal concern of early childhood development. These interests might well begin with continued efforts to refine ideas about the most appropriate units of analysis for studying different kinds of outcomes associated with community influences. Reliance on administrative sources of data provides relatively crude information for making inferences about environmental effects. The PHDCN has invested heavily in creating new measures to observe directly the terrain of neighborhoods and the types of activities that go on within them and to interview systematically residents and people who work in these areas about the quality of life (Raudenbush & Sampson, in press; Sampson, Morenoff, & Earls, in press). But there remain important features of urban life that complicate matters. People move frequently and for a variety of reasons. Parents typically work at some distance from their homes, making commuting a daily stress on family life. It might not be uncommon for a family to have members who work and attend schools, child care facilities, and churches all in different neighborhoods, not to mention where they go to purchase food and other important commodities. This kind of mobility may be conditioned by high levels of affluence and control over resources, so that the meaning of neighborhood decreases as income and education increase. If this is the case, it suggests that neighborhoods may carry less importance for middle-class persons than they do for individuals at the lower rungs of society, but of course that is an empirical question.

A second concern relates to the need to widen standards on the specific resources and types of activities that constitute a habitable environment. Sanitation and housing codes represent the first obvious steps in this direction. To these are added standards for what constitute health risks, such as lead contamination and toxic wastes. But having large numbers of disadvantaged families residing in the same area may produce a social climate in which adult monitoring of children decreases, youth gangs increase in size and authority, and the lack of security seriously diminishes the quality of life. All these undermine the capacity of parents to raise their children and may present opportunities for children to choose deviant options. The possibility that adults and youths who experience this reduced quality of life can transmit hopeless attitudes and insecure feelings to very young children must not be minimized. One of the areas in which the PHDCN has concentrated its efforts is in studying children's exposure

to violence (Kindlon et al., 1996; Selner-O'Hagen et al.,1998). The interview method developed for this purpose asks parents of all children, and older children themselves, about being a victim of violence as well as being a witness to violent events both inside or outside the home environment. Existing data indicate that young children are far from isolated or protected from violent events taking place within neighborhood settings (Buka et al., in preparation).

All of these issues relate to the most important reason to study neighborhoods, and that concerns the way neighborhoods facilitate, constrain, or undermine the healthy and socially competent development of children. Poverty may not act alone in constraining or undermining the capacity of a neighborhood to produce competent children. Thus, observing a variety of settings provides a wider window from which to observe how combinations of formal and informal processes work to define the social organization of a neighborhood. In capturing a broad spectrum, it must be remembered that neighborhood effects extend across a wide socioeconomic range of families, not just those who are poor. Schor (1995) noted:

The lack of participatory civic forums, both formal and informal, coupled with a concentration of political power in a professional elite, has decreased the general sense of civic obligation. There are fewer incentives and opportunities for individuals to take responsibility for themselves, their families and neighbors – not to mention strangers – and a diminished expectation to hold themselves and others accountable for their actions in the social context. (p. 440)

Most of what has been learned or theorized regarding community influences on human development concerns older children and adolescents. The work summarized in this chapter, on theories of social selection and social causation and on the impacts of community social organization on delinquent and prosocial activities, pertains almost exclusively to adolescents and young adults. This results, in part, from differences in the unit of influence and study for adolescents and adults. Although limited, data exist on larger geographic units, such as neighborhoods and communities. Less information is readily available for the contexts that affect the development of preschool children, such as child care settings, apartment buildings, face-blocks, and city blocks. Much work remains to apply and modify existing theories and methods for the study of early childhood development. First, we need to describe those contextual factors that may have a particular salience for this developmental period. New theories involving collective attitudes toward child-rearing and parenting, social support for parenting, local resources for recreation and interaction among families with young children, and related constructs are required. Second, existing measures and constructs that have proven useful for explaining the development of older children must be available for smaller geographic units, such as face-blocks or city blocks. Many variables collected in the U.S. Census are available only at the census tract level – a geographic unit that may be too large to characterize the smaller regions that characterize the world of infants and toddlers. Census data aggregated to the face-block level would further this line of inquiry. Ideally, information on social processes described herein would also be available at this microlevel – including information on reciprocity, trust, support, and the like.

Third, special study designs are required to explain fully the influence of contextual factors on early childhood development. As in the PHDCN, these ideally would include a sufficiently large and diverse number of contexts (such as child care centers or city blocks), a sufficiently large and diverse number of young children within each context, and measures of the individual children and their families as well as the contexts themselves.

Recent work has shown advances in all of these areas as documented in the two volume collections of studies edited by Brooks-Gunn, Duncan, and Aber (1997a,b). A growing number of investigations are including such contextual variables hypothesized to affect the young child, including indices of the physical environment (soil lead levels), indices of the social environment (levels of violence and exposure to violence), attitudes toward parenting, and collective levels of social support. Finally, major new investigations, such as a federally sponsored study on child maltreatment, are implementing new designs with both contextual measures and longitudinal study of children developing within these contexts (Runyan et al., 1998).

It will be interesting to see if any of the types of methods described in this chapter evolve in the direction of strategies that permit rapid assessment of neighborhood social and physical characteristics. Such techniques could be adopted by local organizations to evaluate and monitor their own areas with some degree of autonomy and confidence. Issues such as school safety, access to child care facilities and other human services, levels of trust and reciprocity among neighbors, quality of play and recreational areas, and many others could be assessed, discussed, and acted upon periodically by civic organizations and other groups, including those that might be initiated by children themselves.

Although it deserves a separate and focused inquiry of its own, there are important ethical issues that also should be considered before and after data are collected about communities. At the moment, these matters are not instituted formally in a way that approximates traditional procedures designed to protect individuals engaged in research. But the concept that communities or neighborhoods as organized entities deserve respect and protection will certainly emerge as this kind of research progresses. To advance this concern, four alternative levels of engagement are postulated to guide potential interactions between organized research projects and communities: 1) unrestricted access in which the community/neighborhood is an open field; 2) unrestricted access, but the community/neighborhood provides consultation; 3) informed consent obtained at the community/neighborhood level; and 4) community/neighborhood members serve as co-investigators. Although arguable, the tradition in the social sciences has more closely approximated the first step. A practical reason given frequently by investigators is that deciding who represents the community is a difficult question. In fact, this issue alone may require a type of inquiry that consumes considerable time and effort, and it will be interesting to follow developments in this area of ethics over the next decade.

Although a single study has been emphasized in this chapter, using it as an example does facilitate the study and interpretation of how causal influences operate within the nested and hierarchically arranged relationships among metropolitan systems, neighborhoods, families, and individuals. To this end, a significant investment has been made in designing a multimethod approach to measure neighborhoods as social and physical entities. Findings that indicate the importance of neighborhood are beginning to emerge, but the study is still at an early stage of producing substantive evidence that quality of life in a neighborhood does make a distinctive and important contribution to child development. In light of this, it is important to heed the advice of Aber (1995):

We should not prematurely conclude that individual and family factors matter more than community factors in determining child outcomes (or vice versa!). Rather, strategies are needed to address the issue of the comparative and interactive impacts of individual, family and community factors. In this sense, the practical stakes are high for a new generation of better designed and analyzed studies. (p. 263)

The concepts and methods covered in this chapter represent cutting-edge developments in the study of community influences on human development. It might be anticipated that results from this and similar studies will produce new knowledge that will contribute to policies and practices that enhance standards of living in neighborhoods and their contributions to the well-being of children.

REFERENCES

Aber, J. L. (1995). Poverty, violence, and child development: Untangling family and community level effects. In C. Nelson (Ed.), *Threats to optimal development: Integrating biological, psychological and social risk factors*. The Minnesota Symposium on Child Psychology (Vol. 27, pp. 229–72). Hillsdale, NJ: Erlbaum.

Barker, R., & Wright, H. F. (1949). Psychological ecology and the problem of psychosocial development. *Child Development, 20*, 131–43.

Barnes, J., Sampson, R. J., Kindlon, D., & Reiss, A. J., Jr. (1997). A community approach to ecological assessment: Results from a pilot study. In F. Earls & S. Buka (Eds.), *Project on human development in Chicago neighborhoods: A technical report* (pp. 34–45). Washington, DC: The National Institute of Justice.

Bronfenbrenner, U. (1977). Toward an experimental ecology of human development. *American Psychologist, 32*, 513–31.

Bronfenbrenner, U. (1979). *The ecology of human development*. Cambridge, MA: Harvard University Press.

Brooks-Gunn, J., Duncan, G., & Aber, J. L. (Eds.). (1997a). *Neighborhood poverty: Context and consequences for children* (Vol. 1). New York: Russell Sage Foundation Press.

Brooks-Gunn, J., Duncan, G., & Aber, J. L. (Eds.) (1997). *Neighborhood poverty: Policy implications in studying neighborhoods* (Vol. 2). New York: Russell Sage Foundation Press.

Brooks-Gunn, J., Duncan, G. J., Klebanov, P. K., & Sealand, N. (1993). Do neighborhoods influence child adolescent development? *American Journal of Sociology, 99*, 353–95.

Brooks-Gunn, J., Klebanov, P. K., & Duncan, G. (1996). Ethnic differences in children's intelligence test scores: Role of economic deprivation, home environment, and maternal characteristics. *Child Development, 67*, 396–408.

Buka, S., Birdthistle, I., & Earls, F. The epidemiology of witnessing violence in childhood and adolescence (in preparation).

Cooley-Quille, M. R., Turner, S. M., & Beidel D. C. (1995). Emotional impact of children's exposure to community violence: A preliminary study. *Journal of American Academy of Child and Adolescent Psychiatry, 34*, 1362–8.

Coulton, C. C. (1995). Using community-level indicators of children's well-being in comprehensive community initiatives. In J. P. Connell, A. C. Kubisch, L. B. Schorr, & C. H. Weiss (Eds.), *New approaches to evaluating community initiatives*. Washington, DC: The Aspen Institute.

Coulton, C. C. (1996). Effects of neighborhoods on families and children: Implications for services. In A. J. Kahn & S. B. Kamerman (Eds.), *Children and their families in big cities*. New York: Cross-National Studies Program.

Crane, J. (1991). Effects of neighborhoods on dropping out of school and teenage childbearing. In C. Jencks & P. E. Peterson (Eds.), *The urban underclass*. Washington, DC: The Brookings Institution.

Dohrenwend, B., & Lavav, I. (1992). Socioeconomic status and psychiatric disorder: The causation-selection issue. *Science, 255*, 946–51.

Duncan, G. J. (1993). *Families and neighbors as sources of disadvantage in the schooling decisions of white and black adolescents*. Ann Arbor: University of Michigan.

Earls, F., & Buka, S. (Eds.) (1997). *Project on human development in Chicago neighborhoods: A technical report*. Washington, DC: The National Institute of Justice.

Earls, F., McGuire, J., & Shay, S. (1994). Evaluating a community intervention to reduce the risk of child abuse: Methodological strategies in conducting neighborhood surveys. *Child Abuse and Neglect, 18*, 473–85.

Earls, F., & Reiss, A. J. (Eds.). (1994). *Breaking the cycle*. Washington, DC: The National Institute of Justice.

Ensminger, M. E., Lamkin, R. P., & Jacobson, N. (1996). School leaving: A longitudinal perspective including neighborhood effects. *Child Development, 67*, 2400–16.

Feinleib, M. (1996). Editorial: New directions for community intervention studies. *American Journal of Public Health, 86*, 1696–7.

Figueira-McDonough, J. (1991). Community structure and delinquency: A typology. *Social Service Review, 65*, 69–91.

Freudenburg, W. R. (1986). The density of acquaintance-ship: An overlooked variable in community research. *American Journal of Sociology, 92*, 27–63.

Freudenberg, W. (1997). *Health promotion in the city*. Atlanta, GA: U.S. Centers for Disease Control.

Furstenberg, F. F. (1993). How families manage risk and opportunity in dangerous neighborhoods. In W. J. Wilson (Ed.), *Sociology and the public agenda* (pp. 231–58). Newbury Park, CA: Sage.

Garbarino, J., & Sherman, D. (1980). High-risk neighborhoods and high-risk families: The human ecology of child maltreatment. *Child Development, 51*, 188–98.

Institute of Medicine. (1996). *Youth development and neighborhood influences: Challenges and opportunities.* Washington, DC: National Academy of Sciences Press.

Kindlon, D. J, Wright, B. D., Raudenbush, S. W., & Earls, F. (1996). The measurement of children's exposure to violence. *International Journal of Methods in Psychiatric Research, 6*, 187–94.

Lewin, K. (1954). Behavior as a function of the total situation. In L. Carmichael (Ed.), *Manual of child psychology* (pp. 918–70). New York: Wiley.

Raudenbush, S. (1997). Hierarchical linear models and growth models. In F. Earls & S. Buka (Eds.), *Project on human development in Chicago neighborhoods: A technical report.* Washington, DC: The National Institute of Justice.

Raudenbush, S., & Sampson, R. (in press). "Ecometrics": Toward a science of assessing ecological settings, with application to the systemic social observation of neighborhoods. *Sociological Methodology.*

Reiss, A. J., Jr. (1968). Stuff and nonsense about social surveys and observation. In H. S. Becker, B. Greer, D. Riesman, & R. S. Weiss (Eds.), *Institutions and the person* (pp. 351–67). Chicago: Aldine.

Reiss, A. J., Jr. (1971). Systematic social observation of natural social phenomena. In H. Costner (Ed.), *Sociological methodology* (pp. 3–33). San Francisco: Jossey-Bass.

Reiss, A. J., Jr. (1975). Systematic observation surveys of natural social phenomena. In A. W. Sinaiko & L. A. Broedling (Eds.), *Perspectives on attitude assessment: Surveys and their alternatives* (pp. 132–50). Washington, DC: Smithsonian Institution. Reprinted (1976, pp. 123–41). Champaign, IL: Pendelton Publications.

Reiss, A. J., Jr. (1986). Why are communities important in understanding crime? In A. J. Reiss Jr. & M. Tonry (Eds.), *Communities and crime* (pp. 1–34). Chicago: University of Chicago Press.

Runyan, D. K., Hunter, W. M., Socolar, R. S., Amaya-Jackson, L., English, D., Lansverk, J., Dubowitz, H., Browne, D. H., Bangdiwala, S. I., & Mathew, R. M. (1998). Children who prosper in unfavorable environments: The relationship to social capital. *Pediatrics, 101*, 12–18.

Sampson, R. J. (1992). Family management and child development: Insights from social disorganization theory. In J. McCord (Ed.), *Advances in criminological theory* (Vol. 3, pp. 69–93). New Brunswick, NJ: Transaction.

Sampson, R. J. (1994). The community. In J. Q. Wilson & J. Petersilia (Eds.), *Crime* (pp. 193–216). San Francisco: ICS Press.

Sampson, R. J., Raudenbush, S. W., & Earls, F. (1997). Neighborhoods and violent crime: A multilevel study and collective efficacy. *Science, 277*, 918–24.

Sampson, R. J., Morenoff, J., & Earls, F. (in press). Beyond social capital: Neighborhood mechanisms and structural sources of collective efficacy for children. *American Sociological Review.*

Scarr, S. (1992). Developmental theories for the 1990s: Development and individual differences. *Child Development, 63*, 1–119.

Schor, E. L. (1995). Developing communality: Family-centered programs to improve children's health and well-being. *Bulletin of the New York Academy of Medicine, 72*, 413–42.

Selner-O'Hagen, M. B., Kindlon, D. J., Buka, S. L., Raudenbush, S. W., & Earls, F. (1998). Assessing exposure to violence in urban youth. *Journal of Child Psychiatry and Psychology, 39*, 215–24.

Shaw, C. R., & McKay, H. D. (1942). *Juvenile delinquency and urban areas.* Chicago: University of Chicago Press.

Singer, M. I., Anglin, T. M., Song, L., & Lunghofer, L. (1995). Adolescents' exposure to violence and associated symptoms of psychological trauma. *Journal of the American Medical Association, 273*, 477–82.

Singh, G. K., & Yu, S. M. (1996). Adverse pregnancy outcomes: Differences between US- and foreign-born women in major US racial and ethnic groups. *American Journal of Public Health, 86*, 837–43.

Taylor, L., Zuckerman, B., Harik, V., & Groves, B. (1992). Exposure to violence among inner city parents and young children. *American Journal of the Diseases of Children, 146*, 487.

Tonry, M., Ohlin, L., & Farrington, D. (1991). *Human development and criminal behavior: New ways of advancing knowledge.* New York: Springer-Verlag.

University of Maryland, Department of Criminology and Criminal Justice. (1997). What works, what doesn't, what's promising. *Office of Justice Research Report.* Washington, DC: U.S. Department of Justice.

PART FIVE

SERVICE DELIVERY MODELS AND SYSTEMS

CHAPTER FIFTEEN

Preventive Health Care and Anticipatory Guidance

PAUL H. DWORKIN, M.D.

The field of pediatrics emerged as a medical specialty in response to the realization that children's health problems differ from those of adults. At the beginning of the twentieth century, physicians were concerned only with the treatment of illness and confined their efforts to the child when sick, rather than focusing on the maintenance of health (Cone, 1979). Health supervision of children was limited, at most, to a cursory examination to detect signs of contagious illness. In the United States, the earliest origins of preventive child health care were found in the milk stations and urban child health conferences where infants could be brought to be fed, weighed, examined, and later immunized against contagious diseases (Hoekelman, 1997).

In the middle years of the twentieth century, child health services were altered dramatically by the improved control of infection as a result of the introduction of antibiotic agents, enhanced sanitation, the implementation of effective public health measures, and the development of an array of effective immunizations. With the resultant dramatic reduction in childhood morbidity and mortality (i.e., the childhood mortality rate today is nearly twenty-five times less than it was in 1900), attention shifted from an exclusive focus on the treatment of illness to the promotion of health and the prevention of disease. Indeed, the importance of preventive care was a major impetus for the establishment of the American Academy of Pediatrics (AAP), and it continues to distinguish the discipline of pediatrics from other medical specialties (Hoekelman, 1997). In 1955, the American Public Health Association's Committee on Child Health defined

children's health as "a state of physical, mental, and social well-being, not merely the absence of disease or infirmity." The objective of health supervision for children was identified as keeping "the well child well and to promote the highest possible level of his complete well-being" (Committee on Child Health, 1955). Similarly, the American Academy of Pediatrics has defined the goal of child health supervision as the promotion of the optimal growth and development of children (American Academy of Pediatrics Committee on Standards of Child Health Care, 1972).

Approximately twenty-five years ago, Haggerty and colleagues identified behavioral, developmental, and psychosocial problems as the "new morbidity" of pediatric practice (Haggerty, Roughman, & Pless, 1975). Subsequent studies confirmed the high prevalence of such problems within the primary care practice setting (Hickson, Altemeier, & O'Connor, 1983). As a result, pediatric preventive care has increasingly focused on the behavioral and social aspects of child health.

More recently, the need for child health supervision to acknowledge and respond to profound changes in the family and society has been emphasized through such activities as Bright Futures, a collaborative effort by the Maternal and Child Health Bureau of the U.S. Public Health Service and the Medicaid Bureau of the Health Care Financing Administration to develop guidelines for health supervision of infants, children, and adolescents (Green, 1994). The challenges in delivering comprehensive child health supervision services include the widespread weakening of family relationships, a decrease in the time parents spend with their children, much less direct contact with grandparents and extended family, geographic mobility, and a diminution of neighborhood cohesiveness and social supports (Green & Kessel, 1993). The Bright Futures guidelines emphasize the critical importance of viewing child health in context and being responsive to the individual needs of children and their families.

Studies demonstrate that from one-third to one-half of pediatricians' time in office practice is devoted to well-child care and health supervision (Hoekelman, 1983). Despite this considerable commitment, the extent to which such services successfully promote children's development is uncertain. The goal of this chapter is to examine critically the role of the pediatric practitioner (i.e., pediatrician, family physician, and nurse practitioner) in promoting children's development during child health supervision visits. Discussion focuses on select content of preventive child health services, as well as such aspects as the setting in which care is provided and the process by which it is delivered. Finally, strategies are identified to improve the effectiveness of well-child care.

DEVELOPMENTAL MONITORING

As identified by the AAP's Committee on Practice and Ambulatory Medicine, traditional components of child health supervision services include a health history, physical examination, measurements, sensory screening, developmental and behavioral monitoring, immunization and laboratory procedures, and age-specific counseling, termed *anticipatory guidance* (American Academy of Pediatrics, 1995). While all components are regarded as contributing to health promotion, the content areas that address children's development most specifically are developmental monitoring and anticipatory guidance.

One goal of child health supervision is to identify, as early as possible, developmental disabilities and children at risk for future disabilities to ensure the provision of appropriate services and support (Chamberlin, 1987a). By virtue of their access to young children and families, pediatric practitioners are well positioned to participate in the early detection of developmental problems. However, how to best perform such detection is uncertain.

Pediatricians use a variety of techniques to monitor children's development, including reviewing developmental milestones with parents; using an informal collection of age-appropriate tasks selected from various developmental schedules; relying on clinical judgment based on history, physical examination, and office observation; and performing formal screening with a standardized test (Shonkoff, Dworkin, Leviton, & Levine, 1979; Dobos, Dworkin, & Bernstein, 1994). Past research has documented the infrequent use of developmental screening tests by pediatricians (Smith, 1978). A more recent survey found that only 30% of pediatricians performed formal screening with a standardized instrument such as the Denver Developmental Screening Test (Dobos, Dworkin, & Bernstein, 1994).

Many developmental screening tools have important limitations, including issues of reliability, validity, and the lack of well-established norms (Meisels, 1988). Even the Denver II, the recent restandardization of the Denver Developmental Screening Test, has been criticized for its low specificity (i.e., accuracy in identifying children who do not have delays) and resultant overly high referral rate of children for further evaluation (Glascoe et al., 1992). Instruments such as the Batelle Developmental Inventory Screening Test, the Brigance Screens, and the Early Screening Inventory (ESI) approach, to varying degrees, conventional standards for psychological tests (Glascoe, Martin, & Humphrey, 1990; Glascoe, 1995; Meisels, Henderson, Liaw, Browning, & Ten Have, 1993). However, studies are needed to demonstrate the applicability of such tools to the pediatric office visit, where time is limited and children are often uncooperative.

Developmental Surveillance

The approach to developmental monitoring currently practiced by pediatric providers is most consistent with the process termed *developmental surveillance*. As defined by the British, developmental surveillance is a flexible, longitudinal, continuous process whereby knowledgeable pediatric practitioners perform skilled observations of children during child health encounters (Dworkin, 1989).

Components of surveillance include eliciting and attending to parents' concerns; obtaining a relevant developmental history; making accurate and informative observations of children; and sharing opinions and concerns with other relevant professionals, such as child care providers, visiting nurses, and preschool teachers. Rather than viewing development in isolation during a screening session, emphasis is placed on monitoring development within the context of the child's overall well-being (Dworkin, 1992). Some child health providers choose to supplement their clinical impressions and improve the accuracy of surveillance by periodically administering a screening test, either a professionally administered tool (e.g., Denver II) or a parent-completed measure (e.g., Parents' Evaluation of Developmental Status [PEDS]; Child Development Inventories; Ages and Stages Questionnaires; Glascoe & Dworkin, 1995; Glascoe, Martin, & Humphrey, 1990). Alternatively, pediatric practitioners may use such a test selectively, as a second-stage screening instrument when suspicions arise (Frankenburg, 1973; Meisels, 1988).

One of the most important components of developmental monitoring is to elicit parents' opinions and concerns effectively. Clinical information available from parents may be divided into two broad categories: appraisals and descriptions. Appraisals (i.e., opinions of children's development) include parents' concerns, estimations, and predictions. Descriptions include both recall and report. Each type of information offers distinct advantages and disadvantages in monitoring children's development (Glascoe & Dworkin, 1995).

Parents' concerns for their children's development have been shown to be accurate indicators of true developmental problems (Bagnato & Neisworth, 1991; Henderson & Meisels, 1994). Certain types of concerns are particularly predictive. For example, in one study performed within the pediatric office waiting room, concerns about speech and language, fine motor skills, or more general functioning were accurate indicators of measurable difficulties. In contrast, concerns in such areas as self-help skills and behavior were not found to be as sensitive indicators of developmental problems (Glascoe, Altemeier, & MacLean, 1989).

Parents have also been found to be reasonably accurate in providing estimations of their children's developmental level. When asked, "Compared with other children, how old would you say your child acts now?" parents' responses generally correlate well with children's actual developmental quotients (Glascoe & Sandler, 1995). Parents' predictions, however, are less accurate and are more likely to overestimate their children's future functioning. Recall of developmental milestones is notoriously unreliable and not helpful in the detection of developmental delays. In contrast, parents' contemporaneous reports of their children's current skills and achievements are both accurate and useful (Knobloch, Stevens, Malone, Ellison, & Risemberg, 1979; Sonnander, 1987). Developmental surveillance is consistent with expert opinion on monitoring children's development. Bright Futures emphasizes the importance of health professionals and families observing the emergence of abilities in children over time through developmental surveillance (Green, 1994). The AAP Committee on Children with Disabilities concludes that successful early identification of developmental problems requires the pediatrician to be skilled in the use of screening techniques and developmental surveillance and actively to elicit parental concerns and create linkages with community resources (American Academy of Pediatrics, 1994). The authors of the Denver II, a major revision and restandardization of the Denver Developmental Screening Test, recommend that this instrument be used as an aid to monitoring children's development, much like a growth chart. Results should not be interpreted in isolation but rather over time, within the context of the child's overall functioning and circumstances (Frankenburg et al., 1992).

The validity of developmental surveillance requires examination through large-scale population-based studies. Whether surveillance ultimately achieves the goals of child health supervision depends on the extent to which its implementation is enhanced through clinical practice, training, and research (Dworkin, 1989).

DEVELOPMENTAL FACILITATION THROUGH ANTICIPATORY GUIDANCE

In the primary care setting, child health providers offer parents guidance and support in promoting their children's development through the provision of *anticipatory guidance*. Telzrow (1978) defined anticipatory guidance as the "provision of information to parents or children with the expected outcome being a change in parent attitude, knowledge, or behavior" and emphasized the mutual participation of parents and health providers in discussions of "ideas and opinions about normal parental responses to development" (p. 14). Brazelton (1975) described anticipatory guidance as the mechanism for strengthening a child's developmental potential.

A limited number of studies have evaluated the effectiveness of anticipatory guidance during child health supervision. The majority of these studies have examined the influence of counseling on specific issues, such as injury prevention and parenting behaviors (Miller & Galbraith, 1995; Sege et al., 1997). Even fewer studies have examined the broader influence of anticipatory guidance on children's behavior and development.

In the 1970s, Gutelius and colleagues provided forty-seven mothers and their young infants within inner-city Washington, DC, with extensive child health supervision services, including anticipatory guidance. In comparison to a control group receiving only limited advice, positive effects were noted in children's dietary and eating habits, in some developmental and behavioral domains such as night awakening, toilet training, and separation difficulties, and in children's self-confidence during psychological testing (Gutelius, Kirsch, MacDonald et al., 1977). In addition, parents' perceptions of their child and child-rearing practices, such as the amount of conversing with the child and frequency of outdoor play, were altered favorably.

Several years later, Chamberlin and his colleagues examined the efforts of pediatricians in a variety of practice settings in Rochester, New York, to educate mothers about child development and behavior during well-child care. When the pediatricians made at least a moderate effort to provide such counseling, the mothers reported learning more about their children's development, described more affectionate, developmentally promoting activities with their children, and felt that they were helped more in their child rearing (Chamberlin & Szumowski, 1980; Chamberlin, Szumowski, & Zastowny, 1979).

A third study, conducted in rural North Carolina, also suggested positive effects of anticipatory guidance on children's development. Casey and Whitt (1980) provided thirty-two mothers and their young infants with specific counseling based upon the infant's developmental stage. In contrast to a control group of mothers who received routine care, the intervention group mothers displayed more developmentally stimulating behaviors, including more appropriate interaction, cooperation, and sensitivity with their infants. In addition, the infants displayed developmental advances in their verbal language.

These research findings support the value of anticipatory guidance in promoting children's development. However, the systematic implementation of developmentally oriented anticipatory guidance is made difficult by the variable content of counseling in past studies. For example, in the three previously cited studies, the content of the anticipatory guidance ranged from advice regarding the management of specific day-to-day situations (Gutelius et al., 1977), to planned discussions about child development (Chamberlin et al., 1979), to an emphasis on "normal developmental sequences of infant behaviors in a social context" (Casey & Whitt, 1980, p. 816).

A subsequent study attempted to evaluate specifically the influence of certain recommended content of anticipatory guidance on its effectiveness. Many authors have recommended that discussions of developmental stages be a routine component of anticipatory guidance (Brazelton, 1975; Telzrow, 1978). To examine the effect of such content, eighty-three inner-city mothers and their healthy first-born infants were randomly assigned to either a control or an intervention group. At each well-child visit during the first 6 months of life, anticipatory guidance for all mothers included discussions of such age-appropriate issues as nutrition, safety, sleep, and common problematic behaviors. For the thirty-nine intervention group mothers only, the basis for such information was explained through age-specific discussions of affective, cognitive, and physical development. For example, at the two-week visit, discussing the "predictable unpredictability" of infant behavior illustrates the precariousness of state organization at this age and explains the infant's fluctuating sleep–wake cycles, feeding, and elimination patterns. Parental responses to subtle cues of the infant suggesting hunger, fatigue, or a wet diaper are praised as examples of the increasing synchrony between infant and caregiver. Discussing the importance of secure attachment between infant and parent discourages needless fears of spoiling. Describing the infant's activity level, intensity of cry when hungry, and mood during such activities as bathing illustrates the child's temperament or behavioral style.

No significant effect of these discussions of developmental stages was found on maternal–infant interaction; maternal perceptions of infant temperament, family adaptation and adjustment to the birth of the infant, and satisfaction with the infant's behavior and development; or maternal satisfaction with pediatric services. The researchers concluded that there was no need to routinely emphasize the developmental basis for age-appropriate advice and guidance (Dworkin, Allen, Geertsma, Solkoske, & Cullina, 1987).

Given the lack of evidence to determine the specific content of anticipatory guidance, recommendations continue to be based on a combination of limited research findings and the consensus of experts. Research findings do, however, support the recommendation to individualize the content of anticipatory guidance and to discuss matters at the level of the parents' cognitive, cultural, and psychological readiness (Korsch, 1984). Eliciting parents' opinions and concerns and encouraging them to set the agenda for discussions of their children's development may prove far more effective than adhering to a listing of suggested topics for discussion. Such an open-ended, parent-led format deserves critical study.

INNOVATIVE STRATEGIES FOR EARLY CHILDHOOD INTERVENTION IN THE HEALTH CARE SETTING

Despite the importance of the content of child health supervision services, the circumstances in which such services are provided are also critical determinants of effectiveness (Dworkin, 1993). To this end, Bright Futures encourages the pediatric health professional to use a contextual approach and to be sensitive to the full world of the child (Green, 1995). To enhance children's development optimally, various innovations in the setting, process, and content of child health supervision merit consideration. Examples, supported by preliminary evidence

of their effectiveness, include home visiting, group well-child care, office-based literacy programs, and parent-held child health records.

Home Visiting

In Europe, home visiting programs have existed for more than a century; in many countries, home visits are regarded as an essential component of child health supervision services (European Health Committee, 1985). The provision of preventive services within the home setting by a trained visiting nurse (or health visitor) is routine, for example, in Great Britain and Denmark (Chamberlin, 1987a). In these countries, universal home visiting programs are regarded as an important component of a network of economic and social supports provided to families (Kamerman & Kahn, 1993). In general, such programs are accepted and supported without formal evaluation to prove their effectiveness.

Within the United States, there is no tradition of broad, universal home visiting, although select studies have demonstrated benefits of prenatal and infancy home visitation programs for socially disadvantaged women and children. Such programs, in which providers may be nurses or paraprofessionals, have been found to influence favorably women's health-related behaviors during pregnancy, birth weight and length of gestation, parent–infant interaction, children's developmental status, child behavior problems, and the incidence of child abuse and neglect (Olds & Kitzman, 1990, 1993). Whether such benefits are sustained over years is uncertain (Olds, Henderson, & Kitzman, 1994). Nonetheless, in 1991 the U.S. Advisory Board on Child Abuse and Neglect recommended that the federal government implement a national universal home visiting program during the neonatal period (Krugman, 1993). The increasing requirement by managed care companies that apparently healthy newborns be discharged by twenty-four hours of age has given this recommendation added relevance.

The European experience and positive results from select U.S. studies suggest that home visiting deserves further consideration as a strategy to improve the effectiveness of child health supervision services. Home visiting may be particularly useful as one component of a comprehensive approach to meeting the needs of families at risk because of poverty and limited personal and social resources (Chamberlin, 1989).

Group Well-Child Care

During group well-child visits, four to six parents and their children of similar ages meet with their pediatric practitioner to discuss issues relevant to that age group (Osborn & Wooley, 1981). Following a discussion session of forty-five minutes to an hour, the children are examined individually and receive indicated procedures and immunizations. The format of group well-child care visits is designed specifically to facilitate parental education and to address the limited time available for discussion of parenting and prevention issues during traditional individual visits. Group visits also offer the potential advantage of functioning as a support group for parents.

In small-scale studies conducted in one region of the United States (Salt Lake City, Utah), evaluation of this approach to child health supervision has yielded positive results. As compared with the traditional individual visit format, the group method has been shown to be more efficient, with greater coverage of material considered important by the AAP (Dodds, Nicholson, Muse, & Osborn, 1993). In addition, mothers were noted to be more assertive during the group process, asking more questions, and initiating discussions of more issues, including both recommended topics and others not typically suggested. An earlier study found a decrease in advice-seeking between visits, suggesting the usefulness of group discussions (Osborn & Wooley, 1981).

More recently, a randomized control trial of group versus individual well-child care for high-risk infants was conducted in two urban university pediatric clinics in Seattle, Washington. Mothers and their 4-month-old infants were considered high risk and eligible for the study on the basis of poverty, single marital status, less than a high school education, age less than 20 years at delivery, previous substance abuse, or a history of exposure to substance abuse as a child. No differences were found after the fifteen-month visit in developmental outcomes, maternal–child interaction, health care utilization, or the child's health status (Taylor, Davis, & Kemper, 1997a, 1997b). The investigators concluded that group well-child care is a viable alternative to individual well-child care for high-risk children.

On the basis of these preliminary findings, group well-child visits are worthy of further consideration as a means to improve both the effectiveness and the efficiency of child health supervision services. Furthermore, parents' preference for discussing topics not typically recommended (by a ratio of approximately 2:1) supports the importance of encouraging parents to set the agenda for anticipatory guidance (Dodds, Nicholson, Muse, & Osborn, 1993).

Office-Based Literacy Programs

The promotion of children's school readiness has been identified as a national concern (National Governors' Association, 1990). In 1991, the Carnegie Foundation for the Advancement of Teaching surveyed more than 7,000 kindergarten teachers to learn about children's school readiness and found that, according to the teachers' subjective impressions, 35% of the nation's children (an estimated 1.5 million children) are not ready for academic learning (Boyer, 1991). In an effort to address the problem of early failure in learning to read, an innovative, clinic-based intervention to promote literacy was developed in the Pediatric Primary Care Clinic at Boston City Hospital (Needlman, Fried, Morley, Taylor, & Zuckerman, 1991). The intervention, named *Reach Out and Read*, was based on a finding from educational research that children become literate more easily if their parents read to them (Goldfield & Snow, 1984).

The Reach Out and Read program includes three components: volunteers who read aloud to children in the waiting room; counseling by the pediatrician about literacy development; and the distribution of a free book at each visit from 6 months through 6 years of age. A pilot study found that parents who had previously received a book were more likely to report looking at books with their children or to identify looking at books as a favorite activity (Needlman et al., 1991).

Pending further multisite evaluation, these preliminary findings suggest that the pediatric practitioner can play an important role in enriching children's early literacy experiences. Such an intervention may be especially important for children from impoverished environments, who are at particularly high risk for school failure.

Parent-Held Child Health Records

How to best encourage parents to be active partners with health providers in the provision of pediatric preventive care is uncertain. Parent-held child health records are one possible strategy to promote such a partnership. Parental responsibility for their child's health record acknowledges the key role of parents in meeting their child's health needs and may enhance communication and cooperation between parents and child health professionals (Hall, 1989). These health records may be used as a basis for discussing developmental, behavioral, or common health care issues with pediatric providers (Saffin & Macfarlane, 1988). Records could also serve as a resource for parents by containing useful health promotion and education materials. Preliminary evaluation suggests that such records may improve attendance for health supervision visits and improve immunization rates and the performance of recommended laboratory screening procedures (O'Flaherty, Jandera, Llewellyn, & Wass, 1987).

The potential advantages of parent-held child records have led to their use in Great Britain, France, Portugal, Sweden, Finland, Denmark, New Zealand, Australia, and some African countries (Johnson, 1988; Macfarlane, 1986; O'Flaherty, Jandera, Llewellyn, & Wass, 1987). The World Health Organization has also recommended that parents should retain possession of the records of their children's health and development (World Health Organization European Working Group, 1985).

To date, experience with such records within the United States has been sparse. Implementation has been attempted on a limited basis as one component of child health supervision programs in New York City and Boston (Goldberg, Harris, & Pirani, 1989). The innovative Partners in Health Care Program in Colorado features the implementation of the Denver Child Health Passport, intended for use by parents and health providers (Frankenburg, 1994). Prior to each well-child visit, parents are requested to fill out a form that includes developmental questions and elicits any worries or concerns they may have. Selected sections of the passport include the family social history; family medical history; sixteen health evaluations from the neonatal examination through the six-year health supervision visit; dental evaluations; reports from consultations; lists of

intercurrent illnesses, injuries, surgeries, hospitalizations, allergies, and so forth; and a summary chart documenting the dates when each preventive service was provided. Parents are requested to tear out anticipatory guidance sections, which include a description of expected developmental changes and age-related suggestions about promoting children's development, and to use them as a daily reminder by affixing them to the refrigerator with a magnet. One copy of the health evaluation is retained by the pediatric practitioner, while a second copy may be sent to a local community coordinator who compiles a computerized inventory of provided services.

Parent-held child health records have received limited critical evaluation. International experience has, in general, suggested that such records are enthusiastically received by parents, considered helpful by health professionals, and rarely lost by parents (Saffin & Macfarlane, 1988; O'Flaherty et al., 1987; Macfarlane, 1990). Field studies of the Denver Child Health Passport have found high acceptance rates by parents and providers and 85–90% availability of passports at the time of office visits (Frankenburg, 1994). Use of the passport has been found to substantially increase pediatricians' documentation of children's developmental disorders.

Given their promising but limited evaluation, further research on parent-held child health records is needed. Critical study should determine the extent to which these records achieve such potential benefits as improving parental compliance with visits and procedures during child health supervision and increasing parents' knowledge of successful strategies to promote their children's development and safety.

Other Approaches

Additional approaches to improving the effectiveness of child health supervision also merit consideration. One example is the application of such health promotion and planning methods as the PRECEDE-PROCEED model. The PRECEDE component (Predisposing, Reinforcing, and Enabling Constructs in Educational and Environmental Diagnosis and Evaluation) is a diagnostic or needs-assessment phase that may help the pediatric practitioner to identify multiple factors influencing children's developmental status and to focus on the specific needs of the family and child. The PROCEED component (Policy, Regulatory, and Organizational Constructs in Educational and Environmental Development) provides strategies for intervention, policy development, and evaluation of services (Osborn, 1994).

Incorporating a family-focused, family-systems approach during visits should enable the pediatric provider to better assess family structure and function and to establish more effectively a therapeutic alliance with the parents (Cohen, 1995). Acknowledging and incorporating cultural beliefs and practices when working with ethnic minority families should enhance satisfaction with care and the acceptance of traditional preventive interventions (Pachter, Cloutier, & Bernstein, 1995).

The pediatric primary care clinic or office may be an opportune setting in which to link child health services to other community-based programs. For example, legal aid and advocacy services can ensure that families receive Medicaid benefits, arrange Social Security benefits for children with special needs, and protect families from illegal housing evictions and fuel shutoffs (Zuckerman & Parker, 1995). Early childhood educators can help monitor children's development and suggest how parents may promote school readiness. Alternatively, child health supervision may be provided in community settings where children are already present, such as child care centers and schools (American Academy of Pediatrics Task Force on Integrated School Health Services, 1994). Research is needed to examine the extent to which such innovations enhance the effectiveness of preventive child health services.

CHALLENGES IN AN EVOLVING HEALTH CARE SYSTEM

Innovations in child health supervision deserve consideration to improve the effectiveness of pediatric services. Moreover, research findings suggest potential benefits from changes in the content, setting, and process of preventive child health care. However, successful implementation of such changes requires that formidable obstacles be addressed. Despite the emphasis placed on primary and preventive services by managed care, there is no evidence that financial resources have been realized as a result of the reduced use of emergency rooms and specialty physician services (Freund & Lewitt, 1993). Certain

proposed innovations, such as implementing new strategies for providing anticipatory guidance and developmental monitoring and scheduling parent groups for well-child care, have minimal financial implications. Other innovations, such as office-based literacy-promotion programs, require limited financial support and the commitment of volunteers. More extensive approaches, such as home visiting and parent-held child health records, require a major commitment of financial support and personnel. Demonstration projects that document the extent to which innovations improve the effectiveness of child health supervision are needed to justify funding and support. For example, one health maintenance organization has agreed to pay for the Denver Child Health Passport because it supports high-quality preventive health care and simplifies chart review. Colorado's major liability insurance company provides an incentive to pediatricians who implement the Partners in Health Care program because the program promotes comprehensive, legible, and timely documentation of provided services (Frankenburg, 1994).

It is important to note that efforts to enhance the effectiveness of child health supervision services must be considered within a sociopolitical context. For example, in the late 1990s, welfare reform at the federal and state levels is likely to affect the utilization of child health services and children's health status. Prior to the new legislation, many children eligible for Medicaid coverage for health services did not receive such services. In 1994, for example, 4.8 million eligible children under age 11 were not enrolled in Medicaid. Because welfare enrollment was a primary means for many children to gain access to public health insurance, new restrictions in welfare eligibility increase the likelihood of more insured children and emphasize the need for alternative Medicaid enrollment strategies. Moreover, changes in the Supplemental Security Income (SSI) program, including a new definition of disability that eliminated certain types of behavioral problems of childhood, are likely to eliminate benefits for approximately 10 to 12% of children currently receiving SSI payments (Perrin, 1997). Welfare reform will also affect food accessibility for poor families by reducing funding for the food stamp program and the Special Supplemental Nutrition Program for Women, Infants and Children (WIC Program).

Resulting poor nutrition is likely to contribute to adverse health and developmental outcomes for many children, including an increase in iron-deficiency anemia (Willis, Kliegman, Meurer, & Perry, 1997).

Exciting programs have recently been proposed as new approaches to enhance child health care. Healthy Steps for Young Children, launched in 1994 by the Commonwealth Fund, is now in partnership with other funders to operate and evaluate this innovative approach in approximately twenty sites across the United States (Zuckerman, Kaplan-Sanoff, Parker, & Taaffe Young, 1997). This model adds a new professional, the Healthy Steps Specialist, to the traditional child health team. The specialist's role includes: conducting office visits; assessing children's developmental progress; helping parents to prevent and manage common behavioral concerns; providing families with referrals for helpful community resources; facilitating parents' groups; staffing a telephone information line; and coordinating Reach Out and Read activities. In addition, Healthy Steps encourages child health practitioners to use "teachable moments" to communicate information about children's behavior and development. Written materials include parent handouts, "prompt sheets" sent prior to health supervision visits, and a child health and development record. Training and technical assistance are provided to all participating sites. A national evaluation will assess the effectiveness of this approach and determine the desirability of widespread adoption.

An example of a local approach to enhancing the effectiveness of child health supervision is Child-Serv. Launched in 1998 in Hartford, Connecticut, and supported by the Hartford Foundation for Public Giving Bright Futures initiative, ChildServ includes five components: 1) training child health providers, child care providers, and parents in effective developmental monitoring and promotion; 2) a computerized inventory of community-based programs supporting families and children's development; 3) a case-coordination system to link children and families to resources and support services; 4) data collection on children's developmental status; and 5) dissemination of office-based literacy promotion. Evaluation will determine whether ChildServ is successful in increasing the number of children receiving developmental promotion and monitoring within a medical home, as well as receiving coordinated services that address developmental and medical needs.

The task of enhancing the effectiveness of child health supervision has important implications for pediatric training. Proposed innovations require, for example, that pediatricians be able to support parents as partners in the process of child health supervision, elicit and respond to parents' opinions and concerns, skillfully observe children's behavior and development, meaningfully share observations and impressions with other professionals serving children, apply health education models and family systems theory, and practice culturally sensitive health care. The increasing emphasis on ambulatory and community-based experiences for residents and medical students offers an opportunity to promote the knowledge and skills needed to enhance preventive services for children (Recchia, Petros, Spooner, & Cranshaw, 1995).

Finally, expectations for child health supervision should be tempered by the realization that the most urgent problems confronting today's youth are the result of complex sociopolitical and behavioral factors (Murray-Garcia, 1995). Examples of such problems include intentional and unintentional injuries, substance abuse, suicide, HIV, school-related learning and behavior problems, and violence. The broad-based approaches necessary to address the contemporary needs of children and families clearly exceed the boundaries of traditional preventive child health services (Kamerman & Kahn, 1993). Consequently, pediatric efforts must also include the role of child advocate, supporting those programs at the community, state, and national levels that facilitate development and promote school readiness (Sia, 1992).

Despite past research efforts, how to optimally enhance children's development during pediatric preventive care is uncertain. Various promising strategies are supported by preliminary evidence of their effectiveness and deserve further consideration. Well-designed, prospective studies are needed to determine which innovations should be important components of future child health supervision services.

REFERENCES

American Academy of Pediatrics, Committee on Standards of Child Health Care (1972). *Standards of child health care* (2nd ed.), Evanston, IL: American Academy of Pediatrics.

American Academy of Pediatrics, Committee on Children with Disabilities (1994). Screening infants and young children for developmental disabilities. *Pediatrics, 93,* 863–5.

American Academy of Pediatrics, Committee on Practice and Ambulatory Medicine (1995). Recommendations for pediatric preventive care. *Pediatrics, 96,* 373–4.

American Academy of Pediatrics, Task Force on Integrated School Health Services. (1994). Integrated school health services. *Pediatrics, 94,* 400–2.

Bagnato, S., & Neisworth, J. (1991). *Assessment for early intervention: Best practices for professionals.* New York: Guilford Press.

Boyer, E. (1991). *Ready to learn. A mandate for the nation.* Princeton, NJ: The Carnegie Foundation for the Advancement of Teaching.

Brazelton, T. (1975). Anticipatory guidance. *Pediatric Clinics of North America, 22,* 533–544.

Casey, P., & Whitt, J. (1980). Effect of the pediatrician on the mother-infant relationship. *Pediatrics, 65,* 815–20.

Chamberlin, R. (1987a). Developmental assessment and early intervention programs for young children: Lessons learned from longitudinal research. *Pediatrics in Review, 8,* 237–47.

Chamberlin, R., (Ed.). (1987b). *Beyond individual risk assessment: Community-wide approaches to promoting the health and development of families and children.* Washington, DC: National Center for Education in Maternal and Child Health.

Chamberlin, R. (1989). Home visiting: A necessary but not in itself sufficient program component for promoting the health and development of families and children. *Pediatrics, 84,* 178–80.

Chamberlin, R., & Szumowski, E. (1980). A follow-up study of parent education in pediatric office practices: Impact at age two and a half. *American Journal of Public Health, 70,* 1180–8.

Chamberlin, R., Szumowski, E., & Zastowny T. (1979). An evaluation of efforts to educate mothers about child development in pediatric office practices. *American Journal of Public Health, 69,* 875–86.

Cohen, W. (1995). Family-oriented pediatric care: Taking the next step. *Pediatric Clinics of North America, 42,* 11–20.

Committee on Child Health. (1955). *Health supervision of young children.* New York: American Public Health Association.

Cone, T. Jr. (1979). *History of pediatrics.* Boston, MA: Little, Brown.

Dobos, A., Dworkin, P., & Bernstein, B. (1994). Pediatricians' approaches to developmental problems: Has the gap been narrowed? *Journal of Developmental and Behavioral Pediatrics, 15,* 34–8.

Dodds, M., Nicholson, L., Muse, B., & Osborn, L. (1993).

Group health supervision visits more effective than individual visits in delivering health care information. *Pediatrics, 91,* 668–70.

Dworkin, P. (1989). British and American recommendations for developmental monitoring: The role of surveillance. *Pediatrics, 84,* 1000–10.

Dworkin, P. (1992). Developmental screening: (Still) expecting the impossible? *Pediatrics, 89,* 1253–5.

Dworkin, P. (1993). Ready to learn: A mandate for pediatrics. *Journal of Developmental and Behavioral Pediatrics, 14,* 192–6.

Dworkin, P., Allen, D., Geertsma, A., Solkoske, L., & Cullina, J. (1987). Does developmental content influence the effectiveness of anticipatory guidance? *Pediatrics, 80,* 196–202.

European Health Committee. (1985). *Health: Child health surveillance.* Strassbourg, France: Council of Europe, Publications Section.

Frankenburg, W. (1973). Pediatric screening. *Advances in Pediatrics, 20,* 149–75.

Frankenburg, W. (1994). Preventing developmental delays. Is developmental screening sufficient? *Pediatrics, 93,* 586–93.

Frankenburg, W., Dodds, J., Archer, P., Shapiro, H., & Bresnick, B. (1992). The Denver II: A major revision and restandardization of the Denver Developmental Screening Test. *Pediatrics, 89,* 91–7.

Freund, D., & Lewitt, E. (1993). Managed care for children and pregnant women: Promises and pitfalls. *The Future of Children 3,* 92–122.

Glascoe, F. (1995). *A validation study and the psychometric properties of the Brigance Screens.* (Tech. report). North Billerica, MA: Curriculum Associates, Inc.

Glascoe, F., Altemeier, W., & MacLean, E. (1989). The importance of parents' concerns about their children's development. *American Journal of Diseases of Children, 143,* 855–8.

Glascoe, F., Byrne, K., Ashford, L., et al. (1992). Accuracy of the Denver II in developmental screening. *Pediatrics, 89,* 1221–5.

Glascoe, F., & Dworkin, P. (1995). The role of parents in the detection of developmental and behavioral problems. *Pediatrics, 95,* 829–36.

Glascoe, F., Martin, E., & Humphrey, S. (1990). A comparative review of developmental screening tests. *Pediatrics, 86,* 547–54.

Glascoe, F., & Sandler, H. (1995). The value of parents' age estimates of children's development. *Journal of Pediatrics, 127,* 831–5.

Goldberg, D., Harris, C., & Pirani, S. (1989). *Piloting a parent-held child health record for New York City.* Presented at the annual meeting of the American Public Health Association, Boston, Massachusetts.

Goldfield, B., & Snow, C. (1984). Reading books with children: The mechanics of parental influence on children's reading achievement. In J. Flood (Ed.), *Promoting reading comprehension.* Newark, DE: International Reading Association.

Green, M. (Ed.). (1994). *Bright Futures. Guidelines for health supervision of infants, children, and adolescents.* Arlington, VA: National Center for Education in Maternal and Child Health.

Green, M. (1995). No child is an island. Contextual pediatrics and the "new" health supervision. *Pediatric Clinics of North America, 42,* 79–87.

Green, M., & Kessel, S. (1993). Diagnosing and treating health: Bright Futures. *Pediatrics, 91,* 998–1000.

Gutelius, M., Kirsch, A., MacDonald, S., et al. (1977). Controlled study of child health supervision: Behavioral results. *Pediatrics, 60,* 294–304.

Haggerty, R., Roughman, K., & Pless, I. (1975). *Child health and the community.* New York: John Wiley and Sons.

Hall, D. (Ed.). (1989). *Health for all children: A programme for child health surveillance.* Oxford, England: Oxford University Press.

Henderson, L., & Meisels, S. J. (1994). Parental involvement in the developmental screening of their young children: A multi-source perspective. *Journal of Early Intervention, 18,* 141–54.

Hickson, G., Altemeier W., & O'Connor, S. (1983). Concerns of mothers seeking care in private pediatric offices: Opportunities for expanding services. *Pediatrics, 72,* 619–24.

Hoekelman, R. (1983). Well-child visits revisited. *American Journal of Diseases in Children, 137,* 17–20.

Hoekelman, R. (1997). Child health supervision. In R. Hoekelman (Ed.), *Pediatric primary care.* St. Louis, MO: Mosby-Year Book.

Johnson, F. (1988). Personal health record. *Medical Journal of Australia, 148,* 544.

Kamerman, S., & Kahn, A. (1993). Home health visiting in Europe. *The Future of Children, 3,* 39–52.

Knobloch, H., Stevens, F., Malone, A., Ellison, P., & Risemberg, H. (1979). The validity of parent reporting of infant development. *Pediatrics, 63,* 872–8.

Korsch, B. (1984). What do patients and parents want to know? What do they need to know? *Pediatrics, 74* (suppl), 917–19.

Krugman, R. (1993). Universal home visiting: A recommendation from the U.S. Advisory Board on Child Abuse and Neglect. *The Future of Children, 3,* 184–91.

Macfarlane, A. (1986). Child health services in the community: Making them work. *British Medical Journal, 293,* 222–3.

Macfarlane, A. (Ed.). (1990). *Report of the joint working party on professional and parent-held records used in child health surveillance.* London: British Paediatric Association.

Meisels, S. J. (1988). Developmental screening in early childhood: The interaction of research and social policy. *Annual Review of Public Health, 9,* 527–50.

Meisels, S. J., Henderson, L., Liaw, F., Browning, K., & Ten Have, T. (1993). New evidence for the effectiveness of the early screening inventory. *Early Childhood Research Quarterly, 8,* 327–46.

Miller, T., & Galbraith, M. (1995). Injury prevention counseling by pediatricians: A benefit-cost comparison. *Pediatrics, 96,* 1–4.

Murray-García, J. (1995). African–American youth: Essential prevention strategies for every pediatrician. *Pediatrics, 96,* 132–7.

National Governors' Association (NGA). (1990). *Consensus for change. Educating America: State strategies for achieving the nation's education goals (The Report of the Task Force on Education).* Washington, DC: National Governors' Association.

Needelman, R., Fried, L., Morley, D., Taylor, S., & Zuckerman, B. (1991). Clinic-based intervention to promote literacy. A pilot study. *American Journal of Diseases in Children, 145,* 881–4.

O'Flaherty, S., Jandera, E., Llewellyn, J., & Wass, M. (1987). Personal health records: An evaluation. *Archives of Diseases of Childhood, 62,* 1152–5.

Olds, D., Henderson, C., Jr., & Kitzman, H. (1994). Does prenatal and infancy home visitation have enduring effects on qualities of parental care giving and child health at 25 to 50 months of life? *Pediatrics, 93,* 89–98.

Olds, D., & Kitzman, H. (1990). Can home visitation improve the health of women and children at environmental risk? *Pediatrics, 86,* 108–16.

Olds, D., & Kitzman, H. (1993). Review of research on home visits for pregnant women and parents of young children. *The Future of Children* (Center for the Future of Children), *3,* 53–92.

Osborn, L., & Wooley, F. (1981). The use of groups in well-child care. *Pediatrics, 67,* 701–6.

Osborn, L. (1994). Effective well-child care. *Current Problems in Pediatrics, 24,* 306–26.

Pachter L., Cloutier, M., & Bernstein, B. (1995). Ethnomedical (folk) remedies for childhood asthma in a mainland Puerto Rican community. *Archives of Pediatrics and Adolescent Medicine, 149,* 982–8.

Perrin, J. M. (1997). The implications of welfare reform for developmental and behavioral pediatrics. *Journal of Developmental and Behavioral Pediatrics, 18,* 244–66.

Recchia, K., Petros, T., Spooner, S., & Cranshaw, J. (1995). Implementation of the community outpatient practice experience in a large pediatric residency program. *Pediatrics, 96,* 90–8.

Saffin, K., & Macfarlane, A. (1988). Parent-held child health and development records. *Maternal and Child Health, 13,* 288–91.

Sege, R., Perry, C., Stigol, L., Cohen, L., Griffith, J., Cohn, M., & Spivack, H. (1997). Short-term effectiveness of anticipatory guidance to reduce early childhood risks for subsequent violence. *Archives of Pediatrics and Adolescent Medicine, 151,* 392–7.

Shonkoff, J., Dworkin, P., Leviton, A., & Levine, M. (1979). Primary care approaches to developmental disabilities. *Pediatrics, 64,* 506–14.

Sia, C. (1992). Abraham Jacobi award address, April 14, 1992. The medical home: Pediatric practice and child advocacy in the 1990's. *Pediatrics, 90,* 419–23.

Smith, R. (1978). The use of developmental screening tests by primary care pediatricians. *Journal of Pediatrics, 93,* 524–7.

Sonnander, K. (1987). Parental developmental assessment of 18-month-old children: Reliability and predictive value. *Developmental Medicine and Child Neurology, 29,* 351–62.

Taylor, J., Davis, R., & Kemper, K. (1997a). A randomized controlled trial of group versus individual well child care for high-risk children: Maternal–child interaction and developmental outcomes. *Pediatrics, 99,* 864.

Taylor, J., Davis, R., & Kemper, K. (1997b). Health care utilization and health status in high-risk children randomized to receive group or individual well child care. *Pediatrics, 100,* 379.

Telzrow, R. (1978). Anticipatory guidance in pediatric practice. *Journal of Continuing Education in Pediatrics, 20,* 14–27.

Willis, E., Kliegman, R. M., Meurer, J. R., & Perry, J. M. (1997). Welfare reform and food insensitivity. *Archives of Pediatrics and Adolescent Medicine, 151,* 871–75.

World Health Organization European Working Group. (1985). *Today's health – tomorrow's wealth. New perspectives in prevention in childhood. Summary report. Kiev, 21–25 October 1985.* Geneva, Switzerland: World Health Organization.

Zuckerman, B., Kaplan-Sanoff, M., Parker, S., & Taaffe Young, K. (1997, June/July). The Healthy Steps for Young Children Program. *Zero to Three,* 20–25.

Zuckerman, B., & Parker, S. (1995). Preventive pediatrics – new models of providing needed health services. *Pediatrics, 95,* 758–62.

CHAPTER SIXTEEN

Early Care and Education:

Current Issues and Future Strategies

SHARON L. KAGAN AND MICHELLE J. NEUMAN

Throughout the 1990s, interest in and support for our youngest citizens has expanded considerably in the public and private sectors. Throughout the United States, researchers, policy makers, business leaders, media, and parents have recognized the significance of early care and education to fostering children's early learning and development. Yet, despite recent attention to and activity concerning early care and education, persistent challenges pervade the delivery of services for young children and their families. Historically our nation, while voicing commitment to young children and their families, has layered an insufficient number of piecemeal and idiosyncratic services upon one another, constantly reinforcing – rather than alleviating – an inequitable, nonsystem of early care and education. Although innovative efforts have been launched to redress this situation, like the direct services themselves, these efforts have been without significant coordination or collaboration.

Given the increasing utilization of early care and education services, the significant attention being accorded to young children, and the willingness of the public to act more aggressively on this issue than ever before, how can we create a strategic approach to advancing early care and education in the United States? In this chapter, we tackle these issues, first discussing the status of American early care and education today, particularly recent changes in demographics, service delivery, and attitudes. We then delve into the pervasive problems that have plagued the field throughout its history. Given this context, we describe some current innovative efforts in early care and education. After delineating some of the

limitations of these efforts, we propose an alternative framework for analysis and action. Finally, we conclude by offering some recommendations that, when fully implemented, will achieve a comprehensive, long-term, research-based vision for an early care and education system.

In this chapter we use the term *early care and education programs* to refer to both center-based and home-based services that provide nonparental care and education for young children. Center-based programs include nonprofit and for-profit child care, Head Start and other comprehensive development programs, school-based prekindergarten programs, and part-day nursery schools; home-based programs include family child care. The term *early care and education* indicates that all programs with responsibility for young children necessarily provide both care and education; the question is just how well they do it.

THE STATUS OF AMERICAN EARLY CARE AND EDUCATION TODAY

The present status of early care and education is the product of two major forces: 1) sociodynamic problems that present fresh challenges and 2) persistent, longstanding problems that endure over decades. Sociodynamic problems have been especially pronounced over the past thirty years, reshaping the demand for, and supply of, early care and education services. They include changes in populations and demographics, patterns of service delivery, and attitudes. They are the fluid, contextually responsive variables that conspire with more durable problems to frame the current context. The more persistent problems – those that are historically rooted and more deeply ingrained – characterize the field and include issues of quality, equity, and structure. Although each type of problem is important in its own right, both must be addressed if positive change is to be achieved.

Sociodynamic Problems

The field of early care and education is currently being shaped by sociodynamic problems in three major areas. First, changing populations and demographics of children and families over the past several decades have led to a surge in demand for, and utilization of, early care and education services. Second, changing patterns of service delivery mean that children are being cared for in a variety of constantly changing, loosely configured settings. Third, changing attitudes have resulted in more positive attention focused on young children and their families than at any time in our history, giving the nation the opportunity and the challenge to craft an improved early care and education system.

CHANGING DEMOGRAPHICS. In the United States, about 60% of children under 6 – more than 12.9 million infants, toddlers, and preschool children who have yet to enter kindergarten – receive some type of nonparental early care and education on a regular basis (West, Wright, & Germino Hausken, 1995). This has not always been the case. Indeed, the demand for early care and education services has surged in recent years. Throughout the 1980s and 1990s, enrollments in center-based care have quadrupled (Love, Schochet, & Meckstroth, 1996). This rise can be attributed, in part, to population changes. For example, in the 1980s alone, the nation's population of children under the age of 5 rose by 28% (U.S. General Accounting Office, 1993; West, Germino Hausken, & Collins, 1993). Service demand can also be attributed to changes in employment trends as increasing numbers of women with children enter the paid workforce. More than half of all mothers return to work within a year of their baby's birth, with infants and toddlers constituting the fastest-growing subgroup of children in early care and education programs (Hofferth, Brayfield, Deich, & Holcomb, 1991).

Just who are the children using today's early care and education services? As might be expected, the percentages vary according to the age of the children and a host of family variables (e.g., family income, education and race, and parental employment status). Although, as noted, only half of children under 1 year of age are in care on a regular basis, the percentage of youngsters who receive early care and education services jumps to 78% of 4-year-olds and 84% of 5-year-olds (West et al., 1995). Age is a critical factor, but the percentage of children enrolled in early care and education also varies greatly by maternal employment status, with children more likely to receive early care and education when their mothers work. Of children whose mothers are employed full-time, 88% receive early care and education services. The majority (75%) of children with mothers who are employed part-time also participate in early care and education on a regular basis. In contrast, only 32% of children whose mothers are not in the workforce regularly receive care and education by persons other than their parents (West et al., 1995).

Enrollment in early care and education programs also varies by family income, parental education levels, and race. Participation in early care and education increases as family income rises. Half of children with family incomes less than $10,000 regularly receive early care and education services compared to 77% of children with family incomes over $75,000 (West et al., 1995). Children with mothers who have higher educational attainments are also more likely to participate in early care and education programs. Seventy percent of children whose mothers graduated from college enroll in early care and education, whereas only 38% of children whose mothers did not complete high school or earn a GED do so (West et al., 1995). Enrollment also varies by race: Hispanic children have been found to have fewer early care and education experiences than others, regardless of family income (U.S. Department of Education, 1996; West et al., 1993). Only 46% of Hispanic children receive early care and education services compared to 62% of White children and 66% of Black children (West et al., 1995). In short, one of the key issues in the early care and education context is the vast numbers of children who are participating in care and the variability of participation rates across populations.

CHANGING PATTERNS OF SERVICE DELIVERY.
The nature of services available to these children is also in flux. Today, America's young children are served in their own homes by in-home caregivers, in child-care centers, or in family child-care homes – the latter referring to providers who care for children in their own homes. According to the most current available national supply data, there are approximately 80,000 early care and education centers with a licensed capacity to serve 4.2 million preschoolers that are serving 4 million children (Kisker, Hofferth, Phillips, & Farquhar, 1991). The types of centers vary considerably: approximately two-thirds (65%) of the centers serving preschool children are non-profit, and one-third (35%) are for-profit (Kisker et al., 1991). More specifically, 8% of centers are public school settings and 9% are Head Start programs; 6% are part of a for-profit chain; 29% are independent for-profit; 25% are independent nonprofit; 8% are other sponsored nonprofit; and 15% are under religious auspices (Kisker et al., 1991).

There are approximately 118,000 regulated family child-care providers, who care for children in their own home, with a capacity to serve 860,000 but who are actually serving 700,000 children (Kisker et al., 1991). There is no direct measure of the total number of unregulated family child-care providers, although estimates range from 550,000 to 1.1 million (Hofferth et al., 1991). About 23% of regulated and 2% of nonregulated family child-care homes are sponsored by groups that organize family child-care in the community (Willer et al., 1991).

Distribution of service utilization is instructive. About one-third of children under 6 years participate in center-based care and 18% participate in family child-care on a regular basis (West et al., 1995). But, like child-care utilization in general, participation in different types of early care and education settings is related to children's age. Roughly 17% of infants (under 1 year) are enrolled in family child-care programs, and only 7% are cared for in center-based settings. Two-year-olds are about equally as likely to be receive early care and education in home-based as they are in center-based settings. As children become older, they are more likely to enroll in center-based programs. Participation rates in center-based programs jump to 65% among 4-year-olds who have yet to enter kindergarten, whereas participation rates among these children in family child-care and other

home-based arrangements remain stable (West et al., 1995).

Distribution of utilization also varies by maternal employment status. Families with working mothers rely more on center-based settings (31%) than family child-care providers (17%) for their preschoolers (Casper, 1996). Mothers who work part-time rely slightly less on center-based care (23% versus 34%) and family child care (14% versus 18%) than full-time employed mothers (Casper, 1996). However, compared to mothers who are not in the labor force, mothers who work full-time and part-time are much more likely to use center-based (39 and 35% versus 22%) and family child-care arrangements (27 and 20% versus 3%) for their preschoolers (West et al., 1995).

Enrollment in center-based versus home-based programs varies to some extent by racial-ethnic group. White and Black children under 6 years participate in center-based care at similar rates (33%). However, Hispanic children are much less likely to attend center-based programs (17%) than their counterparts of other races. White children (21%) are more likely to receive care and education from a nonrelative in a private home than children of any other racial-ethnic group (West et al., 1995). Just as demographics have influenced how many children use child care, changes also exist in that nature of child care that is selected and the nature of services that is offered in what is essentially a market-driven nonsystem of early care and education.

CHANGING PUBLIC ATTITUDES. Just as demographics and service utilization are in flux, so are attitudes toward early care and education. Recently, there has been increased public attention accorded the importance of the earliest years of life, and with this has come concern about the conditions in which children spend these earliest years – the quality of early care and education notwithstanding.

Several forces have conspired to produce this increased attention and concern. First, results from research indicate that high-quality early care and education make a marked difference to children's developmental outcomes over the short term and yield savings in social expenditures in the long run. This research has been accompanied by the release of research by neuroscientists that underscores the plasticity of early brain development and the need to intervene early (Carnegie Task Force on Meeting the Needs of Young Children, 1994; Education Commission of the States, 1996; Shore, 1997). Fortified by a White House conference on brain development, the involvement of Hollywood in the early childhood public engagement campaign, and unprecedented press coverage of these issues, more and more parents and policy makers are realizing the importance of the early years to children's long-term development, spiking interest in early care and education.

Second, global competition has escalated the demand for improved academic performance from American education. In response, the first National Education Goal calls for all children to begin school ready to learn and acknowledges the importance of early care and education in preparing children for school success (Kagan, Moore, & Bredekamp, 1995). Prestigious national groups including the Business Roundtable and the Committee for Economic Development (1993) have addressed the education needs of the nation, with many of their leaders participating in planning, funding, and supporting early care and education. States and localities have responded by establishing scores of new programs; in fact, the number of states operating early childhood initiatives actually tripled between 1979 and 1992 (Adams & Sandfort, 1994). Galvanized by corporate and political America's concern about national readiness for global competition, young children's readiness for, and success in school, has become a critical issue.

Third, dramatic changes in America's welfare system have heightened attention to the early care and education of children in low-income families. The new Temporary Assistance for Needy Families (TANF) program, which replaced Aid to Families with Dependent Children (AFDC), requires parents to work in order to receive public assistance and establishes a five-year lifetime limit for the receipt of cash benefits or services. TANF's strict work requirements and time limits will propel millions of low-income women into the training and labor forces, creating unprecedented demand for child care. Although the federal law allocates additional funds to child care in order to support maternal employment or training, the Congressional Budget Office and others predict that this funding is insufficient to meet the expanded need for subsidies (Adams & Poersch, 1996). Moreover, families leaving welfare

face difficulties not only in affording care but also in securing child care because of irregular work schedules; many end up relying on informal care for their children (Hofferth, 1995). Although, for the most part, child care has been approached as primarily a custodial service to enable parents to get off public assistance, the new welfare legislation also has the potential to affect children's growth and development significantly (Collins & Aber, 1997). Specifically, policies that enable families to obtain quality child care could have positive consequences for children, whereas those that push children into low-quality care can have significant harmful effects on children (Collins & Aber, 1997).

Taken together, these forces – changing populations and demographics, changing services, and changing attitudes – have positioned early care and education front and center onto the political and policy agendas. Yet, buried beneath the spotlight's superficial glow are enduring problems that have long faced and framed the field. We turn to a discussion of these, with the understanding that their treatment is necessary to understand the current context.

Persistent Problems

The changes just presented would engender concern in any human service worker. Simply the amount of reform that is being considered in education, health, and social service spheres suggests that the 1990s may be considered an era of social service reform. In early care and education, however, the challenges are compounded because the sociodynamic changes that propel much social reform fall upon a set of persistent, deeply rooted problems – unique to early care and education in that they have been long neglected, if not ignored. In particular, three enduring problems that characterize early care and education need to be acknowledged: quality, equity, and structure. Stated simply, the quality of early care and education programs remains uneven, with services ranging from those that promote children's healthy development and learning to a sizable minority that may harm youngsters. Second, there is little equity in the system, with children and families of different income backgrounds not having equal access to services, much less to quality services. Third, structural challenges prevail; there is no coherent understanding of what constitutes the early care and education system, and there is no infrastructure to support it. Critical to understanding the status of the field, each of these challenges deserves closer examination.

THE CHALLENGE OF QUALITY. Recent studies have linked quality early care and education to the healthy cognitive, social, and emotional development of all young children (Cost, Quality, and Child Outcomes Study Team [CQCO], 1995) and in particular to low-income children's later social and cognitive functioning (Barnett, 1995; Gomby, Larner, Stevenson, Lewit, & Behrman, 1995; Phillips, 1995; Schweinhart, Barnes, & Weikart, 1993; Yoshikawa, 1995). Young children who receive quality early care and education are likely to demonstrate better cognitive and language abilities and experience more positive mother–child interactions in the first 3 years of life (NICHD, 1997). Children who develop reasoning and problem-solving skills within a quality early care and education environment are likely to be more cooperative and considerate of others and have greater self-esteem. Many of these positive effects may linger and contribute to children's increased cognitive abilities, positive classroom learning behavior, long-term school success, and even improved likelihood of long-term social and economic self-sufficiency (Gomby et al., 1995; Poersch, Adams, & Sandfort, 1994; Schweinhart et al., 1993). Children attending lower-quality programs, in contrast, are more likely to encounter difficulties with language and social development and are less likely to have mastered age-appropriate behaviors or expected levels of development (Whitebook, Howes, & Phillips, 1989).

Despite this child development research, quality early care and education are scant. The recent Cost, Quality, and Child Outcomes four-state study found that the vast majority of centers (86%) provides mediocre-to-poor-quality care (CQCO Study Team, 1995). Specifically, seven in ten centers provided mediocre care, meaning services that may compromise children's ability to begin school ready to learn. The quality of care in one in eight centers was so low that it threatened children's health and safety. Only one in seven centers provided a level of quality that promoted healthy development (CQCO Study Team, 1995). The United States also faces a quality

crisis in family child care. Another recent study found that 16% of regulated family child-care homes and up to half of unregulated homes offered substandard care (Galinsky, Howes, Kontos, & Shinn, 1994).

The quality of care is even worse for infants and toddlers. Fully 40% of infant and toddler rooms in centers were found to endanger children's health and safety in the Cost, Quality, and Child Outcomes Study (CQCO Study Team, 1995); a smaller study set this figure at above 60% (Burchinal, Roberts, Nabors, & Bryant, 1995). These figures are particularly disturbing in light of the fact that infants and toddlers constitute the fastest-growing subgroup of children in early care and education programs.

THE CHALLENGE OF EQUITY. Millions of children who could benefit from quality early care and education do not have access to it. The supply of early care and education – of any quality – varies by location and economic capacity. More affluent counties have two to three times the supply of early care and education programs per capita than less affluent counties (Fuller & Liang, 1995). Early care and education are more difficult to find in communities with more families on welfare and with more single-parent families. Children from low-income families are the least likely to attend early care and education programs. In 1990, just 35% of poor 3- and 4-year-olds participated in preschool, compared with approximately 60% of those in the highest income group (U.S. General Accounting Office, 1993).

Government subsidies allow some children from low-income families to enroll in early care and education programs, but funds are limited. For example, Head Start expansion has not kept pace with growing need, as the number of disadvantaged 3- and 4-year-old children increases. In five of six states surveyed in a 1994 study, parents were on waiting lists for subsidies to purchase early care and education, but subsidization was not forthcoming because of limited funding (U.S. General Accounting Office, 1994). Another study found that at least thirty-eight states and the District of Columbia had waiting lists of low-income families who needed financial assistance to enroll the children in early care and education, which would enable the parents to work (Adams & Poersch, 1996).

Moreover, most children (59%) from low-income homes who are enrolled in preschool attend programs that are unlikely to provide the full range of child development, health, and parent services needed to support their school readiness (U.S. General Accounting Office, 1995a). Children from low-income families are two times less likely than upper-income families to use regulated family child-care providers; providers enrolling children from low-income families were found to be less sensitive and have more restrictive child-rearing attitudes (Love et al., 1996). Working-class and lower-middle-income families are also likely to rely on inadequate care (Hofferth, 1995; Phillips, Voran, Kisker, Howes, & Whitebook, 1994). In short, early care and education services are not equitably distributed throughout the population.

THE CHALLENGE OF STRUCTURAL ISSUES. The challenges of poor quality and inequitably distributed programs are better understood than the deeply pervasive structural issues that may give rise to, and perpetuate, the quality–equity problems. Stated most simply, structural challenges take two forms. First, there is no unified field that integrates child care, early education, and early intervention. For reasons we shall soon see, three distinct fields have emerged, with serious negative consequences. The second structural problem, which reinforces the first, is that because these minifields have been so fragmented, no infrastructure exists to support them individually or collectively. We discuss these two facets of the structural problems, in turn.

Care, Education, and Early Intervention: The Unconnected Troika. Child care, early education, and early intervention began with separate purposes that have influenced their destinies. Historically, the care and education of America's young children were considered the primary responsibility of the family. Public and private institutions only intervened when families failed or were deemed deficient. Child care and early intervention services evolved from this deficit-oriented approach. Child care, for example, was designed originally to serve the needs of lower-income parents who needed custodial care so they could work. Being from families of the less fortunate (and less prosperous), the children were enrolled in private infant schools that provided not only care but also instruction in moral education, with the goal of uplifting the next generation from lives of poverty and squalor (Cahan, 1989). The

rise of day nurseries followed in the late nineteenth and early twentieth centuries from a private philanthropic effort to – once again – help poor families balance their maternal employment and child-care needs (Kagan, 1991). For the most part, day nurseries were more concerned with the needs of the parents than those of the children. However, some day nurseries provided social services in addition to custodial care in an effort to prevent the institutionalization of poor children and to preserve families. Because the focus was on the adults – to support their employment – and not the children, it is not surprising that the quality of the services was low. With underqualified caregivers and inadequate facilities (Cahan, 1989), day nurseries began the trend toward poor children receiving poor-quality care.

Although infant schools and day nurseries provided services for poor working parents, another stream of programs evolved to support more privileged children's education and development. Emanating from the nursery school and kindergarten movements, the primary focus of these early education (note the change in nomenclature) programs was to supplement the enrichment that children received at home (Cahan, 1989). While poor children received custodial, low-quality care in child care or day nurseries, a growing number of children from educated, well-to-do families enrolled in Froebelian-influenced kindergartens (Kagan, 1991). In the early twentieth century, the nursery school movement flourished, building on the momentum of child-development research at institutes, colleges, and universities. Most nursery schools – similar to preschools today – had a strong educational focus, were part-day, and served children of middle- and upper-class families (Kagan, 1991). The quality of children's experiences in both kindergartens and nursery schools was generally high (Kagan, 1991) and quite distinct from the quality of services provided to the poor in child care.

Unlike child care or early education, early intervention has a different history, one couched in a third strand of early care and education services. Early intervention drew on the activism of the Civil Rights Movement to provide services to a discrete and targeted population – disabled youngsters. No longer content with having their children isolated and receiving inferior services, parents of disabled children mobilized in the late 1960s and early 1970s. With support from bureaucrats, policy makers, and politicians, new legislation was enacted – the Education for All Handicapped Children Act of 1975 – mandating that free appropriate public education and related services would be available to all handicapped children between the ages of 3 and 21 (Kagan, 1991). With the goal of mainstreaming preschool-aged children into early education settings, the legislation tried to support early childhood largely in the form of school-based programs. For the most part, child care continued to remain separate, and even when children with disabilities were mainstreamed, often the aura of polite accommodation – not fully programmatic integration – reigned.

The structural legacy of this history is a tiered system of inchoate services for young children and their families. With the exception of compensatory programs for children from low-income families – namely, Head Start – affluent children benefited from quality early education and socialization programs, whereas their more disadvantaged counterparts did not. Children with disabilities fared as best as they could within the patchwork system.

Reinforced by differences in intention and nomenclature, child care, early education, and early intervention also conjure quite different images and elicit different public reaction. Programs labeled *child care* are often thought to provide merely a custodial service for children while their parents work, whereas early education programs are associated with providing an enriched learning environment for children. Early intervention suggests another distinct set of programs – services for the disabled, often services that are more richly supported and individually tailored than either child care or early education. In reality, the services intended to be "educational" may be limited to providing custodial care (Carnegie Task Force on Learning in the Primary Grades, 1996), and vice versa. The distinction that needs to be made is not so much in nomenclature but in the quality of services rendered. Quality pedagogy does not differ among child care, early education, and early intervention programs. Although the term *early care and education* is gaining currency in the field, the lack of a clear, widely accepted, and promulgated definition underscores the differences in attitude that continue to exist; the nontroika persists.

Limited Infrastructure to Support Services. To date, most child care, early education, and early intervention public policy has focused on promoting direct services – the programs that touch the lives of children and families day to day. However, accessible quality early care and education programs cannot be achieved in isolation; they must be supported by a set of elements that work behind the scenes to support a quality system. Scholars have identified five key elements or essential functions of the infrastructure: 1) parent information and engagement; 2) professional development; 3) facility licensing, enforcement, and accreditation; 4) funding and financing; and 5) government and planning (Kagan, 1993).

As with any system of services, quality early care and education – the term being used to convey linked child care, early education, and early intervention services – will function effectively only when all of the infrastructural components work together. For example, requiring more professional development without increasing financing (and compensation in particular) will lead to staff turnover and may, in the long run, lower rather than raise program quality (Morgan et al., 1993). Similarly, if facility licensing and accreditation are enhanced without attention to parent information and engagement, parents might fail to discriminate between high- and low-quality programs, providing little incentive for programs to strive toward higher standards. Although it is important to integrate work across elements of the infrastructure, most of the efforts underway today still focus primarily on one area, underutilizing the potential synergy contained in more comprehensive reform.

LOOKING AHEAD: THE URGENT NEED FOR ACTION

The current context is characterized, then, by two challenges: first, the need to address the short-term problems; second, the need to bring about such changes so that the more enduring problems of quality, equity, and structure will be addressed in a comprehensive and visionary manner. How can we best do this in a time of limited resources, when short-term answers are needed to long-term problems? The next section addresses these challenges. It calls for an integrated response, a set of solutions that, when implemented, may have the capacity to bring about fundamental reforms in quality, equity, and structure, as well as improvement in immediate service delivery. Specifically, we address seven critical areas in which change is urgently needed: 1) child results, 2) family engagement, 3) individual licensing, 4) professional development, 5) facility licensing, 6) funding and financing, and 7) governance. For each area, the nature of the problem and some potential solutions are offered.

Inadequate Focus on Results

Recently, the process of gauging quality of services for young children has undergone some reform. In the past, researchers and practitioners focused on assessing quality by studying inputs (e.g., child-to-staff ratios, group size, staff training, and education) and on the manner in which services are delivered (e.g., nature of adult–child interactions, Hofferth & Chaplin, 1994; Phillips, Mekos, Scarr, McCartney, & Abbott-Shim, in press). Currently, there is some interest in linking quality to results – or outcomes – rather than inputs (Council of Chief State School Officers, 1995; Schorr, 1994). The focus on a results orientation is desirable because it meets many purposes: to identify children who may be members of groups at risk for health or developmental problems and to determine appropriate remediation, pedagogical planning and improvement, evaluation, and monitoring (Meisels & Fenichel, 1996). By defining desired goals and results, practitioners who work with young children can plan and tailor their activities to foster individual children's development. In addition, specified goals and results can provide programs with the feedback they need to evaluate their effectiveness and identify areas for improvement. Used for monitoring purposes, results can also assess the overall status of young children in communities, states, and the nation (Schorr, 1994). With this information in hand, parents, practitioners, and the public can hold decision makers at all levels accountable for investing in early care and education (Kagan, Rosenkoetter, & Cohen, 1997).

Despite the advantages of evaluating quality in terms of child-based results, the field has been reluctant to embrace such an approach because of several concerns. First, information generated from assessments of young children has often led to the mislabeling, miscategorizing, and stigmatization of children (Agee & California State Department of Education, 1988; Bredekamp & Rosegrant, 1992; Kagan et al., 1997; Meisels, 1987; National Association for the Education of Young Children, 1988). Second, there is no consensus regarding which results are most important for young children or how to measure results. Third, concern has been raised when measuring results for children younger than age 3 and children who are racially, ethnically, and linguistically diverse; when the data may be used to make "high-stakes" decisions concerning children's placement; and when results may be used as a basis for decisions about resource allocation, such as merit pay for teachers or levels of program reimbursement (Kagan et al., 1997).

Strategies exist, however, to address these concerns. To move toward a results-focused approach – and to safeguard children from the misuses of results – parents, practitioners, policy makers, and the public need to come together to define results and expectations for 3- and 4-year-old children, taking into consideration the child, family, and community conditions that promote young children's development. Results should be specified at the local, state, and national levels, increasing the customization and specificity at each level. Concurrently, developmentally appropriate instruments should be developed to evaluate progress toward the achievement of specified results in all domains of development. Researchers must consider results from the perspective of children – across programs and time – to capture the cumulative impact of early care and experiences. Information also needs to be shared in ways that increase public understanding of the connection among child results, effective services, and the expenditure of public funds (Kagan et al., 1997).

Inadequate Engagement of Families

A second area in which improvement in early care and education is badly needed relates to the engagement of families. Research shows that parent and family engagement in early care and education programs improves results for children, increases the likelihood of children's success and achievement, and decreases the likelihood of negative outcomes, both in school and later in life (Bronfenbrenner, 1974; Bronson, Pierson, & Tivnan, 1984). Intensive parental engagement is particularly important for the development of children whose mothers have relatively low levels of education (Bronson et al.,

1984; Laosa, 1980). When parents are engaged, opportunities exist among parents and staff to share concrete information about children, to develop reciprocal relationships in which parents' values and knowledge are respected and staff are trusted, and to foster communication so that the adults with whom children spend most of their time can agree on basic goals and approaches (Parker et al., 1992; Powell, 1989).

Parents and family members also benefit from their engagement in early care and education programs. When parents and families are involved in programs, they receive direct services and education, and they can develop support networks and ties with other families. Furthermore, when parents are involved in decision-making roles – organizing parent activities, running programs, and making budgetary and policy decisions – they often develop more positive attitudes toward themselves and greater life satisfaction (Powell, 1989). In addition, early care and education programs that meet the needs of adults as well as the needs of children are more likely to promote parents' own well-being and reduce the conflict between work and family life (Shinn, Galinsky, & Gulcur, 1990).

Although desirable, parent engagement as real partners in their children's programs is difficult to achieve for a number of reasons. Many parents are unwilling or unable to become involved in early care and education programs. They may be burdened by work and family responsibilities that prevent them from contributing time and energy to early care and education programs. Parents may also not recognize the value of their participation and involvement to their children's early development and learning. In addition, if parents are not comfortable interacting with program staff or with the teaching approaches followed in the program, they will be less likely to participate in their children's early care and education.

It is also difficult to engage parents as effective consumers because parents face numerous hurdles in finding and selecting programs. They may not have adequate time to conduct the search, and they may not have many convenient, affordable, and quality program options from which to choose. Parents may not know exactly what to look for or may not feel that they are adequate judges of program quality. As a result, they rely on friends and neighbors for information, with only about 9% of parents using resource and referral services to research programs (Hofferth et al., 1991).

To overcome these obstacles, families' diverse needs and interests need to be accommodated in a variety of ways. Programs need to ensure that they have adequate numbers of staff who are interested, trained, and experienced in working with parents (Larner, 1995). Staff need to focus on developing regular communication among practitioners and parents in which both parties feel like equals, adding valuable information to the discussion. Programs need to provide multiple activities to involve parents (Epstein, 1995; Henderson, Marburger, & Ooms, 1986), because parents who are reluctant to engage in one kind of activity may welcome the opportunity to participate in other ways (Larner, 1995). Programs also need to design and schedule activities in ways that take into consideration the diverse logistical needs of parents and families, for example, working parents or at-home parents, dual-parent families and single-parent families, teenage parents and older parents, and parents in school and vocational programs (Lee & Seiderman, 1994). Staff can also better meet parents' needs by including them in the governance of early care and education programs (Kagan, 1994). Skilled staff from both resource and referral agencies and parenting education efforts can assist parents in learning about and evaluating their early care and education options.

Finally, parents need support from employers so that they can become partners in their children's programs, effective consumers of early care and education services, and productive employees (Galinsky, Bond, & Friedman, 1993; Staines & Galinsky, 1991). Employers can and do support these goals by offering benefits to their employees, including flex-time options that enable parents to find, monitor, and participate in their children's early care and education programs and family events. Corporations can and should also offer flexibility in the use of all benefits, including sick/personal days, and job-protected paid maternity and parental leave.

Need for Licensing of Staff

Individual licensure – a third area in which considerable work is needed – has been debated but has not been systematically examined. Today, no individual licensure is required throughout the field and, as a result, there is no established system for conferring such licenses (Mitchell, 1995; Morgan et al., 1993). This situation exists despite the reality that the creation of licenses and a system to confer them would not only help assure the quality of programs (American Public Health Association & American Academy of Pediatrics, 1992) but would also help increase professionalization, staff compensation, opportunities for career advancement and mobility, and the quality of training and education.

It is important to note what is meant by licensure and why it has been so illusive in early care and education. Individual licensure refers to the permission that is granted to an individual person by a competent authority, usually a government, to engage in a business or activity; without this license, practicing the activity would be illegal. If licensure is so necessary, why has it been absent in this field? The responses reflect deeply held attitudes. First, parents and society often equate the teaching of young children with parenting; because parenting demands no particular training or education, why should licenses be created for teachers? Such licenses, it is argued, might make an informal service overly formal. Second, the field itself values open access to all who wish to work in early childhood, recognizing the importance of engaging community members in key early care and education roles. As a result, the field has difficulty reconciling the value of individual licensure and the value of maintaining open access to employment. Third, current staff may have difficulties meeting licensing requirements under today's system of professional development (Morgan et al., 1993). A final barrier to individual licensure is that requiring higher levels of staff training and education could lead to increased salaries and benefits and would likely raise the cost of programs.

Despite these caveats, individual early care and education licensing exists in most Western European nations and Japan, which require significantly more training and education of practitioners (Pritchard, 1996). In Finland, preschool teachers are required to have at least three years of related college-level training (Ojala, 1989); in Japan, they are required to have two years of college-level training (Lassegard, 1993); in Sweden, they are required to have two and one half years at the college level (Gunnarsson, 1993); and in the United Kingdom, the standard is four years of college-level preparation (Pascal, Bertram, & Heaslip, 1991). France is perhaps the pacesetter,

requiring the same masters-level preparation for teachers in primary schools and preschools (Richardson & Marx, 1989). Several countries focus on the qualifications of supervisors and directors of early care and education programs. In New Zealand, supervisors in center-based programs must complete training in either primary school teaching or nursing (Smith & Swain, 1988); in Norway, lead teachers and directors must have three years of early childhood teacher training at the college level (Bo, 1993). Some industrialized nations have standards for practitioners in family child care. In the United Kingdom, family child-care providers are required to complete preservice vocational training (Cohen, 1993); in Finland, they must complete a 16-hour first-aid class and a 250-hour training course (Ojala, 1989). The more rigorous standards for qualification of early care and education workers in other industrialized countries are coupled with a more coordinated and sequenced training delivery system (Pritchard, 1996).

Structures to support licensing individuals are also well established in many other occupations in the United States. State governments require many professionals and nonprofessionals working with the public to be licensed (Mitchell, 1996), including helping professionals (e.g., social workers, registered nurses, licensed practical nurses, and teachers), technical professionals (e.g., architects and engineers), tradespeople (e.g., electricians), and even service workers (e.g., cosmetologists). It is no accident that workers in other occupations earn from two to six times more than early care and education practitioners (Mitchell, 1996). Additionally, the individual licensing requirements have set the goals for training and education and have often promoted career mobility. That other nations, and other professions within the U.S., have successfully established coherent individual licensing systems suggests that the obstacles to establishing a coherent facility licensing system for individuals can be surmounted in order to achieve quality programs for children.

Inadequate Preparation of Practitioners

Closely allied with the licensure issue is a fourth area in which additional efforts are needed: practitioner training and education. Research is clear, the more training and education practitioners have – both general education and early childhood-related training and education – the more skilled they are at helping young children thrive and achieve their potential (Arnett, 1989; CQCO Study Team, 1995; Fosberg, 1981; Phillips & Howes, 1987; Ruopp, Travers, Glantz, & Coelen, 1979; Schweinhart et al., 1993; Whitebook et al., 1989). Well-trained and educated practitioners are less harsh and restrictive than staff with less preparation (Arnett, 1989; Berk, 1985; Howes, 1983; Ruopp et al., 1979; Whitebook et al., 1989). In family child care, increased training has been associated with children who are more securely attached to their providers and who spend more time engaged in activities and less time wandering aimlessly (Galinsky, Howes, & Kontos, 1995). Early childhood-related training and education seem to be particularly important for practitioners working with infants (Phillips et al., in press) and toddlers (Whitebook et al., 1989). Well-trained staff are also more likely to establish positive relationships with parents, communicate with them more regularly, and develop services and activities to meet their needs.

Although preparing early care and education practitioners and supporting their ongoing training are important to program quality, professional development services are inadequate and uncoordinated. About 40% of early care and education teachers in center-based programs have high school degrees or less, and about 10% have just two-year college degrees (Willer et al., 1991). Center-based teachers receive only about ten hours of ongoing training annually, commonly at their own centers or at community colleges (Kisker et al., 1991). Roughly half of the assistant teachers and aides in centers have high school degrees or less (Whitebook et al., 1989). Among family child-care providers who are regulated, the average education is about one year of college, although the coursework is not necessarily related to young children; one-third of regulated providers have never received any specialized training (Kisker et al., 1991). The training and education of unregulated providers – the bulk of all providers – are not known. The field simply does not have the capacity to produce adequate numbers of well-trained individuals: The total number of graduates from all college-level early childhood programs across the country would constitute barely

enough teachers for early care and education centers in Massachusetts and New York (Morgan et al., 1993).

Staff who pursue training typically must negotiate an uncoordinated and unsequenced array of offerings. In many cases, staff do not receive academic credit for the coursework that they complete; even when courses do carry credit, it is often difficult to transfer that credit from one institution to another, making it difficult to earn a degree. Moreover, much training is geared to the lowest common denominator, with entry-level training offered over and over (Morgan et al., 1993) and few opportunities for intermediate and advanced training. In a study conducted by High/Scope Educational Research Foundation, the amount and kind of inservice training (i.e., ongoing professional training and development) was shown to be a significant predictor of program quality (Epstein, 1993). Yet, courses are usually preservice courses that are not geared to practitioners who are already employed in programs. Revamping the education and training for early care and education staff – practitioners, administrators, and leaders – is fundamental to creating a quality early care and education system.

Inadequate Licensing of Facilities

Facility licensing – a fifth domain of work – is essential to the quality of early care and education settings and to the impact of those settings on children. Facility licensing, which complements individual licensing, not only benefits children but can also provide parents with the assurances that their children will be safe and protected from harm. Facility licensing refers to the regulations and rules that must be met for many early care and education programs to operate legally. Research has demonstrated that states with more demanding facility licensing requirements have more centers that enhance the development of children by positively affecting children's cognitive, social, and language development; their behavior; and their secure attachments to teachers (CQCO Study Team, 1995).

Despite its value, current facility licensing is inadequate. In many locales, licensing may be weak or inattentive to major quality variables (U.S. Advisory Commission on Intergovernmental Relations [ACIR], 1994). This variation exists not only in what is regulated but also in what programs are regulated and whether the standards that accompany licensure are enforced. Many states have only minimal requirements, whereas others have regulations that are specific and promote quality. Some states exempt large numbers of family child-care homes, church-sponsored programs, part-day programs, and school-sponsored programs from all licensing requirements. Indeed, it has been estimated that nationwide, more than 40% of all children in early care and education attend programs that are legally exempt from state regulation (Adams, 1990). In thirty-eight states, many family child-care homes are not subject to facility licensing requirements; part-day private nursery schools in twenty-three states and church-run centers in nine states are also exempt (Morgan et al., 1993); and centers run by public schools are totally or partially exempt in thirty states (U.S. ACIR, 1994). With regard to enforcement, studies suggest that decreased monitoring and enforcement are a trend (Morgan et al., 1993; Phillips, Lande, & Goldberg, 1990). Moreover, when programs are inspected and found to be in violation of licensing requirements, states rarely levy significant penalties (Gormley, 1995; Scurria, 1996). This lack of quality and consistency in licensure has led to great state-to-state variability in how well regulations protect children. Any effort to enhance quality must address these regulatory irregularities.

Need for Public Investment

For all children to have access to quality early care and education programs, the system must be funded adequately – the sixth and most critical area in which work is needed. Low public investment in early care and education jeopardizes children by forcing programs to operate with inadequate funds to provide quality. Although the average of $5,800 that governments spend per child on a year of public school pays for just thirty hours of education a week for about forty weeks a year, the combined parent and government spending of $3,000 to $5,000 per child for a year of full-time early care and education pays for thirty-five to fifty hours of early care and education per week for fifty to fifty-two weeks per year (Casper, 1995; CQCO Study Team, 1995; Hofferth

et al., 1991; Sugarman, 1995). Given the relatively large number of hours paid for by the relatively small investment in early care and education compared to school, it should not be surprising that the quality of most early care and education programs is so low.

Inadequate public funding burdens parents with the majority of the costs of early care and education and contributes to inequitable service delivery. Roughly 80% of all early care and education costs are absorbed by families, with the remaining 20% distributed among the government (by means of program and consumer subsidies), foundations, and corporations (CQCO Study Team, 1995). Families with lower incomes bear a disproportionate burden of the early care and education expense – and receive lower quality services in return. A national study found that families with monthly incomes less than $1,200 spent 25% of their incomes on early care and education (averaging $47 per week), whereas families with monthly incomes of $4,500 or more spent 6% of their income on early care and education (averaging $92 per week; Casper, 1995). Those families who cannot afford the full cost of early care and education must rely on the small stream of public subsidies to enroll their children in programs. Limited subsidies constrain parents' early care and education choices. Without financial assistance, lower-income parents are often forced to settle for lower-quality care for their children.

Children of all incomes, races, and needs do better in higher-quality programs than in lower-quality programs, and these programs cost somewhat more (CQCO Study Team, 1995). Furthermore, the components of the infrastructure to support a quality system, as discussed earlier, also depend on adequate funding. Thus, current underinvestment in early care and education prevents a quality early care and education system from developing and prevents children across the United States from obtaining needed services.

Inadequate Governance

Given the fragmented history of early care and education discussed earlier, it is not surprising that no coordinated approach to governance exists in early care and education. Rather than having municipal or quasi-public entities responsible for planning, coordination, equitable service delivery, monitoring, and quality control – as routinely exist in health, welfare, and social services – early education is not governed. Its services are administered by individual programs that fall under the jurisdictions of state departments of education, departments of health, and departments of welfare or social services (Kagan, Goffin, Golub, & Pritchard, 1995). A recent study documented ninety different federal programs concerned with early care and education, residing in eleven federal agencies and twenty separate offices (U.S. General Accounting Office, 1995b).

The multiple programs are unconnected and have few mechanisms for coordination. As a result, there are countless overlaps and gaps in policy, eligibility, fees, and programming. Programs emerge episodically and inconsistently, with firm eligibility cutoffs that often lead to disruptions in services from even slight changes in the child's family income, work status, or residence (U.S. General Accounting Office, 1994). Moreover, scarce funding has led programs to compete for resources and for children. Worse, without linkages to demystify "the system," parents are forced to negotiate the service maze on their own, weakening their potential to choose quality programs and become strong advocates for their children.

In short, an effective system of governance is needed to ensure a good match between the supply of programs in a given state or locality and the needs of the families who live there. Such governance entities can help alleviate gaps between parental needs and community services. They can strengthen and coordinate components of the infrastructure and see that resources are distributed and utilized in an efficient, cost-effective manner. These entities can create incentives to raise quality, foster greater programmatic equity, and engender the results orientation discussed earlier.

Although responsibility for the governance of early care and education has never been clearly differentiated, with roles assigned to the various levels of government varying over time and across locales (Marzke & Both, 1994), a number of exciting governance efforts, as well as efforts to address the other quality enhancement strategies discussed herein, are emerging. They provide a glimpse into a future of opportunity.

CURRENT INNOVATIVE EFFORTS

What has been done to address the current challenges and improve early care and education? Across the country, new efforts have emerged, suggesting inventive strategies and innovative approaches to change. With the goal of providing a sampling of the efforts underway, we turn to a discussion of efforts to achieve quality in the areas, which were previously discussed: professional development and individual licensure; facility licensure; funding and financing; governance, accountability, and planning; and parent engagement. Additionally, some comprehensive efforts are highlighted. These efforts are followed by a discussion of the challenges they pose.

Professional Development and Individual Licensure

Throughout the 1990s, initiatives to improve the professional development of early care and education workers have expanded considerably (Azer, Capraro, & Elliott, 1996). National efforts – such as those by the Center for Career Development in Early Care and Education at Wheelock College – have focused on creating career development systems in individual states and generating models that can benefit other states (Azer et al., 1996). The Center for Career Development in Early Care and Education has also recommended a set of specific requirements that could be included in state licensing requirements to promote a career development approach, including: 1) specialized early childhood preservice and ongoing training; 2) multiple routes for meeting preservice qualifications; 3) multiple roles for practitioners – each with higher qualifications; 4) more than one topic area covered in training (such as child development, special needs, diversity, first aid, parent relations, and age-appropriate programming); and 5) experience requirements (Azer & Eldred, 1997). Massachusetts, Kansas, Vermont, and Colorado are examples of states that have incorporated these concepts in their training requirements (Azer & Eldred, 1997).

The National Black Child Development Institute's efforts have aimed at increasing the number of leaders in early childhood education by developing a comprehensive and integrated approach to leadership development (Moore, 1997). In addition to its annual Early Childhood Leadership Institute, the National Black Child Development Institute has gathered data on the status of African American leadership in early care and education and has developed concrete recommendations for increasing the participation of African Americans in leadership positions in the field (NBCDI, 1993). At the state level, at least eight states are in the process of developing new credentials or certificates for practitioners. One state has developed a set of professional development competencies for early care and education practitioners, administrators, and trainers. Other state efforts have focused on increasing career mobility in the field by improving articulation among community-based training, vocational child care, community colleges, and four-year colleges/universities and by making it easier to transfer credits among these institutions. Connecticut's Charts a Course is one example of such an effort.

Facility Licensure

Improving facility licensing of early care and education settings is the focus of several innovative efforts. One approach is to require programs that are not required to be fully licensed to have certificates that focus on the safety of the facility, supervision, and staffing levels. Differential monitoring of early care and education facilities, basing the number of site visits to individual programs on their track records, and using indicator checklists to gauge quality is another innovative approach to improving the efficacy of facility licensing. Improving licensing of family child-care homes (Gormley, 1995), incentive-based approaches to enforcement, and considering revamping facility licensing regulations to permit teachers with more training to care for a slightly higher number of children (Miller, 1995) are among the range of innovative initiatives around facility licensing at the state level. Efforts are also underway to respond more effectively to consumers in the regulatory process. Some states are taking measures to ensure that more parents become aware of licensing standards and programs' compliance with the requirements, and a few states are also working to ensure that consumers have a contact point where their concerns can be aired and addressed (Kagan & Cohen, 1997).

Funding and Financing

Many policy makers, organizations, and legislators are now addressing funding and financing challenges in early care and education. At the national level, policy research and development, policy-maker forums, and public education activities have focused on improving the effectiveness, efficiency, and equity of public financing for education and other children's services. At the state and local levels, tax incentives are being explored as a way of financing services for young children and their families. The Finance Project (1997) noted the many different forms that tax incentives can take – including deductions, exemptions, credits, and abatements – and that these are efficient ways of providing services to large numbers of people. Colorado, for example, uses tax credits to leverage voluntary contributions to early care and education in enterprise zones (Mitchell, Stoney, & Dichter, 1997). Other examples of innovative tax policies include using a portion of tax revenue to create a child-care trust fund, the interest from which will continue to benefit children's programs in the future (Mitchell et al., 1997), and creating local taxation districts in order to generate additional funds from property taxes for children's services. In several states, bonds and loan guarantee programs raise money to build and renovate early care and education facilities (Mitchell et al., 1997). North Carolina and Ohio have allocated significant new funds for early care and education from state general funds: North Carolina's Smart Start initiative invests $68 million annually, and Ohio spends $145 million to supplement Head Start and $31 million on its preschool program (Knitzer & Page, 1996). In addition, several states provide paid maternity leave, using statewide temporary disability insurance.

Governance, Accountability, and Planning

In the latter part of the 1990s, various innovative governance and accountability efforts have been launched in the field of early care and education (Center for the Study of Social Policy, 1996; Kagan et al., 1995; Knitzer & Page, 1996). At the national level, such efforts include the Families and Work Institute's Early Education Quality

Improvement Project (EQUIP) to assess the quality of early care and education systems. The Families and Work Institute, in collaboration with the National Center for Children in Poverty and the National Governors' Association, provides technical assistance to states as they develop comprehensive systems of programs and services for young children and their families. The Child Care and Education Forging the Link Initiative, the Council of Chief State School Officers, and the Child Care Action Campaign provide technical assistance to state and local efforts to link child care with education and other relevant services, community by community.

Planning efforts are also taking hold across the nation, with many chronicled in the Map and Track document (Knitzer & Page, 1996). Others emanate from an education orientation and are described in the U.S. Department of Education publication titled *Early Childhood Reform in Seven Communities* (1996). These documents highlight the need for advances that are being made to launch more systematic and carefully planned social strategies that advance the provision of community-based, collaborative early care and education services.

Improvements are also being made in efforts to make services more accountable and effective. Data revealing service provision are becoming more routine through Kids Counts efforts in the states – an annual accounting of early care and education data. Related efforts are taking place throughout the country. In California, for example, an outstanding compendium of early childhood services provides a county-by-county overview of the community and the nature of services provided, including the salaries and costs of child care (CCR & RN, 1997).

At the state level, the Oregon Benchmarks (Cutler, Tan, & Downs, 1995) and the Minnesota Milestones (Knitzer & Page, 1996) projects have specified standards for measuring state and community progress toward assuring the well-being of children and families. Partnerships have been formed across government agencies, with citizen involvement at the state and local levels, to work toward achieving standards and to improve service delivery to children and families. Finally, Massachusetts's Community Partnerships for Children gives grants to selected local partnerships of child-care providers, Head Start programs, and schools to enable them to

develop and implement joint plans to integrate services for young children and their families (Kagan & Cohen, 1997).

Parent Engagement

A number of national initiatives have focused on parent engagement (Miller & Anderson, 1995). In more than 300 early care and education programs in six states, the Parent Services Project (PSP) has engaged parents as partners in their children's programs by making existing early care and education programs more supportive of families, for example, by organizing parent and family activities to raise parents' sense of importance, diminish feelings of isolation, increase parenting skills, and help them secure needed resources. At the state and local level, numerous child-care resource and referral agencies are focusing on creative strategies for helping parents become effective consumers of early care and education programs. For example, twelve large child-care resource and referral agencies have collaborated to develop a publication that answers questions the agencies most commonly receive from the parents of young children. In addition, projects are currently working to organize the parents of young children across a community around a range of early care and education issues; for example, the Parent Leadership Institute of the Connecticut Commission on Children provides leadership training for parents as community activists and child advocates in the school system and local government (Kagan & Cohen, 1997).

Comprehensive Efforts

Finally, a few innovative efforts address early care and education as part of a larger effort to provide more comprehensive family-supportive services for young children and their families. The Carnegie Corporation of New York's Starting Points initiative has funded projects in four cities (Baltimore, Boston, Pittsburgh, and San Francisco) and ten states (Colorado, Florida, Georgia, Hawaii, Minnesota, North Carolina, Ohio, Rhode Island, Vermont, and West Virginia) to meet the needs of children in the first 3 years of life (Kagan & Cohen, 1997). These city and state projects address early care and education, comprehensive family support, health care and home visiting, and economic development and employment incentives and utilize a variety of strategies, including public education, community mobilization, new governance mechanisms, creation of statewide benchmarks to assess progress, and program evaluation. More than 500 schools in sixteen states are taking part in the School of the 21st Century initiative (Finn-Stevenson, Desimone, & Chung, in press). The project addresses parent engagement, funding, and governance issues by integrating into schools a range of services for young children and their families: early care and education programs, information and referral for families with young children, and other family support services (Kagan & Cohen, 1997).

The Challenges These Efforts Pose

Despite their inventiveness, some of these efforts have achieved only limited success. A primary weakness is that they are characterized by the same fragmentation as the services themselves. There has been little coordination and communication among initiatives focused on changing early care and education. Typically, the leaders of these efforts are individuals from one sector, such as child development, social policy, health, mental health, education, or social work. Few alliances have formed across institutional and disciplinary boundaries. Although this phenomenon is not surprising, there have been few linkages among early care and education and other reform efforts; for example, health care reform, welfare reform, education reform, and community development. Without collaboration, it is difficult to eliminate the duplication of services and to ensure that target groups are served as efficiently and effectively as possible. In addition, reformers will be unable to share resources, funding, and expertise toward the common goal of helping young children and families.

Second, few reform efforts have used comprehensive strategies to improve early care and education. In general, initiatives have targeted certain components of the problem; for example, compensation, training, licensing, or funding. Less attention has been accorded to how these components can interact to form a system. As noted earlier, to influence comprehensive, durable change, efforts must

approach the field as a whole. They must facilitate the linkages among elements of the infrastructure as well as the linkages among the infrastructure and direct services.

A third weakness is that most of these efforts have been short-term efforts, focusing on delivering short-term solutions. For example, the field has been content to launch new add-on programs without discerning how such programs may contribute to or distract from the long-term goal of creating more systemic change. Funds are made available for short-term in-service training without discerning the long-term needs for a training infrastructure. These efforts, however, are often merely Band-Aids™ for large-scale problems, but they are popular because they can secure adequate financial resources; funders may not be willing to give money to sustain research and initiatives that may not yield positive outcomes for many years. Government also favors short-term solutions to problems (that have taken years to evolve) because they are more palatable to politicians who face frequent reelection. Similarly, long-range planning and strategizing does not capture the media attention because it is not "catchy" enough to be worthy of news coverage. Such shortsightedness on the part of all stakeholders has prevented reformers from conceptualizing and considering approaches that are more likely to take time to implement but also to be innovative and far-reaching. Initiatives that look to the future of the early care and education field are more likely to produce far-sweeping change and long-lasting effects.

Finally, although visions of an early care and education system have been considered (Kamerman & Kahn, 1995; Sugarman, 1993), there has never been a widely shared vision of a quality system of early care and education. This exists despite the fact that many benefits might accrue if such a vision could be constructed. A shared vision can guide the field toward what it wants to become in the future while uniting the field around common purposes and goals. It could begin to address seriously the intransigent problems discussed earlier in a systematic way. Creating and implementing a shared vision for an early care and education system would reap benefits in the process, as well; it would force the field to grapple with issues long swept under the rug and, in so doing, evoke the coordination, comprehensiveness, and long-term perspective needed as the field becomes professionalized.

A FRAMEWORK FOR CHANGE

One framework for change is the Quality 2000 Initiative (Kagan & Cohen, 1997) of the Yale University Bush Center in Child Development and Social Policy. Funded by several private foundations, Quality 2000 was charged with creating a long-range, comprehensive, and integrated vision for early care and education that – when implemented – would significantly improve the quality of children's life experiences and outcomes. Since 1993, hundreds of parents, early childhood educators, psychologists, political scientists, policy analysts, economists, finance experts, community organizers, and media specialists have contributed their knowledge and expertise to the initiative through activities that include a series of commissioned papers, cross-national literature reviews, task forces, and working groups.

Throughout the 1990s, Quality 2000 has considered the changing demographics, patterns of service delivery, and attitudes that characterize the early care and education field today as the context for widespread change. Capitalizing on the changing zeitgeist toward children and families, it has called for dramatic reform. Quality 2000 – as with any successful reform effort – has addressed early care and education's quality, equity, and structural problems. To that end, the initiative developed eight recommendations to assure that by the year 2010, high-quality early care and education programs will be available and accessible to all children from birth to age 5, whose parents choose to enroll them. These services will be supported by a well-funded, coherent, and coordinated infrastructure and will be linked to services that advance children's healthy development (Kagan & Cohen, 1997). Drawing from the work of Quality 2000, the following recommendations – some of many approaches to fostering change – are offered as a framework, with the understanding that any effort to foster serious improvement in the early care and education system must address a variety of essential functions simultaneously and must be characterized by long-term think-

ing. These recommendations were designed to be considered as a set and to be achieved over the next fifteen years.

1. *Achieve high quality in all programs.* Family child care and center-based programs (Head Start, for- and non-profit child care, prekindergartens, nursery schools) must be designed for quality, allowing staff flexibility in using resources creatively and cost-effectively and in using state-of-the-art approaches.
2. *Focus on results.* Clear results and expectations must be specified and used to guide individual planning for all 3- and 4-year-old children, based on all domains of development (social–emotional, physical–motor, cognitive, language, and approaches to learning).
3. *Enlist parents and communities.* Parents of young children must be involved in their children's programs in some way, with programs providing diverse opportunities for such involvement. Parents should have the user-friendly information and support they need to be effective consumers in choosing programs for their children. Business must provide policies that enable parents to become involved in their children's learning and early education.
4. *Credential all staff.* All individuals working with children in early care and education programs must have, or be actively in the process of obtaining, credentials related to the position they hold or seek. Ongoing training and education (lifelong learning) must be encouraged for all staff.
5. *Revamp training–preparation opportunities.* All training for early childhood positions must be child and family focused, reflecting and respecting cultural and linguistic diversity. All approved training must bear credit, lead to increased credentials and compensation, and equip individuals for diverse and advanced roles.
6. *License all programs.* All early care and education programs must be licensed, eliminating legal exemptions. Facility licensing procedures must be streamlined and enforced to assure that all programs promote children's safety, health, and development. Incentives for facility enhancement must be provided.
7. *Invest in quality.* Young children's early care and education must be funded by the public and private sectors at per-child levels, commensurate with funding for elementary-age children. Ten percent of the funds must be set aside for professional and

staff development; enhanced compensation; parent information and engagement; program accreditation; resource and referral services; evaluation, data collection, and research; planning; and licensing and facility enhancement.

8. *Govern early care and education rationally.* Mechanisms (councils and boards) must be established or built upon in every community and state to carry out planning, governance, and accountability roles in early care and education.

CONCLUSION

The field of early care and education has been shaped by recent changes in demographics, service delivery, and public attitudes. These changes have led to a surge in demand for and utilization of services, with children cared for in a variety of constantly changing, loosely configured settings. At the same time, changing public attitudes have brought an unprecedented level of positive attention to the needs of children and families. In addition, early care and education have been challenged throughout history by quality, equity, and structural issues. As a result, the quality of services is uneven, and families do not have equal access to services of any quality. Moreover, there is no unified field that integrates child care, early education, and early intervention, and relatedly, early care and education services are not adequately supported by an infrastructure.

Addressing the sociodynamic problems and the enduring problems that affect early care and education requires immediate action in the following areas: child results, family engagement, individual licensing, professional development, facility licensing, funding and financing, and governance. Fortunately, across the nation, innovative efforts have focused on redressing some of early care and education's long-standing challenges. Although promising and inventive, these efforts have achieved only limited success. In general, the impact of these efforts has been weakened by their fragmentation, lack of comprehensive strategies, short-term focus, and absence of a shared vision for the future of the field. Alternatively, the Quality 2000 initiative has taken an integrated, comprehensive, long-term approach for improving early care and education

services and may serve as a model or partner for other reform efforts.

This chapter suggests that American early care and education are at a crossroads. With increased public support and increased investment in the field, opportunity for advancement exists as it has not before. The challenge before us is not to squander the opportunity but to maximize it by thinking broadly, thinking into the future, and thinking and acting (as the African proverb suggests) as if it is impossible to fail. The recommendations offered herein have attempted to suggest steps to that end.

REFERENCES

Adams, G. (1990). *Who knows how safe? The status of state efforts to ensure quality child care.* Washington, DC: Children's Defense Fund.

Adams, G., & Poersch, N. O. (1996). *Who cares? State commitment to child care and early education.* Washington, DC: Children's Defense Fund.

Adams, G., & Sandfort, J. (1994). *First steps, promising future: State prekindergarten initiatives in the early 1990s.* Washington, DC: Children's Defense Fund.

Agee, J. L., & California State Department of Education. (1988). *Here they come: Ready or not! A report of the School Readiness Task Force.* Sacramento: California State Department of Education.

American Public Health Association and American Academy of Pediatrics. (1992). *Caring for our children: National health and safety performance standards – guidelines for out-of-home child care programs.* Washington, DC, and Elk Grove Village, IL: Author.

Arnett, J. (1989). Caregivers in day care centers: Does training matter? *Journal of Applied Developmental Psychology, 10,* 541–52.

Azer, S. L., & Eldred, D. (1997). *Training requirements in child care licensing regulations.* Boston, MA: The Center for Career Development in Early Care and Education, Wheelock College.

Azer, S. L., Capraro, K. L., & Elliott, K. A. (1996). *Working toward making a career of it: A profile of career development initiatives in 1996.* Boston, MA: The Center for Career Development in Early Care and Education, Wheelock College.

Barnett, W. S. (1995). Long-term effects of early childhood programs on cognitive and school outcomes. *The Future of Children: Long-term outcomes of early childhood programs, 5*(3), 25–50.

Berk, L. (1985). Relationship of educational attainment, child-oriented attitudes, job satisfaction, and career commitment to caregiver behaviors towards children. *Child Care Quarterly, 14,* 103–29.

Bo, I. (1993). Norway. In M. Cochran (Ed.), *International handbook of child care policies and programs* (pp. 391–414). Westport, CT: Greenwood Press.

Bredekamp, S., & Rosegrant, T. (Eds.). (1992). *Reaching potentials: Appropriate curriculum and assessment for young children.* Washington, DC: National Association for the Education of Young Children.

Bronfenbrenner, U. (1974). *A report on longitudinal evaluations of preschool programs, Vol. II: Is early intervention effective?* Washington, DC: Office of Child Development, Department of Health, Education, and Welfare.

Bronson, M. B., Pierson, D. E., & Tivnan, T. (1984). The effects of early education on children's competence in elementary school. *Evaluation Review, 8,* 615–29.

Burchinal, M. R., Roberts, J. E., Nabors, L. A., & Bryant, D. M. (1995). *Quality of center child care and infant cognitive language development.* Unpublished manuscript. Frank Porter Graham Child Development Institute and University of North Carolina at Chapel Hill.

Cahan, E. D. (1989). *Past caring: A history of U.S. preschool care and education for the poor, 1820–1965.* New York: National Center for Children in Poverty, School of Public Health, Columbia University.

California Child Care Resource and Referral Network [CCR and RN]. (1997). *The California child care portfolio.* CA: Author.

Carnegie Task Force on Learning in the Primary Grades. (1996). *Years of promise: A comprehensive learning strategy for America's children.* New York: Carnegie Corporation of New York.

Carnegie Task Force on Meeting the Needs of Young Children. (1994). *Starting points: Meeting the needs of our youngest children: The report of the Carnegie Task Force on meeting the needs of young children.* New York: Carnegie Corporation of New York.

Casper, L. M. (1995). What does it cost to mind our preschoolers? *Current population reports: Household economic studies.* P70-52. Washington, DC: U.S. Department of Commerce.

Casper, L. M. (1996). Who's minding our preschoolers? *Current population reports: Household economic studies* (P70-53). Washington, DC: U.S. Department of Commerce.

Center for the Study of Social Policy. (1996). *Beyond lists: Moving to results-based accountability.* Washington, DC: Author.

Cohen, B. (1993). The United Kingdom. In M. Cochran (Ed.), *International handbook of child care policies and programs* (pp. 515–34). Westport, CT: Greenwood Press.

Collins, A., & Aber, J. L. (1997). *Children and welfare reform issue brief 1: How welfare reform will help or hurt children.* New York: National Center for Children in Poverty.

Committee for Economic Development. (1993). *Why child care matters: Preparing young children for a more productive America.* New York: Committee for Economic Development.

Cost, Quality, and Child Outcomes Study Team. (1995). *Cost, quality, and child outcomes in child care centers.* Denver, CO: Department of Economics University of Colorado at Denver.

Council of Chief State School Officers. (1995, Summer). *Moving toward accountability for results: A look at ten states' efforts.* Washington, DC: Author.

Cutler, I., Tan, A., & Downs, L. (1995). *State investments in education and other children's services: Case studies of financing innovations.* Washington, DC: The Finance Project.

Education Commission of the States. (1996). *Bridging the gap between neuroscience and education. Summary of a workshop.* Denver, CO: Author.

Epstein, A. S. (1993). *Training for quality: Improving early childhood programs through systematic inservice training.* Ypsilanti, MI: High/Scope Press.

Epstein, J. L. (1995, May). School/family/community partnerships: Caring for the children we share. *Phi Delta Kappan,* 701–12.

The Finance Project. (1997). *Revenue generation in the wake of welfare reform: Summary of the pilot learning cluster on early childhood finance.* Washington, DC: Author.

Finn-Stevenson, M., Desimone, L., & Chung, A. (in press). Linking child care and family support services with the school: Pilot evaluation of the School of the 21st Century. *Children and Youth Services Review.*

Fosberg, S. (1981). *Family day care in the United States: Summary of findings – Final report of National Day Care Home Study (Vol. 1).* Cambridge, MA: Abt Associates.

Fuller, B. F., & Liang, X. (1995). *Can poor families find child care? Persisting inequality nationwide and in Massachusetts.* Cambridge, MA: Harvard University Press.

Galinsky, E., Bond, J. T., & Friedman, D. E. (1993). *The changing workforce: Highlights of the National Study.* New York: Families and Work Institute.

Galinsky, E., Howes, C., & Kontos, S. (1995). *The family child care training study: Interim report.* New York: Families and Work Institute.

Galinsky, E., Howes, C., Kontos, S., & Shinn, M. (1994). *The study of children in family child care and relative care.* New York: Families and Work Institute.

Gomby, D. S., Larner, M. B., Stevenson, C. S., Lewit, E. M., & Behrman, R. E. (1995). Long-term outcomes of early childhood programs: Analysis and recommendations. *The future of children: Long-term outcomes of early childhood programs, 5*(3), 6–24.

Gormley, W. T. (1995). *Everybody's children: Child care as a public problem.* Washington, DC: Brookings Institution.

Gunnarsson, L. (1993). Sweden. In M. Cochran (Ed.), *International handbook of child care policies and programs* (pp. 491–514). Westport, CT: Greenwood Press.

Henderson, A. T., Marburger, C. L., & Ooms, T. (1986). *Beyond the bake sale: An educator's guide to working with *parents.* Columbia, MD: The National Committee for Citizens in Education.

Hofferth, S. L. (1995). Caring for children at the poverty line. *Children and Youth Services Review, 17*(1–2), 1–31.

Hofferth, S. L., Brayfield, A., Deich, S., & Holcomb, P. (1991). *National child care survey, 1990.* Washington, DC: The Urban Institute Press.

Hofferth, S. L., & Chaplin, D. (1994). *Child care quality versus availability: Do we have to trade one for the other?* Washington, DC: The Urban Institute Press.

Howes, C. (1983). Caregiver behavior in center and family day care. *Journal of Applied Developmental Psychology, 4,* 99–107.

Kagan, S. L. (1991). *United we stand: Collaboration for child care and early education services.* New York: Teachers College, Columbia University.

Kagan, S. L. (Ed.). (1993). *The essential functions of the early care and education system: Rationale and definition.* New Haven, CT: *Quality 2000,* Yale University.

Kagan, S. L. (1994). *Defining America's commitments to parents and families: An historical-conceptual perspective.* Commissioned paper for The Ewing Marion Kauffman Foundation, Kansas City, MO.

Kagan, S. L., & Cohen, N. E. (1997). *Not by chance: Creating an early care and education system for America's children.* New Haven, CT: Bush Center in Child Development and Social Policy, Yale University.

Kagan, S. L., Goffin, S., Golub, S., & Pritchard, E. (1995). *Toward systemic reform: Service integration for young children and their families.* Falls Church, VA: National Center for Service Integration.

Kagan, S. L., Moore, E., & Bredekamp, S. (Eds.). (1995). *Reconsidering children's early development and learning: Toward shared beliefs and vocabulary.* Washington, DC: National Education Goals Panel.

Kagan, S. L., Rosenkoetter, S., & Cohen, N. E. (Eds.). (1997). *Considering child-based results for young children: Definitions, desirability, feasibility, and next steps.* New Haven, CT: Bush Center in Child Development and Social Policy, Yale University.

Kamerman, S., & Kahn, A. (1995). *Starting right: How America neglects its youngest children and what we can do about it.* New York: Oxford University Press.

Kisker, E., Hofferth, S., Phillips, D., & Farquhar, E. (1991). *A profile of child care settings: Early education and care in 1990: Vol. I.* Princeton, NJ: Mathematica Policy Research.

Knitzer, J., & Page, S. (1996). *Map and track: State initiatives for young children and families.* New York: National Center for Children in Poverty.

Laosa, L. M. (1980). Maternal teaching strategies in Chicano and Anglo-American families: The influence of culture and education on maternal behavior. *Child Development, 51,* 759–65.

Larner, M. (1995). *Linking family support and early childhood programs: Issues, experiences, opportunities.* Chicago: Family Resource Coalition.

Lassegard, E. (1993). Japan. In M. Cochran (Ed.), *International handbook of child care policies and programs* (pp. 313–32). Westport, CT: Greenwood Press.

Lee, L., & Seiderman, E. (1994). *Elements for success: Replicating Parent Services Project.* Fairfax, CA: Parent Services Project.

Love, J. M., Schochet, P. Z., & Meckstroth, A. L. (1996). *Are they in any real danger? What research does – and doesn't – tell us about child care quality and children's well-being.* Princeton, NJ: Mathematica Policy Research.

Marzke, C., & Both, D. (1994). *Getting started: Planning a comprehensive services initiative.* Falls Church, VA: National Center for Service Integration.

Meisels, S. J. (1987). Uses and abuses of developmental screening and school readiness testing. *Young children, 42,* 4–6, 68–73.

Meisels, S. J., & Fenichel, E. (Eds.). (1996). *New visions for the developmental assessment of infants and young Children.* Washington, DC: Zero to Three.

Miller, L. (1995). *Strategies to build and sustain good child care quality during welfare reform.* CCAC Issue Brief #1. New York: Child Care Action Campaign.

Miller, L., & Anderson, C. (1995). *Empowering parents: Developing support, leadership, advocacy, and activism.* CCAC Issue Brief No. 2. New York: Child Care Action Campaign.

Mitchell, A. (1995). *A proposal for licensing individuals who practice early care and education.* New Haven, CT: *Quality 2000,* Bush Center in Child Development and Social Policy, Yale University.

Mitchell, A. (1996). Licensing: Lessons from other occupations. In S. L. Kagan & N. E. Cohen (Eds.), *Reinventing early care and education: A vision for a quality system* (pp. 101–23). San Francisco: Jossey-Bass.

Mitchell, A., Stoney L., & Dichter, H. (1997). *Financing child care in the United States: An illustrative catalog of current strategies.* Kansas City, MO: The Ewing Marion Kauffman Foundation and The Pew Charitable Trusts.

Moore, E. K. (1997). Race, class, and education. In S. L. Kagan & B. T. Bowman (Eds.), *Leadership in early education* (pp. 69–74). Washington, DC: NAEYC.

Morgan, G., Azer, S. L., Costley, J. B., Genser, A., Goodman, I. F., Lombardi, J., & McGimsey, B. (1993). *Making a career of it: The state of the states report on career development in early care and education.* Boston: The Center for Career Development in Early Care and Education, Wheelock College.

National Association for the Education of Young Children. (1988). Position statement on standardized testing of young children 3 through 8 years of age. *Young Children, 43*(3), 42–7.

National Black Child Development Institute. (1993). *Paths to African American leadership in early childhood education: Constraints and opportunities.* Washington, DC: Author.

National Institute of Child Health and Human Development [NICHD]. (1997, April). *Mother-child interaction and cognitive outcomes associated with early child care: Results of the NICHD study.* Poster symposium presented at the biennial meeting of the Society for Research in Child Development, Washington, DC.

Ojala, M. (1989). Early childhood training, care, and education in Finland. In P. P. Olmsted & D. P. Weikart (Eds.), *How nations serve young children: Profiles of child care and education in 14 countries* (pp. 87–118). Ypsilanti, MI: High/Scope Press.

Parker, F. L., Robinson, R., Sambrano, S., Piotrkowski, C., Hagen, J., Randolph, S., & Baker, A. (Eds.). (1992, January). *New directions in child and family research: Shaping Head Start in the 90's.* Conference Proceedings. Washington, DC: Administration on Children, Youth and Families, the Administration for Children and Families, Department of Health and Human Services.

Pascal, C., Bertram, T., & Heaslip, P. (1991). *Comparative directory of initial training for early years teachers.* Worcester, England. Association of Teacher Education in Europe, Early Years Working Group.

Phillips, D. A. (Ed.). (1995). *Child care for low-income families: Summary of two workshops.* Washington, DC: National Academy Press.

Phillips, D. A., & Howes, C. (1987). Indicators of quality in child care: Review of research. In D. Phillips (Ed.), *Quality in child care: What does the research tell us?* (pp. 1–19). Washington, DC: NAEYC.

Phillips, D. A., Lande, J., & Goldberg, M. (1990). The state of child care regulation: A comparative analysis. *Early Childhood Research Quarterly, 5,* 151–79.

Phillips, D. A., Mekos, M., Scarr, S., McCartney, M., & Abbott-Shim, M. (in press). *Within and beyond the classroom door: Defining quality in typical child care.*

Phillips, D. A., Voran, M., Kisker, E., Howes, C., & Whitebook, M. (1994). Child care for children in poverty: Opportunity or inequality? *Child Development, 65,* 440–56.

Poersch, N., Adams, G., & Sandfort, J. (1994). *Child care and development: Key facts.* Washington, DC: Children's Defense Fund.

Powell, D. R. (1989). *Families and early childhood programs.* Washington, DC: National Association for the Education of Young Children.

Pritchard, E. (1996). Training and professional development: International approaches. In S. L. Kagan & N. E. Cohen (Eds.), *Reinventing early care and education: A vision for a quality system* (pp. 124–41). San Francisco: Jossey-Bass.

Richardson, G., & Marx, E. (1989). *A welcome for every child: How France achieves quality in child care – Practical ideas for the United States.* New York: The French–American Foundation.

Ruopp, R., Travers, J., Glantz, F., & Coelen, C. (1979). *Children at the center: Final results of the National Day Care Study.* Boston: Abt Associates.

Schorr, L. B. (1994). The case for shifting to results-based accountability. In N. Young, S. Gardner, S. Coley, L. Schorr, & C. Bruner (Eds.), *Making a difference: Moving to outcome-based accountability for comprehensive service reforms* (pp. 13–28). Falls Church, VA: National Center for Service Integration.

Schweinhart, L. J., Barnes, H. V., & Weikart, D. P., with Barnett, W. S. & Epstein, A. S. (1993). *Significant benefits: The High/Scope Perry Preschool Study through age 27.* Ypsilanti, MI: High/Scope Press.

Scurria, K. L. (1996). Regulation: Alternative approaches from other fields. In S. L. Kagan & N. E. Cohen (Eds.), *Reinventing early care and education: A vision for a quality system* (pp. 142–57). San Francisco: Jossey-Bass.

Shinn, M., Galinsky, E., & Gulcur, L. (1990). *The role of child care centers in the lives of parents.* New York: Department of Psychology, New York University.

Shore, R. (1997). *Rethinking the brain: New insights into early development.* Executive summary. New York: Families and Work Institute.

Smith, A. B., & Swain, D. A. (1988). *Childcare in New Zealand: People, programs, politics.* Wellington, New Zealand: Allen & Unwin/Port Nicholson Press.

Staines, G. L., & Galinsky, E. (1991). *Parental leave and productivity: The supervisor's view.* New York: Families and Work Institute.

Sugarman, J. (1993). *Building local strategies for young children and their families.* Washington, DC: Center on Effective Services for Children.

Sugarman, J. (1995). *Thinking about new strategies for programs that serve children, youth and families.* Washington, DC: Center on Effective Services for Children.

U.S. Advisory Commission on Intergovernmental Relations. (1994). *Child care: The need for federal-state-local coordination.* Washington, DC: Author.

U.S. Department of Education. National Center for Education Statistics. (1994). *National public education financial survey for fiscal year 1993.* Washington, DC: Author.

U.S. Department of Education. Office of Educational Research and Improvement. (1996). *Early childhood reform in seven communities.* Washington, DC: Author.

U.S. General Accounting Office. (1993). *Poor preschool-aged children: Numbers increase but most not in preschool.* Washington, DC: Author (93-111).

U.S. General Accounting Office. (1994). *Child care: Working poor and welfare recipients face service gaps.* Washington, DC: Author. (94-87).

U.S. General Accounting Office. (1995a). *Early childhood centers: Services to prepare children for school often limited.* Washington, DC: Author (95-21).

U.S. General Accounting Office. (1995b). *Early childhood programs: Multiple programs and overlapping target groups.* Washington, DC: Author (95-4FS).

West, J., Germino Hausken, E., & Collins, M. (1993). *Profile of preschool children's child care and early care and education participation.* Washington, DC: U.S. Department of Education (NCES 93-133).

West, J., Wright, D., & Germino Hausken, E. (1995). *Child care and early care and education participation of infants, toddlers, and preschoolers*. Washington, DC: U.S. Department of Education (NCES 95-824).

Whitebook, M., Howes, C., & Phillips, D. (1989). *Who cares? Child care teachers and the quality of care in America: Final report of the National Child Care Staffing Study*. Oakland, CA: Child Care Employee Project.

Willer, B., Hofferth, S., Kisker, E., Divine-Hawkins, P., Farquhar, E., & Glantz, F. (1991). *The demand and supply of child care in 1990: Joint findings from the National Child Care Survey 1990 and a profile of child care settings*. Washington, DC: National Association for the Education of Young Children.

Yoshikawa, H. (1995). Long-term effects of early childhood programs on social outcomes and delinquency. *The Future of Children: Long-term outcomes of early childhood programs, 5*(3), 51–75.

CHAPTER SEVENTEEN

Early Childhood Intervention for Low-Income Children and Families

ROBERT HALPERN

This chapter examines historical experience, recent developments, and ongoing issues facing the field of early childhood intervention for low-income children and families. The discussion includes an assessment of the evidence for the effectiveness of particular approaches; lessons learned and continuing questions about program design; and an assessment of progress made toward the development of coherent early childhood intervention systems at local and state levels. The chapter also examines early childhood intervention in the context of larger trends in the human services.

The chapter focuses principally (though not solely) on services for families with children birth to age 3, whose primary objectives are enhanced child rearing and child development, and in some cases improved maternal well-being and child health. These traditional early childhood intervention objectives, and the services that follow from them, increasingly are combined with others, such as adult literacy and employment, and even community development. In fact, it is becoming more difficult, and in some respects less useful, to distinguish early childhood intervention from related fields of service for young families.

As a discrete field, early childhood intervention is at a critical point in its evolution. A number of new assumptions, program approaches, and specific models were introduced during the 1990s. There is now an abundance of practical wisdom and of lessons learned from scores of large and small initiatives, as well as a renewed preoccupation with the importance of the birth-to-3 period in children's lives. A growing, although still small, number

of infancy theorists and researchers are focusing on poverty-related issues, such as the effects of exposure to violence on infants and their families, as well as on those who work with families (see articles in April/May 1996 issue of *Zero To Three*). A number of states and localities have formed commissions or committees to organize the pieces of the early childhood intervention puzzle. In a few cities and states, clusters of providers are getting together in local coordinating bodies (e.g., local area councils and interagency councils) to discuss rationalizing birth-to-3 services, or early childhood services generally. A handful of initiatives are struggling to develop service approaches that cross the boundaries of maternal and child health, child welfare, and early childhood special education.

At the same time, the quantitative research evidence supporting early childhood intervention remains modest at best regardless of the objectives, scope, or approach of particular programs (see, for example, Halpern, 1990b; Barnes, Goodson, & Layzer, 1996). The situation of poor families with young children, particularly the growing proportion of such families residing in the inner city, is as perilous today as at any period in the past thirty years. The larger child development research community continues to view poverty as a complicating variable in its research, not something that has a profound and pervasive influence on, and is a fundamental organizer of, children's and families' lives. Only a handful of educational institutions around the country remain that prepare professionals to work with vulnerable families with children under 3.

Not a single state or city has developed a coherent system of birth-to-3 services or has provided adequate funding for the services that are available. In fact, services for birth-to-3 poor children do not so much constitute a system as a patchwork of categorical purposes and programs. Few of the numerous comprehensive community initiatives sprouting up in urban areas around the country include concrete plans to develop or strengthen early childhood intervention services. The recent Carnegie Corporation report *Turning Points* noted that "community services for families with children under three are few and fragmentary" (Carnegie Corporation, 1996, p. xvi).

In other words, at the end of the twentieth century, we have made progress but are still far from a well-developed, coherent, adequately differentiated service and support system for young families in poverty. To be fair, it is not clear where leadership for developing a vision and plan for early childhood intervention should reside. We are more sensitive now to the importance of involving local communities in designing, governing, and implementing interventions. Yet it is not clear what the most appropriate roles of different community stakeholders ought to be in these tasks. We know now that we can no longer afford to view early childhood intervention for poor families in isolation from the policies, priorities, and practices of the major family support systems: public aid, child welfare, public health, education, and mental health. Yet historically most early childhood intervention for poor families has occurred outside of these systems. Even were public commitment to our youngest families to increase, key questions remain unresolved. It is not clear which families should be the priority focus of service efforts and dollars. It is not easy to know how to take the complex mixture of available approaches and models, lessons learned, and broad principles (e.g., comprehensive, integrated, empowering and family centered) and turn them into a coherent system. Many of the unanswered questions about the scope and purpose of early childhood intervention have no single answer.

POOR FAMILIES WITH VERY YOUNG CHILDREN: A BRIEF PORTRAIT

At any point in time, there are about 12 million children under the age of 3 in the United States. Of these,

three million are poor by governmental standards (Carnegie Corporation, 1996), and another million to a million and a half hover just above poverty. Pregnant women are also a potential target population for early intervention services; at any point in time, there are slightly more than one million poor women who are pregnant. About two-thirds of poor infants and toddlers live in mother-only families, and until the demise of the AFDC program, about two-thirds lived in families supported by welfare. (From the perspective of the welfare system, at any point in time about 60% of AFDC families had at least one child under age 3.) Over half of poor infants and toddlers live in families in which parents have not completed high school, and about half live in families in which the mother began childbearing in her teens (National Center for Children in Poverty, 1990).

It hardly bears noting that poverty places infants and toddlers at heightened risk for a host of problems, beginning the moment they are conceived. Poverty significantly heightens the risk of exposure to toxic substances in utero, poor birth outcomes, constitutional vulnerabilities (e.g., subtle central nervous system damage, malnutrition, postneonatal mortality, asthma, and other chronic health problems), and elevated blood lead levels, among other health problems (Klerman, 1991). Poverty and its correlates heighten the risk of inattentive or erratic parental care (Halpern, 1993) and, in the extreme, this risk of being removed from home and placed in foster care for reasons of abuse or neglect. Children under age 3, particularly babies, are the fastest-growing category of children entering foster care, and most of those children are poor. Of the 50,000 or so children under age 2 in foster care in the United States, perhaps 70% are from poor families. (A recent study in New York City found the rate of placement into foster care is 1.45 per 100 children in the poorest neighborhoods versus .29 per 100 children in the wealthiest [Wulczyn, 1996].)

A growing proportion of poor families with very young children, close to 40%, live in inner-city neighborhoods with high concentrations of poverty. The majority of such families do what they can under extraordinarily difficult circumstances to assure that their children's developmental needs are met (Anderson, 1994; Hans, Ray, & Halpern, 1995; Nightingale, 1993). Yet the correlates of inner-city poverty can undermine even the most adaptive and resourceful parents' efforts (Halpern, 1993). Moreover, a significant percentage of young inner-city parents – perhaps 20 to 30% – lack even the most minimal personal and social resources to meet their children's needs. These are young adults with personal histories marked by adversity in many spheres, including disruptions in their own early caregiving; inadequate nurturance, rejection, or both; parental substance abuse; family violence; and difficulties in school. The effects of these difficult personal histories carry over into the present, affecting not only parenting but also many other domains, including adult relationships, capacity to finish school and hold on to work, physical and mental health, and managing household resources.

It is no accident that the most vulnerable families – those with the greatest number and severity of difficulties – tend disproportionately to live in inner-city neighborhoods. In a vicious cycle, families with multiple vulnerabilities contribute to the stressfulness of these neighborhoods, and their own difficulties are exacerbated by the fact that so many others around them have serious problems. Poverty does not always create family vulnerabilities, but it almost always exacerbates their effects, and sometimes activates them.

EVOLUTION OF THE EARLY CHILDHOOD INTERVENTION FIELD: 1960–1990

As a rule, children's early experience in the United States "is associated with the home – a private realm into which many policy makers have been reluctant to intrude" (Carnegie Corporation, 1994, p. xiv). For poor families, however, this rule has been followed more in the breach than in the observance. Charity agents, social workers, nurses, home economists, parent educators, child development specialists, and others have been intervening in the lives of poor families with young children for more than 100 years. Poor families' child-rearing practices have been criticized for not reflecting prevailing prescriptions (i.e., middle-class norms) in supervision, management and discipline of young children, feeding, care of illness, toilet training, sleeping arrangements, and verbal interaction (Halpern, 1998). Poor parents have been accused of neglecting their young children, not preparing them for the demands of industrial society, and exposing them to immoral influences (Halpern, 1998). Indeed, poor parents

themselves have been viewed like children, in need of supervision. Crocker (1992, p. 50) quoted Leander Adams, who conducted a 1910 study of living conditions in Indianapolis's immigrant neighborhoods: "Like young children, they [immigrants] should have their actions regulated by authority, until they reach a point of understanding."

Within the framework of this larger history, the conception and practice of early childhood intervention as such is now about 35 years old. The field emerged in the early 1960s with the home visiting programs of Ira Gordon, David Weikart, Phyllis Levenstein, and Martin and Cynthia Deutsch (see Beller, 1979). These programs were premised on two sets of ideas: First, a growing body of basic research in psychology suggesting that early experience had a powerful influence on later ability, that the birth-to-3 period was a critical one in development, and that intelligence was not fixed, as was commonly assumed, but rather malleable or plastic; second, the idea that poor mothers did an inadequate job of stimulating, modeling, and supporting their infants' cognitive and language development and, therefore, of preparing their children for school.

The general approach of these early childhood intervention pioneers was to try to teach mothers to be better teachers of their children, to provide direct stimulation to the children themselves, or both. Mothers were taught games and activities that they could in turn play with their children; were encouraged to view feeding, bathing, diaper-changing, and related activities as opportunities for learning; and encouraged to talk to their children as much as possible. Some programs focused primarily on cognitive development: sensorimotor skills, object permanence, exploratory behavior, and so on. Others focused more on language. For example, Phyllis Levenstein's Verbal Interaction Project focused on "giving information by describing the label, form, color and size of the object . . . eliciting [verbal] response of the child through questions . . ." (Beller, 1979, p. 858). A few of the projects also focused on encouraging mothers to say and do things that strengthened children's sense of efficacy and self-esteem.

The overwhelming majority of families targeted and served by these early programs were African American, leading some observers to suggest that they reflected little more than "institutional racism." Baratz and Baratz (1971) saw an "expanding web of concern" that ultimately questioned the whole pattern of life in poor, African American communities: "Postulation of one deficit which is unsuccessfully dealt with by intervention programs then leads to the discovery of more basic and fundamental deficits. Remediation or enrichment gradually broadens its scope of concern from the fostering of language competence to a broad-based restructuring of the entire cultural system" (p. 117).

In the 1960s, the theories and assumptions of the parent education interventions were influential in framing the new field of early childhood intervention. In practical terms, they were overshadowed by the growth and struggles of the Head Start program. (Although Head Start did not focus on families with children birth to 3 until 1995, its early history provided an important base for developments in services for such families in the 1970s and 1980s.) Some of the premises underlying Head Start were similar to those underlying the experimental home visiting programs (i.e., the research on early childhood as a "critical period" in development and the findings from "culture-of-poverty" researchers on the deficits in poor children's early family lives). Yet Head Start was designed to compensate for inadequate early childhood parenting in poor families as much as to strengthen it. It was assumed that, on their own, poor parents did not have the wherewithal to prepare their children for school.

Head Start emerged from a confluence of events. The Kennedy family supported a foundation that funded the work of Susan Gray's Early Training Project in Nashville, Tennessee, a preschool program designed to prevent "progressive" retardation (i.e., boost IQ) and foster school readiness in poor African American children. Gray's approach is illustrated in this anecdote cited by Zigler and Muenchow (1992, p. 5): "The children loved to ride tricycles, but were only allowed to do so if they asked for them properly and identified the particular tricycle they wished to ride." Teachers in this program also "read to children several times a day." Gray's work was echoed in a number of "experimental" preschool interventions around the country, as well as those being run by the Ford Foundation's Gray Areas programs, the latter of which provided models of what a Head Start program might look like in a poor urban community (Halpern, 1995, pp. 93–100).

Sargent Shriver, head of the Office of Economic Opportunity (OEO) – the agency charged with promulgating the War on Poverty – sensed that a program for preschool children would be attractive, even to the most conservative constituencies. In early 1965, OEO assembled a panel of social scientists and charged them with outlining a model early childhood intervention strategy. The result was a comprehensive program, an ambitious collection of health services (including screening and immunization), nutrition, family social services (principally case management), and community development activities, surrounding a core of preschool education for 3- and 4-year-old children. Parents were to have a significant role in the program, not just as targets of parent education, but as partners with professionals. The advisors recommended a small pilot program, serving at most some hundreds of children. Politics, however, demanded a much more dramatic gesture, and Head Start was launched as an eight-week summer program for nearly a half-million children.

Hundreds of poor communities had to be stimulated to apply for Head Start grants, and some 40,000 teachers had to be trained in a matter of a few months. Most of the initial applicants were school districts. After the first two summers, Head Start was converted to a ten-month program, and, with assistance and prodding from OEO staff, hundreds of community-based organizations, especially the new community action agencies, prepared applications to sponsor Head Start programs. Most local sponsors started from scratch, bringing community representatives together either during or after the application process to elaborate a local program. This new freedom to create programs – combined with the actual need to do so – was both exhilarating and, at times, paralyzing. Community residents charged with program design were often strongly resistant to accepting assistance from early childhood professionals. This was at times painful to the latter group, who felt forced to observe what seemed like a needless struggle to invent and refine that which already had been invented and refined in model programs, with well-developed philosophy, curricula, and teacher-training approaches.

Professionals, usually in the role of resource people, nonetheless had much to learn themselves. At program-planning meetings, they had to learn to let their questions to community people about program design issues "seep and soak through several hundred years of never having been asked" (Greenberg,

1990, p. 96). Head Start was in some ways profoundly different from the professionally run nursery school programs with which they were familiar. It was designed as much to be a vehicle for adult and community development as for child development, and most early childhood professionals had little experience in these former areas. Head Start was intended to be an institution that drew its life and energy from the community and that placed professionals who were not from the community in an ambiguous position.

Tensions about quality pervaded the early years of Head Start (and remain to the present day). Its rapid early growth, primarily for political reasons, made it impossible to build program foundations carefully. Visitors to local Head Start programs in the early years more often than not found either rote, mechanical drill or aimless play with too little structure and purpose (see Zigler & Muenchow, 1992, pp. 40–8). Teachers had little or no repertoire of learning games and activities to draw on to strengthen children's language skills and vocabulary, auditory and visual discrimination skills, problem-solving skills, and others. There were few or no materials for science, math, or art activities. Such administrative functions as program planning, staff supervision, and financial management were also managed erratically.

Underlying concerns about Head Start's quality was the question of which of the many purposes of Head Start was most important: the best possible preschool classroom experience for children, the employment and empowerment of parents and other community members, or the organization of the community? These questions related in one way or another to the purpose of parent involvement and the role of parents in the program. At one extreme was the view that the main purpose of Head Start was to create alternative environments for poor children, different from those of family and even community. A middle position held that it was futile to try to counter children's larger social ecology (parents, home, and community) with a program that served them a few hours a day, a few days a week. Rather, intervention efforts had to try to take that ecology into account and strengthen it. Such efforts would include parent education about child rearing and related matters and support for parents' own efforts to grow and develop. At the other extreme were

those who believed that the most important thing Head Start could do, and the only thing that would make it effective, was to empower parents politically. What would most help poor children would be to see their parents (who after all were their primary role models) as decision makers, organizing and acting collectively to address community problems and meet needs. A variation of the latter two views held that it was critical for parents to be involved in Head Start, but primarily in their children's education. Children would thereby see and feel their parents' commitment to education, and parents would see their children and their children's actions in a new light (Zigler & Muenchow, 1992, p. 101). For example, a parent might observe a teacher praise a child's artwork, and thus see that artwork and her child's skills differently, as well as how positively her child responds to praise.

Beyond problems of classroom and management quality, and tensions about purpose, Head Start was developing numerous strengths. It was a national program – with goals and standards set outside local communities – that nonetheless managed to meet the needs of those communities. It was informal and open to, indeed not differentiated from, its surrounding community. It provided the beginning steps of a career pathway for some parents. Head Start programs provided badly needed health services and nutrition and were helping families with a variety of concrete problems. Head Start programs served as a center for community discussion of important child-rearing issues. Parents joined together to discuss and argue about what their Head Start center should try to accomplish, who their children were after all, what their ideals for their children ought to be, and the implications for their own roles as parents. Head Start was a lively institution that strengthened social connections within poor communities, which it did with chronically inadequate funding. Staff salaries were so low that they rarely lifted poor staff out of poverty.

Too early in its history (1965–1966) Head Start experienced pressure from Congress to evaluate its effects on children. A series of local studies was funded by the Office of Economic Opportunity, mostly of high-quality programs. Despite the breadth of purpose of the program, early studies focused largely on IQ effects, finding modest short-term gains that soon disappeared (see Zigler & Muenchow, 1992, ch. 3).

In 1968, a major national study was launched by the Westinghouse Learning Corporation, using a host of child measures, which seemed to find little positive effect of Head Start in the early elementary school years (Cicirelli, 1969). The study had numerous sampling and methodological flaws; for example, 70% of children sampled had participated only in summer programs, although by then Head Start was a 10-month program.

In retrospect, it was clearly inappropriate to make inferences about Head Start as whole, given the diversity of local programs, and it was inappropriate to seek definitive judgment about impact so early in its life as a program. Nonetheless, Head Start proponents were in a delicate position. In an increasingly conservative, and war-weary, political climate, any vulnerability in a program was an excuse to decrease funding. Despite the obstacles, Head Start would survive. Its Washington managers used the equivocal findings of the early research to argue that to be truly effective Head Start had to become a national laboratory for developing new approaches to helping poor children and families. Perhaps, they reasoned, 3 or 4 years of age was too late to help children living in poverty, and interventions that did not alter children's family environments were destined to be too weak. These lines of thinking suggested the need to develop and test new approaches, which focused on the earliest years and on parents themselves (Skerry, 1983, p. 22). Head Start leadership initiated a program of research and development on birth-to-3 services for poor families that would continue for almost three decades, but which immediately provided the scientific cover needed to keep the larger preschool program alive.

NEW THREADS OF EARLY CHILDHOOD INTERVENTION

The parent education models of Gordon, Weikart, Levenstein, and the Deutches had provided the outline and prototype for a new type of human service intervention. During the 1970s and 1980s, a variety of theoretical developments and social preoccupations contributed in turn to the multiplication of early childhood intervention approaches and its gradual establishment as a distinct, albeit heterogeneous, branch of the human services.

This period brought a virtual explosion of research and clinical attention to infancy, primarily in psychology and psychiatry (see, for example, Call, Galenson, & Tyson, 1983). Research and clinical work highlighted the enormous amount and range of developmental activity occurring during infancy, including not only cognitive but also socioemotional development, development of self-regulatory capacities, and a sense of self in relation to others. It generated a new conception of the infant as an active, perceiving, social being. It identified new sources of risk in infancy (e.g., maternal depression, attachment disorders, and regulatory and sensory disorders). A small group of researchers also explored the contribution of the infant to the parent–child relationship. These new lines of research redirected interventionists' attention to the birth-to-3 period and reinforced the global belief that had emerged in the 1960s – that experience in the earliest years was the most critical determinant of later outcomes for children.

At the same time, led by Urie Bronfenbrenner, a few researchers began applying an ecological framework to child development studies (see, for example, Bronfenbrenner, 1979). They examined how factors beyond the mother–child relationship – other family members, parents' social support networks, community characteristics, and at the broadest level, race, class, and economic arrangements – affected child development and the mother–child relationship and how different kinds of factors mutually influenced each other. Somewhat related to ecological child development research were the relatively new fields of family research and family therapy. The ideas from these fields also suggested less focus on parents, and the parent–child relationship, and more on families as a whole, and provided researchers and interventionists new ways of looking at poor and vulnerable families. As Ooms (1996) pointed out, systems theories were "non-blaming," less linear, and less cause-and-effect oriented than the traditional linear thinking of developmental researchers. This contributed to a growing focus, at least in rhetoric, on family strengths.

Clinical Infant Programs

In the early 1970s, the first line of theory and research led to a new clinical thread of early childhood intervention that focused on therapeutic work in families with vulnerable parent–infant relationships. Although families served by the new clinical infant programs were often poor, poverty was viewed as a compounding stress rather than as a central issue in working with a family. Clinical infant work had a number of pioneers, foremost of whom was Selma Fraiberg and her colleagues at the University of Michigan's Child Development Project. They developed a tripartite intervention approach that included developmental guidance/supportive intervention, brief crisis intervention, and a new helping modality called *parent–infant psychotherapy* (Fraiberg, Shapiro, & Cherniss, 1983). Families received one, two, or all three of these, depending on clinical assessment of the family situation, apparent causes of parenting difficulties, basic parenting capacities, and developmental or psychological readiness to enter a formally therapeutic relationship.

The most innovative of these three modalities, parent–infant psychotherapy, drew on theory from both child development and psychoanalysis. As in traditional psychodynamic therapy, the therapist used the positive and negative transference to the helper as a mechanism to illuminate issues and foster change. One difference was that the goal was not change in personality but in capacity to nurture. The therapist worked to help the parent recognize the effects of such formative experiences as loss, abandonment, and unavailable parenting on her reactions to, "representations" of, and behavior toward her own baby. Through that recognition she could free herself to some degree from that past and find "new solutions to old problems" (Fraiberg et al., 1983, p. 60; see also Fraiberg, Adelson, & Shapiro, 1975). The presence of the baby during therapeutic sessions provided both an additional source of information about the actual qualities of the relationship and another basis for intervention. The therapist took her cue not only from what she learned of the parent's own nurturance history, and the meaning of the baby to the parent (e.g., the feelings that the baby evoked in the parent), but also from close observation of parent and infant together.

Much of the help some families received was at their home during home visits. The team was persistent in reaching out to families who missed scheduled appointments. When necessary, the therapist provided concrete guidance on caring for infants

and helped the family address situational stresses (e.g., problems with public aid or a landlord) and family crises. In other words, the therapist was much more active and flexible in her role than would have been the case in traditional therapy.

Other approaches to clinical infant work did not employ parent–infant psychotherapy but rather infused its principles into supportive work with parents. For example, Sally Provence and colleagues developed the Yale Child Welfare Research Program, in which a highly skilled interdisciplinary team consisting of a clinical social worker, nurse, pediatrician, day-care worker, and psychologist provided an individually tailored mix of supportive services to young families experiencing parenting difficulties (Provence & Naylor, 1983). The program included twice-monthly home visits by a social worker, primary health care, high-quality day care, and developmental exams. During the home visits, and in informal activities in a remodeled house in the neighborhood where participating families lived, the social workers focused on attending to mothers' own "psychological neediness and stress" (Provence & Naylor, 1983, p. 20). The idea was that before some parents would be able to nurture their children, or tolerate their children being cared for by others (i.e., the day-care providers), they had to be nurtured themselves.

The clinical thread of early childhood intervention remained modest in size and impact throughout the 1970s and 1980s and focused in a few clinical/academic centers where the kind of sophisticated training needed for such work was provided. Practitioners from the medical and mental health fields interested in infancy work received some exposure to infant mental health theory, principles, and methods through the activities of the National Center for Clinical Infant Programs (later renamed Zero To Three: The National Center for Infants, Toddlers and Families) and a handful of academic centers. Some of the more accessible elements and insights from this approach – for example, taking one's cue as an interventionist from observation of parent and infant together; helping the parent appreciate the baby's perspective or feelings by speaking for the baby; recognizing that being active and reliable in meeting concrete needs is important both for itself and because it affects the way parents experience relationships – filtered into the broader early childhood intervention field. However, community-based social service and child welfare providers, who had the most contact with the growing numbers of young, multiply vulnerable families in poor communities, had little direct exposure to either the ideas or the model itself.

Ecologically Oriented and Systems Approaches

If clinical attention to and research on infancy suggested the importance of looking deeply into the distinct dynamics and issues in each parent–infant relationship as a basis for intervention, ecological and systems theories suggested looking beyond that relationship. Already in the 1960s, questions had been raised about the decontextualized way in which early parenting interventions had been conceptualized and implemented. Building on that essentially political critique, Bronfenbrenner and others argued for what they called "ecologically valid interventions"; for instance, the need to focus attention on the whole family, the value of strengthening parents' social support networks, and of linking families to community resources (Bronfenbrenner, 1987, p. xiii). Yet systems-oriented theories also implied that everything was connected. This meant, for better or worse, that interventions needed to be more ambitious and holistic (and led eventually to the current preoccupation with comprehensive interventions).

One can trace the growing influence of ecological and family systems theories by comparing the two best-known federal demonstration programs of that era: the Parent Child Development Centers (PCDCs), which involved Parent Child Centers in Birmingham, Houston, and New Orleans, and the Child and Family Resource Programs (CFRPs), an eleven-site demonstration. (The PCDC experiment grew out of the Parent Child Center [PCC] program. The PCCs were envisioned initially to become a nationwide network of multipurpose family centers providing parent education and health and social services to poor families with children birth to 3 years of age. A variety of factors, most notably a deteriorating funding climate, prevented that vision from becoming reality.) In the PCDCs it was possible to see the beginnings of an ecological and systems perspective. Program materials acknowledged

the importance of addressing "the complex of problems of poor families" (Andrews et al., 1982). All three PCDC programs provided or linked families to health, social, and other corollary services. Within a framework of common elements, the three local programs were given flexibility to design their approaches on the basis of local needs and circumstances. At the same time, their interventions were strongly premised and focused on changing maternal knowledge, behavior, and attitudes. The specific approaches included parenting and child development classes for mothers; maternal observation of and participation in infant nursery activities; and home visits (Andrews et al., 1982).

The Child and Family Resource Programs reflected much more fully the influence of ecological theory and systems ideas. The programs were based on the idea that in order for parenting programs to promote child development, they had to concentrate equally on specific parenting competencies and on the full range of family and neighborhood conditions that impinged on parenting (Hewett, 1982). The heart (and for many participating families the extent) of the program was a monthly home visit by specially trained community members, for up to two years. Home visitors tended to focus on helping families gain access to other services and resources, helping with whatever problems preoccupied families at the moment, and generally supporting families' coping efforts. One key assumption of CFRP was that over time, families would be better able to act as their own service brokers and problem managers and that they as well as the home visitors would then be able to shift their attention to parenting and child development. Yet this did not occur. Most home visitors had limited or no preparation for work focused on parenting and child development issues. As such, it was far more comfortable simply to remain preoccupied with the endless stream of immediate, concrete problems experienced by program participants.

In the late 1970s, the idea of early childhood intervention as family support coalesced under the banner of a new program movement by that name. This movement caught and built on a public feeling (common in American history) that the social fabric was unraveling – that family life was breaking down and communal support systems deteriorating. It also drew on growing loss of faith in prevailing helping services and helping professionals.

Services were under fire for being fragmented, incoherent, unresponsive, and crisis-driven; service providers for paternalism, putting self-interest ahead of family interests, pathologizing families, failing to respect families' cultural traditions, and related sins (Halpern, 1998). Family support programs were envisioned as a means of simultaneously strengthening informal support ties among families and creating a new model of helping services. They would bring families together to provide mutual support around parenting and other tasks. The programs would build on family strengths and follow families' lead. Staff would respect families' culture and child-rearing traditions and serve as a bridge between local child-rearing norms and those of the larger society. Programs would be conveniently located, with few barriers to eligibility and participation (Family Resource Coalition, 1996; Weiss & Halpern, 1988).

The family support movement was not focused originally on poor families. Rather, its proponents argued that families across the income spectrum were increasingly isolated from traditional informal sources of support. Nonetheless, this movement quickly began to influence rhetoric and design in the field of early childhood intervention for poor families. Even though somewhat global, family support principles reenergized hundreds of small, community-based programs in low-income communities. They served as the template for a growing number of federal and state initiatives targeted at particular populations, such as teen parents, and parents at risk of child abuse or neglect (see below).

At the same time, the family support movement created new tensions within the early childhood intervention field. For instance, it implicitly questioned the prevailing focus on strengthening child rearing, in some ways obscuring the original reason for being of intervention programs. In its deemphasis on (and devaluing of) professional knowledge, skills, and approaches, the family support movement left the paraprofessional providers operating under its banner unprepared to assess, acknowledge, and deal with the many family vulnerabilities observed or brought to them. Family support programs were ambivalent about whether they even were a formal helping service. Many proponents viewed family support programs as a new community institution that would supplant the historic role of social services. In that light, staff of such programs were viewed as community members helping other community members, with little need for a strong knowledge base, training, or supervision. During the 1980s, as family support programs in low-income communities began to see and serve greater numbers of highly vulnerable families, their ambiguous identity and sense of purpose, and diffuse principles and methods, contributed to growing internal pressures. Without access to the kinds of conceptual tools, detailed "process" descriptions and case vignettes, and intense training and support structures for frontline workers characteristic of clinical infant programs, their staff increasingly felt overwhelmed.

In spite of theoretical differences and practical struggles, the early childhood intervention programs that emerged in the 1970s and 1980s were important for a number of reasons. They infused human development theory and research more directly into the world of social services. In their diversity, from clinical infant programs at one end to family support programs at the other, they suggested a continuum of services for more and less vulnerable young families. Collectively, early childhood intervention programs embodied helping principles useful to all kinds of services and service conditions: They met people where they lived, not only physically but also psychologically. Most programs and providers considered it their responsibility to reach out to isolated or distrustful families and nurture their capacity to use support. In the framework of families' own efforts to master parenting and other developmental tasks, and to cope with the difficulties associated with poverty, the programs provided emotional support, encouragement, and assistance. They had the flexibility to mold to unique patterns of stress and support of different populations in different community contexts. Finally, these programs were inherently optimistic, focused on promoting development rather than treating dysfunction and on working with young families, for whom the future still seemed open.

1990s: NEW ASSUMPTIONS, PURPOSES, APPROACHES

"New" Concepts and Concerns

Although there are always clusters of ideas, and particular language, floating in and out of the vision of the early childhood intervention field, each period has had its key concepts. New concepts do not so much replace older ones as get added in to an increasingly complex mix. As alluded to earlier, in the late 1980s and early 1990s, there was a call for family-centered, empowering or strengths-oriented, and culturally sensitive services. More recently the field has become enamored of comprehensive and continuous services, collaboration among service providers, and the idea of a continuum of services. Some researchers and practitioners are also promoting services that have what is called a two-generation focus.

Perhaps the most widely used of the current service-shaping concepts is that of comprehensive services. Its popularity may derive from its identification as a key principle of effective services by Schorr (1988). The concept also has roots in developments in early intervention for children with disabilities (i.e., P.L. 99-457 called for comprehensive services). The concept of comprehensiveness is translated in widely differing ways in initiatives and programs that subscribe to it. Most commonly, it means directly providing a few services and referring or linking children and families to most others, often under a case-management regime. Less commonly it means developing cooperative agreements with other providers or contracting or otherwise arranging for specialized service providers to provide specific services, hold slots, and so forth. Services provided directly are often either those that one has been providing, or could provide best, given an agency's mission and expertise, or those needed services that cannot be secured from other sources.

Another concept that is found in a number of recent initiatives is that of continuous, or "seamless," service from birth to age 5. (This concept is also found in the language of P.L. 99-457.) The general idea is that poor children and families should not have any gaps in attention or service from the time a child is born to the time he or she enters school and that services to particular families would evolve in relation to their emergent support needs. This concept, which may have originated in the Syracuse Family Demonstration Project (Lally, Mangione, & Honig, 1988), was adopted by the Child and Family Resource Program demonstration and has been a principle in many Head Start–related demonstrations ever since. A related concept, referring more to the service system as a whole, is that of a continuum of local services. This notion refers to the idea that at any moment in time local communities should have a variety of types of services available to young families (e.g., a core of nonspecialized supportive services, surrounded by specialized services such as mental health and substance-abuse treatment).

Still another recent construct influencing the early childhood intervention field is that of two-generation programs (Smith, 1995). From the beginning, there has been a paradox, some might say an inherent limitation, in early childhood intervention: Poor children, like their more advantaged peers, cannot wait for their parents or their family's life situation to change. They need the things they need – love, protection, consistent attention, and regular structure – when they need them. Yet the immediacy of children's developmental needs stands in sharp contrast to the difficulty of influencing the nature and quality of the care they receive, not to mention their family's basic life situation. Moreover, it is neither possible nor desirable to work around the key figures in infants' and toddlers' lives.

In the late 1980s and early 1990s, this paradox rose to the surface in thinking about the design of early childhood intervention. Some observers looked at what they saw as weak evidence in support of discrete intervention approaches – preschool education, parent support and education (and its cousin, family support), and adult development/welfare to work – and concluded that the problem was that each lacked what the other had. Each discrete approach appeared too limited, or indirect, for its own specific reasons. Preschool education did not affect children's basic circumstances and life situation, and these have a far greater influence on children's well-being and future chances than a one- or two-year preschool experience. Parenting intervention alone was viewed as too weak because altering parenting beliefs and practices is complicated and difficult. Even the most skillful interventions, such as those described earlier in the discussion of clinical infant programs, took years to produce modest effects. Preparing poor parents for work, and then helping them learn to become steady workers, likewise was proving a difficult and slow task, often taking years (Herr & Halpern, 1993). There was virtually no literature concerning the effects of parents' struggle to leave welfare on young children's well-being and development.

By implication, it was inferred that if direct developmental services to children, efforts to support and strengthen parenting, and work-preparation approaches were combined, they would complement each other – fill in the efficacy gaps, as it were – to produce an adequately strong approach. This, largely speaking, was the rationale for what came to be called the two-generation programs. Additional, but related, arguments held that two-generation programs addressed a wider range of risk factors more directly, created the possibility for synergistic effects, and created more pathways for positive change in families' lives (Smith & Zaslow, 1995).

From the perspective of the early childhood intervention field, the two-generation approach purportedly put adult goals, particularly movement into the labor force, more squarely and unambiguously in the foreground, adding child care or preschool as an element designed to assure that children's developmental needs were met. Some of the demonstration models of the 1970s and 1980s, such as the CFRPs, had given minor attention to adult development goals. Yet there had been a certain ambivalence about moving parents into the workforce – a fear that such a push would shortchange children.

Recent Initiatives

Along with new concepts, the 1990s have brought a new wave of experimental multisite demonstrations (sponsored by the federal government or major private foundations), as well as waxing and waning program models. The former include the Comprehensive Child Development Program, New Chance, Even Start, the Infant Health and Development Program, and Healthy Start (an infant mortality reduction initiative of the Health Resources Services Administration). New or newly popular program models include AVANCE and Healthy Families America (based on Hawaii's Healthy Start model, designed to prevent child abuse and neglect). As ever, new initiatives and approaches in the early childhood intervention field both reflect the language of the era and remain diverse in assumption, purpose, and content.

COMPREHENSIVE CHILD DEVELOPMENT PROGRAM (CCDP). The CCDP, begun in 1989, was the next in the long line of multisite demonstrations initiated by the federal Administration for Children,

Youth, and Families (Smith & Lopez, 1994). It was a twenty-one-site demonstration (sixteen urban and five rural) intended to provide continuous, comprehensive, integrated services to selected populations of low-income families, from birth to age 5. The general program model mandated a wide range of services: for children, screening and assessment, individual plans, primary health care, child development "experiences," and child care; for parents, health and mental health services, parent education (often using a curriculum), work preparation experiences; and for families, regular home visits and case management. Local CCDP projects "were designed to build on ... existing services instead of creating a wholly new set of services" (St. Pierre, Layzer, Goodson, & Bernstein, 1997, p. 2-1). In other words, mandated services could be provided through referral. The rationale was the desire to avoid duplicating existing services.

Although CCDP was envisioned as a long-term intervention, the majority of families only participated for one or two years. Families received home visits every week or two in the early months, with visits gradually becoming less frequent. Most services beyond home visiting were brokered (as the model had anticipated) rather than provided directly. The majority of service brokering (51%) involved referrals; 26% through contracts; and 23% through cooperative agreements (St. Pierre, Goodson, Layzer, & Bernstein, 1997). In other words, CCDP did not provide a strong test of the efficacy of comprehensive services.

The evaluation of CCDP, which employed an experimental design, was undertaken by Abt Associates (St. Pierre, Goodson, Layzer, & Bernstein, 1997). The evaluators examined a wide range of domains – parenting, parent–child interaction, parental problem-solving strategies, parental mental health, parental employment, child cognitive and language development, child behavior, child socioemotional problems, family self-sufficiency, maternal and child health status, and health care utilization – at various time points from infancy through age 5. Virtually no program favoring outcomes was found. One exception was that treatment mothers reported spending more time with very young children than controls and were observed to be a bit more sensitive to children's cues. Analyses designed to detect positive effects for participants with certain characteristics or higher levels of participation also found no effects; site-level analyses found only one of twenty-one sites with some positive outcomes. It can be argued that the evaluator should have restricted outcomes analyses to families that participated for three or four years, the "intended" length of intervention. Aside from the fact that it is important to examine program effects under average-expectable conditions, that is, with families who participate for the typical length of time, it should be noted that the evaluator did in fact examine effects for the more restricted group and found tiny program-favoring differences that were "not educationally meaningful" (St. Pierre et al., 1997, p. 7-3).

NEW CHANCE. The New Chance demonstration was designed, managed, and evaluated by the Manpower Demonstration Research Corporation (Quint, Polit, Bos, & Cave, 1994). It involved a highly structured, strictly sequenced, intensive eighteen-month intervention for older teen and young adult parents on welfare. During Phase 1, all participants attended a school-like program from 9 A.M. to 3 P.M., five days a week. Classes focused on adult basic education and GED preparation, "employability development," parent education, and some skills training. Phase 2 included vocational preparation, work internships, and job placement assistance. Direct developmental services to children were not emphasized. Onsite developmental child care was "encouraged but not required" (Quint & Egeland, 1995, p. 111). In fact, participants' children received child care of varying quality. Families also received case management services. The goals of New Chance were to prepare parents for work and link them to jobs, improve parenting and child development, and encourage participants to postpone further childbearing.

The evaluation of New Chance, like that of the Comprehensive Child Development program, used multiple measures and covered multiple domains. No effects of New Chance were found on work-related outcomes, parenting, maternal emotional well-being, maternal literacy, or maternal health and health self-care behaviors. The one program-favoring effect found was on GED attainment (43% for participants versus 30% for controls). Rates of absenteeism and attrition were high; the investigators noted that at many sites only half the participants who were still enrolled were present on any given day (Quint, Polit, Bose, & Cave, 1994, p. 61). Because participants could not gain access to phase 2 services until they finished Phase 1, many who wished to seek work were not allowed to do so. There apparently was no effort by MDRC to alter the program model as it became clear that the model was inappropriate for many participants.

INFANT HEALTH AND DEVELOPMENT PROGRAM. This multisite experiment fit into the historic model of efforts to improve the cognitive and language development and increase the IQ of poor and otherwise vulnerable young children. It focused on low-birth-weight infants, on the grounds that this population is at heightened risk for poor cognitive outcomes (Brooks-Gunn, Klebanov, Liaw, & Spiker, 1993; Brooks-Gunn et al., 1994). The intervention included regular home visits (by professionals) from birth to age 3, decreasing in frequency over time; a daily center-based program for children beginning at one year of age and continuing to age three; parent group meetings every three months; and regular pediatric and developmental assessment. Families received an average of sixty-seven home visits during the three-year intervention period, and children attended the center-based program an average of 267 days a year (McCarton et al., 1997, p. 127). The research team found positive effects of the intervention at three years on children's IQ and receptive vocabulary, and on parental reports of their children's behavior, with greater effects for heavier low-birth-weight children. These effects largely disappeared by age 5. An age 8 follow-up, which included measures of cognition, children's behavior, and school progress, found no differences between intervention and control groups (McCarton et al., 1997).

EARLY HEAD START. During the past twenty-five years, Head Start has remained focused primarily on 4-year-old children (two-thirds of those served) and 3-year-olds (another quarter of those served). The program has continued to provide valuable medical and dental care to hundreds of thousands of children and employment to thousands of poor parents, and it has continued to be a critical community institution in thousands of poor communities. At the same time, it has continued to struggle as well with issues of program quality, staff qualifications and compensation; political pressures to serve more 3- and 4-year-old children, and the need to be responsive to working parents. Behind these long-standing pressures has been a nagging awareness of the need to extend the Head Start model downward, to the birth-to-3 period. This need led, early in the Clinton administration, to the establishment of an advisory committee, whose recommendations were converted into a new initiative called Early Head Start (EHS).

Early Head Start is at once a demonstration program, in the spirit of the PCDCs and CFRPs, and is a significant effort to amend the Head Start model in order to create continuous birth-to-5 services. It operates within the framework of the Head Start performance standards, with their emphasis on parent participation in program governance and service provision. The initiative began in 1995 with grants to sixty-eight programs or agencies, including twenty-two Head Start programs, twenty-four "former" Parent Child Centers, and fifteen former Comprehensive Child Development Programs. Each year since then the program has expanded by about that same number. (Three percent of total Head Start funds were set aside for EHS with increasing amounts annually.) Early Head Start has what its designers call a "four-cornered emphasis:" child development, family development, community development, and staff development. Core services include child care/early childhood education, developmental screening/early identification, parent education and family support through home visits and other activities, primary health care, mental health services, and services to promote economic independence. As with other comprehensive two-generation models, some of these services can be provided through contract or referral. A national evaluation of the program, managed by Mathematica Policy Research Institute of Princeton, New Jersey, is underway.

HEALTHY START/HEALTHY FAMILIES AMERICA. In 1975, the Healthy Start program began operation in Hawaii as a then unique child abuse and neglect prevention model (Hawaii Family Stress Center, 1994). In the early 1990s, the National Committee for the Prevention of Child Abuse and Neglect joined with the program leadership from Hawaii to start the Healthy Families America initiative, designed to disseminate the Healthy Start approach throughout the United States. The model begins with a staff member screening hospital records to

identify potentially high-risk families. (Indicators of risk include mother unmarried, partner unemployed, low income, no telephone, maternal education less than twelve years, history of substance abuse, previous abortions, and history of psychiatric care. It is not clear how Healthy Start staff get permission to screen hospital records without first obtaining permission from individual families.) Those deemed to be high risk are then interviewed after the birth of the baby, while the mother and newborn are still in the hospital, using an index of factors thought or known to predict child abuse or neglect. These include parental history of abuse or neglect in their own childhoods, parental history of criminal activity, substance abuse, mental illness, multiple current stressors, anger management problems, unrealistic expectations of the newborn, and beliefs about discipline.

High-risk parents are offered services for up to five years, primarily home visiting by specially trained, carefully supervised paraprofessionals. The paraprofessionals have curricular materials to guide their work with families. Healthy Start programs are supposed to have skilled clinical staff available for consultation, assessment, crisis intervention, or brief counseling (Wallach & Lister, 1995, p. 170). Recreational, support, or therapeutic groups have also emerged in some programs. Clients are classified by level of service need and vulnerability, which determines frequency of home visits. Caseloads, which may vary between fifteen and twenty-five per case worker, are weighted to include higher and lower risk families. Each family is also linked to a medical home (i.e., a clearly defined primary care provider).

AVANCE. This program model, based loosely on that of the Parent Child Development Centers, originated in the late 1970s in San Antonio, Texas, and has now spread to some forty or so sites throughout that state. It serves families with children aged birth to 3, mostly in Hispanic communities (Walker, Rodriguez, Johnson, & Cortez, 1995). AVANCE has two stages: In the first, parents participate in a once-per-week center-based parent education class, while their children receive child care. The weekly class is divided between lecture/discussion on specific child development topics and toy-making. (During the latter activity, there is reportedly a good deal of informal discussion, sharing, and mutual support around parenting and other family issues.) There is also a monthly home visit and some case management. Parents who "graduate" from Stage 1 at the end of nine months (by virtue of participation) then proceed to a stage focused on their own development and education, which could include adult basic education, GED preparation, English-as-a-second-language classes, citizenship classes, and community college. Transportation is provided to and from the AVANCE centers.

In the late 1980s, a two-site evaluation of AVANCE was undertaken (Johnson & Walker, 1991). The investigators used random assignment in one site and a matched control group in the other. The study found modest program-favoring effects on the Caldwell HOME Inventory but few effects on mothers' knowledge of child development (somewhat surprising given the emphasis on such knowledge in the weekly classes); and no effects on children's development, as measured by the Bayley Scales of Infant Development. A high rate of maternal depression was found in the study sample at baseline, but no program effects were found on that variable. Attrition from the program was very high; of 245 families who began the program in the two sites during the study period, 108 completed it. (Families who dropped out were excluded from analyses of program effects.)

HEALTHY START/INFANT MORTALITY REDUCTION INITIATIVE. One distinct line of early childhood intervention during the past quarter century has involved community-based efforts to reduce infant mortality and improve maternal and child health among low-income populations. (This line of intervention overlaps with a similar one that has focused on prevention of low birth weight.) Most such efforts have used lay health workers to reach out to high-risk populations to provide information and social support intended to alter health self-care behaviors and linkage to health services and other resources (e.g., WIC [the Women, Infants' and Children's Food program]). Many efforts take a broad perspective on the causes of infant mortality, including in their focus such indirect factors as maternal emotional well-being, housing conditions, lack of job opportunities, and community social disorganization. In 1991, the federal Health Resources Services Administration launched a significant demonstration along these lines, with a secondary emphasis on improving clinic-based care.

Healthy Start is a sixteen-site demonstration, currently being evaluated by Mathematica Policy Research Institute (Devaney et al., 1996; Howell, 1994). Target sites are all high infant mortality urban neighborhoods, and the original goal called for a 50% reduction in infant mortality in each neighborhood within five years of initial implementation. Program funds in each city go to city, county, or state health departments, which either operate the program themselves or contract with other providers, such as community health centers, to do so. Required elements include: 1) outreach, assessment, and case management, primarily by paraprofessionals backed up by nurses; 2) clinic enhancements (i.e., added nursing staff, expanded hours, more family planning, and added clinic locations); 3) support services, provided directly or contracted, including transportation, substance abuse treatment, mental health services, and health and nutrition education; 4) infant mortality reviews; and 5) public information campaigns. The federal government also mandates community involvement in program planning and governance (Thiel, Van Dyck, & McGann, 1992).

The evaluation of Healthy Start is still underway. Implementation findings indicate that the main service provided through Healthy Start has been outreach and case management, but that high caseloads have contributed to irregularity in home visiting. As in other comprehensive models, ancillary services have been provided mostly through referrals. The initiative has stimulated some local creativity: For instance, some sites have developed mobile approaches to provision of clinical services. There has been some creative use of federal Medicaid matching dollars to fund the necessary administrative machinery for a comprehensive program. Program funding has also provided more medical staff in underserved neighborhoods and communities and longer clinic hours.

LESSONS: WHERE WE STAND

The Overall Effectiveness of Early Childhood Intervention

In 1990, I examined the evidence from twenty-five years of evaluated program experience with early childhood intervention for poor families, focusing especially on well-designed studies of well-conceptualized and implemented programs (Halpern, 1990b). The review included the multisite Parent Child Development Center and Child and Family Resource Program demonstrations (described earlier in this chapter), as well as a number of other local studies with experimental and strong quasi-experimental designs. I found a consistent pattern of modest, short-term, program-favoring effects on selected outcome measures, often those measures most closely related to program emphases, such as maternal praise, responsiveness, restrictiveness, or teaching behavior; parental coping or sense of efficacy, children's language or cognitive development in a few studies. Enduring effects were discernible in two of seven studies that followed children into their school years: the Yale Child Welfare Research Program (Provence & Naylor, 1983; Seitz, Rosenbaum & Apfel, 1985) and the Syracuse Family Development Research Program (Lally, Mangione, & Honig, 1988). In some cases, program strategies made a modest difference. Use of professional staff was associated with larger effects, and provision of direct developmental services to children led, not surprisingly, to stronger short- and long-term child outcomes. The overall picture, though, was only slightly encouraging.

The new generation of demonstrations, models, and approaches reinforces the historic pattern of relatively modest effects. None of the key multisite experimental demonstrations of recent years – Even Start, Comprehensive Child Development Program, New Chance, the Infant Health and Development Project – found much in the way of program-favoring effects on children's development. Effects on parents and parenting are difficult to summarize, given the range of constructs, foci, and measures used; yet they also appear spotty. One study might report program-favoring effects on one or a few Caldwell HOME subscales; another on family use of community resources; and another on parental "attitudes." There is almost no evidence in the literature of program-favoring effects on maternal mental health, subsequent pregnancy, or maternal literacy. Effects on infant–mother attachment have been measured in only a handful of studies and are contradictory (see Gowen & Nebrig, 1997; for an exhaustive recent review of outcomes of early childhood intervention across a range of domains, see Barnes, Goodson, & Layzer, 1995, 1996).

The new findings with respect to program effectiveness, added to the older literature, might seem discouraging, especially to those wishing to identify empirically validated models to replicate throughout a state or even more broadly. There are a number of implications of the recent wave of evaluation findings. The first and foremost relates to the way evaluation is conducted in this field. Clearly, the model of the massive, multisite experimental demonstration is not serving the field well. Most commonly, it leads to premature outcome evaluation and does not (or at least seems not to) allow for demonstrations that promote gradual, trial-and-error program development, field testing, and refinement – demonstrations that also recognize that there is no such thing as a program model, only a program model in its context. For example, it was clear within the first year or two of implementation that New Chance was ill-designed and not meeting the needs of many participants. Yet there was no adjustment of the program model on the basis of what could be learned from the experience of frontline staff and participant feedback, which would have allowed for development of a more appropriate model.

In addition to freezing the research and development process, summative evaluations that begin too soon limit the opportunity of evaluators to spend time coming to understand what is happening in a program and then select site-specific outcome measures that reflect areas in which staff and families are working hardest and most consistently. In contrast, the use of elaborate measurement batteries, sometimes applied at multiple time points, typically yields positive findings for one or two of a large cluster of measures and sometimes different positive findings at different points in time. Even when statistically significant, effects are often modest in absolute terms. The evaluator faces the dilemma of aggregating findings across sites, perhaps in an effort to increase statistical power, which often creates a largely uninterpretable data set, or alternatively of having to draw inferences from multiple programs in very different institutional and community contexts.

The persistent finding across studies and over time of only modest effects on selected dimensions of parenting, and even more intermittent effects on child development, suggest an urgent need to lower expectations of early childhood intervention program effects. Deliberately setting out to alter parenting in a significant way is an uncertain proposition. As noted earlier, the quality and nature of early parent–child relationships are strongly shaped by parents' own nurturance history, which in turn shapes parents' sense of what they are like as people, as well as what their relationships are like. Parent–child relationships are also deeply embedded in and strongly shaped by family and group traditions, as well as by current social milieus that may reinforce existing views of one's self and one's ways of relating and coping. Parent–child relationships and child-rearing patterns cannot be altered in more than the most superficial way by exposure to the contents of a parent education curriculum, by deliberately constructed social support, or by efforts to reduce stresses on families by linking them to needed resources. It is possible that these domains might be strengthened by significant improvement in families' life situations, for instance a parent moving from welfare dependence to steady work. But for many families moving from welfare to work is a long, unsteady process, with many setbacks and reversals of direction, not a one-time discontinuous change. Moreover, we do not yet know enough about the effects of corollary changes in families' lives set in motion by movement from welfare to work, whether the process is steady or not.

This is not to suggest that there are not other valid reasons to provide the kinds of modest supports to young parents typical of most early childhood intervention programs. For instance, when queried about what they valued most about their participation, parents in a number of programs have noted the availability of a supportive and interested figure: someone to talk to, someone who provided encouragement, who listened, and who could be trusted. It also remains possible that some early childhood intervention approaches have positive long-term effects – "sleeper effects" – that may not appear until later childhood or adolescence. But these remain to be seen.

Points of Agreement

Holding aside the problems with prevailing evaluation designs and expectations for change, there is moderate to substantial agreement at this point about a number of issues related to program design and implementation. There is not room enough in

this chapter to mention them all. A few of the more important lessons and continuing issues are highlighted here.

- An earlier review concluded that "some mix of parent support and direct developmental services to young children appears to hold the most promise of promoting improved long-term child development outcomes, while not neglecting parents' own developmental and support needs" (Halpern, 1990b, p. 300). The importance of including direct services to children – if one is interested in supporting child development – is reinforced by subsequent evidence and experience and is one of the central inferences drawn by the evaluators of the Comprehensive Child Development Programs. (Moreover, this finding converges with what is sure to be a growing need for high-quality infant and toddler care for welfare recipients struggling to move from welfare to work.)
- A number of studies (e.g., IHDP and CCDP) have found a relationship between the degree (i.e., duration and regularity) of participation in scheduled program services and the magnitude of program effects for families who did not drop out of a particular program. There may, however, be some confounding of ability to participate fully and family characteristics, with those who can participate most fully gaining the most from these programs. This finding is also difficult to reconcile with the individualized way that families use even the most structured, inflexible interventions. Nonetheless, it suggests also that the very modest average effects reported by most recent demonstrations may be masking more notable effects for some families.
- The recent argument that providing (or arranging for the provision of) a variety of services to achieve a variety of goals leads to more effective services is not supported by the evidence. To be sure, most recent initiatives have been comprehensive in name only, and it seems increasingly clear that trying to achieve comprehensiveness through referral, case management, or cooperative agreements is not working. Nonetheless, it seems perfectly reasonable, and possibly more effective, for programs to choose a few areas of focus and concentrate on doing them well, bearing in mind that developmental domains and roles are interconnected in families' lives. If a program chooses to be more ambitious – if, for example, a program whose main strength is in parenting support is committed to a welfare to work component, or vice versa – the "other" component cannot be treated simply as a kind of vague ancillary service, or a matter of referral,

but must be as well developed and implemented as any other key program service.

- An earlier review of the literature (Halpern, 1990b) suggested that professionals and paraprofessionals each have their strengths and that employing one or the other is a matter of trade-offs. Since then, there has been growing evidence that programs using professional staff tend to have more robust effects than those using paraprofessionals. The conclusions from the available evidence nonetheless assume the greater importance of certain objectives (i.e., child development and parenting effects), rather than others (i.e., providing employment and employment pathways to community residents or building social capital).
- The experience of recent demonstrations, such as the CCDPs, confirms Schorr's (1988) observation that low intensity services (e.g., a home visit every few weeks or a class once a week) are simply inadequate as a base of intervention for growing numbers of poor families. The dilemma is that although it is possible to sustain some vulnerable families' involvement in a demanding intervention, especially when transportation and related assistance are provided, many other families do not accept or cannot cope with more intensive services.
- There is still no agreement on whether relatively higher or lower risk populations benefit more from participation in early childhood intervention services. Findings can be marshaled to make either argument. However, for some programs this is a moot issue – funding requirements, location, and other circumstances compel them to serve very vulnerable families.

More Subtle Lessons

As an extension of these broad design lessons, it is possible to cull from the early childhood intervention literature a growing collection of discrete lessons, which can be articulated as design and helping principles. These derive largely from program developers' and operators' reflections on their experience rather than from the evaluation literature. Some focus on qualities of programs, others on the qualities of individual providers or helping relationships. Some seem self-evident, others a bit abstract. They do nonetheless capture the accumulated wisdom of a field.

The first principle pertains to the importance of an explicit theoretical framework, addressing such issues as what children need, what is most important about parenting and parent–child relationships, what good helping relationships are about, how they develop, and how they help bring about change. At a more specific level, programmatic objectives also need to be thought through, especially the kinds of change that might reasonably be expected to occur in parents or families as a result of particular helping efforts and the mechanisms underlying change (see, for examples, Bromwich, 1978; Provence & Naylor, 1983). Though seemingly abstract, theoretical frameworks help providers make sense of what they are observing and learning about families and decide how and where to intervene. They provide a common language, a kind of shorthand, for staff to use in their work with each other, contributing to shared understanding of helping goals and issues. They provide a tool for interpreting what is happening in helping relationships. When a provider is working from a coherent theory, it helps her communicate to the client that she is making an honest effort to make sense of what she is learning.

Closely related to the importance of a clear theoretical framework is the importance of a clear mission and boundaries, albeit flexibly implemented. When families served have multiple support needs and when (as is common) one feels that other community or societal institutions are not meeting those needs, there is a natural tendency to try to respond to everything. Yet individual helpers, and to a large extent programs and agencies, cannot be all things to all people. If they try to do and be too much, they will find it difficult to establish or maintain an identity, and their staff will be spread too thin and be overwhelmed by the effort. (This principle is being tested as family support programs expand their concern to issues of economic security and community-building. For instance, some programs and agencies are creating and managing neighborhood resource exchanges; others are partnering with community development corporations to prepare people for and find them jobs; still others are assuming leadership in community planning efforts [Stokely, 1996].)

In seeming contradiction to these first two principles, but in reality complementing them, is the idea that interventions have to start where families are developmentally – what parents are capable of investing in and contributing to in the helping relationship and in their own lives – and the related idea that interventions have to begin with parents' own experience of their situation and their own preoccupations. These two ideas have been implemented in some programs through the use of contracts or monthly plans, spelling out mutual expectations. The goal is to elevate expectations gradually, creating a "pathway" for progress in different domains (Herr, Wagner, & Halpern, 1996). Both principles require linking one's agenda as a helper to whatever a family is experiencing. If the helper has a topic in mind, say infant feeding, she may start by asking a parent how this is going from the parent's perspective, what issues regarding feeding may be on her mind, and so forth.

Another principle is found in the idea that individual growth and change are spurred by, or occur through, relationships. Learning, teaching, modeling, problem solving, and growth in self-awareness occur most effectively in and through good relationships. Until an interventionist gets to know a family, she cannot know what information is relevant to that family or the best ways and times to share it. Moreover, how information is taken in and considered depends on the relationship of the information-giver with the recipient. As the helper gains significance for her client, so does what she is trying to accomplish. As a corollary, it is understood that building a good relationship takes time. In discussing their home visiting program for parents at heightened risk of parenting difficulties (because of personal histories of abuse or neglect), Egeland and Erickson (1990, p. 7) noted that the home visitors sometimes worried that they were not doing enough during their early visits. But the slow work of relationship-building was crucial to the important work that would be done later. Many things were in fact going on in the early weeks: testing helpers' reliability and trustworthiness, gaining mutual knowledge, and providing an outlet for expressing feelings.

There is a growing appreciation in the field of early childhood intervention that working from a strengths perspective does not require denial of family vulnerabilities and difficulties. This means helping parents acknowledge and begin wrestling with problems, even as one is recognizing and validating the positive things they are doing. Nor does working from a strengths perspective require helpers to avoid acknowledging and wrestling with their own complex, and not completely positive, feelings toward clients. In fact, not acknowledging these feelings can undermine the capacity to see and appreciate the positive (Musick & Stott, 1990).

There is growing sensitivity in the early childhood intervention field to the importance of not only viewing the child in the context of the family but also of not losing the child when using a family-centered lens. Historically, some sentiment existed that providing alternative care and developmental experiences to infants and toddlers somehow undermined the principle of family-centeredness, bypassed the family, or weakened the parent's sense of identity as a mother or father. A growing number of providers now view direct care for infants as a support to parents as well as a boon for infants themselves.

Collectively, the practice principles being articulated for the field suggest the importance of balance between a program's own world view, mission, and priorities and those of families; between the needs of parents and those of children; between a recognition of strengths and attention to vulnerabilities; and between doing for families and encouraging them to do for themselves. Service providers want to communicate that they are reliable and trustworthy, but at the same time they do not want to undermine parents' motivation to grow and take risks. They want to link their own lives and rhythms partly to those of the community in which they work while also maintaining their own identity. They want to convey to families that they can be a meaningful resource, but they do not want to promise more than they can deliver. These days, many programs have to balance the goal of attracting and maintaining the participation of very vulnerable families with that of not stretching program resources too thinly, thus undermining capacity to serve better-coping families.

Also implicit in the helping ideas and principles discussed earlier is the importance of appropriately modest expectations regarding impacts and change. In all work with families, but particularly in work designed to address such basic issues as parenting, and in work with the growing number of vulnerable young families, change is understood to be gradual, fragile, and reversible. Progress must be conceptualized and measured in small units. Change is understood to take time because, as noted earlier, it occurs partly or largely through the relationships that develop with helpers, and such relationships gain the necessary solidity and significance only gradually.

Change is difficult in part because individuals' ways of thinking and coping are tied to their basic sense of identity. Change is difficult because people are embedded in social milieus that reinforce existing views of self, ways of coping, and relating.

The Challenge of Work with Vulnerable Populations

Providers in the early childhood intervention field, particularly in inner-city communities, report that a growing percentage of the families they serve are affected by substance abuse, family or community violence, complicated histories of adversity in child rearing and other domains, as well as involvement with child welfare authorities. For instance, developers of Family First, a community-based program that provides home visits by specially trained paraprofessionals to young families in Marin City, California, report that the home visitors face two core issues in families served: "Day-to-day survival, including shelter, finances, and food, represents one concern, while the other is substance abuse and its overall effect on children, adults and the environment in which families live" (Stokely, 1996, p. 37).

Interventionists who work with highly vulnerable young families face a number of distinct challenges. They have to deal with parents who may be preoccupied with issues other than the needs of their children; families in which there may be intermittent drug-dealing going on before their eyes, or violent interpersonal interactions. They have to cope with the effects on themselves of working with families that have experienced family members being killed and families in which adults use physical violence with each other and sometimes on their children. Often it is difficult to make and maintain contact with families in such circumstances. Parents in these populations may have difficulty trusting others, including those who offer help, and service providers' commitment may be tested, sometimes repeatedly (see Halpern, 1997). Compounding these difficulties for some providers is the stress of going to work every day in a neighborhood in which their movements are monitored by gang members and their own safety and well-being are threatened.

Those working in community-based programs not surprisingly report feeling ill-equipped to serve the most vulnerable families in their caseloads. In some instances, providers simply avoid acknowledging and discussing these issues fully and directly – whether it be a mother's substance abuse or a pattern of interpersonal violence within a family. Yet they are affected by them in a host of ways: They may have a strong desire to avoid work with a particular parent; they may feel pressure to solve insoluble problems; and they may feel angry, let down, and even come to wonder about their own competence (Provence & Naylor, 1983; Weider, Drachman, & DeLeo, 1992).

Clearly, providers who work with vulnerable families need regular opportunities, through such mechanisms as case conferences and individual supervision, to be validated in their efforts; to figure out how to approach complicated situations; and most of all to reflect on the feelings evoked by particular families and situations (and the effect of those feelings on their helping efforts). As Pawl (1988) put it, frontline workers need time "to gain distance, to slow down, to consider, explore and conceptualize" (p. 291).

It is also worth asking whether community-based providers with notably vulnerable families in their caseloads could benefit from carefully delimited exposure to concepts on helping relationships from the infant mental health literature; for example, transference and countertransference, resistance, and the concept of "holding" the helping relationship (Seligman, 1994). As such, the infant mental health framework embodies a potentially useful theoretical base for work with vulnerable families, combining child development theory, psychodynamic theory, and elements of family systems and crisis intervention approaches. It is built on a sensitivity to the way in which parents' pasts intrude on the present while viewing the present (including the hardships and depredations associated with poverty and the stresses of difficult community contexts) as real and important. The underlying theory usefully reminds helpers that children's and parents' interests overlap but are not identical.

Assuming clear boundaries around what is appropriate to expect from paraprofessional providers, a large part of the problem for community-based programs becomes the dearth of appropriate clinical services for vulnerable families. Nonetheless, building on the principles and approaches of clinical infant work, small clusters of child development clinicians and researchers have focused their attention on the need for distinct intervention models for uniquely vulnerable populations. For instance, there are now a number of approaches for addicted mothers and infants. One example is Project HOPE in Chicago (Samuelson, personal communication), a long-term, 5-day-a-week, outpatient model with multiple components – including a "morning group," individual therapy, parenting support groups, Alcoholics Anonymous groups, medical care, and a therapeutic nursery for infants and toddlers – all integrated in a milieu framework. A multidisciplinary staff come from child development, substance abuse, mental health, and health backgrounds.

Three intertwined principles guide the program: The first is that both the women served and their children are primary clients. The second is that the women are a group of people struggling to master developmental tasks, as is true for anyone. Their problems, although real and requiring the attention of specialized expertise, do not define them and should not negate the importance of support around developmental tasks, especially parenting. The third principle is that the children's developmental needs cannot wait, and yet meeting those needs does not imply bypassing the mothers. On the contrary, the mothers' motivation to meet their children's needs is viewed as an important engine for their growth. Each component, or part of the milieu, and each distinct relationship with a different staff member, provides an opportunity to work on some cluster of developmental issues; whereas the milieu as a whole provides a consistent, stable, integrating backdrop. Unexpectedly, the presence of the therapeutic nursery, and the children, has profoundly shaped the larger program. The nursery has become the anchor for the larger program, for both staff and parents. Staff get a sense of how parents are doing and progressing by observing how the children are doing and how parents relate to their children and the nursery. Parents observe how the nursery staff interact with and relate to their children and have an opportunity to practice their own new skills and feelings in a safe and supportive environment.

Approaches and helping principles for families experiencing violence are at an earlier stage of development. A small group of infancy researchers and interventionists are focusing on the effects of exposure to family and community violence (Osofsky, 1996; Zeanah & Scheeringa, 1996). Combining the theoretical framework of posttraumatic stress literature with their own clinical work and research with young families, these researchers have identified behaviors associated with traumatic experience during infancy (e.g., sleep disturbance and emotional and behavioral withdrawal). They argue that the consequences of very early exposure to violence are enduring and reverberate through the whole family (Lewis, 1996). Yet Zeanah and Scheerina (1996) noted that "few of the thousands of infants and young children in this country who experience or witness violence in their homes or communities come to mental health professionals for evaluation or treatment" (p. 9). For one thing, the very caregivers who might seek help for infants are often implicated as perpetrators or victims of violence and may have a stake in denying its effects on the young child. Even when parents and other caregivers are not involved, they may assume that very young children "can't understand," "won't remember," or "will get over" or outgrow the trauma of witnessing violence in the home or community (Osofsky, 1996, p. 6).

SYSTEMS ISSUES IN EARLY CHILDHOOD INTERVENTION

Early childhood intervention for poor families does not so much constitute a system as a patchwork of categorical purposes and programs. The patchwork differs from state to state, city to city, neighborhood to neighborhood, full in some local contexts, hardly visible in others. It includes some public system activities, primarily within maternal and child health services (under the federal Title V, WIC, and numerous state and city initiatives), and early intervention services that have grown up around Part H of P.L. 99-457; semipublic networks of family support programs in a handful of states; and individual parenting support of child development programs operated by private agencies, funded by a mix of categorical public and private sources. Programs and initiatives wax and wane. New initiatives emerge without reference to existing services. In some states, cities, and neighborhoods multiple initiatives cut across each other. A poor neighborhood may have two, three, or more case management programs, all targeting the same young families, but from slightly different angles. A community agency with a parenting support program may have to draw on a variety of funding streams to support that program or subsidize it out of general operating resources. New money attached to new ideas searches half-blindly for local agencies, while those agencies search the same way for money to operate existing or new programs of their own.

All this is not to imply that early childhood intervention "systems" should look alike from state to state or community to community. As much or more than any service domain, early childhood intervention networks ought to reflect local priorities and realities and build on local, trusted institutions. It seems clear that those coming from outside of particular local communities can no longer walk in and impose their vision of services on those communities. Yet at present, almost no state or locality has developed a vision of what a well-developed, coherent, well-differentiated local early childhood intervention system would look like, let alone what the steps and mechanisms might be for moving toward such a vision. The numerous existing or potential pieces of a coordinated system remain unconnected and sometimes at odds. Knitzer and Page (1996) noted the prevalence of such problems as administrative fragmentation, inconsistent or conflicting eligibility, repetitive reporting requirements, lack of easy access to specialized services (e.g., mental health and substance abuse), and poor use of scarce professional development resources.

State and Local Initiatives

Nonetheless, there has been sporadic support for system-building throughout the 1990s. Governors and state legislators are beginning to respond to the renewed media attention to the birth-to-3 period with new initiatives. As noted earlier, one can observe growing numbers of interagency councils, interinitiative coordinating bodies, partnerships, collaboratives, and the like. The Starting Points initiative of the Carnegie Corporation (1994, 1996) has provided financial support to a number of cities and states for several kinds of efforts, including system-building. Knitzer and Weiss (undated, p. 39) noted that "three states with preexisting systems change efforts not focused specifically on infants and toddlers (Georgia, Rhode Island, and West Virginia) used

Starting Points to develop an explicit focus on young children and families within the context of the larger initiative." A grant to Boston is supporting efforts to develop more integrated birth-to-3 services in selected poor neighborhoods and to bring a number of city- and statewide initiatives together to better coordinate their activities (Knitzer & Weiss, undated, p. 13). A grant to Pittsburgh supplements a $40 million grant from the Howard Heinz Endowment and the United Way for the expansion of early childhood services to reach the majority of poor children birth to 5, with child care as the core of expanded early childhood intervention services to poor infants and their families. A grant to Ohio supports efforts to create local coordinating councils to oversee planning, funding, and growth of early childhood programs.

A number of states are not so much building systems as expanding services by using a core model or type of program. Minnesota is working to adapt its school-system–based, universal access family support and education program (called *Early Childhood Family Education*) to the relatively greater needs of poor families. Challenges include reaching out to nonparticipating families and developing appropriately intense and focused services or service plans for particularly vulnerable families. Missouri relies on Parents as Teachers, Kentucky on school-based family resource centers, Hawaii on its network of Healthy Start sites, and Vermont on its network of Parent–Child Centers. Some states select and disseminate models from others. Oregon and Maine have adopted the Healthy Start/Healthy Families America model. A few states, such as Colorado, Connecticut, and Maryland, use a generic family resource center model as a base for services (Knitzer & Page, 1996).

In each of these examples, local sites or programs may serve as a base for provision of an array of services. For example, Vermont's 16 Parent Child Centers have eight core services, including child care, home visiting, play groups, crisis intervention, information and referral, drop in, and community development work (Knitzer & Page, 1996, p. 136). In some of these cases, there is an explicit or implicit priority target population. Healthy Start/Healthy Families America focuses on families at heightened risk of child abuse and neglect. In Vermont, teen parents and their children are the highest priority population. The strategy of most states that are trying to build statewide networks seems to be to use the cover of universal access to secure public and legislative support for the program, while assuring that the most vulnerable families get reached and served appropriately. This strategy requires the finest of balancing acts but probably is the most realistic politically.

Funding Issues

In part because early childhood intervention for poor families is not a mandated responsibility for any public system, it has no obvious or secure public funding stream. Although state funding for early childhood services is growing, the great bulk of new public money going into such services in most states – perhaps 80% – is going into prekindergarten (pre-K) programs in public schools. For example, in one recent fiscal year Georgia spent $700,000 on its Healthy Families program and $157 million on pre-K programs; Colorado $900,000 on its Family Centers program and $12 million on pre-K; and Illinois $2 million on its Prevention Initiative and $100 million on pre-K (Knitzer & Page, 1996). The exception to this pattern is Kentucky, which spent $37 million on pre-K but a like amount on its school-based family resource centers.

It seems that at some point early childhood intervention system-building efforts will have to draw in or draw on the resources of the major federal maternal and child health programs that still serve poor families with children birth to 3. These include the Women, Infants and Children's Food program (WIC), Early and Periodic Screening, Diagnosis and Treatment (EPSDT), and Medicaid. Also, the potential role of Head Start remains unclear. It is the most well-established and extensive early childhood network for poor children and families in the United States. Its norm of parent involvement and its deep roots in specific neighborhoods are among its great strengths. The Early Head Start demonstration is establishing a beachhead for birth-to-3 services within the Head Start system and building a potentially valuable body of experience on which to draw. A few states already have looked to Head Start as a key institution for young families in poverty and have provided supplemental funding for program expansion. Yet Head Start is still wrestling with problems of quality in its center-based programs for 3- and 4-year-olds. Does it really have the capacity to serve

as a base for birth-to-3 services? Finally, the evolving publicly subsidized child-care system will have to be part of any early intervention funding, not to mention programmatic, strategy. A steadily growing proportion of poor infants and toddlers spend their days in center-based or family child care. By default or occasionally by design, child-care program staff are becoming important sources of social support for poor parents who are working or preparing for work.

It would seem that there is also some potential for early childhood intervention to be able to draw on child welfare resources, but that potential has never been realized. The possibilities are dramatically illustrated by data from the neighborhood of Mott Haven in the South Bronx, in New York city. As noted earlier, vulnerable families tend to be concentrated in the poorest neighborhoods, and that certainly is the case for Mott Haven. During 1990, 299 infants from Mott Haven were removed from their families and placed in some form of care; 182 infants were placed in foster care at a cost of $33,000 per child (including administrative costs); 111 infants were placed in relative foster care at a cost of $43,000 per child; and 6 infants were placed in congregate care at a cost of $51,000 per child (Wulczyn, 1996). That is a total expenditure of over $11 million on infant foster care during one year in just one neighborhood. If a good early childhood intervention program could have prevented placement for even a modest percentage of those infants – say 10 to 20% – it would have saved both money and unnecessary human pain.

Perhaps the most worrisome development in the human services arena with respect to the potential for greater early childhood intervention funding is the growing focus on cost containment. As Drotar (1996) noted, early childhood service providers increasingly may be "called upon to develop specialized, comprehensive services to increasingly complex populations while providing services that are cost-efficient, which is often defined merely as inexpensive or brief" (p. vi). A much discussed, although thus far little-implemented, cost containment strategy is managed care. Loosely speaking, managed care involves the provision of a fixed amount of dollars to a defined network of service providers (or an individual provider) to meet whatever service needs may arise in a defined population (say, any poor family with children birth to 3 in a particular neighborhood or local community). The funding formula is based on historical experience with the incidence of particular risk conditions or vulnerabilities in that defined population, along with the costs of "treating" children and families for those conditions.

One can easily see the difficulty of applying the managed care paradigm to early childhood intervention. We do not have a clear idea which families to serve or how to define and delimit the risk factors and vulnerabilities to be addressed, let alone how to measure their incidence in particular local populations or estimate the cost of providing appropriate services for them. Nor do we have agreement on what services are appropriate for particular families or "conditions." Because experience has taught us that different families use services very differently, have different capacities to use and benefit from help, and benefit in different areas and in different ways, standardizing early childhood intervention services – making the key variables stand still so they can be measured – is exceedingly difficult.

Impact of Welfare Reform

The work of early childhood intervention programs is affected significantly by developments outside the field per se – for example, trends in family circumstances, changing conditions of low-income neighborhoods, and broader developments in the human services. Social problems and populations change, as do policy imperatives and constraints. One of the most important recent developments in the larger context impinging on early childhood intervention is the demise of Aid to Families with Dependent Children and its replacement with the Temporary Assistance to Needy Families Act (TANF). TANF virtually ignores the developmental needs of infants and toddlers as a potential touchstone for welfare to work program design. The only things to be said for sure at this point are that the Act will put immigrant and refugee families at even greater risk than they are now and will most likely increase the demand for infant–toddler child care. Much else is an open question, dependent on how states use the flexibility afforded under the Act. One key question relevant to early childhood intervention is whether states will include as approved activities in satisfying work requirements either meeting specific basic parental responsibilities for care of very young children (e.g., taking infants to "recommended" health

care appointments) or participation in parenting support programs. Another question, noted earlier, is how the newly reorganized streams of child-care money will be deployed. A final unanswered question pertains to the kinds of support strategies that will be developed for the most vulnerable young families, including teen parents.

CONCLUSION

As suggested at the beginning of the chapter, early childhood intervention for poor children and families is at a crossroad. There is much cause for optimism about the future, stemming largely from the richness of knowledge about early childhood development that has accumulated and the hard-won, field-based experience underpinning the field. There is growing consensus around a number of "best-practice" principles – for instance, that early intervention programs should include direct developmental services to children and that they should include mechanisms for supporting frontline service providers in their difficult work. There is a healthy debate about a number of important issues; for instance, prevailing assumptions about the need for programs to be comprehensive and about the strengths of paraprofessionals. (Although there is reason to question the historic and continuing reliance on paraprofessionals, the United States still has but a relatively tiny handful of frontline providers trained specifically to work with families and children birth to 3, and many of them do not work in community-based programs in low-income communities.)

In spite of the rich knowledge and experience base, the field of early childhood intervention faces three important tasks. The first is that of achieving greater coherence. Early childhood intervention is not a system but consists of multiple, overlapping systems with different, sometimes competing, priorities. In part, for this reason, there remains "no clear locus for broad-scale leadership on behalf of young children and families. There are policy-makers, providers and local neighborhood leaders, but typically these different stakeholders do not come together to plan, think strategically, and thrash out a shared vision" (Knitzer & Weiss, undated, p. 42). The field may well remain heterogeneous and fluid and continue evolving idiosyncratically. Consequently, future federal or state initiatives in each system or service area – maternal and child health, mental health, social services, education – will have to pay close attention to how those initiatives fit with innovative efforts in other service areas, as well as with existing neighborhood service arrays. Local (neighborhood-level) planning and governance bodies are likely to play an increasingly prominent role in the coming years and will require financial support and technical assistance.

The second important task is to address honestly the equivocal quantitative evidence in support of early childhood intervention. This evidence raises all kinds of questions about purpose and expectations, program design and implementation, as well as the promises that can and should be made to politicians and funders. Critical to developing a research agenda for the future, and critical to future program design and system-building, will be a workable narrative for the field: a sensible rationale and realistic language of expectations, as well as an accurate model of how early childhood intervention programs work and where they fit in families' lives.

The third task facing the field is to rethink program purposes and strategies, in response to the growing demands on poor parents of very young children to seek and hold on to work. Within this context, it is likely that early childhood intervention programs will feel increased pressure to help parents on welfare begin moving toward stable employment. That pressure will compound questions of purpose and mission. Families will continue to need support with child-rearing, but that support may have to be structured differently. It is possible, and perhaps desirable, that high-quality infant and toddler care might take a more prominent place as a strategy for achieving early childhood intervention goals. This possibility is made more appealing by the accumulated evidence that high-quality child development programs can complement and extend parents' efforts to meet the developmental needs of their infants and toddlers. Especially for families under great stress, a center-based experience can provide young children a predictable daily routine, a safe environment, and the verbal stimulation and focused attention that parents may not have the energy to provide. When parents observe their children thriving, that can serve as an engine for their own commitment to their children. The potential for center-based child

care to serve as a more important element of early childhood intervention is constrained by the enormous cost of providing high-quality care for infants and toddlers. Yet the new combined child-care funding streams created as a by-product of welfare reform may be one source of support, especially for families in which mothers of very young children are being required to work.

REFERENCES

Anderson, E. (1994). The code of the streets. *Atlantic Monthly*, May, 81–94.

Andrews, S., Blumenthal, J., Johnson, D., Kahn, A., Ferguson, C., Lasater, T., Malone, P., & Wallace, D. (1982). The skills of mothering: A study of the Parent Child Development Centers. *Monographs of the Society for Research in Child Development, 47*, 1–81.

Baratz, J., & Baratz, S. (1971). Early childhood intervention: The social science base of institutional racism. *Harvard Education Review*, Reprint Series No. 5, 111–32.

Barnes, H., Goodson, B., & Layzer, J. (1995, 1996). *Review of research on supportive interventions for children and families* (Two volumes). Cambridge, MA: Abt Associates.

Beller, K. (1979). Early intervention programs. In J. Osofsky (Ed.), *Handbook of infant development* (pp. 852–94). New York: Wiley.

Bromwich, R. (1978). *Working with parents and infants*. Austin, TX: Pro-Ed.

Bronfenbrenner, U. (1979). *The ecology of human development*. Cambridge, MA: Harvard University Press.

Bronfenbrenner, U. (1987). Forward: Family support: The quiet revolution. In S. Kagan, D. Powell, B. Weissbourd, & E. Zigler (Eds.), *America's family support programs* (pp. xi–xvii). New Haven, CT: Yale University Press.

Brooks-Gunn, J., Klebanov, P., Liaw, F., & Spiker, D. (1993). Enhancing the development of low birth weight, premature infants: Changes in cognition and behavior over the first three years. *Child Development, 64*, 736–53.

Brooks-Gunn, J., McCarton, C., Casey, P., McCormick, M., Bauer, C., Bernbaum, J., Tyson, J., Swanson, M., Bennett, F., Scott, D., Tonascia, J., & Meinert, C. (1994). Early intervention in low birth weight premature infants. *Journal of the American Medical Association, 272*(16), 1257–62.

Call, J., Galenson, E., & Tyson, R. (1983). *Frontiers of infant psychiatry* (Vols. I & II). New York: Basic Books.

Carnegie Corporation. (1994). *Starting points: Meeting the needs of our youngest children*. New York: Author.

Carnegie Corporation. (1996). *Starting Points: State and community partnerships for young children*. New York: Author.

Cicirelli, V. (1969). *The impact of Head Start*. Athens: Ohio University, Westinghouse Learning Corporation.

Crocker, R. (1992). *Social work and social order: The settlement movement in two industrial cities, 1889–1930.* Urbana: University of Illinois Press.

Devaney, B. et al. (1996). *National evaluation of Healthy Start: Year 2 Annual Report.* Princeton, NJ: Mathematica Policy Research Institute.

Drotar, D. (1996). But where are the data? Planning services for infants and families in an era of managed care. *Infants and Young Children, 9*(2), vi–vii.

Egeland, B., & Erickson, M. (1990). Rising above the past: Strategies for helping new mothers break the cycle of abuse and neglect. *Zero to Three, 11*(2), 29–35.

Family Resource Coalition. (1996). *Guidelines for family support practice.* Chicago: Author.

Fraiberg, S., Adelson, E., & Shapiro, V. (1975). Ghosts in the nursery: A psychoanalytic approach to the problem of impaired infant–mother relationships. *Journal of the American Academy of Child Psychiatry, 14,* 387–422.

Fraiberg, S., Shapiro, V., & Cherniss, D. (1983). Treatment modalities. In J. Call, E. Galenson, & R. Tyson (Eds.), *Frontiers of infant psychiatry* (pp. 56–73). New York: Basic Books.

Gowen, J., & Nebrig, J. (1997). Infant–mother attachment at risk: How early intervention can help. *Infants and Young Children, 9*(4), 62–78.

Greenberg, P. (1990). *The devil has slippery shoes.* Washington, DC: Youth Policy Institute.

Halpern, R. (1990a). Parent support and education programs. *Children and Youth Services Review, 12,* 285–308.

Halpern, R. (1990b). Community-based early intervention. In S. J. Meisels & J. P. Shonkoff (Eds.), *Handbook of early childhood intervention* (pp. 469–98). New York: Cambridge University Press.

Halpern, R. (1993). Poverty and infant development. In C. Zeanah (Ed.), *Handbook of infant mental health* (pp. 73–86). New York: Guilford Press.

Halpern, R. (1995). *Rebuilding the inner city: A history of neighborhood initiatives to address poverty.* New York: Columbia University Press.

Halpern, R. (1997). Good practice for multiply vulnerable young families: Challenges and principles. *Children and Youth Services Review, 19*(4), 253–75.

Halpern, R. (1998). *Fragile families, fragile solutions: A history of supportive services for families in poverty.* New York: Columbia University Press.

Hans, S., Ray, A., & Halpern, R. (1995). *Caregiving in the inner-city.* Chicago: University of Chicago, Unit for Research in Child Psychiatry.

Hawaii Family Stress Center. (1994). *Healthy start.* Honolulu, HI: Department of Health.

Herr, T. & Halpern, R. (1993). Changing what counts: Rethinking the journey out of welfare. *American Behavioral Science Review, 1*(2), 113–64.

Herr, T., Wagner, S., & Halpern, R. (1996). *Making the shoe fit: Creating a work prep system for a large and diverse welfare population.* Chicago: Project Match, Erikson Institute.

Hewett, K. (1982). Comprehensive family service programs: Special features and associated measurement problems. In J. Travers & R. Light (Eds.), *Learning from experience* (pp. 203–53). Washington, DC: National Academy Press.

Howell, E. (1994). *Implementing a community-based initiative: The early years of Healthy Start.* Princeton, NJ: Mathematica Policy Research.

Johnson, D., & Walker, T. (1991). *Final report of an evaluation of the AVANCE parent education and family support program.* San Antonio, TX: AVANCE.

Klerman, L. (1991). *Alive and well?* New York: National Center for Children in Poverty.

Knitzer, J., & Page, S. (1996). *Map and track: State initiatives for young children and their families.* New York: National Center for Children in Poverty, Columbia University.

Knitzer, J., & Weiss, H. (undated). *Starting points: Challenging the quiet crisis.* New York: National Center for Children in Poverty.

Lally, R., Mangione, P., & Honig, A. (1988). The Syracuse University Family Development Research Program: Long range impact of an early intervention with low-income children and their families. In D. Powell (Ed.), *Parent education as early childhood intervention* (pp. 79–104). Norwood, NJ: Ablex.

Lewis, M. (1996). Trauma reverberates: Psychosocial evaluation of the caregiving environment of young children exposed to violence and traumatic loss. *Zero to Three,* April/May, 21–8.

McCarton, C., Brooks-Gunn, J., Wallace, I., Bauer, C., Bennett, F., Bernbaum, J., Broyles, S., Casey, P., McCormick, M., Scott, D., Tyson, J., Tonascia, J., Meinert, C. (1997). Results at age 8 years of early intervention for low-birth-weight premature infants: The Infant Health and Development Program. *Journal of the American Medical Association, 277,* 2, 126–132.

Musick, J., & Stott, F. (1990). Paraprofessionals, parenting, and child development. In S. J. Meisels & J. P. Shonkoff (Eds.), *Handbook of early childhood intervention* (pp. 651–67). New York: Cambridge University Press.

National Center for Children in Poverty. (1990). *Five million children.* New York: Author.

Nightingale, C. (1993). *On the edge.* New York: Basic Books.

Ooms, T. (1996). *Where is the family in comprehensive community initiatives for children and families?* Washington, DC: Family Impact Seminar.

Osofsky, J. (1996). Introduction. *Zero to Three,* April/May, 5–8.

Pawl, J. (1988). Toward a comprehensive infant mental health program for a community. In E. J. Anthony & C. Chiland (Eds.), *The child in his family* (pp. 263–89). New York: Wiley.

Provence, S., & Naylor, N. (1983). *Working with disadvantaged parents and their children: Scientific and practice issues.* New Haven, CT: Yale University Press.

Quint, J., & Egeland, B. (1995). New Chance: Comprehensive services for disadvantaged young families. In S. Smith (Ed.), *Two generation programs for families in poverty* (pp. 91–134). Norwood, NJ: Ablex.

Quint, J., Polit, H., Bos, H. & Cave, G. (1994). *New Chance: Interim findings on a comprehensive program for disadvantaged young mothers and their children.* New York: Manpower Demonstration Research Corporation.

Schorr, L. (1988). *Within our reach: Breaking the cycle of disadvantage.* New York: Doubleday.

Seitz, V., Rosenbaum, L., & Apfel, N. (1985). Effects of family support intervention: A ten year follow up. *Child Development, 56,* 376–91.

Seligman, S. (1994). Applying psychoanalysis in an unconventional context: Adapting infant-parent psychotherapy to a changing population. *Psychoanalytic Study of the Child, 49,* 481–500.

Skerry, P. (1983). The charmed life of Head Start. *The Public Interest, 71,* 18–39.

Smith, A., & Lopez, M. (1994). *Comprehensive Child Development Program.* Washington, DC: U.S. Department of Health and Human Services.

Smith, S. (Ed.). (1995). *Two generation programs for families in poverty.* Norwood, NJ: Ablex.

Smith, S., & Zaslow, M. (1995). Rationale and policy context for two-generation interventions. In S. Smith (Ed.), *Two generation programs for families in poverty* (pp. 1–36). Norwood, NJ: Ablex.

Stokely, J. (1996). *The emerging role of California's family support programs in community economic development.* Oakland, CA: National Economic Development and Law Center.

St. Pierre, R., Goodson, B., Layzer, J., & Bernstein, L. (1997). *National impact evaluation of the Comprehensive Child Development Program.* Cambridge, MA: Abt Associates.

St. Pierre, R., Layzer, J., Goodson, B., & Bernstein, L. (1997). *National impact evaluation of the Comprehensive Child Development Program: Final report.* Cambridge, MA: Abt Associates.

Thiel, K., Van Dyck, P., & McGann, T. (1992). *Healthy Start: Assessing efforts to develop comprehensive systems of perinatal care to reduce infant mortality.* Paper presented at the annual meeting of the American Public Health Association, October 1993.

Travers, J., Nauta, M., & Irwin, N. (1982). *The effects of a social program: Final Report of the Child and Family Resource Program's infant toddler component.* Cambridge, MA: Abt Associates.

U.S. Department of Health and Human Services (1993). *Creating a 21st century Head Start.* Washington, DC. Author.

Walker, T., Rodriguez, G., Johnson, D., & Cortez, C. (1995). AVANCE Parent–Child Education Program. In S. Smith (Ed.), *Two Generation Programs for Families in Poverty* (pp. 67–90). Norwood, NJ: Ablex.

Wallach, V., & Lister, L. (1995). Stages in the delivery of home-based services to parents at risk of child abuse: A Healthy Start experience. *Scholarly Inquiry for Nursing Practice, 9*(2), 159–73.

Weider, S., Drachman, R., & DeLeo, T. (1992). A developmental/relationship in-service training model. In E. Fenichel (Ed.), *Learning through supervision and mentorship* (pp. 100–12). Washington, DC: National Center for Clinical Infant Programs.

Weiss, H., & Halpern, R. (1988). *Family support and education programs: Something old or something new?* New York: National Center for Children in Poverty.

Wulczyn, F. (1996). Child welfare reform, managed care, and community reinvestment. In A. Kahn & S. Kamerman (Eds.), *Children and their families in big cities* (pp. 199–229). New York: Columbia University School of Social Work.

Zeanah, C., & Scheeringa, M. (1996). Evaluation of post-traumatic symptomatology in infants and young children exposed to violence. *Zero to Three,* April/May, 9–14.

Zigler, E., & Muenchow, S. (1992). *Head Start: The inside story of America's most successful educational experiment.* New York: Basic Books.

CHAPTER EIGHTEEN

Services for Young Children with Disabilities and Their Families

GLORIA L. HARBIN, R. A. McWILLIAM, AND JAMES J. GALLAGHER

Remarkable progress has been made in the development of comprehensive and coordinated services to young children with disabilities (Smith & McKenna, 1994). Thirty years ago, early intervention programs were virtually nonexistent; today, families in every community nationwide can make use of services that are designed to meet the developmental needs of their child and to support them in enhancing their child's development. A combination of interacting factors has enabled the growth and evolution of services (Harbin, 1993; Meisels & Shonkoff, 1990). Research, technical assistance, advocacy, as well as the political and social context combined in the enactment of sweeping federal legislation (Garwood & Sheehan, 1989; Harbin, 1993). This public policy, now entitled Part C of the Individuals with Disabilities Education Act (IDEA), is intended to increase the number of children receiving services, to identify children in need of services as early as possible, and to improve services for children and families by making those services more comprehensive, coordinated, and family centered. The legislation required numerous changes in service delivery and modifications in how many professionals perform their jobs (Bailey, 1989; Dokecki & Heflinger, 1989; Gallagher, Harbin, Thomas, Clifford, & Wenger, 1988; Hanft, 1989; Hurley, 1989).

As many policy researchers and advocates discovered, the enactment of legislation and the implementation of that legislation are very different

The authors would like to thank Dave Shaw, Tracey West, and Michele Whiteaker for their valuable contributions to the preparation of this chapter.

processes (Campbell & Mazoni, 1976; Elmore, 1978; Harbin, Gallagher, & Batista, 1992; Meisels, 1985, 1989; Weatherly, 1979). As states began the implementation of this monumental federal policy in 1986, the amount and types of services that were provided varied greatly (Meisels, Harbin, Modigliani, & Olson, 1988). By 1992, all states had developed policies in compliance with the federal legislation, and the process of implementing these policies began at the community level (Harbin et al., 1992; Smith & McKenna, 1994).

This chapter presents a description of the major changes in service delivery required by federal legislation. It also provides a portrait of several current, complex, service delivery models. Data are presented regarding the factors that shaped these service models, as well as the nature of service delivery for children and families resulting from these models. An ecological cluster of interacting factors that appear to influence service delivery helps explain the complexities of service delivery. The chapter concludes with a discussion of future challenges for improving services to young children with disabilities and their families.

FEDERAL POLICY

In a relatively short period of time, early intervention "has been transformed from an emerging service with a primitive empirical base, scant funding, and virtually no public mandate to a robust area of theory, research and practice" (Meisels & Shonkoff, 1990, p. xv). Fundamental changes in beliefs and service delivery occurred as a result of the

TABLE 18.1. Paradigm Shift in Service Delivery as a Result of Enactment of P.L. 99-457

Area	What Services Were Like	How Services Are Supposed to Be
Entitlement	Served only some of the eligible children	Serve all eligible children
Eligibility	Served only disabled children and waited until children evidenced measurable delays	Serve children with diagnosed conditions regardless of whether measurable delays are present May serve at-risk children in order to prevent developmental delay
Early identification	Waited until children came to program	Find children as early as possible
Service array	Confined services to what program offered	Provide an array of services across programs
System	Provided separate, autonomous programs	Provide comprehensive, coordinated, interagency system of services
Focus	Child-centered	Family-centered
Individualization	Offered a package of services	Offer individualized services
Inclusion	Established segregated, self-contained programs	Establish inclusive programs and use of community resources
Disciplines	Disciplines worked autonomously	Disciplines working together to integrate all services (interdisciplinary, transdisciplinary)
Therapies	Provided separate and sometimes insufficient therapies	Provide sufficient integrated therapies
Procedural safeguards	Families had no recourse for complaints	Procedural safeguards in place
Transition	Unplanned traumatic transitions	Planned transition from infant and toddler program to preschool program
Funding	Single primary funding source	Coordinate and use all possible funding sources

complex interactions of five broad factors: 1) conceptual contributions of scholars and theorists; 2) the innovative ideas and concepts of skilled and experienced practitioners; 3) research studies from diverse disciplines (e.g., medicine, psychology, special education, social work, etc.); 4) sociopolitical factors; and 5) the cooperative advocacy of parents, service providers, state and local program administrators, and researchers (Harbin, 1993).

In the 1980s, a federal policy was enacted (P.L. 99-457) that currently guides services to young children with disabilities, requiring substantial changes in service delivery nationwide. In 1988 this legislation was renamed the Individuals with Disabilities Education Act and was given a new number as well, P.L. 102-119. Part H of IDEA was the specific section of the law containing requirements for programs to infants and toddlers with disabilities. In 1997 the law was amended, and Part C of the law

now contains provisions for services to infants and toddlers (IDEA, Amendments of 1997, P.L. 105-107). Table 18.1 presents the major shifts in public policy and service provision required by the law.

Implementation of this federal policy required major changes in thirteen areas mentioned in Table 18.1 that are related to service delivery (Gallagher et al., 1988; Gallagher, Trohanis, & Clifford, 1989; Harbin, Gallagher, Clifford, Place, & Eckland, 1993; Smith & McKenna, 1994). First, prior to this legislation, programs were restricted to serving only those children with identifiable disabilities. Part C of IDEA recognized that there were some conditions such as Down syndrome in which infants might develop normally for a time but eventually would exhibit developmental delays. This legislation instructed providers to begin intervention for children with established conditions on diagnosis. In addition, the law permits states to serve children at risk of developmental delays. The most recent amendments encourage states to expand opportunities for children under three years of age, who would be at risk of having a substantial developmental delay if early intervention services were not provided. However, services to this population remain at the discretion of the states. Second, although many states defined groups of children as eligible to receive services, programs historically provided services to only a portion of these children because of limited funds. This created long waiting lists for services. Currently, all eligible children are entitled to be served.

The third area of change relates to the timing of identification. Prior to this law, most early intervention programs did not conduct aggressive child find activities, relying primarily on other agencies (e.g., health department and social services) to refer children. Early intervention programs now have the responsibility to conduct comprehensive and coordinated child find activities in order to identify children as early as possible. Previously, when children were enrolled in early intervention services, services were confined to those offered by the program. Every agency worked autonomously and had a package of services that it offered to eligible children, and services were fragmented as a result. However, children with disabilities and their families often require services from more than one discipline and agency. Part C of IDEA requires a comprehensive, coordinated, interagency system of early intervention services. This system is to be composed of an array of services and resources to meet the individual needs of both the child and family (Trivette, Dunst, & Deal, 1997) and requires that a service coordinator be assigned to ensure coordination. To encourage further the coordination of services, the law requires that individuals from different disciplines work to integrate all services and therapies.

The law also requires a shift in the recipients of services. Previously, services were provided only to the child. Part C of IDEA establishes not only the child but the child's family as legitimate recipients as well. The law calls for the development of an Individualized Family Service Plan (IFSP) for each recipient of services. Previously, assessment focused on the child, took place in unfamiliar settings, and sometimes used assessment devices inappropriately (e.g., using a criterion-referenced test as if it were a norm-referenced test or using a screening device to make a placement decision; Greenspan & Meisels, 1996; Meisels, 1996). Provisions of the law sought to reverse these practices by assessing the family's strengths and needs in addition to the child's, conducting assessments in multiple environments, and using multiple sources and instruments for the purpose for which they were developed (Meisels & Provence, 1989).

Prior to the legislation, some services were provided in the child's home or in specialized centers in which only children with disabilities received services. The new legislation required children and families to be assessed and served in settings in which children without disabilities are cared for and taught. A justification must be provided when services are not provided in a natural environment.

Part C of IDEA also provides procedural safeguards for the child with disabilities and his or her family. Previously, families had no place to turn if they had complaints about the services or objected to being placed on a waiting list. The procedural safeguards section of the law instructs that parents will be informed of their rights. Before the enactment of this legislation, when the child had to make a transition from one program to a program provided by a different agency, the burden to make this transition was placed on the family. Neither the sending nor receiving agencies had any responsibility; no plan was required. This legislation corrects this situation by instructing that the sending agency will inform the receiving agency (usually the public schools) six months in advance of the child's third birthday and requires the development of a transition plan. Finally, in the past there was little effort to identify and use all possible sources of funds. The current legislation requires the coordination of all possible funding sources into a system of finances so that individual funding sources complement one another, but do not duplicate efforts.

SERVICE DELIVERY MODELS

Many of the descriptions of service delivery models in the literature addressed a single developmental intervention program, often concentrating on the location of intervention – home- or center-based (Bailey & Wolery, 1992; Odom & Fewell, 1983); the target of intervention – child, family, and so forth (Bricker & Veltman, 1990; Gilkerson,

Gorski, & Panitz, 1990; Seitz & Provence, 1990; Simeonsson & Bailey, 1990); the process of intervention – child find, assessment, IFSP, and so on (Bagnato & Neisworth, 1981; Beckman, Robinson, Jackson, & Rosenberg, 1986; Bricker & Veltman, 1990; Frankenburg, Emde, & Sullivan, 1985; Odom & Shuster, 1986; Sheehan, 1982; Vincent et al., 1980); or the philosophical orientation of the early intervention program – behaviorist, Piagetian, ecological, developmental, and so forth (Bagnato & Neisworth, 1981; Bricker & Veltman, 1990).

However, the special needs of young children with disabilities and their families often require the involvement of a multitude of public and private programs and resources. McKnight (1987) and others declared that a variety of programs and organizations exist within the community that also should be thought of as valuable resources (e.g., churches, libraries, YWCA, child care, and civic organizations) in addition to the services provided by traditional public agencies (health, education, social services, etc.). Accordingly, as a result of a broader and more normalized view of service systems, Trivette et al. (1997) divided the array of community resources into twelve broad categories (e.g., child education, health, parent education and information, housing, and legal etc.). The development of a comprehensive and coordinated system of services utilizing all relevant resources requires several key elements: 1) the identification of all relevant programs and resources; 2) the knowledge of the services provided by each, including the manner in which services are provided; and 3) a plan describing how the various services form a holistic system. The federal law provides little guidance to communities regarding what constitutes "comprehensive." Consequently, the task of identifying relevant resources and defining the "system" is reliant on the vision of the local early intervention coordinator and other members of the local council (Garland & Linder, 1994). For example, the inclusion of the Even Start program, which is designed to improve parent and child literacy, depends on whether the local early intervention coordinator or someone else within the local coordinating council knows of the program and, if so, whether he or she sees it as a relevant and important resource.

Just as state policies differed prior to the enactment of IDEA, so too did the service delivery models (Meisels et al., 1988). In many communities, the program that provided developmental intervention (i.e., social, cognitive, motor, and language activities) functioned fairly autonomously, coordinating infrequently with other agencies or community resources around a specified event or circumstance (e.g., surgery, therapies, or health care) regarding a particular child. However, in other communities, professionals from some agencies and programs had begun the arduous process of integrating a variety of health, education, and social services into a more cohesive system. Not surprisingly, in a study of nine diverse communities, despite the federal requirement for a comprehensive and coordinated service delivery system, the current service delivery models varied with regard to the scope of participation in decision making by various agencies and the organization of the service systems (Harbin & West, 1998).

Studying Service Delivery

This study of service delivery models was part of a series of studies conducted to describe several aspects of service delivery to infants, toddlers, and preschool children and their families (Harbin & Kochanek, 1992, 1998). Harbin and Kochanek (1998) selected a sample, which was purposively diverse (Patton, 1980) at the state, community, child, family, and service provider levels. Three states were selected for study that were diverse with regard to sociodemographic factors (e.g., size, region, and economy), eligibility policy, lead agency, history of service provision, and approach to funding and providing services. The three states selected included a large Northeastern agricultural and industrial "rust-belt" state (Pennsylvania), a growing South Atlantic state with a history of textiles and tobacco (North Carolina), and a scenic Western state in the Rockies (Colorado). Each state's study sites included a high, medium, and low population and resource density community and ranged in size from a large urban environment with a population of 2,403,676 to a remote rural community with a population of 2,838.

In each of these communities, case study children ($N = 75$) were selected from a larger purposive sample ($N = 300$) and were followed for a two-year period. In addition to surveys, questionnaires, and service use protocols, other qualitative and quantitative strategies were used to collect data related to service provision and utilization at the state, community, and program levels. These strategies include analysis of public policy and budget documents; analysis of IFSPs and IEPs; and focus groups and interviews with families, service providers, administrators, and important leaders of each community.

Harbin and West (1998) focused specifically on describing and understanding service delivery models, using data from multiple sources (interviews with program administrators, service providers, and families, as well as examination of relevant documents). Through cross-site analysis they identified six qualitatively different organizational models for early intervention service delivery ranging from a traditional single-program oriented model to a comprehensive model designed to provide services to all children in the community. Table 18.2 describes key elements of each of the six models. Several elements are addressed within each model: the overall organizational structure that guides service delivery; the amount and nature of interagency decision making; the scope of the target population; and the scope and nature of service resources that are utilized.

Single-Program Oriented

This model is most similar to the service delivery models existing prior to the enactment of Part H or Part C of IDEA. A single developmental intervention program focuses on addressing the cognitive, social, language, and motor needs of the child. Interventionists in these programs seldom see family needs as part of their domain. They most often work one-on-one with the child, primarily using a direct teaching approach. Occasionally, the interventionist will enlist the parent's help by teaching the parent (usually the mother) some particular educational activity that can be done with the child.

In the single-program oriented service delivery model, all other programs are viewed as supplementary to the program that provides developmental intervention. The interventionist recognizes that the child may have medical needs or that the family has housing needs, but these issues are seen as outside the focus of the early intervention program. There might be some instances in which the developmental interventionist feels the need to converse with a professional or administrator in another agency (e.g., the Health Department); however, these interactions and arrangements with professionals

from other agencies are almost always informal in nature. Because the interventionist spends most of his or her time with the child, little time is available to work and coordinate with other professionals.

In a single-program oriented model, the target for service delivery is children with identifiable disabilities or developmental delays. Therefore, the array of services consists of those services provided by the developmental intervention program and perhaps only a few other specialized programs that are designed primarily for children with disabilities. As a result, the services are specialized and usually offered in segregated settings when not provided in the child's home.

Network of Programs

In this model, a network of programs from a variety of agencies (e.g., health, social services, and mental health) has begun to meet together and engage in some cooperative planning. In many instances, the members of this group are trying to determine how to work together, as well as trying to decide the appropriate focus of their activities. This network often begins by focusing its efforts on some cooperative agreements around public awareness and reciprocal referral procedures. In some communities, the product of these efforts is a cooperatively developed and funded brochure, informing the public about the existence of various services, their location, general information about the services they provide, and the appropriate phone numbers for each program or service agency.

In a network of programs model, each agency or program continues autonomously to plan and carry out its own services; however, each becomes more aware of the services provided by the other agencies as well. The informal linkages and relationships are strengthened and, as a result, this network of programs may develop some formal agreements as well. However, because these agency representatives are accustomed to functioning autonomously, their first efforts at cooperative planning often focus on dividing service responsibilities in order to eliminate overlaps and to operate more efficiently.

The network of programs is primarily interested in serving children with disabilities, and the membership of the group depends on the background of the lead agency and the programs with which they have

TABLE 18.2. Infant–Toddler Service System Models

Model feature	Single program	Network of programs beginning to coordinate	Loosely coupled Primary coordination with intervention, secondary coordination with other agencies
Visual Depiction			
Organizational structure	Single intervention program provides most services and coordinates when necessary with other programs. Links to other programs are weak to moderate. Arrangements–agreements are usually informal.	A network of programs from multiple agencies that plan and implement programs somewhat autonomously but have recently established a Local Interagency Coordinating Council (LICC) and are beginning to do some cooperative and coordinated planning; system and services dominated by lead agency. Agreements and arrangements are usually informal, but many have formalized a few agreements or procedures.	Primary coordination occurs between and among two or more intervention programs designed to provide general developmental intervention either to children of all disabilities or to children with particular disabilities (e.g., language and motor). Local Interagency Coordinating Council (LICC) is instrumental in cooperative design of intervention procedures/components to be used across all providers (e.g., IFSP, assessment, and intervention). Focus is on educational intervention process more than on total coordination of educational intervention with health and welfare programs.
Decision making	Lead agency makes decisions, rarely asks other agencies for input, but primarily informs. Lead agency dominates decision making.	Lead agency dominates decision making. Other agencies participate so that they can be informed of decisions/policies of lead agency. Make some cooperative agreements around public awareness. Decisions often focus on dividing up service responsibilities.	The multiple intervention programs provide leadership/direction for LICC decisions (educational intervention predominates). Other agencies contribute, but secondarily.
Scope of target	Disability oriented in terms of population served.	Disability oriented in terms of population served.	Disability oriented in terms of population served.
Scope of resources	Array consists primarily of those programs designed for disabled children.	Focus of array and links depends upon the nature of the lead agency: poverty, disability, health, education.	Focus of array primarily those programs designed for disabled children.

Moderately coupled	Strongly coupled	Comprehensive System for All
Multiagency system with some leadership coming from lead agency	**Multiagency system – leadership and decision making dispersed among agencies**	**LICC is lead agency for comprehensive and cohesive system for all children**
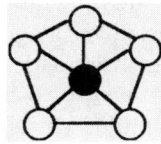	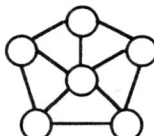	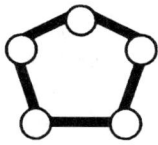
Lead agency or core group of agencies facilitates coordinated planning and service delivery among multiagency group that focuses not only on educational intervention but also to some extent on the health and welfare needs. A formal LICC has developed formal interagency procedures for service delivery.	LICC chair, lead agency, or core group of programs/agencies facilitate coordinated planning and service delivery. Many or most intervention activities are cooperative endeavors. Multiple educational intervention programs work closely as if on same staff or part of single program. Works like a well-oiled machine.	LICC is composed of a broad array of child and family services. All programs and providers (public and private) share common values and have participated in planning equally. System in the focus – all programs are designed to go together to form a cohesive whole. Grants written to supplement what public agencies are not funded to do. Use of a family center for ongoing coordination and co-location of programs.
Agencies contribute fairly equally to decision making. However, leadership and direction come from lead agency.	Strong cooperative LICC is the vehicle for all participants to have equal voice. Private programs and providers are also integrated in decision making.	Cooperative, equal decision making.
Population served can be disability oriented or disability and children at risk. Array of programs designed to meet not only educational needs of child but health and welfare needs of child and potential family needs as well.	Population served can be disability oriented or include children at risk, but some activities focus on all children. The array of programs and resources focuses on meeting educational, health, and welfare needs of children and their families.	Population addressed is all children and their families. Comprehensive array including specialized and natural community programs and resources.

the most natural linkages. For example, if the lead agency previously served children in poverty, then participating agencies are likely to be those programs that also served children in poverty (e.g., Head Start, Even Start, and the Health Department). If, however, the developmental intervention program is one that was developed for children with mental retardation (e.g., an ARC, formerly the Association for Retarded Citizens program), the program is likely to invite other categorical programs for children with disabilities (e.g., United Cerebral Palsy and other programs or clinics that provide specialized services and therapies for children with disabilities). The lead agency (the developmental intervention program) still dominates the decision making by setting the agenda and laying out the parameters regarding the choices and decisions to be made by the group. Accordingly, the network of programs recognizes the lead agency as the responsible agency for abiding by the law and making things work. Other agencies are seen as supplementary to service delivery.

Loosely Coupled System

When multiple programs form themselves into a single, broader organization or system, these newly formed organizations range in terms of how cohesive or how tightly they are bound together. The phrase "loose coupling" was first discussed by Glassman (1973) in the context of biology and then by March and Olson (1975) and Weick (1974, 1976) with regard to organizations in general and educational organizations in particular. In general, these authors delineated several characteristics of such systems: 1) influence is slow to spread among programs, 2) lack of coordination or slow coordination, 3) absence of regulations, 4) planned unresponsiveness, 5) independence, 6) decentralization, and 7) absence of linkages. Harbin and West (1998) showed that the concept of coupling and the degree of coupling were useful in describing the complexities and nuances of interagency coordination among human service agencies. Harbin and West (1998) used the characteristics described previously to distinguish four different levels of coupling of programs within systems, ranging from loosely coupled to a cohesive system for all children.

In this model (i.e., loosely coupled system), once again, developmental intervention with the child remains the focus of service delivery. However, a local interagency coordinating council (LICC) or group that has been meeting over the course of a few years is in existence, and the efforts of this group have moved from public awareness and streamlining the referral process to cooperatively designing and implementing some specific components of the intervention process (e.g., conducting multidisciplinary assessments). Other participating agencies, such as the Health Department, assist with developmental intervention that still focuses primarily on the educational needs of the child, which is still viewed as the responsibility of the lead agency (the developmental intervention program).

Under this type of system, some communities maintain multiple developmental intervention programs. These can be private or quasi-private programs that often initially served children with particular types of disabilities (e.g., United Cerebral Palsy or ARC) and which once also functioned autonomously. In some cases, these programs have received state funds, thus obligating that their practices be based on state requirements. As part of a loosely coupled system, these developmental intervention programs agree to relinquish some of their autonomy in order to meet new federal and state guidelines. The LICC becomes the mechanism to facilitate the agreement among programs in order to ensure that all assessments are conducted according to required procedures and that the individualized plan developed by various programs is referred to as an IFSP (Individualized Family Service Plan). Each program continues to use these assessment instruments and procedures that always have been in place, unless there is an interagency assessment process in which all programs participate. Similarly, each developmental intervention program often designs its own IFSP format. Rarely do other agencies (e.g., Health and Social Services) participate in the development of the IFSPs or the selection of needed resources and placements for the child or family.

Moderately Coupled Interagency System

As noted earlier, Glassman (1973), March and Olson (1975), and Weick (1974) presented the idea that there was a continuum regarding the amount of coupling among programs in a system. To that end, this model possesses a greater amount of coupling with regard to the characteristics outlined by Weick (1976), which were listed earlier. The programs in this model exhibit stronger connections than the loosely coupled system described previously. In this model, a local interagency council has cooperatively developed formal service delivery procedures. Agencies other than those that provide developmental intervention (e.g., Health and Mental Health) are seen as possessing an important perspective for planning the intervention system and as holding resources important to contribute to intervention for the child and his or her family. In the moderately coupled system, several agencies are seen as having an important role – not only the lead agency. Many times the lead agency continues to chair the interagency council, but the agenda is shaped and the leadership is provided by a core group of three or four individuals from different agencies. Agencies contribute fairly equally to decision making. As a result, the array of programs in this model includes those designed to meet not only the educational needs of the child but his or her health and welfare needs as well. This interagency model also recognizes and includes programs and services to meet some of the family's needs.

Strongly Coupled Interagency System

This model exhibits a higher level of connectedness and cohesion among agencies than the two previous models. In this model, several agencies are seen as responsible for coordinated planning and service delivery. The chair of the local interagency council can be a representative from any of the agencies and is usually selected on the basis of his or her leadership skills, not because he or she represents a particular agency. In some instances, the chair of the local council rotates yearly from one agency to another.

Many or most intervention activities in a strongly coupled interagency system are cooperative endeavors with each agency playing an equally important role. All agencies participate in discussions and share common understandings of such terms as *screening, family-centered practice, inclusion,* and *service coordination.* The service delivery system works like a well-oiled machine. Individuals from different programs work closely, as if they were part of a single program.

Private programs and providers are also integrated into the cooperative decision-making and service delivery processes.

The array of programs and resources in this model focuses on meeting the educational, health, and welfare needs of children and their families. The population served includes children with disabilities and often includes children at risk for developmental delay as well. In this model, the interagency council has also begun to focus some of its activities more broadly on all children within the community. The development of a family center to be used by all families, or a health fair, in which screening for developmental delay is only part of the event, is an example of this broader focus. Perhaps the health fair includes a variety of games or a puppet show to entertain the children, along with booths or stations that are designed to inform parents about the variety of useful resources within the community that are available to enhance their child's development and to facilitate family functioning.

Comprehensive System for All Children

This model is different from the previous model in two important ways: 1) the scope of the population to be addressed and hence the number and array of agencies that are involved and 2) the organizational structure. In this model, the participants plan a system of services for all young children and their families within the community. This philosophy of universal services recognizes that all children and families belong to the community, and thus it is the community's responsibility to support and facilitate the development of all children and support all families in this endeavor.

Individuals in these communities believe that providing universal services will result in four important consequences. First, children in need will be identified and receive services as soon as possible (early identification). Second, because all children receive services, developmental problems can be minimized or avoided (prevention). Third, stigma for receiving service is eliminated, because it is viewed as natural in the community to take advantage of resources; there is nothing wrong with help-seekers, help is their right and to their advantage. Fourth, this model makes it easier to access natural settings, resources, and activities. As a result of this broader vision of the service system, more agencies and programs are involved in addressing the scope of needs of all children and families within the community. This model also often includes services from programs or organizations that are clearly embedded in the larger community (e.g., Inter-Faith Council), but that are usually not included in the more disability-focused service delivery models discussed previously.

The second major difference between this model and the strongly coupled system lies in the organizational structure of this endeavor. In this model, the local coordinating council is considered the lead agency and often contains a broader representation of the community (e.g., business sector and city government). In addition to operating as the lead agency for service planning, the group might also receive funding, making it also the fiscal agent at times. The group has visibility within the community, often having a formal name (e.g., Partnership for Children) and is recognized as the primary force and vehicle for meeting family needs, even as individual programs are seen as supplementary and supportive to the cause. To maximize resources, all programs and participants participate cooperatively in decision making; and to supplement the community services (e.g., development of a family center), the council plans and writes grants to foundations, state agencies, and federal agencies for demonstration projects. In addition, when one of the local agencies must submit a grant to its funding agent, the local council has as much or more input into the design and conceptualization of the grant as the submitting agency.

This comprehensive approach requires community acceptance and support, as well as strong linkages between traditional public agencies (health, education, developmental disabilities, and social services), the business community (e.g., chamber of commerce), and the local governmental officials (e.g., town manager and mayor). It also requires a group of cooperative leaders that have the skills to build bridges between groups and constituencies and to develop working teams.

Summary: How Coordinated Are They?

Part C of IDEA requires coordinated programs. The law does not define which programs should be coordinated, how coordination should occur, or the mechanisms through which coordination should be achieved. However, given the types of complaints presented by parents to the congressional subcommittees on the Handicapped (U.S. Senate Report 99-315, 1986), families clearly prefer more coordination rather than autonomous service programs. Three of the previously described service delivery models, then, appear to meet family desires: moderately coupled, strongly coupled, and comprehensive systems for all children and families. However, in the nine communities studied by Harbin and West (1998), only four possessed one of these three models, leaving five communities that have not completely achieved the intent of those who advocated for a more comprehensive and coordinated service system.

The difficulties of coordinating services are described in the literature (Brewer & Kakalik, 1979; Gans & Horton, 1975; Harbin & McNulty, 1990; Kagan, Goffin, Golub, & Pritchard, 1995; Martinson, 1982; Peterson, 1991; Rogers & Farrow, 1983; Weis, 1981). Studies conducted by Harbin and her colleagues (Harbin & McNulty, 1990; Harbin et al., 1995; Harbin et al., 1998) indicate the importance of two factors in developing and implementing a coordinated service delivery structure. First, localities need policy direction from the state regarding how to set up an interagency structure because this task is not part of traditional discipline-specific training. Indeed, in the study by Harbin and West (1998), three of the four communities using one of the more comprehensive and coordinated models came from a single state (North Carolina). Policies in this state provided direction in the development and operation of the interagency structure to be used at the community level. Second, local authorities require training in how to perform the many tasks necessary for achieving the goal of developing a comprehensive and coordinated service system. Prominent among these tasks is taking an array of autonomous programs and resources and forming this disparate collection of services into a holistic system.

ELEMENTS OF SERVICE DELIVERY: WHAT ARE SERVICES LIKE?

In addition to seeking a coordinated and comprehensive service system, federal policy makers sought to make services more family-centered, integrated, and inclusive (see Table 18.1). In addition to being included in federal policy, these elements have been considered best practice for some time (Bruder & Chandler, 1993; McWilliam & Strain, 1993; Odom & McLean, 1993; Vincent & Beckett, 1993). Other aspects of service delivery addressed in this section include family satisfaction with services in general and with transition in particular. Suggested areas of program improvement by families are also included.

Family-Centered

The definition of family-centered practice has evolved over time (Bailey, 1987; Barber, Turnbull, Behr, & Kerns, 1988; Dunst, 1985; Dunst, Johanson, Trivette, & Hamby, 1991; Fewell & Vadasy, 1986; Rosenberg, 1977; Odom & McLean, 1993). More recently, McWilliam, Tocci, and Harbin (1995) utilized the literature, as well as discourse analyses of family interviews, to develop a more comprehensive definition, identifying four dimensions of family-centered principles, policies, and practices: 1) responding to family priorities, 2) empowering family members, 3) employing a holistic (ecological) approach to the family, and 4) demonstrating insight and sensitivity to families.

Kochanek and Brady (1995), Gallagher (1997d), and McWilliam, Tocci, and Harbin (1995), using a questionnaire, focus groups, and in-depth interviews, respectively, found that families expect services to focus on the needs of the child with disabilities. After all, that is why they signed up to participate in early intervention. Analysis of IFSPs revealed that the majority of the goals (86%) contained in these plans do indeed focus on the child (Gallagher, 1997b). Case study interviews of seventy-five families and forty-nine service providers also revealed that services are child-oriented (McWilliam, Tocci, & Harbin, 1995). Thus, despite the legal mandate and the widespread acceptance of the concept of a more ecological, holistic, and family-centered approach to intervention, it appears that most of the emphasis in intervention continues to be child-focused. To understand this phenomenon, McWilliam and his colleagues (1995) conducted a discourse analysis of interview transcripts and concluded that service providers were not "opening the door" to a more family-centered approach. Despite

IDEA's requirements "to assess families' strengths, priorities and concerns," professionals did not routinely or effectively ask families if they needed assistance in other areas. Hence, by not asking, they did not "open the door" to or facilitate a broader intervention focus. Families' early interactions with representatives of the program revolved around the formal assessment of their child's needs, the selection of goals for their child, and the selection of a placement for their child. This led McWilliam and colleagues to conclude, despite potential family needs and desires, that professionals set the stage for a child-centered approach because all of the initial program activities and questions focus on the child.

In fact, because families expect services to focus on their child, addressing child needs is the primary path to opening the door to a family-centered approach. McWilliam and his colleagues (1995) concluded that service providers must demonstrate competencies with the child, laying the foundation for establishing trust with the parents. Through this process, parents are then more willing to reveal their needs (McWilliam, Harbin et al., 1995). However, these revelations came only when parents realized that it might be possible to address family needs. This usually occurred informally. Unfortunately, many families never realized that other services could be accessed because the service provider failed to inform them early in the process, thus access to a more family-centered approach remained unavailable.

If a family-centered approach to service provision is considered best practice (McWilliam & Strain, 1993; Odom & McLean, 1993), then why have service providers been slow to implement this practice? In a survey ($N = 198$) by McWilliam and Lang (1994) and focus groups ($N = 67$) by Gallagher (1997c), service providers described why it was difficult to employ family-centered practices. These include 1) lack of training in how to address complex and sensitive family issues, 2) fear of offending or alienating the families, 3) lack of knowledge of resources within the community to meet family needs, and 4) belief that there are no existing resources to meet family needs within the community (Gallagher, 1997c; McWilliam & Lang, 1994).

However, despite these challenges and the absence of a family-centered approach in general, some of the service providers in case studies conducted by

McWilliam, Tocci, and Sideris (1997) employed family-centered practices. These individuals shared many of the following characteristics: 1) investment in the child and competence in working with the child, 2) respect for families' values and investment in diverse families, 3) connection with families based on something in common, 4) provision of informational and emotional support to the family, and 5) the service providers' style. The style consists of being positive, responsive, friendly, and sensitive. These findings support the characteristics described by Dunst and his colleagues (1994) in their delineation of a help-giving approach, which they contend leads to family-centered practices, in turn resulting in positive outcomes for children and families.

Some program models made more progress than others in implementing the vague and complex construct of family-centeredness. These programs possessed several characteristics in common. They were comprehensive, coordinated, flexible, responsive, and possessed program leaders who were knowledgeable about best practices in the area of family-centered service provision. Not only did these leaders understand this concept but they also valued it, designed aspects of the program and service system to reflect it, hired staff who would be most likely to use family-centered practices, and provided ongoing training and supervision in this area (Harbin & West, 1998).

Integrated Therapies

Some children with disabilities are born with sensory impairments (i.e., vision and hearing), conditions causing motor impairments (e.g., cerebral palsy), or communicative impairments (i.e., speech and language impairments). Congress recognized the need for providing physical therapy, occupational therapy, and speech and language therapy and included these traditional therapies in the list of required early intervention services (Section 1472 (E) P.L. 102-119 of IDEA Amendments, 1991). In addition to these traditional therapies, the law lists a variety of other services as well (e.g., nutrition, audiology, and family counseling). Therefore, each community must have these services available and provide them to the children who need them. The

law does not address the amount of therapy that should be provided. Neither does the law specify how the therapies should be provided.

Much has been written about the scarcity of therapists, particularly physical and occupational therapists (American Occupational Therapy Association, 1985; Dockery, 1988; Hyman, 1985; McWilliam, 1996b; Meisels et al., 1988; *Physical Therapy Bulletin*, 1988; Yoder & Coleman, 1990). The lack of specialized therapists, especially in rural areas, has plagued special education in general and early intervention in particular (Yoder & Coleman, 1990). Given the limited number of individuals prepared each year, it appears there may never be a sufficient number of therapists to provide required amounts of therapeutic intervention (U.S. Department of Education, 1995; Yoder & Coleman, 1990).

As a result of this personnel shortage, coupled with experts' knowledge of the interrelated nature of the child's development (Cicchetti & Wagner, 1990; McCune Kalmanson, Fleck, Glazewski, & Sillari, 1990; Woodruff et al., 1985), many professionals began to recommend a transdisciplinary approach to the provision of therapies (Bailey, 1989; Bruder, 1993; Bruder & Bologna, 1993; Garland, McGonigel, Frank, & Buck, 1989; Gilkerson, Hilliard, Schrag, & Shonkoff, 1987; Haynes, 1976; Klein & Campbell, 1990; Linder, 1990; McGonigel & Garland, 1988; McWilliam, 1991; Woodruff, Hanson, McGonigel, & Sterzin, 1990; Woodruff & McGonigel, 1988; Yoder & Coleman, 1990) or the use of therapists as consultants to those individuals who work more regularly with children (McWilliam, 1996b). Thus, experts in the field have argued that for therapies to be effective, they must be integrated into the child's natural activities and routines (McWilliam, 1991, 1996a; Williamson, 1994). This change requires a shift from traditional therapeutic environments, as well as a change in the way therapy is delivered. Instead of working solely with the child, the therapist must consult with other individuals who spend time with the child (e.g., parents, teachers, and child-care givers), assisting them in integrating therapy goals into normal routines (Bruder, 1996; McWilliam, 1991; Odom & McLean, 1993). Within a transdisciplinary team, members commit to teach, learn, and work across disciplinary boundaries, in both planning and providing integrated services. Families are considered important, participating members of the team.

However, recent studies reveal that children most often continued to receive separate therapies, using a traditional pull-out therapy model (Gallagher, 1997a; McWilliam, 1995; McWilliam, Young, & Harville, 1996). Program administrators attribute this to restrictions regarding the amount of time available from therapists, as well as the therapists' clear desire to continue to use a more traditional approach. Thus, it appears that administrators need assistance in structuring programs and using existing personnel in order to achieve a more integrated approach (Garland & Linder, 1994), as well as strategies to convince therapists that children will not be harmed by this approach (McGonigel, Woodruff, & Roszmann-Millican, 1994). More work by national and state associations to train and influence current therapists would also be helpful (Dunn, 1996; Hanft, 1989; Rainforth & Roberts, 1996). Finally, state policy makers could use the power of the purse to require the provision of integrated therapies in order to receive state funds (Gallagher, 1997a).

Inclusion

Many parents and professionals have long advocated for the provision of services in natural environments, which include both typically and atypically developing children (McWilliam & Strain, 1993; Odom & McLean, 1993). The infant–toddler and preschool sections of the IDEA certainly encourage this practice as well.

A study of nine communities indicates some progress in moving away from self-contained, segregated programs to serving children in more inclusive settings (Kochanek & Buka, 1995b; Kochanek & Buka, 1997). Thirty-four percent of the 300 children participating in this study received some type of developmental intervention in child care, Head Start, or play groups (Kochanek & Buka, 1995b). One of the three states participating in this study (North Carolina) served a higher proportion of children in inclusive settings than the other two states. Policy makers in this state stressed the importance of inclusion in statewide training as well as in policy, requiring segregated centers to become inclusive if they were to continue receiving state funds.

Although several communities are using inclusive settings, others rarely serve children in these settings. These communities continue to use a more traditional approach, focusing primarily on the educational needs of the child. In these programs, interventionists work only with children in home– or center-based settings that serve groups of children with disabilities.

Despite progress in increasing the number of children served in inclusive educational and child-care settings, less progress has been made to integrate the child and his or her family into other community programs and activities used by typically developing children and their families. As discussed earlier, researchers have advocated assisting families in participating in and utilizing the full variety of community resources (McKnight, 1987; Trivette et al., 1997). Examples of these programs for children include, but are not limited to, gymnastics, swimming, horseback riding, libraries, parks, and religious institutions. Possible options for families include religious institutions, civic and political organizations, clubs, YMCAs, and libraries, as well as educational, job training, and recreation programs.

Transition

Despite the similarity in the needs of infants, toddlers, and preschool children, federal policy has separate and different requirements for infants and toddlers (Part C of IDEA) and preschool children with disabilities (Part B of IDEA). Therefore, when children become 3 years of age they are required to leave the early intervention system and enter the preschool system for children with disabilities. Numerous professionals (Harbin et al., 1995) and families (McWilliam, Lang et al., 1995) have decried this situation. The federal law includes some requirements that are designed to facilitate this transition process.

Anticipating problems in transitioning from one program to another, state policy makers in the three states participating in the group of studies conducted by Harbin and Kochanek (1992) and their colleagues desired to develop a seamless system of services from birth through 5 years of age. Despite the local programs' compliance with the legal requirements and state policy makers efforts and intentions, parents participating in focus groups (Gallagher, 1997d; McWilliam, Harbin et al., 1995) and case studies (Tocci, McWilliam, Sideris, Melton, & Clarke, 1997) were extremely unhappy with the process. Families of infants and toddlers explained that it took time for them to learn about the program and services for their child and to begin to feel comfortable in navigating the system. Then, when their child turned 3, they were confronted with a new set of programs, placements, and rules and thus needed new information. Not surprisingly, the result often was frustration and anger.

To families, the requirement for transition from the infant and toddler program to the preschool program seems both unnecessary and ill-informed. The transition process can go smoothly from a bureaucratic point of view but may still be traumatic from a personal perspective for families. The transition process unwillingly severs the therapeutic relationship that took time to develop between the family and the service provider. The family and the service provider are required to terminate this relationship abruptly.

Understandable frustration, coupled with lack of contact, makes the development of a positive relationship between service provider and family difficult in preschool programs for children with disabilities. Some program administrators work to overcome these barriers by holding informational meetings for families, providing a list of possible service and placement options, and accompanying parents when they visit potential placements for their child. In some communities, the preschool special education program coordinator also attempts to play the role of service coordinator when children and families have needs that must be addressed by other agencies. However, to families this feels like applying Band-Aids to cover large wounds that should never have been inflicted.

It appears that this is one area of the law that needs to be changed. Until this occurs, it seems that we should turn to the literature of those professions that have traditionally established emotionally therapeutic relationships (e.g., psychiatry, clinical psychology, and social work) in order to better sensitize providers and administrators to the traumatic effects experienced by families as a result of severing their therapeutic relationship with their primary service provider.

Family Satisfaction

Historically, parent satisfaction with services was seen as an important indicator of program success (Wiegerink & Posante, 1977). Studies of parent satisfaction with early intervention services were conducted in several states since the implementation of Part C of IDEA (Able-Boone, Goodwin, Sandall, Gordon, & Martin, 1992; McWilliam, Lang et al., 1995; Upshur, 1991).

One hundred and ninety-five parents of children in nine early intervention programs across three states completed a twenty-one-item questionnaire that measured the parents' level of satisfaction in three broad areas: 1) providing information to families about their child and the competence of their service provider, 2) parent–service provider communication and engagement, and 3) service access and adequacy. Findings from this questionnaire were similar to those from the previously indicated studies, revealing highly favorable perceptions of the services received and of the individuals who provided the services (Kochanek & Brady, 1995). In particular, mothers reported that participation in early intervention had resulted in a clearer understanding of their child's needs and development and that they had developed knowledge and confidence in using strategies at home to promote their child's development (Kochanek & Brady, 1995). Mothers also viewed their providers as sincere, caring, competent, respectful, truthful, and thoughtful individuals. In addition, interviews with seventy-five families and focus groups with forty-five families revealed that although families thought highly of their service providers and often described the service providers as friends rather than professionals, they often wanted more services than they were receiving (Gallagher, 1997a; McWilliam, Tocci, & Harbin, 1998).

In addition to wanting more services, families' satisfaction was moderated by their knowledge of recommended practices. McWilliam, Lang, Vandiviere, Angell, Collins, and Underdown (1995) concluded that in some instances families would have been less satisfied with some aspects of service delivery if they had been more knowledgeable about best practice. These authors suggested the concept of parents as "uninformed consumers." These findings are similar to those reported in a study of child-care settings

(Cryer, 1994) in which a discrepancy existed between the satisfaction of parents and the ratings of program adequacy by independent observers.

In an earlier study of parent satisfaction with early intervention programs in North Carolina, McWilliam, Lang et al. (1995) identified another important phenomenon. In this study, numerical ratings of program satisfaction were extremely high. However, follow-up interviews with a sample of respondents uncovered areas of dissatisfaction. For example, families described significant barriers to the coordination of services. Similarly, Kochanek and Brady (1995), using a questionnaire, found relatively high program satisfaction in their study with 195 families. However, in focus groups conducted with some of the same families ($N = 45$), participants reported several problems in service delivery (Gallagher, 1997a, 1997b). Although generally satisfied with service provision, many of the seventy-five families participating in in-depth interviews identified three major areas of early intervention that they believe needed considerable improvement: 1) the availability and transmission of information to families, 2) contact with other parents, and 3) service coordination (Tocci et al., 1997). A brief description of parents' views of each of these three areas follows.

Parents want comprehensive, organized information about all available services and resources that are both specialized and nonspecialized, and they want an easily accessible and easy to read, family-friendly directory of resources. Parents often spend a significant amount of time trying to locate resources and services while navigating the service system (Tocci et al., 1997). Parents want to be able to access information on their own when they need it, and they do not want to rely on or depend on professionals to determine what information to give them.

Although parents reported that their service providers were extremely supportive and they valued this support, they also identified the need to speak to and connect with other parents in similar circumstances (Tocci et al., 1997). These parents reported preferences for interactions with individual parents on an as-needed basis or more informal group gatherings such as picnics (Gallagher, 1997c, 1997d; Krauss, Upshur, Shonkoff, & Hauser-Cram, 1993). Many parents viewed the traditional parent support groups as reflecting a clinical or therapy orientation, with which they were uncomfortable (Gallagher, 1997d).

The role of the service coordinator is extremely important in informing parents about available services as well as in assisting in the coordination of relevant services and resources (Zipper, Weil, & Rounds, 1991). In a paper-and-pencil measure of 195 families' satisfaction with services, one of the items asked families to rate their level of satisfaction with service coordination (Kochanek & Brady, 1995). The mean rating by study families was 5.6 on a 7-point scale, with responses ranging from 1 (*low satisfaction*) to 7 (*high degree of satisfaction*), thus indicating relatively high satisfaction when a quantitative measure was used.

However, many of the seventy-five parents participating in the case study interviews indicated that service coordination, as currently practiced, was not an effective vehicle for the provision of information to families or in the coordination of services to children and their families (Tocci et al., 1997). Several families were unable to identify their service coordinator, despite the fact that the name of this individual is supposed to appear on the IFSP.

Four different approaches to service coordination were used across the nine communities studied by Tocci et al. (1997). The service coordinator is 1) the child's/family's primary service provider; 2) someone other than the primary service provider, but who works within the same agency as the primary interventionist; 3) someone who also provides intervention but is from another agency; and 4) someone from an independent agency that does not provide service. The experiences of the families in the case study revealed that the third and fourth approaches were the least effective, because with these approaches the service coordinator saw families infrequently and was too far removed from their experience to be effective.

FACTORS INFLUENCING SERVICE PROVISION

Although the importance of the various components of the broader ecology has widely been accepted (Bronfenbrenner, 1975; Garbarino, 1990; Odom & McLean, 1993), until recently there were few data to support this belief. Harbin et al. (1998) integrated data obtained from 120 families, 116 service providers, 37 program administrators, and 60 community leaders across three states and nine communities. They constructed a community portrait, identifying the most important factors influencing service delivery in each of nine diverse communities. Qualitative cross-site analyses (Yin, 1989) revealed some differences in the results of service delivery across children and, more importantly, to some extent across communities as well. For example, there were differences in the percentage of children served, the array of services provided, and the ease of navigability through the service system by parents. One of the most important findings is that no single factor was sufficient to explain child or community differences. Indeed, differences in service delivery appear to be associated with a combination of factors, supporting those who propose an ecological theory of child development and outcomes (Bronfenbrenner, 1979; Garbarino, 1990). The seven broad interacting factors linked to service delivery identified by Harbin and her colleagues (1997) include 1) state and community context, 2) state policy, 3) service delivery model, 4) leadership, 5) service provider skills and characteristics, 6) family characteristics, and 7) service provider–family relationships. Previous sections of this chapter have already discussed some of these factors. However, because all of these interactive factors play an important role in understanding the nature of service delivery, each of the factors is presented. The "systemic" nature of early intervention requires a systematic appraisal of all these factors in each community in order to improve service delivery significantly.

Context

Community is defined as "a social system composed of people living in some spatial relationship to one another, who share common facilities and services, develop a common psychological identification with the locality symbol, and together frame a common communication network" (Chekki, 1979, p. 5). The milieu within which communities exist is known as the *community context* (Bronfenbrenner, 1979). Previous policy implementation studies of other federal programs aimed at changing the human service system identified several elements of the community context as playing an important role in shaping the nature of policy implementation from

one community to another (Elazar, 1984; Foster, 1978; Mazmanian & Sabatier, 1983; Walker, 1969; Weatherly, 1979).

Factors also exist within the state as a whole that have some bearing on individual communities (Marshall, Mitchell, & Wirt, 1985). For example, when the state economy is experiencing a serious downturn, state fiscal resources to communities are reduced. Similarly, the current devolution of federal governmental functions is likely to result in new expectations of community leaders and community service systems. A change in one part of the state system, such as welfare reform initiatives, will have consequences for other components of the human services system within communities.

Shaw and Harbin (1997) identified seven broad contextual factors within nine communities that were found to have some influence on the resulting services provided to children and their families. These include leadership, culture, history, resources, economy, political climate, and geography. This cluster of contextual factors interacted in unique ways in each of the nine communities. Merely by living in a particular community, service leaders, service providers, and families receive powerful and unique messages influencing the way they think and behave, as well as influencing their expectations of individuals and institutions within the community. For example, as a result of the community context, individuals designing and implementing early intervention may expect to solve problems cooperatively and to generate resources, despite a poor local economy, believing that all people in the community can contribute to solutions. Conversely, in a different community, because of their experience with ineffective community leaders, individuals may feel that human service problems are insurmountable, resulting in lowered expectations and passivity, feeling they must accept what is provided.

Yet, in other communities, the experience of a bureaucratic government that is unresponsive to its citizens prepares families to approach the service system with doubt and skepticism, expecting to have to fight for services. Thus, cultural values and the ability of the leadership within the community provide a powerful framework for initial and subsequent interactions among all of the individuals involved, particularly regarding families' beliefs in the value and quality of services offered to them.

Accordingly, those who seek to make changes in the design of the service system need to understand how the desired changes will fit with the context of the community. If the desired service system changes are different from the attitudes, values, and expectations of the community at large, these differences should be addressed, or those participating in service delivery as providers and recipients will experience significant barriers.

State Policy

Policy is defined as "the rules and standards that are established in order to allocate scarce public resources to meet a particular social need" (Gallagher, Harbin, Eckland, & Clifford, 1994). Three aspects of state policy are linked to service delivery: breadth, emphasis, and specificity. The breadth of the state's eligibility policy, in general, was linked to the percentage of children served in three states (Harbin & West, 1998). The three states had differing levels of eligibility policy (broad, moderate, and narrow). The state with the broadest policy served the highest percentage, whereas the state with the narrowest policy served the lowest percentage of infants and toddlers with disabilities. However, differences were found among the three communities in each state with regard to the percentage of children served, indicating that state policy is only one of the influential factors related to the percentage of children deemed eligible and served.

Although all three states' policies addressed the components contained in the federal legislation (Part C of IDEA), the emphasis of the state policy, as well as the policy areas stressed by policy makers, was linked to variability in service delivery. As reported earlier in this chapter, the state in which policy makers most emphasized serving children in inclusive settings served a higher proportion of children in these settings than the other two states (Kochanek & Buka, 1995b). Similarly, the communities in the state that had a policy specifying particular interagency structures and mechanisms were among the more comprehensive and cohesive interagency service delivery models in the study.

Finally, one of the state's policies was written in bureaucratic language and contained processes that were more bureaucratic than the other two states' policies. This bureaucratic emphasis was associated with community service delivery models that were more insular and cumbersome and that lacked the necessary flexibility to establish an interagency system or to be responsive to families. Families in this state more frequently "ran into the walls" of the system than did families in the other two states.

One state provided more specificity with regard to the assessment process than the other two states. Consequently, assessment practices in this state more closely resembled best practice than in the other two states. Although the policy characteristics of emphasis and specificity were discussed separately, they are usually intertwined. Those aspects that are emphasized in the written policy and by policy makers usually contain more policy specificity as well. The amount and nature of policy specificity and emphasis helped to shape the community service delivery models and processes.

Service System Model

As discussed earlier in this chapter, six different models operated across nine communities studied by Harbin and West (1998). In a cross-site comparative analysis, there seemed to be a link between different models of service delivery and the results of service delivery (e.g., percentage of children served and array of services provided; Harbin, Tocci et al., 1998). Six aspects of the service delivery model appear to contribute to differences in service delivery. These consist of 1) the structure and organization of the model, 2) the linkages between and among programs and resources, 3) flexibility, 4) inclusion of best practice in program policies and procedures, 5) personnel practices, and 6) leadership. Although leadership of the early intervention program is technically part of the service delivery model, the importance of this aspect warrants separate attention and is highlighted later.

In general, the more comprehensive and cohesive the system, the better the results for children and families. The more cohesive the system, the broader the array of services and the better the linkages among programs in the public sector, as well as between the public and private sectors. In cohesive service system models, staff tend to use practices more frequently that are identified as desirable by experts in the field (e.g., family-centered and inclusion). Conversely, the service delivery models that were generally associated with less positive results (e.g., not meeting needs of children and families and families frustrated by the system) were usually more insular, having a narrower array of services and weaker linkages with other programs and resources. These programs did not employ nationally recognized best practices in their policy and procedures and were often described as more bureaucratic and rigid.

It is interesting to note that the characteristics of the service delivery models listed here are nearly identical to those listed in the section of this chapter describing family-centered intervention programs. Thus, it appears in the nine communities studied that the programs that tend to provide family-centered services also tend to be the same programs that result in other enhanced outcomes as well (e.g., broader array of services, more individualized services, increased amount of services, and increased use of inclusive settings).

Leadership

The skills and knowledge of the early intervention leaders were a significant factor in determining the nature and direction of the service delivery model. In those communities in which in general there were more positive outcomes for children and their families, leaders shared several qualities. These successful leaders had a clear sense of mission, a broader and more comprehensive vision of the service system, and the ability to communicate this vision to different groups of stakeholders (Bennis, 1984; Garland & Linder, 1994; Harbin et al., 1993; Larson & LaFasto, 1989). They put together an array of services and resources that spanned the public and private sectors and addressed not only the educational needs of the child but were designed to meet some of the health, recreational, and welfare needs of children with disabilities and their families as well. Successful leaders were knowledgeable about best practice. They established a foundation for the service system on the basis of this knowledge. They also communicated elements of this philosophic base to staff and set expectations for staff to utilize best practice in interactions with children and families. These leaders were also resourceful and flexible. They sought all available resources within the community and when necessary went to outside sources, such as

grants, to bring new resources to the community. In addition, successful leaders were bridge-builders. They communicated well and established good relationships with families, their own program staff, staff from other agencies, other administrators, and community leaders. Successful leaders were adept at understanding complex situations, creating and managing change, and unleashing talent – often described as situational leadership (Garland & Linder, 1994; Harbin et al., 1993; Hersey & Blanchard, 1988; McNulty, 1989).

Service Providers

Cross-site analysis by Harbin et al. (1998) revealed generally that in those communities with more positive service outcomes regarding the amount and nature of service delivery, most service providers shared several important characteristics. These characteristics are similar to those presented earlier with regard to family-centered practices and include 1) sensitivity to families and cultures, 2) knowledge and use of best practice, 3) initiative and resourcefulness, 4) flexibility, 5) responsiveness, and 6) a style of help-giving that enables and empowers families. These help-giving skills and attitudes were consistent with many of those identified by Dunst and his colleagues (1991).

Perhaps one of the most interesting and important findings in the study by Harbin, Shaw, and colleagues (1998) was the link between the qualities and competencies of the service providers and the qualities and competencies of the leadership of the developmental intervention program. (This person is often referred to as the program coordinator.) Consistently, where the leaders were skillful and knowledgeable, so too were all, or most of, the service providers employed by the program. Cross-site analysis revealed that the successful coordinators used hiring practices to select staff who possessed knowledge of best practice (i.e., family-centered, inclusion, and so forth), teamwork and partnership skills and attitudes, and resourcefulness and flexibility (Garland & Linder, 1994). They also used in-service training, ongoing supervision, and the provision of informational and emotional support as mechanisms to continue to facilitate further growth and improvement in the service providers' knowledge and skills.

These coordinators were not the traditional bureaucratic administrators who maintain distance between themselves and their staff by focusing on paperwork and meetings. Instead, successful program coordinators also served as mentors and educational leaders for their staff. One program coordinator, for instance, not only provided opportunities for in-service training but also arranged with one of the universities in the state to have her community serve as an off-campus location for a graduate training program. Because this community is located two and one-half hours from the closest university training program, it otherwise would have been impossible for staff to take classes at night. By bringing this graduate program to the community, this program coordinator advocated for her staff, improved their knowledge and skills, and enhanced service delivery to children and families.

Families

Case studies of seventy-five families conducted by Tocci and her colleagues (1997) revealed three characteristics possessed by families that influenced the amount and nature of service provision, as well as their perceptions of control over service provision: 1) knowledge of the service system and ability to navigate within it; 2) knowledge of resources to meet the needs of their child and family and the ability to go after those resources (i.e., resourcefulness); and 3) the ability to advocate persistently for the needs of their family, including their child with disabilities. These family skills were often associated with increased services or increased service options, whereas the absence of these skills by family members sometimes was associated with fewer or more fragmented services, especially when the families lived in a community that had narrow and uncoordinated early intervention services. Thus, the early intervention system, and the developmental intervention program in particular, act as mediating variables with regard to the families' influence on service provision.

It is important to note that these three family skills can be addressed and strengthened. Program policies and procedures, behaviors of service providers, and changes in federal and state funded parent training centers might increase the likelihood that parents will gain increased competence in these areas.

Service Provider–Family Relationships

Families enter the system with a variety of expectations and competencies; the responsibility for establishing enabling and empowering relationships lies with the service provider (Dunst & Trivette, 1990). Not surprisingly, in those communities in which service providers took the lead in establishing enabling and empowering relationships (Dunst & Trivette, 1990) with families, service outcomes tended to be more positive. Families not only felt positively about their experiences but felt capable as well (Harbin et al., 1998). These relationships were built on mutual trust; partnerships, with each partner contributing; reciprocity; caring; and fostering independence (Harbin, Shaw, McWilliam, Westheafer, & Frazier, 1997).

Conversely, relationships that were built on control, paternalism (i.e., helping by doing for the less fortunate), and staying within the boundaries of the program and the "professional" role, resulted in families who often were more passive, dispirited, or grudgingly resigned to accept what was provided. It is clear from the data on a larger sample of children ($N = 300$) that some similarities between the service provider and the family can result in an increase in the amount of services delivered (Kochanek & Buka, 1995b). Case study data of seventy-two families independently confirmed this. The similarity is described here by one service provider: "I guess one thing is that you kind of find whatever you have in common with them. The biggest bond that you can build is if there is anything that you have that is similar to what they've been through or going through right now....I think that's been the biggest thing, like the ice breaker with families."

Summary: Interacting Influential Factors

Although each of the factors can be discussed individually, many of the factors interact to influence service delivery. Figure 18.1 presents a summary of the factors discussed earlier. Central to the understanding of service delivery is the interaction among 1) the service delivery model, which includes the developmental intervention program and the broader service system in which the program operates; 2) service provider(s); and 3) families. The characteristics of each of these interact, influencing

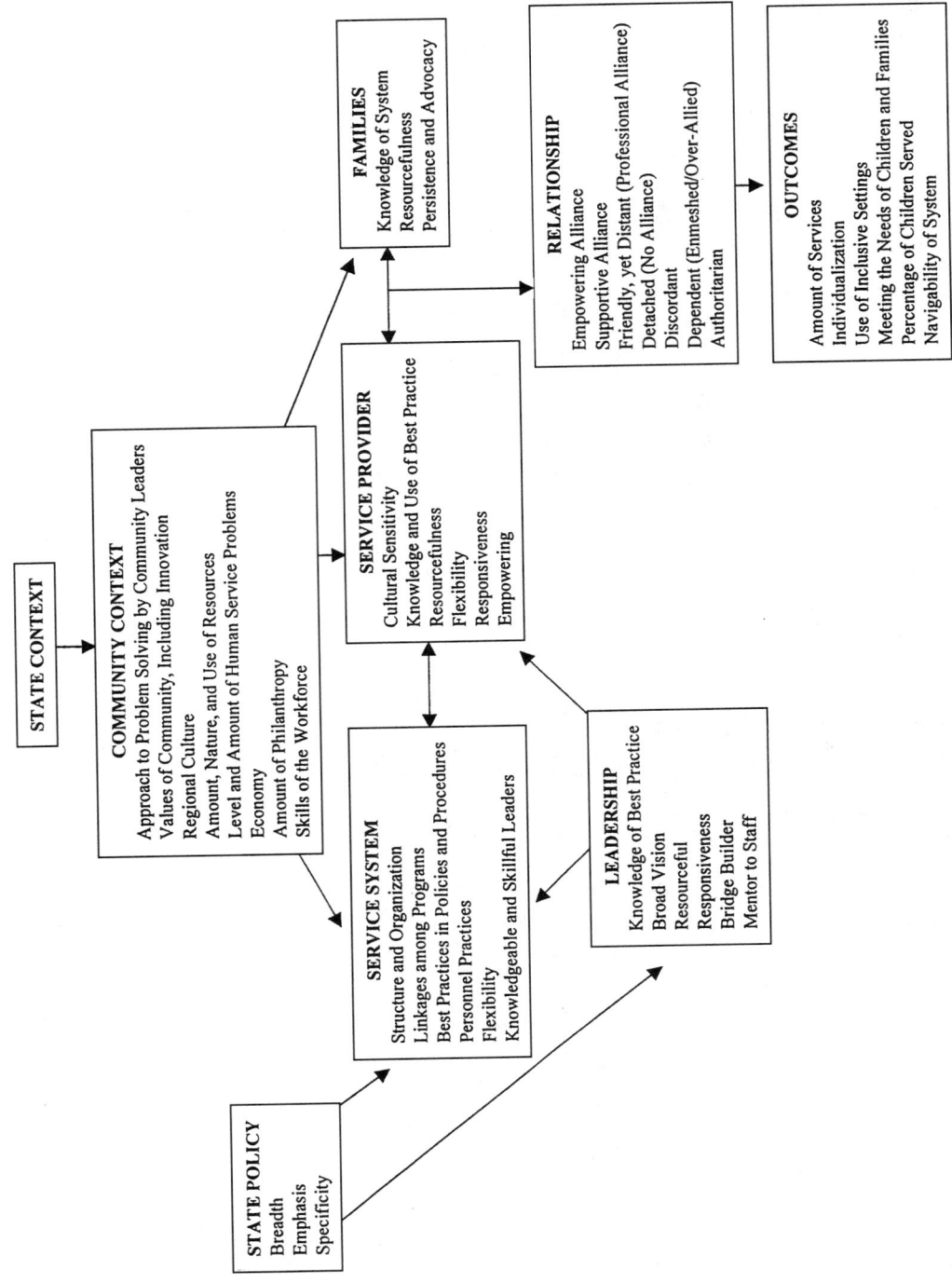

Figure 18.1. Factors Interacting to Influence Service Provision and Service Outcomes

the relationship between the family and the service provider. The nature of this relationship has a significant influence on the services and resources offered and used, as well as on the resulting service outcomes.

The leader of the developmental intervention program, as well as the leaders of the early intervention service system, exert a powerful influence over the program, system, and service providers. The vision, skills, and knowledge of the leaders greatly influence how comprehensive, coordinated, family-centered, and inclusive the service delivery model is. These individuals also have a great deal of influence on the use of best practice (Odom & McLean, 1993), including the help-giving style (Dunst et al., 1994; McWilliam, Tocci, & Sideris, 1997) of the service providers, which is directly linked to the service provider–family relationship.

The program and service system leaders are shaped in part by factors within the community in which they live (e.g., values, priorities, and community leaders' resourcefulness and approach to problem solving). Their vision of the system is partially shaped by state policies, the nature and content of their training, as well as their experiences. State policy also sets up the parameters and emphasis for the service system, thus influencing numerous aspects of the service delivery model. State policies influence service providers directly through credentialing and continuing education requirements.

Clearly, to deny the "systems" properties of service delivery would be shortsighted. According to systems theory, properties of each component must be addressed, because each component exerts influence on the system (Garbarino, 1990). To identify one factor as the most important and to focus exclusively on that factor would not be as effective as systematically addressing each and anticipating the results of the interactions.

CONCLUSION

The Individuals with Disabilities Education Act (IDEA) sought to change and improve services to young children with disabilities and their families, and the provisions of this law created hope in many parents that the dreams for their children might be realized. Studies reviewed in this chapter revealed, in general, that communities have made

progress in the implementation of this federal policy. More children, for instance, are being served, and more children are also being identified earlier (Kochanek & Buka, 1995a). In contrast, these studies indicate that despite this and other progress in implementing components of Part C of IDEA, improvements nonetheless are needed. For example, although more children are being served, the percentage of the total population served indicates that not all eligible children are receiving services. Changes in policy, practice, and training are needed if we are to continue to make progress in providing quality services to all young children with disabilities and their families.

Prior to the implementation of this law at the community level, Shonkoff and Meisels (1990) identified four broad challenges in meeting the intent, as well as the letter of the law: 1) redesigning service delivery systems, 2) rethinking traditional disciplinary boundaries, 3) reconsidering parent-professional relationships, and 4) matching service goals and recipients. Results of the studies reviewed in this chapter indicate that local program developers and implementors continue to struggle with these challenges.

Redesign Service Delivery Models

The service delivery models currently in use in some communities are more complex than models employed previously. In these, community leaders have designed a coordinated system of services composed of many programs. However, in the remaining communities, the development of a comprehensive, coordinated system has yet to be achieved. Results of studies in nine communities indicate that the more comprehensive and cohesive service systems tend to produce better services for children and families. Unfortunately, many community administrators and service providers in this country have received little direction or guidance regarding what a system should contain or how it should be organized. Clearly, individuals charged with developing a comprehensive, coordinated service system would benefit from more direction by means of policy and training. State policy makers (e.g., program administrators and the State Interagency Coordinating Council) could develop a list of programs (e.g., WIC and EPSDT) and resources (child care, YWCA, etc.) that should be considered when developing a comprehensive system. It is possible that the taxonomy of resources developed by Trivette and her colleagues (1997) could be useful in generating a broad array of programs and resources. Local program administrators could also receive training as an interagency team with regard to how to envision a system; how to establish the system, including which structures and mechanisms need to be in place; and what processes are useful to achieve these goals. The process of shared leadership was important in the more coordinated service delivery models and supports earlier findings on the importance of a core group of leaders in the development of a system of services (Bennis, 1984; Dyer, 1987; Ends & Page, 1977; Harbin & McNulty, 1990). Finally, further research is needed to establish a clear link between characteristics of the service delivery model and the outcomes of service delivery (e.g., child progress and increased family competence).

Rethinking Traditional Disciplinary Boundaries

Best practice recognizes the importance and necessity of the team approach in service provision (McGonigel et al., 1994; Odom & McLean, 1993). Perhaps one of the most disappointing findings in the previous reviews is the lack of teams for the provision of services. The coordination of tasks and roles to facilitate the complex development of young children is essential. Attitudinal barriers, high case loads, and inadequate administrative structures are just some of the barriers to a more coordinated integrated and transdisciplinary approach to direct service provision. Agencies can become more coordinated in their service delivery activities, but unless we improve the integration of the activities of the individual service providers who are responsible for the direct provision of services, we will fail to meet the needs of children and families or maximize their development.

Reconsidering Parent–Professional Relationships

Families report that service providers are responsive and provide invaluable support (Gallagher, 1997d; McWilliam, Tocci, & Harbin, 1995). However, it appears for a variety of reasons that service pro-

viders have not opened the door to families' needs that go beyond their concern for their child's disability. This might be due in part to the fact that state policies provide specific guidance with regard to the child: what to assess, how to assess, and so forth. However, these policies lack the same specificity in addressing family needs: which needs to address, when to assess, and how to assess. Perhaps more specificity and focus in state policy or in program guidelines would be helpful to program administrators and service providers, assisting them in knowing how and when to open the door. Because making a more family-centered approach accessible and developing an empowering relationship occur as part of the process of interaction between families and service providers, training that provides the opportunity to learn and practice establishing relationships with different types of families is warranted. (The use of parents as trainers in this process seems essential.) The relationship typologies developed by Harbin, Shaw et al. (1998) might be useful in helping service providers learn how to develop more empowering and capacity-building relationships. The typologies could also be used by supervisors as part of their staff evaluation process. Research could be used to determine the effectiveness of various training strategies, such as the case method of instruction (McWilliam, 1992), role-playing, mentoring, or coaching.

These studies also point to another need that should be addressed. Opening the door to family-centered practice is accomplished only partially through asking families about broader family issues and concerns. Family-centered practice also requires a partnership with families (Dunst & Paget, 1991). Families in these studies echo the sentiments of other families who request more information about all available services and resources; currently, many parents are uninformed consumers and, thus, unequal "partners." It is difficult to be a partner in service delivery by caring adequately and advocating for your child when information and knowledge are lacking.

Matching Service Goals and Recipients

Integration of data by Harbin and colleagues (1997) across several studies also demonstrated the value of designing a system of services and resources to meet the needs of all children and their families. The most comprehensive and coordinated services for disabled children and their families tended to occur in the community that had designed a comprehensive system for all young children and families. It appears from this review that within this broader system it was easier to match the needs of children with the available resources and programs. This broader system seemed to bring greater knowledge to all those involved with service delivery, thus improving their ability to identify and use an array of community resources. Conversely, the greater the fragmentation of services, the more difficult the task of identifying resources to meet the individual needs of children and their families. It is important to note that early intervention program coordinators provided the leadership for developing this broader system of services. It is quite possible that if early intervention leaders are not involved substantively in the design of these broader systems, children with disabilities could be neglected and excluded.

In many communities, multiple initiatives targeted to a variety of specific problem areas exist; creating high quality, coordinated services for children with disabilities is only one of these initiatives. In North Carolina, a state-funded initiative (Smart Start) was proposed to increase and improve a variety of resources for all young children in each community. All interested and relevant stakeholders were to be brought together "around a table" to plan a service system for all young children, determining together what was needed to achieve this goal. As a result, Smart Start created local public–private Partnerships for Children (Bryant, Maxwell, Burchinal, & Lowman, 1997a; Bryant, Maxwell, Burchinal, & Lowman, 1997b; Cornish & Noblit, 1997; Smart Start, 1994; Smart Start, 1995). Recent Smart Start evaluation efforts suggest that the quality of preschool center-based child care has improved as a result of Smart Start activities. Smart Start is only one such initiative. Other states through either their governor's office or initiatives funded by foundations or organizations are also seeking to increase and improve services to our nation's young children (Knitzer & Page, 1996).

Efforts such as Smart Start and the service delivery model described by Harbin and West (1998), which suggested a system of services for all children and their families, require the support of a variety of

community segments and call for an assessment of the community context: its values, issues, barriers, and strengths (Shaw & Harbin, 1997). Leaders must also become knowledgeable about community development strategies, including learning to garner the support and participation of local governmental officials and business leaders. There is, however, a scarcity of adequate community development models to guide community leaders. Clearly, development of these models and research to determine their effectiveness would be beneficial.

Successfully addressing the four challenges outlined earlier will require attention to multiple factors simultaneously. However, this review demonstrates the critical role played by leadership in positively addressing and improving service delivery. The quality of leadership appeared to be linked to the nature of the service delivery model; knowledge, skills, and behaviors of the service providers; and the types of help-giving relationships formed by service providers. The influence of program leadership on service delivery warrants more emphasis in training and research than currently exists.

Current preservice and in-service training programs ignore training in critical leadership skills, focusing instead on aspects of direct services. Many program coordinators need long-term ongoing training that prepares them to be the educational leader within their program (Garland & Linder, 1994), much like the principal is the educational leader of the school. In addition, they must also gain competence working as leaders at the system level, another skill for which they are often unprepared.

If the promises of IDEA are to be realized, continued improvement is needed in both service delivery and the creation of service delivery models for young children with disabilities. Currently, there is variability in service provision, with children and families in some communities better served than children and families in other communities, raising important issues of equity. Review of the various issues raised in this chapter indicate that improvements can be made only by addressing several interacting factors: No single factor is responsible for service provision. Although development of comprehensive, coordinated service delivery systems is a complex and challenging endeavor, meeting this challenge is essential if the hopes and dreams of families and the potential of our nation's youngest citizens are to be realized.

REFERENCES

Able-Boone, H., Goodwin, L. D., Sandall, S. R., Gordon, N., & Martin, D. G. (1992). Consumer-based early intervention services. *Journal of Early Intervention, 16*, 201–9.

American Occupational Therapy Association. (1985). *Occupational therapy manpower: A plan for progress*. Rockville, MD: Author.

Bagnato, S. J., & Neisworth, J. T. (1981). *Linking developmental assessment and curricula: Prescriptions for early intervention*. Rockville, MD: Aspen Systems.

Bailey, D. B. (1987). Collaborative goal-setting with families: Resolving differences in values and priorities for services. *Topics in Early Childhood Special Education, 7*(2), 59–71.

Bailey, D. B. (1989). Issues and directions in preparing professionals to work with young handicapped children and their families. In J. J. Gallagher, P. L. Trohanis, & R. M. Clifford (Eds.), *Policy implementation & P.L. 99-457: Planning for young children with special needs* (pp. 97–132). Baltimore, MD: Paul H. Brookes.

Bailey, D. B., & Wolery, M. (1992). *Teaching infants and preschoolers with disabilities* (2nd ed.). New York: Macmillan.

Barber, P. A., Turnbull, A. P., Behr, S. K., & Kerns, G. M. (1988). A family systems perspective on early childhood special education. In S. L. Odom & M. B. Karnes (Eds.), *Early intervention for infants and children with handicaps* (pp. 198–9). Baltimore, MD: Paul H. Brookes.

Beckman, P. J., Robinson, C. C., Jackson, B., & Rosenberg, S. A. (1986). Translating developmental findings into teaching strategies for young handicapped children. *Journal of the Division for Early Childhood, 10*, 45–52.

Bennis, W. (1984). The four competencies of leadership. *Training and Development Journal, 38*(8), 15–19.

Brewer, G., & Kakalik, J. (1979). *Handicapped children: Strategies for improving services*. New York: McGraw-Hill.

Bricker, D., & Veltman, M. (1990). Early intervention programs: Child-focused approaches. In S. J. Meisels & J. P. Shonkoff (Eds.), *Handbook of early childhood intervention* (pp. 373–99). New York: Cambridge University Press.

Bronfenbrenner, U. (1975). *Influences on human development*. Hinsdale, IL: Dryden Press.

Bronfenbrenner, U. (1979). *The ecology of human development: Experiments by nature and design*. Cambridge, MA: Harvard University Press.

Bruder, M. B. (1993). The provision of early intervention and early childhood special education within community early childhood programs: Characteristics of effective service delivery. *Topics in Early Childhood Special Education, 13*(1), 19–37.

Bruder, M. B. (1996). Interdisciplinary collaboration in service delivery. In R. A. McWilliam (Ed.), *Rethinking pull-out services in early intervention: A professional resource* (pp. 27–48). Baltimore, MD: Paul H. Brookes.

Bruder, M. B., & Bologna, T. (1993). Collaboration and service coordination for effective early intervention. In W. Brown, S. K. Thurman, & L. F. Pearl (Eds.), *Family-centered early intervention with infants and toddlers: Innovative cross-disciplinary approaches* (pp. 103–27). Baltimore, MD: Paul H. Brookes.

Bruder, M. B., & Chandler, L. K. (1993). Transition. In S. L. Odom & M. McLean (co-chairpersons), *DEC recommended practices: Indicators of quality in programs for infants and young children with special needs and their families* (pp. 96–104). DEC Task Force on Recommended Practices: The Council for Exceptional Children.

Bryant, D., Maxwell, K., Burchinal, P., & Lowman, B. (1997a). *North Carolina Smart Start Initiative: 1996–97 annual evaluation report*. Report to the Department of Human Resources by the Smart Start Evaluation Team, University of North Carolina at Chapel Hill.

Bryant, D., Maxwell, K., Burchinal, P., & Lowman, B. (1997b). *The effects of Smart Start on the quality of preschool child care*. Report to the Department of Human Resources by the Smart Start Evaluation Team, Frank Porter Graham Child Development Center, University of North Carolina at Chapel Hill.

Campbell, R., & Mazoni, T. (1976). *State policy making for the public schools*. Berkeley, CA: McCutcheon Publishing Corp.

Chekki, D. A. (1979). *Community development: Theory and method of planned change*. New Delhi, India: Vikas.

Cicchetti, D., & Wagner, S. (1990). Alternative assessment strategies for the evaluation of infants and toddlers: An organizational perspective. In S. J. Meisels & J. P. Shonkoff (Eds.), *Handbook of early childhood intervention* (pp. 246–77). New York: Cambridge University Press.

Cornish, M., & Noblit, G. (1997). *Bringing the community in the process: Issues and promising practices for involving parents and business in local Smart Start partnerships*. University of North Carolina Smart Start Evaluation Report.

Cryer, D. (1994). *Parents as informed consumers of child care: What are their values? What do they know about the product they purchase?* Unpublished doctoral dissertation, University of North Carolina at Chapel Hill.

Dockery, J. L. (1988). *Council on medical education report*. Reported to Reference Committee C, Donald T. Lewers, M. D., Chairman.

Dokecki, P. R., & Heflinger, C. A. (1989). Strengthening families of young children with handicapping conditions: Mapping backward from the "street level." In J. J. Gallagher, P. L. Trohanis, & R. M. Clifford (Eds.), *Policy implementation & P. L. 99-457: Planning for young children with special needs* (pp. 59–84). Baltimore, MD: Paul H. Brookes.

Dunn, W. (1996). Occupational therapy. In R. A. McWilliam (Ed.), *Rethinking pull-out services in early intervention: A professional resource* (pp. 267–314). Baltimore, MD: Paul H. Brookes.

Dunst, C. J. (1985). Rethinking early intervention. *Analysis and Intervention in Developmental Disabilities, 5,* 165–201.

Dunst, C. J., Johanson, C., Trivette, C. M., & Hamby, D. W. (1991). Family-oriented early intervention policies and practices: Family-centered or not? *Exceptional Children, 58,* 115–26.

Dunst, C. J., & Paget, K. D. (1991). Parent–professional partnerships and family empowerment. In M. J. Fine (Ed.), *Collaboration with parents of exceptional children* (pp. 25–44). Brandon, VT: Clinical Psychology Publishing Co.

Dunst, C. J., & Trivette, C. M. (1990). Assessment of social support in intervention programs. In S. J. Meisels & J. P. Shonkoff (Eds.), *Handbook of early childhood intervention* (pp. 328–51). New York: Cambridge University Press.

Dunst, C. J., Trivette, C. M., Davis, M., & Cornwell, J. C. (1994). Characteristics of effective help-giving practices. In C. J. Dunst, C. M. Trivette, & A. G. Deal (Eds.), *Supporting and strengthening families: Volume 1: Methods, strategies and practices* (pp. 171–86). Cambridge, MA: Brookline Books.

Dyer, W. (1987). *Team building: Issues and alternatives* (2nd ed.). Reading, MA: Addison-Wesley.

Education for Handicapped Children Act of 1986, P. L. 99-457.

Elazar, D. J. (1984). *American federalism: A view from the states* (3rd ed.). New York: Harper & Row.

Elmore, R. F. (1978). Organizational models of social program implementation. *Public Policy, 26*(2), 185–228.

Ends, E. J., & Page, C. W. (1977). *Organizational team building.* Cambridge, MA: Winthrop.

Fewell, R., & Vadasy, P. (Eds.). (1986). *Families of handicapped children: Needs and supports across the life span.* Austin, TX: Pro-ed.

Foster, J. L. (1978). Regionalism and innovation in the American states. *The Journal of Politics, 40*(1), 179–87.

Frankenburg, W. K., Emde, R. N., & Sullivan, J. W. (1985). *Early identification of children at risk: An international perspective.* New York: Plenum Press.

Gallagher, J. (1997a). *The million dollar question: Unmet service needs for young children with disabilities.* Chapel Hill, NC: Early Childhood Research Institute: Service Utilization, Frank Porter Graham Child Development Center, University of North Carolina at Chapel Hill.

Gallagher, J. (1997b). *Planning for young children with disabilities and their families: The evidence from IFSP/IEPs.* Chapel Hill, NC: Early Childhood Research Institute: Service Utilization, Frank Porter Graham Child Development Center, University of North Carolina at Chapel Hill.

Gallagher, J. (1997c). The role of the professional working with children with disabilities and their families. In *Services for young children with disabilities: An ecological perspective.* Chapel Hill, NC: Early Childhood Research Institute: Service Utilization, Frank Porter Graham Child Development Center, University of North Carolina at Chapel Hill.

Gallagher, J. (1997d). Service delivery for young children with disabilities: Focus group data from parents and providers. In *Services for young children with disabilities: An ecological perspective.* Chapel Hill, NC: Early Childhood Research Institute: Service Utilization, Frank Porter Graham Child Development Center, University of North Carolina at Chapel Hill.

Gallagher, J. J., Harbin, G. L., Eckland, J., & Clifford, R. (1994). State diversity and policy implementation: Infants and toddlers. In L. J. Johnson, R. J. Gallagher, M. J. Montagne, J. B. Jordan, J. J. Gallagher, P. L. Hutinger, & M. B. Karnes (Eds.), *Meeting early intervention challenges: Issues from birth to three* (2nd ed.) (pp. 235–50). Baltimore, MD: Paul H. Brookes.

Gallagher, J., Harbin, G., Thomas, D., Clifford, R., & Wenger, M. (1988). *Major policy issues in implementing Part H – P. L. 99-457 (Infants and Toddlers).* Chapel Hill, NC: Carolina Institute for Child and Family Policy, The University of North Carolina at Chapel Hill.

Gallagher, J. J., Trohanis, P. L., & Clifford, R. M. (Eds.). (1989). *Policy implementation & P.L. 99-457: Planning for young children with special needs.* Baltimore, MD: Paul H. Brookes.

Gans, S. P., & Horton, G. T. (1975). *Integration of human services: The state and municipal levels.* New York: Praeger.

Garbarino, J. (1990). The human ecology of early risk. In S. J. Meisels & J. P. Shonkoff (Eds.), *Handbook of early childhood intervention* (pp. 78–96). New York: Cambridge University Press.

Garland, C. W., & Linder, T. W. (1994). Administrative challenges in early intervention. In L. J. Johnson, R. J. Gallagher, M. J. Montagne, J. B. Jordan, J. J. Gallagher, P. L. Hutinger, & M. B. Karnes (Eds.), *Meeting early intervention challenges: Issues from birth to three* (2nd ed.) (pp. 133–66). Baltimore, MD: Paul H. Brookes.

Garland, C. W., McGonigel, M. J., Frank, A., & Buck, D. (1989). *The transdisciplinary model of service delivery.* Lightfoot, VA: Child Development Resources.

Garwood, S. G., & Sheehan, R. (1989). *Designing a comprehensive early intervention system: The challenge of Public Law 99-457.* Austin, TX: Pro-ed.

Gilkerson, L., Gorski, P. N., & Panitz, P. (1990). Hospital-based intervention for pre-term infants and their families. In S. J. Meisels & J. P. Shonkoff (Eds.), *Handbook of early childhood intervention* (pp. 445–68). New York: Cambridge University Press.

Gilkerson, L., Hilliard, A. G., Schrag, E., & Shonkoff, J. P. (1987). *Report accompanying the Education of the Handicapped Act Amendments of 1986 and commenting on P. L. 99-457.* Washington, DC: National Center for Clinical Infant Programs.

Glassman, R. B. (1973). Persistence and loose coupling in living systems. *Behavioral Science, 18,* 83–98.

Greenspan, S. I., & Meisels, S. J. (1996). Toward a new vision for the developmental assessment of infants and young children. In S. J. Meisels and E. Fenichel (Eds.),

New visions for the developmental assessment of infants and young children (pp. 11–26). Washington, DC: Zero to Three National Center for Infants, Toddlers and Families.

Hanft, B. (1989). Early intervention: Issues in specialization. *American Journal of Occupational Therapy, 43,* 431–4.

Harbin, G. L. (1993). Family issues of children with disabilities: How research and theory have modified practice in intervention. In N. J. Anastasiow & S. Harel (Eds.), *At-risk infants: Interventions, families and research* (pp. 101–14). Baltimore, MD: Paul H. Brookes.

Harbin, G. L., Gallagher, J., & Batista, L. (1992). *Status of states' progress in implementing Part H of IDEA: Report No. 4. The final status report on state progress towards implementation of Part H.* Chapel Hill, NC: Carolina Policy Studies Program, Frank Porter Graham Child Development Center, University of North Carolina at Chapel Hill.

Harbin, G., Gallagher, J., Clifford, R., Place, P., & Eckland, J. (1993). *Case study report #2: (Systems change: Case studies of six diverse states).* Chapel Hill, NC: Carolina Policy Studies Program, Frank Porter Graham Child Development Center, University of North Carolina at Chapel Hill.

Harbin, G. L., & Kochanek, T. T. (1992). *Service patterns and utilization: A collaborative and systems-based investigation.* (Submitted under Early Education Programs for Children with Disabilities CFDA 84.024.)

Harbin, G. L., & Kochanek, T. (1998). *Early Childhood Research Institute on Service Utilization: Final report.* Chapel Hill, NC: Early Childhood Research Institute: Service Utilization, Frank Porter Graham Child Development Center, University of North Carolina at Chapel Hill.

Harbin, G. L., & McNulty, B. A. (1990). Policy implementation: Perspectives on service coordination and interagency cooperation. In S. J. Meisels & J. P. Shonkoff (Eds.), *Handbook of early childhood intervention* (pp. 700–22). New York: Cambridge University Press.

Harbin, G. L., McWilliam, R. A., Porter, P., Vandiviere, P., Mittal, M., & Munn, D. (1995). *An evaluation of family-centered coordinated Part H services in North Carolina: Part 2-Interagency coordination of services.* North Carolina Department of Human Resources, Division of Developmental Disabilities Section and University of North Carolina at Chapel Hill, Frank Porter Graham Child Development Center.

Harbin, G. L., Shaw, D., McWilliam, R. A., Westheafer, C., & Frazier, H. (1997). Lessons learned about the family–service provider relationship. In *Services for young children with disabilities: An ecological perspective.* Chapel Hill, NC: Early Childhood Research Institute: Service Utilization, Frank Porter Graham Child Development Center, University of North Carolina at Chapel Hill.

Harbin, G. L., Shaw, D., Tocci, L., McWilliam, R. A., Gallagher, J. J., West, T., & Sideris, J. (1998). Lessons learned about the importance of the broader ecological context. In *Services for young children with disabilities: An ecological perspective.* Chapel Hill, NC: Early Childhood Research Institute: Service Utilization, Frank Porter Graham Child Development Center, University of North Carolina at Chapel Hill.

Harbin, G. L., & West, T. (1998). *Early intervention service delivery models: What are they like?* Chapel Hill, NC: Early Childhood Research Institute: Service Utilization, Frank Porter Graham Child Development Center, University of North Carolina at Chapel Hill.

Haynes, U. (1976). The National Collaborative Infant Project. In T. D. Tjossem (Ed.), *Intervention strategies for high risk infants and young children* (pp. 509–34). Baltimore, MD: University Park Press.

Hersey, P., & Blanchard, K. H. (1988). *Management of organizational behavior* (5th ed.). Englewood Cliffs, NJ: Prentice-Hall.

Hurley, O. L. (1989). Implications of PL 99-457 for preparation of preschool personnel. In J. J. Gallagher, P. L. Trohanis, & R. M. Clifford (Eds.), *Policy implementation & P. L. 99-457: Planning for young children with special needs* (pp. 133–45). Baltimore, MD: Paul H. Brookes.

Hyman, C. S. (1985). The 1985 omnibus survey: Implications for strategic planning. *ASHA, 28*(4). Rockville, MD: The American Speech-Language Hearing Association.

Individuals with Disabilities Education Act (IDEA), Amendments of 1991, P. L. 102-119.

Individuals with Disabilities Education Act (IDEA), Amendments of 1997, P. L. 105-17.

Kagan, S. L., Goffin, S. G., Golub, S. A., & Pritchard, E. (1995). *Toward systematic reform: Service integration for young children and their families.* Falls Church, VA: National Center for Service Integration.

Klein, N. K., & Campbell, P. (1990). Preparing personnel to serve at-risk and disabled infants, toddlers, and preschoolers. In S. J. Meisels & J. P. Shonkoff (Eds.), *Handbook of early childhood intervention* (pp. 679–99). New York: Cambridge University Press.

Knitzer, J., & Page, S. (1996). *Map and track: State initiatives for young children and families.* NY: National Center for Children in Poverty, Columbia University School of Public Health.

Kochanek, T., & Brady, A. (1995). *Maternal satisfaction with infant/toddler and preschool services: Components, outcomes, and correlates.* Early Childhood Research Institute: Service Utilization, Rhode Island College.

Kochanek, T. T., & Buka, S. L. (1995a). *The Early Childhood Research Institute on Service Utilization: Study environments and a portrait of children, families and service providers within them.* Early Childhood Research Institute: Service Utilization, Rhode Island College.

Kochanek, T. T., & Buka, S. L. (1995b). *Socio-demographic influences on services used by infants with disabilities and their families.* Early Childhood Research Institute: Service Utilization, Rhode Island College.

Kochanek, T. T., & Buka, S. L. (1997). *Influential factors in inclusive versus non-inclusive placements for preschool children with disabilities.* Early Childhood Research Institute on Service Utilization, Rhode Island College.

Krauss, M. W., Upshur, C. C., Shonkoff, J. P., & Hauser-Cram, P. (1993). The impact of parent groups on mothers of infants with disabilities. *Journal of Early Intervention, 17*(1), 8–20.

Larson, C. E., & LaFasto, F. M. (1989). *Teamwork: What must go right/What can go wrong.* Newbury Park, CA: Sage.

Linder, T. W. (1990). *Transdisciplinary play-based assessment: A functional approach to working with young children.* Baltimore, MD: Paul H. Brookes.

March, J. G., & Olson, J. P. (1975). *Choice situations in loosely coupled worlds.* Unpublished manuscript, Stanford University.

Marshall, C., Mitchell, D. E., & Wirt, F. (1985). Assumptive worlds of education policy makers. *Peabody Journal of Education, 62*(4), 90–115.

Martinson, M. C. (1982). Interagency services: A new era for an old idea. *Exceptional Children, 45*(5), 389–94.

Mazmanian, D. A., & Sabatier, P. A. (1983). *Implementation and public policy.* Glenview, IL: Scott, Foresman and Co.

McCune, L., Kalmanson, B., Fleck, M. B., Glazewski, B., & Sillari, J. (1990). An interdisciplinary model of infant assessment. In S. J. Meisels & J. P. Shonkoff (Eds.), *Handbook of early childhood intervention* (pp. 219–77). New York: Cambridge University Press.

McGonigel, M. J., & Garland, C. W. (1988). The individualized family service plan and the early intervention team: Team and family issues and recommended practices. *Infants and Young Children, 1*(1), 10–21.

McGonigel, M. J., Woodruff, G., & Roszmann-Millican, M. (1994). The transdisciplinary team: A model for family-centered early intervention. In L. J. Johnson, R. J. Gallagher, M. J. Montagne, J. B. Jordan, J. J. Gallagher, P. L. Hutinger, & M. B. Karnes (Eds.), *Meeting early intervention challenges: Issues from birth to three* (2nd ed.) (pp. 95–131). Baltimore, MD: Paul H. Brookes.

McKnight, J. (1987). Regenerating community. *Social Policy* (Winter Issue), 54–8.

McNulty, B. (1989). Leadership and policy strategies for interagency planning: Meeting the early childhood mandate. In J. Gallagher, P. Trohanis, & R. Clifford (Eds.), *Policy implementation & P. L. 99-457: Planning for young children with special needs* (pp. 147–67). Baltimore, MD: Paul H. Brookes.

McWilliam, P. J. (1992). The case method of instruction: Teaching application and problem-solving skills to early interventionists. *Journal of Early Intervention, 17,* 431–44.

McWilliam, R. A. (1991). Integrated therapy: Why are we still debating? *INTAC Tribune, 4*(9), 1–3.

McWilliam, R. A. (1995). Integration of therapy and consultative special education: A continuum in early intervention. *Infants and Young Children, 7*(4), 29–38.

McWilliam, R. A. (1996a). Implications for the future of integrating specialized services. In R. A. McWilliam (Ed.), *Rethinking pull-out services in early intervention: A professional resource* (pp. 343–72). Baltimore, MD: Paul H. Brookes.

McWilliam, R. A. (Ed.). (1996b). *Rethinking pull-out services in early intervention: A professional resource.* Baltimore, MD: Paul H. Brookes.

McWilliam, R. A., Harbin, G. L., Porter, P., Vandiviere, P., Mittal, M., & Munn, D. (1995). *An evaluation of family-centered coordinated Part H services in North Carolina: Part 1-Family-centered service provision.* University of North Carolina at Chapel Hill/Frank Porter Graham Child Development Center and the North Carolina Department of Human Resources/Division of Developmental Disabilities Section.

McWilliam, R. A., & Lang, L. L. (1994). *What North Carolina professionals think of early intervention services.* Report for the Children and Families Committee of the North Carolina Interagency Coordinating Council for Children with Disabilities Ages Birth to 5 and Their Families.

McWilliam, R. A., Lang, L., Vandiviere, P., Angell, R., Collins, L., & Underdown, G. (1995). Satisfaction and struggles: Family perceptions of early intervention services. *Journal of Early Intervention, 16,* 360–73.

McWilliam, R. A., & Strain, P. S. (1993). Service delivery models. In S. L. Odom & M. McLean (co-chairpersons), *DEC recommended practices: Indicators of quality in programs for infants and young children with special needs and their families* (pp. 40–6). DEC Task Force on Recommended Practices: Council for Exceptional Children.

McWilliam, R. A., Tocci, L., & Harbin, G. L. (1995). *Services are child-oriented and families like it that way – but why?* Chapel Hill, NC: Early Childhood Research Institute: Service Utilization, Frank Porter Graham Child Development Center, University of North Carolina at Chapel Hill.

McWilliam, R. A., Tocci, L., & Harbin, G. L. (1998). Family-centered services: Service providers' discourse and providers. *Topics in Early Childhood Special Education, 18*(4), 206–221.

McWilliam, R., Tocci, L., Harbin, G., & Sideris, J. (1997). *Large-sample case studies: The best of both worlds.* Chapel Hill, NC: Early Childhood Research Institute: Service Utilization, Frank Porter Graham Child Development Center, University of North Carolina at Chapel Hill.

McWilliam, R. A., Tocci, L., & Sideris, J. (1997). Case study interpretations of family-service provider relationship. In *Services for young children with disabilities: An ecological perspective.* Chapel Hill, NC: Early Childhood Research Institute: Service Utilization, Frank Porter Graham Child Development Center, University of North Carolina at Chapel Hill.

McWilliam, R. A., Young, H. J., & Harville, K. (1996). Therapy services in early intervention: Current status, barriers, and recommendations. *Topics in Early Childhood Education, 16*(3), 348–74.

Meisels, S. J. (1985). A functional analysis of the evolution of public policy for handicapped young children. *Educational Evaluation and Policy Analysis, 7*, 115–126.

Meisels, S. J. (1989). Meeting the mandate of Public Law 99-457: Early intervention in the nineties. *American Journal of Orthopsychiatry, 59*, 451–60.

Meisels, S. J. (1996). Charting the continuum of assessment and intervention. In S. J. Meisels & E. Fenichel (Eds.), *New visions for the developmental assessment of infants and young children* (pp. 27–52). Washington, DC: Zero to Three: National Center for Infants, Toddlers and Families.

Meisels, S. J., Harbin, G., Modigliani, K., & Olson, K. (1988). Formulating optimal state early childhood intervention policies. *Exceptional Children, 55*(2) 159–65.

Meisels, S. J., & Provence, S. (1989). *Screening and assessment: Guidelines for identifying young disabled and developmentally vulnerable children and their families.* Washington, DC: National Center for Clinical Infant Programs and National Early Childhood Technical Assistance System.

Meisels, S. J., & Shonkoff, J. P. (Eds.). (1990). *Handbook of early childhood intervention.* New York: Cambridge University Press.

Odom, S. L., & Fewell, R. R. (1983). Program evaluation in early childhood special education: A meta-evaluation. *Educational Evaluation and Policy Analysis, 5*, 445–60.

Odom, S. L., & McLean, M. (co-chairpersons). (1993). *DEC recommended practices: Indicators of quality in programs for infants and young children with special needs and their families.* DEC Task Force on Recommended Practices: Council for Exceptional Children.

Odom, S., & Shuster, S. (1986). Naturalistic inquiry and the assessment of young handicapped children and their families. *Topics in Early Childhood Special Education, 6*, 68–82.

Patton, M. (1980). *Qualitative evaluation methods.* Beverly Hills, CA: Sage.

Peterson, N. L. (1991). Interagency collaboration under Part H: The key to comprehensive, multidisciplinary, coordinated infant/toddler intervention services. *Journal of Early Intervention, 15*(1), 89–105.

Physical Therapy Bulletin, March 23, 1988. ASAHP study foretells serious shortage of PT.

Rainforth, B., & Roberts, P. (1996). Physical therapy. In R. A. McWilliam (Ed.), *Rethinking pull-out services in early intervention: A professional resource* (pp. 243–66). Baltimore, MD: Paul H. Brookes.

Rogers, C., & Farrow, F. (1983). *Effective state strategies to promote interagency collaboration: A report of the handicapped public policy analysis project.* Washington, DC: Center for the Study of Social Policy.

Rosenberg, S. (1977). *Family and parent variables affecting outcomes of a parent-mediated intervention.* Unpublished

doctoral dissertation, George Peabody College for Teachers, Nashville, TN.

Seitz, V., & Provence, S. (1990). Caregiver models of early intervention. In S. J. Meisels & J. P. Shonkoff (Eds.), *Handbook of early childhood intervention* (pp. 400–27). New York: Cambridge University Press.

Shaw, D., & Harbin, G. L. (1997). Community contextual influence of service delivery: A multi-method perspective. In *Services for young children with disabilities: An ecological perspective.* Chapel Hill, NC: Early Childhood Research Institute: Service Utilization, Frank Porter Graham Child Development Center, University of North Carolina at Chapel Hill.

Sheehan, R. (1982). Infant assessment: A review and identification of emergent trends. In D. Bricker (Ed.), *Intervention with at-risk and handicapped infants: From research to application* (pp. 47–61). Baltimore, MD: University Park Press.

Shonkoff, J. P., & Meisels, S. J. (1990). Early childhood intervention: The evolution of a concept. In S. J. Meisels & J. P. Shonkoff (Eds.), *Handbook of early childhood intervention* (pp. 3–31). New York: Cambridge University Press.

Simeonsson, R. J., & Bailey, J. B. (1990). Family dimensions in early intervention. In S. J. Meisels & J. P. Shonkoff (Eds.), *Handbook of early childhood intervention* (pp. 428–44). New York: Cambridge University Press.

Smart Start. (May 1994). *Giving North Carolina's children a 'Smart Start' in life.* Raleigh, NC: North Carolina Department of Human Resources, Public Affairs Office.

Smart Start. (Fourth Quarter 1995). *Report to the North Carolina General Assembly.* Raleigh, NC: North Carolina Department of Human Resources.

Smith, B. J., & McKenna, P. (1994). Early intervention public policy: Past, present and future. In L. J. Johnson, R. J. Gallagher, M. J. Montagne, J. B. Jordan, J. J. Gallagher, P. L. Hutinger, & M. B. Karnes (Eds.), *Meeting early intervention challenges: Issues from birth to three* (2nd ed.) (pp. 251–64). Baltimore, MD: Paul H. Brookes.

Tocci, L., McWilliam, R., Sideris, J., Melton, S., & Clarke, B. (1997). *Straight from the source: Enhancers of and barriers to service utilization.* Chapel Hill, NC: Early Childhood Research Institute: Service Utilization, Frank Porter Graham Child Development Center, University of North Carolina at Chapel Hill.

Trivette, C. M., Dunst, C. J., & Deal, A. G. (1997). Resource-based approach to early intervention. In S. K. Thurman, J. R. Cornwell, & S. R. Gottwald (Eds.), *Contexts of early intervention: Systems and settings.* Baltimore, MD: Paul Brookes.

U.S. Department of Education. (1995). *To assure the free appropriate public education of all children with disabilities: 17th annual report to Congress on the implementation of the Individuals with Disabilities Education Act.* Washington, DC: Author.

U.S. Senate Report, Committee on Labor and Human Resources. (1986). *Education of the Handicapped Amendments of 1986 (Report No. 99-315).* Washington, DC: U.S. Government Printing Office.

Upshur, C. C. (1991). Mothers' and fathers' ratings of the benefits of early intervention services. *Journal of Early Intervention, 15,* 345–57.

Vincent, L. J., & Beckett, J. A. (1993). Family participation. In S. L. Odom & M. McLean (co-chairpersons), *DEC recommended practices: Indicators of quality in programs for infants and young children with special needs and their families* (pp. 19–25). DEC Task Force on Recommended Practices: Council for Exceptional Children.

Vincent, L. J., Salisbury, C., Walter, G., Brown, P., Grunewald, L. J., & Powers, M. (1980). Program evaluation and curriculum development in early childhood special education: Criteria of the next environment. In W. Sailor, B. Wilcox, & L. Brown (Eds.), *Methods of instruction for severely handicapped students* (pp. 303–28). Baltimore, MD: Paul. H. Brookes.

Walker, J. (1969). The diffusion of innovation among the American states. *American Political Science Review, 63,* 880–99.

Weatherly, R. A. (1979). *Reforming special education: Policy implementation from state level to street level.* Cambridge, MA: MIT Press.

Weick, K. E. (1974). Middle range theories of social systems. *Behavioral Science, 19,* 357–67.

Weick, K. E. (1976). Educational organizations as loosely coupled systems. *Administrative Science Quarterly, 21,* 1–19.

Wiegerink, R., & Posante, R. (1977). Consumerism. In J. Paul, D. Stedman, & G. Neufield (Eds.), *Deinstitutionalization* (pp 63–79). Syracuse, NY: Syracuse University Press.

Weis, J. A. (1981). Substance vs. symbol in administrative reform: The case of human services coordination. *Policy Analysis, 7,* 21–45.

Williamson, G. (1994). Assessment of adaptive competence. *Zero to Three, 14*(6), 28–33.

Woodruff, G., Hanson, C. R., McGonigel, M., & Sterzin, E. D. (1990). *Community-based services for children with HIV infection and their families: A manual for planners, service providers, families and advocates.* Brighton, MA: South Shore Mental Health Center.

Woodruff, G., & McGonigel, M. (1988). Early intervention team approaches: The transdisciplinary model. In J. B. Jordan, J. J. Gallagher, P. L. Hutinger, & M. B. Karnes (Eds.), *Early childhood special education: Birth to three* (pp. 163–81). Reston, VA: Council for Exceptional Children.

Woodruff, G., McGonigel, M., Garland, C., Zeitlin, S., Chazkel-Hochman, J., Shanahan, K., Toole, A., & Vincent, L. (1985). *Planning programs for infants* (State Series Paper No. 2). Chapel Hill: Technical Assistance Development System, University of North Carolina at Chapel Hill. (ERIC Document Reproduction Service No. ED 266-573.)

Yin, R. K. (1989). *Case study research: Design and methods* (revised edition). Newbury Park, CA: Sage Publications.

Yoder, D. E., & Coleman, P. P. (1990). *Allied health personnel meeting the demands of Part H, P. L. 99-457.* Chapel Hill, NC: Carolina Policy Studies Program, Frank Porter Graham Child Development Center, University of North Carolina at Chapel Hill.

Zipper, I. N., Weil, M., & Rounds, K. (1991). *Service coordination for early intervention: Parents and professionals.* Chapel Hill, NC: Carolina Institute for Research on Infant Personnel Preparation.

CHAPTER NINETEEN

Early Childhood Mental Health Services:

A Policy and Systems Development Perspective

JANE KNITZER

Knowledge about how young children develop and thrive has been growing over the past decades. So too have understandings about how environmental and biological risks can affect their cognitive, physical, and social development (Meisels & Shonkoff, 1990). This knowledge formed the basis of special education laws to create incentives for the development of family-centered services to young children with developmental delays or disabilities or, in some instances, those at risk of delays and disabilities. In theory, these laws include attention to social and emotional problems in young children. Yet, in practice, little policy or practice has focused on family-centered services to young children with emotional or behavioral disabilities or those at high risk of developing them (Knitzer, 1996a,b). Put differently, little attention has been paid to what, for the purposes of this chapter, is called "early childhood mental health." This chapter argues that the need for early childhood mental health services and systems development is critical. To make the case, it draws on knowledge reported by practitioners and on empirical data to the extent that these are available. (Unfortunately, because this is an emerging field of public concern, it has not yet been well studied.) This chapter also highlights the potential connections between meeting publicly espoused early childhood social goals and addressing early childhood mental health issues. Finally, it argues that barriers and obstacles to creating responsive policies and nurturing a field of practice are considerable and pose some general directions for action.

To set the stage, the first section offers a perspective on early childhood mental health, recognizing that there is not yet consensus in the field about specific boundaries or emphases. The second section considers the practice-based, research-based, and policy-based rationales for increased attention to early childhood mental health. The third section examines the current status of the nascent service delivery system, highlighting promising programs as well as system-level initiatives and issues. The chapter concludes with a modest agenda for the future that highlights principles to guide system and program development and offers recommendations to promote early childhood mental health at the national, state, and community levels.

WHAT IS EARLY CHILDHOOD MENTAL HEALTH?

The aim of early childhood mental health programs is to improve the social and emotional well-being of young children and families by strengthening relationships with caregivers and promoting age-appropriate social and emotional skills. Early childhood mental health strategies are built on developmental knowledge about young children and families, enriched by clinical perspectives. Such strategies are needed when the actions of families or caregivers are not effective in promoting positive behaviors and reducing challenging or otherwise disturbing behaviors in young children. Early childhood mental health initiatives can be defined as a set of strategies and perspectives that

- promote the emotional and behavioral well-being of young children, particularly those whose emotional development is compromised by virtue of poverty or other environmental or biological risks;
- help families of young children address whatever barriers they face to ensure that their children's emotional development is not compromised;
- expand the competencies of nonfamilial caregivers and others to promote the emotional well-being of young children and families, particularly those at risk by virtue of environmental or biological factors; and
- ensure that young children experiencing clearly atypical emotional and behavioral development and their families have access to needed services and supports.

Early childhood mental health services, as is true of mental health services for older children and families, recognize that some young children are seriously troubled and have identifiable disturbances. The services also have a strong preventive focus, reflected in a commitment to reach out to children at risk for developing emotional and behavioral impairments (Zeanah, 1993). In this, the mental health services reflect the core tenets of preventive science (Coie et al., 1993; Mrazek & Haggerty, 1994): The belief is that early, intensive interventions for many, if not all, of the most troubled young children can prevent or reduce future impairments, as well as future public and private costs.

The term *early childhood mental health* is used throughout this chapter because terms more commonly used are not sufficiently comprehensive. *Infant mental health* refers primarily to children from birth to 3 years. *Child and adolescent mental health* concerns largely children 6 years or above. Thus, the term early childhood mental health underscores the need for a service system that deals with the emotional, social, and behavioral needs of young children from birth to 6 (and perhaps even 8 years) through both developmental and clinical perspectives.

WHY PAY ATTENTION TO EARLY CHILDHOOD MENTAL HEALTH?

Three sets of arguments support attention to early childhood mental health from a policy and systems development perspective: 1) concerns expressed by teachers, caregivers, and mental health providers;

2) research suggesting that early disruptions in emotional development and caregiving relationships can have long-term negative consequences; and 3) the potential importance of an early childhood mental health perspective in achieving widely accepted social goals, particularly that all children enter school ready to learn. Each of these is discussed briefly.

Practice-Based Perspectives

The romantic picture of young children exploring their worlds in physical safety and emotional security continues to be a reality experienced by most young children. For a sizable minority, though, the experience of childhood is quite different. For these vulnerable children, there is a widespread perception that they are entering a wide range of early childhood settings "with fewer intellectual, social and emotional school readiness skills [and that they] have a precocious knowledge of life issues that they lack the emotional and cognitive ability to understand and integrate" (Edelfsen & Baird, 1994, p. 567). Instead of security and growth, these children face the "double jeopardy" (Kaplan-Sanoff, Parker, & Zuckerman, 1991; Shonkoff, 1982) of poverty compounded by exposure to environmental and biological risks, either alone or in combination.

Head Start, for example, long viewed as a premier example of a preventive developmental program, reports increased concern about the mental health of their children, families, and staff (Yoshikawa & Knitzer, 1997). Most typically, complaints focus on the levels of provocative, inappropriate, and challenging behavior of the children. Family needs too, in some programs, overwhelm the staff and challenge the core of Head Start's commitment to strong parental involvement. High levels of parental depression are not uncommon. In a study of one Head Start program, 47% of the parents reported poverty-related sadness, demoralization, and other indices of despair (Parker, Piotrkowski, Horn, & Greene, 1995) – a pattern found in other non–Head Start samples as well (Johnson & Walker, 1991). In some programs, high levels of parental involvement in substance abuse and familial or community violence also pose enormous challenges to the staff.

Similar reports are emerging from the child care community. For example, although there are no systematic data, child care providers in communities across the country, including Head Start, report that more and more young children are being "expelled" from programs (Knitzer, 1996b). This, like the quest for child care itself, is a private matter. Unlike the situation for older children, no review or referral to either mental health or special education agencies is required. Teacher reports on children entering kindergarten confirm this troubling picture. The reports suggest that increasing numbers of children are less prepared to cope with the demands of that environment than has been true in the past. A national survey of 7,000 kindergarten teachers reported that 35% of their students were not ready for school, with 42% of the teachers reporting a worsening of the situation during the past five years (Boyer, 1991). Data from one state paint a parallel picture: In Vermont, 28% of children entering kindergarten were deemed not ready for school (Vermont Agency of Human Services, 1997). Low-income children and families are the most vulnerable, yet there are signs that other families with young children are also experiencing higher levels of stress (Love & Logue, 1992). Although there are methodological flaws in these studies, nonetheless, the patterns are troubling (and are consistent with anecdotal evidence).

Scattered data from mental health agencies, although not reflecting a representative sample, confirm the levels of risk among young children and parents who become involved with the mental health system. The data clearly challenge the stereotype that mental health problems do not exist in young children. For example, in Vermont, although only 12% of children served by mental health agencies were younger than six years, almost half of these young children (45%) met criteria for serious emotional disturbance (Vermont Agency of Human Services, 1997). An analysis of 1,000 children from birth to 7 years served by twenty-one mental health agencies involved in a special demonstration program found that 38% of the children served were under 5 years (11% were between birth and 3 years, and 27% between 4 and 5 years of age). Seventy-eight percent of the children were in families earning less than the poverty threshold. Perhaps most sobering, though, 56% had a history of parental substance abuse, 51% a history of family violence, 31% had experienced physical abuse, 26% sexual abuse, 20% parental conviction, 19% parental hospitalization, and 9% child

psychiatric hospitalization. Twenty percent already had siblings in foster care (personal communication, MACRO, Spring 1997). Clinical data from early efforts to provide mental health services to infants and toddlers confirm the picture of familial stress and disorder (Luby & Morgan, 1997).

Research Perspectives

Multiple streams of research support the rationale for paying attention to the emotional development of all young children, those with "clinically significant" problems (Campbell, 1996) and those at high risk of developing clinically significant problems. Although it is beyond the scope of this chapter to present a thorough review of these literatures, it is appropriate to suggest the scope of converging evidence.

Recent research on the development of the brain in young children suggests not just the importance of early experience for cognitive development but also, significantly, for emotional development. A child's capacity to control emotions is related to the interaction between his or her biological system and early experiences and attachments. Evidence also suggests that high levels of stress in the earliest years can actually undermine brain development (Perry, Pollard, Blakley, Baker, & Vigilante, 1995; Shore, 1997). Thus, children deprived of early warm and nurturing relationships may experience such lifelong adverse consequences as impaired school performance, inability to manage anger as reflected in higher delinquency rates, disproportionate use of special education, and other negative outcomes. Parents coping with depression are especially vulnerable to difficulties in establishing warm and nurturing relationships with their children (Belle, 1982). Depression has been linked to punitive parenting behaviors, as well as to anxiety and aggression in children (Downey & Coyne, 1990; Lyons-Ruth, Botein, & Grunbaum, 1984). Parents suffering from other mental illnesses, or substance abuse (Luthar & Suchman, 1999), or parents who themselves have not experienced nurturing parenting (Barnard, Morisset & Spieker, 1993) may also be at risk of developing poor relationship patterns with their children. As McLoyd (1990) and others (Halpern, 1993; Hardin, 1997) have argued, poverty itself, and the chronic and episodic crises associated with it, may also negatively affect parenting, as do community-level risks (Aber, 1994; Gephart, 1997).

From the nascent field of infant mental health comes compelling new clinical and theoretical understandings of the many ways in which early relationships between infants and toddlers and those who care for them can be distorted (Greenspan, Wieder, & Nover, 1985; Sameroff & Emde, 1989; Zeanah, 1993), in effect, providing a textured counterpart to the brain research findings. From infant mental health pioneers too come new understandings of how to help families whose relationship patterns appear to be deeply impaired (Greenspan, Wieder & Nover, 1985; Lieberman & Pawl, 1993; Zeanah, 1993). From the developmental psychopathology field comes new understandings of the interaction between developmental stages and the emergence of psychopathology (Luthar, Burack, Cicchetti, & Weisz, 1997; Tolan, Guerra, & Kendall, 1995), although understanding early high-risk behaviors in children before the age of 6, and how this form of behavior relates to later behavior, remains for the most part limited. The partial exception is the evidence for what has been called "early onset conduct disorder." Here data suggest that this dysfunction starts early and lasts long (Kazdin, 1993; Loerber & Hay, 1994; Lochman & Conduct Problems Prevention Research Group, 1995; Patterson, DeBaryshe, & Ramsey, 1989), with consequences reflected in delinquency, emotional and behavioral disabilities, or other ultimately high-cost outcomes to society (Constantino, 1992).

Research on the consequences of specific trauma in young children (e.g., exposure to violence or abuse or the experience of early loss) is also enhancing our understanding of what early experiences can mean for emotional and behavioral development. Clinical data suggest that a wide and disturbing set of behaviors in young children, including babies, can signify exposure to trauma. Signs include dazed, dissociative behaviors; aggressive, acting-out behaviors; inability to concentrate; and distorted attachments to adults (including not expecting that adults can help or protect them; Gaensbauer & Siegel, 1995; Lewis, 1996; Osofsky, 1995; Vig, 1996). There are no conclusive data on the numbers of young children affected by trauma, but research on a sample of children under 6 years treated at Boston City Hospital indicated that 10% had witnessed a knifing or

a shooting by age 6 (Groves, Zuckerman, Marans, & Cohen, 1993).

There is also a body of research that focuses directly on preschoolers who manifest emotional and behavioral disorders. Some of this work explores patterns of behavior in affected preschoolers (Campbell, 1995), and some addresses issues related to screening and assessment (Feil, Walker, & Severson, 1995; Forness & Finn, 1993; Sinclair, Del'Homme, & Gonzalez, 1993). Some research, building on studies of older children (Kupersmidt, Coie, & Dodge, 1990), describes interventions to promote early positive peer relationships, even among high-risk young children and families (Fantuzzo, Coolahan, & Weiss, 1997).

Particularly important, from a practice perspective, is the evidence of the co-occurrence of communication problems and emotional and behavioral difficulties in young children (Prizant, Wetherby, & Roberts, 1993). Recognition of these comorbidity patterns has implications not only for the training of speech and language therapists who work with young children but also for mental health practitioners. This recognition also helps put in perspective a well-known phenomenon: the reluctance to identify emotional and behavioral disturbances in young children and the "labeling down" of such concerns as speech and language problems. Nationally, for example, 67% of Head Start children identified as having a disability are diagnosed as speech impaired, compared to 4% who are diagnosed as having an emotional or behavioral disability. However, in a pattern that appears to be typical, a functional assessment of 159 Head Start children identified as having some kind of disability found that 29% had serious emotional and behavioral disorders, and 18% speech impairments (Sinclair, 1993). This helps explain another pattern, long documented informally, and most recently, formally (Duncan, Forness, & Hartsough, 1995), of the time lag for older children between when problems are first identified and when appropriate services begin.

Theoretical and empirical research on risk, protective, and resiliency factors adds yet another dimension to the case for developing an early childhood mental health system of services. That literature confirms and elaborates on the patterns highlighted almost two decades ago by Rutter (1979). Children experiencing two risk factors were four times as likely to have a psychiatric impairment compared to children not exposed to any risk factor or who were only exposed to one. Children with four risk factors were ten times as likely to have a psychiatric impairment as those with one or none. In Rutter's work, risk factors included marital discord, low SES, large family size, parental criminality, maternal psychiatric disorder, and child welfare involvement. Subsequent efforts have examined the impact of combinations of biological and environmental risk factors, including, for example, lack of prenatal care, substance abuse during pregnancy, parental depression, poor temperamental fit between parent and child, substantiated abuse or neglect, and out-of-home placements. Most important, from a policy and service perspective, the patterns hold regardless of the specific risk factors (Sameroff & Fiese, this volume).

A focus, though, on risk factors tells only part of the story. Rutter and other researchers have also directed attention to protective, or resiliency, factors, finding that the impact of risk factors was lessened for children who experienced "buffers," such as a warm, caring relationship with an adult. This evidence that negative patterns can be transformed has direct implications for the design of general early childhood and family support programs that incorporate a mental health perspective, for the design of intensive preventive intervention initiatives embedded within early childhood programs (Mrazek & Haggerty, 1994), and even for mental health strategies targeted to young children and families with highly challenging problems.

Research is only just beginning to provide data about the prevalence of emotional and behavioral disorders in young children. Epidemiological data to guide estimates of the numbers of young children who have diagnosable problems or who are at risk of developing them are limited. Scattered studies of relatively small samples of preschoolers suggest a range from 7% to 22% (Campbell, 1996; Earls, 1980; Webster-Stratton, 1996). Other studies highlight patterns of underidentification (Beare & Lynch, 1986). Most recently, a large study of a pediatric sample of more than 3,800 preschool-aged children found that 21% met the criteria for a psychiatric disorder, 9.1% of them for a severe disorder (Lavigne et al., 1996). The data also confirm the patterns suggested by other types of research. Levels of risk are not evenly distributed across the population but are concentrated among young children from low-income families (Duncan, Brooks-Gunn, & Aber, 1997; McLoyd, 1990; personal communication, MACRO, Spring 1997). Given the large numbers of low-income young children, this poses a serious challenge. Demographic data indicate that between 1979 and 1996, the number of children under age 6 living in poverty in the United States grew from 3.5 million to 5.5 million (National Center for Children in Poverty, 1998). Furthermore, of those children in poverty, half are growing up in extreme poverty (i.e., families with incomes half or less than half of the poverty line). A stunning 43% of all American children under 6 are growing up with family incomes at or below 185% of the poverty line (National Center for Children in Poverty, 1998). Within this population are large numbers of young children most likely to be at risk for impaired emotional and social development.

Data on the efficacy of different intervention approaches for enhancing the social and emotional functioning of young children are also largely missing from current research literature. Longitudinal research on high quality early childhood programs suggests that the most powerful effects in reducing long-term negative outcomes, such as delinquency, are found in programs that combine a strong child-focused program with a strong family component (Barnett, 1995; Yoshikawa, 1994, 1995). Unfortunately, however, none of these studies had examined specific emotional and behavioral outcomes, nor did they provide an analysis of the levels of problematic behavior in the children when they were young. Furthermore, most of these studies were carried out during the early 1970s, when the economic and social context was quite different, and they lacked the levels of concern about challenging behaviors reported by the field today. This suggests a critical need to design and evaluate a new generation of intensive preventive interventions that are explicitly intended to address the levels of problematic behavior that are almost routinely seen among young children, particularly in programs with concentrations of low-income children. When examining studies conducted in the past fifteen years that focused explicitly on interventions to reduce aggressive behavior in young children, only four studies were found meeting this criterion, which compelled the researchers to extend the age range to 8 and to begin again. This expansion yielded an additional thirteen studies (Bryant, Vizzard, Willoughby, & Kupersmidt, 1998). There does, however, seem to be growing recognition of the need to design and test out specific early childhood mental health approaches. Within the past several years, the national Head Start Bureau has funded a limited number of university–Head Start mental health research partnerships. Similarly, the federal Substance Abuse, Mental Health Services Administration, through an initiative called *Starting Early Starting Smart*, has funded thirteen projects to examine the efficacy of integrating behavioral services (including mental health and substance abuse) into primary health and child care programs. Moreover, evaluation data from a new generation of comprehensive, multi-component preventive interventions with children in the early school years (Conduct Problems Prevention Group, 1992, 1997; Walker et al., 1998) are just emerging. This too will enhance the knowledge base and perhaps yield opportunities to adapt such designs for still younger children.

In summary, findings from these multiple strands of research converge and suggest the importance of developing an early childhood mental health service system with the capacity to respond to young children – and their families – who manifest diagnosable disorders or whose behaviors suggest that they are at high risk for the development of such disorders. The research, however, provides only limited information about the prevalence rates or the efficacy of different types of interventions either to prevent future disorders or to reduce the impact of those identified in young children.

Public Policy Perspectives

A third reason for paying attention to early childhood mental health is that it might facilitate meeting publicly espoused policy goals for young children and families. Two goals in particular implicitly call for a focus on early childhood mental health. The first is the national goal, established by a panel authorized in federal legislation, that "all children shall enter school ready to learn." Although the domains of school readiness adopted by the National Education Goals Panel include personal and social development, activities to promote school readiness have largely been interpreted as a cognitive

challenge (e.g., promoting mathematical and reading literacy) or a community challenge (Love, Aber, & Brooks-Gunn, 1994). That a child's emotional state also affects his or her ability to achieve the level of social and cognitive competence necessary to learn has generally been ignored by most researchers, but with some exceptions (Greenspan & Wieder, 1993; Smith, Brooks-Gunn, & Klebanov, 1997; Zero to Three, 1993). Yet the fact that positive emotional and behavioral patterns can be identified, promoted, or discouraged long before a child enters school along with the high cost of school failure (evident in grade repetition, high use of special education, lower employment potential, and a host of other undesirable outcomes), suggests that an investment in early childhood mental health interventions for those at risk of school failure is likely to pay off in significant ways.

The second link between nationally accepted social goals and early childhood mental health is less obvious, but equally important. In 1996, the United States embraced a policy that requires all low-income women to work as a condition for receiving public benefits (Personal Responsibility and Work Opportunity Reconciliation Act [PRWORA] of 1996, as amended by the Balanced Budget Act of 1997). This includes even those with young children, although states have the option to exempt infants for up to one year. In response, states are seeking to "reduce barriers to employability" among even the most vulnerable populations, including adults affected by substance abuse, mental illness, and domestic violence. These are also the same adults who, as parents of young children, are likely to be in need of extra supports. Ironically, this means that efforts to implement welfare reform successfully might become a rationale for increased attention to family-centered early childhood mental health services. Indeed, as noted later, there is some evidence to suggest that such a course would have clear payoffs.

TOWARD AN EARLY CHILDHOOD MENTAL HEALTH SERVICE DELIVERY SYSTEM

This section explores the current status of the early childhood mental health service delivery system, focused on three sets of questions: 1) What is known about promising early childhood mental health strategies? 2) Are there any examples of community-based and statewide strategies to promote the development of early childhood mental health services? and 3) What systemic issues must be addressed to develop an early childhood mental health service delivery system?

Early Childhood Mental Health Strategies in Child Care, Home Visiting, and Family Support Settings

Evidence suggests that there is growing awareness among policy makers about the importance of investing in child care, Early Head Start, Head Start, prekindergarten programs, home visiting, and family support programs for young children (Knitzer & Page, 1996, 1998). In effect, while far from universally available, there appears to be a growing consensus that a core set of services should be available to either all families or all high-risk families with young children. For the purposes of this chapter, this cluster of services is referred to as the *primary support system* (although, in fact, the services are often disconnected, fragmented at both the community and state level, far from universally available, and typically unevaluated).

It is, in fact, within these kinds of programs that many of the problems facing young children, their families, and staff have been identified. To date, though, there have only been scattered efforts to create an appropriate support system to help these children and families. Although in virtually all instances, these efforts are either small scale research-based efforts or approaches invented by practitioners, taken together they represent a vision of the kinds of efforts that might grow to scale and become the basis for more systematic evaluation.

INTEGRATING MENTAL HEALTH PRINCIPLES INTO CORE HEALTH, HOME VISITING, AND EARLY CARE AND EDUCATION PROGRAMS. One approach to integrating mental health principles into core health, home visiting, and early care and education programs is to construct primary support programs (or program components) that incorporate mental health principles, particularly those focused on relationship building, into their core approach. Some data support this. For example, *Keys to Caregiving* is a home visiting program grounded in mental health relationship-building principles. It was initiated after Barnard, Morisset, and Spieker (1993) identified a group of families for whom traditional home visiting nursing services provided within three months of the birth of a child were determined ineffective. These were largely women with few friends, little support, and many problems. In response, the researchers designed a careful study to test the efficacy of two contrasting service approaches with this population. One, the mental health model, asked the nurses to focus on relationship building to foster social interaction and communication between the mother and child, as well as to decrease the mother's social isolation and to increase her sense of competence as a parent and person. The other service model used the nurses to provide educational and resource information. The findings supported the efficacy of the relationship-focused mental health model. This is an important finding at a time when health related home visiting programs are proliferating rapidly (Center for the Future of Children, 1993), often in the absence of attention to what the home visitors do, the kind of clinical supervision they have, or the intensity of the intervention.

A second example of an effort to integrate core mental health principles into the fabric of a program strategy is the *Parent Services Project* (PSP). Initiated in the 1980s, the PSP is one of the earliest family support programs and still one of the few to try to build a parent component into child care settings. Developed initially by a mental health task force, the goal was to create a nonintrusive prevention strategy to reduce stress on low-income families with young children in child care settings (Link, Beggs, & Seiderman, 1997). The aim was to strengthen child care programs by adding activities to bring parents together to create informal support networks among themselves and to create decision-making opportunities by which parents themselves decide upon the kinds of activities in which they would like to participate (e.g., family social events, activities just for parents, and so forth). Although the PSP has no formal mental health component, early research using a matched set of parents from child care programs without the PSP for comparison found a decline in depression among the parents as well as decreases in isolation among those parents participating in the program (Stein & Associates, 1988). Today, the Parent Services Project has grown enormously; according to a recent report, principles and practices have now been incorporated into more than 500 programs in six states (Link, Beggs, & Seiderman, 1997). Unfortunately, however, there has been no further assessment of its mental health impact.

The third example, the *Partners Project*, highlights an effort to integrate core mental health principles into the parent-involvement component of Head Start (Yoshikawa & Knitzer, 1997). As with the Barnard et al. (1993) model, this intervention strategy is grounded in child development knowledge and relationship-building theory. Here, however, the focus is on efforts to promote positive parent–child relationships among groups of parents by using guided group discussion based on videotaped vignettes of parent–child interactions in common and often troublesome situations. Particularly powerful is the use of a family support approach; parents solve problems together, sharing their reactions, strategies, and frustrations. A total of 362 parents from eight Head Start centers participated in a study; two-thirds were part of the intervention group, and one-third served as the comparison group (Webster-Stratton, 1996). Trained family service workers, initially in teams with clinicians, as well as parents who emerged as natural leaders, facilitated the discussions over eight weeks. There was also a teacher-training component. The evaluation examined both child effects (i.e., the reduction of conduct problems and increased social competence) and parent effects (i.e., better limit-setting, less harsh discipline, and more positive interaction) through written and observational measures. Results at the conclusion of the intervention and six months later were positive, with intervention group mothers showing more gains in measures of parental competence. The rate of parental participation itself was telling, as it was more than ten times the normal response rate to Head Start's monthly parent education events. Furthermore, kindergarten teachers of children in the intervention group reported a significantly higher level of parental involvement in school than did teachers with children from the comparison group, suggesting a link to school readiness issues. Also instructive was the fact that one group of parents did not benefit: parents with already identified mental illness. For them, the intervention was simply not robust enough. What is particularly compelling about this approach is

that it is an adaptation of one of the few empirically tested successful treatment approaches to helping parents of children with early onset conduct disorder in a clinic setting (Bryant, Vizzard, Willoughby, & Kupersmidt, 1998; Webster-Stratton, 1996; Webster-Stratton & Hammond, 1997).

STRENGTHENING CLINICAL SUPERVISION AVAILABLE TO STAFF IN PRIMARY SETTINGS. As noted earlier, many staff working in settings serving families with young children are not well trained or supervised. Yet they are asked to deal with very complex family and child situations, typically with little help. Adding on-site mental health staff to provide continuing help in problem solving about behavioral and emotional issues, and offering clinical supervision, reflect another strategy for establishing a mental health perspective in primary programs for young children and families. The two examples cited here capture both the potential impact of such a strategy and the challenge of funding it. *Hawaii Healthy Start*, whose roots are in the prevention of child abuse and neglect, uses paraprofessional staff as key to its home visiting program (Wallach & Lister, 1995). Widely recognized as a pioneering, high-quality model, efforts are now underway to adapt the model more widely through the work of Healthy Families America. Yet when one of the Hawaii programs carried out a survey of the population it served, it found that about one-third of the mothers had experienced so much grief and trauma in their own lives, so much abuse themselves, and so much depression that the basic home visiting strategy could not meet the needs of the families. An on-site psychologist was hired to help the home visitors understand more about the behaviors they were seeing, as well as to facilitate shared learning and problem solving through group discussions and supervision. In some rare instances, the psychologist also made home visits herself. Although the staff reported great benefits from this clinically enriched supervision and support, the psychologist's role is not built into the basic staffing pattern of Hawaii Healthy Start, and the program has not been able to procure funds to sustain the strategy (Wallach, 1994).

Another example of creating within-program mental health staff comes from a network of Boston Head Start programs serving eighteen centers with over 2,000 children from a variety of different cultures. Family service workers in that program reported that they were having a very difficult time working with parents, particularly parents who were suspected of neglecting or abusing their children. In response, the management team decided to strengthen the clinical supervision available to the workers. To do that, the team made the difficult decision to hire fewer family service workers and instead hire a clinically trained staff member to supervise and support them. Meeting with the family workers in groups, the supervisor was able to address the anxieties and anger of the staff, suggest alternative ways of handling difficult situations, and expand their skills in working with both the children and the parents (Yoshikawa & Knitzer, 1997).

Although there has been no formal evaluation of this initiative, informal reports suggest that, with support from the supervisors, family services workers have shifted their goals. They no longer simply refer children suspected of abuse and neglect to child protection agencies but are willing to work with the families in the context of the Head Start program to teach parents new ways of disciplining and supporting their children. They have also been able to create, with supervision, support groups for families involved in domestic violence (Yoshikawa & Knitzer, 1997), thus more effectively serving a group of Head Start parents and children not previously well served. This approach is important, not because it represents a compelling new treatment advance, but because so few early childhood programs have access to any kind of clinically informed perspectives or expertise, and because the payoff in terms of staff skill improvement in typical programs mounted without rigorous design or development appears to be significant at a time when there is great concern about their overall quality.

USING ONGOING, ON-SITE CONSULTATION. Another way of strengthening the clinical expertise available to staff, children, and families in early childhood programs is to ensure that the programs have access to on-site and ongoing consultation from a mental health professional with expertise in early childhood. Sadly, this happens but rarely, even in Head Start, in which the performance standards require such access (Yoshikawa & Knitzer, 1997). The consultation approaches that have been identified

take many forms (Bernstein, Percansky, & Wechsler, 1996; Donahue, 1997; Johnston, 1990; Yoshikawa & Knitzer, 1997). Some approaches emphasize work with staff to help them meet the needs of children in the context of the program; others focus on families; and others provide a range of services, from individual and family interventions to program consultation, to training and staff development activities, to participation in service teams for the most troubled. One relatively unique approach is now being tested in Cleveland, Ohio. *Day Care Plus* is a collaborative effort that joins the local child care resource and referral agency, Starting Point, the Cuyahoga County Mental Health Board, and the Early Intervention Centers of the Positive Education Program – a local mental health agency (Knitzer, 1996b). (The Early Intervention Center itself is highlighted later.) Using a "train-the-center" approach, which began in 1997, the aim is to provide a group of child care centers with intensive staff consultation for at least one year and then to reduce the intensity of the contact while adding new centers that receive more intensive consultation. One year later, ten centers were being served by two full-time consultants. Consistent with epidemiological findings cited earlier, between 18 and 20% of the children were identified by staff or parents as having behavioral or emotional concerns. Staff training was the area of greatest focus, involving ongoing, classroom-based teacher-to-teacher consultation. In addition, there were group trainings, both within and across centers, mostly dealing with behavioral challenges; the establishment of a resource lending library, with contents chosen by the centers and local early childhood experts; and the convening of a director's network to provide a vehicle for peer support.

Several aspects of the program are noteworthy. First, rather than using typical mental health variables, the evaluation will assess the impact of Day Care Plus in terms of such key program quality variables as reduced staff turnover, decreased staff stress, and increased staff education (e.g., staff enrollments in the Child Development Associate Program). Comparisons will be made with the cohort of ten centers that will be the target for consultation in the anticipated next round of funding. Thus, the evaluation explicitly links the mental health strategy with child care quality improvement indicators. This is significant because although a central policy goal for child care providers and policy makers across the nation is to support quality improvement strategies, mental health consultation or related strategies are not typically seen as having a role to play in such efforts. Second, the program auspices reflect a three-part collaboration that has been key to the project's early success. The involvement of the local child care resource and referral agency has been particularly crucial. Because the resource and referral agency is so trusted by the child care community, it has reduced the time the mental health community has spent in gaining entry and winning trust among child care providers. Third, in addition to the consultants, parent aides are available to help in the classroom and to co–lead parent groups. The aides are parents of children with challenging behaviors who have been successfully served by the Early Intervention Center. Finally, although the majority of the funds were used for staff and operational expenses, additional flexible dollars provided by the Community Mental Health Board have been crucial in enabling the partners to be responsive to what the centers want, such as library resources and meetings between the child care centers and those providing substance abuse and mental health treatment in the community.

USING NONTRADITIONAL MENTAL HEALTH STRATEGIES TO SERVE THE MOST TROUBLED YOUNG CHILDREN IN PRIMARY SETTINGS. Mental health services for children are often defined narrowly: out-patient services, in-patient services (including psychiatric hospitalizations and residential treatment), and day treatment (including therapeutic preschools). During the 1990s, efforts to improve services to older children and adolescents with severe problems led to the development of what are often called "wraparound" services (Lourie, Katz-Leavy, & Stroul, 1996; Vandenburg, 1993). This new approach to treatment is part of a larger effort to transform a pathology-oriented children's mental health treatment approach into a family-centered, strength-based model, and to make treatment planning and service delivery more flexible in order to maximize the opportunities for avoiding high-cost residential placement and needless separation of children from their families and communities (Knitzer, 1996a). Often called "systems of care" (Stroul, 1996), five core principles

undergird these transformation efforts: 1) viewing parents as partners, not problems; 2) collaborating with other systems, rather than providing mental health services in isolation; 3) providing flexible wraparound services based on family goals and needs, instead of being limited to traditional in-patient, out-patient, and day-treatment services; 4) providing treatment, to the extent possible, in everyday settings, rather than "pull-out" therapies in unfamiliar settings; and 5) being responsive to cultural and community contexts (Isaacs-Shockley, Cross, Bazron, Dennis, & Benjamin, 1996; Knitzer, 1996a).

Until recently, most of the efforts to implement these principles focused on school-aged children and adolescents, and, indeed, the bulk of mental health system energy is still focused on this population. However, there are emerging efforts to introduce these concepts to those working with younger children and families. For example, the Child and Family Center in Stark County, Ohio, whose mental health agency pioneered implementation of "system-of-care" efforts for older children and adolescents, has now extended its efforts to younger children. To that end, the center has formed a partnership with the local Head Start agencies and now supports an on-site early intervention team of three paraprofessionals with one master's-level clinician. That team provides both traditional Head Start mental health activities and works with families and staff in ways consistent with a wraparound mental health philosophy. Thus, the team carries out typical Head Start mental health activities, including classroom observation, staff training (in that program especially around discipline and transition issues), and referrals. But they also make home visits and offer nontraditional services to families, including in-home behavioral aides and respite care (Yoshikawa & Knitzer, 1997). Using these new treatment approaches, the Head Start program has been able to avert out-of-home placement of disturbed young children, thus reducing the potential costs to the county and state (personal communication, Poulos, 1996).

Efforts such as the Stark County collaboration are significant for two reasons. First, these programs increase awareness among the early childhood community of family-centered mental health treatment strategies of which the larger early childhood community is largely uninformed (Piotrkowski, Collins, Knitzer, & Robinson, 1994). Second, the efforts illustrate for the early childhood community that principles undergirding these treatment strategies are consistent with the strategies and principles that are more familiar to them through the family support movement (Kagan & Weissbourd, 1994) and early intervention efforts to create a family-driven system (Dunst, Trivette, & Deal, 1989).

Early Childhood Mental Health Strategies in Secondary Support Services

A second cluster of emerging early childhood mental health strategies focuses on young children and families already requiring specialized services from the secondary support system, either because of the child's needs or the parent(s)' needs. For the purposes of this chapter, the secondary support system is defined to include adult-centered programs that focus on mental health, substance abuse, and domestic violence and typically treat adult clients without regard to their status as parents; child protection services; and early intervention services for children with developmental delays and disorders. This second cluster also includes specialized programs for young children with identified emotional and behavioral disorders, such as therapeutic preschool programs. To date, only limited examples of efforts to infuse the secondary support system with early childhood mental health strategies have been reported either in the research literature or by practitioners. Three exceptions are highlighted here.

DEVELOPING EARLY CHILDHOOD MENTAL HEALTH PROGRAMS IN MENTAL HEALTH AGENCIES. *Project Before* involves the development of a home-visiting program for high-risk mothers of infants, toddlers, and preschoolers (Rast, 1997a,b). It is part of an initiative called "Kan Focus," which, similar to Stark County, has been developing a system of care for older troubled children. In 1996, Kan Focus received a grant to create a system of care for young children whose mothers were either mentally ill or abused substances or who were at risk of mental illness or substance abuse. Project goals were to ensure appropriate health care for enrolled children and mothers; provide support for

substance abuse and mental health needs for the parent; reduce risk factors for the families; and build protective factors in the children. Families were assigned home visitor/case managers with experience in substance abuse and mental illness and supplemental training in early childhood issues (Rast, 1997b). Although still preliminary, early project results have met or exceeded expectations about impacts on individual children and families (Rast, 1997b). At intake, 55% of the children were receiving medical care, and 35% had been immunized. Within three months, more than 95% were receiving medical care, and 70% had been immunized. With respect to the mothers, at intake only 60% of the mothers were receiving maternal health care, and fewer than 25% of the pregnant women had any prenatal care. Within three months, health care utilization increased to 85%. Similarly, utilization of therapy and substance-abuse services by the parents increased, with some parents returning to treatment and others entering for the first time. Most significantly, there was an unexpected result with respect to the earlier identified public policy goals of ensuring family self-sufficiency. Within three months, 75% of these mothers, considered the most difficult to serve, had gone to work. All of these mothers had received public assistance and were thought to be unlikely to become ready for work so quickly.

In the process of adapting the system of care concepts to younger children and to their families, rather than to the adolescents with whom they were more familiar, the project leaders report three important lessons. First, the network of collaborators is different, encompassing child health and child care providers, as well as child protection and substance abuse workers. Second, drawing on or creating informal support networks for families with young children is even more important than it is for families with older children. Third, the priority outcomes for the families are different. For older children, the focus is generally on avoiding out-of-home placement, increasing school attendance, and reducing interfamilial stress. Often, these are families who have already been burned out by the efforts to ensure their children appropriate special education, get them to myriad evaluations, and so forth. For younger children, the outcomes center around strengthening parent–child relations; ensuring that parents have access to nutrition services, health care, and child care; and helping the families address both economic and safety issues related to domestic violence for their children and themselves (Rast, 1997a).

PROVIDING FAMILY-CENTERED, SPECIALIZED, EARLY CHILDHOOD MENTAL HEALTH PROGRAMS FOR VERY TROUBLED CHILDREN AND FAMILIES. The second program highlighted here, the *Early Intervention Center* (EIC) of the Positive Education Program (PEP), represents an early intervention program specially designed for children with serious emotional and behavioral problems (Knitzer, 1996b). In general, few such programs exist. Highlighted earlier in connection with Day Care Plus, EIC is a parent-driven early intervention program in Cleveland, Ohio, for young children with emotional and behavioral challenges. Essentially, it uses parents as change agents for their young seriously troubled children. This is in contrast to the traditional pull-out therapeutic nurseries which sometimes include families, sometimes not. The program is a combination of individualized learning for parents, group support, opportunities to participate in formal courses about child development (as co–leaders as well as participants), and group experiences for children staffed by parents and resource coordinators. Parents learn first by rehearsing and role-playing in the observation room with the help of coaches and then by testing out new learnings in real settings, such as the home, grocery store, and classroom. The coaches, typically, are parents who have successfully been through the program, backed up by resource consultants who are either early childhood educators or mental health professionals (Knitzer, 1996b). This staffing pattern sends a powerful message to parents struggling with difficult children. Parents report that the support from the "hands-on" approach, the opportunity to be mentored by other parents and to be honest about their frustration and confusion, and the constant encouragement from the professional staff all result in major long term changes. Funding comes from mental health, social services, and special education agencies. Unfortunately, there has been no formal evaluation of this program. The director reports, however, a high level of diversion from continued special education placements. At intake, typically two-thirds of the children are classified "special needs,"

but only one-third go on to special education placements.

INTEGRATING MENTAL HEALTH AND FAMILY SUPPORT STRATEGIES FOR MOTHERS WHO ABUSE SUBSTANCES. Substance abuse (and often, related violence) among families with young children is widespread. Yet, few programs working with parents addicted to drugs address the challenges of parenting in the context of treatment. Although not focused solely on young children, the *Relational Psychotherapy Mothers' Group* (RPMG) illustrates a still-too-rare effort to incorporate attention to parenting issues in the context of substance-abuse services (Luthar & Suchman, in press). Substance abuse affects all aspects of a family's functioning. Often the children suffer in school, in social relationships, and in their own sense of self-esteem. Observations of infants and mothers show that addicted women, when compared to controls, are relatively disengaged from their babies, respond to their infants' cues less frequently, and make fewer active attempts to elicit responses from them (Luthar, Burack, Cicchetti, & Weisz, 1997). Data suggest that, by adolescence, a stunning 65% of children of mothers who use drugs have a major psychiatric disorder (Luthar, Burack, Cicchetti, & Weisz, 1997). Parents suffer grief, guilt, and a sense that no one believes that they really love their children. Nevertheless, treatment typically focuses only on the addiction rather than on parenting issues.

The RPMG is a data- and theory-based intervention that addresses parenting needs and serves as a supplement to addiction treatment. Its approach recognizes the comorbidity of mental illness among low-income substance abusers (in one study, the authors report 89% of the women had, at some point, been diagnosed with a major affective or anxiety disorder [Luthar & Suchman, 1999]); the impact of trauma, especially violence, in the lives of addicted women; and the fact that drug abuse reflects a constellation of serious problems of which addiction is only one part. The aim of the program is to provide nurturing experiences for women through the group in order to help them become better parents and to validate their strengths. The intervention involves six months of group meetings run jointly by a clinician and a drug counselor. Noteworthy about this approach, and what differentiates it from other structured therapy encounters and more didactic approaches (including parent education), is that for each structured session the mothers actively explore solutions by using brainstorming experiences and role plays that fit their own lifestyle. This approach was found to be effective with a less vulnerable population of Head Start parents through the Partners Project highlighted earlier (Webster-Stratton, 1996). Early results from the RPMG are promising. On key variables assessed (e.g., maternal maltreatment, positive interactions with children, and satisfaction in the maternal role), the target mothers fared significantly better, over time, than the mothers in traditional treatment (Luthar & Suchman, 1999).

Community and State-Level Initiatives

Even as it is crucial to document and evaluate what appear to be the best clinical and program strategies, it is also evident from this review that creating an early childhood mental health system entails a major systems development challenge. Although the systemic issues and challenges in developing early childhood mental health services that provide outreach to existing early childhood programs and that supplement existing secondary support services are highlighted later, here it is useful to describe the few actual examples there are of a systems development strategy at the community level and at the state level.

The community-level project, Project Before, was described earlier in terms of its mental health–based home visiting strategy (Rast, 1997a,b), but it also has a systems-building component. In the process of developing the home visiting model, the project director noted that even in a rural, low-income part of Kansas, there were already multiple home visiting projects that often targeted, with no particular sequence, the same families. As a result, a strategic effort was undertaken to engage the existing primary and secondary support services within the community in a planning and service delivery improvement process, working with an existing early childhood planning group. This effort resulted in training-resource, sharing, reduced service overload on the most vulnerable families in the community and in two target communities, and development of community–wide family resource centers. This effort also facilitated networking among not just the primary early childhood community but also between the community and those providing specialized support services.

Several states have also reported efforts to develop statewide programming concerning early childhood mental health that provide glimpses of how to move to a larger scale response to better meet the emotional and behavioral needs of all young children and families, particularly those at risk for developing poor outcomes (Knitzer & Page, 1998). Of these, the most well developed and evaluated is the Michigan *Infant Mental Health Program* (Tableman, 1995). Based on infant development and attachment theory, this program involves an intensive home visiting approach focused on facilitating behavioral changes in the infant, reinforcing the mother's positive parenting strategies, enhancing the parent's view of herself (or himself) as competent, and reducing stress in the family system. The program now operates at forty-three sites and is funded by a combination of Medicaid, state prevention grants, state mental health funds, and 10% local match money. Eighty percent of the parents served are single, 77% receive cash assistance, and close to 60% are enrolled early in pregnancy or at the time of their child's birth. Families with infants under 1 year of age who are exempted from work requirements under welfare reform may participate as part of a required social contract.

Several other states (e.g., Mississippi and Colorado) report limited grant programs to community mental health centers to promote early childhood mental health, particularly in child care settings (Knitzer & Page, 1998). Vermont is embarking on a regional system development strategy. The state's aim is to join local early childhood providers and family resource centers with local mental health providers, families, those implementing welfare reform, and those addressing domestic violence to develop a better mental health support network for Vermont's families and young children (Vermont Agency of Human Services, 1997). Nevada has developed a program known as *Early Childhood Support Services*, which encompasses intensive services and outreach to developmentally delayed young children as well as young children showing high risk for the development of behavioral and emotional problems, as well as their families and nonrelative caregivers (Knitzer & Page, 1998). Although these efforts are significant, it is also noteworthy that little attention has been devoted to linking these strategies with broader community development initiatives, such as empowerment or enterprise zones or community-focused foundation initiatives. This is an area that is ripe for creative connections, particularly in terms of training local residents to provide the needed supports and skills to the rest of the early childhood community.

Commonalties Across Promising Programs and Practices

The intervention and treatment strategies highlighted in this section cover a range of early childhood contexts (e.g., child care, home visiting programs, and Head Start), as well as more traditional treatment contexts (e.g., early intervention programs and substance abuse programs). These strategies share seven important commonalties. First, they are strength based, assuming that even the most highly stressed parents bring knowledge of their child and their own needs and abilities to the child-rearing task. Second, they assume that helping parents is the most powerful and long lasting way to help young children. Third, they start with parents where they are – responding respectfully to their needs and wishes. Fourth, they recognize the need to offer staff opportunities to explore their own feelings about complex issues (e.g., violence and child abuse), help the staff engage in peer-to-peer problem solving, and build staff expertise in dealing with complex emotional and behavioral issues. Fifth, they seek to meet the needs not just of those with diagnosed emotional and behavioral disorders, but also those at risk for developing them and those in any kind of crisis. Sixth, they rely on traditional medical model pull-out therapy only as a last resort. Seventh, they invent connections across systems that have traditionally not collaborated with one another; for example, linking mental health and substance-abuse agencies with child care programs or engaging child care resource and referral agencies in collaborative partnerships with mental health and substance abuse agencies.

System Development Challenges

The programs and practice initiatives highlighted in this chapter are exceptions. They are scattered across the country and typically lack evaluations. For most young children and their families or caregivers,

there is no readily accessible service delivery system to provide needed help for emotional, behavioral, or related issues. Despite evidence of need and potential efficacy, early childhood mental health is not considered central to the primary support systems for young children and families (i.e., health care preventive home visiting programs, early care and education, and family support programs) or to the existing secondary support systems, such as mental health, substance abuse, and early intervention/special education services. Therefore, a functioning infrastructure to pay for, expand, and evaluate such programs must be invented; it does not exist. This will require that at least five sets of systemic challenges be addressed.

IDEOLOGICAL CHALLENGES. One ideological challenge comes from the early childhood community. The traditional early childhood development perspective is that, except for a small proportion of children, all that is needed to promote the healthy emotional, social, and behavioral development of young children is a rich and stimulating early childhood environment. For example, one recent observer reported that the widely used standards for early childhood programs developed by the National Association for the Education of Young Children (Bredekamp & Copple, 1997) are vague on how to deal with children with challenging behaviors (Bryant et al., 1998). Related to this, many early childhood practitioners are skeptical about incorporating a mental health perspective into early childhood services, fearing that it will result in inappropriate labeling of children and, in effect, do more harm than good (Yoshikawa & Knitzer, 1997). Yet, as this chapter makes clear, typical early childhood practices (even the best), as well as parent support and parent education practices, are not always sufficiently robust to help families whose young children might not demonstrate positive early emotional development or to help early childhood staff trying to work with these children and their families. As a result, opportunities for significant and early intensive prevention and intervention are lost.

A second ideological challenge, ironically, comes from the formal mental health community, as reflected in the policies and procedures of state and community mental health agencies. These procedures and practices have, until recently, almost systematically ignored the fact that young children can have emotional and behavioral problems. In fact, some state agencies clearly note that mental health services for children begin at age 6 (unpublished data collected by Knitzer, 1994). Most typically, the failure to include requirements about meeting the mental health needs of young children and families means that local mental health agencies do not routinely have staff with appropriate clinical and developmental knowledge or skills to help that population. Although there are no empirical data, it is likely that this perspective is a result of the widespread belief that children under 6 do not have emotional or behavioral problems of such significance that they require mental health intervention. Obviously, there is sufficient evidence to refute this view, some of it cited earlier, but from a systems development perspective the myth that young children do not have serious disorders clearly hampers the development of mental health collaborations with the early childhood community.

A third ideological tension is found among both the early childhood and mental health practitioners. It is reflected in a debate about whether the focus of interventions should be on treatment or on preventive intervention. The formal mental health system, if it responds to young children at all, is organized to respond primarily to those with the most severe problems. The early childhood community tends to focus on strategies for early intervention and prevention, but it does so largely without a framework that encompasses the kind of necessary clinical expertise highlighted in this chapter. What is needed is a framework that cuts across these different perspectives and that encompasses a focus on the emotional development of all young children (prevention); high-risk young children (early intervention); and those with already identified severe disorders (treatment). Yet, notwithstanding evidence of need, with few exceptions (Forness, Kavale, MacMillan, Asarnow, & Duncan, 1996; Hoagwood & Koretz, 1996), there is little support for a system of early childhood mental health that encompasses both high-intensity preventive efforts grounded within normal developmental contexts for those already at risk and therapeutic interventions to the extent possible in normal developmental contexts for those with identifiable problems.

CROSS-SYSTEM COLLABORATION CHALLENGES. As this chapter makes clear, few families with young children who have or are at risk of developing emotional and behavioral problems deal with single issues: substance abuse coexists with violence, behavioral and emotional disorders in young children coexist with speech and language problems, and so forth. This means that there must be broad-based interagency collaboration not just for particular children and families but also at the systems level if an early childhood mental health system is to emerge. Yet there has been relatively little effort to build cross-system links around early childhood emotional development and mental health issues in a way parallel to what is expected through Part H (now Part C) or through the child and adolescent mental health service system (Skiba & Polsgrove, 1996; Stroul, 1996). To increase priority attention to young children and families at the community level efforts at developing cross-system links are the emerging strategies. Largely initiated by New York State, Knitzer and Page (1998) found that twenty-seven states report such initiatives, fourteen of which have explicit or exclusive focus on the needs of young children and families. Similarly, building blocks could emerge from existing early intervention networks and collaborations focused on systems of care for older children (Skiba & Polsgrove, 1996).

FISCAL CHALLENGES. Current funding mechanisms do not fit easily with the practices and principles of early childhood mental health. Four issues are especially problematic. First, although consultation and outreach to early childhood programs and to nonfamilial caregivers may be the most important early childhood mental health strategy, ongoing funding mechanisms are not typically in place to provide such interventions. Consultation has not been a formal part of children's mental health services since the 1970s. At that time, community mental health centers were required to provide consultation and education as a form of outreach and prevention for community organizations, which they did, often with a particular focus on early childhood programs (Greenspan, Nover, & Brunt, 1975; Knitzer, 1982).

Second, the gateway to access mental health services is a diagnostic label. This is a dilemma because there is much in the field of early childhood mental health, as defined in this chapter, and by infant mental health practitioners to challenge traditional notions of classification and diagnosis. Access to services and supports for young children, even more than is the case for older children, needs to be related not just to the presence of a disorder but also to the presence of conditions that lead to a disorder. The recent diagnostic classification system proposed by Zero to Three for infants and toddlers offers a framework for such assessment (Zero to Three, 1993, 1994). Yet, to date, no state has adopted this system. Similarly, new screening tools are emerging to identify preschoolers at risk for developing social and emotional problems (Feil, Walker, & Severson, 1995; Wittmer, Doll, & Strain, 1996). Although further refinement is needed, these approaches are intended to provide access to services for young children before their problems become severe. Thus far, though, there has been no concerted effort to design and pay for service entry pathways that reflect the importance of preventive and early intensive mental health interventions for young children.

A third challenge is also a longstanding one. Even for children and adolescents, the mental health system remains in too many places not a family-centered system but a child-centered system, in which the child, not the family, is the indicated client. This barely works for older children. For younger children, it is senseless. Indeed, given the importance to the therapeutic process of strengthening parent–child relationships, this can lead to absurd situations. In one mental health center that did not have a "treatment code" for parent–infant as client, the baby was named the indicated client, but the comptroller was concerned because the baby could not sign the treatment plan. (A proposed thumbprint was rejected [personal communication to Jane Knitzer by the mental health staff, 1996].)

The fourth issue is in some ways the most important; it is the dilemma about who should pay. Past efforts to develop child and adolescent systems of care have been premised on efforts to pool funds from multiple systems (Knitzer, 1996b; Stroul, 1996). The theory is that this approach provides better and more cost-effective services and that cost savings are reflected across systems in increased school attendance, less involvement with juvenile justice systems, and lower out-of-home placement costs. A

similar framework could be used to pool funds across systems serving young children and families, including those at high risk, with benefits tracked in terms of improved adjustment in kindergarten, reduced special education placements, and lower health care costs. To date, there has been no demonstration effort to implement such pooling. To add to the complexity, it is not clear whether managed care represents an opportunity or a risk for the development of early childhood mental health services. The focus on enhancing health services for young children through Medicaid expansions as well as state supplemental child health insurance programs clearly represents a significant opportunity, as long as there are efforts to ensure mental health parity and coverage of services that are appropriate to young children and families.

PERSONNEL CHALLENGES. Early childhood mental health services require an interdisciplinary knowledge base and a unique mix of skills and competencies; a core knowledge of child and family development, with a particular emphasis on the infant, toddler, and preschool years; an understanding of psychopathology and how it develops, as well as a high level of clinical skills; and an understanding of family dynamics and the ability to work collaboratively with families as well as with professionals from other disciplines or systems. Although some of the personnel challenges are the same as for those working with young children with developmental delays in the context of Part H (now Part C), clearly there is also a mental health clinical component that represents the potentially unique contribution of mental health services. Adding to the required mix is a comfort in working with low-income families and families from diverse cultural and ethnic traditions. It is not difficult to see why such programs as Head Start have had a difficult time finding mental health personnel to assist them. There are simply too few incentives and training opportunities to develop the necessary cadre of mental health professionals to master this broad set of competencies. Similarly, notwithstanding significant efforts to enhance the skills of those providing early care and education through state professional development strategies, public quality improvement funds, and public–private partnerships, helping child care directors or home visiting and family support staff to address the predictable emotional and behavioral challenges they will face has not been part of the national early childhood professional development agenda.

RESEARCH CHALLENGES. As this review suggests, there is a good deal of research that is relevant to understanding issues related to early childhood mental health. Nevertheless, it is also clear that there are large gaps, particularly with respect to the efficacy of different types of intensive preventive and treatment interventions for young children and families exposed to different levels of risk as well as the costs and benefits of such interventions. These kinds of issues must be addressed in order to sustain an early childhood mental health service system that can support primary early childhood services and supplement existing secondary services. To understand more fully the pathways to successful and impaired social and emotional functioning early in life, early childhood mental health research must continue.

TOWARD THE FUTURE: PRINCIPLES AND RECOMMENDATIONS

This chapter has argued that there is a compelling need for policy and practice to devote attention to the mental health needs of young children, families, and caregivers. It concludes with a discussion of nine principles to guide the development of an early childhood mental health system, followed by recommendations at the national, state, and community level to advance an early childhood mental health agenda.

Ten Principles of an Early Childhood Mental Health Service System

Growing out of the themes highlighted in this chapter, nine principles provide guidelines for developing a strategic approach to early childhood mental health.

1. *A family-centered early childhood mental health service system, including mental health and related services, should be designed to support parents of young children to nurture and build caring relationships with them.* Implicit in this principle, there are two assumptions of vital importance for early childhood mental health services. First, for young children, the cornerstone of all development appears to be the quality of the care and nurture that they receive. Therefore, a central aim of any early childhood mental health intervention is the assurance that parents have the emotional support and knowledge necessary to promote a nurturing relationship with their child. Even for families with sound psychological and material resources, this is a challenge, given family work patterns and economic realities. For families with limited economic resources, children with special needs, or both, the hurdles can be enormous. Thus, the need for access to family-friendly mental health interventions connected with either the primary early care and education or secondary support system (i.e., substance abuse, mental health, and so forth) is critical.

2. *A family-centered early childhood mental health service system, including mental health and related services, should be designed to support nonparental caregivers of young children to nurture and build caring relationships with them.* Increasingly, young children spend large amounts of time in child care settings or with nonrelative caregivers. Therefore, there is a need not only for consistency across home and caregiving settings in the ways that children are treated but also for the help nonparental caregivers receive in dealing with challenging situations. Communication between parents and caregivers is also necessary and should be facilitated by the service system.

3. *A family-centered early childhood mental health service system, including mental health and related services, should be delivered, to the greatest extent possible, in natural settings, including homes, child care, health care, and family support settings.* There may be some instances when families prefer to be seen in office-based settings but, in general, field reports suggest that families and staff are more likely to be responsive to mental health services delivered in settings in which the families feel comfortable. Yoshikawa and Knitzer (1997) suggested that delivering on-site mental health services in Head Start through either an enhanced clinical supervision or a consultant model tends to trigger a positive snowball effect resulting in enhanced program quality in general and better outcomes for individual children and families in particular. A family-centered early childhood mental health service system should be designed to respect developmental processes and be flexible and individualized to meet the needs of young children.

Two themes are embedded in this principle. Any effective early childhood mental health system must integrate, in a central way, principles of and expertise in early childhood development, as well as understandings of atypical development and developmental psychopathology. As with older children, though, mental health services must be flexible, and designed to meet the needs defined by the families and caregivers. This directly reflects the lessons from the mental health reform efforts on behalf of older children (Stroul, 1996), as well as family support principles (Kagan & Weissbourd, 1994) and clinical practice (Sax, 1997).

4. *A family-centered early childhood mental health and related service system should be sensitive to cultural, community, and ethnic values of families.* Young children and families are among the most culturally diverse in this society. Given the demographics of families with young children (National Center for Children in Poverty, 1998), special sensitivity to issues of ethnicity, cultural diversity, and class is important for building the relationships and trust with families that in turn is key to establishing an effective early childhood mental health service system (Greenfield, & Cocking, 1994; Yoshikawa & Knitzer, 1997).

5. *Caregivers, home visitors, family workers, and administrators working with infants, toddlers, and preschoolers should have access to clinical services, case consultation, and clinical supervision to strengthen their competencies in promoting emotional development in all young children, in young children who are at high risk for developing diagnosable problems, and in young children with already diagnosed problems.* Mental health services have traditionally provided support to family and nonfamily members (e.g., teachers) only as collateral services. That model is not appropriate for young children, for whom relationships with adults are central to healthy emotional development. Furthermore both family members and other caregivers need help in observing and understanding emotional and behavioral cues in young children, and in dealing with difficult situations in order to promote adaptive development and to reduce the impact of unhealthy emotional patterns.

6. *Family service workers, home visitors, and others working with families of infants, toddlers, and preschoolers and their families (including kinship and other foster parents, grandparents, and noncustodial fathers) should have access to mental health program consultation, case consultation, and backup support for families requiring more intensive interventions, particularly if there* are issues of substance abuse, domestic violence, child maltreatment, depression, or other mental illness. Family services workers are frequently asked to deal with enormously complex family issues. Service workers' experiences in the field strongly suggest that helping families develop greater skills and competencies with backup access to clinical support may enhance the efficacy of the core program, as well as help staff to understand when more intensive services are needed.

7. *Caregivers, home visitors, family workers, and administrators working with families of infants, toddlers, and preschoolers should have access to clinical supervision and support in dealing with such staff issues as burnout, cultural, and workplace conflicts.* Child care programs frequently report staff conflicts concerning how to address such ongoing issues as discipline, cultural differences, and stress management, as well as uncertainty about how to deal with crisis situations such as the terminal illness of a child, violence affecting staff members, family violence, or other disasters. Offering staff opportunities for shared reflection and problem solving can be facilitated by a mental health consultant and can thereby enhance the overall program environment.

8. *Young children, families, and programs experiencing crises related to violence, community disasters, or family-specific upheavals should have immediate and as-necessary access to crisis intervention and support.* An early childhood mental health system should help primary caregivers cope with psychological, health, and natural disasters. Primary care settings, particularly early care and education and family support settings, should have crisis plans in place, similar to those that many school districts now use. Special outreach efforts should be made to vulnerable infants, toddlers, and preschoolers and their families who are in shelters, involved with courts, or not in any formal care settings.

9. *Developing a family- and caregiver-centered early childhood mental health service system requires building partnerships among both primary and secondary support services at the community and state level.* This means linking the early childhood community (including child care, prekindergarten, home visiting, etc.), mental health and substance abuse providers, and other secondary support services in a process of strategic planning, goal setting, and resource mapping, with special attention to fiscal issues raised by the new challenges of managed health and behavioral health care.

Recommendations

On the basis of these principles, as well as lessons from the research, programs, and issues reviewed in this chapter, it is possible to craft a modest agenda that can be implemented nationally, within states, and within communities. For example, at the national level, early childhood mental health could be built into federal mental health legislation, promoted by pooling demonstration and research funds across federal agencies, integrated into training and technical strategies to support quality improvement in early childhood programs, and required in planning by substance abuse and mental health agencies that receive federal funds. Similarly, it might be possible to engage national groups involved in early childhood, family support, mental health, and early intervention in public dialogues about strategies to promote early childhood mental health services and systems development. Most important, there need to be specific efforts to develop and promote a research agenda that focuses on the efficacy of a range of interventions, including consultation to staff, multicomponent preventive interventions, wraparound strategies, and other approaches to preventing and reducing emotional and behavioral dysfunction among young children and their families.

Although these kinds of efforts could take place at the state level as well as at the national level, states also represent potential laboratories to develop new policy strategies (e.g., developing state-specific incentives to encourage local collaboration among mental health, substance abuse, early intervention, and early childhood programs). Currently, twenty-four states have funded programs for infants and toddlers, thirty-four states have funded programs for preschoolers, and twenty-five states have funded family support-type programs for children from birth to age 6 (Knitzer & Page, 1998). Given the interest in professional development strategies for early care and education providers, the states are also in a position to strengthen systems of training for child care and early education providers to include a focus on dealing with the most psychologically vulnerable young children and families and to increase attention to early childhood mental health issues in training programs for social work, psychology, and allied disciplines.

At the community level, there is much room for local initiative, building on the networking and community mobilization that is already occurring on behalf of young children and families and on the efforts to apply emerging treatment strategies from mental health to younger children and families.

Conclusion

Emotional and developmental issues confronting young children and families are an arena ripe for service system and social policy development. Research-based data and field-based reports paint a picture of compelling need. The achievement of public policy goals related to welfare and to early success in school could directly benefit from attention to the emotional and behavioral development of young children, particularly those at high risk for developing later emotional and behavioral disorders, or even young children with already identified disorders. Treatment and intervention strategies are emerging that have the potential, if brought to scale, to affect positively both short- and long-term outcomes for large numbers of young children and families. The challenge of transforming these glimpses of what might be into a workable system of services and supports is considerable and will require strategic efforts at multiple levels. Yet, ignoring the challenge is likely to be even more costly in the short term for young children, families, and their caregivers and, in the long term, for the schools and other institutions left to try to transform more hardened patterns of maladaptation.

REFERENCES

Aber., J. L. (1994). Poverty, violence and child development: Untangling family- and community-level effects. In C. Nelson (Ed.), *Threats to optimal development: Integrating biological, psychological and social risk factors.* The Minnesota symposium on child psychology, *27,* Hillsdale, NJ: Erlbaum.

Barnard, K. E., Morisset, C. E., & Spieker, S. (1993). Preventive interventions: Enhancing parent–infant relationships. In C. Zeanah, Jr. (Ed.), *Handbook of infant mental health* (pp. 386–401). New York: Guilford Press.

Barnett, W. S. (1995). Long-term effects of early childhood programs on cognitive and school outcomes. *The Future of Children: Long-term Outcomes of Early Childhood Programs, 5*(3) 25–50.

Beare, P. L., & Lynch, E. C. (1986). Under identification of preschool children at risk for behavioral disorders. *Behavioral Disorders, 11,* 177–83.

Belle, D. (1982). *Lives in stress: Women and depression.* Newbury Park, CA: Sage Publications.

Bernstein, V. J., Percansky, C., & Wechsler, N. (1996). Strengthening families through strengthening relationships: The Ounce of Prevention Fund developmental training and support program. In M. C. Roberts (Ed.), *Model programs in child and family mental health* (pp. 109–33). Hillsdale, NJ: Erlbaum.

Boyer, E. L. (1991). *Ready to learn: A mandate for the nation.* Princeton, NJ: Carnegie Foundation for the Advancement of Teaching.

Bredekamp, S., & Copple, C. (Eds.) (1997). *Developmentally appropriate practice in early childhood programs* (Rev. ed.). Washington, DC: National Association for the Education of Young Children.

Bryant, D., Vizzard, L. H., Willoughby, M., & Kupersmidt, J. (1998). *A review of interventions for preschoolers with aggressive and disruptive behavior.* Unpublished manuscript. University of North Carolina at Chapel Hill, Frank Porter Graham Child Development Center, Maternal and Child Health, Department of Psychology, Chapel Hill, NC.

Campbell, S. B. (1995). Behavioral problems in preschool children: A review of recent research. *Journal of Child Psychology and Psychiatry and Allied Disciplines, 36*(1), 113–49.

Campbell, S. B. (Ed.). (1996). *Journal of Clinical Child Psychology: Special Section on the Development of Psychopathology in Young Children, 25*(4).

Center for the Future of Children. (1993). *Home Visiting (3)3.* Los Altos, CA: Center for the Future of Children, The David and Lucille Packard Foundation.

Coie, J. D., Watt, N. F., West, S. G., Hawkins, J. D., Asarnow, J. R., Markman, J. J., Ramey, S. L., Shire, M. B., & Long, B. (1993). The science of prevention: A conceptual framework and some directions for a national research program. *American Psychologist, 4*(8), 1013–22.

Conduct Problems Prevention Research Group. (1992). A developmental and clinical model for the prevention of conduct disorder. The FAST Track Program. *Development and Psychopathology, 4*, 509–27.

Conduct Problems Prevention Research Group. (1997, April). *Prevention of antisocial behavior: Initial findings from the Fast Track Project.* Symposium presented at the Society for Research in Child Development Biennial Meeting, Washington, DC.

Constantino, J. (1992). On the prevention of conduct disorder: A rationale for initiating preventive efforts. *Infants and Young Children, 5*(2), 29–41.

Donahue, P. J. (1997, June). *Mental health collaborations in Head Start.* Paper presented at the Roundtable on Head Start Research, Washington, DC.

Downey, G., & Coyne, J. C. (1990). Children of depressed parents: An investigative review. *Psychological Bulletin, 108*, 50–76.

Duncan, B. B., Forness, S. R., & Hartsough, C. (1995). Students identified as seriously emotionally disturbed in school-based day treatment: Cognitive, psychiatric, and special education characteristics. *Behavioral Disorders, 20*(4), 238–52.

Duncan, G., Brooks-Gunn, J., & Aber, J. L. (Eds.). (1997). *Neighborhood poverty: Context and consequences for child and adolescent development.* New York: Russell Sage.

Dunst, C. J., Trivette, C. M., & Deal, A. (1989). *Enabling and empowering families: Principles and guidelines for practice.* Cambridge, MA: Brookline Books.

Earls, F. (1980). Prevalence of behavior problems in 3-year-old children: A cross-national replication. *Archives of General Psychiatry, 37*(10), 1153–57.

Edelfsen, M., & Baird, M. (1994). Making it work: Preventive mental health care for disadvantaged preschoolers. *Social Work, 39*, 566–73.

Fantuzzo, J., Coolahan, K., & Weiss, A. (1997). Resiliency partnership-directed intervention: Enhancing the social competencies of preschool victims of physical abuse by developing peer resources and community strengths. In D. Cicchetti & S. L. Toth (Eds.), *Rochester symposium on developmental psychopathology, Vol. 8: Developmental perspectives on trauma* (pp. 463–480). Rochester, NY: University of Rochester Press.

Feil, E. G., Walker, H. M., & Severson, H. H. (1995). The Early Screening Project for young children with behavior problems. *Journal of Emotional and Behavioral Disorders, 3*(4), 194–202.

Forness, S. R., & Finn, D. (1993). Screening children in Head Start for emotional or behavioral disorders. *Severe Behavioral Disorders Monograph, 16*, 6–14. Arizona State University, Teacher Educators for Children with Behavioral Disorders, and Council for Children with Behavioral Disorders.

Forness, S. R., Kavale, K. A., MacMillan, D. L., Asarnow, J. R., & Duncan, B. B. (1996). Early detection and prevention of emotional or behavioral disorders: Developmental aspects of systems of care. *Behavioral Disorders, 21*(3), 226–40.

Gaensbauer, T., & Siegel, C. (1995). Therapeutic approaches to post-traumatic stress disorder in infants and toddlers. *Infant Mental Health Journal, 16*, 292–305.

Gephart, M. (1997). Neighborhoods and communities as contexts for development. In G. Duncan, J. Brooks-Gunn, & J. L. Aber (Eds.), *Neighborhood poverty: Context and consequences for child and adolescent development* (pp. 1–43). New York: Russell Sage.

Greenfield, P. M., & Cocking, R. R. (1994). *Cross-cultural roots of minority child development.* Hillsdale, NJ: Erlbaum.

Greenspan, S. I., Nover, R. A., & Brunt, C. H. (1975). Mental health consultation to early child care. In F. V. Manaino (Ed.), *Mental health consultation.* [DHEW Pub. No. (ADM) 74-112 (pp. 105–27)] Washington, DC: U.S. Government Printing Office.

Greenspan, S. I., & Wieder, S. (1993). Regulatory disorders. In C. H. Zeanah (Ed.), *Handbook of infant mental health* (pp. 280–90). New York: Guilford Press.

Greenspan, S. I., Wieder, S., & Nover, R. A. (1985). Diagnosis and preventive intervention of developmental and emotional disorders in infancy and early childhood: New perspectives. In M. Green (Ed.), *The psychological aspects* of the family: The new pediatrics (pp. 13–52). Lexington, MA: Lexington Books.

Groves, B., Zuckerman, B., Marans, S., & Cohen, D. (1993). Silent victims: Children who witness violence. Journal of the American Medical Association, 269, 262–4.

Halpern, R. (1993). Poverty and infant development. In C. H. Zeanah (Ed.), Handbook of infant mental health (pp. 73–86). New York: Guilford Press.

Hardin, B. (1997, February/March). You cannot do it alone: Home visitation with psychologically vulnerable families and children. Zero to Three: Bulletin of Zero To Three: National Center for Infants, Toddlers, and Families, 17(4).

Hoagwood, K., & Koretz, D. (1996). Embedding prevention services within systems of care: Strengthening the nexus for children. Applied and preventative psychology: Current scientific perspectives, 5(4), 225–34.

Isaacs-Shockley, M., Cross, T., Bazron, B. J. Dennis, K., & Benjamin, M. P. (1996). Framework for a culturally competent system of care. In B. A. Stroul (Ed.), Children's mental health: Creating systems of care in a changing society (pp. 23–39). Baltimore, MD: Paul H. Brookes.

Johnson, D. L., & Walker, T. B. (1991, October). Final report of an evaluation of the AVANCE Parent Education and Family Support Program. Submitted to the Carnegie Corporation.

Johnston, K. (1990, October). Mental health consultation. Paper presented at the Conference on early challenges: Caring for children birth to three, Infant Toddler Consortium of the San Francisco Psychoanalytic Institute, Haywood, CA.

Kagan, S. L., & Weissbourd, B. (Eds.) (1994). Putting families first: America's family support movement and the challenge of change. San Francisco: Jossey-Bass.

Kaplan-Sanoff, M., Parker, S., & Zuckerman, B. (1991). Poverty and early childhood development: What do we know, what should we do? Infants and Young Children, 4(1), 68–76.

Kazdin, A. E. (1993). Treatment of conduct disorder: Progress and directions in psychotherapy research [Special issue]. Toward a developmental perspective on conduct disorder. Development and Psychopathology, 5(1–2) 277–310.

Knitzer, J. (1982). Unclaimed children: The failure of public responsibility to children and adolescents in need of mental health services. Washington, DC: Children's Defense Fund.

Knitzer, J. (1996a). Children's mental health: Changing paradigms and policies. In E. F. Zigler, S. L. Kagan, & N. W. Hall (Eds.), Children, families, and government: Preparing for the twenty-first century (pp. 207–32). New York: Cambridge University Press.

Knitzer, J. (1996b). Meeting the mental health needs of young children and their families. In B. A. Stroul (Ed.), Children's mental health: Creating systems of care in a changing society (pp. 553–72). Baltimore, MD: Paul H. Brookes.

Knitzer, J., & Page, S. (1996). Map and track: State initiatives for young children and families. New York: National Center for Children in Poverty, Columbia University School of Public Health.

Knitzer, J., & Page, S. (1998). Map and track: State initiatives for young children and families. New York: National Center for Children in Poverty, Columbia University School of Public Health.

Kupersmidt, J., Coie, J., & Dodge, K. (1990). The role of poor peer relationships in the development of disorder. In S. Asher & J. Coie (Eds.), Peer rejection in childhood (pp. 274–308). New York: Cambridge University Press.

Lavigne, J. V., Gibbons, R. D., Christoffel, K. K., Arend, R., Rosenbaum, D., Binns, H., Dawson, N., Sobel, H., & Isaacs, C. (1996). Prevalence rates and correlates of psychiatric disorders among preschool children. Journal of the American Academy of Child and Adolescent Psychiatry, 35(2), 204–14.

Lewis, M. D. (1996). Trauma reverberates: Psychosocial evaluation of the caregiving environment of young children exposed to violence and traumatic loss. In J. Osofsky & E. Fenichel (Eds.), Islands of safety: Assessing and treating young victims of violence (pp. 21–8). Arlington, VA: Zero To Three: National Center for Infants, Toddlers, and Families.

Lieberman, A. F., & Pawl, J. H. (1993). Infant-parent psychotherapy. In C. H. Zeanah (Ed.), Handbook of infant mental health (pp. 427–42). New York: Guilford Press.

Link, G., Beggs, M., & Seiderman, E. (1997). Serving families. Fairfax, CA: Parent Services Project, Inc.

Lochman, J. E., & Conduct Problems Prevention Research Group. (1995). Screening of child behavior problems for prevention programs at school entry. Special section: Prediction and prevention of child and adolescent antisocial behavior. Journal of Consulting and Clinical Psychology, 63(4), 549–59.

Loerber, R., & Hay, D. F. (1994). Developmental approaches to aggression and conduct problems. In M. Rutter & D. F. Hay (Eds.), Development through life: A handbook for clinicians (pp. 488–516). Boston: Blackwell Scientific.

Lourie, I. S., Katz-Leavy, J., & Stroul, B. A. (1996). Individualized services in a system of care. In B. A. Stroul (Ed.), Children's mental health: Creating systems of care in a changing society. Baltimore, MD: Paul H. Brookes.

Love, J. M., Aber, J. L., & Brooks-Gunn, J. (1994). Strategies for assessing community progress toward achieving the first national education goal. Princeton, NJ: Mathematica Policy Research Institute.

Love, J. M., & Logue, M. E. (1992). Transitions to kindergarten in American schools: Executive summary. Final report of the National Transition Study. Portsmouth, NH: RMC Research Corporation.

Luby, J., & Morgan, K. (1997). Characteristics of an infant/preschool psychiatric clinic sample: Implications for clinical assessment and nosology. Infant Mental Health Journal, 18(2), 209–20.

Luthar, S. S., & Suchman, N. E. (1999). Developmentally informed parenting interventions: The Relational Psychotherapy Mothers' Group. In D. Cicchetti & S. L. Toth (Eds.), *Rochester symposium on developmental psychopathology, volume X: Developmental approaches to prevention and intervention* (pp. 271–309). Rochester, NY: University of Rochester Press.

Luthar, S. S., Burack, J. A., Cicchetti, D., & Weisz, J. R. (1997). *Developmental psychopathology: Perspectives on adjustment, risk, and disorder.* New York: Cambridge University Press.

Lyons-Ruth, K., Botein, S., & Grunbaum, H. U. (1984). Reaching the hard to reach: Serving isolated and depressed mothers with infants in the community. In B. Cohler & J. Musick (Eds.), *Intervention with psychiatrically disabled parents and their young children* (pp. 95–121). San Francisco: Jossey-Bass.

MACRO. (Spring 1997). Personal communication. Preliminary results for Systems of Care evaluation, Atlanta, GA.

McLoyd, V. C. (1990). The impact of economic hardship on black families and children: Psychological distress, parenting, and socioemotional development. *Child Development, 61,* 311–46.

Meisels, S. J., & Shonkoff, J. P. (Eds.). (1990). *Handbook of early childhood intervention.* New York: Cambridge University Press.

Mrazek, P. J., & Haggerty, R. J. (Eds.). (1994). *Reducing risks for mental disorders: Frontiers for preventive intervention research.* Washington, DC: National Academy Press.

National Center for Children in Poverty. (1998). *Young children in poverty: A statistical update.* New York: National Center for Children in Poverty, Columbia School of Public Health.

Osofsky, J. D. (1995). The effects of exposure to violence on young children. *American Psychologist, 50,* 782–8.

Parker, F. L., Piotrkowski, C. S., Horn, W., & Greene, S. (1995). The challenge for Head Start: Realizing its vision as a two-generation program. In I. Sigel (Series Ed.) & S. Smith (Vol. Ed.), *Advances in applied developmental psychology: Vol. 9. Two-generation programs for families in poverty* (pp. 135–59). New Jersey: Ablex.

Patterson, G. R., DeBaryshe, B. D., & Ramsey, E. (1989). A developmental perspective on antisocial behavior. *American Psychologist, 44,* 329–35.

Perry, B. D., Pollard, R. A., Blakley, T. L., Baker, W. L., & Vigilante, D. (1995). Childhood trauma, the neurobiology of adaptation, and "use-dependent" development of the brain: How "states" become "traits." *Infant Mental Health Journal, 16,* 271–96.

Piotrkowski, C. S., Collins, R. C., Knitzer, J., & Robinson, R. (1994). Strengthening mental health services in Head Start: A challenge for the 1990s. *American Psychologist, 49*(2), 133–9.

Poulos, J. (1996, February). Personal communication. Child and Adolescent Service Center Preschool Community Services Program, Stark County, OH.

Prizant, B. M., Wetherby, A. M., & Roberts, J. E. (1993). Communication disorders in infants and toddlers. In C. H. Zeanah (Ed.), *Handbook of infant mental health* (pp. 260–79). New York: Guilford Press.

Rast, J. (1997a, June). Lessons from the village. *KanFocus,* 4.3.

Rast, J. (1997b, July). More village lessons. *KanFocus,* 4.4.

Rutter, M. (1979). Protective factors in children's responses to stress and disadvantage. *Social competence in children* (pp. 49–74). Hanover, NH: University of New England.

Sameroff, A. J., & Emde, R. N. (1989). *Relationship disturbance in early childhood: A developmental approach.* New York: Basic Books.

Sax, P. (1997). Narrative therapy and family support: Strengthening the mother's voice in working with families with infants and toddlers. In C. Smith & D. Nylund (Eds.), *Narrative therapies with children and adolescents* (pp. 111–46). New York: Guilford Press.

Shonkoff, J. P. (1982). Biological and social factors contributing to mild mental retardation. In K. Heller, W. Holtzman, & S. Messick (Eds.), *Placing children in special education: A strategy for equity* (pp. 133–81). Washington, DC: National Academy Press.

Shore, R. (1997). *Rethinking the brain: New insights into early development.* New York: Families and Work Institute.

Sinclair, E. (1993). Early identification of preschoolers with special needs in Head Start. *Topics in Early Childhood Special Education, 13,* 12–18.

Sinclair, E., Del'Homme, M., & Gonzalez, M. (1993). Systematic screening for preschool behavioral disorders. *Behavioral Disorders, 18,* 177–88.

Skiba, R., & Polsgrove, L. (1996). *Developing a system of care: Interagency collaboration for students with emotional and behavioral disorders.* Reston, VA: Council for Exceptional Children.

Smith, S., Brooks-Gunn, J., & Klebanov, P. (1997). Consequences of living in poverty for young children's cognitive and verbal ability and early school achievement. In G. J. Duncan & J. Brooks-Gunn (Eds.), *Consequences of growing up poor* (pp. 132–89). New York: Russell Sage Foundation.

Stein, A., & Associates. (1988). *Parent services project evaluation: Final report of findings.* Fairfax, CA: Parent Services Project.

Stroul, B. A. (Ed.). (1996). *Children's mental health: Creating systems of care in a changing society.* Baltimore, MD: Paul H. Brookes.

Tableman, B. (1995). *A review of infant mental health services in the context of systems reform.* Lansing: Michigan Department of Mental Health.

Tolan, P. H., Guerra, N. G., & Kendall, P. (1995). A developmental-ecological perspective on antisocial behavior in children and adolescents: Toward a unified risk and intervention framework. *Journal of Consulting and Clinical Psychology, 63*(4), 579–84.

Vandenburg, J. E. (1993). Integration of individualized mental health services into the system of care for children and adolescents. *Administration and Policy in Mental Health, 20*(4), 247–57.

Vermont Agency of Human Services. (1997). *CUPS (Children's UPstream Services).* A proposal to the Department of Health and Human Services, Center for Mental Health Services, for the Child Mental Health Initiative, GFA No. SM 97-007 CFDA No. 93.104. Vermont Agency of Human Services, Department of Developmental and Mental Health Services, Division of Mental Health, Child, Adolescent and Family Unit.

Vig, S. (1996). Young children's exposure to community violence. *Journal of Early Intervention, 20*(4), 319–28.

Walker, H. M., Kavanagh, K., Stiller, B., Golly, A., Severson, H. H., & Feil, E. G. (1998). First step to success: An early intervention approach for preventing school antisocial behavior. *Journal of Emotional and Behavioral Disorders, 6*(3), 66–80.

Wallach, V. A. (1994). Healthy Start Hawaii: A clinical consultation model within a prevention model. In the *First Healthy Families American Conference: Getting Families Off to a Good Start.* Presentation at the meeting of the Healthy Families America Conference, Oakbrook, IL.

Wallach, V. A., & Lister, L. (1995). Stages in the delivery of home-based services to parents at risk of child abuse: A Healthy Start experience. *Scholarly Inquiry for Nursing Practice: An International Journal, 9*(2), 159–73.

Webster-Stratton, C. (1996, November). *Preventing conduct problems in Head Start children: Strengthening parenting competencies.* Paper presented at the APHA Pre-Conference Workshop, New York City.

Webster-Stratton, C., & Hammond, M. (1997). Treating children with early-onset conduct problems: A comparison of child and parent training interventions. *Journal of Consulting and Clinical Psychology, 65*(1), 93–109.

Wittmer, D., Doll, B., & Strain, P. (1996). Assessment of social and emotional development in early childhood: The identification of competence and disabilities. *Journal of Early Intervention, 20*(4), 299–317.

Yoshikawa, H. (1994). Prevention as cumulative protection: Effects of early family support and education on chronic delinquency and its risks. *Psychological Bulletin, 115*(1), 28–54.

Yoshikawa, H. (1995). Long-term effects of early childhood programs on social outcomes and delinquency. *The Future of Children, 5*(3), 51–75.

Yoshikawa, H., & Knitzer, J. (1997). *Lessons from the field: Head Start mental health strategies to meet changing needs.* New York: National Center for Children in Poverty, Columbia University School of Public Health, and American Orthopsychiatric Association.

Zeanah, C., Jr. (Ed.). (1993). *Handbook of infant mental health.* New York: Guilford Press.

Zero To Three. (1993). *Heart Start: The emotional foundations of school readiness.* Arlington, VA: Zero To Three: National Center for Clinical Infant Programs.

Zero To Three. (1994). *Diagnostic classification of mental health and developmental disorders of infancy and early childhood.* Washington, DC: Zero To Three: National Center for Infants, Toddlers and Families.

CHAPTER TWENTY

Paraprofessionals Revisited and Reconsidered

JUDITH MUSICK AND FRANCES STOTT

I think that it is a direct and personal service that I offer my clients. I live in the community I serve; I am available at all hours and on weekends. By living in the community, I am available to provide the same resources as is common in our middle-class communities which often have doctors, lawyers, and other professionals living next door to each other. Individuals such as myself have never been available for the poor community to take advantage of. I believe that my style of handling clients' problems who live in the poor community is the most effective way possible. I'm from the community I serve, I know most of the people, they know me. I know their problems because they are mine also, and I understand the poor people because I am one, and a part of them. (Specht, Hawkins, & McGee, 1968, p. 10)

This chapter examines the roles and effectiveness of staff in community-based, urban, early intervention programs in which the primary goal is improving the caregiving environment and the development of infants and young children considered at risk. In these programs, risk is defined as a consequence of any one, or a combination of, the following factors: growing up in a community with high rates of poverty, violence, crime, unemployment, and so forth; being raised by very young or troubled parents; or manifesting developmental problems or delays. Seldom are those charged with the task of modifying the caregiving environment professionally trained staff such as physicians. Although trained professionals may provide consultation or supervision, most of the direct service in these programs is carried out by paraprofessionals living in or near the community being served. It is these "lay" workers who have personal relationships

with program participants, visit their homes, see them on a regular basis in centers, and make certain they have access to and make use of other necessary health, educational, occupational, or social services. These individuals form the web of structured social support that is the essence of the community-based approach to early intervention in urban settings.

In a chapter for the first edition of this volume (Musick & Stott, 1990), we focused on the role of paraprofessionals as mediators in parent–child relationships and, ideally, as facilitators of parenting change when problems existed. While acknowledging the challenges such workers faced in intervening in such complex processes, we did not question the wisdom of their being assigned such roles. In a later article, reflecting a growing discomfort on our part with this conceptualization, we cautioned against relying too heavily on lay staff, especially on untrained and unsupervised staff in programs for multirisk families of young children. In that chapter, we noted that the problems observed were "less the fault of paraprofessionals than of the unrealistic expectations of program administrators" (Stott & Musick, 1994, pp. 199–200) who ask such workers to take on roles for which they are unprepared.

Continuing concern with this issue has led us to reconsider the notion of paraprofessionals as interventionists in the parenting process and to redirect our attention to more effective and authentic roles for them to fulfill. These roles are more effective and authentic because they build on the strengths of paraprofessionals and take advantage of their life experience and wisdom. They also provide social, personal, and economic development for paraprofessionals and for the families they serve in low-income urban settings.

THE USE OF PARAPROFESSIONALS IN HUMAN SERVICES: THE REAL BENEFITS AND COSTS

Who Are Paraprofessionals?

The paraprofessional, or lay helper, is an individual who has not received training in a traditional baccalaureate, postbaccalaureate, or professional training program. Such workers have always been involved in the delivery of social services, but their widespread use dates only from the mid-1960s' War on Poverty. The initial impetus for using lay workers was the rapid growth of human service programs, with a resultant shortage of trained workers (e.g., Albee, 1968; Austin, 1978; Gartner, 1971). During this era, indigenous workers were employed in health care (with chronic hospitalized patients and substance-abuse programs), mental health agencies, Head Start and other early childhood programs, education, juvenile corrections, welfare and law, and community action programs. At the same time, the use of paraprofessionals was thought to increase the efficiency and effectiveness of services (Austin, 1978) because it freed professionals from duties that could be done as well by persons with less training, skill, or both. Finally, paraprofessionals were thought to provide a more cost-effective system of service delivery. Not only are these rationales still considered valid today but there has also been renewed interest in the deployment of paraprofessionals as a strategy of both good practice and economic development (Nittoli & Giloth, 1998).

WHY USE PARAPROFESSIONALS?

Economic Factors

In considering why contemporary early intervention programs employ paraprofessional workers, we begin with the most obvious factor: It is difficult to find sufficient numbers of trained professionals willing to work in unsafe environments and moreover to do so for low wages and few benefits – circumstances characteristic of many programs serving low-income urban communities. This reluctance appears to be as true for professionals who originally came from

such communities as it is for those who grew up elsewhere. In addition, paraprofessionals are hired to create jobs and opportunities for unemployed local people or to help launch them on new career paths.

For many, the use of paraprofessionals provides a more cost-effective system of service delivery, an especially compelling reason during times of limited resources and funding cuts. In truth, however, programs are unlikely to save much money on paraprofessionals if they do their job conscientiously. Recruiting, training, and retaining competent and effective paraprofessional staff call for significant expenditures of time, effort, and money, especially for programs serving struggling families in very-low-income communities. It takes energy and skill to determine who has the potential to be an effective provider and who does not. Consider, for example, Ida, the program coordinator responsible for recruiting, training, selecting, and overseeing a network of providers for a child-care demonstration program studied by Judith Musick. Although these child-care providers ultimately viewed themselves and functioned as professional providers, none had professional degrees, few had attended college, and some had not completed secondary school. During the first several years of the project, approximately 160 women responded to Ida's recruitment efforts. She eventually interviewed more than 100 women, visited approximately 40, and screened at least 20 to 25. Of these, four were accepted and trained but ultimately did not end up working for the program. Two were screened and rejected, and two dropped out during training (Musick, 1996).

As is apparent, the recruitment process is labor intensive but clearly necessary and worthwhile. Those who completed the process were an able and enthusiastic group of women. The care they provided to children was good, and in some cases, exceptional. Effects on parents' lives were often exceptional as well. Recruiting and retaining such women are significant, although costly, accomplishments (Musick, 1996).

Recent cost analyses of family support programs – programs generally targeting families in the birth to preschool-age range – raise questions about the cost-effectiveness of using paraprofessionals within this domain. For example, analysis of costs in the Child Survival/Fair Start initiative found that the cost differential of using paraprofessionals versus professionals may not be as large as often assumed (Harkavy & Bond, 1992). The cost analysis indicated that the programs expended considerable time and money in providing ongoing training and supervision for paraprofessionals and that there is great variation in local wage structures for paraprofessionals. This pattern has also been found in other home-visiting family support programs (e.g., Olds & Kitzman, 1993).

A "Bridge" to the Broader Community

One of the more compelling reasons for using paraprofessionals is the assumption that they have a better understanding of their clients because their circumstances more closely resemble their own. Paraprofessionals are valued for providing a "bridge" between programs and clients because they share the same cultural backgrounds and live in similar neighborhoods. In a discussion of the Fair Start intervention programs, Harkavy and Bond (1992) stated that "cultural familiarity enabled the workers [paraprofessionals] to read behavioral cues, frame program messages in acceptable and understandable terms, and avoid violating community norms" (p. 186).

Unquestionably, the bridge role casts paraprofessionals as ambassadors of the program's goodwill and good intentions, living symbols of the program's commitment to the community and respect for its members. Furthermore, because paraprofessionals do not rely on the use of role and techniques that produce distance between helper and client, they are able to gain entry and establish rapport with a variety of individuals who might otherwise be unapproachable (Kalafat & Boroto, 1977). These hard-to-reach families are more likely to trust and accept such program staff because they are from the same place; they know the same streets and people and stories. Even troubled parents perceive them as not so different from themselves and can feel accepted as they are, not judged for what they are not.

Paraprofessionals as Beneficiaries

A final major reason for using paraprofessionals in early intervention programs concerns the benefits that accrue to the paraprofessionals themselves.

One such benefit is employment for the poor and chronically unemployed. This goal was implicit in such legislation as the Economic Opportunity Act of 1964 (Austin, 1978) and remains so today. An extension of the employment motive is a "new careers" philosophy that emphasizes continuous employment and personal advancement opportunities (Riessman, 1965). Riessman's "helper therapy principle" holds that through their training and attempts at helping others, nonprofessional helpers themselves often experience significant personal growth. This growth results from increased opportunities to develop and refine skills, as well as improvements in aspects of psychological health such as self-esteem, aspirations, and the ability to engage in effective interpersonal relationships. As the paraprofessional realizes these benefits, she becomes a more effective staff member and this, in turn, has positive effects on program participants.

The children of paraprofessionals may also be beneficiaries not only of their mother's improved economic status but also of her new knowledge and skills. New understandings and competencies gained both through training and experience may lead the paraprofessional to reconsider and make changes in her own parenting behavior (Halpern & Convey, 1983; Musick, 1996). Here two providers from the child-care demonstration project described earlier recount how this took place for them:

I'm not proud of this. What I used to do with my seven-year-old is, I was a spanker. I hit him. I spanked him hard on the butt, on the legs. I got so frustrated with him sometimes, I would shake him, because that's what my family used to do to me. Well, through the workshops, through this agency, through the information...given us, I've learned to use my words, my emotions with my son...I think this did wonders for me...I no longer hit my children...I was hit all the time. So was my husband. So he's also learning through me.

I always believed in the beginning, before I did this, I believed that kids – I'm not saying child abuse, don't get me wrong – I'm saying children had to have a little bit of fear of you to respect and do what they were told. And my oldest son was hyperactive, so like I did give him spankings...and then when I learned something, I learned that spanking didn't do any good....I will sit there and try to reason with them...I've learned to choose my battles...okay, let's work it out. (Musick, 1996)

Such changes in parenting behavior can have profound effects on children's development. Toby Herr, founder and director of Project Match, a nationally recognized welfare-to-work program in Chicago, observes that there are paraprofessionals for whom a community-based program is the first job after many years of being on public assistance. Herr notes that such a job is often an ideal way to make the transition from welfare to work because the new worker need not go abruptly from a familiar to a foreign world. She can remain in the community where she feels comfortable, entering and becoming accustomed to the world of work in company with people similar to herself. She can be herself, surrounded and supported by people who understand her experience, as she allows the work experience to gradually socialize her into a new role and self-image (T. Herr, personal communication, 1997).

PARAPROFESSIONALS IN EARLY CHILDHOOD PROGRAMS: DIFFERENT ROLES AND DIFFERENT GOALS

Parents and Children Together

Two basic types of intervention programs jointly serve parents and children: programs for young children with developmental delays or disabilities (Bricker & Veltman, 1990) and those serving children deemed to be at environmental risk (Barnes, Goodson, & Layzer, 1995, 1996). In considering programs in the first category, one finds paraprofessionals in many community-based (as contrasted, for example, to hospital-based) programs for young children with disabilities or delays. In developing a comprehensive intervention system to maximize the potential of eligible infants, toddlers, and preschoolers with delays or disabilities, and to assist their families (as mandated by the Individuals with Disabilities Education Act, 1990, 1991), individual states and jurisdictions integrate paraprofessionals into their service systems for this population, and some have established new occupational categories at the paraprofessional level. The three main reasons for this are 1) persistent personnel shortages; 2) the movement to more "family-centered" service delivery approaches, including an emphasis on cultural competence; and 3) budget and monetary constraints causing states to examine the cost-efficient

basis of incorporating paraprofessionals into their personnel system (Striffler, 1993).

The goals and tasks of programs working with children with developmental impairments are more straightforward than those of programs seeking to mitigate environmental risk. First, the reasons for enrolling in the program are apparent to parents from the start; second, staff at all levels have a clearer sense of what to do; and third, there are more likely to be noticeable improvements in child outcomes. In such programs, the main emphasis is on the child's difficulties and, when parents need help coping, they tend to be easier to help because the objectives are less abstract and ambiguous (Farran, 1990).

In contrast, by their very nature, programs working with children at environmental risk, including many programs for teen parents (Brown & Eisenberg, 1995; Cohler & Musick, 1996), usually have the more ambiguous and decidedly more ambitious goal of reducing risk by "improving parenting" (Halpern, 1990). The assumption here is that parents will then be better able to foster their children's socioemotional and intellectual development (Musick, 1993). To accomplish this goal, programs in the second category employ such techniques as parent education classes, child development groups, and parent–child activities. Frequently these are facilitated or led by lay workers. To date, such efforts have led to few if any significant or lasting improvements in child outcomes (Barnes, Goodson, & Layzer, 1995, 1996). As noted earlier, intervening in the parenting process is a complex, fundamentally therapeutic, endeavor. Such an endeavor calls for well-trained and sophisticated workers with theoretical as well as practical knowledge of the parenting process and with an understanding of how, and under what circumstances, people change. It calls for excellent supervision as well.

Parenting Struggling Parents

None of this is to say that the only viable and meaningful role for the paraprofessional in community-based programs is as a bridge between the program and the community. There are other equally valuable and practical functions for paraprofessionals to fulfill. These can also have positive effects on parents and parenting, albeit in ways distinct from those described in our earlier chapter in which the emphasis was on paraprofessionals as change agents in the parenting process. Specifically, we viewed providers' relationships with parents as the scaffolds for building or rebuilding parenting strengths – the best means of transforming the caregiving environment for children at risk (Musick & Stott, 1990).

Many community-based family support programs define their mission as prevention or early intervention. In such programs, the work of lay helpers often includes securing a range of material and social resources for stressed and overburdened parents. This might mean helping teenage mothers stay in school by finding good child care for their children, directing them to appropriate educational or training programs, and encouraging their efforts to succeed when others often actively discourage them (Quint, Musick, & Ladner, 1994). Lay workers are also effective in interceding to lessen or stop crisis situations before they escalate and damage parents and children. For example, they may help a struggling young mother extricate herself from destructive relationships, whether these are with boyfriends, peers, or even family members (Musick, 1993).

Similarly, paraprofessionals also provide sustaining support and "mothering" for teenage mothers – emotionally needy young women often searching for the maternal love and approval they were denied as children and youth. Here a Family Child Care Connection provider describes her relationships with the adolescent mothers of the children she cares for in her home.

I have had very young parents, where I have to almost play the role of the mother. And I have this girl's mom call me and said "You are doing a great job," and her daughter obeys me more and listens to me more than her. That makes me feel good. That encourages me to keep on working with her. (Musick, 1996)

Such nurturance is the bedrock of positive change for many young mothers, as was evident among a sample of former teenage mothers in a national welfare-to-work demonstration. In their follow-up study of this sample, Quint and Musick, with Ladner (1994), found that some of the more successful participants had managed to find and attach themselves to male partners with strong, loving mothers. They apparently did this in order to secure a new and more enabling mother for them-

selves – someone able to furnish the guidance, modeling, and encouragement they knew they would need to move ahead – especially, to move ahead without leaving their children behind. Here two young mothers describe their perceptions of how their partners' family differs from their own:

He has someone to sit down and ask, "How do you feel today?... How are things going with you?" I don't have too many people to ask me those questions... It's basically on me to sit down and say to myself, "Well are you O.K. today, Andrea? How do you feel?" Lou's mom, his sisters, they're all really nice to me. They work hard constantly. Always working. [Lou's mom], she's really nice. She's a church lady. I think [she] really raised them up good... She did a good job. I wish I had a mom like that. (Quint & Musick, 1994, p. 106)

These young women not only found themselves new partners but new and better mothers (and families) as well. They understood, intuitively, if not always consciously, that such relationships are key ingredients in the construction of better lives for themselves and their children. When paraprofessionals step in to fulfill surrogate mother roles, much like the work of Selma Fraiberg and colleagues, they help undo past pain, enabling young mothers to break cycles of poor parenting by finding new solutions and "doing it better" than their own mothers did (Fraiberg, Shapiro, & Cherniss, 1983).

Providing Care for Children – and for Their Parents

In addition to programs that clearly define themselves in terms of intervention, there is another kind of "intervention" for very young children, especially those growing up in difficult circumstances. Under the right conditions, high-quality child care (either center- or home-based) can enhance the development of infants and preschoolers and supply their parents with essential supports and assistance (Musick, 1997). It is within this field that one finds another appropriate role for paraprofessionals. The provision of child care is an appropriate match for the skills and experience of community-based staff without professional degrees, affording them work they reasonably can do, and can do well. This assumes, however, that they are well trained and paired with trained professionals who serve as

supervisors and resources. Much of the data presented in this section come from Judith Musick's
(1996) study of child-care providers, parents, and
children in the Family Child Care Connection, a
model program designed to improve the quality of
family child care for infants and toddlers living in
low-income communities in Chicago.

Quality child care is early intervention, affording
low-income parents opportunities to move ahead in
their lives without sacrificing their children. This is
especially the case for the infants and toddlers of
young (often single) mothers completing school and
entering or reentering the world of work. Qualified
and motivated providers do much more than merely
provide care for the children of these stressed and
struggling young parents; they also model effective
parenting practices and they share socializing functions such as toilet training, weaning from the bottle or pacifier, getting along with others, learning
proper table manners, and so forth.

When providers soothe and calm irritable infants
and hyperactive toddlers and alleviate problems
around eating, sleeping, and discipline, they indirectly facilitate positive parent–child relationships
and prevent or reduce conflict (Caldwell, 1991). Parents view such role-sharing as easing their burdens
and are often grateful for the help they receive.

I feel she has really helped with Patricia. I guess because
I raised the three boys on my own and Sheryl [her child-
care provider], it seems like it's made it easier, and she's
taught Patricia so much that my job is not that hard.

Parents value positive changes observed in their
children, and credit their child's provider for such
gains:

She's not scared of bugs anymore because of Rena
[the provider]. I know that Moira doesn't have a pacifier
anymore because of Rena.
The first week, she didn't walk yet. At the end of the
week, she started walking with Ronnie [the provider].
I was, "How did you do that?" And she is so happy
with her. She's learning a lot of things. She gives me a
surprise.
I do attribute a lot of his changes to being with
her . . . things like sharing, and some of the things he
says . . . He's like "I love all of the animals, and I love
all the colors." . . . He can count to ten. He knows all
the colors, he knows all the shapes. I mean he can get
himself completely dressed except for tying his shoes.

Providers also notice such positive changes and
find them personally rewarding.

I've seen changes. What makes me feel good is that the
parents have too . . . the two-year-old, she cried for everything . . . She wanted a bottle all the time. She knew
that once she cried she was going to get the bottle. I
got her off the bottle . . . She has pretty much learned
that she doesn't have to cry for everything. She's talking a lot better and she is doing really good. Her mother
just got a new job. . . . It's kind of going to be out of
her way and take up a lot more time to bring her here
[to the provider's house] . . . . We worked out an arrangement where she can stay here because she does not want
to take her out of here. She has learned so much. Her
grandparents were totally against her bringing her, and
now that they have seen how much she's learned, they
are glad that she did. It makes me feel great. When I got
Gina, the baby, the baby couldn't sit up . . . she was eight
months. . . . That was my prize. I know that I taught her,
even her mom has commented on it. Within two weeks
I had her crawling, sitting up . . . I did all the exercises,
sit her up, stand her up . . . Her sister was a little withdrawn and shy. She opened up a lot . . . That makes me
feel real good, when they run through the door and
grab me every morning and say, "Hi Em."

Most important, good child-care providers organize the day for children whose lives might otherwise lack structure and predictability. Within the
context of warm and nurturing relationships, they
also establish limits.

The children need to know their rules, their limits. You
talk to them and they go along just fine.

In accommodating a schedule that includes
variety within routine, young children come to
internalize a sense of order and an understanding
of sequence – that one thing follows another. This
readies them to adapt to the time-governed context
of school. Qualified child-care providers support
and encourage parents' efforts to balance work and
family life (Musick, 1996). They take care of parents
as well as their children by offering counsel and
assistance:

We [the mother and her children's provider] actually
sit down and we talk about life. Things she's been
through, things I've been through. She gives me advice. She has strong religious beliefs, so I like listening
to her. She is real nice to me. If she has something to
say to me, she will say it to me. She's honest. I like that
about her.

Some also offer meals, to celebrate holidays or birthdays, or simply to give work-weary parents a special treat.

[Child care provider]: When [it's] Christmas or Thanksgiving, or whatever, I'll have a dinner for [parents]. They don't all have to come at the same time, but when they come home from work . . . I don't make a big deal. And I've had different times where I just make macaroni or spaghetti night or whatever . . . . And you could see where they're looking at the other kids. Their kid is interacting with the others. They feel good about it. They feel their responsibility more, the father and the mother.

[Parent]: Like the other day I came in and I sat down at the table with my kids and my kids started eating breakfast. I always spend about ten or fifteen minutes in the morning with them. Rena just came over and handed me breakfast too. And she made me a piece of toast, a cup of coffee. I think a lot of it.

The respectful and nurturing relationships such child-care providers establish with parents are doubly meaningful for parents in difficult circumstances, especially young single mothers. Wise and mature child-care providers act as surrogate mothers, grandmothers, advisors, teachers, and mentors for many parents struggling to work (or finish school) and raise their children with limited social and economic resources. Thus, they are unquestionably family resources in a time and context in which there are woefully few supports for low-income young parents.

Qualified, motivated, and well-trained child-care providers are also vital community resources. One paraprofessional noted:

When [training is] poured into us, it's poured into the community. It's making productive children. We're giving back as much or more than what's given.

When child care is recognized and rewarded as valuable work, and child care programs are well organized and stable, the benefits are experienced more widely by other community members, beyond those directly involved.

Before, I used to care for the people who maybe go to my church, that little circle. Now I care about my community more. Even though I have always been involved in the community, I care more now about my community because I have gotten to know [it] better through this . . . . Because people know the program, they call the

program and they call me and they ask me and they tell me. "We have this need; this is what we would like to do and we want you to help us."

In this way, child-care providers such as these come to view themselves as stewards of all the community's youngest children. Others come to see them that way as well. Similarly, in early intervention programs, paraprofessionals employed as home visitors, parent advocates, and the like perform a community-building service when they help families in low-income areas make use of institutions that are designed to serve them.

USING PARAPROFESSIONALS IN HUMAN SERVICES: WHAT IT TAKES TO DO THE JOB RIGHT

New Goals with Training and Supervision to Match

Once clear reasons for using paraprofessionals are established, successful use of paraprofessionals rests on two central assumptions, the first of which is wise recruitment. Just as professionals and service recipients are a heterogeneous group, so too are their paraprofessional counterparts. For younger staff members, employment in the program may be simply a first step on the journey to choosing and working toward a career. Middle-aged and older women may want to do something for other children in their communities, after having successfully raised their own. They may want to bring additional income into their families, or they may be single parents independent of public assistance for the first time in their lives. Although such variety is desirable, reflecting sensitivity to the diversity of individual communities, there are certain personal qualities about which there should be no compromise. Paraprofessionals, like professionals, should be caring, intuitive people, capable of forming positive relationships with others. Also, they must be open to new ways of thinking and behaving and be able and willing to reflect on themselves and their work. Most of all, as staff working intimately with stressed and struggling families, they need to be emotionally strong people with a good deal of common sense. These qualities must be carefully looked and listened for during the recruitment and early supervisory process. Such qualities constitute the foundation for successful use of paraprofessional staff (Musick & Stott, 1990).

Successful use of paraprofessional staff rests on a second assumption as well: training and supervision that is well conceived, well implemented, and fully integrated with the program and its goals. This model of training and supervision creates a climate in which staff acquire new roles and work identities, as well as new knowledge. It keeps pace with staff members' own learning and personal development and matches their learning styles and experience. For example, role-playing is a highly effective training technique because it offers active learning directly tied to practice. Moreover, a well-conceived model of training and supervision affords opportunities for continuous growth, nourishing the competence and pride that come from using one's knowledge and skills, and reflecting on what one does.

Full implementation of this model rests on the special training of professional-level staff. Community-based paraprofessionals, especially those entering (or reentering) the world of work, often bring a host of practical difficulties with them to their jobs. Some have little support and encouragement from those around them as they cope with the changes and challenges of new roles and obligations. Many also have multiple caretaking responsibilities at home – other demands on their time and energy. Sensitive and informed supervision can serve as timely intervention if the demands of work and home conflict. Unaddressed, such situations are likely to escalate, interfering with a provider's effectiveness with program participants, even with her relationships with fellow staff members. Unchecked, they may ultimately interfere with her mastery and motivation in regard to work. In our 1990 chapter, we raised three key supervisory issues for paraprofessionals working with parents in early intervention programs: domains of silence, countertransference, and lower expectations paraprofessionals might have in regard both to their own children or to parents and children in the program.

Domains of Silence

In many community-based programs, the majority of direct service is carried out by paraprofes-sional staff members living in or near the community that houses the program. Halpern's (1990) notion of "domains of silence" aptly describes a phenomenon much noted among these paraprofessional staff members. This notion refers to those topics or problems paraprofessionals might avoid discussing with program participants because they find them personally threatening or culturally taboo. For example, in many teen parent programs, home visitors and parent-group facilitators seldom deal frankly or consistently with such loaded topics as sexual behavior, family planning, adoption, domestic violence, sexual abuse, or parenting practices and decisions that affect the well-being of children (Musick, 1993).

What are the origins of the domains of silence phenomenon as it manifests itself in staff reluctance to deal with parents in their parenting roles, that is, as caregivers and socializers of children? Certainly, lack of sufficient understanding of this domain, as well as cultural and community norms about what is permissible to discuss openly, is a major factor, particularly with regard to such topics as adoption or physical punishment of children. There may also be personal factors that make these domains intimidating for some staff members. For instance, can a provider break the hold of a young parent's painful past and current circumstances – especially those that negatively affect the parent's child-rearing practices and relationship with the child – if she herself has not dealt with her own similar experiences or pain? Will she effectively deal with a teen parent's harsh child-rearing practices if she has unexamined anger about how she was raised or hidden guilt about how she raised her own children? Will she be able to see or intervene around sexual abuse if she has denied or repressed her own experiences or feelings of victimization? Can she counsel young mothers (and fathers) about healthy, respectful relationships if she has failed to deal with disrespectful relationships in her own life? Will she consistently and straightforwardly teach young parents about responsible sexual behavior and family planning if she is conflicted in these domains herself? In such cases, her unacknowledged inner struggles may keep her silent when she should speak or immobilize her when she needs to act.

Countertransference

The term *countertransference* is used here to describe difficulties paraprofessionals might have maintaining psychological distance in regard to participants and the situations they present. Originally, this term was used to designate the emotional reactions of a psychoanalyst to a patient's transference toward him or her. It was considered to be a disturbing factor in that it interfered with the therapist's ability to be objective in regard to the patient (Gitelson, 1952). Currently, however, the term is used more broadly to refer to distortions or emotional interference on the part of the therapist that may result in failures of empathy, failure to notice, understand, or adequately interpret what is going on with a patient, including idealizing some patients and disliking others. Countertransference phenomena have their roots in a wide variety of external and internal psychological phenomena. For the purposes of this chapter, countertransference refers to the possibility of a provider inadvertently harming or failing to help a client because of his or her unrecognized feelings (Richan, 1978). It may, for example, be particularly painful to acknowledge that a young mother's attitude or behavior toward her child is truly harmful, if that is the way you were raised or the way you felt and behaved toward your own children. Developmental issues around dependency, autonomy, negativism, separation, assertiveness, aggression, and the expression of strong emotions can become spheres of conflict in parent–child relationships, especially in troubled or multiproblem families. Such issues can have powerful psychological reverberations for service providers because they are so heavily affect-laden and may threaten to bring into awareness feelings so painful they have been denied or repressed.

In theory, professional clinical training is expected to take into account such psychological phenomena. The social worker, psychiatrist, or other human service professional is supposed to be armed with the skills to recognize when countertransference is interfering with the helping relationship by preventing the therapist from seeing what is actually going on and by distorting clinical perception and interpretation of behavior. Such training has not generally been part of the paraprofessional experience, nor do we advocate that it should be provided in precisely the same way as for professional-level staff. However, some carefully designed and well-implemented training of this nature is both useful and necessary in order to guard against a lay worker either ignoring or seriously exacerbating a problem when it reverberates with the worker's own issues. Furthermore, such training can be conducted in a manner that will not undermine the real strengths lay helpers bring to high-risk families.

Expectations

A third impediment to the paraprofessional's capacity for dealing with participants as parents is lowered expectations. These are manifested on two levels: 1) the expectations paraprofessionals had or have of their own children and 2) the expectations they have of their clients, both parents and children. Lowered expectations are most likely derived from internalizations of the experience of poverty and discrimination. The sense of powerlessness or helplessness that is the outcome of such internalizations is the result of a number of interconnected factors. It can emerge directly from past and current experiences. It can also be generated indirectly by observing the ways in which one's parents coped with their particular life circumstances.

The psychological experience of being poor or of minority status all too frequently results in lowered expectations for one's children and a dim view of their chances for a different and better life. This is especially the case when a parent's family of origin endured psychologically devastating experiences, repeated trauma, multiple life-event stresses, and limited social support (Clark, 1983). In describing the parents of the low-achieving high school student he studied, Clark noted that these parents "have experienced severe psychologically debilitating events at earlier stages in their lives. Past (and contemporary) experiences in their own family of origin and in the marketplace have had a trickle down effect, which has left mental scars so deep as to have rendered them unable or unwilling to stay deeply committed to quality parental functioning" (p. 192). They have, Clark noted, "sustained immeasurable strain and pain, and they now have an impoverished human spirit" (p. 192). They sense little chance for a better tomorrow and, although they may be interested in their children, they lack hope, a sense of power, and expectations that they can have a positive influence on their children's potential for more than mere survival. Such parents "just can't see how they can do any better" (p. 190). Interestingly, such parents' life circumstances are not always qualitatively worse than those of Clark's contrast group – the parents of successful high school students. Rather, their "sense of powerlessness and hopelessness was markedly different" (p. 191).

In light of such issues, one of the greatest strengths of using lay workers – shared background and understandings between staff and participants – can also be viewed as a potential weakness in the fabric of community-based programs. Many paraprofessionals find themselves working with young mothers who are not too different from the young mother they were in the not-so-distant past. Although they have achieved some success in moving forward in school, work, or community roles, they may have been far less successful in their roles as parents. For example, Brooks-Gunn and Furstenberg (1986) found that although a group of former adolescent mothers had achieved a level of success as adults, their children fared more poorly than the offspring of older childbearers. Furthermore, these differences became increasingly pronounced as the children became older. The monumental effort to pull oneself up out of generations of poverty, with little or no support from near or extended kin, may take its toll on the capacity for being an enabler of one's own children and being able to promote their best interests. The negative self-images established in childhood remain, despite success experiences, and manifest themselves psychologically and behaviorally in lowered expectations. In summary, the challenge for program developers is to utilize effectively paraprofessional helpers as change agents, recognizing that some lay helpers will themselves require strengthening of socioemotional resources that are of critical importance for the task ahead.

Plainly, a service provider who has higher expectations to begin with will be in the best position to facilitate positive growth for parents. Certainly there are paraprofessionals with healthy expectations for themselves, their own children, and for the families they serve. Such persons may have high expectations but nevertheless lack some of the means to fulfill them or enable others to do the same. The fortunate (and skillful) program developer will have

recruited at least some of these individuals whose training and supervision can focus primarily on gaining new knowledge and access to resources and on expanding their existing repertoire of skills. Unfortunately, such characteristics do not typify many paraprofessional service providers. For them, the issue of expectations must be addressed in a meaningful way, because no amount of education about child development or child-rearing principles can be effective if it conflicts with a provider's deeply held views about parents and children. The first step in solving the problem of paraprofessionals' lower expectations (of both parents and children) should come from new training approaches.

Training Issues

In our 1990 chapter, we suggested that well-conceptualized and well-implemented training for lay helpers working with at-risk parents and children offered considerable promise for breaking transgenerational cycles of maladaptive and growth-thwarting parenting patterns. Although we continue to believe that training and supervision can and should address such issues, we no longer find it advisable or appropriate for paraprofessionals to assume what are essentially clinical roles. Although clinical supervision is an indispensable tool for professionals seeking to promote psychological change in troubled parents and troubled parent–child relationships, paraprofessionals working with nonclinical populations have a different set of goals for which clinical models are neither necessary nor suitable. Self-knowledge about such issues as countertransference or domains of silence is fundamental when working with troubled populations, or in supervision when clinical issues arise, as they inevitably do from time to time in early intervention settings. Nevertheless, such competencies should not take center stage in the training and supervision of paraprofessional workers.

The families in community-based early intervention settings may face many challenges and crises in their daily lives, but they are not "clinical" populations. Staff who work with children and parents in family support and teen parent programs, in child-care centers and family child-care homes, and in Head Start and prekindergarten programs need adequate time and opportunities for observation and review of written materials and a knowledge base that is closely tied to program goals. They also require grounded and practical supervision tied to the here and now. In this type of supervision, the supervisor's role entails keeping the staff member's "eye on the ball" – helping her understand what she is supposed to be doing, why she is doing it, and what the anticipated outcomes are. Finally, training and supervision should provide support and information to paraprofessionals in a manner that is direct, systematic, concrete, and mutually respectful, with everything expected made explicit and reinforced through regular meetings.

For programs serving children directly, such as Head Start, Early Head Start, child-care centers, and birth-to-3 interventions for children with developmental problems, training goals are relatively straightforward reflections of program goals. If the goal for children is school readiness and, ultimately, school success, in addition to nurturing care, staff need a body of formal knowledge that they can impart to their young charges in a developmentally appropriate manner. Thus, the wealth of local knowledge and life experience of paraprofessionals should be paired with the formal knowledge and training of professionals. Although paraprofessionals in such settings certainly need knowledge about child behavior and development, parents, and parenting, and about the helping relationship, they cannot by themselves educate young children for success in preacademic subjects. Children growing up in disadvantaged circumstances need every possible advantage – including highly qualified teachers to help them succeed in school.

The benefits of pairing lay and professional staff are reciprocal, with the latter gaining insights from the former that keep them from going astray in their interventions. A professional colleague who regularly consults to a community-based birth-to-3 program comments:

We work in pairs with the parents in this early intervention project, and find that the community-based staff we are paired with lend us credibility with the parents. They also serve another really important role by interpreting the meaning of parents' behavior, which helps us understand what is really going on in any particular situation. That is, we both have learned to check out our assessments of parents' behavior with our community-based partners, who respond by, in a

sense, saying "Yes, that's what was going on when she said (or did) that" or "No, that wasn't what the mother meant." Our partners sometimes reinterpret a situation and clarify its meaning for us, keeping us from saying or doing something that is way off the mark.

Program Structure and Paraprofessionals' Success

A program with a clear philosophy and clear goals, well-articulated role definitions, and job descriptions provides a "holding environment" – a guiding structure for staff at all levels. In such settings, staff know what is expected of them and how to go about accomplishing it; training and supervision are a natural outgrowth of the program's goals. Unfortunately, the purposes, and thus the training and supervision, are often poorly defined in interventions targeting parents and children together, especially programs targeted to children and parents at environmental risk (Stott & Musick, 1994). Staff may not know precisely what is expected of them, because their training and supervision have failed to establish and maintain performance standards, reasonable responsibilities, and attainable goals. The theoretical rationale for community-based family support programs is drawn from the literature on social support that emphasizes helping (e.g., Weiss & Jacobs, 1984) and the tenets of clinical infant intervention that address specific obstacles to adequate parenting (e.g., Fraiberg, 1980; Greenspan, 1981).

Establishing clear roles for paraprofessionals is difficult in such programs. Informal social support and clinical intervention do not easily lend themselves to precise definition. Beyond that, as Halpern and Larner (1988) noted, paraprofessionals need to "invent" their new role, tailoring it to each family in a way that is acceptable to that family. Furthermore, they must do this while balancing personal responsiveness to the needs and concerns expressed by the participants with the agenda and goals of the program.

The overarching goals of most early intervention and prevention programs for environmentally at-risk children have long been to help optimize child development, promote educability, and ensure later educational success (Farran, 1990). To a large degree, programs rely on environmental manipulations to meet these goals. Acknowledging that in infancy and early childhood parents constitute the child's primary environment, the approach has generally been to emphasize parents as the "window" into the life of the child and parenting as the modality that promotes (or inhibits) development. Yet, there is currently little evidence of long-term maintenance of changes in either parental behavior or infant development that is the specific result of intervention programs (Halpern, this volume).

Parenting is a relationship – a way of interacting with, nurturing, and guiding a young and initially dependent human being. As such, it cannot be learned in the same way as an academic discipline, nor can it result from the kinds of training required for vocational competence. This would appear to be self-evident, yet many early intervention programs seem to be predicated on the notion of parenting as analogous to a job; that is, something that can be taught or retaught if it has not been "learned" well initially. In truth, the processes by which the capacity for parenting normally develops are poorly understood. Thus, it is not surprising that failures to bring about significant change are widespread. Scholars and practitioners compare techniques but seldom look at what underlies the goals they have set for bringing about change.

If changing the early caregiving environment involves changing the parent, this can best be accomplished in the context of a relationship with the parent. Where issues revolve around relationships, the change agents are not the methods or curricula, they are other people. It is these other people and the quality of the relationships they are able to establish that will be the critical elements in any intervention. These relationships are the scaffold for building or rebuilding parenting strength. It is, at best, difficult to develop a precise job description when the objective is as amorphous as "developing relationships."

Plainly, paraprofessionals in early intervention programs need a base in both knowledge and practice. This is acquired through pre- and in-service training, as well as through supervision concerning child development, early education, child care, parenting, intervention strategies, and so on. Optimally, training and supervision should move providers forward incrementally in terms of knowledge and skills, keeping them within what Vygotsky (1978) called the "zone of proximal development" in which one's reach exceeds one's grasp in man-

ageable and motivating ways. Paraprofessionals also need a forum and repeated opportunities for reflecting on themselves and their work. Such opportunities can include regular team meetings and interactive workshops, as well as keeping journals of their experiences and observations.

Obviously, the worker's effectiveness is mitigated by her attitudes and behaviors: these might include overidentifying with or projecting her own problems onto a participant, imposing her own values on the participant, or having difficulty sharing power with parents, fellow staff members, or both. Supervision is the mechanism for creating incentives and inculcating skills essential for reflection on oneself and one's work but, again, not the clinical model of supervision typically offered to professionally trained psychologists, social workers, counselors, and the like.

PARAPROFESSIONALS, PARENTING, AND SOCIAL CHANGE

Although we no longer think it best for paraprofessionals to be assigned a clinical role with parents, there are other modes of working with parents that are equally meaningful, especially because most parents in these programs are not ill and thus do not require clinical intervention. Some of these models were described earlier, such as supporting struggling parents, guiding and nurturing young mothers needing mothering themselves, assisting parents whose children they care for, and serving as resources for parents of young children in their community. There is yet another way for paraprofessionals to influence the lives of parents positively: by promoting the kinds of social change that affect young children's development. We use the term *social change* here to refer to such activities as talking and reading to infants and toddlers, seeking out and enrolling preschoolers in Head Start and prekindergarten enrichment programs, and making sure that children are inoculated and seen regularly for well-child checkups. Such behaviors are often best introduced by staff members with backgrounds similar to parents – people better able to make the case for behavioral changes, especially if they have come to believe strongly in such activities themselves. Parents may elect to make these changes, in part, because of the influence of their relationship with a service provider. They accept the values and beliefs she puts forward because of their trust in her and desire to please her and be like her. Changes in child-rearing behavior thus take place through the parent's membership in another social network, one that includes the paraprofessional and the other parents whose lives she touches. The paraprofessional, in turn, will be more or less successful, depending on her relationship with the professionals who trained, supervised, and socialized her into her new role and occupational identity – those who imparted new knowledge to her and inspired her own social changes. When this multilevel process works well, it creates a "chain of enablement" (Musick & Stott, 1990), fostering positive growth in service providers so that they can foster similar growth in parents, who can then use what they gain to further their own growth and that of their children.

If individual social change influences practice and subsequently affects the recipients of services, it is important to understand why this happens more readily in some settings than in others. Why are paraprofessional workers employed more successfully in the health care system than in social services – the system encompassing many early intervention programs? Could it be that health care settings tend to have more clearly articulated and fixed codes of conduct, more clearly articulated roles, rules, and duties? Beginning work in a hospital or clinic, the paraprofessional (e.g., medical assistant and nursing aide) frequently finds herself in a system with different social values and beliefs. For example, while visiting her cousin in the hospital, a woman asked the aide a question but was ignored. A nurse, who was of the same ethnic background as the aide, the patient, and the visitor, spoke firmly and directly to the aide, saying, "You answer a question when a visitor asks" (personal communication, anonymous). To succeed in this new setting, the aide will need to adapt and change, and the nurse knows this. In a sense, the nurse has directed the aide toward making an individual social change that will enable her to do well at the work she has chosen.

In a similar fashion, social service providers who firmly tell teenage mothers to "Feed your baby milk, not soda pop" or "Hold your baby when you feed him" inspire parental social change and help young mothers to succeed at parenting, often the first motivational step to success in other domains (Musick, 1993). Adolescent parents are not always easy to work with, yet some providers see them as challenges and feel compassion for them and their children.

I have one teenager that has two children . . . She was fifteen not long ago. They are not easy . . . You really try with these kids . . . I really make them feel like adults, but yet in the position that they're in, they do still have to listen to their parents. They're living with their parents. They're still their parents' child. (Musick, 1996)

As in the incident with the nurse and aide described earlier, providers working with adolescent mothers are most effective when they are clear and resolute in guiding them toward necessary social changes.

I told her, "Listen, when you cannot make it on time; [to bring her children to child care] if you're going to be late or anything is going to happen, I don't want your mother to call me, I don't want your sister, your father, your uncle, your aunt. You're responsible for those children, and I want to deal with you as an adult." She just smiled, just nodded in a real shy way and said, "All right." That child has not been late again.

Being straightforward in this way is perhaps easier in settings where the objectives are immediately apparent. Child-care settings seem to lend themselves to such directiveness more readily than family support programs and other early intervention programs for parents and children.

CONCLUSION

The thoughts expressed in this chapter have evolved largely from our observations and studies of staff in child and family programs, principally in very low-income urban areas. As noted earlier, it is our reconsidered opinion that paraprofessionals are most effective when their work fills a demonstrable need. That is, when it is real work – unambiguous and rooted in solving actual day-to-day problems and providing actual services, such as child care or health care. As part of an early intervention team, paraprofessionals can affect parenting indirectly by fulfilling such instrumental functions as providing access to material and social resources. Respectful and nurturing relationships are the vehicles for carrying out such instrumental functions and can in themselves be beneficial. At the same time, such relationships should not be viewed as ends in themselves.

This chapter describes how paraprofessionals can be most effective. When they have had less success, it is due not to their own individual shortcomings but rather to two programmatic factors. First, the services paraprofessionals are called on to provide emerge from program philosophies and goals that are often poorly defined or overly ambitious. Goals such as "improved parent–child relationships," "prevention of teen pregnancy," and "strengthening families" are premised on naive notions about social services. A focus on family relationships and individual mental health cannot by itself prevent or cure what are essentially societal problems such as poverty, unemployment, and crime.

The second factor is misuse of paraprofessionals. When help for families or individuals in psychological distress is called for, it is best provided by those who are professionally trained. Clear role boundaries not only benefit program participants but also serve as inspiration to paraprofessionals who may one day choose to further their education to become professionals themselves.

Finally, as is the case for all staff in early childhood intervention programs, paraprofessionals deserve carefully conceived and delivered training and supervision. This means supervision that is fully integrated with the program and its goals, creating an environment in which paraprofessional staff can acquire new work identities in addition to new knowledge and skills. Realistic goals and reflection on one's experiences through supervision are the twin pillars of continuous growth, competence, and pride in one's work.

REFERENCES

Albee, G. W. (1968). Conceptual models and manpower requirements in psychology. *American Psychologist, 23,* 317–20.

Austin, M. J. (1978). *Professionals and paraprofessionals.* New York. Human Sciences Press.

Barnes, H., Goodson, B., & Layzer, J. (1995, 1996). *Review of research on supportive interventions for children and families, 1*(2). Cambridge, MA: ABT.

Bricker, D., & Veltman, M. (1990). Early intervention programs: Child-focused approaches. In S. J. Meisels & J. P. Shonkoff (Eds.), *Handbook of early childhood intervention* (pp. 373–99). New York: Cambridge University Press.

Brooks-Gunn, J., & Furstenberg, F. (1986). Antecedents and consequences of parenting: The case of adolescent motherhood. In A. Fogel & G. Melson (Eds.), *Origins of nurturance* (pp. 233–58). Hillsdale, NJ: Erlbaum.

Brown, S., & Eisenberg, L. (Eds.). (1995). *The best intentions: Unintended pregnancy and the well-being of children and families.* Washington, DC: National Academy Press.

Caldwell, B. (1991, June). Educare: New product, new future. *Journal of Developmental and Behavioral Pediatrics, 12*(3), 199–205.

Clark, R. (1983). *Family life and school achievement: Why poor black children succeed or fail.* Chicago: University of Chicago Press.

Cohler, B., & Musick, J. (1996). Adolescent parenthood and the transition to adulthood. In J. A. Graber, J. Brooks Gunn, & A. Petersen (Eds.), *Transitions through adolescence: Interpersonal domains and context* (pp. 201–31). Hillsdale, NJ: Erlbaum.

Farran, D. C. (1990). Effects of intervention with disadvantaged and disabled children: A decade review. In S. J. Meisels & J. P. Shonkoff (Eds.), *Handbook of early childhood intervention* (pp. 501–39). New York: Cambridge University Press.

Fraiberg, S. (Ed.). (1980). *Clinical studies in infant mental health.* New York: Basic Books.

Fraiberg, S., Shapiro, V., & Cherniss, D. (1983). Treatment modalities. In J. Call, E. Galenson, & R. Tyson (Eds.), *Frontiers of infant psychiatry* (pp. 56–73). New York: Basic Books.

Gartner, A. (1971). *Paraprofessionals and their performance.* New York: Praeger.

Gitelson, M. (1952). The emotional position of the analyst in the psychoanalytic situation. *International Journal of Psycho-Analysis, 33,* 1–10.

Greenspan, S. (1981). *Psychopathology and adaptation in infancy and early childhood: Principles of clinical diagnosis and preventive intervention.* New York: International Universities Press.

Halpern, R. (1990). Community-based early intervention. In S. J. Meisels & J. P. Shonkoff (Eds.), *Handbook of early childhood intervention* (pp. 469–98). New York: Cambridge University Press.

Halpern, R., & Convey, L. (1983). Community support for adolescent parents and their children: The parent-to-parent program in Vermont. *Journal of Primary Prevention, 3,* 160–73.

Halpern, R., & Larner, M. (1988). The design of family support programs in high-risk communities: Lessons from the child survival/fair start initiative. In D. Powell (Ed.), *Parent education as early childhood intervention: Emerging directions in theory, research and practice* (pp. 181–207). Norwood, NJ: Ablex.

Harkavy, O., & Bond, J. T. (1992). Program operations: Time allocation and cost analysis. In M. Larner, R. Halpern, & O. Harkavy (Eds.), *Fair start for children* (pp. 179–97). New Haven, CT: Yale University Press.

Kalafat, J., & Boroto, D. R. (1977). The paraprofessional movement as a paradigm community psychology endeavor. *Journal of Contemporary Psychology, 5,* 3–12.

Olds, D., & Kitzman, H. (1993). Review of research on home visiting for pregnant women and parents of young children. *Future of Children, 3*(3), 53–92.

Musick, J. (1993). *Young, poor and pregnant: The psychology of teenage motherhood.* New Haven, CT: Yale University Press.

Musick, J. (1996). *Uncovering the many sides of family child care: A study of the family child care connection.* Chicago: YWCA of Metropolitan Chicago.

Musick, J. (1997, January). *Having to work and paying to work: Low income parents view day care costs.* A report prepared for the Illinois Department of Public Aid.

Musick, J., & Stott, F. (1990). Paraprofessionals, parenting and child development: Understanding the problems and seeking solutions. In S. J. Meisels & J. P. Shonkoff (Eds.), *Handbook of early childhood intervention* (pp. 651–67). New York: Cambridge University Press.

Nittoli, J. M., & Giloth, R. P. (1998). New careers revisited. In R. P. Giloth & J. M. Nittoli (Eds.), *Jobs and economic development: Strategies and practice* (pp. 152–76). Beverly Hills, CA: Sage.

Quint, J., & Musick, J., with Ladner, J. (1994). *Lives of promise, lives of pain: Young mothers after new chance.* New York: Manpower Demonstration Research Corporation.

Riessman, F. (1965). The "helper" therapy principle. *Social Work, 10,* 26–32.

Richan, W. (1978). Training of lay helpers. In F. Kaslow (Ed.), *Supervision, consultation and staff training in the helping professions* (pp. 115–32). San Francisco: Jossey-Bass.

Specht, H., Hawkins, A., & McGee, F. (1968). Excerpts from the casebooks of subprofessional workers. *Children, 15*(1), 7–12.

Stott, F., & Musick, J. (1994). Supporting the family support worker. In L. Kagan & B. Weissbourd, *Putting families first: America's family support movement and the challenge of change* (pp. 189–215). San Francisco, CA: Jossey-Bass.

Striffler, N. (1993). *Current trends in the use of paraprofessionals in early intervention and preschool services.* Chapel Hill, NC: National Early Childhood Technical Assistance System.

Vygotsky, L. (1978). *Mind in society.* Cambridge, MA: Harvard University Press.

Weiss, H., & Jacobs, F. (1984). *The effectiveness and evaluation of family support and education programs.* Final report to the Charles Stewart Mott Foundation.

CHAPTER TWENTY-ONE

Personnel Preparation for Early Childhood Intervention Programs

NANCY K. KLEIN AND LINDA GILKERSON

The passage of the 1986 Amendments of the Education of All Handicapped Children's Act, P.L. 99-457, including the infant and toddler focus in Part H (now known as Part C) and the preschool focus in Part B, brought new challenges and opportunities to professionals and families alike. Within this legislation resides a philosophical framework emphasizing the family-centered, interdisciplinary, and collaborative nature of early childhood services. Although the legislation created new intervention opportunities for children and families, a major challenge facing the field is the preparation of an adequate supply of highly qualified personnel to deliver services to a diverse group of young children with disabilities and their families in a range of community settings.

Qualified early childhood personnel are those trained to work with infants, toddlers, and preschoolers with disabilities and their families as part of an interdisciplinary team (Bailey, 1996) in inclusive settings (Miller & Stayton, 1996) using a family-centered service delivery model (McCollum & Bailey, 1991). Federal law requires that all personnel, across disciplines, meet the highest entry-level state standards and that states develop a Comprehensive System of Personnel Development (CSPD) to respond to the need for trained professionals from several disciplines. Training programs must assure that personnel not only meet state and federal requirements but also the professional standards of quality that are now accepted by the field as recommended practices (Bredecamp & Copple, 1997; McCollum & Maude, 1992; NAEYC, 1996; Odom & McLean, 1996). Professionals must acquire discipline-specific knowledge and additional specialized knowledge, abilities, and personal capacities to meet the particular needs of the age group of children served: infants, toddlers, or preschoolers and their families (Thorp & McCollum, 1994). Furthermore, ongoing reflective supervision and continuing education for professional growth are needed to increase job satisfaction, performance, and retention of staff at all levels (Fenichel, 1992).

The purpose of this chapter is to explore the opportunities, challenges, and promising practices in the preparation of early childhood intervention professionals. We consider personnel training issues within the differing philosophies of service delivery in infancy and the prevailing practices and controversial issues in early childhood settings. Although the field is interdisciplinary, the focus of this chapter is on the role of the early childhood educator: specifically, the child development specialist in birth-to-3 settings and the early childhood special educator in preschool settings. The reader is referred to Bricker and Widerstrom (1996) for a description of personnel preparation for professionals in eight disciplines and for paraprofessionals involved in community-based early childhood intervention teams.

In this chapter, we document the need for qualified personnel and describe current personnel shortages. We review the philosophical frameworks underlying service delivery in the birth-to-5 period and propose guiding principles for personnel preparation on the basis of the values and practices of the field. Next, we present the roles and competencies of infant and preschool personnel and describe the essential content and formats for preservice and inservice training programs. Innovative practices are highlighted, and special emphasis is placed on the needs of the adult learner. The chapter concludes with challenges and recommendations to the field for initiatives to achieve the personnel preparation goals set forth in the enabling legislation for early childhood intervention services.

NEED FOR QUALIFIED PERSONNEL

The critical shortage of trained personnel to provide infant and preschool services as specified by the Individuals with Disabilities Education Act (IDEA) has been well documented (Bruder, Lippman, & Bologna, 1994; Meisels, 1989; Meisels, Harbin, Modigliani, & Olson, 1988). This shortage is expected to continue into the twenty-first century and is occurring in many areas of special education (Office of Special Education Program/OSERS, 1989), physical and occupational therapy (National Easter Seal Society, 1988), nursing, and speech and language intervention (Yoder, Coleman, & Gallagher, 1990). The shortage is due in part to the requirements under Part H, now Part C, of IDEA, which mandate that personnel employed in programs serving young children with disabilities have the skills and knowledge to work successfully with infants and toddlers as well as preschoolers (Bailey, 1989; Bailey, Farrel, O'Donnell, Simeonsson, & Miller, 1986; McCollum & Thorp, 1988). In addition, Part C requires that professionals from several disciplines (i.e., physical, occupational, and speech therapy, nursing, psychology, and social work) be trained to work collaboratively to assess infants and families and to provide services jointly (Bruder, Lippman, & Bologna, 1994). This requirement presents a particular challenge to states as they search for an adequate statewide supply of fully prepared related service professionals (i.e., speech, occupational, and physical therapists) who are critical to an interdisciplinary team. Shortages of therapists may result from the lower pay scales in early intervention, competition from such new fields as sports medicine, and increasing demand for therapeutic services resulting from the higher incidence of children with complex medical and developmental needs (Widerstrom & Abelman, 1996).

One significant barrier to sufficient numbers of adequately prepared professionals to work in infant programs is that many college and university preservice personnel preparation programs do not offer coursework to address these needs (Bailey, Palsha, & Huntington, 1990; Bailey, Simeonsson, Yoder, & Huntington, 1990) and furthermore do not intend to offer such programs. Gallagher and Staples (1990) surveyed deans of colleges of education and found that the majority reported that they had no program for training personnel to work with infants. There are several explanations for such findings, not the least of which is lack of skills and knowledge among many university faculty to plan and implement programs to train personnel to work with infants and toddlers with special needs and their families (Bailey, 1989; Fenichel & Eggbeer, 1991; Thorp & McCollum, 1988). In addition, many colleges and universities that are preparing early childhood special education (ECSE) personnel do not have speech, occupational, or physical therapy training programs, making interdisciplinary training very difficult (Kilgo & Bruder, 1997).

Another issue that contributes to the lack of well-prepared personnel to work in Part C and Part B programs is the absence of inclusive high-quality field placements. In most communities, the vast majority of programs for infants and toddlers do not yet enroll young children with disabilities. Although there are preschool programs for typically developing youngsters in most communities, high-quality inclusive settings are rare because of lack of staff training, available interdisciplinary consultation, and resources to support collaborative planning (Bricker, 1995). Finally, many universities are unable to commit the resources to support faculty in their efforts to personalize training by providing students with ongoing opportunities for individual and group supervision and guided reflection of trainees' practice. These are labor-intensive, costly activities that require substantial resources at a time of budget reduction in many institutions of higher education (Kilgo & Bruder, 1997).

Target Populations for Early Childhood Intervention

The first question to be addressed in considering the components of personnel preparation in early intervention programs is the nature of the target populations. Children who have and who will be identified for services include the following: 1) infants, toddlers, and preschoolers with established disabilities (e.g., Down syndrome, spina bifida, visual impairments); 2) infants, toddlers, and preschoolers at increased environmental risk (e.g., extreme poverty, and teenage parent); and 3) infants, toddlers, and preschoolers at increased biological risk (e.g., history of extremely low birth weight and asphyxia). Early intervention programs for these groups of children are intended to "enhance development, minimize potential developmental delays, remediate existing problems, and prevent institutionalization by providing developmental and therapeutic services to children and support and instruction to families" (Meisels, 1985, p. 115). An increasing number of children served through Part C programs are also involved with state child protection agencies. The needs of these children and their families cross discipline, program, and service system boundaries, requiring a new integration of the fields of disability, early education, and child welfare.

PHILOSOPHICAL BASE

The field of special education arose out of a commitment to equity and is shaped by a strong philosophical orientation. In this section, we describe three seminal philosophical frameworks that underlie the delivery of early intervention services to children ages birth to 5: 1) family-centered services, 2) interactive approaches to child learning and development, and 3) naturalistic approaches to intervention. We then describe the implications of these philosophical frameworks for personnel preparation.

Family-Centered Services

The most far-reaching shift that has taken place in early childhood intervention is a reconceptualization of the role of the family. Although programs were once at the center of the universe with families orbiting about them, the new paradigm places families in the center with services revolving around them. This philosophical revolution was formalized into legislation (P.L. 99-457 in 1986 and P.L. 102-119, IDEA, in 1991). These laws required that parents and professionals work together to develop individual family service plans (IFSP) and that IFSPs could address the needs of the family as well as the child. Thus, families became respected partners in the early educational process (Bennett, Nelson, & Lingerfelt, 1992). This paradigm shift has had a profound impact on the nature of parent–professional relationships and has resulted in clear implications for personnel preparation practices.

The introduction of a family systems orientation into special education was central to this paradigm shift. The family systems approach challenged interventionists to view the family as a dynamic system in which the interactions of one member of the family have ripple effects on all of the other members (Minuchin, 1974). Family complexity and individuality were stressed. Attention was placed on such multiple determinants of family relationships as family structure and hierarchy, cultural background, and personal resources of family members (Barber, Turnbull, Behr, & Kerns, 1988). Family systems theory introduced the concept of family life cycle (Carter & McGoldrick, 1980). Turnbull (1987) urged interventionists to adopt a longer time frame in order to help families develop "marathon skills" – skills such as knowing yourself and your family, building relationships, loving your child unconditionally, experiencing and benefiting from emotions, anticipating the future, and seeking a balance. Turnbull pointed out that the field of early intervention needs to seek a balance in its goals and methods, because balance is what families seek.

Family systems theory focuses attention on family meanings and on individual family coping and adaptation styles (Olson, McCubbin, Barnes, Larsen, Muxen, & Wilson, 1983; Winton, 1990). The recognition of family diversity and family complexity required that interventionists develop cross-cultural competence (Lynch & Hanson, 1992) through self-awareness, knowledge of information specific to different cultures, and effective application of this knowledge and sensitivity in successful interactions (Chan, 1990). The grief and loss model was challenged as the only framework for understanding the influence of disability on family life (Lynch & Hanson, 1992; Wikler, Wasow, & Hatfield, 1981) and was replaced by a series of affirmations of adaptation (Miller, 1994). A family orientation was incorporated into intervention program models through the implementation of family empowerment and family-centered care frameworks. The primary variables differentiating these models from others are the degree to which 1) families are decision makers; 2) programs are strength-based; and 3) services are targeted at the child or at more broadly based family concerns (Dunst, Johanson, Trivette, & Hamby, 1991). Family-centered approaches are consumer driven and competency enhancing. Summers et al. (1990) found that what parents want most from professionals during the early years is information combined with emotional sensitivity. Thus, the role of professionals is to share their knowledge within the context of respectful, collaborative relationships so that child and family competency is strengthened.

Interactive Approaches to Child Development and Learning

Early efforts at early childhood intervention focused on the amelioration of developmental deficits through child-focused stimulation models (Simeonsson & Bailey, 1990). A "fix-it" approach to disability underlies the traditional view of intervention as building skills in deficit areas. Turnbull and Turnbull (1986) described four elements of this approach: 1) the child is viewed as broken; 2) the child is differentially valued according to how much developmental progress is accomplished; 3) instruction is the dominant mode of everyone's interaction with the child; and 4) the child's full humanness can be reached through approximating normality.

The fix-it approach to disability assumes that a "pouring-in" model is necessary for developmental accomplishment: the child becomes a passive recipient of adult-controlled interventions. This model stands in stark contrast to current developmental theory that emphasizes the transactional nature of development (Sameroff & Chandler, 1975), the responsive quality of early relationships (Sameroff & Emde, 1988; Stern, 1977, 1985), and the inherently social nature of learning (Vygotsky, 1978). With infants and young children, it matters greatly "how" we are with them (Pawl, 1995a). A child's sense of self develops not only from what he or she thinks of him- or herself but also how others see and relate to the child. A child's sense of mastery is fueled not only by his or her accomplishments but also by the expectations and approval of those around him or her. For young children with disabilities, the acquisition of self-initiated behavior appears to

be a particularly vulnerable aspect of development, resulting in more passive behavior and less effective self-generated coping skills (Mahoney & Powell, 1988; Zeitlin & Williamson, 1990).

Greenspan (1992) noted that the primary goal for children who have significant delays is to enable them to form a sense of who they are, that is, their own personhood – a sense of themselves as intentional, interactive individuals. To this end, he proposed that every intervention goal – whether motor, cognitive, language, or self-help – has a corollary social–emotional goal. This proposition underscores the premise that there is no such thing as a purely technical intervention; all goals for child change have a relational base (Kalamson & Seligman, 1992). From the child's perspective, this means that the child's goals and characteristics are taken into consideration. It is important to remember that parents often model their own behavior on the ways that professionals interact with their children. "When parents think of interveners as doing things to the child rather than as understanding what the child is doing, they will model their interactions with the child on this more intrusive style of interaction, even when it feels foreign to them" (Kalamson & Seligman, 1992, p. 50).

Naturalistic Approaches to Intervention

Intervention models are shifting across disciplines and across philosophical lines to a more naturalistic, interactive, and integrated approach to child intervention planning (Bricker & Cripe, 1992; Greenspan, 1992; Linder, 1993; McCollum & Yates, 1994; McWilliam, 1992, 1995; Zeitlin & Williamson, 1994). Zeitlin and Williamson (1994) proposed that specific developmental skill acquisition (e.g., block stacking) serves as a resource to the developmental process rather than as an end point. Bricker and Cripe (1992) proposed an activity-based intervention model that recognizes the active involvement of the learner in functional and meaningful activities that capitalize on the child's motivations, interests, and actions. Following the child's lead is seen as a crucial element of interventions built into routine, planned, and child-initiated activities. Bricker and Cripe (1992) made the case that indirect strategies capitalizing on the child's interest are even more important for children at lower developmental levels with more significant disabilities in which the capacity for generalization and transfer of learning is more limited. Linder's (1993) play-based assessment and intervention approach involves parents and professionals as coinvestigators of the child's development, learning style, and interaction patterns. Linder (1993) and McWilliam (1995) suggested that interventions be organized around pleasurable interactions and functional activities that are a natural part of the child's day.

The developmental therapies – occupational therapy, physical therapy, and speech and language therapy – have experienced a parallel shift in orientation toward more emphasis on naturally occurring learning opportunities that capitalize on more child-motivated activities and on less hands-on facilitation (Harris, 1980, 1997; Kaiser & Hester, 1994; Warren, 1992).

EARLY CHILDHOOD EDUCATION: DEVELOPMENTALLY APPROPRIATE PRACTICE

Within the general field of early childhood education (ECE), developmentally appropriate practices (DAP), which have widely been adopted as a framework for organizing a preschool setting, place similar emphasis on the interactional nature of learning and development (Bredekamp, 1987). DAP classrooms emphasize the process of learning through active exploration and interaction with material, use of play, learning activities that are concrete and of interest to individual children, and provisions for heterogeneous groups of children (Fox, Hanline, Vail, & Galant, 1994). DAP is firmly grounded in the constructivist theories of Vygotsky (1978) and in promoting each child's developing independence. DAP classrooms provide a setting for staff to use a variety of approaches to instruction from didactic to facilitative teaching behaviors, depending on the developmental needs of individual children.

DAP is neither teacher centered nor learner centered, neither lesson or task centered nor child centered in a permissive sense; rather, DAP is child sensitive and interaction centered.

Although there has been widespread support for the use of DAP in classrooms for young children, this perspective is not held by all early childhood educators (Safford, 1989). Provided strong criticism of DAP, which was based primarily on its lack of recognition of members of cultural and linguistically diverse groups as key stakeholders. She also expressed concern that cultural issues are not viewed as contextual but as characteristics, minimizing the degree to which some parental voices in the community might be heard.

ECSE Best/Recommended Practices: A Complement to DAP

Several ECSE writers have urged the wholesale adoption of the DAP approach for programs serving young children with disabilities (Berkeley & Ludlow, 1989; Mahony, Robinson, & Powell, 1992). Others have urged caution and maintain that DAP is acceptable for young children with special needs, but that adaptations and accommodations will be needed (Bredekamp, 1993); concluded that DAP classrooms provide an appropriate setting for children with special needs. However, a program based on the guidelines alone would not be sufficient to meet the special needs of many children at risk and those with special educational needs.

Early Intervention/Early Childhood Special Education: Recommended Practices (Odom & McLean, 1996) provides an overview of recommended practices for practitioners in ECSE. These practices provide for ECSE what the DAP guidelines provided for ECE and can be used as the basis for personnel preparation and classroom practice. The resulting recommended practices describe the essential content, including both knowledge and skills, vital to preparing highly skilled early childhood special education practitioners to work in inclusive settings with young children and should be included in personnel preparation programs.

DAP Revised

The most recent version of *Developmentally Appropriate Practice in Early Childhood Programs*, edited by Bredekamp and Copple (1997), is a collaboration with members of the National Association for the Education of Young Children (NAEYC) and the

TABLE 21.1. Principles of Child Development and Learning that Inform Developmentally Appropriate Practice

Domains of children's development – physical, social, emotional, and cognitive – are closely related. Development in one domain influences and is influenced by development in other domains.

Development occurs in a relatively orderly sequence, with later abilities, skills, and knowledge building on those already acquired.

Development proceeds at varying rates from child to child as well as unevenly within different areas of each child's functioning.

Early experiences have both cumulative and delayed effects on individual children's development. Optimal periods exist for certain types of development and learning.

Development proceeds in predictable directions toward greater complexity, organization, and internalization.

Development and learning occur in and are influenced by multiple social and cultural contexts.

Children are active learners, drawing on direct physical and social experience, as well as culturally transmitted knowledge to construct their own understandings of the world around them.

Development and learning result from interaction of biological maturation and the environment, which includes both the physical and social worlds in which children live.

Play is an important vehicle for children's social, emotional, and cognitive development, as well as a reflection of their development.

Development advances when children have opportunities to practice newly acquired skills, as well as when they experience a challenge just beyond the level of their present mastery representing what they know.

Children demonstrate different modes of knowing and learning and different ways of representing what they know.

Children develop and learn best in the context of a community where they are safe and valued, their physical needs are met, and they feel psychologically secure.

Note: From Bredekamp and Copple (1997), pp. 10–15.

Division for Early Childhood of the Council for Exceptional Children (DEC) and is more inclusive in the presentation of material related to at-risk and atypical young children than was the earlier edition. Specifically, the 1997 position clearly argues for a definition of developmentally appropriate practice that encompasses knowledge of and responsiveness to every child's individuality.

Bredekamp and Copple (1997) presented twelve principles (Table 21.1) that teachers can use to guide their decision making in inclusive classrooms for young children. These principles are based on research in child development, cover a broad range of developmental domains, and apply to all young children, including those at risk and those with disabilities. These principles can provide the organizing theoretical framework for preparing personnel to work with all young children. Specialized intervention strategies, utilizing ECSE recommended practices, can then be designed for children with visual,

hearing, and physical impairments; those with developmental delays; and those at risk within developmentally, culturally, and individually appropriate settings. DAP and its revisions provide a conducive context for the inclusion of young children with special needs in a number of early childhood settings.

Inclusion in Natural Environments

Inclusion in the least restrictive setting as mandated by IDEA has been the catalyst for the reconceptualization of educational practices for preschool-age children with disabilities. Inclusion for preschool children means the placement of a child at risk or with special needs in a community program the child might attend if he or she had no special needs. "Inclusion is about belonging to a community – a group of friends, a school community, or a neighborhood" (Allen & Schwartz, 1996, p. 2). These settings include, but are not limited to, family support programs, child-care programs, nursery and preschool settings, Head Start, and recreational programs. Many children at risk are enrolled in Head Start and other preschool and child-care settings. Inclusion for infants might refer to serving the child in the home, relative care, family child care, or center-based child-care environments.

The goal in inclusive settings is for the child to have the opportunity to become a fully contributing member of the group, thus enjoying social as well as physical integration. Such children participate in all program or classroom activities, with modifications to meet their individual needs and consultation from appropriate specialists to help staff make the necessary modifications (File & Kontos, 1992).

Based on philosophical, ethical, educational, and legal rationales, the integration of children with disabilities has had strong advocates and critics (Fuchs & Fuchs, 1994). Bricker (1995) encouraged careful reflection about inclusion and expressed concern regarding professionals who embrace the term at the conceptual level but seem to ignore the implications for the individual child. She suggested that successful inclusion is influenced by three factors: 1) positive and constructive attitudes of adults toward young children with special needs; 2) resources including collaborative planning time, materials, equipment, and access to resources, and 3) the curriculum.

Inclusive programs provide the opportunity to preserve individualized approaches to developing goals and objectives for children with disabilities, and for assessing outcomes, within the context of developmentally appropriate practices. There have been changes in both early childhood special education and early childhood education in the early 1990s, as previously described, that hold promise for making inclusive classrooms a reality. Early childhood special education classes now incorporate teaching strategies that emphasize more child-initiated activities, with teachers taking a more responsive rather than directive role (Mahoney, Robinson, & Powell, 1992). There is also an openness in DAP classrooms to consider a blend of direct and indirect strategies to meet more fully the learning needs of individual children. Although these changes are occurring slowly, there is evidence that inclusion is increasingly documented as accepted practice (Wolery et al., 1993).

IMPLICATIONS FOR PERSONNEL PREPARATION

The move toward family-centered interactive approaches in inclusive settings significantly influenced personnel preparation in early childhood special education in multiple ways. This shift challenged university faculty and community-based trainers alike to engage in a critical reexamination of their own beliefs and experiences regarding professional–family relationships and their approaches to teaching about families, children, and disability. As a result, personnel preparation efforts adopted new frameworks for learner competencies, curricular content, and instructional formats. Here we describe personnel preparation implications related to working with families, children, and teams in a range of early intervention and early childhood settings. For more extensive reviews of family-centered personnel preparation approaches, see Beckman (1996); Bennett, Nelson, and Lingerfelt (1992); Edelman (1991); McBride and Brotherson (1997); Roberts, Rule, and Innocenti (1998); and Winton (1992).

Developing Respectful, Collaborative Relationships with Families

The move toward family-centered services requires that practitioners have skills in collaboration, support, and negotiation (McBride & Brotherson, 1997). Personnel preparation efforts across disciplines have emphasized a cognitive understanding of family-centered principles paired with explicit training in communication – both listening and speaking. The capacity to listen with empathy and to understand the family's point of view is at the heart of family-centered practice (Seligman & Darling, 1989). Responsiveness to family priorities, preferences, and concerns requires that professionals learn to identify and respect the family's agendas and to become aware of their own goals and motives as well. Thus, training efforts for early childhood special educators have increasingly included self-knowledge as a professional competency (Bowman, 1989). Summers et al. (1990) found that parents preferred relationships that were characterized by an unhurried atmosphere, with an informal conversational style that includes some degree of mutual disclosure. Hence, professional family-centered communication skills include learning to value and enjoy family stories, offering information in engaging and natural ways, and sharing one's self while maintaining a sensitive awareness of interpersonal boundaries within relationships. Involving families as partners in preservice and in-service education has proven to be one of the most effective means for conveying the centrality of families in early intervention and demonstrating the power of parent–professional collaboration (Capone, Hull, & DiVenere, 1997). The mutuality of engagement between parents and professionals in early intervention requires a new definition of professionalism for the early childhood special educator and therefore results in new approaches for personnel preparation.

Working from a Strength-Based Perspective

Central to a family-centered/family empowerment model is the assumption that strengths and competencies already exist within the family and the child and that the job of the interventionist is to match recommendations to these existing and expandable capabilities. Dunst, Trivette, and Deal (1988) defined family strengths as family functioning style; that is, the way that the family is already organized to solve problems and to meet the needs of its members. Part C requires that family strengths be incorporated into the IFSP process. Personnel preparation efforts have focused on family strengths in multiple ways, from teaching about the literature on family strengths, to applied activities such as learning to listen for strengths during family interviews (American Association for Marriage and Family Therapy, 1995), or to learning to ask questions that highlight family strengths (Bennett, Lingerfelt, & Nelson, 1990). A strength perspective does not ignore family or child vulnerability (Hirshberg, 1998); rather, it views vulnerability as one part of the picture, in which strengths are used as starting points for amelioration. The goal of professional education, then, is to increase the comfort of the interventionist with the full range of human emotions and experiences – both the positive and negative – and to prepare the interventionist to work toward an integrated approach in which strengths are emphasized and vulnerabilities are partnered (Shanok,

1992). This learning may best be accomplished on the job through ongoing mentorship and clinical supervision.

Becoming Systems Thinkers

To adopt a family-centered approach, personnel efforts must train interventionists to think systemically. This means preparing child-oriented professionals to understand that a system has to work as a whole; that the benefit of child interventions must be weighed in relation to the impact on each subsystem within the family: spousal, parental, and sibling. Within this framework, interventionists learn not to take sides but to look at the system broadly and to find the best way for change to occur within this particular family system. As noted earlier, interventionists need to be prepared to appreciate and work with the preexisting family style – the way the family communicates, solves problems, challenges child growth, and relates to the community – as a key to understanding how a family can best organize itself to address desired early intervention goals. A systems approach goes hand-in-hand with a strength-based model; within a systems perspective, disability is reframed as an extension of healthy family functioning.

Family-centered services recognize the family role as the ultimate decision maker and require flexible leadership patterns that take advantage of everyone's skills and resources (Turbiville, Turnbull, Garland, & Lee, 1996). Training based on a systems perspective prepares interventionists to share power and avoid polarization. A systems perspective relates the immediacy of current issues to the larger picture. Thus, professionals are trained to consider the intensity and timing of the intervention, as well as the demands of the intervention on the participants in relation to the benefits.

Developing Capacity for Reflection and Self-Knowledge

Reflection is the capacity to conceptualize what one is observing, doing, and feeling continually (Fenichel, 1991). Reflection is both a means and an end. That is, reflection is a way of examining one's work with children and families and a way of approaching the work: "reflection-in-action" and "reflection-on-action" (Schon, 1983). Work with relationships engages the emotions as fully as the intellect. Essential competencies include understanding one's own values and beliefs, cultural practices, and professional biases; developing an awareness of one's personal style (e.g., temperament and coping mechanisms); and learning to recognize and take responsibility for one's own reactions and interactions. When roles are shifting, as they have in family-centered services, it is vital that professionals have a safe place to sort out the complex feelings and dynamics that are inherent in human relationships – a safe place "to recognize the worst and the best of their feelings and capabilities with a partner who helps them get where they need to go" (Shanok, 1992, p. 37). A supervisory relationship can provide the context for this type of discovery and learning. Fenichel (1992) described three elements that must be present in supervision: 1) reliability, 2) collaboration, and 3) opportunity for reflection. Pawl (1995b) points out that supervision in every discipline should, at minimum, give the individual the opportunity to discover his or her own beliefs, attitudes, and characteristic responses and to realize that he or she will be the recipient of similar preformed ideas of others. Opportunities for reflection and supervision can be provided individually or in groups. Journal writing, reflective essays shared with colleagues, and even electronic on-line supervision can provide opportunities for participants to examine their practice. Although a requirement of the mental health disciplines, this type of reflective supervision has traditionally not been included in the preservice or in-service training of educators. Gallacher (1997), in an extensive review of supervision, mentoring, and coaching methods, concluded that such opportunities must be included as part of a comprehensive personnel development program in early intervention and that the success of these processes depends on the skills of the facilitator. "Specialized instruction and continued personnel development must be a priority for individuals who supervise, mentor, and coach" (Gallacher, 1997, p. 209) – another domain for personnel preparation efforts in early intervention. The role of a parent as co-supervisor and mentor has successfully been implemented in graduate preparation in early intervention (McBride, Sharp, Hains, & Whitehead, 1995).

Primary Emphasis on Child Development

The content of training for general and special educators in early childhood should be developmental in orientation, including content/research related to all domains of children's development: cognitive, language, social–emotional, and physical for children with typical development and for children who are at risk or who have disabilities. The developmental approach places each child's developmental progress on a continuum and has relevance for children at risk and those with disabilities, as each is seen along the developmental spectrum. The developmental perspective considers the child's current functioning in relation to ordinary/normative expectations of sequential accomplishment of developmental skills in all domains (Safford, 1989). Teachers trained to use a developmental approach have been characterized as having a strong understanding of the developmental needs and characteristics of young children and the ability to interact appropriately with them (Day & Drake, 1986). A central premise of the developmental approach is that "children are active learners who learn best through direct experiences with developmentally appropriate materials and activities" (Safford, 1989, p. 43).

Respecting the Child's Contribution

The move toward more naturalistic intervention planning requires that professionals learn to consider what is important to the child in organizing their observations and intervention plans: What is the child's developmental agenda (Als, 1978)? What are children trying to accomplish and what means are they currently using? What can children do for themselves and what do they need from the environment? In this framework, disability is understood as one aspect of the developmental process. For students in training to grasp this perspective, direct observation and modeling are essential. Students need ample opportunity to observe and talk about children with faculty and mentor teachers. They need to hear and see what it means to consider the child's viewpoint as an essential feature of the intervention planning process. Observation with the parents is a powerful forum for jointly identifying the child's interests, strengths, motives, and challenges. Helping trainees understand how to deliver family-guided, child-centered services (Slentz & Bricker, 1992) is one of the most challenging tasks confronting ECSE personnel preparation and cannot be left to chance.

Developing Capacity for Attuned Engagement with Children

Naturalistic intervention requires a high degree of attunement and engagement with the child. For many children, this interaction will be at a nonverbal level. Personnel preparation programs must provide multiple opportunities for students to watch skilled practitioners in action and, with support and coaching, to develop their capacity to engage children effectively, first individually and then in small groups. ECSE personnel need to be trained to use specialized observation techniques that enable them to be sensitive to even the most subtle messages and developmental needs of each child (Cohen, Stern, & Balaban, 1997). Students need to have many opportunities to view themselves in action: to see the child's response to their overtures and, conversely, to watch their responses to the child's initiatives. This type of interactional observation and reflection is the foundation upon which all other child intervention skills are based and, as such, should be at the core of preservice training for new professionals and ongoing supervision of experienced practitioners.

Use of Interdisciplinary/Collaborative Teaching and Learning

An interdisciplinary approach is a foundational component of early intervention services during the birth-to-5 period. Full implementation of an IFSP or IEP (individualized educational plan) requires a commitment from all team members to work toward common goals. Thus, the values and practices of interdisciplinary collaboration are essential features of entry-level and ongoing personnel preparation efforts and are best taught through applying these concepts in the context of training (Bailey, 1996). Faculty from ECSE, ECE, and the related service disciplines share the responsibility for preparing professionals who understand the integrative nature of development and the importance of multiple discipline perspectives. Crossing discipline boundaries in higher education provides professionals in training with access to multiple knowledge

bases and with firsthand experience with an inclusive education. Interdisciplinary training can take many forms including, but not limited to, guest lectures, coteaching, shared practicum experiences, interdisciplinary team-based training, and interdisciplinary degree programs (Bailey, 1996; McCollum, Rowan, & Thorp, 1994; Rosenkoetter & Stayton, 1997). In addition to new faculty partnerships, preservice programs must establish new connections with community providers, involving experienced practitioners from a range of disciplines who have created family-centered, inclusive learning environments in the preparation of the next generation of early educators. The involvement of parents, administrators, and related service personnel who have worked together on interdisciplinary teams offers students exposure to examples of successful collaborative practice. Learning to learn from experienced peers and parents is a competency that will support the goal of life-long professional development.

Use of More Applied and Active Teaching/Learning Formats

Preservice and in-service preparation for family-centered, inclusive services involves an exploration of attitudes and values as much as an acquisition of skills and knowledge. When the complexity of synthesis and application is high as in a values-based approach, teaching methods that actively engage the learner with real life problems are required (Harris, 1980). These include role-playing, field application, case studies, guided reflection, self-analysis, and clinical supervision. The involvement of families as partners in these types of personnel preparation activities deepens the learning experience, providing firsthand insights into the intricacies of family-centered services and opportunities to gain feedback from families in a supported environment (Capone, Hull, & DiVenere, 1997; McBride, Sharp, Hains, & Whitehead, 1995).

Equal Emphasis on Preservice, In-Service, and Reflective Supervision

Because of the complexity of child and family roles, and because of the challenges of inclusion, professional education in early intervention must be conceived of as a continuum including preservice, in-service, and ongoing supervision. Fenichel and Eggbeer (1991) identified four elements of professional development in infancy and early childhood: 1) knowledge base built on a framework of concepts common to all disciplines concerned with infants, toddlers, and families; 2) opportunities for direct observation and interaction with children and families with whom one will be working; 3) individualized supervision for trainees to reflect upon their learning; and 4) support from colleagues within and across disciplines that begins early in training and continues throughout one's professional life.

Universities and schools are increasingly adopting the professional development school (PDS) as a model to integrate preservice and in-service training and as a strategy to improve teaching and learning (Darling-Hammond, 1994). The major purpose of the PDS is to enhance children's learning through a planned program of professional development and research. Preservice students are placed in PDSs for all of their field experiences, courses are taught by teams that include teachers, and professional development and research are built into the PDS agenda.

The intent of the PDS model is to create a collaborative instructional experience for preservice and inservice participants with universities and other participants on equal footing. It enables education professionals to contribute to the advancement of quality services for children and families by participating in practicum seminars at the university as well as assisting in the preparation of new practitioners. (Wesley & Buysse, 1997, pp. 68–9)

Although the PDS model has been used primarily in elementary and secondary schools, it holds tremendous potential for use in early childhood settings such as child care and Head Start centers where interdisciplinary training could take place on the site of service delivery.

PROFESSIONAL ROLES, COMPETENCIES, AND ESSENTIAL CONTENT

Although there is general agreement on the core areas of knowledge shared by professionals who work with infants, toddlers, and preschoolers, there are also strong opinions that infant early intervention personnel require information and skills different from preschool personnel and that the training programs that serve these two age groups should reflect these differences (Bricker & LaCroix, 1996; Bricker & Slentz, 1988). In the following section, we focus on the roles, competencies, and essential content for the infant and preschool specializations in early childhood intervention.

Infant Specialization

RATIONALE. The needs of infants and toddlers and their families differ from those of preschool-age children in several important respects that have direct bearing on the roles of professionals and therefore on personnel preparation programs. Infancy is a period of major reorganization in a family's life. Parents are moving toward new identities and new roles as the family system is readjusting to incorporate a new member. The early diagnosis of disability increases the normative crisis of the newborn period. Supporting parental competency and self-worth are essential aspects of any intervention effort (Cardone & Gilkerson, 1990). Because infant development occurs within the context of primary relationships, much of infant intervention is conducted indirectly through primary caregivers (Bromwich, 1997; Weston, Ivins, Heffron, & Sweet, 1997). Hence, supporting the developing relationships with significant adults in the infant's life is an essential aspect of supporting the infant's growth and development. Services to infants, toddlers, and their families are highly individualized, based on the infant's characteristics and family's needs, and should be responsive to cultural considerations of importance to the family. In infancy, there is an increased demand for ongoing interdisciplinary collaboration with health and allied health professionals to address the early diagnosis and management of complex medical needs. The structure of services to infants requires more interagency collaboration and service coordination than during the preschool years. The emotional content of early relationships and the intimacy of home visiting evoke powerful feelings in adults (Fenichel, 1992; Foley, Hochman, & Miller, 1994). Intervention programs must provide the practitioner with opportunities to sort out the complex emotions that arise in infant/family work (Fenichel, 1992; Shanok, Gilkerson, Eggbeer, & Fenichel, 1995). As noted, personnel preparation provides the foundation for this capacity for self-knowledge and reflective practice.

INFANT PERSONNEL. The different staffing patterns usually found in infant–toddler and preschool programs reflect the two distinct components of IDEA (Widerstrom & Abelman, 1996). Part C requires that participating states provide community-based, coordinated interagency services focusing on a range of infant, toddler, and family needs. Reflecting the interagency thrust of Part C, more than half of the states have designated health or social service agencies as the lead agency (Hebbeler, cited in Widerstrom & Abelman, 1996). Part B focuses on the educational needs of children aged 3 to 5. All Part B services are provided under the auspices of state education agencies, although not necessarily in public schools. Who are the personnel involved in these programs?

Widerstrom and Abelman (1996) summarized data collected by the Office of Special Education Programs (OSEP) in 1991 and published in 1993 regarding categories of personnel in infant–toddler intervention programs in forty-seven states and jurisdictions. The two largest groups of infant–toddler service providers (35.2%) are paraprofessionals and special educators. Nurses, speech and language pathologists, social workers, occupational therapists, physical therapists, physicians, psychologists, audiologists, and nutritionists make up the remaining 64.8%. Because of lack of uniformity of reporting categories, particularly special education and paraprofessional, these data serve only as approximations of the actual figures. As noted previously, shortages have been reported in all categories of personnel but particularly for paraprofessionals, special educators, speech and language pathologists, physical and occupational therapists, nurses, and social workers. Results from a survey in Illinois confirm that the child development specialist role (i.e., early childhood/early childhood special educator) is the most consistently represented discipline across programs and the discipline with the widest variety of program functions (McCollum, Cook, & Ladmer, 1993).

In comparison to preschool, staff in infant programs tend to be more interdisciplinary; address more family and noneducational needs; have a higher adult:child ratio, often working individually rather than in groups; and have more complex staffing patterns, including a significant portion of contract service therapists (Widerstrom & Abelman, 1996). Although preschool teachers work primarily in classroom settings, infant professionals must be comfortable with a range of formats including home visiting; center-based or hospital-based individual sessions with the infant or with the infant and parent; parent–child play groups; and toddler groups. Preschool personnel are employed by local school districts, public or private preschool programs, and child-care centers. Infant personnel may be employed by a range of community agencies sponsoring comprehensive programs or by specialized community or regional programs serving one population of children (e.g., children with low incidence disabilities such as vision or hearing). Infant personnel also work in hospital outpatient clinics (e.g., rehabilitation departments or infant follow-up programs) or in in-patient services (e.g., neonatal intensive care units or failure-to-thrive programs). Increasingly in some states, infant services are provided by private, independent agencies offering developmental therapies and, less frequently, child development services. Infant specialists may function as one-person "teams," as members of interdisciplinary direct service teams, or as participants on medically oriented diagnostic teams (Thorp & McCollum, 1994).

The younger the child, the more a provider works with the adult in that child's world. In infancy, the professional must be prepared to work directly with parents, other family members, and family friends. Infant specialists work closely with fellow team members and with professionals and paraprofessionals in other community-based infant–family services (e.g., family and center-based child care; family support programs; family literacy centers; public health clinics and health outreach programs; and hospital clinics, specialized medical services, and child life programs). In addition, infant specialists work with an array of social service, mental health, and public assistance agencies addressing the emotional and self-sufficiency needs of families.

Because of the increased use of early intervention services to address the developmental needs of infants and toddlers who have been abused or neglected, early intervention providers must build alliances with the child protective system. In fact, in such states as Illinois, early intervention providers, particularly those in large urban areas, may have a majority of the families whom they serve living in foster families or living in intact families involved with protective services (Gilkerson, Zvetina, Turbiville, & Turnbull, in preparation). Infant specialists must be prepared to work directly with families who have extremely complex social, developmental–educational, mental health, and health needs. In addition, they must be prepared to cooperate with a system that many of the providers feel increases rather than alleviates family disruption. The responsibility for this aspect of training is shared by preservice programs, in-service initiatives, and employers who provide for the ongoing supervision needs of frontline and administrative staff.

ROLES AND COMPETENCIES. What roles and competencies are essential to the infant specialization? One of the earliest descriptions of roles for the infant early intervention specialist comes from the Wheelock College Early Intervention Master's Program (Geik, Gilkerson, & Sponseller, 1982). Because the program addressed an interdisciplinary audience, the five role and competency areas, as initially conceived, were cross-disciplinary. These roles are 1) facilitator–consultant, 2) infant specialist, 3) parent educator, 4) team collaborator, and 5) program developer and advocate.

In this formulation, two aspects of the infant specialist role were emphasized: 1) supporting the parent–child relationship through indirect, rather than direct, intervention strategies and 2) maintaining a focus on child development through exploration and play designed around the interests and preferences of the child and on the creation of enjoyable environments that meet the play requirements common to all infants. The parent educator role was conceived broadly, including understanding family systems and adult development, parenting from the different perspectives of fathers and mothers, and designing flexible models of services that respect the many roles and individual preferences of families. The team collaborator role addressed the capacity to communicate across disciplines, with special emphasis on collaboration with medical professionals and preschool programs. The program developer and advocate role stressed the leadership responsibilities of the master's prepared specialist

and included knowledge of legislation, supporting research, program design and evaluation methods, and advocacy and community action skills.

ESSENTIAL CONTENT IN INFANT SPECIALIZATION. Thorp and McCollum (1994) proposed a model for conceptualizing the levels of specialized training that infant personnel require. In this model, three levels of training are essential: Level 1: Professional discipline is the general body of knowledge and skill that a professional belonging to a discipline will be assumed to possess; Level 2: Infancy specialization is the more specialized disciplinary content related to the infancy period; and Level 3: Common infancy core is the knowledge and skills needed by all disciplines working in early intervention. Table 21.2 presents the content suggested for the common infancy core for all disciplines. Table 21.3 presents the competencies more specifically focused on the early childhood special education/child development specialist role in infancy. Thorp and McCollum (1994) stressed, as we have in this chapter, that the roles and competencies of the infant specialist are closely intertwined with the unique aspects of the early intervention service delivery system and the unique configuration of services necessitated by the developmental patterns of the infancy period. They also pointed out that, similar to other disciplines involved in early intervention, a final delineation of the competencies needed to work with infants, toddlers, and their families remains elusive. Godfrey noted that "we must constantly remind ourselves and each other that early intervention is a very young specialty. Growth and change are inevitable" (1995, p. 81).

Weston et al. (1997) questioned whether the move to family-centered infant–toddler intervention services constituted a paradigm shift because, in their view, the organizing principles and developmental perspective focusing on child outcomes have not changed. Weston et al. proposed that the centrality of relationships should be the organizing construct for early intervention and that this perspective needs to permeate the whole organization, recognizing the power of relationships to shape behavior and performance at all levels. To accomplish this vision for early intervention, they proposed that the following tenets of an infant mental health perspective should

TABLE 21.2. Common Infancy Core

Infant-related
Ability to learn from observation
Understanding of typical and atypical development
Knowledge of medical complications in infancy

Family-related
Awareness of family systems
Cultural variations in parenting style
Understanding sources of vulnerability
Supporting family strengths and natural systems
Supporting healthy parent–child relationships

Team-related
Common vocabulary
Models of teaming
Ability to integrate knowledge from another
  discipline
Joint planning and problem-solving strategies
Conflict resolution skills

Interagency, advocacy-related
Knowledge of state legislation
Coordination of programs across agencies
Knowledge of parent rights
Ability to "de-discipline" and "deprogram"
  oneself to make use of a wide range of
  community resources

Personal attributes
Capacity for relationships
Flexibility
Maturity
Independence and initiative
Self-knowledge

Note: Thorp and McCollum (1994).

underlie service delivery and staff development efforts:

1. recognition of relationships as both organizers of development and the basis of all intervention,
2. focus on the process of intervention as well as the content, and
3. willingness to respond to the levels of need and readiness of the parent and the child.

These principles imply new competencies for the infant specialist and new content and processes for preservice and in-service training. For example, a willingness to respond to the level of need and readiness of the parent implies that the specialist make an effort to understand how behaviors feel from the inside, not just how they look from the outside (Lieberman, 1998). Hirshberg (1998) described this process as "trying to put yourself in the emotional shoes of another person – with all its complexity, ambiguity, and conflict" (p. 19). This attempt to understand how the world feels to the parent expands the interventionist's capacity to empathize with families; for example, to identify with the pain and the hope of a mother who buys an expensive pair of shoes as the first birthday present for her child who was newly diagnosed with a severe motor impairment. The capacity to empathize with the strivings of others and to contain anxiety-provoking feelings will enable the interventionist to feel connected to the mother, in this instance, and to be more nonjudgmental, emotionally sensitive, and therefore, more helpful.

As noted, the expectations of the capacity of the family-centered practitioner for communication and for relationships is extremely high (McGonigel, Kauffman, & Johnson, 1991). It may not be possible for preservice and in-service training programs to prepare infant specialists for this degree of interpersonal and intrapersonal capacity without drawing from the tenets and practices of the mental health field. Early intervention has embraced an interdisciplinary approach to service delivery and personnel preparation (Bailey, 1996; Bricker & Widerstrom, 1996). Yet, the integration of two major research and clinical practice areas in infancy – Part C early intervention and infant mental health – is just beginning (Foley & Hochman, 1998; Ivins & Sweet, 1992; Moss & Gotts, 1998; Weatherston, 1998). The outcome of these interdisciplinary efforts holds promise for new partnerships in the delivery of service to infants and families and new approaches to preservice and ongoing professional development of infant–family practitioners.

Preschool Specialization

PERSONNEL STANDARDS. Throughout the 1990s, ECSE and ECE professionals involved in professional education of preschool personnel increasingly became aware that a new set of personnel preparation standards and practices was needed to guide the field. In large measure, this awareness arose from

---

TABLE 21.3. Child Development/ECSE Competencies in Infancy

Infant-related
  Knowledge of infant cognitive and social/emotional development
  Understanding of interrelationship of developmental domains
  Capacity to interpret experience from the infant's perspective
  Formal and informal developmental assessment skills
  Capacity to guide parents as assessment partners
  Knowledge of temperament/affective style in infant learning
  Design of learning environments to provide opportunities for infants to accomplish
    parent-identified goals
  Capacity to support parent–child interaction
  Skills in data collection and evaluation

Family-related
  Collaborator and consultant to families
  Strategies for including family members as partners in planning and implementing
    intervention
  Strategies for promoting interaction between parent–child capacity to help families
    identify learning opportunities within parent–child interactions and everyday
    environments
  Home visiting skills
  Confidentiality

Team-related
  Skill in integrating the knowledge and recommendations of multiple disciplines into
    the child's and family's daily routines
  Ability to translate educator's knowledge for other disciplines
  Understanding of the boundaries of educator's role

Agency-related
  Knowledge of special education and early childhood service delivery systems
  Procedural safeguards
  Knowledge of state and federal policies affecting service delivery, transition
    specialists, service coordinators

Note: Thorp and McCollum (1994).

---

the legislative requirements for placement in the least restrictive environments for infants, toddlers, and preschoolers at risk and those with disabilities (Kontos & Diamond, 1997). To this end, four major ECSE, ECE, and teacher certification groups developed a document collaboratively: *Guidelines for Preparation of Early Childhood Professionals* (National Association for the Education of Young Children [NAEYC], 1996). The guidelines were developed by NAEYC, DEC, the Association of Teacher Educators (ATE), and the National Board for Professional Teaching Standards (NBPTS) for professionals in all early childhood settings to serve as the standards for the preparation of personnel in ECE and ECSE. The statement of recommendations evolved from a consensus building process among the ATE, DEC,

and NAEYC "in recognition of their overlapping interests in ensuring high-quality environments for all young children, including those with special needs" (NAEYC, 1996, p. 31). The organizations recommended that personnel standards be derived from "empirically defensible knowledge and philosophical assumptions about what constitutes effective early education and early intervention" (NAEYC, 1996, p. 33). In addition to personnel standards, the guidelines describe roles for three early childhood professionals: early childhood educator, early childhood special educator, and related service professionals (e.g., physical, occupational, and speech and language therapists, nurses, and social workers). These guidelines describe the knowledge, performances, and dispositions that ECE and ECSE personnel are expected to have acquired during their personnel preparation programs.

CHANGING ROLES AND COMPETENCIES. Two major shifts in roles and responsibilities of ECSE personnel have occurred and will continue to change substantially (Bruder, 1993; Buysse & Wesley, 1993). The first is in relation to working with families and the move to a family-centered approach, described earlier in this chapter. Such a focus means that personnel must reconceptualize the way in which they relate to families and the way in which program services, including planning, implementing, and evaluating, are implemented. Professionals now have the responsibility to collaborate with families in ways that empower families rather than assuming an expert–novice relationship (Turnbull & Turnbull, 1996).

The second shift results from changing service delivery models and the enrollment of children with disabilities in community programs (File & Kontos, 1992). To support the inclusion of young children at risk and those with special needs in community settings, ECSE professionals are adopting indirect service roles, including consultation with ECE professionals and paraprofessionals, collaboration with families, and technical assistance and training of other professionals (Bruder, 1993; File & Kontos, 1992). Consequently, ECSE teachers will be working more with adults, rather than working directly with children. ECSE personnel will now move beyond their isolated classrooms and "integrate themselves" into community programs (Peck, Furman, & Helmstetter, 1993) as consultants to their ECE colleagues.

In parallel fashion, ECE professionals – child-care, preschool, and Head Start teachers – will provide more direct service to children at risk and those with special needs. Furthermore, these teachers must collaborate with ECSE and related services professionals in order to implement fully the goals and objectives of the child's individualized education plan (IEP) and to meet the developmental needs of each child (File & Kontos, 1992).

Successful inclusion of children with disabilities in early childhood settings utilizes related service consultation models that facilitate integration (Jones & Meisels, 1987; Klein & Sheehan, 1987; Kontos,

1988). McWilliam (1995) proposed a model of integrated therapy provided by occupational, physical, speech/language therapists, and ECSE. This holistic model crosses traditional disciplines and brings therapists into the classroom to work side-by-side with early childhood educators.

Buysse and Wesley (1993) have referred to these changing roles as an "identity crisis" as ECSE and ECE practices have expanded to include more varied and complex responsibilities in community settings rather than practice in self-contained classrooms. For personnel who have spent many years as ECSE providers in specialized settings, these changes require a newly developed "sense of professional identity," as well as new skills and knowledge to collaborate successfully with their new colleagues in ECE inclusive settings (File & Kontos, 1992). According to Strain (1990), "Integration is not easy because it represents a fundamental change in who does what, to whom, and with what" (p. 94).

Buysse and Wesley (1993) offered several predictions regarding the reconceptualizaton of the professional ECSE roles: 1) ECSE professionals will serve primarily as consultants in inclusive child-care programs within the community; 2) the need for consultants is likely to increase as more families with young children with special needs choose to enroll their children in neighborhood inclusive settings; and 3) ECSE professionals will serve in a variety of direct and indirect roles; that is, as an educator with professionals and families, as a *planner* for developing new service models at the local or state levels, as an *evaluator* gathering information to document the effectiveness of inclusion, and as a *marketer* of the concept of inclusion. The challenge in personnel preparation is to create programs that provide training for new personnel as well as professional development experiences for seasoned personnel that will enable them to assume new professional roles and responsibilities and to meet the interprofessional standards described in the *Guidelines for Preparation of Early Childhood Professionals* (NAEYC, 1996).

ESSENTIAL CONTENT. ECSE personnel working with children 3 to 5 years of age will focus on characteristics and behaviors associated with the preoperational child and learning activities that facilitate cognitive and language development, motivation and inquiry, and basic elements of developmentally appropriate classrooms. Within this framework, trainees learn strategies for modifying activities to accommodate the special needs of at-risk and disabled children, to participate on interdisciplinary teams, and to implement individualized interventions (Kontos & Diamond, 1997). A developmental orientation that reflects an integration of content from DAP and ECSE "recommended practices" provides a solid foundation for curricular development. Students will need to develop competencies in direct and indirect teaching practices in ECE and ECSE settings.

Table 21.4 presents the knowledge bases described in the *Guidelines for Preparation of Early Childhood Professionals* (NAEYC, 1996) and, as such, provides the framework for the identification of the content for preschool personnel preparation programs. Generic content can be supplemented by specialized modules (e.g., sign language, using adaptive equipment, or working with medically complex children). Table 21.5 presents the essential training experiences recommended in the guidelines. The inclusion of the knowledge and processes described in Tables 21.4 and 21.5 will enable ECSE personnel preparation planners to design training programs that prepare well-trained preschool personnel to work in inclusive early childhood settings and that meet the standards described in the guidelines (NAEYC, 1996). Many states are adopting these standards as their licensure requirements for early childhood professionals (Miller & Stayton, 1996).

INSERVICE TRAINING ISSUES AND MODELS

The provision of infant and preschool services using a family-centered, inclusive approach is a relatively new service delivery model that requires innovative, nontraditional approaches to in-service preparation of personnel. Winton, McCollum, and Catlett (1997) described some of the issues, models, and practical strategies for reforming personnel preparation in early intervention in order to meet fully the needs of ECSE personnel in preservice and in-service programs. Although traditional in-service efforts often attract individuals with only a few years of teaching experience, many of those who attend in-service training will be seasoned ECE and ECSE professionals learning to work with children and adults in new ways. To prepare personnel to provide effective services, it will be necessary for them to acquire knowledge, skills, and experiences that go far beyond simply providing ECSE services to young children at-risk and with disabilities and their families in separate settings. ECSE professionals need a firm understanding of the development of young children with varying abilities and how to design programs for them in order to collaborate successfully with ECE professionals in inclusive settings. In addition, they need new competencies in collaborating with families. They must begin to assume the many roles described by Bailey (1989) and Bricker (1989) that are the foundation for the *Early Childhood Special Educator* role described in the DEC/CEC standards (NAEYC, 1996). Clearly, ECE professionals will need opportunities to learn to communicate effectively with their ECE colleagues in order to deliver ECSE services in this new model. The same principles of quality in-service education apply to ongoing training in working with families in infancy and preschool settings (Winton, 1991).

Unlike preservice program models, in-service participants will include a substantial array of professionals and paraprofessionals from several disciplines who have limited time, limited resources, and varying schedules to accommodate (Kontos & Diamond, 1997). Because in-service activities are directed to experienced practitioners in the field, it is important to include them in the planning, implementation, and evaluation of such efforts in order to determine in-service program effectiveness from the broadest possible perspectives.

The need for a community-based training approach to in-service programs in early childhood special and regular education has been described by Buysse and Wesley (1993) and Wesley and Buysse (1997). According to these authors, a community-based training approach brings members from the larger community together for planning staff development activities. In addition, training emphasizes strategic planning and problem-solving skills and brings together participants from diverse backgrounds to receive training. Such community-based training provides an opportunity for a broad range of stakeholders to work together to identify issues of mutual concern in order to meet the needs of both the adults and the children in field settings. Guskey and Peterson (1996) suggested that

TABLE 21.4. Knowledge Bases for Early Childhood Special Education

ECSE Personnel Preparation graduates will demonstrate knowledge of:

The uniqueness of early childhood as a developmental phase.

All developmental domains, the application of developmental theories to at-risk and disabled children, and the role of developmental status in devising interventions.

Family systems theory and dynamics, roles, and relationships within families and the community.

The significant role of families as key decision makers and full partners in early intervention.

Developmentally and individually appropriate practices in ECSE as a framework for organizing classroom activities.

Curriculum development and strategies for implementing appropriate instruction based on the identified needs of individual children.

Culturally competent professional behaviors and cross-cultural differences as they affect interactions with children and families (see Barrera & Kramer, 1997).

The importance of collaborative interpersonal and interprofessional behavior for members of interdisciplinary teams, including how to build and maintain effective teams.

Child and family assessment and program evaluation strategies, including the use of performance-based authentic assessments.

The historical, legal, and philosophical bases of services for typical and atypical children, and strategies for advocacy on behalf of young children.

The meaning and application of professionalism, that is, adherence to the highest levels of professional practice, as it relates to work with parents, children, and other professionals.

including parents and staff in presentations is critical for developing high-quality staff in effective schools.

The determination of in-service training content should be based on needs assessments of potential participants, consideration of the specific settings in which staff development activities will occur, interviews with staff and families, and use of the most innovative approaches culled from research (Snyder & Wolfe, 1997). Whenever possible, a broad range of presenters should be selected from experienced and highly regarded ECSE and ECE practitioners, ECSE and ECE faculty in higher education, specialists in the community and in higher education, and parents. It is important that clearly specified evaluation strategies are used to assess the effectiveness of training efforts and to determine how the instruction can be improved (Wesley & Buysse, 1997). Detailed feedback from participants, and evaluative follow-up of the benefits of in-service training with site visits, consultation, and observation are essential in determining the degree to which in-service training is having an effect on the professional behavior of practitioners and specialists in the field (Wolfe & Snyder, 1997).

The research on staff development in ECSE personnel preparation highlights the central role that follow-up activities play in supporting transfer of training from the workshop setting to the workplace (Caffarella, 1994). However, there has been little published evidence specifying strategies that have systematically been implemented to foster the successful carryover of newly acquired content and skills to the workplace setting (Caffarella, 1994).

Nevertheless, several follow-up strategies have been used to facilitate the transfer of training from the staff development arena to the participants' workplace setting. Among these, peer support groups and coaching have been shown to facilitate transfer of training. Peer support groups bring colleagues together to help each other by providing

TABLE 21.5. Essential Training Experiences for ECSE Personnel

All ECSE personnel preparation participants should have training that:

Includes extensive field-based components to provide participants with the intervention content, processes, and skills needed for meeting the developmental and learning needs of young children at-risk and those with disabilities in an array of settings.

Includes on-site observations, interviews, and interactions with experienced practitioners, hands-on experiences with children, use of materials under supervision, and use of videotaped activities for reflection and feedback.

Enables participants to be active/contributing members of interdisciplinary teams through readings, knowledge of research in early intervention, observations, interviews, and interactions with well-functioning teams.

Stresses the importance of family and community relationships, provides strategies for communicating with professionals, stakeholders, and paraprofessionals in community settings, and includes community representatives in presentations (Wesley & Buysse, 1997).

Provides participants experience in selecting and administering assessments in all child domains, family assessments, and program evaluation, including developmentally based, authentic performance assessment.

Enables ECSE personnel to communicate effectively the assessment and program evaluation data to interdisciplinary team members, parents, and community stakeholders.

Prepares participants to collaborate with early childhood personnel and parents in developing, monitoring, and evaluating Individualized Family Service Plans (IFSP), Individualized Education Plans (IEP), and Individualized Transition Plans (ITP) and prepares them to provide training to early childhood professionals.

Prepares them for planning and monitoring of transitions to the next setting or supplemental services in community settings.

Includes multiple opportunities for engaging in reflective practice and collaborative problem solving as strategies for professional growth and ongoing professional development.

support and feedback to improve each other's professional competence (Killion & Kaylor, 1991). Coaching, on the other hand, involves specifically identified individuals helping participants implement newly acquired skills through analysis and critical feedback of actual observations of classroom behavior (Showers, 1985). There is some research that documents the effectiveness of coaching as a follow-up strategy (Ackland, 1991; Showers, 1985). Wolfe and Snyder (1997) provided several additional strategies that have been used to follow up staff development presentations: back home plans; that is, specific plans for implementing staff development content in participants' home settings, mentors, assignments, job aids, handouts, refresher sessions, follow-up telephone calls, and follow-up letters/packets of information. Clearly, time, money,

and staff resources are factors in selecting follow-up activities that are realistic in terms of resources available and usefulness to participants.

Technology is another vehicle that is currently being developed and holds potential for supporting follow-up of staff development for novice or experienced professionals assuming new roles. Electronic support networks could be created among professionals who wish to share concerns, effective consultation activities, or productive intervention strategies. Such electronic contact will provide access for interaction and collaboration that is often difficult for ECSE and early childhood personnel who are dispersed throughout the community. Special efforts might be directed toward creating electronic support networks for parents as well. Finally, distance education has been shown to be an effective instructional mode for individuals who are unable to make use of more conventional educational models but who are interested in pursuing professional development activities (Hughes & Forest, 1997).

CHALLENGES CONFRONTING THE PREPARATION OF INFANT AND PRESCHOOL PERSONNEL

Several challenges face those who prepare ECSE professionals to work with infants, toddlers, and preschoolers at-risk and those with disabilities and their families. To prepare professionals who have the requisite skills and knowledge to meet the NAEYC/DEC standards and to provide intervention that fosters maximum development for the children they serve, these challenges will need to be addressed in a thoughtful, planned, and timely fashion.

Building the Expertise of University Faculty

Institutions of higher education have a key role to play in the preparation of personnel and in the development and evaluation of effective models of service. In both the fields of infancy and preschool, many faculty face challenges for which they are not prepared. In the infancy area, many faculty have not had the opportunity to work directly with infants and toddlers. Typically, their clinical experience has been with preschool-aged children. In addition, many special education faculty have little experience using family-centered approaches with families who are experiencing a high degree of social–environmental stress, including risk for abuse and neglect or other circumstances that place young children at risk.

In such situations, it will be necessary for institutions of higher education to help faculty identify and access opportunities to acquire new knowledge and skills. In addition to the traditional faculty development activities – sabbaticals, conferences, and self-study – new options will need to be created. Collaborative partnerships with other universities in their local community or elsewhere whose faculty have such expertise may hold particular promise. The program described by Bruder, Lippman, and Bologna (1994) in New York City offers one model

for increasing the capacity of institutions of higher education to offer coursework, practicum, and specialty-course sequences for several disciplines involved in early intervention with infants and toddlers within a given geographic area. This Multidisciplinary Faculty Training Institute could be replicated in other communities with several institutions of higher education, some of which have the expertise for such training. Other federally funded regional faculty institutes have provided rich opportunities for interdisciplinary faculty development, curriculum resource identification, and networking (Winton, 1996). In states in which such opportunities are not available, the Part C lead agency in collaboration with the state department of education (Part B agency) and with universities can establish an annual summer faculty institute at an easily accessible location. The institute can address not only the professional development needs of faculty but also those of local directors and coordinators who provide program-based training and supervision. Furthermore, professional associations such as NAEYC, DEC, and Zero To Three: The National Center for Infants, Toddlers and Families (ZTT) organize faculty institute sessions yearly at their annual conferences.

The establishment of university/service agency partnerships offers the opportunity to create professional development communities benefiting both practitioners and faculty, similar to the PDS model described earlier. In Chicago, the Erikson Institute, a graduate school in child development, and the Ounce of Prevention Fund, a large community service agency, received local foundation funding to conduct a Participatory Action Research Project (Gilkerson & Stott, 1997). This project brought faculty together with mothers, grandmothers, fathers, grandfathers, with Early Head Start staff to identify community views of "good enough parenting" and ways that the program could be most helpful to families. Participation in the study deepened the understanding of the faculty of frontline issues and gave the faculty the opportunity to develop relationships with family members living in a high-risk community. Thus, faculty could move from teaching about families to sharing what they have learned from families.

In the preschool area, ECSE faculty may not have had experience in regular ECE settings. Therefore, cross-fertilization of early childhood and early childhood special education faculty is crucial. Historically, ECE and ECSE have been separate disciplines in terms of the journals in which they publish, the professional meetings they attend, the colleagues with whom they collaborate, and the terminology that they use in planning, implementing, and evaluating programs. Miller (1992) has argued for personnel preparation programs in ECE and ECSE to be merged. Such a strategy can encourage team teaching and provide a model of collaboration for students, simultaneous with faculty development (Kontos & Diamond, 1997). Integration of ECE faculty and ECSE faculty is a critical first step toward achieving high-quality, inclusive personnel preparation programs. At Western Kentucky University, the Interdisciplinary Early Childhood Education (IECE) Program offers a unified certificate in Early Childhood Education and Early Childhood Special Education. Students are qualified as early childhood educators and early childhood special educators and are prepared to work at both the infant–toddler and preschool levels. Courses are interdisciplinary, and program content includes both within- and cross-discipline content (McCollum & Stayton, 1996). Kilgo and Bruder (1997) described several other models for interdisciplinary training that involve all or parts of programs. Although little research exists on the efficacy of personnel preparation models (Bricker & Slenz, 1988; Klein & Campbell, 1990), the adoption of this new paradigm provides an excellent opportunity to undertake such research initiatives.

Identifying and Creating High-Quality Field Settings

Both in infancy and preschool, there is a pressing need for high-quality field placement sites, particularly sites that model effective inclusion. Although the practice of inclusion has been advocated throughout the 1970s, 1980s, and 1990s (Guralnick, 1986; Meisels, 1979), there are many communities in which this has not been implemented. As a result, the opportunity to provide current and future ECSE professionals with field settings in which they can observe high-quality inclusive programs is limited. One solution might be the creation of university/community model programs such as PIWI (Parents Interacting with Infants Practicum; McCollum, Rowan, & Thorp, 1994). PIWI, jointly sponsored by the University of Illinois and the local park district, is an interdisciplinary practicum designed to offer student teams the opportunity to design independently intervention services based on a set of philosophical statements. Families of infants with and without disabilities enjoy this opportunity for parent–child play while students gain experience in supporting parent–child relationships and in interdisciplinary team process. As inclusion increasingly becomes the accepted practice, it is vital that community-based partnerships become established between service providers and universities. Close monitoring of field placements to ensure linkages to coursework and exposure to quality service delivery will ensure that students receive the preparation necessary for delivering high-quality early intervention services. It is through such collaborative efforts that resources and expertise can be merged in ways that benefit children, families, and the profession.

Preparing Infant and Preschool Professionals to Work Effectively with Adults

Working with infants, toddlers, and preschoolers from the perspectives of family-centered, inclusive services requires that the ECSE personnel be as prepared to work with adults as with children. The capacity of the interventionist to engage with parents and with members of their own and other disciplines, as well as with paraprofessionals, must be addressed in preservice preparation and continually reinforced through in-service and continuing education and ongoing opportunities for reflective supervision. This recommendation has several implications for the design of personnel preparation, direct service, and policy initiatives.

First, the important role of ECSE with adults should be explained to candidates when they are recruited into the field. Preservice programs must balance the instructional and practicum time to provide students with beginning competencies in child, family, and interdisciplinary team process. Graduate programs in infancy and early childhood special education must be available to provide the entry-level professional as well as the experienced practitioner with advanced training and specialization (e.g., Erikson Institute's Master's Infant Specialization Program and Wheelock College's two master's programs: Early Intervention and Early Childhood Special Education). More intense focus on working with families and working across settings can be provided at the graduate level. Interdisciplinary graduate programs (e.g., Bank Street's Master's Program in Infancy and Social Work; De-Paul University's Early Intervention Dual Master's Degree in Child Development and Counseling; and Western Kentucky University Program in ECE and ECSE) and Interdisciplinary Practica (e.g., University of Illinois PIWI Program with the Departments of ECSE and Speech and Hearing) offer rich opportunities to blend multiple knowledge bases and cross-disciplinary practice related to working with adults as well as children. Training programs that involve parents in central roles may offer the most promise for providing practitioners with an authentic understanding of family-centered practice (University of Vermont College of Education and Parent to Parent of Vermont). Undergraduate and graduate training programs must assess the nature of their supervision of students (Gallacher, 1997; Gilkerson, 1995) and ensure that each participant has the opportunity to become a reflective practitioner – a professional who can improve his or her practice based on an awareness of self and other.

In-service and continuing education are essential to provide practitioners with opportunities to continue to grow. Bricker (1995) noted that a significant factor contributing to the successful inclusion of children with disabilities in ECE community settings is the attitude of professionals and parents in those settings. In-service training can provide ECSE and ECE professionals with opportunities to explore the roles, practices, attitudes, and beliefs of their own and other disciplines. Such training experiences must include strategies for consultation (File & Kontos, 1992, 1993), sensitivity to cultural and linguistic diversity (Lynch & Hanson, 1992; Mallory & New, 1994), and fostering of interpersonal skills that support effective communication among adults from different disciplines, cultures, and levels of experience. For example, family child-care providers will need a different interaction/collaborative style than the master's-level teacher in a large preschool program. Little data exist regarding specific in-service and consultation strategies that have been effective with home-based providers, as inclusion in these settings is only a fairly recent practice. Providers have expressed concerns regarding whether ECSE professionals will respect them and the work that they do and whether ECSE consultants will help them meet the complex needs of youngsters for whom some care for many hours per day. The task that we face is to design training processes and consultation procedures that foster respect for the frontline, experienced child-care providers who have not had formal training regarding children with disabilities and who are striving to meet their complex needs.

Probably the most relevant source of continuing education for practitioners working with adults is the opportunity for supervision and consultation regarding their ongoing work. Supervision may be a relationship for learning, but it is also one that occurs within an organization. Gilkerson and Young-Holt (1992) described the necessary conditions for supervision to be an ongoing reality in direct service programs: 1) there must be an organizational philosophy and commitment to provide supervision for all staff members; 2) funding and time must be set aside on a regular basis; 3) supervisors must be identified and supported; 4) supervisory relationships should be specified in job descriptions; and 5) reliable support and consultation must be available to the program director as well. Bertacchi and Stott (1992) described a model for a director's support seminar that is offered to directors of practicum sites affiliated with a preservice training program.

Because of the increasing diversity and complexity of family circumstances in early intervention, a pressing need exists for program-based opportunities to build and refine one's capacity to work with parents and with other team members. Increased collaboration between early intervention programs and infant mental health services is providing a new source of consultation and supervision to staff in Part C programs. This collaboration prepares staff to attend more fully to the emotional experiences of family members and, thus, to increase their empathy for and helpfulness to families facing multiple challenges (Foley & Hochman, 1998; Hirshberg, 1998; Ivins & Sweet, 1992; Weatherston, 1998).

Meeting the Needs of Adult Learners

The new roles and responsibilities of experienced infant and preschool professionals will best be acquired through the integration of theory and practice in professional development activities. Throughout the 1980s and the 1990s, a wealth of information has been published in the adult learning and development literature (cf. Knowles, 1980; Lawler, 1992; Schaie & Willis, 1996) that can be used to guide the selection of training processes and strategies for both preservice and in-service participants. Selecting essential content, in conjunction with the use of an array of active learning strategies based on the adult literature, holds promise for enhancing the value of training efforts by making them relevant to participants' developmental needs, interests, and abilities. In large measure, this growing body of research recommends developmentally appropriate practice for adults in much the same way DAP has been developed for children (Knowles, 1980).

Knowles (1980) cited four assumptions about adult learners that set them apart from children and youth. Using the term *andragogy*, meaning that adults learn differently from children and need instruction that is responsive to their needs, he characterized adult learners in the following ways:

1. Having a self-concept that moves from being one of a dependent personality toward being a self-directed human being;
2. Accumulating a growing reservoir of experience that becomes an increasingly rich resource for learning;
3. Orienting their readiness to learn to developmental tasks appropriate to their social roles; and
4. Changing their perspective from one who postpones the application of knowledge to one who sees the immediacy of knowledge application. (pp. 44–5)

The learning characteristics of adults should serve as a framework for structuring training content and processes in professional development initiatives. This premise challenges personnel preparation efforts in several ways:

1. Adults make up a diverse group of students with varying backgrounds, experiences, motivations for becoming learners, responsibilities outside their role as students, and cultural and value systems that have a profound influence on what they learn and how they learn it. These differences have an impact on how each adult learns, and this diversity is an important characteristic that must have a central focus in program planning.
2. Adults come to the learning task feeling competent in many areas of their lives but may feel insecure and anxious about their roles as learners. Thus, understanding and reducing anxiety in the adult learner is a key to successful training (Lawler, 1992). Providing opportunities to discuss their concerns, making the expectations clear, and providing academic assistance may help reduce their anxiety.
3. Adult education is learner centered and, just as with children, it starts with the participants – and where they are – and must take into consideration which type of learning activities will be most meaningful to them and provide opportunities for them to share their experiences and expertise with others.
4. A needs assessment, much like the assessment we do with children, will assist planners in assuring that the material is presented in ways that are relevant to the needs of the learner. This assessment may take the form of interviews, surveys, performance appraisals (Lawler, 1992), or some measure of pre-entry skills and knowledge constructed for each particular situation.
5. Preservice and in-service ECSE experiences should be organized into "clusters of experiences" that are broader than traditional coursework and include opportunities for several types of learning on the basis of the adult development literature (cf. Lawler, 1992): didactic classroom interactions, observations using actual field visits and videotaped presentations, small group discussions, parent and provider interviews, role-play, joint observations in field sites with faculty and peers, case conferences, collaborative problem-solving opportunities, individual supervision, conferences, and use of technology and the Internet. The creation of advisement/support groups similar to those employed by the Bank Street College (Ayers, 1991) and Erikson Institute (Stott & Bowman, 1996) foster cohesion and enable adults to learn with and from each other.
6. Adult learners lead busy lives. While their need for peer support is high, the time available may be limited. For those participants who have access to e-mail, ongoing communication and collaboration can be established electronically, forming a readily accessible problem-solving think tank and support network.

Diversifying the Workforce

Given the complexity and diversity of families involved in early intervention services, it is imperative that personnel preparation programs expand efforts to identify and train people from a range of cultural, racial, and ethnic backgrounds. Targeted recruitment strategies should be developed and implemented to inform persons from traditionally underrepresented groups about careers in early intervention and about preservice and inservice education opportunities. Specialized cooperative agreements with the early childhood and mental health paraprofessional programs at community colleges, including individualized advising and the facilitation of the transfer of credits to four-year institutions, hold strong promise for recruiting a rich new pool of early childhood practitioners. Expanding the availability of financial aid, academic assistance, and careful advising and job placement services are essential to the success of this effort. New linkages among community colleges, undergraduate, and graduate schools will facilitate the identification of promising candidates and the provision of ongoing mentoring that is often needed to launch individuals on a new career path.

Preparing for Change

Personnel preparation efforts mirror and, to a certain extent, stimulate changes in the field. As previously described, the field of early childhood special education is still evolving. Paradigms shift, service delivery models change, and professional roles evolve. Similarly, new models of community-based and higher education instruction emerge, including innovations such as distance learning (Hughes & Forest, 1997; Ludlow, 1994), professional development communities (Darling-Hammond, 1994), and interprofessional education (Kilgo & Bruder, 1997). Faculty and in-service trainers must prepare practitioners to adopt a posture of learning, staying open to change and questioning currently accepted knowledge and practice as well as being guided by them.

Furthermore, faculty and practitioners must be open to the widening circles of influence on children, families, and communities. The boundaries among health, social service, education, employment, and mental health services are diminishing. Welfare reform, for example, affects the availability of families to participate in intervention services, the need for inclusive child care, and the very nature of family support services – what is most helpful and for whom. Understanding the impact of the changes in the larger social system on the specific children and families served is a professional competency that will become increasingly important in personnel preparation for the twenty-first century.

IMPLICATIONS FOR FUTURE RESEARCH

In this chapter, we have attempted to explicate the contrasting philosophies that have prevailed in early childhood special and regular education as family-centered, inclusive early education increasingly becomes the accepted practice. In many ways, these philosophies differ with regard to the central role of development as contrasted to learning in young children. Furthermore, there are different perspectives with regard to the structure and organization of learning environments, roles, expectations, and competencies of teachers and other staff and the freedom and expectations of the child in learning environments. We encourage scholars and practitioners to construct a synthesis of these multiple perspectives into theoretical reformulations that can be evaluated with all children. Such theories would provide a framework for applied research and for testing theories related to child development, family adaptation, family-centered practices, and effective intervention strategies in inclusive settings. The activity-based approaches to early intervention (Bricker & Cripe, 1992; Greenspan & Weider, 1998) exemplify the type of theory-based interventions that hold promise as intervention strategies that are effective for children with varying abilities. More theory-based intervention efforts, accompanied by carefully designed research studies, could provide a valuable research base for both early intervention and personnel preparation.

The dearth of useful research related to teacher effectiveness in schools in general, and teacher effectiveness in inclusive early childhood classrooms in particular, defines a research area in need of attention. In a comprehensive volume entitled *Reforming Personnel Preparation in Early Intervention* (Winton, McCollum, & Catlett, 1997), a rich variety of information for preparing early intervention personnel is presented. These valuable materials must be carefully evaluated to determine the effectiveness of specific personnel preparation strategies for the education of all young children. Systematic efforts are needed to validate personnel preparation models empirically, to explore the relationship of various preservice and in-service training models to professional performance, and to examine the relationship of professional performance to child and family outcomes in inclusive and specialized settings. Empirical descriptions of highly competent infant–family specialists and early childhood teachers could provide guidelines for personnel preparation. The examination of intervention process research also holds promise for identifying qualities of the interventionist and elements of the parent–interventionist relationship that contribute to successful outcomes.

Research efforts should be directed toward the study of theory-based approaches to learning and curricula that foster the inclusion of infants and young children at-risk and those with disabilities. Generating such activities from conceptual models would provide a framework within which to test hypotheses. Similarly, research related to effective consultation strategies to meet the professional development needs of diverse providers and successful models for consultation in rural areas, family child-care homes, and large early childhood centers in urban areas are topics that need an empirical database to guide personnel preparation practices.

Finally, a longitudinal research agenda that specifies appropriate contrast groups, identifies valid and reliable developmental outcome measures, and incorporates cost factors, program characteristics, and ECSE and ECE personnel competencies will permit comparisons across regions of the country and will contribute significantly to our knowledge base in early intervention. Such efforts should differentiate among recipients regarding types of problems (e.g., low birth weight, failure to thrive, visual impairment, and Down syndrome, demographic and family factors) and should identify specific personnel competencies related to child and family outcomes to be included within personnel preparation programs.

The policy mandate for inclusive early childhood education provides a valuable opportunity for professionals and parents to use existing knowledge to help infants and young children at-risk and those with disabilities and to generate new knowledge that will advance current practices regarding ECSE and ECE personnel training. Hopefully, current legislation will serve as a catalyst for the articulation of new theories, creation of innovative interventions, accumulation of new bodies of applied research, and devising databased personnel preparation models that will benefit service recipients directly.

REFERENCES

Ackland, R. (1991). A review of the peer coaching literature. *Journal of Staff Development, 12,* 276–8.

Allen, K., & Schwartz, I. (1996). *The exceptional child: Inclusion in early childhood education* (3rd ed.). Boston: Delmar Publishing.

Als, H. (1978). Assessing an assessment. In A. Sameroff (Ed.), Organization and stability of newborn behavior: A commentary on the Brazelton neonatal behavioral assessment scale. *Monographs of the Society for Research in Child Development, 43,* 14–29.

American Association for Marriage and Family Therapy. (1995). *Listening to families: Videotape series.* Van Nuys, CA: Author.

Ayers, W. (1991). Spreading the roots: Bank Street advisement and the education of teachers. *Thought and Practice, 3*(1), 25–8.

Bailey, D. (1989). Issues and directions in preparing professionals to work with young handicapped children and their families. In J. Gallagher, P. Trohanis, & R. Clifford (Eds.), *Policy implementation and P.L. 99-457: Planning for young children with special needs* (pp. 97–132). Baltimore, MD: Paul H. Brookes.

Bailey, D. (1996). An overview of interdisciplinary training. In D. Bricker & A. Widerstrom (Eds.), *Preparing personnel to work with infants and young children and their families: A team approach* (pp. 3–21). Baltimore, MD: Paul H. Brookes.

Bailey, D., Farrel, A., O'Donnell, K., Simeonsson, R., & Miller, C. (1986). Preparing infant interventionists: Interdepartmental training in special education and maternal and child health. *Journal of the Division for Early Childhood, 11,* 67–77.

Bailey, D., Palsha, S., & Huntington, G. (1990). Pre-service preparation of special educators to serve infants with handicaps and their families. Current status and training needs. *Journal of Early Intervention, 14*(1), 43–54.

Bailey, D., Simeonsson, R., Yoder, D., & Huntington, G. (1990). Preparing professionals to serve infants and toddlers with handicaps and their families: An integrative analysis across eight disciplines. *Exceptional Children, 57*(1), 26–35.

Barber, P. A., Turnbull, A. P., Behr, S. K., & Kerns, G. M. (1988). A family systems perspective on early childhood special education. In S. L. Odom & M. B. Karnes (Eds.), *Early intervention for infants and children with handicaps: An empirical base* (pp. 179–98). Baltimore, MD: Paul H. Brookes.

Barrera, I., & Kramer, L. (1997). Monologues to skilled dialogues: Teaching the process of crafting culturally competent early childhood environments. In P. Winton, J. McCollum, & C. Catlett (Eds.), *Reforming personnel preparation in early intervention: Issues, models, and practical strategies* (pp. 217–51). Baltimore, MD: Paul H. Brookes.

Beckman, P. (Ed.). (1996). *Strategies for working with families of young children with disabilities*. Baltimore, MD: Paul H. Brookes.

Bennett, T., Nelson, D. E., & Lingerfelt, B. (1992). *Facilitating family-centered training in early intervention*. Tucson, AZ: Communication Skill Builders.

Bennett, T., Lingerfelt, V. V., & Nelson, D. E. (1990). *Developing individualized family support plans*. Cambridge, MA: Brookline Books.

Berkeley, J., & Ludlow, B. (1989). Toward a reconceptualization of the developmental model. *Topics in Early Childhood Special Education, 9*(3), 51–66.

Bertacchi, J., & Stott, F. (1992). A seminar for supervisors in infant/family programs: Growing versus paying more for staying the same. *Zero To Three, 12*(2), 34–9.

Bowman, B. T. (1989). Self-reflection as an element of professionalism. *Teachers College Record, 90*(3), 444–451.

Bredekamp, S. (Ed.). (1987). *Developmentally appropriate practice in early childhood programs serving children from birth through age 8*. Expanded edition. Washington, DC: NAEYC.

Bredekamp, S. (1993). The relationship between early childhood education and early childhood special education: Healthy marriage or family feud. *Topics in Early Childhood Special Education, 13*(3), 258–273.

Bredekamp, S., & Copple, C. (Eds.). (1997). *Developmentally appropriate practice in early childhood programs* (rev. ed.). Washington, DC: NAEYC.

Bricker, D. (1989). *Early intervention for at-risk and handicapped infants, toddlers, and preschool children* (2nd ed.). Palo Alto, CA: VORT Corp.

Bricker, D. (1995). The challenge of inclusion. *Journal of Early Intervention, 19*(3), 179–94.

Bricker, D., & Cripe, J. (1992) *An activity-based approach to early intervention*. Baltimore, MD: Paul H. Brookes.

Bricker, D., & LaCroix, B. (1996). Training practices. In D. Bricker & A. Widerstrom (Eds.). *Preparing personnel to work with infants and young children and their families: A team approach* (pp. 43–67). Baltimore, MD: Paul H. Brookes.

Bricker, D., & Slentz, K. (1988). Personnel preparation: Handicapped infants. In M. Wang, M. C. Reynolds, &

H. J. Walberg (Eds.), *Handbook of special education: Research and practice* (Vol. 3, pp. 319–45). Elmsford, NY: Pergamon Books.

Bricker, D., & Widerstrom, A. (1996). *Preparing personnel to work with infants and young children and their families: A team approach*. Baltimore, MD: Paul H. Brookes.

Bromwich, R. (1997). *Working with families and their infants at risk* (2nd ed.). Austin, TX: Pro-Ed.

Bruder, M. B. (1993). The provision of early intervention and early childhood special education within community early childhood programs: Characteristics of effective service delivery. *Topics in Early Childhood Special Education, 13*, 19–37.

Bruder, M., Lippman, C., & Bologna, T. (1994). Personnel preparation in early intervention: Building capacity for program expansion within institutions of higher education. *Journal of Early Intervention, 18*(1), 103–10.

Buysse, V., & Wesley, P. (1993). The identity crisis in early childhood education: A call for professional role clarification. *Topics in Early Childhood Special Education, 13*(4), 418–29.

Caffarella, R. S. (1994). *Planning programs for adult learners: A practical guide for educators, trainers, and staff developers*. San Francisco: Jossey-Bass.

Capone, A., Hull, K. M., & DiVenere, N. J. (1997). Parent–professional partnerships in preservice and inservice education. In P. J. Winton, J. A. McCollum, & C. Catlett (Eds.), *Reforming personnel preparation in early intervention: Issues, models and practical strategies* (pp. 435–52). Baltimore, MD: Paul H. Brookes.

Cardone, I., & Gilkerson, L. (1990). Family administered neonatal activities: An exploratory method for the integration of parental perceptions and newborn behavior. *Infant Mental Health Journal, 11*(2), 127–41.

Carter, E. A., & McGoldrick, M. (Eds.). (1980). *The family life cycle: A framework for family therapy*. New York: Gardner Press.

Chan, S. Q. (1990). Early intervention with culturally diverse families of infants and toddlers with disabilities. *Infants and Young Children, 3*(2), 78–87.

Cohen, D. H., Stern, V., & Balaban, N. (1997). *Observing and recording the behavior of young children* (4th ed.). New York: Teachers College Press.

Darling-Hammond, L. (1994). *Professional development schools*. New York: Teachers College Press.

Day, B., & Drake, K. (1986). Developments in experimental programs: The key to quality education and care for young children. *Educational Leadership, 44*(3), 24–7.

Dunst, C. J., Johanson, C., Trivette, C. M., & Hamby, D. (1991). Family-oriented early intervention policies and practices: Family-centered or not? *Exceptional Children. 58*, 115–26.

Dunst, C. L., Trivette, C. M., & Deal, A. G. (1988). *Enabling and empowering families: Principles and guidelines*. Cambridge, MA: Brookline Books.

Edelman, L. (Ed.). (1991). *Getting on board: Training activities* to promote the practice of family-concerned care. Bethesda, MD: Association for the Care of Children's Health.

Fenichel, E. (1991). Learning through supervision and mentorship to support the development of infants, toddlers and their families. *Zero to Three, 12*(2), 1–26.

Fenichel, E. (Ed.). (1992). *Learning through supervision and mentorship to support the development of infants, toddlers and their families.* Arlington, VA: Zero to Three.

Fenichel, E. S., & Eggbeer, L. (1991). Preparing practitioners to work with infants, toddlers, and their families: Four essential elements of training. *Infants and Young Children, 4*(2), 56–62.

File, N., & Kontos, S. (1992). Indirect service delivery through consultation: Review and implications for early intervention. *Journal of Early Intervention, 16*(3), 221–33.

File, N., & Kontos, S. (1993). The relationship of program quality to child's play in integrated early intervention settings. *Topics in Early Childhood Special Education, 13*(1), 1–18.

Foley, G. M., & Hochman, J. D. (1998). Programs, parents and practitioners: Perspectives on integrating early intervention with infant mental health. *Zero to Three, 18*(3), 13–18.

Foley, G., Hochman, J., & Miller, S. (1994). Parent–professional relationships: finding an optimal distance. *Zero to Three, 14*(4), 19–22.

Fox, L., Hanline, M., Vail, C., & Galant, K. (1994). Developmentally appropriate practice: Applications for young children with disabilities. *Journal of Early Intervention, 18* (3), 243–57.

Fuchs, D., & Fuchs, L. (1994). Inclusive school movement and the radicalization of special education reform. *Exceptional Children, 60,* 294–309.

Gallacher, K. K. (1997). Supervision, mentoring, and coaching. In P. Winton, J. A. McCollum, & C. Catlett (Eds.), *Reforming personnel preparation in early intervention: Issues, models, and practical strategies* (pp. 191–224). Baltimore, MD: Paul H. Brookes.

Gallagher, J., & Staples, A. (1990). *Available and potential resources for personnel preparation in special education: Dean's survey.* Chapel Hill: Carolina Policy Studies Program, University of North Carolina at Chapel Hill.

Geik, I., Gilkerson, L., & Sponseller, D. (1982). An early intervention training model. *Journal of the Division for Early Childhood, 5,* 42–52.

Gilkerson, L. (1995). Reflections on the process of supervision. In R. Shanok, L. Gilkerson, L. Eggbeer, & E. Fenichel, *Reflective supervision: A relationship for learning.* Arlington, VA: Zero to Three.

Gilkerson, L., & Stott, F. (1997). Listening to the voices of families: Learning through caregiving consensus groups. *Zero to Three, 18*(2), 9–16.

Gilkerson, L., & Young-Holt, C. (1992). Supervision and the management of programs serving infants, toddlers, and their families. In E. Fenichel (Ed.), *Learning through supervision and mentorship to support the development of infants,*

toddlers, and their families: A source book. Arlington, VA: Zero to Three.

Gilkerson, L., Zvetina, D., Turbiville, V., & Turnbull, R. (in preparation). Abuse and neglect of young children with disabilities: Issues for the early intervention specialist.

Godfrey, A. B. (1995). Preservice interdisciplinary preparation of early intervention specialists in a college of nursing: Faculty reflections and recommendations. *Infants and Young Children, 7*(3), 74–82.

Greenspan, S. I., & Weider, S. (1998). *The child with special needs: Encouraging intellectual and emotional growth.* Reading, MA: Addison-Wesley.

Greenspan, S. I. (1992). *Infancy and early childhood: The practice of clinical assessment and intervention with emotional and developmental challenges.* Madison, CT: International University Press.

Guralnick, M. J. (1986). Recent developments in early intervention efficacy research: Implications for family involvement in P.L. 99-457. *Topics in Early Childhood Special Education, 9*(1), 1–17.

Guskey, T. R., & Peterson, K. D. (1996). The road to classroom change. *Educational Researcher, 15*(5), 5–11.

Harris, B. M. (1980). *Improving staff performance through inservice education.* Needham, MA: Allyn & Bacon.

Harris, S. R. (1997). The effectiveness of early intervention for children with cerebral palsy and related motor disabilities. In M. J. Guralnick (Ed.), *The effectiveness of early intervention* (pp. 327–348). Baltimore, MD: Paul H. Brookes.

Hirshberg, L. M. (1998). Infant mental health consultation to early intervention programs. *Zero to Three, 18*(3), 19–23.

Hughes, M., & Forest, S. (1997). Distance education in early intervention personnel preparation. In P. Winton, J. McCollum, & C. Catlett (Eds.), *Reforming personnel preparation in early intervention: Issues, models, and practical strategies* (pp. 453–74). Baltimore, MD: Paul H. Brookes.

Ivins, B., & Sweet, N. (1992). Supervision as a catalyst in the evolution of an integrated infant mental health/developmental intervention program. In E. Fenichel (Ed.), *Learning through supervision and mentorship to support the development of infants, toddlers and their families: A source book* (pp. 76–83). Arlington, VA: Zero to Three.

Jones, S., & Meisels, S. J. (1987). Training family day care providers to work with special needs children. *Topics in Early Childhood Special Education, 7,* 1–12.

Kaiser, A. P., & Hester, P. P. (1994). Generalized effects of enhanced milieu teaching. *Journal of Speech and Hearing Research, 37,* 1320–40.

Kalmanson, B., & Seligman, S. (1992). Family–provider relationships: The basis of all interventions. *Infants and Young Children, 4*(4), 46–52.

Kilgo, J., & Bruder, M. (1997). Creating new visions of higher education: Interdisciplinary approaches to personnel preparation in early intervention. In P. Winton,

J. McCollum, & C. Catlett (Eds.), *Reforming personnel preparation in early intervention: Issues, models, and practical strategies* (pp. 81–101). Baltimore, MD: Paul H. Brookes.

Killion, J. P., & Kaylor, B. (1991). Follow up: The key to training for transfer. *Journal of Staff Development, 12*(1), 64–7.

Klein, N., & Campbell, P. (1990). Preparing personnel to serve at-risk and disabled infants, toddlers, and preschoolers. In S. J. Meisels & J. P. Shonkoff (Eds.), *Handbook of early childhood intervention* (pp. 679–99). New York: Cambridge University Press.

Klein, N., & Sheehan, R. (1987). Staff development: A key issue in meeting the needs of young handicapped children in day care settings. *Topics in Early Childhood Special Education, 7*, 13–27.

Knowles, M. (1980). *The modern practice of adult education* (rev. ed.). Cambridge, MA: Adult Education Co.

Kontos, S. (1988). Family day care as an integrated early intervention setting. *Topics in Early Childhood Special Education, 8*, 1–15.

Kontos, S., & Diamond, K. (1997). Preparing practitioners to provide early intervention services in inclusive settings. In P. Winton, J. McCollum, & C. Catlett (Eds.), *Reforming personnel preparation in early intervention: Issues, models, and practical strategies* (pp. 393–410). Baltimore, MD: Paul H. Brookes.

Lawler, P. (1992). *The keys to adult learning: Theory and practical strategies*. Philadelphia: Research for Better Schools.

Lieberman, A. (1998). An infant mental health perspective. *Zero to Three, 18*(3), 3–5.

Linder, T. W. (1993). *Transdisciplinary play-based intervention: Guidelines for developing meaningful curriculum for young children*. Baltimore, MD: Paul H. Brookes.

Ludlow, B. L. (1994). Using distance education to prepare early intervention personnel. *Infants and Young Children, 7*(1), 51–9.

Lynch, E., & Hanson, M. (1992). Steps in the right direction: Implications for interventions. In E. Lynch & M. Hanson (Eds.), *Developing cross-cultural competence: A guide for working with young children and their families* (pp. 355–70). Baltimore, MD: Paul H. Brookes.

Lynch, E. W., & Hanson, M. J. (1992). *Developing cross-cultural competence: A guide for working with young children and their families*. Baltimore, MD: Paul H. Brookes.

Mahoney, G., & Powell, A. (1988). Modifying parent–child interaction: Enhancing the development of handicapped children. *Journal of Special Education, 22*, 82–96.

Mahoney, G., Robinson, C., & Powell, A. (1992). Focusing on parent–child interaction: The bridge to developmentally appropriate practices. *Topics in Early Childhood Special Education, 12*(1), 105–20.

Mallory, B., & New, R. (1994). *Diversity and developmentally appropriate practices: Challenges for early childhood education*. New York: Teachers College Press.

McBride, S. L., & Brotherson, M. J. (1997). Guiding practitioners toward valuing and implementing family-centered practices. In P. J. Winton, J. A. McCollum, & C. Catlett (Eds.), *Reforming personnel preparation in early intervention: Issues, models and practical strategies* (pp. 253–76). Baltimore, MD: Paul H. Brookes.

McBride, S. L., Sharp, L., Hains, A. H., & Whitehead, A. (1995). Parents as co-instructors in pre-service training: A pathway to family centered practice. *Journal of Early Intervention, 19*, 377–89.

McCollum, J., & Bailey, D. (1991). Developing comprehensive personnel systems: Issues and alternatives. *Journal of Early Intervention, 15*(1), 51–6.

McCollum, J. A., Cook, R. J., & Ladmer, L. A. (1993). The staffing of early intervention programs in Illinois: A descriptive study of current personnel. *Illinois Council for Exceptional Children Quarterly, 43*(1), 15–28.

McCollum, J., & Maude, S. (1992). *Comparison of professional competencies for early intervention personnel*. Reston, VA: Division of Early Childhood, Council for Exceptional Children.

McCollum, J., Rowan, L., & Thorp, E. (1994). Philosophy as training in infancy personnel preparation. *Journal of Early Intervention, 18*, 216–26.

McCollum, J., & Stayton, V. (1996). Preparing early childhood special educators. In D. Bricker & A. Widerstrom (Eds.), *Preparing personnel to work with infants and young children and their families: A team approach* (pp. 67–90). Baltimore, MD: Paul H. Brookes.

McCollum, J., & Thorp, E. (1988). Training of infant specialists: A look to the future. *Infants and Young Children, 1*(2), 55–65.

McCollum, J. A., & Yates, T. (1994). Dyad as focus, triad as means: A family-centered approach to supporting parent–child interactions. *Infants and Young Children, 6*(4), 54–63.

McGonigel, M., Kauffman, R., & Johnson, B. (1991). *Guidelines and recommended practices for the individualized family service plan* (2nd ed.). Bethesda, MD: Association for the Care of Children's Health.

McWilliam, R. (1992). *Family-centered intervention planning: A routines-based approach*. San Antonio, TX: Communication Skill Builders.

McWilliam, R. (1995). Integration of therapy and consultative special education: A continuum in early intervention. *Infants and Young Children, 7*(4), 29–38.

Meisels, S. J. (Ed.). (1979). *Special education and development: Perspectives on young children with special needs*. Baltimore, MD: University Park Press.

Meisels, S. J. (1985). A functional analysis of the evolution of public policy for handicapped young children. *Educational Evaluation and Policy Analysis, 7*, 115–26.

Meisels, S. J. (1989). Meeting the mandate of Public Law 99-457: Early childhood intervention in the nineties. *American Journal of Orthopsychiatry, 59*, 451–60.

Meisels, S. J., Harbin, G., Modigliani, K., & Olson, K. (1988).

Formulating optimal state early childhood intervention policies. *Exceptional Children, 55*(2), 159–65.

Miller, N. (1994). *Nobody's perfect: Living and growing with children who have special needs.* Baltimore, MD: Paul H. Brookes.

Miller, P. (1992). Segregated programs of teacher education in early children: Immoral and inefficient practice. *Topics in Early Childhood Special Education, 11*(4), 39–52.

Miller, P., and Stayton, V. (1996). Personnel preparation in early education and intervention: Recommended pre-service and inservice practices. In S. Odom & M. McLean (Eds.), *Early intervention/early childhood special education: Recommended practices* (pp. 329–58). Austin, TX: Pro-Ed.

Minuchin, S. (1974). *Families and family therapy.* Cambridge, MA: Harvard University Press.

Moss, B., & Gotts, E. A. (1998). Relationship-based early childhood intervention: A progress report from the trenches. *Zero to Three, 18*(3), 24–32.

National Association for the Education of Young Children. (1996). *Guidelines for preparation of early childhood professionals.* Washington, DC: Author.

National Easter Seal Society. (1988). *Crisis ahead: Recruitment and retention of rehabilitation professionals in the nineties and beyond.* Chicago: Author.

Odom, S., & McLean, M. (1996). *Early intervention/early childhood special education: Recommended practices.* Austin, TX: Pro-Ed.

Office of the Special Education Program/OSERS. (1989). *Eleventh annual report to Congress on the implementation of the Education of Handicapped Act.* Washington, DC: U.S. Department of Education.

Olson, D. H., McCubbin, H. I., Barnes, H., Larsen, A., Muxen, M., & Wilson, M. (1983). *Families: What makes them work.* Beverly Hills, CA: Sage.

Pawl, J. (1995a). The therapeutic relationship as human connectedness: Being held in another's mind. *Zero to Three, 15*(4), 2–5.

Pawl, J. (1995b). On supervision. In R. Shanok, L. Gilkerson, L. Eggbeer, & E. Fenichel, *Reflective supervision: A relationship for learning* (pp. 41–9). Arlington, VA: Zero to Three.

Peck, C., Furman, G., & Helmstetter, E. (1993). Integrated early childhood programs: Research on the implementation of change in organizational contexts. In C. Peck, S. Odom, & D. Bricker (Eds.), *Integrating young children with disabilities into community programs: Ecological perspectives on research and implementation* (pp. 187–206). Baltimore, MD: Paul H. Brookes.

Roberts, R. N., Rule, S., & Innocenti, M. S. (1998). *Strengthening the family-professional partnership in services for young children.* Baltimore, MD: Paul H. Brookes.

Rosenkoetter, S. E., & Stayton, V. (1997). Designing and implementing innovative, interdisciplinary practice. In P. J. Winton, J. A. McCollum, & C. Catlett (Eds.), *Reforming personnel preparation in early intervention: Issues, models and practical strategies* (pp. 453–74). Baltimore, MD: Paul H. Brookes.

Safford, P. L. (1989). *Integrating teaching in early childhood: Starting in the mainstream.* White Plains, NY: Longman.

Sameroff, A., & Chandler, M. (1975). Reproductive risk and the continuum of caretaking causality. In F. D. Horowitz, M. Hetherington, S. Scarr-Salapatek, & G. Siegel (Eds.), *Review of child development research* (Vol. 4, pp. 187–244). Chicago: University of Chicago Press.

Sameroff, A., & Emde, R. (1988). *Relationship disturbances in early childhood.* New York: Basic Books.

Schaie, K., & Willis, S. (1996). *Adult development and aging* (4th ed.). New York: HarperCollins.

Schon, D. A. (1983). *The reflective practitioner: How professionals think in action.* New York: Basic Books.

Seligman, M., & Darling, R. (1989). *Ordinary families, special children. A systems approach to childhood disability.* New York: Guilford Press.

Shanok, R. S. (1992). The supervisory relationship: Integrator, resource, guide. In E. Fenichel (Ed.), *Learning through supervision and mentorship: A sourcebook.* Arlington, VA: Zero to Three.

Shanok, R., Gilkerson, L., Eggbeer, L., & Fenichel, E. (1995). *Reflective supervision: A relationship for learning.* Arlington, VA: Zero to Three.

Showers, B. (1985). Teachers coaching teachers. *Educational Leadership 42*(7), 43–8.

Simeonsson, R., & Bailey, D. (1990). Family dimensions in early intervention. In S. J. Meisels & J. P. Shonkoff (Eds.), *Handbook of early childhood intervention* (pp. 428–44). New York: Cambridge University Press.

Slentz, K., & Bricker, D. (1992). Family-guided assessment for the IFSP development: Jumping off the family assessment bandwagon. *Journal of Early Intervention, 16* (1), 11–19.

Snyder, P., & Wolfe, B. (1997). Needs assessment and evaluation in early intervention personnel preparation: Opportunities and challenges. In P. Winton, J. McCollum, & C. Catlett (Eds.), *Reforming personnel preparation in early intervention: Issues, models, and practical strategies* (pp. 127–71). Baltimore, MD: Paul H. Brookes.

Stern, D. N. (1977). *The first relationship: Infant and mother.* Cambridge, MD: Harvard University Press.

Stern, D. N. (1985). *The interpersonal world of the infant: A view from psychoanalysis and developmental psychology.* New York: Basic Books.

Stott, F., & Bowman, B. (1996). Child development knowledge: A slippery base for practice. *Early Childhood Research Quarterly, 11,* 169–83.

Strain, P. (1990). LRE for preschool children with handicaps: What we know, what we should be doing. *Journal of Early Intervention, 14*(4), 291–6.

Summers, J. A., Dell'Oliver, C., Turnbull, A. P., Benson, H. A., Santelli, E., Campbell, M., & Siegel-Causey, E. (1990). Examining the individual family service plan process: What are family and practitioner preferences? *Topics in Early Childhood Special Education 10*(1), 78–99.

Thorp, E. K., & McCollum, J. A. (1988). Defining infancy specialization in early childhood special education. In J. Jordan, J. Gallagher, P. Hutinger, & M. Karnes (Eds.), *Early childhood special education: Birth to three* (pp. 147–60). Reston, VA: Council for Exceptional Children.

Thorp, E. K., & McCollum, J. A. (1994). Defining the infancy specialization in early childhood special education. In L. J. Johnson, R. J. Gallagher, M. J. Montagne, et al. (Eds.), *Meeting early intervention challenges: Issues from birth to three* (pp. 167–83). Baltimore, MD: Paul H. Brookes.

Turbiville, V., Turnbull, A., Garland, C., & Lee, I. (1996). Development and implementaion of IFSPs and IEPs: Opportunity for empowerment. In S. Odom & M. McLean (Eds.), *Early intervention/early childhood special education recommended practices* (pp. 77–100). Austin, TX: Pro-Ed.

Turnbull, A. (1987). *Accepting the challenge of providing comprehensive support to families*. Paper presented at Early Childhood Development Association of Washington annual conference, Seattle, WA.

Turnbull, A. P., & Turnbull, H. R. (1986). Stepping back from early intervention: An ethical perspective. *Journal of Division of Early Childhood, 10*(2), 106–17.

Turnbull, A., & Turnbull, H. (1996). *Families, professionals, and exceptionality: A special partnership*. Columbus, OH: Merrill.

Vygotsky, L. S. (1978). *Mind in society*. Cambridge, MA: Harvard University Press.

Warren, S. F. (1992). Facilitating basic vocabulary acquisition with milieu teaching procedures. *Journal of Early Intervention, 16*(3), 235–51.

Weatherston. D. (1998). She needed to talk and I needed to listen: An infant mental health intervention. *Zero to Three, 18*(3), 6–12.

Wesley, P. W., & Buysse, V. (1997). Community based approaches to personnel preparation. In P. Winton, J. McCollum, & C. Catlett (Eds.), *Reforming personnel preparation in early intervention: Issues, models, and practical strategies* (pp. 53–80). Baltimore, MD: Paul H. Brookes.

Weston, D. R., Ivins, B., Heffron, M. C., & Sweet, N. (1997). Formulating the centrality of relationships in early intervention: An organizational perspective. *Infants and Young Children, 9*(3), 1–12.

Widerstrom, A., & Ableman, D. (1996). Team training issues. In D. Bricker & A. Widerstrom (Eds.), *Preparing personnel to work with infants and young children and their families: A team approach* (pp. 23–42). Baltimore, MD: Paul H. Brookes.

Wikler, L., Wasow, M., & Hatfield, E. (1981). Chronic sorrow revisited: Attitude of parents and professionals about adjustment to mental retardation. *American Journal of Orthopsychiatry, 51*(1), 63–70.

Winton, P., McCollum, J., & Catlett, C. (Eds.). (1997). *Reforming personnel preparation in early intervention: Issues, models, and practical strategies*. Baltimore, MD: Paul H. Brookes.

Winton, P., & DiVenere, N. (1995). Family professional partnerships in early intervention personnel preparation: Guidelines and strategies. *Topics in Early Childhood Special Education, 15*, 296–313.

Winton, P. J. (1990) Promoting a normalizing approach to families: Integrating theory with practice. *Topics in Early Childhood Special Education, 10*(2), 90–103.

Winton, P. J. (1991). *Working with families in early intervention: Interdisciplinary perspectives*. Chapel Hill: University of North Carolina, Frank Porter Graham Child Development Center.

Winton, P. J. (1992). *Communicating with families in early intervention: A training module*. Chapel Hill: University of North Carolina at Chapel Hill, Frank Porter Graham Child Development Center.

Winton, P. J. (1996). A model for supporting higher education faculty in their early intervention personnel preparation roles. *Infants and Young Children, 8*(3), 56–67.

Wolery, M., Holcombe-Ligon, A., Brookfield, J., Huffman, K., Schroeder, C., Martin, C., Venn, M., Werts, M., & Fleming, S. (1993). The extent and nature of preschool mainstreaming: A survey of general early educators. *Journal of Special Education, 27*, 222–34.

Wolfe, B., & Snyder, P. (1997). Follow up strategies: Ensuring that instruction makes a difference. In P. Winton, J. McCollum, & C. Catlett (Eds.), *Reforming personnel preparation in early intervention: Issues, models, and practical strategies* (pp. 173–90). Baltimore, MD: Paul H. Brookes.

Yoder, D. E., Coleman, P. P., & Gallagher, J. J. (1990). *Personnel needs: Allied health personnel meeting the demands of Part H, P.L. 99-457*. Chapel Hill: University of North Carolina, Carolina Policies Study Program.

Zeitlin, S., & Williamson, G. G. (1990). Coping characteristics of disabled and non-disabled young children. *American Journal of Orthopsychiatry, 60*, 404–11.

Zeitlin, S., & Williamson, G. G. (1994). *Coping in young children: A model for early intervention*. Baltimore, MD: Paul H. Brookes.

PART SIX

MEASURING THE IMPACT OF SERVICE DELIVERY

An Expanded View of Program Evaluation in Early Childhood Intervention

PENNY HAUSER-CRAM, MARJI ERICKSON WARFIELD, CAROLE C. UPSHUR, AND THOMAS S. WEISNER

Beginning with the first quantitative evaluations of the Head Start program (e.g., Westinghouse Learning Corporation, 1969), there have been lively discussions about the usefulness and limitations of quantitative evaluations of early childhood programs. Questions have emerged about the types of outcomes and magnitude of change that can be expected from a wide range of interventions and the value of such outcomes to children, parents, schools, and the society as a whole (Center for the Future of Children, 1995; Farran, 1990; Hamburg, 1994). Conflicting views and beliefs about the efficacy of early childhood interventions have made it necessary to broaden evaluations so that they provide meaningful information to the necessary audiences.

This challenge to expand evaluation studies has emerged from fundamental questions about 1) the nature of developmental change, 2) the inviolability of the traditional scientific paradigm, and 3) the dichotomy between quantitative and qualitative methodologies. Simultaneously, evaluations have benefited from a growing sophistication about how systems operate within political contexts and how programs themselves evolve over time. In this

chapter, we explore each of these areas with a view toward expanding the scope of early childhood intervention program evaluations through the incorporation of multimethod approaches.

BELIEFS ABOUT DEVELOPMENTAL CHANGE

Program evaluators, similar to other researchers, are guided by their theoretical and metatheoretical perspectives and assumptions about the nature and process of developmental change (Lerner, Hauser-Cram, & Miller, 1998). Beliefs about key principles of development are likely to affect the perspective of the evaluation team and lead to decisions about the research design and methodology employed. In particular, evaluators' beliefs about four critical aspects of developmental functioning are likely to affect evaluation designs: 1) the extent to which mechanistic or constructivist theories adequately describe children's learning, 2) the degree to which the acquisition of cognitive processes is universal, 3) the extent to which plasticity occurs in developmental functioning, and 4) the degree to which development is embedded in a social and cultural context. We maintain that while seldom made explicit, these beliefs affect the way in which researchers conceptualize evaluations of early intervention (EI) and other early childhood programs.

Models of Learning

Different views of the process of children's learning have long existed in educational psychology. Mechanistic models tend to be elementalistic and

The preparation of this chapter was supported in part by Maternal and Child Health Bureau, Health Resources Administration, U.S. Health and Human Services Grant MCJ-250644. Thomas S. Weisner completed his portions of the chapter while at the Center for Advanced Study in the Behavioral Sciences and received financial support at the Center from the National Science Foundation Grant SBR-9022192 and the William T. Grant Foundation Grant 95167795. The authors express appreciation to Jennifer C. Greene, Richard M. Lerner, and George F. Madaus for their comments on a draft of this chapter.

emphasize quantitative accretion of skills (Lerner & Tubman, 1989). Such models are well represented, especially in special education settings (e.g., Snell, 1987), by behavioral approaches (e.g., stimulus, response, and reinforcement) proposed by Skinner (1953) and applied to child development by Bijou and Baer (1966). In contrast, constructivist models tend to be broad in scope and focus on changes in the way children think about and understand phenomena (Lerner & Tubman, 1989). Such models guide early childhood settings that center on developmentally appropriate practice (Bredekamp & Copple, 1997). These models have different implications for the types of outcomes evaluators may consider appropriate. For example, evaluators working from the mechanistic tradition may choose to focus on specific skill acquisition, such as children's ability to count a series of objects. In contrast, those operating from the constructivist viewpoint might choose outcomes that illustrate how children "make meaning" in their school environment, such as the type of social play in which children engage.

Universality of Development

A longstanding debate in developmental psychology focuses on questions of the universality of the development of cognitive processes. Much of this debate has centered around the notion of invariant stages of development proposed by Piaget (1952) and whether the proposed stages are acquired in all cultures (Dasen & Heron, 1981; Jahoda, 1980). From this perspective, the concept of universality is viewed as a question of whether a phenomenon, such as the acquisition of conservation of mass, occurs within all cultures.

A different but equally important view of universality involves our understanding of the development of children with disabilities (Hodapp & Burack, 1990). In this regard, there is considerable debate, first generated in the late 1960s, about whether the development of children with mental retardation is structurally different or delayed but organized similarly to that of other children (Cicchetti & Beeghly, 1990; Weisz, Yeates, & Zigler, 1982; Zigler, 1969). Evaluators operating from a perspective that children with disabilities, such as mental retardation, are developmentally delayed tend to focus on the selection of different outcome measures from those

who consider the development of such children to be qualitatively different from that of other children. For example, the former may select measures assessing the organization and structure of development, such as Piagetian-based measures of cognition (e.g., Cicchetti & Pogge-Hesse, 1982), whereas the latter may select measures that are seldom used to evaluate typically developing children, such as measures of perseveration (Sandson & Albert, 1984).

Plasticity of Developmental Function

Another central and long-term debate in psychology focuses on questions about the plasticity of development. Historically, this discussion has engendered investigations on both biological and behavioral indicators of change in developmental trajectory (Lerner, 1984). Studies on the capacity of the central nervous system to recover function after insult, damage, or complications associated with premature birth have indicated the extent to which the organism can modify or adapt behavior. For example, investigations of children's recovery of function after head injury have been optimistic, depending on the age of the child and the extent of the injury (Spreen, Risser, & Edgell, 1995). Furthermore, studies of children born prematurely indicate that those from middle-income families display signs of "catching up" developmentally with chronological age peers by around 2 years of age (e.g., Greenberg & Crnic, 1988). Evaluators who believe that early development is quite malleable might choose to focus on such aspects of development as social development, in which great variability has been shown to occur (Damon, 1983). In contrast, those who subscribe to a view of early development as resistant to outside influence might choose to focus on psychomotor skills, in which maturational functions appear to outweigh experiential effects during the early years of life (McCall, 1987).

Sociocultural Context

In addition to these three issues, a fourth has emerged, however, that has critical implications for evaluating intervention programs: the question of how extensively development (and developmental change) is embedded within a social and cultural context. Throughout the 1980s and 1990s, developmental psychologists increasingly recognized the importance of the multiple systems in which a child develops. Bronfenbrenner (1979), using an ecological perspective, maintained that development occurs within multiple contexts, from proximal interactions within the family to distal policies established by governmental agencies. Sameroff (1995) emphasized the interplay (i.e., transactions) among various forces in development in his description of the transactional model. Lerner (1991) advanced a bidirectional and transforming model, developmental contextualism, in which children both affect and are affected by the multiple and changing systems in which they develop.

One implication of the systems perspective of either Bronfenbrenner (1979) or Lerner (1991) is that any intervention program is just one of the many influences on children's development and may be best understood as expressing its effectiveness in interaction with other systems. Although some programs may have direct influences on children through individual services, they are more likely to have indirect effects on children through the microsystem of the family or the mesosystem of the family–program relationship (McCartney & Howley, 1991). From a systems perspective, viewing an intervention or early childhood program as the sole or most direct influence on development would be overly simplistic. Thus, researchers operating within a systems perspective would construct evaluation designs that incorporate the web of relations among various systems in which the child, family, and program operate. Weiss and Greene (1992) described several examples of program evaluations that reflect the complex relations among family support programs and the sociocultural milieu in which they are embedded. Understanding the effectiveness of such programs requires an understanding of the milieu, because change in one aspect of the system may involve changes in other aspects as well (Hetherington & Baltes, 1988). Guralnick (1997) has termed the refocusing of evaluation studies on this type of contextual understanding as *second generation* research.

In contrast, evaluators who view a program as having a discrete influence on children's development tend to approach evaluations from an experimental, rather than ecological, framework. Casto and White (1993) described a series of studies of EI undertaken to determine the effectiveness of specific program

components. For example, Boyce, White, and Kerr (1993) studied the effect of an additional component of service, parent meetings, on children and families across two sites. Although this program component was found to have no direct effect on child or family outcomes, its relation to the multiple systems in which children and families develop was not a critical feature of the investigation. Thus, although no main effect was evident, the possibility of contextual effects was not explored.

The value of understanding culture as an integral part of the context in which children are nurtured has achieved increasing importance in current views of development (Rogoff & Morelli, 1989). This emphasis in part reflects the growing variability in the families served by many early childhood programs. Increasing numbers of Latino and Asian populations, as well as social and economic changes in communities (e.g., single parenthood and chronic unemployment; Hanson & Carta, 1995), have resulted in evolving and multidimensional child-rearing patterns that need to be understood by those who want to provide services to young children and their families.

Several researchers have proposed an ecocultural framework for understanding how development occurs within the activity settings of everyday life (Super & Harkness, 1986; Tharp & Gallimore, 1988; Weisner, 1984, 1996b; Weisner, Gallimore, & Jordan, 1988). They have stressed the importance of understanding parents' goals and aspirations for their children and how these are revealed through the activities in which children and parents engage. For example, Reese, Balzano, Gallimore, and Goldenberg (1991) described the determination of low-income parents of Mexican American children to keep their child on the *buen camino* (good path) and described some of the ways in which parents directed children's activities to achieve this goal. Some investigators have found that ecocultural factors (such as maternal and paternal workload, integration into both disabled and nondisabled social networks, or parents' information seeking about services for children with disabilities) predict children's developmental status above and beyond more traditional measures of the home environment (Nihira, Weisner, & Bernheimer, 1994).

At a macrolevel, the sociocultural context specifies the values and beliefs about what is important and worthwhile. Institutions, such as the family, serve to organize behaviors around those values and beliefs (Gordon & Armour-Thomas, 1991). At a microlevel, the sociocultural context mediates the processes of teaching and learning through social interaction (Rogoff, 1990). Such interactions occur most frequently for young children within the family or neighborhood, although children in child care, early education, or early intervention programs also have these as additional settings in which teaching and learning occurs.

What are the implications for designing program evaluations if we view development from the perspective of the importance of the sociocultural context? First, evaluators need to consider the community in which the program is situated. This would mean understanding how a program is viewed within that culture (Nieto, 1992). Cultural views of the meaning of disabilities and the value attributed to such services as early intervention vary considerably (Lynch & Hanson, 1992). For example, families may regard services as a benefit, burden, or stigma. Next, the belief systems and values espoused by parents and other community members would be considered important. Sigel, Stinson, and Flaugher (1991) described how parents vary in their beliefs regarding how children learn and become socialized. Some parents believe that children learn best through direct instruction, whereas others believe that children learn best by figuring out solutions on their own. Such different beliefs have implications for how parents might work with service providers in structuring activities for children. Sociocultural discontinuities between children's home and school settings have been explored in the educational literature (e.g., Heath, 1982) and also require consideration by those evaluating any social program targeting children. Finally, evaluators need to consider the teaching–learning transactions that occur among children, parents, service providers, and other significant adults or siblings in the child's life.

Although evaluation of intervention programs has never been a simple task, evaluators who operate from a framework that incorporates the ecological and sociocultural systems that form the context of development take on an even more complex, yet in our view, necessary, task. They must attempt to understand the effect and meaning of a program within the cultural niches in which children and families live (Weisner, Matheson, & Bernheimer, 1996). Their selection of measures must be true to the program's goals as well as to an understanding of parental aspirations and community culture. What is studied and how it is studied needs to integrate a range of perspectives. The assumption of "mainstream" – largely White, middle-class – goals and aspirations for all children and families does not hold in all contexts.

In summary, as theoretical models of human development attempt to incorporate the cultural embeddedness of human lives, the task of program evaluation becomes increasingly complex. Evaluators need to examine their own assumptions about development – as well as the assumptions of those implementing an intervention, delivering services, and participating in a program – if they are to design evaluations that will produce valid and useful information.

The move toward more contextual models of development within the child development community raises critical questions about the fundamental nature of designing evaluations. If we believe that development and change are embedded in context, the standard models of evaluation appear inadequate. Fundamental to those models are assumptions about the nature of scientific inquiry.

BELIEFS ABOUT THE NATURE OF SCIENTIFIC INQUIRY

The majority of evaluations of early childhood programs use traditional models of scientific inquiry, including experimental, quasi-experimental, and correlational designs. Although valuable information has accrued on the effectiveness of early childhood intervention programs in general, the methods of scientific inquiry used to generate that information are increasingly questioned by the public and policy makers. There is a growing skepticism about the truth of science and a concomitant belief that the positivist paradigm (i.e., traditional experimental design) is inadequate to reflect current reality (Humphries & Truman, 1994; Lincoln, 1994; Meenaghan & Kilty, 1994). The debate about the usefulness of the scientific–experimental method has been rooted in the empowerment of undervalued groups (Fetterman, 1994); discussions about contextual metatheories (Overton, 1998); new discoveries in the physical sciences that call into question whether it is possible to conduct uncontaminated experiments (Meenaghan & Kilty, 1994; Shadish, 1995); and a recognition of value biases in all evaluation and research (Fischer, 1995; Lincoln & Guba, 1989).

The traditional primacy of the experimental paradigm, especially when entitlement to services has been established in most states or where ethical reasons dictate that services cannot be denied to eligible individuals, renders the conduct of evaluations of early childhood programs quite challenging. Random assignment to different treatment conditions for the purposes of experimental control is the basis of the scientific paradigm. Once held as sacrosanct, there is a growing movement within science to acknowledge the limitations of this feature of the traditional positivist paradigm.

A positivist framework for evaluation of early childhood intervention programs suggests that it is possible through scientific methods to determine definitively what works and does not work in intervention strategies, what effect sizes (standardized differences between intervention and nonintervention groups) are obtainable, and thus whether a program is worth continuing. This notion of objective truth, however, has been criticized by ongoing debates in the philosophy of science (Boyd, 1984; Dolby, 1979; Knorr-Cetina, 1984). What has come to be known as a postpositivist paradigm is now at the cutting edge of scientific discourse (Overton, 1998). The postpositivist paradigm acknowledges that science is not value free; that knowledge is socially constructed and constrained by history, culture, and time; and that there are multiple possible views of truth. In essence, the postpositivists argue that context and values are important in conducting and understanding scientific inquiry and are no less important in contributing to an understanding of the phenomenon under study (Fischer & Forester, 1987; Habermas, 1973).

Within the postpositivist framework, essential questions include for whom an evaluation is being conducted and for what purpose it is taking place. As Fischer (1995) pointed out, an intervention program can be evaluated at many different levels. At the first level, verification, the traditional scientific–technical paradigm, may be used to address the question of whether the program fulfills its stated objectives. For example, are the services

being delivered appropriately to the intended population and are proposed impacts being achieved? At the second level, validation, the question as to whether the objectives themselves are useful or valid is addressed. That is, do the specific objectives meet the identified need or problem? They may be fulfilled perfectly well but miss the mark in terms of what is most useful for the target population. A good example of this level of analysis comes from the debate about whether changing children's IQ scores or helping them be better prepared for the challenging tasks of the school environment is more important in promoting lasting school achievement among children with disabilities (Hauser-Cram & Shonkoff, 1995).

At the third level, one must examine the social vindication of the program. Does it have value for the participants, other stakeholders, and their collective community? Does it have value for the society as a whole? Does it promote commonly agreed upon values? In the case of early childhood education, strong arguments can be made in support of the broad and perhaps unmeasurable benefits gained by including children with disabilities in normative activities and by providing respite and support for parents, regardless of other measurable benefits. Is it enough that parents value the services and rate them positively (Upshur, 1991)?

Finally, programs can be viewed within a social choice framework, in terms of whether they support the broadly competing goals of equity, liberty, and community. To what extent does the program contribute to a vision of a civil society, and what precise vision is being supported? The debate here focuses on utilities and rights: whether, for example, disproportionate expenditures and services for children with disabilities compromise resources available for other children. Analysis at this level often engenders a theoretical debate but importantly links the mundane considerations of program documentation to considerations of the world view that certain interventions imply.

Fischer's (1995) framework suggests that there are many types of inquiry that are relevant to the evaluation of programs and policies. Several new models of evaluation practice have recently been proposed that address the concerns of the postpositivists, as well as acknowledge the fundamental values questions raised by Fischer's framework. Three examples are a constructivist paradigm of evaluation, an empowerment evaluation, and a participatory evaluation. Guba and Lincoln (1989) argued for a constructivist paradigm of evaluation. Their approach suggests that the role of an evaluator is to identify carefully the goals, needs, and issues of staff, managers, funders, policy makers, and recipients and to produce information for all of these groups with the goal of obtaining consensus and agreement on what is happening in the program. The constructivist paradigm has direct applicability in early childhood programming because the field has moved away from professionally centered to parent-centered models of service delivery (Dunst, Trivette, & Deal, 1988; Friedman, 1996). For example, parents' goals for their children and parental assessments of success in achieving those goals may be as important a component of evaluating programs as using standardized developmental assessments. Parents may rate a program as highly successful if it helps a distractible child increase his or her attention span, even though a standardized assessment might not show measurable progress. In summary, the constructivist model acknowledges that there are various perspectives on how well a program may be performing. Each perspective is a valid and important viewpoint that should be included in the evaluation.

Similar and related evaluation strategies to the framework proposed by Guba and Lincoln (1989) are those of empowerment evaluation (Fetterman, 1994; Fetterman, Kaftarian, & Wandersman, 1995; Weiss & Greene, 1992) and participatory evaluation (Cousins & Earl, 1992; Upshur & Baretto-Cortez, 1995). Empowerment models seek to involve recipients in conducting their own evaluations. The essential focus is to give voice to those who are intended to be changed by the intervention so that they can identify their needs and the ways in which the intervention is or is not meeting those needs. Criteria for success are generated by the recipients, not outside researchers. Empowerment models have been slow to come to the field of disabilities but have been central to the family support movement (Weiss & Greene, 1992). Philosophically, empowerment evaluation recognizes the inherent ability of recipients to help themselves and to shape programs and resources to meet their own needs. Fundamentally, empowerment evaluation discounts the deficit

model for children and families who utilize early childhood intervention services.

Participatory evaluation is related to empowerment evaluation and has explicit roots in the work of Paolo Freire (Fals-Borda & Rahman, 1991) and W. F. Whyte (1991). Participatory evaluation is grounded in the experience of staff and recipients of services and seeks to provide practical, formative, and useful information to improve program outcomes. Like empowerment evaluation, participatory evaluation also results in the empowerment of participants but seeks to derive activities not just from the evaluation experience but through the development of a critical consciousness that explicitly deals with the issues of power and knowledge through the implementation of the evaluation findings. Participatory evaluation, similar to empowerment evaluation, values the views of the recipients of services more than those of funders or outside policy makers.

These new evaluation paradigms represent a variety of approaches that seek to address the inherent limitations of the traditional experimental designs and their derivatives in program evaluation. Another essential feature of these new approaches, however, is a rethinking of the presumed distinctions between quantitative and qualitative methodologies.

BELIEFS ABOUT THE DISTINCTION BETWEEN QUALITATIVE AND QUANTITATIVE METHODS OF INQUIRY

In current discourse, quantitative and qualitative methodologies are considered paired opposites. Qualitative research, in its everyday academic folk model, is typically opposed to its presumed opposite – quantitative research. Naturalistic research is paired with its presumed opposite – experimental research. Contextual, cultural, or comparative research is contrasted with its assumed opposite – monocultural work (which is, impossibly, somehow culture-free). In contrast, we propose a more useful way of conceptualizing these methods, one that assumes complementarity (Weisner, 1996a, 1997).

Qualitative, or holistic, research can more usefully be contrasted with *particularistic*, or specifically focused, research. Qualitative refers to capturing more of the whole of a phenomenon, in context, including the meanings and interpretations of actors.

Particularistic methods select out for analytical reasons, or for reasons of time, money, design, and so forth, specific aspects of a phenomenon, intentionally assessed out of context, in order to better understand that particular aspect of them. Quantitative is not the opposite of qualitative but has to do with the level of measurement available or appropriate for a study. Quantitative levels of measurement (ordinal, interval, and ratio) could be more accurately and usefully contrasted with *nominal* or categorical levels of measurement. For example, a community might divide the seasons into dry and rainy, or summer, fall, winter, and spring, or recognize a single diety, or call dogs and cats and some goldfish pets. These are all cultural categories with meaning and significance that are not inherently ranked or scaled.

One epistemological approach that requires complementary methods is outlined by Shweder (1996), who proposed that a useful and powerful assumption to make about the world is that it consists of "quanta" and "qualia." Quanta are objects, events, and processes in the world minus the subjective; they are things that have power independent of our experience and awareness of them. Examples of quanta include demographic circumstances (e.g., fertility rates, and migration cycles), resource availability (e.g., climate and ecology), social processes (e.g., attachment and self and other appraisal), cognitive or mental abilities (e.g., memory processes and neurological maturation), historical and path-dependent conditions (the prior existence in a community of clans, economic classes and castes, and trading networks, for instance, which, although social conditions with meaning and significance, are also in part fixed features from the past, shaping inevitably the way things are done in the present). In contrast, qualia are things that can only be understood with or through the subjective, that is, by what they mean, signify, or imply to persons in a particular place; how they are experienced, remembered, and enacted. Quanta typically are studied by using procedures such as pointing, counting, measuring, sampling, and calculating; qualia typically are studied by using empathy, interpretation, thematization/emplotment, narration, contextualization, and exemplification. Quanta and qualia are useful analytic distinctions, but they are not pure. For example, demographic and resource conditions (such as population density, gross domestic product,

and wealth and income distributions) are structural constraints but are always understood through our interpretations of them and actions in response to them. Qualia are influenced by social regularities and lawful general conditions, even if those regularities and conditions are not directly known to or experienced by actors. For example, memory processes and the varying kinds of memory constrain what we can recall and how we recall events, even though we are not directly aware of these processes. Public health conditions (e.g., lower infection rate due to better sanitation) influence how we protect children and what we worry about regarding their health and safety, but we may not be consciously aware of the public health environment. Indeed, we may take much of this environment for granted as if it were "natural." Hence, complementary methods are needed to represent and understand a world filled with both quanta and qualia.

Exclusive use of quantitative measurement can inadvertently close off understanding of phenomena vital to evaluation even before a study gets underway. Hence, we believe that complementary quantitative and qualitative methods should be the default standard (i.e., what is normally and routinely expected) for the design of evaluations of early childhood programs.

Paradoxically, then, the design of meaningful *quantitative* evaluations of early childhood programs may require methods other than those conventionally viewed as the traditional quantitative measurement strategies (i.e., questionnaires, tests and assessments, surveys, observer ratings, precoded behavioral observations, and the like). Not that these quantitative measures are not useful in evaluation work; to the contrary, they are essential. However, quantitative methods alone are unlikely to be sufficient without complementary methods that are effective in understanding subjective experience, context, representation, meaning, and interpretation.

Although perspectivistic, participatory, and empowerment models may highlight the importance of subjective experience, the general point applies to all evaluation models to varying degrees. Perspectivist, participatory, and empowerment models for evaluation have a common theme: the views of certain stakeholders matter most. Stakeholders include all individuals and groups who are affected, either directly or indirectly, by the implementation and results of an evaluation (i.e., staff, managers, funders, policy makers, and recipients; Rossi & Freeman, 1993). The perspectivist, participatory, and empowerment models take most seriously the point of view of the participants in a program, compared to conventional evaluation designs and measures that have been motivated more often by the concerns of policy makers and funders. What do program participants experience? What cultural beliefs do staff and parents use regarding domains such as gender, ethnicity, or competence? What is the meaning and moral significance of program goals and personal involvement? How do different participants interpret the activities of a program? How reflexive and critical are staff and participants about aspects of the program? How ambivalent are they about some elements? These kinds of questions involve understanding at least three fundamental features of any social inquiry, including evaluations of early childhood interventions: 1) the subjective experiences of the participants in a program; 2) the local contexts in which these experiences occur; and 3) the representation of the program and experience in the form of cultural models and scripts (i.e., patterned shared schemas about why and how the world works) held in the mind of participants and others (D'Andrade & Strauss, 1992; Harkness & Super, 1996; Holland & Quinn, 1987).

Qualitative methods are holistic and include the qualia of events and experience. These can include any text, interview or interview transcript, vignette, or story or experience that is either told to a researcher or observed. Ethnographic methods are more comprehensive in topic as well as methods. Ethnographic methods include participant and nonparticipant observation, a variety of kinds of interviews (casual, informal, probing, structured, etc.), as well as the use of more formal methods such as network sampling, use of archival materials, and community analysis. An ethnographer attempts to capture the life of an individual, family, and community in context – to understand the social and cultural world surrounding the particular family or individuals or intervention program one is studying. Qualitative and ethnographic methods are especially useful in understanding these subjective experiences, contexts, and representations. Hence, it is no accident that qualitative and ethnographic methods are more

often associated with perspectivist and related evaluation models than are purely quantitative methods.

A similar point regarding these evaluation models holds for the use of naturalistic contexts for performing evaluations. Naturalistic studies, conducted in the everyday context of our lives, contrast with research that is in some way contrived by the researcher or others. Experimental work, which attempts to infer cause, is usefully contrasted with correlational studies, which attempt to discover coherence, relations, and patterns. Both qualitative and quantitative methods can include contrived, manipulated interventions that attempt to infer cause, and both include the analysis of patterns and relationships for which cause can perhaps be inferred but not directly.

Both quantitative and qualitative measures have a context. The most useful contrast is between studies in which there are context-examined procedures and those with little or no careful examination of the context in which the procedures were conducted. Questionnaires completed by a particular group have a context that is usually unexamined. It is rarely known in any depth what was going on in the mind of the informant or participant when he or she circled a number on a page or said yes to a predetermined question. Ethnographic studies have a visible context, usually much more carefully considered but much less contrived or controllable than other methods. All studies have an implicit comparative frame of reference of some sort – a meaning in a context relevant to some cultural place, whether for the purpose of cultural comparison or not. In this sense, all studies have an *ethnographic* component embedded in them, even if ethnography was not done or even considered by the researcher (Weisner, 1996a).

Complementarity has also been proposed by evaluators as one type of "mixed-methods" design. Caracelli and Greene (1997) described several types of mixed-method approaches to evaluation that attempt to integrate quantitative and qualitative methods to produce comprehensive evaluation plans. These styles include the following: triangulation, complementarity, development, initiation, and expansion (Greene, Caracelli, & Graham, 1989). Although only a few evaluations have been conducted using this framework (e.g., Mark, Feller, & Button, 1997), the concepts suggest useful new strategies that should be explored in future evaluations of early childhood programs.

Triangulation involves identifying how results from different methodologies converge to produce similar findings. For example, in-depth, open-ended interviews with parents may indicate that they find some of the physical tasks of caring for a child with a motor impairment the most taxing of all child care tasks, whereas a more standardized instrument of caretaking burden may also indicate greater levels of impact related to this domain of parenting.

Complementarity of methods, as defined by Greene et al. (1989), describes designs in which one method is used to enhance or clarify the results of another. For example, suppose results of a quantitative analysis indicated that participation in a parent support group was associated with decreases in stress for some parents and increases for others. Observations of parent support group sessions combined with focus groups conducted with samples of families who experienced different stress outcomes may elucidate that finding.

Development designs are constructed so that different methods are used sequentially. For example, suppose an evaluator was interested in conducting participant observations of a range of home visits conducted by early intervention professionals who serve children with a variety of disabilities and their families. Quantitative data previously gathered on various aspects of the home visit sessions, such as the length of the session, the type of service provided (e.g., primarily counseling to the parent or predominantly therapy to the child), and the number of family members involved in the visit, could be analyzed so that a representative sample of visits could be selected for observation.

A different approach to the use of mixed methods is constructed when the two different methods are used to discover contradictions and paradoxical findings that generate hypotheses to be tested in future evaluations. Termed *initiation designs* (Greene et al., 1989), these are intended to use one method to provoke questions of data collected with a different methodology. For example, suppose parents report in interviews that greater learning occurs for their child with home-based services, but analyses of data gathered by means of standardized performance measures indicate greater increases with center-based services. Several hypotheses could be generated from such a finding: parents might have greater opportunity to observe their child's learning during home visits, parents may themselves benefit from the interaction during home visits and believe that it is beneficial to the child as well, or both.

Finally, *expansion designs* (Greene et al., 1989) occur when either methodology is used to expand the breadth and depth of inquiry. As Caracelli and Greene (1993) pointed out, quantitative evaluations are usually the principal method for examining outcomes, whereas qualitative approaches examine processes. An evaluation could be expanded if both approaches were used for both types of examination. For example, quantitative analyses could elucidate the program components that parents and providers believe are most valuable for promoting peer interaction and interviews could probe why they consider these to be valuable. Furthermore, observational studies of peer interaction and content analyses of children's drawings might reveal the extent to which experience in child groups during early intervention relates to more successful peer interactions in preschool. Finally, analyses of "extreme cases" (e.g., children who are quite successful in making friends or who have great difficulty in peer relationships) could be selected for in-depth study, which will lend understanding to how children negotiate such relationships.

In summary, we take the scientific tradition seriously but include holistic, nominal, contextual, comparative, context-examined, subjectively rich data and conceptions in our notion of science. Such approaches provide knowledge essential to understanding children and the programs intended to assist them. Quantitative methods emphasize certain criteria for accuracy and believability, particularly reliability and validity. However, reliability and validity criteria can also be applied usefully to qualitative data as well (Bernard, 1988; Maxwell, 1992; Miles & Huberman, 1994). These are important for science but are not the only important standards for believability. Other criteria important to science are found in qualitative work but are often absent or weak in quantitative methods (Becker, 1996). These include breadth of coverage of a problem; depth of understanding across levels (including subjective experience), time, and multiple contexts; convergence of observation and interpretations across researchers and participants; veridicality or accuracy of data in context (i.e., how phenomena actually appear in real context and real time); and precision of observations. We contend that early childhood evaluations that are designed from the outset to meet as many of these criteria as possible will produce greater understanding and better, truer science.

THE VALUE OF UNDERSTANDING THE POLITICAL CONTEXT OF EVALUATIONS

The different assumptions about human development and approaches to scientific inquiry made by the various individuals and groups interested in social programs are critical ingredients in designing evaluations. After all, evaluations are conceived, designed, and conducted in response to a demand made by program stakeholders to make some judgment about a social program or service delivery strategy. Although stakeholders often request "unbiased" evaluations of programs, they bring subjective judgment to the evaluation process.

Stakeholders include four main groups of individuals and organizations: 1) sponsors of the program; 2) program managers and staff; 3) participants in the program; and 4) evaluators and other members of the research, policy, and academic community (Rossi & Freeman, 1993). Each of these groups has something different "at stake" in an evaluation, be it their financial resources, their reputation as effective providers, their desire for a particular service to continue to be accessible and responsive to their needs, and their career aspirations, to name only a few (Guba & Lincoln, 1981). Given that these stakeholder groups have a different relationship to the program being evaluated, they often have conflicting perspectives regarding what the objectives of an evaluation should be and how an evaluation should be conducted (Thomas & Palfrey, 1996). Therefore, the ultimate form and design of an evaluation are influenced by the political context in which it is developed (Weiss, 1975).

Stakeholders and Their Information Needs

The political dynamics surrounding an evaluation will differ depending on the origin of the demand for the evaluation, the types of stakeholders who become involved, and the nature and extent of individual stakeholder participation. The demand for an evaluation may come from a variety of different sources. Historically, evaluation practice developed in response to the needs of high-level policy makers for proof of a program's efficacy (i.e., Did it achieve its goals?) and efficiency (i.e., Did it achieve its goals at a given level of expenditure, Weiss & Greene, 1992). Over the past twenty years, however, evaluation practice has expanded to consider questions regarding program implementation and operation in addition to efficacy and efficiency and to use a greater variety of methodological approaches. This expansion has encouraged other stakeholders to demand evaluations that meet their specific information needs. To understand the political context of evaluations, we must describe the way in which each of the four stakeholder groups is affected by the program being evaluated, their information needs, and the extent to which they are able to influence the objectives of an evaluation.

SPONSORS OF THE PROGRAM. This group of stakeholders includes three distinct sets of individuals or organizations. First, policy makers and decision makers are government officials who not only decide whether to implement a program initially but also make determinations regarding how long the program will be in operation and when it should be expanded or cut back. Second, program sponsors are organizations such as private foundations that initially fund the program to be evaluated. Third, evaluation sponsors are organizations such as private foundations or the federal government that initiate and fund the evaluation. In some cases, the individuals and organizations in these groups may overlap. For example, the original Head Start program and its evaluation were funded by the federal government, but the evaluation was conducted by the Westinghouse Learning Corporation and Ohio University (Westinghouse Learning Corporation, 1969).

This group of stakeholders is often interested primarily in knowing whether the services that it is paying for are being provided to the target population, whether the services are having the desired effect, and whether the program is economically efficient. Their focus on these bottom-line concerns stems from the financial resources they have invested and the need to be accountable to the public, in the case of elected officials, or to board members of private organizations (Usher, 1995). These stakeholders can have a considerable amount of input in the design and structure of an evaluation by tying the receipt of future funds to certain performance standards or other evaluation requirements (Thomas & Palfrey, 1996).

PROGRAM MANAGERS AND STAFF. These stakeholders are responsible for both overall program operation and the actual delivery of services to the program's participants. Although both managers and staff may view evaluation as a way potentially to improve the services they provide, their specific information needs may differ because each is accountable primarily to a somewhat different audience (Chambers, Wedel, & Rodwell, 1992). Managers and administrators are accountable to program funders and must often focus on demonstrating positive outcomes that justify the program's expenditures and its allocation of staff and resources. In general, managers are interested in evaluations that enable them to compare the efficiency of alternative approaches to service delivery and monitor the operation of the program to ensure that particular models of service are being implemented and reaching those they are designed to serve (Usher, 1995).

Program staff are accountable not only to their supervisors but are also focused on how the intervention influences the participants both positively and negatively. These "street level bureaucrats" (Lipsky, 1980) are likely to be most interested in evaluations that concentrate on understanding whether services are acceptable to participants and relevant to their needs (Thomas & Palfrey, 1996).

Program managers and staff can influence the objectives of an evaluation in a variety of ways. As the individuals with the most knowledge about the day-to-day operation of the program as well as access to program records and other documentation, they possess information that is critical to the development of an evaluation plan. Therefore, these stakeholders provide needed input regarding those aspects of the program that can be studied and the types of questions that are most important to address. In addition, program staff hold beliefs about the principles of intervention, and such beliefs are

likely to affect the process of engagement with program participants. For example, in a study of utilization rates of early intervention services, Kochanek and Buka (1996) found that service providers had stronger beliefs about family-centered principles of service than did the mothers in their program. Finally, as gatekeepers of program information, staff cooperation is vital to any evaluation effort.

PROGRAM PARTICIPANTS. Although program participants may have the most at stake in an evaluation's outcome, they have often had little influence on the direction and nature of evaluations because they are typically not well organized as a group (Rossi & Freeman, 1993) and because traditional models of evaluation denied the importance of their voice. Most evaluations that have attempted to assess participants' concerns have focused simply on measuring client satisfaction (Thomas & Palfrey, 1996).

However, newer approaches to evaluation, as described earlier, have been designed to empower participants by involving them in the evaluation process (Greene, 1988). These evaluation approaches are particularly salient for early intervention services provided under the Individuals with Disabilities Education Act (IDEA) Amendments of 1990, 1991, and 1997 (P.L. 101-476, P.L. 102-119, and P.L. 105-17, respectively) and family support services in general because these programs emphasize participant empowerment and parent–professional collaboration as a central goal (Weissbourd & Kagan, 1989).

EVALUATORS AND THE RESEARCH AND POLICY COMMUNITY. This group of stakeholders includes the evaluator(s) responsible for the design and conduct of a particular evaluation as well as other individuals and organizations concerned with public policy, social science research, and program development. As discussed in prior sections, the assumptions of evaluators about the nature of developmental change, modes, and methods of inquiry, as well as their experience and skills, influence the scope and shape of any individual evaluation plan.

In summary, just as programs operate within sociocultural contexts, evaluations themselves reflect the political context in which they are developed and conducted. The main objective of an evaluation will be influenced by the degree to which individuals within the various stakeholder groups advocate successfully for a study that meets their particular information needs. Evaluations may be undertaken to address questions of accountability, gather information for program improvement, develop and test model programs, gain a better understanding of how programs and services influence the behavior and development of children and families, or empower participants.

THE VALUE OF UNDERSTANDING THE EVOLUTION OF A PROGRAM

Programs vary not only in terms of the sociocultural and political contexts in which they operate but also in terms of their evolution. The fact that not every program categorized with a particular label (e.g., family support program and early intervention program) is the same in its organization, operation, level of resources, and population served suggests that evaluations must be tailored according to the characteristics of individual programs.

Weiss (1988) captured the vast differences in programs labeled as *family support programs* by distinguishing the few "flagship" programs from others in the larger "fleet." Flagship programs are those that have been set up as well-funded research and demonstration models whose purpose is to test the efficacy of specific service delivery strategies. In contrast, the fleet is made up of smaller community-based programs with uncertain funding that provide a variety of often innovative services in an attempt to meet the diverse needs of local families.

Although many early childhood programs may lie somewhere on the continuum between the flagship and the fleet, this metaphor emphasizes the importance of designing evaluations that take into consideration each program's unique characteristics such as how long it has been in operation, how clearly its goals and services are defined, and its data collection capabilities (Jacobs, 1988). This information is critical in determining whether a program is ready to be evaluated.

Evaluability Assessment

One systematic way to examine evaluation readiness is through evaluability assessment. Evaluability assessment involves gathering information in three areas: 1) purpose, 2) program, and 3) technical feasibility (Chambers et al., 1992).

ASSESSMENT OF PURPOSE. The rationale for a program evaluation emanates from the information needs of different stakeholder groups. Conflicts among these groups, however, may arise. For example, Usher (1993) described a program in which the evaluability assessment found that the delivery of services was inconsistent. Therefore, although state and local policy makers had wanted to conduct an evaluation to assess program effectiveness, discussions with program managers resulted in a decision to postpone that type of outcome study in favor of designing a more precise model of service, developing a database to track implementation information, and assessing the targeting and delivery of services. Ideally, the purpose of an evaluation is determined by this type of negotiation between groups of stakeholders (Chen, 1989). The other two areas of evaluability assessment (i.e., program and technical feasibility assessment) can inform this negotiation process and help to resolve conflict regarding the objective of an evaluation.

PROGRAM ASSESSMENT. The purpose of program assessment is to identify how well program components are defined, how clearly program goals are specified, and whether there is a discrepancy between how the program was conceived and designed and how it actually operates in the field. This phase of an evaluability study provides the "situation-specific knowledge" and qualitative judgments that are important in determining the type of evaluation to conduct (Campbell, 1987, p. 349). Four iterative steps are used to gather data that allow for a complete program assessment. First, all written documentation (e.g., authorizing legislation, grant proposals, brochures, and so forth) about the program must be reviewed. These documents will identify broadly the mandate for the program and its mission and goals.

Second, a more detailed program description must be developed by interviewing policy makers as well as program managers and administrators. Key questions focus on understanding the informant's views of the short- and long-term objectives of the program, what mechanisms are in place to make it possible to achieve these goals, why the program's inputs and activities will cause the goals to be achieved, what kinds of information are available, and what different types of information are unavailable but necessary to assess the program's performance.

Third, a flow model can be constructed to depict visually how each component of a program and the program as a whole are thought to work based on data gathered from documents and interviews. This model, which serves as a program's "theory of change," should spell out in great detail the assumptions that link each aspect of the program in order to chart how and why the intervention will produce the expected effects (Weiss, 1995). Fourth, the accuracy of the flow model should be tested by visiting the program, observing it in operation, interviewing staff responsible for its day-to-day operation, and interviewing program participants.

The program assessment phase should generate a clear definition of the program to be evaluated and an explication of the theory or theories behind the program. Although defining the program may be obvious in some cases, it is important to identify clearly the boundaries around what will and will not be evaluated. For example, EI programs often provide a variety of different services. It is important to establish whether the evaluation will focus on one component (e.g., home visits) or on all services that the program provides to children and families directly. Furthermore, EI programs under P.L. 102-119 are mandated to coordinate services with other local providers so that the full range of needs demonstrated by eligible children and families can be met. Whether the evaluation will focus on all of the services (both inside and outside of EI) that are received by a selected sample of children and families, or on only those services provided directly to the children and families by one program, has important implications for who the stakeholders are, what contextual features of the service system should be assessed, and how the evaluation results should be interpreted.

The flow model developed during the program assessment stage should underscore the theories on which the program is based. Evaluations grounded in a theoretical framework are more likely to provide important information for program improvement (Chen & Rossi, 1989). Improvement may occur in

two ways. First, by asking policy makers, administrators, service providers, and participants to make explicit what their assumptions are regarding how the program is expected to produce the desired changes, conflicting perspectives can be revealed. Discussions to resolve these conflicts can highlight whether they result in a lack of consistency in the delivery of services and what changes should be made (Weiss, 1995). Second, by designing the evaluation to examine the extent to which the different assumptions hold, the results can identify which specific aspects of the program should be modified (Weiss, 1995).

TECHNICAL FEASIBILITY ASSESSMENT. Four main technical feasibility issues must be examined. First, the availability of information that can be used in an evaluation must be assessed. It is critical to determine the type of data the program currently collects, the accuracy and completeness of those data, how long the data have been collected, on whom the data are recorded, and how relevant the data are to the evaluation questions being asked. Second, the feasibility of using different research designs and methodologies must be assessed in light of a variety of issues such as intrusion into program processes, burden on staff and participants, sampling procedures, and the integrity of control or comparison groups.

Third, the technical expertise and computer facilities required to analyze the data that will be gathered must be assessed. Finally, the resources necessary to conduct the program evaluation must be estimated. The cost of evaluation is influenced heavily by the amount of original data that must be gathered to supplement information already maintained by the program, the scope of the evaluation plan, and the technology required to conduct the study.

In summary, evaluability assessment is a useful technique for gaining a clear understanding of the goals of a program, how its day-to-day activities are organized to reach its goals, and the extent to which the program documents its activities in a systematic way. This information serves to identify unique aspects of a particular program so that an appropriate and useful evaluation can be designed and conducted. Evaluators using this approach recognize that programs are not static but change over time and that an evaluation of a program during its maturity should differ from one conducted during its early phases.

WHAT HAVE WE LEARNED FROM EVALUATIONS?

While we contend that it is desirable for evaluations developed within a variety of political contexts to broaden their scope beyond traditional views based on positivism and the aura of numbers and to construct meaningful ways to recognize how change is embedded within a sociocultural context, we also recognize that no single evaluation, either currently or in the future, will be able to incorporate all of the ideal features we have delineated. In this section, we present a few examples of evaluations that, while largely quantitative, have used a range of methodologies and yielded valuable findings. These illustrations demonstrate how a broad array of strategies can be used to address similar questions in the following four topic areas: 1) the entrance of participants into a program, 2) the operation of a program, 3) program effectiveness, and 4) program cost and efficiency. We also identify newer techniques and approaches that can supplement and enhance the findings generated by future evaluations.

Entrance of Participants Into a Program

One critical question that concerns program staff is whether the target population is being reached. Individuals are considered to be underserved if they are eligible for services but do not enter the system or use services to the full extent of their eligibility (Arcia, Keyes, Gallagher, & Herrick, 1993). Because it can be difficult to estimate precisely the size of the target population and therefore compare who does and does not participate, studies have employed different strategies to get an estimate of those who are likely to be underserved.

Sontag and Schacht (1993) analyzed questionnaires on service utilization completed by 536 families enrolled in early intervention programs. They investigated differences in the type of services received based on ethnicity, income, and the age of the child and found barriers to early intervention service utilization for ethnic minorities, low-income families, and children under 18 months of age. These markers for underutilization are important because

Arcia et al. (1993) found that the percentage of children under 5 years of age from ethnically diverse backgrounds and the percentage of young children from low-income families are increasing. Furthermore, many families are experiencing increasing and persistent risk conditions (Dunst & Trivette, 1997). This suggests that a portion of the target population is both increasing in size and is at risk for underutilization of early intervention services.

One way to understand how to improve recruitment of families at risk of being underserved is to use a perspectivist model to identify those aspects of service provision that attract individuals to a program. For example, Pharis and Levin (1991) interviewed thirty mothers who were at high risk for difficulties in parenting about their participation in the Clinical Infant Development Program (CIDP). Using open-ended questions, researchers asked the mothers to describe how the program worked for them and what it meant to them. Using content analysis to categorize the responses, Pharis and Levin found that the mothers especially liked program components that gave them opportunities to talk to their primary clinician and to view infant assessment sessions. In general, participants preferred the relationship aspect of the services more than the concrete assistance that they received around transportation, housing, and money management.

Future evaluations that are designed to understand how programs can increase participation among all members of their target population might benefit from involving a greater variety of stakeholders (e.g., current participants and local community leaders) in developing, implementing, and assessing various outreach strategies. These strategies might use different methods to advertise the components of a program that participants view most favorably. This type of evaluation may also elucidate what successful participation means to those whom the program is trying to reach (McNaughton, 1994).

Program Operation

Evaluations of how programs for young children and their families operate can focus on a variety of important issues. The Early Intervention Collaborative Study (EICS) is a longitudinal investigation of the development of children with disabilities and the adaptation of their families (Shonkoff,

Hauser-Cram, Krauss, & Upshur, 1992). A sample of 190 children and families was followed during their first year in early intervention programs in Massachusetts and New Hampshire, and the type and amount of services they received each month were documented.

Analyses of the services received by the EICS sample revealed that the total amount of services received per month averaged a modest seven hours. Although children and families received, on average, three hours of home visits per month, they received less than two hours per month of each of the other service types (e.g., child group, parent support group, and center-based individual services). There was, however, a tremendous amount of variability in the amount and types of services received. For example, the average quantity received per month ranged from a few minutes to twenty-one hours. The child's type of disability and level of severity of impairment contributed to the observed variability in the intensity of services received. In addition, the analysis of variation in service types revealed substantial differences in both the intensity and the combinations of services received by a given child and family on a month-to-month basis over the course of the one-year study period (Erickson, 1991).

The modest level of services received and the variability in service provision offer important insights for other evaluations of early intervention that focus on estimating service impact. Although individualization of services is one of the hallmarks of early intervention programs, it strains traditional approaches to evaluation (Powell, 1988). Questions about the type of effects that can be expected from this level of intervention for children with different characteristics as well as queries about the types and amounts of services received outside of early intervention are important to consider in light of these findings (Guralnick, 1993).

Evaluations of program operation can also focus on observing how participants react to different features of an intervention in order to identify whether the model is working as designed. Brinker (1992) described an experimental program in which public aid–supported families were randomly assigned to either an intervention group that received tangible incentives when they attended the program (e.g., individualized help with housing, food, baby formula, baby clothes, and so forth) or a comparison

group that received no tangible incentives. Preliminary results indicated that there was no difference in the rate of attendance between the incentive families and the comparison participants as families in both groups attended approximately 40% to 50% of the weekly sessions. Because incentives appeared to have no effect, staff attempted to make the program more receptive to participants' needs. For example, the program staffing was expanded to include community leaders and individuals with experience conducting self-help programs for families on public aid. Expanding the intervention team increased staff knowledge about the infrastructure of resources within the community and ways in which families could stretch their limited resources. These changes resulted in greater success in establishing relationships with families and in increasing the rate of participation in the program. This approach to evaluation contains some elements of the development style of a mixed-method design in that the lack of positive results from the experimental phase motivated the staff to better understand participants' needs through outreach into the community. The knowledge gained was then put to use in the next round of implementation and evaluation.

Another important aspect of program operation that evaluations can examine concerns the factors that influence how service providers interact with families. DeGangi, Wietlisbach, Poisson, Stein, and Royeen (1994) interviewed twenty-six early intervention professionals to assess their perceptions of the effects of cultural diversity and socioeconomic status (SES) on family–professional collaboration. The interview included both closed and open-ended questions as well as two case vignettes. DeGangi et al. found that service providers responded differently to families whose cultural background varied from their own and that families from lower, in comparison to higher, income groups differed in their response to providers. These insights indicate further how varied each family's experience is in early intervention.

These three studies underscore the complexities of measuring the actual treatment received by children and families. Beyond counting the number and types of services received, treatments between individuals vary in more subtle ways, depending on the training, attitudes, and goals of the provider(s); the evolving needs of the child and family; and the interactions among the system and its providers, the community, and the family and child (Telzrow, 1993). If the evaluation is meant ultimately to elucidate the way services affect the multiple systems in which children and families develop, careful attention to the content of actual sessions with children and families will be needed.

Empowerment models of evaluation that focus on understanding the participants' point of view about how different interventions affect them and influence their behavior may help evaluations to identify specific aspects of the treatment that need to be measured in future studies. Such models are also critical in bringing together the assets needed to sustain an effective and valued program.

Program Effectiveness

Other chapters in this volume (see Farran, Brooks-Gunn, Berlin, & Fuligni) provide extensive reviews of studies assessing the impact of services on both child and family outcomes. This section, therefore, focuses briefly on the following three questions that are central to assessing program effectiveness: 1) In what domains will the program have an effect? 2) How will the outcomes be measured? and 3) How will change be measured?

IN WHAT DOMAINS WILL THE PROGRAM HAVE AN EFFECT? The ecological model of human development suggests that programs may influence child, family, and community-level outcomes (Bronfenbrenner, 1979; Bronfenbrenner & Morris, 1998). Until recently, evaluations of programs for young children and their families concentrated on child outcomes (Shonkoff & Hauser-Cram, 1987), although studies have begun to focus on family-level effects as well (e.g., Shonkoff et al., 1992; Trivette, Dunst, Boyd, & Hamby, 1995). Flow models that underscore the theories on which a particular program is operating should be developed and consulted in the process of identifying areas in which effects may be expected (LeLaurin & Wolery, 1992).

HOW WILL THE OUTCOMES BE MEASURED? Once the areas of potential program effect have been identified, decisions must be made regarding the appropriate instruments and techniques to use to measure each outcome. The strengths and weaknesses of different assessment strategies that may be used with infants, parents, families, and communities are described in detail in other chapters in this volume (see Meisels & Atkins-Burnett; Kelly & Barnard; Krauss; and Earls & Buka). Evaluations may further benefit from current interest in early education on authentic assessment methods, which use children's typical work and activities as a way of recognizing change. Schwartz and Olswang (1996) proposed that early childhood special education programs consider developing portfolios of children's activities, including documents such as videotapes of children's play, observational data collected on children's peer interactions using time-sampling techniques, parent reports, and teachers' notes. Meisels's (1993) Work Sampling System offers a comprehensive approach to authentic assessment for children in early childhood and primary classrooms. Although not yet well used in program evaluations, such approaches offer promise to those who demand that outcomes of evaluation efforts have meaning for the program participants.

HOW WILL CHANGE BE MEASURED? Accurately quantifying the amount of change in an outcome measure over time and being able to attribute some portion of the total change to a particular intervention or treatment have always been a challenge for evaluators of early childhood programs. A variety of approaches to measuring change and then partitioning it into its various components have been proposed and applied. These methods include norm-referenced models, indices of change, difference scores, and residual change scores. The strengths and weaknesses of these approaches have been discussed elsewhere (Hauser-Cram, 1990; Hauser-Cram & Krauss, 1991).

A relatively new and useful approach to understanding change that is increasingly being applied to longitudinal studies is hierarchical linear modeling (HLM). Bryk and Raudenbush (1992) have contended that to really understand change, data must be collected over more than two time points (see also Baltes, Reese, & Nesselroade, 1977). HLM makes maximum use of data gathered over several time points and utilizes a two-step process. First, an estimate is made of the growth trajectory and overall rate of growth for each individual in the sample being analyzed. Second, differences in these growth rates across individuals are assessed. This analysis involves examining whether differences in change are a function of selected characteristics of the child (such as gender and type of disability), the family (such as income), or services (such as intensity).

The advantage of HLM applied to the evaluation of early intervention services is that it allows ways of testing whether development occurs in a linear or curvilinear fashion. This is in contrast to other approaches that assume a linear model. Moreover, HLM allows researchers to test whether development approaches an asymptote (i.e., levels off) at a certain point, and if so, whether this occurs for certain subgroups and not others (Burchinal, Bailey, & Snyder, 1994).

Dunst and Trivette (1994) used HLM to examine the predictors of growth in mental age for children with chromosomal abnormalities (mostly children with Down syndrome) and physical impairments (mostly children with cerebral palsy), the majority of whom were receiving EI services. Mental age was measured using the Bayley Scales of Infant Development and the Stanford–Binet Intelligence Scale. Data were gathered on the subjects between birth and 48 months of age. Each child was assessed using the Bayley or Stanford–Binet between four and five times during this period.

Three sets of variables were included in the model as predictors of growth in mental age: 1) background variables, including mothers' education, marital status, occupation, race, and number of siblings; 2) stressor-related variables, including the number of family members or relatives with mental health problems and the number of child hospitalizations; and 3) intervention variables, including age of entry into EI and length of intervention. Controlling for both the background and stressor-related variables, age of entry was a significant predictor of growth in mental age for children with chromosomal abnormalities but not for children with physical impairments. Children with chromosomal abnormalities who entered EI at younger ages demonstrated a faster rate of progress than children who entered EI at older ages.

Future evaluations of early childhood programs may also benefit from utilizing another feature of HLM: assessing accurately the influence on

development of specific characteristics of a child's environment. For example, Lee and Bryk (1989) employed HLM to examine whether differences in school outcomes for children in different classrooms or school systems may be accounted for by variations in specific features of those environments.

Program Cost and Efficiency

Most cost and benefit-cost analyses of early childhood programs have employed traditional experimental or quasi-experimental research designs in which children and families are assigned, using various methods, to intervention, control, or comparison groups and are provided a predetermined and unchanging package of services for a set period of time (Barnett & Escobar, 1990). Economic evaluations of services provided by programs operating with limited resources under federal or state legislative rules and regulations, however, face unique analytic challenges. The inability to standardize service delivery and maintain a control or comparison group requires that these evaluations address somewhat different but important questions. The purpose of this section is to describe the three objectives of a cost-effectiveness study that was conducted in conjunction with the Early Intervention Collaborative Study (EICS; Shonkoff et al., 1992). As noted earlier, EICS examined the services provided by publicly supported EI programs. Each child and family received services that were tailored to meet their particular needs and be responsive to their changing circumstances.

The first objective of the cost-effectiveness study was to identify the predictors of service cost (Erickson, 1992). Most cost studies focus simply on determining the average cost per client in a particular program or state. In a system in which services are provided in accordance with individualized needs, however, this approach can mask the potentially large differences in the cost required to serve children and families who vary on a wide range of characteristics.

Erickson (1992) developed models using actual service utilization data to identify the child and family characteristics that significantly influence service cost. The findings indicated that differences in the age at which a child enters an EI program and variation in the severity of a child's disability significantly influence cost. The estimates produced for subgroups of children who differed on these two characteristics revealed a considerable amount of variability in the expenditures associated with providing one year of EI services.

The second objective was to compare the gains made by children across the various outcome measures to a set level of resources (Warfield, 1994). By holding the resource level constant, the estimated gains made by children with different characteristics were compared to identify the domains in which the greatest amount of change had occurred. The findings indicated that children classified as having mild disabilities experienced greater improvement in adaptive behavior, whereas children with more severe disabilities made greater gains in child–mother interaction. These results underscore the ways in which children with different characteristics move toward different goals relative to a common investment of resources. This information will help service providers and family members set priorities as to the relative importance of achieving certain outcomes.

The third objective was to compare the efficiency of home-visiting versus center-based group services for subgroups defined by severity of disability and age at entry (Warfield, 1995). The service identified as most cost-effective varied by subgroup and outcome measure. For example, home visits were more cost-effective in reducing parenting stress across all of the subgroups. In terms of improvements in mother–child interaction, however, group services were more cost-effective for children entering EI at less than 1 year of age, whereas home visits were more cost-effective for children entering after 1 year of age.

Therefore, the results associated with the three objectives of the EICS cost-effectiveness study indicate that critical questions about cost and efficiency can be addressed by disaggregating findings across subgroups that differ by selected child and family characteristics. Future studies conducted on more diverse samples utilizing a broader array of outcome measures will enhance the usefulness of this technique.

THE FUTURE OF EVALUATION RESEARCH

Our knowledge of evaluation results and our approach to evaluation design have grown immensely since the days of the first Head Start studies. We have developed methods to model growth over time and to test the effects of critical predictors of development. We have learned to recognize the various audiences who attend to evaluation results and appreciate the political context in which evaluations occur. We have realized that programs themselves change and that evaluations need to fit with their stage of evolution. We have also come to question the limits of positivism, the foundation upon which quantitative evaluations have been built. We are on the threshold of change in evaluation approaches.

The challenge now is to find ways to incorporate these lessons successfully and consistently into evaluation plans. Meeting this challenge will require that new partnerships be forged among those who have different beliefs about developmental change, those who have different information needs, and those who champion different methods of scientific inquiry. Evaluations that involve a variety of stakeholders and take advantage of the vast array of methodologies will best be able to generate necessary and meaningful information about early childhood intervention programs in the future.

REFERENCES

Arcia, E., Keyes, L., Gallagher, J. J., & Herrick, H. (1993). National portrait of sociodemographic factors associated with underutilization of services: Relevance to early intervention. *Journal of Early Intervention, 17*, 283–97.

Baltes, P. B., Reese, H. W., & Nesselroade, J. R. (1977). *Life-span developmental psychology: Introduction to research methods.* Monterey, CA: Brooks/Cole.

Barnett, W. S., & Escobar, C. M. (1990). Economic costs and benefits of early intervention. In S. J. Meisels & J. P. Shonkoff (Eds.), *Handbook of early childhood intervention* (pp. 560–82). New York: Cambridge University Press.

Becker, H. S. (1996). The epistemology of qualitative research. In R. Jessor, A. Colby, & R. Shweder (Eds.), *Ethnography and human development: Context and meaning in social inquiry* (pp. 53–71). Chicago: University of Chicago Press.

Bernard, R. H. (1988). *Research methods in cultural anthropology.* Newbury Park, CA: Sage.

Bijou, S. W., & Baer, D. M. (1966). *Child development. Vol 2: The universal stage of infancy.* New York: Appleton-Century-Crofts.

Boyce, G. C., White, K. R., & Kerr, B. (1993). The effectiveness of adding a parent involvement component to an existing center-based program for children with disabilities and their families. *Early Education and Development, 4,* 327–45.

Boyd, R. N. (1984). The current status of scientific realism. In J. Leplin (Ed.), *Scientific realism* (pp. 41–82). Berkeley, CA: University of California Press.

Bredekamp, S., & Copple, C. (1997). *Developmentally appropriate practice in early childhood programs.* Washington, DC: National Association for the Education of Young Children.

Brinker, R. P. (1992). Family involvement in early intervention: Accepting the unchangeable, changing the changeable, and knowing the difference. *Topics in Early Childhood Special Education, 12,* 307–32.

Bronfenbrenner, U. (1979). *The ecology of human development: Experiments by nature and design.* Cambridge, MA: Harvard University Press.

Bronfenbrenner, U., & Morris, P. A. (1998). The ecology of developmental processes. In R. M. Lerner (Ed.), *Theoretical models of human development: The handbook of child psychology* (*Vol. I,* 5th ed., pp. 993–1028). New York: Wiley.

Bryk, A. S., & Raudenbush, S. W. (1992). *Hierarchical linear models for social and behavioral research: Applications and data analysis methods.* Newbury Park, CA: Sage.

Burchinal, M. R., Bailey, D. B., & Snyder, P. (1994). Using growth curve analysis to evaluate child change in longitudinal investigations. *Journal of Early Intervention, 18,* 403–23.

Campbell, D. T. (1987). Problems for the experimenting society in the interface between evaluation and service providers. In S. L. Kagan, D. R. Powell, B. Weissbourd, & E. F. Zigler (Eds.), *America's family support programs: Perspectives and prospects* (pp. 345–51). New Haven, CT: Yale University Press.

Caracelli, V. J., & Greene, J. C. (1993). Data analysis strategies for mixed-method evaluation designs. *Educational Evaluation and Policy Analysis, 15,* 195–207.

Caracelli, V. J., & Greene, J. C. (1997). Crafting mixed-method evaluation designs. In J. C. Greene & V. J. Caracelli (Eds.), *Advances in mixed-method evaluation: The challenges and benefits of integrating diverse paradigms* (pp. 19–32). San Francisco: Jossey-Bass.

Casto, G., & White, K. R. (1993). Longitudinal studies of alternative types of early intervention: Rationale and design. *Early Education and Development, 4,* 224–37.

Center for the Future of Children. (1995). *The future of children: Long-term outcomes of early childhood programs.* Los Altos, CA: David and Lucile Packard Foundation.

Chambers, D. E., Wedel, K. R., & Rodwell, M. K. (1992). *Evaluating social programs.* Boston: Allyn & Bacon.

Chen, H. T. (1989). The conceptual framework of the theory-driven perspective. *Evaluation and Program Planning, 12,* 391–6.

Chen, H. T., & Rossi, P. H. (1989). Issues in the theory-driven perspective. *Evaluation and Program Planning, 12,* 299–306.

Cicchetti, D., & Beeghly, M. (1990). An organizational approach to the study of Down syndrome: Contributions to an integrative theory of development. In D. Cicchetti & M. Beeghly (Eds.), *Children with Down syndrome: A developmental perspective* (pp. 29–62). Cambridge, England: Cambridge University Press.

Cicchetti, D., & Pogge-Hesse, P. (1982). Possible contributions of the study of organically retarded persons to developmental theory. In E. Zigler & D. Balla (Eds.), *Mental retardation: The developmental-difference controversy* (pp. 277–318). Hillsdale, NJ: Erlbaum.

Cousins, J. B., & Earl, L. M. (1992). The case for participatory evaluation. *Educational Evaluation and Policy Analysis, 14,* 397–418.

Damon, W. (1983). *Social and personality development: Infancy through adolescence.* Cambridge, England: Cambridge University Press.

D'Andrade, R., & Strauss, C. (Eds.). (1992). *Human motives and cultural models.* New York: Cambridge University Press.

Dasen, P. R., & Heron, A. (1981). Cross-cultural tests of Piaget's theory. In H. Triandis & A. Heron (Eds.), *Handbook of cross cultural psychology: Vol. 4. Developmental psychology* (pp. 295–341). Boston: Allyn & Bacon.

DeGangi, G. A., Wietlisbach, S., Poisson, S., Stein, E., & Royeen, C. (1994). The impact of culture and socioeconomic status on family–professional collaboration: Challenges and solutions. *Topics in Early Childhood Special Education, 14,* 503–20.

Dolby, R. G. A. (1979). Reflections on deviant science. In R. Wallis (Ed.), *On the margins of science: The social construction of rejected knowledge.* Sociological Review Monograph 27 (pp. 9–47). Keele, Staffordshire, England: University of Keele.

Dunst, C. J., & Trivette, C. M. (1997). Early intervention with young children and their families. In R. Ammerman and M. Hersen (Eds.), *Handbook for the prevention and treatment of children and adolescents: Intervention in real world context* (pp. 157–80). New York: Wiley.

Dunst, C. J., & Trivette, C. M. (1994). Methodological considerations and strategies for studying the long-term effects of early intervention. In S. L. Friedman and H. C. Haywood (Eds.), *Developmental follow-up: Concepts, domains, and methods* (pp. 277–313). San Diego, CA: Academic Press.

Dunst, C. J., Trivette, C. M., & Deal, A. (1988). *Enabling and empowering families.* Cambridge, MA: Brookline Books.

Erickson, M. (1991). *Evaluating early intervention services: A cost-effectiveness analysis.* Unpublished doctoral dissertation, Brandeis University, Waltham, MA.

Erickson, M. (1992). An analysis of early intervention expenditures in Massachusetts. *American Journal on Mental Retardation, 96,* 716–29.

Fals-Borda, O., & Rahman, M. A. (Eds.). (1991). *Action and knowledge: Breaking the monopoly with participatory action research.* New York: Apex Press.

Farran, D. C. (1990). Effects of intervention with disadvantaged and disabled children: A decade review. In S. J. Meisels & J. P. Shonkoff (Eds.), *Handbook of early childhood intervention* (pp. 501–39). New York: Cambridge University Press.

Fetterman, D. M. (1994). Empowerment evaluation. *Evaluation Practice, 15,* 1–15.

Fetterman, D. M., Kaftarian, S. J., & Wandersman, A. (Eds.). (1995). *Empowerment evaluation: Knowledge and tools for self-assessment and accountability.* Thousand Oaks, CA: Sage.

Fischer, F. (1995). *Evaluating public policy.* Chicago: Nelson-Hall.

Fischer, F., & Forester, F. (Eds.). (1987). *Confronting values in policy analysis: The politics of criteria.* Newbury Park, CA: Sage.

Friedman, D. (1996). *Parenting in public: A study of help-giving practices to support parenting and child well-being in Massachusetts' congregate family shelters.* Unpublished doctoral dissertation, Brandeis University.

Gordon, E. W., & Armour-Thomas, E. (1991). Culture and cognitive development. In L. Okagaki & R. J. Sternberg (Eds.), *Directors of development: Influences on the development of children's thinking* (pp. 83–99). Hillsdale, NJ: Erlbaum.

Greenberg, M. T., & Crnic, K. A. (1988). Longitudinal predictors of developmental status and social interaction in premature and full-term infants at age two. *Child Development, 59,* 554–70.

Greene, J. C. (1988). Stakeholder participation and utilization in program evaluation. *Evaluation Review, 12,* 91–116.

Greene, J. C., Caracelli, V. J., & Graham, W. F. (1989). Toward a conceptual framework for mixed-method evaluation designs. *Educational Evaluation and Policy Analysis, 11,* 255–74.

Guba, E. G., & Lincoln, Y. S. (1989). *Fourth generation evaluation.* Newbury Park, CA: Sage.

Guba, E. G., & Lincoln, Y. S. (1981). *Effectiveness evaluation: Improving the usefulness of evaluation results through responsive and naturalistic approaches.* San Francisco: Jossey-Bass.

Guralnick, M. J. (1993). Second generation research on the effectiveness of early intervention. *Early Education and Development, 4,* 366–78.

Guralnick M. J. (1997). Second generation research in the field of early intervention. In M. J. Guralnick (Ed.), *The effectiveness of early intervention* (pp. 3–20). Baltimore, MD: Paul H. Brookes.

Habermas, J. (1973). *Legitimation crisis.* Boston: Beacon Press.

Hamburg, D. A. (1994). *Today's children: Creating a future for a generation in crisis.* New York: Times Books.

Hanson, M. J., & Carta, J. J. (1995). Addressing the challenges of families with multiple risks. *Exceptional Children, 62,* 201–12.

Harkness, S., & Super, C. M. (Eds.). (1996). *Parents' cultural belief systems: Their origins, expressions, and consequences.* New York: Guilford Press.

Hauser-Cram, P. (1990). Designing meaningful evaluations of early intervention services. In S. J. Meisels & J. P. Shonkoff (Eds.), *Handbook of early childhood intervention* (pp. 583–602). New York: Cambridge University Press.

Hauser-Cram, P., & Krauss, M. W. (1991). Measuring change in children and families. *Journal of Early Intervention, 15,* 288–97.

Hauser-Cram, P., & Shonkoff, J. P. (1995). Mastery motivation: Implications for intervention. In R. H. MacTurk & G. A. Morgan (Eds.), *Mastery motivation: Origins, conceptualizations, and applications* (pp. 257–72). Norwood, NJ: Ablex.

Heath, S. B. (1982). Questioning at home and at school: A comparative study. In G. Spindler (Ed.), *Doing the ethnography of schooling: Educational anthropology in action* (pp. 102–31). New York: Holt, Rinehart and Winston.

Hetherington, E. M., & Baltes, P. B. (1988). Child psychology and life-span development. In E. M. Hetherington, R. M. Lerner, & M. Perlmutter (Eds.), *Child development in life-span perspective* (pp. 1–19). Hillsdale, NJ: Erlbaum.

Hodapp, R. M., & Burack, J. A. (1990). What mental retardation teaches us about typical development: The examples of sequences, rates, and cross-domain relations. *Development and Psychopathology, 2,* 213–36.

Holland, D., & Quinn, N. (Eds.). (1987). *Cultural models in language and thought.* New York: Cambridge University Press.

Humphries, B., & Truman, C. (1994). Rethinking social research: Research in an unequal world. In B. Humphries & C. Truman (Eds.), *Rethinking social research: Antidiscriminatory approaches in research methodology* (pp. 1–21). Aldershot, England: Avebury.

Jacobs, F. H. (1988). The five-tiered approach to evaluation: Context and implementation. In H. B. Weiss & F. H. Jacobs (Eds.), *Evaluating family programs* (pp. 37–68). Hawthorne, NY: Aldine.

Jahoda, G. (1980). Theoretical and systematic approaches in cross-cultural psychology. In H. C. Triandis & W. W. Lambert (Eds.), *Handbook of cross-cultural psychology* (Vol. 1, pp. 69–142). Boston: Allyn & Bacon.

Knorr-Cetina, K. (1984). The fabrication of facts: Toward a microsociology of scientific knowledge. In N. Steher & V. Meja (Eds.), *Society and knowledge: Contemporary perspectives in the sociology of knowledge* (pp. 223–4). New Brunswick, NJ: Transaction Books.

Kochanek, T. T., & Buka, S. L. (1996). *Utilization rates of early intervention services by infants/toddlers and their families.* Rhode Island College, RI: Early Childhood Research Institute.

Lee, V. E., & Bryk, A. S. (1989). A multilevel model of the social distribution of high school achievement. *Sociology of Education, 62,* 172–92.

LeLaurin, K., & Wolery, M. (1992). Research standards in early intervention: Defining, describing, and measuring the independent variable. *Journal of Early Intervention, 16,* 275–87.

Lerner, R. M. (1984). *On the nature of human plasticity* (2nd ed.). New York: Random House.

Lerner, R. M. (1991). Changing organism–context relations as the basic process of development: A developmental contextual perspective. *Developmental Psychology, 27,* 27–32.

Lerner, R. M., Hauser-Cram, P., & Miller, E. (1998). Assumptions and features of longitudinal designs. Implications for early childhood education. In B. Spodek, O. N. Saracho, & A. D. Pelligrini (Eds.), *Yearbook in early education* (Vol. 8, pp. 113–138). New York: Teachers College Press.

Lerner, R., & Tubman, J. G. (1989). Conceptual issues in studying continuity and discontinuity in personality development across life. *Journal of Personality, 57,* 343–73.

Lincoln, Y. S. (1994). Tracks toward a postmodern politics of evaluation. *Evaluation Practice, 13,* 299–309.

Lincoln, Y. S., & Guba, E. G. (1989). *Fourth generation evaluation.* Newbury Park, CA: Sage.

Lipsky, M. (1980). *Street level bureaucracy.* New York: Russell Sage.

Lynch, E. W., & Hanson, M. J. (1992). *Developing cross-cultural competence: A guide for working with young children and their families.* Baltimore, MD: Paul H. Brookes.

Mark, M. M., Feller, I., & Button, S. B. (1997). Integrating qualitative methods in a predominantly quantitative evaluation: A case study and some reflections. In J. C. Greene & V. J. Caracelli (Eds.), *Advances in mixed-method evaluation: The challenges and benefits of integrating diverse paradigms* (pp. 47–59). San Francisco: Jossey-Bass.

Maxwell, J. A. (1992). Understanding and validity in qualitative research. *Harvard Educational Review, 62,* 279–300.

McCall, R. (1987). Developmental function, individual differences, and the plasticity of intelligence. In J. Gallagher & C. Ramey (Eds.), *The malleability of children* (pp. 25–35). Baltimore, MD: Paul H. Brookes.

McCartney, K., & Howley, E. (1991). Parents as instruments of intervention in home-based preschool programs. In L. Okagaki & R. J. Sternberg (Eds.), *Directors of development: Influences on the development of children's thinking* (pp. 181–202). Hillsdale, NJ: Erlbaum.

McNaughton, D. (1994). Measuring parent satisfaction with early childhood intervention programs: Current practice, problems, and future perspectives. *Topics in Early Childhood Special Education, 14,* 26–48.

Meenaghan, T. M., & Kilty, K. M. (1994). *Policy analysis and research technology: Political and ethical considerations.* Chicago: Lyceum Books.

Meisels, S. J. (1993). Remaking classroom assessment with the Work Sampling System. *Young Children, 48,* 34–40.

Miles, M., & Huberman, A. M. (1994). *Qualitative data analysis* (2nd ed.). Thousand Oaks, CA: Sage.

Nieto, S. (1992). *Affirming diversity: The sociopolitical context of multicultural education.* New York: Longman.

Nihira, K., Weisner, T. S., & Bernheimer, L. P. (1994). Ecocultural assessment in families of children with developmental delays: Construct and concurrent validities. *American Journal on Mental Retardation, 98,* 551–66.

Overton, W. F. (1998). Developmental psychology: Philosophy, concepts, and methodology. In R. M. Lerner (Ed.), *Theoretical models of human development: The handbook of child psychology* (Vol. I, 5th ed. pp. 107–88). New York: Wiley.

Pharis, M. E., & Levin, V. S. (1991). "A person to talk to who really cared": High-risk mothers' evaluations of services in an intensive intervention research program. *Child Welfare, 70,* 307–20.

Piaget, J. (1952). *The origins of intelligence in children.* New York: International Universities Press.

Powell, D. (1988). Challenges in the design and evaluation of parent-child intervention programs. In D. R. Powell (Ed.), *Parent education as early childhood intervention: Emerging directions in theory, research and practice* (pp. 229–37). Norwood, NJ: Ablex.

Reese, L., Balzano, S., Gallimore, R., & Goldenberg, C. (1991). *The concept of "educacion": Latino family values and American schooling.* Paper presented at the annual meeting of the American Anthropological Association, Chicago.

Rogoff, B. (1990). *Apprenticeship in thinking: Cognitive development in social context.* New York: Oxford University Press.

Rogoff, B., & Morelli, G. (1989). Perspectives on children's development from cultural psychology. *American Psychologist, 44,* 343–8.

Rossi, P. H., & Freeman, H. E. (1993). *Evaluation: A systematic approach* (5th ed.). Newbury Park, CA: Sage.

Sameroff, A. J. (1995). General systems theories and developmental psychopathology. In D. Cicchetti & D. J. Cohen (Eds.), *Developmental psychopathology, Vol. I: Theory and methods* (pp. 659–95). New York: Wiley.

Sandson, J., & Albert, M. L. (1984). Varieties of perseveration. *Neuropsychologia, 22,* 715–32.

Schwartz, I. S., & Olswang, L. B. (1996). Evaluating child behavior change in natural settings: Exploring alternative strategies for data collection. *Topics in Early Childhood Special Education, 16,* 82–101.

Shadish, W. R. (1995). The quantitative–qualitative debates: "DeKuhnifying" the conceptual context. *Evaluation and Program Planning, 18,* 47–9.

Shonkoff, J. P., & Hauser-Cram, P. (1987). Early intervention for disabled infants and their families: A quantitative analysis. *Pediatrics, 80,* 650–8.

Shonkoff, J. P., Hauser-Cram, P., Krauss, M. W., & Upshur, C. C. (1992). Development of infants with disabilities and their families: Implications for theory and service delivery. *Monographs of the Society for Research in Child Development, 57*(6, Serial No. 230).

Shweder, R. A. (1996). Quanta and qualia: What is the "object" of ethnographic method? In R. Jessor, A. Colby, & R. Shweder (Eds.), *Ethnography and human development. Context and meaning in social inquiry* (pp. 175–82). Chicago: University of Chicago Press.

Sigel, I., Stinson, E. T., & Flaugher, J. (1991). Socialization of representational competence in the family: The distancing paradigm. In L. Okagaki & R. J. Sternberg (Eds.), *Directors of development: Influences on the development of children's thinking* (pp. 121–44). Hillsdale, NJ: Erlbaum.

Skinner, B. F. (1953). *Science and human behavior.* New York: Appleton-Century-Crofts.

Snell, M. E. (Ed.). (1987). *Systematic instruction of persons with severe handicaps* (3rd ed.). Columbus, OH: Merrill.

Sontag, J. C., & Schacht, R. (1993). Family diversity and patterns of service utilization in early intervention. *Journal of Early Intervention, 17,* 431–44.

Spreen, O., Risser, A. H., & Edgell, D. (1995). *Developmental neuropsychology.* New York: Oxford University Press.

Super, C. M., & Harkness, S. (1986). The developmental niche: A conceptualization at the interface of child and culture. *International Journal of Behavior Development, 9,* 1–25.

Telzrow, C. F. (1993). Commentary on comparative evaluation of early intervention alternatives. *Early Education and Development, 4,* 359–65.

Tharp, R. G., & Gallimore, R. (1988). *Rousing minds to life: Teaching, learning, and schooling in social context.* New York: Cambridge University Press.

Thomas, P., & Palfrey, C. (1996). Evaluation: Stakeholder-focused criteria. *Social Policy and Administration, 30,* 125–42.

Trivette, C. M., Dunst, C. J., Boyd, K., & Hamby, D. W. (1995). Family-oriented program models: Helpgiving practices and parental control appraisals. *Exceptional Children, 62,* 237–48.

Upshur, C. C. (1991). Mothers' and fathers' ratings of the benefits of early intervention services. *Journal of Early Intervention, 15,* 345–57.

Upshur, C., & Barreto-Cortez, E. (1995). What is participatory evaluation (PE)? What are its roots? In *The evaluation exchange: Emerging strategies in evaluating child and family services.* Cambridge, MA: Harvard Family Research Project.

Usher, C. L. (1993). *Building capacity for self-evaluation in family and children's services reform efforts.* Paper presented at the annual meeting of the American Evaluation Association, Dallas, TX.

Usher, C. L. (1995). Improving evaluability through self-evaluation. *Evaluation Practice, 16,* 59–68.

Warfield, M. E. (1995). The cost-effectiveness of home visiting versus group services in early intervention. *Journal of Early Intervention, 19,* 130–48.

Warfield, M. E. (1994). A cost-effectiveness analysis of early intervention services in Massachusetts: Implications for policy. *Educational Evaluation and Policy Analysis, 16,* 87–99.

Weisner, T. S. (1984). A cross-cultural perspective: Ecocultural niches of middle childhood. In A. Collins (Ed.), *The elementary school years: Understanding development during middle childhood* (pp. 335–69). Washington, DC: National Academy Press.

Weisner, T. S. (1996a). Why ethnography should be the most important method in the study of human development. In R. Jessor, A. Colby, & R. Shweder (Eds.), *Ethnography and human development. Context and meaning in social inquiry* (pp. 305–24). Chicago: University of Chicago Press.

Weisner, T. S. (1996b). The 5 to 7 transition as an ecocultural project. In A. Sameroff & M. Haith (Eds.), *The five to seven shift: The age of reason and responsibility* (pp. 295–326). Chicago: University of Chicago Press.

Weisner, T. S. (1997). The ecocultural project of human development: Why ethnography and its findings matter. *Ethos, 25,* 177–90.

Weisner, T. S., Gallimore, R., & Jordan, C. (1988). Unpackaging cultural effects on classroom learning: Native Hawaiian peer assistance and child-generated activity. *Anthropology and Education Quarterly, 19,* 327–51.

Weisner, T. S., Matheson, C., & Bernheimer, L. (1996). American cultural models of early influence and parent recognition of development delays: Is earlier always better than later? In S. Harkness, C. M. Super, & R. New (Eds.), *Parents' cultural belief systems* (pp. 496–531). New York: Guilford Press.

Weiss, C. H. (1975). Evaluation research in the political context. In E. L. Struening & M. Guttentag (Eds.), *Handbook of evaluation research* (pp. 2–26). Beverly Hills, CA: Sage.

Weiss, C. H. (1995). Nothing as practical as good theory: Exploring theory-based evaluation for comprehensive community initiatives for children and families. In J. P. Connell (Ed.), *New approaches to evaluating community initiatives: Concepts, methods, and contexts* (pp. 65–92). Queenstown, MD: Aspen Institute.

Weiss, H. B. (1988). Family support programs: Working through ecological theories of human development. In H. B. Weiss & F. H. Jacobs (Eds.), *Evaluating family programs* (pp. 3–36). Hawthorne, NY: Aldine.

Weiss, H. B., & Greene, J. C. (1992). An empowerment partnership for family support and education programs and evaluations. *Family Science Review, 5,* 131–48.

Weissbourd, B., & Kagan, S. L. (1989). Family support programs: Catalysts for change. *American Journal of Orthopsychiatry, 59,* 32–48.

Weisz, J. R., Yeates, K. O., & Zigler, E. (1982). Piagetian evidence and the developmental-difference controversy. In E. Zigler & D. Balla (Eds.), *Mental retardation: The developmental-difference controversy* (pp. 213–76). Hillsdale, NJ: Erlbaum.

Westinghouse Learning Corporation. (1969). *The impact of Head Start: An evaluation of the effects of Head Start on children's cognitive and affective development.* Athens, OH: Ohio University.

Whyte, W. F. (Ed.). (1991). *Participatory action research.* Newbury Park, CA: Sage.

Zigler, E. (1969). Developmental versus difference theories of mental retardation and the problem of motivation. *American Journal of Mental Deficiency*, *73*, 536–56.

CHAPTER TWENTY-THREE

Another Decade of Intervention for Children Who Are Low Income or Disabled:

What Do We Know Now?

DALE C. FARRAN

The decade from 1987 through 1996 witnessed an explosion in services for young children who were presumed to need specialized preparation before attending school. Head Start was reauthorized and provided its largest increase in funding in twenty years. In 1988, Even Start was funded at a national level. In fact, all sorts of starts were initiated (Fair Start, Healthy Start, Bright Start, and, even, Smart Start in North Carolina). P.L. 99-457 mandated intervention services for children with disabilities and encouraged states to develop intervention programs for children from birth to age 3. Funds from Title I (or Chapter 1, as it was called from 1980 to 1992) of the Elementary and Secondary Education Act (ESEA) were increasingly spent on establishing preschool classrooms in Title I elementary schools, and many states began spending state money on prekindergarten programs for children at risk (Marx & Seligson, 1988).

At the same time, it became harder to obtain research funding for experimental work on intervention practices; two decades of model demonstration classrooms and support for the programs themselves in which research occurred drew to a close. Research results reported in the 1990s have been primarily follow-up reports from programs begun in the 1970s, general evaluations of programs implemented on a national scale, small studies of a few new approaches for children with disabilities, and one major, extensively reported intervention program for low-birth-weight babies.

The 1990s has also been called the "Decade of the Brain," with a focus on increased understanding of the importance of early experience on brain organization and development (Carnegie Task Force on Meeting the Needs of Young Children, 1994; Shore, 1997). With increasingly sophisticated research techniques, neuroscientists demonstrated how responsive the young child's brain is to stimulation early in life. This work has been primarily descriptive, as in Neville's (1991) comparative study of deaf children born to deaf parents, hearing children of deaf parents, and hearing children of hearing parents. Her research on the differential responsivity of these three groups to sensory, cognitive, and language tasks provided support for the idea that children's brains undergo a rapid increase in the number of synapses formed from birth to 2 years of age, with the period from 2 to 15 years marked by subsequent "pruning" of synapses. The pruning takes place to stabilize certain connections and to eliminate or suppress others on the basis of continuing and repeated sensory stimulation. In other words, infants appear to be primed to be maximally responsive to the stimulation in the world around them initially and then to spend a good portion of the preschool and early school years organizing the stimulation to be more precisely in tune with their environments. Experimental work with rats suggests that placement in the deprived environment of a simple laboratory cage may be linked directly to lower brain weight (e.g., Greenough et al., 1993).

Special appreciation goes to Cindy McGaha, who helped locate and summarize articles in the section on intervention for children with disabilities. Much gratitude also goes to Laura Flower, who tenaciously located and corrected citations and provided very helpful editing.

Nevertheless, just as the scientific community is beginning to better understand the crucial importance of the nature of early experiences, the United States appears to be putting more of its youngest citizens in risky environments. The percentage of children under age 6 living in poverty increased yearly until 1995 before stabilizing at 24% (Children's Defense Fund, 1996). Poverty is a major high-risk environment that exerts a profound adverse effect on many aspects of development in ways that are not completely understood (Starfield, 1992). An increasing number of children are spending their earliest years in group care situations; the Cost, Quality and Child Outcomes in Child Care Centers' national study found group care for infants to be particularly poor, with only one in seven centers surveyed deemed to be developmentally sound environments (Helburn et al., 1995). The Carnegie Corporation issued a call for action in *Starting Points*, a document linking infant care practices and the new information on brain growth and development (Carnegie Task Force on Meeting the Needs of Young Children, 1994). Several years before, Clarke and Clarke (1989) cautioned that "we have to face the sad fact that an unknown number of children in advanced countries live in conditions which place them at risk for malevolent environments as well as suboptimal constitutions" (p. 294).

Throughout the 1990s, the number of children diagnosed as requiring specialized education has increased steadily, most notably in the areas of learning disabilities and behavior disorders (Farran & Shonkoff, 1994). It is safe to say, however, that the field of special education is not any more united in its understanding of the most appropriate interventions than it was in the past decade (Brantlinger, 1997). There is currently discussion of the need for "etiologic specificity" in intervention efforts (Meisels, Dichtelmiller, & Liaw, 1993) – one size does not fit all, despite the fact that for the most part treatments of children with varying types of disabilities are indistinguishable (Reynolds, Wang, & Walberg, 1987; Salisbury, 1991). In the absence of data about effectiveness, programs are avidly supported on the basis of ideology rather than on demonstrated outcomes (Siegel, 1996).

Thus, the context in which this review is being written is different in many ways from the last decade review (see Farran, 1990). The amount of scientific information being generated that should be directly relevant to enhancing environments for young children is increasing dramatically while the conditions in which children exist are more grave and threatening to their optimal development than ever before. Despite Baumeister's (1997) caution that science does not determine public policy, perhaps continuing careful reviews can set the stage for a more purposeful blending of science and practice in the next decade.

As in the previous review, I first discuss programs for children from economically disadvantaged backgrounds. I then review research regarding programs for children with disabilities. The chapter concludes with a review of themes that are common to both groups of children. With a few exceptions for major, but unpublished, reports of large interventions, this chapter focuses on studies that were published in journals, books, or monographs. The publication dates reviewed are from 1987 through 1997, and, as in the first review, the studies covered early intervention projects with children who were either disadvantaged by virtue of poverty or who had disabilities, with a focus at least partly on cognitive outcome data. Children's ages ranged from birth through age 6, and the interventions occurred before they formally entered first grade, most often before kindergarten. Before a review of the past decade's research, the major findings of the first review are listed briefly.

SUMMARY OF CONCLUSIONS FROM FIRST REVIEW

Children Disadvantaged by Poverty

Children disadvantaged by poverty included in research studies during the decade from 1977 to 1986 were almost exclusively Black. The type of intervention varied, but the focus of all these projects was cognitive remediation or support. The intervention efforts were most often delivered by educational staff, frequently in centers. Parents were less often the source of the intervention. Reviewing published data that involved more than 5,000 children who received intervention along with 2,000 control subjects, the first review drew the following conclusions:

• Experience with preschool intervention and school-like tasks appeared to raise tested performance immediately – especially at age 3 when early intervention seems to produce an inflated, unsustainable developmental test score – but not to have continued effects into the school years.

- Children who served as control subjects gradually "caught up to" experimental subjects so that by the second, third, or fourth grades, the differences between them were neither statistically nor educationally significant.
- Home visiting alone did not appear to be an effective intervention strategy for disadvantaged children. In fact, there was some suggestion that it could sometimes have a negative effect.
- Early intervention in infancy did not appear to have more significant effects on later school performance than intervention efforts begun in the preschool years.
- Social outcomes (e.g., better grade advancement and less juvenile delinquency) might be promising avenues for future study but they had not been studied sufficiently, and the effects found were not strong enough to conclude that they represent an alternative benefit of intervention for disadvantaged children.

Children with Disabilities

The previous review covered forty-two intervention projects for children with disabilities: twenty-nine of these served a mixed population of disabilities and thirteen were exclusively created for children with Down syndrome (children with Down syndrome were increasingly reared in homes instead of institutions, and interventionists were interested in them as a unique population). For all of the intervention programs, age of entry varied widely, and, consequently, so did the length of treatment. In contrast to the studies of impoverished children, little information was provided about the families of children with disabilities, despite the fact that they were much more often the locus of the intervention effort. The following conclusions were drawn in the first review:

- In general, studies that used at least a pre–post assessment on the intervention group showed gains in the children's skills at the end of the program. These gains were not always reflected in increased developmental quotients nor were they found in all areas of development.
- Determining if programs were successful was extremely difficult for many reasons:

1. There was no agreement about how to measure gain for children whose development is not typical, and all of the proposed approaches were fraught with difficulties.
2. The programs served mixed groups of children; effects that may have been strong for one type of disability could have been lost in the statistical noise generated by all of the other groups involved.
3. Programs used widely varying assessment instruments, some standardized and some created by the programs themselves. Most of the standardized tests had not included children with disabilities in their standardization samples.
4. It was difficult to apply a scientific research design to intervention programs for children with disabilities – strategies such as random assignment to treatment and establishing control groups for comparison were not possible.
5. Little follow-up past the provision of the intervention itself took place.

- No particular approach for working with children with disabilities emerged as being more successful than any other, although it was clear that families responded well to the support provided through early intervention teams in general.

REVIEW OF INTERVENTION FOR CHILDREN DISADVANTAGED BY POVERTY: 1987–1997

General Organization

Several major programs established in the 1970s, and included in the first review, continued to follow their graduates in order to provide more long-term information about their effectiveness. Those studies are reviewed first. New information about Head Start has also emerged from further studies; these data are reviewed next. Finally, several new programs were implemented and reported throughout the 1990s, including the Infant Health and Development Program, which fits in this category because of the disproportionate prevalence of low birth weight among the offspring of women in poverty. Such two-generation programs as Even Start and Parents as Teachers, and data from the Chapter 1–funded Child Parent Centers in Chicago are reviewed as new initiatives. Finally, the review focuses on both old programs with new data and on data from new programs.

Old Programs for Poor Children: New Data

ABECEDARIAN/PROJECT CARE. The *Abecedarian Project* consisted of early infant intervention for four cohorts of children in center-based care at a university (Campbell & Ramey, 1994). Children were selected for intervention on the basis of a maternal interview covering a high-risk index that combined various risk factors (low income, no father present in the home, low maternal education, and so forth) and were then randomly assigned to intervention and control groups at birth. In the southern university town in which the intervention took place, selecting on the basis of risk yielded a sample that was 97% African American.

Data have now been presented on the children through ages 12 (Campbell & Ramey, 1994) and 15 (Campbell & Ramey, 1995). The experimenters have been indefatigable in finding and assessing children who move often – changing home addresses, schools, and sometimes even states. The Abecedarian Project represents center-based intervention beginning in infancy, an intervention approach that seems to create an immediate positive effect on children's developmental test scores. The scores of children in center-based intervention began to plateau about age 4, when the control group's scores started to increase steadily. For the Abecedarian children, the two groups entered the public schools about a half a standard deviation apart. Most of the effects of preschool intervention on tested intelligence had disappeared by age 12, but at age 15 there was a nonsignificant mean difference in the full-scale Wechsler Intelligence Scale for Children (WISC–R) of 4.6 points favoring the intervention group. At age 12, the group who had preschool intervention scored significantly higher on an individually administered achievement test, the Woodcock Johnson Psychoeducational Battery, on the Reading and Knowledge subtests. At age 15, the preschool group scored significantly higher on the Woodcock Johnson Reading and Mathematics subtests. In terms of grade retention and the need for special education, there was a trend for the preschool group to have fewer retentions and special education placements at age 12, which were reported to be significant differences by age 15. It is important to note that only the preschool intervention continued to have an effect; intervention at school age (a version of home-school coordination) never showed any additional positive effect.

These data suggest that one of the most highly publicized intervention projects of the 1970s, with large numbers of publications (e.g., Campbell, Goldstein, Schaefer, & Ramey, 1991; Campbell & Ramey, 1990; Feagans & Farran, 1994; Feagans, Fendt, & Farran, 1995; Horacek, Ramey, Campbell, Hoffmann, & Fletcher, 1987), was moderately successful in demonstrating the value of early intervention for children from very poor homes. Although many of the early effects dissipated fairly rapidly, some persisted into early adolescence. One of the most interesting publications to emerge from the project is the recent book by Vernon-Feagans (1996), which includes a complete description of project findings and a presentation of the evolving perspectives of the researchers engaged in the project. She concluded that the philosophical orientation of the 1960s and 1970s may have led to an incorrect focus for the preschool intervention and a poor grasp of the power of the subsequent public school experience for these very poor children in a university community. Vernon-Feagans argued that the focus of the Abecedarian Project was on "fixing" the child's deficits, making children prepared academically for school. She documented clearly how devastatingly unprepared the school system was to interact with the Abecedarian children to foster their continuing development. Vernon-Feagans's book provides strong support for the importance of changing the venues in which children must function rather than just focusing on the children alone.

A review of the extensive journal publications related to the Abecedarian Project raises some cautions. First, in many of the later publications, mean scores on the assessment measures are not provided by the researchers. Instead, data are often presented graphically, in figures that have a visual tendency to inflate small group differences. The presentation of straightforward tables would allow one to compare not only the means but also the variances of the groups involved. Similarly, the number of children assessed varies across different measures within the same publication; because the graphs appear to be of everyone who had a score on that measure (even if they were not available for other years), it is difficult to determine the mean scores for the groups on whom the longitudinal analyses were actually conducted.

These may seem like trivial concerns. They are important, however, because as one examines the full corpus of publications on this project, the number of subjects reported has not been consistent. At a minimum, some explanation of the differences would be helpful. These variations can lead to an impression of manipulation of readers rather than straightforward reporting of an important project. Spitz (1992) and others have voiced concerns about the interpretation of the Abecedarian data, which can best be answered by presenting means and standard deviations and conducting the analyses only on the groups for whom complete data exist.

Because the Abecedarian Project has been researched so completely, from many different perspectives, it is an invaluable source of information about the effects of poverty on young African American children's development in the South. The importance of the school system as a receiving environment has only recently received any sustained attention, and evidence suggests it is not a positive environment for poor children. For the Abecedarian children, the school system was dominated by White, university-related families, creating a cultural chasm between their language styles and the other children in their school classes. The sequence of events for this population is one that has great implications for future intervention efforts, and one hopes that planners will take into account the information available from this project. Early intervention can improve the skills of poor children entering school; the subsequent school environment must be able to maintain the growth trajectory established in preschool. Little research has been done on the critical juncture between experiences and skills developed before school and the experiences that occur after school entry.

Project Care is a second-generation Abecedarian project involving the addition of a family education component to center-based intervention begun in early infancy, as well as the creation of a new type of intervention package – one that included only family education through home visiting (Ramey, Bryant, Campbell, Sparling, & Wasik, 1990). Data

on this variation of the program were presented through fifty-four months by Wasik, Ramey, Bryant, and Sparling (1990), who reported that those families whose children did not receive center-based care were visited by home visitors on the average of 2.5 times per month; center-based care families were also visited an average of 2.7 times per month. When the children were 4 and 5 years old, home visiting decreased for both groups to approximately once a month.

The results suggest that the center-based program with the addition of home visiting was successful in affecting children's development through age 36 months. It was more successful than either the provision of family education alone or doing nothing at all (the control group), but it was not more successful than the original Abecedarian center-based-only project. At eighteen months, the mean scores for the group that received family education alone were actually lower than the control group, though no significance data have been reported for this comparison. (Again, as in the Abecedarian Project, results are presented graphically; means and standard deviations for the three groups are not provided.) By forty-eight and fifty-four months, the center-based plus family-education group has been reported as scoring significantly higher than the group of children for whom only family education was provided but not significantly higher than the control group. Given no difference between the developmental test scores of the center-based, family education group and the control group, it would appear that the control group had begun to catch up with the center-based intervention group. Because of the significant difference reported between the center-based group and the home-visit-only group, the second inference would seem to be that the home-visit-only group had been negatively affected, scoring lower than the control group, and that these negative effects continued through the preschool years.

The family education component should be scrutinized carefully in this program. Surprisingly, it appears to have diminished the effect of the center-based program, which when given alone in the Abecedarian Project had a stronger effect than when combined with home visitation, at least through the preschool years. Moreover, it appears to have had a negative effect when provided alone (reported previously in Ramey, Bryant, Sparling, & Wasik, 1985).

Wasik et al. (1990) described the family education program as a problem-solving approach in which the home visitors discussed with parents ongoing family concerns and ways to use strategies to solve their own problems. Given that many of the problems associated with poverty are fairly intractable (too little money, inadequate housing, poor health, lack of transportation, and too few employment opportunities), one can only speculate that this approach may have been more frustrating to the parents than helpful. Even so, it is sobering indeed to think that it might actually have slowed the children's development, proof that one needs to be cautious in intervening in high-risk situations. (Clearly, this is a small sample, and the effect could be a non-replicable one, although researchers might be hesitant to study this.)

In summary, the Abecedarian and Project Care programs are perhaps the most scientifically controlled and thoroughly reported early intervention efforts in social science, certainly more so than any other programs implemented in the 1960s and 1970s. Overall, their findings show modest success in altering the cognitive test scores of children from low-income, high-stress environments with a center-based preschool intervention beginning in infancy. The parent component does not appear to have provided any particular additional benefit to the center-based program. No data beyond preschool have been provided for Project Care. Some effects of the preschool intervention for Abecedarian children persist through age 15, but no effects were found for the school-age program. Much of the attenuation in the group differences appears to be accounted for by the improvement of the control group children when they encountered ordinary preschool and school experiences, albeit at a later date than the experimental group children.

PARENT CHILD DEVELOPMENT CENTERS. The Parent Child Development Centers (PCDC) were an intervention program for poor children and their parents that began in several sites around the country in the early 1970s. The Texas sites (Houston, San Antonio, and AVANCE) have remained the most active. In San Antonio and AVANCE, continued funding allowed the programs to enroll children through 1991; researchers assessing these programs

also conducted follow-up studies of the effects of the Houston PCDC. The Texas programs primarily served Hispanic families. The program's general goal was to "foster the development of competence in young children by helping parents become effective teachers of their young children" (Walker & Johnson, 1988, p. 378).

Program effects reviewed in the earlier version of this chapter (Farran, 1990) were modest, weaker than several of the other programs reviewed (e.g., the Syracuse group by Honig & Lally, 1982, and the Abecedarian Project by Ramey & Campbell, 1984). That pattern persisted in the follow-up assessments. Walker and Johnson (1988) followed up with a younger and an older sample and concluded there were "no significant effects of the PCDC on intelligence when the children were followed 1 to 6 years after the program's conclusion" (p. 380). Both groups tested as having normal intelligence, and, for the older children, the group means were nearly identical. In a subsequent publication, Johnson and Walker (1991) reported on the children in the second through fifth grades. The early intervention group did not differ from the control group on school grades in any subject, grade retention, referral to special education, or teacher-reported contacts with parents during the school year. The intervention group scored higher, however, than the control group on three subtests of the Iowa Tests of Basic Skills (Vocabulary, Reading, and Language), and fewer of the intervention children were enrolled in bilingual classes. The researchers concluded that overall both groups were doing reasonably well in school with an overall percentile level of 50.1 and C+ grades.

Data on the continuing PCDC program are reported in Walker, Rodriguez, Johnson, and Cortez (1995), a chapter that concentrates on the effects on the parents; no child effect data are presented. The chapter does contain a detailed description of the program itself. Parent education classes were provided to participants weekly for the first nine months of the child's life followed by the second stage of intervention in which adult basic education, English as a second language, and preparation for the GED were provided. Child care and transportation continued during this stage. The authors provided data on attrition from the project, which for the experimental group were nearly double those of the control group. In the first year of the program, 53% of the experimental group was retained compared to 90% of the control group. More of the control group dropped out the next year, but additional loss also occurred in the experimental group. This program used the CES-D (depression scale) as a mediator variable; Walker et al. reported that about half of the population of mothers tested as depressed. Perhaps this mental state made them less interested in a parenting class focused on child development.

Despite the fanfare that greeted the creation and funding of Parent Child Development Centers and the continued support for some of them, the data have not shown either a powerful or a lasting effect on the children and have indicated only modest effects on the mothers. It would be useful to conduct a more objective and systematic analysis of the programs offered and the family characteristics of those enrolled to determine why a program that seemed so right to so many people has had such a minimal impact.

HIGH/SCOPE. Another "old" program for which data continue to be published is the High/Scope program located in Ypsilanti, Michigan. Two separate samples were followed. One is the Perry Preschool, a project whose data were included in the Consortium for Longitudinal Studies (Lazar & Darlington, 1982), and the other is the three curriculum comparison study, originally reported by Schweinhart, Weikart, and Larner (1986). As described by Schweinhart, Barnes, and Weikart (1993), the High/Scope approach is explicitly Piagetian in focus with children viewed as active learners. To encourage active learning, the children engage in a set daily routine that includes a plan-do-review sequence. The High/Scope Foundation certifies curriculum trainers and teachers. By the end of 1992, the foundation had certified 1,100 trainers in eleven countries, and those trainers had trained an estimated 28,500 teachers and assistants in the High/Scope approach (Schweinhart et al., 1993).

In 1993, the High/Scope Foundation published a monograph that detailed the follow-up of the Perry Preschool graduates through age 27 (Schweinhart et al., 1993). The staff has been remarkably persistent in locating and interviewing the graduates so

that attrition has been relatively low. At age 27, 117 of the original 123 subjects were located and interviewed. Although differences in tested intelligence on several measures had disappeared by age 8, the interview at age 27 revealed that the Perry Preschool graduates had completed almost a full year more of schooling (11.9 years compared to 11.0 years) than the comparison group. No difference was reported in the rate of grade retention between the two groups, and each made use of an equal amount of special educational services while in school. But the experimental preschool students tended to spend more time in compensatory education programs in contrast to the control children, who were more likely to be placed in classes for children with educational mental impairment. While in school, the experimental preschool students achieved a significantly higher grade point average and scored significantly better on the subtests of California Achievement Test in reading, arithmetic, and language than the control children. It is important to note that the GPA achieved by the experimental preschool students was 2.09 compared to 1.68 for the control group, and the achievement test results for both groups were well below the 20th percentile, even though they differed from one another. Tested intelligence never rose above the low average level for either group.

The data from this project that have received much attention are those related to criminality. It is apparent that this was a group at substantial risk for criminal behavior; about one-quarter of the intervention group and one-third of the control group had spent time in jail by the time they were 27. The control group had been arrested twice as often as the intervention group (4.6 arrests compared to 2.3); however, no F statistic or p value is reported for these findings, leading one to suspect that the variance in the groups prevented this apparently large mean difference from achieving statistical significance.

Following a group into adulthood has meant that project staff can investigate employment histories, which, according to some, is the ultimate test of an early intervention project. The data indicate that the intervention graduates were earning higher monthly incomes at age 27 than the comparison group. Oddly, there were no differences between the groups in the percentage currently employed or the percentage that had been employed in the previous five years. The difference in these two figures suggests a checkered employment history with many job changes for both groups. The control group made more use of social services throughout the ten years prior to the interview than the program group, although they were not getting more of any particular type of assistance when interviewed at 27.

The amount of data collected from various sources and the detailed nature of the interview conducted with the experimental preschool graduates and their controls at age 27 are impressive. In many categories, there are significant differences favoring the program group as well as a fairly consistent trend in their favor. Publishing the data in books with mainstream publishers or in peer-reviewed journals, or both, might lead to analysis strategies revealing other important information about the effects of early intervention on this group. For example, Schweinhart et al. (1993) did not report the standard deviations for any of the means, and the p value was only listed when there was a significant difference in the means (but no F value was ever given). Much of their analyses focused on chi-square comparisons of percentages in multiple categories. There are several problems with this approach. Using multiple chi-squares with a small number of subjects carries with it the danger of capitalizing on chance. There is also an ipsative problem – changes in the percentages in one category must necessarily affect the percentages in the other categories. Finally, it seems as if the variance in both groups must be high, and one would like to see an investigation of possible subgroups. For example, was there a group for whom the intervention was more highly effective (e.g., female subjects versus male subjects), and are they the people also likely to finish school, have higher grade point averages, get better jobs, stay out of jails, and not use social services? If so, finding out about their characteristics would be helpful.

A related study has followed three groups of children exposed to different curricula during preschool, comparing High/Scope, a direct instruction approach, and a traditional nursery school approach. In both this study and the Perry project, groups were intended to be randomly assigned, an important component for scientific acceptance. In each, violations of random assignment occurred. Siblings were assigned to the same treatment group in both studies. This affected nine of the original sixty-eight children in the curriculum study (Schweinhart & Weikart, 1997). In the Perry Preschool study, single parents who had jobs were assigned to the control group. In the curriculum study, the nursery group was composed of those from a significantly higher socioeconomic background, suggesting that there might have been some alterations at parents' behest in this group's assignment as well.

The follow-up curriculum study interviewed and collected data from fifty-two of the original sixty-eight participants when they were 23 years old. Varying amounts of data were accessible for each participant so that the sample size fluctuates from measure to measure. Dividing fifty-two subjects among three intervention groups results in a small number of individuals representing each group. There are no outcome differences among the groups at age 23 in number of years of schooling completed, years of special education, or the likelihood of failing a grade and being retained. They did differ in the type of special education placement, with the direct instruction students more likely to have been identified as having an emotional impairment. The direct instruction members were also more likely to have been arrested, but not significantly so. Overall, in fact, there are remarkable similarities among the outcomes for the groups, many more similarities than there are significant differences. There was no nonintervention group in this study and thus no way to know what might have happened with no intervention at all.

In summary, the High/Scope Perry Preschool program is the early intervention program with the most extensive longitudinal data. It is a program that has become a minor industry with its own foundation, publishing system, and training program for teachers. The High/Scope curriculum is used widely in this country and elsewhere. Although the initial small research samples have been extremely helpful in identifying likely strengths of the High/Scope approach to intervention, its widespread use would seem to demand a larger, systematic investigation of effects. The High/Scope curriculum was developed in the early 1960s; much has changed for children in poverty in the nearly forty years since its inception. It is important to determine what the effects of the curriculum are now; Schweinhart and Weikart

(1997) are some of the few in the country who could find out.

HEAD START. Head Start is another program that began in the mid-1960s in an era of buoyant optimism about ending poverty by means of education. Unfortunately, poverty did not end in the 1960s. Quite the contrary, poverty among young children has increased since then at an alarming rate. Determining the effects of Head Start as it is implemented today is so difficult as to be almost impossible. For one thing, evaluations are performed in the overpowering political atmosphere that surrounds the program – belief in what it was meant to do, a strong desire that it be able to accomplish its goals, and an unwillingness to challenge congressional faith in the program. As Kassebaum (1994) has said, Head Start is "one of the few prevention programs for children in which Congress has confidence" (p. 126). It is difficult for researchers to keep congressional faith while providing the kind of objective information the program needs to improve.

Other problems in evaluating Head Start's effects involve the fact that Head Start programs around the country use a variety of curricular approaches, programs are of variable quality without readily available quality indicators, there are very few longitudinal data available on the graduates, and valid assessment instruments and assessors are not available to most Head Start programs. Many of these problems were illustrated in a study of variations in quality among thirty-two Head Start classrooms conducted by Bryant, Burchinal, Lau, and Sparling (1994). Only three of the thirty-two classrooms met standards that would be considered developmentally appropriate (using the Early Childhood Environmental Rating Scale [Harms, Cryer, & Clifford, 1990]). Moreover, children in higher quality classrooms scored better on outcome measures related to achievement and preacademic skills, no matter what the quality of their home environments, demonstrating that these variations in classroom quality are important.

Analyzing data from the Head Start Longitudinal Study, Lee, Brooks-Gunn, and Schnur (1988) examined the progress of Head Start graduates from Trenton, New Jersey, and Portland, Oregon. Within the database were the scores of children from the same catchment areas who had either not attended any preschool or attended a preschool other than Head Start. The three groups of children were not really comparable: the Head Start attendees were made up of many more Black children than the other two groups, and the Head Start children were considerably behind the other two groups on all of the initial measures administered to them. All subsequent analyses of effects were analyses of covariance, taking into account entering characteristics of the children. Lee et al. (1988) concluded that Head Start produced gains on some measures, but these gains were more likely to occur for Black children and for those who were more cognitively delayed when they had entered. In a subsequent follow-up of the same children, Lee, Brooks-Gunn, Schnur, and Liaw (1990) found that Head Start graduates scored significantly higher on a preschool competency test at the end of kindergarten, but that these strong effects were attenuated somewhat by the end of first grade.

Two important issues are involved in understanding the long-term effects of Head Start as an intervention program. The first relates to the demographic conditions in which Head Start enrollees spend both their preschool and public school lives. As Takanishi and DeLeon (1994) noted, the "current consensus is that the social and economic conditions within which Head Start was originally created in 1965 have worsened" (p. 120). Using the National Education Longitudinal Study of 1988, Lee and Loeb (1995) drew a sample of current eighth graders who had been Head Start graduates. On every measure considered, the children who attended Head Start were demographically disadvantaged compared to the rest of the sample. Head Start graduates were also found in schools that were of much poorer quality, measured by such aspects as safety and school academic quality. "No matter how strong the early boost received by these children from their Head Start experience, the fact that their subsequent education is in lower quality schools (and that learning is likely to be inferior in those schools) would seem to undermine any early advantage" (Lee & Loeb, 1995, p. 74).

The second troubling issue relates to the Head Start curriculum, one that was constructed in the mid-1960s from a model provided by Susan Gray (Sargent Shriver, October, 1996, personal communication). Gray's DARCEE project was located in the South in rural isolated communities (Gray & Klaus, 1968), at a time when television was not omnipresent. The focus of the curriculum was on basic school-related information: colors, numbers, street signs, and school-appropriate behavior. This curriculum continues to have positive effects for those children who test the farthest behind on cognitive and school readiness measures (Lee et al., 1988). It may not, however, be as effective for children who are exposed to violence and grow up in fear (Takanishi & DeLeon, 1994) or those who have access to much more information from television and the like but less stress-free time in which to process and synthesize it. New attention may need to be given both to the curricular focus most appropriate for Head Start classrooms in the new century and to monitoring and evaluating how well the curriculum is being implemented in Head Start programs (Kassebaum, 1994).

New Programs for Poor/At-Risk Children

INFANT HEALTH AND DEVELOPMENT PROGRAM
General description. One of the most remarkable events in early childhood intervention during the 1990s was the creation, implementation, and extensive reporting of the Infant Health and Development Program (IHDP). Although this program was not explicitly designed for poor children, low birth weight is a more common phenomenon among impoverished mothers, and the intervention approaches used were based on the Abecedarian Project and Project Care – both of which are programs for poor children and families. Unlike previous intervention efforts, IHDP was conceived as a "randomized clinical trial" (Spiker, Kraemer, Scott, & Gross, 1991) in which the same intervention would be delivered in monitored sites in many places simultaneously. The belief underlying such a strategy was that enough was known about intervention to deliver it in a systematic fashion, much as one would a new drug being considered for release. The potential contribution this strategy could make to science appears to have been recognized from the outset.

Eight medical institutions were selected to participate in a "randomized and controlled efficacy trial of early intervention to enhance the cognitive, behavioral and health status of low-birth-weight, premature infants" (Ramey et al., 1992, p. 454). All of the medical institutions were teaching hospitals connected to large universities, most in big cities (New York, Boston, Dallas, Little Rock, Miami, New Haven, Philadelphia, and Seattle). Stanford University was selected as the coordinating center, and the Frank Porter Graham Child Development Center at the University of North Carolina at Chapel Hill was to be responsible for program development and monitoring. The investigators at the Frank Porter Graham Center who had developed the curricular approaches for Project Care and the Abecedarian Project also developed the modifications used for the home visiting component in IHDP (Wasik, Bryant, & Lyons, 1990; Wasik & Lyons, 1984) and the center-based curriculum that all were required to implement (Sparling & Lewis, 1984; Sparling, Lewis, & Neuwirth, in press). The Abecedarian Project and Project Care together served as the "prototype for the IHDP intervention program," according to Ramey et al. (1992, p. 460). Thus, it was an intervention program developed for children in poverty that was applied to the new samples.

Children involved. As Brooks-Gunn, Liaw, and Klebanov (1992) described, the focus of the intervention was on infants with low birth weight (LBW), defined as a birth weight equal to or less than 2,500 grams, and premature babies, defined as equal to or less than 37 weeks gestational age. Meeting those criteria at the eight sites were 1,302 infants of whom 75.7% (985 infants) accepted the program. Refusals were primarily due to an unwillingness on the part of the parents to accept random assignment to each aspect of the program, according to the Infant Health and Development Program, 1990. One-third of the recruits were randomly assigned to the intervention group, and two-thirds to medical follow-up only. The resulting population of children had an average birth weight of 1,800 grams and an average of 33 weeks gestational age; half of the population was male, 53% was Black, and 10% was Hispanic (Ramey et al., 1992). The infants were disproportionally from poor families and thus at "double risk from both biologic and environmental factors" (Spiker et al., 1991, p. 388).

Intervention. Ramey et al. (1992) described the intervention and its monitoring across the sites in detail. The plan was for intervention infants to be visited in their homes every week for the first twelve months and bimonthly thereafter. The home visitors were college graduates with previous home visiting experience (unlike Project Care in which home visitors for the original parent education component were indigenous to the population of the parents). At twelve months gestational age, infants were to begin attending a Child Development Center; most infants were transported to the site. Center-based intervention using the Partners for Learning curriculum (Sparling & Lewis, 1984) continued until the children were 36 months of age, at which time intervention ceased. A final component was a parent group that met every two months when the child was enrolled in the Child Development Center.

Unlike other intervention programs, because this was a randomized clinical trial in which the exact intervention was to be delivered at each site, careful monitoring of adherence to the program was undertaken. Thus, IHDP can report the participation rate fairly completely (Ramey et al., 1992). Each child who participated in the home visit component (98% of the sample) received an average of sixty-seven home visits (of a possible eighty-four); 86% attended the Child Development Center for an average of 267 days out of a possible 498 days; 78% of the parents attended parent group meetings for an average attendance of 3.7 meetings out of a possible 12. It is clear from these statistics that a small group of families did not participate at all in one or more of the intervention components; moreover, participation among the intervention modalities was not highly correlated. Ramey et al. (1992) professed to being perplexed by the variations in participation, given the high level of initial acceptance.

Early outcomes. The effects of the intervention program measured when the children were 2 and 3 years old were reported extensively (Bradley et al., 1994; Brooks-Gunn, Gross, Kraemer, Spiker, & Shapiro, 1992; Brooks-Gunn, Liaw, & Klebanov, 1992; Brooks-Gunn, Klebanov, Liaw, & Spiker, 1993; McCormick, McCarton, Tonascia, & Brooks-Gunn, 1993; Ramey et al., 1992). At age 24 months, children in the intervention program scored significantly higher on the Mental Development Index of the Bayley Scales, a difference that continued at 36 months on the Stanford-Binet and the Peabody Picture Vocabulary Test (Brooks-Gunn, Liaw, & Klebanov, 1992). Developmental and intellectual quotients obtained over the first three years actually declined in both the intervention and

follow-up groups, but the decline was steeper for the comparison children (Brooks-Gunn et al., 1993).

Because the sample size was large enough, and contained some diversity, subgroup analyses were possible. The differences between the intervention group and the control children could be compared within educational and racial subgroups (Brooks-Gunn, Liaw, & Klebanov, 1992). The intervention appears to have been more successful for the Black and Hispanic children in that there was a greater difference between the intervention and control groups for those children. It should be noted, however, that the intervention-group Black children obtained a mean score on the PPVT at 36 months some ten points lower than the control White children. Intervention generally was more effective for heavier LBW babies, girls, and children whose mothers had more college education (Ramey et al., 1992). Further analyses showed that children whose mothers had a higher education scored better whether they had intervention or not, and White children scored higher regardless of whether their mothers attended college (Brooks-Gunn, Gross, Kraemer, Spiker, & Shapiro, 1992). Even at age 3 years, children whose mothers were college educated did not show any positive (or negative) effects of the intervention.

Postintervention outcomes. IHDP children have been followed through age 8 with major publications emerging from the assessments at age 5 (Brooks-Gunn et al., 1994) and age 8 (McCarton et al., 1997). At the age 5 assessment, the investigators had retained 82% of the sample. The 9.4 IQ points difference between the intervention and control children at age 3 attenuated to a difference on the WPPSI of 0.02 points at age 5. The scores of the intervention group had decreased by about two points, but most of the early difference found between the groups was erased by the control group's scoring about seven points higher (as has been reported consistently from other early intervention projects; see Farran, 1990). The greatest difference between intervention and control children at age 3 had been found for the heavier infants, and it was the heavier infants in the control group who showed the most gain from ages 3 to 5 (from a score of 83.6 at age 3 to 91.7 at age 5). For the lower birth weight group, by age 5, the mean score of the intervention group was actually lower than that of the control children.

Many measures other than global tests of intelligence were obtained for the children. Scores on the PPVT, for example, were a little different from the more general intelligence tests – both the intervention and follow-up groups lost ground on the PPVT between ages 3 and 5, but the difference between them at age 5 was at a $p = .07$ level of significance favoring the intervention children. Behavioral and health measures showed no differences as an effect of intervention. The evaluation at age 8 was actually conducted on more children than were available at age 5 (89% of the original sample was tested at age 8). No differences were found between the intervention and control groups of children on the WPPSI, PPVT, or Woodcock Johnson Psycho-Educational Battery, nor were there differences between the groups in the number of children retained in grade or referred for special education. The two groups were not different in behavioral ratings obtained from the mother or in such measures of health as hospitalizations, surgical procedures, and school absences. The one difference obtained indicated that the intervention group was rated significantly lower than the control group on a scale of physical functioning, meaning that the intervention children were perceived as more limited in their physical activities.

The age 8 follow-up article presents the only cost estimates for the IHDP intervention program. McCarton et al. (1997) reported figures from an analysis at the Miami site that estimated the cost of delivering the three programmatic components at $15,146 per child per year, although it is not clear if they were using 1997 dollars or those corresponding to 1988, when the program began. Whichever, the cost of the program was clearly high.

Explanations of findings. The lack of effect for such an ambitious, well-run, and expensive program was unanticipated and troubling. Because so many sites were involved and so much data were collected, there have been many publications related to various aspects of the program that may provide some understanding of the "no-effect" finding.

One possible explanation is that the intervention itself was not appropriate for the sample because the sample consisted of families who were impoverished generally in addition to having a child with low birth weight. In an analysis of the risks faced in the follow-up only group, Liaw and Brooks-Gunn (1994) argued that intervention may need to be tailored to

the number of risks families face, becoming more intensive as the risks increase. In an important article relevant to this possible explanation, Liaw, Meisels, and Brooks-Gunn (1995) reported extensive analyses of the intervention program, who participated in it, and their different test scores at age 3. For the first time in any of the large number of publications on this project, they revealed that eighty-one children effectively dropped out of the intervention – they did not attend at least one day at the center and did not receive at least one home visit. This group had disproportionally more White families in it.

The value of the extensive data collected relevant to participation in the program is demonstrated in this Liaw et al. (1995) article. During home visits, the home visitors rated the parents' responsivity to each of the activities presented; during the center-based intervention, the teachers rated whether the children responded to each classroom activity. Liaw et al. then divided the sample into a 2×2 matrix: high/low parent response and high/low child response. As might be suspected, the group with the best child outcomes was characterized by high parent responsivity and high child responsivity, although it was not significantly different from the low parent responsivity/high child responsivity group. Relevant to the point Liaw and Brooks-Gunn (1994) made about targeted intervention, Liaw et al. found that degree of responsivity was related to level of poverty for the families. In the lowest participation group, 84% were the most impoverished of the sample, suggesting that the intervention was least appropriate for this group. Liaw et al. concluded that "simply providing an opportunity to participate in an intervention does not necessarily bring about changes in LBW children and their parents" (p. 426). Similarly, Yogman, Kindlon, and Earls (1995) examined the effect of father involvement using IHDP data (measured by whether the father was present in the home during assessment sessions). Less involved fathers were poor, young, Black, and involved with teenaged mothers.

One reason this intervention may not have been effective is that the particular form and content of the interventions were based on approaches developed for nonurban poor children and families with no health risks in a single area of the country. In the IHDP sample, the ordinary difficulties caused by poverty for the families were compounded by giving birth to a child with health problems. The description of the curriculum provided in the Child Development Center makes it clear that it was maturationally based, oriented around traditional domains of development, but lacking any theoretical rationale for which experiences might be the most important foundations for later functioning (Liaw et al., 1995). The home visiting curriculum used in IHDP was an adaptation of the program developed by Project Care according to the Infant Health and Development Program, 1990. Subsequent reported analyses of the progress of children involved in Project Care have shown this curriculum to have, at a minimum, no effect for poor families (Wasik et al., 1990), with the possibility of significant negative effects (Ramey et al., 1985).

An explanation tendered by the group itself is that the intervention may have been appropriate for the higher weight babies but not for the very low- and extremely low-birth-weight babies (McCormick, McCarton, Tonascia, & Brooks-Gunn, 1993). The higher birth weight babies in the intervention group continued to have a Wechsler score four points higher than the control group at age 8 (McCarton et al., 1997). Birth weight was a significant predictor of IQ test scores for the total group (Duncan, Brooks-Gunn, & Klebanov, 1994). The research group concluded that babies with lower birth weight may have had neurologically based problems and required a "more structured and professionally designed situation" (McCarton et al., 1997, p. 131).

Another argument put forward by McCarton et al. (1997) is that the intervention did not last long enough. Stopping the intervention at age 3 was never defensible from either a theoretical or empirical viewpoint. It is true that other intervention programs had shown the greatest effects at age 3, but this finding has been assumed to be an artifact of the content of the tests at that age (Farran, 1990) and not a justification for discontinuing intervention after age 3. Although there might have been more effects had the intervention continued, it must be remembered that the lack of group difference was created by the strong surge of the control group rather than a large loss by the experimental group. One can only assume that the increased scores for the control group would have occurred no matter what, and it is not clear, using the precedents of other intervention

efforts continuing through age 5, that continued improvements could have been brought about for the intervention group if the form of the intervention had remained the same.

Too much data were collected at too great a cost for the scientific and educational community not to learn more about what is advisable for future intervention. Lately, subgroups of IHDP researchers have published separately and not often with exactly the same figures on sample size and attrition (note inconsistencies in the Blair, Ramey, & Hardin, 1995, article compared to Liaw et al., 1995). One would hope that this project could serve as the catalyst for an open, searching discussion on what the scientific community now knows about children from disadvantaged backgrounds who have health risks and what the next steps should be.

CHAPTER 1: CHILD PARENT CENTERS. Reynolds and his colleagues (1995, 1996, 1998) investigated a "Head Start-like" preschool program conducted in twenty Child Parent Centers (CPC) in the Chicago public schools for one to two years beginning at ages 3 or 4. Entry into the programs required that families be eligible for Chapter 1 (now Title I) educational services; enrollment was voluntary, and no comparison group for evaluation was established at the outset. Although there was no uniform curriculum, the focus of Chapter 1 preschools was on general school readiness, with special attention to reading and language skills (Reynolds, Mehana, & Temple, 1995). Parental involvement was required – parents had to attend the school for half a day per week.

Reynolds et al.'s (1995, 1996; Reynolds, 1995) investigations began in 1992 at the end of six years of school for the children. To assess the effects of preschool enrollment in the CPC, the investigators drew a sample of 130 children who attended the same kindergartens but who had no preschool experience. They reported that children with preschool experience scored higher in mathematics and reading achievement six years later in school (Reynolds et al., 1995), there was no further effect for two years of preschool experience over one year (Reynolds, 1995), and cognitive measures taken at kindergarten entry plus subsequent parental involvement mediated the effects of preschool preparation.

One would like to be able to make practical and theoretical use of the reports of Reynolds and his colleagues (Reynolds, Mavrogenes, Bezrucko, & Hagemann, 1996). Many school systems are using Chapter 1/Title I funds to provide preschool experiences, and little is known about the effectiveness of these programs (Farran, Son-Yarbrough, Silveri, & Culp, 1993). Reynolds described the control group he used (Reynolds, 1995; Reynolds et al., 1995), but it is clearly a sample of convenience. In extremely low-income urban neighborhoods when preschool experiences are provided by the public schools at no cost to the parents, who are the children who would not have attended? They are very likely those whose parents were too disorganized or whose living situations were too unstable to enable them to attend. Moreover, Reynolds's publications are more confusing than necessary. In each of the three publications, the samples are a different size, (Ns of 887, 757, and 360) even though they are described the same way; no explanation of the relation among these numbers is provided.

A more recent publication corrects some of these earlier problems of clarity (Reynolds & Temple, 1998). It is apparent in this paper that the intervention group had preschool, kindergarten, and subsequent follow-on services through Grades 2 or 3, and the comparison children were those who left after completing the kindergarten intervention. Continued program participation for two or three years following kindergarten was associated with higher reading achievement test scores through seventh grade. Those with continuing intervention were also less likely to be retained in grade or to be placed in special education. It is encouraging to realize that a school system can create a sustained intervention effort through the first few grades of school that will show continuing effects in middle school. Perhaps this effort could be modeled by other school systems.

TWO-GENERATION PROGRAMS. Almost all of the newly created programs reviewed so far are different from most of the 1970s intervention programs in that they included a parenting intervention component. Widening the lens of intervention for children from disadvantaged circumstances is one of the hallmarks of the intervention efforts of the 1980s and 1990s. This new focus became known as *two-generation programs* (Smith & Sigel, 1995), and its effects will be reviewed next.

Even Start. In 1991 the Even Start authorization (of the Elementary and Secondary Education Act of 1965 as amended by the Hawkins-Stafford Elementary and Secondary School Improvement Amendments of 1988) was amended by Congress to require the program to blend early childhood education and adult education for parents as a cooperative project among agencies in the community (St. Pierre, Swartz, Murray, & Deck, 1996). The Even Start program combines early childhood education, adult literacy, and parenting education. To participate, a family must have an adult who is eligible for adult education (typically without a high school education and in need of the GED) and a child less than 8 years old, and they must live in a Chapter 1/Title I elementary school attendance area. The majority of Even Start families (71%) had an income under $10,000 in the 1989–90 and 1990–91 program years; and 77% of the adults had not finished high school (St. Pierre & Swartz, 1996).

A major evaluation of the Even Start programs was conducted by Abt Associates. The reports from this evaluation (St. Pierre et al., 1996; St. Pierre & Swartz, 1996) provide the only available overview of Even Start's effects; it will be important to have this information in research journals to be more readily accessible. Abt Associates selected 200 families from five Even Start projects; families were randomly assigned to attend the program or serve as controls. Data were collected on the children's achievement and parental accomplishments before the program began and again at 9 and 18 months afterward.

Initially, Even Start child participants gained more than the control group children (St. Pierre et al., 1996), but those advantages were lost 18 months later as the control group caught up with the participating children on both the PPVT and the Preschool Inventory, a measure of school readiness developed by Abt Associates. For the parents, the only difference between participants and controls was that more adults in Even Start (22.4%) completed their GED than among the control group families (5.7%). However, measures of literacy gains showed no differences between the groups. There were no effects from participation in Even Start on such measures as the quality of the home environment, parent–child interactions during book reading, and parental expectations for their children. No effects for program participation on employment or income were found. Moreover, 46% of Even Start mothers were classified as having high levels of depressive symptoms at the outset, and those symptoms were not affected by program participation. "Even Start's services did result in gains in several domains for children and their parents, but in general, the gains were not greater than those that similarly motivated families obtained for themselves using locally available services" (St. Pierre et al., 1996, p. 18).

Again, as with other programs of marginal or disappearing effects, explaining why the effect dissipated is crucial. In general, St. Pierre and colleagues found that all three programmatic elements were ill-defined. Local sites had control over the early childhood education component, hence no structure or content was specified (St. Pierre & Swartz, 1996). About one-third of the programs chose to use the High/Scope curriculum in the first year. The adult education component was also unspecified and not systematically implemented across sites. Programs could hold adult education classes during the day when the children were in school or at night to accommodate working adults. They could focus on the GED or on general instruction in basic skills. No philosophy guided the parent education component; many sites used a combination of commercially available materials. At least 14% of the families left Even Start in the first year of their enrollment because of a "general lack of interest" (St. Pierre & Swartz, 1995, p. 25). To retain families, many programs resorted to such tangible rewards as books, fans, T-shirts, and credits for attendance that could be used at an Even Start store stocked with such necessities as food. Most parents were drawn to the program for the school readiness component for their children. "Participating in parenting education rarely seems to be a drawing card for Even Start" (St. Pierre & Swartz, 1995, p. 63).

Attrition from a program with a heavy parent education component is reminiscent of the high rates of loss from the Parent Child Development Centers (Walker et al., 1995). Similar also are the high rates of maternal depression found in both groups of mothers. One wonders how appropriate "commercially available" parenting programs are for depressed mothers living in poverty with no job

prospects and a fairly bleak future and what these parents must have thought of the educated, employed program coordinators whose approach could have conveyed the impression that poor parenting created poverty rather than the other way around.

Parents as Teachers. The Parents as Teachers (PAT) program originated in Missouri and is widely implemented there (Winter & Rouse, 1990). It is not a classic early intervention program; rather, it is a universal program of support for any new parents in the state who choose to participate in it (Ehlers & Ruffin, 1990). All participation is voluntary; it is difficult to find any definitive, objective evidence regarding its effectiveness. Although PAT or NPAT (New Parents as Teachers) may be one of the first programs with its own web site that includes a section labeled "evaluation," everything included there is unpublished. No data are actually presented, and no evidence is given in the summaries of evaluations for how parents who were evaluated were chosen or with whom they were compared.

The basis for the approach taken by PAT is the research conducted by Burton White in the 1960s and early 1970s (Hausman, 1989; Meyerhoff & White, 1986). The original intervention involved home visits by parent educators once every month, but the Missouri legislature passed a much diluted version that guaranteed only a minimum of four individual visits and four group meetings. Parent educators provide information about child development, and they help parents become observers of their children (Ehlers & Ruffin, 1990). Widespread implementation of the model was supported by the legislature after a 1985 evaluation conducted on a contractual basis by the Research and Training Associates of Overland Park, Kansas (described by Ehlers & Ruffin, 1990). This evaluation compared the performance of seventy-five 3-year olds who had been enrolled in the project with seventy-five control children. No actual data are reported in accessible publications from this evaluation; Ehlers and Ruffin (1990) summarized the findings as showing that the PAT children were significantly advanced over controls in language, problem solving, and other intellectual abilities, as well as being advanced in coping skills and positive relationships with adults. These may be the same data that are reported in Pfannenstiel and Seltzer (1989). Pfannenstiel and Seltzer also reported that it was very difficult to form a comparison group and that the PAT group was from a higher socioeconomic status than the control group.

Universal, but voluntary, programs of support for parents with a new baby are an excellent service for a state to offer and need not necessarily be burdened with the stress of establishing their effectiveness. As Hausman (1989) asserted, models of intervention are not easily bought by states – "*adaptation* rather than *replication* is the essential lesson" (p. 39). This sort of modest statewide support, however, should not be equated with intervention programs aimed at helping children for whom school failure is a distinct possibility. The danger of the Missouri PAT program lies in trying to make more of it than it is, and other states coming to believe that voluntary support for new parents is the same as intervening with children from families beset by chronic poverty and disorganization.

Summary

Reviewing the work related to intervention for children from disadvantaged backgrounds over this past decade is somewhat disheartening. A great deal of money was spent on programs that have not been shown to be more effective than doing nothing at all (IHDP and Even Start); it is hard to believe that researchers and educators will be able to engage congressional imagination and attention again to fund other large intervention efforts. Yet the situations for children and families remain the same or may, in fact, be growing worse – the 1996 federal welfare reform legislation requires that poor mothers go to work, but no money has been allocated for creating adequate child care for their young children.

It is possible that the primary problem with the intervention efforts mounted so far is that they do not take a contextual focus. Even when parents have been enlisted, the objective has been to "fix" their parenting as well as the child's development. There is a lack of recognition of the intimate relationship between parenting and context; parenting grows out of the contexts in which families are functioning. Change the context and parenting itself will change. None of the programs reviewed here made any difference to the income, housing conditions, or employment of the parents involved, despite the fact that the families were often chosen because they

had extremely low incomes. If such issues are not going to be addressed by intervention programs, then the best intervention may be to provide clean, positive, enriched child-care centers with adequate adult:child ratios for the children to attend until school entry. Having such centers in place and with a guarantee of their availability would allow at least some parents to plan and organize their lives (e.g., going back to school and finding a job) without having to worry about child care.

Finally, the scientific and educational community needs to create and then assess alternative ideas about which foundational skills and experiences are required in order to be successful in school when the school curriculum profoundly changes at third and fourth grades (Chall, Jacobs, & Baldwin, 1990; Snow, Barnes, Chandler, Goodman, & Hemphill, 1991). Most of the intervention programs reviewed appear to have taught children concrete skills and pieces of information that enabled them to perform better on readiness tests when they entered school. An entirely different set of skills is needed in order to be successful later in school when an understanding of the content of the materials is required. Development is not a linear accretion of facts, skills, and information. To do well, children must know how to access and relate information and how to synthesize across contents, not just understand what individual words mean. Little theoretical attention has been paid by intervention researchers to preparing children for these later skills; one would hope that the next decade of intervention research will be devoted to such an enterprise.

REVIEW OF INTERVENTION FOR CHILDREN WITH DISABILITIES: 1987–1997

Changes in Intervention Context Since Last Review

A major event related to services for young children with disabilities occurred in 1986 with the passage of the Education of the Handicapped Act Amendments (P.L. 99-457). This bill contained two essential parts. Part B (Section 619) created funding incentives for states to provide public education for all eligible 3- to 5-year-old children with disabilities by 1991–92; Part H (now known as Part C) offered encouragement and assistance to states to implement early intervention for birth to 3-year-old children with disabilities, but it did not require them to do so (Trohanis, 1994).

The assumption that lies behind P.L. 99-457 is that early intervention is cost-effective, saving money on services that would be required in the future. The 1985 Seventh Annual Report to Congress on the Implementation of the Education of the Handicapped Act, published by the U.S. Department of Education, estimated savings of $16,000 per child if intervention began at birth instead of age 6 (USDOE, 1985). The following quotes relate to the implications of this estimate:

Widespread belief that early intervention would result in lower special education costs over the school years formed the basis for the argument that the savings to be derived would more than offset the cost of the program. (Florian, 1995, p. 248)

What stands ultimately behind the national policy is the conventional wisdom that early intervention services represent a "good" investment of public funds. (Chambers, 1991, p. 144)

It is important to realize that this was a different basis for a law than was the case for the passage of P.L. 94-142 – a difference with potentially important consequences. P.L. 94-142 was rooted in the Civil Rights argument for the provision of a free and appropriate education for children with disabilities (Allen, 1992). Even though a publicly funded system of education existed, children were being excluded from it because of their disabilities. Due process and legal definitions of appropriate education followed the passage of P.L. 94-142; the courts have generally upheld the law on constitutional grounds related to the Fourteenth Amendment.

P.L. 99-457 was passed as a prevention measure. No publicly funded universal system of care for young children existed in the United States, then or now. Generally, school systems were not responsible for the education of 3- to 5-year-old children, and services for children from birth to 3 years were rare. Concerns were expressed right away: "Despite a large literature in early intervention, not enough is currently known or understood about what combination of programs and resources will lead to long term benefits for certain kinds of children" (Chambers, 1991, p. 171). To provide universal services for

children with disabilities, school systems have had to invent a system of services as well as to figure out how to identify and enroll children.

The ideology of the 1980s reflected strongly held beliefs in the efficacy of early intervention and a societal commitment to children with disabilities and their families (Shonkoff & Meisels, 1990). The battle over the reauthorization of IDEA in 1996 and 1997 was fueled in part by a potential retreat from this ideological basis for P.L. 99-457. If the ideological support erodes, it might be difficult to find a constitutional basis for the law, although the United States Justice Department has ruled that community child care centers are a public accommodation (like restaurants) and, as such, cannot discriminate against children with disabilities (U.S. Department of Justice, Civil Rights Division, Disability Rights Section, 1998). A heavier burden, however, is on researchers and advocates in the 1990s to prove cost effectiveness in order to buttress support for the law (Guralnick, 1991). Unfortunately, little research in the past decade has addressed the issue of cost-benefit; no one has demonstrated the savings projected by the 1985 U.S. Department of Education report to Congress.

In the late 1980s and early 1990s, several prominent researchers issued strong calls for a second generation of intervention research. Shonkoff, Hauser-Cram, Krauss, and Upshur (1988) suggested moving "beyond asking such simple (and relatively meaningless) questions as Does early intervention work? and pose more important (and more instructive) questions such as, What kinds of services have what kinds of impacts on which kinds of children in which kinds of families?" (p. 87). Marfo and Dinero (1991) characterized the 1980s as a decade of critical analysis of early intervention and asserted that the 1990s would launch a "generation of efficacy research that will be conceptually and methodologically richer" (p. 301). Meisels et al. (1993) asserted that given the heterogeneity of families and disabilities, focus should be put on the family and child in context. This assertion was echoed by Guralnick (1991), who argued that existing research, prior to the 1990s, was global and inexact. Shonkoff (1992) called for "asking why some children and families do better than others" (p. 9). What was needed according to all of these researchers was, in effect, an assessment of aptitude by treatment or investigations into those types of programs that are most appropriate for specific families and disabilities.

The next few sections review work published since 1987. First, a set of studies that examines the implementation of P.L. 99-457, especially services within Part H (now Part C), is presented. Next a review of a series of smaller studies of a variety of intervention programs, most of which have not been replicated, is provided. Third, studies that focus on childhood autism as a detailed example of intervention for a particular type of disability are featured. The final section reviews three programmatically focused and systematic investigations that address the complexities of intervention research.

Implementation of P.L. 99-457

PART B (3- TO 5-YEAR-OLDS). A comprehensive analysis of services provided for young children with disabilities was conducted in the late 1980s in Montgomery County, Maryland (Markowitz, Hebbeler, Larson, Cooper, & Edmisten, 1991). Early intervention for children, birth to age 5, was coordinated by the Montgomery County Public School system. They assessed 489 children who received services; their diagnostic categories provide information about who is likely to be identified during the preschool years. Of the 489 children, almost half (220) were language impaired and 123 were speech impaired; 146 were labeled multihandicapped with significant delays in two or more areas. The latter group was on average a year and a half younger than the first two groups.

The three diagnostic groups received different types of services. Almost all (98%) of the multihandicapped group received classroom-based services (two to five days per week, two to five hours per day) with additional therapies. Approximately half of the language-impaired group was served in a classroom setting. The other half received itinerant speech/language therapy one to three times a week for thirty minutes each time. Of those classified as speech impaired, 96% received speech therapy one to three times per week as their only intervention. In the entire sample of 498, three children received home-based services; no other mention of parental involvement is included in the descriptions of intervention services. Classrooms do not appear to have

been integrated with disabled and nondisabled children.

Markowitz et al. (1991) assessed effectiveness through a value-added analysis. Value-added analysis is the same as many other methods of comparing rate of growth on a posttest to the rate of growth on a pretest. Rosenberg, Robinson, Finkler, and Rose (1987) demonstrated that all of these methods yielded similar results, with no method superior to another. Children were assessed following a year's intervention with the Battelle Developmental Inventory. (The wide variability in developmental measures used in research in the 1970s and 1980s was replaced in the 1990s by an almost exclusive reliance on the Battelle; see the review of this instrument by Meisels, Atkins, & Barnett this volume.)

The group making the most progress by far was language impaired. The least progress was made by the children with speech impairments. The multihandicapped group made more progress than expected in all developmental areas except fine and gross motor skills. Given that the three groups had such different interventions, these results are difficult to interpret. One thing of note is that the group making the least progress was the one whose members spent the least time in classroom settings. The intervention for these children with speech impairments was fairly minimal, as was their progress. Unfortunately, no data are provided beyond the twelve-month intervention. Thus, there is no way to know how many of these children were mainstreamed into the public schools or were classified later as no longer eligible for services (i.e., what the savings might have been).

Two other studies focused on defining and describing the implementation of intervention provided as a consequence of Part B. Schwartz, Carta, and Grant (1996) demonstrated that the amount of gain that children with language impairment attained was directly related to the extent to which the language practices were implemented in the classrooms. In a related study, Liebman and Goodman (1995) demonstrated that even when the objectives of individualized educational plans (IEP) are met, maintenance and generalization of these skills are highly variable and related to developmental age.

This variability raises questions about the appropriateness of the IEP objectives. As public schools assume responsibility for educating younger children, caution must be observed to be sure that the goals established for children are actually appropriate. Liebman and Goodman (1995) found the least generalization was achieved for mathematics objectives (i.e., counting to twenty or counting ten objects) and teaching the concepts of big and little; these are concepts that typically developing children of the same preschool age find difficult. Clearly, special education teachers accustomed to instructing older children will need assistance in identifying appropriate goals for preschool children with disabilities.

The studies cited earlier involved segregated classroom-based intervention administered by a school system. The next series of studies investigated how to provide intervention for preschool children within community-based child-care programs. Although community-based programs have a variety of funding sources and administrative structures (about half are private, for profit, [Deiner, 1997]), they represent what is available to preschool children without disabilities.

Two studies used the Early Childhood Environmental Rating Scale (ECERS; Harms et al., 1990) as an assessment for classrooms into which children with disabilities were placed. The ECERS is the only published, standardized early childhood classroom rating scale (Deiner, 1997); scores of five or above on this seven-point criterion-referenced scale are considered appropriate. File and Kontos (1993) assessed community-based classrooms that enrolled children with disabilities. They found that teachers were more involved with all children in the class and better supported cognitive play in those classrooms with higher ECERS scores (the average for the classrooms was 4.6).

Bruder (1993) used scores on the ECERS as part of the procedure for selecting classrooms in which children with disabilities could be placed, but she did not specify the cut-off point she used or how well the classrooms scored. Bruder's program appears to be quite similar to one developed by Brown, Horn, Heiser, and Odom (1996), known as Project BLEND. Both of these approaches provide support staff who trained the preschool staff, modeled intervention strategies for them, and interacted with families. Neither model has provided comprehensive, detailed evaluation data in published form yet. Both assert that their programs have been successful

with children, parents, and staff. Brown et al. (1996) indicated that the cost of their model was comparable to a center-based early intervention program, an important point for school systems that may believe that community-based intervention will be less costly to conduct.

A final issue affects Part B intervention services and their effectiveness. Parents of preschool children may wish their children to participate in early intervention because they believe, as Congress did, that early intervention will allow their child to "catch up" (Harry, Allen, & McLaughlin, 1995). The transition between Part B services and school entry is one that has received much less attention than one would expect. Harry et al. interviewed parents longitudinally through this transitional period and found them to be increasingly disillusioned. Instead of helping their children catch up, early labeling appeared to solidify the child's permanent participation in special education over the school years. If this is a genuine trend, it may mean that the total cost of early intervention will actually combine the cost of early intervention plus the cost of school-age special education placement.

PART C (BIRTH-TO-3 SERVICES). In contrast to the relative paucity of studies related to Part B, children and families served through Part H (now Part C of IDEA) received more attention. Several large-scale surveys of parents were completed since the passage of P.L. 99-457, and one major longitudinal study has charted utilization of services over a year's time.

Surveys of families were conducted in Colorado, North Carolina, and Pennsylvania (Kochanek & Buka, 1995), Michigan (Thompson, Lobb, Elling, & Herman, 1997), the Southwest (Sontag & Schacht, 1994), and North Carolina, South Carolina, Virginia, Georgia, and Florida (Mahoney & Filer, 1996). Responses from families were fairly consistent across the country, leading to the following conclusions.

- Families with high education, positive family characteristics, and few needs for support were likely to receive the greatest amount of services (Kochanek & Buka, 1995; Mahoney & Filer, 1996; Sontag & Schacht, 1994). Parents with more education and a more secure economic base are apparently more likely both to be aware of and to demand services for their children. Low-income mothers with less education probably had greater need for service co-ordination but seem much less likely to receive it.

- Families indicated that they wanted the early intervention system to provide more organized and coherent information about the services that exist (Sontag & Schacht, 1994) and a more timely response from service coordinators (Thompson et al., 1997). In two of the four surveys, parents were asked about assessment of family needs, a part of the individualized family service plan (IFSP). In each survey, a majority of families did not wish to have their needs surveyed as part of the intervention process, leading Sontag and Schacht (1994) and Mahoney and Filer (1996) to question whether Part H should be considered family-needs-driven or should be reconceptualized as a family decision-making model.

The most comprehensive description of families whose children received intervention services through Part H is provided in the longitudinal study of Shonkoff, Hauser-Cram, Krauss, and Upshur (1992). They followed 190 children and families from twenty-nine community-based early intervention programs (twenty-five in Massachusetts and four in New Hampshire) for twelve months. The sample reflected the three most common problems of children referred to early intervention during the birth-to-3 period: Down syndrome ($N = 54$), motor impairment ($N = 77$), and developmental delay ($N = 59$). Children with Down syndrome tended to be enrolled in early intervention quite young (3.4 months); children who were developmentally delayed were much older at first enrollment (16 months).

Overall, Shonkoff et al. (1992) found that children with similar types and severity of disability received markedly different amounts of intervention. As the other surveys showed, some of the variation in services delivered was related to family status – mothers with low education received fewer services. On average, families received three different types of service for a total of 6.9 hours of intervention per month. Families whose children had more severe psychomotor impairment participated in more early intervention services than families of children with milder levels of severity. In addition, children with more severe impairments made less progress over the year than those with milder impairments.

The relationship between intensity of intervention and severity of disability seems logical, but it is also one of the reasons it is so difficult to demonstrate the effectiveness of early intervention. If children who are more severely delayed or who have more severe impairments are likely to change less even though they receive more intervention, early intervention could appear ineffective. Careful consideration of this interaction is necessary as intervention programs are evaluated by policy makers.

The Shonkoff et al. (1992) study provides a detailed, comprehensive description of changes in children and families and relates these changes to early intervention services. In general, few of their measures predicted changes in children's development over the year. Positive family changes were predicted more by family characteristics than by anything else. Of these family characteristics, initially higher maternal education and higher quality of home environments were associated with more positive change than was predicted. Child and family characteristics were much stronger predictors of child and family change than particular aspects of early intervention services.

Several aspects of intervention were found to be important in unexpected ways. More positive changes for children and families were obtained if children received services from a single discipline rather than multiple disciplines. In addition, more positive child and family changes were achieved when the service format was individualized rather than mixing group and individualized services. No differences in outcome were found to be associated with the location of service delivery, whether primarily center-based or primarily home-based.

Shonkoff et al.'s (1992) study provides a wealth of information regarding the potential impact of Part C services, and it highlights the numerous difficulties in evaluating the implementation of a new public policy. For example, the authors point out in their conclusion that in order to assess the value of enhancing the early caregiving environment, long-term follow-up is required. Assessments during the period of sensorimotor development are notoriously unreliable predictors of later development (Farran & Harber, 1989; McCall, Eichorn, & Hogarty, 1977). Thus, what may appear to be low rates of progress, or even lack of responsivity to early intervention as assessed during the first 3 years of life, may be the foundation for much better outcomes at school age. The complexity of the relationship between child and family characteristics and early intervention services is apparent. More studies like this would provide service providers and coordinators with much vital information to aid their planning.

Single Intervention Programs

Most of the studies reviewed in this section assessed the effects of intervention over a short time frame, typically seven to twelve months. Only two of the studies included a follow-up assessment. Thus, these studies cannot effectively address the concerns identified by Guralnick (1991), Marfo and Dinero (1991), Meisels, Dichtelmiller, and Liaw (1993), and Shonkoff et al. (1988) concerning the interface between specific programs and characteristics of children and families. The programs themselves differed in the socioeconomic levels and mix of disabilities of the children they served and in the intervention each delivered. In most cases, the descriptions of the intervention provided were too sparse to enable one to know if differences in outcome were related to differences in treatment. The programs also do not address the issue of cost-effectiveness, although several assessed related issues, such as age of onset of intervention and alternative models of intervention. The studies tend to cluster into two types that are based on the site of service delivery: those in which the intervention was primarily delivered in classroom settings and those in which the delivery site was primarily home-based.

CLASSROOM-BASED INTERVENTION. Several studies assessed the effects of intervention delivered in classroom settings. Four programs served small numbers of young children in classrooms for twenty to forty hours per week. Apparently contradictory results were obtained by Fewell and Glick (1996) and Rose and Calhoun (1990) in terms of who most benefited from the intervention. Fewell and Glick demonstrated that for the total group, progress during the intervention (seven months) was about the same as progress before the intervention, but when the forty-four children were separated by severity level, the more mildly involved made more progress than the more severely disabled. In contrast, the Charlotte Circle Project served infants and toddlers with severe and profound disabilities, and Rose and Calhoun found that the children progressed at

twice the developmental rate than would have been expected. This difference highlights the difficulty of drawing conclusions about the effectiveness of intervention for different types of children from these small, diverse samples and programs.

In a comparison of full- and part-time intervention for birth to three-year-old children eligible for intervention services, Dihoff et al. (1994) also found that children with less severe biologically based symptoms improved more in each of the intervention models, giving credence to the Fewell and Glick (1996) conclusion. Dihoff et al. discovered an interesting set of relations in their assessments of the children at six and twelve months during the intervention. First, neither group (full- or part-time) outscored the other in cognitive development after twelve months; this includes a comparison to a waiting-list control group of similar children. The groups differed in their development of motor skills, with the full-time group showing gains after six months of intervention that the part-time group only showed at twelve months. A similar lag in effects for the part-time group was demonstrated in expressive and receptive language skills. Social adaptation skills did not show significant improvement for either group until after twelve months. This is a well-conceptualized study that raises important issues regarding when intervention assessments should be conducted. Many of the interventions in which the results are published assess program effects after periods of five to seven months. The results obtained by Dihoff et al. (1994) suggest that, depending on the intensity of the intervention, such a time frame may be much too brief to indicate effects.

Two other studies were also designed to yield internal comparisons. This could be an important strategy in intervention research. Control or comparison groups are so difficult to obtain and justify that investigating variations in intervention models within the population of children with disabilities might be preferable. Burchinal, Bailey, and Snyder (1994) compared the developmental progress of 1- to 4-year-old children with disabilities who were placed either with same-aged children or in a mixed-age class. Both types of classes also enrolled typically developing peers. Children in the two treatment groups did not show different patterns of change over time. These were, however, small classes (class size of six) in a university-based program with much individualized attention, which may not have been an adequate test of the mixed-age versus same-age classmates question. Rittenhouse, White, Lowitzer, and Shisler (1990) compared the progress of severely hearing-impaired children aged 18 months–5 years who were divided into two instructional groups. One group received instruction in English sign language, and the other received instruction in an oral-aural only method. Both groups were in a classroom 2 1/2 hours a day, four days per week, and each classroom had four to five children with a teacher and an aide. No differences were found between the groups on the Battelle Developmental Inventory at the end of nine months. From the description provided, it is not clear how segregated the two instructional groups were from one another. In addition, nine months seems like a small amount of time to assess the effects of intervention choices that are so emotionally laden within the deaf education community.

Intervention models must always deal with the "generation effect" (Farran, 1990). Almost all programs are effective when they are initially developed, especially if they are established during a heightened period of belief that a new solution to a developmental problem has been found. As soon as programs pass beyond the hands of the originators into a second generation, few have proven to have lasting significance. Important lessons are to be learned from this phenomenon. The first is that belief in the efficacy of a program and in children's potential to learn and progress rapidly may be the most critical element in any intervention strategy. Belief, however, is difficult to export. In training new implementors, it may be less important to train them in the fine points of the curriculum than to imbue them with a strong sense that they will be effective and that change is possible.

Two studies by Fewell and Oelwein (1990, 1991) represent efforts to take a developed model of intervention and use it in other sites to determine if the same effects can be obtained. The Model Preschool Program (MPP) was developed by Fewell as one of the twenty-four original experimental early intervention programs funded by the Handicapped Children's Early Education Assistance Act of 1968. The MPP was a classroom-based model with what could best be characterized as a teacher-directed focus. The fourteen replication sites served an extremely wide

age range, from 8 months to 12 years (Fewell & Oelwein, 1991). Overall, the children made more gains on the Battelle Developmental Inventory during the nine months they participated in the intervention than prior to the intervention. The picture was more mixed for the children with Down syndrome in the sample who showed significantly increased rates of progress on only three of the seven Battelle subtests. Another aspect of this replication effort may help explain this finding. As Fewell and Oelwein reported in 1990, the replication sites also varied by the degree of mainstreaming or access to typical peers. In that study, children with Down syndrome made more progress in expressive language skills if they were in sites without integration.

Finally, one study followed up children who had participated in early intervention services delivered in a classroom setting (Urwin, Cook, & Kelly, 1988). The classroom enrolled preschool children with severe receptive or expressive language disabilities (not the result of neurological impairment or hearing loss) whose IQ scores were above 80. The program met daily for two hours each morning for four ten-week sessions. Urwin et al. located twenty-five of the original thirty-eight children when they were 8 years old and found that 84% of them were functioning in mainstream education and were well integrated in their classrooms. Parents reported that the children continued to have some difficulties expressing complex ideas and were slower in reading, but they had no serious concerns. "The major finding of this study was to show that children who had suffered serious language difficulties early in life were almost exclusively within the mainstream of education with minimal support" (Urwin et al., 1988, p. 142). Interestingly, Urwin et al.'s findings are similar to those of the short-term effects obtained by Markowitz et al. (1991) with language-impaired preschool children whose early intervention was provided by the school system in Montgomery County, Maryland. These findings suggest that there may be good reasons to attend closely to the language skills of children between the ages of 2 and 3 years as others have suggested (Rescorla, Roberts, & Dahlsgaard, 1997). Focused services for that particular group of children appear to be beneficial to their later development.

HOME-BASED INTERVENTION. The next section reviews six small studies conducted to assess various forms of intervention delivered in the home. All of the children involved were quite young, ranging in age from 9–22 months when intervention began. Studies by both Diamond and LeFurgy (1992) and Mahoney and Powell (1988) did not cite the intervention results as their primary focus, although both presented pre- and posttest data. Neither demonstrated changes in mental development as assessed by the Bayley Scales over the course of the intervention. In fact, Diamond and LaFurgy actually showed a significant decrease in psychomotor development on the Bayley. Neither study explains the lack of effect. It gives one pause to realize how little the intervention itself seems to have changed the children's development.

Palmer and his colleagues (Palmer et al., 1990; Palmer et al., 1998) investigated two types of intervention with children diagnosed with cerebral palsy. One group received twelve months of neurodevelopmental therapy (NDT) beginning in the second year of life. The other group received six months of general infant stimulation activities and six months of NDT. Parents were taught how to deliver both forms of intervention, with the infant stimulation intervention involving interactive games rather than physical therapy. Parents were instructed to work with their infants daily; they and the child saw a therapist every other week. At the end of six months, the children in the second group had better cognitive and motor development. Oddly enough, at the end of twelve months, the second group of children continued to score higher on motor development, although the two groups were equivalent on cognitive development. This outcome was unexpected and difficult to explain. In a follow-up study, Palmer et al. (1990) investigated whether changes in the parents accounted for changes in the children (i.e., if the second group of parents had changed their parenting behaviors significantly as a consequence of learning the infant stimulation approach). They found no differences in the two treatment groups on the HOME scale, the Carey Temperament Scales, or measures of maternal responsivity. In a 1997 review of neuromotor interventions, Pakula and Palmer asserted that this work showed that "the routine use of NDT was concluded to offer no short-term advantage over infant stimulation in infants presenting with apparent spastic diplegia" (Pakula & Palmer, 1997, p. 103). This was an interesting

study that tested an important aspect of intervention. Additional studies examining the interaction between clinical physical therapy approaches and general infant stimulation would seem to be in order.

The next two studies of home-based intervention are more difficult to evaluate. One is a study of the implementation of a family-focused intervention model as conceptualized by Bailey et al. (1986). Infants began the program when they were 22 months old chronologically but 8 months of age developmentally (Caro & Derevensky, 1991). Over the course of the intervention, composed of one two-hour visit to the family each week for five months, children gained an average of four months developmentally, prompting Bailey et al. to assert that "most of these infants approximated near normal rates of progress over the 5-month period" (p. 76). It is not clear, however, which services these children were receiving before the family-focused intervention began. All of the children's diagnoses were those commonly identified in infancy including Down syndrome, tuberous sclerosis, cerebral palsy, and other severe disabilities. If, indeed, these 22-month-old children received no intervention before Caro and Derevensky initiated their family-focused program, it is possible that the gain was the kind of burst that often accompanies the initial impact of intervention. It would be important to determine what happened after the five-month intervention and whether the developmental trajectories of these children continued to show improvement.

In contrast, Behl, White, and Escobar (1993) showed no stronger effects for an early intervention program that involved an hour of intervention services once a week in the home compared to a low intensity program in which parents merely participated in a monthly support group. The children involved were all visually impaired. Behl et al. followed the children's progress for three years. Unfortunately, as was true for other intervention models, there is a confound in this study between severity and intensity. Children who received the more intense program had more severe developmental problems as initially measured by the Battelle. No information was provided about comparability of visual status. The less intense intervention group had significantly more children in child care and more mothers who worked at higher level jobs. Because of these initial differences, it is hard to know how to make use of their findings, demonstrating again how complex early intervention can be.

Three studies assessed the issue of whether beginning intervention earlier is better; all were home-based (Boyce, Smith, Immel, Casto, & Escobar, 1993; Mastropieri, 1987; Watkins, 1987). Earlier intervention appears generally to be associated with more positive changes in children's development, but it does not make an overwhelming difference or even a significant one in some cases. Using an available sample, Mastropieri found a negative correlation between length of intervention and posttest scores, suggesting, as would be reasonable, that children with more severe problems or those who were not making progress remained in the intervention longer. Further investigation should try to disentangle starting age from length of intervention, controlling for severity of disability.

CONCLUSION. These studies are so disparate that general conclusions are somewhat difficult to derive. Nevertheless, it appears that for the types of disabilities identified during the preschool years, intervention of all types and in all locations produces more gains on standardized tests for those participating children who are more mildly impaired than for those more severely impaired. Second, intervention focused on preschool children (3–5 years of age) who are speech and language impaired appears to be generally effective and associated with participation in mainstreamed education in elementary school. Third, focused clinical intervention during the sensorimotor period appears to be less effective than general global infant intervention focused on positive family interactions. Less experimentation occurred during the 1990s with alternative forms of intervention than occurred in the 1980s. Perhaps motivation for the earlier experimentation and the high volume of published studies was the Handicapped Children's Early Education Assistance Act that funded the experimental programs, the results of which were published mostly in the 1970s and 1980s. With rare exceptions, one does not see in the recent set of published studies tests of philosophically different orientations toward intervention. Nor does one see many efforts to dissociate the various contributions to intervention effectiveness in a way that would advance the field.

Research Focused on Specific Disabilities: The Example of Autism

OVERVIEW. A comprehensive set of reviews of intervention strategies for children with different types of disabilities is to be found in the edited book by Guralnick (1997), *The Effectiveness of Early Intervention*. The research studies reviewed vary from case studies and single-subject designs to small interventions focused on particular groups. Individual chapters are devoted to such specific disability categories as Down syndrome, cerebral palsy, conduct disorder, hearing loss, visual impairments, autism, and communication disorders. Although the book itself does not include a summary chapter, Gallagher (1997) has helpfully provided generalizations that he thinks the chapters illustrate, two of which are particularly relevant to the issue of differential effects of intervention for different disabilities. First, the results of the interventions reviewed across the disability groups are positive but modest. Children with disabilities make some improvement but remain for the most part well below average. Second, a major gap continues to exist between what has been established by research and what is actually practiced; programs should be more "research sensitive" (Gallagher, 1997, p. 90).

Most of the disability groups reviewed individually in chapters in Guralnick's (1997) book actually receive intervention in groups of children of mixed disabilities. Often, specialized therapists (e.g., physical, speech, or occupational therapists and mobility specialists) work with the child one-on-one either in the classroom or in a clinic setting or the home. The general form of the intervention, though, tends to be similar to that described in the previous section concerning small intervention programs. All of the children, whatever their categorization, receive similar intervention. However, one disability for which that is often not the case is childhood autism. This disorder has received much more attention as a separate group this past decade. It is this group about which the most vociferous philosophical differences exist in current programs. This section reviews the research on autism during the 1990s.

CHILDHOOD AUTISM. In their recent review of autism, or pervasive developmental disorder (PDD), of which autism is considered to be a subtype,

Dawson and Osterling (1997) estimated the prevalence as 15 in 10,000 children. Children who are diagnosed with PDD tend to be diagnosed later than children with other disabilities. Thus, they enter preschool intervention programs between the ages of 3-1/2 and 4 years. Dawson and Osterling reviewed the major approaches to PDD and concluded that it is difficult to make meaningful comparisons among programs. Some of the programs provide placement data and information on developmental gains and assert that about half of their graduates are later served in general educational settings and that children are gaining an average of 20 IQ points (from an average initial IQ in the mid-50s). However, the programs usually do not provide descriptions of the general educational settings or the extent to which children require special supports within the setting. Moreover, developmental gains are provided in such a variety of ways that the programs are difficult to compare. Dawson and Osterling concluded their review by stating that "more specific answers to questions such as whether one intervention approach is more effective than another and what is the optimal intensity of intervention will have to await the next generation of intervention research" (1997, p. 314).

The common characteristic among intervention approaches to autism is that they are more intense than interventions for other disability groups. All programs typically involve more than twenty hours per week, and they almost always involve the parents in a cotherapist role, thus extending the intervention into the home. The interventions vary in the approach each group believes will work, with the most radical disagreements occurring between a behavioral approach represented by Lovaas (1987) and his colleagues and a play-based approach represented by Rogers and Dunlap and Fox. Because these perspectives take such a different view of the intervention that will be successful for children with autism and because parents often become staunch, emotionally committed advocates of one view or the other, each of these approaches is reviewed here.

The fundamental assumption behind the behavioral approach of Lovaas (1987) is that normal children learn from their everyday environments but autistic children do not. Thus, in order for autistic children to "catch up" with their peers by the first grade, a special, intense, and comprehensive training environment must be created. This training

environment takes place in "almost all of the subjects' waking hours" (Lovaas, 1987, p. 5). Therapists are involved with the children for forty hours per week, and parents are trained to continue the system at home. This intensity is maintained for two or more years. During the first year, the intervention focuses on reducing self-stimulating and aggressive behaviors. The second year focuses on teaching language and play with peers, and the third year on preacademic tasks and expressing emotions. Lovaas believes that the laws of learning apply to autistic children who can learn like other human beings; their problems result from a mismatch of their central nervous system and the environment, resolved by manipulating the environment (Lovaas & Smith, 1989).

The original study instituted by Lovaas (1987) included his experimental group receiving the full intervention and two control groups: one that received minimal intervention (ten hours or less of the treatment) and one that received no intervention. Although the groups were not randomly assigned (a fact about which there has been controversy from opponents to this approach; for example, Schopler, Short & Mesibov, 1989), other behaviorists and such methodologists as Baer (1993) have argued that the original design was legitimate and convincing. Lovaas has followed the children's progress through age 13. At an age 6 follow-up, the experimental group scored significantly higher than the control group, with an average IQ gain of 30 points. Nine of the experimental group (termed the *best outcome group*) were successfully enrolled in regular first grades in public schools. Lovaas argued that the original experimental group actually contained two distinct groups with different etiologies, although their presenting characteristics were the same at intake. One group of recovered children showed no permanent intellectual, language, or behavioral deficits after intervention; the other group was less responsive. At age 13, the experimental group continued to score 30 points higher than controls and to perform better on the Vineland Adaptive Behavior Scales (McEachin, Smith, & Lovaas, 1993). Of the nine best-outcome children, one had been moved to special education, and one of the less initially responsive experimental children had moved from special to regular education. None of the control group children was in regular education. These follow-up findings were deemed a "triumph of behavioral science and behaviorally scientific clinical application" (Baer, 1993, p. 373).

Despite the response of some that the Lovaas (1987; Lovaas & Smith, 1989) work is a triumph, the behavioral nature of the intervention is antithetical to what others believe is best practice for young children with disabilities. Klinger and Dawson (1992) contended that developing skills in autistic children should be modeled on naturally occurring patterns in typical social interactions and not explicitly taught. In their alternative model, the child is in control of the stimulation he or she receives and is not a passive recipient of intense manipulation by adults as in the Lovaas (1987) model. The model developed by Rogers and colleagues (Rogers & DiLalla, 1991; Rogers & Lewis, 1988) reflects this alternative point of view. Rogers and Lewis (1988) believe that there is an "all-encompassing" (p. 207) social deficit in autistic children that can best be remediated by the use of play, interpersonal relationships, and special activities to foster language and symbolic thinking. They argued against behavioral models: "Failure to tie treatment goals to a developmental framework may result in the accrual of isolated skills that have poor transfer to other situations and which have limited generalizability to other skill areas" (Rogers & Lewis, 1988, p. 212). Unfortunately, they had no control group, they had not followed up their children for as long as Lovaas, nor did they provide information on the later educational placement of the children. Assessing the rate of development during treatment compared with rates projected at intake, Rogers and Lewis found significant differences in the areas of cognition, language, social–emotional, and motor development. Their data indicate an initial steep rise in developmental rates when intervention is instituted followed by a slowing of the acceleration.

A variation of the developmental approach was proposed by Dunlap and his colleagues (Dunlap, Johnson, & Robbins, 1990; Dunlap, Robbins, Morelli, & Dollman, 1988; Fox, Dunlap, & Philbrick, 1997; Robbins & Dunlap, 1992). The premise behind this approach is that the odd social behaviors exhibited by autistic children are not deficits but are, in fact, functional and communicative. The goal of the intervention is to establish alternative communication signals that serve the same function as

effectively and efficiently as the problem behavior. Dunlap and colleagues' intervention approach involves the entire family; the support is highly individualized without a predetermined sequence or script, based on the resources, values, and preferences of the family itself. Their approach involves an intense intervention phase, but this phase only lasts four to five months and for an average of twelve hours per week. Follow-up of children from this program has been less intense than that of Lovaas. They argued that the state of Florida, where this program takes place, provides few opportunities for children with significant disabilities to be included in regular education classrooms. In general, Dunlap and colleagues asserted that the program has improved parent interaction skills substantially and increased rates of child development, while reducing problem behaviors (Fox et al., 1997).

REMEDIATION VERSUS DEVELOPMENTAL MODELS OF INTERVENTION. The serious philosophical disagreement between the intervention approach developed by Lovaas and those of Rogers and Dunlap illustrates a more pervasive rift in early childhood special education generally. The developmental approach tends to be exemplified by early childhood education; the remedial approach is characteristic of early childhood special education (Stafford & Green, 1996). Special education has its roots in the behavioral approaches developed with older populations, many of which have been institutionalized. As the field involves younger and younger children who are increasingly placed in inclusive early childhood settings, the conflicts between teacher-directed and child-initiated perspectives have become more apparent (Goodman, 1994; Lifter, 1995). Adherents of one perspective or another (see Winter, 1997) tend to be absolute in their beliefs, many of which are not actually substantiated by data. As Bricker (1995) asserted, in the field of early childhood special education, "Advocacy for the cause was often obscuring individual child and family needs" (p. 179).

The important contribution that the field of early intervention must make in the future is to combine these two approaches. Children with specific disabilities may not, in fact, be able to make use of conventional early experiences, because of motoric, linguistic, or cognitive differences. Those children with childhood autism, for example, may be exposed to "normal" environments but have behaviors that actively interfere with their understanding and assimilating social cues. In contrast, isolating children assures that they will have difficulty generalizing what they have learned to more typical environments. The next series of research projects demonstrates the importance of careful, systematic investigations of the components of various forms of intervention, isolating which factors work for whom, and may yield the kind of information needed to inform practitioners how to combine the remedial and the developmental approach.

Systematic Investigations: Three Examples

EARLY CHILDHOOD RESEARCH AND INTERVENTION PROGRAM. A small program with a complex design and a philosophical focus based on a transactional approach to development (Sameroff & Fiese, 1990) was created by Seifer, Clark, and Sameroff (1991), the results of which are also reported in Brinker, Seifer, and Sameroff (1994). This is a center-based model in which children with disabilities (whose average initial age was 10 months) and their families participated for ten months, two hours per week. In the first hour, mothers interacted with their children under the guidance and tutelage of a transdisciplinary team of interventionists. Every intervention session was followed by a meeting of the full team to share information and to plan further intervention. During the second hour, parents participated in a parent support group while the classroom intervention team worked directly with the child.

The 144 infants who participated in the research represented the usual types of disabilities identified early in a child's life: 40% had Down syndrome, 33% had cerebral palsy, and the remaining infants were divided between genetic anomalies and serious developmental delay of unknown causes. The socioeconomic and ethnic mix, however, was more diverse than many intervention programs, including more Black (27%) and Hispanic (12%) families as well as those from middle and low SES backgrounds. Attrition from the program was more likely by those without intact marriages, of lower SES, and whose children had indeterminant diagnoses (matching the attrition trends from other intervention programs for children from poor backgrounds).

The analyses of the data collected by this project could serve as a model for investigating intervention. Brinker et al. (1994) argued that the data support a complex relation among family systems, family adaptation, and child outcomes. Overall, the children did not make significant progress in the intervention. The developmental rate over the course of the ten-month intervention appears to be the same as before the intervention began, with the Bayley MDI mean scores actually decreasing. Participation in the intervention had a complex relationship with socioeconomic status and family stress. Contrary to expectations, when low SES mothers who were experiencing high amounts of stress participated actively, their children scored less well than their initial MA would have predicted. On the other hand, the participation of low SES mothers under low stress was linked to children having a better than predicted outcome. For middle SES mothers, participation in the intervention had a positive effect on the child's outcome, regardless of initial stress levels. Middle SES mothers who were least stressed and who did not participate in the intervention had poorer child outcomes. It is clear that the intervention was incorporated into the lives of mothers differently, depending on their existing circumstances. It appears as though early intervention (at least as delivered in a center setting) was an additional stressor for already stressed mothers in impoverished circumstances and may have served as a risk factor rather than as a help for their children. These analyses represent a good example of designing evaluations of interventions to take into account different family and child characteristics, the results of which should affect the practice of providing intervention.

MILIEU TEACHING AND PRELINGUISTIC MILIEU TEACHING INVESTIGATIONS. One of the most systematic investigations of early intervention during the 1990s has been that of Yoder, Warren, Kaiser, and their students. Their focus has been on language development in children with developmental disabilities (not exclusively language impaired, although delays in development typically affect language as well as other areas of development), and their interest has been in milieu teaching. *Milieu teaching* is a naturalistic intervention strategy that incorporates the following elements: following the child's lead or interest, explicit prompts for the child's language, rewards within naturally occurring consequences, and intervention embedded in ongoing interactions between the interventionist and the child (Kaiser, Yoder, & Keetz, 1992).

Exploration of the effects of milieu teaching on the language acquisition of children with developmental disabilities has been systematic, with the results embedded in and expanding on the original theoretical framework. In two studies, the milieu teaching approach was compared to an alternative strategy. Yoder, Kaiser and Alpert (1991) randomly assigned forty preschool children (communication age [CA] of 52 months; mean length of utterance [MLU] of 2.19) to two language intervention treatments, either milieu teaching or the communication training program (CTP). CTP is a direct instruction model with a predetermined protocol, drill, and practice. Comprehension is explicitly taught, and concrete rewards are used. Staff were randomly assigned to the method of intervention, and two staff members administered both types. Contrary to expectations, the highest scoring children were in the CTP group. More detailed comparisons revealed that the milieu language approach benefited children who did not talk much, did not self-initiate often, and were not very intelligible at the outset; whereas the CTP approach worked better for children whose initial language capabilities were better.

Further investigations of the milieu teaching approach contrasted it with another naturalistic language intervention method, *responsive interaction* (Yoder et al., 1995). This comparison was carried out in classrooms in Nashville and Pittsburgh and involved 102 preschool children whose MLU averaged about 2.4. No significant overall group differences were found to favor either intervention approach; however, the previous results obtained by Yoder et al. (1991) were corroborated. Children who were in the earlier stages of language development responded better to the milieu teaching approach. Yoder et al. (1995) speculated that milieu teaching might be difficult to implement for children with more syntactically complex language and that therefore any other method of intervention (direct instruction or responsive interaction) would be more effective with children at more advanced stages of language acquisition.

Yoder and colleagues then investigated a particular stage of language acquisition, the transition from prelinguistic to linguistic communication, as described in detail by Warren and Yoder (1998):

The transition from pre-intentional to intentional communication may represent a period during which transactional effects can have a substantial impact on development. Adults have relatively dramatic changes to respond to and the child's behavior and brain development may be most susceptible to alteration, both positive or negative, by environmental input and social responsiveness. (p. 371)

The intervention Warren and Yoder developed became a modified form of milieu teaching called *prelinguistic milieu teaching* (PMT). The focus of two investigations has been the transactional effects that occur from providing language intervention during this particular developmental moment. Intervention with the children creates changes in the children's behaviors that could lead to changes in the adults with whom they interact. Those adults, in turn, could become more language facilitating, thus stabilizing the changes in the children.

Warren, Yoder, Gazdeg, Kim, and Jones (1993) found that PMT increased children's prelinguistic intentional requesting behaviors within the intervention sessions. Intentional requesting behaviors were also found to generalize to the classroom setting and were demonstrated toward classroom teachers who had not been part of the intervention. Moreover, the teachers were observed to engage in more linguistic mapping of the children's communication acts after the intervention. In a replication and extension of these findings, Yoder, Warren, Kim, and Gazdag (1994) selected four children from a university-based intervention program who were mentally retarded, without speech, and delayed in intentional requesting behaviors. Training sessions were conducted for twenty-five minutes per day, four days per week; the number of sessions ranged from thirty-five to sixty-one. Generalization sessions were conducted with the children's mothers. Intervention and generalization effects were observed in the number of intentional requests made by the children, demonstrating generalization to mothers as well as to teachers, as found in the previous study. Contingency analyses of both sets of data indicated that naive adults (teachers and mothers) were more likely to map linguistically (attach meaningful words to the child's behaviors) children's intentional communicative acts rather than preintentional ones, lending credence to the pathway the group is proposing. The implications are that intervention timed to work with a child during this transition is much more likely to be supported by consequent behaviors from the natural environment.

APTITUDE × TREATMENT INTERACTIONS. Another long, productive research partnership exists among Cole, Dale, and Mills. Their longitudinal investigation of contrasting forms of early intervention for preschool children with disabilities began in the late 1980s (Dale & Cole, 1988). In the first study, eighty-three children with mild disabilities between the ages of 3 and 8 were assigned to preschool ($N = 61$) or kindergarten classrooms ($N = 22$) at a university-based experimental laboratory school. Students were randomly assigned to receive mediated learning (ML), a cognitively-oriented program that emphasizes generalization, or direct instruction (DI), a program that explicitly and systematically teaches academic skills.

To assure that the different instructional programs were being implemented with fidelity, Dale and Cole (1988) devised a classroom observational system. On nine of fourteen categories, the classrooms were significantly different in the predicted directions. The effects of the two forms of instruction were different for the two age groups. For the preschool children, ML produced higher scores after six to ten months of intervention on four of six subscales of the McCarthy and on MLU. Direct instruction led to greater gains for preschool children on the Test of Early Language Development and the Basic Language Concepts test. At kindergarten, however, only two significant differences were found between the groups on the posttests, the General Cognitive Index and the Perceptual subtests of the McCarthy Scales, both favoring the DI group. In this early study, the investigators concluded that both forms of intervention were effective but noted that DI might be more appropriate for kindergarten, when children are ready for academic content. They also observed more behavioral disruption in the ML kindergarten program.

A second study extended the investigation of ML and DI as alternative forms of early intervention. More children were added to the sample for a total of 110 who had participated in the intervention for one to three years. In a follow-up comparison, eighty-four of the entire sample of 110 who had completed one year of intervention were located and tested; forty-six of the seventy-six who had completed two years were tested. (All subjects in the two-year sample were also in the one-year group.) Although the one-year posttest scores were in the predicted directions, few significant differences were found, with even fewer obtained at two years postintervention. ML tended to produce higher scores on the Stanford Binet at one-year postintervention, and DI tended to produce higher PIAT scores, a finding consistent with their predictions. Cole, Mills, and Dale (1989) concluded that both programs were effective in slightly different areas and that a prudent teacher might use elements of each. They also noted a washout effect over the early grades similar to that found in intervention efforts with low-income children.

Subsequent analyses and further follow-up of augmented samples in the same randomly assigned comparison instructional groups yielded a clearer understanding of the effects of these two approaches (Cole, Dale, & Mills, 1991; Cole, Dale, Mills, & Jenkins, 1993; Mills, Dale, Cole, & Jenkins, 1995). These researchers have investigated the issue of aptitude (i.e., child characteristics) by treatment (i.e., ML or DI) interactions. Over the four years of the experiment, 206 children were enrolled in one of the two forms of instruction. The subsequent studies were based on subsamples of this total group. Cole et al. (1991) selected 107 children who were language delayed and assessed their response to six to ten months of the contrasting forms of intervention (ML versus DI). Although significant gains were achieved by the entire group across many of the measures (favoring neither form of intervention), the interesting findings were the Aptitude × Treatment interactions. Unexpectedly, higher-performing students at pretest responded better to DI, whereas lower-performing students gained more from ML intervention.

Again drawing from the 206 students in the total sample, Cole et al. (1993) examined the response of a more diverse group of 164 children with disabilities (80% were language impaired, some of whom were part of the 1991 study). They confirmed that higher-performing students gained more from direct instruction, and lower-skilled children responded better to the more process approach of mediated learning. "In these studies, higher functioning students benefitted more from interventions that maximized learning time, whereas lower functioning students benefitted more from interventions that targeted specific learning strategies" (Cole et al., 1993, p. 26). From the original sample, Mills et al. (1995) were able to follow up 141 children at age 9 and found the same Aptitude × Treatment effects in the same directions. Because this is one of the few follow-up studies of children who participated in early intervention, it is important to note that there were no differences between the two groups in their likelihood of being placed in special education. By age 9, two-thirds of the sample was in a special education placement. Follow-up mean IQ scores averaged around 80, just as they did before the intervention began in preschool or kindergarten.

Cole, Mills, Dale, and Jenkins (1991) also used a subset of this same sample to compare integrated and segregated early intervention settings. A group of 100 children with disabilities was randomly assigned to integrated or segregated classrooms. A group of twenty-four typically developing children was randomly assigned to the integrated classes. Overall, no significant differences were obtained on the posttests favoring either type of intervention. Aptitude × Teatment interactions were obtained, however, with the higher-functioning students doing better in integrated classrooms and the lower-functioning students responding better to the segregated situation. Cole et al. concluded that the "effects of integration may be complex," and may be influenced by individual student characteristics.

This line of research demonstrates not just the old adage that one size doesn't fit all. The results are more interesting than that. For years, researchers and interventionists have speculated that the same intervention does not have the same effects for different children. Cole et al. (1991) have helped identify the types of children who respond to different forms of intervention. Unfortunately, all of this work was done on the same sample of children, and at some point one begins to capitalize on the chance characteristics of a particular sample. The important next step is to replicate and extend these findings in the same systematic way that the work on milieu teaching has proceeded. Cole et al. (1989) have identified which characteristics should be pursued.

It appears that lower-functioning children may need a different form of intervention. Their argument is that for direct instruction to be successful, children must be able to follow and attend to a teacher's lead. In mediated learning, the child's lead more often forms the basis for teacher action (Cole et al., 1993). If lower-functioning children are more dependent on the teacher's reading their cues, the greater diversity of the integrated classrooms may make this more difficult to achieve and account for their slower progress in that setting.

CONCLUSION. These examples demonstrate the difficulty and complexity of engaging in research related to early intervention for children with disabilities. Systematic, step-by-step theoretically grounded programs of research such as the three sets of studies reviewed here are the only ones likely to yield the answers the field now requires. Somehow, these efforts need to be highlighted and funded so that the work can continue and the findings can be applied to the actual practice of intervention.

Conclusion

This review makes clear that the largest intervention effort for children with disabilities and their families has received little systematic attention concerning its effectiveness. Part C is now implemented in all of the states. In most, the public schools are responsible for intervention services for children with disabilities who are 3 to 5 years of age. Responsibility for younger children varies. Unfortunately, very little information exists as to the effectiveness of this massive effort. At least some attention over the next several years must be devoted to understanding what various school systems are doing across the country to meet the demands of Part C and what outcomes the alternative strategies are producing. School systems in different states are having difficulty determining what the components of an instructional program for preschool children should be and how much intervention they must actually be responsible for and can afford to provide. Similar wide differences exist in intervention systems for children younger than 3 years, but associating these differences with outcomes has not taken place.

Parent surveys of the implementation of Part C (formerly Part H of P.L. 99-457) highlight the important issue of how to define early intervention. How intensive does it have to be? Intervention for children in poverty and for those with autism tends to be much more intensive than for children with other vulnerabilities. Most children with disabilities receive a few hours of intervention a month (with the most severely affected receiving more). As Part C is implemented on a widespread basis, it may ironically result in more children being served with much less intervention. At what point intervention ceases to be useful because it is just too limited becomes a critical question to address for families dependent on school systems and other agencies for services.

Another point concerning the various programs surveyed here is that evaluations uniformly occur over such a very short period that they rarely have enough time to show effects. Most have no follow-up data of even the most rudimentary kind. With school systems now responsible for intervention services for preschool children, it should be possible to access records to determine at least where children who received preschool services are subsequently placed and what kinds of services they continue to need.

One outcome of such follow-up efforts might be to identify approaches that are more effective than others. An additional irony is that school systems responsible for preschool intervention services might not want specific intervention approaches to be identified that parents believe to be effective. For example, parents who believe in the Lovaas approach to early intervention for children with autism are emotionally, irrevocably, and stridently committed to having that service provided for their children. As long as the interventions are roughly the same for all types of disabilities and no one in particular is established as effective, the extreme advocacy of committed families who believe in one form of intervention can be avoided.

The last three systematic approaches reviewed in this section provide testimony as to how complex the interaction actually is among family, child, and intervention characteristics. Providing the right intervention might not be so much finding a single approach to adopt (as in Lovaas) but in determining when in the developmental sequence it is appropriate and facilitating to administer certain forms of intervention. Both of the last two groups of researchers have demonstrated that younger, less competent children may require a specialized kind of intervention, delivered at critical times in their development. Whether that kind of Aptitude × Treatment implementation can be mounted by a school system has yet to be established. Finally, whether intervention on a broad scale can be tailored to the ecological context of the family also remains unknown.

COMMON ISSUES

Ignored/Undertreated Populations

A phenomenon found both in studies of intervention for children disadvantaged by poverty and those with disabilities is that no approach seems to have found a way to be effective with families experiencing significant personal stress, especially those from low-income groups. Parents appear to be expressing their resistance to various intervention programs with their feet. In every situation in which attrition has been reported, low-income, single, and minority parents are disproportionally likely to leave the program. Most of the studies reviewed on intervention for children with disabilities contained higher numbers of White middle-class families than expected from population statistics. Although in the intervention programs for disadvantaged or LBW babies and children, final samples still include high numbers of poor families, in fact, attrition was high in all the two-generation programs and in IHDP. Thus, it is difficult to know if the findings from the reactions of those remaining would actually generalize to other populations.

Although it may be that the stressors in their lives and their geographic instability are major deterrents for poor families, it also could be that the programs have not been designed well to meet their needs. None of the programs for poor families affected any of the major adverse ecological factors that interfere with parenting – factors such as stress (leading to depression), doing without (leading to anger at the system), the absence of employment, and so forth. Almost half of the PCDC mothers and Even Start mothers had elevated clinical levels of depression. Yet no specific attention was paid by these programs to how one can help depressed mothers who cannot escape from poverty. Obtaining a GED in Even Start did not appear to help, perhaps because the job market requires more than a GED for employment beyond minimum wage. It has been established internationally that higher levels of maternal education have dramatically positive effects on children (Stein, 1997) – no matter what the base rate of maternal education is in the country. In the IHDP program, maternal education predicted children's outcomes as a main effect and did not interact with intervention. This suggests that the next round of intervention efforts should take an ecological approach seriously, investigating how to change the child-rearing context for the families rather than focusing primarily on changing the child. Changing this context could, in fact, include the provision of well-run, universally available, and easy-to-access child-care programs, as well as other parent-support measures.

Similarly, for children with disabilities, the families who are able to garner the most services are middle class and educated. Children who have disabilities and who come from impoverished family situations are in double jeopardy. They have the threats that the stresses associated with poverty impose on families as well as more limited access to interventions specifically focused on the disability. The early intervention system currently depends on knowledgeable and demanding parents who know how to obtain those services to which their children are entitled. Those parents who either do not know about the services or who may be distracted by other stressors are less likely to receive much intervention for their children.

Program Specificity

The premise underlying IHDP, expressed explicitly by the authors at the outset, was that the fields of developmental psychology and early intervention are sufficiently well developed that they could deliver programs as one would a new medication. Social intervention may never, in fact, be able to approach medical interventions in exactitude of administration; in contrast, interventions in the lives of children and families are more typically complex clinically and dependent on powerful ecological circumstances. Few of the comparison studies of intervention approaches either for economically disadvantaged or disabled children showed a significant advantage for one approach over another. A more reasonable conclusion may be that we must look to

the specific form of the intervention delivered at a particular time (Warren & Yoder, 1998) or alter the form and intensity of intervention for poor children on the basis of an analysis of the risks their families face (Liaw & Brooks-Gunn, 1994).

The danger that comes from recognizing that intervention is complicated and may have to be matched much more explicitly to the characteristics of children and families in order to be effective is that policy makers may give up on social interventions altogether. For example, one treatment that has received no attention in the early intervention literature relies almost exclusively on changing the internal characteristics of the child. Specifically, Ritalin is being administered increasingly to younger and younger children, especially those who are poor and highly active, as a substantial intervention to change the child's behavior (Brett, 1997; McGinnis, 1997). Just between 1990 and 1995, there has been a 250% increase in the administration of Ritalin to youths (Safer, Zito, & Fine, 1996). In 1997, the Food and Drug Administration announced publicly that it had begun to investigate a liquid form of Prozac that can be administered to children who were thought to be depressed (Strauch, 1997). Given what is now known about the lengthy postnatal period of brain development, experimenting with such drugs early in children's lives would seem indefensible (Livingston, 1997), particularly if the reason for doing so is that more substantial ecological interventions are not currently supported by the political will needed to enact them.

CONCLUSION

Unfortunately, many of the conclusions reached in a previous review of early intervention (Farran, 1990) must be echoed at the end of this review of a subsequent decade of research on intervention for children disadvantaged by poverty or disabilities. Clarke and Clarke (1988) espoused two developmental trajectories: the biological and the social. For children with physical disabilities, the biological trajectory may limit their response to interventions, as this review demonstrated by finding consistently that children with more severe disabilities made less progress and were less responsive to intervention. Families of more severely impaired children, however, required and obtained more services, as would be appropriate.

Families of children with more significant biological needs will need more help from the social and educational service systems if their children are to remain at home. In the future, it might be more appropriate to investigate the intervention needs of these children as a separate group. Judging whether intervention has been effective by whether a mixed group of children make progress is inappropriate. In fact, there may be more effective interventions for children with more severe needs, but that must be demonstrated within the group of severely disabled children and their families. In a larger mixed group, the potential effectiveness of interventions for subgroups can be lost.

For children who are potentially at risk from a social environment that is less than adequate, most intervention efforts are focused on changing the child. When families have been included in the intervention, they have continued to be viewed as part of the problem. They are placed in parenting education classes (which they rarely attend), visited in their homes to help them learn to solve problems, or both. There continues to be a persistent lack of recognition of the parenting context of poverty. One of the reasons that the Abecedarian Project may have been more effective than Project Care, although the latter included a home visit component, is that Abecedarian parents knew their children were being well cared for in the center, and from infancy to school entrance, the stress of finding adequate child care was removed. The 1990 review called for a focus on "job training for parents, adult literacy sessions, parental support groups, and PTA groups in low-income schools that empower parents rather than disenfranchise them" (Farran, 1990, p. 533). Although some efforts were made to mount adult literacy programs during the 1990s, little else on this list has received attention.

Finally, for both trajectories (biological and social), much more needs to be understood about the reception of the public schools to these children. No studies of children with disabilities actually followed them into schools and examined the kind of responses and educational programs the children received once they made the transition. The one study of poor children that demonstrated continuing effects from intervention actually achieved the effects from the intervention over the first two to three years of elementary school, not preschool or

kindergarten (Reynolds & Temple, 1998). Vernon-Feagans's (1996) eloquent description of the mismatch between the Abecedarian children's skills and those of their teachers in the early elementary grades brings home the critical necessity of thinking beyond the preschool years for children at risk. Somehow, our nation has to move beyond thinking of the problems of young children as being something someone else fixes at an earlier age or in a different place so that other systems do not have to change. A developmental focus that covers the first 12 to 15 years of life would be a good start.

REFERENCES

Allen, K. (1992). *The exceptional child: Mainstreaming in early childhood education* (2nd ed.). Albany, NY: Delmar Publishers, Inc.

Baer, D. (1993). Quasi random assignment can be as convincing as random assignment: Commentaries on McEachin, Smith and Lovaas. *American Journal on Mental Retardation, 97*, 373–5.

Bailey, D., Simeonsson, R., Winton, P., Huntington, G., Comfort, M., Isbell, P., O'Donnell, K., & Helm, J. (1986). Family-focused intervention: A functional model for planning, implementing, and evaluating individualized family services in early intervention. *Journal of the Division for Early Childhood, 10*, 156–71.

Baumeister, A. (1997). Behavioral research: Boom or bust? In W. MacLean (Ed.), *Ellis' handbook of mental deficiency, psychological theory and research*. Hillsdale, NJ: Erlbaum.

Behl, D., White, K., & Escobar, C. (1993). New Orleans early intervention study of children with visual impairments. *Early Education and Development, 4*, 256–74.

Blair, C., Ramey, C., & Hardin, M. (1995). Early intervention for low birthweight, premature infants: Investigating the age-at-start question. *Early Education and Development, 4*, 290–305.

Boyce, G., Smith, T., Immel, N., Casto, G., & Escobar, C. (1993). Early intervention with medically fragile infants: Investigating the age-at-start question. *Early Education and Development, 4*, 290–305.

Bradley, R., Whiteside, L., Mundfrom, D., Casey, P., Caldwell, B., & Barrett, K. (1994). Impact of the Infant Health and Development Program (IHDP) on the home environments of infants born prematurely and with low birthweight. *Journal of Educational Psychology, 86*, 531–41.

Brantlinger, E. (1997). Using ideology: Cases of nonrecognition of the politics of research and practice in special education. *Review of Educational Research, 67*, 425–59.

Brett, V. (1997, November 2). Today's school routine: Readin', ritin', and Ritalin. *The Los Angeles Times*, p. 30.

Bricker, D. (1995). The challenge of inclusion. *Journal of Early Intervention, 19*, 179–194.

Brinker, R., Seifer, R., & Sameroff, A. (1994). Relations among maternal stress, cognitive development and early intervention in middle- and low-SES infants with developmental disabilities. *American Journal on Mental Retardation, 98*, 463–80.

Brooks-Gunn, J., Gross, R., Kraemer, H., Spiker, D., & Shapiro, S. (1992). Enhancing the cognitive outcomes of low birth weight, premature infants: For whom is the intervention most effective? *Pediatrics, 89*, 1209–15.

Brooks-Gunn, J., Klebanov, P., Liaw, F., & Spiker, D. (1993). Enhancing the development of low-birthweight, premature infants: Changes in cognition and behavior over the first three years. *Child Development, 64*, 736–53.

Brooks-Gunn, J., Liaw, F., & Klebanov, P. (1992). Effects of early intervention on cognitive function of low birth weight preterm infants. *The Journal of Pediatrics, 120*, 350–9.

Brooks-Gunn, J., McCarton, C., Casey, P., McCormick, M., Bauer, C., Bernbaum, J., Tyson, J., Swanson, M., Bennett, F. C., Scott, D., Tonascia, J., & Meinert, C. (1994). Early intervention in low birth-weight premature infants. *Journal of the American Medical Association, 272*, 1257–62.

Brown, W., Horn, E., Heiser, J., & Odom, S. (1996). Project BLEND: An inclusive model of early intervention services. *Journal of Early Intervention, 20*, 364–75.

Bruder, M. (1993). The provision of early intervention and early childhood special education within community early childhood programs: Characteristics of effective service delivery. *Topics in Early Childhood Special Education, 13*, 19–37.

Bryant, D., Burchinal, M., Lau, L., & Sparling, J. (1994). Family and classroom correlates of Head Start children's developmental outcomes. *Early Childhood Research Quarterly, 9*, 289–304.

Burchinal, M., Bailey, D., & Snyder, P. (1994). Using growth curve analysis to evaluate child change in longitudinal investigations. *Journal of Early Intervention, 18*, 403–23.

Campbell, F., Goldstein, S., Schaefer, E., & Ramey, C. (1991). Parental beliefs and values related to family risk, educational intervention, and child academic competence. *Early Childhood Research Quarterly, 6*, 167–82.

Campbell, F., & Ramey, C. (1990). The relationship between Piagetian cognitive development, mental test performance, and academic achievement in high-risk students with and without early educational experience. *Intelligence, 14*, 293–308.

Campbell, F., & Ramey, C. (1994). Effects of early intervention on intellectual and academic achievement: A follow-up study of children from low-income families. *Child Development, 65*, 684–98.

Campbell, F., & Ramey, C. (1995). Cognitive and school outcomes for high risk African-American students at middle adolescence: Positive effects of early intervention. *American Educational Research Journal, 32*, 743–72.

Carnegie Task Force on Meeting the Needs of Young Children. (1994). *Starting points*. New York: Carnegie Corporation of New York.

Caro, P., & Derevensky, J. (1991). Family-focused intervention model : Implementation and research findings. *Topics in Early Childhood Special Education, 11*, 66–80.

Chall, J., Jacobs, V., & Baldwin, L. (1990). *The reading crisis: Why poor children fall behind*. Cambridge, MA: Harvard University Press.

Chambers, J. (1991). A cost analysis of the federal program for early intervention services: A case study of Part H of PL 99-457 in California. *Journal of Education Finance, 17*, 142–71.

Children's Defense Fund. (1996). New data show gains. *Children's Defense Fund Reports, 17*(12), 5–6.

Clarke, A. M., & Clarke, A. D. (1988). The adult outcome of early behavioral abnormalities. *International Journal of Behavioral Development, 11*, 3–19.

Clarke, A. M., & Clarke, A. D. (1989). The later cognitive effects of early intervention. *Intelligence, 13*, 289–97.

Cole, K., Mills, P., & Dale, P. (1989). A comparison of the effects of academic and cognitive curricula for young handicapped children one to two years post-program. *Topics in Early Childhood Special Education, 9*, 110–27.

Cole, K., Dale, P., & Mills, P. (1991). Individual differences in language delayed children's responses to direct and interactive preschool instruction. *Topics in Early Childhood Special Education, 11*, 99–124.

Cole, K., Dale, P., Mills, P., & Jenkins, J. (1993). Interaction between early intervention curricula and student characteristics. *Exceptional Children, 60*, 17–28.

Cole, K., Mills P., Dale, P., & Jenkins, J. (1991). Effects of preschool integration for children with disabilities. *Exceptional Children, 58*, 36–45.

Dale, P., & Cole, K. (1988). Comparison of academic and cognitive programs for young handicapped children. *Exceptional Children, 54*, 439–47.

Dawson, G., & Osterling, J. (1997). Early intervention in autism. In M. J. Guralnick (Ed.), *The effectiveness of early intervention* (pp. 307–26). Baltimore, MD: Paul H. Brookes.

Deiner, P. (1997). *Infants and toddlers: Development and program planning*. Fort Worth, TX: Harcourt Brace.

Diamond, K., & LeFurgy, W. (1992). Relations between mothers' expectations and the performance of their infants who have developmental handicaps. *American Journal on Mental Retardation, 97*, 11–20.

Dihoff, R., Brosvic, G., Kafer, L., McEwan, M., Carpenter, L., Rizzuto, G., Farrelly, M., Anderson, J., & Bloszinsky, S. (1994). Efficacy of part- and full-time early intervention. *Perceptual and Motor Skills, 79*, 907–11.

Duncan, G., Brooks-Gunn, J., & Klebanov, P. (1994). Economic deprivation and early childhood development. *Child Development, 65*, 296–318.

Dunlap, G., Johnson, L., & Robbins, F. (1990). Preventing serious behavior problems through skill development and early intervention, In A. C. Repp & N. N. Singh (Eds.), *Positive behavioral support: Including people with difficult behavior in the community* (pp. 31–50). Baltimore: Paul H. Brookes.

Dunlap, G., Robbins, F., Morelli, M., & Dollman, C. (1988). Team training for young children with autism: A regional model for service delivery. *Journal of the Division for Early Childhood, 12*, 147–60.

Ehlers, V., & Ruffin, M. (1990). The Missouri Project – Parents as Teachers. *Focus on Exceptional Children, 23*, 1–14.

Farran, D. C. (1990). Effects of intervention with disadvantaged and disabled children: A decade review. In S. J. Meisels & J. P. Shonkoff (Eds.), *Handbook of early intervention* (pp. 501–39). New York: Cambridge University Press.

Farran, D. C., & Harber, L. (1989). Responses to a learning task at 6 months and I.Q. Test performance during the preschool years. *International Journal of Behavioral Development, 12*, 101–14.

Farran, D. C., & Shonkoff, J. P. (1994). Developmental disabilities and the concept of school readiness. *Early Education and Development, 5*, 141–51.

Farran, D. C., Son-Yarbrough, W., Silveri, B., & Culp, A. (1993). Measuring the environment in public school preschools for disadvantaged children: What is developmentally appropriate? In S. Reifel (Ed.), *Advances in early education and day care* (pp. 75–93). Greenwich, CN: JAI Press.

Feagans, L., & Farran, D. C. (1994). The effects of daycare intervention in the preschool years on the narrative skills of poverty children in kindergarten. *International Journal of Behavioral Development, 17*, 503–23.

Feagans, L., Fendt, K., & Farran, D. C. (1995). The effects of day care intervention on teacher's ratings of the elementary school discourse skills in disadvantaged children. *International Journal of Behavioral Development, 18*, 243–61.

Fewell, R., & Glick, M. (1996). Program evaluation findings of an intensive early intervention program. *American Journal on Mental Retardation, 101*, 233–43.

Fewell, R., & Oelwein, P. (1990). The relationship between time in integrated environments and developmental gains in young children with special needs. *Topics in Early Childhood Special Education, 10*, 104–16.

Fewell, R., & Oelwein, P. (1991). Effective early intervention: Results from the model preschool program for children with Down syndrome and other developmental delays. *Topics in Early Childhood Special Education, 11*, 56–68.

File, N., & Kontos, S. (1993). The relationship of program quality to children's play in integrated early intervention settings. *Topics in Early Childhood Special Education, 13*, 1–18.

Florian, L. (1995). Part H early intervention program: Legislative history and intent of the law. *Topics in Early Childhood Special Education, 15*, 247–62.

Fox, L., Dunlap, G., & Philbrick, L. (1997). Providing individual supports to young children with autism and their families. *Journal of Early Intervention, 21*, 1–14.

Gallagher, J. (1997). We make a difference: No Nobel Prizes though. *Journal of Early Intervention, 21*, 88–91.

Goodman, J. (1994). Early intervention for preschoolers with developmental delays: The case for increased child collaboration. *Psychological Reports, 75*, 479–96.

Gray, S., & Klaus, R. (1968). The early training project and its general rationale. In R. D. Hess & R. M. Bear (Eds.), *Early education: Current theory, research and action* (pp. 63–70). Chicago: Aldine.

Greenough, W., Wallace, C., Alcantara, A., Anderson, B., Hawrylak, N., Sirevaag, A., Weiler, I., & Withers, G. (1993). Development of the brain: Experience affects the structure of neurons, glia, and blood vessels. In N. Anastasiow & S. Harel (Eds.), *At-risk infants: Interventions, families, and research* (pp. 173–85). Baltimore, MD: Paul H. Brookes.

Guralnick, M. (1991). The next decade of research on the effectiveness of early intervention. *Exceptional Children, 58*, 174–83.

Guralnick, M. (Ed.). (1997). *The effectiveness of early intervention*. Baltimore, MD: Paul H. Brookes.

Harms, T., Cryer, D., & Clifford, R. (1990). Early childhood environmental rating scale. New York: Teachers College Press.

Harry, B., Allen, N., & McLaughlin, M. (1995). Communication vs. compliance: African-American parents' involvement in special education. *Exceptional Children, 61*, 364–77.

Hausman, B. (1989). Parents as teachers: The right fit for Missouri. *Educational Horizons, 67*, 35–9

Helburn, S., Culkin, M., Morris, J., Mocan, N., Howes, C., Phillipsen, L., Bryant, D., Clifford, R., Cryer, D., Peisner-Feinberg, E., Burchinal, M., Kagan, S., & Rustici, J. (1995). *Cost, quality and child outcomes in child care centers*. Final report available from R. Clifford, University of North Carolina at Chapel Hill.

Honig, A., & Lally, R. (1982). The family development research project: A retrospective review. *Early Child Behavior and Care, 10*, 41–62.

Horacek, J., Ramey, C. T., Campbell, F., Hoffmann, K., & Fletcher, R. (1987). Predicting school failure and assessing early intervention with high-risk children. *Journal of Child and Adolescent Psychiatry, 26*, 758–63.

Johnson, D., & Walker, T. (1991). A follow-up evaluation of the Houston Parent–Child Development Center: School performance. *Journal of Early Intervention, 15*, 226–36.

Kaiser, A., Yoder, P., & Keetz, A. (1992). Evaluating milieu teaching. In S. F. Warren & J. Reichle (Eds.), *Communication and language intervention series: Vol. 1. Causes and effects in communication and language intervention* (pp. 9–47). Baltimore, MD: Paul H. Brookes.

Kassebaum, N. (1994). Head Start: Only the best for America's children. *American Psychologist, 49*, 123–6.

Klinger, L., & Dawson, G. (1992). Facilitating early social and communicative development in children with autism. In S. F. Warren & J. Reichle (Eds.), *Communication and language intervention series: Vol. 1. Causes and effects in communication and language intervention* (pp. 157–86). Baltimore, MD: Paul H. Brookes.

Kochanek, T., & Buka, S. (March, 1995). *Socio-demographic influences on services used by infants with disabilities and their families*. Unpublished paper from the Early Childhood Research Institute on Service Utilization. (available from Thomas T. Kochanek, Early Childhood Research Institute: Service Utilization, Rhode Island College, Providence.)

Lazar, I., & Darlington, R. (1982). Lasting effects of early education: A report from the Consortium for Longitudinal Studies. *Monographs of the Society for Research in Child Development, 47* (2–3, Serial No. 195).

Lee, V., Brooks-Gunn, J., & Schnur, E. (1988). Does Head Start work? A 1-year follow-up comparison of disadvantaged children attending Head Start, no preschool, and other preschool programs. *Developmental Psychology, 24*, 210–22.

Lee, V., Brooks-Gunn, J., Schnur, E., & Liaw, F. (1990). Are Head Start effects sustained? A longitudinal follow-up comparison of disadvantaged children attending Head Start, no preschool, and other preschool programs. *Annual Progress in Child Psychiatry and Child Development*, 600–18.

Lee, V., & Loeb, S. (1995). Where do Head Start attenders end up? One reason why preschool effects fade out. *Educational Evaluation and Policy Analysis, 17*, 62–82.

Liaw, F., & Brooks-Gunn, J. (1994). Cumulative familial risks and low birthweight children's cognitive and behavioral development. *Journal of Clinical Child Psychology, 23*, 360–72.

Liaw, F., Meisels, S. J., & Brooks-Gunn, J. (1995). The effects of experience of early intervention on low birth weight, premature children: The Infant Health and Development Program. *Early Childhood Research Quarterly, 10*, 405–31.

Liebman, J. L. & Goodman, J. F. (1995). Learning in early intervention programs: The generalization and maintenance of IEP objectives. *Early Education and Development, 6*, 127–43.

Lifter, K. (1995). Strategies that make sense. *Journal of Early Intervention, 19*, 106–7.

Livingston, K. (1997). Ritalin: Miracle drug or cop-out? *Public Interest* (pp. 3–18). Washington DC: National Affairs.

Lovaas, O. I., (1987). Behavioral treatment and normal educational and intellectual functioning in young autistic children. *Journal of Consulting and Clinical Psychology, 55*, 3–9.

Lovaas, O. I., & Smith, T. (1989). A comprehensive behavioral theory of autistic children: Paradigm for research and treatment. *Journal of Behavior Therapy and Experimental Psychiatry, 20*, 17–29.

Mahoney, G., & Filer, J. (1996). How responsive is early intervention to the priorities and needs of families? *Topics in Early Childhood Special Education, 16*, 437–57.

Mahoney, G., & Powell, A. (1988). Modifying parent–child interaction: Enhancing the development of handicapped children. *Journal of Special Education, 22*, 82–96.

Marfo, K., & Dinero, T. (1991). Assessing early intervention outcomes: Beyond program variables. *International Journal of Disability, Development and Education, 38*, 289–303.

Markowitz, J. B., Hebbeler, K., Larson, J. C., Cooper, J. A., & Edmisten, P. (1991). Using value-added analysis to examine short term effects of early intervention. *Journal of Early Intervention, 15*, 377–89.

Marx, F., & Seligson, M. (1988). *The public school early childhood study: The state survey*. New York: Bank Street College of Education.

Mastropieri, M. A. (1987). Age at start as a correlate of intervention effectiveness. *Psychology in the Schools, 24*, 59–62.

McCall, R. B., Eichorn, D. H., & Hogarty, P. S. (1977). Transitions in early mental development. *Monographs of the Society for Research in Child Development, 42* (3, Serial No. 171).

McCarton, C., Brooks-Gunn, J., Wallace, I., Bauer, C., Bennett, F., Bernbaum, J., Broyles, S., Casey, P., McCormick, M., Scott, D., Tyson, J., Tonascia, J., & Meinert, C. (1997). Results at age 8 years of early intervention for low-birth-weight premature infants. *Journal of the American Medical Association, 277*, 126–32.

McCormick, M., McCarton, C., Tonascia, J., & Brooks-Gunn, J. (1993). Early educational intervention for very low birth weight infants: Results from the Infant Health and Development Program. *The Journal of Pediatrics, 123*, 527–33.

McEachin, J., Smith, T., & Lovaas, O. I. (1993). Long term outcome for children with autism who received early intensive behavioral treatment. *American Journal on Mental Retardation, 97*, 359–72.

McGinnis, J. (1997, September 18). Attention deficit disaster. *Wall Street Journal*, pp. A, 14:4.

Meisels, S. J., Dichtelmiller, M., & Liaw, F. R. (1993). A multidimensional analysis of early childhood intervention programs. In C. H. Zeanah (Ed.), *Handbook of infant mental health* (pp. 361–85). New York: Guilford Press.

Meyerhoff, M., & White, B. (1986). New parents as teachers. *Educational Leadership, 44*, 42–6.

Mills, P., Dale, P., Cole, K., & Jenkins, J. (1995). Follow-up of children from academic and cognitive preschool curricula at age 9. *Exceptional Children, 61*, 378–93.

Neville, H. (1991). Neurobiology of cognitive and language processing: Effects of early experience. In K. R. Gibson &

A. Peterson (Eds.), *Brain maturation and cognitive development*. New York: Aldine de Gruyter.

Pakula, A., & Palmer, F. (1997). Early intervention for children at risk for neuromotor problems. In M. Guralnick (Ed.), *The effectiveness of early intervention* (pp. 99–108). Baltimore, MD: Paul H. Brookes.

Palmer, F. B., Shapiro, B. K., Allen, M. C., Mosher, E., Bilker, S. A., Harryman, S. E., Meinart, C. L., & Capute, A. J. (1990). Infant stimulation curriculum for infants with cerebral palsy: Effects on infant temperament, parent–infant interaction and home environment. *Pediatrics, 85*, 411–15.

Palmer, F. B., Shapiro, B. K., Wachtel, R. C., Allen, M. C., Hiller, J. E., Harryman, S. E., Mosher, B. S., Meinert, C. L., & Capute, A. J. (1988). The effects of physical therapy on CP: A controlled trial in infants with spastic diplegia. *New England Journal of Medicine, 318*, 803–8.

Pfannenstiel, J., & Seltzer, D. (1989). New parents as teachers: Evaluation of an early parent education program. *Early Childhood Research Quarterly, 4*, 1–18.

Ramey, C., Bryant, D., Campbell, F., Sparling, J., & Wasik, B. (1990). Early intervention for high-risk children: The Carolina Early Intervention Program. *Prevention in Human Services, 7*, 33–57.

Ramey, C., Bryant, D., Wasik, B., Sparling, J., Fendt, K., & LaVange, L. (1992). Infant Health and Development Program for low birth weight, premature infants: Program elements, family participation, and child intelligence. *Pediatrics, 3*, 454–65.

Ramey, C., Bryant, D., Sparling, J., & Wasik, B. (1985). Project CARE: A comparison of two early intervention strategies to prevent retarded development. *Topics in Early Childhood Special Education, 5*, 12–25.

Ramey, C., & Campbell, F. (1984). Preventive education for high-risk children: Cognitive consequences of the Carolina Abecedarian Project. *American Journal of Mental Deficiency, 88*, 515–23.

Rescorla, L., Roberts, J., & Dahlsgaard, K. (1997). Late talkers at 2: Outcomes at age 3. *Journal of Speech, Language and Hearing Research, 40*, 556–66.

Reynolds, A. (1995). One year of preschool intervention or two: Does it matter? *Early Childhood Research Quarterly, 10*, 1–31.

Reynolds, A., Mavrogenes, N., Bezrucko, N., & Hagemann, M. (1996). Cognitive and family support mediators of preschool effectiveness: A confirmatory analysis. *Child Development, 67*, 1119–40.

Reynolds, A., Mehana, M., & Temple, J. (1995). Does preschool intervention affect children's perceived competence? *Journal of Applied Developmental Psychology, 16*, 211–30.

Reynolds, A., & Temple, J. (1998). Extended early childhood intervention and school achievement: Age thirteen findings from the Chicago Longitudinal Study. *Child Development, 69*, 231–46.

Reynolds, M., Wang, M., & Walberg, H. (1987). The necessary restructuring of special and regular education. *Exceptional Children, 53*, 391–8.

Rittenhouse, R., White, K., Lowitzer, C., & Shisler, L. (1990). The costs and benefits of providing early intervention to very young, severely hearing-impaired children in the United States: The conceptual outline of a longitudinal research study and some preliminary findings. *British Journal of Disorders of Communication, 25*, 195–208.

Robbins, F., & Dunlap, G. (1992). Effects of task difficulty on parent teaching skills and behavior problems of young children with autism. *American Journal on Mental Retardation, 96*, 631–43.

Rogers, S., & DiLalla, D. (1991). A comparative study of the effects of a developmentally based instructional model on young children with autism and young children with other disorders of behavior and development. *Topics in Early Childhood Special Education, 11*, 29–47.

Rogers, S., & Lewis, H. (1988). An effective day treatment model for young children with pervasive developmental disorders. *Journal of the American Academy of Child and Adolescent Psychiatry, 28*, 207–14.

Rose, T. L., & Calhoun, M. L. (1990). The Charlotte Circle Project: A program for infants and toddlers with severe/profound disabilities. *Journal of Early Intervention, 14*, 175–85.

Rosenberg, S. A., Robinson, C., Finkler, D., & Rose, J. (1987). An empirical comparison of formulas evaluating early intervention program impact on development. *Exceptional Children, 54*, 213–19.

Safer, D., Zito, J., & Fine, E. (1996). Increased methylphenidate usage for attention deficit disorder in the 1990s. *Pediatrics, 98*, 1084–8.

Salisbury, C. (1991). Mainstreaming during the early childhood years. *Exceptional Children, 58*, 146–55.

Sameroff, A., & Fiese, B. (1990). Transactional regulation and early intervention. In S. J. Meisels & J. P. Shonkoff (Eds.), *Handbook of early childhood intervention* (pp. 119–49). New York: Cambridge University Press.

Schopler, E., Short, A., & Mesibov, G. (1989). Relation of behavioral treatment to "normal functioning": Comment on Lovaas. *Journal of Consulting and Clinical Psychology, 57*, 162–4.

Schwartz, I., Carta, J., & Grant, S. (1996). Examining the use of recommended language intervention practices in early childhood special education classrooms. *Topics in Early Childhood Special Education, 16*, 251–72.

Schweinhart, L., Barnes, H., & Weikart, D. (1993). *Significant benefits: The High/Scope Perry Preschool study through age 27*. Monographs of the High/Scope Educational Research Foundation, number 10. Ypsilanti, MI: The High/Scope Press.

Schweinhart, L., & Weikart, D. (1997). The High/Scope preschool curriculum comparison study through age 23. *Early Childhood Research Quarterly, 12*, 117–44.

Schweinhart, L., Weikart, D., & Larner, M. (1986). Consequences of three preschool curriculum models through age 15. *Early Childhood Research Quarterly, 1*, 15–45.

Seifer, R., Clark, G., & Sameroff, A. (1991). Positive effects of interaction coaching in infants with developmental disability and their mothers. *American Journal on Mental Retardation, 96*, 1–11.

Shonkoff, J. P. (1992). Early intervention research: Asking and answering meaningful questions. *Zero To Three, 12* (3), 7–9.

Shonkoff, J.P., Hauser-Cram, P., Krauss, M., & Upshur, C. (1988). Early intervention efficacy research – what have we learned and where do we go from here? *Topics in Early Childhood Special Education, 8*, 81–93.

Shonkoff, J. P., Hauser-Cram, P., Krauss, M., & Upshur, C. (1992). Development of infants with disabilities and their families. *Monographs of the Society for Research in Child Development, 57* (6, Serial No. 230).

Shonkoff, J. P., & Meisels, S. J. (1990). Early childhood intervention: The evolution of a concept. In S. J. Meisels and J. P. Shonkoff (Eds.), *Handbook of early childhood intervention* (pp. 3–31). New York: Cambridge University Press.

Shore, R. (1997). *Rethinking the brain: New insights into early development.* New York: Families and Work Institute.

Siegel, B. (1996). Is the emperor wearing clothes? Social policy and the empirical support for full inclusion of children with disabilities in the preschool and early elementary grades. *Society for Research in Child Development Social Policy Report, 10*, 2–17.

Smith, S., & Sigel, I. (Eds.). (1995). *Two generation programs for families in poverty: A new intervention strategy* (pp. 251–70). Norwood, NJ: Ablex.

Snow, C., Barnes, W., Chandler, J., Goodman, I., & Hemphill, L. (1991). *Unfulfilled expectations: Home and school influences on literacy.* Cambridge, MA: Harvard University Press.

Sontag, J. C., & Schacht, R. (1994). An ethnic comparison of parent participation and information needs in early intervention. *Exceptional Children, 60*, 422–33.

Sparling, J., & Lewis, I. (1984). *Partners for learning.* Lewisville, NC: Kaplan Press.

Sparling, J., Lewis, I., & Neuwirth, S. (in press). *Partners for learning: Curriculum kit.* Lewisville, NC: Kaplan Press.

Spiker, D., Kraemer, H., Scott, D., & Gross, R. (1991). Design issues in a randomized clinical trial of a behavioral intervention: Insights from the Infant Health and Development Program. *Developmental and Behavioral Pediatrics, 12*, 386–93.

Spitz, H. (1992). Does the Carolina Abecedarian Early Intervention Project prevent sociocultural mental retardation? *Intelligence, 16*, 225–37.

St. Pierre, R., & Swartz, J. (1995). The Even Start Family Literacy Program. In S. Smith & I. Sigel (Eds.), *Two generation programs for families in poverty: A new intervention strategy* (pp. 37–66). Norwood, NJ: Ablex.

St. Pierre, R., & Swartz, J. (1996). *The Even Start family literacy program: Early implementation.* Cambridge, MA: Abt Associates.

St. Pierre, R. G., Swartz, J., Murray, S., & Deck, D. (1996). *Improving family literacy: Findings from the national Even Start evaluation.* Cambridge, MA: Abt Associates, Inc.

Stafford, S., & Green, V. (1996). Preschool integration: Strategies for teaching. *Childhood Education, 72*, 214–18.

Starfield, B. (1992). Effects of poverty on health status. *Bulletin of the New York Academy of Medicine, 68*, 17–24.

Stein, J. (1997). *Empowerment and women's health: Theory, methods and practice.* London, UK: Zed Books.

Strauch, B. (1997, August 10). Use of antidepression medicine for young patients has soared. *New York Times*, p. 1.

Takanishi, R., & DeLeon, P. (1994). A Head Start for the 21st century. *American Psychologist, 49*, 120–2.

Thompson, L., Lobb, C., Elling, R., & Herman, S. (1997). Pathways to family empowerment: Effect of family-centered delivery of early intervention services. *Exceptional Children, 64*, 99.

Trohanis, P. (1994). Early intervention: A national overview. *The Exceptional Parent, 24*, 18–20.

United States Department of Justice, Civil Rights Division, Disability Rights Section (1998) (on-line). Commonly asked questions about child care centers and the Americans with Disabilities Act. (Http://www.usdoj.gov/crt/ada/chldq%26a.htm)

United States Department of Education. (1985). *Seventh annual report on the implementation of the Education of the Handicapped Act.* Washington, DC: U.S. Government Printing Office.

Urwin, S., Cook, J., & Kelly, K. (1988). Preschool language intervention: A follow-up study. *Child Care, Health and Development, 14*, 127–46.

Vernon-Feagans, L. (1996). *Children's talk in communities and classrooms.* Cambridge, MA: Blackwell.

Walker, T., & Johnson, D. (1988). A follow-up evaluation of the Houston Parent–Child Development Center: Intelligence test results. *Journal of Genetic Psychology, 149*, 377–81.

Walker, T., Rodriguez, G., Johnson, D., & Cortez, C. (1995). AVANCE Parent-Child Education Program. In S. Smith & I. Sigel (Eds.), *Two generation programs for families in poverty: A new intervention strategy* (pp. 67–90). Norwood, NJ: Ablex.

Warren, S., & Yoder, P. (1998). Facilitating the transition from preintentional to intentional communication. In A.M. Wetherby, S. Warren, & J. Reichle (Eds.), *Communication and language intervention series: Vol. 7. Transitions in prelinguistic communication.* Baltimore, MD: Paul H. Brookes.

Warren, S., Yoder, P., Gazdeg, G., Kim, K., & Jones, H. (1993). Facilitating prelinguistic communication skills in young children with developmental delay. *Journal of Speech and Hearing Research, 36,* 83–97.

Wasik, B., Bryant, D., & Lyons, C. (1990). *Home visiting.* Newbury Park, CA: Sage.

Wasik, B., & Lyons, C. (1984). *A handbook on home visiting.* Chapel Hill, NC: Frank Porter Graham Child Development Center, University of North Carolina.

Wasik, B., Ramey, C., Bryant, D., & Sparling, J. (1990). A longitudinal study of two early intervention strategies: Project CARE. *Child Development, 61,* 1682–96.

Watkins, S. (1987). Long term effects of home intervention with hearing-impaired children. *American Annals of the Deaf, 132,* 267–71.

Winter, M., & Rouse, J. (1990). Fostering intergenerational literacy: The Missouri Parents as Teachers program. *The Reading Teacher, 43,* 382–6.

Winter, S. (1997). "SMART" planning for inclusion. *Childhood Education, 73,* 212–18.

Yoder, P., Kaiser, A., & Alpert, C. (1991). An exploratory study of the interaction between language teaching methods and child characteristics. *Journal of Speech and Hearing Research, 34,* 155–67.

Yoder, P., Kaiser, A., Goldstein, H., Alpert, C., Mousetis, L., Kaczmarek, L., & Fischer, R. (1995). An exploratory comparison of milieu teaching and responsive interaction in classroom applications. *Journal of Early Intervention, 19,* 218–42.

Yoder, P., Warren, S., Kim, K., & Gazdag, G. (1994). Facilitating prelinguistic communication skills in young children with developmental delay. II: Systematic replication and extension. *Journal of Speech and Hearing Research, 37,* 841–51.

Yogman, M., Kindlon, D., & Earls, F. (1995). Father involvement and cognitive/behavioral outcomes of preterm infants. *Journal of the American Academy of Child and Adolescent Psychiatry, 34,* 58–66.

CHAPTER TWENTY-FOUR

Early Childhood Intervention Programs:

What About the Family?

JEANNE BROOKS-GUNN, LISA J. BERLIN, AND ALLISON SIDLE FULIGNI

Early childhood development (defined as occurring from birth, or before birth, through ages 6 to 7) is increasingly being viewed as the foundation of adolescent and young adult cognitive and emotional functioning. In the first half of the 1990s, evidence of the interest in enhancing early development included the Carnegie Corporation's pair of reports, *Starting Points* (1994) and *Years of Promise* (1996), the creation in 1990 of a National Goals Panel and the Goals 2000 legislation of 1994 (centering on the goal that "by the year 2000 all children will start school ready to learn"), and President Clinton's Early Childhood Initiative. A theme common to each of these endeavors is the importance of early experiences – especially supportive relationships and intellectual stimulation – for later development (Brooks-Gunn, 1997).

We wish to thank the Administration on Children, Youth, and Families (ACYF) and the National Institute of Mental Health (NIMH) for their support through the ACYF–NIMH Head Start-Mental Health Research Consortium. We are appreciative of the support by the National Institute of Child Health and Human Development Research Network on Child and Family Well-Being, the Administration on Children, Youth, and Families' Early Head Start Research and Evaluation Project, the Robert Wood Johnson Foundation, and the Pew Charitable Trust. We also wish to thank our many colleagues in the field of early childhood education and health for their insights – especially Cecelia McCarton, Marie McCormick, April Benasich, John Love, Helen Raikes, Ellen Kisker, Craig Ramey, Ruth Gross, Kathryn Barnard, JoAnn Robinson, Robert Emde, Urie Bronfenbrenner, Beatriz Chu Clewell, Hirokazu Yoshikawa, and Jeffrey Evans. The editors of this volume, Jack Shonkoff and Samuel Meisels, were also very helpful, and we appreciate their support. The assistance of Colleen O'Neal, Christy Brady, So-Yun Lee, and Claudia O'Brien on manuscript preparation is also appreciated.

By the fall of 1997, excitement surrounding the early childhood years was palpable. The President and First Lady had just completed two White House Conferences on early childhood, the first on early development, with a focus on brain growth and the importance of stimulation and relationships, and the second on child care, with a focus on the need for quality care. An entire issue of *Newsweek* was devoted to the early years. Scholars who usually toiled in relative anonymity were showing up on television talk shows, becoming, if only for a moment, famed "talking heads." A documentary on early development by actor and director Rob Reiner was aired on prime-time television.

THE ROLE OF PARENTS IN CURRENT EARLY CHILDHOOD INITIATIVES

Amidst all of this publicity, a critical element was missing from the discourse. Where were parents and families? Of course they were mentioned, but they were almost taken for granted. The U.S. Department of Education's Goals 2000 program had among its goals not only school readiness but also supporting parents as the first educators of their children. Nevertheless, several family-related themes were missing or perhaps distorted.

First, almost all of the discussion was framed around school readiness as illustrated by the first National Educational Goal, "All children will enter school ready to learn." The implicit assumption was that programs are designed primarily for children, ignoring the fact that almost all early childhood programs target not only the child but also the family. That is, services are provided that do more than prepare environmentally or biologically vulnerable children to enter schools on an equal footing with children at lesser risk. They are also intended to benefit parents and families in a variety of ways (Clarke-Stewart & Fein, 1983; Olds & Kitzman, 1993; Yoshikawa, 1995). As a consequence, school readiness can be interpreted as preparing families and parents as well as children for school. (We are leaving aside, for the purposes of this chapter, the important debate about whether school readiness should be viewed as schools being ready for the range of children that come to them versus children and parents being ready for what the school staff believe is necessary for success in kindergarten and the primary grades [Kagan, 1995; Lewitt & Baker, 1995; Love, Aber, & Brooks-Gunn, 1994].)

Little was said during the 1997 media blitz about whether early childhood programs enhance parental and family well-being. In contrast, a strong plea for a focus on the family in such programs has been made by scholars and practitioners (Benasich, Brooks-Gunn, & Clewell, 1992; Bronfenbrenner, 1979; Brooks-Gunn, 1995). But questions remain concerning the eventual impact of beliefs about the importance of family well-being as a goal of early intervention. How is success in these efforts to be defined? Will policy makers be satisfied if a program (or set of programs) lowers child abuse, punitive and harsh child-rearing practices, parental depressive symptomology, welfare dependency, or social isolation (aspects of family and parental well-being that early intervention programs have targeted, as discussed in this chapter)? How much importance will be placed on such family outcomes if programs do not also increase children's achievement test scores or reduce grade retention? One heartening sign is the increased attention focused on universal home visiting (or targeted home visiting to families at heightened risk of either child abuse or harsh parenting); the goal of such home visiting during pregnancy or the first year of life is to support and enhance parenting behavior, not to influence child behavior per se (Council on Child and Adolescent Health, 1998; Gomby Larson, Lewitt, & Behrman, 1993; Krugman, 1993; U.S. Advisory Board on Child Abuse and Neglect, 1991).

Second, in 1997, economics received more attention in the discourse about early childhood programs than has occurred previously. For example, after years of publication, the journal published by the Institute for Research on Poverty of the University of Wisconsin (*Focus*) showcased early childhood for the first time. Given the readership of this journal, the theme of "Investing in Young Children" provided a more economically oriented perspective than is typically seen in the early childhood education literature (the notable exception being the work of Barnett, who is an economist, 1993, 1995). Another possible first was the interest in early childhood demonstrated by the Council of Economic Advisors, which prepared material for the two White House Conferences in 1997. The economic perspective emphasizes the role of parents, as does the perspective from developmental psychology. Parents make choices that influence young children's well-being; these choices are often made in light of constraints (i.e., parents with low incomes have limitations placed on the purchase of materials and opportunities for enhancing the development of their children) as well as conflicting goals (i.e., parents have to juggle many trade-offs, such as spending more time in the workforce versus spending more time with their children; Duncan & Brooks-Gunn, 1997; Haveman & Wolfe, 1994; Wilson, Ellwood, & Brooks-Gunn, 1995). Haveman and Wolfe (1994) summarized the concerns that come into play when looking at choices and investments:

The success of a child is determined by three primary factors: the choices made by the society, primarily the government, regarding the opportunities available to children and their parents (the "social investments in children"); the choices made by the parents regarding the resources to which their children have access (the "parental investments in children"); and the choices that the child makes given the investments in and opportunities available to him or her. (p. 26)

Choices to invest in young children, then, are contingent on government decisions as well as parental decisions, which are determined in part by the set of services or programs available in a community as well as parental investment in these programs on behalf of their children. The array of public supports available to parents has been divided into two groups: in-kind transfer programs and cash programs (Brooks-Gunn & Duncan, 1997; Currie, 1997). This chapter focuses on in-kind transfer programs rather than on cash programs. In-kind programs include those that focus on health, parenting education, literacy programs, family support, and preschool education. All depend in part on the parents to procure the health services offered, to engage in the programs requiring parental participation, or to ensure that the children get to center-based educational sources (Leventhal, Brooks-Gunn, McCormick, & McCarton, in press). However, the focus on parent choice and preference is often missing in the early childhood literature (although complementary themes do exist, such as availability of services, access to interventions, and parental knowledge about programs).

Third, the national discourse has not focused sufficiently on how early childhood programs benefit children. The educational programming literature has generally been criticized as being a "black box" (Berlin, 1998; Berlin, O'Neal, & Brooks-Gunn, 1998). This is true of preschool as well as school-age intervention efforts. What are the pathways through which programs actually work? Although Bronfenbrenner (1979) has characterized parents as engines of change in early intervention, the workings of this complex machinery have not been tapped to any great extent (Brooks-Gunn, 1995). In this chapter, we ask, as have other scholars, Do programs have direct effects on parents, and do programs influence children indirectly through their impact on parents? These frequently asked questions have not received significant attention in the recent national discussions of young children. Nor are they answered extensively by extant research, rendering it one of those perennial pleas made to the field for additional research.

Because parents and families are integral to any early childhood education, child care, or other child-focused investment strategy, our chapter highlights both the ways in which families are critical to program access and the ways in which programs influence parental well-being. We see the success of interventions as mirrored in enhancing parental skills and competencies as much as in helping children acquire and maintain competencies. Another premise is that program effects upon children are more likely to be sustained if parental well-being has been influenced; that is, effects on child outcomes will be mediated in part through program effects upon parents. Finally, we believe that parental involvement

(or investment) in early childhood programs is the foundation upon which any good program rests, which is in part reflected by the relationships among parents, staff, and children.

This chapter is divided into four sections. In the first, effects of four general types of programs are reviewed, with respect to parental and family outcomes. These program types are labeled as follows: 1) parent-focused home-based programs, 2) parent-focused combination center- and home-based programs, 3) intergenerational family literacy programs, and 4) parent-focused literacy programs. In the second section, we examine more deeply the premise that parents are engines of change in early intervention programs. Three issues are considered. The first concerns three of the family outcomes that may be the most likely candidates to be mediators of change. The second focuses on actual empirical tests of these outcomes as mediators of the intervention-to-child-outcome link. The third examines parental involvement or engagement as a prerequisite for program efficacy. The next section focuses on policy and practice implications of early intervention program effects on parents, and the concluding section provides recommendations for the next wave of programs and their evaluations.

EFFICACY OF EARLY INTERVENTION PROGRAMS FOR PARENTS

The review of early childhood program effects on parents is divided into four general service types: 1) parent-focused home visiting programs, 2) parent-focused combined center- and home-based programs, 3) intergenerational literacy programs, and 4) parent-focused literacy programs. Other classifications are possible, of course. This chapter differs from previous reviews (most notably those of Benasich et al., 1992 and Yoshikawa, 1995) in considering only programs that have a parent focus. Consequently, center-based programs that do not include home visiting or regularly scheduled parenting groups are not reviewed. In addition, intergenerational literacy and parent literacy programs are reviewed because of their emphasis on parental as well as child skill development.

Program effects are reviewed in terms of several classes of outcomes, specifically: 1) parent education/employment/self-sufficiency; 2) parent mental and physical health; 3) observed parent–child interaction/relationship quality; 4) use of child-related services; 5) parenting attitudes, knowledge, and quality of the home environment; and 6) child maltreatment indicators. Virtually all of this evaluation research focuses on the mother, rather than on the father or the mother and father. Slightly different categorizations are found in previous reviews. Parent behavior is separated from home environment because in the former the focus is usually on actual parent–child interaction; whereas measures of the home environment, often based on the Home Observation Measure of the Environment (HOME) Inventory (Caldwell & Bradley, 1984), include interviewer ratings augmented by direct parent questioning. Such measures are not analogous to the interactions observed between parents and children when researchers have used structured or semistructured situations to learn about the dyad (Berlin, Brooks-Gunn, Spiker, & Zaslow, 1995). Unlike some reviews, a separate category is included for use of services, given our concerns with parent investment and choice. Parents need to take their children to doctors during acute illness episodes, to well-baby clinics, to Womens, Infants, and Children (WIC) classes, and the like. Parents decide whether to go to a doctor or emergency room when their child is ill, although their choices are constrained by service availability, income, neighborhood norms, and a host of other factors (Brooks-Gunn, McCormick, Klebanov, & McCarton, 1998). A separate category is used for maternal education and employment in order to highlight the importance of these outcomes in center-based education programs that provide child care for working parents in addition to focusing on child outcomes (Chase-Lansdale & Brooks-Gunn, 1995; Hofferth, 1995).

All programs reviewed began in the prenatal period or in the first 3 years of life. Preschool programs initiated in the fourth or fifth year are not examined (see Clarke-Stewart & Fein, 1983; Lazar, Darlington, Murray, Royce, & Snipper, 1982; Lazar, Hubbell, Murray, Rosche, & Royce, 1977; McKey et al., 1985, for previous reviews of such programs). Additionally, the vast majority of the programs included in our review employed random assignment. Those programs that did not use an experimental design are marked by an asterisk in the appendix

tables. The review is also limited to programs that offered their services to families for at least six months, based on the premise that short-term programs are not likely to alter families' lives significantly (see, for one notable exception, the home visiting program conducted by Achenbach, Phares, Howell, Rauh, & Nurcombe, 1990, and Rauh, Achenbach, Nurcombe, Howell, & Teti, 1988).

Parent-Focused Home-Based Programs

Many experts believe that the long-term success of programs depends not on their capacity to alter child development directly but on their capacity to alter the environment in which the child lives, especially in terms of parental and familial functioning (see Bronfenbrenner, 1979; Woodhead, 1988). In this section, we consider a specific body of programs, parent-focused home-based interventions and their effects on several aspects of parent and family functioning (see Appendix 24.A for an overview). We first examine intervention programs beginning prenatally or within the child's first year and then turn to programs that get underway between the child's first and third birthdays. As mentioned earlier, to be included in this review a program must have delivered services for at least six months and evaluation findings must have been published no earlier than 1975 (see also the 1999 special issue of *Future of Children* on home visiting [Behrman, 1999].)

As illustrated in Appendix 24.A, the programs that we examined varied considerably in scope and mode of service delivery. Some interventions, such as the Johns Hopkins Children and Youth Program (Hardy & Street, 1989), the Prenatal and Early Infancy Project (e.g., Olds et al., 1997), and the Memphis New Mothers Project (Kitzman et al., 1997; Olds et al., 1999) emerged from a public health tradition and delivered a comprehensive array of services aimed at the "whole person" (i.e., parent). Others focused more on parent education and parental mental health as a pathway to enhanced early child development (see, e.g., Barrera, Rosenbaum, & Cunningham, 1986; Booth, Mitchell, Barnard, & Spiker, 1989; Larson, 1980; Madden, O'Hara, & Levenstein, 1984). A few programs targeted child–parent attachment (e.g., Erickson, Korfmacher, & Egeland, 1992; Jacobson & Frye,

1991; Lieberman, Weston, & Pawl, 1991; Lyons-Ruth, Connell, Grunebaum, & Botein, 1990).

Considerable variation in the ways that program outcomes were evaluated was also found. Some studies examined program processes and the mechanisms underlying their programs' successes and failures, whereas many did not. Thus, an important caveat concerning the findings is that the programs' impacts (or the lack thereof) are not always well documented.

We examined fourteen parent-focused home-based programs that began prenatally or within the child's first year and three parent-focused home-based programs that began between ages 1 and 3. Program effects on all six aspects of parental and familial functioning are considered.

EFFECTS ON MATERNAL EDUCATION AND EMPLOYMENT. Of the seventeen programs reviewed, three examined influences on parent education, employment, and self-sufficiency, and each had at least some impact. The strongest effects come from the most comprehensive program – Olds's Prenatal and Early Infancy Project. Participation was associated with reduced use of welfare and food stamps, greater maternal workforce participation, and fewer subsequent pregnancies (Olds, Henderson, Chamberlin, & Tatelbaum, 1986, 1988; Olds, Henderson, & Kitzman, 1994; Olds, Henderson, Kitzman, & Cole, 1995; Olds, Henderson, Tatelbaum, & Chamberlin, 1986; Olds et al., 1997, 1999). Similar though less consistent findings emerged from a subsequent urban version of the Prenatal and Early Infancy Project, the Memphis New Mothers Project (see Kitzman et al., 1997). Participation in Project STEEP, which focused on the developing infant–parent attachment, was associated with the development of greater maternal "life management" skills (Erickson et al., 1992).

EFFECTS ON MATERNAL MENTAL AND PHYSICAL HEALTH. Of the seventeen programs reviewed, five examined effects on parental mental and physical health. Findings as often as not indicated no significant treatment-control group differences (Barth, Hacking, & Ash, 1988; Lyons-Ruth et al., 1990). In one case, a negative treatment effect was found because treatment mothers had higher blood pressure than did the controls (Field, Widmayer, Stringer, &

Ignatoff, 1980). In the Prenatal and Early Infancy Project, however, in the two years following the end of the intervention, physicians' reports indicated fewer "coping problems" in treatment mothers than in the control group (Olds et al., 1994). In Project STEEP, treatment group mothers showed fewer symptoms of depression and anxiety than did controls (Erickson et al., 1992).

EFFECTS ON OBSERVED PARENT–CHILD INTERACTION/RELATIONSHIP QUALITY. Observed parent–child interaction or relationship quality was the familial outcome most likely to be assessed in the program evaluations reviewed here. Of the seventeen programs, thirteen examined parent–child interactions/relationships, and only two did not indicate at least some treatment benefits in this domain (Erickson et al., 1992; Gray, Cutler, Dean, & Kempe, 1979). The other eleven programs demonstrated at least some positive effects on parent–child interaction. Effects favoring the treatment group(s) were revealed in terms of less harsh or negative parenting behaviors (Olds et al., 1988, 1994); more sensitive, supportive, or positive parenting behaviors (e.g., Barrera et al., 1986; Field et al., 1980; Gray & Ruttle, 1980; Larson, 1980; Lieberman et al., 1991; Madden et al., 1984; Olds et al., 1988, 1994); and greater likelihood of infant–parent attachment security (Jacobson & Frye, 1991; Lieberman et al., 1991; Lyons-Ruth et al., 1990). It is notable that the majority of program relationship effects centered on greater degrees or incidence of sensitive parenting. This pattern fits with that revealed in a recent review and meta-analysis of attachment-based program effects (van Ijzendoorn, Juffer, & Duyvesteyn, 1995). van Ijzendoorn et al. found that these programs were more effective in altering parental insensitivity than in changing the quality of the relationship attachment per se.

Two evaluations reported program effects on parent–child interaction to be contingent upon the quality of program participation. Specifically, in the Menninger Infancy Project (Osofsky, Culp, & Ware, 1988), laboratory assessments conducted at six, thirteen, and twenty months comparing the treatment and control groups on several measures of mother–infant interaction initially revealed no group differences. However, a second series of analyses compared home-visited mothers who "took" the intervention to those who did not, with "taking" defined as both keeping home visiting appointments and following through on established goals and activities. At both six and thirteen months, "taker" mothers received more positive scores in both feeding and play interactions with their infants than did their "nontaker" counterparts. An attempt to identify the factors that may have contributed to whether the mothers actively participated in (took) the home intervention indicated that the nontakers were significantly younger than the takers and were more likely than the takers to have smaller infants with shorter gestational ages.

Similarly, in the Clinical Nursing Models study (Barnard, Magyary, Booth, Mitchell, & Spieker, 1988; Booth et al., 1989), which contrasted an "information/resource" program with a "mental health" intervention, initial analyses revealed no group differences in mother–child interactions. Further analyses drawing on the home-visitor records, however, indicated that almost half of the mothers in the information/resource treatment group actually received services more consonant with the mental health approach. Subsequent analyses then examined participants on the frequency of therapeutic visits received and treatment goals attained. Analyses revealed that it was the attainment of treatment goals that predicted posttreatment social skills, and posttreatment social skills, in turn, predicted more positive mother–child interactions. Furthermore, when pretreatment social skills were considered, these results were significant for mothers who had begun the program with low social skills, but they faded out for mothers who had entered the program with initially better social skills.

Taken together, the findings from these two programs highlight the importance of the quality of program participants' engagement in program services as well as the interaction between participant characteristics and their potential to benefit from intervention (see also Berlin et al., 1998; Liaw, Meisels, & Brooks-Gunn, 1995). In summary, quality of the mother–child interaction is a frequent family outcome. The processes underlying program effects on the mother–child relationship, however, have not been specified in great detail.

EFFECTS ON THE USE OF CHILD-RELATED SER-VICES. Of the seventeen evaluations reviewed, five examined effects on the use of child-related services.

Early intervention programs can ostensibly be expected to increase as well as decrease parental use of child-related services. One could expect increases in well-baby visits and in immunizations, for example, and decreases in acute care visits and hospitalizations. Although only two of five evaluations revealed treatment effects on the use of child-related services, both of these effects were observed in the studies reviewed here (Barth et al., 1988; Hardy & Street, 1989).

EFFECTS ON PARENTING KNOWLEDGE, ATTITUDES, AND QUALITY OF THE HOME ENVIRONMENT. Parenting knowledge and attitudes and the quality of the home environment were the second most likely family outcomes to be assessed in the program evaluations reviewed here. Of the seventeen programs reviewed, twelve examined these variables. Eleven evaluations used the HOME Inventory (Caldwell & Bradley, 1984), and eight demonstrated at least some treatment influence on the quality of the home environment (Barrera et al., 1986; Erickson et al., 1992; Field et al., 1980; Gray & Ruttle, 1980; Larson, 1980; Olds et al., 1994; Osofsky et al., 1988; Ross, 1984). Impacts on parents' knowledge of child development and child-rearing attitudes were less frequent, with only one of the four programs demonstrating a treatment effect (Field et al., 1980).

EFFECTS ON INDICATORS OF CHILD MALTREATMENT. The presence of child maltreatment or indicators of child maltreatment was an outcome examined by six of the seventeen programs reviewed here. All six found treatment effects on signs and symptoms such as untreated severe diaper rash, closed head injuries, and emergency room visits, if not on substantiated maltreatment reports per se (Barth et al., 1988; Gray et al., 1979; Hardy & Street, 1989; Kitzman et al., 1997; Larson, 1980; Olds, Henderson, Chamberlin et al., 1986; Olds et al., 1988, 1994, 1995, 1997; see also Duggan et al., 1999). A striking exception is the Prenatal and Early Infancy Project (Olds et al., 1988), which, in a fifteen-year follow-up, found fewer verified reports of child maltreatment in treatment group families than in control group families (although the findings are based on a small number of families with records of child maltreatment).

Parent-Focused Combined Center- and Home-Based Programs

A second group of early intervention programs combines home visiting or other parent-focused services with a center-based component for the young child. The theoretical underpinnings of this type of intervention can be found in the ecological model propounded by Bronfenbrenner and the family support movement (e.g., Zigler & Weiss, 1985). These interventions strive to promote the healthy development of children and families who are environmentally at risk by providing treatments to both children and their parents (in the multiple settings of the home and early childhood center) and by seeking to increase access to social support for these families.

Appendix 24.B outlines ten studies of programs that included both a center-based early childhood education or developmental child care component and a parent-focused component: either home visiting or other forms of parenting education and support. Studies are included in the appendix only if they examined some form of parental outcome. Three types of family outcomes were examined: 1) parent education, employment, and self-sufficiency; 2) observed parent–child interaction/relationship quality; and 3) parenting attitudes, knowledge, and the quality of the home environment.

A number of programs begin serving families before the child is born or sometime during the first year of the child's life. Some provide different services based on the age of the child, starting out with home visits during the first year of life and then providing center-based service in later years; whereas other programs provide ongoing center-based service concurrently with home visiting or other parent-focused services. One of the first models of this comprehensive type of service delivery was the federal Parent Child Development Centers (PCDC) project, which began in 1970. The PCDC model introduced the concept of using parent education to help parents promote and sustain their children's development. PCDCs employed three principal methods to achieve their goals: 1) parent education to increase parents' knowledge about typical child development, 2) promotion of the mother's personal development, and 3) appropriate family support services (Andrews et al., 1982). At the three different demonstration sites (in Birmingham,

Houston, and New Orleans), the particular services offered varied (see Appendix 24.B).

Although the PCDC services tended to begin when the target child was a few months old, other programs begin during pregnancy or immediately following the child's birth. In 1985 the Infant Health and Development Program (IHDP) began to provide weekly home visits after the child's birth that continued through the child's first year, with visits tapering to biweekly during the second and third years when children began receiving center-based preschool services (Brooks-Gunn, Klebanov, Liaw, & Spiker, 1993; Brooks-Gunn et al., 1994; McCormick, McCarton, Brooks-Gunn, Belt, & Gross, 1998; Ramey et al., 1992). Similarly, the Teenage Pregnancy Intervention Program (Field, Widmayer, Greenberg, & Stoller, 1982), Project CARE (Wasik, Ramey, Bryant, & Sparling, 1990), and the Milwaukee Project (Garber, 1988) began with home visiting services from the birth of the child through the first several months, then provided center-based early childhood education for the children and job training or other parent support services for the mothers. The High/Scope Perry Preschool program is the only program of this type that did not begin providing services until the child was 3 years old; however, families were visited weekly in their homes during the year or two that children attended a developmental preschool four days per week.

Some programs in this category represent true comprehensive family support programs (as described by Zigler & Weiss, 1985), because in addition to home visits focused on parenting and the provision of center-based child care their services included several additional social supports. For instance, the Yale Child Welfare Project (Seitz & Apfel, 1994) provided social work, psychological services, and personalized pediatric care services to participating families. The Brookline Early Education Project (BEEP; Weiss, 1979; Zigler & Weiss, 1985) also included pediatric exams and developmental screenings in addition to its parent education and support services.

EFFECTS ON MATERNAL EDUCATION AND EMPLOYMENT. With their focus on improving personal outcomes for the mother as a pathway for improving the well-being and functioning of the child's family, several program evaluations monitored employment, education, and self-sufficiency outcomes for participating mothers. One pathway through which these comprehensive parenting support programs hope to benefit children and families is through increasing the educational and occupational opportunities of parents, which should in turn improve the socioeconomic resources of the family as a whole. All of the studies reporting on these outcomes found positive effects of program participation. Mothers who participated in the Birmingham PCDC were more likely to return to school and had a better grasp of the resources available in their communities for handling problems (Andrews et al., 1982). Rates of maternal employment were higher among IHDP mothers at the end of program participation than among control group mothers (Brooks-Gunn, McCormick, Shapiro, Benasich, & Black, 1994), and an increase in continued education and lower rates of subsequent childbearing were found for mothers in the Teenage Pregnancy Intervention Program (Field et al., 1982) and the Yale Child Welfare Project (Seitz & Apfel, 1994).

EFFECTS ON MATERNAL MENTAL AND PHYSICAL HEALTH. In addition to the positive findings in the areas of parenting, home environment, and maternal education and employment, the Birmingham PCDC findings showed that program mothers had higher levels of general life satisfaction than control mothers, and the High/Scope Perry Preschool evaluation reported more positive child-rearing attitudes immediately following program participation (Schweinhart, Barnes, Weikart, Barnett, & Epstein, 1993). In addition, lower depressive symptom scores were reported by mothers in the intervention group in the IHDP when the children were 1 and 3 years of age (Klebanov, Brooks-Gunn, Lee, & McCormick, in press). These effects were most pronounced in the IHDP mothers who had experienced a large number of negative life events.

EFFECTS ON OBSERVED PARENT–CHILD INTERACTION RELATIONSHIP/QUALITY. Of the seven studies reviewed that reported on parenting behaviors, six found positive program effects, and one (Project CARE; Wasik et al., 1990) found no difference between program and control parents. The PCDC evaluation (Andrews et al., 1982) administered extensive measures of mother–child interactions and found more positive interaction qualities

among program mothers. At the three- and four-year follow-ups at the Birmingham site, program mothers showed more use of reason and less use of physical punishment in their child control techniques than did control group mothers. In the New Orleans PCDC, follow-up at two and three years revealed that program mothers interacted in more sensitive, accepting, and cooperative ways and used more positive and less negative language with their children than control group mothers. The Houston PCDC found more affection, praise, use of appropriate control techniques, and encouragement of child verbalizations among mothers in the treatment group.

In the Teenage Pregnancy Intervention Program (Field et al., 1982), mother–infant interactions were measured at the four-month assessment, when families were close to the end of service receipt. Significant program effects were found on all assessments of the interactions: mothers' and infants' eye contact, facial expressions, vocalizations, and sensitivity; mothers' verbalizations; and the amount of time infants' gaze was averted from the mother. Garber (1988) also found significant effects of participation in the Milwaukee Project on measures of parenting. In the Infant Health and Development Program, mothers in the treatment group had higher quality of assistance and supportive presence scores, based on rating videotapes of problem-solving tasks when the children were 30 months of age (Spiker, Fergusson, & Brooks-Gunn, 1993).

EFFECTS ON PARENTING KNOWLEDGE, ATTITUDES, AND QUALITY OF THE HOME ENVIRONMENT. The effect of program participation on the child's home environment was assessed in four studies, with two finding very modest program effects (IHDP and Houston PCDC; Andrews et al., 1982; Bradley et al., 1989; Brooks-Gunn et al., 1994). Project CARE (Wasik et al., 1990) and the Teenage Pregnancy Intervention Program (Field et al., 1982) found no differences in the home environments of treatment and control families. One reason for both the low rates of assessment and the significant findings on this outcome is that the home environment may be considered to be only indirectly related to the intervention programs. Whereas parenting skills and interaction techniques were usually direct foci of the parenting education components of these programs, it can be argued that the provision of stimulating, enriched home environments was usually addressed more generally (with the exception of IHDP and Project CARE). Therefore, few researchers chose to look at home environments when measuring program effects, and those that did found mixed results (although none found control families to have higher home environment scores).

EFFECTS ON INDICATORS OF CHILD MALTREATMENT. None of the studies reviewed here reported on child maltreatment; however, in the IHDP, the incidence of physical discipline was lower for mothers of boys who were in the treatment group, as compared to mothers of boys in the follow-up group (Smith & Brooks-Gunn, 1997).

Intergenerational Literacy Programs

The group of early childhood interventions labeled *family literacy programs* or *intergenerational literacy programs* evolved out of recognition of two separate but complementary issues: 1) the relative lack of success of traditional adult education programs in reducing adult illiteracy, low education, and unemployment and 2) the theory behind the comprehensive services provided by many successful early childhood programs. The notion that the needs of young children who are environmentally at risk for poor school and future outcomes can be better met by providing services to other family members in addition to the child has been broadened in family literacy programs. In these programs, adult family members are explicit targets of educational services as well as other support services. Thus, family literacy programs are designed to provide educational and literacy training to both children and adult family members in order to improve the well-being and future prospects for the entire family (St. Pierre, Lazyer, Goodson, & Bernstein, 1997).

Traditional family literacy programs offer at least three main types of services to families: 1) early childhood education, 2) adult education, and 3) parenting education. The theoretical rationale for family literacy programs is that children are expected to benefit directly from early childhood education and indirectly from the two parent-focused services. Adult education is also expected to improve the educational and occupational status of the adults who have participated in the program, thus

improving the family's material resources and general well-being. The parenting education component is generally designed to improve the literacy-related interactions and activities in which parents and children engage and increase the amount of literacy-related materials available in the home environment (St. Pierre et al., 1997). Thus, family literacy programs emphasize improving children's lives and future prospects by helping their families become more self-sufficient (through increased education and, optimally, employment) and providing more supportive learning environments for their children.

Benefits to parents or other adult caregivers participating in family literacy programs are seen to be ends in themselves and pathways through which children's experiences and prospects are improved. Research evaluating the efficacy of family literacy programs has focused not only on the effects on young children but also on parent and family outcomes due to program participation. These include such education and literacy-related outcomes for the adult as educational attainments and achievement test performance; employment outcomes (affecting family income and environment); and changes in parental behaviors, including parent–child literacy and teaching activities and the provision of literacy-supportive home environments.

Generally, a two-generation early intervention program is considered to be a family literacy program if it provides educational components directly to both a young child and an adult caregiver of the child, as well as some form of parenting education (Smith, 1995a, 1995b). This model is relatively new, with the first family literacy programs appearing in the mid- to late-1980s. Some programs that do not specifically provide an adult education component also describe themselves as family literacy programs because they aim to improve children's literacy and academic achievements by enhancing parent–child literacy interactions and family literacy environments. Such programs typically focus their intervention on parents alone or on parent–child interactions; this topic is addressed here in a later section. In this section, a brief background on the evolution of the family literacy model is presented, and family literacy programs are described briefly (see Appendix 24.C).

Kentucky's Parent and Child Education (PACE) program, created in 1986, is considered to be one of the original family literacy programs and has since been replicated in numerous local-level family literacy initiatives, as well as by the Federal Even Start Family Literacy Program (Heberle, 1992). Because of its early success, the Kenan Charitable Trust established the Kenan Family Literacy Project, now commonly known as the *PACE/Kenan model*, to help replicate and extend family literacy programs nationally and to conduct evaluations of their implementation and efficacy. The National Center for Family Literacy (NCFL) was created to support advocacy, research, technical assistance, and dissemination activities (including the *Toyota Families for Learning* family literacy programs, which operate in more than fifty sites in fifteen U.S. cities; Philliber, Spillman, & King, 1996).

Federal legislation in 1988 (the Hawkins–Stafford Elementary and Secondary School Improvement Amendments, P.L. 100-297), amended in 1991 with the National Literacy Act (P.L. 102-73), called for the institution of a federal family literacy program. The 1991 legislation initiated Even Start, which was guided by three goals: 1) helping parents become full partners in the education of their children; 2) assisting children in reaching their full potential as learners; and 3) providing literacy training for parents. These goals are addressed through the provision of three core services: early childhood education services for children from birth to 8 years of age, adult education instruction, and parent education services. Families are eligible to receive Even Start services if they have a child under age 8, an adult qualifying for adult basic education services, and live in a school district receiving Title I funds. As of the 1994–95 program year, there were a total of 513 local Even Start projects, serving approximately 31,000 families (St. Pierre & Swartz, 1995). Taken together, NCFL and Even Start family literacy projects represent hundreds of individual intervention programs united in their focus on providing adult literacy training and parenting education in addition to early childhood education services. Yet each program is uniquely different, tailored to address the specific needs and services available in specific communities.

The activities of the NCFL have helped make many family literacy program evaluation activities possible. The Even Start legislation mandates ongoing evaluation of program implementation and effectiveness. However, research on family literacy effectiveness that has included control or comparison groups is not extensive. PACE, Kenan Trust, and Toyota Families for Learning projects conducted smaller evaluations, which are reported here, but these tend to lack a rigorous controlled methodology, limiting the conclusions that can be drawn from them. These and two national Even Start evaluations are the primary source of outcome data. The evaluations reported here include studies lacking randomly assigned control groups, because so few studies on family literacy programs included a control group. The main exception is the first national Even Start evaluation (St. Pierre & Swartz, 1995), which contained an in-depth study of ten Even Start Programs and five randomly assigned control groups. Most other evaluations report changes in measured competencies from before program participation to the close of program participation, and some compare these changes to what would be expected or has already been measured in other nonparticipating groups.

EFFECTS ON MATERNAL EDUCATION AND EMPLOYMENT. In terms of program effects for parents and families, by far the most commonly assessed outcome is the parents' educational gain. Because family literacy programs include direct educational intervention for adult family members, gains in adult literacy skills and other educational endeavors are one of the primary areas of interest for program designers and participants alike. These are generally measured through standardized tests (see St. Pierre et al., 1997) such as the Comprehensive Adult Student Assessment System (CASAS; Rickard, Stiles, & Martois, 1989) and the Test of Adult Basic Education (TABE; CTB/McGraw-Hill, 1987). Other program impact measures on adult education are the attainment of a GED certificate, or high school diploma, or participation in activities toward this goal. Evaluations tend to report small but significant improvements based on these indicators. The first national Even Start evaluation (St. Pierre & Swartz, 1995) reported that rates of GED attainment were higher in the Even Start group (22%) than in the control group (6%) but that reading scores measured by the CASAS were not significantly higher for the Even Start enrollees.

The national Even Start evaluation for the second four-year funding cycle recently released an interim report (Tao, Swartz, St. Pierre, & Tarr, 1997). This study does not include control groups but has pretest and outcome data for a subsample of fifty-seven Even Start projects (the Sample Study). Literacy scores in this sample showed improvement in both reading and math achievement tests. In all Even Start programs, the GED attainment rate was 8%; for those in the Sample Study, the rate was 24% (for reasons unclear to the researchers, obtaining a GED was an educational goal for a higher proportion of these participants, which may explain their higher rate of attainment).

Gains in adult literacy scores were also documented in evaluations of Kentucky's PACE program and a model Even Start project called the *Family Intergenerational Literacy Model* (FILM; Richardson & Brown, 1997). Parents in the PACE program showed gains in TABE scores of .22 *SD* in reading, .16 *SD* in math, and .16 *SD* in language (Heberle, 1992). Parents participating in FILM gained seven points on the CASAS reading test – a significant improvement and one larger than the 4.9 point gain reported in the national Even Start Sample Study for the same program year (Richardson & Brown, 1997). FILM also documented a steadily increasing rate of GED attainment, from 10% of participating adults in 1991–92 to over 40% in 1996–97.

One important question for researchers interested in adult literacy is whether family literacy programs are any more successful than adult education programs that do not include a more comprehensive family focus. A few studies have addressed this question by comparing pre- and posttest gains in traditional adult education programs with those for adults participating in family literacy programs. In such a comparison for Kentucky's PACE program, significant differences were documented in adults' rates of GED attainment (37% in PACE versus 15% in Adult Basic Education; Heberle, 1992). Similarly, Philliber, Spillman, and King (1996) reported data on adults participating in the Toyota Families for Learning Program in comparison with adult-focused education programs in California and New York City. More than 1,500 adults in California gained an average of 2.3 points on the CASAS reading scale, whereas of 111 adults measured on the CASAS in the Toyota program, the average gain was 4.5 points – a statistically significant difference. The TABE was used to assess an unreported number of adults in a New York adult literacy program and 133 adults in the Toyota program. The adults in the family literacy program gained 1.15 grade equivalents in reading; the gain for adults in the adult-focused program was only .75 grade equivalents. Although the samples compared here differ in many respects, both adult education samples were older than the family literacy samples; furthermore, because age tends to be correlated with achievement in adult education, the claim of larger gains for the family literacy adults is strengthened.

EFFECTS ON MATERNAL MENTAL AND PHYSICAL HEALTH. Most family literacy programs assume that they will have positive effects on the family as a whole, but only a few programs have chosen to document some of these effects. The first national Even Start evaluation assessed program effects on maternal well-being by measuring depression and locus of control in mothers after program participation. No differences between Even Start and control group mothers were observed on these variables. In some Even Start evaluations, pre- and postparticipation levels of family income, perceived social support, adequacy of family resources, and parental employment status were measured. No significant program effects for any of these family-level variables were found.

EFFECTS ON OBSERVED PARENT–CHILD INTERACTION/RELATIONSHIP QUALITY. Almost no research on the family literacy programs focused on observing parent–child interactions. St. Pierre and Swartz (1995), who conducted the national evaluations of Even Start, made an interesting point about changes in parenting related to participation in the program. They noted that although the parenting support and education component is not the component that tends to attract families into the program (most are drawn for the adult education and the rest for the early childhood component), some parents report that they have seen the greatest program impact on their own parenting. St. Pierre and Swartz also noted that the parents have more patience with their children, use less physical punishment, and have learned new ways of playing with their children.

EFFECTS ON PARENTING, KNOWLEDGE, ATTI-
TUDES, AND QUALITY OF THE HOME ENVIRON-
MENT. In the first national Even Start evaluation,
St. Pierre and Swartz (1995) found that the largest
program effect for parenting was on the number
of reading materials for children in the home. The
Even Start group had larger gains than control families on this measure, with an effect size of .40.
Other Even Start/control group comparisons in this
study found no significant differences on measures
of parent–child reading interactions or changes in
educational expectations. The ongoing Even Start
evaluation employed a smaller battery of parenting
measures, based on the lack of significant findings
in the earlier evaluation. Parenting is assessed in
the current evaluation in which the HOME Screening Questionnaire (HSQ; Coons, Gay, Fandal, Ker, &
Frankenburg, 1981), was used, which is a self-report
measure of home environment and parent–child activities. Even Start parents of children under age 3
had standardized gains on the HSQ from pretest to
posttest of .60, and parents of children 3–6 years had
gains of .48 (Tao et al., 1997).

Summaries of research conducted by the NCFL indicate a number of qualitative gains in the parenting domain for participants in family literacy programs. For instance, parents reported feeling that
they are better equipped to be good parents (Brizius & Foster, 1993); spend more time helping their
children with homework and reading to them; attend more school functions and teacher–parent conferences; and have a better understanding of education, teachers, and administrators (Potts & Paull,
1995). Parents also reported that they have become
more dedicated to keeping their children in school
(Potts & Paull, 1995). Parents in the Kentucky PACE
program showed significant increases in their expectations for their children's educational attainment,
with the proportion of parents believing their child
would finish high school increasing from 44% before
PACE program participation to 57% after (Heberle,
1992). In addition, program staff noted that virtually all parents showed improvement in parenting,
and they rated 40% of parents as "much improved"
in being better role models for their children (Brizius
& Foster, 1993).

Evaluation of sixty-seven families across several
Toyota Families for Learning programs in three cities
found several areas of improvement in learning

experiences after just four to six months of program
participation (Mikulecky, Lloyd, & Brannon, 1994).
The only measured areas in which significant increases were not found were in parents' knowledge
of child development concepts and parental modeling of literacy behaviors.

Parent-Focused Family Literacy Programs

As mentioned earlier, a number of other programs
may be described as family literacy programs in that
they recognize the importance of family interactions and environments in promoting literacy development. However, these programs do not meet
a strict definition of intergenerational family literacy programs because they do not provide the full
complement of services (i.e., early childhood education, adult education, and parenting education and
support). Rather, these programs focus on parenting education, with the goal of helping to enhance
parent–child learning activities in the home. The
programs described below are two examples of these
parenting education programs with a family literacy focus. They are the Home Instruction Program
for Preschool Youngsters (HIPPY; Baker, Piotrkowski,
& Brooks-Gunn, 1998, 1999) and the Parents as
Teachers (PAT) program (see Wagner & Clayton,
1999; Winter & Rouse, 1990). Each has had outcome
evaluations that include comparison or control
groups.

HIPPY is an early intervention program designed
to give parents of 2- or 3- to 5-year-olds concrete
tools for interacting with their children in educationally supportive ways. The centerpiece of the program is a weekly home visit by a trained paraprofessional, who brings a packet of scripted activities
and instructs the parent how to use the materials
with the child. The program is unique in that it
hopes to improve children's school readiness and
school success but does not provide services directly
to the child. Additional and complementary goals
of HIPPY are to raise parents' expectations for their
children's educational attainment and to increase
the frequency of parent–child activities that are associated with school success.

A two-site two-cohort evaluation of HIPPY began
in 1990 and 1991 and followed HIPPY and control
group families from the beginning of program participation through a follow-up after the children had

been in kindergarten for one year (Baker et al., 1998, 1999). Control groups were randomly assigned at one site but not at the other. The second site used a comparison sample from the same community because random assignment was not feasible. Although the evaluation focused on children's academic outcomes (finding some significant effects), a few measures of the home literacy environment and parental expectations were assessed. The findings were not strong but were suggestive of positive program effects. In one site, HIPPY families had a larger variety of literacy materials in their homes after program participation than did controls. At the other site, parental expectations for children's educational attainment and performance were positively affected, although none of these results was consistent across the two cohorts. Program effects obtained at this second site are especially interesting, because at this site both HIPPY and control children participated in the same high-quality developmental preschool program. Thus, parent expectations were enhanced for HIPPY parents over and above the effects of the early childhood enrichment.

The PAT program originated in Missouri as a parent education and support program for families with children from birth to age 3 from all socioeconomic backgrounds. It has enjoyed strong support in some policy circles and is now a statewide program in Missouri and Minnesota and exists on a smaller scale in many other states. The central component of the PAT program is a series of home visits by a certified parent educator who provides information and support to parents to help enhance their children's development across social, emotional, intellectual, and physical domains. Many parents begin the program before the birth of their child, and home visitors provide guidance to help prepare the parents for having a new baby in their home (Wagner & Clayton, 1999; Winter & Rouse, 1990). The home visits follow a set curriculum of learning activities, which the educator models with the child. The home visits include discussions of what parents can expect from children at each age and how to deal with different parenting situations. In addition to the home visits, PAT families participate in group meetings with other parents, receive child developmental screenings through the first 3 years, and are provided referrals to any needed community services. Enrollment is open to all families in participating public school districts, with no income or other risk-related requirements for eligibility.

An evaluation of three pilot PAT sites in Texas is unique in that it used baseline measures of parent characteristics, included comparison groups of families with similar backgrounds who did not receive PAT services, followed families longitudinally across the three years of program participation, and assessed both parent and child outcomes (Owen & Mulvihill, 1994). Measures of family effects included parent knowledge of child development, parent attitudes toward child rearing, parenting stress, perceptions of social support and parenting satisfaction, and quality of the home environment. For most of these outcomes, there were no measurable PAT program effects in this middle-class sample. However, there was a significant difference in home environment assessed using the HOME scales. Even though both PAT and comparison families had high scores on the HOME, families participating in PAT received significantly higher scores at the end of program participation. Owens and Mulvihill also commented that the sample was middle-class with motivated parents already providing developmentally stimulating environments for their children. Families with lower baseline levels of knowledge of child development and fewer resources for providing stimulating home environments (in other words, with more need of assistance and information on parenting) may be more likely to benefit from the parenting education and support provided by PAT (Owen & Mulvihill, 1994). A more recent evaluation of two randomized trials of PAT revealed similar findings (Wagner & Clayton, 1999). This evaluation also indicated effects on children's motor, cognitive, and language development, especially for children of Spanish-speaking Latino families and for children whose families received more intensive services (Wagner & Clayton, 1999).

Summary

The programs reviewed here indicate some positive and some mixed findings with regard to effects of early intervention programs on parents. Several factors that may interact contribute to these varied findings. First, although all of the programs are parent-focused, or include parent-focused components, the interventions for parents vary widely.

Some programs focus on parenting, aiming to increase parents' confidence in themselves as parents and as the first teachers of their children, improve understanding of child development, and encourage positive and stimulating parent–child interactions. Other programs focus more on improving parents' skills in other arenas of their lives, such as their academic and occupational attainments or their access to multiple social services. Many programs attempt to address both parenting and adult life skills to varying degrees. Effects on parenting attitudes, behaviors, home environments, and self-sufficiency would be expected to be contingent upon the extent to which a particular intervention program focused its services on each area.

Second, questions about method of service delivery, service intensity, participant engagement, and staff–participant relationships all have bearing on the effectiveness of the programs for parents. These issues have been discussed in-depth in a recent special issue of *Zero to Three* (Berlin et al., 1998) and are described later in this chapter.

Third, the field continues to be constrained by the research that has been conducted, as many early interventions lack rigorous, controlled, empirical evaluations. Furthermore, those researchers who do conduct evaluations often fail to measure (or perhaps report) outcomes for parents.

FAMILIES AS ENGINES OF CHANGE FOR EARLY INTERVENTION

It has been two decades since Bronfenbrenner (1979) described families as engines of change for early intervention programs. He meant, of course, that early intervention programs were unlikely to be successful unless they involved parents and perhaps the entire family. However, quite surprisingly, almost no evaluation research has examined this premise. It is almost as though the primacy of parental change has been reified to the point that empirical verification is not considered necessary. An alternative explanation is that the majority of evaluations do not have the data available to test the premise. Our belief is that parental engagement is seen as axiomatic to early intervention, which has led to an implicit acceptance of its importance.

The *Statement of the Advisory Committee on Services for Families with Infants and Toddlers* (DHHS, 1994) urges Early Head Start programs to support the infant–parent relationship. The family is one of the four cornerstones of the program (with the child, the staff, and the community being the other three). Indeed, Head Start is predicated on parental involvement and has been very successful in promoting such engagement. For example, the Head Start Bureau reports that in 1996 almost one-third of the Head Start staff were parents of current or former Head Start children and that almost all parents of children enrolled in Head Start volunteer in their local Head Start programs.

At least three issues need to be addressed when considering the role of parents in early intervention, the first having to do with the effects of programs on the family, the second with the links between the efficacy of intervention on the family and the child, and the third with parental engagement in programs and programs' roles in enhancing parental involvement. The previous sections provide detailed reviews of the effects of program participation upon parents. Here we discuss, albeit briefly, three of the major dimensions of family change that have been studied that are likely to be affected by participation in programs and that are known to influence child outcomes. These are 1) maternal mental health, 2) provision of stimulating home experiences (primarily cognitive and literacy activities), and 3) maternal sensitivity/responsiveness in interactions. Then we examine whether the effects of early intervention upon children are in part mediated through effects on these three family dimensions through the few studies that address this issue. Finally, the importance of parental involvement in the program is considered. The emphasis is not only on how to measure parental involvement but also on the characteristics of programs and staff that might enhance parental engagement.

Program Effects on Parents: Mental Health, Learning Experiences, and Parenting

Early intervention programs – whether they be home visiting (by a nurse, social worker, or educator), center-based child care, or access to family resource centers – are all predicated on the belief that programs can alter parental behavior, as has been discussed in this review. Some programs have focused on the family system and on relationships among members of the family as central to altering parent and child outcomes (Barnard et al., 1988; Booth et al., 1989; Egeland & Erikson, 1990; Greenspan, 1990; Ramey & Ramey, 1998). Outcomes of interest include parental mental health, learning experiences in the home, and parental interactions with children.

MATERNAL MENTAL HEALTH. Parental mental health may be targeted as an outcome because depressive symptoms have been linked to child outcomes. Children of mothers with high scores on depressive symptoms are likely to exhibit higher levels of behavior problems (Downey & Coyne, 1990; Egeland, Kalkoske, Gottesman, & Erickson, 1990; Lyons-Ruth, Zoll, Connell, & Grunebaum, 1986); similar findings are reported for adolescents with conduct disorder (Fergusson, Lynskey, & Horwood, 1993) and depressive symptoms or disorder in older children and adolescents (Downey & Coyne, 1990; Hammen, Burge, & Adrian, 1991). A smaller number of studies found significant associations between maternal depressive symptoms and children's cognitive and school competence (Downey & Coyne, 1990; Goodman & Brumley, 1990; Klebanov, et al., 1998; Zahn-Waxler, Iannotti, Cummings, & Denham, 1990).

Few early intervention programs reported effects on maternal depressive symptoms. Our assumption is that most evaluations did not include such a measure (instead of examining depressive symptoms, finding no differences, and not reporting this fact). Three studies are noteworthy, however. In a program targeting pregnant women who had low amounts of social support, two home visitation models were implemented (Barnard et al., 1988; Booth et al., 1989). One model focused on the home visitor establishing a therapeutic relationship with the mother through which mothers would learn more effective ways to deal with interpersonal situations and more adaptive problem solving. The other model relied strictly on providing information and resources to mothers in the promotion of a healthy lifestyle. Mothers who received the mental health curriculum reported significantly fewer depressive symptoms than those who received the educational curriculum. The mental health treatment was most beneficial for mothers with multiple risks.

In the Infant Health and Development Program, depressive symptom scores were lower in the intervention than the follow-up only group when the children were 1 and 3 years of age, with these effects being seen in the mothers with the lowest education levels (Klebanov et al., in press). IHDP mothers in the treatment group received a problem-solving curriculum during the home visits (Wasik, Bryant, Lyons, Sparling, & Ramey, 1997). A third, nonrandomized study, which focused on mothers with high depressive symptoms, also found significant effects of emotional support upon depressive symptoms (Lyons-Ruth et al., 1990). Thus, programs that focus on mothers' daily lives – which help them learn more adaptive problem-solving skills, lend emotional support, or both – have the potential for reducing depressive symptoms.

LEARNING EXPERIENCES. Providing learning experiences in the home has been demonstrated repeatedly to be associated strongly with child cognitive and school competencies (Bradley, 1995; Bradley et al., 1989; Duncan, Brooks-Gunn, & Klebanov, 1994; Klebanov et al., 1997; Klebanov et al., 1998). The studies cited here used the HOME Inventory, which is based on observation and interview during a home visit (i.e., types of play materials in the home are observed, and mothers are asked about reading materials and amount of time spent reading to the child). Early provision of cognitive stimulation was examined in some studies by means of observing teaching strategies, with links to child well-being reported as well. For example, the ways in which parents read to their children are associated with their preschooler's language skills, over and above the amount of reading that occurs in the home (e.g., Snow, 1986; Whitehurst et al., 1994). In a related vein, "help and support" provided by mothers during a problem-solving assessment was associated with young children's enthusiasm and persistence toward the task (Bornstein, 1989; Crowell & Feldman, 1988; Spiker et al., 1993).

Many program evaluations include measures of home stimulation, with the HOME being the most frequent measure (see Appendixes 24.A, 24.B, and 24.C). Program effects on the HOME were reported by some (but not all) of the evaluations. Additionally, family literacy programs provide some evidence for enhancements in reading and other literacy activities in the home. Programs that target literacy and learning games are most likely to alter HOME scores.

MOTHER–CHILD INTERACTION. Parenting behavior is linked to children's well-being, as demonstrated in literally hundreds of studies (Bornstein, 1995; Lamb, 1998; Maccoby, 1992; Maccoby & Martin, 1983). Not surprisingly, more program evaluations examined mother–child interactions than other aspects of family life, as noted earlier in this chapter. In some cases, evaluations used relatively straightforward measures, such as maternal warmth and punitiveness, which can be derived from the HOME Inventory or from survey questions. Generally, treatment effects are not found on the HOME Warmth subscale (Bradley, Casey, & Caldwell, 1997). Few studies examined punishment and spanking; however, in those that did study these behaviors, significant effects were reported (Olds et al., 1994; Smith & Brooks-Gunn, 1997).

The quality and tone of mother–child interactions are most likely to be mentioned as an engine of change in many programs (Berlin et al., 1998; Clarke-Stewart & Fein, 1983; Woodhead, 1988; Yoshikawa, 1995). Parental emotional support, especially sensitivity, is a major dimension believed to contribute to secure infant–parent attachment as well as to later child well-being (Ainsworth, Blehar, Waters, & Wall, 1978; Belsky & Cassidy, 1994; Thompson, 1998). Within the infant–parent relationship, sensitivity refers to two dimensions: 1) the parent's awareness of the infant's needs and accuracy in reading the infant's cues and 2) the parent's contingent responsiveness to the infant's cues and needs. Parental insensitivity can take a number of forms, including intrusiveness, detachment, and negative regard/hostility. As reviewed earlier, many programs report positive effects on measures of maternal sensitivity.

Indirect Effects of the Parent Dimensions Upon Child Outcomes

The rationale for targeting maternal mental health, parenting behaviors, and provision of learning and literacy experiences in early intervention programs derives in large part from the expected benefits for children. To test this premise, it is necessary to demonstrate that an intervention influences parental outcomes and that these outcomes are associated with child outcomes. That is, a portion of the intervention effect on the child would have to be mediated through a treatment effect upon the parent (see Baron & Kenny, 1986). Given that this modeling is straightforward, the paucity of such analyses is startling and perhaps even disturbing. To our knowledge, only three relevant analyses have been conducted.

Using the Abecedarian and Project CARE early intervention data from North Carolina, Burchinal and her colleagues (1997) presented an elegant demonstration of mediating processes upon the cognitive test scores of poor children. Their proposed model suggests that the home visiting component of their program might influence child cognitive test scores by influencing the parent's authoritarian attitudes and the quality of the home environment. Furthermore, the child-care component of their program is hypothesized to have direct effects upon child test scores as well as an indirect effect through the responsiveness of the infant (responsiveness being defined by means of the assessor's ratings of activity level, sociability, and task orientation during administration of the Bayley Scales of Infant Development [the Infant Behavior Record]). Growth curve analyses were employed using HLM (hierarchical linear modeling), and mediated treatment effects were found for infant responsivity. Infant responsivity scores increased from 6 to 18 months for the infants in the treatment but not for those in the control group (i.e., those receiving center-based care), and this treatment effect was significant (i.e., it reduced the coefficient between child responsivity and child test score). Quality of the home environment had a direct effect on child test scores, but none of this effect was mediated through the effect of the intervention upon the home environment. Parental authoritarian attitudes had no direct effect on child outcome (so that mediation effects could not be examined). Thus, parenting did not seem to be an engine of change, given the lack of mediating effects. Whether this was due to the parenting measures used (i.e., no observational assessments were included), sample characteristics, or the intervention services provided (home visits alone, home visits and center-based, and center-based alone, rendering the size of the sample in any treatment group quite small) is not known. However, this study stands as an exemplar of the type of work that needs to be replicated in the early intervention field.

Using the Infant Health and Development Program data set, we also examined whether the effects on parents contribute a pathway through which early intervention influences children (Brooks-Gunn et al., 1993; Brooks-Gunn et al., 1994). The first model is based in part on the work by McLoyd (1990, 1998) and Conger and colleagues (1994, 1997), in which the pathways through which economic conditions (poverty, job loss, and financial strain) might influence children are explored (see also Elder, 1998). Child outcomes (with most of the work focusing on emotional and social competencies rather than on cognitive and school achievement competencies) are thought to be influenced by parent emotional functioning and parent behavior; mental health is thought to operate primarily through its impact on parent behavior. With respect to early intervention, we have altered this model to see whether treatment effects on children are mediated through maternal depressive affect and parenting behavior (Linver, Brooks-Gunn, & Kohen, 1999). Strong evidence was found for the premise that parents are a pathway through which early intervention programs influence children, controlling for demographic characteristics and family income. The treatment influenced maternal depressive symptoms, which in turn influenced parenting behavior, which affected child test scores. Parenting behavior was also influenced by participation in the treatment group. The findings with respect to parenting behavior differ somewhat from those of Burchinal and colleagues (1997). We suspect that the parenting measures that were included in our models (videotaped observations of parental authoritarian and authoritative behavior during free play) are more sensitive to early intervention effects (Berlin et al., 1995; Chase-Lansdale, Brooks-Gunn, & Zamsky, 1994).

Another set of analyses examined links among depressive symptoms, coping skills, and life events (Brooks-Gunn, Smith, Berlin, & Lee, in press; Klebanov, Brooks-Gunn, McCarton, & McCormick, 1998). The premise is based on the literature suggesting that depressive symptoms are in part a function of stressful life events and that the response to such events is moderated by coping skills (Park & Folkman, 1997). Participation in a family-oriented,

supportive, problem-centered early intervention program might influence mothers' emotional health directly or indirectly, by means of enhancing maternal coping skills. Direct effects of the intervention were found on depressive symptoms but not on coping skills, and no interaction between coping and treatment was found for maternal depressive symptoms. Thus, direct but not indirect effects were seen on maternal emotional health. In addition, the intervention only influenced emotional health in those mothers with a large number of stressful life events. With regard to child outcomes (child test scores and depressive symptoms at age 3), a parental pathway was found such that intervention children whose mothers had a high number of stressful life events and high depressive scores had higher test scores and lower depressive/anxious symptoms than did the follow-up children whose mothers had similar profiles. These analyses controlled for a variety of social, economic, and demographic characteristics.

In brief, one of the pathways through which early intervention programs influence child well-being involves the parent. Of the three relevant analyses, two provide support for the parent as mediator of treatment effects, and one does not.

Parent Engagement in Programs

Unless parents are engaged in a program, it is unlikely that direct benefits to the parents, or indirect effects upon the child by means of the parent, will be realized. Engagement, in our view, is based on the relationships between the family members and the program staff. In the first edition of the *Handbook of Early Childhood Intervention*, Simeonsson and Bailey (1990) discuss the critical nature of involvement between participants and those whom they termed the *interventionists*. They suggest that involvement might be measured using six categories or scales, which range from elective non-involvement to psychological involvement. The last category involves interactions in which value conflicts are defined and addressed by the participant and the program staff as progress is made toward behavioral change (change may be at the individual, dyadic, or family level). Such engagement is believed to be most likely to result in change, especially change that is enduring.

Engagement within the context of staff–family relationships has not been studied with any frequency.

Involvement is often inferred from the number of home visits or number of days at the center – the assumption being that participation is in large part dependent upon psychological involvement. So-called dose-related studies, whose findings draw solely on program (treatment) group(s), are vulnerable to the possibility that some preexisting characteristics of the participants rather than the program itself account for participant outcomes (i.e., selection effects). Consequently, it is not completely clear why some families have higher participation rates than others (i.e., factors other than psychological involvement might account for the variation; see the articles written from the IHDP, which collected extensive data on attendance in center-based care and number of home visits completed; Liaw, Meisels, & Brooks–Gunn, 1995; Ramey et al., 1992; Sparling et al., 1991). These three studies indicate that demographic characteristics account for a small amount of the variance in participation rates. Program dosage, however, is linked to child outcomes, even after controlling for demographic characteristics of the families. These findings suggest that program quantity (or amount of services) is important above and beyond some family characteristics that are associated with the extent of services that families receive.

Because dosage is only a rough proxy for involvement, what are alternative methods for assessing engagement? In one of the IHDP studies, we defined "active participation" in center-based child care and in the home visiting program (Liaw, Meisels, & Brooks–Gunn, 1995). Home visitors rated the mother on a three-point scale in terms of how involved she was in that day's activities. Summing these ratings over all of the home visits resulted in an involvement scale. Children whose mothers were rated as highly involved during the home visits had higher IQ scores at 3 years of age, even when controlling for demographic characteristics (maternal age, education, marital status, and race), child characteristics (gender, birth weight, and neonatal health), and participation (number of home visits and number of days at the child-care center). Involvement was also rated for the children in the child-care center, with scores being summed over all days at the center. High child involvement was associated with cognitive test scores at age 3, again controlling for a variety of possible covariates (keeping in mind that these findings are not based on randomization so that selection bias caused by unmeasured characteristics may be accounting for some or all of these effects). It is notable that the highest child test scores were obtained in the group with high mother and child involvement, suggesting that both were contributing to the outcome. We have suggested that participants' active engagement in programs should be one of the primary goals of early intervention efforts (Berlin et al., 1998).

Yet another approach to examining engagement focuses on the relationship between staff and parents. The term *therapeutic alliance* has been applied to this relationship, especially in programs with an emphasis on psychological involvement (Horvath & Luborsky, 1993; Kazdin, 1997). In fact, a number of programs have targeted the staff–parent relationship as the means through which enhanced parenting may be achieved (Egeland & Erickson, 1990, 1993; Erickson et al., 1992; Lieberman et al., 1991). Although the limited results to date are mixed (see van Ijzendoorn et al., 1995), programs such as the one developed by Barnard and colleagues (1988), discussed earlier, hold great promise. Interestingly, the Early Head Start program has defined staff as one of their cornerstones, and the national evaluation of the Early Head Start is studying staff–parent relationships (see Elicker, Noppe, Noppe, & Fortner-Wood, 1997; Pianta, 1992).

Characteristics of staff members may also be linked to participant engagement. Wasik et al. (1997) identified the following characteristics as central for high-quality home visiting: communication and interpersonal skills, maturity, warmth, and openness. It is likely that home visitors with this set of competencies would be perceived as more emotionally supportive than home visitors without these characteristics. Although little data exist to test this premise, the Memphis New Mothers' Study provides an intriguing finding (Korfmacher, Kitzman, & Olds, 1998). Specifically, mothers rated the nurse home visitors at the end of the program by using the Helping Relationship Inventory (tapping perceptions of trust, understanding, and sensitivity of the home visitor) (Barnard, 1998). For mothers who had high levels of psychological resources, maternal ratings of nurse empathy were associated with maternal empathy directed toward the child (both measures, however, were maternal report). The Home Visiting 2000 Program in Denver will be examining these links in more detail (Olds et al., 1997).

Relationships between staff and children also need to be considered. The early intervention literature has not concentrated on these relationships, at least in terms of evaluations. We suspect that this is related to an assumption that teachers and other staff are responsive, nonpunitive, warm, and cognitively stimulating toward the children in their care. The child care literature paints a different picture, however, because great variation is seen in teacher–child interactions across centers (Hayes, Palmer, & Zaslow, 1990; Love et al., 1994; Phillips, 1995). There is reason to suspect that variation is also common in early intervention programs (and it is time to document such variation). Higher quality teacher–child relationships are associated with better child outcomes (Howes, 1997; Love et al., 1994).

The final point in our discussion of participant engagement has to do with the match between participant needs and program services (Berlin et al., 1998). As Meisels (1992) and Barnard (1998) have pointed out, parental engagement and program success are no doubt linked to whether program services are relevant to a child's or family's specific vulnerabilities as well as to the parent's perceived needs. An example of a possible match comes from the program developed by Barnard (1998). Higher-risk mothers benefited more from a mental health curriculum than an educational curriculum, whereas lower-risk mothers benefited more from the educational curriculum. In an analysis of the IHDP (Liaw & Brooks-Gunn, 1994), when poor families were characterized by number of risk factors (i.e., low maternal education, unemployed head of household, single marital status, teenage mother, high levels of depressive symptoms, and low social support), the intervention was efficacious for poor children whose families had a few or a moderate number of additional risk factors. However, the poor children whose families had a high number of risk factors were not influenced by the set of intervention services provided by this program. It is possible that these multiproblem poor families needed a different set of services, a more intensive set, or a more extensive dose of services.

PRACTICE AND POLICY IMPLICATIONS FOR EARLY CHILDHOOD PROGRAMS

The implications of the findings on parents and families for practice and policy are briefly considered in this section. The perspective of program staff suggests the ways in which parents and families are incorporated into early childhood education efforts. This perspective might also indicate a disconnection between evaluations and program goals. From a policy perspective, we raise the issue of the possible implications of welfare reform on early childhood education.

Practice Implications: Theories of Change

Early intervention programs generally have multiple goals, some of which are made explicit and others of which are implicit. In this chapter, we have argued that the focus on parents is often taken for granted. Being more deliberate about specifying the goals of programs and the pathways through which positive outcomes are generated is a means of unpacking the black box of early intervention (Berlin, 1998; Klebanov et al., 1998). At least five components of a program need to be examined: 1) the program's philosophy or theory of change; 2) the principal targets, or recipients, of services; 3) the program's curriculum or specific activities; 4) the program's method of service delivery; and 5) the quantity and timing of services (Berlin et al., 1998). The first component – theory of change – is discussed here. Other chapters in this volume discuss the other components (see Halpern; Harbin, McWilliams, & Gallagher; Kagan & Neuman; Knitzer; Musick & Stott).

A program's philosophy refers to its emphases, goals, expected outcomes, and specific practices for achieving its defined impacts. A program's particular philosophy and the extent to which the program has articulated this philosophy are important program characteristics. Explicit program goals, expectations, and practices should facilitate service delivery as well as service receipt. This has been termed a *program's theory of change*, which guides the work of practitioners (Weiss, 1995). Much of the attention to theories of change has been generated from community-based initiatives, which often have many different goals, various constituencies, and multiple programmatic efforts aimed at integrating and coordinating services (Leventhal, Brooks-Gunn, & Kamerman, 1997). This approach is becoming increasingly evident in the early childhood field (Kagan & Pritchard, 1996).

In a sense, programs usually have more than a single theory of change. Often, the target of service, and the pathways through which change is expected, are perceived differently by different staff members within one program. For example, home visitors in a particular program might perceive the major pathway to enhanced parent–child interaction to be the provision of emotional support or problem-solving skills (although home visitors within a program might often differ in their emphases on support or skill enhancement as most crucial to promoting parenting competence). Case managers might stress the reduction of financial strain as most critical for parenting, arguing that sensitive parenting is not possible (or is difficult to achieve) when families are under economic duress. A speech and language therapist might focus on the improvement of parent–child communication skills as the key to sensitive parenting. All, of course, could be correct in that the pathway each emphasizes may alter parenting. The question, from a programmatic perspective, is how to forge an integrated philosophy that takes into account the strengths and interests of various program staff. We suspect that programs in which staff members have a coherent philosophy about how families are influenced are likely to be the most successful. Although no current data exist to test this premise, the national evaluation of Early Head Start is conducting interviews and group meetings with staff in the seventeen sites in the evaluation to obtain information on perceived theories of change (Mathematica Policy Research, Inc., 1998).

The theories of change approach has the potential to alter how evaluation research is conducted (Berlin et al., 1998; Green & McAllister, 1998). If a program articulates a set of pathways and goals, this theory provides a blueprint for building an evaluation. For example, our experience in talking with Early Head Start Program staff about expected pathways and outcomes suggests that the parent–child relationship is often central both as a pathway to child outcome and as an outcome in and of itself. Consequently, more detailed measures of

relationships have been included in the national evaluation than originally planned. Another example may be taken from the four cornerstones of Early Head Start, which recognize staff, child, family, and community. In this context, little work has focused on staff outcomes or on the relationships between staff and parents, even though program staff recognize them as central to success (Greenstein, 1998; Korfmacher, 1998). Consequently, as a result of this focus, measures of staff–parent relationships are being collected from both staff and parents.

Perhaps even more critical to the evaluation process is the co-construction of evaluation goals among research and practice partners (Chen & Rossi, 1983). Green and McAllister (1998) have termed this *theory-based, participatory evaluation*. They combine aspects of two approaches to evaluation – "(a) theory-based evaluation, which is based on careful articulation of the program model and use of this model as a guiding framework for evaluation; and (b) participatory evaluation, which involves close collaboration between evaluators and program administrators, staff, and families in developing, implementing, and interpreting the evaluation" (p. 30). In presenting an example from their work on family support programs, these authors suggest that such evaluations are more comprehensive, more grounded in the reality of program operation and in the context of families' lives, and less static than more traditional evaluations. We expect that the adoption of this type of approach will highlight even more boldly the ways in which families and parents are influenced by programs.

Policy Implications: Welfare Reform and Early Intervention

The vast majority of programs reviewed in this chapter have as their focus families who are poor or near poor. Federal programs such as Early Head Start use the federal poverty thresholds as guidelines for eligibility (keeping in mind that 10% of the Head Start slots are reserved for children with disabilities, who may or may not meet the income eligibility requirements). Other programs target families whose parents have low education, are teenagers at the time of the birth of the child, are unemployed, are single, or all of these. All of these demographic characteristics are associated with income poverty and welfare receipt (Brooks-Gunn & Duncan, 1997; Duncan & Brooks-Gunn, 1997; Duncan et al., 1994; Liaw & Brooks-Gunn, 1994; McLoyd, 1998). Consequently, many families served by early childhood programs are likely to be affected by welfare reform (Brooks-Gunn et al., in press). Changes in welfare rules (term limits and work requirements), child-care provisions, and Medicaid may affect the way that parental early intervention programs are run, the services that families receive, and the engagement that programs expect from parents (Brooks-Gunn & Duncan, 1997; Chase-Lansdale & Brooks-Gunn, 1995; Currie, 1997; Devaney, Ellwood, & Love, 1997; Duncan & Brooks-Gunn, 1998).

In the near future, many more poor mothers with young children are expected to enter the workforce because the welfare reforms of 1996 have ended the entitlement to a stipend for single parents not in the workforce. Welfare, or Temporary Assistance to Needy Families (TANF), is now limited to sixty months in a parent's lifetime. States have the option of shortening this limit, and many have done so. At the same time, eligible parents must enter the workforce or acceptable job programs after twenty-four months of TANF assistance. Again, many states have much more stringent requirements for finding work. The implementation of welfare reform is proceeding at a rapid pace (in part because thirty-five states already had waivers in place prior to the passage of the 1996 reforms to make welfare requirements more restrictive than allowed in the Family Support Act of 1988).

As more mothers enter the workplace, what happens to their relationships with early childhood program staff? How do they sustain high participation rates in program activities, given their time constraints? How do programs react to such constraints (i.e., in terms of home visiting, parent support groups, referrals to other services, and so on)? Will programs be reconfigured to take into account the expected increases in poor parents' labor market participation? Will parent engagement drop, as evidenced by lower rates of home visit completions, fewer parenting support groups, and diminished numbers of parent volunteers?

Changes might even occur in the numbers of parents enrolling their children in early intervention programs. For example, programs that do not offer full-time child care, flexible hours, or both will not be practical for working mothers. The majority of Head Start programs are half-day and are not geared to the needs of mothers in the labor force. Many programs for infants and toddlers provide home visiting services and parent–infant groups at centers. These services may become less attractive to mothers. Clearly, these changes must be monitored closely, both in terms of the choices that parents are making and the level of engagement in services.

In the spirit of providing more integrated and comprehensive programs for poor families, policy attention has been focused on combining adult-focused and family-focused programs (Aber, Brooks-Gunn, & Maynard, 1995; Smith, 1995a,b; St. Pierre et al., 1997). We reviewed some of these approaches under intergenerational family literacy programs. These programs might be characterized as adult- and family-focused programs because their focus is typically on women as adults entering the workforce and on women as mothers rearing children (Chase-Lansdale & Brooks-Gunn, 1995; Smith, Brooks-Gunn, & Jackson, 1997). It is possible that more programs that include family and work components will be implemented in the wake of welfare reform.

CONCLUSION

Virtually all early childhood intervention programs take some form of a family-oriented approach. Evaluations of these programs have a distinguished thirty-five-year history. The programs for infants and toddlers designed and implemented in the 1960s and 1970s uniformly included enhancing parent (and parenting) functioning as primary goals. However, published evaluations were much less likely to report findings on parents, as opposed to children (Benasich et al., 1992; Clarke-Stewart & Fein, 1983; Lazar et al., 1982; McKey et al., 1985). The reasons for this omission are not clear, but in all likelihood reflect a number of factors: the emphasis on getting children ready for elementary school; the lack of attention generally for social and emotional competence (in children as well as parents); the relative paucity of well-established, universally recognized measurement instruments for parental outcomes (when compared with the widespread use of infant cognitive tests); (Clarke-Stewart & Fein, 1983; Lewis, 1983); and the variety of program approaches used when working with parents. In addition, there is a certain logic to looking at child outcomes. The early program designers wished to demonstrate that significant effects on children could be generated; the question of what some saw as intermediary effects (i.e., effects on parents) was of less short-term policy relevance.

With the early results of the possible efficacy of early childhood programs having been demonstrated, however, efforts turned in the evaluations of the 1980s and 1990s toward a more rigorous examination of intervention effects on parents, as reviewed in this chapter. In part, this emphasis may be due to the fact that in the late 1980s and early 1990s evaluators found that some program designs were less likely to result in enhanced child language and cognitive function than were others. For example, the success of the Abecedarian Program was not replicated when home visiting alone, rather than in conjunction with center-based care, was examined in Project CARE (Campbell & Ramey, 1994). The reviews by Olds and colleagues (1994) of home visiting programs also suggested that children's cognitive test scores were usually not altered. At the same time, a review of the effects of home visiting and combination home- and center-based programs indicated that parent outcomes were enhanced (Benasich et al., 1992).

Another possible contributing factor had to do with the development of new curriculum materials to be used with parents. Programs were developed that focused on maternal problem-solving and coping skills, maternal responsivity, maternal child-rearing knowledge (including health, safety, and attitudes toward child rearing), maternal support, maternal emotional health, and learning games – to mention some of the most widely used approaches (Barnard et al., 1988; Benasich et al., 1992; Lyons-Ruth et al., 1990; Olds et al., 1997; Sparling et al., 1991; Wasik et al., 1997). Intergenerational literacy curricula were also developed (Brizius & Foster, 1993; Potts & Paull, 1995; St. Pierre et al., 1997), and parental behaviors were a target of the programs. As reviewed in this chapter, these approaches resulted in enhanced mother–child interaction, quality of the home environment, and use of child-oriented services.

The realization that families served in most early intervention programs were often the target of other educational and welfare services may also be contributing to a focus on parent outcomes (Smith, 1995a,b). So-called two-generational (child and parent) programs are being initiated, in the hopes of combining the best of early intervention with the best of training and work programs. It was believed that an escape from the ill effects of poverty would be best accomplished by focusing on the child and the family together (Brooks-Gunn, 1995; Chase-Lansdale & Brooks-Gunn, 1995). These ideals are akin to those espoused by the pioneers in early childhood education, who saw the programs serving families, not just children (Zigler & Valentine, 1979).

Our predictions for the early childhood programs to be initiated in the next century include the following. First, at least two types of programs will emerge. One will have as the primary focus child care, because maternal employment, especially among low-income families, is severely constrained by the lack of such care (Kisker & Ross, 1997). The movement of Head Start to full-day programs and to "wraparound" care is an example of this trend. It is unclear as to what the nature and extent of parent involvement in these programs will be, given the expected increase in mothers' participation in the workforce. If coupled with parent engagement, such programs have the greatest potential to impact children, given the possibility of direct effects as well as indirect effects on the child by means of the parents. Two examples of such mediated pathways are presented in this chapter (Linver et al., 1999; Klebanov et al., in press). Another strand will emphasize parenting practices, reduction of family stress, and enhancement of parent mental health and coping. These programs will be based on home visiting models, with parent involvement expected. Effects on the parents are anticipated, as illustrated throughout this chapter. At the same time, it is unclear as to what the impacts of such programs might be on the children. To date, no evidence exists as to the effects of home visiting on parents acting as a pathway through which home visiting influences children.

Second, the integration of child, family, and adult components into a single program will continue; however, the early enthusiasm for these so-called two-generational programs might need to be tempered. It is extremely difficult to offer these components simultaneously. The programs that have done so, with the exception of Even Start and other intergenerational literacy programs, have provided minimal services related to parenting practices (Aber et al., 1995; Brooks-Gunn, Berlin, Aber, & Carcagno, 1998). Unless early childhood educators become equal partners in the work programs, then the chances of altering parent behavior (as opposed to adult work behavior) are not high.

Third, as program staff make more explicit their theories of change, they will be working with both researchers and families to articulate program emphases, goals, expected outcomes, and specific practices for achieving these expectations. This approach, moreover, gives families a more central role in contributing to program design and evaluation, and highlights the importance of the relationships between program staff and family members. The benefits of program services will not be fully realized unless participants are genuinely engaged. This engagement, we have argued, hinges on the relationships between the program and its participants, especially vis-à-vis the extent to which program services match families' needs. The theory of change approach also helps maximize researchers' abilities to detect program effects, with explicit ideas about program functioning providing the basis for increasingly theory-based program evaluation.

In summary, program staff always have ideas about the impact of their services on families and children. When made explicit, the formulation of theories of change allows for evaluation of the pathways through which individual programs are expected to influence outcomes. Hopefully, such initiatives will result in greater specificity of program approaches and more targeted intervention strategies.

REFERENCES

Aber, J. L., Brooks-Gunn, J., & Maynard, R. (1995). Effects of welfare reform on teenage parents and their children. *The Future of children: Critical issues for children and youth*, 5, 53–71.

Achenbach, R. M., Phares, V., Howell, C. T., Rauh, V. A., & Nurcombe, B. (1990). Seven-year outcome of the Vermont Intervention Program for Low-Birthweight Infants. *Child Development*, 61, 1672–81.

Ainsworth, M., Blehar, M. C., Waters, E., & Wall, S. (1978). *Patterns of attachment*. Hillsdale, NJ: Erlbaum.

Andrews, S. R., Blumenthal, J. B., Johnson, D. L., Kahn, A. J., Ferguson, C. J., Lasater, T. M., Malone, P. E., & Wallace,

D. B. (1982). The skills of mothering: A study of Parent–Child Development Centers (New Orleans, Birmingham, Houston). *Monographs of the Society for Research in Child Development*, 47 (6, Serial No. 198).

Baker, A., Piotrkowski, C. S., & Brooks-Gunn, J. (1998). Home Instruction Program for Preschool Youngsters: A multi-site longitudinal evaluation. *Early Childhood Research Quarterly*, 13, 571–88.

Baker, A., Piotrkowski, C., & Brooks-Gunn, J. (1999). The Home Instruction Program for Preschool Youngsters (HIPPY). *The Future of Children*, 9, 116–33.

Barnard, K. E. (1998). Developing, implementing, and documenting interventions with parents and young children. In L. J. Berlin (Ed.), Opening the black box: Understanding how early intervention programs work [Special Issue]. *Zero To Three*, 18, 23–9.

Barnard, K. E., Magyary, G. S., Booth, C. L., Mitchell, S. K., & Spieker, S. (1988). Prevention of parenting alterations for women with low social support. *Psychiatry*, 51, 248–53.

Barnett, W. S. (1993). Economic evaluation of home visiting programs. *The Future of Children*, 3(3), 93–112.

Barnett, W. S. (1995). Long-term effects of early childhood programs on cognitive and school outcomes. *The Future of Children*, 5, 25–50.

Baron, R. M., & Kenny, D. A. (1986). The moderator–mediator variable distinction in social psychological research: Conceptual, strategic, and statistical considerations. *Journal of Personality and Social Psychology*, 51, 1173–82.

Barrera, M. E., Rosenbaum, P. L., & Cunningham, C. E. (1986). Early home intervention with low-birth-weight infants and their parents. *Child Development*, 57, 20–33.

Barth, R. P., Hacking, S., & Ash, J. R. (1988). Preventing child abuse: An experimental evaluation of the Child Parent Enrichment Project. *Journal of Primary Prevention*, 8, 201–17.

Behrman, R. E. (Ed.). (1999). Home visiting: Recent program evaluations. *The Future of Children*, 9(1).

Belsky, J., & Cassidy, J. (1994). Attachment: Theory and evidence. In M. Rutter, D. Hay, & S. Baron-Cohen (Eds.), *Developmental principles and clinical issues in psychology and psychiatry* (pp. 373–402). Oxford, England: Blackwell.

Benasich, A. A., Brooks-Gunn, J., & Clewell, B. C. (1992). How do mothers benefit from early intervention programs? *Journal of Applied Developmental Psychology*, 13, 311–62.

Berlin, L. J. (1998). Introduction. In L. J. Berlin (Ed.), Understanding intervention processes in early interventions [Special issue]. *Zero To Three*, 18, 1–3.

Berlin, L. J., Brooks-Gunn, J., McCarton, C., & McCormick, M. C. (1998). The effectiveness of early intervention: Examining risk factors and pathways to enhanced development. *Preventive Medicine*, 27, 238–45.

Berlin, L. J., Brooks-Gunn, J., Spiker, D., & Zaslow, M. J. (1995). Examining observational measures of emotional support and cognitive stimulation in black and white mothers of preschoolers. *Journal of Family Issues, 16,* 664–86.

Berlin, L. J., O'Neal, C. R., & Brooks-Gunn, J. (1998). Understanding the processes in early intervention programs: The interaction of program and participants. In L. J. Berlin (Ed.), Opening the black box: Understanding how early intervention programs work [Special issue]. *Zero To Three, 18,* 4–15.

Booth, C. L., Mitchell, S. K., Barnard, K. E., & Spieker, S. J. (1989). Development of maternal social skills in multiproblem families: Effects on the mother–child relationship. *Developmental Psychology, 25,* 403–12.

Bornstein, M. H. (1989). Between caretakers and their young: Two models of interaction and their consequences for cognitive growth. In M. H. Bornstein & J. S. Bruner (Eds.), *Interactions in human development* (pp. 197–214). Hillsdale, NJ: Erlbaum.

Bornstein, M. H. (Ed.). (1995). *Handbook of parenting.* Mahwah, NJ: Lawrence Erlbaum Associates.

Bradley, R. H. (1995). Environment and parenting. In M. Bornstein (Ed.), *Handbook of parenting* (pp. 235–61). Mahwah, NJ: Lawrence Erlbaum Associates.

Bradley, R. H., Caldwell, B. M., Rock, S. L., Ramey, C. T., Barnard, K. E., Gray, C., Hammond, M. A., Mitchell, S., Gottfried, A. W., Siegel, L., & Johnson, D. (1989). Home environment and cognitive development in the first three years of life: A collaborative study involving six sites and three ethnic groups in North America. *Developmental Psychology, 25,* 217–35.

Bradley, R. H., Casey, P. H., & Caldwell, B. M. (1997). Quality of home environment. In R. T. Gross, D. Spiker, & C. W. Haynes (Eds.), *Helping low birth weight, premature babies: The Infant Health Development Program* (pp. 242–56). Stanford, CA: Stanford University Press.

Brizius, J. A., & Foster, S. A. (1993). *Generation to generation: Realizing the promise of family literacy.* Ypsilanti, MI: High/Scope Press.

Bronfenbrenner, U. (1979). *The ecology of human development.* Cambridge, MA: Harvard University Press.

Brooks-Gunn, J. (1995). Children and families in communities: Risk and intervention in the Bronfenbrenner tradition. In P. Moen, G. H. Elder, & K. Lusher (Eds.), *Examining lives in context: Perspective on the ecology of human development* (pp. 467–519). Washington, DC: American Psychological Association Press.

Brooks-Gunn, J. (1997). Introduction. *Focus, 19.* Madison, WI: University of Wisconsin, Institute for Research on Poverty.

Brooks-Gunn, J., Berlin, L. J., Aber, J. L., & Carcagno, G. J. (1998). *Moving from welfare to work: What about the family?* Manuscript submitted for publication.

Brooks-Gunn, J., & Duncan, G. J. (1997). The effects of poverty on children. *The Future of Children, 7,* 55–71.

Brooks-Gunn, J., Klebanov, P. K., Liaw, F., & Spiker, D. (1993). Enhancing the development of low birth weight, premature infants: Changes in cognition and behavior over the first three years. *Child Development, 64,* 736–53.

Brooks-Gunn, J., McCarton, C., Casey, P., McCormick, M., Bauer, C., Bernbaum, J., Tyson, J., Swanson, M., Bennett, F., Scott, D., Tonascia, J., & Meinert, C. (1994). Early intervention in low birth weight, premature infants: Results through age 5 years from the Infant Health and Development Program. *Journal of the American Medical Association, 272,* 1257–62.

Brooks-Gunn, J., McCormick, M. C., Klebanov, P. K., & McCarton, C. (1998). Health care use of 3-year-old low birthweight premature children: Effects of family and neighborhood poverty. *The Journal of Pediatrics, 132,* 971–975.

Brooks-Gunn, J., McCormick, M. C., Shapiro, S., Benasich, A. A., & Black, G. (1994). The effects of early education intervention on maternal employment, public assistance, and health insurance: The Infant Health and Development Program. *The American Journal of Public Health, 84,* 924–31.

Brooks-Gunn, J., Smith, J., Berlin, L. J., & Lee, K. (in press). Familywork: Welfare changes, parenting, and young children. In G. R. Brookins (Ed.), *Exits from poverty.* New York: Cambridge University Press.

Burchinal, M. R., Campbell, F. A., Bryant, D. M., Wasik, B. H., & Ramey, C. T. (1997). Early intervention and mediating processes in cognitive performance of children of low-income African American families. *Child Development, 68,* 935–54.

Caldwell, B., & Bradley, R. H. (1984). *Home observation for measurement of the environment (HOME).* Little Rock, AR: University of Arkansas at Little Rock.

Campbell, F. A., & Ramey, C. T. (1994). Effects of early intervention on intellectual and academic achievement: A follow-up study of children from low-income families. *Child Development, 65,* 684–98.

Carnegie Task Force on Learning in the Primary Grades. (1996). *Years of promise: A comprehensive learning strategy for America's children. The report of the Carnegie Task Force on Learning in the Primary Grades.* New York: Carnegie Corporation of New York.

Carnegie Task Force on Meeting the Needs of Young Children. (1994). *Starting points: Meeting the needs of our youngest children. The report of the Carnegie Task Force on Meeting the Needs of Young Children.* New York: Carnegie Corporation of New York.

Chase-Lansdale P. L., & Brooks-Gunn, J. (1995). *Escape from poverty: What makes a difference for children?* New York: Cambridge University Press.

Chase-Lansdale, P. L., Brooks-Gunn, J., & Zamsky, E. S. (1994). Young African–American multigenerational families in poverty: Quality of mothering and grandmothering. *Child Development, 65,* 373–93.

Chen, H., & Rossi, P. (1983). Evaluating with sense: The theory-driven approach. *Evaluation Review, 7,* 283–302.

Clarke-Stewart, K. A., & Fein, G. G. (1983). Early childhood programs. In P. H. Mussen (Series Ed.), *Handbook of child psychology, Vol. 4*. Socialization, personality, and social development (pp. 918–99). New York: Wiley.

Conger, R. D., Conger, K. J., & Elder, G. (1997). Family economic hardship and adolescent academic performance: Mediating and moderating processes. In G. J. Duncan & J. Brooks-Gunn (Eds.), *Consequences of growing up poor* (pp. 288–310). New York: Russell Sage Foundation.

Conger, R. D., Ge, X., Elder, G., Lorenz, F., & Simons, R. (1994). Economic stress, coercive family process and developmental problems of adolescents. *Child Development, 65*, 541–61.

Coons, C. E., Gay, E. C., Fandal, A. W., Ker, C., & Frankenburg, W. K. (1981). *The Home Screening Questionnaire reference manual*. Denver, CO: John F. Kennedy Child Development Center, School of Medicine, University of Colorado Health Sciences Center.

Council on Child and Adolescent Health. (1998). The role of home-visitation programs in improving health outcomes for children and families. *Pediatrics, 101*, 486–9.

Crowell, J. A., & Feldman, S. S. (1988). Mothers' internal models of relationships and children's behavioral and developmental status: A study of mother-child interaction. *Child Development, 59*, 1273–85.

CTB/McGraw-Hill. (1987). *Tests of Adult Basic Education: Examiner's Manual*. Monterey, CA: CTB/McGraw-Hill.

Currie, J. M. (1997). Choosing among alternative programs for poor children. *The Future of Children, 7*, 113–31.

Department of Health and Human Services (1994). *Statement of the advisory committee on services for families with infants and toddlers* (DHHS Publication No. 1994-615-032/03062). Washington, DC: U.S. Government Printing Office.

Devaney, B. L., Ellwood, M. R., & Love, J. M. (1997). Programs that mitigate the effects of poverty on children. *The Future of Children, 7*, 88–112.

Downey, G., & Coyne, J. C. (1990). Children of depressed parents: An integrative review. *Psychological Bulletin, 108*, 50–76.

Duggan, A. K., McFarlane, E. C., Windham, A. M., Rohde, C. A., Salkever, D. S., Fuddy, L., Rosenberg, L. A., Buchbinder, S. B., & Sia, C. C. J. (1999). Evaluation of Hawaii's Healthy Start program. *The Future of Children, 9*, 66–90.

Duncan, G. J., & Brooks-Gunn, J. (Eds.). (1997). *Consequences of growing up poor*. New York: Russell Sage Foundation Press.

Duncan, G. J., & Brooks-Gunn, J. (1998). Welfare's new rules: A pox on children. *Issues in Science & Technology, 14*, 67–72.

Duncan, G. J., Brooks-Gunn, J., & Klebanov, P. K. (1994). Economic deprivation and early-childhood development. *Child Development, 65*, 296–318.

Egeland, B., & Erickson, M. F. (1990). Rising above the past: Strategies for helping new mothers break the cycle of abuse and neglect. *Zero To Three, 11*, 29–35.

Egeland, B., & Erickson, M. (1993). Attachment theory and findings: Implications for prevention and intervention. In S. Kramer & H. Parens (Eds.), *Prevention in mental health: Now, tomorrow, ever?* (pp. 21–50). Northvale, NJ: Jason Aronson.

Egeland, B., Kalkoske, M., Gottesman, N., & Erickson, M. F. (1990). Preschool behavior problems: Stability and factors accounting for change. *Journal of Child Psychology and Psychiatry, 31*, 891–909.

Elder, G. H., Jr. (1998). The life course and human development. In W. Damon (Ed.), *Handbook of child psychology. Vol. 1: Theoretical models of human development* (pp. 939–92). New York: Wiley.

Elicker, J., Noppe, I. C., Noppe, L. D., & Fortner-Wood, C. (1997). The Parent-Caregiver Relationship Scale: Rounding out the relationship system in infant child care. *Early Education and Development, 8*, 83–100.

Erickson, M. F., Korfmacher, J., & Egeland, B. (1992). Attachments past and present: Implications for therapeutic intervention with mother–infant dyads. *Development and Psychopathology, 4*, 495–507.

Fergusson, D. M., Lynskey, M. T., & Horwood, L. J. (1993). The effect of maternal depression on maternal ratings of child behavior. *Journal of Abnormal Child Psychology, 21*, 245–69.

Field, T., Widmayer, S., Greenberg, R., & Stoller, S. (1982). Effects of parent training on teenage mothers and their infants. *Pediatrics, 69*, 703–7.

Field, T. M., Widmayer, S. M., Stringer, S., & Ignatoff, E. (1980). Teenage, lower-class, black mothers and their preterm infants: An intervention and developmental follow-up. *Child Development, 51*, 426–36.

Garber, H. L. (1988). *The Milwaukee Project: Preventing mental retardation in children at risk*. Washington, DC: American Association on Mental Retardation.

Gomby, D. S., Larson, C. S., Lewitt, E. M., & Behrman, R. E. (1993). Home visiting: Analysis and recommendations. *The Future of Children, 3*, 6–22.

Goodman, S. H., & Brumley, H. E. (1990). Schizophrenic and depressed mothers: Relational deficits in parenting. *Developmental Psychology, 26*, 31–9.

Gray, J. D., Cutler, C. A., Dean, J. G., & Kempe, C. H. (1979). Prediction and prevention of child abuse and neglect. *Journal of Social Issues, 35*, 127–39.

Gray, S. W., & Ruttle, K. (1980). The Family-Oriented Home Visiting Program: A longitudinal study. *Genetic Psychology Monographs, 102*, 299–316.

Green, B. L., & McAllister, C. (1998). Theory-based, participatory evaluation: A powerful tool for evaluating family support programs. *Zero To Three, 18*, 30–6.

Greenspan, S. I. (1990). Comprehensive clinical approaches to infants and their families: Psychodynamic and developmental perspectives. In S. J. Meisels & J. P. Shonkoff (Eds.), *Handbook of early childhood intervention* (pp. 150–72). New York: Cambridge University Press.

Greenstein, B. (1998). Engagement is everything. *Zero To Three, 18*, 16.

Gross, R. T., Spiker, D., & Haynes, C. W. (Eds.). (1997). *Helping low birth weight, premature babies: The Infant Health and Development Program*. Stanford, CA: Stanford University Press.

Hammen, C., Burge, D., & Adrian, C. (1991). Timing of mother and child depression in a longitudinal study of children at risk. *Journal of Consulting & Clinical Psychology*, *59*, 341–5.

Hardy, J. B., & Street, R. (1989). Family support and parenting education in the home: An effective extension of clinic-based preventive health care services for poor children. *Journal of Pediatrics*, *115*, 927–31.

Haveman, R. H., & Wolfe, B. L. (1994). *Succeeding generations: On the effects of investments in children*. New York: Russell Sage Foundation.

Hayes, C., Palmer, J. L., & Zaslow, M. J. (Eds.). (1990). *Who cares for America's children?* Washington, DC: National Academy Press.

Heberle, J. (1992). PACE: Parent and child education in Kentucky. In T. B. Sticht, M. J. Beeler, & B. A. McDonald (Eds.), *The intergenerational transfer of cognitive skills. Vol. I: Programs, policy and research issues* (pp. 1261–348). Norwood, NJ: Ablex.

Hofferth, S. L. (1995). Caring for children at the poverty line. *Children and Youth Services Review*, *17*, 61–90.

Horvath, A. O., & Luborsky, L. (1993). The role of the therapeutic alliance in psychotherapy. *Journal of Consulting and Clinical Psychology*, *61*, 561–73.

Howes, C. (1997). Teacher sensitivity, children's attachment, and play with peers. *Early Education and Development*, *8*, 41–9.

Jacobson, S. W., & Frye, K. F. (1991). Effect of maternal social support on attachment: Experimental evidence. *Child Development*, *62*, 572–82.

Kagan, S. L. (1995). *By the bucket: Achieving results for young children*. Issue Brief. Washington, DC: National Governor's Association.

Kagan, S. L., & Pritchard, E. (1996). Linking services for children and families: Past legacies, future possibilities. In E. F. Zigler, S. L. Kagan, & N. W. Hall (Eds.), *Children, families, and government: Preparing for the twenty-first century* (pp. 378–93). New York: Cambridge University Press.

Kazdin, A. E. (1997). A model for developing effective treatments: Progression and interplay of theory, research, and practice. *Journal of Clinical Child Psychology*, *26*, 114–29.

Kisker, E., & Ross, C. (1997). Arranging child care. *The Future of Children*, *7*, 99–109.

Kitzman, H., Olds, D. L., Henderson, C. R., Hanks, C., Cole, R., Tatelbaum, R., McConnochie, K. M., Sidora, K., Luckey, D. W., Shaver, D., Engelhardt, K., James, D., & Barnard, K. (1997). Effect of prenatal and infancy home visitation by nurses on pregnancy outcomes, childhood injuries, and repeated childbearing: A randomized controlled trial. *Journal of the American Medical Association*, *278*, 644–52.

Klebanov, P. K., Brooks-Gunn, J., Chase-Lansdale, L., & Gordon, R. (1997). The intersection of the neighborhood and home environment and its influence on young children. In J. Brooks-Gunn, G. Duncan, & J. L. Aber (Eds.), Neighborhood poverty: Context and consequences for children. *Six studies of children in families in neighborhoods* (Vol. 1). New York: Russell Sage Foundation Press.

Klebanov, P. K., Brooks-Gunn, J., McCarton, C., & McCormick, M. C. (1998). The contribution of neighborhood and family income upon developmental test scores over the first three years of life. *Child Development*, *69*, 1420–36.

Klebanov, P. K., Brooks-Gunn, J., Lee, K., & McCormick, M. C. (in press). Enhancing maternal social and emotional health via family-oriented early intervention. *Developmental Psychology*.

Korfmacher, J. (1998). Examining the service provider in early intervention. *Zero To Three*, *18*, 17–22.

Korfmacher, J., Kitzman, H. K., & Olds, D. L. (1998). Intervention processes as conditioners of home visitation program effects. *Journal of Community Psychology*, *26*, 49–64.

Krugman, R. D. (1993). Universal home visiting: A recommendation from the U.S. Advisory Board on Child Abuse and Neglect. *The Future of Children: Home Visiting*, *3*, 184–91.

Lamb, M. E. (1998). Nonparental child care: Context, quality, correlates, and consequences. In W. Damon (Ed.), *Handbook of child psychology. Child psychology in practice* (Vol. 4), (pp. 73–134). New York: Wiley.

Larson, C. P. (1980). Efficacy of prenatal and postpartum home visits on child health and development. *Pediatrics*, *66*, 191–7.

Lazar, I., Darlington, R., Murray, H., Royce, J., & Snipper, A. (1982). Lasting effects of early education: A report from the Consortium for Longitudinal Studies. *Monographs of the Society for Research in Child Development*, *47*, (2–3, Serial No. 195).

Lazar, I., Hubbell, R., Murray, H., Rosche, M., & Royce, J. (1977). *The persistence of preschool effects: A long-term follow-up of fourteen infant and preschool experiments* (Final report to Office of Human Development Services, Grant No. 18-76-07843). Ithaca, NY: Community Services Laboratory, Cornell University.

Leventhal, T., Brooks-Gunn, J., & Kamerman, S. (1997). Communities as place, face, and space: Provision of services to poor, urban children and their families. In Brooks-Gunn J., Duncan G. J., & Aber, J. L. (Eds.), *Neighborhood poverty: Context and consequences for children. Conceptual, methodological, and policy approaches to studying neighborhoods* (Vol. 2), (pp. 181–205). New York: Russell, Sage Foundation Press.

Leventhal, T., Brooks-Gunn, J., McCormick, M. C., & McCarton, C. M. (in press). Patterns of service use in preschool children: Correlates, consequences, and the role of early intervention. *Child Development*.

Lewis, M. (1983). *Origins of intelligence: Infancy and early childhood*. New York: Plenum Press.

Lewitt, E. M., & Baker, L. S. (1995). School readiness. *The Future of Children, 5*, 128–39.

Liaw, F., & Brooks-Gunn, J. (1994). Cumulative familial risks and low birth weight children's cognitive and behavioral development. *Journal of Clinical Child Psychology, 23*, 360–72.

Liaw, F., Meisels, S. J., & Brooks-Gunn, J. (1995). The effects of experience of early intervention on low birth weight, premature children: The Infant Health and Development Program. *Early Childhood Research Quarterly, 10*, 405–31.

Lieberman, A. F., Weston, D. R., & Pawl, J. H. (1991). Preventive intervention and outcome with anxiously attached dyads. *Child Development, 62*, 199–209.

Linver, M., Brooks-Gunn, J., & Kohen, D. (1999). *Parenting behavior and emotional health as mediators of family poverty effects upon young low birth weight children's development*. Manuscript submitted for publication.

Love, J. M., Aber, L., & Brooks-Gunn, J. (1994). *Strategies for assessing community progress toward achieving the first national educational goal*. Princeton, NJ: Mathematica Policy Research, Inc.

Lyons-Ruth, K., Connell, D. B., Grunebaum, H., & Botein, S. (1990). Infants at social risk: Maternal depression and family support services as mediators of infant development and security of attachment. *Child Development, 61*, 85–98.

Lyons-Ruth, K., Zoll, D., Connell, D., & Grunebaum, H. (1986). The depressed mother and her one-year-old infant: Environmental context, mother–infant interaction and attachment, and infant development. In E. Tronick & T. Field (Eds.), *Maternal depression and infant disturbance* (pp. 61–82). San Francisco: Jossey-Bass.

Maccoby, E. E. (1992). The role of parents in the socialization of children: An historical overview. *Developmental Psychology, 28*, 1006–17.

Maccoby, E. E., & Martin, J. A. (1983). Socialization in the context of the family: Parent–child interaction. In P. H. Mussen & E. M. Hetherington (Eds.), *Handbook of child psychology, Vol. 4: Socialization, personality, and social development* (pp. 1–102). New York: Wiley.

Madden, J., O'Hara, J., & Levenstein, P. (1984). Home again: Effects of the mother-child home program on mother and child. *Child Development, 55*, 636–47.

Mathematica Policy Research, Inc. (1998, January). *Overview of the Early Head Start research and evaluation project*. Princeton, NJ: Author.

McCormick, M., McCarton, C., Brooks-Gunn, J., Belt, P., & Gross, R. T. (1998). The Infant Health and Development Program: Interim summary. *Journal of Developmental and Behavioral Pediatrics, 19*, 359–70.

McKey, R. H., Condelli, L., Granson, H., Barrett, B., McConkey, C., & Plantz, M. (1985). The impact of Head Start on children, families and communities. *Final report of the Head Start Evaluation, Synthesis and Utilization Project*. Washington, DC: CSR, Inc.

McLoyd, V. C. (1990). The impact of economic hardship on black families and children: Psychological distress, parenting, and socioemotional development. *Child Development, 61*, 311–46.

McLoyd, V. (1998). Children in poverty: Development, public policy, and practice. In W. Damon (Ed.), *Handbook of child psychology: Child psychology in practice* (Vol. 4), (pp. 135–210). New York: Wiley.

Meisels, S. J. (1992). Early intervention: A matter of context. *Zero To Three, 12*, 1–6.

Mikulecky, L., Lloyd, P., & Brannon, D. (1994, May). *Evaluating parent/child interactions in family literacy programs*. Paper presented at the National Conference on Family Literacy, Louisville, KY.

Olds, D. L., Eckenrode, J., Henderson, C. R., Kitzman, H., Powers, J., Cole, R., Sidora, K., Morris, P., Pettitt, L. M., & Luckey, D. (1997). Long-term effects of home visitation on maternal life course and child abuse and neglect: Fifteen-year follow-up of a randomized trial. *Journal of the American Medical Association, 278*, 637–43.

Olds, D. L., Henderson, C. R., Chamberlin, R., & Tatelbaum, R. (1986). Preventing child abuse and neglect: A randomized trial of nurse home visitation. *Pediatrics, 78*, 65–78.

Olds, D. L., Henderson, C. R., Chamberlin, R., & Tatelbaum, R. (1988). Improving the life-course development of socially disadvantaged mothers: A randomized trial of nurse home visitation. *American Journal of Public Health, 78*, 1436–45.

Olds, D. L., Henderson, C., & Kitzman, H. (1994). Does prenatal and infancy nurse home visitation have enduring effects on qualities of parental caregiving and child health at 25–50 months of life? *Pediatrics, 93*, 89–98.

Olds, D. L., Henderson, C., Kitzman, H., & Cole, R. (1995). Effects of prenatal and infancy nurse home visitation on surveillance of child maltreatment. *Pediatrics, 95*, 365–72.

Olds, D. L., Henderson, C. R., Tatelbaum, R., & Chamberlin, R. (1986). Improving the delivery of prenatal care and outcomes of pregnancy: A randomized trial of nurse home visitation. *Pediatrics, 77*, 16–28.

Olds, D. L., Henderson, C. R., Kitzman, H. J., Eckenrode, J. J., Cole, R. E., & Tatelbaum, R. C. (1999). Prenatal and infancy home visitation by nurses: Recent findings. *The Future of Children, 9*, 44–65.

Olds, D. L., & Kitzman, H. (1993). Review of research on home visiting for pregnant women and parents of young children. *The Future of Children, 3*, 53–92.

Osofsky, J. D., Culp, A. M., & Ware, L. M. (1988). Intervention challenges with adolescent mothers and their infants. *Psychiatry, 51*, 236–41.

Owen, M. T., & Mulvihill, B. A. (1994). Benefits of a parent education and support program in the first three years. *Family Relations, 43*, 206–12.

Park, C. L., & Folkman, S. (1997). Meaning in the context of stress and coping. *Review of General Psychology, 1*, 115–44.

Philliber, W. W., Spillman, R. E., & King, R. E. (1996). Consequences of family literacy for adults and children: Some preliminary findings. *Journal of Adolescent & Adult Literacy, 39*, 558–65.

Phillips D. A. (Ed.). (1995). *Child care for low-income families: Summary of two workshops.* Steering Committee on Child Care Workshops, Board on Children and Families, Commission on Behavioral and Social Sciences and Education, National Research Council and Institute of Medicine. Washington DC: National Academy Press.

Pianta, R. C. (1992). *Beyond the parent: The role of other adults in children's lives. New directions in Child Development, Volume 57.* San Francisco: Jossey-Bass.

Potts, M. W., & Paull, S. (1995). A comprehensive approach to family-focused services. In L. M. Morrow (Ed.), *Family literacy: Connections in schools and communities* (pp. 167–83). International Reading Association.

Ramey, C. T., Bryant, D. M., Wasik, B. H., Sparling, J. J., Fendt, K. H., & LaVange, L. M. (1992). Infant Health and Development Program for low birth weight, premature infants: Program elements, family participation, and child intelligence. *Pediatrics, 89*, 454–65.

Ramey, C. T., & Ramey, S. L. (1998). Early intervention and early experience. *American Psychologist, 53*, 109–20.

Rauh, V. A., Achenbach, T. M., Nurcombe, B., Howell, C., & Teti, D. M. (1988). Minimizing adverse effects of low birthweight: Four-year results of an early intervention program. *Child Development, 59*, 544–53.

Richardson, D. C., & Brown, M. (1997). *Family Intergenerational Literacy Model. Fact sheet and impact statements.* Oklahoma City, OK: National Diffusion Network.

Rickard, P., Stiles, R., & Martois, J. (1989). *Psychometric background and measurement issues related to the development of the CASAS.* San Diego, CA: CASAS.

Ross, G. S. (1984). Home intervention for premature infants of low-income families. *American Journal of Orthopsychiatry, 54*, 263–70.

Schweinhart, L. J., Barnes, H. V., Weikart, D. P., Barnett, W. S., & Epstein, A. S. (1993). *Significant benefits: The High/Scope Perry Preschool Study through age 27.* Ypsilanti, MI: High/Scope Press.

Seitz, V., & Apfel, N. (1994). Parent-focused intervention: Diffusion effects on siblings. *Child Development, 65*, 677–83.

Simeonsson, R. J., & Bailey, D. B. (1990). Family dimensions in early intervention. In S. J. Meisels & J. P. Shonkoff (Eds.), *Handbook of early childhood intervention* (pp. 428–43). New York: Cambridge University Press.

Smith, S. (1995a). *Two generation programs for families in poverty: A new intervention strategy.* Norwood, NJ: Ablex Publishing.

Smith, S. (1995b). Two generation programs: A new intervention strategy and directions for the future. In P. L. Chase-Lansdale & J. Brooks-Gunn (Eds.), *Escape from poverty: What makes a difference for children?* (pp. 299–314). New York: Cambridge University Press.

Smith, J. R., & Brooks-Gunn, J. (1997). Correlates and consequences of mother's harsh discipline with young children. *Archives of Pediatric and Adolescent Medicine, 151*, 777–86.

Smith, S., Brooks-Gunn, J., & Jackson, A. (1997). Parental employment and children. In R. Hauser, B. Brown, W. Prosser, & M. Stagner (Eds.), *Social indicators of children's well-being* (pp. 279–308). New York: Russell Sage Foundation Press.

Snow, C. E. (1986). Conversations with children. In P. Fletcher & M. Garman (Eds.), *Language acquisition: Studies in first language development* (pp. 69–89). New York: Cambridge University Press.

Sparling, J., Lewis, I., Ramey, C. T., Wasik, B. H., Bryant, D. M., & LaVange, L. M. (1991). Partners, a curriculum to help premature, low birth weight infants get off to a good start. *Topics in Early Childhood Special Education, 11*, 36–55.

Spiker, D., Ferguson, J., & Brooks-Gunn, J. (1993). Enhancing maternal interactive behavior and child social competence in low-birth-weight, premature infants. *Child Development, 64*, 754–68.

St. Pierre, R., Layzer, J. I., Goodson, B. D., Bernstein, L. S. (1997). *National impact evaluation of the Comprehensive Child Development Program: Final Report.* Cambridge, MA: Abt Associates, Inc.

St. Pierre, R. G., & Swartz, J. P. (1995). The Even Start Family Literacy Program. In S. Smith (Ed.), *Advances in applied developmental psychology: Two generation programs for families in poverty: A new intervention strategy* (Vol. 9), (pp. 37–66). Norwood, NJ: Ablex.

Tao, F., Swartz, J., St. Pierre, R., & Tarr, H. (1997). *National evaluations of the Even Start Family Literacy Program.* Washington, DC: U.S. Department of Education.

Thompson, R. A. (1998). Sequelae of early attachment experiences. In J. Cassidy & P. Shaver (Eds.), *Handbook of attachment theory and research.* New York: Guilford Press.

U.S. Advisory Board on Child Abuse and Neglect. (1991). *Creating caring communities.* Washington, DC: U.S. Department of Health and Human Services.

van Ijzendoorn, M. H., Juffer, F., & Duyvesteyn, M. G. C. (1995). Breaking the intergenerational cycle of insecure attachment: A review of the effects of attachment-based interventions on maternal sensitivity and infant security. *Journal of Child Psychology and Psychiatry, 36*, 225–48.

Wagner, M. M., & Clayton, S. L. (1999). The Parents as Teachers program: Results from two demonstrations. *The Future of Children, 9*, 91–115.

Wasik, B. H., Bryant, D. M., Lyons, C., Sparling, J. J., & Ramey, C. T. (1997). Home visiting. In R. T. Gross, D. Spiker, & C. W. Hayes (Eds.), *Helping low birth weight, premature babies: The Infant Health and Development*

Program (pp. 27–41). Stanford, CA: Stanford University Press.

Wasik, B. H., Ramey, C. T., Bryant, D. M., & Sparling, J. J. (1990). A longitudinal study of two early intervention strategies: Project CARE. *Child Development, 61,* 1682–96.

Weiss, H. (1979). *Parent support and education: An analysis of the Brookline Early Education Project.* Harvard Graduate School of Education, unpublished doctoral dissertation.

Weiss, C. H. (1995). Nothing as practical as a good theory: Exploring theory-based evaluation for Comprehensive Community Initiatives for children and families. In J. P. Connell, A. C. Kubisch, L. B. Schorr, & C. H. Weiss (Eds.), *New approaches to evaluating community initiatives: Concepts, methods, and contexts.* Washington, DC: The Aspen Institute.

Whitehurst, G. J., Arnold, D. S., Epstein, J. N., Angell, A. L., Smith, M., & Fischel, J. E. (1994). A picture book reading intervention in day care and home for children from low-income families. *Developmental Psychology, 30,* 679–89.

Wilson, J. B., Ellwood, D. T., & Brooks-Gunn, J. (1995). Welfare to work through the eyes of children: The impact on parenting of movement from AFDC to employment. In P. L. Chase-Lansdale & J. Brooks-Gunn (Eds.), *Escape from poverty: What makes a difference for children?* (pp. 63–86). New York: Cambridge University Press.

Winter, M., & Rouse, J. (1990). Fostering intergenerational literacy: The Missouri Parents as Teachers program. *The Reading Teacher, 43,* 382–6.

Woodhead, M. (1988). When psychology informs public policy: The case of early childhood intervention. *American Psychologist, 43,* 443–54.

Yoshikawa, H. (1995). Long-term effects of early childhood programs on social outcomes and delinquency. *The Future of Children, 5,* 51–75.

Zahn-Waxler, C., Iannotti, R. J., Cummings, E. M., & Denham, S. (1990). Antecedents of problem behaviors in children of depressed mothers. *Development and Psychopathology, 2,* 349–66.

Zigler, E. F., & Valentine, J. (Eds.). (1979). *Project Head Start: Legacy of the war on poverty.* New York: Free Press.

Zigler, E. F., & Weiss, H. (1985). Family support systems: An ecological approach to child development. In R. Rapoport (Ed.), *Children, youth, and families: The action-research relationship* (pp. 166–205). New York: Cambridge University Press.

Appendixes

Appendixes A, B, and C summarize findings on the efficacy of three types of early childhood programs for parental/familial outcomes. Appendix A summarizes the efficacy of parent-focused home-based programs for parental/familial outcomes. Appendix B summarizes the efficacy of parent-focused center- and home-based programs. Appendixes A and B are divided into two parts: 1) programs that begin prenatally or within the child's first year of life and 2) programs that begin when the child is 12–36 months old. Appendix C summarizes the efficacy of intergenerational and parent-focused family literacy programs. In all appendixes, the following outcomes are reported when data are available: parental education/employment/self-sufficiency; parental mental and physical health; observed parent-child interaction/relationship quality; use of child-related services; parenting attitudes, knowledge, and quality of the home environment; and maltreatment indicators. Studies that used random assignment are indicated with an asterisk (*).

APPENDIX 24.A Efficacy of Early Childhood Programs for Parental/Familial Outcomes: Parent-Focused Home-Based Programs

Part A1: Intervention programs beginning prenatally or within the child's first year of life

Study (* = random assignment)	Age of child/ Duration of intervention	Description of intervention	Outcomes (T = Treatment group; C = Comparison group; T1, T2 = Time 1, Time 2, etc.)
*Barrera et al., 1986	birth/12 months	Weekly home visits for 1 to 4 months, biweekly visits for 5 to 8 months, monthly visits for 9 to 12 months; average of 23 visits T1: Parent-infant interaction intervention T2: Child development intervention	*Observed parent-child interaction/relationship quality*: At 16 months, T1 & T2 > C on maternal responsivity *Parenting attitudes, knowledge, and quality of the home environment*: At 16 months, T1 > C on HOME
*Barth et al., 1988; (Child-Parent Enrichment Project)	pregnancy/6 months	Two home visits per month	*Parental mental and physical health*: T = C on maternal well-being and social support *Use of child-related services*: At post-test, T > C on well-baby care *Maltreatment indicators*: T < C on ER visits, removal of child from home, and child care by neighbor; T = C on reports of child abuse
*Field et al., 1980	birth/1 year	Biweekly home visits	*Parental mental and physical health*: At 8 months, T > C on maternal blood pressure *Observed parent-child interaction/relationship quality*: T > C on "optimal" face-to-face interaction *Parenting attitudes, knowledge, and quality of the home environment*: At 4 months, T > C on realistic developmental expectations and child-rearing attitudes; At 8 months, T > C on HOME (maternal responsivity and involvement)
*Gray et al., 1979	birth/2 years	Weekly home visits; biweekly visits to pediatrician; biweekly calls to pediatrician	*Observed parent-child interaction/relationship quality*: At 17 & 35 months, T = C on "abnormal parenting" *Use of child-related services*: T = C on immunizations *Maltreatment indicators*: At 17 & 35 months, T = C for reported accidents and child maltreatment; T < C on child hospitalization for serious injuries
*Hardy & Street, 1989 (Johns Hopkins Children and Youth Program)	birth/2 years	Comprehensive community-based program including 10 home visits for parenting education	*Use of child-related services*: At 2 years, T > C on child immunizations; T < C for hospital admissions *Maltreatment indicators*: At 2 years: T < C for severe diaper rash, closed head trauma

(continued)

APPENDIX 24.A (*continued*)

Part A1: Intervention programs beginning prenatally or within the child's first year of life

Study (* = random assignment)	Age of child/ Duration of intervention	Description of intervention	Outcomes (T = Treatment group; C = Comparison group; T1, T2 = Time 1, Time 2, etc.)
*Jacobson & Frye, 1991	3rd trimester/ 1 year	30 home visits	*Observed parent-child interaction/relationship quality*: At 14 months, T > C on Q-Sort "attachment ratings" *Parenting attitudes, knowledge, and quality of the home environment*: T = C on HOME
*Larson, 1980	T1: Seventh month of pregnancy to 15 months old T2: 6 weeks to 15 months old	T1: One prenatal and one postpartum visit; seven visits from 6 weeks to 6 months; three visits from 6 to 15 months T2: Seven visits from 6 weeks to 6 months; three visits from 6 to 15 months	*Observed parent-child interaction/relationship quality*: At 12 & 15 months, T1 < T2 on mother-infant interaction 'problems' and on father participation in caregiving; at 6 weeks, 6 & 18 months, T1 > T2 = C on Maternal [Sensitive] Behavior Scale; at 12 months, T1 = T2 = C on Maternal [Sensitive] Behavior Scale *Use of child-related services*: At 18 months, T = C on well-child visits, immunizations *Parenting attitudes, knowledge, and quality of the home environment*: At 6 weeks, 6, 12, & 18 months, T1 > T2 = C on HOME *Maltreatment Indicators*: At 6 & 12 months, T1 & T2 < C on accident rates; at 18 months, T = C on emergency room visits
*Lyons-Ruth et al., 1990	birth to 9 months/ending at child's 18th month	Approximately weekly home visits C1: High risk C2: Low risk	*Parental mental and physical health*: T = C on mother's social isolation *Observed parent-child interaction/relationship quality*: At 18 months, T < C1 on disorganized infant-mother attachment; T = C1 = C2 on mother-child interaction
*Kitzman et al., 1997 (Memphis New Mothers Project)	pregnancy/2 years	Average of 7 home visits during pregnancy and 26 home visits from birth to 24 months	*Parental education/employment/self-sufficiency* : T < C on subsequent pregnancies; T = C on educational achievement and labor force participation; T = C on use of public assistance *Maltreatment indicators*: T < C on children's injuries and ingestions
*Olds, Henderson, Chamberlin et al., 1986; Olds, Henderson, Tatelbaum et al., 1986; Olds et al., 1988, 1994, 1997, 1999; (Prenatal and Early Infancy Project)	pregnancy/24 months	One home visit per week for the first 6 weeks postpartum, gradually decreasing to one visit every 6 weeks; average of 31 visits	*Parental education/employment/self-sufficiency*: For poor, unmarried teens: First 24 months, T < C on days of public assistance; at 46 months, T > C on participation in workforce and T < C on number of subsequent pregnancies; at 15-year follow-up, T < C on number of subsequent children, T > C on spacing between 1st and 2nd births, T < C on use of AFDC or Food Stamps *Parental mental and physical health*: Between 25 and 50 months, T < C on physician's reports of parental coping problems *Observed parent-child interaction/relationship quality*: For poor, unmarried teens: At 10, 22, and 46 months, T < C on punishment and restriction; T > C on providing appropriate play materials; at 34 months, T = C on maternal warmth and control and T > C on maternal involvement; at 46 months, T = C on maternal warmth, control, and involvement *Use of child-related services*: Between 25 and 50 months, T = C on number of hospitalizations

Study (* = random assignment)	Age of child/ Duration of intervention	Description of intervention	Outcomes (T = Treatment group; C = Comparison group; T1, T2 = Time 1, Time 2, etc.)

Part A1: Intervention programs beginning prenatally or within the child's first year of life

Study (* = random assignment)	Age of child/ Duration of intervention	Description of intervention	Outcomes (T = Treatment group; C = Comparison group; T1, T2 = Time 1, Time 2, etc.)
			Parenting attitudes, knowledge, and quality of the home environment: At 34 and 46 months, T = C on HOME; at 46 months, T < C for home hazards; T > C on HOME language stimulation and provision of learning materials *Maltreatment indicators*: At 24 months, T < C on child maltreatment (p = .07); between 25 and 50 months, T = C on child maltreatment; T < C on injuries, ingestions; during 1st year, T < C on ER visits; during 2nd year, T < C on ER visits, accidents, and poisonings; at 46 months, T = C on child exposure to poisons; T < C on ER visits; at 15-year follow-up, T < C on verified reports of maltreatment
*Osofsky et al., 1988 (The Menninger Infancy Project)	birth/18 months	21 home visits	*Observed parent-child interaction/relationship quality*: At 6 and 13 months, for "takers" (those more engaged in services): T > C on maternal [sensitive] behaviors in play and feeding *Parenting attitudes, knowledge, and quality of the home environment*: At 36 months, for "takers": T > C on HOME
Ross, 1984	birth/12 months	15 home visits	*Parenting attitudes, knowledge, and quality of the home*: At 12 months, T > C on HOME; T = C on maternal child-rearing attitudes
*Barnard et al., 1988; Booth et al., 1989 (Clinical Nursing Models Intervention)	< 22 weeks pregnant/12 months	T1: Information/ resource model (average of 13.7 visits) T2: Mental health model (average of 19.1 visits)	*Observed parent-child interaction/relationship quality*: At 12 months, for mothers with low social skills: T1 & T2: Treatment goals attained => more supportive maternal teaching
*Erickson et al., 1992 (Project STEEP)	2nd trimester pregnancy/18 months	Approximately 36 home visits	*Parental education/employment/self-sufficiency*: T > C on maternal life management skills *Parental mental and physical health*: T < C on maternal depressive symptoms and anxiety *Observed parent-child interaction/relationship quality*: T = C on infant-mother attachment security *Parenting attitudes, knowledge, and quality of the home*: T > C on HOME

(continued)

APPENDIX 24.A (*continued*)

Part A2: Intervention programs beginning when child is 12–36 months old

Study (* = random assignment)	Age of child/ Duration of intervention	Description of intervention	Outcomes (T = Treatment group; C = Comparison group; T1, T2 = Time 1, Time 2, etc.)
*Gray & Ruttle, 1980 (DARCEE Family-Oriented Program)	17 to 24 months/ 9 months	Weekly home visits	*Observed parent-child interaction/relationship quality*: At 1 year, T > C on quality of teaching strategies *Parenting attitudes, knowledge, and quality of the home environment*: At 10, 20, and 32 months, T > C on HOME
*Lieberman et al., 1991	1 year old/1 year	Weekly home visits	*Observed parent-child interaction/relationship quality*: At 12 months, T > C for maternal empathy, maternal initiation of interaction; at 24 months, T = C on Q-Sort of child-mother attachment quality *Parenting attitudes, knowledge, and quality of the home environment*: At 12 months, T = C on maternal child-rearing attitudes
*Madden et al., 1984 (Mother-Child Home Program)	2 to 3 years old/ 2 years	Home visits twice each week (~46 visits per year for 2 years)	*Observed parent-child interaction/relationship quality*: In 2 out of 3 cohorts at 2-year follow-up, T > C on labeling and verbalizing in mother-child interactions; T = C on demonstrations of affection and verbal praise

APPENDIX 24.B. Efficacy of Early Childhood Programs for Parental/Familial Outcomes: Parent-Focused Center- and Home-Based Programs

Part B1: Intervention programs beginning prenatally or within the child's first year of life

Study (* = random assignment)	Age of child/ Duration of intervention	Description of intervention	Outcomes (T = Treatment group; C = Comparison group; T1, T2 = Time 1, Time 2, etc.)
*Andrews et al., 1982 (Birmingham PCDC)	3 to 5 months old/3 years	*Year 1*: three to four half days per week with mothers and infants together in center; *15 to 36 months*: four half days per week, mothers as understudies to teachers; fifth day in classes	*Parental education/employment/self-sufficiency*: At posttest, T > C on likelihood to return to school; T > C on grasp of community resources as available for handling problems *Parental mental and physical health*: At posttest, T > C on general life satisfaction *Observed parent-child interaction/relationship quality*: At 36 and 48 months, T > C on positive behaviors in mother-child interaction; at posttest T > C on child control techniques: more use of reason and less use of physical punishment
*Andrews et al., 1982 (New Orleans PCDC)	2 months/3 years	Two half days per week in center; child care and parenting groups	*Observed parent-child interaction/relationship quality*: At 36 and 48 months, T > C on parenting measures; at 24 & 36 months, T > C on positive maternal interaction: more sensitive, accepting, & cooperative; at 24 months, T < C on use of negative language
*Andrews et al., 1982 (Houston PCDC)	1 year old/2 years	*Year 1*: 30 90-minute home visits *Year 2*: Four half days per week of educational child care plus classes for parents Optional weekly English classes; 4 weekend family workshops	*Observed parent-child interaction/relationship quality*: At posttest, T > C on parenting measures: affection, praise, appropriate control, and encouragement of child verbalization *Parenting knowledge, attitudes, and home environment*: At 36 months, T > C on HOME
*Brooks-Gunn et al., 1994; Gross, Spiker, & Hayes, 1997; McCormick et al., 1998; Smith & Brooks-Gunn, 1997; Berlin, Brooks-Gunn, McCarton, & McCormick, 1998; Klebanov, Brooks-Gunn, & McCormick, in press (Infant Health and Development Program)	hospital discharge/ 3 years	*Year 1*: Weekly home visits *Years 2 & 3*: Biweekly home visits; at least 5 half days of preschool per week; bimonthly parent group meetings	*Parental education/employment/self-sufficiency*: At 3 years, T > C on maternal employment; T > C on maternal problem solving *Parental mental and physical health*: At 1 year, T > C on mothers' depressive symptoms *Observed parent-child interactions*: At 30 months, T > C on maternal quality of assistance during problem solving and on mother-child "mutuality" *Use of child-related services*: T > C on illness-related visits to physicians; T = C on hospitalizations, days in hospital care, outpatient surgical procedures, ER visits *Parenting attitudes, knowledge, and quality of the home environment*: At 3 years, T > C on HOME; T = C on maternal child-rearing knowledge and attitudes *Maltreatment indicators*: At 3 years (for boys only), T < C on hitting and harsh scolding

(continued)

APPENDIX 24.B (continued)

Part B1: Intervention programs beginning prenatally or within the child's first year of life

Study (* = random assignment)	Age of child/ Duration of intervention	Description of intervention	Outcomes (T = Treatment group; C = Comparison group; T1, T2 = Time 1, Time 2, etc.)
*Field et al., 1982 (Teenage Pregnancy Intervention Program, T2 group only)	birth/6 months	*T1*: Biweekly home visits; caregiving training *T2*: Job training – paid teacher's aides in infant nursery	*Parental education/employment/self-sufficiency*: At 1 & 2 years, T1 & T2 < C for repeat pregnancies; T2 > T1 > C for maternal employment, schooling *Observed parent-child interaction/relationship quality*: At 4 months, T1 = T2 > C on "optimal" face-to-face interaction; T2 > T1 = C on mother talking to infant *Parenting attitudes, knowledge, and quality of the home environment*: At 8 months, 1 & 2 years, T = C on HOME
Garber, 1988 (Milwaukee Project)	birth/5 years	Intensive home visiting (9–15 hrs/wk) at program onset; full-day child care, five days per week; job counseling and paid training for parents	*Parental mental and physical health*: At posttest, T > C on maternal internal locus of control *Observed parent-child interaction/relationship quality*: At posttest, T > C on parenting measures: more verbal and physical positive feedback on structured interaction; T = C on maternal teaching ability
Seitz & Apfel, 1994 (Yale Child Welfare Project)	pregnancy/30 months postpartum	Average of 28 home visits; optional educational child care; social work, psychological services; personalized pediatric care; developmental exams	*Parental education/employment/self-sufficiency*: At 10-year follow-up, T > C on maternal education and delay to next pregnancy; T < C on AFDC receipt and family size
*Wasik et al., 1990; Burchinal et al., 1997 (Project CARE)	birth/5 years	*T1*: 107 home visits *T2*: 110 home visits and full-day child care five days per week	*Parenting knowledge, attitudes, and home environment*: At 6, 12, 18, 30, 42, 54 months and 7 years, T1 & T2 = C on HOME inventory; at 36 months and 8 years, T1 & T2 = C on child-rearing attitudes
*Weiss, 1979; Zigler & Weiss, 1985 (Brookline Early Education Project- BEEP)	newborn/school entry	Home visits, play groups, prekindergarten programs, developmental and pediatric exams, parent education and support	*Observed parent-child interaction/relationship quality*: During kindergarten and 2nd grade, T > C initiating contact with teachers

Part B2: Intervention program beginning when child is 12–36 months old			
Study (* = random assignment)	Age of child/ Duration of intervention	Description of intervention	Outcomes (T = Treatment group; C = Comparison group; T1, T2 = Time 1, Time 2, etc.)
*Schweinhart et al., 1993 (High/Scope Perry Preschool)	3 to 4 years old/until age 5	Weekly home visits; preschool classes 2.5 hours per day, five days per week	*Parenting knowledge, attitudes, and home environment*: At age 4 to 5, T > C on child-rearing attitudes

APPENDIX 24.C. Efficacy of Early Childhood Programs for Parental/Familial Outcomes: Intergenerational and Parent-Focused Family Literacy Programs

Study (* = random assignment)	Age of child/ Duration of intervention	Description of intervention	Outcomes (T = Treatment group; C = Comparison group; T1, T2 = Time 1, Time 2, etc.)
*St. Pierre et al., 1995 (Even Start)	birth to 7 years/one or more years	Early childhood education for children from birth through 7 years; adult education services including Adult Basic Education, English as a Second Language, and GED preparation; parent education services	*Parental education/employment/self-sufficiency*: At posttest, T > C on rates of GED attainment; T = C on CASAS reading scores *Observed parent-child interaction/relationship quality*: At posttest, T = C on parent-child reading interactions; pretest-posttest improvements on parent-child interactions, parenting, learning activities in the home, and 'Parent As a Teacher' scale *Parenting attitudes, knowledge, and quality of the home environment*: At posttest, T > C on increase in number of reading materials for children in the home; T = C on parents' educational expectations for children but significant pretest-posttest improvements in parental expectations for child's school performance and high school graduation rates
Tao et al., 1997 (Even Start)	birth to 7 years/one or more years	Early childhood education for children from birth through 7 years; adult education services including Adult Basic Education, English as a Second Language, and GED preparation; parent education services	*Parental education/employment/self-sufficiency*: Pretest-posttest improvements on CASAS reading and math tests; pretest-posttest improvements on TABE scores; 8% overall (24% sample study) GED completion rate *Parenting attitudes, knowledge, and quality of the home environment*: Pretest-posttest standardized gains on HSQ: .60 for parents of children under 3 and .48 for parents of children 3–6
Heberle, 1992 (PACE)	3 to 5 years/one to two years	Early childhood classes with High/Scope curriculum; adult education classes; parent-child activity time in the early childhood classroom; parenting support and education	*Parental education/employment/self-sufficiency*: T > C in GED attainment; 37% GED attainment rate; significant gains in TABE scores *Parenting attitudes, knowledge, and quality of the home environment*: Pretest-posttest increase on parents' educational expectations for their children
Brizius & Foster, 1993 (Kenan/ Toyota Families for Learning)	unspecified	Early childhood education; adult education; parenting support and education	*Parental education/employment/self-sufficiency*: Progress in individual educational goals: GED attainment, identification of specific further education necessary for desired employment, pursuit of advanced education *Observed parent-child interaction/relationship quality*: Staff report improvements in parenting and rate 40% of parents as better role models for children after program participation *Parenting attitudes, knowledge, and quality of the home environment*: Parents report feeling better equipped to be good parents

Study (* = random assignment)	Age of child/ Duration of intervention	Description of intervention	Outcomes (T = Treatment group; C = Comparison group; T1, T2 = Time 1, Time 2, etc.)
Richardson & Brown, 1997 (Family Intergenerational Literacy Model-Even Start – FILM)	unspecified- preschool age	Adult education; parent discussion group; home visits; parent/child interaction playgroup; early learning center	*Parental education/employment/self-sufficiency*: Pretest-posttest gains on CASAS; over 40% GED attainment rate *Parenting attitudes, knowledge, and quality of the home environment*: Pretest-posttest improvements on Home Screening Questionnaire (HSQ) and HOME; majority of parents report having learned the importance of reading to children, developmentally appropriate games and their benefits, and new skills and strategies in guiding and disciplining children
Philliber, Spillman, & King, 1996 (Toyota Families for Learning)	3–4 years/1 to 2 years	Early childhood education; adult literacy training; parent support groups; parent-child interaction Comparison groups were unmatched groups of adults participating in traditional adult literacy programs in New York and California	*Parental education/employment/self-sufficiency*: T > C on CASAS reading scores and TABE scores
Mikulecky, Lloyd, & Brannon, 1994 (Toyota Families for Learning)	3–4 years/4–6 months	Early childhood education; adult literacy training; parent support groups; parent-child interaction	*Observed parent-child interaction/ relationship quality*: Pretest-posttest increases in time parent spends reading with child and frequency of library visits *Parenting attitudes, knowledge, and quality of the home environment*: Pretest-posttest increases in literacy materials in the home, parent displaying of child's work, and parents' value of child learning through active play; no gains in parental modeling of literacy activities or knowledge of child development
Owen & Mulvihill, 1994 (Parents as Teachers)	birth or prenatal to 3 years/3 years	Home visits; parent group meetings; child development screenings and referrals	*Parental mental and physical health*: T = C on parenting stress, perceptions of social support, or parenting satisfaction *Parenting attitudes, knowledge, and quality of the home environment*: T > C on HOME environment and parenting scores; no program effects on knowledge of child development or attitudes toward child-rearing

(continued)

APPENDIX 24.C (*continued*)

Study (* = random assignment)	Age of child/ Duration of intervention	Description of intervention	Outcomes (T = Treatment group; C = Comparison group; T1, T2 = Time 1, Time 2, etc.)
*Baker, Piotrkowski, & Brooks-Gunn, 1998, 1999 (Home Instruction Program for Preschool Youngsters)	4 and 5 years/1 to 2 years	Weekly home visits by parent educator	*Parenting attitudes, knowledge, and quality of the home environment*: At one site, T > C on variety of literacy materials in home at posttest; at the other site, T > C on parental expectations for children's educational attainment and performance

CHAPTER TWENTY-FIVE

Economics of Early Childhood Intervention

W. STEVEN BARNETT

Public policy choices regarding early intervention can be viewed from a variety of perspectives, one of which is economics. The unique contribution of the economic perspective is that it insists that policy makers take into account the trade-offs involved in decisions about how to provide early intervention services, including all of the benefits produced and all of the resources consumed. Most often, economic analysis has been used to provide information about the costs and, to a lesser extent, the benefits of early intervention services. This type of information can help inform policy makers regarding the level of funding required to support a set of early intervention services and to decide what types of early intervention programs are desirable. Economic analysis can also be used to address the question of how government should fund and administer with the available resources a system of early intervention services that will produce the greatest benefits for children and families.

This chapter introduces the methods and findings of economic research on early intervention and explores the implications for research, policy, and practice. The chapter begins with an overview of methodology and terminology. This is followed by an introduction to cost analysis and a review of cost estimates for early intervention programs. The next section introduces benefit-cost analysis by way of a detailed example and a brief review of the literature on the long-term benefits of early intervention emphasizing studies that examined both costs and benefits. In a final section, conclusions are drawn regarding the economics of early intervention, and recommendations are made for policy, practice, and

promising future applications of economic analysis to early intervention.

WHAT IS ECONOMIC ANALYSIS?

From an economic perspective, early intervention is an investment in young children and their families that can yield both immediate and long-term benefits. Economic analysis can be used to measure the net economic gain or loss from early intervention and to describe the distribution of gains and losses within society. If an activity provides a net gain to society as a whole, it is said to be "economically efficient." Economics provides specific criteria for judging efficiency. However, it does not provide criteria for assessing the fairness, or equity, of distribution. Economics merely provides a description of the distribution of gains and losses produced by a program or policy. Policy makers must use their own values (or those of their constituents) to judge the fairness of a distribution.

Practically, economic analysis is an extension of underlying evaluations of program operation and program effectiveness. Cost analysis is possible only if there is an adequate program description. Economic analysis that goes beyond costs is desirable only if there is evidence of program effectiveness. Ideally, economic analyses are built upon data from ecological or systems studies (e.g., Bronfenbrenner, 1986; Sameroff, 1983) because economic analysis is concerned with all costs and effects of a program or policy, no matter who bears the costs or receives the benefits and whether or not the results were intended. Thus, economic analysis is concerned with costs that early intervention programs may impose on children and their families as well as the costs that appear in the program budget. For example, cost analyses should take into account the resources parents use in providing transportation to a center. Program effectiveness measures should include not just effects on the children receiving services but also effects on other family members and the broader society, including the schools children enter after early intervention. Researchers might even consider effects on program staff; for example, if one approach is less stressful than another or results in greater job satisfaction.

In educational research, various terms are used more or less interchangeably to refer to economic analysis (Levin, 1983): cost analysis, cost-effectiveness analysis, and cost-benefit analysis. However, these terms have distinctly different meanings in economics. The term *cost analysis* properly refers to studies of only the resources used by an activity. *Benefit-cost* (or *cost-benefit,* these terms are interchangeable) *analysis* and *cost-effectiveness analysis* make possible study of the resources used and the results produced by a program or policy. These two techniques differ in their treatment of results and in the circumstances in which they are most useful.

In benefit-cost analysis, monetary values are estimated for both the resources used (costs) and the effects produced (benefits). For example, it might be determined that the economic value of benefits from Program A is $5,000 per child more than its cost. In cost-effectiveness analysis, programs are evaluated on the basis of program costs and effects alone; there is no attempt to estimate the monetary value of program effects. For example, it might be determined that children in Program A gain ten points on a standardized test at a cost of $3,000 per child, and children in Program B gain five points at a cost of $2,500. This type of analysis is obviously easier to perform because, practically speaking, it is an incomplete benefit-cost analysis.

Whether benefit-cost analysis or cost-effectiveness analysis should be used in a particular situation depends on the resources available to conduct the analysis, the program outcome measures, and the amount of information required by the decision makers. Benefit-cost analysis is more time consuming and costly to perform. The underlying effectiveness study may or may not yield outcome measures

that can be translated into monetary terms. For example, reductions in the need for special education can be assigned a dollar value quite easily; increases in self-esteem cannot. On the other hand, cost-effectiveness results alone may provide less information than decision makers want. If a single program is studied, is it enough to conclude that later special education needs are reduced, or will decision makers want to compare the cost of the program to the cost savings? If two programs are compared, will the decision makers be satisfied with cost estimates and a specified number of program outcome measures for each program, or will they want some summation that says how much those outcomes are worth?

COSTS AND COST ANALYSIS

The most basic question in the economics of early intervention is: How much does early intervention cost? This is not a simple question to answer. One reason is that early intervention programs are extremely diverse. A wide range of programs exists to serve a wide range of children and families who vary greatly in their needs. Local variations in salaries, rents, and other prices are also a source of differences in costs (Grubb, 1987). For example, teacher salaries differ considerably from New York to Mississippi. Another reason is that relatively few cost studies have been conducted, and many of these have not followed standard practices of economics. Thus, the lack of information makes it difficult to generalize about average national costs, and inconsistencies across studies compound the problem and make it difficult to compare accurately the costs of different approaches to early intervention.

Cost-Analysis Methodology

The goal of cost analysis is to determine the economic value of all resources used in the activity or program studied (Barnett, 1994). Levin (1983) has described the standard economic approach to cost analysis as an "ingredients model." The first step in the use of this model is to develop a list of all the ingredients and the amounts of each that are needed by the program. One can think of this as a recipe for producing the program. The second step is to determine the cost of each ingredient. When the cost of each ingredient has been established, these costs can be summed to produce a measure of the total cost of the intervention.

The first step in the ingredients model is straightforward if one is careful not to omit any of the ingredients. A program description can be used to produce a list of the ingredients needed to produce all of the intervention's activities, and the ingredients can then be categorized by type. Almost all early intervention program ingredients will fall into one of the following categories: personnel, facilities, equipment, materials and supplies, utilities, communications, and insurance. Programs also tend to have a few small items left for a miscellaneous ingredients category. Transportation is sometimes thought of as an additional category, but the ingredients used to provide transportation can be sorted into the various categories already listed.

The second step in the model is to determine the cost of each ingredient. The key to correctly determining costs is understanding that the true cost of an ingredient is its *opportunity cost*; that is, the value of an ingredient in its best alternative use. When a resource is used in an early intervention program, its cost is the value of the forgone opportunity to use that resource in another way. Most people understand and apply the concept of opportunity cost in daily life. For example, people often say that they "can't afford the calories" in something. The cost of an afternoon snack is giving up dessert after dinner, running an extra mile, or gaining weight. The amount paid for the snack is only of secondary importance. Opportunity cost is important in determining the cost of early intervention programs precisely because what is paid does not always represent the full cost there as well.

Costs of Early Intervention

The early intervention research literature was reviewed to bring together the most relevant published information on the costs of early intervention. Cost estimates are presented for major government programs such as Head Start, preschool special education, early intervention for children with disabilities and their families, and programs that have been the subject of important studies such as the Comprehensive Child Development Program (CCDP; St. Pierre, Layzer, & Barnes, 1995), Infant Health and Development Program (IHDP;

Gross, Spiker, & Haynes, 1997), Abecedarian Program (Campbell & Ramey, 1994, 1995), and Perry Preschool Program (Schweinhart, Barnes, Weikart, Barnett, & Epstein, 1993). The results are summarized in Table 25.1, which describes programs in terms of the ages of children served, the primary criterion by which the target population is identified (poverty, disability or developmental delay, and low birth weight) and the primary mode of service delivery (in a center, through home visits, or both). To make the various estimates as comparable as possible, all estimates were converted to 1995 dollars using a price index for state and local government purchases to correct for inflation (Bureau of Economic Analysis, 1996a, 1996b).

As shown in Table 25.1, early intervention programs vary widely in their costs for a year of services. Much of the variation in cost across programs is due to differences in the amounts and types of services provided. Another important source of variation in cost is the characteristics of the personnel providing the services – the more highly trained and qualified the staff, the higher the cost. It is also the case that the model programs with strong evidence of program effectiveness for children in poverty (e.g., Perry Preschool and Abecedarian programs) are much more expensive than such public programs as Head Start and urban prekindergartens that have been funded to try to reproduce their results on a large scale. Programs for children with disabilities and developmental delay tend to have more funding per child than programs for children in poverty. The most expensive programs are programs that serve children in classrooms all day, all year, or that provide a wide menu of services to families. Programs that are more comprehensive in their approach to serving children and their families are not necessarily more expensive, but this is because they make trade-offs, reducing the quantity or quality of direct services to children to increase service coordination and services to parents.

Some of the variation in cost among programs in Table 25.1 is the result of differences in what is included in costs. This is most clearly demonstrated by the estimates for the annual costs of state-sponsored early intervention for children under 3 with disabilities and developmental delays (and their families) under the Individuals with Disabilities Education Act (IDEA). The average estimate from a

TABLE 25.1. Cost per Child and Family for One Year of Early Intervention (in 1995 dollars)

Program	Age	Target	Mode	Cost
1. Head Start: Federal cost	3–5	Poverty	Center	$4,680
plus 20% local matching funds				$5,616
2. Early Head Start: Federal cost	0–3	Poverty	Mixed	$4,539
plus 20% local matching funds				$5,446
3. Home Start	3–5	Poverty	Home	$5,484
4. IDEA Preschool (Part B)	3–5	Disability	Center	$8,073
5. IDEA Infant/Toddler (Part H)	0–3	Disability	Mixed	
a. NEC*TAS 19 state survey:				
Low				$3,582
High				$12,778
Average				$7,098
b. California				$5,702
c. Florida				$5,349
d. Massachusetts				$5,936
e. Nebraska				$7,341
f. New Jersey				
Program only				$6,036
Total system				$7,441
6. Perry preschool	3–5	Poverty	Both	$8,110
7. CCDP	0–5	Poverty	Mixed	$8,891
8. IHDP	0–3	LBW	Both	$23,000
9. Abecedarian	0–2	Poverty	Center	$11,108
	2–5			$10,386
10. Yale Family Support	0–3	Poverty	Center	$11,201
11. HCEEP	0–6	Disability	Mixed	
Low cost				$2,012–$4,681
Medium cost				$5,378–$7,666
High cost				$8,795–$23,460

Note: (1) Verzaro-O'Brien, Powell, & Sakamoto, 1996. (2) St. Pierre, Layzer, & Barnes, 1995. (3) Love, Nauta, Coelen, Hewlett, & Ruopp, 1976. (4) Kakalik, Furry, Thomas, & Carney, 1981. (5a.) Coakley, 1995. (5b.) American Institutes for Research, 1990. (5c.) Zervigon-Hakes, Graham, & Hall, 1991. (5d.) Erickson, 1992. (5e.) Parrish, 1990. (5f.) Tarr, 1997. (6) Barnett, 1996. (7) St. Pierre, Layzer, & Barnes, 1995. (8) Fewell & Scott, 1997. (9) Escobar & Barnett, 1986. (10) Seitz, Rosenbaum, & Apfel, 1985. (11) Stock et al., 1976.

nineteen-state survey conducted by the National Early Childhood Technical Assistance System (NEC*TAS; Coakley, 1995) is about $7,100. Estimates for several other states are considerably below this level. One reason for this is suggested by the two estimates for New Jersey. The lower estimate is for the cost of services from early intervention provider organizations. The higher estimate contains many of the other costs of the early intervention system including state and regional administration and support services for programs and families, training and professional development, state interagency coordinating council, research and evaluation, procedural safeguards, service co-

ordination, identification, initial evaluations, and referrals. Researchers often estimate only costs for the direct provision of services and do not include the other aspects of an early intervention system.

Program characteristics that affect cost are matters of choice and should explicitly be considered when designing early intervention programs. Four program characteristics were identified that can significantly influence program cost: duration, intensity, number of services, and reliance on parents to bear part of the cost. Each of these influences on cost is discussed on the following pages. The incentive structure of the early intervention system is one other factor that influences cost, in a somewhat different fashion. The ways in which early intervention service providers are paid for their services can affect the efficiency with which services are delivered.

COST AND DURATION OF SERVICES. One source of variation in the cost of early intervention is the duration of intervention services. Programs that serve children in classroom settings vary according to the length of day and number of days per year. The day may be 2 1/2 hours (half-day), 6 hours (full school day), or 8 or more hours (child care). The number of days per year may reflect a school year or year-round program. Head Start and public school programs for children ages 3 to 5 most often provide a half-day during the school year. By contrast, the Abecedarian program provided year-round child care. Programs that serve children through home visitors vary in the length of visits and the number of visits per year. The number of hours of service can vary from less than an hour per week (50 hours per year) to nearly 50 hours per week (2,500 hours per year) in full-day child care.

One way to compare the cost of services in which variations in the amount of time that services are provided is taken into account is to estimate cost per hour. Escobar and Barnett (1994) estimated cost per hour for twenty-three programs serving children with disabilities and developmental delays. About half the programs served children in classrooms, and half in home visits or one-on-one in centers. Although the average cost per child for the home visit and other one-on-one services was considerably lower than for the classroom programs, the cost-per-hour was much lower for the classroom programs. Generally, classroom programs deliver services to groups of children using lower staff: child ratios for longer periods of time. Home visits and one-to-one sessions in centers are used much more frequently for infants and toddlers; classroom programs are used much more often for older preschoolers. As the age of the child decreases, the staff: child ratio rises increasing the cost of each hour of service (reducing the cost disadvantages of one-on-one services), and there are obvious advantages to serving children in their homes.

An aspect of duration not captured in Table 25.1 is the number of years of intervention received. All of the cost estimates in Table 25.1 are for one full year of service. However, programs vary considerably in the number of years of service they provide. Programs that begin at birth and continue until school entry can be expected to cost much more than programs that begin at 3 or 4 years of age and last only a year or two. Some programs that focus on parents may not need to be continuous until school age if they prevent harm to the child (e.g., by preventing smoking, drinking, or other substance abuse during pregnancy) or transfer to parents knowledge or other resources necessary to continue the intervention's success. For other programs, it may be important to ensure continuity of service delivery until school entry (Barnett, 1998b). Early intervention for children with disabilities and delays under the age of 3 is unusual in that there is no standard starting age. Children can enter at any age under 3. Thus, some children receive services for nearly three years, many receive services for one or two years, and others receive services for less than a year (Barnett, Frede, Hasbrouck, Spain, & Yarosz, 1997). These variations in duration could affect program benefits as well as costs (Barnett, 1998b).

COST AND INTENSITY OF SERVICES. Variation in the intensity of services is another important source of variation in the cost of early intervention. Program intensity, defined in terms of the quality and quantity of service delivered in a given period of time, is largely determined by the number of personnel and their qualifications. Direct service personnel account for 50% or more of program costs (Escobar & Barnett, 1994; Coelen, Glantz, & Calore, 1979; Kakalik, Furry, Thomas, & Carney, 1981; Ruopp, Travers, Glantz, & Coelen, 1979). Thus, substantial increases in program intensity imply substantial increases in program cost.

Program intensity tends to vary with the characteristics of the children served. The two most important characteristics in this respect are age and the nature of a child's disability. Younger children and children with more severe disabilities require higher staff: child ratios. It is instructive to examine the cost estimates provided by Kakalik et al. (1981) for public school preschool special education programs by type of disability. The cost estimates have been adjusted for inflation and are presented in Table 25.2. Children in these programs tend to receive the same number of hours of services, but the staff: child ratio

TABLE 25.2. Preschool (ages 3–5 years) Special Education in Public Schools, Cost per Child by Disability (in 1995 dollars)

Disability	Cost per child
Speech impairment	$5,701
Learning disability	7,766
Educable mental retardation	7,933
Trainable mental retardation	10,796
Severe mental retardation	12,254
Emotional impairment	7,464
Deaf	17,575
Partial hearing loss	13,402
Blind	15,118
Partial sight loss	7,451
Orthopedic impairment	11,670
Other health impairment	5,310
Multiple disabilities	21,481
All conditions	8,073

Note: Kakalik, Furry, Thomas, and Carney (1981, p. 34).

varies greatly. It has also been found that cost varies with type and severity of disability for children with disabilities and developmental delays under the age of 3, but in this case the cost variations are primarily due to differences in the numbers of hours of services received (Erickson, 1992; Shonkoff, Hauser-Cram, Krauss, & Upshur, 1992).

The information in Table 25.1 covers the range of likely policy options but does not provide clear guidance regarding the appropriate cost of early intervention programs. Indeed, it cannot because the appropriate duration and intensity depends on benefits as well as costs. The programs included in the cost review that were specially designed for research projects have high staff:child ratios and exceptionally qualified (and well-paid) staff. For example, the Perry Preschool had a 1:6 ratio with two teachers per classroom compared to many public programs provided on a large scale. State initiatives providing preschool programs for economically disadvantaged preschoolers commonly set much lower ratios, 1:10 with one teacher and an aide per classroom (Grubb, 1987). Head Start programs tend to have staff with much lower educational qualifications as well as lower ratios. Comparisons by Barnett and Camilli (in press) suggested that less intensive programs produce smaller benefits, although the benefits may remain large relative to costs. A similar issue arises

for early intervention programs for children under age 3 with disabilities that may provide only a few hours per month of services to each child and family.

The National Day Care Study (NDCS; Ruopp et al., 1979) sheds some light on the importance of intensity in center-based programs. The NDCS investigated the links between cost, program characteristics, and program quality that were measured by observing caregiver and child behavior and by administering standardized tests at the beginning and end of the year. The NDCS researchers concluded that staff:child ratio was the most important influence on cost per child, but it was not strongly related to caregiver behavior, child behavior, or test scores of 3- to 5-year-old disadvantaged children. Class size and staff training were strongly related to caregiver and child behavior and children's test scores, but not to cost. Their conclusions were similar for infant and toddler programs, except that staff:child ratio was more strongly related to caregiver behavior (the only outcome measure because assessments were not given to infants). This study's findings have been confirmed by a number of more recent studies investigating the relationships linking child outcomes, process measures of quality, and group sizes and ratios (Helburn & Howes, 1996).

These findings require cautious interpretation. As the NDCS researchers recognized, in practice it is difficult to decrease class size without increasing staff:child ratio (Ruopp et al., 1979, pp. 137–57). Although it might be possible to trade two classes with a teacher and an aide in each for three classes with one teacher in each, this arrangement might create problems for safety or for responding to individual needs and could preclude integration of children with disabilities into a class. Also, the meaning of the findings depends on the types of comparisons on which they were based. Was the comparison that of one teacher and an assistant with twenty children to one teacher with twelve children, or was it of two teachers who work as a team with fourteen children to one teacher with seven children? The latter comparison seems unlikely. Finally, the modest relationship between staff qualifications and compensation can be expected to hold over only a very limited range and is a likely cause of high turnover. Although there are always a small number of highly qualified persons willing to work in early intervention programs no matter how poor the pay, it is unreasonable to expect to attract and keep large numbers of highly qualified staff unless salaries are competitive.

COST AND NUMBER OF SERVICES. Other things being equal, programs that provide more services are more costly. Thus, early intervention programs that provide classroom services for children together with home visit services for children, parents, or both tend to cost more than programs that deliver only one or the other of these options to each family. Costs are also increased by offering health care, nutrition, family counseling, transportation, and other services that support child and family health and development more generally. Head Start is one example of a program that offers a wide range of services. To keep costs down, Head Start has tended to offer low salaries, a short year, and part-day educational programs for children. The Yale Family Support Project (Seitz, Rosenbaum, & Apfel, 1985) provides an example of comprehensive and intensive services. It offered prenatal care, pediatric care, social work, and infant day care. Not surprisingly, the Yale program is among the most expensive reviewed.

COSTS TO PARENTS. The costs of programs may appear to vary because parents bear part of the costs in some programs. The cost estimates in Table 25.1 include only the costs borne by the public. In such developed countries as the United States, fees for early intervention services are rare and, when used, they are quite low. Two concerns with fees are that the administrative costs of collecting and accounting for fees could consume much of the fee income and that fees may discourage participation. However, when fees are low and ability to pay is taken into account, a family's unwillingness to pay sends an important signal about the perceived value of services. More important than fees are the unseen costs when parents are used as intervenors at home or in classrooms, in other volunteer roles, or as providers of transportation for their children. Yet, the opportunity cost to parents of the time consumed by these activities is frequently overlooked. Omitting such costs causes some programs to appear more economical than they really are. Escobar and Barnett (1994) estimated costs to parents in early intervention programs for children with disabilities and developmental delays. They found that parent time

contributions to programs were substantial for ten out of twelve home-based programs and five of eight center-based programs. The value of parent time varied from a few hundred dollars to over $1,500 per year. Parents also had considerable out-of-pocket costs for transportation in many programs.

Early intervention programs that provide services to children in classrooms for substantial periods each day provide child care services that have value to families apart from their contributions to the child's development. Child care is increasingly important as a facilitator of maternal employment and contributes to the financial and personal well-being of families with young children. Yet, the quality of much of the available child care is quite poor (Helburn & Howes, 1996). Not surprisingly, many parents of young children with disabilities are unable to find child care that they believe can address the special needs of their children (Barnett, Frede, Hasbrouck, Spain, & Yarosz, 1997). Parents of children with disabilities have long reported that the time demands of a child with a disability are a major problem (Dunlap & Hollinsworth, 1977). Barnett and Boyce (1995) have documented the magnitude of the time burden associated with caring for a child with a disability and found that mothers of children with disabilities significantly reduce their time in the labor force.

An overlooked insight from economics about the costs of early intervention is that the costs of child care are borne by society whether or not child care is provided by an early intervention program. One approach to early intervention may have lower costs to the public than another program because one provides child care and the other does not. However, such a comparison is not accurate from the perspective of society as a whole unless the costs of providing child care in both situations (and the benefits) are taken into account, as well. If decisions are made on the basis of the public costs alone, programs that do not provide child care such as home-visiting and center-based programs of one or two hours per week (for children up to age 3) or even two to three hours a day (for children ages 3 to 5) appear much less costly than programs that provide substantial amounts of child care. Programs that do not provide child care may impose additional costs on parents if the limited service schedules offered make it difficult for parents to arrange work. One approach to facilitating child care while limiting cost to the program is to provide early intervention services in community child care settings that are paid for by other government agencies, community organizations, or the parents (e.g., Rule et al., 1987; Weiss, 1981). However, the poor quality of many community child care programs is a limiting factor. It is difficult to determine how much this explains the reluctance of early intervention programs for young children with disabilities to work with community child care providers to the same extent that they have worked with parents.

Whether parents should bear part of the cost of intervention is an ethical, practical, and legal question on which economics can shed some light. Parent involvement is often desirable, and, in some cases, the use of parents as intervenors may be more effective and economically efficient than the alternatives. Yet, the costs to parents of participating in an intervention program can be substantial, even when there is no fee for services. Policy makers and the public should not confuse cost shifting, which decreases the public cost but increases the costs to parents, with cost reduction; the total cost to society can be higher for a program that has lower public costs. Moreover, imposing costs on parents (whether or not they are "invisible") can have undesirable effects such as increasing family stress, decreasing the time and money that parents can devote to their children, and discouraging participation so that children do not receive the desired type or amount of service. Requirements that parents bring their children to a center for services, participate in home visits, or conduct specific activities with their children to enhance the child's development all impose costs on parents that must be taken into account. Recognition that there is a cost to parents when parents are required or persuaded to conduct intervention activities with children may lead to the development of intervention activities that are integrated into the natural interactions of parents and children and do not require setting aside a special time (e.g., Barnett, Escobar, & Ravsten, 1988).

The cost of transportation is an important related issue because transportation costs can be high, and many programs rely on parents to provide transportation. Escobar and Barnett (1994) found the average cost of transportation for 3-to-5-year-old children receiving preschool special education

exceeded $1,000. A study of transportation costs for young children with disabilities in Utah found a range of $500 to $2,500 per child for one school year, with a significant number of programs reporting costs toward the high end (Escobar, Peterson, Lauritzen, & Barnett, 1987). For younger children with disabilities, transportation costs can represent an even larger percentage of total costs because such programs may provide only 30 to 90 minutes of services per visit. Relying on parents to provide transportation holds down costs to the public and makes programs appear more efficient than they would otherwise. It may be that parental provision of transportation is the lowest cost approach from a societal perspective; however, relying on parents may present barriers to participation for some families and impose undesirably large costs on others.

COST AND INCENTIVE STRUCTURE. When government sets up early intervention systems, it tends to fund programs rather than children and families. This can be the case even in systems in which an entitlement to services is created. For example, some states fund early intervention programs on the basis of program capacity or numbers of children enrolled. When this is the case, programs have no financial incentive to operate efficiently by providing the maximum amount of services to the child and family given the resources available. We should not be surprised if high rates of missed or canceled appointments are found or if programs close frequently because of inclement weather, vacations, or other reasons and make-up services are not scheduled. By contrast, if programs are paid only for services actually delivered (tracked individually or as average daily attendance), they may be expected to go to greater lengths to ensure that children and families receive scheduled services. Tying payments to services delivered also provides an incentive for programs to be more solicitous of parental needs in terms of schedules, transportation, and types of services, particularly if programs must compete for clients because families have choices among service providers.

BENEFITS AND BENEFIT-COST ANALYSIS

From an economic perspective, early intervention is an activity with two conceptually distinct products: child development services and family support services. The primary product is child development services because the definitive aim of early intervention is to improve child outcomes. At the same time, many early intervention programs also include family support services that aim to improve family functioning and well-being. Child care is the most common form of family support. Child care relieves parents from custodial responsibilities so that they can pursue such other activities as work, rest, and recreation without distraction. There has been a movement toward broader family support programs that address a variety of family needs (Kagan, Powell, Weissbourd, & Zigler, 1987; Kysela & Marfo, 1983; Weissbourd, 1983).

Family support services are provided for a variety of reasons. Family support may be viewed as an important indirect avenue of intervention for the child. An intervention program also may have goals for family outcomes in their own right (Bristol, Reichle, & Thomas, 1987; Brooks-Gunn et al., this volume; Kelly & Barnard, this volume; St. Pierre, Layzer, & Barnes, 1995). Family support can even be an incidental by-product of child-directed intervention, as when programs provide out-of-home child care because they use a classroom model to deliver intervention. However, from an economic perspective, the rationale for family support services is irrelevant. Family support services produce outcomes that are economically valuable, and estimates of program benefits should include the value of services to all family members whenever it is possible.

Benefit-Cost Analysis Methodology

Benefit-cost analysis is essentially the application of economic theory, primarily microeconomics, to the problem of estimating the economic value of a program's effects. A complete introduction to the methodology of benefit-cost analysis is beyond the limits of this chapter, and the reader is referred to the excellent texts by Levin (1983) and Thompson (1980). As the application of economic methods to the study of early intervention has been discussed in detail elsewhere (Barnett, 1986), only a brief outline of the procedures involved is presented prior to our consideration of research findings regarding the benefits of early intervention. Cost-effectiveness analysis may be viewed as an incomplete benefit-

cost analysis and is not discussed separately (Barnett, 1994, provides examples).

The process of conducting a benefit-cost analysis of an early intervention program can be described in a series of steps. The first is to identify and estimate the resources used and the effects produced by the program. The second is to translate resource and effect estimates into monetary measures of costs and benefits. The third is to aggregate those monetary estimates of costs and benefits to depict the net economic value of the program to society as a whole. The fourth is to describe the distributional consequences; that is, who gains and who loses. The final step is to consider how the underlying assumptions and any other limitations of the analysis might affect the findings. An example using these steps is presented, which serves a dual purpose, illustrating the methodology and describing the benefits of early intervention.

Benefits of Early Intervention: The Perry Preschool Project

The most extensive evidence to date of the benefits of early intervention is provided by a benefit-cost analysis based on the Perry Preschool Project (Barnett, 1993, 1996). The Perry Preschool Project is a longitudinal study of the effects of a preschool program that was begun with 3- and 4-year-olds in the early 1960s. It has published findings through age 27 (Schweinhart, Barnes, Weikart, Barnett, & Epstein, 1993). The 123 subjects of the study were children with low IQs from low-income African American families. Many of the children had IQs that would classify them as mentally retarded, and half of the control group eventually received special education. Thus, this study is relevant to early intervention for children with disabilities as well as for economically disadvantaged children.

PROGRAM RESOURCES. The Perry Preschool program ran from October to June and consisted of a 2 1/2 hour daily classroom program that met five days per week and 1 1/2 hour weekly home visits by the teachers. Children attended the program at ages 3 and 4, except for a small group of children the first year who attended only at age 4. Two public school teachers with early childhood and special education training served each classroom of eight

TABLE 25.3. Major Findings of the Perry Preschool Project

Category	Number of subjects[a]	Preschool group	No preschool group	p
Mean IQ at age 5	123	95	83	<.001
Age 15 achievement test	95	122.2	94.5	<.001
Precentage of all school years in special education	112	16%	28%	.039
High school graduation (or equivalent)	121	67%	49%	.034
Postsecondary education at age 19	121	38%	21%	.029
5 or more arrests by age 27	121	7%	35%	.004
Females only: teen pregnancies per 100	49	64	117	.084
Received welfare by age 27	121	59%	80%	.010
Monthly earnings at age 27 (1993 dollars)	115	$1,219	$766	.007

Note: Berrueta-Clement, Schweinhart, Barnett, Epstein, and Weikart (1984); Schweinhart, Barnes, Weikart, Barnett, and Epstein (1993).
[a]Maximum N = 123

to thirteen children. Teachers taught in the morning and conducted home visits in the afternoon. A cognitive-developmental curriculum was used as described by Weikart, Kamii, and Radin (1967). Study subjects entered public kindergarten at age 5.

PROGRAM EFFECTS. The Perry Preschool Project employed an experimental design to study immediate and long-term effects. Subjects were assigned in a manner approximating random assignment either to an experimental group that entered the program or to a control group that did not enter the program (Schweinhart et al., 1993). Analyses indicate that no biases were introduced by incidental initial differences between the groups of subsequent attrition (Berrueta-Clement, Schweinhart, Barnett, Epstein, & Weikart, 1984). Thus, comparison of the two groups can be considered to yield unbiased estimates of the effects of the preschool program. Measures of child development and success in a variety of areas have been obtained periodically since the first year of preschool. Most recently, the findings of the project were reported through age 27 (Schweinhart et al., 1993).

The Perry Preschool Project found a chain of lasting effects that stretches from preschool to adulthood. Some of the most important effects are displayed in Table 25.3 as comparisons of means for the experimental and control groups. As can be seen, the intervention's effects were pervasive as well as persistent. The intervention's first measured effects were IQ gains for the experimental group at ages 3 and 4. The IQ differences between experimental and control groups began to decline after school entry and ceased to be statistically significant by second grade. Despite the decline in IQ, the initial IQ gains were associated with later success. The experimental group performed better on achievement tests and on teacher ratings throughout the school years and was less likely to be placed in special education (Schweinhart et al., 1993). By the time they were young adults, it was clear that the experimental group was also experiencing nonacademic as well as academic advantages. They were not only more likely to be pursuing higher education, but they also had higher employment rates and higher incomes, less involvement in crime and delinquency, and as teenagers, girls had borne fewer children (Berrueta-Clement et al., 1984). At age 27, benefits in the form of higher earnings, increased financial assets, less crime, and less dependency on welfare were still apparent (Schweinhart et al., 1993).

THE MONETARY VALUE OF COSTS AND BENEFITS. The heart of the economic analysis was an estimation of the program's economic value based on the resources used by the program and estimated program effects. For comparability, all figures are presented in 1995 dollars. A complete cost estimate was produced on the basis of program records. As reported in Table 25.1, annual cost was about $8,000 per child. As some children attended for only one year, a weighted average based on the number incurring one and two years of costs was employed in the analysis. The economic value of benefits was estimated for child care, elementary and secondary education, postsecondary education, earnings and employment, crime and delinquency, and welfare. The estimated value of benefits was in each case based on observed program effects, although in some cases it was necessary to predict continued benefits beyond age 27.

The value of child care was estimated on the basis of the number of hours of center-based care provided. For the Perry Preschool program, this was relatively small because it was only a morning program. Moreover, because the parents' potential wage rates and incomes were low, their ability and willingness to pay for child care was low. With these limitations, the estimated value of child care to parents was only $928 per year. By comparison, the value of full-day, year-round child care to low-income parents might be $3,000 to $4,000 per year.

The effect of intervention on the costs of elementary and secondary education was estimated by calculating the cost of each year of education for each child on the basis of school placement and by comparing average costs for the experimental and control groups. The intervention reduced total educational costs by about $10,000 per child as the result of two opposing effects. First, cost was reduced because children who attended preschool required less expensive placements (e.g., less special education). Second, cost was increased because preschool attendees were less likely to drop out and therefore had more total years of schooling. Thus, the overall cost savings was achieved despite the cost of increased educational attainment.

The effect of intervention on the costs of postsecondary education demonstrates that it is possible to have negative benefits. The intervention increased the estimated costs of public higher education by about $1,500 per child because experimental subjects were more likely to enter postsecondary education. To some extent this increased cost was offset by cost savings from lower rates of adult remedial and adult secondary education (compared to the control subjects) after leaving high school. Note that neither of these estimated effects was statistically significant through age 27. However, in producing the best estimate of benefits it is important to include all estimated effects. This is especially the case when dealing with small samples in which effects can be quite large without statistical significance and when the summation of benefits from a set of small effects (possibly because each involves a low incidence condition or activity) is potentially large. In this instance, inclusion of the estimated benefit is also important in order to avoid giving the impression of bias toward a positive estimate.

The Perry Preschool program increased the employment rate and earnings of the experimental group. The effect on total compensation (wages plus fringe benefits) was based on actual earnings data through age 27 and was predicted from educational attainment beyond age 27. Total earnings were roughly $25,000 higher per experimental subject through age 27. Obviously, they had many years remaining in their earning careers, and some had postponed work in order to continue their education. The effect on total compensation over the balance of the lifetime was estimated by using U.S. Census data that linked educational attainment to earnings by race, age, sex, and data on fringe benefit rates. The estimated lifetime benefit was nearly $90,000 per child.

Crime and delinquency were reduced as a result of the preschool program. This finding was based on self-report data and police and court records. Because official records data were gathered later than interview data, information concerning involvement with the criminal justice system was available through age 28. Costs to victims and costs to the police, court, and prison systems were estimated for each arrest. Data on the ratio of arrests to crimes by type of crime were used to estimate the total benefits from crime reduction. A comparison of average cost of the two groups indicated that the cost of crime and delinquency had been reduced by about $95,000 per child by age 28. National data on patterns of arrests by age were used to project arrest rates and crime costs beyond age 28, producing an estimate of more than $60,000 per child in additional cost reductions over the subjects' lifetimes.

The Perry Preschool program's effect on welfare costs was estimated from the subjects' reports of welfare payments through age 27. The estimated effect on welfare payments through age 27 was roughly $4,000 per child. The effect of the program on welfare payments beyond age 27 was a difficult task because much less is known about long-term patterns of welfare assistance than about other patterns over the life cycle and because welfare reform is changing the rules. Thus, this estimate is the least certain of those made in the benefit-cost analysis. However, the estimated cost savings to society is only a small fraction of the reduction in welfare payments. This is because welfare is primarily a shift of resources from one person to another. Only the administrative cost of welfare is a cost to society as a whole, which amounts to roughly 10% of the payments.

AGGREGATION AND INTERPRETATION. A summary of the Perry Preschool program's costs and benefits is presented in Table 25.4. The figures in Table 25.4 are not simply the sums of all the dollar values from each year for each cost and benefit, for it would be incorrect to add dollars across years as if they were perfectly comparable. Two adjustments are required to produce comparable values across the years. One corrects dollar values for the effects of inflation, which robs dollars of their buying power over the years. All dollar amounts in the Perry Preschool benefit-cost analysis were converted to constant 1995 dollars using a price index – the Gross Domestic Product Deflator for State and Local Purchases of Goods and Services (Bureau of Economic Analysis, 1996b). The other adjustment takes into account the time value of money, which may be most easily understood as the opportunity cost of waiting. Even without the effects of inflation, a dollar today is more valuable than a dollar to be received next year or in 10 or 20 years. A dollar received today can be spent on something that is enjoyed now or it can be invested to yield more than a dollar next year or at some later time. Everyone understands the necessity for this adjustment, at least intuitively: Who would pay $1,000 today to receive $1,000 (even inflation adjusted) in 20 years?

There are several ways to adjust constant dollars from different years so that they are equivalent in terms of their value to society at a single point in time (Gramlich, 1981; Thompson, 1980). The one used in this study converts all constant dollars into

TABLE 25.4. Present Value of Costs and Benefits of the Perry Preschool Project Discounted at 3% (in 1995 dollars)

Benefits	Amount
Through age 27	
Child care	$787
School cost savings K–12	7,332
Adult and higher education	−624
Earnings increase	15,469
Crime reduction	52,330
Welfare reduction	234
TOTAL	75,528
Beyond age 27	
Earnings increase	16,894
Crime reduction	22,767
Welfare reduction	49
TOTAL	39,710
Total	
Benefits	115,238
Cost	13,184
Net benefits	$102,054

Note: Adult and higher education benefits are on balance negative, that is, a cost, due to estimated increased participation in higher education. Barnett (1993, p. 504).

their *present value*, which is their equivalent value at the beginning of the project. Present value is calculated by discounting dollars in every year beyond the start of the project by the annual interest rate at which people are willing to trade a dollar today for a dollar next year. This annual interest rate is called the *discount rate*, and in this study it was assumed to be 3%. In other words, society is assumed to regard as fair trades for a $1.00 today $1.03 in one year, $1.03 squared in two years, and $1.03 to the 25th power in 25 years. Thus, present value converts $1.00 in benefits received one year in the future to $1.00/1.03, $1.00 received two years in the future to $1.00/(1.03)^2$, and $1.00 received 25 years in the future to $1.00/(1.03)^{25}$. When all of the present values of costs and benefits are summed, a simple decision rule can be applied. If the present value of benefits exceeds the present value of costs, then the project is a good investment for society. When two projects are compared, the one with the greatest net present value (present value of benefits minus present value of costs) is more economically efficient and is a better investment.

The bottom line in Table 25.4 indicates that the net present value of the Perry Preschool program to society was positive and large. It is notable that this can be established on the basis of observed benefits through age 27 alone and does not depend on less certain predictions about benefits in later years. Thus, it can be concluded that the Perry Preschool program was a sound economic investment. In fact, the rate of return on the Perry Preschool program was higher than the long-term rate of return on investments in the U.S. stock market (Barnett, 1996). However, the results also indicate that early intervention is the kind of investment that requires a long time horizon. The investment in this fairly expensive program was not "paid off" until some years after the participants left school and became adults. This may present a problem if the public or its representatives are shortsighted. However, the public invests in many activities – from highways and bridges to higher education and scientific research – that pay off only over similarly long time horizons, and early intervention does generate immediate benefits.

One of the questions that was not answered by the Perry Preschool Project is: Are two years of preschool needed to generate the long-term benefits or would one year be sufficient? There was no statistically significant difference in effects between the one-year and two-year subjects, but because the one-year sample was so small, the power to detect differences was relatively slight. Obviously, this is an important question from an economic perspective. One year would cost just about half as much as two years (slightly more because such costs as screening tests are incurred just once), which is a large savings. However, it is also possible that even two years is too little. Even greater benefits may be produced by beginning intervention prior to age 3 (Barnett & Camilli, in press). Further research on this issue that estimates costs and benefits is greatly needed.

DISTRIBUTIONAL CONSEQUENCES. Having determined that society as a whole gained as a result of this program, further analysis was directed to the question of the distribution of costs and benefits from the Perry Preschool program. Barnett (1996) investigated the distribution of costs and benefits to two conceptually distinct groups: taxpayers (i.e., people in the role of taxpayer) who paid for the program and participants who attended the program (and their families). It was found that most of the present value of the benefits accrued to the taxpayers, and that taxpayers' benefits more than justified the program's cost. The participants and their families received a relatively small share of the monetary benefits.

There are two salient public policy implications of the distributional analysis. First, the Perry Preschool program appears to have been a social program in which everybody was a winner. Both participants and taxpayers came out ahead. Such a program should be very popular politically. Second, the distribution of benefits offers a strong rationale for public funding. Families such as those in the Perry Preschool Project cannot afford to buy high-quality preschool services on their own. The economic ability to fund early intervention lies with the taxpayers who can receive more than enough economic benefits to make it an attractive investment at the same time as they improve the educational and economic success of children born into poverty. Apparently a society can do well by doing good.

ASSUMPTIONS AND LIMITATIONS. Extensive analyses were conducted to investigate the effects of departures from the various assumptions required to conduct the benefit-cost analysis of the Perry Preschool program. One of the most crucial assumptions in any benefit-cost analysis is the rate used in discounting, and economists disagree about the most appropriate rate. Some argue for rates below 3%, and others argue for higher rates. Thus, net present value was calculated by using a wide range of discount rates. The estimated net present value of the program was positive for real (without inflation) discount rates up to 11%, far beyond the reasonable range. Extensive analyses were also conducted by varying the assumptions used to estimate benefits to age 27 and to project benefits beyond age 27. Even radical changes in assumptions did not alter the conclusion that the program was a sound investment. Barnett (1996) has provided details of all of the alternative analyses.

Perhaps the most serious limitation of the benefit-cost analysis was that cost was more completely estimated than benefits. This tends to be true generally in benefit-cost analysis of early intervention because the economic value of many benefits is difficult to assess. In the Perry Preschool study, some benefits could not be valued at all: 1) early IQ gains and school success, per se; 2) increased satisfaction with high school; and, 3) reduced teenage pregnancy, fewer abortions, and increased rates of marriage for women. Nevertheless, this analysis demonstrates that benefit estimates for early intervention programs can be more complete than many have thought possible. For example, because of advances in research on the economics of crime, it was possible to estimate benefits from crime reductions that included the effects on pain and suffering and the risk of death as well as the direct losses from stolen or damaged property, hospitalization and time lost from work, and cost-savings to the criminal justice system. This still does not capture the value of increased feelings of safety or decreased expenditures on locks, guards, and other security measures, but it is remarkably complete.

Other Longitudinal Studies

Although the Perry Preschool study is the most comprehensive of its kind, its findings are supported by the results of a large number of other studies of the long-term effects of early intervention for children in poverty (Barnett, 1998b; Farran, this volume; Halpern, this volume). A few of these studies have included economic analyses. Several studies have follow-ups that extend through adolescence. Similar studies have not been conducted with children with disabilities that are attributed primarily to biological impairments. The extent to which studies with disadvantaged children contribute to the knowledge of the economics of early intervention for children with disabilities more generally is a matter that is discussed later in the chapter. Two studies that estimated the economic value of benefits are briefly summarized here.

Weiss (1981) conducted a benefit-cost analysis of the effects of adding INREAL, which is a language intervention program, to ordinary preschool and kindergarten classrooms. The study's subjects were 3- to 5-year-old disadvantaged children in seven matched pairs of classrooms. One classroom from each pair was randomly assigned to receive INREAL. The INREAL program was delivered by language specialists who were assigned to classrooms for one school year. Each specialist worked with one preschool class in the morning and one or two

kindergartens in the afternoon. A major goal of the INREAL program is to provide language therapy in the classroom in a way that minimizes the stigmatizing of children needing therapy. A three-year follow-up of study participants revealed that children in the intervention group repeated fewer grades and had fewer and less restrictive special education placements than children in the control group.

To assess the intervention program's economic value, Weiss (1981) compared the program's cost to the benefits from reductions in later educational costs over the three-year follow-up period. Despite some flaws in the economic analysis and the inclusion of only three years of benefits, it is clear that the present value of benefits exceeded that of costs. This finding suggests that early intervention programs for disadvantaged children (17% of the sample was identified as having a disability at study entry) can have a substantial economic impact (Weiss & Heublein, 1981). Of course, the INREAL study did not measure the economic benefits of the preschool and kindergarten programs alone, but its results indicate that there are substantial economic benefits to be obtained from early intervention (beyond those already yielded by the basic programs) and that ordinary early childhood programs serving disadvantaged children might significantly increase their economic value by adopting such language interventions as INREAL.

Seitz et al. (1985) reported the results of a ten-year follow-up study of economically disadvantaged families who participated in the Yale Family Support Project. The intervention program provided medical and social services and an educational childcare program for about 2 1/2 years beginning at birth. Some parents received prenatal services as well. A comparison group was obtained by applying the procedures used to select the treatment group to later births at the hospital from which the treatment group was drawn. Comparison families were matched with treatment families on sex of child, income, number of parents in the home, and mother's ethnicity. Together, the two groups contained twenty-eight families. Program effects were measured by comparing parent and child outcomes of the two groups.

Seitz et al. (1985) found evidence of positive effects on parent and child at the age 10 follow-up. Treatment-group mothers had a higher employment rate, a higher level of educational attainment, and a lower birth rate. Children had better school attendance records and fewer special education placements. Although a complete benefit-cost analysis was not conducted, the monetary value of costs and some benefits was estimated. Cost was reported to be approximately $20,000 (1982 dollars) per family over the program's 2 1/2 year life. The estimated value of benefits from increased employment and reduced special services in the follow-up year was $2,125 (1982 dollars) per family. The present value of those benefits discounted at 5% was $1,337. It would be difficult to extrapolate accurately the value of benefits from a single follow-up year, although the effect on lifetime income might be estimated on the basis of educational attainment. It is interesting that the educational cost savings accounted for about half of the one-year benefit and were similar in magnitude to the average annual educational cost savings estimated for the Perry Preschool program.

Olds et al. (1993) investigated the costs, long-term effects, and economic benefits of a home visiting program conducted prenatally through the first two years of life for first-born children and their mothers. Results fifteen years later have been reported, and the study has been replicated elsewhere (Olds et al., 1997). Effects of the intervention for low-income mothers and children at the original site include reductions in reported child abuse and neglect, increased spacing between first and second children, fewer subsequent children, and fewer months on welfare (Kitzman et al., 1997). Most strikingly, mothers were arrested and convicted of crimes less often, and as adolescents the children were less likely to have been arrested (Olds et al., 1997). Replication of this study conducted in another state, with a heavily minority population (the original study sample was mostly White), found in the first two years postpartum the following: For children, fewer health care encounters and fewer hospitalizations related to injuries and ingestions; for mothers, fewer second pregnancies and live births and less use of governmental subsidies such as Aid To Families With Dependent Children (Kitzman et al., 1997). Estimates of costs and benefits indicate that the program paid off as an intervention with low-income families within four years (Olds et al., 1993).

Additional evidence of benefits comes from early intervention studies that have found long-term

effects similar to those of the Perry Preschool Project. The Consortium for Longitudinal Studies (1983) conducted analyses of pooled data from eleven long-term studies of early intervention (including the Perry Preschool Project). Eight studies provided information about school success at Grade 7, and four studies provided information about school success through Grade 12. Pooled analyses across studies indicated that there was significantly less grade retention and special education placement for children who had received early intervention, and the results were not dependent on the inclusion of the Perry Preschool results in the analyses. Barnett (1998b) reviewed thirty-five studies of early intervention for children in poverty that followed children at least through Grade 3 and found consistent evidence of effects on achievement, grade retention, and special education. A longitudinal study of the Chicago Child Parent Centers through age 15 (Reynolds, 1997) has found substantial effects on achievement, grade retention, and special education. In a long-term follow-up study of children who received intervention from birth through age 5, Lally, Mangione, and Honig (1988) found effects on juvenile delinquency. Finally, the Abecedarian study, a true experiment with full-day care from the first year of life through age 5, has found large effects on achievement, grade retention, and special education placement persisting through age 15 (Campbell & Ramey, 1994, 1995).

The evidence that early intervention with children in poverty increases school success (and thereby reduces the costs of schooling) is quite strong. This finding has been replicated in a variety of locations and times with programs that differed in theoretical approach, service delivery model, and the age at which intervention begins. It has also been found outside the United States in Brazil, France, Germany, India, Ireland, and Turkey (Boocock & Larner, 1998; Kagitcibasi, 1996; Myers, 1992). Support for the other economic benefits found in the Perry Preschool study is less broad-based, but a substantial body of research in economics links educational success to key variables for economic benefits: earnings and employment, criminal activity, childbearing, and health (Haveman & Wolfe, 1984). However, studies of longer lasting programs such as Abecedarian and the Chicago Child Parent Centers suggest that some academic benefits of early intervention could be even greater than in the Perry Preschool study.

Generalizations must be developed cautiously because the benefits of early intervention vary to some extent with the design and delivery of the intervention, the characteristics of the children and families served, and the broader social and economic environments (Barnett, 1993; Frede, 1998). For example, effects on grade repetition and special education placements obviously depend on the rates at which these occur for the target population, which is determined by both the characteristics of the children and the policies of the schools. The conditions of primary education in developing countries not only differ from conditions in industrialized countries but also differ considerably from each other in ways that can influence the long-term consequences of early intervention (Myers, 1992). Efforts to improve health and nutrition in conjunction with early education take on added importance when rates of mortality, serious illness, and malnutrition for young children are high and hunger and illness present serious problems for child development and learning (Myers, 1992). In industrialized countries, not all programs found to increase school success have had the same positive effects on crime and delinquency (Boocock & Larner, 1998; Clarke & Campbell, 1997; Schweinhart & Weikart, 1996). Why this should be so is unclear. However, one possibility is that early intervention programs differ in the extent to which they provide opportunities to learn social problem solving.

Benefits for Nonpoor Children with Disabilities

Longitudinal studies comparable to the studies with disadvantaged children have rarely been conducted on early intervention for children with disabilities or developmental delays who are not poor, and information is most scarce regarding interventions for young children with moderate-to-profound disabilities (Casto & Mastropieri, 1986; Dunst, 1986; Guralnick, 1997; Shonkoff & Hauser-Cram, 1987). One reason for this is that services are mandated for all young children with disabilities. Thus, the case for long-term benefits to children with the most severe disabilities generally rests on other kinds of evidence including single case studies, program

comparison studies, and studies relying on natural variation in early intervention experiences (which are less supportive of strong causal inferences). Some of these studies have included information on costs and provide a basis for cost-effectiveness comparisons (Erickson, 1992; White & Boyce, 1993).

This evidence is reviewed extensively elsewhere, with generally positive conclusions (Guralnick, 1997; Guralnick & Bennett, 1987). There appears to be a substantial basis for concluding that early intervention can produce immediate benefits for the general population of children with disabilities and that these are of the same order of magnitude as initial benefits for disadvantaged children (Casto & Mastropieri, 1986; Farran, this volume; Shonkoff & Hauser-Cram, 1987). This at least leaves open the possibility of substantial long-term benefits for these children, although the nature of the long-term benefits may well vary with type and severity of disability and may differ from those for children in poverty. Program comparisons suggest that improving services through increases in duration and intensity is more complex than simply increasing the number of home visits, increasing the length of time in a classroom, or adding new services (Barnett & Pezzino, 1987; Burkett, 1982; Goetze & Yang, 1997; Shonkoff et al., 1992; White & Boyce, 1993).

One of the more interesting studies of an intervention that did not target poor children is the Infant Health and Development Program (IHDP). This study is a multisite randomized trial of intensive early intervention during the first three years of life for low-birth-weight (LBW) premature children (Gross, Spiker, & Haynes, 1997). The intervention provided home visits in the first year of life, educational child care in the second two years, and pediatric follow-up. The treatment group had substantially higher IQ scores at age 3. At age 5, the treatment group as a whole showed no advantages in IQ, behavior problems, or health. However, in the higher LBW stratum (>2,000 grams), the treatment group had an advantage of 4 IQ points. This pattern was repeated at age 8 in which no effects were found within the lower LBW stratum, but effects in the higher LBW stratum included higher IQ, higher achievement test scores, and a marginally significant ($p = .09$) decrease in special education placements (McCarton et al., 1997). Some evidence indicates that children of mothers with the least formal education receive the largest cognitive gains from intervention (Ramey & Ramey, 1998).

Although benefits to children and their families can be expected to vary with type and severity of disability, some useful generalizations may be made regarding potential economic benefits to nonpoor children with disabilities. The costs of special education are high and tend to increase with the severity of the disability. Even modest decreases in the intensity of required special education might generate significant cost savings. Substantial benefits from decreases in crime and delinquency are less likely because of low rates of such problems. Increases in cognitive and social abilities, and in daily living skills in particular, might generate significant benefits to families of children with disabilities and generally reduce costs to society to the extent that the ability for independent living (even if not completely independent) is increased. Child care provided by center-based programs probably has a relatively high value. Child care is likely to be more difficult and costly to obtain for these children, and better educated parents have higher earnings potential.

On the whole, it seems quite possible that early intervention for nonpoor children with disabilities and developmental delays can be economically efficient. This may be the case, even if the costs of early intervention for these children are higher than for disadvantaged children. In evaluating the benefits, it is important not to slight potential benefits of early intervention that are difficult to value economically. Parents may highly value such benefits as an increased understanding of their child, improved family relationships, reduced stress, and relatively small improvements in their child's abilities that might hardly be noticed by others – especially if these improvements directly contribute to a higher quality of life for the child and family. The value of increased and more successful participation in family, school, work, and community activities could be quite high. The magnitude and economic value of such benefits is an important area for future research on the economics of early intervention.

CONCLUSION

Early intervention for disadvantaged children and their families can be a sound economic investment. Moreover, it is an investment that should be undertaken by taxpayers because they are the primary economic beneficiaries. Currently, the United States underinvests in early intervention because it fails to accommodate all children in poverty for even one year prior to kindergarten. Less is known about the economic benefits of early intervention for nonpoor children with disabilities and developmental delays and their families, but there is clear potential for benefits that would more than justify the costs. These conclusions are broad generalizations over highly diverse populations and may not hold true for every subpopulation. However, this is the level of generality at which policy decisions are made.

Early intervention is an expensive investment, which makes cost an important policy consideration. The challenge is to restrain cost without jeopardizing benefits. From an economic perspective, the objective is to set cost at the level that yields the maximum net gain to society, regardless of how high or low that cost. In other words, rather than seeking to maximize benefits to children and families at whatever the cost, the goal is to increase quality and quantity of early intervention services to the point at which the value of the additional benefits just equals the additional cost. This perspective recognizes not only that there are competing priorities for society's resources but also that children with disabilities and their families have needs and interests other than the child's disability. The key policy variables with respect to cost and benefits are 1) duration, age at start and length of service; 2) intensity, quantity and quality of staff time devoted to each child and family; 3) number of services, how broadly the child and family are served; 4) target population, how programs are targeted and eligibility for services defined; and 5) cost shifting, particularly the extent to which costs are borne by families. Policy makers need more information on the effects of these variables on costs and benefits, and this review suggests directions for future research.

The costs of current public programs for disadvantaged preschoolers are considerably lower than the costs of the programs that provide most of the evidence for long-term benefits. Costs are lower because Head Start and other programs tend to have lower staff: child ratios and lower staff qualifications and provide only one year at age four (Grubb, 1987; Administration for Children and Families

1997; Hofferth, 1996; Verzaro-O'Brien, Powell, & Sakamoto, 1996). The precise effects of the reductions in intensity and duration on child outcomes are uncertain, but the potential for substantially reduced benefits cannot be ignored. Within-study and cross-study comparisons (Barnett, 1998a,1998b) indicate that important benefits are lost as a result of underinvestment in intensity and duration in current programs. Careful research on the effects of amount of service (including number of years), staff: child ratio, and staff qualifications should be assigned a high priority. Such studies should build on past work by recognizing that much larger sample sizes are required to measure the effects of program improvements than to detect the effect of a program compared to no program, that detailed measurement of program implementation is critical when comparing alternatives, and that effective use of increased resources may require qualitative changes in programs rather than simple expansions.

Given the high costs of early intervention, low-cost options that have some demonstrated success should be the subject of research and practical experiments. Home-based programs are one low-cost option and are particularly well-suited for early intervention with infants. However, some high-cost models such as the Abecedarian program have also proven to be highly successful. No program is a panacea, and home visitor programs do not address needs for child care and may provide quite different benefits than programs that work much more extensively with the child. Researchers and early intervention advocates must counsel policy makers not to jump to the conclusion that a single intervention, even a highly successful one, suffices for all families (Meisels, Dichtelmiller, & Liaw, 1993). Some children and families may not respond to a particular intervention or may find it difficult to participate because of its design, but some may benefit from multiple interventions, and it may be that the advantages of specialization are such that multiple programs (in parallel or in series) are more effective than a single program that tries to do it all.

Early intervention for children with disabilities and developmental delays has a high enough cost that questions are raised about the efficiency of common modes of service delivery. Infants and toddlers with disabilities often receive only a few hours of services per week, whereas children ages 3 to 5 may receive only ten to twelve hours per week when public schools are in session. Yet the costs of these services approach the cost of such full-day, year-round programs as Abecedarian. When the child care needs and the potential contribution to the well-being of children and families from child care are considered, it seems reasonable that it might be more efficient to provide early intervention services for many children in the context of developmentally appropriate child care programs operated by early intervention providers or other community organizations. Given the evidence that more extensive services can have larger impacts on child development, shifts in the ways in which services are provided might have important payoffs (Blair, Ramey, & Hardin, 1995). Research comparing the two approaches is another area that should have a high priority. One specific focus for such research would be the costs and benefits of providing early intervention services through the School of the Twenty-First Century, which integrates child care and education (Zigler & Finn-Stevenson, 1996).

Early intervention programs for children with disabilities tend to limit enrollment to children who already manifest the outcome that is to be prevented. For many children at risk of developing a disability that is due to environmental conditions associated with poverty, this means that they are not served by early intervention or are served later for a more limited time. Most of the children who are in special education programs did not receive early intervention or preschool special education (Barnett, 1988). Despite recent increases in funding for Head Start and other programs for disadvantaged children, these programs remain less well funded than programs for children with disabilities, and they do not serve all of the eligible population. With the provision of early intervention services so limited, a great many of the potential benefits of early intervention are forgone. State and federal governments should be encouraged to serve all children in poverty and to expand eligibility for early intervention to all children at risk of developing a disability as well as those already exhibiting a disability or substantial delay. Policies need to be developed that take into account the overlap between programs targeting children in poverty and programs targeting children with, or at risk of developing, a disability. Further research on risk factors is warranted, although poverty clearly is an important risk factor for current use in policy development.

Despite great progress, much remains to be learned regarding the economics of early intervention. In addition to the topics suggested earlier, useful research on costs and benefits can be conducted on issues ranging from alternative approaches to intervention for children with the most severe disabilities to alternative ways of organizing and paying for early intervention services. Advances in the economics of early intervention will require support from government and other sponsors of early intervention research, but it is not solely the province of academic researchers. State governments can increase their own abilities to examine these issues by refining their administrative data systems to collect information on unit cost of services by program, quality and quantity of services (by child and family), and duration of service and dropout (Are families entering as soon as we would like? Do families leave early intervention because it does not meet their needs? Do families that move find it difficult to re-enroll?). Economic research has demonstrated its usefulness to both policy and practice in the past. Future research can be equally valuable in supporting policy and program improvement if it is based on sound research designs and adheres to accepted economic methods.

REFERENCES

Administration for Children and Families. (1997). *Head Start Statistical Fact Sheet*. Washington, DC: Administration on Children Youth and Families, Administration on Children and Families, Department of Health and Human Services.

American Institutes for Research. (1990). *California's early intervention program (PL 99-457) cost evaluation study*. Palo Alto, CA: Author.

Barnett, W. S. (1986). Methodological issues in economic evaluation of early intervention programs. *Early Childhood Research Quarterly, 1*, 249–68.

Barnett, W. S. (1988). The economics of early intervention under P.L. 99-457. *Topics in Early Childhood Special Education, 8*, 12–23.

Barnett, W. S. (1998a). Long-term cognitive and academic effects of early childhood education on children in poverty. *Preventive Medicine, 27*(2), 204–7.

Barnett, W. S. (1998b). Long-term effects on cognitive development and school success. In W. S. Barnett & S.S. Boocock (Eds.), *Early care and education for children in poverty: Promises, programs, and long-term results* (pp. 11–44). Albany, NY: SUNY Press.

Barnett, W. S. (1993). Benefit-cost analysis of preschool education: Findings from a 25-year follow-up. *American Journal of Orthopsychiatry, 63*(4), 500–8.

Barnett, W. S. (1994). Cost effectiveness and cost-benefit analysis. In W. S. Barnett (Ed.), *Cost analysis for education decisions: Methods and examples* (pp. 257–76). Greenwich, CT: JAI Press.

Barnett, W. S. (1996). *Lives in the balance: Age-27 benefit-cost analysis of the High/Scope Perry Preschool Program*. Ypsilanti, MI: High/Scope Press.

Barnett, W. S., & Boyce, G. C. (1995). Effects of children with Down syndrome on parents' activities. *American Journal on Mental Retardation, 100*(2), 115–27.

Barnett, W. S., & Camilli, G. (in press). Compensatory preschool education, cognitive development, and "race." In J. Fish (Ed.), *Understanding race and intelligence*. Northvale, NJ: Jason Aronson.

Barnett, W. S., Escobar, C. M., & Ravsten, M. (1988). Parent and clinic early intervention for children with language handicaps: A cost-effective analysis. *Journal of the Division for Early Childhood, 12*, 290–8.

Barnett, W. S., Frede, E. C., Hasbrouck, S., Spain, A., & Yarosz, D. (1997). *Early intervention systems study annual report*. New Brunswick, NJ: Rutgers University Graduate School of Education.

Barnett, W. S., & Pezzino, J. (1987). Cost-effectiveness analysis for state and local decision making: An application to half-day and full-day preschool special education programs. *Journal of the Division for Early Childhood, 11*, 171–9.

Berrueta-Clement, J. R., Schweinhart, L. J., Barnett, W. S., Epstein, A. S., & Weikart, D. P. (1984). *Changed lives: The effects of the Perry Preschool program on youths through age 19*. Ypsilanti, MI: High/Scope.

Blair, C., Ramey, C. T., & Hardin, J. M. (1995). Early intervention for low birthweight, premature infants: Participation and intellectual development. *American Journal on Mental Retardation, 99*(5), 542–54.

Boocock, S. S., & Larner, M. (1998). Long-term outcomes in other nations. In W. S. Barnett & S. S. Boocock (Eds.), *Early care and education for children in poverty: Promises, programs, and long-term results* (pp. 45–76). Albany, NY: SUNY Press.

Bristol, M., Reichle, N., & Thomas D. (1987). Changing demographics of the American family: Implications for single-parent families of young handicapped children. *Journal of the Division for Early Childhood, 12*, 56–69.

Bronfenbrenner, U. (1986). Ecology of the family as a context for human development: Research perspectives. *Developmental Psychology, 22*, 723–42.

Bureau of Economic Analysis. (1996a). *The national income and product accounts of the United States: Statistical tables.* Washington, DC: U.S. Government Printing Office.

Bureau of Economic Analysis. (1996b, November). *Survey of current business.* Washington, DC: Author, U.S. Department of Commerce.

Burkett, C. W. (1982). Effects of frequency of home visits on achievement of preschool students in a home-based early childhood education program. *Journal of Educational Research, 76,* 41–4.

Campbell, F. A., & Ramey, C. T. (1995). Cognitive and school outcomes for high-risk African-American students in middle adolescence: Positive effects of early intervention. *American Educational Research Journal, 32*(4), 743–72.

Campbell, F. A., & Ramey, C. T. (1994). Effects of early intervention on intellectual and academic achievement: A follow-up study of children from low-income families. *Child Development, 65,* 684–98.

Casto, G., & Mastropieri, M. A. (1986). The efficacy of early intervention programs: A meta-analysis. *Exceptional Children, 52,* 417–24.

Clarke, S. W., & Campbell, F. A. (1997, April). *The Abecedarian Project and youth crime.* Paper presented at the biennial meeting of the Society for Research in Child Development, Washington, DC.

Coakley, T. (1995, November 15). A profile of Part H program costs in 19 states. NEC*TAS Part H Update, p. 35.

Coelen, C., Glantz, F., & Calore, D. (1979). *Day care centers in the U.S.A.: National profile 1977-1977.* Cambridge, MA: Abt Associates.

Consortium for Longitudinal Studies. (1983). *As the twig is bent.* Hillsdale, NJ: Erlbaum.

Dunlap, W. R., & Hollinsworth, J. S. (1977). How does a handicapped child affect the family? Implications for practitioners. *The Family Coordinator, 26,* 286–93.

Dunst, C. J. (1986). Overview of the efficacy of early intervention programs. In L. Bickman & D. L. Weatherford (Eds.), *Evaluating early intervention programs for severely handicapped children and their families* (pp. 79–147). Austin, TX: Pro-Ed.

Erickson, M. (1992). An analysis of early intervention expenditures in Massachusetts. *American Journal on Mental Retardation, 96*(6), 617–29.

Escobar, C. M., & Barnett, W. S. (1986, October). *Benefit-cost analysis of the Abecedarian preschool program.* Paper presented at the Council for Exceptional Children, Division of Early Childhood Annual National Conference, Louisville, KY.

Escobar, C. M., & Barnett, W. S. (1994). Early childhood special education. In W. S. Barnett (Ed.), *Cost analysis for education decisions: Methods and examples* (pp. 183–202). Greenwich, CT: JAI Press.

Escobar, C. M., Peterson, A., Lauritzen, V., & Barnett, W. S.

(1987). *Transportation options and costs for preschool special education in Utah* (Report to the Utah State Office of Education). Logan: Utah State University, Early Intervention Research Institute.

Fewell, R. R., & Scott, K. G. (1997). Cost of implementing the intervention. In R. T. Gross, D. Spiker, & C. W. Haynes (Eds.), *Helping low birth weight, premature babies: The Infant Health and Development Program* (pp. 479–504). Stanford, CA: Stanford University Press.

Frede, E. C. (1998). Preschool program quality in programs for children in poverty. In W. S. Barnett & S. S. Boocock (Eds.), *Early care and education for children in poverty: Promises, programs, and long-term results* (pp. 77–98). Albany, NY: SUNY Press.

Goetze, L. D., & Yang, Y. N. (1997, July). *The long-term effects of alternative types of early intervention on public school services.* Paper presented at the annual meetings of the Western Economics Association, Seattle.

Gramlich, E. M. (1981). *Benefit-cost analysis of government programs.* Englewood Cliffs, NJ: Prentice-Hall.

Gross, R. T., Spiker, D., & Haynes, C. W. (Eds.). (1997). *Helping low birth weight, premature babies: The Infant Health and Development Program.* Stanford, CA: Stanford University Press.

Grubb, W. N. (1987). *Young children face the states: Issues and options for early childhood programs.* Center for Policy Research in Education (CPRE) Joint Note. New Brunswick, NJ: Rutgers, Eagleton Institute of Politics, CPRE.

Guralnick, M. J. (Ed.). (1997). *The effectiveness of early intervention.* Baltimore, MD: Paul H. Brookes.

Guralnick, M. J., & Bennett, F. C. (Eds.). (1987). *The effectiveness of early intervention for at-risk and handicapped children.* Orlando, FL: Academic Press.

Haveman, R. H., & Wolfe, B. L. (1984). Schooling and economic well-being: The role of nonmarket effects. *Journal of Human Resources, 19,* 377–407.

Helburn, S. W., & Howes, C. (1996). Child care cost and quality. *The Future of Children, 6*(2), 62–82.

Hofferth, S. L. (1996). Child care in the United States today. *The Future of Children, 6*(2), 41–61.

Kagan, S. L., Powell, D. R., Weissbourd, B., & Zigler, E. F. (Eds.). (1987). *America's family support programs: The state of the art.* New Haven, CT: Yale University Press.

Kagitcibasi, C. (1996). *Family and human development across cultures.* Hillsdale, NJ: Erlbaum.

Kakalik, J. S., Furry, W. S., Thomas, M. A., & Carney, M. F. (1981). *The cost of special education* (Report No. N-1792-ED). Santa Monica, CA: The Rand Corporation.

Kitzman, H., Olds, D., Henderson, C., Hanks, C., Cole, R., Tatelbaum, R., McConnochie, K., Sidora, K., Luckey, D., Shaver, D., Engelhardt, K., James, D., & Barnard, K. (1997). Effect of prenatal and infancy home visitation by nurses on pregnancy outcomes, childhood injuries, and repeated childbearing in low-income families:

a randomized controlled trial. *Journal of the American Medical Association, 278*(8), 644–52.

Kysela, G., & Marfo, K. (1983). Mother-child interactions and early intervention programmes for handicapped infants and young children. *Educational Psychology, 3,* 201–12.

Lally, J. R., Mangione, P. L., & Honig, A. S. (1988). The Syracuse University Family Development Program: Long-range impact of an early intervention with low-income children and their families. In D. Powell (Ed.), *Parent education as early childhood intervention: Emerging directions in theory, research, and practice* (pp. 79–104). Norwood, NJ: Ablex.

Levin, H. (1983). *Cost-effectiveness: A primer.* Beverly Hills, CA: Sage.

Love, J., Nauta, M., Coelen, C., Hewlett, K., & Ruopp, R. (1976). *National Home Start evaluation final report: Findings and implications.* Cambridge, MA: Abt Associates.

McCarton, C. M., Brooks-Gunn, J., Wallarce, I. F., Bauer, C. R., Bennett, F. C., Bernbaum, J. C., Broyles, S., Casey, P. H., McCormick, M. C., Scott, D. T., Tyson, J., Tonascia, J., & Meinert, C. L. (1997). Results at age 8 years of early intervention for low-birth-weight premature infants. *Journal of the American Medical Association, 277*(2), 126–32.

Meisels, S. J., Dichtelmiller, M., & Liaw, F. R. (1993). A multidimensional analysis of early childhood intervention programs. In C. H. Zeanah (Ed.), *Handbook of infant mental health* (pp. 361–85). New York: Guilford Press.

Myers, R. G. (1992). *The twelve who survive: strengthening programmes of early childhood development in the Third World.* London: Routledge.

Olds, D., Henderson, C., Phelps, C., Kitzman, H., & Hanks, C. (1993). Effect of prenatal care and infancy nurse home visitation on government spending. *Medical Care, 31*(2), 155–74.

Olds, D., Eckenrode, J., Henderson, C., Kitzman, H., Powers, J., Cole, R., Sidora, K., Morris, P., Pettitt, L. M., & Luckey, D. (1997). Long-term effects of home visitation on maternal life course, child abuse and neglect: Fifteen-year follow-up of a randomized trial. *Journal of the American Medical Association, 278*(8), 637–43.

Parrish, T. (1990). *Nebraska Financing Study, PL 99-457: Part H, EHA.* Palo Alto, CA: American Institutes for Research.

Ramey, C. T., & Ramey, S. L. (1998). Prevention of intellectual disabilities: Early interventions to improve cognitive development. *Preventive Medicine, 27*(2), 224–32.

Reynolds, A. J. (1997, April). *Long-term effects of the Chicago Child–Parent Center Program through age 15.* Paper presented at the biennial meeting of the Society for Research in Child Development, Washington, DC.

Rule, S., Stowitschek, J., Innocenti, M., Striefel, S., Killoran, J., Swezey, K., & Boswell, C. (1987). The Social Integration Program: An analysis of the effects of mainstreaming handicapped children into day care centers. *Education and Treatment of Children, 10,* 175–92.

Ruopp, R., Travers, J., Glantz, F., & Coelen, C. (1979). *Children at the center: Summary findings and policy implications of the National Day Care Study.* Cambridge, MA: Abt Associates.

Sameroff, A. J. (1983). Developmental and theory systems: Contexts and evolution. In P. Mussen (Ed.), *Handbook of child psychology: Vol. I. History, theory, and methods* (pp. 263–88). New York: Wiley.

Schweinhart, L. J., Barnes, H. V., Weikart, D. P., Barnett, W. S., & Epstein, A. S. (1993). *Significant benefits: The High/Scope Perry Preschool study through age 27.* Ypsilanti, MI: High/Scope Press.

Schweinhart, L. J., & Weikart, D. P. (1996). *Lasting differences: The High/Scope Preschool Comparison Study through age 23.* Ypsilanti, MI: High/Scope Press.

Seitz, V., Rosenbaum, L. K., & Apfel, N. H. (1985). Effects of family support intervention: A 10-year follow-up. *Child Development, 56,* 376–91.

Shonkoff, J. P., & Hauser-Cram, P. (1987). Early intervention for disabled infants and their families: A quantitative analysis. *Pediatrics, 80,* 650–8.

Shonkoff, J. P., Hauser-Cram, P. Krauss, M. W., & Upshur, C. C. (1992). Development of infants with disabilities and their families: Implications for theory and service delivery. *Monographs of the Society for Research in Child Development, 57*(6, Serial No. 230).

St. Pierre, R. G., Layzer, J. I., & Barnes, H. V. (1995). Two-generation programs: Design, cost, and short-term effectiveness. *The Future of Children, 5*(3), 76–93.

Stock, J. R., Wnek, L. L., Newborg, J. A., Schenck, E. A., Gabel, J. R., Spurgeon, M. S., & Ray, H. W. (1976). *Evaluation of the Handicapped Children's Early Education Program.* Columbus, OH: Battelle Memorial Institute.

Tarr, J. E. (1997). *A cost analysis of Part H early intervention services in New Jersey. Dissertation Proposal.* New Brunswick: Rutgers Graduate School of Education.

Thompson, M. A. (1980). *Benefit-cost analysis for program evaluation.* Beverly Hills, CA: Sage.

Verzaro-O'Brien, M., Powell, G., & Sakamoto, L. (1996). *Investing in quality revisited: The impact of the Head Start Expansion and Improvement Act of 1990 after five years of implementation.* Alexandria, VA: National Head Start Association.

Weikart, D. P., Kamii, C. K., & Radin, N. L. (1967). Perry Preschool Project progress report. In D. P. Weikart (Ed.), *Preschool intervention: A preliminary report of the Perry Preschool Project* (pp. 1–61). Ann Arbor, MI: Campus Publishers.

Weiss, R. S. (1981). INREAL intervention for language handicapped and bilingual children. *Journal of the Division for Early Childhood, 4,* 40–51.

Weiss, R. S., & Heublein, E. A. (1981). Colorado school district INREAL experimental study. In B. A. McNulty, D. B. Smith, & E. W. Soper (Eds.), *Effectiveness of early special education for handicapped children* (Appendix). Denver: Colorado Department of Education.

Weissbourd, B. (1983). The family support movement: Greater than the sum of its parts. *Zero to Three, 4,* 8–10.

White, K. R., & Boyce, G. C. (Eds.). (1993). Special Issue: Comparative evaluations of early intervention alternatives. *Early Education and Development, 4*(4), 221–378.

Zervigon-Hakes, A., Graham, M., & Hall, J. (1991). *Florida's cost implementation study for Public Law 99-457, Part H, Infants and Toddlers. Phase II findings.* Tallahassee, FL: Center for Prevention and Early Intervention Policy, Florida State University.

Zigler, E. F., & Finn-Stevenson, M. (1996). Funding child care and public education. *The Future of Children, 6*(2), 104–21.

PART SEVEN

NEW DIRECTIONS FOR THE TWENTY-FIRST CENTURY

CHAPTER TWENTY-SIX

Early Childhood Intervention Policies:

An International Perspective

SHEILA B. KAMERMAN

The United States is known worldwide for its leadership role in child development theory and research. Included in this is considerable theory and research about early intervention. The United States is also well-known for its laggard status in the development of proactive and preventive child policies. In contrast, the European countries do not announce new theories of effective intervention, nor do they emphasize intervention research. There is not much discussion of the value of early intervention, and what there is seems borrowed from the United States. Nonetheless, many European countries have been at the forefront of promoting what in the United States would be considered early intervention through the design and implementation of social policies that embody the concept. Family policies, generally, and parental leave, child care, home-health visiting, and family support policies and programs, in particular, are illustrations of these developments. Apart from those programs traditionally thought of in the United States as early intervention, the Europeans have developed also, for a variety of reasons, an elaborate social policy infrastructure, including income transfers, health care, and housing assistance, that provides a strong foundation for those policies targeted on young children and their families. This whole policy and program "package" also appears to reduce the need for treatment services and crisis interventions (Kamerman & Kahn, 1988, 1989, 1995).

In this chapter I contrast the U.S. and European perspectives on early intervention, describe the main European early intervention policies, and refer to other elements of their social policy infrastructure. Finally, I offer some concluding comments about what these policies have achieved.

EARLY INTERVENTION POLICIES: CONTRASTING PERSPECTIVES

Early childhood intervention, as defined by Shonkoff and Meisels, consists of "multidisciplinary services provided for developmentally vulnerable or disabled children form birth to age 3 years and their families" (Meisels & Shonkoff, 1990, p. xvi). Over the last two decades of the twentieth century, this concept has become increasingly popular in the United States, whether among child development psychologists convinced of the importance of the first few years of life (Brooks-Gunn, 1995; Kagan, 1996; Zigler & Styfco, 1993, 1996), pediatricians and public health experts concerned with healthy development (Behrman, 1994, 1995; Hamburg, 1992; Krugman, 1993) or social workers (Guterman, 1997), early childhood educators (Campbell & Ramey, 1994; Lally et al., 1995; Young, 1996), and others concerned with alleviating the problems of troubled families (Carnegie Task Force, 1994; Harris, 1996; Sawhill, 1993). The concept of intervening early in the life cycle to prevent later problems has become almost conventional wisdom.

Several legislative initiatives enacted during these years reflect this conviction, targeting high-risk and vulnerable young children and their families (U.S. House of Representatives [USHR], Committee on Ways and Means, 1996, 1998). For example, in the mid- and late 1980s, Congress expanded Medicaid coverage for poor, pregnant women and young children under age 6 (and later phased in coverage for all poor children beginning with those born in September 1983). Federal legislation enacted in 1993 provided funding for family support services, going beyond the provisions of the earlier P.L. 99-457, which established a new discretionary program (Part H, now known as Part C) for states to facilitate the development of early intervention services for infants and toddlers with developmental delays or disabilities. With the reauthorization of Head Start in 1993, significant attention was given to expanding coverage of children under 3 in addition to the 3- to 4-year-olds – the primary participants – in the program.

A Carnegie Corporation Task Force report (1994) stressed the importance of intervening in the early years, identifying and recommending effective strategies for preventing problems, and promoting healthy child development. However, this report went beyond a focus on high-risk and vulnerable children to include all young children. A report on recent brain research (Shore, 1997) underscored the importance and efficacy of prevention and early intervention, once again stressing the universality of the findings. The report pointed out how the quality of care that young children receive affects how they develop subsequently, their ability to learn, and their capacity to control their emotions. A major dissemination effort has been underway to bring this information to all parents. Our own research (Kamerman & Kahn, 1995) on the need for policy attention to 3-year-olds and under and "lesson-learning" from relevant European policies culminated in the book *Starting Right: How Americans Neglect Their Youngest Children and What We Can Do About It*. Its major focus is the importance of the early years, the value of early intervention, and the universal policies and programs that exist in other countries that facilitate positive and early interventions.

Clearly, awareness of the importance of the first 3 years of life is growing in the United States, at least with regard to the importance of prenatal care, maternal and child health care, prevention of developmental disabilities, preparation for school, and prevention of child abuse and severe neglect. Nevertheless, other developments during the 1990s in the United States suggest that this knowledge has not been integrated into public policy or into the discussions of decision makers.

Public awareness of the implications of recent research documenting the importance of the early years for optimal physical, emotional, social, and cognitive development of all children and the cost-effectiveness of early intervention is still inadequate. For example, recent research has strongly emphasized the negative consequences of poverty for young children (Chase-Lansdale & Brooks-Gunn, 1995; Duncan & Brooks-Gunn, 1997; Duncan, Brooks-Gunn, & Klebanov, 1994; Huston, 1991). Yet children in the United States are more likely to be poor than children in nineteen other major industrialized countries (Rainwater & Smeeding, 1995; Smeeding, 1997). Moreover, the younger the children are, the more likely they are to be poor in the United States, although the reverse is true in most of Europe (Kamerman & Kahn, 1995). Nor is there a policy response in the United States. Infant mortality rates remain far higher in the United States than those in other countries, whereas immunization rates for preschoolers are still relatively lower in the United States (UNICEF, 1997). Here, too, the policy response has been inadequate. Access to health care is still not assured to all young children and their mothers (Kamerman & Kahn, 1996). The recently enacted welfare legislation (The Omnibus Personal Responsibility and Work Opportunity Reconciliation Act of 1996) requires women receiving assistance to be ready for work outside the home when their children are aged 1 and older; it also permits states to require that these women go to work when their babies are as young as 13 weeks (Kamerman & Kahn, 1996, 1996/1997, 1997). Despite the increased funding for child care, the legislation offers little protection for the quality of care infants and toddlers will receive while their mothers are at work.

Thus, despite the growing knowledge base underscoring the importance of the early years, early childhood intervention policies in the United States remain limited, often inconsistent, and at best are narrowly targeted on children who are at high risk of developmental delays and their families. Despite a rhetoric of comprehensiveness, the interventions stress services rather than income and community-based strategies rather than national policies and aim at preventing problems rather than enhancing development (Kamerman & Kahn, 1990, 1995). Moreover, they are often only demonstration projects.

Early childhood intervention is not yet a slogan in the other advanced industrialized countries. Yet many countries invest in what Americans would view as early childhood interventions (albeit not explicitly labeled as such). These investments are far greater in several countries than in the United States and reflect a very different perspective. Among the European countries, only Britain focuses primarily on "children in need" or "children at risk" (Gaskins, 1993; Pugh, 1992). The British Children Act of 1989, implemented in 1991, clearly reflects this focus, stressing interventions targeted on children with special needs (Gaskins, 1993). In contrast to a focus on vulnerable, deprived, and high-risk populations, the other major OECD countries (Organization for Economic Cooperation and Development established in 1961 and based in Paris) stressed a universal thrust. These countries have enacted policies targeting all children rather than concentrating on particular problem categories. The OECD countries include the advanced industrialized countries of Europe plus Japan and Korea. In 1997, with the recent addition of the Czech Republic, Hungary, and Poland, there were twenty-nine member countries in the OECD. Many stress a developmental orientation and try to ensure optimum development rather than limiting their goals to the prevention of problems.

Finally, in contrast to an emphasis on a services strategy, most other industrialized Western countries stress a more comprehensive policy and program package, one that includes economic and financial support as well as services. When fully developed, the European early intervention strategy includes three essential components: adequate family income, sufficient time for parenting, and supportive and care services (Kamerman & Kahn, 1994a,b 1995). Thus, in addition to maternal and child health care, child care, and other supportive and treatment services, these countries provide generous financial help and extensive paid and job-protected leaves from work for employed parents with child-related needs. It is this tripartite early childhood intervention policy package of money, time, and services that is described in the next section.

EARLY CHILDHOOD INTERVENTIONS IN EUROPE

Brooks-Gunn (1995) pointed out that the three most important types of early childhood interventions in the United States are home-visiting programs, center-based child-care programs, and parent education and training programs. She also noted that "the goal of most programs for young poor children is not one of eradicating poverty. Instead, services are provided in order to ameliorate the effects of poverty on children" (p. 107). The first two are important early childhood interventions in several other countries, too, as are parent support and education, but parent-work-training programs are not thought of this way in other countries (although perhaps they should be). At least as important elsewhere, however, are income transfer programs that assure incomes above the poverty threshold, compensate parents somewhat for the costs of child rearing, assure parents time off from work to care for a new baby (or an ill one), and provide support for parents adjusting to the arrival of a new baby (Kamerman & Kahn, 1995).

Income Transfers

As already indicated, there is extensive research now that highlights the negative consequences for children of living in poverty, especially when they are young (Chase-Lansdale & Brooks-Gunn, 1995; Duncan & Brooks-Gunn, 1997; Duncan, Brooks-Gunn, & Klebanov, 1994; Huston, 1991). Despite this well-documented finding, the economic situation of children is far worse in the United States than in the other major industrialized countries and especially so with regard to children in lone-mother families (Rainwater & Smeeding, 1995; Smeeding, 1997). A higher proportion of children live in lone-mother families in the United States than elsewhere, and this is certainly a contributing factor to higher U.S. child poverty rates, but it is not the major factor. As recent research has found, the major factor leading to higher rates of child poverty in the United States is inadequate government policies, in particular the inadequacy of welfare payments, the most important government income transfer targeted on poor children and their families (Hernandez, 1993; USHR, Committee on Ways and Means, 1993). Welfare for poor families was first enacted in 1935 as Aid to Dependent Children, a provision of the original Social Security Act. Benefits were provided to the children of selected poor single mothers but not to their mothers until 1950; the title of the program was changed to Aid to Families with Dependent Children (AFDC) in 1962, and Temporary Assistance to Needy Families (TANF) in 1996. The real value of AFDC benefits declined between the mid-1970s and early 1990s by more than 40%, as inflation occurred and benefit levels were cut or remained level. Even when coupled with Food Stamps (the federal benefit that is indexed to inflation), the total benefit package declined in real value by about 30%, leaving the children in those mother-only families needing assistance far more likely to be poor.

In contrast, which policies account for the lower child poverty rates in these other countries? Rainwater and Smeeding (1995) found that "broadly similar child poverty problems face most advanced national governments. What differs is national governments' abilities to address these problems" (p. 16). Using a measure that defines poverty as income below 50% of the median, and acknowledging that children in lone-mother families always do less well than those living with both parents, Rainwater and Smeeding concluded that

most societies provide a mix of tax and transfer benefits that, when coupled with market earnings, reduce child poverty to very low levels. But not all nations do so well. In particular, the overall high rate of both pre- and post-government poverty in the United states is troubling. (p. 18)

It is especially troubling when one recognizes that this pattern continues despite much higher unemployment rates throughout Europe.

Among the most important income transfers protecting the economic situation of families with children, especially during periods of economic recession, are the generous unemployment benefits provided to qualified workers. These benefits are part of the social infrastructure in the European countries that also help children living in families with an unemployed head of household (Smeeding, 1997). In most of Europe, unemployment insurance benefits (UIB) include dependents' benefits too. In the United States, UIB are provided at a very low level and for a far shorter period of time than in Europe. Moreover, only ten states provide dependents' benefits along with UIB. Several other countries provide unemployment assistance as well – a means-tested benefit available when low-income, unemployed workers have exhausted their insurance benefits (Bradshaw et al., 1993; Eardley et al., 1996; Kahn & Kamerman, 1983). In addition, there are important child-specific income transfers that play a significant role as well. The most important are briefly described here.

CHILD OR FAMILY ALLOWANCES. Cash benefits provided to families based on the presence and number of children, regardless of family income, are provided in some eighty-six countries around the world, about half of all countries (United States Social Security Administration, 1997). Although the financial significance of these benefits varies across nations, all industrialized countries except the United States and South Africa, and even many less developed countries, supplement family incomes to take into account the economic costs of rearing children.

The rationale for providing these benefits varies among the countries (Kamerman & Kahn, 1995, 1998). Some hope that the benefits will encourage parents to have more children, whereas others view this as an investment in improved "child quality" (an "investment in human capital"). Still others aim at reducing the gap between wages and family needs without burdening employers. Regardless, all recognize that bearing and rearing children carries an economic burden. These cash benefits, usually in the form of a flat rate for each minor child, generally constitute about 5 to 10% of a country's average wage in manufacturing for one child but amount to a significantly larger share of family income for large families or families headed by lone mothers or young parents who are likely to earn less. Countries often supplement the basic allowance for children with disabilities; some countries provide additional income-tested supplements for low-income families. All of these child and family benefits are far more important to families than tax allowances (e.g., the dependents' exemption in the United States) because they are available whether or not families have taxable income (Kahn & Kamerman, 1983). The poverty reduction impact may be modest, but nonetheless it is present (Kamerman & Kahn, 1997; Rainwater & Smeeding, 1995; Smeeding, 1997).

Most European countries also provide a guaranteed minimum child support benefit (a payment of child support or child maintenance by a government agency) for those children growing up in lone-parent families when their noncustodial parent fails to provide financial child support or provides it irregularly or not at all (Kahn & Kamerman, 1988). Under such circumstances, the society assumes responsibility for providing a basic level of support because it has a vested interest in protecting the well-being of children, regardless of their parents' behavior. A government agency enforces parental payment of support when the absent parent is able to pay, but the child is not penalized by the father's incapacity or irresponsibility. Some countries (e.g., Germany and Austria) phased in this policy by beginning with younger children.

Many countries provide various kinds of housing subsidies for families with children (Bradshaw, Ditch, Holmes, & Whiteford, 1993; Kahn & Kamerman, 1983). Housing allowances are cash benefits that cover part of the cost of housing and are provided on an income-tested basis. In contrast to the U.S. policy of providing a tax deduction for the payment of interest on mortgages, these benefits are a key policy in assuring modest income families access to decent housing, including rental housing. Given the dramatic rise in housing costs during the 1980s and 1990s throughout the industrialized countries, such a benefit achieves this goal without creating a crushing economic burden for families with children.

Children cannot have a decent start in life without some protection against the risk of being born into poverty. Most other advanced industrialized countries recognize this and have enacted policies that protect children against such risk. Whether stemming from a child-, family-, or individual-focused policy, this protection against being born into poverty is among the most important of the European early intervention policies, even if not explicitly labeled as such. Even when unemployment rates are high, as they were in France and Germany during the 1990s, the government social protection system still functions as a basic safety net for children and their families, and the society at large continues to assure political support. Protection against income poverty may not be sufficient, by itself, to assure children of a good start in life, but clearly it is a precondition if other early intervention policies are to be effective.

Time

In addition to receiving economic protection and security, for children to develop well, they need an opportunity to begin their lives with a parent who has the time to relate to them and care for them (Kamerman & Kahn, 1991, 1995). The ongoing caretaker, father or mother, needs time to provide physical care, to learn and understand the baby's signals, and to respond and talk to the baby. A newborn is best protected physically and developmentally if his or her earliest months are at home with a parent or other consistent caregiver. Mothers need time for physical and emotional recovery after pregnancy and childbirth, fathers need time to learn what their babies are all about, and both need time to learn how to become nurturing parents.

Throughout the advanced industrialized world, mothers are increasingly likely to be in the labor force (Bradshaw et al., 1996; Ditch, Barnes, & Bradshaw, 1996a, 1996b; Ditch, Barnes, Bradshaw, Commaille, & Eardley, 1995a, 1995b; Ditch, Barnes, & Kilkey, 1997a, 1997b; European Commission Network on Childcare, 1996; Kamerman & Kahn, 1995). Although female labor force participation rates are higher in some countries than in others, the U.S. pattern (63% of mothers of children under age 6 were in the labor force in 1997, and 60% of those with children under age 3) is not unique. Canada, France, and Norway have similar rates; there are countries with far higher rates as well. For example, about 85% of mothers of preschool-aged children in Denmark, Finland, and Sweden are in the labor force.

Most other countries have recognized the changes that have occurred in gender roles and have initiated policies in response. More than 100 countries around the world, including almost all of the major industrialized nations and many developing countries as well, provide a paid and job protected leave to employed mothers following childbirth or adoption (Ditch et al., 1995a, 1995b; European Commission Network on Child Care, 1994; Kamerman & Kahn, 1991, 1995; USSSA, 1997). The typical leave in Europe is six months. Several countries have enacted extended parental leaves of one year (Italy), one to one and a half years (Denmark, Sweden), and two or three years (Austria, Finland, and Germany). With wages replaced in full or part, or a flat-rate cash benefit provided, family income is protected while parents have time off from work to adjust to and care for a new baby. Canada provides a six-month paid leave, available in part to fathers as well as mothers.

The European Union has mandated a three-month paid maternity leave as the absolute minimum and is urging provision of another three months as a parental leave benefit. (If not for British objections, this parental leave would have been a requirement as well. The British Labour Party has recently announced that it will support this policy when it is next brought up.) All countries assume that women will be in the labor force throughout all or almost all of their pregnancies and that they will return to work after a brief hiatus at home, caring for their new baby (or sharing that care with their husband/partner). Parents who take time off from work after childbirth not only have their jobs and income protected but also have seniority, fringe benefits, and pension entitlements protected while on leave as well.

The Swedish parenting policy is an exemplar. It provides an 18-month, job-protected parental leave that includes one year paid by a cash "parent insurance" benefit (a social insurance benefit) worth 80% of prior wages, three months paid at a modest flat rate, and three months that are unpaid but job protected (Ditch et al., 1995a, 1995b; Kamerman, forthcoming; Kamerman & Kahn, 1994a,b, 1995). Almost half of the eligible fathers make some use of the leave, although mothers continue to make greater use. Swedish policy also provides parents the right to paid time off from work if a child is ill and paid time off from work to accompany a child to school for the first time or to visit a child's school.

All countries share a common goal in establishing these policies: support for parental care for young children at home for some time following childbirth – making infant care by a parent a viable option for those who wish it, while protecting family income against significant loss as a result. The results are clear. Take-up rates of parental leaves by working parents are extraordinarily high wherever such policies exist, and the demand for infant care is therefore reduced. Even in countries in which high proportions of mothers of infants are in the labor force, as in all the Nordic countries, infants are cared for,

primarily, by a parent at home. Swedish fathers, as a result of their country's parental leave policy, spend more time with their young children than fathers in any other country. Assuring babies adequate time and attention from their working parents is a second important early intervention policy.

Services

HEALTH CARE AND HOME HEALTH VISITING. All European nations (as well as Australia, New Zealand, Canada, and Japan) and several somewhat less developed countries (e.g., South Korea and Taiwan) have either national health services or national health insurance systems as the foundation for child and family health care and the base on which preventive child health services are developed (USA, 1997). Such physical and social health services are viewed as one component of the larger cluster of economic and social supports provided by government to families with children. Preventive child health services are delivered through two interrelated components: what in the United States are called "well-baby" clinics or services and home health visiting services. The well-baby clinic/service may be either freestanding or a service provided by the family's primary care physician. The clinic service usually lasts until the child reaches school age, when the school health service then takes over. In cases in which the family physician is the main provider, the service continues indefinitely.

The home health visiting service (HHV) may be a service that is linked to the clinic, physician, or local social service agency (Kamerman & Kahn, 1994, 1995). The service may be limited to the time immediately after childbirth, may cover the baby's first year of life, or continue throughout the early years. All such services are voluntary, free, and cover all new babies, not just those born to poor or low-income parents. Although the United States has such services, they are neither free nor do they cover all young children (Behrman, 1993; Gomby, Culross, & Behrman, 1999). Indeed, although all poor babies are supposed to have access to health care, they do not. Although HHV services have become increasingly popular in the United States, few states can claim full coverage for even one visit.

In Denmark, Ireland, Great Britain, and the Netherlands, in addition to universal health care, nearly all newborns and their mothers are visited at home by a public health nurse at least several times during the first year (Kamerman & Kahn, 1993, 1995; Williams & Miller, 1991). In several other countries, mandatory visits are limited to one or two following childbirth, but additional visits are provided on a discretionary basis, and there is no "cap" on these visits if they are deemed necessary. Despite growing concern about limited resources to expend on social programs in many European countries, HHV programs continue to be universal (available to all families) in all of these countries. They are popular, generously supported, and viewed as effective.

Every country that provides HHV services focuses its programs on children under the age of 3. The services include preventive care, health education, and social support services, including parent education. The HHV also links the family, as needed, to health care, income transfer programs, child care services, housing, assistance, and access to other social services. All of the countries offering the service see the home locus as essential for effective early intervention. Programs vary across nations as to whether the focus is on all families with a new baby or on particular categories of vulnerable families (e.g., those with first babies, very young or much older mothers, and minority or immigrant families), whether visits begin prenatally or only after birth, whether visits are supplemented by support groups, and the frequency of the visits.

HHV services are designed to meet both health and social objectives: to help produce an optimally developed young child. The HHV's primary focus is to ensure that the baby develops normally, that the mother knows and understands what normal development is and what to expect of her child at different ages and stages of development, that the mother and father feel competent in their maternal/paternal/parenting roles, and that if help is needed it is readily available. This is particularly important for first-time mothers/parents who increasingly come to parenting with little prior experience or exposure to young children.

Initially, the HHV service was begun as a strategy for identifying problems and lags in a child's physical, emotional, cognitive, and social development, carrying out regular examinations of children, and ensuring that they obtain essential inoculations in timely fashion. In both Britain and Denmark, for example, the countries with the most comprehensive programs, the service began in response to concerns about high infant mortality rates and interest in assuring access to good medical care for poor high-risk populations (Danish National Health Service, 1970; Goodwin, 1990a, 1990b). Over time, as national health care systems were established and community-based health care clinics became more available, the definition of *health* was broadened. Program goals shifted from the narrowly health-oriented toward a broader social focus (Goodwin, 1990a, 1990b; USHR Select Committee, 1990).

In recent years, although the health orientation of HHV has continued, there is less emphasis on monitoring health problems. Instead, there is a growing stress on detecting social problems (e.g., child abuse or neglect, developmental lags, inadequate parenting, or maternal difficulties such as postpartum depression) and linking parents with the local health clinic. HHVs offer treatment or referrals, as appropriate, for children, mothers, or other family members. Similar to all professionals working with children and their families, HHVs must report incidents of child abuse to the appropriate authorities. However, they are not involved in the investigation of these situations nor in subsequent court proceedings; if they occur, protective service social workers perform this role.

In recent years, family-focused goals have increasingly emerged as equally important to child health goals. HHVs are now trained to be more knowledgeable about children's social and emotional development and are more skilled in helping parents to enhance their parenting roles. In Britain and Denmark, there is increased emphasis on the goals of "empowering" mothers: providing family support, educating parents about their children's needs and developmental patterns, helping parents to have more realistic expectations regarding their children's behavior, and providing parents with referrals to needed services. In this way, HHVs help mothers and fathers to be more effective parents.

In contrast to the emphasis in the United States on formal summative evaluations of policy and program interventions, there are no formal evaluations of HHV services in either Britain or Denmark. Nonetheless, in 1970, a Danish report concluded that HHV services were both effective and viewed positively by the public (Danish National Health

Service, 1970). However, if priorities are to be set, this and subsequent reports recommended that efforts should be concentrated on "homes with a first child and on the about 15% of the families in which the children are either not quite well or are living under conditions which may influence their physical and/or mental development" (p. i). This is not meant to eliminate universal coverage, however. Instead, the finding led to a subsequent curtailment of first year visits from twelve to about six, with more frequent visits to families with first children or those living in situations requiring special attention. HHV remains universal.

In Britain, too, despite the absence of rigorous evaluation studies, policy makers view HHV as an effective intervention (Goodwin, 1990a, 1990b). There is evidence that accidental deaths within the home can be reduced significantly by health information and education strategies provided by HHVs. Another study reported by Goodwin concluded that HHV is an effective way to empower parents. Finally, HHVs play an important role in assuring immunization. By 1989, 87% of 2-year-olds were immunized against the major childhood diseases, a significant increase in previous rates and a result attributable in no small part to the work of HHVs.

HHV is viewed as an effective preventive service. For example, inadequate parenting of a young baby is often linked to maternal depression, a problem that HHVs are especially sensitive to. Apart from referring mothers with severe depression for treatment, HHVs may also offer increased visits and support to mothers who would appear to need and benefit from extra help. Similarly, child abuse is often linked to parents' unrealistic expectations of their young children, and it is within this context that HHV is explicitly designed to educate and inform parents about how their child is developing, what to expect, and how to prepare for new stages. Moreover, of particular importance, HHVs are increasingly organizing mother–baby and parent groups that breach the social isolation of mothers with young children and provide support and companionship. In Britain and Denmark, despite the absence of formal evaluations, officials believe that all of these characteristics of HHV reduce child abuse and neglect.

Policy scholars and decision makers in Britain and Denmark also point to data on low rates of infant mortality, high rates of prenatal care, low rates of low birth weight, and high rates of early and timely immunizations as evidence of the success of their overall maternal and child health system. HHV is viewed as a key part of this system but not as a discrete intervention.

There is widespread conviction in Europe that, despite their effectiveness, HHV programs are but one piece of an essential network of economic and social supports provided by the government to families. The achievement of child health goals requires not only access to health services but also economic support, housing supports, child care services, parental leaves, and social services as needed by the family. In essence, HHV and other child health-related policies and programs are integral to and interdependent with the other elements of social policy for children and their families. These are the basic building blocks which together provide the social infrastructure for supplementary interventions for children and families with special needs (Goodwin, 1990a, 1990b; Manciaux, Jestin, Fritz, & Bertrand, 1990; Verbrugge, 1990; Wagner, 1990). Without such an infrastructure, it is believed that HHV would be just one more program, perhaps effective for some, but plagued by many gaps and deficits. There is the danger that implementation of HHV without these broader systems in place will be seen as a general panacea and divert attention from the need to progress on a broader child and family policy front. It is generally feared that HHV will disappoint because case finding – the identification of problems – will not necessarily ensure the availability of treatment and other service resources.

CHILD CARE SERVICES. In the United States, when the concept of early intervention is applied to child care or to early childhood care and education, as the field is sometimes called, Head Start is the focal point. Head Start has become a world-renowned exemplar of effective early intervention for the problems of young children. Head Start is a compensatory education program that was launched in 1965 at the onset of the War on Poverty, first as a summer program and then as an all-year, part-day preschool program for poor children, with links to health care and other social services. Initially targeted to 5-year-olds, almost all children of this age now attend kindergarten, largely under public auspices. By now, the program's major target is poor 4-year-olds, although some 3-year-olds are enrolled as well. In the mid-1990s, some modest efforts were launched to serve children under 3 years of age as well. Nonetheless, as one of the founders and strongest advocates of Head Start has stated, for the most part, it is still only "a one-year treatment delivered at the age of four" (Zigler & Styfco, 1993). In 1995, about 751,000 children were enrolled in Head Start out of a total of about 6 million potentially eligible poor children under age 6 (USHR, 1996). Despite acknowledged variations in quality (Zigler & Styfco, 1993, 1996) and debates about its long-term effectiveness (Berreuta-Clement et al., 1984; Haskins, 1995), Head Start and other high-quality preschool programs are viewed as significant early interventions, leading to children with fewer problems subsequently, especially at school age.

In addition to those enrolled in Head Start, about 40% of 3- to 4-year-olds attended preprimary school programs in the early 1990s, disproportionately from affluent families with well-educated parents. These are largely part-day programs, under private auspices, and with parents paying most of the costs. For children under 3 years old, about 14% (20% of those with working mothers) were in centers, and another 14% were in family day care, largely unregulated.

In contrast, the European countries almost unanimously have elected universal but voluntary preschool for children from the age of 2, 2 1/2, or 3 until age 5, 6, or 7, varying with the age that compulsory schooling begins (European Commission Network on Childcare, 1996; Kamerman, 1998; Kamerman & Kahn, 1994a, 1994b, 1995; Moss, 1990). The infant–toddler care developments need to be understood within this context. These preschool programs are variously justified as preparing children for school, enhancing child socialization and development, and, somewhat less frequently, offering good quality care while parents work. So important are the school readiness concerns and so highly valued are the socialization and developmental opportunities that in most countries participation is unrelated to parental employment status, family income, cultural background, or judgments about parental capacities. All children in the 3 to 5 year age range attend in some countries (95% or more of the cohort in Belgium, France, and Italy), and almost all in others (at least 75–85% in Germany, Denmark, Finland, and Sweden). These programs are heavily subsidized, operate largely in the public sector or in the voluntary sector with extensive public subsidy, and cover at least the normal school day. In the Nordic countries, the full workday is covered. Although different nations have various arrangements for supplementary care to match parental work hours, the countries in which the preschool and school day is short (e.g., Germany), there are problems for working parents.

In most of Europe, the preschools are part of the education sector. There is an alternative pattern, however, as seen in Denmark, Finland, and Sweden, in which a separate child care system covers all children until age 7, when elementary school begins. Canada, Britain, and, to some extent, the United States, represent still a third pattern in which some children in care (ages 2–4 in Britain where compulsory school begins at age 5, 3–5 in Canada where school begins at age 6, and 3–4 in the United States) are in what has been known as "day care" in the social welfare sector, whereas others attend preschool or nursery school under educational auspices (usually part-day or full school day). Both of these programs may be publicly subsidized but not necessarily so; in the United States, a significant portion is under private auspices, both nonprofit and for profit. The programs under social welfare auspices give priority and subsidy to children alleged to have special needs because of abuse, neglect, or parental and familial problems.

With this backdrop, an important distinction for Europe may be introduced. If child care for the 3- to 5-year-olds is now universal and has a large school readiness and socialization–developmental rationale, care for the under-2-year-olds remains limited in most societies and is an essential response to female labor force participation (Kamerman & Kahn, 1995). Yet there is also an increasing affirmation of the importance of offering even the youngest children an experience providing cognitive stimulation and socialization with peers and other adults, even if there is a parent at home during the day.

In this context, three other differences between the United States and Europe should be noted. First is the explicit and special concern in Europe with child care policy for 3-year-olds and under, dating from the mid-1970s and reflecting a consensus regarding universal preschool for 3–6-year-olds. Second is the distinction between infant and toddler care, with infant care increasingly defined as care by a parent at home, as a result of the policy of postchildbirth leaves described earlier. Third are the innovations in toddler care now emerging, beginning at the age when parental leaves from work terminate and non-parental infant care is needed by a working parent.

A REVIEW OF POLICIES IN SIX COUNTRIES

A brief summary of the infant and toddler care policies in six European countries follows.

Denmark has the highest coverage of child care for children under 3 years in all of the West, combining high-quality center care and family day care. About 60% of 1- and 2-year-olds are in out-of-home care, about half in centers and half in supervised family day care. Children are guaranteed a place in a publicly subsidized child care program from the age of 1. Infant–toddler care is delivered under social services auspices, with programs including children from the age of about 9 months (the Danish paid parental leave currently lasts one year) through 6 years, when compulsory schooling begins. Given the high rates of female labor force participation, virtually all children attend 8–10 hours a day. Some programs are age-segregated, and some are integrated. Active parent involvement is emphasized.

Danish child care, similar to that in Sweden, is of consistently high quality, with high staff:child ratios, small groups, well-trained staff, and low staff turnover. However, the programs are not inexpensive. In the early 1990s, when Danish wages and median family income were somewhat higher than in the United States, the operating costs for a place in toddler care was about $12,500 a year. Parent fees cover a little more than one-fifth of the costs, are income-related, and equal about 5% of family income for an average two-earner family. Services are free to low-income families and are heavily subsidized for all participating families.

Recognizing that many children spend long days in care most of the week while their parents spend a full day at work, Danish child care program staff realize that they are part of a dual socialization experience for children. Yet they do not wish to replace the family or take over the child's socialization. As a result, the staff have developed a program philosophy that emphasizes psychological and social development rather than formal instruction. The emphasis is on creativity, the attainment of social maturity through group activities, language development, relationships, and overall stimulation of the children with the help of a wide range of materials and activities. Acknowledging the need for organization at home in two-earner families with young children, there is a deliberate effort at compensating for this by avoiding a formal curriculum and too much structure in their child care programs.

France has the highest preschool coverage for 3- to 5-year-olds internationally and the highest proportion of 3-year-olds and under in care after Denmark. Its services for children under age 3 are under health auspices, while its preschool program serving children aged 2–5 is under education auspices. Two-year-olds may be served in either system but most of those in out-of-home care are in the preschool. France also subsidizes in-home care and family day care for children younger than 3 years of age.

Italy has almost all its 3- to 5-year-olds enrolled in preschool, but only limited coverage for 3-year-olds and under. Infant care is largely maternal care, by mothers at home, mothers on leave from work, or care provided by a grandmother or "nurse." Program creativity in north-central Italy with regard to the 3- to 5-year-olds has inspired early care and education developments in many other countries. In particular, the preschool "Diana" in Reggio Emilia has been visited by more than 8,000 foreign child care and early childhood education experts during the 1990s. It serves seventy-five children aged 3–6 in three age-specific groups of twenty-five children each, with each group staffed by two teachers and an extra teacher assigned specifically to help with the three children with disabilities. There is also a special teacher in charge of the studio art workshop, which is a special feature of this program. The facility is structured so that all of the group rooms open from a large central area that functions as a kind of village square, used by all children at the start and end of the day and for special activities. Here, in contrast to the Danish programs, there is a deliberate curriculum, but it is heavily individualized; here too, creativity is stressed.

In this same part of Italy there is recent and significant expansion in programs serving 3-year-olds and under (largely aged 9 months and older, when the Italian maternity leaves end), and a strong case is made for ensuring access for infants and toddlers even if a full-time adult caregiver is available at home. Of special interest, all child care programs in several regions in north-central Italy are under education auspices, even though there is a clear distinction made between services for 3-year-olds and under and those for 3- to 5-year-olds; the programs for the 3-year-olds and under include both full workday child care and a variety of family support services (described later).

Finland and *Sweden*, in systems covering all children to age 7, are considered pioneers for offering parental at-home options for infant care, while also legislating a right to guaranteed child care (in the Finnish case, for 3-year-olds and under; in Sweden, for those aged 12 months and older). Like Denmark, their child care services are all under social service auspices, in a separate system; like Denmark, their programs are of exceptionally high quality. Here, too, operating costs are high, parent fees are income-related, and the services are expensive and heavily subsidized for all participating families.

England, along with Germany in this group of countries, has the smallest proportion of young children in out-of-home child care, perhaps in part because of its low (but recently rising) labor force participation rates for women with children of this age. Although compulsory school begins at age 5, and almost all 4-year-olds are in a program somewhat similar to U.S. kindergarten, coverage for 3-year-olds and under, and especially for 2-year-olds and under, is almost nonexistent, apart from informal child minding (family day care). Moreover, England provides child care through two parallel systems: one a social service for children "in need" – who are deprived, disadvantaged, or troubled – and a second, an education-based program for middle-class children whose parents seek an enrichment experience for them. England is of special interest because several local jurisdictions are now attempting to integrate the education and social service programs into a unified child care system, under education auspices.

Summary

Despite a growing conviction about the importance of group experiences for young children for optimum child development, the supply of infant and toddler care remains limited in most of Europe (Broberg & Hwang, 1991; European Commission Network on Child Care, 1996; Kamerman & Kahn, 1994a, 1994b, 1995; Leprince, 1991; New, 1993; Vedel-Petersen, 1992). Even high-coverage countries, such as the Nordic countries, France, and the north-central part of Italy, continue to have significant gaps between demand and supply, even if the target is limited to the children of working parents. In the light of continued scarcity, priorities are similar across countries: children of single working mothers; disabled, immigrant, disadvantaged, or deprived children, or others with special needs; and children with working parents.

What then is known about the effectiveness of these early intervention child care/preschool programs (Melhuish & Moss, 1991)? Extensive research in France documents the effectiveness of the French preschool (the Ecole Maternelle) in preventing a wide range of school problems, particularly primary school failure (Baudelot, 1988; Boocock, 1995; Norvez, 1990). Less extensive and systematic research suggests that various types of toddler programs facilitate subsequent adjustment to preschool (Kamerman & Kahn, 1995).

Scandinavian research, summarized in a Danish report (Vedel-Pedersen, 1992), by and large has concluded that children who attend the high-quality child care centers in these countries "find it easier to make the transition to school, . . . do well . . . are outspoken, independent, and competent in social situations" (p. 23). The results for children in Scandinavian supervised family day care are similar, but parents prefer centers especially for children aged 2 or 3 and older.

One influential Swedish longitudinal study (Andersson, 1986, 1992) found more positive social and cognitive impacts from early entry into Swedish child care (about 9 months) than from late entry (5 years) and generally positive consequences from the overall experience. Hwang, Broberg, and Lamb (1991) found that for toddlers enrolled in child care in Sweden, there were no clear-cut effects on diverse aspects of children's development and that the quality of home care these children received was the factor most predictive of developmental variations among children. It should be noted that most Swedish children do not enter out-of-home child care now until they are over the age of 1, and the lack of measurable effects may derive from the fact that the programs are of uniformly high quality and almost all children participate. Thus, there are no adequate contrast groups for the research.

Finally, in a recent review of the long-term outcomes of early childhood programs in other countries, Boocock (1995) summarized the research findings as follows: "There is widespread evidence that participating in a preschool program promotes cognitive development in the short term and prepares children to succeed in school" (p. 96). Other conclusions are as follows:

- There is no strong or consistent evidence that the form of the preschool experience (pedagogic approach, daily schedule, or setting) influences long-term outcomes for children.
- Preschool attendance appears to be a stronger force in the lives of low-income than more advantaged children.
- Preschool attendance can narrow the achievement gaps faced by disadvantaged children, although most of these effects appear to diminish over time.

Unfortunately, this review does not distinguish between those programs serving 3- to 5-year-olds only and those serving younger children as well, or younger children only. Andersson (1986, 1992) and Hwang et al. (1991) have addressed the experiences of younger children. Nonetheless, despite the effectiveness of these programs in Europe, they too must be seen as part of a larger cluster of interventions. The European programs are closely linked to the health care and HHV services described earlier and the family support services described next.

FAMILY SUPPORT SERVICES

Paralleling the emergence of infant and toddler programs in the United States is a growing interest in providing supportive services to families with young children, in particular those with special needs. These so-called family support services do not constitute a single, specific, uniformly delivered intervention but a cluster of services, delivered in a variety of ways and under different auspices (Brooks-Gunn, 1995; Kagan, Weissbourd, & Zigler, 1987; Kamerman & Kahn, 1994b, 1995; Schorr, 1988). Together, they are a developing component

of preventive services for children and their families and are potentially an important early intervention for childhood problems.

Family support services are broad-brush programs, often with multiple goals, that employ multiple, and somewhat diffuse interventions. Their major focus is on educating and helping parents to be more successful in their child-rearing roles. The ultimate goal is to improve child and parent outcomes. More specific goals may include better physical health of children, enhanced child development (cognitive and social), greater school readiness, better parenting skills, facilitation of parents' independence, and prevention of child abuse. Most U.S. programs are targeted primarily on preventing the kinds of family crises that result in child abuse or severe neglect and that lead to removal of a child from his or her home or on decreasing adolescent out-of-wedlock pregnancy, especially recidivism.

Family support services are usually community-based and voluntary, often involve parents as volunteers, and variously emphasize close links with the health, education, child care, and social welfare systems. In the United States, these services usually provide all or some of the following services: information and referral, parent education classes, adult education and training programs, home visiting, drop-in child care, and occasionally counseling.

During the latter part of the 1980s, a series of new and parallel initiatives began to emerge in several European nations, linked to child care in some countries but independent in others (Kamerman & Kahn, 1994b, 1995). These developments suggest the formation of a more extensive system of child and family services. The objective is to meet the diverse needs of young children and the preferences of parents who might not need or want to participate in a formal child care center because they do not work outside of the home, work part-time, or have a relative who provides care. Many, however, are convinced that they do need and want a group experience for their children and, often, for themselves, too.

Leading French and Italian child development researchers and child care policy and program experts who see themselves as working for the enhancement of childhood rather than just the improvement of child care services have taken a new and different approach (Anolli & Mantovani, 1991; Musatti, 1992). These experts see their agenda as improving the conditions of childhood; responding to social change, including changes in family structure and gender roles; facilitating the new interest in educational reform; trying to be sensitive to the needs of parents who have limited knowledge of parenting; and, most of all, responding to the needs of children.

These new developments are also seen as providing opportunities for parents and other caregivers to exchange experiences and concerns; to obtain expert guidance from professionals if they wish, including information, help, and support in their parenting role; and ultimately to enhance parents' socialization and education as well as that of their children through peer interaction and interaction with staff. None of this is proposed as an alternative to "traditional" quality center care but rather as a supplement to and extension of such programs, for those with more circumscribed needs – and at lower costs than a full-day program.

Recent Italian research documents the need for such developments. Musatti and her colleagues (1992) found that children from economically better-off families are the most likely to be provided with intellectual and social stimulation by their parents and also the most likely to be in an infant–toddler center and thus benefit from this experience as well. These children end up better prepared for preschool and later for primary school than those who come from families with fewer resources, whose mothers have more limited education and lower-status jobs, are less likely to have knowledge about child development, and are most likely to use informal child care or poorer quality child care offering less stimulation. Inevitably, these latter children are less likely to be prepared for school.

These and other child development researchers are convinced that given small family size and the paucity of children in neighborhoods, the social isolation of many of these mothers and their children can be devastating. In such circumstances, supplementary and supportive group experiences are essential. These experiences need not be full day, but they must provide opportunities for children to play with other children separately from their mothers and for mothers/parents/caregivers to interact with one another as well as with their own and other children and staff. Unfortunately, these developments are too recent for there to be any systematic data regarding even supply, let alone outcome, data. No longitudinal studies are planned, nor are any rigorous evaluations anticipated.

In contrast to these Italian developments and others in France, the British "family centers" are more similar to U.S. programs (Kamerman & Kahn, 1994b, 1995; Walker & Family Centres, 1991). They are focused on high-risk and vulnerable children and their families, on young parents, and (like many in the United States) are equally diffuse in the ways in which they "intervene" and in their impacts. The more interesting developments have something of the quality of a settlement house. Almost all programs characterize their mission as strengthening family functioning through services designed to help and enhance parenting skills. And almost all are located in communities with high rates of social pathology, poverty, and unemployment. The interventions used vary, some focusing on intensive "family preservation" type work and crisis intervention, and others carrying out remedial and treatment interventions with abusing parents or very disorganized families. These are problem-oriented, treatment services rather than the developmental and supportive services of the Italian programs. They appear to focus primarily on case finding and the monitoring of families who have failed.

A British exemplar, the Pen Green Centre for children 5 years and under and their families, is located in a heavily industrialized region that experienced high unemployment in the 1970s and 1980s. It is described now as a "women's working town" because many of the men remain unemployed, and the women are working irregularly, off-hours, or doing shift work in the service sector. The program began as a child care center and expanded to include an extensive parent education program; a mother–toddler program; a home-visiting program; a child health center where the local HHV holds a regular weekly clinic and a mothers' group; and extensive supportive, educational, and work-training programs. Parent involvement is extensive, and the community has a strong sense of "ownership."

Whether in Britain, France, Italy, or elsewhere, it seems clear that these programs constitute one more form of early intervention in a larger policy/program cluster. The link with health care, HHV, parental leaves, and child care is obvious, but there are also important links with parent education, training, and employment as well as other forms of government aid to families with children. Family support may be an important early intervention but it is not sufficient by itself.

CONCLUSION

Clearly, a wide range of programs in Europe directly target very young children and their families or provide a strong foundation of support for families generally. Without the label, they include all that we in the United States would consider "early intervention" programs and more. They are popular and are considered successful in achieving positive outcomes.

In reviewing early childhood programs in other countries, Boocock (1995) and Gustafson and Stafford (1995) confirmed what we had found earlier (Kamerman & Kahn, 1981): These early childhood policies and programs are effective both as preventive interventions and as strategies for promoting child and family well-being, and other countries have established such policies and programs based on far less research than exists in the United States as the result of political will, not necessarily rigorous research. Building on commonly held values about children and their families, these countries have invested in these policies and programs on the assumption that children are important, that they must be well cared for, that the society has a large stake in the future of its children, and that over time there will be lessons from the program experiences that will lead to improvements. (We could say the same for the United States, but we lack the political will.)

It is clear that the European interventions – their early childhood policies and programs – would be understood as even more effective if a broader concept of early intervention were applied (Kamerman & Kahn, 1995). This would lead to the inclusion of the effects of income transfer policies benefiting families with children, housing benefits, and access to health care, in addition to adequate time for parenting (without loss of income) and supportive and caring service interventions. Young children in many of the European countries are much less likely to be born poor than American children and are far less likely to experience poverty and economic insecurity as they grow up. They are assured of more time with their parents as infants and

toddlers and of far greater access to health care and child care/preschool – both of which are universal in these countries (and in Japan as well).

Looking at conventional childhood social indicators, whether linked causally with these interventions or not, poor and disadvantaged children are clearly better launched in these other countries and are far less likely to experience the marginalization and social exclusion that are increasingly becoming their lot in the United States. However conceptualized, these are clearly highly valued policies. Even in the current climate of constraints in social programs, there is no indication that these countries will cut back significantly on what is done for their children – even if they cut elsewhere. In the end, it is simply a matter of priorities and values.

REFERENCES

Andersson, B.-E. (1986). *Home care or external care*, Report No. 2 from the Stockholm Institute of Education.

Andersson, B.-E. (1992). Effects of day care on cognitive and socioemotional competence of 13-year-old Swedish schoolchildren. *Child Development, 63*, 20–36.

Anolli, L., & Mantovani, S. (1991). Oltre il Nido: Il Tempo per le Famiglie. In A. Bandioli. & S. Mantovani (Eds.), *Manuale Critica Dell Asilo Niddo*. Milan, Italy: FrancoAngelia.

Baudelot, O. (1988). *Child care in France*. Paper presented to the National Academy of Science/National Research Council, Commission on Behavioral and Social Sciences and Education, Committee on Child Development Research and Public Policy, Panel on Child Care Policy. Paris: Institute for Pedagogical Research, 1988.

Behrman, R. E. (Ed.). (1993). U.S. health care for children [Special issue]. *The Future of Children, 2*(2).

Behrman, R. E. (Ed.). (1994). Home visiting [Special issue]. *The Future of Children, 3*(3).

Behrman, R. E. (Ed.). (1995). Long term outcomes of early childhood programs [Special issue]. *The Future of Children, 5*(3).

Berrueta-Clement, J. R., Schweinhart, L. B., Barnett, W. S., Epstein, A. J., & Weikart, D. P. (1984). *Changed lives: The effects of the Perry Preschool Program on youths through age 19*. Ypsilanti, MI: The High/Scope Press.

Boocock, S. S. (1995). Early childhood programs in other nations: Goals and outcomes. In R. E. Behrman (Ed.), Long term outcomes of early childhood programs [Special issue]. *The Future of Children, 5*(3), 94–114.

Broberg, A., & Hwang, P., (1991). Day care for young children in Sweden. In E. C. Lemhuish & P. Moss (Eds.), *Day care for young children: International perspectives* (pp. 75–101). London: Tavistock/Routledge.

Bradshaw, J., Ditch, J., Holmes, H., & Whiteford, P. (1993). *Support for children: A comparison of arrangements in 15 countries.* London: HMSO.

Bradshaw, J., Kennedy, S., Kilkey, M., Hutton, S., Corden, A., Eardley, T., Holmes, H., & Neale, J. (1996). *Policy and the employment of lone parents in 20 countries.* York, England: University of York, European Observatory on National Family Policies.

Brooks-Gunn, J. (1995). Strategies for altering the outcomes of poor children and their families. In P. L. Chase-Lansdale & J. Brooks-Gunn (Eds.), *Escape from poverty* (pp. 87–120). New York: Cambridge University Press.

Campbell, F. A., & Ramey, C. T. (1994). Effects of early intervention on intellectual and academic achievement: A follow-up study of children from low-income families. *Child Development, 65*(2), 684–98.

Carnegie Task Force on Meeting the Needs of Young Children. (1994). *Starting points: Meeting the needs of our youngest children.* New York: Author.

Carnegie Task Force On Learning in the Primary Grades. (1996). *Years of promise.* New York: Author.

Chase-Lansdale, P. L., & Brooks-Gunn, J. (Eds.). (1995). *Escape from poverty.* New York: Cambridge University Press.

Danish National Health Service. (1970). *Health visiting: Summary of Report I.* Copenhagen, Denmark: Author.

Ditch, J., Barnes, H., & Bradshaw, J. (1996a). *Developments in national family policies in 1995.* York, UK: University of York, SPRU.

Ditch, J., Barnes, H., & Bradshaw, J. (1996b). *A synthesis of national family policies in 1995.* York, England: University of York, SPRU.

Ditch, J., Barnes, H., Bradshaw, J., Commaille, J., & Eardley, T. (1995a). *Developments in national family policies in 1994.* York, England: University of York, SPRU.

Ditch, J., Barnes, H., Bradshaw, J., Commaille, J., & Eardley, T. (1995b). *A synthesis of national family policies in 1994.* York, England: University of York, SPRU.

Ditch, J., Barnes, H., Bradshaw, J., & Kilkey, M. (1997a). *Developments in national families policies in 1996.* York, England: University of York, SPRU.

Ditch, J., Barnes, H., Bradshaw, J., & Kilkey, M. (1997b). *A synthesis of national family policies in 1996.* York, England: University of York, SPRU.

Duncan, G. J., Brooks-Gunn, J., & Klebanov, P. K. (1994). Economic deprivation and early childhood development. *Child Development, 65,* 296–318.

Duncan, G. J., & Brooks-Gunn, J. (Eds.). (1997). *Consequences of growing up poor.* New York: Russell Sage.

Eardley, T., Bradshaw, J., Ditch, J., Gough, I., & Whiteford, P. (1996). *Social assistance in OECD countries: Synthesis report.* London: HMSO.

European Commission Network on Child Care and Other Measures to Reconcile Employment and Family Responsibilities. (1993). *Mothers, fathers, and employment, 1985–1991.* Brussels, Belgium: European Commission, DGV, Equal Opportunities Unit.

European Commission Network on Child Care and Other Measures to Reconcile Employment and Family Responsibilities. (1994). *Leave arrangements for workers with children.* Brussels, Belgium: European Commission, DGV, Equal Opportunities Unit.

European Commission Network on Child Care and Other Measures to Reconcile Employment and Family Responsibilities. (1996). *A review of services for young children in the European Union, 1990–1995.* Brussels, Belgium: European Commission, DGV, Equal Opportunities Unit.

Gaskins, R. (1993, March). Comprehensive reform in child welfare: The British Children Act, 1989. *Social Services Review, 67*(1), 1–15.

Gomby, D., Culross, P., & Behrman, R. (1999). Home visiting: Recent program evaluations – analysis and recommendations. *The future of children: Home visiting: Recent program evaluations, 9.*

Goodwin, S. (1990a). Child health services in Britain and Wales: An overview. *Pediatrics, 86*(6), 1032–6.

Goodwin, S. (1990b). Statement. U.S. House of Representatives, Select Committee on Children and Youth. *Hearing on Child Health: Lessons from Developed Nations.* 101st Congress, 2d Session.

Gustafsson, S., & Stafford, F. P. (1995). Links between early childhood programs and maternal employment in three countries. In R. E. Behrman (Ed.), Long term outcomes of early childhood programs [Special issue]. *The Future of Children, 5*(3), 161–74.

Guterman, N. B. (1997). Early prevention of physical child abuse and neglect: Existing evidence and future directions. *Child Maltreatment, 2*(1), 12–34.

Hamburg, D. A. (1992). *Today's children.* New York: Times Books.

Harris, I. B. (1996). *Children in jeopardy: Can we break the cycle of poverty?* New Haven, CT: Yale University Press.

Haskins, R. (1995). Future policy and research directions. In P.L. Chase-Lansdale & J. Brooks-Gunn (Eds.), *Escape from poverty* (pp. 241–71). New York: Cambridge University Press.

Hernandez, D. (1993). *America's children: Resources from family, government, and the economy.* New York: Russell Sage.

Huston, A. (Ed.). (1991). *Children in poverty.* New York: Cambridge University Press.

Hwang, C. P., Broberg, A., & Lamb, M. E. (Eds.). Swedish childcare research. In E. C. Lemhuish & P. Moss (1991), *Day care for young children: International perspectives* (pp. 102–20). London: Tavistock/Routledge.

Kagan, S. L. (1996). America's family support movement: A moment of change. In E. Zigler, S. L. Kagan, & N. W. Hall (Eds.), *Children, families and government: Preparing for the twenty-first century* (pp. 156–70). New York: Cambridge University Press,.

Kagan, S. L., Weissbourd, B., & Zigler, E. F. (Eds.). (1987). *America's family support programs.* New Haven, CT: Yale University Press.

Kahn, A. J., & Kamerman, S. B. (Eds.). (1983). *Income transfers for families with children: An eight-country study.* Philadelphia: Temple University Press.

Kahn, A. J., & Kamerman, S. B. (Eds.). (1988). *Child support: from debt collection to social policy.* Newbury Park, CA: Sage.

Kahn, A. J., & Kamerman, S. B. (1994). *Social policy and the under 3s: A six country study.* New York: CUSSW.

Kamerman, S. B. (1994). *Child care policies and programs: An international overview.* International Encyclopedia of Education Research. Tarrytown, NY: Pergamon.

Kamerman, S. B. (1998, May). *Early childhood intervention and care: An international overview.* Paris: OECD.

Kamerman, S. B. (forthcoming). From maternity to parenting policies: Women's health and child well-being. *Journal of the American Women's Medical Association.*

Kamerman, S. B., & Kahn, A. J. (1981). *Child care, family benefits, and working parents.* New York: Columbia University Press.

Kamerman, S. B., & Kahn, A. J. (Eds.). (1983). *Family policy: Government and families in fourteen countries.* New York: Columbia University Press.

Kamerman, S. B., & Kahn, A. J. (1988). Social policy and children in the United States and Europe. In J. L. Palmer, T. Smeeding, & B. B. Torrey (Eds.), *The vulnerable* (pp. 351–80). Washington, DC: The Urban Institute Press.

Kamerman, S. B., & Kahn, A. J. (1989, Spring). Family policy: Has the United States learned from Europe? *Policy Studies Review, 8*(3) 581–98.

Kamerman, S. B., & Kahn, A. J. (1990). Social services for children, youth, and families in the United States. *Children and Youth Services Review, 12*(1–2).

Kamerman, S. B., & Kahn, A. J. (Eds.). (1991). *Child care, parental leaves, and the under 3s.* Westport, CT: Auburn.

Kamerman, S. B., & Kahn, A. J. (1993). Home health visiting in Europe. *The Future of Children, 3*(3), 39–52.

Kamerman, S. B., & Kahn, A. J. (1994a). Family policy and the under 3s: Money, time, and services in a policy package. *International Social Security Review, 47*(3–4), 31–44.

Kamerman, S. B., & Kahn, A. J. (1994b). *A welcome for every child: Care, education, and family support for infants and toddlers in Europe.* Washington, DC: Zero To Three.

Kamerman, S. B., & Kahn, A. J. (1995). *Starting right: How Americans neglect their youngest children and what we can do about it.* New York: Oxford University Press.

Kamerman, S. B., & Kahn, A. J. (1996). Coping with the changes in U.S. child and family policies: Exploring the choices. In S. B. Kamerman & A. J. Kahn (Eds.), *Confronting the new politics of child and family policies: Report I, Whither American social policy?* (pp. 93–115). New York: CUSSW.

Kamerman, S. B., & Kahn, A. J. (Eds.). (1996/1997). *Confronting the new politics of child and family policies: Report I,*

Whither American social policy? Report III, Child health and Medicaid in the context of welfare reform. Report IV, Child care in the context of welfare reform. Report VI, P.L. 104-193: Challenges and opportunities. New York: CUSSW.

Kamerman, S. B., & Kahn, A. J. (1997). Investing in children: Government expenditures for children and their families in advanced industrialized countries. In G. A. Cornia & S. Danziger (Eds.), *Child poverty and deprivation in industrialized countries.* Oxford, England: Oxford University Press.

Kamerman, S. B., & Kahn, A. J. (Eds.). (1998). *Family policy: Government and families in fourteen countries.* New York: Columbia University Press.

Krugman, R. (1993). Universal home visiting: A recommendation from the U.S. Advisory Board on Child Abuse and Neglect. *The Future of Children, 3*(3), 184–91.

Lally, J. R., Griffin, A., Finichel, E., Segal, M. M., Szanton, E. S., & Weissbaurd, B. (1995). *Caring for infants and toddlers in groups.* Washington, DC: Zero To Three.

Leprince, F. (1991). Day care for young children in France. In E. C. Lemhuish & P. Moss, *Day care for young children: International perspectives* (pp. 10–26). London: Tavistock/Routledge.

Manciaux, M., Jestin, C., Fritz, M., & Bertrand, D. (1990). Child health care policy and delivery in France. *Pediatrics, 86*(6), 1037–43.

Meisels, S. J., & Shonkoff, J. P. (Eds.). (1990). *Handbook of early childhood intervention.* New York: Cambridge University Press.

Melhuish, E., & Moss, P. (1991). *Day care for young children: International perspectives.* London: Tavistock/Routledge.

Moss, P. (1990). *Childcare in the European community, 1985–1990.* Brussels, Belgium: European Commission, DGV, Equal Employment Opportunities Unit.

Musatti, T. (1992). *La Giornata Del Mio Bambino.* Bologna: Italy: Il Mulino.

National Institute of Child Health and Human Development (NICHD), Child Care Network. (1997). *Report.*

New, R. (1993). Italy. In M. Cochran (Ed.), *International handbook of child care policies and programs* (pp. 291–312). Westport, CT: Greenwood Press.

Norvez, A. (1990). *De La Naissance a L'Ecole.* Paris, France: Presses Universitaires de France, Institut National D'Etudes Demographiques.

Pugh, G. (Ed.). (1992). *Contemporary issues in the early years: Working collaboratively for children.* London: The National Children's Bureau. Paul Chapman Publishing.

Rainwater, L., & Smeeding, T. M. (1995). *Doing poorly: The real income of American children in a comparative perspective.* Luxembourg Income Study, Working Paper No. 127. Luxembourg: CEPS.

Sawhill, I. (1993). *Young children and families: Setting national priorities.* Washington, DC: Brookings Institution.

Schorr, L. (1988). *Within our reach*. New York: Doubleday.

Shore, R. (1997). *Rethinking the brain: New insights into early development*. New York: Families and Work Institute.

Smeeding, T. (with the assistance of Katherine Ross). (1997). *Financial poverty in developed countries: The evidence from LIS*. In UNDP Human Development and Poverty, 1997. Background Paper.

UNICEF (1997). *State of the child*. Oxford, UK: Oxford University Press.

U.S. House of Representatives, Committee on Ways and Means. (1993, January). *Sources of the increase in poverty, work effort, and income distribution data*. Washington, DC: U.S. Government Printing Office.

U.S. House of Representatives, Committee on Ways and Means. (1996). *The green book: An overview of entitlement programs*. Washington, DC: U.S. Government Printing Office.

U.S. House of Representatives, Committee on Ways and Means. (1998). *The green book: An overview of the entitlement programs*. Washington, DC: U.S. Government Printing Office.

U.S. Social Security Administration. (1997). *Social security programs throughout the world – 1995*. Washington, DC: U.S. Government Printing Office.

U.S. House of Representatives, Select Committee on Children and Youth. (1990). *Hearing on child health: Lessons from developed nations*. 101st Congress, 2d Session. Washington, DC: U.S. Government Printing Office.

Verbrugge, H. (1990). Statement. *U.S. House of Representatives, Select Committee on Children and Youth*. Hearing on child health: Lessons from developed nations. 101st Congress, 2d Session. Washington, DC: U.S. Government Printing Office.

Vedel-Petersen, J. (1992). *Day care for children under school age in Denmark*. Copenhagen, Denmark: Danish National Institute of Social Research.

Wagner, M. (1990). Statement. *U.S. House of Representatives, Select Committee on Children and Youth*. Hearing on child health: Lessons from developed nations. 101st Congress, 2d Session Washington, DC: U.S. Government Printing Office.

Walker, H., & Family Centres. In P. Carter, T. Jeffs, & M. Smith (Eds.), (1991). *Social work and social welfare yearbook 3*. London: Open University Press.

Williams, B. C., & Miller, C. A. (1991). *Preventive health care for young children*. Washington, DC: Zero to Three.

Young, M. E. (1996). *Early child development: Investing in the future*. Washington, DC: The World Bank.

Zigler, E., & Styfco, S. (1993). *Head Start and beyond*. New Haven, CT: Yale University Press.

Zigler, E., & Styfco, S. (1996). Head Start and early childhood intervention: The changing course of social science and social policy. In E. Zigler, S. L. Kagan, & N. W. Hall (Eds.), *Children, families, and government: Preparing for the twenty-first century* (pp. 132–55). New York: Cambridge University Press.

CHAPTER TWENTY-SEVEN

Evolution of Family–Professional Partnerships:

Collective Empowerment as the Model for the Early Twenty-First Century

ANN P. TURNBULL, VICKI TURBIVILLE, AND H. R. TURNBULL

In this chapter we present four models of parent–professional partnerships, including a discussion of the power relationships within each. The approaches that we discuss include 1) parent counseling/psychotherapy, 2) family involvement, 3) family-centered services, and 4) collective empowerment. The research and professional literature upon which we base our analysis is drawn from the early childhood special education field. That literature has been constructed primarily since the 1950s with a focus on young children with developmental disabilities. Family–professional partnership trends in other areas of early childhood services have differed from those that we are presenting; however, it is beyond the scope of a single chapter to analyze partnership models within all early childhood fields.

We begin the chapter with a discussion of the type of power – power-over, power-with, and power-through – that are generally inherent in each of the four family–professional partnership models. The models are further portrayed through the use of a what-might-have-been vignette. We begin the chapter with a vignette of an imaginary family, one that prototypically might be known to any service provider. As we discuss each of the models and the power relationships within those models, we suggest how that model may have been brought to bear on that family.

Jeanette A. is a 37-year-old African American woman who lives in a community of approximately 65,000 people in an eastern state. Her daughter, Tisha, was born at 26 weeks gestation, weighing 1 pound, 12 ounces. Tisha has multiple disabilities including hydrocephaly, a heart defect, and cerebral palsy. Jeanette also has an older son, Lenny, who is a 19-year-old high school dropout and is intermittently employed. Jeanette's mother lives about 25 miles away but often is called upon for child care and is a source of emotional support for Jeanette.

Jeanette and Tisha usually live by themselves in a two-bedroom duplex, but Jeanette's former husband, who is also Tisha's father, sometimes lives with her, as does Lenny. Jeanette works as a nurse's aide, 11:00 a.m. till 3:00 p.m., five days a week, at a nursing center in a community 30 miles away from her home.

Lenny and Jeanette have a stormy relationship, with frequent verbal and physical altercations over both relatively minor and significant issues. Lenny is a good care provider for his younger sister, Tisha, and is often called upon to provide child care for her.

Jeanette's relationship with her husband and her son have on occasion been physically abusive. Jeanette has some learning disabilities and requires medication for a bipolar disorder. She also regularly attends AA meetings because of her drug and alcohol addiction.

POWER AND FAMILY–PROFESSIONAL PARTNERSHIPS

The evolution in developing and implementing family–professional partnerships within early childhood special education can be described as an evolution along a power continuum, as illustrated in Figure 27.1.

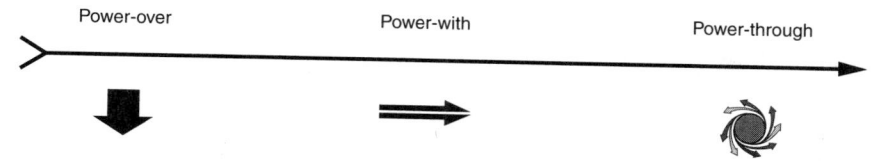

Power-over   Power-with   Power-through

Figure 27.1. Power Continuum

Forty years ago, the professionally driven parent counseling/psychotherapeutic model with the professionals in a power-over relationship with parents was most common (Wolfensberger, 1967). Today, an empowerment model, one that enables power to be generated and to grow through relationships, is emerging (Dunst, Trivette, Gordon, & Starnes, 1993; Turnbull & Turnbull, 1997).

Power, which is the "ability and willingness to affect the behavior, thoughts, physical well-being, and/or feelings of another" (Claus & Bailey, 1977, cited in Kisthardt, 1992, p. 76), is a critical element of all relationships. Natiello (1990) suggested that power in and of itself is neither good nor bad; it is how it is used that can lead to either destructive or creative growth. She further suggested that, traditionally, authoritarian power has been most common in human relationships.

The use of authoritarian power can result in feelings of distrust, competition, loss of control, and dependency by subordinates on those who are in the dominant role (Natiello, 1990). For the subordinates in authoritarian power relationships, there is often low self-esteem; loss of social and personal potential; and feelings of anger and unrest. In these relationships, there is little room for emotional expression, personal openness, intimacy, or interconnectedness (Crais, 1993; Natiello, 1990).

Parent–professional partnerships have been traditionally marked by the presence of these dominant-subordinate power structures, with the service provider in the dominant role and parents or family members in the subordinate role. Professionals most often have had control of information and resources that were needed by families in order to help their children. This power structure is referred to as a *power-over* relationship (Follett, 1924; Natiello, 1990; Turnbull & Turnbull, 1997). Power-over relationships are characterized by professionals exerting decision-making control over parents through perceived higher competence, professionalized communication, and control of environmental resources. The goal is often to define parental problems on the basis of the professional's "diagnosis" and to enforce compliance through authoritarian control with "treatment." Parent counseling/psychotherapy and parent training/involvement partnership models are built on these traditional authoritarian power relationships. Table 27.1 identifies the characteristics of power-over relationships.

In recent years, relationships and the power distribution between service providers and families have begun to change. Emerging partnerships began to reflect the principles of family-centered practice in which families are actively involved in decision making and services meet family and child needs (Bailey, Buysse, Edmondson, & Smith, 1992; Kjerland & Kovach, 1990; McBride, Brotherson, Joanning, Whiddon, & Demmitt, 1993; Turnbull & Summers, 1985).

Family-centered partnerships are marked by power-with relationship between providers and family members. Service providers and family members recognize the value of the knowledge and expertise each brings to the table. Ultimate decision making is a responsibility of the family, although the decision might be to avoid making a decision or to delegate decision making to the service provider (Turbiville, Turnbull, Garland, & Lee, 1996). *Power-with* partnerships arise when collaborative decision making is used among parents and professionals through perceived equal competence, contextual communication, and sharing of environmental resources. In family-centered partnerships, professionals respect family members' competence, listen to their perspectives, and are influenced by the knowledge and resources inherent in their family system and community ecology. Because they are not the primary decision makers in most instances, professionals in power-with relationships are collaborators with families through information sharing and problem solving (Crais, 1993). Table 27.1 highlights the characteristics of these partnerships.

TABLE 27.1. Evolution of Relationships

Type of power	Family–professional partnership model	Type of decision making	Participants	Communication	Resources
Power-over	Parent counseling/ psychotherapy; parent training involvement	Exerting control	Professionals, with parents (usually mothers)	Full of clinical jargon, maintenance of professional distance, and directive	Often limited to existing service-system resources within professionals' control
Power-with	Family-centered services	Collaborating	Parents (usually mothers) and professionals	Courteous and candid	Existing service-system resources, plus family resources
Power-through	Collective empowerment	Synergizing	Parents, family members, friends, community citizens and professionals	Insightful ("head"), caring ("heart"), and dynamic	Creation of new and preferred resources

One might presume that a balancing of power or power-with partnerships would be the desired outcome of any relationship. As knowledge about family/professional partnerships has progressed, however, an even more productive way for families and professionals to relate has emerged. That relationship, which we refer to as collective empowerment, is a *power-through* partnership. Power-through partnerships incorporate synergistic decision making among family members, professionals, friends, and community citizens through perceived group competence, "mind and heart" communication, and the creation of new and preferred environmental resources. Synergistic decision making infuses the traditional individual and dyadic decision making with group energy and creativity so that the combined effect is substantially greater than what individuals or dyads could have constructed. In more common vernacular language, it means "that the whole is greater than the sum of the parts."

By defining power in terms of capacity rather than control, partnerships are moved to a different plane. On that plane, power becomes a synergistic resource for everyone who is involved in the partnership. No longer is control of communication, resources, decision making, or other people the issue. In these partnerships, there is a synergy that creates power

(and empowerment) for all participants. Power is not finite within collective empowerment partnerships; instead, it is generative and available to all (Wagner, 1992). This partnership creates the context in which all participants can access and influence the resources they need to achieve their goals (Kalyanpur & Rao, 1991; Katz, 1984; Kieffer, 1984).

Service providers sometimes fear the loss of control or power in power-with or power-through partnerships. In fact, particularly in power-through partnerships, power increases. Here, through the synergy of the relationships, more resources are made available to all members of the partnerships (Turnbull & Turnbull, 1997; Wagner, 1992). Power-through partnerships based on synergistic power are characterized by openness, responsiveness, dignity, personal empowerment for each member, alternating influence, and cooperation (Katz, 1984; Kieffer, 1984; Natiello, 1990). These partnerships generate win-win outcomes: each partner gains (Turnbull & Turnbull, 1997).

MODELS OF FAMILY–PROFESSIONAL PARTNERSHIPS

As we stated at the outset, we want to reiterate that our focus is on family–professional partnerships

TABLE 27.2. Time Periods of Primary Emphasis of Family–Professional Partnership Models within Early Childhood Special Education Field

Time of primary emphasis	1950s–1960s	1960s–1970s	1980s	1990s and into 21st century
Models	Counseling/psychotherapy model	Parent training/involvement	Family-centered model	Collective empowerment

within the early childhood special education field. The literature that we cite comes from the early childhood special education field with a primary emphasis on serving children with developmental disabilities and their families. We highlight each of the four family–professional partnership models (parent counseling/psychotherapy, family involvement, family-centered services, and collective empowerment) in a sequential order in terms of the period of time in which the model has had or continues to have most influence. Table 27.2 illustrates the four models and the general time period most associated with their primary emphasis within the field of early childhood special education.

We want to caution readers against generalizing our analysis of practices within the early childhood special education field to all applications of parent counseling–psychotherapy, family involvement, family-centered services, and collective empowerment in other fields and with other populations. We briefly highlight 1) an overview of the model, 2) the type of power that generally characterizes the model, 3) assumptions, 4) professional roles and perspectives, 5) parent perspectives, and 6) expected outcomes.

Overview of Parent Counseling–Psychotherapy Model

Counseling–psychotherapy models were particularly prevalent with mothers of young children with mental retardation in the 1950s and 1960s (Beddie & Osmond, 1955; Bowlby, 1960; Dalton & Epstein, 1963; Emde & Brown, 1978; Goshen, 1963; Mandelbaum & Wheeler, 1960; Ross, 1964; Sieffert, 1978; Solnit & Stark, 1961; Wolfensberger, 1967). Wolfensberger's (1967) comprehensive review of the 300-plus articles that constituted the bulk of the par-

ent counseling/psychotherapy literature highlights the psychoanalytic framework and clinical orientations of this period. The literature primarily emphasizes 1) the impact of the child with mental retardation on the mother's "adjustment" and 2) clinically observed stages of grieving.

A passage from Solnit and Stark (1961), a frequently cited article illustrative of this model and time period, characterizes the model's psychoanalytic framework:

The theoretical approach to our work is founded on the psychoanalytic explanation of the process of the mourning as applied to the mother's reactions to the birth of a defective child (Bibring, 1959; Bibring, Dwer, Huntington, & Valenstein, 1961; Freud, 1917, 1923; Janis, 1958a,b). Freud's contributions to the understanding of narcissism and its vicissitudes (1914) are essential for the study of object loss – in our case, the loss of the longed-for healthy child. (Solnit & Stark, 1961, p. 524)

Parents frequently became the "cases" for counseling and psychotherapeutic treatment. This treatment focused almost exclusively on mothers.

Although the mother's reactions to her defective child are to a significant extent shaped by the type and degree of defect, they also are greatly influenced by her own past experiences with parents and siblings as well as by other significant life events. Conflicts in the woman's relationship to her own mother and in regard to her own femininity are often reawakened during the psychological work during the pregnancy…an awareness of the preparatory developments in the mother will heighten understanding of the impact of the disappointment, feeling of helplessness, and sense of failure that the individual woman experiences when the child she bears is obviously blighted. (Solnit & Stark, 1961, p. 525)

Grief models hypothesized a sequence of stages, beginning with initial shock and concluding with the final acceptance of reality (Wolfensberger, 1967). A pervading sense of pathology characterizes this literature. "Treatment" attempted to "fix" mothers' personal pathologies and their relationships with their child with mental retardation and other family members. Parent counseling/psychotherapy was often the sole intervention, with children with mental retardation receiving no or limited services.

Although this view of parents (i.e., mothers) as needing counseling or psychotherapy is less frequently seen in the 1990s than in the 1950s and 1960s, it is still cited today. Seitz and Provence (1990), in depicting caregiver-focused models of early intervention in the infant mental health field, described Fraiberg's work in which "the problem of the infant is seen to be a result of conflict between parent and infant arising from the mother's unresolved problems with her own past – the 'ghosts' that have invaded the nursery" (p. 404). Such caregiver models, however, are essentially absent from contemporary early childhood special education literature on family–professional partnerships (Odom & Karnes, 1988; Odom & McLean, 1996; Stayton & Karnes, 1994).

TYPE OF POWER. Skrtic (1995) suggested that one of the principal uses of professional power, so illustrative of the parent counseling–psychotherapy model, is the power to define "normalcy." Because of their expert knowledge, professionals have the power to decide who is normal and who is not. Once classified as abnormal, parents are then prescribed treatment, which can only be provided by professionals, according to the counseling/psychotherapy model. An example of the "diagnosis" and "prognosis" reflecting power relationships is exemplified in how Jeannette might have been characterized through the lens of a counseling/psychotherapeutic model.

Mrs. A. was referred to therapy by the child protective services agency. Early on, intensive counseling with this mother revealed a deeply disturbed personality. Her postnatal feelings of guilt, worthlessness, helplessness, hopelessness, and self-blame justify a finding of narcissistic disequilibrium. When I recommended that she place the child in foster care or put the child up for adoption, she manifested denial and avoidance of acceptance of the reality of Tisha's deviancy. Her vituperative response prompted her to engage in typical shopping-around behavior, evidencing her continued denial and incapacity for acceptance. Whatever the results of her shopping behavior, she returned to therapy only after our clinical social worker contacted her with the non-negotiable ultimatum that she resume therapy or else have to justify, in a child neglect/custody hearing, why her child should not be taken from her home and put into child protective services custody.

The power within this therapeutic relationship can be characterized as unequal, with the professional having power-over communication, resources, and outcomes.

ASSUMPTIONS. Assumptions of the counseling/psychotherapy model (Darling, 1989; Saleebey, 1992) include the following:

1. Children with disabilities create family pathology and counseling/psychotherapy is the appropriate treatment.
2. The professional refers to the child and family as "my case."
3. Diagnostic categorizations and clinical judgment result in an expert diagnosis that serves as the basis of treatment.
4. The professional's treatment consists of working to change the mother's reaction to the child and the child's diagnosis, with negligible attention to changing the family's environmental ecology by building on strengths and enhancing preferred formal and informal resources.
5. Emphasis is placed on finding "an optimal distance" (Foley, Hochman, & Miller, 1994, p. 19) in the therapeutic relationship through focusing on problems associated with managing transference and countertransference.

By transference, we mean the feelings, impulses and behaviors repeatedly experienced by the client in relation to the psychotherapist, which arise not out of the "real" but out of recapitulations of earlier relationships (Freud, 1912; Sander, 1993). By countertransference, we mean the unconscious reactions directed toward their clients in the present that are experienced by the psychotherapists and which have their origins in the past. (Foley et al., 1994, p. 19)

PROFESSIONAL PERSPECTIVE. The counseling/psychotherapy model assigns professionals, particularly those with medical backgrounds, the role as experts. Not surprisingly, the term *medical model* – which frequently refers to an expert making a diagnosis and providing treatment to a patient or case – pervades the professional literature describing the counseling/psychotherapy model (Weick, 1983). Interactions with professionals typically occur within their clinics or offices, with few community resources.

Kanner (1953) described the challenge of providing counseling/psychotherapy to parents:

Whenever parents are given an opportunity to express themselves, they invariably air their emotional involvement in the form of questions, utterances of guilt, open and sometimes impatient rebellion against destiny, stories of frantic search for causes, pathetic accounts of matrimonial dissensions about the child's condition, regret about the course that has been taken so far, anxious appraisals of the child's future, and tearful pleas for reassurance. It takes a considerable amount of cold, hard-boiled, pseudo-professional detachment to turn a deaf ear on the anxieties, self-incriminations, and concerns about past, present, and future contained in such remarks. (p. 375)

In a description of the clinical interviewing process, Hirshberg (1996) stressed the importance of building a relationship between the provider and the family members. "[T]he critical point is that what is learned about the infant and family is a picture or account which is constructed in the course of an active, dynamic exchange between family members and evaluator" (p. 91).

Although parents are encouraged to participate in the process by telling their story, the purpose of hearing the story is to enable the provider to identify and address the family's problems and underlying issues. The provider uses his or her relationship with the family as a context for assessment and diagnosis of problems (no mention is made of strengths as well), not as a context for collaboration.

It is important to assess how the parents perceive, experience, and interpret the infant's behavior.... This...usually opens up for exploration the parents'

own early experiences and how they may be involved in the problems of the baby. Here again, it is crucial not to pass by or gloss over any areas of anxiety or conflict which may emerge, but instead to focus incisively on them in a persistent but respectful manner. (Hirshberg, 1996, pp. 116–17)

PARENT PERSPECTIVES. Families have frequently described the traumatic way that the diagnosis of mental retardation (Roos, 1985) and autism (Akerley, 1985) was delivered to them by professionals – particularly during the height of the counseling/psychotherapeutic model in the 1950s and 1960s. One parent of a child with Down syndrome described the following situation:

About 8 P.M. the doctor came in and said abruptly: "Read the numbers of the baby's ID bracelet, and the one on your wrist. See, it's the same. This baby is yours. This happens to women your age. You may want genetic counseling, and you'll probably want to put it in a home." (Turnbull & Turnbull, 1997, p. 137)

Paradoxically, there is very little in the research literature of this period concerning the impact of the professional's diagnosis on parent perspectives.

Parents of children with autism were particularly subject to a counseling–psychotheraputic orientation (Bettelheim, 1950, 1967). Mary Akerley (1985), a parent of a son with autism, describes in some detail the ordeal that she and her husband encountered in their "enforced" therapy (i.e., for their son to receive treatment in the late 1960s, they were required to be recipients of psychotherapy).

One of Eddy's favorite play things was a set of wooden dowels that were part of a construction-type toy. His way of enjoying them was to stand them on end, lie down, and move his head back and forth behind them....I chose to see his little game, after trying it myself, as an independent discovery of the theory of relativity. Not so. The learned doctor, who patiently explained to me that I had clearly kept Eddie in his crib and play pen too much because he was now reliving the behind-bars trauma! My response was really more innocent than sarcastic, although it was not perceived that way. "If it was so awful, why is he reliving it with such obvious pleasure?" No answer came. (Akerley, 1985, p. 28)

Another parent told of her interactions with the psychologist sent to her home. This parent describes how her concerns about her two young children were addressed. Her older child had autism, and her younger child had microcephaly, and had begun to projectile vomit.

A psychologist...began visiting my house. [He] told me [he] could find nothing physically wrong with my child. Then [he] said I wasn't bonding properly, and I had given my child infantile depression....During one of the psychologist's visits, my son started acting up, pushing the baby. When I corrected him before comforting my baby, the psychologist said, "That's a perfect example. You paid attention to the older child and neglected the baby." (Autism National Committee, 1996, p. xviii)

EXPECTED OUTCOMES. The primary outcome of the counseling/psychotherapy model was for mothers to reach the final stage of adjustment, namely, acceptance of and adaptation to their child with a disability (Wolfensberger, 1967). To reach that result, mothers had to be helped by treatment to pass through the sequential stages of shock, denial, anger, guilt, or depression so that they could reach acceptance (Grays, 1963; Koegler, 1963; Rosen, 1955). Obviously, in this model, power remained in the hands of the professionals. Because professionals frequently recommended institutionalization of children with mental retardation or other obvious disabilities (Farrell, 1957; Gordon & Ullman, 1956; Koch, Graliker, Sands, & Parmelee, 1959), professional intervention sought the parental outcome of making the institutional placement without suffering negative reactions.

Little emphasis in the parent counseling/psychotherapeutic literature of the 1950s and 1960s was given to any kind of outcome for the infants and toddlers with disabilities. Because this model was particularly prevalent before the time children with developmental disabilities acquired a legal right to early childhood services or elementary–secondary education, it was often assumed that children were not educable and that services and intervention for children was relatively futile.

Parent Training/Involvement Model

OVERVIEW. Two perspectives on parent training and involvement were evidenced in the compensatory education programs for disadvantaged children (a term used in the 1960s and 1970s that today is considered to be culturally insensitive) of the 1960s (Zigler & Valentine, 1979). These parent involvement perspectives, in turn, strongly influenced early intervention for children with disabilities. Based on evidence that family environment influences children's intelligence (Hunt, 1972), the first perspective viewed parents as being in need of remediation to improve their child's development. This is a *parent-deficit model*. This model leads to parent involvement activities that "adopt a primary, didactic, instructional role as a part of the intervention program" (Guralnick, 1989, p. 12) and treat parents as learners so that, in turn, they could be their children's teachers.

The second perspective, based in President Kennedy's New Frontier and President Johnson's Great Society programs and characterized as a *political model*, regarded parents as disenfranchised and in need of an opportunity to increase their decision-making power. Accordingly, parent involvement elements of early Head Start programs gave parents opportunities to be decision makers, not just recipients of services.

TYPE OF POWER. The parent training/involvement model usually continued the power-over relationship of the parent counseling/psychotherapy model. Professionals still had control of communication and resources. In the parent training/involvement model, the parents, primarily mothers, were not necessarily viewed as emotionally deficient but as lacking the specific skills needed to raise their child with a disability.

Professionals used their expert power (Kisthardt, 1992; Skrtic, 1995) to make and prescribe the intervention for children who had disabilities. More significantly, this exercise of power by the providers had an impact on the family system. Family functions and interactions could be interrupted by the demands of intervention activities that parents were expected to complete. Jeannette, for example, might find herself making a choice between working with Tisha to practice picking up puzzle pieces and going to an AA meeting scheduled in the evening. Jeannette would be caught in the dilemma of doing the intervention program that she had been told to do to help Tisha's fine motor skills or working to keep her commitment to long-term sobriety.

ASSUMPTIONS. The assumptions of the parent training/involvement model are as follows:

1. Children with disabilities will learn more and will be more likely to minimize or overcome their disability if their parents teach them at home, supplementing professionals' teaching. Parents need training to be effective teachers.

2. Because parents are viewed as being disenfranchised from program input, they need explicit opportunities to be decision makers regarding program operation. Parents who learn to be effective decision makers within the program will be more effective decision makers at home, and their children will benefit from this enhanced parental skill.

3. Parents have time and energy to be involved in their child's training and educational program.

4. Parent involvement is oriented toward enhancing program and child outcomes, as contrasted to parental outcomes (e.g., helping parents get a job or access to economic resources) or system outcomes (e.g., creating greater access to community participation on the part of children with disabilities).

5. Parent training/involvement typically is mother training/involvement, with little evidence in the literature that fathers have been highly involved in these kinds of activities.

6. Parents should act as agents of professionals, which will result in children receiving the benefit of educational programs that are delivered by professionals, as well as their parents. When parents carry out professional roles at home, it should not interfere with their parenting role, so this approach is additive for the child as contrasted to the child "losing a parent" to "gain another teacher."

PROFESSIONAL PERSPECTIVES. With compensatory education programs as a precursor, Congress authorized the Handicapped Children's Early Education Program (HCEEP) in 1968 for children from birth to 8. HCEEP projects were expected to demonstrate methods and techniques for enhancing the development of preschoolers with disabilities (Harvey, 1977). In addition, they were expected to enlist parents as allies of early intervention specialists, as the chairman of the Select Committee on Education, Congressman Dominick V. Daniels, made clear:

Few parents are prepared to take care of a child who looks different, behaves in grossly unacceptable ways or fails to respond even to the sound of a mother's voice.

Parents of handicapped children have fears and are often frustrated and bewildered. They need help in understanding their child's disability. They need help in working with their handicapped child.

This bill will bring us into a new era of educating handicapped children. In addition, it is anticipated that this legislation will enlist the help of the parents as allies and associates of educators to provide a total program. (Lavor & Krivit, 1969, p. 381)

Federal regulations implementing the HCEEP network specified four parent involvement modes:

1. parent assistance in project planning, development, operation, and evaluation;
2. parent training;
3. parent participation in educational and therapeutic project components; and
4. parent participation in advising and assisting in information dissemination related to the project.

A major impetus for parent involvement came from P.L. 94-142, now titled the Individuals with Disabilities Education Act (IDEA). P.L. 94-142 required that parents be invited to attend their child's IEP conference. Comprehensive reviews of research on the nature of parent involvement in the IEP process is beyond the scope of this chapter and can be found in other sources (Smith, 1990; Turnbull & Turnbull, 1997; Wood, 1995). In brief, however, research reveals that the IEP process is a passive experience for most parents: parents, such as Jeanette, typically listen to professionals describe to them an already developed IEP. The professionals still hold the power over the family to determine the child's needs and to prescribe the best approach to addressing those needs. Notwithstanding this fact, the IEP model served as a precursor for the IFSP, which was implemented with the intention of incorporating a family-centered approach (which is discussed in the next section).

PARENT PERSPECTIVES. Jeannette was no longer targeted for intervention because of deficiencies as a parent or person; she now was recognized as "extra hands" for the provider. She and other parents were enlisted as assistants to the teacher or therapist. Jeannette often heard the phrase, "We can only teach her five hours of the day; you have her the rest of the time. You have more opportunity to teach her than we." So each time Jeannette met with a provider, she went home with a list of discrete therapy or teaching activities. These activities often included a sheet for keeping "data" as she worked with Tisha.

For Jeannette, the parent involvement model meant that most activities with Tisha had a teaching component designed by the teacher or therapist to work on deficit areas. Jeannette was given training to incorporate speech and language skills into the family dinner hour and to teach Tisha to stack blocks during the time Jeannette had in her schedule for playing with Tisha. Jeannette did not see these as priorities for Tisha. She thought that Tisha's learning to entertain herself so that she could be less dependent on parental attention was a higher priority, given their family style. The teacher, however, said "home therapy" had to be done, so Jeannette was trying valiantly to follow through with the program.

For many parents the parent training/involvement model presented a conflict in role expectations. Often, parents did not want to take on a pedagogical role but instead wanted to be "just" parents, not teachers (Seligman & Darling, 1997). Martha Blue-Banning, whose son Ryan is 20 years old and has Down syndrome, often relates her regret at the loss of Ryan's toddler years. Martha remembers that everything she did with Ryan was "therapy"; there was not even a recognition that he was a baby and then a toddler who could be played with and enjoyed for himself (M. J. Blue-Banning, personal communication).

EXPECTED OUTCOMES. There has been a strong expectation within the early childhood special education field that higher quantity and quality of parent training/involvement result in better outcomes for children. There has been some disagreement over whether this outcome has been actualized, however. Casto and Lewis (1984) reported that programs involving parents were not necessarily more effective than programs that did not involve parents. Others, however, found benefits to parents and children from parent involvement. Shonkoff, Hauser-Cram, Krauss, and Upshur (1992) reported positive outcomes in the Early Intervention Collaborative Study for both parent and child as a result of the mother's involvement in early intervention. In one stage of this study, mother–child interactive skills were corre-

lated positively with the cognitive performance and adaptive behavior of their children (Krauss, 1993). During this period of the study, the children demonstrated "relatively accelerated growth in adaptive behavior and play skills" (Krauss, 1997, p. 615). It is important to note that parent involvement was a means to achieving child outcomes – not a means for achieving parent or family outcomes. Jeannette's role was to help remediate Tisha's deficits. That role was dictated to her without regard for other family demands or circumstances. Service providers still maintained a position of power over Jeannette and the rest of the family.

Family-Centered Model

MODEL OVERVIEW. At the core of the family-centered approaches is the recognition of the centrality of the family – not just the mother – in the life of the child (Bailey & McWilliam, 1993; Shelton, Jeppson, & Johnson, 1989). Conceptually, family-centered intervention also recognizes the relationships between individual family members, the nuclear family, the extended family, and community as factors affecting the functioning of the family and the development of the child. The goal of family-centered intervention is one of improving the well-being of the family as a whole (Bailey & McWilliam, 1993). Family-centered models became more prevalent in the mid-to-late 1980s.

It is difficult to define the specific characteristics of family-centered services. Despite varying definitions, however, two elements are consistently included as nonnegotiable in the delivery of family-centered services: family choice and a family strengths perspective (Allen & Petr, 1996).

Family Choice. Support for family decision making is central to definitions of family-centered services (Allen & Petr, 1996; McBride, Brotherson, Joanning, Whiddon, & Demmitt, 1993; Raver & Kilgo, 1991). The family choice component of family-centered services is expressed in many different ways but has at its core the concept that a family is the final decision maker when it comes to issues related to their child or family. It is Jeannette's decision to include issues related to her participation in AA in her IFSP, not the service provider's. Some definitions refer to this as *consumer-driven services* (Dunst, Johnson, Trivette,

& Hamby, 1991) or as responsiveness to families' priorities and choices (Lee, 1993; Leviton, Mueller, & Kauffman, 1992). The role of the professional in this decision-making process is to be the agent or instrument of the family in the promotion of family decision making (Dunst et al., 1991).

Choices for Jeannette and other families begin with their decision to participate in the process and their level of participation (Simeonsson & Bailey, 1990). Other choices include but are not limited to: 1) family membership; 2) decision maker; 3) unit of attention; 4) nature of the family–professional relationship; 5) sharing of information; 6) identification of needs, goals, and intervention; and 7) limits of choice (Allen & Petr, 1996). The choice-making component recognizes that the decisions families make may vary from opportunity to opportunity and depend on their perceptions of their resources, concerns, and priorities and on the resources, concerns, and priorities of those around them.

Family Strengths Perspective. The second constant in family-centered intervention is the adoption of a strengths perspective in working with families (Allen & Petr, 1996). Family-centered intervention includes the belief that every family has strengths (Bailey & McWilliam, 1993) that arise from the family's capacities, talents, possibilities, visions, values, and hopes that have survived circumstance, oppression, and trauma (Saleebey, 1996). Often, the environment around the individual or family is such that their strengths cannot be used effectively to address a problem. One professional role is to facilitate the availability of environments where those strengths can be recognized and used (Dunst, Trivette, & Deal, 1988). Another role is to focus on the strengths and resources of the family rather than on their pathology, deficits, or needs (Bailey & McWilliam, 1993).

Focusing on the family's strengths and resources requires the professional to look at those things that will enable the family to carry out their responsibilities effectively. Building on family strengths also mandates that services enhance families' knowledge, skills, and abilities to make decisions about their child; mobilize social resources and supports; protect the family from unwarranted intrusion; and enable parents to make choices by providing a variety of information and options (Dokecki & Heflinger, 1989).

POWER AND THE FAMILY-CENTERED MODEL. The move to family-centered services also marks a change in the power relationships between families and service providers. Its emergence is accompanied by a power realignment. In a shift from a power-over relationship to a power-with partnership, parents and service providers each have some power to determine what issues should be included and addressed and what resources should be provided.

For Jeanette, this means that she chooses the team members who can contribute the most to the outcomes she wishes. She requested parenting help, and efforts were made to move her to the top of the list for the local Parents as Teachers program. With the shared power of family-centered services, she also took a role in identifying sources of funding for the medications she needed. She called several agencies with which she was familiar while her service coordinator called those she knew.

In family-centered services, parents share power with providers while maintaining their role as ultimate decision maker by determining outcomes, resources, and allocation (Turbiville et al., 1996). Some providers oppose sharing power because they view it as a loss of power on their part (Ross, 1995).

Although power is shared with families in this model, this model still assumes a limited amount of power available in a partnership. In previous models, in which the service providers had power over families, the providers had all the power. With the implementation of a family-centered model, service providers and families share power – service providers have power with families.

ASSUMPTIONS. The assumptions underlying family-centered service delivery were first articulated by Shelton, Jeppson, and Johnson in 1989 as principles of family-centered care and were later modified in recognition of the racial, ethnic, cultural, and economic diversity of families (Johnson, 1990). Although other people have suggested different principles, most formulations have their foundation in those listed here (Johnson, 1990).

1. The family is a constant in the child's life, whereas the service systems and personnel within those systems fluctuate.
2. Family–professional collaboration at all levels of care is facilitated.

3. The racial, ethnic, cultural, and socioeconomic diversity of families is honored.
4. Family strengths, individuality, and methods of coping are recognized and respected.
5. Complete and unbiased information is shared with families on a continuing basis and in a supportive manner.
6. Family-to-family support and networking are encouraged and facilitated.
7. Systems of care understand and include the developmental needs of infants, children, and adolescents and their families.
8. Comprehensive policies and programs are implemented that provide emotional and financial support to meet their family needs.
9. Accessible systems of care are designed that are flexible, culturally competent, and responsive to family identified strengths and needs.

PROFESSIONAL PERSPECTIVES. For some professionals, the shift to family-centered services has been difficult. Because most were trained to provide services to children, providing services to the children within the family system framework presents numerous challenges. These challenges include a lack of familiarity, experience, and training in including families in early intervention (Bailey et al., 1992) and time to pursue a holistic, family-centered approach (McWilliam, Tocci, & Harbin, 1995).

The movement toward the family-centered model requires professionals not only to expand their resource knowledge from child-focused to family-focused priorities but it also requires them to change their decision-making approaches (Bailey et al., 1992; Dunst et al., 1993; Seligman & Darling, 1997; Turnbull & Turnbull, 1997). Because professionals have traditionally been the primary decision makers concerning any intervention, implementing a family-centered model requires that decision-making power reside with the family. Collaboration becomes the operating mode in identifying and achieving child and family outcomes (Turbiville et al., 1996).

A challenge for professionals working in the family-centered model is answering satisfactorily the question "What's in it for me?" Family-centered services are values based; if professionals do not value collaborative partnerships and mutual responsibility, the answer to this question is problematic.

FAMILY PERSPECTIVES. For families, the shift to family-centered services has also been challenging. Families have been conditioned by professionals to be the recipients of professional expertise, particularly when they first learn of their child's disability (Seligman & Darling, 1997). McWilliam, Tocci, and Harbin (1995) reported that services to infants and toddlers continue to be far more child- than family-oriented, perhaps because of parent preferences for this emphasis. Families, however, are now expecting their preferences and expertise to be respected as services are made available to their children and family. For families such as Jeannette's, the implementation of the family-centered model means that issues such as getting to AA meetings, finding housing for Lenny, and securing money for her medications could be part of the intervention effort.

Parents report a greater sense of control and direction when services are family centered (Turbiville, Schaffer, Schaffer, & Brammel, 1997). Families find that sharing information and decision making helps them maintain equal footing in the partnership:

The staff at the early intervention center knew we wanted Aric to attend a regular kindergarten class...They gave us ideas to get him into the setting. They never took control out of our hands, and we always did the steps ourselves. They were there as a resource and support. (Leifield & Murray, 1995, cited in Seligman & Darling, 1997)

EXPECTED OUTCOMES. Family-centered early intervention services are expected to generate outcomes for both the child and the family. The family outcomes include an increase in their abilities to meet the needs of their children (McGonigel, Kaufmann, & Johnson, 1991; Pearl, 1993) and an increase in their sense of competence in meeting those needs (Allen & Petr, 1996). Although family-centered services are designed to address family and child issues, the family issues to be addressed relate to those that would increase the family's ability to meet the child's needs. For Jeannette, family-centered services meant she could choose the professionals with whom she wanted to work most closely without being "accused" of shopping around. Furthermore, when she was not interested in placing her child in foster care or adoption, her preference for providing care herself is respected.

Other anticipated outcomes of family-centered services include the involvement of family and kin and the coordination of service delivery (Dokecki & Heflinger, 1989). These outcomes can be achieved through the utilization of a systems approach in planning and implementing intervention services, primarily at the micro- and meso-system levels or in the immediate setting and environment of the child and family members (Bronfenbrenner, 1979).

Although rhetoric within the family-centered model focuses on family outcomes, the actual outcomes of family-centered intervention have been primarily child-centered (Boone, Moore, & Coulter, 1995; Guralnick, 1989; Mahoney & O'Sullivan, 1990; McWilliam et al., 1995). That is, the outcomes written most often are for child skill development. In spite of family-centered assumptions, providers are still trained to work with children rather than with their families and have found it very difficult to shift their focus from the individual child to the child within a family (Bailey et al., 1992).

Moreover, family-centered services still primarily include the mother (Able-Boone, 1993). Turnbull (1993) reported that even in research on parents and families, twelve times as many mothers as contrasted to fathers were involved as participants. Only two percent of outcomes written for the IFSP address paternal issues (Sparling, Berger, & Billing, 1992). Grandparents or brothers and sisters are also usually absent from the early intervention process (Able-Boone, 1993). Most services and support to families come from the formal rather than informal support network (Boone et al., 1995; Crnic & Stormshak, 1997) and from agencies charged with early intervention service delivery rather than from resources throughout the community ecology (Polmanteer & Turbiville, 1997).

Another outcome has been the extra effort made by service providers to provide family-centered intervention when families represent diverse cultural groups. Each family must dictate its membership (Brinker, 1992) and its way of performing family functions (Turnbull & Turnbull, 1997). The assumptions underlying family-centered approaches must be individually tailored for families in a manner that is consistent with their culture and family traditions.

Collective Empowerment Model

OVERVIEW. Definitions of empowerment vary across disciplines, including sociology (Alinsky, 1969; Freire, 1973); psychology (Rappaport, 1987; Zimmerman, 1990, 1992); social work (Gottlieb, 1992; Gutiérrez & Nurius, 1994; Kaplan & Girard, 1994; Pinderhughes, 1994); and education (Turnbull & Turnbull, 1997). The central element in the many definitions, however, is the process of taking action to get what one wants and needs. The outcome of the empowerment process is gaining mastery or control over the challenges that one faces on a daily basis.

Early views of empowerment in early intervention addressed the empowerment of families. Families were viewed as lacking the competence to achieve the outcomes they desired for their child or family. Service providers were assumed to have this competence and therefore were already regarded as empowered. They needed to use their own skills and power to facilitate or enable the empowerment of the family. Unfortunately, it appears that many service providers perceive that they, too, are unable to access the resources they need (Epstein, 1995; Mlawer, 1993; Skrtic, 1991). It would seem to be difficult for service providers who perceive themselves to be unable to access the resources they need to achieve the desired outcomes of actively facilitating or enabling family empowerment. This realization of the sense of disempowerment by service providers has provoked a revision of the thinking on family empowerment. Currently, the contemporary focus is on collective empowerment, in which all participants (i.e., professionals and families) increase their capacity and mastery over the resources needed to achieve mutually desired outcomes (Epstein, 1995; Gutiérrez & Nurius, 1994; Pinderhughes, 1994; Turnbull & Turnbull, 1997).

Indeed, there are three elements of a collective empowerment program philosophy that surpass a singular family focus. One element relates to the families; they represent one group of beneficiaries of an empowerment approach. Another element relates to the professionals; they too are beneficiaries of an empowerment approach. The third element relates to the context in which the families and professionals interact and collaborate. The context is also a beneficiary, because collective empowerment has the outcome of making contexts more responsive.

TYPE OF POWER. The essence of the collective empowerment model is synergistic power, not monopolized power (Bond & Keys, 1993; Epstein, 1995; Katz, 1984; Turnbull & Turnbull, 1997). The new model assumes power-through family–professional partnerships. The collaboration itself creates its own power and then radiates that power synergistically throughout the contexts of community ecology. By contrast, some of the previous models assume power-over in which professionals control the relationship for the purpose of fixing the patient or a power-with situation in which the available power is shared.

In the collective empowerment model, not only is power gained for all participants through the partnerships but the very nature of the power generated is also transformed. Power is no longer only to control events and resources. Power has become capacity building, with participants gaining in competence, abilities, resource acquisition, and capability without taking any power from others (Wagner, 1992). Kanter (cited in Wagner, 1992) stated that power is the ability to get things done and is not domination or control over others. With the collective empowerment model, power or capacity also becomes a limitless resource for everyone in the partnership (Katz, 1984). It is not a scarcity to be hoarded by any member; there is power, as capacity, for all.

ASSUMPTIONS. Many of the assumptions of the collective empowerment model are consistent with the previously discussed assumptions of the family-centered model. As applied to early intervention, the collective empowerment model assumes 1) centrality of the family, 2) family choices as the basis of decision making, and 3) family strengths and capabilities as the focus of intervention. The major additional assumptions within a collective empowerment model focus on 1) access to resources, 2) participation, and 3) changing community ecology.

Access to Resources. Taking action to achieve what one wants and needs requires that families and professionals have access to resources. Two key components of the collective empowerment approach are that 1) participants must be knowledge-able about the resources that would make the most substantial difference to them in gaining a sense of control in their lives and 2) they should participate in the decision-making process about the nature and extent of resources allocated to them. For example, family support programs provide monetary resources to families that they may spend to meet a wide variety of needs; their choices are not limited by the restrictions of the service agency or professional (Agosta & Melda, 1995; Bradley, Knoll, & Agosta, 1993; Garlow, Turnbull, & Schnase, 1991). The role of the professional is to facilitate or guide the family in the process of obtaining preferred resources within both formal and informal systems (see Figure 27.2).

Although the traditional view of service delivery has been that families primarily need formal services (e.g., counseling, psychotherapy, and training) delivered by professionals, a collective empowerment approach focuses on resources available from the informal system as well. Families are encouraged to network with other family members, friends, neighbors, and community providers in gaining resources in the least restrictive environment of their family life.

Jeannette would determine preferred resources in an empowerment model. Working with her providers and friends, who also know the system, she would decide where best to obtain those resources that would work for her. The timing and the use of these resources would also be her decision to make or delegate. Through this collaboration and dialogue about the resources, her service providers and friends gain information about and access to new assets. Thus, all involved increase their capacity and therefore their power.

Participation. A key element of a collective empowerment approach is opportunities for families and providers to participate in a decision-making process in which power is shared and family roles vis-à-vis professionals are characterized as being equal rather subordinate or hierarchical (Kieffer, 1984; Prestby, Wandersman, Florin, Rich, & Chavis, 1990). If, for example, a preschool program advisory board consists almost entirely of professionals and only one or two parents, then the parents are deemed to have unequal participation. Similarly, if an early childhood organization assembles a training manual in which all chapters are written by

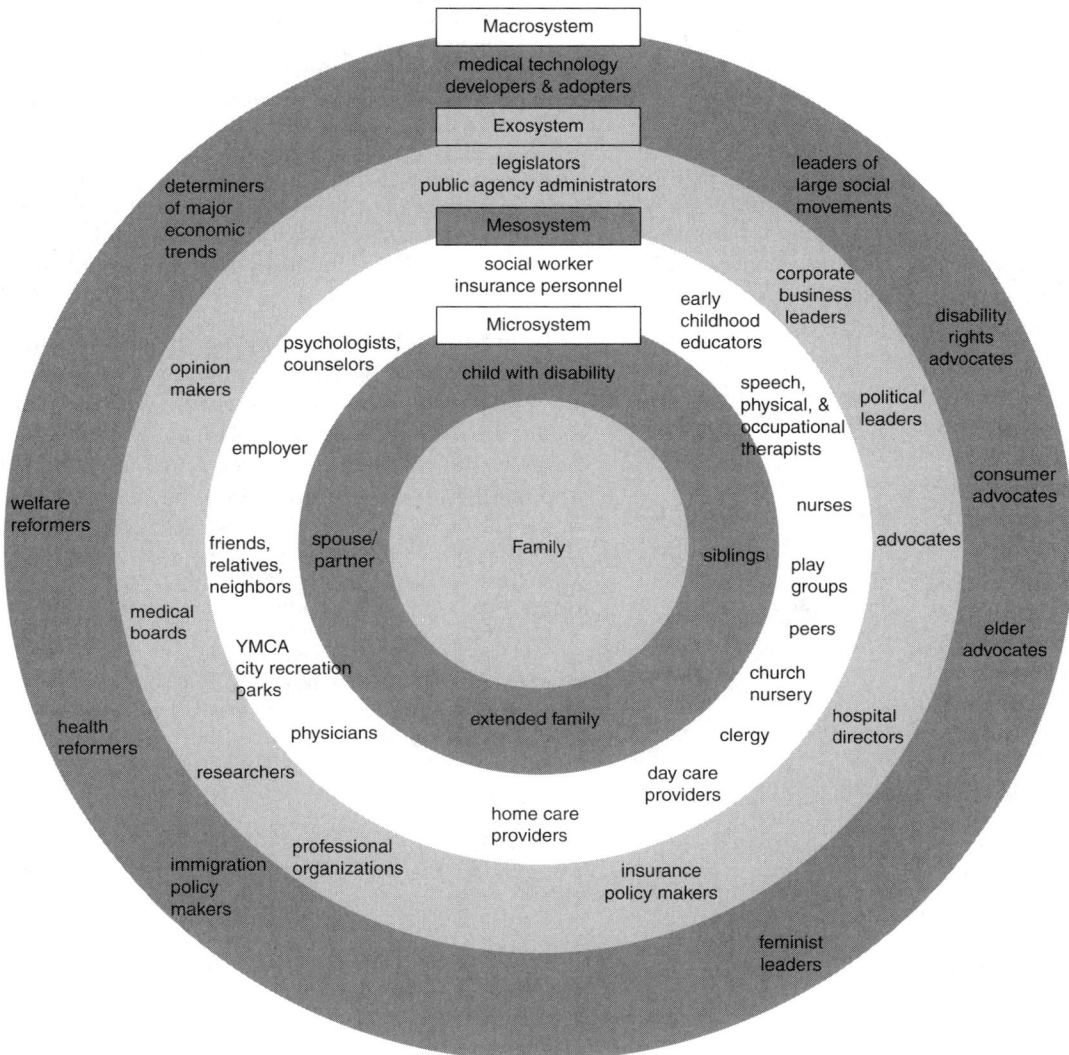

Figure 27.2. Bronfenbrenner's (1979) Ecological Model Applied to Families of Young Children

Adapted from: Singer, G. H. S. (1996). Introduction: Trends affecting home and community care for people with chronic conditions in the United States. In G. H. S. Singer, L. E. Powers, & A. L. Olson (Eds.), *Redefining family support: Innovations in public/private partnerships* (pp. 3–38). Baltimore: Paul H. Brookes Publishing Company.

professionals with the sole exception of one that is written by a mother, it cannot be assumed by the professionals that they have collaborated with families in writing their manual. Participation in an empowerment approach recognizes that power in these types of activities is inherently unequal and that genuine participation requires that there is a sufficient presence of families so that the numbers and respective contributions of families and professionals are roughly equal. Thus, in the development of a training manual, all chapters might be coauthored by a professional and family member (e.g., mothers, fathers, siblings, grandparents). Fam-

ilies thus fully participate in the development of the product, and their views are pervading rather than segmented. (We do not mean to imply here that all products should be developed equally by professionals and families. Our point is that many professionals dominate the writing of products and then "claim" that the products were written in collaboration with families. This claim should only be made when there has been equal participation.)

Moreover, equal participation should occur from the initiation of project planning through project completion (Turnbull, Friesen, & Ramírez, 1995; Whitney-Thomas, 1997; Whyte, 1991). It is insufficient to bring parents into a project after the project has already been conceptualized and key decisions have been made by professionals. Genuine participation means being at an even table (Kritek, 1994) from the outset so that the nature of the project can be shaped from a family as well as a professional perspective.

Finally, because families choose to participate at different levels, at different times, and in different ways, participatory involvement in a collective empowerment model means that family choice pervades the process and decisions about family participation are made by families rather than professionals.

Changes in Community Ecology. The parent counseling–psychotherapy model assumes that the mother is broken and needs to be "fixed" within the mother–child microsystem relationship. Functioning competently at all levels of community ecology (see Figure 27.2) is largely ignored. Rather than viewing the "problem" as solely residing within the mother-child relationship, however, the collective empowerment model views "needs" as largely residing within all four levels of ecological context (see Table 27.2).

PROFESSIONAL PERSPECTIVES. Within the collective empowerment approach, professionals primarily assume the roles of facilitator, collaborator, or partner rather than expert or specialist (Gutiérrez & Nurius, 1994; Turnbull, Turbiville, Schaffer, & Schaffer, 1996; Turnbull & Turnbull, 1997). Bailey (1994) described the concept of dialogue within an empowerment approach, on the basis of the work of Paulo Freire (1981), a Brazilian educator whose work focuses on overcoming oppression.

Briefly, Freire conceives a dialogue is more than a conversation between two people. Dialogue is truly an act of creation. For example, you and I come together and discuss a certain topic. I have opinions "B," and you have opinions "A." In true dialogue, we both are willing to *share* our opinions and simultaneously be *open* to the opinions of the other. In true dialogue, there is mutuality of *respect* (of self and other), *trust* (in self and other), and *caring* (of self and other). Freire talks about these as elements of dialogue – humility, faith, hope, and love. So in true dialogue, we risk being changed as we take on some of the opinions of the other. We are transformed; we have engaged in critical thinking and mutually created an opinion "C" on this topic. (Bailey, 1994, pp. 38–9)

According to Freire (1981), this type of exchange can take place only when there is equality among the parties involved. This equality must be established by working to counterbalance the natural imbalance that often occurs between the professionals and families, the powerful and the powerless.

[P]ractitioners' readiness to empower clients, to value strengths, to respect cultural meaning, to take one-down positions when appropriate, and to engineer larger system change is heavily dependent on practitioner capacity to manage personal power need. Knowledge of how power operates in the helping encounter and how it influences personal motivation and behavior is key. This is so because the power differential that exists between practitioners and their clients is such that it can be and has too often been exploited by practitioners who intend to engage clients but who instead meet their own needs for personal power and esteem through the intervention process (Pinderhughes, 1989; Heller, 1985). (Pinderhughes, 1994, p. 27)

PARENT PERSPECTIVES. Because the collective empowerment model is relatively new in the evolution of family–professional partnership approaches and is being presented here as a direction for the future, there are few published reports from parents who have participated in early intervention programs with this orientation. One such report describes the perspectives of Hortense Walker and the early intervention services she received for her son Eric in south-central Los Angeles. She characterizes her best experience in an early intervention program as being provided by a teacher, Marlene, who visited her home when Eric was 18 months old. Asked how Marlene was encouraging, Hortense responded:

We came to see Marlene as a person whose first objective was to meet the needs of our family as a whole. She emphasized the positives of the program for us and for Eric. We just ate up her time and her knowledge.

She felt appreciated by us, and she was. That made the difference.

Synergy occurs in collective empowerment when parents feel appreciated by professionals, and professionals feel appreciated by parents. The positive energy can enhance capacities for all participants. Susan Rocco, the mother of a young adolescent with autism, compares and contrasts other models of parent–professional partnerships with the empowerment approach as follows:

As the parent of a teenager with both medical and educational challenges, I had experienced most points on the power continuum. The unequal power relationship with Jason's teachers and therapists generally put the burden on me to wheedle, cajole, threaten, flatter – in essence, work harder at the relationship than anyone else – to get the desired outcome. The few times I have experienced true synergy, when we partners are working from our strengths and shared values, the burden has fallen away. The beauty of the synergistic model is that there is no more "them" and "us." "We" pool our resources and our creative juices, and "we" all celebrate in the success.

EXPECTED OUTCOMES. A number of outcomes have been identified as resulting from collective empowerment (Bond & Keys, 1993; Katz, 1984; Kieffer, 1984; Natiello, 1990; Saleebey, 1992). Three of these seem particularly relevant as outcomes of collective empowerment in family–professional partnerships. These include 1) synergy (Bond & Keys, 1993), 2) creation of renewable and expandable resources (Saleebey, 1992), and 3) increased satisfaction by participants (Natiello, 1990). Although these outcomes are separate, they are also strongly linked.

Synergy is commonly discussed as the outcome of collective empowerment (Bond & Keys, 1993; Katz, 1984; Kieffer, 1984; Saleebey, 1992). The synergy in collective empowerment results in the effectiveness of the group being greater than the sum of the individual parts (Bond & Keys, 1993). Synergy is an outcome of collective empowerment through the interaction of the empowerment of the individuals and their collaboration with each other (Bond & Keys, 1993). When only individuals are empowered, without collaboration, there can be little agreement on direction and united effort. Each empowered individual proceeds in his or her own manner and course. On the other hand, if there is collabo-

ration without empowerment, collaboration can become co-option by the strongest individual or group (Bond & Keys, 1993). Synergy, therefore, can be an outcome only when there is both collaboration and empowerment, as in collective empowerment.

A second outcome of collective empowerment is the accessibility of new and renewable resources. These resources are created from the synergy of the partnership. Traditionally, we have viewed resources as scarce and, in many instances, unavailable (Katz, 1984). Through the implementation of collective empowerment, however, resources are constantly being created and re-created by the interaction and synergy of the group members.

Finally, collective empowerment results in an increase in satisfaction for all who participate. Because individuals feel able to meet their needs and are more self-efficient, self-satisfaction increases (Swick, 1988). The increased energy and creativity released through the collective empowerment process may also contribute to the increased sense of satisfaction (Turbiville et al., 1997).

For Jeannette, the collective empowerment of Tisha's intervention group and her family has meant more creative solutions to old problems. These solutions are more stable because of the support of all concerned. Tisha is attending a community preschool as a result of group action planning (Turnbull, Turnbull, & Blue-Banning, 1994; Turnbull, Turbiville, Schaffer, & Schaffer, 1996) by Jeannette, her family, and the intervention team to put together an intervention program that is not overwhelming to the preschool staff or to the early childhood staff. The two staffs believe they share the responsibilities of Tisha's participation in the preschool. The occupational therapist implements the speech-language pathologist's goals two days a week, and they reverse roles the other two days (Rainforth & York-Barr, 1997). Consequently, Tisha receives both services four days a week without adding to either therapy schedule. The preschool staff observes all of the sessions and use the same approaches, and they also take responsibility for sharing those strategies with Jeannette on a daily basis. Tisha's consistent participation in the program allows Jeannette to get to her AA meetings and also to spend time with her mother and Lenny. Jeannette and her group have recently begun to discuss the possibility of applying for a place on the Habitat for

Humanity housing list in the community. They plan to share in the "sweat equity" that Jeannette will be required to contribute. Everyone thinks it will open a whole new set of available resources for each of them.

CONCLUSION

In this chapter, we presented four different models of interaction and power distribution in parent–professional partnerships. Through the vision and advocacy of many, primarily family members and advocates, the partnership orientation of service providers and families has evolved along a developmental continuum from a psychotherapeutic/counseling partnership to parent involvement, family-centeredness, and finally, collective empowerment.

In reality, all four models continue to be used in early intervention. Possibly because their needs and resources change, family preferences for their relationship with early intervention providers change. If family choice is indeed the reason for the continued use of the various models, this continued usage may indicate that the partnerships are based on the principles of family-centeredness or collective empowerment. As Allen and Petr (1996) suggested, one of the choices available to families in family-centered service delivery is that of the relationship between the family and the service providers.

Unfortunately, more often than not, the decision on the partnership model is probably made unilaterally by the service provider. If queried, the provider may respond that the family is satisfied with the partnership. This satisfaction, however, may be similar to the findings regarding the family's preferences for child outcomes (McWilliam et al., 1995). McWilliam et al. suggested that the family may not be aware of other approaches and options. Applied to partnership decisions, the family may not know that models other than the provider as the expert are available. Providers need to reflect on their partnerships with families and ensure that families truly have choices in how these critical relationships evolve.

The evolution of family–professional partnerships from an emphasis on parent (mother) counseling/psychotherapy to an emphasis on the collective empowerment of families and professionals has

represented change and challenge to the field of early childhood special education since the 1950s. Continued change and challenge are inevitable and welcome as we move into the new millennium. We invite the reader to stand in Jeannette's shoes and experience the life she lives. How does she develop the resources, the motivation, and the supportive environment she needs in order to participate in a collective empowerment model? Similarly, how do her providers learn to embrace the inherent values of a collective empowerment approach and the associated skills? Must her service providers first subscribe to collective empowerment and facilitate the development of her philosophy and skills? Can Jeannette facilitate the development in her providers? What is the impact on Jeannette, Tisha, Lenny, other family members and on providers of the partnership model?

The field of early intervention and early childhood special education has an opportunity to answer these questions and to continue to create even more responsive contexts for families and service providers. For now, and into the twenty-first century, we believe the model of collective empowerment holds the best promise for growth for infants, toddlers, and young children who have disabilities, their families, and their providers.

REFERENCES

Able-Boone, H. (1993). Family participation in the IFSP process: Family or professional driven? *Infant–Toddler Intervention, 3*(1), 63–72.

Agosta, J. M., & Melda, K. (1995). *Supplemental security income for children.* Boston: Human Services Research Institute.

Akerley, M. S. (1985). False gods and angry prophets. The loneliness of the long distance swimmer. In H. R. Turnbull & A. P. Turnbull (Eds.), *Parents speak out: Then and now* (2nd ed., pp. 23–38). Columbus, OH: Charles E. Merrill.

Alinsky, S. B. (1969). *Reveille for radicals.* New York: Vintage Books.

Allen, R. I., & Petr, C. G. (1996). Toward developing standards and measurements for family-centered practice in family support programs. In G. H. S. Singer, L. E. Powers, & A. L. Olson (Eds.), *Redefining family support: Innovations in public-private practice* (pp. 57–85). Baltimore, MD: Paul H. Brookes.

Autism National Committee. (1996). *New stories for a new day.* Ardmore, PA: Author.

Bailey, D. (1994). Organizational empowerment: From self to interbeing. In L. Gutiérrez & P. Nurius (Eds.), *Education and research for empowerment practice* (pp. 37–44). Seattle: University of Washington, School of Social Work, Center for Policy and Practice Research.

Bailey, D. B., Buysse, V., Edmondson, R., & Smith, T. M. (1992). Creating family-centered services in early intervention: Perceptions of professionals in four states. *Exceptional Children, 58*(4), 298–309.

Bailey, D. B., & McWilliam, P. J. (1993). The search for quality indicators. In P. J. McWilliam & D. B. Bailey (Eds.), *Working together with children and families* (pp. 3–20). Baltimore, MD: Paul H. Brookes.

Beddie, A., & Osmond, H. (1955). Mothers, mongols, and mores. *Medical Association Journal, 73*, 167–70.

Bettelheim, B. (1950). *Love is not enough.* Glencoe, NY: Free Press.

Bettelheim, B. (1967). *The empty fortress: Infantile autism and the birth of the self.* London: Collier-Macmillan.

Bibring, G. L. (1959). Some consideration of the psychological processes in pregnancy. *Psychoanalytic Study of the Child, 14*, 113–21.

Bibring, G. L., Dwyer, T. F., Huntington, D. S., & Valenstein, A. F. (1961). A study of the psychological processes in pregnancy and of the earliest mother–child relationships. I: Some propositions and comments. *Psychoanalytic Study of the Child, 16*, 9–24.

Bond, M., & Keys, C. (1993). Empowerment, diversity, and collaboration: Promoting synergy on community boards. *American Journal of Community Psychology, 21*(1), 37–57.

Boone, H. A., Moore, S. M., & Coulter, D. K. (1995). Achieving family-centered practice in early intervention. *Infant–Toddler Intervention, 5*(4), 395–404.

Bowlby, J. (1960). Grief and mourning in infancy and early childhood. *Psychoanalytic Study of the Child, 15*, 1–9.

Bradley, V. J., Knoll, J., & Agosta, J. M. (Eds.). (1993). *Emerging issues in family support* (Monograph No. 18, pp. 99–150). Washington, DC: American Association on Mental Retardation.

Brinker, R. (1992). Family involvement in early intervention: Accepting the unchangeable, changing the changeable, and knowing the difference. *Topics in Early Childhood Special Education, 12*(3), 307–32.

Bronfenbrenner, U. (1979). *The ecology of human development: Experiments by nature and design.* Cambridge, MA: Harvard University Press.

Casto, G., & Lewis, A. C. (1984, Fall). Parent involvement in infant and prechool programs. *Journal of the Division for Early Childhood*, 49–56.

Crais, E. R. (1993). Families and professionals as collaborators in assessment. *Topics in Language Disorders, 14*(1), 29–40.

Crnic, K., & Stormshak, E. (1997). The effectiveness of providing social support for families of children at risk. In M. Guralnick (Ed.), *The effectiveness of early intervention.* Baltimore, MD: Paul H. Brookes.

Dalton, J., & Epstein, H. (1963, November). Counseling parents of mildly retarded children. *Social Casework*, 523–30.

Darling, R. B. (1989). Using the social system perspective in early intervention: The value of a sociological approach. *Journal of Early Intervention, 13*(1), 24–35.

Dokecki, P. R., & Heflinger, C. A. (1989). Strengthening families of young children with handicapping conditions. In J. J. Gallagher, P. L. Trohanis, & R. M. Clifford (Eds.), *Policy implementation and PL 99-457: Planning for young children with special needs* (pp. 59–84). Baltimore: Brookes.

Dunst, C. J., Johnson, C., Trivette, C., & Hamby, D. (1991, October-November). Family- oriented early intervention policies and practices: Family-centered or not? *Exceptional Children, 58*(2), 115–26.

Dunst, C., Trivette, C., & Deal, A. (1988). *Enabling and empowering families: Principles and guidelines for practice.* Cambridge, MA: Brookline.

Dunst, C. J., Trivette, C. M., Gordon, N. J., & Starnes, L. (1993). Family-centered case management practices: Characteristics and consequences. In G. H. S. Singer & L. E. Powers (Eds.), *Families, disability, and empowerment: Active coping skills and strategies for family interventions* (pp. 89–118). Baltimore, MD: Paul H. Brookes.

Dunst, C. J., Trivette, C. M., & LaPointe, N. (1992). Toward clarification of the meaning and key elements of empowerment. *Family Studies Review, 5*(1 & 2), 111–30.

Emde, R. N., & Brown, C. (1978). Adaptation to the birth of a Down's syndrome infant. *Journal of the American Academy of Child Psychiatry, 17*, 299–323.

Epstein, J. L. (1995, May). School/family/community partnerships: Caring for the children we share. *Phi Delta Kappan*, pp. 701–12.

Farrell, M. (1957). The adverse effects of early institutionalization of mentally subnormal children. *American Journal of Disturbed Children, 61*, 675–8.

Foley, G. M., Hochman, J. D., & Miller, S. (1994). Parent–professional relationships: Finding an optimal distance. *Zero to Three, 14*(3), 19–22.

Follett, M. P. (1924). *Creative experience.* London: Longmans, Green.

Freire, P. (1973). *Education for critical consciousness.* New York: Seabury Press.

Friere, P. (1981). *Pedagogy of the oppressed.* New York: Continuum.

Freud, S. (1912/1953). Papers on technique. The dynamics of transference. In *The standard edition of the complete psychological works of Sigmund Freud* (Vol. 12, pp. 97–108). London: Hogarth Press.

Freud, S. (1914/1953). On narcissism: An introduction. In *The standard edition of the complete psychological works of Sigmund Freud* (Vol. 14, pp. 73–104). London: Hogarth Press.

Freud, S. (1917/1953). Mourning and melancholia. In *The standard edition of the complete psychological works of Sigmund Freud* (Vol. 14, pp. 243–60). London: Hogarth Press.

Freud, S. (1923/1927). *The ego and the id*. London: Hogarth Press.

Garlow, J. E., Turnbull, H. R., & Schnase, D. (1991). Model disability and family support. *Kansas Law Review, 39,* 783–815.

Gordon, E. W., & Ullman, M. (1956). Reactions of parents to problems of mental retardation in children. *American Journal of Mental Deficiency, 61,* 158–63.

Goshen, C. E. (1963). Mental retardation and neurotic maternal attitudes: A research report. *Archive of General Psychiatry, 9,* 168–74.

Gottlieb, N. (1992). Empowerment, political analyses, and services for women. In Y. Hasenfeld (Ed.), *Human services as complex organizations* (pp. 301–19). Newbury Park, CA: Sage.

Grays, C. (1963). At the bedside: The pattern of acceptance in parents of the retarded child. *Tommorrow's Nurse, 4*(3), 30–4.

Guralnick, M. (1989). Recent developments in early intervention efficacy research: Implications for family involvement in P.L. 99-457. *Topics in Early Childhood Special Education, 9,* 1–17.

Gutiérrez, L., & Nurius, P. (Eds.). (1994, October). *Education and research for empowerment practice* (Monograph No. 7). Seattle: University of Washington, School of Social Work, Center for Policy and Practice Research.

Harvey, J. (1977). The enabling legislation: How did it all begin? In J. B. Jordan, A. H. Hayden, M. B. Karnes, & M. M. Wood (Eds.), *Early childhood education for exceptional children: A handbook of ideas and exemplary practices*. Reston, VA: Council for Exceptional Children.

Heller, D. (1985). *Power in psychotherapeutic practice*. New York: Human Services Press.

Hirshberg, L. (1996). History-making, not history taking: Clinical interviews with infants and their families. In S. J. Meisels & E. Fenichel (Eds.), *New visions for the developmental assessment of infants and young children* (pp. 85–124). Washington, DC: Zero To Three: National Center for Infants, Toddlers and Families.

Hunt, J. (Ed.). (1972). *Human intelligence*. New Brunswick, NJ: Transaction Books.

Individuals with Disabilities Education Act (IDEA), 20 U. S. C. §§1400–1485 (1990).

Janis, I. L. (1958a). *Psychological stress*. New York: Wiley.

Janis, I. L. (1958b). Emotional inoculation: Theory and research on the effects of preparatory communications. In *Psychoanalysis and the social sciences* (Vol. 5, pp. 119–54). New York: International Universities Press.

Johnson, B. H. (1990). The changing role of families in health care. *Children's Health Care, 19*(4), 234–41.

Kalyanpur, M., & Rao, S. S. (1991). Empowering low-income black families of handicapped children. *American Journal of Orthopsychiatry, 61,* 523–32.

Kanner, L. (1953). Parents' feelings about retarded children. *American Journal on Mental Deficiency, 57,* 375–83.

Kaplan, L., & Girard, J. L. (1994). *Strengthening high-risk families: A handbook for practitioners*. Lexington, MA: Lexington Books.

Katz, R. (1984). Empowerment and synergy: Expanding the community's healing resources. *Prevention in Human Services, 3*(2 & 3), 201–26.

Kieffer, C. H. (1984). Citizen empowerment: A developmental perspective. *Prevention in Human Services, 3*(2 & 3), 9–36.

Kisthardt, W. E. (1992). A strengths model of case management: The principles and functions of a helping partnership with persons with persistent mental illness. In D. Saleebey (Ed.), *The strengths perspective in social work practice* (pp. 59–83). White Plains, NY: Longman.

Kjerland, L., & Kovach, J. (1990). Family–staff collaboration for tailored infant assessment. In E. P. Gibbs & D. M. Teti (Eds.), *Interdisciplinary assessment of infants: A guide for early intervention professionals* (pp. 287–97). Baltimore, MD: Paul H. Brookes.

Koch, R., Graliker, B. V., Sands, R., & Parmelee, A. H. (1959). Attitude study of parents with mentally retarded children: I. Evaluation of parental satisfaction with medical care of a retarded child. *Pediatrics, 23,* 582–4.

Koegler, S. J. (1963). The management of the retarded child in practice. *Canadian Medical Association Journal, 89,* 1009–14.

Krauss, M. W. (1993). *Stability and change in the adaptation of families of children with disabilities*. Paper presented at the Society for Research in Child Development Annual Meeting, New Orleans, LA.

Krauss, M. W. (1997). Two generations of family research in early intervention. In M. J. Guralnick (Ed.), *The effectiveness of early intervention* (pp. 611–24). Baltimore, MD: Paul H. Brookes.

Kritek, P. B. (1994). *Negotiating at an uneven table*. San Francisco: Jossey-Bass.

Lavor, M., & Krivit, D. (1969). The Handicapped Children's Early Education Assistance Act, Public Law 90-538. *Exceptional Children, 35,* 379–83.

Lee, I. M. (1993). *A validation study of the Family-Centered Program Rating Scale*. Unpublished doctoral dissertation, University of Kansas, Lawrence.

Leviton, A., Mueller, M., & Kauffman, C. (1992). The family-centered consultation model: Practical applications for professionals. *Infants and Young Children, 4*(3), 1–8.

Mahoney, G., & O'Sullivan, P. (1990). Early intervention practices with families of children with handicaps. *Mental Retardation, 28,* 169–76.

Mandelbaum, A., & Wheeler, M. E. (1960). The meaning of a defective child to parents. *Social Casework, 43,* 360–7.

McBride, S. L., Brotherson, M. J., Joanning, H., Whiddon, D., & Demmitt, A. (1993). Implementation of family-centered services: Perceptions of families and professionals. *Journal of Early Intervention, 17*(4), 414–30.

McGonigel, M. J., Kaufmann, R. K., & Johnson, B. H. (Eds.). (1991). *Guidelines and recommended practices for the Individualized Family Service Plan.* Bethesda, MD: Association for the Care of Children's Health.

McWilliam, R., Tocci, L., & Harbin, G. (1995, August). *Services are child-oriented and families like it that way – But why?* Chapel Hill, NC: Early Childhood Research Institute, Service Utilization.

Mlawer, M. A. (1993). Who should fight? Parents and the advocacy expectation. *Journal of Disability Policy Studies, 4*(1), 105–15.

Natiello, P. (1990), The person-centered approach, collaborative power, and cultural transformation. *Person-Centered Review, 5*(3), 268–86.

Odom, S. L., & Karnes, M. B. (Eds.). (1988). *Early intervention for infants and children with handicaps: An empirical base.* Baltimore, MD: Paul H. Brookes.

Odom, S. L., & McLean, M. E. (Eds.). (1996). *Early intervention/early childhood special education: Recommended practices.* Austin, TX: Pro-Ed.

Pearl, L. (1993). Providing family-centered early intervention. In W. Brown, S. K. Thurman, & L. F. Pearl (Eds.), *Family-centered early intervention with infants & toddlers* (pp. 81–102). Baltimore, MD: Paul H. Brookes.

Pinderhughes, E. (1989). *Understanding race, ethnicity, and power: Keys to efficacy in clinical practice.* New York: Free Press.

Pinderhughes, E. (1994). Empowerment as an intervention goal: Early ideas. In L. Gutiérrez & P. Nurius (Eds.), *Education and research for empowerment practice* (pp. 17–30). Seattle: University of Washington, School of Social Work, Center for Policy and Practice Research.

Polmanteer, K., & Turbiville, V. (1997, February). *Partners and promises: Where are we and where should we go next?* Paper presented at the meeting of the Kansas Division of Early Childhood, Lawrence, Kansas.

Prestby, J. E., Wandersman, A., Florin, P., Rich, R., & Chavis, D. (1990). Benefits, costs, incentive management and participation in voluntary organizations: A means to understanding and promoting empowerment. *American Journal of Community Psychology, 18*, 117–50.

Rainforth, B., & York-Barr, J. (1997). *Collaborative teams for students with severe disabilities: Integrating therapy and educational services* (2nd ed.). Baltimore, MD: Paul H. Brookes.

Rappaport, J. (1987). Terms of empowerment/exemplars of prevention: Toward a theory for community psychology. *American Journal of Community Psychology, 15*(2), 121–48.

Raver, S. A., & Kilgo, J. (1991). Effective family-centered services: Supporting family choices and rights. *Infant–Toddler Intervention, 1*(3), 169–76.

Roos, P. (1985). Parents of mentally retarded children –

Misunderstood and mistreated. In H. R. Turnbull & A. P. Turnbull (Eds.), *Parents speak out: Then and now* (2nd ed., pp. 245–60). Columbus, OH: Charles E. Merrill.

Rosen, L. (1955). Selected aspects in the development of the mother's understanding of her mentally retarded child. *American Journal of Mental Deficiency, 59*, 522–8.

Ross, A. O. (1964). *The exceptional child in the family: Helping parents of exceptional children.* New York: Grune & Stratton.

Ross, K. (1995). Speaking in tongues: Involving users in day care services. *British Journal of Social Work, 25*, 791–804.

Saleebey, D. (1992). *The strengths perspective in social work practice: Extensions and cautions.* New York: Longman.

Saleebey, D. (1996). The strengths perspective in social work practice: Extensions and cautions. *Social Work, 41*(3), 296–306.

Sander, A. M. (1993). An inquiry into the fate of transference in psychoanalysis. *Journal of the American Psychoanalytic Association, 41*, 627–51.

Seitz, V., & Provence, S. (1990). Caregiver-focused models of early intervention. In S. J. Meisels & J. P. Shonkoff (Eds.), *Handbook of early childhoood intervention* (pp. 400–27). New York: Cambridge University Press.

Seligman, M., & Darling, R. B. (1997). *Ordinary families, special children.* New York: Guilford Press.

Shelton, R. L., Jeppson, E. S., & Johnson, B. H. (1989). *Family-centered care for children with special health care needs.* Washington, DC: Association for the Care of Children's Health.

Shonkoff, J. P., Hauser-Cram, P., Krauss, M. W., & Upshur, C. C. (1992). Development of infants with disabilities and their families. *Monographs of the Socity for Research in Child Development, 57*(6, Serial No. 230).

Sieffert, A. (1978). Parents' initial reactions to having a mentally retarded child: A concept and model for social workers. *Clinical Social Work Journal, 6*(1), 33–43.

Simeonsson, R., & Bailey, D. (1990). Family dimensions in early intervention. In S. J. Meisels & J. P. Shonkoff (Eds.), *Handbook of early childhood intervention* (pp. 428–44). New York: Cambridge University Press.

Skrtic, T. M. (1991). *Behind special education: A critical analysis of professional culture and school organization.* Denver, CO: Love.

Skrtic, T. M. (1995). The crisis in professional knowledge. In E. L. Meyen & T. M. Skrtic (Eds.), *Special education & student disability* (pp. 569–607). Denver, CO: Love.

Smith, S. W. (1990, September). Individualized Education Programs (IEPs) in special education: From intent to acquiescence. *Exceptional Children*, 6–14.

Solnit, A. J., & Stark, M. H. (1961). Mourning and the birth of a defective child. *Psychoanalytic Study of the Child, 16*, 523–37.

Sparling, J., Berger, R., & Billing, M. (1992). Fathers: Myth, reality, & Public Law 99-457. *Infants & Young Children, 4*(3), 9–19.

Stayton, V. D., & Karnes, M. B. (1994). Model programs for infants and toddlers with disabilities and their families. In L. J. Johnson, R. J. Gallagher, M. J. LaMontagne, J. B. Jordan, R. J. Gallagher, P. L. Hutinger, & M. B. Karnes (Eds.), *Meeting early intervention challenges: Issues from birth to three* (2nd ed., pp. 33–58). Baltimore, MD: Paul H. Brookes.

Swick, K. (1988, Fall). Parental efficacy and involvement. *Childhood Education,* 37–42.

Turbiville, V., Schaffer, V., Schaffer, R., & Brammel, J. (1997). *The IFSP: Beyond the promise through group action planning.* Paper presented at the meeting of the Kansas Divison of Early Childhood, Lawrence, KS.

Turbiville, V. P., Turnbull, A. P., Garland, C. W., & Lee, I. M. (1996). Development and implementation of IFSPs and IEPs: Opportunities for empowerment. In S. L. Odom & M. E. McLean (Eds.), *Early intervention/early childhood special education: Recommended practices* (pp. 77–100). Austin, TX: Pro-Ed.

Turnbull, A. P. (1993, November). *Fathers as "less apparent" in early childhood special education research and service delivery.* Paper presented at the meeting of the National Research Council/Institute of Medicine, Washington, DC.

Turnbull, A. P., Friesen, B. J., & Ramírez, C. (1995, April). *Forging collaborative partnerships with families in the study of disability.* Paper presented at the National Institute on Disability and Rehabilitation Research Conference on Participatory Action Research, Washington, DC.

Turnbull, A. P., & Summers, J. A. (1985). *From parent involvement to family support: Evolution to revolution.* Paper presented at the Down Syndrome State-of-the-Art Conference, Boston.

Turnbull, A. P., Turbiville, V., Schaffer, R., & Schaffer, V. (1996). "Getting a shot at life" through Group Action Planning. *Zero to Three, 16*(6), 33–40.

Turnbull, A. P., & Turnbull, H. R. (1997). *Families, professionals, and exceptionality: A special partnership* (3rd ed.). Upper Saddle River, NJ: Merrill/Prentice-Hall.

Turnbull, A. P., Turnbull, H. R., & Blue-Banning, M. J. (1994). Enhancing inclusion of infants and toddlers with disabilities and their families: A theoretical and programmatic analysis. *Infants & Young Children, 7*(2), 1–14.

Wagner, M. K. (1992). Information as power in personal social service transactions. (Doctoral dissertation, University of Illinois, Urbana–Champaign, 1992). *Dissertation Abstracts International.*

Weick, A. (1983). Issues in overturning a medical model of social work practice. *Social Work, 28,* 467–71.

Whitney-Thomas, J. (1997). Participatory action research as an approach to enhancing quality of life for individuals with disabilities. In R. L. Schalock (Ed.), *Quality of life: Application to persons with disabilities* (Vol. II, pp. 181–97). Washington, DC: American Association on Mental Retardation.

Whyte, W. F. (Ed.). (1991). *Participatory action research.* Newbury Park, CA: Sage.

Wolfensberger, W. (1967). Counseling the parents of the retarded. In A. A. Baumeister (Ed.), *Mental retardation: Appraisal, education, and rehabilitation* (pp. 329–400). Chicago: Aldine.

Wood, M. (1995). Parent-professional collaboration and the efficacy of the IEP process. In R. L. Koegel & L. K. Koegel (Eds.), *Teaching children with autism: Strategies for initiating positive interactions and improving learning opportunities* (pp. 147–74). Baltimore: Paul H. Brookes.

Zigler, E., & Valentine, J. (Eds.). (1979). *Project Head Start: A legacy of the war on poverty.* New York: Free Press.

Zimmerman, M. A. (1990). Taking aim on empowerment research: On the distinction between individual and psychological distinctions. *American Journal of Community Psychology, 18*(1), 169–76.

Zimmerman, M. A. (1992). *The measurement of psychological empowerment: Issues and strategies.* Unpublished paper, University of Michigan, Ann Arbor.

CHAPTER TWENTY-EIGHT

Resilience Reconsidered: Conceptual Considerations, Empirical Findings, and Policy Implications

MICHAEL RUTTER

During the first half of the twentieth century, as part of the *mental hygiene movement*, extensive attention was paid to associations between children's experiences of stress and adversity and their development of various forms of psychopathology or mental disorder. Bowlby's (1951) WHO monograph emphasized the extent to which the important risk experiences included disturbed parent–child affectional relationships. Although not all of his postulates regarding "maternal deprivation" have proved valid, most have (Rutter, 1995a), and there is abundant evidence that disturbed parent–child relationships do indeed constitute an important risk factor for psychopathology (Rutter, 1995b). During the second half of the twentieth century, the investigations of risk experiences considerably broadened to include the disruptions of family life associated with parental mental disorder (Rutter, 1989); coercive patterns of family interaction and inadequate parental monitoring/supervision of children's activities (Patterson, 1982; Patterson, Reid, & Dishion, 1992); parental divorce (Chase-Lansdale & Hetherington, 1990; Emery & Forehand, 1994; Hetherington, 1997); and both acute and chronic stresses carrying long-term threat (Brown & Harris, 1978, 1989; Goodyer, 1990).

It has been a universal finding, however, in all studies of risk experiences, that there is enormous variation in children's responses. At one extreme, some children succumb with the development of persistent severe psychopathology. At the other extreme, some children seem to escape unscathed, and a few even appear to be strengthened by their adverse experiences. Even with the most severe stressors and adversities, it is unusual for more than half of the children to develop significant psychopathology (Rutter, 1979). For many years, this striking phenomenon received surprisingly little research attention. For the most part, individual differences tended to be attributed to some undefined constitutional factor and were dismissed as of little interest (Ainsworth, 1962), partly because the phenomenon appeared to be largely inexplicable, and partly because psychosocial researchers seemed to fear that a focus on successful outcomes following adverse experiences might distract the attention of policy makers from the need to pay attention to the reality of the damage to psychological development that derived from psychosocial stresses and adversities. The issue, however, would not go away and, indeed, an early review of maternal deprivation singled out the study of individual differences as the most important single research challenge (Rutter, 1972). Research since then has amply confirmed the reality of individual differences (Paykel, 1978).

During the 1970s, the research climate changed and the concept of invulnerable children became popular (Anthony, 1974, 1978). Misleadingly, it came to be thought that there were some children so constitutionally tough that they could not give way under the pressures of stress and adversity. The notion proved to be mistaken in at least three respects: children's resistance to stress is relative, rather than absolute; the origins of stress resistance are both environmental and constitutional; and the degree of resistance is not a fixed individual characteristic. Rather resistance varies over time and according to circumstances (Felsman & Vaillant, 1987; Luthar &

651

Zigler, 1991; Masten & Garmezy, 1985; Rutter, 1985, 1990, 1995c). The relative concept of resilience has taken the place of the absolute notion of invulnerability.

CONCEPT OF RESILIENCE

This topic of individual resilience is one of considerable importance with respect to public policies focused on the prevention of either mental disorders or developmental impairment in young people. In planning preventive policies, it is important to ask whether it is more useful to focus on the risks that render children vulnerable to psychopathology or on the protective factors that provide for resilience in the face of adversity. Thus, for example, should we focus on the steps needed to eliminate family conflict and breakup, or would we do better to focus on how children cope successfully with conflict and disruption of family life? Of course, we may well seek to do both, but choices are needed on priorities, and decision making is likely to be facilitated by an improved understanding of the risk and protective mechanisms involved in vulnerability and resilience in relation to psychosocial adversity. The issue is tackled in this chapter through a brief consideration of what is meant by the concept of resilience, a discussion of some key methodological considerations, a review of empirical findings from studies focusing directly on resilience, and then an account of the inferences that may be drawn on the processes associated with resilience. Each of the eight processes that emerge from the research findings is discussed briefly with respect to policy implications.

As shown by several reviews (see, for example, Anthony & Cohler, 1987; Egeland, Carlson, & Sroufe, 1993; Fonagy, Steele, Steele, Higgitt, & Target, 1994; Haggerty, Sherrod, Garmezy, & Rutter, 1994; Luthar, 1993; Rolf, Masten, Cicchetti, Nuechterlein & Weintraub, 1990; Seifer, 1995; Werner, 1990, this volume), the concept of resilience has remained broad. Four general areas of interest may be identified. First, many investigators emphasize the value of focusing on positive outcomes, and not just on psychopathology. Thus, Masten et al. (1995) and Luthar (1991) investigated the factors associated with the development of social competence. Similarly, Bandura (1995, 1997) and others fostered numerous studies of the causes and consequences of self-efficacy. Second, there has been attention to the effects of positive experiences of various kinds. Thus, particularly in the field of depression, there has been much interest in the protective effect of social support (see Thoits, 1983). Similarly, Stouthamer-Loeber et al. (1993) sought to identify variables that promoted normality but were not associated with variations in deviance. That is to say, they examined dimensional variables and tested whether there were significant effects at the positive end of a variable but no effects at the negative end. They found little evidence supporting this notion. The idea that there may be variables whose presence fosters particularly good functioning but whose absence carries no particular risk of psychopathology is not in itself an unreasonable one. It has not, however, proved a particularly fruitful area of research for two rather different reasons. To begin with, there are immense difficulties in the conceptualization and measurement of supernormal psychosocial functioning (see, for example, Ryff & Singer, 1998). Although it might seem desirable to focus on positive mental health, rather than just the absence of psychopathology, the concept has proved elusive and value-laden. Also, most risk and protective factors function as dimensional variables. Accordingly, it has been somewhat artificial to label positive and negative ends in a different fashion. Thus, divorce has often been treated as a stressor and the presence of a confiding marital relationship as a positive support, but, in reality, both deal with the same basic variable.

The third area of interest has concerned the study of the process of how individuals cope with stress and adversity. Murphy's (Murphy, 1962; Murphy & Moriarty, 1976) studies of coping and mastery during the 1960s and 1970s drew attention to the importance of variations in the ways people deal with threat and challenge. This has led to a major research endeavor investigating the processes involved in coping with stress (see Haggerty et al., 1994; Lazarus & Folkman, 1984; Vaillant, 1977, 1990). The field has been productive in its differentiation of the tasks involved in dealing with the practical situations created by stress and challenge and the parallel need to find effective ways of dealing with the emotions engendered by the life experiences. It has become clear that there is a substantial range of effective coping mechanisms (or psychological defenses), that the coping style that works best for one sort of stress experience may not work equally well with a different kind of adversity, and that there are substantial individual differences in the coping styles with which people are most comfortable (Rutter, 1981). The research has been most crucial in its demonstration that stress and adversity cannot usefully be viewed as passive experiences that simply impinge on people; instead, they involve an active process by which people deal with their environments. On the whole it has appeared advantageous for people to have a varied repertoire of coping strategies in order to deal with the range of adaptive responses required by contrasting life challenges. Although there are certainly a few styles of coping that are usually maladaptive, it has not proved easy to come up with a valid differentiation between effective and ineffective coping styles.

Fourth, research has focused on the features or the processes that differentiate people's responses to serious stress or adversity. In this connection, resilience is operationally defined in terms of a relatively good outcome despite the experience of situations that have been shown to carry a major risk for the development of psychopathology. The focus in this case is strictly on relative resistance to psychosocial risk experiences. The interest is on a range of outcomes, and not just an unusually positive one, there is no necessary expectation that protection should lie in positive experiences, and there is no assumption that the answer should lie in what the individual does about the negative experience at the time (i.e., in how he or she copes with it). This is the concept of resilience considered here. The other three approaches are considered only insofar as they have proved informative in understanding the mechanisms involved in resistance to stress or adversity.

METHODOLOGICAL CONSIDERATIONS

Although, as operationally defined earlier, the topic of resilience would seem reasonably straightforward to study, in practice it has become clear that there are numerous methodological hazards to be circumvented or overcome. Unfortunately, many research reports are uninterpretable because crucial methodological issues have not been dealt with adequately.

Validity of Environmental Risk Mediation

Clearly, the starting point for the investigation of resilience has to be the demonstration that the individuals being studied have truly experienced an environmental risk that carries a major increase in the risk for psychopathology. Unless this first step is satisfactorily dealt with, there is a very real danger that the supposed phenomenon of resilience may turn out to be purely artifactual and mean nothing more than that the individual has not really had a risk experience. It is crucial to differentiate between risk *indicators* and risk *mechanisms*. There are numerous examples in the literature of the problems created by a failure to differentiate between the two. Thus, for example, for many years it was assumed that a child's separation from his or her parents created a major psychopathological risk. Once, however, the circumstances of separation were investigated, it became clear that the main risk derived not from separation per se but rather from the family conflict and discord that accompanied some varieties of separation but not others (Rutter, 1971). This was initially evident in relation to childhood psychopathology, but exactly the same has been found with respect to risks for adult depression (Harris, Brown, & Bifulco, 1986). Thus, parent–child separation in childhood is statistically associated with an increased risk of adult depression, but this is mainly mediated by poor parenting. Poor parenting constitutes a substantial risk factor even in the absence of parent–child separation, and, conversely, parent–child separation does not carry a risk for psychopathology if there is no associated poor parenting. Similar findings have emerged from more sophisticated statistical analyses dealing with the same issue (Fergusson, Horwood, & Lynskey, 1992). Closely comparable findings have applied to the study of poverty and social disadvantage (Brody et al., 1994; Conger et al., 1992; Conger & Elder, 1994; Conger, Ge, Elder, Lorenz, & Simons, 1994; Sampson & Laub, 1994). That is, poverty and social disadvantage are indeed statistically associated with an increased risk of mental disorder. It seems, however, that this is largely because these broad social features predispose to poor parenting. The proximal risk mechanism lies in the poor parenting rather than in poverty or social disadvantage as such. Much the same applies to obstetric and perinatal risk factors (Casaer, de Vries, & Marlowe, 1991;

Meisels & Plunkett, 1988). Obstetric and perinatal risks can directly be involved in risk mediation if they lead to brain damage, but most obstetric and perinatal complications do not lead to brain damage. Much of the association with psychopathology derives from the fact that psychosocial disadvantage is associated with lower birth weight and with a raised rate of other obstetric and perinatal complications. In these circumstances, it seems that the main risk mediation derives from associated psychosocial adversity rather than from the obstetric and perinatal factors as such.

The message from research of this kind is straightforward. Resilience cannot be studied satisfactorily in the absence of the prior demonstration that the individuals concerned have actually experienced substantial risk. That means, among other things, that there must be considerable reservation about studies of resilience that are based on supposed risks that are broadly defined in terms of social disadvantage or obstetric complications. With respect to social policies and strategies for early childhood intervention, the implications are clear and point to the need for greater specificity regarding the reason for the intervention as well as the presumed mediating mechanisms of both risk and protection.

A further challenge to the study of psychosocial risk factors has stemmed from the demonstration, through twin and adoptee studies, that genetic factors are implicated both in individual differences in exposure to environmental risk and in the mediation of risks associated with factors defined in environmental terms (Plomin, 1994a, 1995b; Plomin & Bergeman, 1991). The implication is that some of the risks that have been attributed to environmental risk factors are actually due to genetic rather than environmental mediation. The challenge is real and has to be taken seriously. Nevertheless, there can be no doubt that the findings have been overinterpreted to dismiss environmental risk mediation in a misleading fashion (Rutter, Silberg, O'Connor, & Simonoff, 1999), thereby supporting policy makers who view constitutional problems as inevitable and who consider interventions futile. Certainly, it is necessary to put environmental risk hypotheses to the test and not simply assume that the risks are environmentally mediated just because the risk factor is labeled *environmental*. A range of research designs may be used to test environmental risk hypotheses, and

these have shown the reality and importance of environmentally mediated psychosocial risks (Rutter et al., 1997a; Rutter, Giller, & Hagell, 1998).

Multiple Outcomes

Many studies of resilience have been based on a rather restricted range of outcome measures. It is evident that this can give rise to misleading conclusions. Thus, Farrington, Gallagher, Morley, St. Ledger, and West (1988) found that, for boys in high-risk inner-city families, social isolation provided a protection against delinquency. It was not, however, associated with a generally good outcome. Socially isolated boys from high-risk families tended to be functionally impaired in a number of ways in adult life, despite the fact that they were not involved in crime. Similarly, Luthar (1991, 1993) defined resilience in terms of social competence but found that the resilient children from high-risk backgrounds often showed emotional distress and psychopathology. These findings have sometimes been interpreted (Luthar, 1991) as indicating that a "price" may need to be paid for resilience. This implication does not follow from the findings. The point is that the risk and protective factors associated with one mental disorder are not necessarily the same as those that apply to others.

Thus, for example, the causal processes involved in the genesis of depression are not synonymous with those involved in the genesis of delinquency. It cannot be assumed that because some individuals do not show one particular psychopathological outcome they will not show another, if they have experienced substantial risks predisposing to cause it. Thus, no one supposes that because someone has not developed, say, cancer, he or she is thereby protected against coronary artery disease. The causal processes for the two diseases need to be considered separately because they are not the same. Equally, however, the fact that some individuals have survived a risk for cancer (e.g., despite being a heavy smoker, they have not developed lung cancer) does not mean that they have paid the price of an increased risk for some other condition. It all depends on the risk processes involved. Thus, continuing with the smoking example, smokers who have "escaped" lung cancer probably do have an increased risk for coronary artery disease simply because smoking carries a risk for this as well as for lung cancer. On the other hand, they do not have an increased risk for, say, malignant melanoma or Alzheimer's disease because both of these involve different risk mechanisms and different risk factors. The implication is that it is almost certainly misleading to seek a general answer on resilience. Rather, it is necessary to focus on resilience with respect to particular risk experiences and particular psychopathological outcomes. Some risk and protective factors operate across a wide range, and others are quite specific in their effects. Both possibilities need to be considered and examined rigorously in the formulation of policy initiatives designed to address such interrelated yet distinct long-term outcomes as school performance, teenage pregnancy, economic independence, substance abuse, and delinquency.

Nevertheless, that does not dispose of the concept of paying a price for resilience. The concept does have meaning if it is redefined as a negative outcome that is directly or indirectly caused by the processes leading to resilience. Thus, if someone copes with stress through reliance on drugs or alcohol, there may well be adverse effects from the excessive use of these substances. Alternatively, some may deal with career stresses by working long hours and thereby putting their marriage and family life at risk. The need, however, is to hypothesize a mechanism that derives from resilience processes, which can then be tested empirically. A finding of "success" with respect to one sort of outcome but "failure" on another is, in itself, completely uninformative with respect to the concept of price.

Measurement Error

All measurement involves a substantial degree of error (both random error and errors deriving from bias of one sort or another). Research in recent years has emphasized the major extent to which this constitutes a potential problem in the study of resilience. Thus, there has been much interest in the study of cognitive or behavioral gains and losses following particular experiences. Moffitt, Caspi, Harkness, and Silva (1993), using data from the Dunedin longitudinal study, showed that much of the fluctuations over time are due to errors in measurement rather than real change. Fergusson, Horwood, and Lynskey (1995; Fergusson, Horwood,

Caspi, Moffitt, & Silva, 1996), pooling data from the Dunedin and Christchurch longitudinal studies, both confirmed this finding and showed that it extended broadly across behavioral and cognitive domains. The need, clearly, is for both multiple measurements and methods of analysis that take into account measurement error (such as through a focus on latent constructs).

Random error is certainly something that needs to be taken into account seriously, but it may well not constitute such a serious hazard as that which derives from variations in findings according to informant source. Thus, for example, there has been a concern over the extent to which an awareness of children's educational difficulties may lead to biases in teachers' ratings of behavior (e.g., Goodman, Simonoff, & Stevenson, 1995) or that parents' ratings may be influenced by their own psychopathology or circumstances (e.g., Chilcoat & Breslau, 1997; Fergusson, Lynskey, & Horwood, 1993). These biases are probably not as great as are sometimes assumed (see Boyle & Pickles, 1997; Maughan & Rutter, 1997; Richters, 1992), but nevertheless they do exist and do need to be considered. There are also differences according to the availability of information for different informants. Thus, for example, children will have direct access to their own emotional states, whereas parents and teachers necessarily have to be reliant on the behavioral changes associated with such emotions. Similarly, young people will know about their own involvement in covert antisocial activities that may well be hidden from parents and teachers. The recognition that this is so has often led to a coding convention, whereby psychopathology that is reported by any informant is regarded as valid, even if it is not reported by others (Bird, Gould, & Staghezza, 1992). Unfortunately, the issues and their resolution are not as simple as that. Thus, for example, for reasons that remain totally obscure, it has been a general finding that psychopathology reported by children or adolescents themselves shows a lower genetic component than that reported by parents (Eaves et al., 1997). This is not a function of a lesser reliability for child–adolescent measures (Topolski et al., in press), and it is not at all clear what gives rise to the disparity in the genetic component for child–parent measures. The matter certainly requires systematic investigation, but, in the meantime, the implication is that it is most important to use both multiple informants and multiple measurements over time in order to circumvent measurement error and measurement bias.

Processes of Resilience Over Time

Initially, resilience research tended to assume that either the factors promoting resilience resided in some enduring characteristic of the individual or, alternatively, they derived from the specifics of the interplay between the person and the environmental stress or adversity at the time. Neither assumption has proved to be justified. Longitudinal studies have been crucial in their demonstration of three important features. First, it has been shown that major experiences in adolescence or early adult life can bring about major changes in behavior in individuals who have shown previous psychopathology (Rutter, 1996; Rutter et al., 1997b; Sampson & Laub, 1993). Thus, for example, it has been found that a stable harmonious marriage to a nondeviant spouse is accompanied by a much reduced tendency for antisocial behavior that began in childhood and continued into adult life. Peer group experiences, similarly, can make a substantial impact, bringing about changes of behavior for the better or worse (Rowe, Wouldbroun, & Gulley, 1994). Similar beneficial turning point effects have been reported for army experiences (Elder, 1986; Sampson & Laub, 1996) and for moving one's home somewhere outside the inner city (Osborn, 1980). The evidence is clear-cut that recovery, partial or complete, following early stress or adversities may derive from experiences that take place well after the initial risk experience.

Longitudinal studies have also shown the importance of indirect chain effects by which behavior or experiences at one age predispose to the occurrence of risk or protective experiences at a later age. Thus, numerous studies have shown that antisocial behavior in childhood, associated with early psychosocial risk experiences, is followed by a markedly increased likelihood of psychosocial risks and adversities in adolescence and adult life (Rutter, Champion, Quinton, Maughan, & Pickles, 1995; Rutter et al., 1997a, 1997b). Pawlby, Mills, and Quinton (1997a; Pawlby, Mills, Taylor, & Quinton, 1997b) found that girls from a psychosocial high-risk background were much more likely

than other girls, in adolescence, to develop friendships with individuals showing deviant behavior, to engage in risky sexual behavior, and to fall out with friends. Quinton, Pickles, Maughan, and Rutter (1993) showed that girls who had spent some years being reared in an institutional setting showed a much increased tendency to become a teenage parent, to marry or cohabit with a deviant individual, and to experience marital breakdown. Maughan, Collishaw, and Pickles (1998) found that girls born out of wedlock and reared in psychosocial disadvantage, as compared with adopted children from a similar background, were much less likely to acquire educational qualifications. Robins (1966), in her long-term follow-up of children attending a child guidance clinic, found that those who exhibited antisocial behavior in childhood had much higher rates of unemployment in adult life, were less likely to have social support, and were more likely to have fallen out with friends, as well as having experienced multiple marriage breakdowns.

One of the important ways in which the sequelae of early adversity persists is through negative chain effects by which one negative experience predisposes to another. Conversely, positive turning points, by which a negative life trajectory is turned into a more adaptive one, is associated with experiences or happenings that break this vicious cycle (Rutter, 1996). In similar fashion, both naturalistic and experimental studies have shown how children's oppositional–defiant or antisocial behavior may elicit negative responses from other people (e.g., Brunk & Henggeler, 1984; Ge et al., 1996; Maccoby & Jacklin, 1983; O'Connor, Deater-Deckard, Fulker, Rutter, & Plomin, 1998; Patterson, 1980, 1982; Pike, McGuire, Hetherington, Reiss, & Plomin, 1996; Rutter et al., 1997a). The findings clearly point to the likelihood that at least some aspects of the processes promoting resilience may lie in the nature of the interpersonal interactions that occur over time.

Thirdly, research findings have shown a need to take into account people's experiences before they encounter the stress or adversity that put them at risk for psychopathology. The findings on this point are much more limited, but, for example, Quinton and Rutter (1976) found that children who had experienced chronic psychosocial adversity were more likely to develop disorder following acute stress experiences. In a small-scale study, Stacey, Drearden, Pill, and Robinson (1970) found that happy separation experiences appear to provide some protection in relation to later stressful separation experiences. Animal studies, too, have shown that acute stresses may, in some circumstances, lead to changes in neuroendocrine structure and frontal structure and function that are protective in their effects in relation to the experience of later stresses (Hennessey & Levine, 1979; Hunt, 1979). Protective adaptation to stress has also been observed in humans. Thus, the neuroendocrine response of experienced parachute jumpers is quite different from that of novices. The initial hormonal response for first-time jumpers is that of an acute stress reaction, whereas that of an old hand is rather different (Ursin, Baade, & Levine, 1978).

Considerations for findings such as these have led numerous reviewers to emphasize that resilience is a process and not a trait (Felsman & Vaillant, 1987). As Cohler (1987) concluded, it is "less an enduring characteristic than a process determined by the impact of particular life experiences on persons with particular conceptions of their own life history or personal narrative" (p. 406). This issue is particularly important for interpreting data on long-term impacts of early childhood programs and for setting realistic policy goals for short-term interventions.

Multifactorial Causation

The reason for the difference between these two approaches is that it is distinctly unusual for risks to occur truly in isolation. It is much more common for children experiencing one kind of risk factor also to have a variety of other risk experiences. Other research has confirmed the generally low risks associated with single adversities and the extent to which the risk rises markedly with the accumulation of adverse experiences (Biederman et al., 1995; Fergusson & Lynskey, 1996; Sameroff, Seifer, & Bartko, 1997; Stattin, Romelsjö, & Stenbacka, 1997; Kolvin, Miller, Fleeting, & Kolvin, 1988a, 1988b). Thus, Fergusson and Lynskey (1996) developed an adversity index based on thirty-nine measures of family life that covered such variables as economic disadvantage, maladaptive parent-child interaction, marital conflict, and parental separation. Outcome at 15 to 16 years was assessed on the basis of multiple measures of antisocial behavior and drug or alcohol misuse. Just over half of the sample had a family adversity score of six or less. In this large subgroup, the rate of multiple problems was only 0.2%. The rate in those with a score of seven to eleven was substantially higher at 2.5%; for those with scores of thirteen to eighteen, it was higher still at 8.3%; for those with scores of nineteen or more it was 21.6%. In other words, there was an extremely steep risk gradient with the odds of severe multiple problem behaviors in adolescence being over 100 times higher for those with very high family adversity as compared with those who experienced little family adversity.

Many studies of psychosocial risk have involved the investigation of children's responses to some single particular risk experience – such as hospital admission, parental divorce, bereavement, or physical illness. Resilience is then defined in terms of either the presence of social competence or the absence of psychopathology following this single risk experience. The assumption is that single negative experiences carry a major risk of later psychopathology. The empirical evidence indicates that this is not the case. Thus, in their epidemiological studies of 10-year-old children, Rutter and Quinton (1977) identified six family variables, all of which were strongly and significantly associated with child psychiatric disorder. These comprised severe marital discord, low social status, overcrowding or large family size, paternal criminality, maternal psychiatric disorder, and admission into the care of a local authority. What was striking, and perhaps surprising, was that children with just one of these risk factors (i.e., those with a truly isolated negative experience) were no more likely to have psychiatric disorder than children with no risk factors at all. Even with chronic family stresses, it seemed that the children were not particularly at psychiatric risk so long as it was really a single stress on its own. On the other hand, when any two of the stresses occurred together, the risk went up fourfold. With yet more concurrent stresses, the risk climbed several times further still. At first sight, this finding seems to contradict the abundant research evidence that each of these risk factors is associated with a major increase in the likelihood of psychopathology. The explanation lies in the fact that the evidence that each of these factors is associated with a marked increase in risk is based on analyses that may take into account the presence of other stresses but do not focus on the small subgroup of individuals who truly have only one risk factor. It might appear that these two approaches are the same, but they are not (Rutter, 1983a).

Similarly, although less dramatically, Stattin et al. (1997) found that those with no home background risks had an 11% crime recidivism rate. The recidivism rate then rose progressively according to the number of home background risks through 15%, 18%, 23%, 33%, and 47% with those with five risks. Numerous studies of antisocial behavior have produced similar findings. The clear implication is that the main risk lies in the experience of many adversities, the increased risk being quite low in relation to any single adverse experience. It immediately follows that one of the major factors (probably the major factor) accounting for individual differences in responses to adversity is the extent of adversity experienced. The findings are strongest in relation to antisocial behavior, but it is quite likely that similar considerations apply to other forms of psychopathology.

It will be appreciated that these findings exactly mirror those with respect to genetic risk factors. There is abundant evidence that genetic factors account for a substantial proportion of population variance in psychopathology of all kinds, usually accounting for some 30–70% of the variance (Plomin, De Fries, McClearn, & Rutter, 1997; Rutter et al., 1999). The strength of genetic influences varies considerably according to the type of psychopathology – strongest in the case of disorders such as autism, schizophrenia, bipolar affective disorder, and hyperkinetic disorder and weakest in the case of juvenile delinquency. Nevertheless, it is apparent that genetic factors play a major role in the risk processes for most mental disorders. What is beginning to become evident from molecular genetic research is that although that is true with respect to the cumulative effect of all genetic factors, the risk associated with any single susceptibility gene is small (Plomin et al., 1997). Moreover, it seems probable that much of the genetic risk is mediated through diagnostically nonspecific risk dimensions involving temperamental qualities such as emotionality or novelty-seeking rather than through genes that have a direct effect on a particular disorder. There is also growing evidence that, in some cases, there may be synergistic interactions among genes.

It is necessary to conclude, therefore, that a key need in the study of resilience involves the investigation of the ways in which multiple genetic and environmental risk factors combine in the causal processes leading to disorder. Similarly, public policies that link eligibility for early intervention programs exclusively to child-based diagnostic indicators, and which ignore the role of family characteristics, are fraught with considerable difficulty (Shonkoff & Meisels, 1991).

Risk and Protective Mechanisms

As indicated in the introduction to this chapter, the rising interest in the overall field of resilience was accompanied by a parallel concern to identify protective factors that led to stress resistance. Thus, Garmezy (1985; Masten & Garmezy, 1985) concluded that there were three broad sets of protective factors: 1) personality features such as autonomy, self-esteem, and a socially positive orientation; 2) family cohesion, warmth, and an absence of discord; and 3) the availability of external support systems that encourage and reinforce a child's coping efforts. As Rutter (1990) pointed out, this list basically consists of the antonyms of risk variables. High self-esteem protects; low self-esteem puts one at risk. A negative parent–child relationship is a risk factor, and a good parent–child relationship is a protective one. In seeking to determine the factors promoting resilience, a key issue concerns the overall level of risk and also particular patterns of risk factors. Nevertheless, there is nothing much to be gained, apart from the introduction of unhelpful confusion, calling the low risk end of a risk dimension a protective factor. Rather, it seems preferable to confine the concept of protective mechanisms to some process that modifies a person's response to a risk situation. In other words, what is postulated is some kind of indirect, interactive, catalytic effect. For a whole variety of statistical and conceptual reasons, it would be highly misleading to regard what is proposed as synonymous with a statistical interaction effect (Pickles, 1993; Rutter, 1983a; Rutter & Pickles, 1991; Rutter, 1990). The power to detect statistical interaction effects is notoriously weak (McClelland & Judd, 1993), and it is generally preferable to translate the interactive concept into something more specific that can be put to the test in ways that directly deal with the hypothesized mechanism. The interest lies in the possibility that there are variables that modify people's responses to risk mechanisms through processes that are separate from those that are directly implicated in the risk itself.

In that connection, however, two further points need to be made. First, the protective quality lies in the mechanism and not in the variable as such. There are plenty of examples of features that constitute a risk for one sort of outcome but yet serve as a protection against another one. In the field of internal medicine, heterozygote status for thalassaemia provides a well-known example. It is an abnormal feature involved in susceptibility to sickle cell disease, but it also happens to be a protective factor against malaria. In the behavioral arena, high physiological reactivity to stress constitutes a parallel example. It is a risk factor for anxiety disorders, but it is a protective factor against antisocial behavior. In the realm of experiences, adoption may perhaps also be seen in these terms. For children born into a high-risk family, adoption into a good home may well be a protective experience. On the other hand, the experience of being adopted carries with it its own challenges, and sometimes stresses, and to that extent it may also be a risk feature, albeit a mild one (Sullivan, Wells, & Bushnell, 1995). Similarly, the family breakup that accompanies parental divorce or separation is a stressful experience and thereby a risk factor for many children. Although the main risks for psychopathology derive from the family conflict that precedes and follows the divorce, the breakup of the family also contributes to the risk (Rutter, 1995b). On the other hand, insofar as the divorce serves to bring family conflict to an end, it may also act as a protective feature. The point is that it is necessary to consider the mechanisms involved and not see protection as an inherent attribute of the variable itself.

A related consideration is that whether an experience is hedonically positive is no necessary guide to whether it will operate protectively. Examples given earlier all illustrate this point, but others will be evident throughout the rest of this chapter. It should be added that the personal qualities associated with resilience may not always be attractive ones (Hultsch & Plemons, 1979; Rutter, 1981). Thus, for example, Hinkle (1974) noted that people who seemed most immune to stress had an almost "sociopathic" flavor

to their personality in that they seemed to have a shallow attachment to people, goals, or groups and that they readily shifted to other relationships when established relationships were disrupted. It seemed that they had an awareness of their own needs and limitations and avoided situations that made demands on them that they did not want or felt they could not meet. This may well have been protective for them, but it was not necessarily conducive to positive regard from their peers. Somewhat similar comments have been noted by Lieberman (1975) with respect to the elderly and by Jenkins (1979) in his air traffic controllers study.

STUDIES DIRECTLY FOCUSING ON RESILIENCE

Kauai Study

Although there are many studies with findings that are informative with respect to considerations in relation to resilience, the number of investigations that focused directly on factors promoting resilience through comparisons of resilient and nonresilient children who have experienced comparable psychosocial adversity is much more limited. In many ways, the first systematic investigation to focus explicitly on the features that seem to enable children from high-risk backgrounds to develop into competent well-functioning adolescents and adults was the Kauai study undertaken by Werner and her colleagues (Werner, Bierman, & French, 1971; Werner & Smith, 1977, 1982, 1992). High risk was defined in terms of four or more risk factors, experienced before the age of 2, from a list that included features such as perinatal adversity, chronic poverty, parents with little formal education, a disorganized family environment, and parental alcoholism or mental disorder. About one-third of the cohort was vulnerable in this way, and the follow-up findings confirmed that they did indeed show a much higher rate of psychosocial problems in middle childhood and adolescence.

Several features stand out from the findings. First, there was some consistency in the types of variables that operated across the life span to foster resiliency. These included temperamental characteristics that elicited positive social responses from other people; a lifestyle of planfulness associated with self-efficacy and self-esteem; the availability of competent caregivers and supportive adults who fostered trust and a sense of coherence; and second-chance opportunities at school, work, church, or in the military that led to new experiences likely to foster competence and self-esteem. Second, both risk and protective factors appear to operate through the course of development. That is to say, new influences in middle childhood or adolescence or early adult life had important effects, just as did those in early childhood. Positive turning points in early adult life included marriage or entering into a long-term committed relationship, the birth of a first child, establishment of a career, additional education, the gaining of vocational skills, and becoming an active member of a church or religious community. Third, there were many examples of indirect chain effects. Thus, for example, children's early temperamental features, or their exhibition of behavioral problems, were associated with the likelihood that they would experience social support at a later age. Fourth, there were several variables, particularly cognitive skills and high achievement motivation, that tended to have greater effects on those from high-risk backgrounds, although there were some effects throughout the sample. It seemed that army service was sometimes important for boys from disadvantaged backgrounds in its provision of opportunities for educational advancement and the acquisition of skills. A stable marriage to a nondeviant spouse also appeared protective in relation to earlier adversities.

The overall research strategy was a good one, but it is evident that the risk factors included those that are likely to operate genetically as well as environmentally (e.g., alcoholism or mental disorder), as well as some (such as perinatal risk factors) that may have little direct effect on psychosocial outcomes. Nevertheless, multivariate analyses on longitudinal data extending into adult life have sought to disentangle the complicated set of relationships as they operated over time. Children who had experienced four or more cumulative risk factors but who were nevertheless without serious learning or behavioral problems in childhood and adolescence constituted the resilient subsample. They were compared with two other groups, both of whom had also experienced four or more of the risk factors. The first comparison group comprised those who had developed serious learning or behavioral problems by the age of 10 years. The second group was made

of those with a record of serious delinquency, mental health problems by the age of 18, or both. All three groups had been exposed to chronic poverty. Although the resilient children and their two comparison groups had all experienced substantial stress and adversity, the overall burden of negative experiences was significantly lower in the resilient group. Unfortunately, this difference in level of risk was not adequately taken into account in the examination of protective factors. Nevertheless, there was a range of positive features that was more frequent in the resilient group.

Werner and Smith (1982) summarized protective factors in terms of three clusters: 1) at least average intelligence and dispositional qualities that elicited positive responses from other people; 2) affectional ties with parent substitutes such as grandparents and older siblings; and 3) an external support system, in church, youth groups, or school, that rewarded competence and provided the individuals with a sense of coherence. It was also noted that resilient individuals from a high-risk background often felt the need to detach themselves from their parents and siblings. Quantitative assessment of this process was not obtained, but when children's own families provided pervasively negative experiences, it appeared that it was often helpful for them to develop social ties outside the family and to seek pleasures and rewards from extrafamilial activities. Werner and Smith (1982) argued that the central component of effective coping was a sense of coherence, a feeling of confidence that one's internal and external environment was predictable and that things would probably work out as well as could reasonably be expected.

The Christchurch and Stockholm Studies

In many respects, the two strongest studies of resilience were those undertaken by Fergusson and Lynskey (1996) and Stattin et al. (1997). Fergusson and Lynskey used the Christchurch longitudinal study data to examine resilience in relation to multiple family adversity. The top 20% of their family adversity index (described earlier) was taken as indicating high risk. This sample was subdivided according to the presence of antisocial or drug problems. Resilience was dealt with as both a categorical and a dimensional variable. The first finding was that the resilient youngsters had significantly lower family adversity scores. Nevertheless, when that was taken into account statistically, three main features stood out. First, resilient youngsters tended to have a higher IQ at 8 years. There was a 14-point IQ difference between the top and bottom resilience quintiles. Second, they had lower rates of novelty-seeking at 16 years, and third, they were less likely, on both maternal and self-reports, to have affiliations with delinquent peers. It is noteworthy that these protective factors span both cognitive and behavioral features, as well as the quality of the peer group, and that the main effect on resilience derived from their combination. Just as few individual risk factors carry a major risk when they occur in isolation, it seemed that few factors exerted much protection on their own.

Stattin et al. (1997) examined resilience in a large-scale Swedish records study. When they were conscripted into the armed forces, the men responded to two questionnaires on their background and behavior. Data on criminality were available from the official crime register. Behavioral risks were considered in relation to such variables as frequent truancy, conduct problems at school, drug abuse, and heavy drinking. Home background risks included items such as parental divorce, fathers' heavy drinking, and low family income. Personal competencies were considered in relation to variables such as intelligence, emotional control, and physical health. All three clusters of variables showed substantial associations with recidivist delinquency, the effects being greatest with behavioral risks and least with personal competencies or resources. A main focus of the analyses concerned the interplay between these three sets of variables, and the most striking findings concerned interactions. It might have been expected that interactions would have been most evident in relation to home background risks, but that is not what was found. Rather, they appeared in the interplay between behavioral risks and personal competencies. Behavioral risks had the greatest effect in relation to crime, irrespective of the presence or absence of the other two sets of variables. When individuals had several behavioral risks, however, the presence of personal competencies exerted a substantial protective effect. By contrast, they had little effect on convictions in men who did not also have behavioral risks. The implication is that certain sorts

of personal qualities, such as high intelligence and good emotional control, may exert a protective effect when other risk factors are present, but the absence of these personal qualities on its own does not provide an increased risk for antisocial behavior in adult life. The analysis of the data was systematic and searching, and the authors' discussion of their findings was thoughtful. Nevertheless, the results need to be treated with some caution because they are based on retrospective recall. They provide important clues regarding possible processes involved in resilience, but they are inevitably limited in not being able to examine the interplay during the years of childhood and adolescence.

Interaction Processes

Interaction effects have sometimes been studied as if they were important in their own right, but they are not. That is because interactions may arise for a variety of reasons and reflect a diverse range of mechanisms (Rutter & Pickles, 1991). The mere fact that a statistical interaction between two variables has been found is, on its own, uninformative about the mechanisms involved. The interest lies in the questions that are posed as to why a feature has an effect in one circumstance but not in another. Quinton and Rutter's (Quinton & Rutter, 1988; Rutter, Quinton, & Hill, 1990; Zoccolillo, Pickles, Quinton, & Rutter, 1992) studies of the adult outcome for children who had experienced much of their upbringing in an institutional setting illustrate the point. The results showed that the rate of poor social functioning in adulthood was much higher than in a general population comparison group. The rate of antisocial behavior in childhood and adolescence was particularly high, and its presence had a strong mediating effect on adult outcome. The effect was greater, however, in male subjects than in female subjects.

Despite the marked elevation in the risk of poor social functioning in adult life, and the strong continuities between antisocial behavior in childhood–adolescence and personality disorder in adult life, there were important individual differences in outcome. Some individuals with serious adverse experiences in childhood, including those who exhibited antisocial behavior when young, nevertheless functioned well as adults. The findings showed that one of the most important factors associated with such resilience was a harmonious marriage (or cohabiting relationship) with a nondeviant spouse. Of course, this was an infrequent occurrence in those who had experienced most adversity and who had shown antisocial behavior in childhood. Nevertheless, when it occurred, it was clear that it exerted a substantial effect associated with the development of good social functioning. Moreover, this important "turning point" effect held up after taking full account of measurement error of the individual's previous behavior and of risk experiences (Rutter & Pickles, 1991; Rutter et al., 1997b; Zoccolillo et al., 1992). It was notable, however, that the beneficial effect of a supportive marriage operated only when the individual had shown antisocial behavior when younger. An unsupportive marriage to a deviant spouse was not a risk factor for the development of antisocial behavior in adult life. The reason was evident in the findings on the development of antisocial behavior and its continuation in the form of personality disorder in adult life. The risk process almost always began during childhood and adolescence; it was quite uncommon for antisocial behavior to begin for the first time in adulthood. By no means did all antisocial adults have an official crime record in childhood, but it was distinctly unusual for there not to be evidence of some form of disruptive behavior when young. It does not follow, however, that an unhappy marriage cannot constitute a risk factor for other forms of psychopathology. Indeed, it is clear that it is an important risk factor for the development of depression in adult life (Brown & Harris, 1978).

Given that the resilience in this case seemed to derive from an adult experience (viz., a supportive marriage), despite the fact that the initial risks arose from adverse experiences in childhood, it is necessary to ask how it came about that some high-risk children succeeded in having a successful marriage to a nondeviant spouse. The findings from several longitudinal studies all point to important chain effects (Quinton et al., 1993). Moving backward in time from adult life, it was evident that the characteristics of young people's peer group was important. Those who were part of an antisocial peer group were more likely to take someone showing antisocial behavior or drug or alcohol problems as a partner, and such partnerships were much less likely

to be harmonious and supportive. The finding reflects the fact that partners are likely to be found within one's social group, and if most of one's peers are deviant, it follows that the likelihood of choosing a deviant partner is bound to be much higher. Studies during the adolescent age period itself have confirmed the extent to which youngsters tend to choose friends from a similar high-risk background, many of whom show antisocial behavior (Pawlby et al., 1997a, 1997b).

Nevertheless, that is not the whole story because it is necessary to ask why some high-risk individuals do not end up in an antisocial peer group. Quinton and Rutter's (1988; Quinton et al., 1993; Rutter & Quinton, 1984; Rutter et al., 1990) studies showed that a tendency to exert planning in relation to key life decisions constituted an important protective factor. Many of the children from a high-risk background, particularly those reared in institutions, tended to act as if they could exert no control over what happened to them. Some, however, did make deliberate choices in relation to their careers and choice of marriage partner. Interestingly, this tendency to exercise foresight and take active steps to deal with environmental challenges showed a much weaker protective effect in the general population comparison group than in the sample of institution-reared individuals. It was fairly obvious why planning might be protective in the risk sample. It was associated, for example, with a significantly lower rate of teenage pregnancy; therefore, the pressures to make a hasty marriage were less. Why did this not apply within the comparison group? Rutter (1990) suggested that there were likely to be two reasons. First, the youngsters in the comparison group mainly lived in supportive families so that parents exerted a degree of direction of planning in relation to their children's lives. Also, young people were less likely to be involved in a deviant peer group, so that even if they married by random allocation they were likely to end up with a well-functioning partner.

How, then, did this protective planning tendency develop in some children from high-risk backgrounds? The findings showed that positive school experiences exerted the main effect. Once more, this was not evident in the control group. Only rarely did the positive experiences include exam success, and it does not seem likely that the variable was simply a proxy for high IQ. Probably, the experiences of pleasure, accomplishment, and success at school had helped the young people acquire a sense of self-worth and a feeling that they had the ability to control what happened to them. The reason this was not found in the comparison group was that most of the young people had ample sources of support in the family so that the additional experiences of success in the school merely reinforced self-esteem and self-efficacy, rather than creating these self-concepts.

Perhaps the four main general messages that derive from this body of research are 1) the importance of a planning tendency in shaping young people's later experiences; 2) the important effects of experiences outside of the home (at school and in the peer group); 3) the need to consider the possibility that protective effects may arise only when there is a need and opportunity to counteract the lack of positive experiences deriving from other sources; and 4) the importance of indirect chain effects over time. All four features are also evident in other research.

Planful Competence

Clausen (1991, 1993) reported findings from the archival data set formed by the three main California longitudinal studies together with more intensive retrospective interview data on a randomly selected subsample of sixty cases. Planful competence was assessed in adolescence by Q-sort methods and comprised features of dependability, productivity, and effective use of one's own intelligence, as well as self-esteem and the ability to react positively with others. Planful competence was significantly associated with higher educational attainments and occupational level and a lower rate of multiple marriage breakdowns. In general, men who were less planful, mature, and confident in adolescence had less orderly lives. Planful competence was, however, a less powerful predictor in women (the reverse of the finding in the Quinton and Rutter [Quinton & Rutter, 1988; Rutter et al., 1990; Zoccolillo et al., 1992] studies).

Connell, Spencer, and Aber (1994) examined resilience in relation to outcome in a cross-sectional study of American adolescents experiencing poverty, unemployment, and life in an underclass neighborhood. Modeling suggested that the youths' experiences of their family's support for them, of their own sense of control over their success and failure

at school, and of their feelings of self-worth and emotional security with others regulated their actions, even after taking into account the influence of their background. It was noteworthy, too, that the findings suggested that the youths' own disaffected behavior lessened parental involvement, which in turn contributed to negative appraisals of the self. In other words, a vicious cycle was set up.

Luthar (1991) studied socially disadvantaged adolescents (mostly from ethnic minorities) living in an inner-city area. Negative life events were used as risk variables and peer and teacher ratings of competence as the outcome. She found that an internal locus of control, or the belief that one could control one's life, was a protective factor for assertiveness in the classroom. Contrary to many other studies, high intelligence served as a vulnerability factor in that, at low stress levels, intelligence was positively related to competence but, when stress was high, intelligent children seemed to lose their advantage. It should be noted that the outcome variable here was different from that employed on other studies, and it may be that the role of intelligence varies according to the psychological process or psychopathological outcome being considered. A further study (Luthar, Doernberger, & Zigler, 1993), based on the same general design, showed that highly sociable children tended to show more symptomatology in relation to stress than did less sociable children. Once more, it was evident that individuals who appeared resilient on one outcome measure did not necessarily appear resilient on others.

Lösel and Bliesener (1994) compared resilient and deviant children drawn from residential institutions. They found that the resilient youngsters were more intelligent, more flexible in temperamental style, more approach-oriented, had stronger expectations of self-efficacy and of achievement, considered themselves to be less helpless, had more positive self-esteem, and had a more active and less avoiding coping style. These children differed also in their social resources, having a larger social network and more satisfaction with the social support they received. Intelligence came out as a protective factor only when educator assessments were used to designate groups, not when they were defined entirely in terms of youths' self-reports. Interestingly, these resilient youngsters from highly troubled backgrounds did not report a more positive relationship with one of their parents; rather, they tended to identify more strongly with their residential home and school. That constituted the main context for their lives at the time. The effect sizes in this sample were quite small throughout.

Turning Points in Adult Life

Laub, Nagin, and Sampson (1998) undertook a particularly powerful reanalysis of the Gluecks's data set. They found that a harmonious marriage was an important factor making it much less likely that antisocial activities would continue in adult life. Particular care was taken to ensure that this finding was not a finding of measurement error or of the prior characteristics of the individuals making a harmonious marriage. Sampson and Laub (1993) suggested that the mediation of the protective effect might lie in the informal controls implicit in adult social bonds. Also, however, the harmonious marriage may have been important because involvement in work and family activities reduced the opportunities for crime. In addition, a change in internal cognitions may have played a role. Thus, people's images of themselves, their views of life and opportunities, and their attitudes and expectations may have changed as a result of their experiences of a harmonious marriage. Stable employment in adult life similarly fostered good social functioning, and the continuation of antisocial behavior was more likely when employment opportunities were diminished either because of prison experiences and a prison record or because of the ill-effects of alcohol abuse.

Elder (1986), in his reanalysis of the California longitudinal studies, found that for socially deprived youths who entered the army at an early age immediately after leaving school, the experience proved beneficial in terms of their psychosocial functioning in later adult life. It provided them with the opportunity to continue their education in a more adult environment, it tended to postpone marriage until after they had established careers, and it was accompanied by changes in their self-image. Sampson and Laub (1996), using the Gluecks's data, confirmed Elder's (1986) finding that army experiences could provide an important protective effect for youths from a disadvantaged background. The benefits particularly applied to delinquents who entered the army at an early age before they became established in work and marriage. The effects held up in analyses that took into account a wide range of risk features, as well as childhood antisocial behavior. The reality of the effects was shown by the demonstration that the benefits were largely mediated by on-the-job training and educational opportunities provided by the GI bill. Sampson and Laub further suggested that overseas duties may have helped by knifing off past social disadvantages and criminal stigmatization, as well as by the provision of experiences that broadened perspectives and opened up horizons. In more anecdotal fashion, Long and Vaillant (1984) noted that for some youngsters from multiproblem families, joining the armed forces was instrumental in providing further educational and vocational training. The Kauai study (Werner & Smith, 1992) suggested the same. It should be noted that in all of these studies, army experiences did not have a particularly beneficial effect in those from nondisadvantaged backgrounds or for those who entered the army after getting established in their career and marriage. It was not that army experiences as such were beneficial, but rather that, in particular circumstances, they could be protective through the new opportunities they provided.

Self-Definitions of Resilience

The studies considered thus far have taken as their starting point children who have experienced stress and adversities of some kind. An alternative approach is provided by using people's own concepts and perceptions. Thus, Watt, David, Ladd, and Shamos (1995) studied a volunteer sample of individuals who considered that they had transcended adversity. A sample of twenty-seven women and four men was compared with nineteen control subjects with a similar gender distribution, selected by transcenders as being people from a similar (not disadvantaged) background. The data were obtained through questionnaires and audiotapes for answers to open-ended questions. The resilient subjects had experienced a much higher level of life stress than the controls. Nearly two-thirds reported emotional abuse in childhood, and 16% gave an account of sexual abuse. Those who had transcended adversity emphasized the importance of the feeling that they were able to control the course of their lives, and four-fifths mentioned support from some other person (usually not a relative). For all of them, the process of overcoming adversity was something that happened over a substantial period of time, often with multiple steps involved, rather than through any particular happening at one point in time. Nearly all spoke about their own inner drive, with just over half attributing this to some religious source. Nearly one-third had sought psychotherapy. This seemed to have helped them achieve constructive orientation in their lives. These resilient subjects were assertive on their own self-worth and, as expectable on the basis of the way the sample was recruited, many showed a missionary zeal about the possibility of resilience in the absence of serious adversity. Clearly, there must be considerable caution about any generalizations from a volunteer sample, but the findings provide some useful leads.

Stress-Buffering Effects

Stress-buffering effects were evident in Gore and Aseltine's (1995) questionnaire study of the effects of stress in over 1,000 high school students. As expected, life stresses, strains, and relationships were associated with higher levels of depressed mood a year later, whereas the presence of social resources related to lower levels. Perhaps surprisingly, negative family events and relationship problems with parents were not significantly related to depression; the positive effects of mastery and of social integration were particularly strong. The findings are provocative in their indication that protective effects of social support were more strongly evident when individuals reported high levels of stress. Also, the protective effects were mainly evident within domains. That is to say, support from friends did not ameliorate the effects of family stresses, or vice versa. Support from friends showed a buffering effect with boys, but no such effect in girls. It seemed that it was not so much a gender difference in the availability of resources but that boys and girls differed in their mobilization of support. Gore and Aseltine suggested that it is possible that the support and emotional investment in social relationships may be more closely entwined in girls. Belle (1982) has also drawn attention to the extent to which the greater tendency of girls to exchange emo-

tional confidences (Maccoby, 1998) means that the people who provide support are likely also to bring their own stresses to the relationship, so that it is a two-edged sword. Gore and Aseltine rightly noted important limitations of their study in terms of a reliance on questionnaires and the problems of relatively weak measurement. It would be unjustified to draw strong conclusions on either the synergistic interactions in relation to stress buffering or gender differences. Nevertheless, the findings are provocative in drawing attention to possibly important mediating processes.

Indirect Chain Effects

The probable importance of indirect chain effects is evident in the findings from several other studies. For example, Furstenberg, Brooks-Gunn, and Morgan (1987) found that economic independence was a key factor in leading to successful adaptation and that the elements that fostered such independence were successful graduation from high school, restriction of further childbearing, and making a stable marriage. Masten, Morrison, Pellegrini, and Tellegen (1990), in their summary of findings on Garmezy's Project Competence Program, noted that individual attributes (such as IQ), demographic features (such as family disruption), and parenting qualities (such as organization and cohesion) were all related to both outcome variables such as disruptive behavior and also to negative life events in adolescence. In other words, it seemed that risk characteristics increased maladaptive outcomes in part because they led directly or indirectly to further risk experiences at a later age. Baldwin, Baldwin, and Cole (1990), reporting findings from the Rochester Longitudinal Study, noted that the good quality parenting that was associated with successful outcomes in children from a high-risk background included restrictiveness. It seemed that one of the important features of good parenting in these circumstances was the protection of children from risks in the environment that predisposed to the use of drugs, engagement in delinquency, and early pregnancy. Small (1995), in a large-scale survey of adolescents, similarly found that binge drinking was quite strongly associated with a lack of parental monitoring of children's activities. Neighborhood monitoring showed a similar protective effect. Binge drinking was particularly frequent when there was low monitoring by both parents and the neighborhood.

Long-term follow-up studies of children who have experienced parental divorce when they were young have demonstrated effects on various measures of mental health and social functioning in adult life (Cherlin et al., 1991). The findings, however, have also drawn attention to the importance of considering various mediating factors. Thus, for example, using the British Child Development Study, Chase-Lansdale, Cherlin, and Kiernan (1995) showed that parental divorce that occurred when the children were aged between 7 and 16 years was accompanied by a 20% increase of scores on the Malaise Inventory, a questionnaire measure of distress and disturbance. What at first sight seemed unexpected was that divorce had the most negative impact on children with the least emotional and behavior problems at age 7. It may be that those with problems at age 7 were likely to come from more dysfunctional families, and that divorce, at least in some cases, may actually have had a beneficial effect by its constituting a means of reducing family conflict and discord. The finding highlights the possibility that the same variable may serve as a risk factor in some circumstances but a protective one in others.

Kuh and Maclean (1990), using an earlier British national cohort study, also examined the effects on adult functioning and the experience of parental divorce or separation before the age of 16 years. Parental divorce was associated with lower educational attainment and occupational status, poor mental health, higher alcohol consumption, an increased likelihood of teenage marriage, an increased likelihood of breakdown in their own marriage, and a higher rate of remarriage. It was evident that many of the later sequelae were mediated or moderated by the earlier consequences of parental divorce. Thus, for example, the increased rate of marital breakdown was most evident in those who had married as teenagers. Parental divorce was associated with an increased likelihood of mental disorder in adult life but also a greater tendency to resort to the use of alcohol in the presence of psychiatric disorder. Alcohol abuse, in turn, was associated with an increased likelihood of the persistence or reoccurrence of mental health problems.

Supportive Family Relationships

Numerous studies have noted the positive effects of emotionally responsive care-giving, confident parenting, and warm, supportive parent–child relationships (e.g., Cowen, Work, & Wyman, 1997; Dubow & Luster, 1990; Egeland et al., 1993; Fonagy et al., 1994; Masten et al., 1990; McCord, 1986; Pianta, Egeland, & Sroufe, 1990; Seifer, Sameroff, Baldwin, & Baldwin, 1992). Of course, such positive effects are expectable on the grounds that this is the other end of the risk dimension of family discord, poor parenting, and disturbed parent–child relationships (see Patterson, 1995, 1996; Reiss et al., 1995; Rutter et al., 1997b). However, that is not the whole story. For example, Jenkins and Smith (1990) found that a good relationship with one parent seemed protective in the context of general family discord. Masten et al. (1988) found that girls who had experienced high-quality parenting showed less negative effects from increasing stress exposure (although parenting quality had little protective effect in boys).

Cognitive–Affective Processing of Experiences

Several other points warrant mention. It has long been clear that children actively process their experiences, thinking about what has happened to them and attaching meaning to events. What is to one child a positive challenge to be welcomed may be to another child a situation carrying threat and an expectation of failure. Various writers have argued that the style of cognitive and affective processing of experiences may be crucial to whether resilience results. Thus, Main, Kaplan, and Cassidy (1985), writing about childhood attachment experiences, argued that the effects were a consequence, not so much of what the experiences were actually like in childhood, but of the way that they were thought about in adult life. It was suggested that it was protective for people to accept the reality of their negative experiences rather than to deny or distort what happened to them and to be able to focus on positive aspects in order to incorporate the whole into their own personal schema. Empirical findings show that there is indeed a meaningful distinction between objective experiences and the ways in which they are conceptualized later (van Ijzendoorn, 1995), but few data are available on the relative importance of each. Fonagy et al. (1994) showed that security in a parent (as measured by the Adult Attachment Interview) was associated with an increased likelihood of security in the mother–infant relationship. Negative experiences in the childhood of the mother constituted a risk factor predisposing to insecurity, but a self-reflective style was a protective factor, with its effect greatest in those who had experienced deprivation. As already discussed, self-reports of resilient individuals usually emphasize the importance of their own positive self-concept and their attitude toward and conceptualization of their negative experiences. It certainly seems reasonable to suppose that the style of cognitive processing is likely to be an important moderator of the effects of stress and adversity, but evidence is lacking on the extent to which this is so. Even less is known about the features that predisposed to different styles of cognitive processing.

Sensitizing and Steeling Effects

A related consideration concerns the processes involved in determining whether stress or adversity has a sensitizing or steeling effect, that is, whether it increases or decreases vulnerability to later negative experiences. As already indicated, both effects can occur. There has been little systematic research on the features that make one or other response more likely. It may be, however, that the key feature is whether the initial stress experience is felt to be manageable, results in successful coping, and gives rise to a feeling of mastery, self-efficacy, and self-confidence. For example, in Elder's (1974, 1979) study of children growing up during the period of the Great Depression, he found that the need to take on domestic responsibilities and to undertake part-time work proved strengthening for many of the older children, although it tended to have the reverse effect in younger ones. It seemed that coping successfully and accepting productive roles for responsibility, in which this was associated with cohesive family ties, could lead to personality strengths. In a possibly similar fashion, studies of the treatment of fears and phobias have shown that avoidance of the feared stimulus tends to perpetuate the

phobia, whereas successful encounters with it, however brought about, tend to lead to its diminution and loss (Ollendick, King, & Yule, 1994). Possibly there is a parallel, too, with people's responses to physical hazards of various kinds (Rutter, 1995c). It is obvious that in medicine, and in biology more generally, resilience does not usually reside in positive health characteristics or experiences. Rather, resilience seems to stem from having the encounter with stress at a time, and in a way, that the body can cope successfully with a noxious challenge to its system. Thus, immunity to infections, whether naturally or therapeutically induced through immunization, derives from controlled exposure to the relevant pathogen and not through avoidance of it. The evidence is much too fragmentary for any firm conclusions with respect to the possibility of comparable processes in relation to psychosocial stresses in adversity, but it may well be that the same applies.

Positive Experiences

A further issue concerns the role of positive experiences in the genesis of resilience. Such limited evidence as there is suggests that neither acute nor chronic positive experiences as such exert much protective effect (Rutter & Sandberg, 1992; Sandberg et al., 1993). The evidence, however, mainly comes from comparing clinical samples and controls and finding no difference in the rate of positive experiences. It may be, however, that there are benefits if the positive experiences are of a kind that directly counter, or compensate for, some risk factor. Thus, Asendorpf and van Aken (1997), in an interview study of 139 sixth graders, found that children with low social support from their parents or classmates reported low general self-worth. Low support by a parent was compensated for by a supportive relationship by the other parent, but not by supportive relationships from others. The findings were interpreted to indicate the specificity of relationship support. The already discussed findings from Gore and Aseltine (1995) are consistent with that inference. In studies of life stress as a precipitant of adult depressive disorder, there are comparable findings with respect to so-called neutralizing or fresh-start life events (Brown, Adler, & Bifulco, 1988; Brown, Lemyre, & Bifulco, 1992; Craig, Drake,

Mills, & Boardman, 1994; Tennant, Bebbington, & Hurry, 1981) that negate or counteract the impact of an earlier threatening event or difficulty. Such neutralizing events appear to be associated with an increased likelihood of remission of depression, whereas this is not found for positive events that do not have this neutralizing quality.

Genetic Influences

As already indicated, there is extensive evidence of the important role of genetic factors in the overall liability to all forms of psychopathology and especially in relation to its persistence or recurrence over time (Rutter et al., 1999). It follows, therefore, that genetic factors are bound to play a significant role in relation to resilience, as part of the overall pattern of multifactorial determination. From the point of view of understanding causal mechanisms and developing effective programs of intervention, however, it is necessary to move beyond this rather general inference to a more discriminating appreciation of how genetic factors may work in relation to resilience. As molecular genetic advances begin to make it possible to identify genetic risks at an individual level, it should be possible to take this field much further forward (Plomin & Rutter, 1998). Meanwhile, quantitative genetic findings provide some important leads.

First, it is evident that passive gene–environment correlations are likely to be influential (Rutter et al., 1997b). That is, genetically influenced parental psychopathology is associated with a marked increase in the likelihood of an adverse pattern of rearing that causes a substantial environmental risk. Parents not only pass on genes but they also shape the family environment of their children (and to a lesser extent their extrafamilial experiences). This is most evident in the case of parental personality disorder and parental drug abuse and alcoholism (associated with high rates of family discord and disruption), but it is also apparent with chronic or recurrent parental depression and with other forms of mental disorder (Rutter, 1989; Rutter & Quinton, 1984; Rutter et al., 1997b). Several studies have shown that the main risks to the offspring derive from the association between parental mental disorder and a seriously maladaptive family environment, the direct effects of parental mental disorder being much

less in the absence of environmental risk (Bank, Forgatch, Patterson, & Petrow, 1993; McCord, 1986; Roy, Pickles, & Rutter, in press; Rutter & Quinton, 1984; Vorria, Rutter, Pickles, Wolkind, & Hobsbaum, 1998a, 1998b). Nevertheless, in several of these studies, there was some direct effect of parental mental disorder that was not entirely mediated through the maladaptive environment.

Particularly in the case of antisocial problems, there is also growing evidence of the likely importance of gene–environment interactions. That is to say, some of the genetic effect derives from the role of genes in increasing people's vulnerability or susceptibility to high-risk environments (Rutter et al., 1998). The main evidence derives from adoptee studies that show that environmental effects tend to be greater for individuals who are also genetically at risk as a result of criminality or drug or alcohol problems in biological parents who did not rear them (Bohman, 1996; Cadoret, 1985; Cadoret, Yates, Troughton, Woodworth, & Stewart, 1995; Crowe, 1974). In other words, it is the combination of genetic risk in the biological parents and an adverse environment in the adoptive home that predispose to antisocial behavior.

There is also some evidence that the susceptibility genes involved in depressive and anxiety disorders may also operate through sensitivity to the environment. At least with respect to unipolar disorders, it seems that much of the genetic risk derives from an effect on the personality trait of emotionality or neuroticism rather than directly on some specific psychiatric disorder (Kendler, 1996; Kendler, Neale, Kessler, Heath, & Eaves, 1993). Using an ingenious application of the twin strategy, Kendler et al. (1996) showed that twins with an inferred higher genetic risk were the most likely to respond to a negative life event with the onset of a new affective disorder (as compared with those with an inferred lower genetic risk).

A third route through which genetic factors may operate in relation to resilience, or the lack of it, derives from active and evocative gene–environment correlations (Rutter et al., 1997a). As already discussed, people (through their behavior) influence other people's reactions to them and also shape and select the environments they experience. This effect applies regardless of whether the behavior is genetically or environmentally influenced or both.

Nevertheless, adoptee studies do show that genetic effects operate in this way in part (Ge et al., 1996; O'Connor, Deater-Deckard, Fulker, Autter, & Plomin, 1998). Thus, it has been shown that there are significant associations between genetic risk in the biological parents and negative parenting by the adoptive parents – the intermediate mediating variable being some form of disruptive behavior shown by the child. We know very little about the developmental consequences of this form of person effect on the environment, but there is limited evidence that disturbed behavior in a child is more likely to persist when it engenders negative or maladaptive responses in other people (Maccoby & Jacklin, 1983). Sometimes it is assumed that if the child behavior is strongly genetically influenced, this vicious cycle cannot be modified, but the evidence indicates that is not so. For example, hyperkinetic disorder is one of the more strongly genetically influenced of child psychiatric disorders (Rutter et al., 1999), but when medication improves the child behavior, this is accompanied by consequent beneficial effects on parent–child interaction (Schachar, Taylor, Wieselberg, Thorley, & Rutter, 1987).

We have long since moved past the point of the misleading assumption that "constitutional" factors are irrelevant because we cannot do anything about them (Ainsworth, 1962). To the contrary, there is an active dynamic interplay between nature and nurture; many of the mechanisms are susceptible to modification, given appropriate forms of intervention. It is not, of course, that the genes themselves are alterable (other than through the rather drastic remedy of gene therapy) but rather that, because so many of the effects are indirect, there are ways of influencing the indirect chain reactions involved in the causative processes.

As discussed earlier, it is also important to consider the role of genetic influences in relation to effects that appear on the surface to be environmentally mediated but which, nevertheless, may reflect genetic mediation in part. Thus, individual variations in people's experience of negative and positive life events and their experience of social support of various kinds have been shown to involve a degree of genetic influence (Plomin, 1994a, 1994b; Plomin et al., 1997). The key question, however, is not whether genetic influences play a role in the origins of these different experiences, but whether they play

a role in the mediation of their effects in relation to risk and resilience. In that connection, Kessler, Kendler, Heath, Neale, and Eaves (1992), using the Virginia Twin Study of some 800 same-sexed twin pairs, examined the associations between a questionnaire measure of perceived support (from various relatives and friends) and a questionnaire measure of depression. The findings were complex but informative and important. In brief, the initial analyses showed that higher levels of some form of social support were accompanied by a lower risk of depression and that there appeared to be a stress-buffering effect, with the effects of stress on depression less in the presence of a high level of support. Curiously, in contradiction of other studies, however, the reverse was found for spouse support. But what complicated the picture was that the genetic factors influencing susceptibility to depression were to some extent the same as the genetic factors that underlie individual differences in social support. Statistical modeling showed that in the case of four key support measures, the apparent stress-buffering effect was a result of the fact that the direct effects of genetic and environmental factors that influenced success in developing supportive friendship networks also had a direct effect on depression during conditions of high stress. The implication is that some of the stress-buffering effect was spurious, but there was also evidence suggesting that some was real. Kessler et al. pointed out, however, that there may well be two-way effects. That is, although high levels of support may have a protective effect against depression at times of high stress, so also the effects of depressive disorder may serve to erode social support.

PROCESSES ASSOCIATED WITH RESILIENCE: POLICY IMPLICATIONS

As is clear from all reviews of the topic (see, for example, Compas, Hinden, & Gerhardt, 1995; Gore & Eckenrode, 1994; Hetherington & Blechman, 1996; Luthar, 1993; Rutter, 1994; Wang & Gordon, 1994), despite its critical importance as an organizing construct for the design of early childhood intervention policies for vulnerable children, resilience is not a unidimensional construct that is susceptible to succinct summary. In a real sense, although it focuses on a particular issue (viz., relative success despite the experience of stress and adversity), it involves an understanding of the whole of risk processes for psychopathology. For obvious reasons, that necessarily means that there may well be different processes involved in resilience in relation to different psychopathological outcomes. Although it is the case that there are some features that tend to be relevant to a wide range of outcomes, there are others that are much more diagnosis specific. It would be absurd to suppose that it made any sense to summarize the features promoting resilience in general. As has been apparent in this review, the majority of the studies have focused on one or other aspect of disruptive or antisocial behavior; much more is known about resilience in relation to these outcomes than it is with respect to, say, depressive disorders, anxiety states, or eating disorders. It is also clear, whatever the outcome being considered, that resilience is not an individual trait or characteristic. Rather, it reflects a process or range of processes. These involve mechanisms that are operative before, during, and after the encounter with the stress experience or adversity that is being studied. A range of somewhat diverse mechanisms is involved. Because, as has been evident in the studies considered earlier, the samples, measures, concepts, risk factors, and outcomes have been heterogeneous in the field of resilience research, it is not possible to put the findings together to derive a firm set of conclusions. Nevertheless, the evidence does allow a set of inferences on some of the key types of processes that are likely to be involved in resilience in relation to a range of outcomes (see Rutter, 1999).

Overall Level of Risk

Almost all forms of common psychopathology are multifactorially determined. That is, they are due to a complex interplay among both multiple genes and multiple psychosocial (and physical) risk factors. With but few exceptions, the risks for mental disorder associated with any single risk experience are relatively low, and a key explanation for individual differences in responses to psychosocial risk concerns the number of risk factors involved and the duration of the individual's exposure to them. On the whole, children showing resilience are those who have been exposed to fewer risk factors for a shorter period of time. Although the finding is, in a sense, theoretically unexciting, it does have three

important policy implications. First, the main focus needs to be on children exposed to multiple adversities, and not on those suffering a single major risk experience. Second, a reduction in the overall level of risks may make a substantial difference in promoting resilience, even if considerable risks remain. Third, attention needs to be paid to experiences at school and in the peer group, as well as in the family.

Sensitivity to Risk

It is also evident, however, that for any given degree of risk exposure, there are substantial individual differences in vulnerability or susceptibility. These derive from several different sources. One important source concerns genetic influences. To an important extent, genetic factors operate through their impact on individual differences in susceptibility to environmental hazards. One key implication is that environmental interventions may be most important for those people who are also genetically at risk. Genetic and environmental etiologies do not usually provide alternative routes to psychopathology; rather, the causative processes involve a complex interplay between the two. Obviously, personal qualities, such as those involving temperament or personality, will be implicated in the genetically influenced features that are associated with individual variations in susceptibility to stress or adversity (see, for example, Tschann, Kaiser, Chesney, Alkon, & Boyce, 1996). One characteristic that is fairly consistently associated with risk and resilience is a person's IQ or level of overall cognitive functioning. With but a few exceptions (e.g., Luthar, 1991), a lower IQ is associated with an increased risk of a range of negative outcomes, and a higher IQ with a lower likelihood of maladaptive functioning. The consistency with which it appears as a risk–resilience dimension is strongest in the case of antisocial behavior. The findings in relation to depression, anxiety, or other forms of emotional disturbance are more variable. What is much less clear, however, is how IQ operates in relation to risk processes. In relation to antisocial behavior, it seems that a relatively lower IQ constitutes a risk factor that is not dependent on any association with psychosocial adversity. Its role is partially mediated through educational failure, and the social consequences of such failure, but that seems to be only a part (perhaps a small part) of what is involved. Also, in some studies, the effects of IQ have seemed greater than in others in relation to psychosocial stress–adversity situations (see, for example, Moffitt, 1990).

Goodman et al. (1995) analyzed data on an epidemiological sample of some 400 13-year-old twins in an attempt to determine the mechanisms that might be involved. They found that both parents and teachers reported more disruptive behavior among children with lower IQs. This was not attributable to the effects of parental IQ or social class and was not entirely mediated by lower scholastic attainments. As measured by teacher report, higher levels of emotional symptoms were also related to lower IQ, but this was not found on parental reports. It has often been suggested that the effects of a lower IQ depend on a contrast with the performance of others. On that basis, one might expect that the main risks would occur when a child's IQ was lower than that of his co-twin or siblings. The findings, however, showed that the main effect stemmed from the child's absolute IQ and not the IQ in relation to the co-twin. It was apparent, as it has been in studies over the years (see, for example, Rutter, 1979; Rutter, Tizard, & Whitmore, 1970) that the effects of IQ in relation to risk and resilience apply across the entire IQ range, and not just at lower levels. It must be concluded that cognitive functioning is implicated in an important way in risk–resilience processes, and that this is not simply because of its role in relation to educational attainment, but precisely what mechanism it does reflect remains uncertain.

The other personal qualities that stand out most strongly as associated with resilience are high self-esteem, self-efficacy, and planful competence. The ways in which they promote resilience also remain somewhat uncertain. It is possible that the positive self-concept makes people less vulnerable to the emotional pain, threats to self-confidence, or social rebuffs that some forms of stress and adversity involve. Equally, however, it may be that as Bandura (1995, 1997) has suggested, it is not so much feeling good about oneself that is crucial, but the sense of being in control of one's destiny and feeling able to take effective actions to do whatever is required by challenging situations. Insofar as that is the case, it may be that it is not the particular coping skills that matter most but an attitude of mind that leads to the application of an appropriate range of coping strategies. Of course, it is necessary to go on to ask what kind of experiences tend to foster these seemingly protective self-concept qualities. The evidence suggests two types of experiences are important: the presence of secure intimate relationships (those with caregivers being particularly important during the years of development) and the experience of pleasurable success in one arena or another.

Previous experiences are also probably important. Although there are few empirical findings that directly address the matter, it seems that previous experiences of successfully dealing with challenge or of overcoming adversity may well be protective (see, for example, Elder, 1974, 1979; Phelps, Belsky, & Crnic, 1998). It seems probable that the effects on self-concept are at least as important as the particular coping strategies acquired during the previous encounter with stress or adversity.

Studies of institution-reared children have emphasized the high frequency with which the young people feel at the mercy of fate and the lack of a sense of purpose or control over their lives (Quinton & Rutter, 1988; Pawlby et al., 1997a, 1997b). Although it is not known whether it is the relevant aspect of their institutional experiences in this connection, it is certainly striking that most residential facilities for adolescents provide remarkably few opportunities for the young people to exercise responsibility, autonomy, and control over their lives. Conversely, studies of effective schools (e.g., Maughan, 1994; Mortimore, 1995; Rutter, 1983b; Rutter, Maughan, Mortimore, Ouston, with Smith, 1979; Stipek, 1997) have commented on the fact that school success was often associated with good opportunities for children to exercise responsibility. The ways in which schools did this varied considerably, but it did seem important that they were available in one form or another. Probably similar features apply within ordinary families. Clearly, it is important that the responsibilities available are appropriate to children's developmental level and personal qualities. Equally, it does seem important that children are given an appropriate level of opportunity to make decisions for themselves and to learn through their mistakes, as well as through their successes. Once more, the evidence linking this firmly with resilience is fragmentary, but there is some suggestion that this probably constitutes an important part of children's experiences as they grow up.

Several somewhat different implications for preventive policies arise from considerations of sensitivity to risk. First, it is evident that schools need to provide an ethos that provides opportunities for all children to exercise autonomy and responsibility and to achieve success in some area of their lives (Maughan, 1994; Mortimore, 1995; Stipek, 1997). Such success need not necessarily involve high scholastic achievement, although this is important, too, in its own right. Part of the school ethos should also involve good teacher–pupil relationships, ample sources of encouragement and reward, and a focus on positive features and appropriately high expectations. Second, these same features apply to parenting in the home but with the difference that warm, supportive relationships are particularly important for the provision of security. There have been few systematic evaluations of programs to aid good parenting in high-risk groups, but it seems that such programs may be beneficial (Rutter et al., 1998). Third, there may be value in preventive programs in schools to foster effective social problem solving (see Pellegrini, 1994).

In summary, there are four main policy implications from the findings on sensitivity to risk. First, environmental interventions may be most needed for children who are genetically at risk. Second, to an important extent, the qualities that provide resistance to stress–adversity may be acquired through appropriate experiences. Such experiences include successful coping with life's challenges (attempts to shield children completely from stress may be damaging as well as futile); taking responsibility and exercising autonomy and decision taking; and having secure, harmonious, personal relationships. Third, with respect to such relationships, preventive programs to foster good parenting may well be worthwhile. Fourth, social, as well as pedagogic, experiences at school have an important role to play.

Reduction of the Impact of Stress or Adversity

Many studies have shown the importance of the extent to which risk experiences directly impinge on the individual child rather than just being present as some general part of background experiences. Thus, for example, it seems clear that although general family discord and conflict constitutes a risk (particularly for antisocial behavior), hostility, criticism, and negative feelings that are directly focused on the individual child, as through scapegoating, are the more potent risk factors (see, for example, Reiss et al., 1995). Studies of person–environment correlations indicate that the extent to which negative experiences are focused in this way is influenced by qualities in the children themselves. The interplay is two-way. Nevertheless, it does seem important that this negative individual focus be kept to a minimum in any given high-risk situation. Some of the studies of resilient youths noted that young people may take action themselves to seek rewards outside of the family and to distance themselves to a degree from the risk situation in the family. Therapeutic programs that have proved successful in reducing oppositional–defiant and antisocial behavior (as, for example, those developed by Patterson and his colleagues [Patterson, Dishion, & Chamberlain, 1993] and Webster-Stratton [1991]) include strategies and tactics designed to help families avoid these coercive patterns of interpersonal interchange. Of course, high-risk experiences arise outside of the family, with those in the peer group and at school being likely to be particularly influential. Many studies suggest that appropriate monitoring and supervision by parents, teachers, and neighbors may be valuable in helping young people avoid getting entangled with deviant group activities. Obviously, it is not just a matter of "policing" young people's activities and preventing their engaging in negative activities. It is likely to be just as important to ensure that there are equally attractive alternative activities both inside and outside of the family.

The policy implications, therefore, are 1) that therapeutic interventions with troubled families need to be concerned to help parents avoid scapegoating and drawing children into family conflict, as well as to reduce the overall level of family discord and 2) that attention needs to be paid to the appropriate monitoring and supervision of children's experiences outside of the home.

Reduction of Negative Chain Reactions

Although there may not be universally effective coping strategies, there certainly are responses to stress and adversity that tend to be maladaptive in their consequences. Thus, there is abundant evidence that reliance on drug or alcohol abuse to relieve stress, dropping out of education, or leaping into a teenage pregnancy or marriage as a way of escaping from family conflict all carry potential long-term adverse sequelae. It is evident that a resilient outcome is more likely if young people, either through their own actions or through support, guidance, and supervision of others, are able to avoid these maladaptive coping strategies and find more constructive ways of dealing with stress and adversity. The qualities of self-efficacy and planful competence mentioned earlier are likely to be important in that connection, in addition to adult guidance, supervision, and monitoring. The policy implication is that young children need to be helped to gain a repertoire of coping strategies that do not have these maladaptive consequences. Most of the research focus has been on adolescents, but it is happily likely that styles of coping are first acquired in early childhood and, therefore, that this should constitute a focus in preventive programs in the early years as well as later.

Increasing Positive Chain Reactions

One of the important aspects of research into the effects of different temperamental qualities have been the findings on the effects of temperament on other people. For the most part, the focus has been on the role of negative temperamental or disruptive behavior in eliciting critical, hostile, or punitive responses from other people (see Rutter, 1990; Rutter et al., 1997a). These effects have been shown in a range of both naturalistic and experimental studies (Engfer, Walper, & Rutter, 1994). The opposite pole of the same mechanism is that positive personality features are likely to elicit warm and supportive responses from other people. This aspect of temperament was emphasized in Werner and Smith's (1982) study, and Masten (1982) similarly brought out the protective role of humor. This positive side of temperament has been little studied up to now, but it is a common clinical experience to find that even some children with marked emotional–behavioral disturbance nevertheless tend to elicit positive responses from those about them. A response of distress or unhappiness in the presence of stress or adversity is likely to bring

about more supportive responses from other people than oppositional–defiant responses to the same environmental situation. This aspect of resilience has been neglected but probably warrants further attention. The policy implication is that there needs to be a shift from a view that temperamental features are just within-the-person characteristics to an appreciation that much of their importance lies in their effects on interpersonal interactions. Children need to be helped to use their personal qualities in ways that are socially positive rather than disruptive.

Experiences Opening Up New Opportunities

It is clear from numerous studies that one of the reasons that psychopathology that develops after adverse experiences persists over time is that the adverse environments also continue. It is not so much that the environments are unchanging, although that may sometimes be the case, but that for a variety of reasons one negative environment tends to predispose to the occurrence of later stresses and adversities. Accordingly, one of the potentially important features fostering resilience are happenings that end damaging experiences and open up new opportunities and a change of environment. Army experiences for disadvantaged youths provide a striking example of just this kind of turning point experience. It is not that being in the army was in itself a positive or protective factor, and it certainly is not the case that an absence of army experience is a risk factor for psychopathology. For many youngsters, joining the army can be disruptive because of the negative effects to career and family life, quite apart from any stresses that may be brought about by armed conflict or group living. Nevertheless, when army experience was instrumental in providing more adult-type education and vocational training for disadvantaged youths who had become disenamored with schooling, it could provide a new start. Similarly, if postponing marriage until a later age meant that the potential pool of marriage partners was much widened beyond the delinquent peer group from which the individual had come, that too could be positive. Putting behind stigma and a negative reputation might also aid in fostering a new start.

Many studies have shown the negative effects of dropping out of schooling and of failing to obtain scholastic qualifications and credentials. Conversely, it is clear that persistence in education provides a widening of job opportunities and increases the possibility of economic security. It seems that marriage as such is neither a risk nor a protective experience, because much depends on the quality of the marriage, the sort of person who is involved as partner, and what marriage does to the person's social group and social experiences. However, when these are positive, the effect can be a beneficial opening up of opportunities and entry into a more prosocial peer group. The acquisition of family responsibilities may also be protective through increasing bonds to society. It should be emphasized, as is the case with many of the features being considered here, that the findings mainly apply to antisocial behavior and the situation with respect to, say, depression may be different. Nevertheless, it is clear that attention needs to be paid to the value of turning point experiences in adolescence and adult life and to the steps that may foster their occurrence for youths from high-risk backgrounds.

It might be thought that these turning point experiences in adolescence/early adult life are of little relevance for those primarily concerned with psychosocial risks in the preschool years, but that is not so. It is striking to observe the benefits applied to youths from a high-risk background whose adversities began in the early years. The crucially important implication is that even seriously damaging experiences in early childhood do not necessarily have enduring effects. Much of the persistence of negative sequelae derives from the continuation of adverse experiences. This means that radical changes for the better in life circumstances can do much to ameliorate early risks, even when the changes occur later in life.

Neutralizing or Compensatory Experiences

Although pleasant experiences as such do not appear to play any substantial role in fostering resilience, nevertheless, success, approval from other people, and feelings of accomplishment are important for everyone in terms of fostering self-esteem and self-efficacy. When these are generally lacking,

their provision in one domain or another may be important because they compensate for a lack of such experiences that are normally available in many different settings. Good experiences at school were mentioned as one possible example of this kind. Similarly, close, intimate relationships are important for optimal psychological development. The particular types of relationship that provide this vary over the life span. Selective attachments, usually within the family, are critical in early childhood, and loving, confiding relationships play a somewhat comparable role in adult life (Rutter, 1995a; Rutter & O'Connor, 1999). The lack of such relationships constitutes a risk factor for various forms of psychopathology and, when such relationships are generally lacking, their provision by a new relationship may be quite protective. The evidence does suggest, however, that there is a degree of domain specificity in this connection. That is to say, although a good friendship with a peer may be positive, it provides a rather unsatisfactory substitute for poor parent–child relationships. The evidence on compensatory experiences is too fragmentary for strong policy implications. Nevertheless, it seems that the provision of happy experiences (desirable though that is in its own right) will not, in itself, do much to foster resilience. Rather, what seems important are experiences that may be instrumental in countering a risk mechanism. The findings on the value of a close, confiding relationship suggest that this may be supportive, especially when other relationships are in trouble, but there are substantial limits to the extent to which one good relationship can compensate for difficulties in others.

Cognitive Processing of Experiences

The last feature that may promote resilience is probably the one about which we know least, namely, how people think about their experiences and how they incorporate them into their overall schema of themselves, their environment, and their relationships with other people. It is certainly obvious that there are marked individual differences in how people do this; it seems reasonable to suppose that this will make a difference to how the effects of experiences are carried forward. The investigation of the ways in which different styles of cognitive processing affect the consequences of adverse early

ant research pri-
nically, it proba-
, but there is in-
 deal with what
n is that it may
think positively,
experiences, but
de their control,
pects there may
in their success-
finding adaptive

t a fixed charac-
epresents several
nic processes op-
y opened up the
the findings may
preventive poli-
factors involved
outcome are not
es leading to re-
context, it is not
into a single co-
herent program. In the past, there has sometimes
been a wish to search for the hallmarks of resilience,
as if once one knew what it "looked like," it should
be a relatively straightforward matter to design interventions to bring it about. That no longer appears
a sensible aim. Further research is much needed to
test the ideas that derive from the set of findings reviewed in this chapter. As has been clear from the
outline of the research, some findings are much better established than others. Nevertheless, although a
lot has still to be learned, there is now a much better
understanding of the different sorts of processes that
are likely to be implicated. Already these provide at
least provisional guidelines for possible preventive
policies.

REFERENCES

Ainsworth, M. D. (1962). The effects of maternal deprivation: A review of findings and controversy in the context
of research strategy. In *Deprivation of maternal care: A reassessment of its effects* (pp. 97–165). Public Health Papers
#14. Geneva: World Health Organization.

Anthony, E. J. (1974). The syndrome of the psychologically invulnerable child. In E. Anthony & C. Koupernick
(Eds.), *The child in his family: Vol. 3. Children at psychiatric
risk* (pp. 529–44). New York: Wiley.

Anthony, E. J. (1978). A new scientific region to explore.
In E. J. Anthony & C. Koupernik (Eds.), *The child in his
family: Vulnerable children* (pp. 3–15). New York: Wiley.

Anthony, E. J., & Cohler, B. J. (Eds.). (1987). *The invulnerable
child*. New York: Guilford Press.

Asendorpf, J. B., & van Aken, M. A. G. (1997). Support
by parents, classmates, friends, and siblings in pread-
olescence: Covariation and compensation across relationships. *Journal of Social and Personal Relationships,
14*, 79–93.

Baldwin, A. L., Baldwin, C., & Cole, R. E. (1990).
Stress-resistant families and stress-resistant children. In
J. Rolf, A. S. Masten, D. Cicchetti, K. H. Nuechterlein, &
S. Weintraub (Eds.), *Risk and protective factors in the devel-
opment of psychopathology* (pp. 257–80). New York: Cam-
bridge University Press.

Bandura, A. (Ed.). (1995). *Self-efficacy in changing societies*.
Cambridge, UK: Cambridge University Press.

Bandura, A. (1997). *Self-efficacy: The exercise of control*. New
York: Freeman.

Bank, L., Forgatch, M. S., Patterson, G. R., & Petrow, R. A.
(1993). Parenting practices of single mothers: Mediators
of negative contextual factors. *Journal of Marriage and the
Family, 55*, 371–84.

Belle, D. (Ed.). (1982). *Lives in stress: Women and depression*.
Beverley Hills, CA: Sage.

Biederman, J., Milberger, S., Faraone, S. V., Kiely, K.,
Guite, J., Mick, E., Ablon, S., Warburton, R., & Reed, E.
(1995). Family-environment risk factors for attention-
deficit hyperactivity disorder: A test of Rutter's indicators of adversity. *Archives of General Psychiatry, 52*,
464–70.

Bird, H. R., Gould, M. S., & Staghezza, B. (1992). Aggregating data from multiple informants in child psychiatry and epidemiological research. *Journal of the American
Academy of Child and Adolescent Psychiatry, 31*, 78–85.

Bohman, M. (1996). Predisposition to criminality: Swedish
adoption studies in retrospect. In G. R. Bock & J. A.
Goode (Eds.), *Genetics of criminal and antisocial behaviour.
Ciba Foundation Symposium 194* (pp. 99–114). Chichester,
England: Wiley.

Bowlby, J. (1951). *Maternal care and mental health*. Geneva:
World Health Organization.

Boyle, M. H., & Pickles, A. P. (1997). Influence of maternal
depressive symptoms on ratings of childhood behavior.
Journal of Abnormal Child Psychology, 25, 399–412.

Brody, G. H., Stoneman, Z., Flor, D., McCrary, C.,
Hastings, L., & Conyers, O. (1994). Financial resources, parent psychological functioning, parent co-
caregiving and early adolescent competence in rural two-
parent African-American families. *Child Development, 65*,
590–605.

Brown, G. W., Adler, Z., & Bifulco, A. (1988). Life events, difficulties and recovery from chronic depression. *British Journal of Psychiatry, 152,* 487–98.

Brown, G. W., & Harris, T. O. (1978). *Social origins of depression: A study of psychiatric disorders in women.* London: Tavistock Publications.

Brown, G. W., & Harris, T. O. (1989). *Life events and illness.* New York: Guilford.

Brown, G. W., Lemyre, L., & Bifulco, A. (1992). Social factors and recovery from anxiety and depressive disorders: A test of the specificity hypothesis. *British Journal of Psychiatry, 161,* 44–54.

Brunk, M. A., & Henggeler, S. W. (1984). Child influences on adult controls: An experimental investigation. *Developmental Psychology, 20,* 1074–81.

Cadoret, R. J. (1985). Genes, environment and their interaction in the development of psychopathology. In T. Sakai & T. Tsuboi (Eds.), *Genetic aspects of human behavior* (pp. 165–75). Tokyo: Igaku-Shoin.

Cadoret, R. J., Yates, W. R., Troughton, E., Woodworth, G., & Stewart, M. A. (1995). Genetic–environmental interaction in the genesis of aggressivity and conduct disorders. *Archives of General Psychiatry, 52,* 916–24.

Casaer, P., de Vries, L., & Marlowe, N. (1991). Prenatal and perinatal risk factors for psychosocial development. In M. Rutter & P. Casaer (Eds.), *Biological risk factors for psychosocial disorders* (pp. 139–74). Cambridge, UK: Cambridge University Press.

Chase-Lansdale, P. L., Cherlin, A. J., & Kiernan, K. E. (1995). The long-term effects of parental divorce on the mental health of young adults: A developmental perspective. *Child Development, 66,* 1614–34.

Chase-Lansdale, P. L., & Hetherington, E. M. (1990). The impact of divorce on life-span development: Short and long term effects. In P. B. Baltes, D. L. Featherman, & R. M. Lerner (Eds.), *Life-span development and behavior* (Vol. 10, pp. 107–50). Hillsdale, NJ: Erlbaum.

Cherlin, A. J., Furstenberg, F. F., Jr., Chase-Lansdale, P. L., Kiernan, K. E., Robins, P. K., Morrison, D. R., & Teitler, J. O. (1991). Longitudinal studies of effects of divorce on children in Great Britain and the United States. *Science, 252,* 1386–9.

Chilcoat, H.D., & Breslau, N. (1997). Does psychiatric history bias mothers' reports? An application of a new analytic approach. *Journal of the American Academy of Child and Adolescent Psychiatry, 36,* 971–9.

Clausen, J. S. (1991). Adolescent competence and the shaping of the life course. *American Journal of Sociology, 96,* 805–42.

Clausen, J. S. (1993). *American lives: Looking back at the children of the Great Depression.* New York: Free Press.

Cohler, B. J. (1987). Adversity, resilience, and the study of lives. In E. J. Anthony & B. J. Cohler (Eds.), *The invulnerable child* (pp. 363–424). New York: Guilford Press.

Compas, B. E., Hinden, B. R., & Gerhardt, C. A. (1995). Adolescent development: Pathways and processes of risk and resilience. *Annual Review of Psychology, 46,* 265–93.

Conger, R. D., & Elder, G. (1994). *Families in troubled times: Adapting to change in rural America.* Hillsdale, NJ: Aldine.

Conger, R. D., Conger, K. J., Elder, G. H., Jr., Lorenz, F. O., Simons, R. L., & Whitbeck, L. B. (1992). A family process model of economic hardship and adjustment of early adolescent boys. *Child Development, 63,* 526–41.

Conger, R. D., Ge, X., Elder, G. H., Jr., Lorenz, F. O., & Simons, R. L. (1994). Economic stress, coercive family process, and developmental problems of adolescents. *Child Development, 65,* 541–61.

Connell, J. P., Spencer, M. B., & Aber, J. L. (1994). Educational risk and resilience in African-American youth: Context, self, action, and outcomes in school. *Child Development, 65,* 493–506.

Cowen, E. L., Work, W. C., & Wyman, P. A. (1997). The Rochester Child Resilience Project (RCRP): Facts found, lessons learned, future directions divined. In S. S. Luthar, J. A. Burack, D. Cicchetti, & J. R. Weisz (Eds.), *Developmental psychopathology: Perspective on adjustment, risk, and disorder* (pp. 527–47). New York: Cambridge University Press.

Craig, T. K., Drake, H., Mills, K., & Boardman, A.P. (1994). The South London Somatisation Study: Influence of stressful life events and secondary gain. *British Journal of Psychiatry, 165,* 248–58.

Crowe, R. R. (1974). An adoption study of antisocial personality. *Archives of General Psychiatry, 31,* 785–91.

Dubow, E. F., & Luster, T. (1990). Adjustment of children born to teenage mothers: The contribution of risk and protective factors. *Journal of Marriage and the Family, 52,* 393–404.

Eaves, L., Silberg, J., Meyer, J., Maes, H., Simonoff, E., Pickles, A., Rutter, M., Neale, M. C., Reynolds, C. A., Erikson, M. T., Heath, A. C., Loeber, R., Truett, T. R., & Hewitt, J. K. (1997). Genetics and developmental psychopathology: Vol. 2. The main effects of genes and environment on behavioral problems in the Virginia Twin Study of Adolescent Development. *Journal of Child Psychology and Psychiatry, 38,* 965–80.

Egeland, B., Carlson, E., & Sroufe, L. A. (1993). Resilience as process. *Development and Psychopathology, 5,* 517–28.

Elder, G. H. (1974). *Children of the Great Depression.* Chicago: University of Chicago Press.

Elder, G. H., Jr. (1979). Historical change in life patterns and personality. In P. B. Baltes & O. G. Brim (Eds.), *Life span development and behavior* (Vol. 2, pp. 117–59). New York: Academic Press.

Elder, G. H., Jr. (1986). Military times and turning points in men's lives. *Developmental Psychology, 22,* 233–45.

Emery, R. E., & Forehand, R. (1994). Parental divorce and children's well-being: A focus on resilience. In R. J. Haggerty, L. R. Sherrod, N. Garmezy, & M. Rutter (Eds.), *Stress, risk, and resilience in children and adolescents* (pp. 64–99). New York: Cambridge University Press.

Engfer, A., Walper, S., & Rutter, M. (1994). Individual characteristics as a force in development. In M. Rutter & D. F. Hay (Eds.), *Development through life: A handbook for clinicians* (pp. 79–111). Oxford: Blackwell.

Farrington, D. P., Gallagher, B., Morley, L., St. Ledger, R. J., & West, D. J. (1988). Are there any successful men from criminogenic backgrounds? *Psychiatry, 51,* 116–30.

Felsman, J. K., & Vaillant, G. E. (1987) Resilient children as adults: A 40-year study. In E. J. Anthony & B. J. Cohler (Eds.), *The invulnerable child* (pp. 289–314). New York: Guilford Press.

Fergusson, D. M., Horwood, L. J., Caspi, A., Moffitt, T. E., & Silva, P. A. (1996). The (artifactual) remission of reading disability: Psychometric lessons in the study of stability and change in behavioral development. *Developmental Psychology, 32,* 132–40.

Fergusson, D. M., Horwood, L. J., & Lynskey, M. T. (1992). Family change, parental discord, and early offending. *Journal of Child Psychology and Psychiatry, 33,* 1059–75.

Fergusson, D. M., Horwood, L. J., & Lynskey, M. T. (1995). The stability of disruptive childhood behaviors. *Journal of Abnormal Child Psychology, 23,* 379–96.

Fergusson, D. M., & Lynskey, M. T. (1996). Adolescent resiliency to family adversity. *Journal of Child Psychology and Psychiatry, 37,* 281–92.

Fergusson, D. M., Lynskey, M. T., & Horwood, L. J. (1993). The effects of maternal depression on maternal ratings of child behavior. *Journal of Abnormal Child Psychology, 21,* 245–69.

Fonagy, P., Steele, M., Steele, H., Higgitt, A., & Target, M. (1994). The Emanuel Miller memorial lecture 1992. The theory and practice of resilience. *Journal of Child Psychology and Psychiatry, 35,* 231–57.

Furstenberg, F. F., Jr., Brooks-Gunn, J., & Morgan, S. P. (1987). *Adolescent mothers in later life.* New York: Cambridge University Press.

Garmezy, N. (1985). Stress-resistant children: The search for protective factors. In J. E. Stevenson (Ed.), *Recent research in developmental psychopathology* (pp. 213–33). Oxford, England: Pergamon Press.

Ge, X., Conger, R. D., Cadoret, R. J., Neiderhiser, J. M., Yates, W., Troughton, E., & Stewart, M. A. (1996). The developmental interface between nature and nurture: A mutual influence model of child antisocial behavior and parenting. *Developmental Psychology, 32,* 574–89.

Goodman, R., Simonoff, E., & Stevenson, J. (1995). The relationship between child IQ, parent IQ and sibling IQ on child behavioural deviance scores. *Journal of Child Psychology and Psychiatry, 36,* 409–25.

Goodyer, I. (1990). *Life experiences, development and childhood psychopathology.* Chichester, England: Wiley.

Gore, S., & Aseltine, R. J., Jr. (1995). Protective processes in adolescence: Matching stressors with social resources. *American Journal of Community Psychology, 23,* 301–27.

Gore, S., & Eckenrode, J. (1994). Context and process in research on risk and resilience. In R. J. Haggerty, L. R. Sherrod, N. Garmezy, & M. Rutter (Eds.), *Stress, risk, and resilience in children and adolescents* (pp. 19–63). New York: Cambridge University Press.

Haggerty, R. J., Sherrod, L. R., Garmezy, N., & Rutter, M. (Eds.). (1994). *Stress, risk, and resilience in children and adolescents: Processes, mechanisms, and interventions.* New York: Cambridge University Press.

Harris, T., Brown, G. W., & Bifulco, A. (1986). Loss of parent in childhood and adult psychiatric disorder: The role of lack of adequate parental care. *Psychological Medicine, 16,* 641–59.

Hennessey, J. W., & Levine, S. (1979). Stress, arousal and the pituitary-adrenal system: A psychoendocrine hypothesis. In J. M. Sprague & A. N. Epstein (Eds.), *Progress in psychobiology and physiological psychology* (pp. 133–78). New York: Academic Press.

Hetherington, E. M. (1997). Teenaged childbearing and divorce. In S. S. Luthar, J. A. Burack, D. Cicchetti, & J. R. Weisz (Eds.), *Developmental psychopathology: Perspective on adjustment, risk, and disorder* (pp. 350–73). New York: Cambridge University Press.

Hetherington, E. M., & Blechman, E. A. (Eds.). (1996). *Stress, coping, and resiliency in children and families.* Hillsdale, NJ: Erlbaum.

Hinkle, L. E. (1974). The effect of exposure to culture change, social change, and changes in interpersonal relationships on health. In B. S. Dohrenwend & B. P. Dohrenwend (Eds.), *Stressful life events: Their nature and effects* (pp. 9–44). New York: Wiley.

Hultsch, D. F., & Plemons, J. K. (1979). Life events and life span development. In P. B. Baltes & O. G. Brim (Eds.), *Life-span development and behavior* (Vol. 2, pp. 1–36). New York: Academic Press.

Hunt, J. McV. (1979). Psychological development: Early experience. *Annual Review of Psychology, 30,* 103–43.

Jenkins, C. D. (1979). Psychosocial modifiers of response to stress. *Journal of Human Stress, 5,* 3–15.

Jenkins, J. N., & Smith, M. A. (1990). Factors protecting children living in disharmonious homes: Maternal reports. *Journal of the American Academy of Child and Adolescent Psychiatry, 29,* 60–9.

Kendler, K. S. (1996). Major depression and generalised anxiety disorder: Same genes, (partly) different environments – revisited. *British Journal of Psychiatry, 168* (Suppl. 30), 68–75.

Kendler, K. S., Neale, M., Kessler, R., Heath, A., & Eaves, L. (1993). A longitudinal twin study of personality and major depression in women. *Archives of General Psychiatry, 50,* 853–62.

Kendler, K. S., Neale, M. C., Prescott, C. A., Kessler, R. C., Heath, A. C., Corey, L. A., & Eaves, L. J. (1996). Childhood parental loss and alcoholism in women: A causal analysis using a twin-family design. *Psychological Medicine, 26,* 79–95.

Kessler, R. C., Kendler, K. S., Heath, A., Neale, M. C., & Eaves, L. J. (1992). Social support, depressed mood, and adjustment to stress: A genetic epidemiologic investigation. *Journal of Personality and Social Psychology, 62,* 257–72.

Kolvin, I., Miller, F. J. W., Fleeting, M., & Kolvin, P. A. (1988a). Social and parenting factors affecting criminal-offence rates: Findings from the Newcastle Thousand-Family Study (1947–1980). *British Journal of Psychiatry, 152,* 80–90.

Kolvin, I., Miller, F. J. W., Fleeting, M., & Kolvin, P. A. (1988b). Risk/protective factors for offending with particular reference to deprivation. In M. Rutter (Ed.), *Studies of psychosocial risk: The power of longitudinal data* (pp. 77–95). Cambridge, England: Cambridge University Press.

Kuh, D., & Maclean, M. (1990). Women's childhood experience of parental separation and their subsequent health and socioeconomic status in adulthood. *Journal of Biosocial Science, 22,* 121–35.

Laub, J. H., Nagin, D. S., & Sampson, R. J. (1998). Trajectories of change in criminal offending: Good marriages and the desistance process. *American Sociological Review, 63,* 225–38.

Lazarus, R. S., & Folkman, S. (1984). *Stress, appraisal and coping.* New York: Springer.

Lieberman, M. A. (1975). Adaptive processes in late life. In N. Datan & L. H. Ginsberg (Eds.), *Life-span developmental psychology: Normative life crises* (pp. 135–59). New York: Academic Press.

Long, J. V. F., & Vaillant, G. E. (1984). The natural history of male psychological health, IX: Escape from the underclass. *American Journal of Psychiatry, 141,* 341–6.

Lösel, F., & Bliesener, T. (1994). Some high-risk adolescents do not develop conduct problems: A study of protective factors. *International Journal of Behavioral Development, 17,* 753–77.

Luthar, S. S. (1991). Vulnerability and resilience: A study of high-risk adolescents. *Child Development, 62,* 600–16

Luthar, S. S. (1993). Annotation: Methodological and conceptual issues in research on childhood resilience. *Journal of Child Psychology and Psychiatry, 34,* 441–53.

Luthar, S. S., Doernberger, C. H., & Zigler, E. (1993). Resilience is not a unidimensional construct: Insights from a prospective study of inner-city adolescents. *Development and Psychopathology, 5,* 703–17.

Luthar, S. S., & Zigler, E. (1991). Vulnerability and competence: A review of research on resilience in childhood. *American Journal of Orthopsychiatry, 61,* 6–22.

Maccoby, E. E. (1998). *The two sexes: Growing up apart, coming together.* Cambridge, MA: Belknap Press.

Maccoby, E. E., & Jacklin, C. N. (1983). The "person" characteristics of children and the family as environment. In D. Magnusson & V. Allen (Eds.), *Human development: An interactional perspective* (pp. 75–91). New York: Academic Press.

Main, M., Kaplan, N., & Cassidy, J. (1985). Security in infancy, childhood and adulthood. In I. Bretherton &

E. Waters (Eds.), *Growing points of attachment theory and research. Monographs of the Society for Research in Child Development, 50* (1–2, Serial No. 209), 66–106.

Masten, A. S. (1982). *Humor and creative thinking in stress-resistant children.* Unpublished doctoral dissertation, University of Minnesota.

Masten, A. S., Coatsworth, J. D., Neeman, J., Gest, S. D., Tellegen, A., & Garmezy, N. (1995). The structure and coherence of competence from childhood through adolescence. *Child Development, 66,* 1635–59.

Masten, A. S., & Garmezy, N. (1985). Risk, vulnerability and protective factors in developmental psychopathology. In B. B. Lahey & A. E. Kazdin (Eds.), *Advances in clinical child psychology* (Vol. 8, pp. 1–52). New York: Plenum.

Masten, A. S., Garmezy, N., Tellegen, A., Pellegrini, D. S., Larkin, K., & Larsen, A. (1988). Competence and stress in school children: The moderating effects of individual and family qualities. *Journal of Child Psychology and Psychiatry, 29,* 745–64.

Masten, A. S., Morrison, P., Pellegrini, D., & Tellegen, A. (1990). Competence under stress: Risk and protective factors. In J. Rolf, A. S. Masten, D. Cicchetti, K. H. Nuechterlein, & S. Weintraub (Eds.), *Risk and protective factors in the development of psychopathology* (pp. 236–56). New York: Cambridge University Press.

Maughan, B. (1994). School influences. In M. Rutter & D. Hay (Eds.), *Development through life: A handbook for clinicians* (pp. 134–58). Oxford, England: Blackwell Scientific.

Maughan, B., Collishaw, S., & Pickles, A. (1998). School achievements and adult qualifications among adoptees: A longitudinal study. *Journal of Child Psychology and Psychiatry, 39,* 669–85.

Maughan, B., & Rutter, M. (1997). Retrospective reporting of childhood adversity: Some methodological considerations. *Journal of Personality Disorders, 11,* 19–33.

McClelland, G. H., & Judd, C. M. (1993). Statistical difficulties of detecting interactions and moderator effects. *Psychological Bulletin, 114,* 376–90.

McCord, J. (1986). Instigation and insulation: How families affect antisocial aggression. In D. Olweus, J. Block, & M. Radke-Yarrow (Eds.), *Development of antisocial and prosocial behavior: Research, theories, and issues* (pp. 343–57). Orlando, FL: Academic Press.

Meisels, S. J., & Plunkett, J. W. (1988). Developmental consequences of pre-term birth: Are there long-term effects? In P. B. Baltes, D. L. Featherman, & R. M. Lerner (Eds.), *Life-span development and behavior* (Vol. 9, pp. 87–128). Hillsdale, NJ: Erlbaum.

Moffitt, T. E. (1990). Juvenile delinquency and attention deficit disorder: Developmental trajectories from age 3 to 15. *Child Development, 61,* 893–910.

Moffitt, T. E., Caspi, A., Harkness, A. R., & Silva, P. A. (1993). The natural history of change in intellectual performance: Who changes? How much? Is it meaningful? *Journal of Child Psychology and Psychiatry, 34,* 455–506.

Mortimore, P. (1995). The positive effects of schooling. In M. Rutter (Ed.), *Psychosocial disturbances in young people: Challenges for prevention* (pp. 333–63). Cambridge, England: Cambridge University Press.

Murphy, L. B. (1962). *The widening world of childhood: Paths towards mastery.* New York: Basic Books.

Murphy, L. B., & Moriarty, A. E. (1976). *Vulnerability, coping and growing.* New Haven, CT: Yale University Press.

O'Connor, T. G., Deater-Deckard, K., Fulker, D., Rutter, M. & Plomin, R. (1998). Genotype–environment correlations in late childhood and early adolescence: Antisocial behavioral problems and coercive parenting. *Developmental Psychology, 34*(5), 970–81.

Ollendick, T. H., King, N. J., & Yule, W. (1994). *International handbook of phobic and anxiety disorders in children and adolescents.* New York: Plenum.

Osborn, S. G. (1980). Moving home, leaving London and delinquent trends. *British Journal of Criminology, 20,* 54–61.

Patterson, G. R. (1980). Mothers: The unacknowledged victims. *Monographs of the Society for Research in Child Development, 45* (5, Serial No. 186), 1–64.

Patterson, G. R. (1982). *Coercive family process.* Eugene, OR: Castalia.

Patterson, G. R. (1995). Coercion as a basis for early age of onset for arrest. In J. McCord (Ed.), *Coercion and punishment in long-term perspectives* (pp. 81–105). Cambridge, England: Cambridge University Press.

Patterson, G. R. (1996). Some characteristics of a developmental theory for early onset delinquency. In M. Lenzenweger & J. J. Haugaard (Eds.), *Frontier of developmental psychopathology* (pp. 81–124). New York: Oxford University Press.

Patterson, G. R., Dishion, T. J., & Chamberlain, P. (1993). Outcomes and methodological issues relating to treatment of antisocial children. In T. R. Giles (Ed.), *Handbook of effective psychotherapy* (pp. 43–87). New York: Plenum.

Patterson, G. R., Reid, J. B., & Dishion, T. J. (1992). *Antisocial boys: A social interactional approach.* Eugene, OR: Castalia.

Pawlby, S. J., Mills, A., & Quinton, D. (1997a). Vulnerable adolescent girls: Opposite sex relationships. *Journal of Child Psychology and Psychiatry, 38,* 909–20.

Pawlby, S. J., Mills, A., Taylor, A., & Quinton, D. (1997b). Adolescent friendships mediating childhood adversity and adult outcome. *Journal of Adolescence, 20,* 633–44.

Paykel, E. S. (1978). Contribution of life events to causation of psychiatric illness. *Psychological Medicine, 8,* 245–53.

Pellegrini, D. (1994). Training in interpersonal cognitive problem-solving. In M. Rutter, E. Taylor, & L. Hersov (Eds.), *Child and adolescent psychiatry: Modern approaches* (pp. 829–43). Oxford, England: Blackwell Scientific.

Phelps, J. L., Belsky, J., & Crnic, K. (1998). Earned security, daily stress, and parenting: A comparison of five alternative models. *Development and Psychopathology, 10,* 21–38.

Pianta, R. C., Egeland, B., & Sroufe, L. A. (1990). Maternal stress and children's development: Prediction of school outcomes and identification of protective factors. In J. Rolf, A. S. Masten, D. Cicchetti, K. H. Nuechterlein, & S. Weintraub (Eds.), *Risk and protective factors in the development of psychopathology* (pp. 215–35). New York: Cambridge University Press.

Pickles, A. (1993). Stages, precursors and causes in development. In D. F. Hay & A. Angold (Eds.), *Precursors and causes in development and psychopathology* (pp. 23–49). Chichester: John Wiley & Sons.

Pike, A., McGuire, S., Hetherington, E. M., Reiss, D., & Plomin, R. (1996). Family environment and adolescent depressive symptoms and antisocial behavior: A multivariate genetic analysis. *Developmental Psychology, 37,* 590–603.

Plomin, R. (1994a). *Genetics and experience: The interplay between nature and nurture.* Thousand Oaks, CA: Sage Publications.

Plomin, R. (1994b). Genetic research and identification of environmental influences: Emanuel Miller Memorial Lecture (1993). *Journal of Child Psychology and Psychiatry, 35,* 817–34.

Plomin, R., & Bergeman, C. S. (1991). The nature of nurture: Genetic influence on 'environmental' measures. *Behavioural and Brain Sciences, 14,* 373–427.

Plomin, R., De Fries, J. C., McClearn, G. E., & Rutter, M. (1997). *Behavioral genetics* (3rd ed.). San Francisco: Freeman.

Plomin, R., & Rutter, M. (1998). Child development, molecular genetics and what to do with genes once they are found. *Child Development, 69*(4), 1223–42.

Quinton, D., & Rutter, M. (1976). Early hospital admissions and later disturbances of behaviour: An attempted replication of Douglas' findings. *Development Medicine and Child Neurology, 18,* 447–59.

Quinton, D., & Rutter, M. (1988). *Parenting breakdown: The making and breaking of inter-generational links.* Aldershot, England: Avebury.

Quinton, D., Pickles, A., Maughan, B., & Rutter, M. (1993). Partners, peers and pathways: Assortative pairing and continuities in conduct disorder. *Development and Psychopathology, 5,* 763–83.

Reiss, D., Hetherington, M., Plomin, R., Howe, G. W., Simmens, S. J., Henderson, S. H., O'Connor, T. J., Bussell, D. A., Anderson, E. R., & Law, T. (1995). Genetic questions for environmental studies: Differential parenting and psychopathology in adolescence. *Archives of General Psychiatry, 52,* 925–36.

Richters, J. E. (1992). Depressed mothers as informants about their children: A critical review of the evidence for distortion. *Psychological Bulletin, 112,* 485–99.

Robins, L. N. (1966). *Deviant children grown up: A sociological and psychiatric study of sociopathic personality.* Baltimore, MD: Williams & Wilkins.

Rolf, J., Masten, A., Cicchetti, D., Nuechterlein, K., & Weintraub, S. (Eds.). (1990). *Risk and protective factors in the development of psychopathology*. New York: Cambridge University Press.

Rowe, D. C., Wouldbroun, E. J., & Gulley, B. L. (1994). Peers and friends as nonshared environmental influences. In E. M. Hetherington, D. Reiss, & R. Plomin (Eds.), *Separate social worlds of siblings* (pp. 159–73). Hillsdale, NJ: Erlbaum.

Roy, P., Rutter, M., & Pickles, A. (in press). Institutional care: Risk from family background or pattern of rearing. *Journal of Child Psychology and Psychiatry*.

Rutter, M. (1971). Parent–child separation: Psychological effects on the children. *Journal of Child Psychology and Psychiatry, 12*, 233–60.

Rutter, M. (1972). *Maternal deprivation reassessed*. Harmondsworth, Middlesex: Penguin.

Rutter, M. (1979). Protective factors in children's responses to stress and disadvantage. In M. W. Kent & J. E. Rolf (Eds.), *Primary prevention of psychopathology: Vol. 3. Social competence in children* (pp. 49–74). Hanover, NH: University Press of New England.

Rutter, M. (1981). Stress, coping and development: Some issues and some questions. *Journal of Child Psychology and Psychiatry, 22*, 323–56.

Rutter, M. (1983a). Statistical and personal interactions: Facets and perspectives. In D. Magnusson & V. Allen (Eds.), *Human development: An interactional perspective* (pp. 295–319). New York: Academic Press.

Rutter, M. (1983b). School effects on pupil progress: Research findings and policy implications. *Child Development, 54*, 1–29.

Rutter, M. (1985). Resilience in the face of adversity: Protective factors and resistance to psychiatric disorder. *British Journal of Psychiatry, 147*, 598–611.

Rutter, M. (1989). Psychiatric disorder in parents as a risk factor for children. In D. Shaffer, I. Philips, & N. B. Enzer (Eds.), with M. M. Silverman & V. Anthony (Assoc. Eds.), *Prevention of mental disorders, alcohol and other drug use in children and adolescents* (pp. 157–89). OSAP Prevention Monograph 2. Rockville, Maryland: Office for Substance Abuse Prevention, US Department of Health & Social Services.

Rutter, M. (1990). Psychosocial resilience and protective mechanisms. In J. Rolf, A. Masten, D. Cicchetti, K. Nuechterlein, & S. Weintraub (Eds.), *Risk and protective factors in the development of psychopathology* (pp. 181–214). New York: Cambridge University Press.

Rutter, M. (1994). Stress research: Accomplishments and tasks ahead. In R. J. Haggerty, L. R. Sherrod, N. Garmezy, & M. Rutter (Eds.), *Stress, risk, and resilience in children and adolescents* (pp. 354–85). New York: Cambridge University Press.

Rutter, M. (1995a). Clinical implications of attachment concepts: Retrospect and prospect. *Journal of Child Psychology and Psychiatry, 36*, 549–71.

Rutter, M. (1995b). Maternal deprivation. In M. H. Bornstein (Ed.), *Handbook of parenting: Vol. 4. Applied and practical parenting. Part I: Applied issues in parenting* (pp. 3–31). Hillsdale, NJ: Erlbaum.

Rutter, M. (1995c). Psychosocial adversity: Risk, resilience and recovery. *Southern African Journal of Child and Adolescent Psychiatry, 7*, 75–88.

Rutter, M. (1996). Transitions and turning points in developmental psychopathology: As applied to the age span between childhood and mid-adulthood. *International Journal of Behavioral Development, 19*, 603–26.

Rutter, M. (1999). Reslience concepts and findings: Implications for family therapy. *Journal of Family Therapy, 21*, 119–44.

Rutter, M., Champion, L., Quinton, D., Maughan, B., & Pickles, A. (1995). Understanding individual differences in environmental risk exposure. In P. Moen, G. H. Elder Jr., & K. Luscher (Eds.), *Examining lives in context: Perspectives on the ecology of human development* (pp. 61–93). Washington, DC: American Psychological Association.

Rutter, M., Dunn, J., Plomin, P., Simonoff, E., Pickles, A., Maughan, B., Ormel, J., Meyer, J., & Eaves, L. (1997a). Integrating nature and nurture: Implications of person-environment correlations and interactions for developmental psychopathology. *Development and Psychopathology, 9*, 335–64.

Rutter, M., Giller, H., & Hagell, A. (1999). *Antisocial behavior by young people*. New York: Cambridge University Press.

Rutter, M., Maughan, B., Meyer, J., Pickles, A., Silberg, J., Simonoff, E., & Taylor, E. (1997b). Heterogeneity of antisocial behavior: Causes, continuities, and consequences. In R. Dienstbier (Series Ed.) & D. W. Osgood (Vol. Ed.), *Nebraska symposium on motivation: Vol. 44. Motivation and delinquency* (pp. 45–118). Lincoln: University of Nebraska Press.

Rutter, M., Maughan, B., Mortimore, P., Ouston, J., with Smith, A. (1979). *Fifteen thousand hours: Secondary schools and their effects on children*. London: Open Books; Cambridge, MA: Harvard University Press.

Rutter, M., & O'Connor, T. (1999). Implications of attachment theory for child care policies. In P. Shaver & J. Cassidy (Eds.), *Handbook of attachment* (pp. 823–44). New York: Guilford Press.

Rutter, M., & Pickles, A. (1991). Person–environment interactions: Concepts, mechanisms, and implications for data analysis. In T. D. Wachs & R. Plomin (Eds.), *Conceptualization and measurement of organism-environment interaction* (pp. 105–41). Washington, DC: American Psychological Association.

Rutter, M., & Quinton, D. (1977). Psychiatric disorder – ecological factors and concepts of causation. In H. McGurk (Ed.), *Ecological factors in human development* (pp. 173–87). Amsterdam: North-Holland.

Rutter, M., & Quinton, D. (1984). Parental psychiatric

disorder: Effects on children. *Psychological Medicine, 14*, 853–80.

Rutter, M., Quinton, D., & Hill, J. (1990). Adult outcomes of institution-reared children: Males and females compared. In L. N. Robins & M. Rutter (Eds.), *Straight and devious pathways from childhood to adulthood* (pp. 135–57). Cambridge, UK: Cambridge University Press.

Rutter, M., & Sandberg, S. (1992). Psychosocial stressors: Concepts, causes and effects. *European Child & Adolescent Psychiatry, 1*, 3–13.

Rutter, M., Tizard, J., & Whitmore, K. (1970). *Education, health and behaviour*. London: Longmans.

Rutter, M., Silberg, J., O'Connor, T., & Simonoff, E. (1999). Genetics and child psychiatry. Vol. I: Advances in quantitative and molecular genetics. Vol. II: Empirical research findings. *Journal of Child Psychology and Psychiatry, 40*, 3–55.

Ryff, C. C., & Singer, G. (1998). The contours of positive human health. *Psychological Inquiry, 9*, 1–28.

Sameroff, A. J., Seifer, R., & Bartko, W. T. (1997). Environmental perspectives on adaptation during childhood and adolescence. In S. S. Luthar, J. A. Burack, D. Cicchetti, & J. R. Weisz (Eds.), *Developmental psychopathology: Perspective on adjustment, risk, and disorder* (pp. 507–26). New York: Cambridge University Press.

Sampson, R. J., & Laub, J. H. (1993). *Crime in the making: Pathways and turning points through life*. Cambridge, MA: Harvard University Press.

Sampson, R. J., & Laub, J. H. (1994). Urban poverty and the family context of delinquency: A new look at structure and process in a classic study. *Child Development, 65*, 523–40.

Sampson, R. J., & Laub, J. H. (1996). Socioeconomic achievement in the life course of disadvantaged men: Military service as a turning point, circa 1940–1965. *American Sociological Review, 61*, 347–67.

Sandberg, S., Rutter, M., Giles, S., Owen, A., Champion, L., Nicholls, J., Prior, V., McGuinness, D., & Drinnan, D. (1993). Assessment of psychosocial experiences in childhood: Methodological issues and some illustrative findings. *Journal of Child Psychology and Psychiatry, 34*, 879–97.

Schachar, R. J., Taylor, E., Wieselberg, M., Thorley, G., & Rutter, M. (1987). Changes in family function and relationships in children who respond to methylphenidate. *Journal of the American Academy of Child and Adolescent Psychiatry, 26*, 728–32.

Seifer, R. (1995). Perils and pitfalls of high-risk research. *Developmental Psychology, 31*, 420–4.

Seifer, R., Sameroff, A. J., Baldwin, C. P., & Baldwin, A. (1992). Child and family factors that ameliorate risk between 4 and 13 years of age. *Journal of the American Academy of Child and Adolescent Psychiatry, 31*, 893–903.

Shonkoff, J. P., & Meisels, S. J. (1991). Defining eligibility for services under Public Law 99-457. *Journal of Early Intervention, 15*, 21–5.

Small, S. A. (1995). Enhancing contexts of adolescent development: The role of community-based action research. In L. J. Crockett & A. C. Crouter (Eds.), *Pathways through adolescence: Individual development in relation to social contexts* (pp. 211–34). Hillsdale, NJ: Erlbaum.

Stacey, M., Drearden, R., Pill, R., & Robinson, D. (1970). *Hospitals, children and their families: The report of a pilot study*. London: Routledge & Kegan Paul.

Stattin, H., Romelsjö, A., & Stenbacka, M. (1997). Personal resources as modifiers of the risk for future criminality: An analysis of protective factors in relation to 18-year-old boys. *British Journal of Criminology, 37*, 198–223.

Stipek, D. (1997). Success in school – for a head start in life. In S. S. Luthar, J. A. Burack, D. Cicchetti, & J. R. Weisz (Eds.), *Developmental psychopathology: Perspective on adjustment, risk, and disorder* (pp. 75–92). Cambridge, England: Cambridge University Press.

Stouthamer-Loeber, M., Loeber, R., Farrington, D. P., Zhang, Q., van Kammen, W., & Maguin, E. (1993). The double edge of protective and risk factors for delinquency: Interrelations and developmental patterns. *Development and Psychopathology, 5*, 683–701.

Sullivan, P. F., Wells, J. E., & Bushnell, J. A. (1995). Adoption as a risk factor for mental disorders. *Acta Psychiatria Scandinavica, 92*, 119–24.

Tennant, C., Bebbington, P., & Hurry, J. (1981). The short-term outcome of neurotic disorders in the community: The relation of remission to clinical factors to "neutralizing" life events. *British Journal of Psychiatry, 139*, 213–20.

Thoits, P. (1983). Dimensions of life events that influence psychological distress: An evaluation and synthesis of the literature. In H. B. Kaplan (Ed.), *Psychosocial stress: Trends in theory and research* (pp. 33–103). New York: Academic Press.

Topolski, T. D., Hewitt, J. K., Eaves, L. J., Silberg, J. L., Meyer, J. M., Rutter, M., Pickles, A., & Simonoff, E. (in press). Genetic and environmental influences on child reports of manifest anxiety, and symptoms of separation anxiety and overanxious disorders: A community-based twin study. *Journal of Anxiety Disorders*.

Tschann, J. M., Kaiser, P., Chesney, M. A., Alkon, A., & Boyce, W. T. (1996). Resilience and vulnerability among preschool children: Family functioning, temperament, and behavior problems. *Journal of the American Academy of Child and Adolescent Psychiatry, 35*, 184–92.

Ursin, H., Baade, E., & Levine, S. (1978). *Psychobiology of stress: A study of coping men*. New York: Academic Press.

Vaillant, G. E. (1977). *Adaptation to life*. Boston: Little, Brown.

Vaillant, G. E. (1990). Avoiding negative life outcomes: Evidence from a forty-five-year study. In P. B. Baltes & M. M. Baltes (Eds.), *Successful aging: Perspectives from the behavioral sciences* (pp. 332–58). Cambridge, England: Cambridge University Press.

van Ijzendoorn, M. H. (1995). Adult attachment representations, parental responsiveness, and infant attachment: A meta-analysis on the predictive validity of the adult attachment interview. *Psychological Bulletin, 117,* 387–403.

Vorria, P., Rutter, M., Pickles, A., Wolkind, S., & Hobsbaum, A. (1998a). A comparative study of Greek children in long-term residential group care and in two-parent families: I. Social, emotional, and behavioral differences. *Journal of Child Psychology and Psychiatry, 39,* 225–36.

Vorria, P., Rutter, M., Pickles, A., Wolkind, S., & Hobsbaum, A. (1998b). A comparative study of Greek children in long-term residential group care and in two-parent families: II. Possible mediating mechanisms. *Journal of Child Psychology and Psychiatry, 39,* 237–46.

Wang, M. C., & Gordon, E. W. (1994). *Educational resilience in inner-city America: Challenges and prospects.* Hillsdale, NJ: Erlbaum.

Watt, N. F., David, J. P., Ladd, K. L., & Shamos, S. (1995). The life course of psychosocial resilience: A phenomenological perspective on deflecting life's slings and arrows. *Journal of Primary Prevention, 15,* 209–46.

Webster-Stratton, C. (1991). Annotation: Strategies for helping families with conduct disordered children. *Journal of Child Psychology and Psychiatry, 32,* 1047–62.

Werner, E. E., Bierman, J. M., & French, F. E. (1971). *The children of Kauai.* Honolulu: University of Hawaii Press.

Werner, E. E., & Smith, R. S. (1977). *Kauai's children come of age.* Honolulu: University of Hawaii Press.

Werner, E. E., & Smith, R. S. (1982). *Vulnerable but invincible: A longitudinal study of resilient children and youth.* New York: McGraw-Hill.

Werner, E. E., & Smith, R. S. (1992). *Overcoming the odds: High risk children from birth to adulthood.* Ithaca, NY: Cornell University Press.

Zoccolillo, M., Pickles, A., Quinton, D., & Rutter, M. (1992). The outcome of childhood conduct disorder: Implications for defining adult personality disorder and conduct disorder. *Psychological Medicine, 22,* 971–86.

Name Index

Aase, J. M., 45, 53
Abbott-Shim, M., 346, 349, 359
Abel, E. L., 45, 50
Abel, V., 43, 51
Aber, J. L., 309, 322, 323, 342, 357, 419, 420, 421, 434, 435, 436, 550, 567, 569, 571, 572, 575, 663, 676
Abernathy, S. R., 15, 30, 265, 266, 289
Able-Boone, H., 281, 282, 400, 410, 641, 647
Ableman, D., 455, 465, 483
Ablon, S., 657, 675
Aboagye, K., 46, 53
Achenbach, T. M., 64, 70, 150, 151, 156, 158, 169, 176, 234, 237, 248, 253, 256, 280, 287, 552, 571, 576
Ackland, R., 472, 478
Adams, G., 342, 343, 350, 356, 359
Adelman, A., 70, 73
Adelson, E., 56, 72, 147, 152, 157, 168, 177, 367, 385
Adelstein, D., 65, 66, 72
Adler, Z., 667, 676
Adrian, C., 563, 574
Agee, J. L., 346, 356
Ager, J. W., 61, 72
Aggleton, J. P., 212, 222
Agosta, J. M., 642, 647
Ainsworth, M. D. S., 12, 26, 259, 260, 261, 282, 283, 564, 571, 651, 669, 675
Akerley, M. S., 635, 636, 647
Aksan, N., 165, 177
Alarcon, O., 97, 114
Albee, G. W., 14, 26, 80, 91, 440, 452
Albert, M. L., 488, 507
Albin, R. W., 185, 202
Alcantara, A., 510, 544
Alford, C., 43, 51, 53
Alinsky, S. B., 641, 647

Alkon, A., 670, 681
Alkon-Leonard, A., 121, 131
Allen, D., 331, 336
Allen, K., 459, 478, 526, 542
Allen, M. C., 532, 546
Allen, N., 528, 544
Allen, R. I., 639, 641, 646, 647
Allred, K. W., 302, 306
Alper, T. T., 45, 51
Alpert, C., 537, 548
Als, H., 150, 156, 462, 478
Altemeier, W., 327, 329, 336, 337
Altman, J., 37, 50
Altshuler, J., 175, 178
Alvarez, C., 211, 212, 223
Alvord, E. C., 36, 43
Amaro, H., 46, 53
Amato, P. R., 59, 72
Amaya-Jackson, L., 322, 324
Anastasiow, N. J., 3, 26
Anders, T. T., 277, 289
Anderson, B., 510, 544
Anderson, C., 353, 358
Anderson, E. R., 116, 120, 124, 126, 131, 362, 384, 666, 672, 679
Anderson, J., 530, 543
Andersson, B.-E., 623, 626
Andrew, L., 277, 288
Andrews, R., 262, 285
Andrews, S. R., 368, 384, 555, 556, 571, 583
Andrews, T. J., 241, 253,
Angell, A. L., 563, 577
Angell, R., 399, 400, 401, 413
Anglin, T. M., 312, 324
Anolli, L., 624, 626
Anrolick, L. L., 216, 225
Anthony, E. J., 116, 122, 125, 127, 130, 651, 652, 675
Anthony, L., 187, 201

Antonovsky, A., 125, 130
Apfel, N. H., 375, 386, 555, 556, 576, 584, 592, 595, 602, 609
Appelbaum, M. I., 63, 64, 71, 266, 284
Archer, P., 329, 336
Arcia, E., 500, 504
Ard, W. R., 183, 201
Arend, R., 248, 255, 420, 436
Aries, P., 4, 8, 26
Arlman-Rupp, A., 259, 288
Armour-Thomas, E., 490, 506
Arndorfer, R. E., 185, 199
Arnett, J., 349, 356
Arnold, D. S., 563, 577
Arthur, C. A., 244, 245, 255
Arunkumar, R., 115, 132
Asarnow, J. R., 417, 430, 435
Aschbacher, P. R., 250, 255
Aseltine, R. J., Jr., 665, 667, 677
Asendorpf, J. B., 667, 675
Ash, J. R., 553, 554, 571, 579
Ashe, M. L., 265, 266, 289
Ashford, L. G., 247, 255, 328, 336
Ashworth, C. D., 263, 288
Astley, S. J., 45, 50
Astone, N. M., 95, 111, 135, 158
Atherton, C. R., 80, 91
Atkins-Burnett, S., 20, 502
Atwood, G. E., 65, 75
Ault, M. J., 183, 185, 186, 187, 203
Austin, M. J., 440, 441, 452
Avery, B., 98, 106, 112
Ayers, W., 476, 478
Azer, S. L., 345, 348, 349, 350, 351, 356, 358
Azrin, N. H., 184, 201

Baade, E., 657, 681
Bachevalier, J., 211, 212, 222, 223, 225, 226

Bachmann, J., 170, 176
Baer, D. M., 181, 184, 199, 200, 488, 504, 534, 535, 542
Bagnato, S. J., 149, 156, 239, 242, 244, 248, 250, 252, 253, 254, 256, 329, 336, 390, 410
Bailey, D. B., 180, 182, 184, 186, 188, 198, 199, 200, 201, 203, 234, 244, 246, 253, 291, 294, 295, 296, 297, 299, 301, 302, 303, 304, 305, 308, 387, 389, 397, 398, 410, 454, 455, 457, 463, 467, 470, 478, 481, 482, 503, 505, 530, 532, 542, 543, 576, 631, 638, 639, 640, 641, 644, 647, 650
Bailey, E., 280, 283
Bailey, J. B., 390, 414
Bain, J., 247, 253
Baird, M., 417, 435
Bakeman, R., 258, 282
Baker, A., 347, 359, 560, 561, 571, 588
Baker, E. L., 39, 52, 252, 255
Baker, L. S., 550, 575
Baker, W. L., 418, 437
Balaban, N., 463, 479
Baldwin, A. L., 11, 30, 68, 70, 116, 117, 122, 123, 132, 140, 159, 665, 666, 675, 681
Baldwin, C. P., 11, 30, 116, 117, 122, 123, 132, 140, 159, 665, 666, 675, 681
Baldwin, D., 68, 70
Baldwin, L., 525, 543
Baldwin, W., 266, 282
Balla, D. A., 235, 257
Baltes, P. B., 489, 502, 504, 506
Balzano, S., 489, 507
Balzer-Martin, L., 42, 52
Bamforth, A., 61, 71
Bandura, A., 652, 671
Bangdiwala, S. I., 322, 324
Bank, L., 668, 675
Banks, J. A., 96, 111
Baratz, J., 363, 384
Baratz, S., 363, 384
Barbarin, O. A., 101, 111
Barber, P. A., 397, 410, 456, 479
Barclay-McLaughlin, G., 87, 91
Barker, R., 309, 311, 323
Barnard, K. E., 20, 67, 69, 74, 151, 153, 156, 159, 234, 237, 253, 418, 422, 423, 434, 502, 552, 553, 554, 556, 563, 564, 566, 567, 570, 571, 572, 574, 580, 581, 597, 603, 608
Barnes, C. L., 215, 225
Barnes, H. V., xi, xii, 69, 75, 343, 349, 359, 361, 375, 384, 442, 452, 456, 482, 517, 546, 556, 576, 591, 592, 597, 598, 609, 617, 618, 627

Barnes, J., 318, 323
Barnes, S., 260, 266, 282
Barnes, W., 525, 547
Barnett, D. W., 240, 241, 243, 252, 253, 255, 256
Barnett, W. S., xii, 3, 6, 19, 26, 343, 356, 420, 434, 503, 504, 550, 556, 571, 576, 621, 626
Barnwell, D. A., 299, 305
Barocas, R., 85, 93, 137, 138, 159, 191, 202, 237, 238, 257, 266, 287
Baron, R. M., 564, 571
Barr, R. G., 116, 121, 130
Barrera, I., 236, 253, 471, 479
Barrera, M. E., 552, 553, 554, 571, 579
Barreto-Cortez, E., 508
Barrett, B., 552, 569, 575
Barrett, K., 520, 542
Barringer, K., 242, 243, 255
Barron-Sharp, B., 303, 307
Barsh, E. T., 297, 306
Barth, R. P., 553, 554, 571, 579
Bartholomew, P. C., 186, 200
Bartko, W. T., 140, 159, 657, 681
Basham, R. B., 150, 157, 234, 237, 254, 294, 306
Bashir, A., 40, 51
Bates, J. E., 109, 111, 259, 261, 287
Batista, L., 387, 412
Batts, V., 106, 113
Bauchner, H., 46, 53, 66, 75
Baudelot, O., 623, 626
Bauer, C. R., 150, 157, 372, 384, 385, 520, 521, 522, 543, 545, 555, 556, 565, 572, 583, 604, 609
Bauer, P., 213, 223
Bauman, K. E., 185, 201
Baumeister, A. A., 180, 202, 511, 542
Bayer, S. A., 37, 50
Bayles, K., 259, 261, 287
Bayley, N., 231, 251, 254
Bazron, B. J., 425, 436
Beardslee, W. R., 47, 50
Beare, P. L., 420, 434
Bebbington, P., 668, 681
Becker, H. S., 495, 504
Beckett, J. A., 397, 415
Beckman, P. J., 247, 254, 296, 298, 299, 305, 390, 410, 460, 479
Beckwith, L., 55, 70, 237, 254, 258, 259, 260, 261, 263, 266, 282, 284
Beddie, A., 633, 647
Bedi, G., 220, 226
Bedi, K. S., 47, 50
Bee, H. L., 258, 259, 260, 261, 262, 266, 277, 282, 283
Beebe, B., 259, 264, 283, 288
Beeghley, M., 61, 70, 488, 505
Beggs, M., 422, 423, 436

Behl, D., 532, 542
Behr, S. K., 294, 308, 397, 410, 456, 479
Behrman, R. E., 150, 159, 343, 357, 550, 552, 571, 573, 613, 618, 626, 618, 627
Beidel, D. C., 312, 323
Belgredan, J. H., 248, 254
Bell, R. Q., 11, 26, 259, 283, 303, 307
Bell, S. M., 259, 283
Belle, D., 418, 434, 665, 675
Beller, K., 363, 384
Belsky, J., 54, 55, 70, 78, 87, 91, 258, 261, 283, 564, 571, 671, 679
Belt, P., 555, 575, 583
Benasich, A. A., 550, 551, 556, 569, 570, 571, 572
Benedek, T., 161, 177
Benjamin, M. P., 425, 436
Bennett, F. C., 21, 28, 372, 384, 385, 520, 521, 522, 543, 545, 555, 556, 565, 572, 583, 604, 608, 609
Bennett, L. A., 146, 156
Bennett, S. L., 264, 288
Bennett, T., 456, 460, 461, 479
Bennis, W., 404, 408, 410
Benowitz, S., 242, 243, 255
Benson, H. A., 457, 460, 482
Benveniste, S., 46, 51
Berg, W., 185, 203
Bergeman, C. S., 654, 679
Berger, B., 211, 212, 223
Berger, J., 264, 266, 283
Berger, R., 641, 650
Bergholz, T., 216, 223
Bergman, A., 163, 165, 177
Berk, L., 349, 356
Berkeley, J., 458, 479
Berlin, L. J., 22, 502, 597
Berman, C., 267, 269, 283, 298, 305
Bernard, R. H., 495, 504
Bernbaum, J. C., 372, 384, 385, 520, 521, 522, 543, 545, 555, 556, 565, 572, 583, 604, 609
Berney, C., 170, 176
Bernheimer, L. P., 97, 114, 299, 306, 489, 490, 507, 508
Bernstein, A., 161, 177
Bernstein, B., 328, 334, 336, 337
Bernstein, L. S., 371, 372, 386, 557, 558, 569, 570, 576
Bernstein, V. J., 59, 60, 75, 237, 254, 258, 270, 283, 424, 435
Berrueta-Clement, J. R., 598, 607, 621, 626
Berry, P., 262, 285
Bertacchi, J., 475, 479
Bertram, T., 348, 359

Bertrand, D., 620, 628
Besson, G., 170, 176
Best, K. M., 67, 68, 73, 115, 131
Betancourt, H., 97, 98, 111
Bettelheim, B., 635, 647
Bezrucko, N., 522, 523, 546
Bhavnagri, N. P., 144, 158
Bhide, P. G., 47, 50
Biafora, F. A., 107, 111
Bibring, G. L., 633, 647
Biederman, J., 657, 675
Bien, E., 12, 27
Bierman, J. M., 11, 12, 30, 659, 682
Bifulco, A., 653, 667, 676, 677
Bijou, S. W., 181, 190, 197, 200, 488, 504
Bilker, S. A., 532, 546
Billing, M., 641, 650
Bingol, N., 45, 51
Binns, H. J., 248, 255, 420, 436
Birbaumer, N., 219, 223
Birch, H., 259, 284
Bird, H. R., 655, 675
Birdthistle, I., 312, 321, 323
Biringen, Z., 163, 167, 176, 232, 254
Blacher, J., 293, 306
Black, B., 258, 283
Black, G., 556, 572
Black, J. E., 217, 218, 223, 224
Black, K., 3, 31
Blackard, M. K., 297, 306
Blackwell, P., 277, 283
Blair, C., 522, 542, 605, 607
Blake, J., 266, 283
Blakeslee, S., 116, 122, 124, 126, 132
Blakley, T. L., 418, 437
Blanchard, K. H., 404, 412
Blasco, P. M., 297, 302, 304, 305
Blechman, E. A., 669, 677
Blehar, M. C., 12, 26, 261, 282, 283, 564, 571
Bliesener, T., 663, 678
Block, J., 122, 125, 130
Bloom, B. S., 14, 26, 101, 111
Bloom, F. E., 35, 52, 219, 225, 226, 227
Bloszinsky, S., 530, 543
Blue-Banning, M. J., 294, 308, 646, 650
Blum, R. W., 100, 113
Blumenthal, J. B., 368, 384, 555, 556, 571, 583
Bo, I., 348, 357
Boardman, A. P., 667, 668, 676
Bohman, M., 668, 675
Boliek, C. A., 245, 254
Boll, T., 43, 51
Bologna, T., 398, 410, 455, 473, 479
Bond, J. T., 347, 357, 441, 453

Bond, M., 642, 645, 647
Boocock, S. S., 603, 604, 607, 623, 624, 626
Boone, H. A., 641, 647
Booth, C. L., 258, 259, 260, 261, 262, 267, 277, 282, 283, 285, 286, 552, 554, 563, 564, 566, 570, 571, 572, 581
Bornstein, M. H., 61, 73, 258, 287, 288, 563, 564, 572
Boroto, D. R., 441, 453
Bos, H., 372, 386
Boswell, C., 596, 609
Botein, S., 418, 437, 553, 563, 570, 575, 580
Both, D., 351, 358
Bouchard, C., 88, 91
Boudykis, Z., 94, 113
Boulding, K., 161, 176
Bourgeois, J.-P., 209, 212, 217, 223, 225
Bourne, E., 161, 178
Bowe, F. G., 21, 26
Bowen, M., 144, 156
Bowlby, J., 12, 26, 27, 55, 65, 70, 163, 168, 176, 633, 647, 651, 675
Bowman, B. T., 460, 476, 479, 482
Boyce, G. C., 264, 267, 275, 279, 280, 283, 286, 288, 489, 504, 533, 542, 604, 607, 610
Boyce, W. T., 116, 121, 130, 131, 670, 681
Boyd, K., 502, 508
Boyd, R. D., 245, 246, 254, 257
Boyd, R. N., 491, 505
Boyer, E. L., 332, 336, 418, 435
Boyer, K. M., 44, 52, 53
Boykin, A. W., 95, 107, 111
Boyle, M. H., 655, 675
Brachfeld, S., 263, 285
Bracken, B. A., 240, 243, 244, 254
Bradley, R. H., 259, 283, 520, 542, 552, 554, 556, 563, 564, 572
Bradley, V. J., 642, 647
Bradshaw, J., 616, 617, 618, 627
Brady, A., 397, 400, 401, 412
Brady, M. P., 185, 200
Brammel, J., 640, 646, 650
Brandchaft, B., 65, 75
Brandt, L. J., 60, 74
Brannon, D., 560, 575, 587
Branston, M. B., 189, 200
Brantlinger, E., 511, 542
Brassard, J., 58, 71
Braun, S. J., 5, 27
Braungart, J. M., 162, 178
Brayfield, A., 340, 341, 347, 350, 358
Brazelton, T. B., 25, 65, 71, 170, 176, 258, 259, 261, 262, 283, 330, 336

Bredekamp, S., 5, 27, 342, 346, 352, 357, 358, 429, 435, 454, 458, 459, 479, 488, 505
Brem, F. S., 266, 286
Bremner, J. D., 216, 223
Brennan, J., 151, 158
Brent, D., 247, 254
Breslau, N., 655, 676
Bresnick, B., 329, 336
Bretherton, I., 12, 27, 109, 111, 175, 176
Brett, V., 541, 542
Brewer, G., 396, 410
Bricker, D., 4, 27, 235, 247, 254, 257, 262, 280, 283, 291, 297, 298, 307, 389, 390, 410, 442, 452, 454, 455, 457, 460, 463, 464, 467, 470, 474, 475, 477, 479, 482, 535, 543
Bricker, D. D., 149, 156
Bridges, L. J., 258, 283
Brillon, L., 99, 112
Brinker, R. P., 501, 505, 536, 543, 641, 647
Bristol, M. M., 299, 305, 597, 607
Britt, W., 43, 51
Brittenham, G., 47, 52
Britton, H., 64, 72, 277, 283
Brizius, J. A., 560, 570, 572, 586
Broberg, A., 623, 624, 626, 627
Brock, D. J. H., 39, 50
Brody, G. H., 653, 675
Broman, S. H., 12, 27, 78, 93, 137, 156
Bromwich, R. M., 265, 267, 283, 284, 294, 306, 377, 384, 464, 479
Bronen, R. A., 216, 223
Bronfenbrenner, U., 11, 27, 54, 55, 58, 60, 70, 71, 77, 78, 79, 81, 82, 83, 85, 91, 92, 94, 100, 101, 111, 135, 138, 156, 191, 192, 194, 196, 200, 258, 284, 290, 292, 294, 306, 309, 311, 323, 346, 357, 366, 368, 384, 401, 402, 410, 489, 502, 505, 550, 551, 552, 562, 572, 589, 607, 641, 643, 647
Bronson, M. B., 346, 357
Brookfield, J., 460, 483
Brookins, G. K., 97, 111
Brooks, C. S., 61, 71
Brooks-Gunn, J., 12, 22, 29, 63, 64, 65, 71, 72, 116, 117, 122, 123, 124, 127, 131, 150, 153, 154, 156, 157, 159, 241, 254, 261, 263, 265, 266, 284, 285, 286, 309, 311, 322, 323, 372, 384, 385, 420, 421, 435, 436, 437, 448, 452, 502, 518, 519, 520, 521, 522, 541, 543, 545, 597, 604, 609, 613, 614, 615, 624, 627, 665, 677
Brosterman, N., 4, 27

Brosvic, G., 530, 543

Brotherson, M. J., 149, 159, 295, 307, 460, 481, 631, 639, 649

Brown, C., 44, 52, 633, 648

Brown, F., 116, 117, 122, 123, 124, 126, 132

Brown, G. W., 651, 653, 662, 667, 676, 677

Brown, J. V., 258, 282

Brown, L., 189, 200

Brown, M., 559, 576, 587

Brown, P., 390, 415

Brown, S., 442, 452

Brown, W. T., 210, 224, 528, 543

Browne, D. H., 322, 324

Browning, K., 247, 256, 328, 337

Broyles, S., 372, 385, 520, 521, 522, 545, 604, 609

Bruder, M. B., 280, 283, 397, 398, 410, 455, 469, 473, 474, 477, 479, 480, 528, 543

Brumley, H. E., 563, 573

Bruner, J. S., 94, 111, 145, 157, 164, 175, 176

Brunk, M. A., 656, 676

Brunt, C. H., 430, 435

Brust, J. C. M., 46, 50

Bryant, D. M., 59, 71, 179, 190, 200, 343, 357, 409, 410, 421, 423, 429, 435, 511, 514, 515, 518, 519, 520, 522, 543, 544, 546, 548, 555, 556, 563, 564, 565, 566, 570, 572, 576, 577, 584

Bryk, A. S., 502, 503, 505, 507

Buch, G., 190, 201

Buchan, K., 186, 200

Buchbinder, S. B., 554, 573

Buck, D., 398, 411

Bucy, J. E., 296, 297, 307

Buie, J. D., 184, 202

Buka, S. L., 21, 22, 28, 239, 240, 255, 399, 403, 405, 407, 412, 413, 497, 502, 506, 528, 545

Burack, J. A., 419, 427, 437, 488, 506

Burchinal, M. R., 59, 71, 180, 201, 343, 357, 503, 505, 511, 518, 530, 543, 544, 564, 565, 572, 584

Burchinal, P., 409, 410

Burge, D., 563, 574

Burgess, P., 211, 226

Buriel, R., 95, 112

Burkett, C. W., 604, 608

Burnette, E., 116, 131

Burns, A., 60, 72

Burns, B. J., 247, 254

Burrell, B., 302, 307

Bush, E. G., 146, 157

Bushnell, J. A., 659, 681

Bussell, D. A., 666, 672, 679

Butler, J. A., 16, 21, 27, 30

Butler, M., 39, 51

Buttenwieser, E., 87, 92

Butterfield, P. M., 167, 176

Button, S. B., 494, 507

Buysse, V., 291, 305, 464, 469, 470, 471, 472, 479, 483, 631, 640, 641, 647

Byma, G., 220, 226

Byng-Hall, J., 145, 157, 169, 176

Byrne, K. E., 247, 255, 328, 336

Cabral, H., 46, 53, 66, 75

Cadoret, R. J., 656, 668, 669, 676, 677

Caffarella, R. S., 471, 479

Cahan, E. D., 344, 357

Cahan, S., 241, 254

Cahill, D., 270, 286

Cain, V., 266, 282

Cairns, R. B., 11, 27

Calderon, A., 103, 107, 114

Caldwell, B. M., 3, 10, 13, 27, 28, 259, 260, 283, 288, 444, 452, 520, 542, 552, 554, 556, 563, 564, 572

Caldwell, N. K., 187, 203

Calfee, R., 250, 254

Calhoun, M. L., 530, 546

Call, J., 366, 384

Calloway, D., 47, 52

Calore, D., 593, 608

Cameron, A. M., 216, 225

Camilli, G., 601, 607

Campbell, D. T., 27, 498, 505

Campbell, F. A., 259, 260, 265, 266, 287, 289, 513, 514, 515, 543, 544, 546, 564, 565, 570, 572, 584, 591, 603, 604, 608, 613, 627

Campbell, M., 457, 460, 482

Campbell, P. H., 298, 306, 398, 412, 474, 481

Campbell, R., 387, 410

Campbell, S. B., 418, 419, 420, 435

Campos, J., 56, 75, 162, 176, 178

Cao, Y., 218, 223

Caplan, G., 86, 91

Caplan, N., 94, 111

Capone, A., 461, 463, 479

Capraro, K. L., 351, 356

Capute, A. J., 532, 546

Caracelli, V. J., 494, 495, 505, 506

Carcagno, G. J., 571, 572

Cardon, L. R., 237, 254

Cardone, I., 464, 479

Carey, K. T., 241, 243, 253

Carison, L., 116, 117, 123, 131

Carlson, E., 652, 666, 676

Carlson, L., 262, 283

Carnahan, S., 103, 107, 114, 296, 297, 307

Carney, M. F., 592, 593, 594, 508

Caro, P., 532, 543

Carpenter, I., 39, 53

Carpenter, L., 530, 543

Carr, E. G., 183, 185, 200

Carrell, T. D., 220, 222, 224

Carruth, B. R., 153, 157

Carta, J. J., 191, 202, 489, 506, 527, 546

Carter, B., 144, 158

Carter, C., 40, 51

Carter, E. A., 456, 479

Carter, L., 265, 286

Carter, S., 65, 66, 71

Casaer, P., 653, 676

Casey, P. H., 330, 336, 372, 384, 385, 520, 521, 522, 542, 543, 545, 555, 556, 564, 565, 572, 583, 604, 609

Casey, R. J., 165, 177

Casper, L. M., 341, 350, 357

Caspi, A., 116, 117, 123, 125, 127, 131, 655, 677, 678

Cassidy, J., 564, 571, 666, 678

Cassidy, S., 39, 51

Castino, R. J., 64, 72

Casto, G., 3, 27, 275, 280, 283, 289, 489, 505, 533, 542, 604, 608, 638, 647

Catalano, R., 83, 93

Catlett, C., 470, 477, 483

Catlin, F., 43, 53

Cauce, A. M., 60, 72

Cave, G., 372, 386

Celano, D., 4, 29

Certo, N., 189, 200

Chaille, S., 10, 27

Chalk, R., 69, 71

Chall, J., 525, 543

Chalmers, M., 87, 92

Chamberlain, P., 672, 679

Chamberlain, R., 66, 67, 69, 74

Chamberlin, R., 81, 92, 328, 330, 331, 332, 336, 553, 554, 575, 580

Chambers, D. E., 497, 498, 505

Chambers, J., 526, 543

Champion, L., 656, 667, 680, 681

Chan, S. Q., 95, 112, 456, 479

Chandler, J., 525, 547

Chandler, L. K., 397, 410

Chandler, M. J., 11, 30, 137, 142, 159, 237, 256, 457, 482

Chang, B., 247, 255

Chang, P., 47, 51

Chaplin, D., 346, 358

Chapman, M., 66, 74

Charney, D. S., 216, 223

Chase, A., 8, 9, 27

Chase, H., 47, 51
Chase, J. H., 294, 302, 303, 306
Chase-Lansdale, P. L., 14, 27, 63, 64, 65, 71, 72, 552, 563, 565, 569, 570, 572, 574, 614, 615, 627, 651, 666, 676
Chatters, L. M., 60, 75
Chavez, L. R., 107, 111
Chavis, D., 644, 649
Chazan, R., 266, 284
Chazkel-Hochman, J., 398, 415
Chekki, D. A., 402, 410
Chen, H. T., 498, 499, 505, 568, 572
Chen, K. T. H., 150, 158
Chen, S., 212, 224
Chen, T., 12, 29
Cheng, H., 218, 223
Cherlin, A. J., 83, 91, 666, 676
Cherniss, D., 367, 385, 443, 452
Chesney, M. A., 121, 131, 670, 681
Chess, S., 44, 51, 259, 284
Chesterman, E. A., 121, 131
Chiarello, L. A., 276, 287
Chiesa, J., 3, 19, 28
Chilcoat, H. D., 655, 676
Chiriboga, C. A., 46, 51
Christoffel, K. K., 248, 255, 420, 436
Chugani, H. T., 212, 214, 223, 224
Chung, A., 354, 357
Cicchetti, D. V., 55, 65, 73, 75, 146, 157, 235, 257, 262, 284, 398, 410, 419, 427, 437, 488, 505, 652, 680
Cicirelli, V., 366, 384
Cielinski, K. L., 264, 284
Claflin, C. J., 301, 306
Clark, B., 258, 259, 282
Clark, E. G., 136, 158
Clark, G., 536, 547
Clark, R., 276, 278, 279, 284, 287, 447, 452
Clarke, A. D. B., 3, 27, 511, 541, 543
Clarke, A. M., 3, 27, 511, 541, 543
Clarke, A. S., 216, 223
Clarke, B., 400, 401, 405, 414
Clarke, S. W., 239, 256, 604, 608
Clarke-Stewart, K. A., 4, 14, 27, 57, 71, 144, 157, 259, 266, 284, 550, 552, 564, 569, 572
Clarren, S. K., 35, 45, 50, 51
Clarren, S. T., 45, 53
Clausen, J. S., 663, 676
Clayton, S. L., 560, 561, 576
Cleghorne, M., 4, 28
Clewell, B. C., 550, 551, 569, 570, 571
Clifford, R. M., 20, 27, 387, 388, 403, 404, 411, 412, 511, 518, 528, 544
Cloutier, M., 334, 337
Clyman, R. B., 163, 166, 176, 232, 254
Coakley, T., 592, 608

Coates, D. L., 258, 259, 261, 284, 286
Coatsworth, J. D., 652, 678
Cobb, S., 219, 227
Cochran, M., 58, 59, 60, 71
Cocking, R. R., 433, 435
Coe, R., 91
Coelen, C., 349, 359, 592, 593, 594, 608, 609
Cohen, B., 348, 357
Cohen, D. H., 45, 53, 419, 436, 463, 479
Cohen, F., 121, 131
Cohen, G., 62, 74
Cohen, L., 330, 337
Cohen, N. E., 241, 254, 346, 352, 353, 354, 355, 358
Cohen, S. E., 259, 261, 263, 266, 282, 284
Cohen, W., 334, 336
Cohler, B. J., 266, 278, 287, 288, 442, 452, 652, 657, 675, 676
Cohler, B. S., 127, 131
Cohn, J. F., 66, 71
Cohn, M., 330, 337
Coie, J. D., 417, 419, 435, 436
Cole, C. G., 298, 307
Cole, J., 61, 71
Cole, K., 538, 539, 543, 545
Cole, M., 94, 111
Cole, R. E., xi, xii, 67, 68, 69, 70, 74, 81, 92, 552, 553, 554, 567, 570, 574, 575, 580, 603, 608, 609, 665, 675
Coleman, H. L. K., 110, 112
Coleman, P. P., 398, 415, 455, 483
Collins, A., 86, 91, 342, 357
Collins, L., 399, 400, 401, 413
Collins, M., 340, 359
Collins, R. C., 426, 437
Collins, W. A., 57, 71
Collis, G. M., 264, 288
Collishaw, S., 656, 678
Colombo, M., 46, 51
Colozzi, G. A., 184, 201
Comenius, 4
Comeroff, J., 104, 111
Comfort, M., 301, 306, 532, 542
Comfort-Smith, M., 301, 306
Commaille, J., 617, 618, 627
Compas, B. E., 669, 676
Conboy, T. J., 43, 51
Condelli, L., 552, 569, 575
Cone, T., Jr., 327, 336
Conger, K. J., 565, 573, 653, 676
Conger, R. D., 565, 573, 653, 656, 669, 676, 677
Connell, D. B., 67, 73, 553, 563, 570, 575, 580

Connell, J. P., 171, 176, 258, 283, 663, 676
Connolly, P., 43, 51
Connor, E. M., 44, 51
Connors, R. E., 59, 72
Constantino, J., 419, 435
Convey, L., 441, 452
Conyers, O., 653, 675
Cook, J., 531, 547
Cook, R. J., 465, 481
Cook, T., 138, 139, 157
Coolahan, K. C., 129, 131, 419, 435
Cooley-Quille, M. R., 312, 323
Cools, A. R., 218, 226
Coombs, J. B., 277, 286
Coons, C. E., 560, 573
Cooper, C. S., 95, 96, 98, 99, 106, 112, 294, 302, 303, 306
Cooper, J. A., 527, 531, 545
Cooper, J. O., 181, 182, 186, 200
Cooper, L. Z., 43, 51
Cooper, P., 65, 66, 73
Copple, C., 5, 27, 429, 435, 454, 458, 459, 479, 488, 505
Corden, A., 617, 627
Cordero, M. E., 46, 51
Cordisco, L. K., 187, 191, 202
Corey, L. A., 668, 677
Corley, R., 162, 176, 178
Cornelius, W. A., 107, 111
Cornish, M., 409, 410
Cornwell, J. C., 398, 407, 411
Cortez, C., 373, 386, 515, 524, 547
Costello, E. J., 247, 254
Costley, J. B., 345, 348, 349, 350, 358
Coulter, D. K., 641, 647
Coulton, C. C., 311, 312, 323
Courtney, M., 77, 91
Cousins, J. B., 492, 505
Couvreur, J., 44, 51
Covitz, F. E., 259, 289
Cowen, E. L., 666, 676
Coyne, J. C., 418, 435, 563, 573
Craddock-Watson, J. E., 43, 52
Craft, M., 13, 28
Cragg, B. G., 46, 51
Craig, T. K., 667, 668, 676
Crais, E. R., 631, 647
Cramer, B. G., 65, 71, 170, 176
Crane, J., 311, 323
Cranshaw, J., 335, 337
Crawley, S. B., 263, 275, 276, 279, 280, 284, 288
Cremin, L., 5, 27
Crimmins, D. B., 185, 200
Cripe, J., 457, 477, 479
Crissey, M. S., 9, 27

Crnic, K. A., 59, 71, 150, 157, 234, 237, 254, 260, 284, 293, 294, 306, 488, 506, 641, 647, 671, 679
Crockenberg, S. B., 58, 59, 60, 63, 71, 261, 284
Crocker, R., 363, 384
Crockett, L. J., 57, 71
Cross, A. H., 149, 157, 292, 306
Cross, A. W., 238, 255
Cross, T., 425, 436
Cross, W. E., 60, 71
Crouter, A. C., 60, 71, 79, 82, 83, 87, 88, 91, 92
Crowe, R. R., 668, 676
Crowell, J. A., 152, 157, 563, 573
Cryer, D., 401, 410, 511, 518, 528, 544
CTB/McGraw-Hill, 558, 573
Cuban, L., 4, 27
Cuffs, M. S., 187, 202
Culkin, M., 511, 544
Cullina, J., 331, 336
Culp, A. M., 64, 72, 258, 285, 523, 544, 553, 554, 575, 581
Culp, R. E., 63, 64, 71, 266, 284
Culross, P., 618, 627
Cummings, E. M., 66, 74, 563, 577
Cunningham, C. C., 264, 266, 280, 283, 284
Cunningham, C. E., 552, 553, 554, 571, 579
Cunningham, S., 82, 91
Currie, J. M., 550, 569, 573
Cushing, G., 115, 131
Cutler, C. A., 553, 554, 573, 579
Cutler, I., 353, 357
Czyzurski, D., 42, 52

D'Acuna, E., 46, 51
Dahlsgaard, K., 531, 546
Dale, P., 538, 539, 543, 545
Dalianis, M. K., 116, 123, 125, 126, 131
Dalton, J., 633, 647
Daly, P., 4, 29
Damasio, A., 211, 223
Damon, W., 488, 505
D'Andrade, R., 494, 505
Daniels, D. V., 637
D'Arcis, U., 170, 176
Darkes, L. A., 295, 297, 305
Darling, R. B., 460, 482, 634, 638, 640, 641, 647, 650
Darling-Hammond, L., 464, 477, 479
Darlington, R., 15, 28, 516, 545, 552, 569, 574
Das, R., 278, 288
Das Eiden, R., 61, 71
Dasen, P. R., 488, 505

David, J. P., 664, 682
Davidson, C. E., 266, 284
Davis, A., 101, 111
Davis, B., 265, 286
Davis, C. A., 185, 200
Davis, H., 263, 284
Davis, M., 398, 407, 411
Davis, R. H., 247, 255, 332, 338
Dawson, G., 534, 535, 543
Dawson, N., 420, 436
Day, B., 462, 479
Day, H. M., 183, 185, 200, 201
Day, M., 299, 305
Day, N., 45, 51
De Fries, J. C., 658, 669, 679
de Kloet, E. R., 218, 226
de St. Aubin, E., 145, 158
de Vries, L., 653, 676
Deal, A. G., 194, 195, 196, 200, 202, 292, 294, 295, 302, 303, 306, 389, 390, 399, 408, 414, 426, 435, 461, 479, 492, 505, 639, 648
Dean, J. G., 553, 554, 573, 579
Deater-Deckard, K., 109, 111, 656, 669, 679
DeBaryshe, B. D., 419, 437
DeCesare, L. D., 187, 202
Deck, D., 523, 524, 547
DeFries, J. C., 162, 176, 178
DeGangi, G. A., 501, 505
Deich, S., 340, 341, 347, 350, 358
Deinard, A., 47, 51
Deiner, P., 528, 543
Deitz, S. M., 184, 202
del Valle, C., 66, 72
Delaney, R. C., 216, 223
Delaney, S., 146, 157
DeLeo, T., 379, 386
deLeone, P., 15, 30, 518, 519, 547
Del'Homme, M., 419, 437
Dellinger, J., 244, 246, 253
Dell'Oliver, C., 457, 460, 482
deLone, R. H., 14, 27
Demmitt, A., 295, 307, 631, 639, 649
Demmler, G. J., 38, 43, 51, 53
DeMuralt, M., 170, 176
Denham, S., 563, 577
Dennis, K., 425, 436
Dennis, W., 12, 27
Derevensky, J., 532, 543
DeSantis, L., 104, 111
Desimone, L., 354, 357
Desmonts, G., 44, 51
Detterman, D. K., xi, xii
Deutsch, Martin, 363
Deutsch, Cynthia, 363
Devaney, B. L., 374, 385, 569, 573
Devine, P., 105, 111

DeWeerd, J., 15, 27
Dewey, J., 5
Diamond, A., 214, 223
Diamond, K. E., 248, 254, 468, 470, 474, 481, 532, 543
Dias, L., 41, 52
Diaz, R. M., 110, 111
Dichtelmiller, M., 3, 19, 29, 511, 526, 530, 545, 605, 609
Dichter, H., 352, 358
Dickerson, J. W. T., 215, 223
Dickstein, S., 146, 157
Dihoff, R., 530, 543
DiLalla, D., 535, 546
DiMauro, S., 40, 53
Dinero, T., 526, 530, 545
Dinnebeil, L. A., 281, 284
Disbrow, M. A., 277, 282
Dishion, T. J., 651, 672, 679
Ditch, J., 616, 617, 618, 627
DiVenere, N. J., 461, 463, 479, 483
Divine-Hawkins, P., 341, 349, 360
Divitto, B., 263, 284, 285
Dix, T., 55, 71, 167, 176
Doar, B., 214, 223
Dobbing, J., 46, 51, 215, 223
Dobos, A., 328, 336
Dockery, J. L., 398, 410
Dodds, J., 329, 336
Dodds, M., 332, 336
Dodge, K. A., 109, 111, 419, 436
Dodge, P. R., 46, 51
Dodson, W. E., 216, 223
Doernberger, C. H., 663, 678
Dohrenwend, B., 313, 323
Doi, T., 161, 176
Doke, L. A., 184, 200
Dokecki, P. R., 101, 111, 294, 307, 387, 410, 639, 641, 647
Dolby, R. G. A., 491, 505
Dolezol, S., 167, 176
Doll, B., 431, 438
Dollman, C., 535, 544
Dominquez, R., 46, 51
Donahue, P. J., 424, 435
Donnellan, A. M., 185, 200
Dooley, D., 83, 93
Dorfman, A., 250, 256
Dorsey, M. F., 185, 201
Dovidio, J. F., 105, 111
Dow, M., 149, 156
Downey, G., 418, 435, 563, 573
Downs, L., 353, 357
Doyle, P. M., 183, 185, 186, 187, 203
Drachman, R., 379, 386
Drake, H., 667, 668, 676
Drake, K., 462, 479
Drearden, R., 657, 681

Drell, M., 62, 74
Drinnan, D., 667, 681
Drotar, D., 382, 385
Dubow, E. F., 265, 266, 284, 666, 676
Dubowitz, H., 322, 324
Dubrow, N., 62, 72, 86, 91
Duckitt, J., 94, 111
Duggan, A. K., 554, 573
Dulcan, M. K., 247, 254
Dunbar, S. B., 252, 255
Duncan, B. B., 419, 430, 435
Duncan, G. J., 91, 241, 254, 309, 311, 322, 323, 420, 435, 522, 543, 550, 563, 569, 572, 573, 614, 615, 627
Dunlap, G., 185, 187, 191, 200, 201, 535, 544, 546
Dunlap, W. R., 595, 608
Dunn, J., 165, 176, 654, 656, 668, 671, 680
Dunn, W., 399, 410
Dunst, C. J., 85, 91, 149, 157, 186, 188, 191, 194, 195, 196, 197, 198, 200, 202, 262, 280, 284, 292, 293, 294, 295, 302, 303, 306, 389, 390, 397, 398, 399, 404, 405, 407, 408, 410, 411, 414, 426, 435, 457, 461, 479, 492, 500, 502, 503, 505, 508, 604, 608, 631, 639, 640, 647, 648
Durand, V. M., 185, 200
Duyvesteyn, M. G. C., 553, 566, 576
Dworkin, P. H., 21, 25, 247, 254
Dwyer, T. F., 633, 647
Dye, H. B., 12, 30
Dyer, K., 185, 200, 201
Dyer, W., 408, 411

Eardley, T., 616, 617, 618, 627
Earl, L. M., 492, 505
Earls, F., 22, 218, 223, 258, 289, 420, 435, 502, 521, 548
East, P. L., 64, 71
Easterbrooks, M. A., 152, 157, 164, 165, 176, 266, 284
Eaton, A. P., 21, 28
Eaves, L. J., 654, 655, 656, 668, 669, 671, 676, 677, 680, 681
Eberhart-Wright, A., 63, 64, 65, 66, 74
Eccles, J., 95, 96, 98, 99, 106, 112, 138, 139, 157
Eckenhoff, M. F., 209, 212, 213, 217, 223, 225
Eckenrode, J., xi, xii, 81, 83, 92, 116, 131, 552, 553, 554, 567, 570, 575, 580, 603, 609, 669, 677
Eckland, J., 20, 28, 388, 403, 404, 411, 412
Edelbrock, C. S., 247, 248, 253, 254
Edelfsen, M., 417, 435

Edelman, L., 460, 479
Edelman, M. W., 3, 16, 27
Edgell, D., 488, 508
Edmisten, P., 527, 531, 545
Edmondson, R., 291, 296, 297, 305, 307, 631, 640, 641, 647
Edwards, E. P., 5, 27
Egeland, B., 116, 117, 120, 123, 124, 131, 260, 284, 372, 378, 385, 386, 552, 553, 554, 563, 566, 573, 581, 652, 666, 676, 679
Eggbeer, L., 455, 464, 480, 482
Eggebeen, D. J., 57, 71
Egolf, B., 116, 122, 123, 124, 131
Eheart, B. K., 263, 284
Ehlers, V., 524, 544
Eichenwald, H. G., 44, 51
Eichorn, D. H., 529, 545
Eisenberg, L., 442, 452
Elazar, D. J., 402, 411
Elbert, T., 219, 221, 223
Elder, G., 565, 573, 653, 676
Elder, G. H., Jr., 77, 83, 91, 116, 117, 123, 125, 127, 131, 138, 139, 157, 565, 573, 653, 656, 667, 671, 676
Eldred, D., 351, 356
Eliason, M. J., 244, 245, 255
Elicker, J., 566, 573
Elkind, D., 5, 27
Ellenberg, J. H., 36, 48
Eller, E., 4, 27
Elling, R., 528, 529, 547
Elliot, A., 105, 111
Elliot, S. N., 245, 254
Elliott, K. A., 351, 356
Ellison, P., 329, 337
Ellwood, D. T., 550, 577
Ellwood, M. R., 569, 573
Elmore, R. F., 387, 411
Else, J. G., 216, 226
Elster, A. B., 57, 64, 73
Emde, R. N., 13, 22, 56, 71, 75, 152, 158, 232, 254, 266, 284, 390, 411, 419, 437, 457, 482, 633, 648
Emery, R. E., 116, 131, 651, 676
Emlen, A., 86, 91
Ends, E. J., 408, 411
Engel, M., 259, 285
Engelhardt, K., 67, 69, 74, 552, 553, 554, 574, 580, 603, 608
Engfer, A., 673, 677
English, D., 322, 324
Ensminger, M. E., 309, 311, 323
Entwisle, D. R., 95, 111
Epstein, A. J., 621, 626
Epstein, A. S., 349, 357, 556, 576, 591, 597, 598, 607, 609
Epstein, H., 633, 647

Epstein, J. L., 347, 357, 642, 648
Epstein, J. N., 563, 577
Epstein, L. H., 184, 200
Erickson, R. V., 103, 104, 112
Erickson, M. F., 378, 385, 501, 503, 505, 552, 553, 554, 563, 566, 573, 581, 592, 594, 604, 608
Erikson, E. H., 56, 63, 71, 145, 157, 161, 165, 177
Erikson, J., 233, 235, 249, 254, 256
Erikson, M. T., 655, 676
Erkut, S., 97, 114
Ernhart, C. B., 13, 28
Ershler, J., 245, 254
Escobar, C. M., 503, 504, 532, 533, 542, 592, 593, 595, 596, 607, 608
Esser, G., 65, 73
Everingham, S. S., 3, 19, 28
Everitt, B. J., 218, 225
Eyres, S. J., 258, 259, 277, 282

Fagan, J. F., 231, 254
Fall, M. Z., 39, 53
Faller, H. S., 103, 111
Fals-Borda, O., 492, 506
Fandal, A. W., 560, 573
Fantuzzo, J., 129, 131, 419, 435
Faraone, S. V., 657, 675
Farber, E. A., 116, 120, 124, 131
Farel, A., 277, 285
Farquhar, E., 341, 349, 358, 360
Farran, D. C., 15, 19, 258, 259, 260, 266, 285, 287, 301, 306, 442, 449, 452, 487, 502, 506, 602, 604
Farrel, A., 455, 478
Farrell, M., 636, 648
Farrelly, M., 530, 543
Farrington, D. P., 140, 159, 315, 324, 652, 654, 677, 681
Farrow, F., 396, 414
Fassbender, L. L., 185, 200
Feagans, L., 513, 544
Feil, E. G., 419, 431, 435, 438
Feil, L., 143, 159, 292, 307
Fein, G. G., 4, 14, 27, 550, 552, 564, 569, 572
Feinleib, M., 310, 323
Feldman, M. A., 266, 285
Feldman, R., 61, 73
Feldman, S. S., 152, 157, 563, 573
Felice, M. E., 64, 71
Feller, I., 494, 507
Felsman, J. K., 651, 657, 677
Fendt, K. H., 513, 519, 520, 544, 546, 555, 566, 576
Fenichel, E., 12, 27, 62, 68, 74, 232, 235, 256, 346, 358, 454, 455, 461, 462, 464, 480, 482, 613, 628

Fenichel, O., 174, 177
Ferguson, 279, 280, 288
Ferguson, C. J., 368, 384, 555, 556, 571, 583
Ferguson, J., 150, 153, 154, 159, 556, 563, 576
Fergusson, D. M., 563, 573, 653, 655, 657, 677
Fernandez, T., 100, 114
Ferrarese, M. J., 74
Ferrell, K. A., 180, 201
Ferry, P. C., 3, 21, 27, 28
Fetterman, D. M., 490, 492, 506
Fewell, R. R., 21, 28, 280, 285, 389, 397, 411, 414, 530, 531, 544, 592, 608
Fick, A. C., 62, 63, 64, 72, 74
Fiedler, M., 78, 93
Field, T. M., 63, 65, 66, 72, 150, 157, 262, 263, 265, 266, 285, 553, 554, 555, 556, 573, 579, 584
Fielding, D. W., 41, 53
Fiese, B. H., 13, 22, 94, 234, 237, 257, 536, 546
Figueira-McDonough, J., 312, 323
File, N., 460, 469, 475, 480, 528, 544
Filer, J., 528, 529, 545
Filla, A., 187, 201
Fincham, F. D., 144, 145, 157
Fine, E., 541, 546
Finger, I., 264, 279, 286
Finkler, D., 527, 546
Finn, D., 419, 435
Finnegan, D., 264, 286
Finn-Stevenson, M., 354, 357, 606, 610
Fischel, J. E., 563, 577
Fischer, F., 491, 506
Fischer, R., 537, 548
Fisher, G., 47, 52
Fisher, K., 82, 91
Fishler, K., 13, 27
Fishman, M. A., 46, 51
Fisk, K. B., 116, 125, 131
Flaugher, J., 490, 508
Fleck, M. B., 233, 256, 398, 413
Fleeson, J., 173, 178
Fleeting, M., 657, 678
Fleischer, K. H., 248, 254
Fleishchmann, T. B., 218, 224
Fleming, J., 161, 177
Fleming, L. A., 187, 202
Fleming, S., 460, 483
Fletcher, A., 96, 113
Fletcher, R., 513, 544
Flint, D., 265, 286
Flor, D., 653, 675
Flor, H., 219, 223
Florian, L., 526, 544

Florin, P. R., 101, 111, 644, 649
Foley, G. M., 464, 467, 475, 480, 634, 635, 648
Folkman, S., 121, 131, 565, 576, 652, 678
Follett, M. P., 631, 648
Follmer, A., 59, 71
Foltz, A. M., 8, 27
Fonagy, P., 69, 72, 172, 177, 652, 666, 667, 677
Forbes, G., 47, 52
Forehand, R., 116, 131, 651, 676
Forest, S., 473, 477, 480
Forester, F., 491, 506
Forgatch, M. S., 668, 675
Forness, S. R., xi, xii, 419, 430, 435
Forrester, J., 77, 91
Fors, S., 264, 286
Fortner-Wood, C., 566, 573
Fosberg, S., 349, 357
Foster, J. L., 402, 411
Foster, M., 247, 255
Foster, S. A., 560, 570, 572, 586
Fowler, K., 43, 51
Fowler, M. G., 238, 255
Fowler, S. A., 191, 202
Fox, L., 187, 191, 200, 201, 458, 480, 535, 544
Foxx, R. M., 184, 201
Fraiberg, S., 56, 72, 147, 152, 157, 163, 168, 170, 177, 264, 285, 367, 385, 443, 449, 452, 634
Frank, A., 398, 411
Frank, D. A., 46, 53
Frank, N., 298, 305
Frankenburg, W. K., 329, 333, 334, 336, 390, 411, 560, 573
Frazier, H., 402, 405, 408, 412
Frazier-Thompson, M. D., 59, 72
Frede, E. C., 6, 26, 593, 595, 604, 607, 608
Freedman, M., 126, 131
Freeman, H. E., 494, 496, 497, 507
Freeman, J., 48, 51
Freeman, V. A., 277, 285
Freire, P., 492, 641, 644, 648
French, F. E., 11, 12, 30, 659, 682
Freud, S., 161, 174, 177, 633, 634, 648
Freudenburg, W. R., 310, 312, 323
Freund, D., 334, 336
Fridhandler, B., 166, 177
Fried, A. O., 80, 91
Fried, L. E., 46, 53, 332, 337
Friedman, D. E., 347, 357, 492, 506
Friedman, D. P., 211, 225
Friedman, R. J., 60, 72
Friedrich, W. N., 293, 306
Friesen, B. J., 644, 650

Frison, S., 43, 51
Fritz, J., 59, 60, 73
Fritz, M., 620, 628
Froebel, F., 4, 5
Frye, K. F., 552, 553, 574, 580
Fuchs, D., 242, 243, 255, 460, 480
Fuchs, L. S., 242, 243, 255, 460, 480
Fuchs, M., 45, 51
Fuddy, L., 554, 573
Fukamoto, A., 165, 177
Fuligni, A. S., 22, 502, 597
Fulker, D. W., 162, 176, 178, 237, 254, 656, 669, 679
Fuller, B. F., 343, 357
Funk, S. G., 247, 257
Furman, G., 469, 482
Furry, W. S., 592, 593, 594, 508
Furstenberg, F. F., Jr., 63, 64, 71, 72, 116, 117, 122, 123, 124, 127, 131, 138, 139, 157, 265, 266, 285, 312, 324, 448, 452, 665, 666, 676, 677
Fuster, J. M., 215, 224

Gabel, J. R., 592, 609
Gaensbauer, T. J., 170, 177, 419, 435
Gaertner, S. L., 105, 111
Gaev, L., 43, 51
Gaffaney, T., 185, 199
Galant, K., 458, 480
Galbraith, M., 330, 337
Galenson, E., 366, 384
Galinsky, E., 343, 347, 349, 357, 359
Gallacher, K. K., 462, 475, 480
Gallagher, B., 654, 677
Gallagher, J. J., 20, 21, 25, 27, 28, 180, 201, 455, 480, 483, 500, 504, 533, 544, 567
Gallagher, P., 4, 28
Gallen, C. C., 219, 226, 227
Gallimore, R., 489, 507, 508
Gans, S. P., 396, 411
Ganzel, B., 13
Garbarino, J., 13, 62, 72, 135, 157, 311, 324, 401, 402, 407, 411
Garber, H. L., 555, 556, 573, 584
García-Coll, C. T., 13, 64, 72, 266, 285, 317
Garcia, R., 150, 157
Gardiner, A., 49, 53
Garland, C. W., 390, 398, 399, 409, 411, 413, 414, 415, 461, 483, 631, 639, 640, 650
Garlow, J. E., 642, 648
Garmezy, N., 67, 68, 69, 72, 73, 74, 115, 116, 131, 140, 157, 652, 658, 666, 677, 678
Garnett, M., 239, 257
Garraghty, P. E., 219, 225
Garry, P., 47, 53

Garshelis, J. A., 295, 297, 306
Gartner, A., 10, 21, 28, 440, 452
Garwood, S. G., 21, 28, 387, 411
Gaskins, R., 615, 627
Gaudin, J., 87, 92
Gavin, L. A., 152, 158
Gay, E. C., 560, 573
Gazdag, G., 187, 203, 537, 548
Ge, X., 565, 573, 653, 656, 676, 677
Geertsma, A., 331, 336
Geik, I., 466, 480
Gelber, R., 44, 51
Gelfand, D. M., 65, 72
Genser, A., 345, 348, 349, 350, 358
Gephart, M., 419, 435
Gerhardt, C. A., 669, 676
Gerkin, K. C., 244, 245, 255
Germino Hausken, E., 340, 341, 359, 360
Gerton, J., 110, 112
Gesell, A., 10, 28
Gest, S. D., 67, 68, 73, 652, 678
Geyer, M. A., 218, 224, 226
Gianino, A. F., Jr., 65, 66, 75
Gibbons, R. D., 420, 436
Giles, S., 667, 681
Gilkerson, L., 22, 389, 398, 411
Giller, H., 654, 680
Gilles, F. H., 48, 51
Gilligan, C., 145, 157, 161, 177
Gilman, E., 15, 31, 137, 159
Giloth, R. P., 440, 453
Giovannoni, J., 77, 92
Girard, J. L., 641, 648
Girolametto, L., 258, 285
Gisel, E., 262, 285
Gitelson, M., 447, 452
Gjerde, P., 125, 130
Glantz, F., 341, 349, 359, 360, 593, 594, 608
Glascoe, F. P., 247, 255, 328, 329, 336
Glass, G. V., x, xiii
Glassman, M. B., 116, 125, 131
Glassman, R. B., 394, 411
Glazewski, B., 233, 256, 398, 413
Glick, M., 530, 544
Gliedman, J., 15, 16, 28
Glovinsky, I., 258, 270, 285
Goddard, H., 9
Godfrey, A. B., 466, 480
Goerge, R., 83, 93
Goetz, E. M., 186, 201
Goetze, L. D., 592, 608
Goffin, S. G., 351, 358, 396, 412
Goldberg, D., 333, 336
Goldberg, M., 350, 359
Goldberg, S., 11, 28, 237, 255, 259, 261, 263, 265, 284, 285, 286
Goldenberg, C., 489, 507

Goldfield, B., 332, 336
Golding, E., 57, 72
Goldman, P. S., 214, 224
Goldman, S., 116, 120, 124, 126, 131
Goldman-Rakic, P. S., 209, 211, 212, 214, 217, 223, 224, 225
Goldson, E., 39, 51
Goldstein, H., 537, 548
Goldstein, S., 66, 72, 513, 543
Goldwyn, R., 144, 147, 152
Golly, A., 438
Golub, S. A., 351, 358, 396, 412
Gomby, D. S., 343, 357, 550, 573, 618, 627
Gomez, H., 47, 52
Gomez, I., 47, 52
Goncu, A., 97, 113
Gonzales, J., 66, 72
Gonzales, N. A., 60, 72
Gonzalez, M., 419, 437
Goode, M., 258, 283
Goodman, I. F., 345, 348, 349, 350, 358, 525, 547
Goodman, J. F., 234, 244, 246, 251, 255, 527, 528, 535, 544, 545
Goodman, R., 655, 671, 677
Goodman, S. H., 563, 573
Goodnow, J. J., 60, 72, 143, 146, 157, 159
Goodson, B. D., 361, 371, 372, 375, 384, 386, 442, 452, 557, 558, 569, 570, 576
Goodwin, L. D., 400, 410
Goodwin, S., 619, 620, 627
Goodyer, I., 651, 677
Gopaldas, T., 47, 53
Gopfert, M., 65, 72
Gordon, E. W., 490, 506, 636, 648, 669, 682
Gordon, I., 363
Gordon, J., 46, 53
Gordon, N. J., 194, 200, 400, 410, 631, 640, 648
Gordon, R., 563, 574
Gore, S., 116, 131, 665, 667, 669, 677
Gorman, K. S., 216, 225, 238, 253, 255
Gormley, W. T., 350, 352, 357
Gorski, P. N., 390, 411
Goshen, C. E., 633, 648
Gottesman, N., 563, 573
Gottfried, A. W., 556, 563, 372
Gottlieb, B. H., 294, 306
Gottlieb, G., 161, 162, 177
Gottlieb, N., 641, 648
Gottman, J. M., 146, 158
Gotts, E. A., 467, 482
Gough, I., 616, 627
Gould, M. S., 170, 172, 178, 655, 675

Gowen, J., 375, 385
Grace, J., 277, 285
Graham, F. K., 13, 28
Graham, J. M., 39, 40, 51, 52
Graham, M., 592, 610
Graham, S., 101, 112
Graham, W. F., 494, 495, 506
Graliker, B. V., 13, 27, 636, 649
Gramlich, E. M., 600, 608
Granger, R. H., 61, 73
Granson, H., 552, 569, 575
Grant, S., 527, 546
Gray, C. A., 258, 259, 282, 372, 556, 563
Gray, J. D., 553, 554, 573, 579
Gray, S. W., 364, 518, 544, 553, 554, 573, 582
Grays, C., 636, 648
Green, B. L., 568, 573
Green, J. A., 247, 257
Green, L., 263, 284
Green, M., 21, 28, 327, 328, 329, 331, 337
Green, V., 535, 547
Greenberg, F., 39, 51
Greenberg, M. T., 59, 71, 150, 157, 234, 237, 254, 260, 284, 293, 294, 306, 488, 506
Greenberg, P., 364, 385
Greenberg, R., 555, 556, 573, 579, 584
Greene, J. C., 489, 492, 494, 495, 496, 497, 505, 506
Greene, S., 417, 437
Greenfield, P. M., 110, 112, 433, 435
Greenman, M., 13, 28
Greenough, W. T., 217, 218, 223, 224, 510, 544
Greenspan, S. I., 85, 93, 137, 159, 170, 177, 191, 202, 232, 234, 235, 237, 238, 255, 257, 258, 266, 269, 270, 285, 287, 389, 411, 419, 421, 430, 435, 449, 452, 457, 477, 480, 563, 573
Greenstein, B., 568, 573
Greenswag, L., 39, 51
Greenwood, P. W., 3, 19, 28
Greven, P., 4, 28
Griffin, A., 613, 628
Griffith, J. P. C., 6, 28, 330, 337
Grimshaw, J., 167, 176
Gringlas, M. B., 58, 75
Groce, N. E., 96, 102, 112
Gromish, D. S., 45, 51
Gronwaldt, V., 277, 283
Groom, J. M., 21, 28
Gross, G., 216, 226
Gross, R. T., 519, 520, 543, 547, 555, 574, 575, 583, 591, 604, 608
Grossman, F. K., 57, 72

Grossman, J. B., 132
Groves, B. M., 70, 72, 312, 324, 419, 436
Grubb, W. N., 590, 594, 605, 608
Gruen, G. E., 258, 289
Gruenewald, L., 189, 200
Grunebaum, H. U., 67, 73, 418, 437, 553, 563, 570, 575, 580
Grunewald, L. J., 390, 415
Grych, J. H., 144, 145, 157
Guba, E. G., 491, 492, 496, 506, 507
Guerra, N. G., 419, 437
Guess, D., 184, 185, 201
Guidabaldi, J., 243, 246, 256
Guite, J., 657, 675
Gulcur, L., 347, 359
Gulley, B. L., 656, 680
Gunderson, V., 144, 158
Gunn, P., 262, 285
Gunnarsson, L., 59, 71, 348, 357
Guralnick, M. J., 12, 19, 21, 28, 179, 192, 193, 194, 196, 197, 198, 201, 290, 292, 306, 474, 480, 489, 501, 506, 526, 530, 533, 544, 604, 608, 636, 641, 648
Guskey, T. R., 470, 480
Gustafsson, S., 626, 627
Gutelius, M., 330, 337
Guterman, N. B., 613, 627
Gutfreund, M., 260, 266, 282
Guthertz, M., 66, 72
Gutiérrez, L., 641, 642, 644, 648
Gutierrez, J., 100, 104, 112
Guttmann, E., 79, 92

Haber, A., 137, 158
Habermas, J., 491, 506
Hacking, S., 553, 554, 571, 579
Hadfield, W., 211, 225
Hagedorn, T., 4, 29
Hagell, A., 654, 680
Hagemann, M., 522, 523, 546
Hagen, J., 347, 359
Hagen, V., 262, 288
Hagerman, R. J., 39, 51, 53
Hagger, C., 212, 223
Haggerty, R. J., 327, 337, 417, 420, 437, 652, 677
Hains, A. H., 462, 463, 481
Hale, L. M., 281, 284
Haley, S. M., 276, 287
Hall, D., 333, 337
Hall, F. S., 218, 226
Hall, G. S., 5
Hall, J. D., 240, 255, 592, 610
Halpern, L., 97, 112
Halpern, R., 14, 19, 25, 418, 436, 441, 442, 446, 449, 452, 567, 602
Hamburg, D. A., 487, 506, 613, 627

Hamby, D. W., 194, 200, 397, 404, 411, 457, 479, 502, 508, 639, 647
Hammen, C., 563, 574
Hammond, M. A., 258, 259, 260, 261, 262, 266, 267, 282, 286, 372, 423, 438, 556, 563
Hampson, S., 219, 223
Hamre-Nietupski, S., 189, 200
Hanchett, J., 39, 51
Hancock, T., 187, 201
Hanft, B., 387, 399, 412
Hanks, C., 67, 69, 74, 552, 553, 554, 574, 580, 603, 608, 609
Hanline, M. F., 22, 28, 458, 480
Hann, D. M., 62, 63, 64, 65, 66, 71, 72, 74, 258, 266, 285, 287
Hans, S. L., 59, 60, 75, 237, 254, 258, 270, 283, 362, 385
Hansen, D. F., 238, 248, 255
Hansen, R. L., 61, 75
Hanshaw, C., 59, 72
Hanshaw, J., 43, 51
Hanson, C. R., 398, 415
Hanson, J., 216, 224
Hanson, M. J., 241, 255, 262, 269, 285, 287, 456, 475, 481, 489, 490, 506, 507
Harber, L., 301, 306, 529, 544
Harbin, G. L., 20, 21, 25, 28, 29, 296, 306, 455, 481, 567, 640, 641, 646, 649
Hardee, B. B., 106, 113
Hardin, B., 418, 436
Hardin, G., 77, 92
Hardin, J. M., 605, 607
Hardin, M., 522, 542
Hardy, J. B., 552, 554, 574, 579
Harik, V., 312, 324
Haring, N. G., 185, 201
Harkavy, O., 441, 453
Harkness, A. R., 655, 678
Harkness, S., 94, 97, 112, 114, 489, 494, 506, 508
Harmon, R. J., 164, 170, 177, 258, 287
Harms, T., 518, 528, 544
Harris, B. M., 458, 463, 480
Harris, C., 333, 336
Harris, I. B., 613, 627
Harris, R., 41, 53
Harris, S. R., 262, 285, 458, 480
Harris, T. O., 651, 653, 662, 676, 677
Harrison, A. O., 95, 112
Harry, B., 106, 112, 236, 255, 528, 544
Harryman, S. E., 532, 546
Hartmann, A. T., 13, 28
Hartsough, C., 419, 435
Harvey, J., 637, 648
Harville, K., 399, 413

Harwood, A., 103, 112
Harwood, R. L., 97, 112
Hasbrouck, S., 593, 595, 607
Hashima, P. Y., 59, 72
Haskins, R., 621, 627
Hassing, Y., 259, 288
Hastings, A., 47, 52
Hastings, L., 653, 675
Hatfield, E., 297, 308, 456, 483
Hatton, D. D., 180, 201
Hauser-Cram, P., 4, 6, 19, 20, 22, 23, 28, 30, 258, 262, 275, 277, 280, 288, 291, 307, 401, 413, 526, 529, 530, 547, 594, 604, 609, 638, 650
Hausman, B., 524, 525, 544
Haveman, R. H., 550, 574, 603, 608
Havighurst, R. J., 116, 131
Hawaii Family Stress Center, 373, 385
Hawkins, A. J., 57, 71, 439, 453
Hawkins, J. D., 417, 435
Hawrylak, N., 510, 544
Hay, D. F., 419, 436
Hayes, C., 567, 574
Hayes, S. C., 252, 255
Hayford, J. R., 248, 255
Haynes, C. W., 574, 583, 591, 604, 608
Haynes, K., 277, 288
Haynes, O. M., 61, 73
Haynes, U., 398, 412
Healy, A., 22, 28
Healy, B., 66, 72
Heaslip, P., 348, 359
Heath, A. C., 655, 668, 669, 676, 677
Heath, S. B., 490, 506
Hebbeler, K., 295, 297, 305, 527, 531, 545
Heberle, J., 558, 559, 560, 574, 586
Heffron, M. C., 233, 235, 257, 464, 466, 483
Heflinger, C. A., 387, 410, 639, 641, 647
Heiman, M., 144, 158
Heiser, J., 528, 543
Heiser, K. E., 21, 28
Helburn, S. W., 511, 544, 594, 595, 608
Helfen, C. S., 184, 201
Heller, D., 645, 648
Heller, M., 184, 201
Helm, J., 532, 542
Helms, K. A., 4, 28
Helmstetter, E., 184, 185, 201, 469, 482
Helu, B., 47, 53
Hembroke, H., 82, 85, 92
Hemmeter, M. L., 258, 286
Hemphill, L., 525, 547
Henderson, A. T., 347, 357

Henderson, C. R., Jr., xi, xii, 59, 66, 67, 69, 71, 74, 81, 92, 331, 337, 552, 553, 554, 564, 567, 570, 574, 575, 580, 603, 608, 609
Henderson, L. W., 247, 248, 255, 256, 295, 296, 305, 328, 329, 337
Henderson, S. H., 666, 672, 679
Henggeler, S. W., 656, 676
Hennessey, J. W., 657, 677
Herman, A. A., 98, 106, 112
Herman, J. L., 250, 255
Herman, S., 528, 529, 547
Hermans, H. J. M., 161, 177
Hernandez, T. D., 218, 224, 615, 627
Heron, A., 488, 505
Heron, T. E., 181, 182, 186, 200
Herr, T., 370, 378, 385
Herrenkohl, F. C., 116, 122, 123, 124, 131
Herrenkohl, R. C., 116, 122, 123, 124, 131
Herrick, H., 500, 504
Hersey, P., 404, 412
Hersher, L., 260, 288
Hess, E. H., 259, 285
Hess, R., 101, 111
Hesse, E., 64, 73
Hester, P. P., 187, 201, 458, 480
Hetherington, E. M., 116, 120, 124, 126, 131, 489, 506, 651, 656, 666, 669, 672, 676, 677, 679
Heublein, E. A., 602, 610
Heward, W. L., 181, 182, 186, 200
Hewett, K., 368, 385
Hewitt, J. K., 655, 676, 681
Hewlett, K., 592, 609
Heydeman, P., 44, 52
Hickson, G., 327, 337
Higgins, G. O., 115, 131
Higgitt, A., 652, 666, 667, 677
Hill, J., 661, 662, 663, 681
Hill, M., 91
Hiller, J. E., 532, 546
Hilliard, A. G., 398, 411
Hinde, R. A., 161, 177
Hinden, B. R., 669, 676
Hingson, R., 45, 46, 51, 53
Hinkle, L. E., 659, 677
Hinton, V. J., 210, 224
Hirsch, E. D., 5, 28
Hirshberg, L. M., 233, 255, 268, 270, 285, 300, 306, 461, 467, 475, 480, 635, 648
Hoagwood, K., 430, 436
Hoang, G. N., 103, 104, 112
Hobbs, N., 10, 16, 28, 294, 307
Hobsbaum, A., 668, 682
Hochman, J. D., 467, 475, 480, 634, 635, 648

Hodapp, R. M., 292, 307, 488, 506
Hoehn, T. P., 180, 202
Hoekelman, R., 327, 328, 337
Hofferth, S. L., 340, 341, 342, 344, 346, 347, 349, 350, 358, 360, 552, 574, 606, 608
Hoffman, J., 64, 72, 266, 285
Hoffmann, K., 513, 544
Hogarty, P. S., 231, 256, 529, 545
Holcomb, P., 340, 341, 347, 350, 358
Holcombe, A., 187, 201
Holcombe-Ligon, A., 460, 483
Holland, D., 494, 506
Hollinsworth, J. S., 595, 608
Holm, V., 39, 51
Holman, K., 39, 52
Holmes, D., 6, 28
Holmes, H., 616, 617, 627
Holpel, P., 44, 52
Holt, L. E., 7, 28
Homel, R., 60, 72
Honig, A. S., 47, 53, 69, 73, 370, 375, 385, 515, 544, 603, 609
Honzik, M. P., 231, 255
Hooker, K. A., 145, 146, 157
Hoover-Dempsey, K. V., 294, 307
Hopps, K., 57, 64, 73
Horacek, J., 513, 544
Horn, E., 528, 543
Horn, W., 57, 72, 417, 437
Hornby, G., 184, 202
Horner, R. H., 183, 185, 200, 201, 202
Horowitz, M. J., 166, 177
Horton, G. T., 396, 411
Horvath, A. O., 566, 574
Horwood, L. J., 563, 573, 653, 655, 677
Hossain, Z., 66, 72
Hoube, J., 3, 19, 28
Houck, G. M., 277, 285
Houston, H. L. A., 247, 255
Howanitz, P., 47, 53
Howe, G. W., 666, 672, 679
Howell, C. T., 150, 151, 156, 158, 234, 237, 256, 280, 287, 552, 571, 576
Howell, D. C., 151, 158
Howell, E., 374, 385
Howes, C., 343, 344, 349, 357, 358, 359, 360, 511, 544, 567, 574, 594, 595, 608
Howes, S. R., 218, 225
Howley, E., 489, 507
Hoyson, M., 187, 191, 201
Hubbard, J. J., 67, 68, 73
Hubbell, R., 15, 28, 552, 574
Huber, C., 277, 285
Huberman, A. M., 495, 507
Hudson, M., 39, 51
Huffman, K., 460, 483

Hughes, M., 473, 477, 480
Hull, C. E., 39, 53
Hull, K. M., 461, 463, 479
Hultsch, D. F., 659, 677
Human, M. T., 236, 255
Humby, T., 218, 224, 226
Humphrey, S., 328, 329, 336
Humphrey, T., 211, 224
Humphries, B., 490, 506
Hunt, J. McV., 14, 28, 47, 51, 259, 289, 636, 648, 657, 677
Hunter, A. G., 60, 72
Hunter, W. M., 322, 324
Huntington, D. S., 633, 647
Huntington, G. S., 301, 306, 455, 478, 532, 542
Hurlburt, N., 231, 256
Hurley, O. L., 387, 412
Hurry, J., 668, 681
Hurwitz, I., 47, 50, 52
Huston, A., 96, 106, 112, 614, 615, 627
Hutchins, D. E., 298, 307
Hutchison, T., 247, 255
Huttenlocher, P. R., 210, 214, 217, 224
Hutton, S., 617, 627
Hwang, C. P., 623, 624, 626, 627
Hyman, C. S., 398, 412

Iannaleone, S. T., 39, 51
Iannotti, R. J., 563, 577
Idjradinata, P., 48, 52
Ignatoff, E., 63, 72, 266, 285, 553, 554, 573
Immel, N., 533, 542
Innis, R. B., 216, 223
Innocenti, M. S., 460, 482, 596, 609
Ireton, H., 235, 248, 255
Ireys, H. T., 21, 28
Irwin, N., 386
Isaacs, C., 420, 436
Isaacs-Shockley, M., 425, 436
Isbell, P., 532, 542
Isoub, S., 45, 51
Itard, 9
Ito, J., 40, 52
Ivins, B., 233, 235, 257, 464, 466, 467, 475, 480, 483
Iwata, B. A., 185, 201

Jaccard, J., 144, 158
Jacklin, C. N., 656, 669, 678
Jackson, A., 569, 576
Jackson, B., 390, 410
Jacobs, B., 212, 224
Jacobs, F. H., 291, 294, 296, 301, 307, 449, 453, 498, 506
Jacobs, V., 525, 543

Jacobson, J. L., 61, 72
Jacobson, N., 309, 311, 323
Jacobson, S. W., 61, 72, 552, 553, 574, 580
Jaffe, J., 264, 288
Jahoda, G., 488, 506
James, C. B., 70, 74
James, D., 67, 69, 74, 552, 553, 554, 574, 580, 603, 608
Jamieson, B., 187, 191, 201
Janas, M. S., 211, 224
Jandera, E., 333, 337
Janis, I. L., 633, 648
Jarosinski, J., 64, 72
Jarrett, R. B., 109, 112, 252, 255
Jenkins, C. D., 659, 677
Jenkins, J. N., 538, 539, 543, 545, 666, 677
Jenkins, V., 303, 306
Jenkins, W. M., 220, 225, 226
Jennings, K. D., 59, 72
Jens, K. G., 188, 199, 262, 285
Jeppson, E. S., 638, 650
Jeremy, R. J., 237, 254
Jerger, S., 43, 51
Jernigan, T. L., 214, 224
Jessell, T. M., 206, 207, 208, 224
Jestin, C., 620, 628
Jimenez, E., 47, 52
Joanning, H., 295, 307, 631, 639, 649
Jobse, J., 259, 288
Jodry, W., 293, 294, 306
Johanson, C., 397, 404, 411, 457, 479
Johnson, B. H., 467, 481, 638, 640, 641, 648, 649, 650
Johnson, C., 639, 647
Johnson, D. L., 417, 436, 555, 556, 571, 583
Johnson, D. R., 44, 52, 94, 95, 113, 368, 373, 374, 384, 385, 386, 515, 524, 544, 547, 556, 563, 572
Johnson, F., 333, 337
Johnson, H. L., 116, 125, 131, 184, 202
Johnson, J. L., 116, 132
Johnson, L. F., 14, 185, 200, 535, 544
Johnson, L. L., 247, 255
Johnson, N., 188, 199, 262, 285
Johnson, W. F., 164, 165, 176
Johnson-Crowley, N., 153, 159, 277, 282
Johnston, K., 424, 436
Johnston, M., 104, 105, 112
Johnston, P., 220, 225
Johnston, W. P., 41, 52
Jones, B., 212, 224
Jones, G. H., 216, 218, 224, 226

Jones, H., 537, 548
Jones, K., 216, 224
Jones, O. H. M., 263, 285
Jones, O. W., 107, 111
Jones, S., 469, 480
Jones, T. A., 218, 223
Joosten, J., 259, 288
Jordan, C., 489, 508
Judd, C. M., 658, 678
Juffer, F., 553, 566, 576
Juraska, J. M., 218, 224

Kaas, J. H., 219, 225
Kaczmarek, L., 537, 548
Kafer, L., 530, 543
Kaftarian, S. J., 492, 506
Kagan, J., 162, 165, 176, 177, 178
Kagan, S. L., 22, 25, 90, 92, 396, 412, 426, 433, 436, 497, 508, 511, 544, 550, 567, 568, 574, 597, 608, 613, 624, 627
Kagitcibasi, C., 603, 608
Kahn, A. J., 6, 28, 83, 92, 331, 335, 337, 354, 358, 368, 384, 555, 556, 571, 583, 613, 614, 615, 616, 617, 618, 619, 621, 623, 624, 625, 626, 628
Kaiser, A. P., 181, 186, 187, 201, 202, 203, 458, 480, 537, 544, 548
Kaiser, M., 277, 283
Kaiser, P., 121, 131, 670, 681
Kakalik, J. S., 396, 410, 592, 593, 594, 608
Kalafat, J., 441, 453
Kalkoske, M., 563, 573
Kalmanson, B., 233, 256, 267, 268, 286, 398, 413, 457, 480
Kalyanpur, M., 236, 255, 632, 648
Kamerman, S. B., 6, 28, 83, 92, 331, 335, 337, 354, 358, 568, 574
Kamii, C. K., 598, 609
Kamin, L., 9, 28
Kaminski, R., 247, 254
Kammradt, G., 211, 224
Kanawati, A. A., 216, 227
Kandel, E. R., 206, 207, 208, 224
Kang, R. R., 263, 286, 288
Kanner, L., 635, 648
Kaplan, L., 641, 648
Kaplan, N., 666, 678
Kaplan, W. E., 41, 52
Kaplan-Sanoff, M., 61, 62, 71, 72, 154, 159, 335, 338, 417, 436
Karnes, M. B., 634, 649, 650
Karoly, L. A., 3, 19, 28
Karrer, B., 100, 112
Kasari, C., 301, 306
Kashden, J., 43, 51

Kassebaum, N., 518, 519, 545
Kaston, A. J., 97, 113
Katz, L. F., 146, 158
Katz, R., 632, 642, 645, 646, 648
Katz-Leavy, J., 425, 436
Kauffman, C., 639, 649
Kauffman, R., 467, 481
Kaufmann, R. K., 641, 649
Kavale, K. A., 430, 435
Kavanagh, K., 438
Kaye, K., 164, 177, 261, 262, 286
Kaylor, B., 472, 481
Kayne, H., 46, 53
Kazdin, A. E., 419, 436, 566, 574
Keane, W. M., 259, 285
Keenan, N. L., 277, 285
Keener, M. A., 277, 289
Keesee, P., 22, 28
Keetz, A., 186, 201, 537, 544
Kelley, J. B., 116, 120, 122, 124, 126, 132
Kelly, J. F., 20, 502, 597
Kelly, K., 531, 547
Kempe, C. H., 553, 554, 573, 579
Kempen, H. J. G., 161, 177
Kemper, K. J., 238, 248, 255, 332, 338
Kemper, M., 39, 51
Kendall, D. A., 218, 224
Kendall, K. A., 185, 202
Kendall, P., 419, 437
Kendler, K. S., 668, 669, 677
Keniston, K., 81, 92
Kennedy, C. H., 185, 201
Kennedy, J. F., 14
Kennedy, S., 617, 627
Kennedy, W. A., 12, 27, 137, 156
Kenny, D. A., 564, 571
Keogh, B. K., xi, xii, 299, 306
Ker, C., 560, 573
Kernberg, O. F., 163, 177
Kerns, G. M., 22, 28, 397, 410, 456, 479
Kerr, B., 489, 504
Kessel, S., 328, 337
Kessler, R. C., 668, 669, 677
Ketterlinus, R. D., 60, 74
Kettler, K., 298, 299, 307
Kety, S., 40, 52
Key, T., 40, 52
Keyes, L., 500, 504
Keys, C., 642, 645, 647
Kieffer, C. H., 632, 644, 645, 648
Kiely, K., 657, 675
Kiernan, K. E., 666, 676
Kihlstrom, J. F., 166, 177
Kilborn, P. T., 82, 92
Kilburn, M. R., 3, 19, 28

Kilgo, J., 455, 474, 477, 480, 639, 649
Kilkey, M., 617, 627
Killcross, S. S., 218, 226
Killion, J. P., 472, 481
Killoran, J., 596, 609
Kilty, K. M., 490, 491, 507
Kim, K., 537, 548
Kindlon, D. J., 258, 289, 318, 321, 323, 324, 521, 548
King, N. J., 667, 679
King, P., 69, 71
King, R. A., 165, 178
King, R. E., 558, 559, 576, 587
King, T. L., 47, 53
Kirgis, C. A., 277, 286
Kirk, S. A., 12, 28
Kirsch, A., 330, 337
Kisker, E., 341, 344, 349, 358, 359, 360, 570, 574
Kisthardt, W. E., 631, 636, 648
Kitzman, H. K., xi, xii, 67, 69, 74, 81, 92, 331, 337, 441, 453, 550, 552, 553, 554, 564, 566, 567, 570, 574, 575, 580, 603, 608, 609
Kitzman, R. N., 66, 69, 74
Kjerland, L., 631, 649
Klaus, R., 518, 544
Klebanoff, M. A., 224
Klebanov, P. K., 153, 156, 231, 241, 254, 309, 311, 323, 372, 384, 421, 437, 519, 520, 522, 543 552, 555, 563, 565, 567, 569, 570, 572, 573, 574, 583, 614, 615, 627
Klein, N. K., 22, 398, 412
Klein, P., 47, 52
Klerman, L., 362, 385
Kliegman, R. M., 335, 338
Klinger, C., 110, 111
Klinger, L., 535
Klinnert, M. D., 56, 75
Klohnen, P. C., 115, 131
Knapp, D. S., 187, 202
Knauer, D., 170, 176
Knecht, S., 219, 223
Knitzer, J., 21, 25, 352, 353, 358, 381, 383, 385, 409, 412, 567
Knobloch, H., 329, 337
Knoll, J., 642, 647
Knoll, J. H. M., 39, 52
Knorr-Cetina, K., 491, 506
Knowles, M., 476, 481
Knowlton, A., 22, 28
Knowlton, S., 184, 185, 201
Knox, R. M., 167, 176
Koch, D. B., 220, 222, 224
Koch, R., 13, 27, 30, 636, 649
Koch, T., 44, 45, 52

Kochanek, T. T., 21, 28, 239, 240, 255, 390, 397, 399, 400, 401, 403, 405, 407, 412, 413, 497, 506, 528, 545
Kochanska, G., 66, 75, 165, 177
Koegel, L. K., 185, 201
Koegel, R. L., 185, 201
Koegler, S. J., 636, 649
Kohen, D., 565, 570, 575
Kohler, F. W., 187, 201
Kohn, M. L., 60, 72, 143, 158
Kohut, H., 65, 73
Kolb, B., 218, 224
Koller, H., 12, 29
Kolvin, I., 657, 678
Kolvin, P. A., 657, 678
Koniak-Griffin, D., 270, 286
Kontos, S., 15, 29, 343, 349, 357, 460, 464, 468, 469, 470, 474, 475, 480, 481, 528, 544
Koplow, L., 101, 112
Kopp, C., 262, 286
Korbin, J. E., 104, 105, 112
Koretz, D., 430, 436
Korfmacher, J., 552, 553, 554, 566, 568, 573, 574, 581
Korner, A. F., 259, 286
Korsch, B., 331, 337
Koslowski, B., 259, 261, 283
Kostelny, K., 62, 72, 87, 89, 92
Kotary, L., 145, 146, 157
Kotulak, R., ix, xii
Kovach, J., 631, 649
Kozloff, M. A., 181, 184, 187, 201
Kraemer, H., 519, 520, 543, 547
Krakow, J., 262, 286
Kram, K., 47, 53
Kramer, E. J., 39, 52
Kramer, J. J., 239, 257
Kramer, L., 471, 479
Kraus, N., 220, 222, 224
Krauskoph, D., 47, 52
Krauss, M. W., 4, 19, 20, 22, 23, 28, 30, 258, 262, 275, 277, 280, 288, 401, 413, 501, 502, 503, 506, 507, 526, 529, 530, 547, 594, 604, 609, 638, 649, 650
Kraut, A. M., 102, 107, 112
Krauthausen, I., 211, 224
Kremen, A. M., 122, 130
Kretschmann, J.-J., 211, 224
Krieger, N., 98, 106, 112
Kritek, P. B., 644, 649
Krivit, D., 637, 649
Kromkowski, J., 86, 89, 92
Krugman, R. D., 331, 337, 550, 574, 613, 628
Krugman, S., 43, 51
Krupnick, J., 66, 75

Kuban, K., 48, 49, 52
Kubicek, L., 175, 176
Kubisch, A. T., 171, 176
Kuczynski, L., 66, 74, 165, 177
Kuh, D., 666, 678
Kuhl, P. K., 221, 224, 225
Kuhn, C. M., 150, 157
Kuhnert, P., 47, 52
Kupersmidt, J., 419, 421, 423, 429, 435, 436
Kurtines, W. M., 95, 100, 114
Kysela, G., 597, 609

Lacerda, F., 221, 225
LaCroix, B., 464, 479
Ladd, K. L., 664, 682
Ladmer, L. A., 465, 481
Ladner, J., 443, 453
LaDue, R. A., 45, 53
LaFasto, F. M., 404, 413
LaForme, C., 298, 306
LaFromboise, T., 110, 112
Lalande, M., 39, 52
Lally, J. R., 69, 73, 370, 375, 385, 515, 544, 603, 609, 613, 628
Lamb, M. E., 57, 64, 73, 564, 574, 623, 624, 627
Lamkin, R. P., 309, 311, 323
Lande, J., 350, 359
Landesman, S., 144, 158
Landesman-Ramey, S., xi, xii
Lang, K. A., 39, 53
Lang, L. L., 397, 399, 400, 401, 413
Lange, L., 262, 285
Langer, S. N., 185, 202
Lansverk, J., 322, 324
Laosa, L. M., 100, 101, 112, 347, 358
LaPointe, N., 648
Larbig, W., 219, 223
Larkin, K., 666, 678
Larner, M. B., 103, 114, 343, 347, 357, 358, 449, 452, 516, 547, 603, 604, 607
Larsen, A., 456, 482, 666, 678
Larson, C. E., 404, 413
Larson, C. P., 552, 553, 554, 574, 580
Larson, C. S., 550, 573
Larson, J. C., 527, 531, 545
Larsson, E. V., 185, 201
Lasater, T. M., 368, 384, 555, 556, 571, 583
Lassegard, E., 348, 358
Latt, S. A., 39, 52
Lau, C., 216, 225
Lau, L., 518, 543
Laub, J. H., 653, 656, 664, 678, 681
Laucht, M., 65, 73
Laudet, A. B., 61, 73

Lauritzen, V., 596, 608
LaVange, L. M., 519, 520, 546, 555, 566, 570, 576
Lavav, I., 313, 323
Lave, J., 110, 112
Lavee, Y., 293, 307
Lavigne, J. V., 248, 255, 420, 436
Lavin, R., 61, 73
Lavor, M., 637, 649
Law, T., 666, 672, 679
Lawler, P., 476, 481
Lawson, S., 246, 257
Layzer, J. I., 361, 371, 372, 375, 384, 386, 442, 452, 557, 558, 569, 570, 576, 591, 592, 597, 609
Lazar, I., 15, 28, 516, 545, 552, 569, 574
Lazarus, L., 47, 53
Lazarus, R. S., 652, 678
Leach, P., 25
Leavell, H. R., 136, 158
Leavitt, L. A., 262, 288
Leckie, M. S., 266, 283
LeCours, A.-R., 214, 226
Lee, I. M., 461, 483, 631, 639, 640, 649, 650
Lee, K., 565, 569, 570, 572, 574, 583
Lee, L., 347, 358
Lee, V. E., 503, 507, 518, 519, 545
Leech, R. W., 36, 43
Leet, H. E., 302, 306
LeFurgy, W., 532, 543
Legg, S. M., 252, 256
LeLaurin, K., 502, 507
Lemann, N., 81, 92
Lemire, P. J., 36, 43
Lemyre, L., 667, 676
Lennard, H. L., 161, 177
Lentz, F. E., Jr., 187, 202
Leonard, G., 266, 285
Leonard, K. E., 61, 71
Leoser, J. D., 36, 43
Leprince, F., 623, 628
Lerman, R. I., 57, 73
Lerner, M., 59, 71
Lerner, R. M., 487, 488, 489, 507
Lesser, A. J., 7, 8, 16, 29
Lester, B. M., 61, 62, 73, 94, 113, 266, 286
Levene, M. I., 49, 52
Levenson, S. M., 46, 53
Levenstein, P., 363, 552, 553, 575, 582
Leventhal, T., 551, 568, 574
Levin, H., 590, 597, 609
Levin, V. S., 500, 507
Levine, J. A., 57, 73
Levine, M., 328, 338
Levine, R., 94, 108, 112, 113

Levine, S., 216, 218, 226, 657, 677, 681
Leviton, A., 48, 49, 52, 328, 338, 639, 649
Levy, D. R., 107, 113
Levy, J. A., 63, 64, 71, 266, 284
Lewin, K., 309, 311, 324
Lewis, A. C., 638, 647
Lewis, C. C., 248, 257
Lewis, E., 60, 75
Lewis, H., 535, 546
Lewis, I., 519, 520, 547, 566, 570, 576
Lewis, M., 258, 259, 261, 263, 284, 286, 380, 385, 569, 575
Lewis, M. D., 419, 436
Lewis, M. L., 63, 72
Lewitt, E. M., 334, 336, 343, 357, 550, 573, 575
Lewontin, R. C., 98, 113
Liang, X., 343, 357
Liaw, F. R., 3, 12, 19, 29, 153, 156, 247, 256, 261, 286, 328, 337, 372, 384, 511, 518, 519, 520, 521, 522, 526, 530, 541, 543, 545, 554, 555, 565, 566, 567, 569, 572, 575, 605, 609
Liberty, K. A., 185, 201
Lieberman, A. F., 152, 154, 158, 261, 283, 419, 436, 467, 481, 553, 563, 570, 575, 580
Lieberman, M. A., 293, 307, 659, 678
Liebman, J. L., 527, 528, 545
Lifter, K., 535, 545
Lilienfeld, A. M., 11, 29
Lillie, T., 20, 28
Lincoln, Y. S., 490, 491, 492, 496, 506, 507
Lindblom, B., 221, 225
Linder, T. W., 232, 234, 235, 241, 255, 390, 398, 399, 413, 414, 409, 411, 457, 458, 481
Lindgren, B., 47, 51
Lingerfelt, B., 456, 460, 479
Lingerfelt, V. V., 461, 479
Link, G., 422, 423, 436
Linn, R. L., 252, 255
Linver, M., 565, 570, 575
Lippman, C., 455, 473, 479
Lipsey, M., x, xii
Lipsky, D. K., 10, 21, 28
Lipsky, M., 497, 507
Lipton, E. L., 260, 288
Lipton, R. C., 12, 29
List, A., 47, 51
Lister, L., 373, 386, 423, 438
Little, C., 64, 72
Little, R. E., 45, 50
Little, W. J., 48
Livingston, K., 541, 545

Livingston, R., 47, 52
Llada, V., 212, 224
Llewellyn, J., 333, 337
Lloreda, P., 47, 52
Lloyd, J. W., 185, 202
Lloyd, P., 560, 575, 587
Lloyd-Still, J. D., 47, 52, 216, 225
Lobb, C., 528, 529, 547
Lobo, M. L., 277, 282, 286
Lochman, J. E., 419, 436
Locke, J., 4
Loeb, S., 518, 545
Loeber, R., 140, 159, 652, 655, 676, 681
Loerber, R., 419, 436
Loewald, H. W., 174, 177
Logan, A., 258, 283
Logue, M. E., 418, 436
Lombardi, J., 345, 348, 349, 350, 358
Long, B., 417, 435
Long, J. V. F., 664, 678
Longstreth, L. E., 265, 286
Lopez, M., 371, 386
Lopez, S. R., 97, 98, 111
Lorber, J., 42, 52
Lorenz, F. O., 565, 573, 653, 676
Lorion, R., 62, 73
Lösel, F., 663, 678
Lourie, I. S., 425, 436
Lovaas, O. I., 190, 201, 202, 534, 535, 545
Love, J. M., 340, 344, 358, 418, 421, 436, 550, 567, 569, 573, 575, 592, 609
Lowe, J., 47, 53
Lowe, L. W., 186, 200
Lowitzer, C., 531, 546
Lowman, B., 409, 410
Lozoff, B., 47, 52
Lubin, A., 47, 53
Luborsky, L., 566, 574
Luby, J., 418, 436
Luckey, D. W., xi, xii, 67, 69, 74, 81, 92, 552, 553, 554, 567, 574, 575, 580, 603, 608, 609
Ludlow, B. L., 458, 477, 479, 481
Luiselli, J. K., 184, 201
Lunghofer, L., 312, 324
Luria, A. R., 215, 225
Luster, T., 265, 266, 284, 666, 676
Luthar, S. S., 115, 131, 140, 157, 418, 419, 427, 428, 437, 651, 652, 654, 663, 669, 670, 678
Lynch, E. C., 420, 434
Lynch, E. W., 241, 255, 269, 285, 456, 475, 481, 490, 507
Lynch, M., 39, 52, 55, 73
Lynskey, M. T., 563, 573, 653, 655, 657, 677

Lyons, C., 519, 548, 563, 566, 570, 576
Lyons, N. B., 262, 277, 286
Lyons-Ruth, K., 67, 73, 418, 437, 553, 563, 570, 575, 580

Maccoby, E. E., 109, 113, 564, 575, 656, 665, 669, 678
MacDonald, R. F., 185, 202
MacDonald, S., 330, 337
Mace, F. C., 184, 201
Macfarlane, A., 333, 337
MacGregor, J., 47, 52
Mack, D., 44, 52
MacLean, E., 329, 336
Maclean, M., 666, 678
MacMann, G. M., 241, 243, 253
MacMillan, D. L., xi, xii, 430, 435
MacMillan, R. and M., 5
MacPhee, D., 59, 60, 73, 265, 289
MACRO, 418, 420, 437
MacTurk, R. H., 164, 177
Madden, J., 552, 553, 575, 582
Madden, T. C., 218, 224
Maes, H., 655, 676
Magee, E. M., 7, 29
Magenis, R. E., 39, 52
Magito-McLaughlin, D., 183, 200
Magnuson, K., 13, 317
Maguin, E., 140, 159, 652, 681
Magyary, G. S., 554, 563, 566, 570, 571, 581
Mahler, M. S., 163, 165, 177
Mahoney, A. W., 216, 227
Mahoney, G., 186, 200, 264, 267, 275, 276, 279, 280, 283, 286, 457, 458, 460, 481, 528, 529, 532, 545, 641, 649
Main, M., 64, 73, 144, 147, 152, 172, 177, 259, 261, 283, 666, 678
Mallory, B., 475, 481
Malone, A., 329, 337
Malone, D. M., 4, 28
Malone, P. E., 368, 384, 555, 556, 571, 583
Malphurs, J., 66, 72
Manciaux, M., 620, 628
Mandelbaum, A., 633, 649
Mangione, P. L., 69, 73, 370, 375, 385, 603, 609
Mann, E., 19, 29
Mansergh, G. P., 3, 26
Mantovani, S., 624, 626
Marans, S., 70, 73, 419, 436
Marburger, C. L., 347, 357
March, J. G., 394, 413
Marcus, J., 237, 254
Marfo, K., 263, 275, 279, 280, 283, 286, 526, 530, 545, 597, 609

Margolis, L. H., 8, 29
Margura, S., 61, 73
Marjinksy, K. A. T., 147, 157
Mark, M. M., 494, 507
Markman, J. J., 417, 435
Markowitz, J. B., 527, 531, 545
Marks, N. F., 135, 158
Marlowe, N., 653, 676
Marquis, J. G., 294, 308
Marsden, C. A., 218, 224
Marsden, D. B., 247, 256
Marshall, C., 402, 413
Marshall, P. C., 13, 21, 217
Marshall, R., 103, 107, 114
Martell, L. K., 262, 282
Martier, S. S., 61, 72
Martin, C., 460, 483
Martin, D. G., 400, 410
Martin, E. W., 15, 29, 328, 329, 336
Martin, H., 87, 92
Martin, J. A., 109, 113, 564, 575
Martin, N., 121, 131
Martinez, P., 62, 74
Martinson, M. C., 413
Martois, J., 558, 576
Marx, E., 348, 359
Marx, F., 510, 545
Marzke, C., 351, 358
Mason, C. A., 60, 72
Masten, A. S., 67, 68, 69, 73, 74, 115, 116, 131, 140, 157, 652, 658, 665, 666, 673, 678, 680
Mastropieri, M. A., 533, 545, 604, 608
Matheson, C., 490, 508
Mathew, R. M., 322, 324
Mattis, S. G., 266, 286
Maude, S., 454, 481
Maughan, B., 654, 655, 656, 662, 666, 668, 671, 672, 678, 679, 680
Mavrogenes, N., 522, 523, 546
Maxwell, J. A., 495, 507
Maxwell, K., 179, 190, 200, 409, 410
Mayes, L. C., 61, 62, 73
Maynard, R., 569, 571
Mazmanian, D. A., 402, 413
Mazoni, T., 387, 410
McAdams, D. P., 145, 158
McAdoo, H. P., 60, 73, 97, 113
McAllister, C., 568, 573
McAuley, J. B., 44, 52
McAvity, K. J., 146, 156
McBride, S. L., 295, 307, 460, 462, 463, 481, 631, 639, 649
McCall, R. B., 173, 177, 231, 256, 488, 507, 529, 545
McCarthy, G., 216, 223
McCartney, K., 489, 507
McCartney, L., 123, 128, 132
McCartney, M., 346, 349, 359

McCarton, C. M., 372, 384, 385, 520, 521, 522, 543, 545, 551, 552, 555, 556, 562, 563, 564, 565, 566, 567, 568, 571, 572, 574, 575, 583, 604, 609
McCauley, E., 40, 52
McClearn, G. E., 658, 669, 679
McClelland, G. H., 658, 678
McClelland, P., 82, 83, 92
McClish, D., 47, 52
McClone, D. G., 41, 42, 52
McCollum, J. A., 258, 268, 286, 288, 454, 455, 457, 463, 465, 466, 467, 468, 470, 474, 477, 481, 483
McConahay, J. B., 106, 113
McConkey, C., 552, 569, 575
McConnell, S. R., 186, 191, 202, 295, 297, 306
McConnochie, K. M., 552, 553, 554, 574, 580, 603, 608
McConnochie, M., 67, 69, 74
McCord, J., 666, 668, 678
McCormick, K., 245, 257, 258, 287
McCormick, M. C., 372, 384, 385, 520, 521, 522, 543, 545, 551, 552, 555, 556, 562, 563, 564, 565, 566, 567, 568, 570, 571, 572, 574, 575, 583, 604, 609
McCrary, C., 653, 675
McCubbin, H. I., 97, 113, 293, 307, 456, 482
McCubbin, M. A., 97, 113
McCullough, P., 42, 52
McCune, L., 233, 256, 398, 413
McDermott, R., 99, 102, 113
McDonough, S. C., 94, 113, 153, 154, 158, 270, 287
McEachin, J. J., 190, 202, 534, 545
McEvoy, M. A., 186, 202
McEwan, M., 530, 543
McFarland, C., 43, 51
McFarlane, E. C., 554, 573
McGann, T., 374, 386
McGee, F., 439, 453
McGee, T. J., 220, 222, 224
McGillicuddy-De Lisi, A. V., 143, 159
McGimsey, B., 345, 348, 349, 350, 358
McGinnis, J., 541, 545
McGoldrick, M., 144, 158, 456, 479
McGonigel, M. J., 398, 399, 408, 411, 413, 415, 467, 481, 641, 649
McGrath, M. M., 266, 286
McGrath, S. K., 231, 254
McGuide, P. A., 248, 255
McGuinness, D., 667, 681
McGuire, J., 311, 323
McGuire, S., 656, 679
McKay, A., 47, 52
McKay, H. D., 47, 52, 313, 324

McKenna, P., 180, 202, 387, 388, 414
McKey, R. H., 552, 569, 575
McKnew, D., 66, 75
McKnight, J., 390, 399, 413
McLanahan, S. S., 135, 158
McLaren, D. S., 216, 227
McLaughlin, M., 528, 544
McLaughlin, T. F., 184, 203
McLean, M. E., 245, 257, 258, 287, 397, 398, 399, 401, 407, 408, 414, 454, 458, 482, 634, 649
McLeod, R., 44, 52, 53
McLinden, S. E., 245, 256
McLoyd, V. C., 57, 59, 60, 73, 95, 96, 106, 112, 113, 266, 287, 418, 420, 565, 569, 575
McNaughton, D., 500, 507
McNulty, B. A., 396, 404, 408, 412, 413
McQuire, P., 104, 111
McWilliam, P. J., 408, 413, 638, 639, 647
McWilliam, R. A., 21, 25, 295, 297, 305, 457, 458, 469, 481, 567, 640, 641, 646, 649
McWorter, G. A., 101, 113
Meckstroth, A. L., 340, 344, 358
Meenaghan, T. M., 490, 491, 507
Meezan, W., 77, 92
Mehana, M., 522, 523, 546
Meier, P., 44, 52
Meinart, C. L., 372, 384, 385, 520, 521, 522, 532, 543, 545, 546, 555, 556, 565, 572, 583, 604, 609
Meisels, S. J., 103, 261, 269, 270, 285, 286, 301, 306, 328, 329, 337, 346, 358, 387, 389, 390, 398, 407, 411, 414, 416, 437, 455, 456, 469, 474, 480, 481, 502, 507, 511, 521, 522, 526, 527, 530, 545, 547, 554, 566, 567, 575, 605, 609, 613, 628, 654, 658, 678, 681
Mejta, C. L., 61, 73
Mekos, M., 346, 349, 359
Melda, K., 642, 647
Melhuish, E., 623, 628
Melton, S., 400, 401, 405, 414
Meltzer, L., 243, 256
Menaghan, E., 293, 307
Merritt, J. D., 41, 52
Merzenich, M. M., 220, 225, 226
Mesaros, R. A., 185, 200
Mesibov, G., 534, 546
Messick, S., 252, 256
Messinger, E., 101, 112
Metheson, C. C., 97, 114
Mets, M., 44, 52
Meunier, M., 211, 225

Meurer, J. R., 335, 338
Meyer, E. C., 94, 99, 100, 102, 103, 104, 105, 108, 112, 113
Meyer, J. M., 654, 655, 656, 662, 666, 668, 671, 676, 680, 681
Meyer, K. A., 185, 201
Meyerhoff, M., 524, 545
Michael, J., 183, 202
Mick, E., 657, 675
Miedel, W., 19, 29
Mikulecky, L., 560, 575, 587
Milberger, S., 657, 675
Miles, M., 495, 507
Miller, A., 83, 87, 92
Miller, C. A., 455, 478, 619, 629
Miller, E., 43, 52, 487, 507
Miller, F. J. W., 657, 678
Miller, J. H., 87, 93, 246, 254
Miller, L. J., 267, 287, 352, 353, 358
Miller, M., 184, 202
Miller, M. D., 252, 256
Miller, N., 456, 482
Miller, P., 145, 158, 454, 474, 482
Miller, S. L., 220, 225, 226, 464, 480, 634, 635, 648
Miller, T., 330, 337
Miller-Heyl, J., 59, 60, 73
Milliken, G. W., 219, 220, 225
Mills, A., 656, 662, 671, 679
Mills, K., 667, 668, 676
Mills, P., 538, 539, 543, 545
Miltenberger, R. G., 185, 199
Minuchin, S., 170, 177, 456, 482
Miranda, P. L., 185, 200
Mishkin, M., 212, 219, 222, 223, 224, 225
Mistry, J. J., 94, 97, 110, 113
Mitchell, A., 348, 352, 358
Mitchell, D. E., 402, 413
Mitchell, S. K., 259, 260, 261, 262, 263, 282, 283, 288, 552, 554, 556, 563, 564, 566, 570, 571, 572, 581
Mito, T., 210, 226
Mittal, M., 396, 397, 399, 400, 412, 413
Mlawer, M. A., 642, 649
Mocan, N., 511, 544
Modigliani, K., 21, 29, 387, 390, 398, 414, 455, 481
Moen, P., 82, 91
Moffitt, T. E., 655, 671, 677, 678
Montessori, M., 5
Montie, J. E., 231, 254
Moore, B. B., 145, 158
Moore, E. K., 342, 352, 358
Moore, S. M., 641, 647
Mora, L., 47, 52

Morelli, G., 94, 109, 110, 113, 489, 507
Morelli, M., 535, 544
Morenoff, J., 321, 324
Morgan, B. L. G., 215, 225
Morgan, G. A., 6, 29, 164, 177, 258, 287, 345, 348, 349, 350, 358
Morgan, K., 418, 436
Morgan, P., 63, 72
Morgan, S. P., 116, 117, 122, 123, 124, 127, 131, 157, 265, 266, 285, 665, 677
Moriarty, A. E., 68, 74, 117, 120, 131, 652, 679
Morisset, C. E., 151, 156, 234, 237, 253, 256, 258, 260, 265, 267, 276, 277, 282, 286, 287, 418, 422, 423, 434
Morley, D., 332, 337
Morley, L., 654, 677
Moroney, R. M., 294, 307
Morris, A., 187, 202
Morris, J., 511, 544
Morris, P., xi, xii, 81, 82, 85, 92, 552, 553, 554, 567, 570, 575, 580, 603, 609
Morris, P. A., 502, 505
Morrison, D. R., 666, 676
Morrison, P., 665, 666, 678
Morrow, C., 65, 66, 72
Mortimore, P., 671, 672, 679, 680
Moser, H., 40, 52
Mosher, E., 532, 546
Mosier, C., 97, 113
Moskovitz, S., 116, 123, 124, 125, 126, 131
Moss, B., 467, 482
Moss, H. A., 259, 287
Moss, P. A., 252, 256, 621, 623, 628
Moss, V., 3, 30
Most, R., 258, 283
Mounts, L., 247, 254
Mousetis, L., 537, 548
Moxley, A., 43, 51
Mozaffarian, D., 216, 226
Mrazek, P. J., 417, 420, 437
MRC Vitamin Study Research Group, 41, 52
Mueller, M., 639, 649
Muenchow, S., 15, 31, 364, 365, 386
Mullan, J., 292, 293, 294, 307
Mullick, J. A., 241, 253
Mulvihill, B. A., 561, 575, 575, 587
Mundfrom, D., 520, 542
Munn, D., 244, 246, 253, 396, 397, 399, 400, 412, 413
Munson, L. J., 275, 287
Munson, S. M., 244, 253
Murphy, D. L., 294, 308

Murphy, L. B., 68, 70, 74, 120, 131, 652, 679
Murphy, L. O., 248, 257
Murray, E. A., 211, 225
Murray, H., 552, 569, 574
Murray, L., 65, 66, 73
Murray, S., 523, 524, 547
Murray-Garcia, J., 335, 337
Murrow, N. S., 164, 177
Musatti, T., 624, 628
Muse, B., 332, 336
Musick, J. S., 22, 116, 120, 124, 126, 131, 278, 287, 378, 385, 567
Muxen, M., 456, 482
Myers, G., 43, 53
Myers, R. G., 603, 604, 609

Nabors, L. A., 343, 357
Nader, P., 47, 52
Nagarajan, S. S., 220, 226
Nagin, D. S., 664, 678
Nakagawa, K., 94, 95, 113
Nakagawa, M., 278, 288
Nakashima, C., 95, 96, 98, 99, 106, 112
Naqvi, M., 277, 288
Nathanielsz, P. W., 150, 158
Natiello, P., 631, 632, 645, 649
Nauta, M., 386, 592, 609
Naylor, A., 6, 29
Naylor, N., 367, 375, 377, 379, 385
Neale, J., 617, 627
Neale, M. C., 655, 668, 669, 676, 677
Nebrig, J., 375, 385
Needelman, R., 332, 337
Neeman, J., 652, 678
Neiderhiser, J. M., 656, 669, 677
Neill, A. S., 4, 29
Neisworth, J. T., 21, 28, 149, 156, 191, 202, 239, 242, 244, 248, 250, 252, 253, 256, 329, 336, 390, 410
Nelson, C. A., 13, 25, 35, 38, 50, 52
Nelson, D. E., 456, 460, 461, 479
Nelson, D. L., 39, 53
Nelson, K. B., 36, 48, 51, 52, 259, 287
Nelson, M., 184, 202
Nelson, R. O., 252, 255
Nelson, R. P., 21, 28
Nelson, S. D., 94, 111
Nesselroade, J. R., 502, 504
Neuman, M. J., 22, 25, 567
Neuman, S. B., 4, 29
Neuwirth, S., 519, 547
Neville, H., 510, 545
Nevin, N. C., 41, 52, 53
New, R., 475, 481, 623, 628
Newborg, J. A., 243, 246, 256, 592, 609
Newcomb, S., 298, 299, 305, 307

Nicholls, J., 667, 681
Nichols, P. L., 12, 27, 29, 137, 156
Nichols, R. D., 39, 52
Nicholson, L., 332, 336
Nickel, R., 247, 257
Nicoll, A., 247, 255
Niego, S., 58, 59, 60, 71, 490, 507
Nightingale, C., 362, 385
Nihira, K., 489, 507
Niman, C., 262, 285
Nittoli, J. M., 440, 453
Nitz, K., 60, 74
Noblit, G., 409, 410
Noppe, I. C., 566, 573
Noppe, L. D., 566, 573
Nord, C. W., 239, 256
North, K., 37, 52
Northup, J., 185, 203
Norvez, A., 623, 628
Nover, R. A., 419, 430, 435
Nudo, R. J., 219, 220, 225
Nuechterlein, K., 652, 680
Nunez, J. A., 46, 51
Nurcombe, B., 150, 151, 156, 158, 234, 237, 256, 280, 287, 552, 571, 576
Nurius, P., 641, 642, 644, 648
Nyman, B. A., 266, 283
Nystrom, J., 150, 157

Obrzut, J. E., 245, 254
O'Connor, S., 327, 337
O'Connor, T. G., 654, 656, 666, 669, 672, 674, 679, 680, 681
Odom, S. L., 186, 202, 275, 287, 389, 390, 397, 398, 399, 401, 407, 408, 414, 454, 458, 482, 528, 543, 634, 649
O'Donnell, K., 455, 478, 532, 542
Oelwein, P., 531, 544
O'Flaherty, S., 333, 337
Ogbu, J. U., 95, 107, 108, 113
Ogier, R., 184, 202
Ogonosky, A. B., 248, 254
Oh, W., 64, 72, 94, 113, 266, 285
O'Hara, J., 552, 553, 575, 582
Ohlin, L., 315, 324
Ohlson, C., 8, 18, 29
Oitzl, M. S., 218, 226
Ojala, M., 348, 359
Olds, D. L., xi, xii, 66, 67, 69, 74, 81, 92, 331, 337, 441, 453, 550, 552, 553, 554, 564, 566, 567, 570, 574, 575, 580, 603, 608, 609
Ollendick, T. H., 667, 679
Oller, D. K., 262, 288
Olson, D. H., 293, 303, 307, 456, 482
Olson, J. P., 394, 413

Olson, K., 21, 29, 387, 390, 398, 414, 455, 481
Olson, L., 218, 223
Olson, S. L., 259, 261, 287
Olswang, L. B., 502, 507
Omaye, S. T., 216, 225
Ommaya, A. K., 219, 225
O'Neal, C. R., 551, 554, 567, 572
O'Neil, J. B., 211, 225
O'Neill, R. E., 185, 200, 202
Ooms, T., 347, 357, 366, 385
Oppenheim, D., 152, 158, 163, 175, 176, 232, 254
O'Reilly, C. D., 187, 202
Ormel, J., 654, 656, 668, 671, 680
Orzhekhovskaya, N. S., 215, 225
Osborn, L. M., 238, 248, 255, 332, 334, 336, 337
Osborn, S. G., 656, 679
Oski, F., 47, 53
Osmond, H., 633, 647
Osofsky, H. J., 64, 74
Osofsky, J. D., 13, 22, 25, 36, 258, 266, 284, 285, 287, 380, 385, 419, 437, 553, 554, 575, 581
Osterling, J., 534, 543
Ostrosky, M. M., 186, 202
O'Sullivan, P., 641, 649
Ouston, J., 671, 680
Overton, W. F., 490, 491, 507
Owen, A., 667, 681
Owen, G., 47, 53
Owen, J., 265, 286
Owen, M. T., 561, 575, 575, 587

Pachter, L., 334, 337
Pagano, B., 167, 176
Page, C. W., 408, 411
Page, S., 352, 353, 358, 381, 385, 409, 412, 422, 428, 430, 434, 436
Paget, K. D., 408, 411
Pakula, A., 532, 546
Palacio-Espapa, F., 170, 176
Paldino, A. M., 212, 225
Palfrey, C., 496, 497, 508
Palisano, R. J., 276, 287
Palkoff, R. L., 63, 71
Palm, G. F., 57, 74
Palmer, F. B., 532, 546
Palmer, J. L., 567, 574
Palmeri, S., 233, 235, 249, 256
Palsha, S., 455, 478
Pancoast, D., 86, 91
Pandya, D. N., 215, 225
Paneth, N., 49, 53
Panitz, P., 390, 411
Pantell, R. H., 248, 257
Pantev, C., 219, 221, 223

Papousek, H., 151, 158, 164, 177, 258, 287
Papousek, M., 151, 158, 164, 177
Pardo, 62, 72
Pargament, K. I., 146, 157
Park, C. L., 565, 576
Parke, R. D., 57, 74, 144, 147, 158
Parker, F. L., 347, 359, 417, 437
Parker, S. J., 46, 53, 66, 75, 154, 159, 233, 256, 334, 335, 338, 417, 436
Parkhurst, E., 11, 29
Parmelee, A. H., 137, 158, 294, 306, 636, 649
Parrish, T., 592, 609
Parson, G., 264, 288
Pasamanick, B., 11, 29, 76, 92
Pascal, C., 348, 359
Pascoe, J. M., 238, 248, 255
Pass, R. F., 43, 51
Pass, R., 43, 51, 53
Patel, D., 44, 52
Patterson, D. L., 260, 265, 286
Patterson, G. R., 148, 158, 419, 437, 651, 656, 666, 668, 672, 675, 679
Patterson, J. M., 6, 29, 293, 294, 307, 308
Patterson, M., 100, 113
Patton, D., 44, 52
Patton, M., 390, 414
Paull, S., 560, 570, 576
Pavenstedt, E., 87, 92
Pawl, J. H., 152, 154, 158, 379, 385, 419, 436, 457, 462, 482, 553, 563, 570, 575, 580
Pawlby, S. J., 656, 662, 671, 679
Paykel, E. S., 651, 679
Pearl, L., 641, 649
Pearlin, L., 292, 293, 294, 307
Peck, C., 469, 482
Peebles, C. D., 266, 287
Peebles-Wilkins, W., 59, 75
Peisner-Feinberg, E., 511, 544
Pellegrini, D. S., 74, 665, 666, 672, 678, 679
Pelton, L., 83, 92
Pennoyer, M. M., 13, 28
Percansky, C., 237, 254, 258, 270, 283, 424, 435
Percy, A. K., 40, 43, 53
Perez, J., 241, 248, 257, 303, 307
Perrin, J. M., 334, 337
Perry, A., 40, 53
Perry, B. D., 418, 437
Perry, C., 330, 337
Perry, J. M., 335, 338
Peters, D. L., 15, 29
Peterson, A., 596, 608
Peterson, C. R., 184, 202

Peterson, K. D., 470, 480
Peterson, L. M., 103, 107, 114
Peterson, N. L., 4, 5, 6, 29, 396, 414
Petit, G. S., 109, 111
Petr, C. G., 639, 641, 646, 647
Petrides, M. P., 211, 225
Petros, T., 335, 337
Petrow, R. A., 668, 675
Pettibone, T., 15, 30
Pettitt, C., xi, xii
Pettitt, L. M., 81, 92, 552, 553, 554, 567, 570, 575, 580, 603, 609
Pezzino, J., 604, 607
Pfannenstiel, J., 524, 546
Phares, V., 150, 151, 156, 552, 571
Pharis, M. E., 500, 507
Phelps, C., 603, 609
Phelps, J. L., 671, 679
Phelps, M. E., 212, 214, 223, 224
Philbrick, L. A., 187, 191, 201, 535, 544
Philliber, W. W., 558, 559, 576, 587
Phillips, D. A., 341, 343, 344, 346, 349, 350, 358, 359, 360, 567, 576
Phillips, G. D., 218, 225
Phillips, M. T., 98, 106, 112
Phillipsen, L., 511, 544
Phinney, J. S., 95, 98, 99, 113
Piaget, J., 11, 164, 177, 488, 507
Pianta, R. C., 566, 576, 666, 679
Pickens, J., 66, 72
Pickles, A. P., 654, 655, 656, 658, 661, 662, 663, 666, 668, 671, 675, 676, 678, 679, 680, 681, 682
Piercy, M., 220, 226
Pierson, D. E., 6, 28, 346, 357
Pike, A., 656, 679
Pill, R., 657, 681
Pinderhughes, E., 641, 642, 645, 649
Pine, C. J., 95, 112
Pine, F., 163, 165, 177
Pinto-Martin, J., 49, 53
Piotrkowski, C. S., 347, 359, 417, 426, 437, 560, 561, 571, 588
Pirani, S., 333, 336
Place, P., 388, 404, 412
Plantz, M., 552, 569, 575
Platt, J. R., 161, 178
Plecke, J. H., 57, 73
Plemons, J. K., 659, 677
Pless, I. B., 130, 131, 327, 337
Plomin, P., 654, 656, 668, 671, 680
Plomin, R., 130, 132, 162, 176, 178, 654, 656, 658, 66, 668, 669, 672, 679
Plunkett, J. W., 654, 678
Poersch, N. O., 342, 343, 356, 359
Pogge-Hesse, P., 488, 505

Poisson, S., 501, 505
Polansky, N., 87, 92
Polit, H., 372, 386
Pollack, E., 234, 244, 246, 251, 255
Pollack, W. S., 57, 72
Pollacls, D. B., 212, 224
Pollard, R. A., 418, 437
Pollitt, E., 46, 48, 52, 53, 216, 225, 238, 253, 255
Pollock, T. M., 43, 52
Pollow, R. S., 184, 201
Polmanteer, K., 641, 649
Polsgrove, L., 430, 437
Pons, T. P., 219, 225
Porter, P., 396, 397, 399, 400, 412, 413
Portner, J., 303, 307
Posante, R., 400, 415
Poth, R. L., 252, 256
Potts, M. W., 560, 570, 576
Poulos, J., 425, 437
Powell, A., 264, 279, 286, 457, 458, 460, 481, 532, 545
Powell, D. R., 90, 92, 347, 359, 501, 507, 597, 608
Powell, G., 592, 605, 609
Power, T. G., 57, 74
Powers, J., xi, xii, 81, 92, 552, 553, 554, 567, 570, 575, 580, 603, 609
Powers, M., 390, 415
Prado, R., 46, 51
Pratt, M. W., 7, 29
Pratt, S. S., 187, 202
Prensky, A. L., 46, 51
Prescott, C. A., 668, 677
Prestby, J. E., 644, 649
Price, C., 264, 279, 280, 283, 288
Priestly, B. L., 42, 52
Prince, C., 239, 256
Prior, V., 667, 681
Pritchard, E., 348, 351, 358, 359, 396, 412, 568, 574
Pritchard, M., 39, 52
Prizant, B. M., 419, 437
Prothrow-Stith, D., 69, 74
Provence, S., 6, 12, 27, 29, 233, 235, 238, 248, 249, 256, 367, 375, 377, 379, 385, 389, 390, 414, 634, 650
Pueschel, J., 39, 53
Pugh, G., 615, 628
Pumpian, I., 189, 200
Purpura, D. P., 210, 212, 225
Pynoos, R. S., 70, 74

Quince, C., 39, 53
Quinn, N., 494, 506
Quint, J., 372, 386, 443, 453
Quinton, D., 656, 657, 661, 662, 663, 668, 671, 679, 680 681, 682

Rachman, S., 125, 132
Radin, N. L., 57, 74, 598, 609
Radke-Yarrow, M., 66, 74, 116, 117, 122, 123, 124, 126, 132, 165, 178
Ragozin, A. S., 150, 157, 234, 237, 254, 260, 284, 294, 306
Rahman, M. A., 492, 506
Raimondi, A. J., 42, 52
Rainforth, B., 399, 414, 646, 649
Rainwater, L., 614, 615, 616, 628
Rakic, P., 209, 212, 213, 217, 223, 225, 226
Raleigh, M. J., 212, 224
Ramírez, C., 644, 650
Ramachandran, V. S., 219, 220, 226, 227
Ramey, C. T., xi, xii, 12, 19, 29, 179, 190, 202, 258, 259, 260, 265, 266, 280, 285, 287, 289, 513, 514, 515, 519, 520, 522, 542, 543, 544, 546, 548, 555, 556, 563, 564, 565, 566, 570, 572, 576, 572, 577, 584, 591, 603, 605, 607, 608, 609, 613, 627
Ramey, S. L., 12, 19, 29, 179, 190, 202, 293, 307, 417, 435, 563, 576, 605, 609
Ramirez, M., 67, 68, 73, 110, 113
Ramos, A., 97, 112
Ramsey, E., 419, 437
Randall, P., 216, 223
Randeis, S. P., 45, 53
Randolph, S., 347, 359
Rao, S. S., 632, 648
Rapaport, D., 161, 178
Rappaport, J., 294, 307, 641, 649
Rast, J., 426, 427, 428, 437
Raudenbush, S. W., 318, 320, 321, 324, 502, 505
Rauh, V. A., 150, 151, 156, 158, 234, 237, 256, 280, 287, 552, 571, 576
Raver, S. A., 639, 649
Ravsten, M., 596, 607
Ray, A., 362, 385
Ray, H. W., 592, 609
Raymond, G. T., 80, 91
Read, A. P., 41, 53
Reagan, R., 16
Recanzone, G. H., 220, 226
Recchia, K., 335, 337
Redding, R., 258, 287
Reed, E., 657, 675
Reese, C., 15, 29
Reese, H. W., 502, 504
Reese, L., 489, 507
Reeve, C. E., 183, 200
Reichle, J., 185, 200
Reichle, N., 597, 607
Reid, D. K., 243, 256

Reid, J. B., 651, 679
Reimers, T., 185, 203
Reis, J., 266, 287
Reiss, A. J., Jr., 309, 315, 317, 318, 323, 324
Reiss, D., 145, 147, 158, 165, 178, 656, 666, 672, 679
Remington, J. S., 44, 52, 53
Rende, R., 130, 132
Renouf, A. G., 152, 158
Repp, A. C., 184, 185, 202
Resch, N. L., 132
Rescorla, L., 280, 289, 531, 546
Reynolds, A. J., xi, xii, 19, 29, 522, 523, 546, 603, 609
Reynolds, B. A., 218, 226
Reynolds, C. A., 655, 676
Reynolds, D. W., 44, 53
Reynolds, M., 511, 546
Reznick, J. S., 162, 176, 178
Rheams, T., 241, 248, 257, 303, 307
Ribak, C. E., 212, 224
Ricciotti, H. A., 150, 158
Rich, R., 644, 649
Richan, W., 447, 453
Richard, N. B., 262, 287
Richards, R. I., 39, 52
Richardson, D. C., 559, 576, 587
Richardson, G., 348, 359
Richardson, H. B., 21, 28
Richardson, S. A., 12, 29
Richman, G. S., 185, 201
Richman, N., 116, 132
Richmond, J. B., 14, 260, 288
Richters, J. E., 62, 74, 655, 679
Rickard, P., 558, 576
Rickert, M., 265, 286
Riessman, F., 441, 453
Riley, D., 59, 71, 74
Rimmer, M., 145, 157
Rincover, A., 184, 202
Risemberg, H., 329, 337
Risley, T., 181, 199
Risser, A. H., 488, 508
Rittenhouse, R., 531, 546
Rizzuto, G., 530, 543
Robbins, F. R., 185, 200, 535, 544, 546
Robbins, T. W., 211, 216, 218, 224, 225, 226
Roberts, J. E., 343, 357, 419, 437, 531, 546
Roberts, P., 399, 414
Roberts, R. N., 460, 482
Robert-Tissot, C., 170, 176
Robins, L. N., 656, 679
Robins, P. K., 666, 676
Robinson, C. C., 264, 267, 287, 390, 410, 458, 460, 481, 527, 546

Robinson, D., 657, 681
Robinson, J. L., 13, 22, 64, 72
Robinson, N. M., 150, 157, 234, 237, 254, 260, 284, 294, 306
Robinson, R., 347, 359, 426, 437
Robson, K. S., 259, 287
Rock, S. L., 556, 563, 372
Rockstroh, B., 219, 221, 223
Rodning, C., 258, 282
Rodriguez, G., 373, 386, 515, 524, 547
Rodwell, M. K., 497, 498, 505
Roff, L. L., 80, 91
Rogers, C., 396, 414
Rogers, S., 535, 546
Rogers-Ramachandran, D., 219, 220, 226
Rogoff, B., 94, 97, 109, 110, 113, 144, 158, 240, 256, 489, 490, 507
Rogosch, F. A., 65, 75
Rohde, C. A., 554, 573
Roizen, N., 44, 52
Rolf, J., 652, 680
Roman, R., 87, 92
Romelsjö, A., 657, 658, 660, 661, 681
Roos, P., 635, 649
Rortvedt, A. K., 185, 199
Rosche, M., 552, 569, 574
Rose, J., 527, 546
Rose, T. L., 530, 546
Rosegrant, T., 346, 357
Rosen, L., 636, 649
Rosen, M. G., 48, 53
Rosen, T. S., 116, 125, 131
Rosenbaum, D., 248, 255, 420, 436
Rosenbaum, L. K., 375, 386, 592, 595, 602, 609
Rosenbaum, P. L., 552, 553, 554, 571, 579
Rosenberg, L. A., 554, 573
Rosenberg, R. N., 39, 51
Rosenberg, S. A., 264, 287, 390, 397, 410, 414, 527, 546
Rosenblum, L. A., 259, 286
Rosenfeld, P., 216, 218, 226
Rosenkoetter, S. E., 346, 358, 463, 482
Roskies, E., 151, 158
Ross, A. O., 633, 649
Ross, C., 570, 574
Ross, G. S., 554, 576, 581
Ross, K., 639, 649
Rossi, P. H., 494, 496, 497, 499, 505, 507, 568, 572
Rosso, P., 216, 226
Rosvold, H. E., 224
Roszmann-Millican, M., 399, 408, 413
Roth, W., 15, 16, 28
Rothbart, M. K., 262, 287
Rots, N. Y., 218, 226

Roughman, K., 327, 337
Rounds, K., 401, 415
Rouse, J., 524, 548, 560, 561, 577
Rouse, L., 305
Rousseau, J., 4
Rovee-Collier, C., 213, 226
Rovet, J., 40, 53
Rovine, M., 261, 283
Rowan, L., 463, 474, 481
Rowe, D. C., 656, 680
Rowley, D. L., 98, 106, 112, 113
Roy, P., 668, 680
Royce, J., 552, 569, 574
Royeen, C., 501, 505
Rubin, L., 115, 132
Ruff, C., 277, 287
Ruffin, M., 524, 544
Rule, S., 281, 284, 460, 482, 596, 609
Runyan, D. K., 322, 324
Ruoff, P., 151, 158
Ruopp, R., 349, 359, 592, 593, 594, 609
Russell, A., 57, 75
Russell, G., 48, 53, 57, 71, 75
Russman, B., 21, 28
Rutter, M., 13, 67, 68, 69, 72, 75, 115, 116, 132, 137, 140, 158, 169, 170, 172, 178, 238, 256, 266, 287, 419, 437
Ruttle, K., 553, 554, 573, 582
Rydell, C. P., 3, 19, 28
Ryff, C., 293, 307, 652, 681
Rygh, J., 175, 178

Sabatier, P. A., 402, 413
Sabbach, S., 216, 227
Sachs, B. P., 150, 158
Safanda, J., 39, 53
Safer, D., 541, 546
Saffin, K., 333, 337
Safford, P. L., 458, 462, 482
Sakamoto, L., 592, 605, 609
Saleebey, D., 634, 639, 645, 649
Salisbury, C., 390, 415, 511, 546
Salkever, D. S., 554, 573
Saltzman, W., 62, 73
Sambrano, S., 347, 359
Sameroff, A. J., 11, 13, 22, 30, 85, 93, 94, 100, 104, 112, 116, 117, 122, 123, 132, 161, 169, 178, 191, 202, 234, 237, 238, 256, 257, 266, 287, 292, 307, 419, 437, 457, 482, 489, 507, 536, 543, 546, 547, 589, 609, 657, 666, 681
Sampson, E. E., 161, 178
Sampson, R. J., 312, 313, 318, 320, 321, 323, 324, 653, 656, 664, 678, 681

Sandall, S. R., 400, 410
Sandberg, S., 667, 681
Sander, A. M., 634, 650
Sander, L. W., 165, 178, 261, 262, 287
Sanders, M., 3, 19, 28
Sandfort, J., 342, 343, 356, 359
Sandler, H., 329, 336
Sands, J., 46, 51, 215, 223
Sands, R., 636, 649
Sandson, J., 488, 507
Sanford, D., 113
Santelli, E., 457, 460, 482
Sapolsky, R. M., 216, 226
Sara, V. R., 47, 53
Sarnat, H. B., 35, 37, 53
Sasso, G., 185, 203
Satterly, D., 260, 266, 282
Sattin, D., 87, 93
Sauer, B., 211, 224
Savin, M. H., 218, 223
Sawhill, I., 613, 628
Sax, P., 433, 437
Scafidi, F., 150, 157
Scarr, S., 123, 128, 132, 162, 178, 312, 324, 346, 349, 359
Schachar, R. J., 669, 681
Schacht, R., 500, 508, 528, 529, 547
Schaefer, E., 513, 543
Schaffer, H. R., 264, 288
Schaffer, R., 640, 644, 646, 650
Schaffer, V., 640, 644, 646, 650
Schaie, K., 476, 482
Schanberg, S. M., 150, 157
Scharff, D. E., 169, 170, 178
Scharff, J. S., 169, 170, 178
Schay, W., 44, 52
Scheeringa, M., 380, 386
Scheiner, A., 43, 51
Scheiner, B., 43, 51
Schell, J., 81, 93
Schellenbach, C., 89, 92
Schenck, E. A., 592, 609
Scheper-Hughes, N., 87, 93
Schiller, M. M., 146, 157
Schlesinger, D., 39, 52
Schmidt, M. H., 65, 73
Schnase, D., 642, 648
Schneider, M. L., 216, 223, 226
Schnur, E., 518, 519, 545
Schochet, P. Z., 340, 344, 358
Schoelmerich, A., 97, 112
Schoen, S. F., 187, 202
Schoenborn, C. A., 135, 159
Schon, D. A., 462, 482
Schooler, C., 293, 307
Schopler, E., 534, 546
Schor, E. L., 321, 324
Schorah, C. J., 41, 53

Schore, A. N., 13, 30, 214, 215, 226
Schorr, L. B., 3, 16, 17, 30, 132, 346, 359, 370, 377, 386, 624, 629
Schottenfeld, R., 61, 73
Schrag, E., 398, 411
Schreinder, C. E., 220, 226
Schreiner, C., 220, 225, 226
Schroeder, C., 460, 483
Schulze, P. A., 97, 112
Schwagler, J., 145, 146, 157
Schwart, B., 219, 227
Schwartz, B. J., 219, 226, 227
Schwartz, I. S., 459, 478, 502, 507, 527, 546
Schwartz, J. H., 206, 207, 208, 224, 523, 524, 547
Schweinhart, L. B., 621, 626
Schweinhart, L. J., xi, xii, 69, 75, 137, 159, 343, 349, 359, 516, 517, 546, 547, 556, 576, 591, 597, 598, 604, 607, 609
Scott, C., 104, 105, 113
Scott, D. T., 372, 384, 385, 519, 520, 521, 522, 543, 545, 547, 555, 556, 565, 572, 583, 604, 609
Scott, K. G., 592, 608
Scott, T. M., 216, 223
Scott-Jones, D., 95, 96, 98, 99, 106, 112
Scrimshaw, N., 46, 53
Scurria, K. L., 350, 359
Sealand, N., 311, 323
Searle, M., 48, 53
Seeley, J., 79, 92
Seeman, M. V., 65, 72
Segal, M. M., 234, 235, 257, 267, 288, 613, 628
Segall, H. M., 95, 113
Sege, R., 330, 337
Seguin, E., 9
Seibyl, J. P., 216, 223
Seiderman, E., 347, 358, 422, 423, 436
Seifer, R., 11, 30, 85, 93, 116, 117, 122, 123, 132, 137, 138, 140, 146, 147, 157, 159, 191, 202, 237, 238, 257, 266, 287, 536, 543, 547, 652, 657, 666, 681
Seitz, V., xi, xiii, 375, 386, 390, 414, 555, 556, 576, 584, 592, 595, 602, 609, 634, 650
Sekul, E. A., 40, 53
Seligman, M., 460, 482, 638, 640, 641, 650
Seligman, S., 268, 286, 379, 386, 457, 480
Seligson, M., 510, 545
Seller, M. J., 41, 53
Sells, C. J., 42, 53
Selner-O'Hagen, M. B., 321, 324

Seltzer, D., 524, 546
Seltzer, M. M., 293, 307
Semple, S., 292, 293, 294, 307
Seraphine, A. E., 252, 256
Seress, L., 212, 226
Serpa-Rusconi, S., 170, 176
Seshadri, S., 47, 53
Severson, H. H., 419, 431, 435, 438
Sexton, D., 241, 245, 246, 248, 254,
    257, 302, 303, 307
Shadish, W. R., 491, 507
Shallice, T., 211, 226
Shamos, S., 664, 682
Shanahan, K., 398, 415
Shanok, R. S., 461, 462, 464, 482
Shapira, H. V., 40, 53
Shapiro, B. K., 532, 546
Shapiro, H., 329, 336
Shapiro, S., 520, 543, 556, 572
Shapiro, T., 168, 178
Shapiro, V., 56, 72, 147, 152, 157,
    168, 177, 367, 385, 443, 452
Share, J., 13, 30
Sharp, L., 248, 257, 462, 463, 481
Shaughnessy, P., 12, 27
Shaver, D., 67, 69, 74, 552, 553, 554,
    574, 580, 603, 608
Shaw, C. R., 313, 324
Shaw, D., 396, 401, 402, 403, 404,
    405, 408, 412
Shaw, E., 267, 269, 283, 298, 305
Shay, S., 311, 323
Shayne, M. W., 294, 307
Shaywitz, B., 45, 53
Shaywitz, S., 45, 53
Shearer, D. D., 187, 201
Sheehan, R., 387, 390, 411, 414, 474,
    481
Shelton, R. L., 638, 650
Shepard, L. A., 250, 257
Shepherd, P. A., 231, 254
Sheppard, S., 41, 53
Sherman, D., 82, 88, 89, 92, 311, 324
Sherrod, L. R., 652, 677
Shields, A., 65, 75
Shinn, M., 343, 347, 357, 359
Shiono, P. H., 150, 159
Shire, M. B., 417, 435
Shisler, L., 531, 546
Shonkoff, J. P., 103, 217, 258, 262,
    275, 277, 280, 288, 328, 338, 387,
    398, 401, 407, 411, 413, 414, 416,
    417, 437, 491, 500, 502, 503, 506,
    507, 511, 526, 529, 530, 544, 547,
    594, 604, 609, 613, 628, 638, 650,
    658, 681
Shore, R., ix, xiii, 342, 359, 418, 437,
    510, 547, 614, 629
Short, A., 534, 546

Short, E., 280, 287
Showers, B., 472, 482
Shriver, M. D., 239, 257
Shriver, S., 364
Shuster, S., 390, 414
Shwachman, H., 47, 52
Shweder, R. A., 161, 178, 493, 508
Sia, C. C. J., 335, 338, 554, 573
Sideris, J., 396, 398, 400, 401, 403,
    404, 405, 407, 408, 412, 413, 414
Sidman, R. L., 212, 226
Sidora, K., xi, xii, 67, 69, 74, 81, 92,
    552, 553, 554, 567, 570, 574, 575,
    580, 603, 608, 609
Sieffert, A., 633, 650
Siegel, B., 511, 547
Siegel, C., 419, 435
Siegel, L., 556, 563, 372
Siegel-Causey, E., 457, 460, 482
SiFuentes, F., 219, 220, 225
Sigel, I. E., 101, 113, 143, 159, 490,
    508, 523, 547
Sigesmund, M. H., 187, 202
Silberg, J. L., 654, 655, 656, 662, 666,
    668, 676, 680, 681
Silbert, A., 40, 51
Sillari, J., 233, 256, 398, 413
Silva, P. A., 655, 677, 678
Silverberg, S. B., 262, 288
Silveri, B., 523, 544
Simeonsson, R. J., 293, 294, 295, 296,
    297, 300, 301, 302, 303, 305, 307,
    390, 414, 455, 457, 478, 482, 532,
    542, 576, 639, 650
Simmens, S. J., 666, 672, 679
Simonoff, E., 654, 655, 656, 662, 666,
    668, 671, 676, 677, 680, 681
Simons, R. L., 565, 573, 653, 676
Sinclair, E., 419, 437
Singer, G., 652, 681
Singer, J., 16, 30
Singer, L. T., 231, 254
Singer, M. I., 312, 324
Singh, G. K., 320, 324
Singh, N. N., 184, 185, 202
Sinisterra, L., 47, 52
Sirevaag, A. M., 218, 223, 510, 544
Skaff, M., 292, 293, 294, 307
Skeels, H. M., 12, 30, 162, 178
Skerry, P., 366, 386
Skiba, R., 430, 437
Skinner, B. F., 181, 202, 488, 508
Skinner, J. D., 153, 157
Skrtic, T. M., 634, 636, 642, 650
Slater, M. A., 277, 288
Slaughter, D. T., 101, 113
Slaughter-Defoe, D. T., 94, 95, 113
Slentz, K. L., 4, 27, 291, 297, 298,
    307, 463, 464, 474, 479, 482

Slifer, K. J., 185, 201
Slopis, J. M., 46, 51
Slough, N., 59, 71
Small, S. A., 665, 681
Smeeding, T. M., 614, 615, 616, 628,
    629
Smith, A. B., 348, 359, 371, 386, 671,
    680
Smith, B. J., 21, 22, 28, 30, 180, 202,
    387, 388, 414
Smith, B. L., 262, 288
Smith, D. F., 35, 45, 51, 53, 216,
    224
Smith, J. R., 557, 564, 565, 569, 572,
    576, 583
Smith, K., 248, 255
Smith, L., 115, 262, 288
Smith, M. A., 563, 577, 666, 677
Smith, M. L., x, xiii
Smith, R., 328, 338
Smith, R. J. H., 43, 51
Smith, R. S., 11, 13, 30, 68, 69, 75,
    116, 117, 120, 122, 123, 124, 125,
    126, 127, 132, 137, 159, 659, 660,
    664, 682
Smith, S. W., 370, 371, 386, 421, 437,
    523, 547, 557, 569, 570, 576, 637,
    650
Smith, T. M., 190, 202, 291, 296, 297,
    305, 307, 533, 534, 535, 542, 545,
    631, 640, 641, 647
Smithells, R. W., 41, 53
Smokowski, P., 19, 29
Snell, M. E., 488, 508
Snipper, A., 552, 569, 574
Snow, C. E., 259, 288, 332, 336, 525,
    547, 563, 576
Snyder, C., 258, 259, 277, 282
Snyder, E. D., 187, 201, 203
Snyder, K. D., 294, 302, 303, 306
Snyder, P., 246, 257, 303, 307, 471,
    472, 482, 483, 503, 505, 530, 543
Sobel, H., 420, 436
Socolar, R. S., 322, 324
Sokol, R. J., 45, 50, 61, 72
Solkoske, L., 331, 336
Solnick, J. V., 184, 202
Solnit, A. J., 633, 650
Solomon, J., 64, 73
Sommers, M. W., 41, 52
Sommers, R. C., 42, 52
Song, L., 312, 324
Sonnander, K., 329, 338
Sontag, J. C., 292, 307, 500, 508, 528,
    529, 547
Son-Yarbrough, W., 523, 544
Soraci, S. A., 180, 202
Sorce, J., 56, 75
Soto, A., 216, 223

Southwick, S. M., 216, 223
Spain, A., 593, 595, 607
Sparling, J. J., 514, 515, 518, 519, 520, 522, 543, 546, 547, 548, 555, 556, 563, 566, 570, 576, 577, 584, 641, 650
Sparrow, S. S., 235, 257
Specht, H., 439, 453
Spencer, K. K., 116, 120, 124, 126, 131
Spencer, M. B., 113, 663, 676
Sperling, R. S., 44, 51
Spieker, S. J., 64, 75, 151, 156, 234, 237, 253, 259, 260, 261, 262, 277, 282, 283, 288, 418, 422, 423, 434, 552, 554, 563, 564, 566, 570, 571, 572, 581
Spietz, L. A., 153, 159, 258, 259, 276, 282, 288
Spiker, D., 150, 153, 154, 156, 159, 263, 264, 267, 275, 276, 279, 280, 283, 284, 286, 288, 295, 297, 305, 372, 384, 519, 520, 543, 547, 552, 555, 556, 563, 565, 571, 572, 574, 576, 583, 591, 604, 608
Spillman, R. E., 558, 559, 576, 587
Spitz, H. H., 12, 30, 514, 547
Spitz, R. A., 12, 30, 55, 75, 163, 165, 168, 178, 260, 262, 288
Spivack, H., 330, 337
Sponseller, D., 466, 480
Spooner, S., 335, 337
Sprague, J. R., 185, 202
Spreen, O., 488, 508
Spurgeon, M. S., 592, 609
Squires, J., 247, 248, 254, 257
Sroufe, L. A., 12, 30, 116, 117, 123, 131, 173, 178, 260, 262, 284, 652, 666, 676, 679
St. Andre, M., 146, 157
St. Ledger, R. J., 654, 677
St. Pierre, R. G., 371, 372, 386, 523, 524, 547, 557, 558, 559, 560, 569, 570, 576, 586, 591, 592, 597, 609
Stacey, M., 657, 681
Stafford, A., 105, 113
Stafford, F. P., 626, 627
Stafford, S., 535, 547
Stagg, V., 59, 72
Staghezza, B., 655, 675
Stagno, S., 43, 44, 51, 53
Staines, G. L., 347, 359
Staley, L. W., 39, 53
Stanley-Ragan, M., 116, 120, 124, 126, 131
Stanton, E. E., 216, 225
Staples, A., 455, 480
Starfield, B., 21, 27, 511, 547

Stark, M. H., 633, 650
Stark, R., 40, 51
Starnes, A. L., 194, 200, 631, 640, 648
Stattin, H., 657, 658, 660, 661, 681
Stayton, V. D., 454, 463, 470, 474, 481, 482, 634, 650
Steege, M., 185, 203
Steele, D., 250, 256
Steele, H., 652, 666, 667, 677
Steele, M., 652, 666, 667, 677
Stein, A., 422, 437
Stein, E., 501, 505
Stein, J., 541, 547
Stein, L., 44, 52
Stein, M., 44, 52
Stein, R. E. K., 130, 131
Steinberg, L., 83, 93, 96, 113
Steiner, G. Y., 7, 30
Stenbacka, M., 657, 658, 660, 661, 681
Stenmark, S., 21, 27
Stepanek, J. S., 298, 299, 307
Stern, D. N., 56, 65, 75, 145, 148, 159, 164, 169, 170, 176, 178, 259, 260, 261, 262, 264, 283, 288, 457, 482
Stern, G. G., 260, 288
Stern, V., 463, 479
Sternberg, R. J., 253, 257
Stern-Bruschweiler, N., 170, 178
Sterzin, E. D., 398, 415
Stevens, F., 329, 337
Stevens, J. H., Jr., 75
Stevens, K. N., 221, 225
Stevenson, C. S., 343, 357
Stevenson, J., 655, 671, 677
Stevenson, M. B., 262, 288
Stewart, M. A., 219, 220, 226, 656, 668, 669, 676, 677
Stich, F., 265, 266, 289
Stigol, L., 330, 337
Stile, S., 15, 30
Stiles, R., 558, 576
Stiller, B., 438
Stinson, C., 166, 177
Stinson, E. T., 490, 508
Stipek, D., 671, 672, 681
Stock, J. R., 243, 246, 256, 277, 288, 592, 609
Stocking, S. H., 86, 92
Stokely, J., 377, 379, 386
Stoller, S., 555, 556, 573, 579, 584
Stolorow, R. D., 65, 75
Stoneman, Z., 653, 675
Stoney, L., 352, 358
Storey, K., 185, 202
Stormshak, E., 641, 647
Stott, F. M., 22, 116, 120, 124, 126, 131, 378, 385, 473, 475, 476, 479, 480, 482, 567

Stouthamer-Loeber, M., 140, 159, 652, 681
Stowitschek, J., 596, 609
Strain, B. A., 261, 288
Strain, P. S., 21, 30, 180, 187, 191, 201, 202, 203, 397, 399, 413, 431, 438, 469, 482
Strauch, B., 541, 547
Strauss, C., 494, 505
Stray-Pedersen, B., 44, 53
Street, R., 552, 554, 574, 579
Streissguth, A. P., 45, 53, 266, 283
Strickland, B., 247, 255, 298, 306
Stricklin, S., 246, 257
Striefel, S., 596, 609
Striffler, N., 442, 453
Stringer, S., 63, 72, 266, 285, 553, 554, 573
Stroud, A., 263, 284
Stroul, B. A., 425, 430, 431, 433, 436
Struthers, J. M., 61, 75
Sturner, R. A., 247, 257
Styfco, S. J., 15, 31, 137, 159, 613, 621, 629
Suchecki, D., 216, 218, 226
Suchman, N. E., 418, 427, 428, 437
Sugai, G. M., 182, 184, 186, 203
Sugarman, J., 350, 354, 359
Suleman, M. A., 216, 226
Sullivan, J. W., 390, 411
Sullivan, M. C., 266, 286
Sullivan, P. F., 659, 681
Summers, J. A., 149, 159, 457, 460, 482, 631, 650
Sumner, G. A., 153, 159, 276, 288
Super, C. M., 94, 97, 112, 114, 489, 494, 506, 508
Suppa, R. J., 187, 202
Sutanto, W., 218, 226
Sutherland, G. R., 39, 52
Svinicki, J., 243, 246, 256
Swain, D. A., 348, 359
Swanson, M., 372, 384, 520, 543, 555, 556, 565, 572, 583
Swartz, J. P., 523, 524, 547, 558, 559, 560, 576, 586
Sweet, N., 233, 235, 257, 464, 466, 467, 475, 480, 483
Swezey, K., 596, 609
Swick, K., 646, 650
Swisher, C. N., 44, 52, 53
Symons, F. J., xi, xiii
Szanton, E. S., 613, 628
Szapocnik, J., 95, 100, 114
Szumowski, E., 330, 336

Tableman, B., 428, 437
Taft, L., 21, 28

Takanishi, R., 15, 30, 94, 95, 113, 518, 519, 547
Takashima, S., 210, 226
Talbot, M. E., 9, 30
Tallal, P., 214, 220, 224, 225, 226
Tamis-LeMonda, C., 258, 288
Tan, A., 353, 357
Tannock, R., 258, 263, 285, 288
Tao, F., 559, 560, 576, 586
Tarara, R., 216, 226
Target, M., 652, 666, 667, 677
Tarr, H., 559, 560, 576, 586
Tarr, J. E., 592, 609
Tatelbaum, R., 66, 67, 69, 74, 81, 92, 552, 553, 554, 574, 575, 580, 603, 608
Taub, E., 219, 221, 223, 225
Taussig, C., 3, 31
Tawney, J. W., 187, 202
Taylor, A. K., 39, 53, 656, 662, 671, 679
Taylor, D. G., 261, 283
Taylor, D. L., 107, 111
Taylor, E., 265, 286, 656, 662, 666, 668, 669, 680, 681
Taylor, J., 184, 202, 332, 338
Taylor, L., 312, 324
Taylor, M. J., 3, 30, 275, 279, 280, 283
Taylor, R. D., 60, 75
Taylor, R. J., 60, 75
Taylor, S., 332, 337
Teglasi, H., 236, 255
Teitler, J. O., 666, 676
Tellegen, A., 67, 68, 73, 116, 131, 140, 157, 652, 665, 666, 678
Telzrow, C. F., 502, 508
Telzrow, R. W., 263, 288, 330, 338
Temple, J., 522, 523, 546
Ten Have, T., 247, 256, 328, 337
Tennant, C., 668, 681
Terman, L., 9
Terrell, F. T., 106, 114
Terrell, S., 107, 114
Teti, D. M., 65, 72, 151, 158, 234, 237, 256, 278, 280, 287, 288, 552, 576
Tharp, R. G., 489, 508
Thelen, E., 161, 178
Thiel, K., 374, 386
Thoits, P., 652, 681
Thoman, E. B., 261, 262, 288
Thomas, A., 259, 284
Thomas, D. D., 100, 114, 387, 388, 411, 597, 607
Thomas, M. A., 592, 593, 594, 508
Thomas, P., 496, 497, 508
Thompson, A. I., 97, 113
Thompson, B., 241, 245, 246, 248, 257, 302, 307

Thompson, E. A., 97, 113
Thompson, L. A., xi, xii, 528, 529, 547
Thompson, M. A., 597, 605, 609
Thompson, M. D., 13, 22, 25, 36
Thompson, M. S., 59, 75
Thompson, R. A., 564, 576
Thomson, A. J., 48, 53
Thorley, G., 669, 681
Thorne, B., 95, 96, 98, 99, 106, 112
Thorp, E. K., 258, 268, 288, 454, 455, 463, 465, 466, 467, 468, 471, 481, 483
Thurman, S. K., 188, 189, 190, 192, 197, 202
Thurston, D. L., 13, 28
Tierney, J. P., 132
Tietjen, A., 60, 75
Timperi, R., 46, 53
Tinsley, B. J., 147, 158
Tivnan, T., 6, 28, 346, 357
Tizard, J., 671, 681
Tjossem, T., 22, 30
Tocci, L., 396, 397, 398, 400, 401, 403, 404, 405, 407, 408, 412, 413, 414, 640, 641, 646, 649
Tolan, P. H., 419, 437
Tolson, T. F. J., 60, 75
Tolstoy, L., 4, 30
Toms, F. D., 95, 107, 111
Tonascia, J., 372, 384, 385, 520, 521, 522, 543, 545, 555, 556, 565, 572, 583, 604, 609
Tonry, M., 315, 324
Toole, A., 398, 415
Topolski, T. D., 655, 681
Toth, S. L., 65, 75, 146, 157
Touchette, P. E., 185, 202
Travers, J., 349, 359, 386, 593, 594
Trice, H., 87, 92
Trickett, P. K., xi, xiii
Trivette, C. M., 85, 91, 149, 157, 194, 195, 196, 197, 198, 200, 202, 292, 293, 294, 295, 302, 303, 306, 389, 390, 397, 398, 399, 404, 405, 407, 408, 410, 411, 414, 426, 435, 457, 461, 479, 492, 500, 502, 503, 505, 508, 631, 639, 640, 647, 648
Trohanis, P. L., 20, 27, 388, 411, 526, 547
Tronick, E. Z., 61, 62, 65, 66, 70, 71, 73, 75
Tropp, L., 97, 114
Troughton, E., 656, 668, 669, 676, 677
Truett, T. R., 655, 676
Truman, C., 490, 506
Tschann, B., 121, 131
Tschann, J. M., 670, 681
Tubman, J. G., 488, 507

Tucker, M. B., 60, 75
Tulkin, S. R., 87, 93, 259, 266, 288, 289
Tuma, A. H., 169, 178
Turbiville, V., 10, 22, 294, 461, 466, 480, 483
Turnbull, A. P., 3, 10, 22, 30, 149, 159, 233, 257, 292, 294, 297, 302, 305, 308, 397, 410, 456, 457, 460, 461, 469, 479, 482, 483
Turnbull, H. R., iii, 3, 10, 22, 30, 184, 185, 201, 233, 257, 292, 294, 297, 302, 308, 457, 466, 469, 480, 483
Turner, S. M., 312, 323
Twyman, J. S., 184, 202
Tyson, J., 372, 384, 385, 520, 521, 522, 543, 545, 555, 556, 565, 572, 583, 604, 609
Tyson, R., 366, 384

Ullman, M., 636, 648
Ulrich, B. D., 161, 178
Underdown, G., 399, 400, 401, 413
Ungerleider, L. G., 211, 212, 225, 226
Uno, H., 216, 226
Upshur, C. C., 4, 19, 20, 23, 28, 30, 258, 262, 275, 277, 280, 288, 400, 401, 413, 415, 526, 529, 530, 547, 594, 604, 609, 638, 650
Urbano, R. C., 277, 289
Urrutia, J., 47, 52
Ursin, H., 657, 681
Urwin, S., 531, 547
Usher, C. L., 497, 498, 508
Utley, C. A., 180, 202
Uzgiris, I. C., 259, 289

Vadasy, P. F., 280, 285, 397, 411
Vail, C., 458, 480
Vaillant, G. E., 651, 652, 657, 664, 677, 678, 681
Valcarel, M., 97, 112
Valenstein, A. F., 633, 647
Valentine, J., 14, 15, 31, 570, 577, 636, 650
van Aken, M. A. G., 667, 675
Van Dyck, P., 374, 386
Van Egren, L. F., 266, 283
van Ijzendoorn, M. H., 553, 566, 576, 667, 682
van Kammen, W., 140, 159, 652, 681
van Loon, R. J. P., 161, 177
Van Nguyen, T., 116, 117, 123, 125, 127, 131
Vandenburg, J. E., 425, 438
Vandiviere, P., 244, 246, 253, 396, 397, 399, 400, 401, 412, 413
Varenne, H., 99, 102, 113
Vasquez García, H. A., 97, 114

Vater, S., 233, 235, 249, 256
Vaughn, B. J., 183, 201
Vedel-Petersen, J., 623, 629
Vega, W. A., 107, 111
Vega-Lahr, N., 150, 157
Veltman, M., 389, 390, 410, 442, 452
Venn, M. L., 186, 187, 202, 460, 483
Ventura, S., 239, 256
Verbrugge, H., 620, 629
Vernon-Feagans, L., 513, 547
Verzaro-O'Brien, M., 592, 605, 609
Verzemnieks, I., 270, 286
Vietze, P. M., 261, 265, 266, 288, 289
Vig, S., 419, 438
Vigilante, D., 418, 437
Vila-Coro, A. A., 46, 51
Vincent, L. J., 390, 397, 398, 415
Vinci, R., 46, 53
Vinovskis, M. A., 14, 15, 27, 30
Viteri, F., 47, 52
Vizzard, L. H., 421, 423, 429, 435
Voight, J. D., 59, 60, 75
Volkmar, F. R., 218, 224
Volpe, J. V., 36, 38, 41, 48, 49, 53, 205, 209, 210, 226
von Bertalanffy, L., 161, 176
von Windeguth, B. J., 277, 289
Voran, M., 344, 359
Vorria, P., 668, 682
Vorster, J., 259, 288
Vygotsky, L. S., 78, 93, 450, 453, 457, 458, 483

Wachs, T. D., 258, 259, 289
Wachtel, R. C., 532, 546
Wachtel, W., 15, 30
Wacker, D., 185, 203
Waddell, K., 109, 113
Wagner, M. K., 295, 297, 305, 620, 629, 632, 642, 650
Wagner, M. M., 560, 561, 576
Wagner, S., 378, 385, 398, 410
Walberg, H., 511, 546
Walker, B., 298, 307
Walker, D. K., 6, 28
Walker, H. M., 419, 431, 435, 438, 625, 629
Walker, J., 402, 415
Walker, T. B., 373, 374, 385, 386, 417, 436, 515, 524, 544, 547
Wall, S., 12, 26, 261, 282, 564, 571
Wallace, C. S., 218, 223, 510, 544
Wallace, D. B., 368, 384, 555, 556, 571, 583
Wallace, I. F., 372, 385, 520, 521, 522, 545, 604, 609
Wallach, V. A., 373, 386, 423, 438
Wallerstein, J. S., 116, 120, 122, 124, 126, 132

Walper, S., 673, 677
Walter, G., 390, 415
Walters, V., 44, 52
Walzer, S., 40, 51
Wamboldt, F. S., 152, 158
Wandersman, A., 492, 506, 644, 649
Wang, M. C., 511, 546, 669, 682
Wang, X., 220, 226
Wara, D., 121, 131
Warburton, R., 657, 675
Ware, L. M., 63, 64, 74, 553, 554, 575, 581
Warfield, M. E., 3, 20, 30
Warheit, G. J., 107, 111
Warren, S. F., xi, xiii, 181, 187, 203, 458, 483, 537, 541, 547, 548
Warren, S. T., 39, 52, 53
Wasik, B. A., 21, 22, 29
Wasik, B. H., 14, 515, 519, 520, 522, 546, 548, 555, 556, 563, 564, 565, 566, 570, 572, 576, 577, 584
Wasow, M., 297, 308, 456, 483
Wass, M., 333, 337
Waters, E., 12, 26, 27, 109, 111, 261, 282, 564, 571
Watkins, S., 533, 548
Watson, J., 11, 30
Watt, N. F., 417, 435, 664, 682
Wayman, K. I., 269, 285
Weatherly, R. A., 387, 402, 415
Weatherston, D., 467, 475, 483
Webb, A., 13, 30
Webber, N. T., 234, 235, 257, 267, 288
Webster, J., 65, 72
Webster, M. J., 212, 226
Webster-Stratton, C., 420, 423, 428, 438, 672, 682
Wechsler, N., 424, 435
Wedel, K. R., 497, 498, 505
Weeks, K. H., 294, 307
Weeldreyer, J. C., 294, 302, 303, 306
Weick, A., 635, 650
Weick, K. E., 394, 395, 415
Weider, S., 234, 257, 379, 386, 477, 480
Weikart, D. P., xi, xii, 69, 75, 137, 159, 343, 349, 359, 363, 516, 517, 546, 547, 556, 576, 591, 597, 598, 604, 607, 609, 621, 626
Weil, M., 401, 415
Weiler, I., 510, 544
Weinberg, K., 65, 66, 75
Weinraub, M., 58, 75, 231, 254
Weintraub, S., 652, 680
Weis, J. A., 396, 415
Weisner, T. S., 20, 97, 114
Weiss, A. D., 129, 131, 419, 435
Weiss, C. H., 496, 499, 508, 567, 577

Weiss, H. B., 102, 114, 369, 381, 383, 385, 386, 449, 453, 489, 492, 496, 498, 508, 555, 577, 584
Weiss, R. S., 596, 602, 609, 610
Weiss, S., 218, 226
Weissbourd, B., 90, 92, 426, 433, 436, 497, 508, 597, 608, 610, 613, 624, 627, 628
Weisz, J. R., 419, 427, 437, 488, 509
Welge, P., 246, 254
Wells, G., 260, 266, 282
Wells, J. E., 659, 681
Wenger, M., 387, 388, 411
Werner, E. E., 11, 12, 13, 30, 67, 68, 69, 75, 137, 159, 238, 257, 266, 289, 652, 659, 660, 664, 682
Werner, H., 161, 178
Werts, M. G., 187, 202, 203, 460, 483
Wesley, P. W., 464, 469, 470, 471, 472, 479, 483
West, D. J., 654, 677
West, J., 340, 341, 359, 360
West, S. G., 417, 435
West, T., 390, 391, 394, 396, 398, 401, 403, 404, 405, 408, 409, 412
Westheafer, C., 402, 405, 408, 412
Westinghouse Learning Corporation, 487, 496, 509
Weston, D. R., 152, 158, 233, 235, 257, 464, 466, 483, 553, 563, 570, 575, 580
Wetherby, A. M., 419, 437
Wewers, S., 62, 64, 74
Wheeler, M. E., 633, 649
Whiddon, D., 295, 307, 631, 639, 649
Whishaw, I. Q., 218, 224
Whitbeck, L. B., 653, 676
White, B., 524, 545
White, K. R., 3, 27, 30, 280, 289, 489, 504, 505, 531, 532, 542, 546, 604, 610
White, O. R., 185, 201
Whitebook, M., 343, 344, 349, 359, 360
Whiteford, P., 616, 617, 627
Whitehead, A., 462, 463, 481
Whitehurst, G. J., 563, 577
Whitelaw, R. B., 218, 225
Whiteside, L., 520, 542
Whiting, B. B., 94, 95, 114
Whiting, J. W. M., 94, 114
Whitman, B., 39, 51
Whitmore, K., 671, 681
Whitney-Thomas, J., 644, 650
Whitt, J., 330, 336
Whittaker, J., 79, 86, 93
Whyte, W. F., 492, 509, 644, 650

Widerstrom, A. H., 188, 189, 190, 202, 454, 455, 465, 467, 479, 483
Widmayer, S. M., 63, 72, 103, 107, 114, 266, 285, 553, 554, 555, 556, 573, 579, 584
Wieder, S., 419, 421, 435
Wiegerink, R., 400, 415
Wienbruch, C., 219, 221, 223
Wieselberg, M., 669, 681
Wietlisbach, S., 501, 505
Wiggins, G., 250, 257
Wikler, L., 297, 308, 456, 483
Wilbers, J. S., 199, 203
Wilfong-Grush, E., 275, 283
Wilkinson, L. S., 216, 218, 224, 225, 226
Wille, D. E., 152, 159
Willer, B., 341, 349, 360
Willerman, L., 78, 93
Williams, B. C., 619, 629
Williams, D., 87, 92
Williams, K. A., 221, 225
Williamson, G. G., 233, 257, 398, 415, 457, 483
Williamson, W., 43, 51, 53
Willis, E., 335, 338
Willis, S., 476, 482
Willoughby, M., 421, 423, 429, 435
Wilson, C. B., 44, 53
Wilson, D. B., x, xii
Wilson, E., 76, 93
Wilson, J. B., 550, 577
Wilson, M. N., 60, 72, 75, 95, 112, 456, 482
Wilson, S. P., 97, 112
Wilson, W., 81, 83, 93
Windham, A. M., 554, 573
Wingerd, J., 103, 107, 114
Wingert, F., 211, 224
Winick, M., 215, 216, 225, 226
Winnicott, D., 55, 62, 65, 75
Winter, M., 524, 548, 560, 561, 577
Winter, S., 535, 548
Winterling, V., 185, 200
Winters, L., 250, 255
Winters, S., 44, 52
Winton, P. J., 299, 303, 305, 308, 456, 460, 470, 472, 477, 483, 477
Wirt, F., 402, 413
Wirth, O., 278, 288
Wise, B. M., 219, 220, 225
Wishy, B., 4, 31

Wiske, M. S., 247, 256
Wisniewski, J. J., 241, 253
Wisniewski, K., 210, 224
Withers, G., 510, 544
Wittmer, D., 431, 438
Wittmer, P. S., 69, 73
Wnek, L. L., 243, 246, 256, 592, 609
Wolery, M., 13, 22, 25, 389, 410, 460, 483, 502, 507
Wolf, A., 47, 52
Wolf, D. P., 175, 178
Wolf, M. M., 181, 199
Wolfe, B. L., 471, 472, 482, 483, 550, 574, 603, 608
Wolfensberger, W., 631, 633, 634, 636, 650
Wolff, P. H., 47, 50, 52
Wolin, S. J., 146, 156
Wolkind, S., 668, 682
Wolraich, M. L., 247, 255
Wood, M., 637, 650
Wood, S., 264, 286
Woodhead, M., 552, 564, 577
Woodruff, G., 398, 399, 408, 413, 415
Woodworth, G., 668, 676
Wooley, F., 332, 337
Work, W. C., 666, 676
Workerl, J. O., 218, 226
Woster, S. H., 185, 199
Wouldbroun, E. J., 656, 680
Wright, B. D., 321, 324
Wright, D., 340, 341, 360
Wright, H. F., 309, 311, 323
Wulczyn, F., 83, 93, 362, 382, 386
Wyman, P. A., 666, 676

Yakovlev, P. I., 214, 226
Yancey, A. K., 77, 93
Yang, T. T., 219, 226, 227
Yang, Y. N., 592, 608
Yarosz, D., 593, 595, 607
Yates, T., 457, 481
Yates, W. R., 656, 668, 669, 676, 677
Yatkin, U. S., 216, 227
Yeager, C., 184, 203
Yeates, K. O., 265, 280, 287, 289, 488, 509
Yin, R. K., 402, 415
Yip, R., 48, 53
Yoder, D. E., 398, 415, 455, 478, 483
Yoder, P., 186, 201, 301, 306, 537, 541, 544, 547, 548

Yogman, M. W., 57, 75, 258, 289, 521, 548
York-Barr, J., 646, 649
Yoshikawa, H., 343, 360, 417, 420, 423, 424, 425, 429, 432, 433, 438, 550, 551, 564, 577
Young, H. J., 399, 413
Young, K. T., 100, 114, 154, 159, 335, 338
Young, M. E., 613, 629
Young-Holt, C., 475, 480
Yu, S. M., 39, 52, 320, 324
Yule, W., 667, 679

Zahn-Waxler, C., 66, 75, 162, 165, 176, 178, 563, 577
Zaslow, M. J., 371, 386, 552, 565, 567, 571, 574
Zastowny, T., 330, 336
Zax, M., 85, 93, 137, 138, 147, 159, 191, 202, 237, 238, 257, 266, 287
Zeanah, C., Jr., 277, 289, 380, 386, 417, 419, 438
Zecevic, N., 209, 217, 225
Zecker, S. G., 220, 222, 224
Zeitlin, S., 398, 415, 457, 483
Zeltzer, L. K., 116, 121, 130
Zervigon-Hakes, A., 592, 610
Zhang, D., 216, 227
Zhang, Q., 140, 159, 652, 681
Zigler, E. F., 3, 14, 15, 31, 90, 92, 115, 131, 137, 140, 157, 159, 280, 289, 364, 365, 386, 488, 509, 555, 570, 577, 584, 597, 508, 606, 610, 613, 621, 624, 627, 629, 636, 650, 651, 652, 663, 678
Zill, N., 135, 159, 239, 256
Zimmerman, M. A., 115, 132, 641, 650
Zimmerman, R. S., 107, 111
Zipper, I. N., 401, 415
Zito, J., 541, 546
Zoccolillo, M., 661, 662, 663, 682
Zola, I. K., 96, 102, 112
Zoll, D., 563, 575
Zuckerman, B., 46, 53, 61, 66, 70, 71, 72, 75, 154, 159, 312, 324, 332, 334, 335, 337, 338, 417, 419, 436
Zuckerman, D. S., 233, 256
Zuravin, S. J., 66, 75
Zvetina, D., 466, 480

Subject Index

A

abandonment, 61, 62
Abecedarian project, 513–515, 519, 564, 570, 591, 592, 603–604, 606
Abt Associates, 371, 523
academic achievement/success, 238, 239, 342, 672 (*see also* educational attainment)
acceptance, 190
accountability
  and evaluations of interventions, 496–498
  public, 19–20, 24, 84, 352–353
acculturation, 99–100, 101
action cycles, 260, 262
activism, by parents, 353
activity
  adolescent involvement, 139, 140
  disabled children's participation in, 181
  infant, 163
  sleep–wake, 263
adaptation
  assessment of, 266–267, 303
  brain, 38, 42, 49–50, 217, 220–221
  caregiver, 293
  culture and, 99, 101, 161, 172
  to disabled child, 151–153, 293, 500–501, 633–634, 636
  by families, 146, 303, 456, 500–501
  imagination and, 174–176
  maternal, 263
  measures of, 117, 172
  parent–child interaction, 12, 63–64, 167, 261, 262, 263, 266–267, 638
  protective factors and, 67, 116, 127–128, 140–141, 657
  severity of disability and, 504, 530
adaptive fit, 189–190

Administration for Children and Families, 605, 607
Administration for Children, Youth, and Families, 371
adolescent mothers
  affect, 266
  African American, 123, 127
  child characteristics, 68, 116
  community influences, 311, 363
  depression in, 66
  interaction with infants, 63–64, 66, 70, 266, 277
  interventions, 64–65, 70, 372, 381, 443, 451
  poverty, 362, 363
  resilience in, 122, 124, 127
adolescent parenting
  paraprofessional role, 451
  punitive, 266
  resilient infants, 118–119, 123
  risks, 59, 61, 63–65, 456
adolescents
  CNS development, 210, 214
  ecological risk factors, 138–140, 141, 663
  involvement in activities, 139–140
  protective factors within, 122, 663, 665–666
  substance abuse, 665–666
adoption, 260, 659, 668, 669
Adult Attachment Interview, 667
adversity index, 657, 660–661
advocacy (*see also* parent advocacy), 26, 335
AEPS Family Report, 235
affect
  assessment, 301
  attunement, *see* attunement
  disabled infants, 263

matching, 70
misregulated patterns of, 64, 66, 146
monitoring, 164
in parent–infant relationship, 55–56, 64, 65, 146–147, 154, 164, 262, 263, 266
affiliation, and control, 160, 166
African Americans, 60, 63
  adolescent mothers, 123, 127
  benefits of interventions, 597–602
  child care utilization, 341
  classification of disabilities of, 241
  early care and education, 351–352, 513, 514, 520
  leadership roles, 351–352
  infant mortality, 106
  intervention targeting, 363–364
  parenting practices, 108–109, 363–364
  poverty, 82, 85, 317, 364, 513, 514, 520
  research focus, 101
  resilience, 117, 123, 127
  stereotypes, 96, 241
age factors
  in acculturation levels, 99
  in assessments, 243, 245–246
  developmental disabilities, 47, 48
  in early care and education, 340, 511
  in resilience, 127, 656
agenesis of the corpus callosum, 37, 43, 46, 209
Ages and Stages Questionnaires, 247, 329
aggression, 66, 109, 312, 418
Aid to Families with Dependent Children (AFDC), 17, 77, 81, 342, 362, 383, 603, 616

Ainsworth Strange Situation paradigm, 278
alcohol
  binge drinking by adolescents, 665–666
  children of alcoholic parents, 122, 125, 127, 659, 666
  fetal effects, 35, 45–46, 61, 216
American Academy of Pediatrics, 327
  Committee on Children with Disabilities, 329, 336
  Committee on Practice and Ambulatory Medicine, 328, 336
American Academy of Pediatrics, Committee on Standards of Child Health Care, 327, 335
American Academy of Pediatrics, Task Force on Integrated School Health Services, 334, 336
American Association for Marriage and Family Therapy, 461, 478
American Association for the Study of the Feeble-Minded, 9
American Association on Mental Deficiency, 9
American Association on Mental Retardation, 9, 184
American Institutes for Research, 592, 607
American Occupational Therapy Association, 398, 410
American Psychiatric Association, 170, 176
American Public Health Association and American Academy of Pediatrics, 348, 356
American Public Health Association, Committee on Child Health, 327
amygdala, 211, 212, 213
anaclitic depression, 55–56, 636
andragogy, 476–477
androgynous model, 121–122
anemia, 47–48
anencephaly, 36, 205
Angelman syndrome, 39
anoxia, 13
anticipatory guidance, 328, 329–331, 333, 334
antipoverty programs (see also impoverished children; low-income families; socioeconomic status; welfare reform)
  income transfers, 615–617

public policy changes, 14, 15, 17–18
antisocial personality, 62
anxiety, 165, 418, 659, 668
Apgar scores, 48
applied behavior analysis, 181
aptitude–treatment interactions, 538–539, 540
aquaductal stenosis, 42
arborization, dendritic, 37, 46
arousal (learning condition), 57, 66, 167, 265
Asian Americans, 96, 101, 117, 123, 489
asphyxia, 36, 456
assessment (see also cognitive assessment; family assessment; specific instruments)
  of adaptation process, 266–267, 303
  affect, 301
  age factors in, 243, 245–246
  authentic, 250–251, 502
  behavioral, 181, 185, 187, 235–236, 269, 301, 303
  best practices, 403
  case vignettes, 271–275
  of child characteristics, 269
  classification issues, 241
  of communication, 276–277
  of community characteristics, 89–91, 309–323
  context-based, 235, 239–242, 250, 252–253, 267
  cost-effectiveness, 247
  cues, 240, 272
  cultural considerations in, 100, 103, 233, 234, 235–236, 240–241, 268, 269, 270
  curriculum-based, 244, 250
  definition, 232
  developmental continuum framework, 234, 238
  of developmental problems, 103, 241–242, 279–280, 328
  diagnosis/placement model, 239
  ecological approach, 89–91, 239–240, 241–242
  elements, 233, 237–251
  feedback stage, 242, 270, 272, 273, 278
  functional approach, 222, 234–235, 236, 241–242, 419
  goals, 231, 232, 233
  historical roots, 10–11
  inappropriate devices, 389
  instruments, 275–280, 301–304

integrated/multidimensional, 170–174, 232, 233, 235, 237–239, 242, 253, 394
intervention fused with, 236, 249–251, 252–253, 268, 271–272
judgment-based, 248–249
of moral development, 164, 165
multidisciplinary team approach, 246–249
needs-based, 301–302, 333–334
neurological, 49, 222
norm-referenced/standardized, 236, 241, 242–246, 248, 249, 250, 252, 267–268, 295, 328, 389, 492
of parent characteristics, 269
of parent–child interaction, 170, 233–235, 237, 265, 266, 267–282, 301
parent participation in, 233–234, 235–236, 242, 246–247, 249, 267, 269–270, 329
parent–professional relationship, 235–236, 268, 272
by pediatricians, 328–329
performance-based, 250–251, 252, 253
play-based, 232, 234–235, 241–242, 458
predictive value, 277
principles, 231–237
psychometric problems with, 243–246, 252
reassessment, 236–237
of reciprocity, 164, 266, 269
recommendations, 267–268
relational, 278–279
reliability, 244, 252, 328
risk indexes, 239
screening models, 239, 240, 247–248, 328, 329
sequence of, 233
setting for, 267, 268
of social support, 59, 303–304
social utility of, 239, 252–253
target, 237–239
validity, 233, 236, 239–240, 241, 242, 243, 247, 252, 267–268, 301–304, 328, 329
assimilation ideology, 102
Association for Behavior Analysis, 185
Association for Retarded Citizens, 22, 26, 394
Association of Medical Officers of American Institutions for Idiotic and Feeble-Minded Persons, 9

Association of Persons with Severe
    Handicaps, 185
Association of Teacher Educators
    (ATE), 468
attachment
    to alternative caregivers, 124, 674
    anxious, 152
    assessment, 67, 277–278, 375
    child care and, 349
    child maltreatment and, 120, 124,
        127, 152
    construct, 12
    developmental influences, 57–58,
        109
    disorders, 64, 152, 366
    environmental influences, 62
    insecure, 152, 667
    intervention model, 67, 428
    mental illness in parents and, 67,
        124, 277–278, 428
    parent–child interaction and, 260,
        261, 266, 331
    parenting and, 57–58, 64, 109, 147,
        163, 565
    preterm birth and, 152
    social support and, 60, 65, 67
attention
    deficits, 40, 45, 47, 61, 541
    disabled infants, 264
    neural development and, 211
attrition, 4, 374, 515–516, 536, 540,
    598
attunement
    maternal depression and, 65
    parent–infant relationship, 56,
        64–65, 167, 259, 260–261, 262
    transactional model, 148
auditory tract, development, 205,
    210
Australia, 333
Austria, 618
autism, 44, 190, 533–536, 540,
    635–636, 658
Autism National Committee, 636,
    647
autonomy, 63
    in parent–infant relationship,
        261
    in parental decision making,
        281
AVANCE program, 371, 373–374
aversive stimuli, 184–185
avoidance behavior, 64

B
Balanced Budget Act of 1997, 421
Barrier Box task, 120
Basic Language Concepts test, 538

Battelle Developmental Inventory
    (BDI), 243, 244–246, 328, 527,
    530, 531, 532
Bayley Scales of Infant Development
    II, 161, 265, 374
    at-risk infants, 67
    BDI compared, 244–246
    cognitive assessment, 103, 503
    Infant Behavior Record, 564
    Mental Development Index, 245,
        263, 279, 520, 532, 536
    Mental Scale, 275
    predictive value, 231, 244
    uses, 231
behavior
    antisocial, 656–657, 658, 659,
        660–662, 664, 668, 670, 672
    assessment of, 181, 185, 187,
        235–236, 269, 301, 303
    avoidance, 64
    competence, 188
    coping, 259
    delinquent, 419, 654–655, 658,
        660, 661
    experience and, 182
    family, 303
    genetics and, 162
    intentional requesting, 537
    modification, 9, 105, 144
    monitoring, 211
    moral development and, 166
    operant, 182
    oppositional–defiant, 656, 672
    parent–child interactive, 259–264,
        266, 269, 271, 292, 301
    parental code of, 143, 147–148,
        151–153, 154
    parenting, 36, 58–60, 63, 65, 68,
        69, 376
    protective, 86
    reciprocity and, 55, 214, 260–261
    resistance, 60
    respondent, 182
    response-contingent, 186
    self-initiated, 457
behavior-consequence relationship,
    182–183
behavioral/emotional disorders in
    children
    adolescent parenting and, 64
    assessments of, 139, 419
    brain development and, 44, 418
    child abuse and, 65, 135, 146–147
    in child care settings, 417, 424
    child-focused programs, 420
    in classroom settings, 538
    and communication problems,
        419

costs of treatment, 594
    early onset conduct disorder, 419,
        423, 563
    effectiveness of interventions,
        420–421
    family-focused interventions, 420
    in Head Start settings, 417, 418,
        419
    malnutrition and, 216
    multiple risk factors and, 266,
        419–420, 661
    parental psychopathology and,
        65–66, 563
    parenting style and, 109, 418
    pharmacological interventions,
        541
    poverty and, 418–419, 420
    prevalence, 135, 420, 424, 511
    protective factors, 117–120, 420,
        661–663, 670–671
    research initiatives, 421
    substance abuse and, 61
    violence exposure and, 64, 135,
        312, 419
behavioral perspective
    basic principles, 181–184
    challenges of, 187–192, 311
    contributions of, 184–187
    ecological approach integrated
        with, 191–197, 198, 311
    in education, 184–187, 417
    environmental interactions,
        190–191
    intervention implications,
        182–187, 197–198, 417
    negative perceptions of, 191
    in parent–child interaction, 55,
        168, 259–260, 262–264
    research implications, 198–199
behavioral synchrony, *see* synchrony
behaviorism, 11
Belgium, 621
Benchmarks project, 353
benefit-cost analysis, *see* cost-benefit
    analysis
Berkeley Study of Ego-Resiliency,
    125
best-practice principles, 377–380,
    383, 397–398, 403, 404, 408, 458,
    470, 534
biculturalism, 101, 110
Big Brother/Big Sisters, 129–130
bilingualism, 101, 110
biological screening indexes, 222
biologically impaired children,
    at-risk, 22
biracial heritage, 98
birth order, protective effects, 123

birth weight, *see* low-birth-weight infants; very low birth weight infants
Blacks, *see* African Americans
blind children, 264
block grants, 16, 17, 77
Board on Children, Youth and Families, 25
brain development (*see also* central nervous system)
  adaptation to injury, 38, 42, 49–50, 217, 220–221
  anatomical features, 205–206, 211–215
  cellular development, 37–38, 45, 46, 48, 49
  critical periods, 25, 204
  early intervention implications, 13, 25, 204, 211–215
  environmental influences, 14–15, 35–36, 37, 38, 40–41, 45, 46–48, 210, 215–217, 510
  experience and, 25, 204, 217–220
  injury and, 48–49
  malformation consequences, 41–43
  malnutrition and, 46–48, 215–216
  normal, 19, 35, 205–215
  plasticity, *see* neural plasticity
  size, 215–216
  stress and, 216, 218, 418
  synaptogenesis, 37–38, 46–47, 209–211, 510
  teratogens and, 45–46, 216
  ventricular system, 205
  weight, 46, 510
Brazil, 603
Brigance Screens, 328
Bright Futures initiative, 327, 328, 329, 335
Bright Start, 510
British Child Development Study, 666
Brookline Early Education Project (BEEP), 555, 584
Brown v. Board of Education, 106
Bulgaria, 88
Bureau of Economic Analysis, 591, 600, 608
Bureau of Education for the Handicapped, 10, 15
Bureau of Labor Statistics, 84
Bureau of Maternal and Child Health, 21
Business Roundtable, 342

C
California Achievement Tests, 516
California Child Care Resource and Referral Network, 353, 357

California initiatives, 353, 559, 592, 663
California Psychological Inventory, 122
California State Department of Education, 346, 356
Canada, 617
cardiovascular reactivity, 121
caregiver-child relationship (*see also* father–child relationship; mother–infant interaction; parent–child interaction)
  assessment of, 234–235
  intervention considerations, 168–169
  moral development, 164
caregiver-focused interventions for adolescent mother, 64–65, 70
Carey Temperament Scales, 532
Carnegie Corporation, ix, xii, 81, 353, 362, 363, 381, 384, 511, 549, 614
Carnegie Foundation for the Advancement of Teaching, 332
Carnegie Task Force on Learning in the Primary Grades, 345, 357, 549, 572, 627
Carnegie Task Force on Meeting the Needs of Young Children, 3, 27, 342, 357, 510, 511, 549, 572, 613, 614, 627
case management, 22, 370, 372, 373, 376, 380–381, 426
case method of instruction, 408
case study interviews, 401
Cattell Infant Intelligence Scale, 120, 260
ceiling effects, 243
center-based interventions
  evaluation of, 504, 529, 536
  intensity of service, 190–191
  outcome studies, 372, 504, 513–515
  parent-focused, 373, 555–557, 583–585
  plus home-based, 555–557, 583–585
  preterm/low-birth-weight infants, 153–154, 372, 520
  transactional model, 536
Center for Career Development in Early Care and Education, 351
Centers for Disease Control, 43, 51
Center for the Future of Children, xi, xii, 422, 435, 487, 505
Center for the Study of Social Policy, 352, 357
Center on Addiction and Substance Abuse, 85

central nervous system (*see also* brain development)
  adolescent development, 210, 214
  dysfunction origins, 38–41
  environmental mismatch, 534
  genetic disorders, 36, 38–41
  infections, 43–45
  malnutrition effects, 46–48
  normal development, 35, 36–38
  perinatal insults, 35, 48–49
  recovery from injury, 50
  toxicity, 45–46
cerebellum, 205, 209
cerebral palsy, 36, 43, 48–49, 181, 274, 398, 503, 532, 536, 630
cerebral white matter hypoplasia, 211
certification standards
  special education teachers, 15, 516
chain effects, 451, 665–666, 672–673
chain of enablement, 451
challenge model, 116
Chapter 1/Title I programs, 510, 512, 522–523
Charlotte Circle Project, 530
Charts a Course, 352
Chiari malformation, 41
Chicanas, 100
child abuse, *see* child maltreatment
child allowances, 616–517
Child and Family Center, 425
Child and Family Resource Programs (CFRP), 368, 370, 371, 375
Child Behavior Checklist, 64, 248
child care, 84, 87 (*see also* early care and education)
  adaptation to stressors, 116, 121
  behavioral/emotional problems of children in, 417, 424
  community-based programs, 528, 596
  cost considerations, 595–596, 597, 605
  demand for, 383, 525, 541
  European services, 621–622, 623
  family providers, 341, 343, 344, 348, 349, 350, 352, 443–445, 475
  historical roots, 6
  and intensity of services, 532–533
  linkages with other services, 353, 354, 372, 373, 515
  mental health principles in, 422, 424–425, 428
  paraprofessional role, 440, 443–445
  public policies, 18, 614

child care (*contd.*)
    quality of, 345–351, 372, 376, 409,
        443–445, 511, 541, 595
    regulation, 348, 349–350
    research needs, 199
    resource and referral initiatives, 353
    publicly subsidized, 382, 383, 525
    train-the-center approach, 424
    utilization trends, 341, 343
    welfare reform and, 525
Child Care Action Campaign, 353
Child Care and Education: Forging
    the Link Initiative, 353
Child Development Inventories, 329
child-focused programs
    economic perspective, 596–597
    in family-centered practice, 397,
        408, 462–463
    service delivery, 391, 392, 397, 408
    utilization, 554, 579–580, 583
child maltreatment
    assessment, 271
    and attachment, 120, 124, 127, 152
    and brain development, 221
    child-focused interventions, 77
    community influences, 311
    family-focused interventions, 371,
        373, 381
    home-based interventions, 81, 423,
        603, 620
    intergenerational effects, 56, 146,
        152
    mental health effects, 418
    parent-focused interventions, 152,
        424, 554, 557, 579–581, 583
    parents' characteristics, 65–67
    poverty and, 82–83, 84, 87–88, 362
    protective factors, 60, 118–120,
        122, 123, 124, 127, 664–665
    and reciprocity, 55–56
    risk factors for, 59, 60–69, 82–83,
        116, 373, 672
    sociology, 85–91
Child Parent Centers, 512, 522–523,
    603–604
Child–Parent Enrichment Project, 579
child protection agencies, 456,
    465–466, 634
Child Protection Block Grants, 77
child rearing, *see* discipline;
    parenting
child support benefits, 617
Child Survival/Fair Start initiative,
    441
Child Welfare Services, 7–8
Children's Bureau, 7
Children's Defense Fund, 3, 27, 135,
    157, 511, 543

ChildServ, 335
China, one-child policy, 80–81
chorioretinitis, 43, 44
Christchurch study, 660–661
chromosomal abnormalities, 36, 38,
    39–40
Circumplex Model, 303
Civil Rights Movement, 14, 16, 180,
    344, 526
classical conditioning, 182
classification systems, 169–170, 241
classroom-based interventions, 528,
    530–531, 538–539
cleft lip/palate, 43, 277
Clinical Infant Development Program
    (CIPD), 500
clinical infant programs, 366–368,
    500
Clinical Nursing Models study, 554,
    581
Clinton administration, 373, 549
cocaine, 45, 46, 61, 77, 216
cognitive assessment
    age-based norms, 241
    cultural issues, 110, 241, 488
    multidisciplinary perspective, 238
    outcome measures, 488
cognitive assimilation, 164, 165
cognitive development
    adolescent parenting and, 63, 64
    constructivist view of, 250, 458
    culture and, 103, 109–110, 488
    emotional deprivation and, 162
    ecological risk factors, 137, 216
    institutionalization and, 12
    in low-birth-weight infants, 372
    malnutrition and, 46–48, 216
    maternal depression and, 563
    mother–child interaction and,
        259–260, 266, 638
    motivation and, 163, 164
    neural systems, 204, 218
    Piagetian-based measures, 488
    stress and, 216
cognitive–affective processing,
    666–667, 674–475
Collaborative Perinatal Project, 12–13
Colorado initiatives, 351, 352, 353,
    381, 382, 390–391, 428, 528
Committee for Economic
    Development, 342, 357
Committee on Child Health, 327, 336
Committee on Integrating the
    Science of Early Childhood
    Development, 25
Commonwealth Fund, 335
communication
    with autistic children, 534

by blind infants, 264
development of, 167, 175, 237,
    260, 261, 276–277
disorders, 181, 398, 419
interhemispheric, 209, 218
mean length of utterance, 537
professionals' skills, 269, 467
structure and process assessment,
    276–277
training, 185, 460–461, 475, 537
community-based interventions
analytical strategies, 89–91, 320
antipoverty, 87–88
associational groups, 195
capacity building, 196, 198, 310
child-oriented, 310, 528, 529
data collection methods, 317–320
design, 313–320
effectiveness, 310, 529
family support, 90, 379
government linkages to, 310, 334
health care linked to, 334
for maladaptive parenting, 69–70,
    379
measurement units, 315–317
mental health, 428, 433, 434
paraprofessionals in, 379, 439,
    441, 443
programs and professionals,
    195–196
resource-based model, 194–197,
    198, 390
for substance abuse, 379
theoretical bases for, 311–313
violence-related, 69–70
community factors
adolescent mothers, 311, 363
contextual issues, 321–322
data collection, 315, 316, 321
ethical issues, 322
habitable environments, 321–322
in mental health services, 428
measurement and analysis,
    313–320
protective, 125–126, 312
in service delivery, 402–403
research needs, 320–323
risk, 85–91, 138–139, 312
social organization, 312, 318,
    321–322
unit of analysis, 314, 315–317,
    321
violence, 24, 86–87, 106, 172,
    312, 321
Community Partnerships for
    Children, 353
competence
    behavioral, 188

critical development periods, 25
cultural, 24, 240, 241
of fathers, 57
mutuality construct, 237
social, 314–315
resilient children, 50, 663–664
risk factors, 135–136
Comprehensive Adult Student
    Assessment System (CASAS), 558,
    559
Comprehensive Child Development
    Program (CCDP), 371–372, 373,
    375, 376, 377, 591, 592
Compehensive System of Personnel
    Development (CSPD), 454
Conduct Problems Prevention
    Research Group, 419, 421, 435,
    436
congenital HIV-1 infection, 44–45
congenital hypothyroidism, 216
congenital rubella, 36, 43–44
Connecticut initiatives, 352, 353, 381
conscience formation, 164
Consortium for Longitudinal Studies,
    516, 603, 608
constant time delay, 187
constructivist theories, 250, 458,
    488
contextualism, 11–12
    in assessment, 235, 239–242, 267,
        250, 252–253, 267
    in community studies, 321–322
    in development, 489, 490
    in service delivery, 331–334,
        402–403, 525
contingency analysis, 537–538
contingency-based stimulation, 182
contingent observation, 184
continuum of caretaking casualty, 11
continuum of reproductive casualty,
    11
coping
    bicultural competencies and, 110
    family mechanisms, 292, 293,
        294
    with maternal depression, 66
    with pain, 121
    parent–child interaction and, 259
    protective effects of, 652–653, 667,
        671
    theories, 293–294
Coping Project, 68, 120
corpus callosum, 37, 43, 46, 209, 211,
    217–218
cortical
    dysplasia, 37
    magnetoencephalography, 219–220
    reorganization, 219–221

cost analysis
    definition, 590
    of family support programs,
        440–441
    methodology, 589, 590–591
cost-benefit analyses, 596–597
    aggregation and interpretation,
        600–601
    assumptions and limitations,
        601–602
    definition, 590, 597
    of developmental screening, 247
    distributional consequences,
        601
    of evaluations of interventions,
        503–504
    key policy variables, 605–606
    limitations of, 590
    longitudinal studies, 602–605
    methodologies, 503–504, 597
    monetary value of costs and
        benefits, 590, 598–600
    for nonpoor disabled children,
        604–605
    Perry Preschool Project, 597–602
    for poor disabled children,
        602–604
    program effects, 526–527, 598
    program resources, 597–598
cost containment, 382–383
cost-effectiveness analysis, 530
    definition, 590, 597
    of developmental screening, 247
    limitations of, 590
    objectives of, 503–504
    of paraprofessional employment,
        377, 383, 440–441
Cost, Quality, and Child Outcomes in
    Child Care Centers study, 343,
    511
Cost, Quality, and Child Outcomes
    Study Team, 343, 349, 350, 357
costs of early intervention, 591–593
    duration of services and, 593
    and incentive structure, 596
    health care, 84, 150
    Infant Health and Development
        Program, 521
    intensity of services and, 84,
        593–595
    number of services and, 595
    to parents, 595–596
    special education, 17
Council for Exceptional Children,
    Division for Early Childhood
    (DEC), 15, 459
Council of Chief State School
    Officers, 346, 353, 357

Council of Economic Advisers, 3, 19,
    27, 550
Council on Child and Adolescent
    Health, 550, 573
countertransference, 168, 379, 447,
    634–635
criminality, 516, 598, 599, 603–604,
    605, 658, 661, 668
crisis intervention and support, 433
criterion-referenced measures, 246
critical periods, brain, 25, 204
cultural code, 99, 143, 144, 148, 151,
    153, 154, 166, 269
cultural deprivation, 14, 87, 101
cultural mismatches
    in assessment, 240, 241
    home and school settings, 490
    in parents' values, 102–105
    service provider–client, 96–97, 269,
        501
cultural mistrust, 106–107
Cultural Mistrust Inventory, 107
cultural risk factors
    conceptual framework, 95
    as independent variables, 95
    intervention implications, 23–24
    historical construction of, 100–102
    minority status as, 96, 97, 105–107
culture
    and adaptation, 99, 101, 161, 172
    and assessment, 100, 103, 233,
        235–236, 240–241, 268, 269,
        270, 299–300
    evaluation considerations, 488,
        501
    growth-promoting influences, 60,
        107–110, 160, 489
    individuality, 95, 98–100, 161
    and intervention, 166, 363–364,
        431, 514
    and moral development, 166
    paraprofessional bridge role, 441
    and parenting style, 102–105, 269,
        280, 363–364, 369, 489
    race/ethnicity distinguished, 95,
        96, 97–98
    sensitivity training, 475
    service delivery considerations,
        334, 335, 369, 402, 431, 433,
        441, 456, 458, 464
    as social class, 96
curriculum content
    behavioral-ecological perspective,
        188–190
    High/Scope approach, 516, 524
    Partners for Learning, 520
Cuyahoga County Mental Health
    Board, 424–425

cystic fibrosis, 47
cytomegalovirus (CMV), 38, 43

D

DARCEE project, 518–519, 582
Danish National Health Service, 619, 620, 627
Day Care Plus, 424–425, 427
DC: 0–3 system, 170
Decade of the Brain, 510
delay trials, 187
delayed non-match to sample (DNMS) task, 212
delayed-response (DR) tasks, 214
delinquent behavior, 419, 654–655, 658, 660, 661
demographic context, 55
  for child development, 95, 31, 313–320
  for early care and education, 340, 518–519
  for family participation rates, 566
  for resilience, 665
dendrites, 37, 46, 50, 210, 211–212
Denmark, 331, 333, 617, 618–620, 621, 622, 623
dentate gyrus, 209, 211, 212, 213
Denver Child Health Passport, 333, 334
Denver Developmental Screening Test II, 247, 328, 329
depression
  anaclitic, 55–56, 636
  in children, 541, 563
  genetic factors, 658
  intervention effects, 556, 565
  maternal, 61, 65–67, 85, 146, 238–239, 266, 366, 374, 515, 524, 540, 556, 563, 653
  and parent education, 515, 524
  poverty and, 417
  protective factors, 652, 665, 667–668, 669, 670
  substance abuse and, 61, 62
  violence and, 63
determinism, 11
  genetic, 4, 11
developmental change
  beliefs affecting evaluations, 487–490
  experience and, 366
  milestones, 234, 328, 329
  normative processes of, 102, 161, 163, 366
  motivation and, 163–164
  sociocultural contexts, 234, 488–489

transition periods, 173–174
developmental continuum approach, 169, 233, 238, 462
developmental delays, 20
  assessment of, 244, 275–276, 279
  definition, 21
  effectiveness of interventions, 529
  prevalence, 135
  at-risk children, 21–22, 181
  services for, 389, 395, 428
  socioemotional development, 457
developmental disabilities (*see also* disabled infants)
  age factors, 47, 48
  assessment of, 239, 241–242, 279–280, 328
  and cognitive development, 172
  definition, 334
  and emotional development, 172
  ethno-theories of, 104–105
  fix-it approach, 457, 525
  genetic causes, 39–41
  malnutrition and, 46–48
  parent reaction to, 193
  premature infants, 36
  public policies, 15–16
  screening for, 328
  severity considerations, 503–504, 529, 530, 532–533
  stressors due to, 193–194
  substance abuse and, 61
developmental guidance, 329–331
developmental monitoring, 247–248, 328–329, 334
developmental psychopathology, 419, 651
developmental surveillance, 247–248, 328–329
developmental therapies, 398–399, 422–423, 427–428, 455, 458, 465, 469, 527, 532
developmentally appropriate practice
  definition, 459
  inclusive settings, 459–460
  principles, 458–459, 488
  in special education, 458, 470
diagnosis (*see also* assessment)
  classification system, 430–431
  process, 169–170
dialectic approaches to development, 188
direct instruction methods, 516–518, 524, 537, 538–539
disabled infants/children (*see also* developmental delays; developmental disabilities)

adaptation of parents to, 151–153, 293, 500–501, 633–634, 636
affect, 263
assessment instruments, 279–280, 389
community-based interventions, 528, 529
effectiveness of interventions, 512, 525–540
family-centered practice, 397–398
inclusive settings, 399
interactive behaviors, 262–264
parent involvement, 13, 59
Part B services, 527–528
service delivery models, 389–396
special education, 8–10, 21
therapies, 398–399
transition between services, 399–400
utilization of services, 500
discipline, 4, 59, 60, 78
  authoritative, 312, 564, 565
  cultural considerations, 103, 109
  and externalizing behaviors of children, 109
  punitive, 85, 109, 266, 418, 556, 557, 564
distance learning, 477
distractor coping style, 121
divorce, 116, 118–119, 120–121, 122, 124, 125–126, 652, 659, 663, 666
Domestic Volunteer Service, 129
dorsolateral prefrontal cortex, 214
Double ABCX Model, 293
Down syndrome, 456
  assessment instruments, 10, 275
  attention duration, 264
  brain development, 38, 210
  developmental growth, 388, 503
  effectiveness of interventions, 529, 531, 532, 536, 638
  genetics, 39
  interactive behaviors, 262, 263, 264–265, 271–272, 275
  language development, 264–265
  outcomes studies, 13, 511
  parent–professional relationship, 635–636, 638

E

Early and Periodic Screening, Diagnosis, and Treatment Program (EPSDT), 8, 382, 407
early care and education (*see also* child care; Early Head Start; Head Start; preschool; special education)

accountability, 352–353
African Americans, 351–352, 513, 514, 520
age considerations, 340, 511
and attachment, 349
attitudes toward, 341–342, 348
demographic changes and, 340
developmental outcomes, 341–342, 343, 346, 355, 511
equity in, 342, 343–344, 351
evaluation of, 346, 515–517
finding and selecting, 347
funding and financing, 342, 343–344, 348, 350, 352, 354, 355–356
governance, 350–351, 352–353, 354, 356
infrastructure, 344, 345, 350
licensing issues, 345, 347–348, 349–350, 351–352, 355
mental health principles integrated with, 422, 423
parent education component, 523–524
parent engagement in, 345, 346–347, 353, 354, 355, 423
quality of services, 341, 343, 346–356
reform efforts, 353–355
and school readiness, 343–344
service delivery patterns, 339, 341
sociodynamic problems, 339–342
state initiatives, 348, 349–350, 351, 352
structural issues, 342–343, 344–345
training and education of staff, 345, 347, 348–349, 351–352, 355
welfare reform and, 342
early childhood education (see also special education)
developmentally appropriate practice, 458–460
remedial and compensatory, 101, 535
Early Childhood Environmental Rating Scale, 518, 528
Early Childhood Family Education, 381
Early Childhood Initiative, 549
Early Childhood Leadership Institute, 352
Early Childhood Longitudinal Study, 18
Early Childhood Research and Intervention Program, 536
Early Childhood Support Services, 428

Early Development and Risk Factors Model, 192–194, 196–197, 198
Early Education Program for Children with Disabilities, 180
Early Education Quality Improvement Project (EQUIP), 352–353
Early Head Start, 18–19
  core services, 373
  costs, 592
  eligibility, 568
  evaluation, 171–174, 373, 566, 568
  financing, 373, 382
  mental health principles in, 168, 422
  parent participation, 373, 562, 566
  parenting initiative, 473, 562
  staff–parent relationships, 566
Early Intervention Centers of the Positive Education Program, 424, 427
Early Intervention Collaborative Study (EICS), 500–501, 504, 638
early onset conduct disorder, 419, 423, 563
Early Screening Inventory (ESI), 328
Early Training Project, 364
ecobehavioral analysis, 241, 242
ecocultural development framework, 489
ecological congruence model, 188–190, 192, 197, 199
ecological perspective
  assessment, 89–91, 239–240
  in collective empowerment model, 644
  definition, 76
  early intervention implications, 79, 81, 368–369, 555
  exosystems, 79–80, 84, 643
  family support programs, 368–369
  instructional strategies, 188–190
  macrosystems, 80–81, 84, 489–490, 643
  mesosystems, 79, 489, 643
  microsystems, 54, 78–79, 84, 138, 489, 490, 643
  on neighborhood social organization, 313–314, 318
  resource-based approach, 194–196, 198
  risk factors, 89–91, 137–140, 141, 192–194, 198
  systems approach, 77–81, 192, 489, 643
  theory, 311

Economic Opportunity Act, 15, 441
economic analysis of interventions (see also cost analysis)
  and developmental risk, 81–85, 106
  definition, 589–590
Education Commission of the States, 342, 357
Education for All Handicapped Children Act, 16, 345
Education of the Handicapped Act, see Public Law 99-457
education of practitioners, see training
educational attainment
  and child rearing practices, 100
  and early care and education participation, 340
  family-centered programs and, 372, 540–541
  and IQ of children, 85
  maternal, 13, 100, 122, 123, 238, 265, 340, 541, 553, 555–556, 558–559
  as outcome measure, 172, 237, 238, 372, 540–541, 558
  parent-focused interventions and, 523–524, 553, 555–556, 558–559
  and parent–infant interaction, 265–266, 277
  and resilience of children, 123, 659, 663, 665, 674
  and social support, 60
educational interventions
  (see also early care and education; parent education; preschool education; special education)
  behavioral perspective in, 184–192
  developmentally appropriate practice, 458–460
  environmental perspective in, 188–190
  historical roots, 4–6, 179–180
  intensity of, 190–191
  nature of disabilities and, 180–181
  for parent–child interaction, 167
  rationale for, 179–181, 673
Elementary and Secondary Education Act, (ESEA), 510, 523
eligibility for services
  assessment of, 244–246
  definition, 334
  and disability prevalence, 18
  under IDEA Part C, 21–22
  and service coordination, 351, 403
  welfare reform and, 334–335, 568–569

emotional
  assessment, *see* socioemotional
    assessment
  associations, 212, 214
  availability, 56, 57, 61, 62, 64, 65,
    66, 163, 164, 165, 166–168, 266,
    273
  deprivation, 162
  development, 5–6, 62, 418
  disorders (*see* behavioral/emotional
    disorders)
  expressions, 214
  referencing, 56
  regulation, 55, 61, 65, 66, 165,
    166–168, 277
empathy
  bicultural competency and, 110
  genetic influence, 162
  moral development and, 165
  in parent-child relationship, 262,
    265
  in parent–professional relationship,
    167–168, 268, 271, 460, 467, 475
employers, parent support by, 347
employment
  and early care and education, 340,
    341, 599
  family intervention, 15, 370–371
  as outcome measure, 172, 516–517
  parent-focused interventions and,
    524, 553, 555–556, 558–559
  protective effects, 553, 664, 667
  public assistance tied to, 17, 18,
    370–371
empowerment, *see* parent
  empowerment
encephalitis, 43
encephalopathy, 44, 48
entorhinal cortex, 211, 212
environmental influences, 13 (*see also*
  ecological perspective)
  on brain development, 14–15,
    35–36, 37, 38, 40–41, 45, 46–48,
    210, 215–217
  cumulative, 137–140, 237
  family, 137, 138, 192–194, 292,
    295
  genetic interactions with, 40–41,
    161–162, 654
  indexes of, 322
  intervention implications, 11, 172,
    188–190
  minority status and, 106
  promotive factors, 140–141
  on parenting, 54–56, 59, 68,
    265–267, 274, 653–654
  resilience and, 653–654, 673–674
  risk factors, 22, 68, 456, 653–654

environmental manipulation, 11,
  449–450
environtype, 143–149
epithalamus, 205
equity issues, 343–344, 456
ethical issues
  in community studies, 322
  parents' costs of intervention, 596
  untreated control groups, 4
ethnicity
  assessment issues, 241
  concept, 97–98
  neighborhood structural effects,
    313–314, 316–317
  and resilience, 123
ethnographic studies, 317–318, 319
ethno-theories, 97
  of disease and treatment, 104–105
ethology, 163
eugenics movement, 9
European Commission Network on
  Child Care and Other Measures
  to Reconcile Employment and
  Family Responsibilities, 617, 621,
  623, 627
European Health Committee, 331,
  336
European interventions (*see also*
  individual countries)
  early intervention policies, 613
  income transfers, 615–617
  parental leave programs, 617–618
  services, 618–622
euthanasia, 8
evaluability assessment, 498–500
evaluation of interventions (*see also*
  outcome measures)
  accountability and, 496–498
  average-expectable conditions, 372
  beliefs about developmental
    change and, 487–490, 497
  complementarity approach, 492,
    494–495
  constructivist paradigm, 488,
    491–492
  cost-benefit analyses, 503–504
  demonstration projects, 14, 21, 334
  development designs, 495
  ecological perspective, 502
  effectiveness of programs, 170–174,
    280–281, 334, 502–503, 511–515,
    522–523, 590
  empowerment models, 491–492,
    493–494, 497, 501–502
  epistemological approach, 493
  ethnographic methods, 494
  evolution of program and, 498–500
  expansion designs, 495

experimental (positivist) approach,
  489, 490–491, 492, 494
family-centered programs,
  371–372, 400–401, 498
follow-up assessment, 530,
  538–539, 540, 560–561
Head Start, 365–366, 487, 496,
  518–519
initiation designs, 495
internal comparisons, 530–531
latent effects of early interventions,
  280
measurement of change, 280,
  502–503, 512, 513–514
mechanistic paradigm, 487–488
methodological problems, 512,
  513–514, 517, 523, 530
mixed-methods design, 494–495,
  501
naturalistic contexts for, 492, 494
neurophysiological, 38
of operation of programs, 500–502
of parent–professional
  collaboration, 501
parent-satisfaction measure,
  400–401
participatory models, 491–492,
  493–494, 568
particularistic research, 492–493
perspectivistic models, 493–494,
  500
political context of, 365–366,
  496–498, 518
postpositivist paradigm, 491
of program components and goals,
  498–499
qualitative (holistic) methods,
  492–493, 494
quantitative methods, 492, 493,
  494–495
readiness of program for, 375,
  498–500, 540
reliability and validity criteria,
  495–496
"sleeper effects," 376
social choice framework, 491–492
social value of programs, 491
sociocultural contexts for, 488–490,
  501
stakeholders' influence, 493–494,
  496–498, 499
technical feasibility, 499–500
theories of change approach,
  170–174, 499, 502, 567–568
traditional frameworks for, 491,
  490–492
triangulation of results, 495
utilization of services, 500, 503–504

value-added analysis, 527
verification paradigm, 491
Even Start, 371, 375, 390, 394, 510, 512, 523–524, 525, 540, 558–559, 560, 586
event-related potential, 222
exclusionary time out, 184
executive functions, neural systems, 204, 211, 213–215
exosystems, 79–80, 84
expectations, 217, 377–378, 439
  in counseling/psychotherapy model, 634
  lowered, in paraprofessionals, 379–380, 439, 448–449
  parental, 524
experiences
  active, 262
  and behavior, 182
  cognitive–affective processing of, 666–667, 674–675
  developmental effects, 10–11, 14–15, 25, 50, 79, 204, 217–220
  family-orchestrated, 192–193
  neutralizing or compensatory, 674
extended family, decision making process, 103
externalities, 84

F
failure to thrive, 39, 44, 277
Fair Start, 510
faith, see religious values/beliefs
Families and Work Institute, 352–353
family
  adaptability, 146, 303, 456, 500–501
  allowances, 616–517
  alternative caregivers in, 123–124
  chores and responsibilities of children, 125
  cohesion, 303
  decision-making role, 457, 461, 631, 639
  definition, 23
  functioning, 144, 300, 302–303, 461
  high-risk, 87
  income, 340, 616–617
  influential characteristics, 193, 292–293, 405
  interaction patterns, 192–193, 292
  management of community, 138–139
  needs and priorities, 301–301
  practices and representations, 144–145, 146–147, 152, 154

relationships, 169, 666
rituals, 146, 148–149, 165
size, 85, 266, 625
stories, 145–146, 148–149, 152–153, 299, 461
values and beliefs, 97, 143, 145, 166, 236, 489–490
Family Adaptability and Cohesion Evaluation Scales (FACES), 303
family assessment (see also assessment; Individualized Family Service Plan)
  advantages, 290
  constraints, 291, 296–298, 304–305
  eco-cultural approach, 299–300
  empowerment model, 294–295
  essential domains, 297, 299
  formal methods, 297, 300–304
  guidelines, 296, 297, 298–299
  informal approaches, 297, 298–300
  instruments and measures, 294, 295, 300–304
  intervention implications, 297, 298, 299, 300
  legal/programmatic frameworks, 291, 296
  parent–professional relationship, 294–295, 304
  theoretical bases, 292–296
  training/competency of professionals, 296, 297, 298, 305
family-centered interventions, 12 (see also parent-focused programs)
  assumptions in, 640
  best-practice principles, 377–380, 383, 397–398, 404, 408
  challenges, 397–398
  characteristics common to, 398
  choice component, 639
  community-based, 90, 379, 380
  cultural considerations, 103, 105, 369, 462, 534, 640
  definition of, 397
  direct services for infants in, 378, 397, 534
  ecological model, 95, 138, 368–369
  education programs, 514–515
  empowerment model, 251, 292, 294–295, 461, 631 (see also parent empowerment)
  evaluation of, 371–372, 532, 562–567
  expectations, 378–379, 397, 641
  family perspectives, 640–641
  home visits, 368, 379, 514

implementation trends, 397–398
literacy programs, 557–560, 563–564
long-term, 371–372
mental health services, 379–380, 416, 421, 425, 427, 431, 432–433
mission and boundaries, 377, 379–380
outcomes, 371–372, 555
parent-professional relationship, 294–295, 405, 456, 630–632, 638–641
pediatric health services, 333–334
parents' role in, 377–378, 456–457
personnel training, 368, 369, 408
philosophical base, 456–457
power aspects of, 639–640
professional perspectives, 457, 640
risk factors model, 192–194
service delivery systems, 371, 397–398, 404, 408, 427
strengths perspective, 457, 461, 639
theoretical frameworks, 377, 380
two-generation approach, 370–371
family centers, 368, 381, 382, 395, 522–523, 625, 629
Family Child Care Connection, 443, 444
family child care providers, 341, 343, 344, 348, 349, 350, 352, 443–445, 475
family code
  intervention implications, 151, 152, 153, 154
  transactional model, 143, 144–147, 148
family environment
  assessment, 292–293
  community influences, 311–312, 313
  developmental implications, 192–194, 292–293, 636
  maternal, 238–239
  protective factors, 36, 123–125, 127–128, 129, 659
Family First, 379
Family Functioning Style Scale, 302–303
Family Information Preference Inventory (FIPI), 302
Family Intergenerational Literacy Model (FILM), 559, 587
family involvement (see parent participation)
Family Life Development Center, 83, 92
Family Needs Scale (FNS), 302, 303

Family Needs Survey, 297, 301–302, 303, 304
family resource centers, 381, 382, 428
Family Resource Coalition, 369, 385
Family Resource Scale, 302
family service plans, see Individualized Family Service Plan
Family Support Act of 1988, 569
family support programs, 624–626
    cost analyses, 440–441, 597
    evaluation, 491
    flagship, 498
    historical background, 368–369, 614
    mental health services, 422–423, 426
    paraprofessionals in, 440–441
Family Support Scale, 303
family systems approaches
    advantages, 366
    to assessment, 170
    in preventive health care, 335
    relationship strengthening, 169
    theory, 368–369, 456
    therapy, 366
family workers (see also home visitor programs, paraprofessionals)
    clinical supervision of, 423
    education of, 361
father–child relationship, 56–57, 258–259
fathers
    absent, 85, 96, 124
    of low-birth-weight babies, 521
    maternity leave, 618
    role of, 56–58, 66, 641
    social networks, 59
feedback (see also reciprocity)
    in assessment, 242, 270, 272, 273, 278
    reeducation component, 153
    in systems, 77
fetal alcohol syndrome, 35, 45–46, 216
Finance Project, 352
Finland, 333, 348, 617, 618, 621, 623
fix-it approach, 457, 513, 525, 634, 644
Florida, 353, 528, 534, 592
flow models, 499, 502
FMR-1 gene, 39
Food Stamps, 616
Ford Foundation, 364
forebrain, 205–206, 208
foster care, 77, 82, 129, 362, 382, 466
fragile X syndrome, 39, 210

France, 333, 348, 603, 617, 621, 622, 623, 624–625
friendships, 125–126, 186
Froebelian approach, 6, 344
Functional Emotional Assessment Scale (FEAS), 232, 234, 235
functional communication training, 185
functional magnetic resonance imaging, 222

G
gaze behavior, 262
gender differences
    in family stories, 145
    in resilience, 125, 126, 127, 662, 663, 665, 666
General Cognitive Index, 538
generalization
    of community influences, 315, 317
    of cost–benefit analyses, 603
    of skills, 185–186, 537, 538
    within-group differences and, 95, 107
generation effect in efficacy of programs, 530
generational middle-class status, 96
genetic determinism, 4, 11, 14, 76
genetic disorders, 38–41, 211, 503
genetic risk factors, 654, 658
genotype, 40–41, 128, 143, 161–162, 660, 668–669, 670
Georgia initiatives, 353, 381, 382, 528
Germany, 603, 618, 621
germinal matrix hemorrhage, 49
"ghosts in the nursery," 56, 152, 168, 634
glial cells, 37, 38, 208, 209, 210, 215
Goals 2000 program, 549
goodness of fit, environmental, 188–189
graduated guidance, 187
grandparents, 60, 67, 103, 105, 124, 129
Gray Areas programs, 364
Great Depression, 6, 9, 123, 125, 127, 667
Great Society, 636
Greek Civil War survivors, 116, 126
grief, parental, 273, 633–634
grief and loss model, 456
Gross Domestic Product Deflator for State and Local Purchases of Goods and Services, 600
group friendship activities, 186
group well-child visits, 332
growth retardation, 12, 43, 45, 46, 49, 61

Guatemalan children, 238
gyral development, 210
    errors, 209

H
habitable environments, standards for, 321
habituation paradigm, 260
Haitians, 103, 107
handicapped infants, see disabled infants/children
Handicapped Children's Early Education Assistance Act, 14
Handicapped Children's Early Education Program (HCEEP), 21, 180, 281, 531, 592, 637
Happy Puppet syndrome, 39–40
Hartford Foundation for Public Giving, 335
Hawaii initiatives, 353, 371, 381, 423
Hawkins-Stafford Elementary and Secondary School Improvement Amendments of 1988, 523, 558
head size, 40, 42, 44, 46
Head Start (see also Early Head Start), 345, 394
    behavioral and emotional problems of children, 417, 418, 419, 421
    costs, 591, 592, 593, 594, 595, 605–606
    curriculum, 364–365, 515–516
    disabled children in, 15
    enrollments, 341, 621
    evaluation, 365–366, 487, 496, 512, 518–519
    funding, 352, 353, 382, 510, 614
    mental health component in, 422, 423–424, 425, 428, 431, 432
    outcome studies, 137, 365–366, 518–519
    parent participation in, 364, 382, 417, 423, 569, 636
    peer treatment program, 129
    performance standards, 424
    principles, 370
    purposes, 365, 620–621
    quality issues, 365, 372, 382, 518, 621
    research and development on services, 366, 421
    roots, 14–15, 16, 17, 180, 364, 620–621
    services offered, 15, 137, 372
    settings, 399, 460
    strengths, 365, 382
    teacher training, 364, 365, 372, 423, 594
    waiting lists, 343

Head Start Act, 18
Head Start Longitudinal Study, 518
health care (see also pediatric
    preventive health care)
    access to, 614
    European services, 618–620
    paraprofessionals in, 451
Health Care Financing
    Administration, 327
health fairs, 395
Health Resources Services
    Administration, 371, 374
Healthy Families America, 371, 373,
    382, 423
Healthy Start programs, 371, 373,
    374, 381, 423
Healthy Steps for Young Children,
    335
hearing impairments, 43, 44, 120,
    510, 530, 594
helper therapy principle, 441
Helping Relationship Inventory,
    566–567
helping relationships, 195, 377–379
Heschl's gyrus, 210
hierarchical linear modeling,
    502–503, 564
High/Scope Educational Research
    Foundation, 349, 516–518, 524,
    555, 556, 585
hindbrain, 205
hippocampus, 209, 211–212, 213,
    216, 218
Hispanics
    child care utilization, 340, 341
    family ecology, 60, 97, 99, 103,
        489
    interventions, 373, 515, 561
    parent–child interaction, 277
    poverty, 82
HIV infection
    congenital, 44–45
    maternal, 46
Hmong parents, 103
holding environment, 62, 379, 449
holocaust survivors, 116, 124, 126
holoprosencephaly, 36
home-based interventions, 153,
    531–533
    behavioral aides, 425
    center-based with, 555–557,
        583–585
    costs, 606
    effectiveness, 527, 529
    parent-focused, 552–555, 560–561,
        563–564, 579–582
home environment, 50
    assessment in, 267, 268, 273, 301

and cognitive development, 47
and effectiveness of interventions,
    529
parent-focused interventions and,
    523–524, 554, 556–557, 560,
    579–588
Home Instruction Program for
    Preschool Youngsters (HIPPY),
    560–561, 588
Home Observation for Measurement
    of the Environment (HOME)
    Inventory, 103, 374, 375, 532, 552,
        554, 561, 563–564
    Screening Questionnaire, 560
Home Start, 592
Home Visiting 2000 Program, 567
home visitor programs, 69, 464
    child abuse prevention, 373, 423,
        620
    for depressed mothers, 66–67
    education component, 514–515,
        524
    effectiveness, 511, 514–515, 564,
        624
    European services, 618–620, 624
    evaluation of, 504
    health supervision services,
        331–332, 618–620, 624
    historical background and
        purposes, 363, 364
    interdisciplinary team approach,
        367
    intervention models, 66–67, 368,
        373–374
    for low birth weight premature
        infants, 519–522
    mental health services, 66–67,
        367, 422–423, 426–427, 428,
        563, 620
    outcome studies, 66–67, 81, 504
    paraprofessionals, 373, 379, 423,
        441
    premature/low-birth-weight
        infants, 153, 372
    relationship building, 378, 379
    staff characteristics, 566–567
    for substance abuse, 379
homelessness, 12, 61
Hospice des Incurables, 9
hospitalism, 12
hostility, children, 109
housing subsidies, 617
Howard Heinz Endowment, 381
hydrocephaly, 41, 42, 44, 49, 630
hyperactivity, 40, 216, 218, 658, 669
hypothalamus, 205, 218
hypoxic–ischemic encephalopathy,
    48

I
Illinois initiatives, 382, 465–466
imagination, 174–176
immigrants, 110
    mistrust of intervention services,
        107
    neighborhood composition, 319
    research needs, 130
    resocialization of, 101–102
    undocumented, 107
    welfare reform effects, 383
immune competence, stress and,
    121
immunity model, 116
immunizations, 43
implementation of programs/services,
    19, 21, 24, 407–408
impoverished children
    community influences, 313–314
    costs of interventions, 594
    cultural influences, 96, 106, 241
    effectiveness of interventions,
        511–525, 540
    evaluation of programs, 172,
        522–523
    infant mortality, 84
    lowered expectations in adulthood,
        447–448
    low birth weight, 512, 519–521
    malnutrition, 46–48
    mental health, 417, 418–419
    protective factors, 57–58, 116,
        118–119, 122, 123, 659
    number of, 82, 135, 362, 511, 518
    risk source, 23, 46–48, 81–83, 84,
        96, 141, 266, 362, 456
imprinting, genomic, 39
inborn errors of metabolism, 40
income transfer programs,
    615–617
incidental teaching, 187
inclusive settings, 469, 474, 478
    (see also naturalistic)
    advantages, 460
    definition, 459–460
    determinants of success, 460
    developmentally appropriate
        practice, 459–460, 470
    goals of, 460
    IDEA mandate, 399, 459–460
    and outcomes, 531
    training in, 454, 455, 470, 474
    transition to, 528
independence, in disabled children,
    180, 181, 190, 458
India, 603
indirect chain effects, 656–657, 660,
    662, 665–666, 669, 672–673

individuality
  and assessment, 166
  culture and, 95, 98–100, 161
  genetics and, 161–162
  strengths of, 161–163
Individualized Education Plan (IEP)
  appropriateness of objectives,
    527–528
  assessment issues, 246
  history, 16
  interdisciplinary approach, 463,
    469
  parent involvement in, 637
Individualized Family Service Plan
  (IFSP), 199
  assessment implications, 291,
    303–304, 389, 394, 529
  child-focused, 397
  coordination goal, 394
  cultural considerations, 103
  development and content, 291,
    296
  family strengths-based perspective,
    461
  interdisciplinary approach, 463
  interviews, 303–304
  parent contribution to, 298, 456,
    637–638, 641
  P.L. 99-457, 22, 291
  programmatic challenges, 291
Individuals with Disabilities
  Education Act, see Public Law
  102-119, 398, 412
Infant Health and Development
  Program, 153, 157
Infant Health and Development
  Project (IHDP), 153, 154, 371,
    372–373, 375, 376, 512, 519–522,
    525, 541, 555, 556, 557, 563,
    565, 566, 567, 583, 591, 592, 604
Infant Mental Health Program, 428
infant mortality, 7, 41–42, 44, 49, 82,
  106, 107, 371, 620
infant–parent psychotherapy, 152,
  163, 168
infant specialization
  content of training, 466–467
  personnel, 465–466
  rationale for, 464–465
  roles and competencies, 466
Infant–Toddler Assessment Scale, 249,
  250
Infant–Toddler Developmental
  Assessment (IDA), 232, 235, 249
infantile amnesia, 213
inferior colicus, 205
inferior temporal cortex, 211,
  212–213

ingredients model, 590–591
INREAL program, 602
Institute for Research on Poverty, 550
Institute of Medicine, 25, 313, 324
institutional racism, 363–364
institutionalization, 12, 218,
  663–664, 671
instructional strategies
  case method, 408
  direct, 516–518, 524, 537, 538–539
  sign language, 531
intelligence/IQ
  brain malformations and, 41, 43
  community influences, 311
  environmental risks and, 138
  experience and, 14–15, 363
  family environment and, 636
  fetal alcohol syndrome and, 45
  genetic disorders and, 39, 40
  low-birth-weight infants, 372,
    520–522, 604–605
  maternal, 265
  as outcome measure, 138, 372, 515,
    520, 534, 538, 539
  parent education programs and,
    515
  predictors, 85, 238, 241, 503
  preschool programs and, 364,
    365–366, 513–515, 516, 597–598
  and resilience, 67, 68, 122–123,
    127, 660, 663, 665, 670–671
  socioeconomic status and, 78,
    241
  testing, 9, 242–246, 252, 503
intensity of services, 84, 190–191,
  501, 529, 530, 532–533, 534,
  593–595
interaction processes, 661–663
interagency cooperation
  local interagency coordinating
    council, 392, 393, 394
  mental health services, 426–427
  in service delivery, 389, 392–393,
    394–395, 396, 403, 430, 464
Interdisciplinary Early Childhood
  Education (IECE) Program, 474
intergenerational
  effects, 24, 56, 62, 70, 146, 151
  literacy programs, 557–560,
    563–564, 570
  research, 130
interprofessional education, 477
intervention planning
  assessment issues, 244
  community involvement, 374
  cultural considerations in, 166
  ecological congruence model,
    189–190

environtype considerations,
  143–149
future-oriented, 174–175
long-term perspective, 170–174
for low-birth-weight infants,
  150–154
network-of-programs model, 391,
  392, 394
parent participation in, 297
transactional model of, 141–143,
  148–155
target identification, 141, 149
interventionist approach, 11
intracortical microstimulation, 219
intrauterine growth retardation, 43,
  46, 49, 216
intraventricular hemorrhage, 49, 222,
  237
Inventory of Social Support, 303
invulnerable child, 651–652, see also
  resilience
Iowa Tests of Basic Skills, 515
IQ (see intelligence/IQ)
Ireland, 603, 618–619
iron-deficiency anemia, 47–48, 216,
  335
irritability
  in children, 44, 47, 66
  and parenting, 63
ischemia, 222
Italy, 617, 621, 622–623, 624–625
item gradients, 243

J
Japan, 348
Johnson administration, 14, 101,
  636

K
Kan Focus, 426
Kansas initiatives, 351, 428
Kauai Longitudinal Study, 12–13, 67,
  117, 120–127, 659–660, 664
Kenan Charitable Trust, 558
Kenan Family Literacy Project, 558,
  586
Kennedy administration, 14, 636
Kentucky initiatives, 381, 382,
  557–558, 559, 560
Keys to Caregiving, 153, 422
Kids Count, 353
kindergarten, 4–5, 344, 418, 538–539
Klinefelter syndrome, 40
Kwashiorkor, 215

L
labeling, 18, 429, 528
laissez-faire approach, 4, 84

language development
  bilingualism and, 110
  communication disorders and, 181
  cortical reorganization and, 220, 221
  disabled infants, 264–265, 527, 530, 536
  early intervention and, 372, 522–523, 527, 530, 536–539, 602
  in low-birth-weight infants, 372
  maladaptive parenting and, 64
  transition from prelinguistic to linguistic, 537
language learning impairments, 220, 221, 222
language teaching, 186, 187
Lanham Act of 1940, 6
Laura Spelman Rockefeller Memorial Fund, 10
lay home visitors, see home visitor program, paraprofessionals
lead exposure, 48, 216, 312
learned helplessness, 180
learning
  adult characteristics, 476–477
  constructivist models, 488
  disabilities, 40, 45, 117, 135, 241, 266, 511, 594
  experience and, 190, 217
  mechanistic models of, 487–488
  mediated, 538–539
  observational, 181
  phases, 185–186
  play-based, 4, 457–458
  respondent, 182
  trials, 187
Lehigh Longitudinal Study, 122
licensure
  facility, 345, 349–350, 352
  in early care and education, 345, 347–348, 349–350, 351–352, 470
life satisfaction, 556
linguistic mapping, 537
Lissencephaly-pachygyria, 209
literacy programs, 332, 390
  intergenerational, 557–560, 563–564, 570
  parent-focused, 560–561
local interagency coordinating council, 392, 393, 394
logical reasoning, 109
longitudinal studies, 4, 12–13
  of contrasting interventions, 538–539
  cost-benefit analyses in, 602–605
  disabled children, 264, 528, 529, 602–605
  ecological risk factors, 137–140

intervention evaluation, 172, 264
resilience in children, 67–68, 115, 117–120
school readiness, 18
of service utilization, 528, 529
socioemotional development, 162
low-birth-weight infants, 456
  (see also premature infants)
  brain injury, 49
  causes, 46, 153
  community influences, 311
  health care costs, 150
  intervention strategies, 150–154, 261–262, 372, 604–605, 620
  minority status and, 106
  parent–child interaction, 261–262
  poverty and, 512, 519–521
  prevention services, 84, 150
  survival rates, 49
low-income families (see also antipoverty programs; poverty; single parents, socioeconomic status), 23
  challenges of work with, 379–380, 383–384
  characteristics, 362–363
  child care issues, 343–344, 350
  child maltreatment, 66, 82–83, 84, 87–88, 362, 418–419
  clinical infant programs, 366–368
  consensus on program design, 376–377
  continuum of services, 370–371, 376-377, 383–384
  cost-benefit analysis of interventions, 602–604
  ecological perspective, 368–369, 489, 540
  education of family workers, 361, 377
  effectiveness of interventions, 190, 361, 372–376, 540
  funding, 381, 382–383
  historical context of interventions, 363–366
  inner-city neighborhoods, 362–363, 379, 380
  intensity of interventions, 190, 377
  lessons learned, 377–379
  longitudinal studies, 602–604
  mental health problems, 418, 422
  parenting patterns, 489
  risks associated with, 362, 379
  secure attachment in, 58
  state and local initiatives, 381–382
  systems approach, 368–369, 380–381

utilization of services, 500
  with very young children, 362–363
  welfare reform effects, 362, 383
lumbosacral myelomeningocele, 41

M
MacArthur Longitudinal Twin Study, 162
macroregulation, 148
macrosystems, 80–81, 84, 107, 312
magnetic source imaging, 219
magnetoencephalography, 219–220
Maine initiatives, 381
maladaptive social relationships, 12
Malaise Inventory, 666
male identitiy, 82
malnutrition, developmental sequelae, 46–48, 215–216
managed care, 331, 334, 382–383
mand-model procedure, 187
Manpower Demonstration Research Corporation, 372
Map and Track, 353
marasmus, 215
marathon skills, 456
marginal zone, 207–208
marriage, 65, 146, 662, 664, 665, 673, 674
Maryland initiatives, 381
Massachusetts initiatives, 351, 353, 501, 529, 592
mastery, 190, 457, 652, 665
mastery motivation, 164
match–mismatch negativity, 222
maternal (see also mothers)
  adaptation, 263
  behavior, 153
  competence, 123, 138, 422
  deprivation, 12, 216, 218, 238, 651, 667
  education, 13, 138, 153, 265, 340, 368, 520, 529, 541, 553, 555–556, 558–559, 620
  employment, 340, 341, 553, 555–556, 558–559
  family history, 238–239
  intelligence, 265
  interventions, 427–428, 515
  nutrition, 41, 215–216
  mental health, 65–67, 85, 146, 238–239, 266, 366, 374, 426–427, 515, 540, 553, 556, 559, 563, 579–581, 583–584, 587
  responsivity, 532
  substance abuse, 237, 238–239, 380, 426–428
Maternal and Child Health Block Grant, 16, 21

Maternal and Child Health Bureau, 327
Maternal and Child Health Services, 7–8, 15, 16
Maternity and Infant Care Projects, 14
Maternal Behavior Rating Scales, 275, 276, 279
Mathematica Policy Research Institute, 373, 374
Mathematica Policy Research Institute, Inc., 568, 575
maturational theory, 188
maturationist view, 10–11
McCarthy Scales, Perceptual subtests, 538
measurement, *see* assessment
measurement error, 655–656
measures (*see also* outcome measures) of adaptation, 117, 172
medial temporal lobe, 211–213
mediated learning, 538–539
Medicaid, 8, 18, 21, 327, 334, 374, 382, 428, 613–614
medical-educational collaboration, 5
medulla oblongata, 205
megalencephaly, 42–43
melting-pot ideology, 102
memory, 47, 61, 109
    assessment, 110, 212, 214, 222
    explicit/declarative, 211–213
    milestones, 213
    neural systems, 204, 211–215, 222
    stress and, 216
    working, 213–215
Memphis New Mothers Project, 552, 553, 566–567, 580
meningitis, 43
Menninger Foundation, 68, 120
Menninger Infancy Project, 553–554, 581
mental age, predictors of growth in, 503
mental health services, early childhood
    agency-centered, 426–427
    clinical supervision of staff, 423–424, 425, 432–433
    common elements of, 429
    community-level, 428, 433, 434
    consultation models, 424–425, 430, 432
    in core health programs, 422
    cross-system collaboration, 430
    cultural considerations, 425, 431, 433
    definition, 416–417
    delivery system, 421–432

diagnostic classification system, 430–431
    in early care and education, 422, 423, 432
    evaluation of, 424–425
    family-centered, 379–380, 416, 421, 425, 427, 431, 432–433
    funding, 425, 427, 430–431, 434
    in home visiting, 66–67, 367, 422–423, 425, 426–427, 428
    ideological challenges, 429–430
    in natural settings, 432–433
    nontraditional strategies in primary settings, 425–426
    out-of-home placements, 425
    parent participation in, 425, 427
    parent-professional relationship, 635–636
    parenting interventions, 427–428
    personnel, 425, 431–432, 433, 434
    practice-based perspectives, 417–418
    principles, 425, 432–433
    public policy perspectives, 421
    rationales for, 416, 417–421
    recommendations, 434
    research, 418–421, 432, 434
    secondary support, 426–428, 432
    state-level, 428–429, 433
    system development challenges, 429–432
    for substance abusing mothers, 379, 427–428
    wraparound, 425
mental hygiene movement, 651
mental illness, parental (*see also* depression)
    and competence of children, 137
    parent-focused interventions and, 553, 556, 559, 563, 579–581, 583–584, 587
    and parenting, 65–67, 116, 278–279
    protective factors in children, 118–119, 120, 122, 123, 125, 668, 670
mental retardation, 216
    assessment, 241
    brain injury and, 42, 43, 48, 209, 210
    costs of intervention, 594
    genetics and, 37, 39–40, 210
    infections and, 44
    institutionalization for, 12
    malnutrition and, 46, 216
    maternal adjustment to, 633–634
    and parent–infant interaction, 263
    poverty and, 14

screening programs, 14
    special education, 8–10, 14
mentors, 126, 129
Merrill-Palmer Scales, 47
mesencephalon, 205
mesosystems, 79, 293, 489, 641
metachromatic leukodystrophy, 38
metencephalon, 205–206
Mexican Americans, 99, 100, 103, 489
Michigan initiatives, 428, 528
microcephaly, 37, 42, 43, 45, 216, 636
microregulations, 148
microsystems, 54, 78–79, 84, 293, 322, 489, 490, 641, 644
midbrain, 205–206
Milestones initiative, 353
milestones models, 11
milieu teaching, 186, 536–537, 539
military service, 660, 664, 673
Milwaukee Project, 555, 556, 584
miniregulations, 148
Minnesota initiatives, 353, 381, 561
Minnesota Child Development Inventory, 235
Minnesota Mother–Child Project, 120, 124
minority groups (*see also* ethnicity; race; *specific minorities*)
    resocialization of, 101–102
    population shifts, 98
    problemization of, 100–101
    recruitment of personnel from, 477
    utilization of services, 500
minority status as cultural risk factor, 96, 97, 105–107
Mississippi initiatives, 428
Missouri initiatives, 381, 524–525, 561
mitochondrial disorders, 40
Model Preschool Program, 531
Montessori method, 5, 9
Montreal studies, 88
moral development, 164–166, 314–315
moral education, 344
Mother–Child Home Program, 582
Mother–Child Rating Scale, 275, 279–280
mother–infant interaction (*see also* caregiver–child relationship; parent–child interaction)
    addiction and, 61
    adolescent mothers, 63–64, 66, 70, 266, 277
    and affect, 55, 64
    assessment, 237
    attachment construct, 12, 64

and cognitive development, 259–260
infant characteristics and, 259–260
maternal characteristics and, 259–260
maternal depression and, 65–67
psychotherapy interventions, 152, 163, 168
reciprocity, 259
severity of disability and, 504
mothers (*see also* adolescent mothers; maternal)
categorical, 100
emotional availability, 266
home visit effects, 422
perspectivistic, 100
substance abuse intervention, 426–428
working, 135
motivation
assessment, 185
impaired, 47
moral, 164–166
to perform, 188
to practice, 184
theory, 160, 163–164
motor development
assessment, 240, 242, 275
brain injury and, 48, 205, 209, 220
costs of intervention, 594
effectiveness of interventions, 527, 529, 530, 532
motor impairment, 44, 205, 209, 219, 274, 275, 398
Multidisciplinary Faculty Training Institute, 473
multifactorial causation, 657–658
multifactorial disorders, 40–41
Multi-pass system, 275
multiple-factor screening approaches, 139
mutuality, 86, 153, 237, 267, 269, 461
myelencephalon, 205–206
myelination, 38
errors of, 211
environmental effects, 215
process, 210–211, 214–215
myelodysplasia, 36, 41–42
myelomeningocele, 41–42, 205

N
National Academy of Sciences, 81, 92
National Association for the Education of Young Children (NAEYC), 346, 358, 429, 454, 458–459, 468, 469, 470, 473, 482

National Black Child Development Institute, 351–352, 358
National Board for Professional Teaching Standards (NBPTS), 468
National Center for Children in Poverty, 353, 362, 385, 420, 433, 437
National Center for Clinical Infant Programs, 16, 367
National Center for Education Statistics, 18
National Center for Family Literacy (NCFL), 558, 560
National Commission on Children, 3, 29
National Committee for the Prevention of Child Abuse and Neglect, 373
National Day Care Study, 594
National Early Childhood Technical Assistance System, 592
National Easter Seal Society, 455, 482
National Education Association, 4
National Education Goals, 18, 342, 549–550
National Education Goals Panel, 18, 29
National Education Longitudinal Study, 518
National Governors' Association, 332, 337, 353
National Incidence Study, 83
National Institute of Child Health and Human Development, 12, 29, 343, 358, 628
National Institute of Neurological Diseases and Blindness, 12
National Literacy Act, 558
National Longitudinal Study of Youth, 239
National Research Council, 25
National Survey of Children and Parents, 62, 74
Native Americans, 60, 101, 107
naturalistic
observations, 12
intervention approaches, 457–458, 536–538
therapy settings, 399, 432–433
nature-nurture debate, 10–12, 13
Nebraska initiatives, 592
needs-based assessment, 301–302, 333–334
negative reinforcement, 182
negentropy, 161
negotiation, by children, 165, 167

neighborhood influences (*see also* community influences)
direct, 311
face-block unit of analysis, 316, 322
inner-city poverty, 362–363, 374, 379
on parenting, 311, 322
risk assessment, 86, 87, 89
social organization scales, 318–319
socioeconomic composition, 311–312
on substance abuse, 665–666
neonatal home visiting program, 331
neonatal intensive care unit, 84, 150–151
neonatal stroke, 46
nervous system, *see* brain development; central nervous system
nested models, 315–316
Netherlands, 618–619
neural plasticity, 25, 38, 172
in developing organisms, 218
evaluation implications, 488
intervention implications of, 220–222, 341–342
in mature organisms, 219–220, 221
mechanisms, 217–218
models, 217
in premature infants, 488
and recovery from brain injury, 212, 218, 219–220, 488
neural reorganization, 219–220
neural tube
defects, 40–41, 205, 216
development, 206–207, 208
neurodevelopmental therapy, 532
neurofibromatosis, 37
neurons
abnormalities, 45, 209, 215
destruction, 48, 209, 217, 510
intermediate zone, 208–209
migration, 208–209, 212
normal development, 37–38, 46, 49, 208
overproduction, 209, 214, 217
regeneration, 218
replacement, 50
types, 209
neurotransmitters, 212, 218
neurulation, 205
New Chance, 371, 372, 375
New Frontier, 636
New Jersey initiatives, 592
New Parents as Teachers, 524

New Zealand, 333, 348
non-exclusionary time out, 184
norm-referenced models, 243,
    245–246, 502
North Carolina initiatives, 330, 352,
    353, 390–391, 396, 399, 401, 409,
    510, 528, 564
Norway, 348, 617
nurse home visitation program, 81,
    566–567
nursery schools, 5–6, 344, 365, 517
    (see also early care and education;
    preschool; child care)
Nursing Child Assessment Satellite
    Training
    Feeding Scale, 234, 265, 276–277
    Teaching Scale, 234, 260, 275–277
nutrition
    and CNS development, 40–41,
        46–48, 210, 211, 215–216
    interventions, 334–335

O
observational methods
    classroom, 538
    ecological perspective, 317–320
    parent education on, 524–525
odds-ratio analysis, 139–140
oedipal period, 164
Office of Child Development, 15
Office of Economic Opportunity, 14,
    364, 365
Office of Special Education and
    Rehabilitation Services, 10
Office of Special Education
    Programs/OSERS, 21, 455, 465,
    482
Ohio initiatives, 352, 353, 381
oliogodendroglia, 210, 211
Omnibus Budget Reconciliation Act,
    16
Omnibus Personal Responsibility and
    Work Opportunity Reconciliation
    Act, 17, 77, 421, 614
operant behavior, 182
operant conditioning, 11
operant learning, 182
opportunistic surveillance, 247
opportunity cost, 591
opportunity factors, 195, 196,
    198
orbitoprefrontal cortex, 214–215
Oregon initiatives, 353, 381
Organization for Economic
    Cooperation and Development,
    615
orphanages, 218
Ounce of Prevention Fund, 473

Ounce of Prevention Scale, 249,
    250
outcome expectations
    in collective empowerment model,
        644
    on counseling/psychotherapy
        model, 636
    in family-centered model, 640–641
    on parent participation model,
        637–638
outcome measures, 4, 502
    of adolescent competence, 139–140
    cultural considerations, 488
    for disabled children, 488
    family-level effects, 502
    intermediate, 171, 173–174
    IQ scores as, 138, 372, 515, 520
    learning models and, 488, 516
    long-term, 171–173
    norm-referenced models, 243,
        245–246, 502
    perseveration, 488
    Piagetian-based, 488, 516
    quantification methods, 502–504
    parent satisfaction as, 400–401
    resilient children, 67
    special education placements as,
        515, 517, 523, 539
outcome studies, 374–376, 403–404
overcorrection, 184
overlearning, 186
overprotectiveness, 125
overstimulation, see sensory
    stimulation

P
PACE/Kenan model, 558–559
pain tolerance, 121
panencephalitis, 44
paraprofessionals
    advantages, 440–442, 448
    as beneficiaries, 441–442
    bridge role, 441, 442
    child care providers, 440, 443–445,
        451
    clinical supervision and support of,
        379, 423, 425, 433, 448, 449,
        450
    community-based, 446
    concerns about, 439–440, 446–449
    cost-effectiveness, 377, 383,
        440–441
    countertransferrence, 448
    domains of silence, 447, 448
    in early childhood programs,
        442–445, 448–449, 465
    expectations, 379–380, 439,
        448–449

in health services, 331, 374
    home visits, 373, 379, 423, 441
    in human services, 440, 445–450
    knowledge base, 448–449, 450
    parenting behavior, 441–442
    in parenting interventions, 439,
        442–443, 448–449, 450, 451
    personal qualities, 445–446
    recruitment, 440, 445–446
    role development, 449–450
    training, 383, 440, 441, 446–447,
        448–449, 450, 470
parent advocacy, 295, 353
Parent and Child Education (PACE),
    557–558, 559, 560, 586
parent attitudes
    anticipatory guidance and, 330
    in collective empowerment model,
        644
    on counseling/psychotherapy
        model, 635–636
    in family-centered model, 640–641
    family intervention effects, 397
    on inclusive settings, 475
    on parent participation models,
        637–638
    parent-focused interventions and,
        554, 556–557, 560, 563–564,
        579–588
    on parenting interventions, 524
Parent/Caregiver Involvement Scale
    (P/CIS), 301
Parent Child Development Centers
    (PCDC), 368, 373, 375, 381,
    515–516, 524, 540, 555, 556,
    583
Parent–Child Early Relational
    Assessment, 278–279
parent–child interaction (see also
    caregiver–child relationship;
    father–child relationship;
    mother–child interaction)
    adaptation process, 12, 63–64, 167,
        261, 262, 263, 266–267, 271,
        293, 638
    affect, 55–56, 64, 65, 146–147, 154,
        164, 262, 263, 266
    assessment of, 170, 233–234, 237,
        265, 266–275, 280–281, 301
    attunement, 56, 64–65, 167, 259,
        260–261, 262
    and attachment, 260, 261
    behavioral repertoires, 259–260,
        262–264, 266, 269, 271
    case vignettes, 271–275
    child care and, 343
    communication structure and
        process, 237, 260, 261, 276–277

cultural differences, 101, 268, 269, 280
developmental effects, 259–261, 268, 332, 418, 638
disabled infants, 262–267, 271–275, 279–280, 534
elements of, 259–262
emotional development, 166–168, 651
environmental influences on, 192–193, 265–267, 274
evaluation of interventions, 280, 376, 523–524, 532, 536
family patterns and, 192–193
measures of, 275–280
mental health and, 65–67, 422
models, 167–168, 457
moral development, 164
paraprofessionals' role, 439
parent-focused interventions and, 553–554, 556, 559, 564, 579–584, 586–587
professional training, 268, 277, 278, 280–281, 474
psychotherapy, 367
scales, 275–280
socioeconomic status and, 86, 260
research needs, 266–267, 280
reciprocity in, 61, 258, 260–262, 264–265, 266, 269, 274
and resiliency, 266, 658, 666
transactional model, 54–55, 142–143, 151–152, 536
parent costs, 595–596
parent education
anticipatory guidance, 329–331
assumptions about, 637
disabled infants, 193–194
effectiveness of programs, 515–516, 523–524
evaluation of programs, 332, 335, 376, 523–524
expected outcomes, 638
in family-focused approach, 153–154, 368, 370, 373
in home visits, 153, 363–364
instructional materials, 153, 335
interactions with infants, 167
literacy programs, 523–524, 557–562, 563–564, 586–588
for minorities, 101, 363–364, 365
parent perspectives, 638
parent-professional relationship, 636–638
power aspects, 636–637
and prevention, 69, 332, 335

professional perspectives, 637–638
in well-child visits, 332
parent empowerment
access to resources and, 642–644
assessment process and, 251, 292, 294–295
in child care, 353
collective model of, 641–646
ecological aspect, 644
expected outcomes, 645–646
family involvement approach and, 195, 291, 294–295, 353, 408, 644
in interventions, 281, 365
parent perspectives, 645
parent–professional relationship and, 461, 469, 497, 630–632
procedural safeguards, 389
professional perspectives, 461, 644–645
rationale and strategies, 292
and service outcomes, 405, 408
types of power and, 642
parent-focused interventions (see also parent education; parenting interventions)
center-based plus home-based, 555–557, 583–585
and child maltreatment, 554, 557, 579–581, 583
efficacy of, 551–562, 579–588
home-based, 552–555, 563–563, 579–582
and home environment, 554, 556–557, 560, 579–588
indirect effects on child outcomes, 564–565
and maternal education and employment, 553, 555–556, 558–559
and maternal mental and physical health, 553, 556, 559, 563, 579–581, 583–584, 587
and parent–child interaction, 553–554, 556, 559, 564, 579–584, 586–587
and parenting knowledge and attitudes, 554, 556–557, 560, 563–564, 579–588
and utilization of child-related services, 554, 579–580, 583
parent–infant relationship, see parent–child interaction
Parent–Infant Relational Assessment, 276
Parent–Infant Relationship Global Assessment Scale, 170
parent interviews, 235, 270, 297, 299, 300, 495

parent involvement, see parent participation
Parent Leadership Institute, 353
parent participation
in anticipatory guidance, 331
appropriate level of, 233–234, 262, 377–378
in assessment process, 233–234, 235–236, 242, 246–247, 249, 262, 267, 269–270, 329
assumptions about, 637
categories, 565
cultural considerations, 105
in decision-making process, 281, 644
in early care and education programs, 5, 15, 345, 346–347, 353, 522
effects on children, 261–262
effects on parents, 551–564
evaluation of, 565–568
expected outcomes, 638
in Head Start, 364, 373, 417, 423, 636
in intervention process, 269–270, 549–551, 565–568
in mental health services, 425, 427
monetary value of, 595
in nursery activities, 368
parent perspectives, 638
parent-professional relationship, 636–638
P.L. 99-457 and, 281, 291
P.L. 105-17, 22
power aspects, 636–637
professional perspectives, 637–638
rates of, 423, 501, 520, 566
in training, 353, 462, 463, 475, 636–638
welfare reform and, 568–569
parent–professional relationship
in assessment, 233, 235–236, 268, 270, 271, 271–275, 294–295
boundaries, 461
collective empowerment model, 497, 632, 633, 641–646
consumer-driven services, 639
in counseling–psychotherapy, 633–636, 644
in early care and education, 347
empathy in, 167–168, 268, 271, 460, 467, 475
evaluation of, 501, 566
evolution of, 632
family-centered model, 294–295, 405, 456, 630–632, 633, 638–641

parent–professional (contd.)
  in health care, 333
  intervention issues, 167–168, 268, 281
  medical model, 635
  models of, 632–646
  and outcome expectations, 636
  parent-deficit model, 636
  parent perspectives, 635–636, 638, 640–641, 645
  parent training/involvement model, 633, 636–638
  paternalistic, 195, 197, 369, 405
  partnership, 15, 195, 197, 235–236, 268, 281, 335, 364, 378, 408, 425, 461
  political model, 636
  power relationships, 630–631, 634, 636–637, 639–640, 642
  professional perspectives, 635, 637–638, 640, 644–645
  professional training, 269, 335, 408, 460, 461, 465, 474–475
  sociocultural issues, 501
  in special education, 456–457, 460–461, 632–636
  transition between programs and, 400
parent reports, 235, 240, 247, 329
parent satisfaction, 154
  parental participation and, 346
  program evaluation measure, 400–401
Parent Services Project (PSP), 353, 422–423
parent support groups, 273, 401, 422, 495, 532, 536
Parent to Parent, 475
parent training
  as activists and advocates, 353
  observation skills, 265
  as-therapist, 191, 534
parental leave programs, 617–618
parentification, 61
parenting, 11, 89 (see also adolescent parenting; child maltreatment; discipline; parent–child interaction)
  adaptive, 54, 55–60, 151, 293–294
  code of behavior, 143, 147–148, 151–153, 154
  cultural values and, 97, 100–101, 102–105, 108, 489
  educational attainment and, 100
  environmental influences on, 54–55, 362
  generational factors, 145, 146, 172–174

"good enough," 65, 67–68, 69, 473
infant temperament and, 70, 259
knowledge base, 25, 554, 556–557, 560, 563–564, 579–588
maladaptive, 59, 60–69, 362, 653
mental illness and, 65–67, 116, 620, 653
minority differences in, 108–109, 363–364
normative standard, 100–101
as outcome measure, 172–174
paraprofessional role, 441–443
poverty and, 363
protective strategies, 109, 665–666
reeducation strategies, 153–154, 330, 368, 376, 523–524
religious values and, 4
resilience and, 67–69
resources, 59
social support and, 58–60, 68, 69
structural dimension of, 68
substance abuse and, 60–62, 70
violence and, 62–63, 69–70
parenting interventions (see also parent education)
  for adolescents, 70
  community-based, 69–70, 428
  cost-effectiveness, 504
  Head Start programs, 365
  historical roots, 363–364
  home visitation programs, 69, 364, 428
  outcomes, 69, 450
  paraprofessionals' role, 439, 442–443, 448–449, 450
  parents teaching parents, 69
  preventive, 69–70
  professional training, 466
  settings for, 69
  for substance abusers, 427
  systems approach, 69–70
Parents as Teachers program, 381, 512, 524–525, 560, 561, 587, 639
Parents' Evaluation of Developmental Status, 329
Part C (Part H) services, 20, 21, 258, 380, 387, 388, 389, 396, 454, 455, 456, 465, 525–526, 528–530, 539–540, 591, 592, 614
  definitional issues, 20, 21, 23
  description, 20–23
  eligibility criteria, 21–22, 23
  Individualized Family Service Plan, 22, 389
  family's role, 22, 497
  lead agency, 20–21, 23, 465

medical–educational collaboration, 21
procedural safeguards, 389
programmatic decisions, 21–22
recipients of services, 388–389
transition across service systems, 22, 23
Participatory Action Research Project, 473
Partners for Learning, 520
Partners in Health Care program, 333, 334
Parents Interacting with Infants Practicum (PIWI), 474, 475
Partners Project, 423, 428
Partnership in Parenting Education, 167
partnership model, 194–196
paternalism, 195, 197, 369, 405
Peabody Picture Vocabulary Test (PPVT), 520, 521, 523
Pediatric Practice Research Group, 248, 255
pediatric preventive health care
  anticipatory guidance, 328, 329–331, 333, 334
  challenges in, 334–335
  community-based programs linked to, 334
  cultural sensitivity in, 334, 335
  developmental monitoring and surveillance, 247–248, 328–329, 334
  evaluation of interventions, 334
  family-focused approach, 333–334, 335
  financial considerations, 334
  group well-child visits, 332, 334
  guidelines, 327–328
  history, 327
  home visiting, 331–332, 334
  office-based literacy programs, 332, 335
  parent-held child health records, 333, 334
  training, 335
  welfare reform and, 334–335
peer-mediated education strategies, 186, 187
peer interaction in play, 242
peer relationships, 138, 181, 662, 674
peer treatment program, 129
Pen Green Centre, 625
Pennsylvania initiatives, 390–391, 528
perinatal insults, 10, 13, 48–49, 116, 659

peripheral nervous system, 210, 219
periventricular leukomalacia, 48–49, 211
Perry Preschool Project
    cost-benefit analysis, 591, 592, 598–602, 603
    description, 585
    effects, 516–518, 598, 555, 556, 585
    resources, 597–598
perseveration, measures of, 488
personal social network, 58, 60
personnel (see also disability specialists; paraprofessionals; professionals; training)
    for family support programs, 368, 369
    infant specialists, 465–466
    licensing of, 347–348, 470
    interdisciplinary team approach, 367, 380, 454, 465
    preschool standards, 347–348, 467–469
    recruitment, 477
    reflection and self-knowledge, 461–462
    shortages, 398, 454, 455, 465
    staffing patterns, 465
    standards, 467–469
    transdisciplinary approach, 398–399, 408
pervasive developmental disorder, 533–535
phantom limb phenomenon, 219
pharmacological interventions, 150, 541
phenylketonuria (PKU), 13, 14, 40, 136
Philadelphia Study, 138–140, 141
phobias, 667
Piagetian A not B task, 214
PIAT scores, 538
planful competence, 663–664, 671, 673
plasticity, see neural plasticity
play
    assessment of, 232, 234, 241–242
    cultural differences, 97
    disabled children, 181, 242, 263, 534
    nonstructured, 232, 234, 242
    parent–child, 242, 263, 532, 565
    peer interaction, 242
    structured, 186, 232, 234–235, 242
    supervised, 4, 153–154
playpens, 108
policy making, see public policy
pons, 205
Portugal, 333

positive practice, 184
positive reinforcement, 182, 183, 251
posttraumatic stress syndrome, 216, 312, 380
pouring-in model, 457
poverty (see also impoverished children; low-income families
    adolescent mothers, 362, 363
    cycle, 14, 24, 61, 84, 363, 364
    episodic, 82
    and mental disorder, 653
    race and, 82, 85, 317, 364, 511, 513, 514, 520
    war on, 14, 15, 101, 364, 440
power
    authoritarian, 631
    in collective empowerment model, 631, 642
    continuum, 630–631
    in counseling/psychotherapy model, 631, 634
    definition, 631
    to define normalcy, 634
    in family-centered model, 631, 639–640
    in parent training/involvement model, 636–637
powerlessness, 80
practice
    motivation for, 186
    positive, 184
    principles, 377–379
Prader-Willi syndrome, 39
PRECEDE-PROCEED model, 333–334
prefrontal cortex, 211, 213–215, 222
prelinguistic milieu teaching, 537–538
premature infants, 10 (see also low-birth-weight infants)
    Bayley scores, 151
    brain injury, 48–49, 210, 488
    causes, 46
    home visitor programs, 153, 519–521
    minority status and, 106
    neonatal intensive care units, 150–151
    and neural plasticity, 488
    parent-infant interaction, 151–152, 261–262, 263, 277
    parenting effect, 36, 68
    prevention services, 150
    resilience in, 120
    sensory stimulation, 150–151, 262, 265
Prenatal and Early Infancy Project, 81, 552, 553, 554, 580–581
prenatal brain injury, 49

prenatal care, 84, 87, 620
preschool (see also early care and education; child care; Early Head Start; Head Start; special education)
    child care, 409
    education programs, 5–6, 14–15, 22, 382, 522–423, 538–539
    effectiveness, 511, 513–515, 522–523, 624
    European programs, 621, 622, 623, 624
    funding, 382, 510
    limitations of, 370
    for low-income families, 343–344, 364, 511, 522–523
    mental health principles in, 422
    professional training, 348, 465, 467–470, 473–474
Preschool Inventory, 523
President's Panel on Mental Retardation, 14
preterm birth (see also premature infants)
    prevention, 150
prevention
    definition, 136–137
    infant mortality, 374
    legislative focus, 526
    low birth weight, 150
    maladaptive parenting, 69–70, 266
    mental health interventions, 136, 170, 171
    premature births, 150
    primary, 136
    systems view, 69–70
Prevention Initiative, 382
preventive health care, see pediatric preventive health care
primary support programs, 422
professional–child relationship, 567
professional development communities, 477
professional development school (PDS), 464, 473
professional–parent relationship, see parent–professional relationship
professionals (see also parent–professional relationship)
    assessment staff competency, 240, 268, 277, 278, 280–281, 296, 297, 298, 301
    attitudes, 475
    in collective empowerment model, 644
    communications skills, 269, 467
    community-based interventions, 195–196

professionals (*contd.*)
    congruence between parents and, 297
    disability specialists, 196, 335, 398
    effectiveness of interventions, 375, 376
    in family-centered model, 457, 639–640
    knowledge base, 454, 460–461, 470, 471
    mental health, 423, 635
    minority distrust of, 107
    parent–child interaction, 268, 277, 278, 280–281
    parent training/education, 637–638
    physical therapists, 398
    standards of quality, 454
    training, 268, 277, 278, 280–281, 296, 361, 454, 460–461, 470
    value judgments by, 236
progressive time delay, 187
Project Before, 426–427, 428
Project BLEND, 528
Project CARE, 514–515, 519, 520, 522, 555, 556, 557, 564, 570, 584
Project Competence, 67, 665
Project HOPE, 380
Project LEAP, 190–191
Project Match, 442
Project on Human Development in Chicago Neighborhoods, 310, 311, 313–320, 321
Project STEEP, 553, 581
prosencephalon, 205–206, 208
protective behaviors, 86
promotive factors, 140–141
protective factors (*see also* resilience)
    and adaptation by high-risk children, 67, 116, 127–128, 140–141, 657
    and adaptation, 67, 116, 127–128, 140–141
    in adolescence and adulthood, 122
    community-related, 125–126
    concept, 116–117, 658–659
    in depression, 652
    in early childhood, 120–121
    family-related, 123–125, 127–128, 129
    gender differences in, 125, 126, 127
    in infancy, 117–120
    interaction among, 127, 658–659
    longitudinal studies, 659–660
    methodological issues, 117
    in middle childhood, 121–122
    in neurological development, 35–36
    in parenting process, 55, 658

Prozac, 541
pruning, synaptic, 37–38, 217, 510
psychiatric disorders, 61, 62, 312
psychoanalytic interventions (*see also* mental health services, child-related)
    alternatives fostered in, 174–176
    assumptions in, 634–635
    caregiver–child relationship, 168–169
    diagnostic process, 169–170
    emotional regulation, 166–168
    expected outcomes, 636
    imaginative abilities, 174–176
    individuality focus, 161–163
    infant–parent psychotherapy, 152, 163, 367
    long-term perspective, 170–174
    moral development, 164–166
    motivational theory and, 163–166
    parent perspective, 635–636
    parent–professional relationship, 631, 633–636
    power aspects of, 634
    prevention perspective, 170, 171
    professional perspective, 635
psychobiologic moderators, 121
psychological adjustment of adolescents, 139
psychological stress
    and adaptive parenting, 293–294
    and brain development, 216, 218, 220, 418
    in caregivers, 292, 293–294
    in low-income families, 422
    maladaptive responses to, 672–673
    new opportunities and, 673–674
    and participation rates, 536
    protective factors, 58–59, 116–117, 121, 294, 659, 665
    and psychosocial disorders, 656–657
    sensitizing and steeling effects, 667, 670–672
    therapeutic interventions, 672
psychometric tests, 242–246, 252
psychomotor development, 44, 45, 488
psychopathology
    genetic component, 655–656, 658
    parental, 65–67, 119, 122, 124, 651
    protective factors, 119, 122, 124, 651
psychosocial disorders
    screening for, 247–248
public assistance, 82, 426, 501

public attitudes, early care and education, 341–342, 348
Public Law 88-156, 14
Public Law 90-538, 14
Public Law 92-424, 15
Public Law 93-112, 16
Public Law 93-516, 16
Public Law 94-142, 15, 17, 22, 180, 246, 526, 637
Public Law 99-457 (*see also* Part C (Part H))
    changes in service delivery, 388, 456
    ideological basis, 526
    lead agency, 21
    parent role in intervention, 281, 291, 296
    Part B services, 454, 455, 465, 525, 527–528, 539
    personnel preparation requirements, 454, 455, 465
    services envisioned by, 17, 20, 370, 510
    state responsibilities under, 22–23
Public Law 100-297, 558
Public Law 101-476, 497
Public Law 102-73, 558
Public Law 102-119, 237, 291, 442
    (*see also* Individuals with Disabilities Education Act)
    implementation, 387, 407
    Part B, 591, 592
    inclusive settings, 399, 459–460
    program emphasis, 497
    reauthorization, 526
    therapies, 398
Public Law 104-193, 77, 82
Public Law 105-17
public policies
    accountability, 19–20, 24, 84, 352–353
    challenges, 24, 421
    conventional economic thinking and, 83–85
    on disabled children, 387–389, 525–527
    ecological perspective, 80, 83–85, 87, 258
    funding of early care and education, 350, 352
    international perspective, 615–626
    level of risk and, 670
    long-term perspective, 170–174
    on mental health services, 421
    on minority education, 102
    single-factor targets, 141
    trends, 13–23, 613–615
    welfare reform, 17–18, 77

Public/Private Venture, 129
public school
    desegregation, 106, 180
    early care programs, 341
    prekindergarten, 382
    programs, 4, 9–10, 16, 20, 179–180
Puerto Ricans, 97, 103, 104
punishment, 184 (*see also* discipline)
Puritan influence, 4
pyloric stenosis, 47

Q

qualia, 493
quality issues
    in child care, 345–351, 372, 376,
        409, 443–445, 511, 541, 595
    in early care and education, 341,
        343, 346–356, 365
quality of life, 318
Quality 2000 initiative, 355–356
quanta, 493

R

race, 23–24
    culture distinguished from, 95, 96,
        98
    and child care utilization, 340,
        341
    as independent variable, 95
    neighborhood structural effects,
        313–314, 316–317
    one-drop rule, 98
    and social support, 60
racism, 98, 100–101, 105–107,
    363–364
Rand Corporation, 19
Reach Out and Read program, 332,
    335
reading programs, 332, 522–523, 560,
    563–564
reading skills, 122
Reagan administration, 16
reciprocity
    assessment of, 266, 269
    cultural, 235–236
    and development, 55–56
    by disabled infants, 264–265
    maternal depression and, 65
    moral development and, 164–165
    negative perceptions of, 86
    in parent–child interaction, 61, 65,
        260–262, 264–265, 266, 269
    in parent–professional interaction,
        347, 405
    and social competence, 314–315
    substance abuse and, 61
    systems approach, 78

redefinition intervention, 149–150,
    151–153, 154, 155
reeducation intervention, 149, 150,
    153–154, 155
reflection capacity, 461–462
reflective supervision, 454, 461–462,
    463–464
regression, developmental, 40
regulation, transactional, 143–144,
    148–149
reinforcement, 182, 183, 184–185,
    186, 251, 260
relational deprivation, 293
Relational Psychotherapy Mothers'
    Group, 427–428
relationship
    disorder, 170
    formation, 145
    helping, 195
    intimacy as outcome measure, 172
    power-over, 631, 634, 636, 637, 639
    power-through, 632, 642
    power-with, 631, 632, 639–640, 643
    strengthening, 168–169, 422, 423
religious values/beliefs, 4, 5, 58, 125
remediation strategies, 101, 149,
    150–151, 154, 155, 535–536
representativeness principle, 244
research (*see also* longitudinal studies)
    funding, 510
    minority families, 101
    mental health services, 418–420
    opportunity factors, 198
    professional development, 471
Research and Training Associates,
    524
residential mobility, 313–314, 322
residential placements, 9, 663
residential stability, 319
resilience (*see also* protective factors)
    adolescent parenting and, 118–119,
        122, 123, 124, 127
    age factors, 127
    alternative caregivers and,
        123–124, 127, 129
    to biological insult, 50, 659
    child characteristics, 35–36, 67, 68,
        117–123, 126, 128
    concept, 67, 115–116, 652–653
    environmental risk mediation,
        653–654, 673–674
    friendships and, 125–126
    genotype-environment effect, 128,
        660, 668–669, 670
    indirect chain effects, 656–657,
        660, 662, 665–666, 669, 672–673
    intelligence and, 67, 68, 122–123,
        127, 666–667, 670–671, 674–675

interaction processes, 658–659,
    661–663
intervention implications of
    studies, 128–130, 669–675
longitudinal studies, 67–68, 115,
    117–127, 659–669
maternal competence and, 123
measurement error, 655–656
methodological issues, 117,
    653–659
multifactorial causation and,
    657–658, 670
outcome measures, 654–655
parent–child interaction and, 266,
    666
parenting and, 36, 55, 66, 67–69,
    123–124, 666
planful competence, 663–664, 671,
    673
positive experiences and, 667–668,
    674
promotive factors, 658–659
race/ethnicity and, 117, 123, 127
religious values/beliefs and, 125
required helpfulness and, 125
research needs, 130
school experience and, 126
self-definitions of, 664–665
sensitizing and steeling effects of
    stress, 667, 670–672
socialization practices and, 125
social supports and, 68
stress-buffering effects, 665, 669,
    672
teachers/mentors and, 126, 127,
    129
temporal processes, 656–657
turning points in adulthood, 127,
    656, 660, 662, 664, 673, 674
resistance behavior, 60
resocialization of ethnic minorities,
    101–102
resource-based intervention
    approaches, 193–197, 198
resources
    access to, 642–644
    directory of, 401
    services distinguished from, 195
respite care, 425
respondent behavior, 182
respondent conditioning, 182
response-contingent behaviors, 186
response shaping, 186
respondent learning, 182
responsive interaction, 537
restitution, 184
Rett syndrome, 40
rhinal cortex, 211, 213

rhombencephalon, 205
risk
  adolescent parenting, 59, 61,
    63–65, 456
  biological, 456
  classification, 58
  cumulative effect, 85, 136,
    137–140, 198, 237, 419–420,
    654–655, 658, 660
  definition, 88, 439
  of developmental delays, 21–22
  ecological perspective, 89–91,
    137–140, 141, 192–194, 198
  environmental, 22, 68, 456,
    653–654
  family perspective, 192–194
  indexes, 239, 657, 660–661
  indicators, 653
  level of, 658, 670
  mechanisms, 653
  mediation, 653–654
  research, 12–13
  sensitivity to, 670–672
  single-factor approaches, 141
Risk and Recovery Study, 120
Ritalin, 541
rituals, family, 146
Rochester Longitudinal Study, 122,
  137–138, 665
rubella, congenital, 43–44

S
St. Louis Risk Project, 122
schizencephaly, 209
schizophrenia, 40, 218, 312, 658
school attendance, 238
school completion, 311
school experience, 126, 662–663,
  672, 674
School of the Mother, 4
School of the 21st Century initiative,
  354
school readiness
  African Americans, 364
  assessment of, 239
  child care quality and, 444,
    621–622
  early care and education programs
    and, 342, 343, 344, 364, 522–523
  literacy programs, 332, 335,
    560–561
  measures of, 523
  mental health considerations, 417,
    418, 421, 423
  National Education Goals, 18, 421,
    549–550
  parent participation and, 423
  pediatrician's role, 335

screening
  child-centered, 239
  family-centered, 239
  by pediatricians, 328–329
  parent-completed measures, 329
  PKU, 14
  population-based model, 239, 240
  risk identification, 239
second generation research, 489
secondary support services, mental
  health, 426–428, 432
Section for Exceptional Children, 10
segregation, 106, 313–314
seizures, 37, 39, 40, 44, 48, 209, 211,
  275
Select Panel for the Promotion of
  Child Health, 47, 53
self-assertion, 261
self-care, 241
self competence, 139
self-control, 165, 167, 240
self-directedness, 165
self-efficacy, 314–315, 652, 663, 671,
  673
self-esteem, 658, 671
self-help programs, 501
self-knowledge
  in paraprofessionals, 461–462
  in professionals, 460–462
self-regulation, 148, 163, 167
sensitivity (psychology)
  parental behavior, 65, 565
  and security of attachment, 57, 64,
    565
sensorimotor gating, 218
sensory impairments, 120, 366,
  398
sensory processing, 214
sensory stimulation
  and cognitive development, 47,
    144
  by child-care providers, 66
  effectiveness of interventions,
    532
  play, 57, 263
  prenatal, 144
  premature infants, 150–151, 262,
    263
separation effects, 55, 216, 218, 653,
  657
service delivery systems, 19,
  20–21, 24
  bureaucratic model, 403
  brokering, 371
  collective empowerment model,
    642–643
  community context, 402–403, 409,
    428

comprehensiveness concept,
  370–371, 376, 390, 393, 395–396,
  409
consultation models, 424–425, 430,
  432, 469
contextual approaches, 331–334,
  525
coordination of programs, 390,
  391–396, 401, 464, 499
cultural considerations, 334, 335,
  369, 402, 431, 433, 441, 456,
  458, 464
early care and education, 341, 342,
  344, 350–351, 423
elements of, 396–401, 429
evaluation of models, 390–396,
  403–404, 492
family-centered, 371, 397–398,
  404, 408, 427, 492
family influences, 405
family satisfaction with, 400–401
federal policy, 387–389
fiscal challenges, 430–431
fragmentation of, 25, 341, 344,
  350–351, 354, 369, 380–381,
  383–384, 389, 390
ideological challenges, 429–430
inclusive settings, 399, 403
influential factors, 401–407
interagency collaboration, 389,
  392–393, 394–395, 396, 403,
  430, 464
leadership, 392–394, 395, 404,
  409
matching goals and recipients,
  408–409
mental health, 422–432, 466–467
models, 389–396, 403–404,
  407–408
multidisciplinary services, 529
network-oriented, 391, 392, 394,
  426–427
and outcomes, 403–404
pediatric health care, 327–328
procedural safeguards, 389
principles, 466–467
provider–family relationships,
  103–104, 405, 408
provider characteristics, 404–405
recommendations, 376, 407–409
secondary support services,
  426–428
single-program oriented, 391, 392
staff-related issues, 398, 423–424,
  431–432
state context, 394, 399, 402, 403,
  428–429
studies of, 390–391

team approach, 149, 408, 465, 467, 536
therapies, 398–399, 422–423, 427–428, 458, 469
training of authorities, 396
transition, 389, 399–400
services
    resources distinguished from, 195
    specialized professional, 196
Services for Crippled Children, 7
setting events, 183, 185
settlement houses, 625
severity of disability
    and adaptation, 504, 530
sex differences, see gender differences
shared meaning, 166
Sheppard-Towner Act, 7
shunts, 42
siblings, 67, 124, 130, 187
sign language, 530
single-gene defects, 40
single parents (see also adolescent mothers; adolescent parenting)
    community influences on, 312
    home visitation, 81
    participation in interventions, 105, 272–273
    poverty, 82, 362
    prevalence, 135
    at-risk status, 58, 82, 141
skills
    acquisition of, 185–186, 214
    generalization of, 185–186, 190, 244
    transfer of, 186–187, 190
sleep–wake activity, 263
Smart Start, 409, 414
Smart Start Initiative, 352, 409, 510
social biology, 76
social causation, 312–314, 321
social change, individual, 450–451
social choice, 491
social class effect, 96, 137, 316–317
social cohesion, 318–319
social competence, 314–315, 652
social development, 5–6, 488, 511
social–ecological process, 241, 318
social ecology, demographic characteristics and, 315–316
social environment, 76–77, 312
social fittedness, 163–164, 167
social isolation, 59, 61, 181, 422, 625, 654
social networks, 58–60, 66, 77, 105, 195, 295, 303, 422, 489, 663
social policy, see public policy
social referencing, 56, 164, 165

Social Security Act, 7, 8 (see also Title V programs)
social selection models, 312–314, 321
social service utilization, 517
social skills, deficits, 40
social stimulation, 162 (see also sensory stimulation)
social support
    assessment, 60, 303–304
    and caregiver stress, 294, 295
    community intervention programs, 195, 311
    dimensions, 58
    and depression, 652
    evaluation of interventions, 376
    interventions, 69
    and parenting behavior, 36, 58–60, 63, 65, 68, 69, 376
    protective effects, 667, 669
social toxicity, 77
social validity, 239, 491
socialization, resilient children, 125
sociobiology, 76
sociocultural contexts (see also culture)
    for developmental change, 234, 488–489
    for evaluation of interventions, 488–490, 501
    of risks, 77 (see also cultural risk factors)
sociocultural influences, 94–95
sociocultural opportunities, 77
sociodynamic problems, 340–342
socioeconomic status (see also impoverished children; low-income families; poverty)
    and child maltreatment, 87–88
    developmental effects, 49, 78, 137, 237
    and discriminatory practices, 96
    and effectiveness of interventions, 529
    and genetic defects, 41
    and IQ, 78
    neighborhood composition, 311–312, 316–317
    and parent–child interactions, 86, 260, 266
    and parent–professional interaction, 501
    and parenting patterns, 489
    and participation rates, 536
    and perceptions of development, 100
    and perinatal injury, 49
    and school readiness, 625

socioemotional development, 12, 25, 63, 138, 457
sociology of developmental risk, 85–91
somatosensory cortex, 219–220
spasticity, 209, 532
special education
    behavioral approaches, 488
    best/recommended practices, 458
    costs, 17, 593–594, 596, 605
    cultural considerations, 241
    effectiveness, 511
    eligibility for, 245
    family-centered services, 456–457
    historical roots, 8–9, 14, 535
    interactive approaches, 457
    naturalistic approaches, 457–458
    personnel roles, 465, 469
    personnel training, 15, 455, 460–464, 467–470, 478
    philosophical base, 456–458
    placements as outcome measure, 515, 517, 523, 539
Special Supplemental Nutrition Program for Women, Infants, and Children (WIC), 334–335, 374, 380, 382, 407, 552
speech discrimination task, 222
speech impairment, 220, 221, 419, 527, 594
spina bifida, 36, 40–42, 205, 456
spoiling, 331
SPRANS grants, 8
staff-child ratios, 190–191, 199, 465, 593–594, 605–606
standardized tests, 242–246
Stanford-Binet Intelligence Scale, 245, 246, 503, 520, 538
Starting Early Starting Smart, 421
Starting Points initiative, 353, 381, 424
State Children's Health Insurance Program, 8
state programs
    child care and education, 348, 349–350, 351, 352, 353
    child protection agencies, 456
    mental health, 428–429, 433, 434
    parent education, 524–525
    personnel development, 454
    service delivery role, 394, 402, 428–429
    system building, 381–382
statistical metropolitan reporting area, 316
stereotypes and prejudices, 96, 105, 241

stigmatization, 18, 181, 346, 664
still-face paradigm, 65–66
stimulation, *see* sensory stimulation
stimulus
    aversive, 184–185
    conditioned, 182
    control, 183–184, 186–187
    unconditioned, 182
Stockholm study, 660–661
strabismus, 120
stress, *see* psychological stress
stressors
    caregiver, 293
    disability-related, 193–194
    primary, 293
    secondary, 293–294
structural equation modeling, 238
subependymal zone, 208
substance abuse (*see also* alcohol)
    community factors, 313
    and developmental outcomes,
      45–46, 85, 216
    and IQ, 85
    interventions, 379, 380, 426,
      427–428
    maternal, 237, 238–239, 380, 426,
      427–428
    and parenting, 60–62, 70, 427–428
    poverty and, 85–86
    and resilience in children, 116,
      118–119, 123, 660–661, 668
    and violence, 427
Substance Abuse, Mental Health
    Services Administration, 421
superego, 164
superior colliculus, 205
Supplemental Security Income (SSI)
    insurance, 18, 334
supplemental stimulation, *see* sensory
    stimulation
support
    groups, *see* parent support groups;
      social support
    networks, electronic, 472–473
    sources of, 195
Sweden, 333, 348, 617, 618, 621,
    623–624
synaptogenesis
    in animals, 209, 210, 212, 218
    errors of, 210
    experience-dependent, 217
    experience-expectant, 217
    malnutrition and, 46–47
    normal, 37–38, 210, 212, 214,
      217, 510
synchrony, parent–infant
    relationship, 259, 262, 331

Syracuse Family Demonstration
    Project, 370, 375, 515
system of least prompts, 187
systematic social observation (SSO),
    317–318
systems approach (*see also*
    contextualism; ecological
    perspective; family systems
    approaches; transactional model)
    cross-system collaboration
      challenges, 430
    ecological perspective, 54, 78–81,
      489, 643, 644
    funding issues, 382–383, 430–431
    high-risk environments, 87
    ideological challenges, 429–430
    mental health service delivery, 425,
      428, 429–432
    parenting interventions, 69–70,
      155, 428
    personnel challenges, 431–432
    preventive services, 69–70
    service coordination, 380–383, 641
    state and local initiatives, 381–382
    training for, 461
systems of care, 425, 426
systems sensitivity, 161

T
tabula rasa, 4
tax policies and incentives, 352
Tay-Sachs disease, 40
teachers (*see also* personnel)
    competency-based training,
      464–470
    effectiveness, 477–478, 528, 531
    interactive relationship with
      children, 567, 672
    as role models, 126
    special education, 15, 455,
      460–464, 467–470, 478
    training, 15, 423, 455, 460–464,
      467–470, 478
teenage pregnancy, *see* adolescent
    mothers
Teenage Pregnancy Intervention
    Program, 555, 556, 584
telencephalon, 205–206
temperament, child
    disabled children, 262, 277
    and parenting, 70, 259
    resilient, 663, 673
Temporary Assistance to Needy
    Families (TANF), 17, 18, 342, 383,
    569, 616
teratogens, 45–48, 216
Test of Adult Basic Education (TABE),
    558, 559

Test of Early Language Development,
    538
testing, *see* assessment
Texas initiatives, 515, 561
thalamus, 205
thalassaemia, 659
The Finance Project, 352, 357
theories of change approach,
    171–174
therapeutic alliance, 168, 566
therapeutic nursery, 380
therapies, integrated, 398–399
    (*see also* developmental
      therapies)
time delay procedures, 187
time out, 184
Title V programs, 7–8, 14, 380
tolerance for difference, 188–189
toxicity, central nervous system,
    45–48
toxoplasmosis, 44
Toyota Families for Learning, 558,
    559, 560, 586, 587
training (*see also* personnel; special
    education)
    assessment professionals, 268, 277,
      278, 280–281, 296, 301
    challenges, 473–477
    coaching, 462, 463, 471–472
    in communication, 185, 460–461,
      475
    community-based approach,
      470–471
    continuing education, 454, 475
    in cultural sensitivity, 475
    developmental orientation, 462,
      470
    distance education, 472–473, 477
    early care and education staff, 15,
      345, 347, 348–349, 351–352,
      365, 434
    electronic support networks,
      472–473
    evaluation of effectiveness, 471,
      478
    family-centered model, 296, 409,
      408, 460–461, 469, 474–475
    follow-up strategies, 471–472
    guidelines, 468, 469, 470
    in inclusive settings, 454, 455, 470,
      474, 478
    infant specialists, 466–467,
      474–475
    in-service, 25, 180, 349, 409, 450,
      461, 463–464, 467, 470–473, 474,
      475, 476
    interdisciplinary approach, 455,
      463, 474, 475

learning characteristics of adults, 476–477
mentoring, 462
observational technique, 462–463
paraprofessionals, 383, 440, 446–447, 448–449, 450
parent–child relationship, 268, 277, 278, 280–281, 474
parent–professional relationship, 269, 335, 408, 460, 465, 474–475
parent involvement in, 353, 462, 463, 470–471, 475, 636–638
PDS model, 464, 473
pediatricians, 335
peer support groups, 471–472
preschool specialists, 365, 423, 469–470, 474–475
preservice, 348, 409, 450, 455, 461, 463–464, 467, 474, 476, 477
principles, 466–467
in reflective supervision, 454, 461–462, 463–464
research needs, 477–478
role-playing technique, 446
and service coordination, 22, 396
special education personnel, 15, 467–470, 455
for systems perspective, 461
target populations, 455–456
temporal processing of speech, 220, 221
team-based service delivery, 423
university faculty, 473–474
transactional model, 489
center-based intervention, 536
cultural code in, 144, 489
definition, 141–143
diagnosis decision tree, 154–155
family code in, 144–147
in intervention planning, 11, 62, 135, 149–155
of language intervention, 537
for low-birth-weight infants, 150–154
of minority children, 106
organizational perspective, 143–149
parental code in, 147–148
parent–child interaction, 54–55, 142–143, 536
regulatory processes in, 136, 143–144, 148–149
uncertainty in, 160
validation, 12–13

Transdisciplinary Play-Based Assessment (TPBA), 232, 234, 235, 241–242, 249
transfer of stimulus control, 186–187
transfer programs, in-kind, 550–551
transferrence, 168, 367, 379, 634
transportation assistance, 374, 377, 515, 589, 596
tuberous sclerosis, 37, 532
Turkey, 603
turn taking
    disabled infants, 264–265
    parent–infant relationship, 164–165, 261, 262, 264–265
turning points in adulthood, 127, 656, 660, 662, 664, 673, 674
Turner syndrome, 40
twins, 49, 162, 238, 654, 668, 669, 671
two-generation programs, 370–371, 373, 523–525, 557, 570
Type I punishment, 182
Type II punishment, 182

U
unconditioned stimulus, 182
UNICEF, 614, 629
United Cerebral Palsy, 394
United Kingdom, 331, 333, 348, 615, 618–620, 623, 625
United Way, 381
University of Chicago study, 120
U.S. Advisory Board on Child Abuse and Neglect, 331, 550, 576
U.S. Advisory Commission on Intergovernmental Relations, 349, 350, 359
U.S. Bureau of the Census, 316
U.S. Centers for Disease Control and Prevention, 41
U.S. Department of Commerce, 75
U.S. Department of Education, 17, 21, 353, 398, 414, 526, 547, 549,
U.S. Department of Education, National Center for Education Statistics, 359
U.S. Department of Education, Office of Educational Research and Improvement, 340, 353, 359
U.S. Department of Health and Human Services, 21, 135, 159, 168, 176, 266, 284, 386, 573
U.S. Department of Justice, Civil Rights Division, Disability Rights Section, 526, 547
U.S. General Accounting Office, 340, 343, 344, 351, 359

U.S. House of Representatives, Committee on Ways and Means, 613, 615, 621, 629
U.S. House of Representatives, Select Committee on Children and Youth, 619, 629
U.S. Office of Education, 10
U.S. Public Health Service, 21, 327
U.S. Senate Report, Committee on Labor and Human Resources, 414
U.S. Social Security Administration, 616, 617, 618, 629
utilization of services, 500, 503–504, 528–529, 554

V
validity
    of assessment instruments, 243, 244–245, 252, 253
    evaluation paradigm, 491
value-added analysis, 527
values
    family, 97, 143, 145, 166, 236
    in professional interpretations, 236
Verbal Interaction Project, 363
verification paradigm, 491
Vermont
    intervention initiatives, 151, 351, 353, 381
    Intervention Program for Low Birthweight Infants, 151
    mental health problems of children, 418, 428
Vermont Agency of Human Services, 418, 428, 438
very low birth weight, 211, 522
videotapes
    in community analysis, 318
    feedback, 270, 272, 273, 278, 565
    for guided group discussions, 423
Vineland Scales of Adaptive Behavior, 235, 534
Vineland Social Maturity Scale, 120
violence
    and aggression, 312
    community, 24, 86–87, 106, 172, 312, 321, 380
    domestic, 135, 380, 424
    behavioral and emotional effects, 64, 135, 312, 321, 380, 418, 419
    crisis intervention and support, 433
    and Head Start outcomes, 519
    helping principles for families, 380
    interpersonal, 319–320

and parenting, 61, 62–63, 64,
    69–70, 427–428
  prevention interventions, 69–70
  protective factors, 116
Virginia initiatives, 528
Virginia Twin Study, 669
visiting nurses, 331
visual system
  critical period, 205
  development, 205, 210, 212,
    217
  impairments, 43, 44, 217, 269, 456,
    532–533, 594
vocalization, 262, 264–265
Vocational Rehabilitation Act, 16
vulnerability
  cultural differences and, 96–97,
    100–102, 105
  at developmental transition times,
    173–174
  financial, 82
  resiliency balanced with, 127
  to stress, 121

W
War on Poverty, 14, 15, 101, 364,
    440, 620

washout effect, 538
Wechsler Intelligence Scale for
    Children – Revised, 47, 245, 246,
    513, 522
Wechsler Preschool and Primary
    Scales of Intelligence (WPPSI),
    276, 521
welfare costs, 599–600
welfare reform, 17–18, 77, 82, 84,
    342, 402
  and child care, 525, 614
  and eligibility for services,
    334–335, 568–569
  personnel preparation and,
    477
  work preparation programs,
    370–371, 383, 421, 426, 441, 442,
    569, 614
well-baby care, 87, 332, 334, 618–619
Westinghouse Learning Corporation,
    366, 496
White House Conferences, 7, 19, 342,
    549, 550
Whites
  child care utilization, 340, 341
  mistrust by Blacks, 107
  poverty, 82

Woodcock Johnson Psycho-
    Educational Battery, 513, 521
work preparation programs, 370–371,
    383, 421, 426, 441, 442, 569
Work Sampling System, 502
World Health Organization, 12, 333
World Health Organization, European
    Working Group, 333, 338

Y
Yale Child Welfare Research Program,
    367, 375, 555, 584
Yale Family Support Project, 592, 595,
    602–603
Young Autism Project, 190

Z
zero-second trials, 187
Zero to Three: National Center for
    Infants, Toddlers and Families,
    16, 170, 178, 367, 421, 431, 438,
    473
Zero to Three Working Group on
    Developmental Assessment,
    231–232
zone of proximal development, 78,
    450